CONTROL SYSTEMS

PRINCIPLES AND DESIGN

Second Edition

About the Author

M. Gopal is presently Professor, Department of Electrical Engineering, Indian Institute of Technology (IIT), Delhi. His teaching and research stints span over three decades at institutes such as IIT Delhi; IIT Bombay; BITS Pilani; REC Jaipur; City University London; and Universiti Teknologi Malaysia. He has won international recognition as a distinguished individual in the field of education.

Dr. Gopal is the author/co-author of six books, a video course in Control Engineering, and a large number of research publications.

His current research interests are in the areas of Robust Control, Neural and Fuzzy Technologies, Process Control and Robotics.

CONTROL SYSTEMS
PRINCIPLES AND DESIGN
Second Edition

M Gopal

Professor
Department of Electrical Engineering
Indian Institute of Technology
New Delhi

Boston   Burr Ridge, IL   Dubuque, IA   Madison, WI   New York   San Francisco   St. Louis
Bangkok   Bogotá   Caracas   Kuala Lumpur   Lisbon   London   Madrid   Mexico City
Milan   Montreal   New Delhi   Santiago   Seoul   Singapore   Sydney   Taipei   Toronto

McGraw-Hill
A Division of The *McGraw-Hill* Companies

CONTROL SYSTEMS: PRINCIPLES AND DESIGN, SECOND EDITION
International Edition 2003

10 09
20 09 08 07
CTF   BJE

ISBN 0-07-048289-6

When ordering this title, use ISBN 0-07-123127-7

Printed in Singapore

To
my
Lakshmi

Preface to the Second Edition

In developing this edition of *Control Systems: Principles and Design*, the goal was to improve the textbook without disturbing its basic foundation. We continue to emphasize frequency-domain design methods for using root locus and Nyquist/Bode/Nichols plots; augmented with state variable methods for control system analysis. To prepare the student for industrial practice, the basics of digital control have been included. This has been achieved without using the z-transforms; increasing the breadth of coverage by including z-transform theory would have been at the cost of the depth of the subject covered in the book.

Most of the textbooks on control theory include primarily motion-control application examples. This background is appropriate for control engineering practice in manufacturing industry. To prepare a student for practice in process industry, additional knowledge on slow and complex nature of industrial processes, and their control using tunable PID controllers, is essential. A balanced presentation of motion-control and process-control application case studies is a unique feature of this book. The real-life problems have been suitably tailored to the level of the text, unlike many other presentations wherein the problems are more advanced than the text itself.

The use of Computer-Aided Design (CAD) is universal for practising engineers in this field, as in most other fields. An appendix has been added to integrate learning of control system analysis and design material with learning of how to compute the answers with MATLAB—the most widely used CAD software package in universities. The appendix is not meant to be a substitute for the MATLAB software manuals; rather, it will help guide the reader to the appropriate places in the manuals for specific computations. The manuals are the best source of learning the package; our attempt in the book is only to expedite the process of making full use of the power of the package for control system design problems. MATLAB problems included in the appendix will help the student practice problem-solving using computers.

Recently some authors have integrated MATLAB with the text. We have pushed MATLAB-aided learning environment to an appendix; the main flow of the text is not MATLAB based. This decision is based on the belief that to use CAD software packages effectively, the student must first understand the basics of the method being used so that the results from the computer can be evaluated and checked for reasonableness by independent analysis. It is mandatory that the student retain the ability to compute simple answers by hand.

The book is decidedly longer than what can be covered in a semester. But all topics covered in the book contribute to the subject. In fact, the complete coverage and balance offered by the book is its characteristic feature, and putting it in students' hands is of great value from the point of view of industrial practice.

Many suggestions have been made by the instructors for reorganizing the book in a way that basic material usually covered by most undergraduate first level courses on controls will be retained and other topics shifted to the companion book. In the light of these suggestions, the chapter on Nonlinear Systems has been shifted to the companion book : Gopal M., *Digital Control and State Variable Methods*: *Conventional and Neural-Fuzzy Control Systems,* 2nd edition, Tata McGraw-Hill, New Delhi, 2002.

Certain topics which interrupt the main flow without substantially adding to the knowledge, have been deleted. Review Questions, and a Control Theory Quiz comprising questions with multiple-choice answers have been added; this material should serve the purpose of self-appraisal for the reader.

I appreciate the efforts of students, faculty, and other users who have kept in touch with me. Certain technical points which needed clarification were brought to my attention. I have attempted to address each concern and have corrected every known error. An instructor using this text may obtain the *Solution Manual* from the accompanying website. The URL of the website is www.tatamcgraw-hill.com/digital_solutions/gopal/controls.

M. GOPAL

mgopal@ee.iitd.ac.in

Preface to the First Edition

This text provides an integrated treatment of all those aspects of control systems engineering that prepare the student for early productivity upon entering industrial practice. Important aspects of the subject that help realise this objective arc:

(a) Knowledge of the basic control configurations that have been devised and the characteristic performance features of each. This helps one in initially selecting one or more alternative configurations that have potential for success.

(b) Knowledge of the tools of 'control system design tool box' comprising time-tested design procedures; a particular application needs intelligent selection of tools from this box.

(c) Familiarity with available hardware so that commercially available components to implement the design can be selected.

(d) Competence in modelling of physical systems using judicious assumptions.

This text attempts to provide detailed description of basic control configurations since this storehouse is what one draws on when conceiving a design for a new application. The vast majority of practical systems are designed in this way rather than by some mathematical synthesis procedure. The list of topics includes fundamental control modes: on-off, proportional, integral, derivative, phase-lead, phase-lag; and specialised control schemes: command and disturbance feedforward, cascade control, state-variable feedback.

The 'control system design tool box' comprises extensive collection of results based on the so-called 'classical' and 'modern' control concepts. The *classical control theory* is characterised by frequency-domain methods developed during the period of about twenty years—from the early 1940s through the early 1960s. It has a large body of use-tested knowledge covering linear, nonlinear and sampled-data systems. This theory is still going strong; it provides an efficient framework for the design of feedback controls in all areas of applications, though the term 'classical control' appears to suggest that it is out-of-date. In fact classical design methods have been greatly enhanced by the availability of low-cost computers for system analysis and simulation. The graphical tools of classical design can now be more easily used with computer graphics and the effects of nonlinearities and model approximations evaluated by computer simulation. Coupled with hardware developments such as microprocessors and electro-optic measurement schemes, the classical control theory today provides useful design tools in the hands of practising control engineers.

The *modern control theory* (which is not so modern any longer) refers to a collection of state-space based methods developed in the late 1950s and early 1960s, which deals with matrix methods, eigen analysis, and applications of optimisation methods such as calculus of variations. Modern control methods initially enjoyed a great deal of success in academic circles, but they did not perform very well in many areas of application. Modern control provided a lot of insight into system structure and properties, but it masked other important feedback properties that could be studied and manipulated using classical control. During the past two decades, a body of methods, which is a combination of modern state-space methods and classical frequency-domain methods, has emerged. These techniques are commonly known as *robust control*.

In this text, major emphasis is on frequency-domain design methods based on transfer function representation of systems. State-space based design methods (eigenstructure assignment, optimal control) and the advanced robust control methods are beyond the scope of the book. A conscious and persistent effort has, however, been made to relate these topics to their proper role in the larger scene of engineering design.

Compared to transfer functions, the response of state variable equations is easy to programme. For this reason, many computer-aided design packages use state-space and matrix notation, and therefore it is helpful for control engineers to be familiar with it. An adequate coverage of state variable representation, and its relationship with transfer function representation is within the scope of the book. This limited augmentation of the frequency-domain methods will also provide a smooth transition to the study of advanced control system design techniques.

The practice of using digital hardware for controller implementation has been widely accepted. However, it does not mean that control theory and practice is now concerned with sampled-data system theory, microcomputer programming and electronic design of interface hardware. Digital control, in fact, contributes relatively few basic control concepts of its own to the control system design tool box. The vast majority of digital systems in operation today are implementing well-known design principles, conceived before digital computers were used in control system practice. Most of these principles were actually used in analog systems. Digital control theory adds little to one's expertise in the initial conceptual phase of design. An introductory course in control systems engineering, therefore, must provide an adequate coverage of various analog methods of control system analysis and design. Investment in digital methods is also required so that the control engineer can work well in the increasingly digital environment. Depending upon the availability of curriculum space, the objective of preparing the student for practical control system design in industry may be realised through modest investment in digital methods in an introductory course or a substantial investment in a second course. This spirit has guided the preparation of this text.

Real-life control engineering practice requires extensive knowledge in instrumentation and process dynamics in addition to the knowledge in control systems design. The process dynamics which may vary greatly from one process to another, can only be effectively mastered during practice; the coverage to the topic in this textbook is limited to basic principles for modelling simple mechanical, electrical, fluid, and thermal systems. In-depth coverage of instrumentation physics is also not possible in a control text. This, however, is not a major problem as the required instrumentation knowledge can be readily acquired in practice from experienced engineers or through vendor courses. Nevertheless, an exposure to commercially available hardware is important. In this book, innumerable realistic (but simple) application examples are included to develop familiarity with available hardware.

A modern development that is significant to practical design is the wide availability and low cost of Computer-Aided-Design (CAD) software. Although a practical designer is handicapped without access to such tools, and students definitely benefit from their hands-on use, the text has been designed in such a way that personal access to CAD software facility is not essential. It is advisable to first create a firm knowledge-base of the fundamental results of feedback control theory without any diversion to other domains of learning; this knowledge can then be supplemented by CAD facility to solve practical design problems wherein it is desirable to vary several parameters during the design stage to investigate their effect on the system performance. Some problems for computer solution may be assigned to familiarise the students with CAD tools. This book offers computer-aided learning environment with any commercially available CAD software.

The material in the book has been class-tested. The sequencing and internal organisation of various chapters is such that it permits flexibility of adaptation to the variations in students' prior training and curricula. A judicious selection of a set of case studies from innumerable application examples given in the book, makes the book comprehensible for all engineering disciplines that have control courses as part of their curricula. Practical flavour with careful and complete explanations makes the book appealing for self-study by practising engineers. The book should also serve as a guide for applying design techniques to industrial control problems.

There are fourteen chapters in the book. Chapter 1 gives on overview of all the important application areas and all the basic categories of control systems. A brief account of major historical landmarks in the development of the fascinating area of control systems engineering is also given. The chapter concludes with an outline of scope and organisation of the book.

Chapters 2-11 are devoted to hardware familiarity, concepts of feedback control theory, and the frequency-domain tools of control system design. The material in these chapters forms the core of the introductory course in control engineering. Depending upon the curriculum time and plan of the follow-up courses, additional material from Chapters 12-14 may be used.

The familiarity with the theory of functions of a complex variable, the Fourier transforms, the Laplace transforms, and elementary matrix algebra is helpful but not necessary; these mathematical techniques are reviewed at appropriate places to the extent needed in the book.

Generous participation of instructors, students, and practising engineers to eliminate errors in the text and to refine the presentation, will be gratefully acknowledged.

M. GOPAL

Contents

chapter 1

Introduction to the Control Problem

1.1 CONTROL SYSTEMS: TERMINOLOGY AND BASIC STRUCTURE

In recent years, control systems have assumed an increasingly important role in the development and advancement of modern civilization and technology. Practically every aspect of our day-to-day activities is affected by some type of control system. A bathroom toilet tank is a control system. A home-heating system, a refrigerator, an air-conditioner, and an automobile are all control systems. Control systems are indispensable in modern industrial processes. We find control systems in all sectors of industry, such as quality control of manufactured products, automatic assembly line, machine-tool control, space technology and weapon systems, transportation systems, power systems, robotics, and many others. Even such problems as inventory control, and socio-economic systems control may be approached from the theory of feedback control. In this book we will deal with the control of *engineering systems* that are governed by the laws of physics and are therefore called *physical systems*.

In control parlance, the system to be controlled is given various names: *process*, *plant*, and *controlled system* being perhaps the most common. In the so-called process industries (chemicals, petroleum, steam power, fuel, etc.), one repeatedly encounters the need to control temperature, flow rate, liquid-level in vessels, pressure, humidity, chemical composition, and the like; such applications are generally considered *process control* applications. Historically, the wide practical application of control first took place in the process area. Most of the basic concepts were developed and brought to successful realization by the intuitive and experimentally-oriented engineering methods typical of the 1900 to 1940 era.

Around the time of the Second World War, the technical needs of military systems—automatic airplane pilots, gun-positioning systems, radar antenna control systems, and the like—led to more scientific approaches in the control engineering field. A comprehensive mathematical theory—the theory of *servomechanism*[1]—aimed mainly at applications wherein the need is to control mechanical motions (position, velocity, or acceleration), was developed around 1940 to 1950. Since this time, the design methods of the process-control area, and the servomechanism area have gradually converged. The terminology of the two areas is also converging. The word 'process' is now in use for all types of controlled systems. Also, irrespective of the area of application, the word 'servomechanism' (or *servo system*) is used for a *command following system* wherein the controlled attribute of the system is required to follow a given command.

Figure 1.1 shows the input–output configuration of a process (or plant). Process *outputs* are the response variables which we require to behave in some specified fashion. Process *inputs* are flows of energy and/or material that cause the process to react or respond. The inputs are classified into *manipulated inputs* (subject to our control) and *disturbance inputs* (undesirable and unavoidable effects beyond our control, generated from outside process-environment, and from within). The presence of the disturbance is one of the main reasons of using control. Clever management of manipulated variables so as to counteract the effects of disturbances is the primary role of the *controller*. Figure 1.2 shows the input–output configuration of a *control system*.

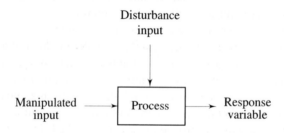

Fig. 1.1   *Process input–output configuration*

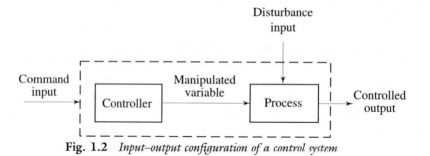

Fig. 1.2   *Input–output configuration of a control system*

---

1. The word servomechanism originated from the words servant (or slave) and mechanism.

When the desired value of the controlled outputs is more or less fixed and the main problem is to reject disturbance effects, the control system is sometimes called a *regulator*. The command input for a regulator becomes a constant and is called *set-point*, which corresponds to the desired value of the controlled output. The set-point may however be changed in time from one constant value to another, and the need for the control of manipulated variables arises from the requirements of both the set-point changes and the disturbance rejection. The control problem is then called *resetting control problem*.

In the *follow-up* or *tracking system*, the controlled output is required to follow or track a time-varying command input. For such systems, the need for the control of manipulated variables arises from the requirements of command-following as well as disturbance rejection.

In the configuration of Fig. 1.3, the controller receives information about the desired value of the controlled output and uses this information as a means of control of the manipulated variables. In contrast to this configuration, the configuration of Fig. 1.4 utilizes measurement of the controlled output in order to compare the actual output with the desired output response. The controller then uses this difference as a means of control of manipulated variables. The configuration of Fig. 1.3 is that of an *open-loop control system* while that of Figure 1.4 is that of *closed-loop control system* or *feedback control system*.

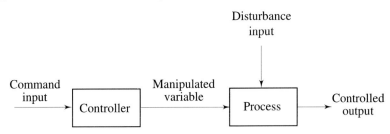

Fig. 1.3 *Input–output configuration of an open-loop control system*

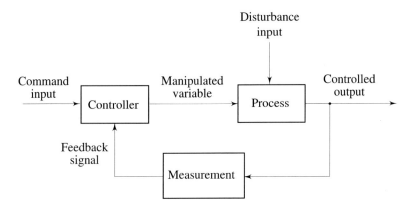

Fig. 1.4 *Input–output configuration of a closed-loop control system*

To make these definitions more concrete, let us consider some familiar examples of control systems.

Example 1.1

A Bathroom Toilet Tank

It is a regulator system that maintains the water level H at a preset height $\overline{H}$. Water level is thus the controlled variable of interest and is clearly affected by the main disturbance input—the outflowing water stream. The manipulated variable is the inflowing water stream. The task of the controller can be defined as the automatic cancelling of the error ($\overline{H} - H$) due to the disturbance. The principle of operation of the system involves making the manipulated variable dependent on the error, and hence on the feedback of the controlled variable. Figure 1.5 gives the schematic diagram and the functional block diagram of the toilet tank.

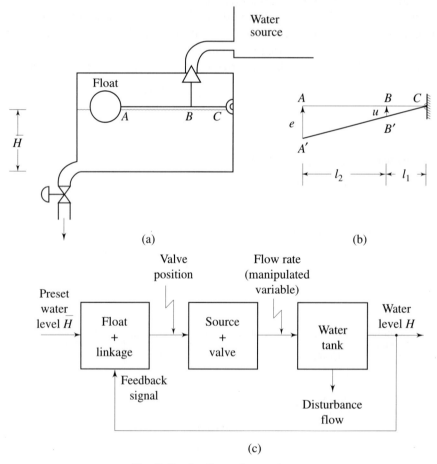

Fig. 1.5 *A toilet tank control system*

If because of disturbance, the water level H has decreased, then the float and the points A and B of the lever move down. The inlet valve allows the inflow of water, thus bringing about a gradual growth in the water level H. The inflow of water is stopped automatically whenever the water level reaches the preset height.

The float and linkage in Fig. 1.5a perform the functions of error detection and generation of the correcting signal. This is clear from the geometry of the linkage shown in Fig. 1.5b. For small movements,

$$\frac{AA'}{AC} = \frac{AA'}{AB + BC} = \frac{BB'}{BC} \qquad \text{or} \qquad \frac{e}{l_2 + l_1} = \frac{u}{l_1}$$

Therefore,
$$u = \frac{l_1}{l_1 + l_2} e$$

where
e = error signal produced by the float; and
u = control signal produced by the linkage.

The control signal u is thus proportional to the error signal e (*control logic*); the gain $K = \dfrac{l_1}{l_1 + l_2}$ can be varied by shifting the lever axis (point B): the shift of the lever axis towards the float (point A) corresponds to an increase in the gain. The functional block diagram of the toilet tank control system (Fig. 1.5c) has been redrawn in Fig. 1.6, showing the error detector and control logic blocks separately.

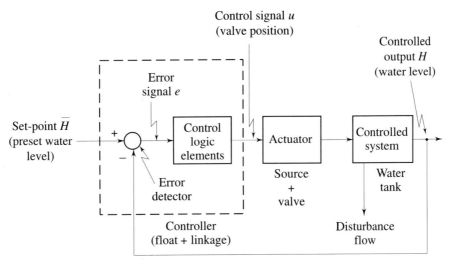

Fig. 1.6 *Functions of controller in control system of Fig. 1.5c*

Although a toilet tank is a very simple mechanism, it has all the ingradients of a closed-loop system.

Example 1.2

Automobile Driving System

The system to be controlled has two inputs (steering, and acceleration/braking) and two controlled outputs (heading, and speed). The two command inputs are the direction of the highway, and speed limits with traffic signals. A block diagram of this two-input, two-output system is shown in Fig. 1.7.

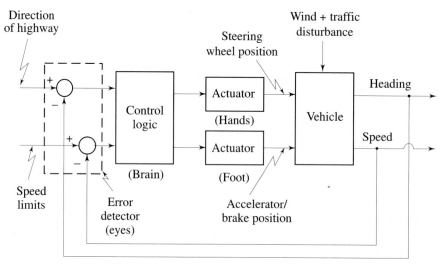

Fig. 1.7 *Automobile driving control system*

Systems with more than one controlled output and command input are called *multivariable* or *multi-input, multi-output* (MIMO) systems. On the other hand, in *single-input, single-output* (SISO) systems, a single output is controlled by single input. In multivariable systems, an input that is meant to control a particular output, also affects the other controlled outputs. This coupling is called *interaction*.

The automobile-driving system is a MIMO system. We can *decouple* this system into two SISO systems for the purpose of design because the interaction is negligible. Steering control affects the heading and not speed, and accelerator control affects the speed and not the heading. However, braking of the vehicle for speed control decreases the side forces at the tyre-road interface for directional control, and with locked wheels the directional control is completely lost. If we consider this interaction negligible, we can consider the vehicle-heading control system as a decoupled SISO system, with no interaction with vehicle-speed control system.

The command inputs for an automobile on the road cannot be constant setpoints. These inputs depend on the traffic and road conditions and vary in an uncontrolled manner. The actual signal inputs to the system are derived by the driver from the actual road and traffic conditions. The human operator subsystem will therefore be a component in the overall control system of the automobile, as shown in Fig. 1.7. The desired course and speed are compared with a measurement of the actual course and speed in order to generate a measurement of the error. The human operator then controls the manipulated variables (steering wheel position, accelerator/brake position) in a manner (control logic) which reduces the absolute error.

Comparison of Figs 1.6 and 1.7 gives many common features of the two closed-loop systems. However, the two systems differ clearly in one aspect. In Fig. 1.7, both the feedback of the controlled outputs (actual course, and speed of travel) for comparison with command inputs (desired course, and speed of travel), and the control actions (rotation of steering wheel, and acceleration/braking) take place through the human operator. In Fig. 1.6, the human operator has been replaced by automatic error detecting and correcting devices; both the feedback of the controlled output (actual water level in the tank), and the correcting action (control of the valve position) take place without the need of a human operator. Such systems, therefore, are *automatic closed-loop control systems*. The systems with human operators included into the closed-loop are *man-machine control systems*.

Example 1.3

Hydraulic Power Steering Mechanism

Many automobiles have power steering which utilizes hydraulic amplifiers for the amplification of the force applied to the wheels. A schematic diagram of the hydraulic power steering mechanism is shown in Fig. 1.8a. The command input to the system is the rotation of the steering wheel by the driver and the controlled output is the vehicle heading, in a command-following mode (note that the hydraulic power steering mechanism is a sub-system of the automobile driving system shown in Fig. 1.7).

When the steering wheel is in the zero position, i.e., the cross bar is horizontal, the tyre wheels are directed parallel to the longitudinal axis of the vehicle. For this condition, the spool is in the neutral position and the oil supply to the power cylinder is cutoff. When the steering wheel is turned anti-clockwise through an angle θ_r, the spool is made to move towards right by an amount x with the help of the gear mechanism. The high-pressure oil enters on the left-hand side of the power cylinder causing the power piston and hence the power ram to move towards right by an amount y. Through a proper drive linkage, a torque is applied to the wheels causing a displacement θ of the wheels.

A rigid linkage bar connects the power ram and the movable valve housing. Movement y of the power ram towards the right causes a movement z of the valve housing in such a direction as to seal off the high pressure line.

A simple model of the load on the power piston is shown in Fig. 1.8b. The wheel-and-axle mass M, tyre stiffness K, and viscous friction coefficient B are the parameters of the assumed model. A nominal load is included in the plant

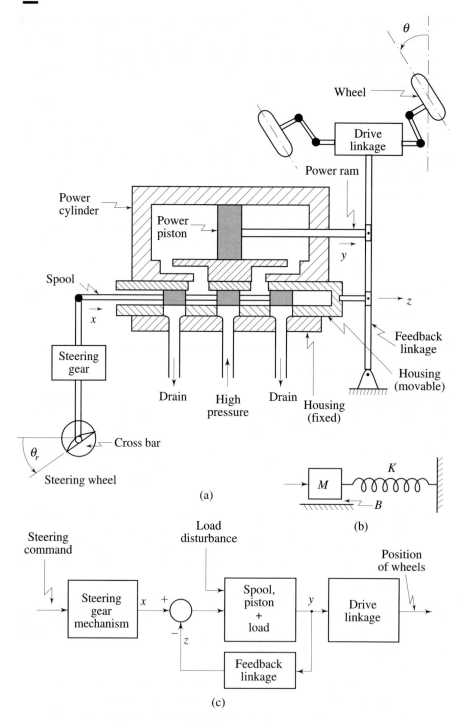

(a)

(b)

(c)

Fig. 1.8   *Hydraulic power steering mechanism*

model for the control design. The main disturbance input is the deviation of the load from the nominal estimated value as a result of uncertainty in our estimate, effect of road conditions, and wind power.

Figure 1.8c shows the functional block diagram of the hydraulic power steering mechanism; sub-blocks corresponding to control logic, actuator, etc., have not been shown. Identification of these blocks requires modelling of the system. Detailed study of the system will be taken up in Chapter 3.

Example 1.4

Residential Heating System

In this system, the indoor temperature is the response variable of interest, and it is affected by the main disturbance input—the outdoor temperature. In the scheme of Fig. 1.9, the desired temperature, which is the command-input temperature, is set on a calibrated dial. This positions the valve that admits the steam for circulation through the radiator. The valve dial is calibrated when the environment temperature has certain value. When this value changes significantly, the controlled temperature will deviate from the desired value by a large error and hence precise control will not be realized. The open-loop scheme of Fig. 1.9 is used when performance requirements for heating of a residential building are not very stringent.

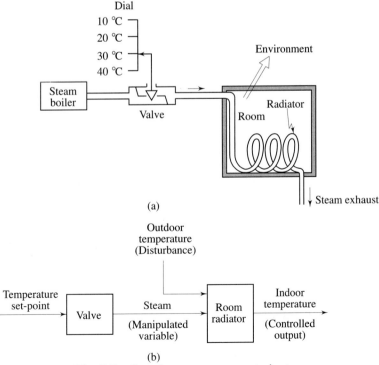

Fig. 1.9 *Open-loop temperature control system*

The open-loop control system of Fig. 1.9 can be converted to a closed-loop system by adding the functions of measurement of the controlled temperature, comparison of measured and desired values of the controlled temperature, and control logic to make changes in the heating rate when the desired and measured values differ.

Most residential heating (or cooling) systems utilize one form or another of on–off control. For example, a thermostat with a bimetallic temperature sensor and a snap-action switch to control a simple solenoid-actuated steam valve is often used for this purpose. In a thermostat, two materials with grossly different thermal expansion coefficients are bonded together. When heated, the different expansion rates cause the assembly curve shown in Fig. 1.10a. This effect is used to control power supply to the solenoid (Fig. 1.10b). When the solenoid coil is energized, the plunger becomes magnetized and mutual attraction takes place between the coil and the plunger. If the force required by the load on the plunger does not exceed the force developed by the solenoid, the plunger will pull in. In the temperature control scheme of Fig. 1.10b, position 1 of the switch corresponds to the opening of the steam valve and position 2 corresponds to the closing of the valve.

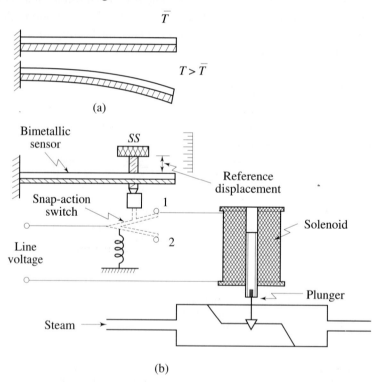

Fig. 1.10   *Closed-loop temperature control system*

The position of the set-screw SS (reference displacement) determines the desired temperature $\overline{T}$. The principle of operation of the temperature control system is that the actuator (solenoid + steam valve) is made to operate according to the sequence in which one of the two possible situations specified below has come about at a given time.

- *Situation* 1: The controlled variable T assumes a value below the desired temperature $\bar{T}$, or in other words, the error $e = (\bar{T} - T)$ is positive. In this situation, the snap-action switch is in position 1, the solenoid is in energized state and the steam valve is open. The controlled variable T gradually increases (with the error e decreasing).
- *Situation* 2: The controlled variable T assumes a value above the desired temperature $\bar{T}$, i.e., the error e is negative. In this situation, the bimetallic strip curls, the snap-action switch is thrown to position 2, the solenoid is de-energized, and the steam valve is closed. The controlled variable T is gradually decreasing (the absolute error is also decreasing) due to the heat transfer from the room to the colder surroundings.

Figure 1.11 shows the functional block diagram of the closed-loop temperature control system. Note that the control signal can assume only two values corresponding to the two states of the snap-action switch. The thermostat is serving as the sensing element as well as the controller—it performs the task of automatic reduction of the error to zero, irrespective of the situation created by the disturbance.

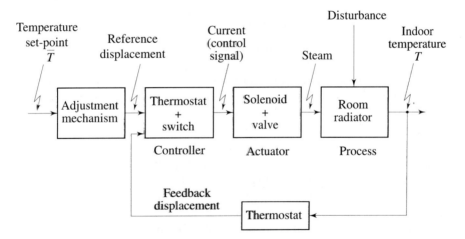

Fig. 1.11 *Functional block diagram of the system of Fig. 1.10*

Basic Structure of a Feedback Control System

The familiar examples of feedback control cited earlier, fit into the basic structure shown in Fig. 1.12 (all functional components identified in Fig. 1.12 do not show up as separate physical elements in Figs 1.6, 1.8, and 1.11).

To understand Fig. 1.12, we begin with the *command signal* y_r—the desired value of the *controlled variable y*. This signal has the same units as the controlled variable, but may or may not exist as an actual physical quantity. For

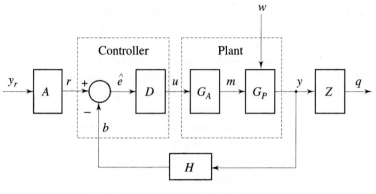

Elements		Signals	
A	: Reference input elements	b	: Feedback signal
D	: Control logic elements	y	: Controlled variable (output)
G_A	: Actuator elements	w	: Disturbance input
	(Final control elements)	$\hat{e}$	: Actuating error signal
G_P	: Controlled system elements	u	: Control signal
Z	: Indirectly controlled	m	: Manipulated variable
	system elements	r	: Reference input
H	: Feedback elements	y_r	: Command input
		q	: Indirectly controlled variable

Fig. 1.12 *Basic structure of a feedback control system*

example in the residential heating system of Fig. 1.10, y_r is the desired room temperature but this is not an actual measurable temperature; it exists only 'mathematically' as the numbers printed on the thermostat dial. In fact, the actual physical input to the control system is a displacement of the set-screw, which is *reference input r* for the residential heating system. The functional block of *reference input elements* represents conversion of the command signal to the reference input signal. In the hydraulic power steering mechanism of Fig. 1.8, the steering gear mechanism corresponds to the reference input elements; it converts the steering command (command input) to the spool displacement (reference input). The reference input element can, when necessary, perform a more sophisticated function such as noise filtering (y_r might be voltage signal contaminated by high-frequency noise).

The *summing junction* is a symbol for the *error detector* which compares the reference input r with the *feedback signal b* and generates a signal $\hat{e} = (r - b)$. The *feedback elements block* is often a sensor for measuring y, but since its functions sometimes include more than simple measurement (e.g., noise filtering), the name feedback element rather than sensing element has been chosen. The signal $\hat{e}$ defines the *actuating error signal*, and not the *system error signal*, which is logically defined as $e = (y_r - y)$. Note that r, b and $\hat{e}$ always have exactly the same dimensions.

The *control logic elements block* produces the *control signal u* which has the knowledge about the desired control action. The *controller* is generally thought of as a system that compares the reference input with the feedback signal and is also responsible for suitable control action. In the toilet-tank system of Fig. 1.6, the control logic is simple *proportional control*; the control signal u is proportional to the error signal e. In the residential heating system of Fig. 1.10, the control logic is simple *on-off control*. In general, the control signal is a function of the actuating error signal, which in turn is a function of the reference input r and controlled output y; the functional relationship may therefore be expressed as $u = f(r, y)$. The primary objective set for this book is to study this functional relationship.

The *actuator elements block* (*final control elements*) consists of devices that develop enough torque, pressure, heat, etc. (*manipulated variable m*), to influence the objects under control. Thus, the actuator elements are the 'muscle' of a control system while the control logic elements are the 'brain'.

Disturbance inputs w are the variables over which the designer has no control, and perhaps little information is available on their magnitude, functional form, or time of occurrence. The controlled variable y is influenced by both the manipulated variable m and disturbance w.

In those situations where the quantity q, which we really wish to control, is not used to generate feedback signal, the path from y (the quantity which is used to generate feedback signal) to q is provided through the *indirectly controlled system elements block*. For example, in the hydraulic power steering mechanism of Fig. 1.8, the drive linkage block corresponds to indirectly controlled system elements.

The structure shown in Fig. 1.12 defines the basic types of signals and components necessary for the description of any feedback control system; however it must be adapted to the needs of each specific design. Alternative feedback structures will be introduced in Section 1.3.

1.2 THE GENESIS AND ESSENCE OF THE FEEDBACK CONTROL THEORY

From the simple and familiar examples of automatic control systems presented in Section 1.1, conclusions can be derived regarding the characteristics common to these systems, notwithstanding their manifestable heterogeneity. Automatic control systems share the following general features:

1. The principle of operation of the system uses the feedback idea, i.e., there exists a closed loop: error → manipulated variable → controlled variable → error.
2. The primary objective of the system is error self-nulling.

In all practical control systems, the objective of error self-nulling is required to be realized with a prescribed accuracy (steady-state errors, speed of response, etc.). A demand on accuracy, as we shall shortly see, may result in the loss of *stability*.[2] The reconciliation of the requirements of satisfactory accuracy and adequate stability margin is the principal accomplishment of the feedback control theory. Detailed quantitative study of the effects of feedback on control system performance will be taken up in Chapter 4. The objective of the brief qualitative study in this section is to introduce the basic principles of the feedback control theory.

A brief consideration of the origins of the feedback control theory will be in order here. Examples of feedback control systems have been identified dating back to the third century BC. Ktesibios, a Greek living in Alexandria, is credited with building a self-regulating flow device for use in water clocks. Several examples of feedback control systems appear in windmill designs used by the Dutch in the fifteenth century.

The arrival of the machine age was accompanied by a large increase in the number of control system designs. The development of the steam engine led to the requirement for a speed control device to maintain constant speed in the presence of changes in load torque or steam pressure. In 1788, James Watt of Glasgow developed his now famous flyball governor for this purpose. The principle of the flyball governor is still used for speed control applications.

Analytical tools for control problems were first developed by J. C. Maxwell in 1868. Maxwell utilized a linear differential equation approach and derived stability conditions for a third-order system. In 1876, Edward John Routh was able to determine the stability conditions for higher-order systems. A solution to the stability problem was also obtained by Adolf Hurwitz and reported in 1895. Routh and Hurwitz were unaware of each other's work. In 1911, equivalence of the Routh and Hurwitz criteria was established.

From 1900 to 1940, significant developments occurred in large-scale power generation, aeronautics, chemical industries, and electronics. The development of the vacuum-tube amplifier, in particular, resulted in many analytical techniques for the design of feedback systems.

One of the key problems in electronics, especially since its application to long-distance telephony, was to develop amplifiers with good gain stability. The difficulty stemmed from the considerable scattering of characteristics in the mass-produced electronic tubes and from changes in characteristics taking place in time (e.g., due to emission loss). In 1927, Harold S. Black discovered the negative feedback amplifier as a solution to this problem. Figure 1.13a shows the idea of operation. A potential-dividing resistor delivers a part of the amplifier's output voltage y to the amplifier's input, where it is subtracted from input voltage r. Figure 1.13b gives the equivalent block diagram of the system. It follows from this diagram that

---

2. Stability is a notion that describes whether the system will be able to follow the input command (Chapter 5). In a nonrigorous sense, a system is said to be unstable if its output is out of control or increases without bound.

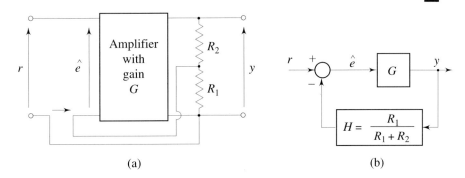

(a)   (b)

Fig. 1.13 *Amplifier with feedback*

$$y = G(r - Hy)$$

The closed-loop gain

$$M = \frac{y}{r} = \frac{1}{\dfrac{1}{G} + H}$$

This equation, specifying the relationship between the closed-loop gain M, the open-loop gain G, and the feedback gain H, is crucial for the feedback theory which was developed in electronics (the studies of Harry Nyquist and Hendrik W. Bode in the 1930s) and which relied heavily on the then widely fostered frequency methods of analysis. The most important observation from this equation which determines feedback performance is that

$$M \cong \frac{1}{H} = \frac{R_1 + R_2}{R_1} \quad \text{for} \quad \frac{1}{G} \ll H \quad \text{or} \quad GH \gg 1$$

where GH denotes the feedback-loop gain. It follows that under the conditions of strong feedback ($GH \gg 1$), the closed-loop gain M does not depend upon the open-loop gain G; it depends only on the potential-dividing resistor. The gain M is practically constant even if gain G varies to a considerable extent, as long as it remains sufficiently high. Thus, by making use of feedback, it has become possible to convert an amplifier with very high but unsteady gain into an amplifier with a lower but steady gain, and furthermore the higher the gain G, the more steady is M. On the other hand, an excessive increase of G results in the loss of stability. The reconciliation of the requirements of satisfactory performance and adequate stability margins was first the central problem and later the principal accomplishment of the feedback control theory.

During World War II, electronics engineers noticed an analogy between the feedback amplifier and the servomechanism of a radar command post, both in structure and principle of operation, and also with respect to the goal and the basic problem, i.e., reconciliation of the requirements of accuracy and stability. The feedback theory was then successfully applied to the design of servomechanisms, becoming more advanced in the process, and, in this way the *theory* of *servomechanisms* came into being.

The application of the theory of servomechanisms to the process industry led to the *feedback control theory*. At about the same time, Norbert Wiener founded *cybernetics* as the new field of study which transplanted elements of the feedback theory to economics, biology and other sciences.

Frequency-response methods have dominated the control systems area since the late 1940s as analysis and design tools. The Nyquist and Bode diagrams became indispensable for assessing closed-loop stability of feedback control systems. Evans' root-locus method brought the complex variable based approach to a fully developed state by 1948. A mature *classical* control systems engineering area thus evolved.

Further advances in control systems engineering resulted from the space programme and associated challenges—launching, maneuvering, guidance, and tracking of space vehicles. The emergence of a *modern* control theory based on state-space ideas is generally traced back to the early 1960s.

After this brief consideration of the origins of the feedback control theory, let us focus our attention on the requirement of reconciling accuracy and stability, which makes the existence of a uniform feedback control theory fully justifiable. We have already considered one example—the electronic amplifier, wherein strong feedback results in insensitivity to variations in parameters of electronic tube. There is however an upper limit on the improvement of performance beyond which stability suffers. In the following we consider more examples.

Example 1.5

Servomechanism for Steering of Antenna

One of the earliest applications of radar tracking was for anti-aircraft fire control, first with guns and later with missiles. Today many civilian applications exist as well, such as satellite-tracking radars, navigation-aiding radars, etc.

The radar scene includes the radar itself, a target, and the transmitted waveform that travels to the target and back. Information about the target's spatial position is first obtained by measuring the changes in the back-scattered waveform relative to the transmitted waveform. The time shift provides information about the target's range, the frequency shift provides information about the target's radial velocity, and the received voltage magnitude and phase provide information about the target's angle[3] [1].

In a typical radar application, it is necessary to point the radar antenna toward the target and follow its movements. The radar sensor detects the error between the antenna axis and the target, and directs the antenna to follow the target. The servomechanism for steering the antenna in response to commands from radar sensor is considered here. The antenna is designed for two inde-

---

3. The bracketed numbers are keyed to the list of references given at the end of the book.

pendent angular motions, one about the vertical axis in which the azimuth angle is varied, and the other about the horizontal axis in which the elevation angle is varied (Fig. 1.14). The servomechanism for steering the antenna is described by two controlled variables—the azimuth angle β and the elevation angle α. The desired values or commands are the azimuth angle β_r and the elevation angle α_r of the target. The feedback control problem involves error self-nulling under conditions of disturbances beyond our control (such as wind power).

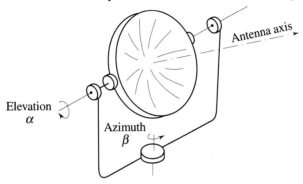

Fig. 1.14 *Antenna configuration*

The control system for steering antenna can be treated as two independent systems—the azimuth-angle servomechanism, and the elevation-angle servomechanism. This is because the interaction effects are usually small. The operational diagram of the azimuth-angle servomechanism is shown in Fig. 1.15. The steering command from the radar sensor which corresponds to the target azimuth angle is compared with the azimuth angle of the antenna axis. The occurrence of the azimuth-angle error causes an error signal to pass through the amplifier, which increases the angular velocity of the servomotor in a direction towards an error reduction. In the scheme of Fig. 1.15, the measurement and processing of signals (calculation of control signal) is digital in

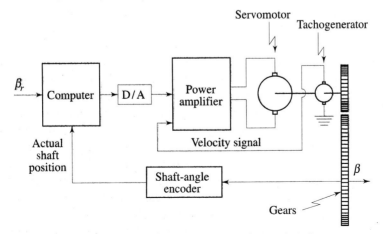

Fig. 1.15 *Azimuthal servomechanism for steering of antenna*

nature and is based on proportional control logic. Figure 1.16a gives the functional block diagram of the control system. A simple model of the load (antenna) on the motor is shown in Fig. 1.16b. The moment of inertia J and the viscous friction coefficient B are the parameters of the assumed model. The nominal load is included in the plant model for the control design. The main disturbance input is the deviation of the load from the nominal estimated value as a result of uncertainty in our estimate, effect of wind power, etc.

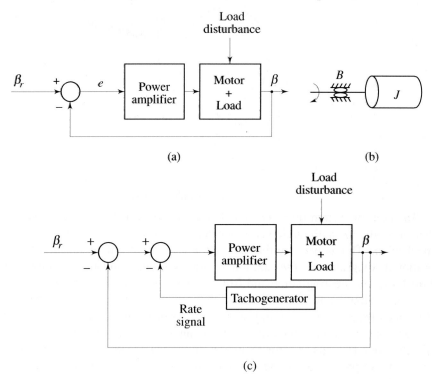

Fig. 1.16 *Functional block diagram of azimuthal servomechanism*

In the tracking system of Fig. 1.16a, the occurrence of error causes the motor to rotate in a direction favouring the dissolution of error. Note that the components of our system cannot respond instantaneously since any real-world system cannot go from one energy level to another in zero time. Thus, in any real-world system there is some kind of dynamic lagging behaviour between the input and the output. In the servosystem of Fig. 1.16a, the control action on the occurrence of the deviation of the controlled output from the desired value (the occurrence of error) will be delayed by the cumulative dynamic lags of the shaft angle encoder, digital computer and digital-to-analog converter, power amplifier, and the servomotor with load. Eventually, however, the trend of the controlled variable deviation from the desired value will be reversed by the action of the amplifier output on the rotation of the motor, returning the controlled variable towards the desired value. Now, if a strong correction (high amplifier gain) is applied (which is desirable from the point of view of control system performance, e.g., strong correction improves the speed of response (Chapter 4)), the controlled variable overshoots the desired value (the 'run-out' of the motor towards an error with the opposite rotation), causing a reversal in the algebraic sign of the system error. Unfortunately, because of system dynamic lags, a reversal of correction does not occur immediately and the amplifier output (acting on 'old' information) is now actually driving the controlled variable in the same direction as it is already going, rather than opposing its excursions, leading to a larger deviation. Eventually, the reversed error does cause a reversed correction but the controlled variable overshoots the desired value in the opposite direction and the correction is again in the wrong direction. The controlled variable is thus driven alternatively in opposite directions before it settles to an equilibrium condition. This oscillatory state is unacceptable as the behaviour of the antenna-steering servomechanism. The considerable amplifier gain, which is necessary if the high accuracies are to be obtained, aggravates the described unfavourable phenomenon.

The occurrence of these oscillatory effects can be controlled by the application of special compensation feedback. When a signal proportional to motor's angular velocity (called the rate signal) is subtracted from the error signal (Fig. 1.16c), the braking process starts sooner before the error reaches a zero value. The 'loop within a loop' (velocity feedback system embedded within a position feedback system) configuration utilized in this application is a classical scheme called *cascade control* in the process field and *minor-loop feedback* (or *state variable feedback*) in servomechanisms.[4]

Example 1.6

Variable Speed dc Drive

Many industrial applications require variable speed drives. For example, variable speed drives are used for pumping duty to vary flow rate or pumping pressure, rolling mills, harbour cranes, rail traction, etc. [2–4].

The variable speed dc drive is the most versatile drive available. The silicon controlled rectifiers (SCR) are almost universally used to control the speed of dc motors because of the considerable benefits that accrue from the compact static controllers supplied directly from the ac mains.

Basically all the dc systems involving the SCR controllers are similar but with different configurations of the devices, different characteristics may be obtained from the controller. Figure 1.17 shows a dc motor driven by a full-wave rectified supply. Armature current of the dc motor is controlled by an SCR which is in turn controlled by the pulses applied by the SCR trigger control circuit.

---

4. This and other compensation schemes will be discussed in Chapter 4.

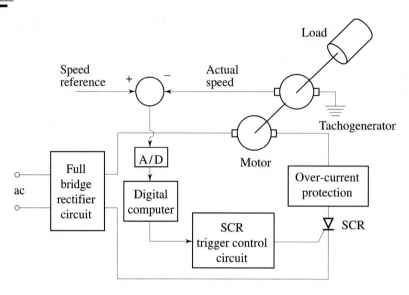

Fig. 1.17 *Variable speed dc drive*

Firing angle of the SCR controls the average armature current which in turn controls the speed of the dc motor. The average armature current (speed) increases as the trigger circuit reduces the delay angle of firing of the SCR, and the average armature current (speed) reduces as the delay angle of firing of the SCR is increased.

In the scheme of Fig. 1.17, the reference voltage which corresponds to the desired speed of the dc motor, is compared with the output voltage of the tachogenerator corresponding to the actual speed of the motor. The occurrence of the error in speed causes an error signal to pass through the trigger circuit which controls the firing angle of the SCR in a direction towards an error reduction. When the processing of the error signal (calculation of the control signal) is based on the proportional control logic, a steady-state error between the actual speed and the desired speed exists (Chapter 4). The occurrence of the steady-state error can be eliminated by generating the control signal with two components: one component proportional to the error signal, and the other proportional to the integral of the error signal. This proportional-integral control logic will be examined in detail in Chapter 4.

▲▲

A point which needs a special mention here is that the presence of disturbances is the main reason for using feedback control. Without disturbances, there is probably no need for feedback control. Table 1.1 gives the details of commonly occurring disturbances in the control system examples considered earlier.

Table 1.1 *Disturbances in specific feedback control systems*

Feedback control system	Disturbance in controlled system	Measurement noise
Bathroom toilet tank	Outflow	Float swaying
Hydraulic power steering mechanism	Vehicle load, resistance to motion	Mechanical vibrations
Residential heating system	Ambient temperature	Mechanical vibrations of bimetallic strip
Servomechanism for steering of antenna	Wind power	Target surface fluctuations
Variable speed dc drive	Variations in load on dc motor	Mechanical vibrations

Other disturbances which affect the performance of control systems are:

(i) uncertainty in our estimate of the hardware parameters of the process and other components of the control system (the estimates of the parameters arc used for the design of controller); and

(ii) changes in the parameters taking place in time (due to wear, ageing, environmental effects, etc.), thereby affecting the dynamic characteristics of the system.

As we shall see later in this book, feedback control systems:

(i) greatly reduce the effect on the controlled variable of all external disturbances except those associated with the sensor (measurement system); and

(ii) are tolerant of variations in hardware parameters other than those of the sensor.

The feedback signal coming from the sensor of controlled variable contains useful information related to disturbances (external disturbances and variations in hardware parameters), which is usually of relatively low frequency. It may often include high frequency 'noise' introduced by the measurement sensors. Such noise signals are too fast for the control system to correct; *low-pass filtering* is often needed to allow good control performance.

1.3 FEEDFORWARD-FEEDBACK CONTROL STRUCTURE

This section presents the principle of one of the most profitable control schemes: *feedforward control*. In earlier sections, we studied the principle of feedback control; a very simple technique that compensates for any disturbance affecting the controlled variable. When a disturbance enters the process, the controlled variable deviates from its desired value (set-point) and, on sensing the error, the feedback controller manipulates the process input in a way favouring the dissolution of error. The main limitation of a feedback control system is that in order for it to compensate for disturbances, the controlled variable must first deviate from its desired value. Feedback control acts upon an error between the set-point and the controlled variable. This means that once a disturbance enters a process, it must propagate through the process and force the controlled variable to deviate from the set-point before corrective action can be taken.

Feedforward control compensates for disturbances before they affect the controlled variable. In this scheme, the disturbances are measured before they enter the process and required value of the manipulated variable to maintain the controlled variable at its desired value is calculated; implementation of such a control results in undisturbed controlled variable. Design of this type of control scheme does not generally require any specialized control theory; basic system dynamics are sufficient in most cases. Success of *disturbance feedforward* control schemes depends on our ability to:

(i) measure the disturbance; and
(ii) estimate the effect of the disturbance on the controlled variable, so that we can compensate for it.

Let us consider an example of disturbance-feedforward.

Example 1.7 _____

Heat Exchanger

The schematic diagram of a heat exchanger is shown in Fig. 1.18. The process fluid flows inside the tubes of the heat exchanger and is heated by steam condensing on the outside of the tubes. The objective is to control the outlet temperature θ of the process fluid in the presence of variations[5] in process fluid flow Q and its inlet temperature θ_i. The objective of controlling the outlet temperature in the presence of disturbances can be accomplished by setting up a feedback control loop as shown in Fig. 1.18a. The flow controller consists of an electronic amplifier and an electropneumatic transducer, which converts the voltage corresponding to the error between the controlled temperature and its set-point value to a pneumatic pressure variable (based on proportional control

---

5. In a typical application, the heat exchanger is a part of the overall system; disturbances in Q and θ_i are caused by other processing operations taking place in the system (in the next section, we will study a distillation system wherein the heat exchanger is a sub-system). ·

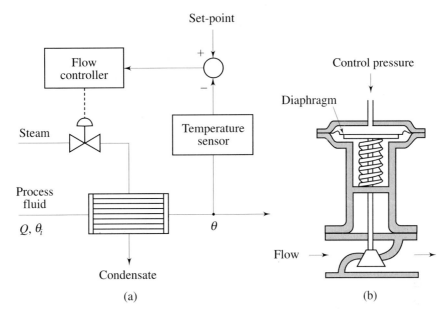

Fig. 1.18   *Feedback control loop for heat exchanger*

logic). The error voltage is derived from the output voltage of the temperature sensor (corresponding to the output temperature θ) and the set-point voltage corresponding to the desired temperature. The pneumatic pressure actuates a pneumatic valve[6], whose essential features are shown in Fig. 1.18b. The actuator section of the valve comprises a diaphragm whose position is set by the balance between the force exerted by a spring and the controller output pressure on the diaphragm.

In the control scheme of Fig. 1.18a, the feedback controller, which manipulates the heat input to the heat exchanger, will not act until an error has developed. If the system involves large time lags, it will take some time before any corrective action takes place.

If feedforward control is provided in such a system, then as soon as a change in Q and/or θ_i occurs, a corrective measure will be taken simultaneously by manipulating the heat input to the heat exchanger. Figure 1.19 shows the disturbance-feedforward control scheme.

Feedforward control can minimize the transient error. However, since it is an open-loop control, there are limitations to its functional accuracy. Feedforward control will not cancel the effects of unmeasurable disturbances.

---

6. By far, the most common form of valve used in process control is the pneumatic actuating valve which can provide large power output. Pneumatic systems use a readily available working medium—compressed air supplies, and are commonly used in process industry because of their explosion-proof characteristics, simplicity and ease of maintenance.

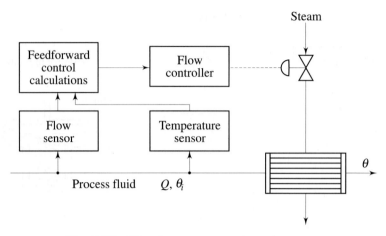

Fig. 1.19 *Disturbance compensated open-loop system*

It is therefore necessary that a feedforward control system include a feedback loop as shown in Fig. 1.20. Essentially, the feedforward control minimizes the transient error caused by measurable disturbances, while the feedback loop compensates for any imperfections in the functioning of the feedforward control and provides corrections for unmeasurable disturbances.

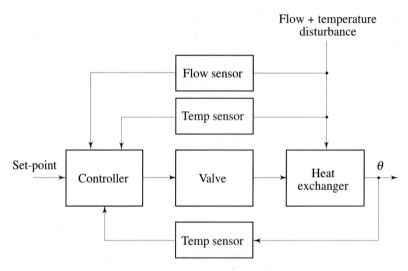

Fig. 1.20 *Feedforward–feedback control structure for the heat exchanger*

▲▲

Another control scheme using the feedforward concept is the *command-feedforward* in combination with feedback loop (Fig. 1.21). Here, based on the knowledge of process characteristics, the command is augmented by command-compensator to produce improved performance. Command-feedforward has been used in several ways for servo applications. In the next section, we will give a combined feedforward-feedback scheme employing command feedforward for the angular motion control of a robot manipulator.

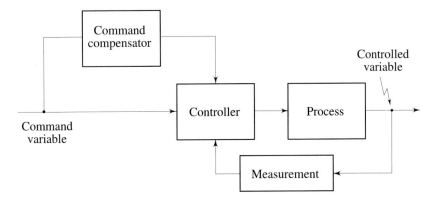

Fig. 1.21 *A control scheme employing command feedforward*

1.4 | MULTIVARIABLE CONTROL SYSTEMS

Complex processes and machines often have several variables (outputs) that we wish to control, and several manipulated inputs available to provide this control. Sometimes the control situation is simple; one input affects primarily one output and has only weak effect on the other outputs. In such situations, it is possible to ignore weak *interactions* (*coupling*) and design controllers under the assumption that one input affects only one output. Input–output pairing to minimize the effect of interactions and application of SISO control schemes to obtain separate controllers for each input–output pair, results in an acceptable performance. This, in fact, amounts to considering the multivariable system as consisting of an appropriate number of separate SISO systems. Coupling effects are considered as disturbances to the separate control systems and may not cause significant degradation in their performance if the coupling is weak. We have already discussed examples of multivariable systems of this nature—the automobile driving system (Example 1.2), and the antenna stabilization system (Example 1.5).

A multivariable system is said to have strong interactions (coupling) if one input affects more than one output appreciably. There are two approaches for the design of controllers for such systems.

1. Design a *decoupling controller* to cancel the interactions inherent in the system. Consider the resulting multivariable system as consisting of an appropriate number of SISO systems, and design a controller for each system.
2. Design a single controller for the multivariable system taking interactions into account.

In this section, we give examples of multivariable systems with strong interactions. These and many other important applications are difficult to present convincingly in an introductory text since their dynamic modelling is too complex to be accommodated. We will therefore only highlight salient features of these control systems. Selected titles for detailed study are [123–134].

Example 1.8

Distillation System

The purification of materials is a prominent operation of the chemical industry. There is scarcely any chemical process which does not require preliminary purification of raw materials or final separation of products from by-products. The towers of a modern petroleum refinery are the evidence of the important role played by these separations in a processing plant.

Figure 1.22 is a schematic diagram of a bubble-cup tray tower used for distillation [13].

Distillation is a method of separating the components of a liquid mixture by the repeated systematic application of vaporization and condensation. For example, if a liquid solution of ammonia and water is partially vaporized by heating, it is found that the newly created vapour phase and residual liquid both contain ammonia and water, but in proportions which at equilibrium are different for the two phases and different from those in the original solution. The vapour phase is richer in the more volatile component (ammonia) and the residual liquid is richer in the less volatile component (water), compared to the original solution. If the vapour and liquid are separated from each other and the vapour condensed, two solutions, one richer in ammonia and the other richer in water, are obtained. If the process of vaporization and condensation is continued over a number of stages, it eventually produces a product with a very high degree of purity in the more volatile component.

The thermal efficiency of this staged operation can be greatly improved if the energy released when the vapour is condensed in one stage is used to vaporize the liquid in an adjacent stage. If the heat required to vaporize one mole of liquid is equal to the heat that is released when one mole of vapour condenses and is independent of composition, then it is evident that a heat source and sink are needed only at the ends of the cascade.

In the distillation column, the necessary heat transfer is accomplished by the direct contact between vapour and liquid by trays (perforated plates) which are designed so that vapour stream bubbles directly through the liquid as illustrated in Fig. 1.22. The feed (multicomponent, in general) is introduced into a vertical cascade of stages close to its centre. The feed mixes with the 'downcoming' liquid. The liquid at every stage is stripped of the more volatile component by the rising vapour, originally produced at the bottom by partial vaporization of the bottom liquid in the reboiler. The liquid residue at the bottom is rich in the less volatile component and is removed. The rising vapour gets progressively enriched in the more volatile component. It is condensed and stored in the reflux accumulator. The material returned at the top of the tower is the reflux and the material removed from the reflux accumulator is the distillate which is rich in more volatile component.

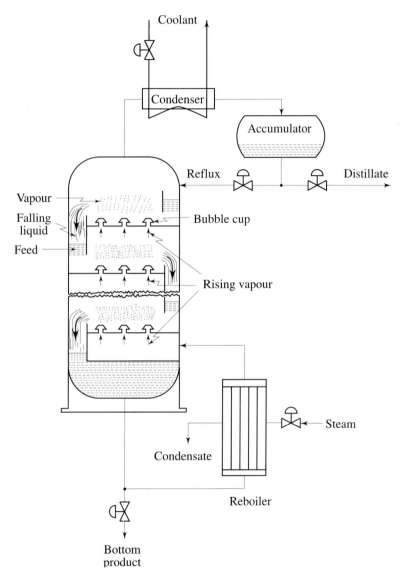

Fig. 1.22 *A distillation column with five primary controlled variables: two compositions, two levels, and pressure*

Let us now consider a simple control scheme for the distillation system. The two main objectives of the control are to maintain two product compositions, x_D (overhead (distillate) product composition) and x_B (bottom product composition), at their set points. The three secondary objectives are to maintain the vapour balance by controlling the column pressure and the liquid balances by controlling the levels in the reflux accumulator and the column bottom.

In the control scheme shown in Figs 1.23–1.24, the distillate rate is manipulated to control the level of reflux accumulator, and the bottom rate is manipulated to control the bottom level. The two variables do not affect the operation of the column directly; the level control systems may therefore be treated as independent SISO systems.

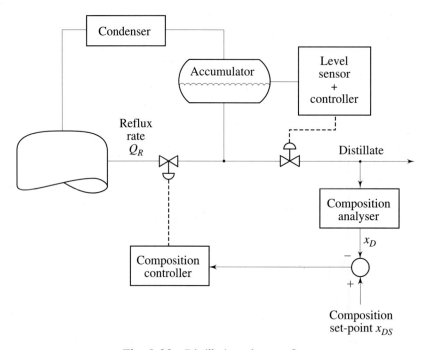

Fig. 1.23   *Distillation-column reflux*

In a column, the pressure is determined solely by the heat balance. If heat is supplied in the reboiler at a higher rate than it is removed in the condenser, the pressure in the column rises with time. Column pressure can be controlled by manipulating the reboiler heating rate or condenser cooling rate. We will assume that the pressure controller manipulates the condenser cooling rate and results in a non-interacting control loop (not shown in figures).

This reduces the problem to a two-by-two multivariable control problem: the manipulated variables are steam rate Q_S and reflux rate Q_R, and the controlled variables are the bottom product composition x_B and the distillate composition x_D. Figure 1.25 shows a block diagram representation of the resulting two-input, two-output system. Changes in the input variable Q_R cause responses in both the outputs, x_D and x_B. Similarly, input variable Q_S affects x_B as well as x_D.

In this book we will consider many examples of liquid-level, temperature, pressure, and composition control systems. SISO design techniques will provide control logic in large number of cases.

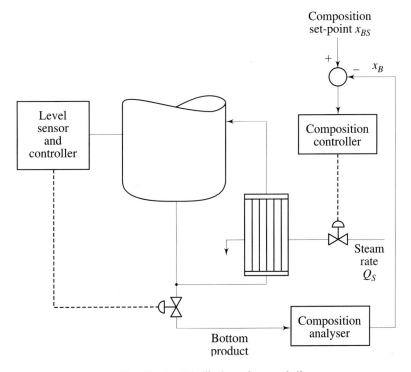

Fig. 1.24 *Distillation-column reboiler*

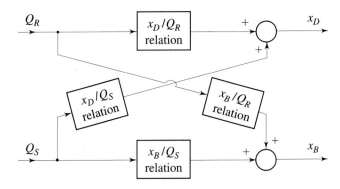

Fig. 1.25 *Block diagram representation of the multivariable control of a distillation column*

Example 1.9

Aircraft Stability and Control

Aircraft control is one of the most important applications through which control system techniques have developed. In aircraft control systems, the 'airframe' acts as a 'plant'; the behaviour of which is to be controlled. Main parts of an airframe include (Fig. 1.26):

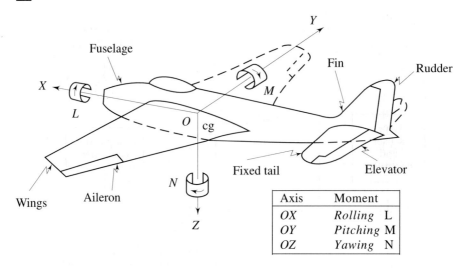

Fig. 1.26 *Control surfaces of an airframe*

Axis	Moment
OX	*Rolling* L
OY	*Pitching* M
OZ	*Yawing* N

 (i) fuselage or mainbody;
(ii) wings with ailerons;
(iii) horizontal tail plane with elevator; and
(iv) fin or vertical tail plane with rudder.

Ailerons, elevators and rudders are the control surfaces. A control surface is a movable (hinged) flap which forms a portion of the fixed aerodynamic surface (wing, horizontal tail, vertical tail) and which is employed to vary the lift coefficient of the surface. Figure 1.27 shows aileron deflection; the aileron angle δ_a is defined as the mean value of the angular displacements of the two ailerons. The other two controls which can be manipulated by the pilot are the elevator deflection δ_e and rudder deflection δ_r.

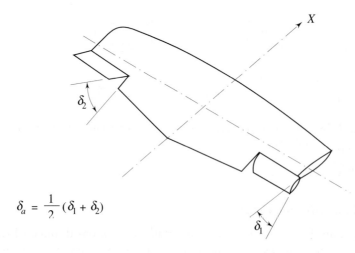

$$\delta_a = \frac{1}{2}(\delta_1 + \delta_2)$$

Fig. 1.27 *Aileron deflection*

In examining the stability and control of a rigid aircraft, it is customary to separate the six degrees of freedom into two groups of three each. One group describes the longitudinal dynamics of the aircraft and comprises the translational motions along the OX- and OZ-axes, and the pitching motion. The other group describes the lateral dynamics of the aircraft and comprises the remaining three degrees of freedom, namely, the translational motion along the OY-axis, and the yawing and rolling motions. The elevator control forces and the throttle affect the longitudinal motion, whereas the aileron and rudder primarily affect the lateral motion. It has been found that for preliminary design work, the coupling of the lateral motion into longitudinal motion can be ignored.

In general, a control functions by causing a change in the pressure distribution on a surface, which results in a change in the lift coefficient of the surface. This change in the lift coefficient causes a change in the moment balance of the aeroplane and results in angular moment about one or more of the axes. The principal control actions of the three control surfaces are :

   (i) the rudder controls yawing, i.e., motion about the OZ-axis;
   (ii) the ailerons control rolling, i.e., motion about the OX-axis; and
   (iii) the elevator controls pitching, i.e., motion about the OY-axis.

The actual positioning of control surfaces is obtained by electric or hydraulic motors which are controlled by the pilot.

Later in this book we shall analyse aircraft motions (SISO systems) under assumptions which neglect many details but preserve the essential nature of the problem. The servo problem of positioning the control surfaces in response to pilot commands will also be considered. Mathematical modelling of aircraft dynamics is beyond the scope of this book. References [14-18] give a good treatment of the subject.

Example 1.10

Robotic Control System

Machines that automatically load and unload, cut, weld or cast are used by industry in order to obtain accuracy, safety, economy, and productivity. Programmable computers integrated with machines that often substitute for human labour in specific repeated tasks, are the modern *robots*.[7] Such devices even have anthropomorphic mechanisms, including what we might recognize as mechanical arms, wrists, and hands.

A *robot manipulator* is made of several links connected usually in series by the joints to form an arm. A link is revolute or prismatic depending upon the type of motion caused by the actuator attached to its joint. When the actuator of a joint causes rotational motion, the link is *revolute*, and when the actuator produces translational motion, the link is called *prismatic*. A gripper, which is

---

7. The word robot seems to originate from the Czech language: robota means compulsory service.

referred to as a hand or an end-effector, is attached to the arm by means of wrist joints. The function of the wrist is to orient the end-effector properly.

The motion of a manipulator end-effector is caused by the movements of the actuators driving the joints. The joint actuators are electric or hydraulic motors, or pneumatically driven devices. The positions of the joints determine the *configuration of the arm*, which places the end-effector at a specific location in the environment. The motion of the joints produced by the actuators determines the position and orientation of the end-effector at any time. Transducers such as encoders and tachometers can be used to provide information for determining the position and orientation of the end-effector and to control the manipulator motion.

The set of all points that can be reached by the end-effector of a manipulator arm forms the *workspace* of the manipulator. A particular position of the end-effector is specified by three independent coordinates, which represent three degrees-of-freedom. Similarly, a specific orientation of the end-effector is determined by three independent variables. Thus, six independent variables are needed to describe the position and orientation of the end-effector. Commercially available robots have typically six joints giving six degrees-of-freedom. However, robots with less than six joints, designed for specific tasks, are also available. Figure 1.28 shows a picture of the PUMA (Programmable Universal Manipulator for Assembly), a revolute manipulator.

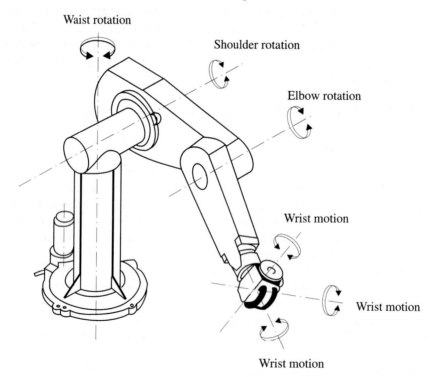

Fig. 1.28   *An industrial robot: PUMA*

The objective in providing position control for a robot manipulator is to design an appropriate controller for the robot motors so that the position and the orientation of the end-effector follow the desired trajectory with no errors even in the presence of disturbances. A multi-link manipulator is a highly complex system—each link of the robot arm has varying inertia and exerts varying torques on all the other links as the configuration of the robot arm changes. The equations of motion for a multi-link manipulator describe a MIMO system; the equations are coupled representing the effects of interactions of the joints. For a six-joint robot, joint positions θ_i, $i = 1, \ldots, 6$ (represented by the position vector θ in Fig. 1.29) are the controlled outputs, and actuator torques u_i, $i = 1, \ldots, 6$ (represented by the input vector $\mathbf{u}$ in Fig. 1.29) are the manipulated variables. θ_r is the position vector corresponding to the desired trajectory.

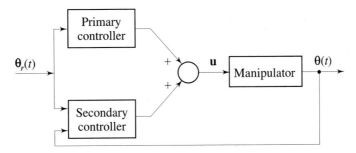

Fig. 1.29 *Manipulator system with primary and secondary controllers*

Perfect tracking can be achieved by a scheme employing command feedforward. Let $\theta_r(t)$ be the input to a feedforward controller with dynamics which are inverse of the dynamics of the manipulator. When the manipulator is driven by the output of such a controller, we get $\theta(t) = \theta_r(t)$. The command-tracking based on this *inverse dynamics* concept can be perfect only if we can exactly determine the dynamic model of the manipulator.

The robotic system is too complex to allow exact identification of the dynamic model. Also, the system is subject to unmeasurable disturbances. Undesirable deviations of the actual motion of the manipulator from the desired trajectory can be corrected by means of feedback control. A block diagram showing the total control system (primary controller (feedforward) and secondary controller (feedback)) is displayed in Fig. 1.29.

The problem of control of the multi-link manipulator is too complex to be included in this introductory text. To bring robot application into our range, we will consider the problem of control of a single-link manipulator (SISO system). Selected titles for further reading are [19–24].

1.5 | SCOPE AND ORGANIZATION OF THE BOOK

This text is concerned with basic concepts of feedback control theory, frequency-domain design tools, and analog/digital implementation of design. We do not intend to solve all the control problems that can be posed under the defined category. In fact, we primarily study a special class of control systems, namely linear, time-invariant, lumped, and deterministic systems. For this class of systems, a fairly complete treatment of the control problem has been given in this book. The development of the material has been influenced by several existing books mentioned in the references given at the end of this text.

There are 11 chapters in the book in addition to this introductory chapter. In each chapter, analysis/design examples are interspersed to illustrate the concepts involved. At the end of each chapter, there are a number of review examples and questions; some of these also serve the purpose of extending the text material. The same approach is followed in unsolved problems. Answers have been given to inspire confidence in the reader.

The examples we have considered in this book are generally low-order systems. Such a selection of examples helps in conveying the fundamental concepts of feedback control without the distraction of large amounts of computations inherent in high-order systems. Many of the real-life design problems are more complex than the ones discussed in this book; high-order systems are common and, in addition, several parameters are to be varied during the design stage to investigate their effect on the system performance. Computer-Aided-Design (CAD) tools are extremely useful for complex control problems. Several software packages with computer graphics are available commercially for CAD of control systems [169–179]. Access to the CAD software is helpful, but not necessary, to solve the control problems discussed in this book. Let us now go through the organization of the chapters in sequence.

Chapter 2 combines some mathematical background with physical system modelling. Basic principles for modelling simple mechanical, electrical, hydraulic and thermal systems are treated, and transfer function and state variable models are derived. The analysis of transfer function models is also given. The analysis of state variable models, and their relationship to transfer functions is deferred to Chapter 12. References for Chapter 2 are [37–43].

Chapter 3 covers the mathematical models of different devices currently in use in industrial control practice. Models of typical industrial control systems are also included. The choice of examples is based on a desire to cover as many different application areas as possible. Devices used in computer-based control systems are covered later in Chapter 11. References for Chapter 3 are [44 – 57].

Chapter 4 introduces the basic modes of feedback control—proportional (P), integral (I), and derivative (D). A suitable combination of the three basic modes can improve all aspects of system performance. Characteristic performance features of commonly used control structures are also included in this chapter.

The material on stability has been progressively built in this book at three places. Chapter 5 introduces the two basic concepts of stability—BIBO (bounded-input, bounded-output) stability and asymptotic stability, as applied to linear time-invariant systems and presents the Routh stability criterion for stability analysis. More on stability analysis appears later in Chapters 8 and 12.

Chapter 6 gives control system performance specifications in time-domain. A number of performance measures for speed of response, relative stability, and steady-state accuracy are introduced.

Control system design has always relied heavily on graphical methods. Chapter 7 develops the root-locus method. Although computer programs are readily available for generating these plots, designers must be able to sketch them first, at least roughly, in order to use the programs efficiently and interpret the results. The material in Chapter 7 has been organized in this spirit. This chapter also uses the root-locus method for compensation; lead, and lag compensation are covered in detail.

Chapter 8 describes the Nyquist stability criterion. Robust stability measures—the gain margin and the phase margin—are introduced in this chapter.

Chapter 9 gives control system performance specifications in the frequency-domain. Correlation between time- and frequency-response is also established.

Chapter 10 uses frequency-response plots—Bode plot, and Nichols chart, for compensator design. Lead and lag compensation are covered in detail. References for the material in Chapters 4–10 are [58–77].

Chapter 11 is concerned with implementation of compensators by physical devices—passive electrical networks, op amp based networks, and digital computers. A modest investment in digital methods has been made so that the control engineer can work well in increasingly digital environment. References for digital control are [78–101].

The practice of selecting a certain class of controller (P, PI, PID) based on past experience with certain classes of processes (pressure, flow, liquid-level, temperature, etc.) and then setting controller parameters by experiment once the controller is installed, has come to be known as controller tuning. Chapter 11 also includes this 'experimental' design method for both analog and digital controllers. References for process control are [5–13].

Many computer aided design packages use state-space and matrix notation, and therefore it is helpful for control engineers to be familiar with it. Chapter 12 on state variable analysis meets this objective. It deals with the problems of state variable representation, solution, controllability, and observability. Relationship between transfer function and state variable models is also given. Although it is assumed that the reader has necessary background on vector-matrix analysis, a reasonably detailed account of vector-matrix analysis is provided in the chapter for convenient reference. References for state variable methods are [102–115].

The text presumes on the part of the reader some knowledge of basic tools like complex variables, and the Laplace transform. However, Appendix A on mathematical background has been included to make the book reasonably self-contained. Appendix B provides an introduction to the MATLAB environment for computer-aided control system design. MATLAB problems included in the appendix give the student practice with problem solving using computers. Multiple choice questions given in Appendix C serve the purpose of self-appraisal review of control theory.

chapter 2
Dynamic Models and Dynamic Response

2.1 | INTRODUCTION

Modelling of physical systems is an important component of the control system design procedure. The present chapter reviews the basic laws of physics used to develop mathematical models of mechanical, electrical, hydraulic, and thermal systems that are commonly encountered in control systems as plant models or as models of control logic elements. The next chapter deals with the models of actuators, measurement sensors, and error detectors. The models of overall control systems are then developed by considering the interaction of these devices. Models of digital devices used in automatic control systems are discussed in Chapter 11.

An alternative approach of modelling is to regard the physical system as merely a 'black box', into which one can inject inputs and from which one can obtain measurements of the corresponding outputs. We then use this data to obtain a mathematical model of the system which produces the same outputs from the given inputs. This approach of modelling is known in the literature as *system identification*. Some simple identification methods will appear in later chapters.

▲▲

Different types of dynamic models used to represent control systems are classified below:

Distributed-parameter and Lumped-parameter Models

The significant variables in a system are distributed in space and they vary with the spatial coordinates and time. The resulting dynamic models, called *distributed-parameter models*, consist of partial differential equations with time and space coordinates as independent variables.

In *lumped-parameter models*, the matter is assumed to be lumped at some discrete points of the space, or the space is subdivided into cells and the matter is assumed to be lumped at these cells. The resulting dynamic models are ordinary differential equations with time as the only independent variable. For example, the assumption that a solid is a rigid body permits lumping all its mass at its mass centre and results in lumped-parameter models of dynamics.

Considerable simplification is achieved in mathematical models when lumped-parameter models are used. In this book, we employ lumped-parameter models for control system design.

Stochastic and Deterministic Models

In physical systems, every signal (inputs, external disturbances, measured outputs) has associated with it certain amount of randomness (usually referred to by the generic term 'noise'). These uncertainties are inconsequential in many practical cases, and we proceed as though all signals are known functions of time. This assumption gives us a *deterministic model* of the system. When signals must be treated as random functions of time, *stochastic models* are used to characterize the system behaviour. In this book, we will make the assumption of deterministic signals.

Time-varying and Time-invariant Models

When the parameters of the mathematical model are varying with time, the model is called *time-varying* or non-stationary. For example, in the guidance and control of a rocket, the mass of the rocket changes with time due to the depletion of fuel, and also the aerodynamic damping can change with time as the air density changes with altitude. The complexity of the control system design increases considerably when the parameters are time-varying.

In this book, we shall concern ourselves with those applications where the time-invariance assumption can safely be made, and therefore the models we use will have constant parameters.

Nonlinear and Linear Models

The mathematical model of a system is *linear*, if it obeys the principle of *superposition and homogeneity*. This principle implies that if a system model has responses $y_1(t)$ and $y_2(t)$ to any two inputs $r_1(t)$ and $r_2(t)$ respectively, then the system response to the linear combination of these inputs, i.e.,

$$\alpha_1 r_1(t) + \alpha_2 r_2(t); \; \alpha_1, \alpha_2 \text{ constants},$$

is given by the linear combination of the individual outputs, i.e.,

$$\alpha_1 y_1(t) + \alpha_2 y_2(t)$$

Powerful mathematical tools that provide general methods of analysis and design are available for *linear systems*. For *nonlinear systems*, general methods are not available and each system must be studied as one of a kind. Practically none of the systems is completely linear, but a linear model is often appropriate over certain ranges of operation.

In control systems, nonlinearities can be classified as *incidental* and *intentional*. Incidental nonlinearities are those which are inherently present in the system and are introduced by the controlled process, sensors, actuators, controllers, etc. The designer strives to design the system so as to limit the adverse effects of these nonlinearities. The intentional nonlinearities, on the other hand, are those which are deliberately inserted in the system to modify system characteristics. The most common example is that of on-off control systems.

Linearization over desired ranges of operation is usually possible and we will mostly employ linear models for systems with incidental nonlinearities. For situations where this approximation becomes too crude to be employed and/or nonlinearities are deliberately introduced, powerful mathematical tools—the *describing function method* and the *phase-plane method*, may be employed [180].

In this book, we will be mainly concerned with linear, time-invariant, lumped systems. Application of physical laws to such a system, as we shall see in this chapter, results in a set of ordinary differential equations which directly provide us with the rates of change of significant variables characterizing the dynamics of the system. These differential equations when rearranged in the form of a set of first-order differential equations, are called *state equations*. Laplace transformation of these differential equations with zero initial conditions gives us *transfer function* representation.

Through the examples given in this chapter, it will become clear that to obtain a transfer function model, one first writes the state equations of the system which 'naturally' arise from the application of physical laws. State variable modelling is thus a 'natural' step required for transfer function modelling.

State variable analysis and design methods use matrix theory and are, to some extent, different from those based on transfer function models. We have separated state variable methods from those based on transfer functions. State variable methods are covered in Chapter 12 while rest of the book uses the transfer function approach.

The presence of disturbances is one of the main reasons for using feedback control. Without disturbances, there is probably no need for feedback control. The character of the disturbances imposes fundamental limitations on the performance of a control system.

The disturbances may be classified as load disturbances, measurement errors, and parameter variations. *Load disturbances* are external disturbances from the process environment which influence the process variables. *Measurement errors* enter through the measuring instruments (sensors). Disturbances also enter in the form of *variations in the parameters* due to wear and tear, ageing, environmental effects, etc., or due to unmodelled dynamics. In Chapter 4, we will study the effects of these disturbances on control system performance.

In the present chapter simple, yet effective, models of load disturbances are given. Transfer functions of disturbance variables (uncontrolled inputs) on the output variables of industrial plants have been derived for commonly occurring load disturbances.

A review of the study of dynamic response of linear time-invariant systems using Laplace transforms has also been given in this chapter.

2.2 | STATE VARIABLE MODELS

In this and the next two sections, three different forms of mathematical models for linear time-invariant lumped systems will be introduced. Depending upon the requirements of analysis or the design techniques used, one form of model might be preferable to another in describing the same system. Since we study only time-invariant systems, we shall assume, without loss of generality, that the initial time is zero ($t_0 = 0$) and that the time interval of interest is $[0, \infty)$, i.e., $\{0 \leq t < \infty\}$.

Consider the resistance-inductance-capacitance (RLC) network shown in Fig. 2.1. The input is a voltage source. The desired output information is usually the voltages and currents associated with various elements of the network. This information at time t can be obtained if the voltage across the capacitor and the current through the inductor of the network at that time are known, in addition to the values of the input. The voltage $e(t)$ across the capacitor and the current $i(t)$ through the inductor thus constitute a set of *characterizing variables* of the network. The selection of characterizing variables is linked with the energy concept. At time t, energy stored in the capacitor is $\frac{1}{2}Ce^2(t)$ and energy stored in the inductor is $\frac{1}{2}Li^2(t)$. Dynamical changes in characterizing variables are caused by the redistribution of energy within the network. The number of independent energy storage possibilities thus equals the number of characterizing variables of the network. The values of the characterizing variables at time t describe the *state* of the network at that time; these variables are therefore called *state variables* of the network.

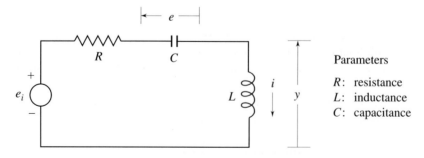

Fig. 2.1 *An RLC network*

Network analysis usually requires setting up of dynamical equations (using Kirchhoff's voltage and current laws) in terms of rates of change of capacitor voltages and inductor currents. The solution of these equations describes the state of the network at time t. Desired output information is then obtained from the state using an algebraic relation.

Let us set up dynamical equations for the RLC network of Fig. 2.1, by using Kirchhoff's voltage law. The governing equations of the system are

$$Ri(t) + e(t) + L\frac{di(t)}{dt} = e_i(t); \quad C\frac{de(t)}{dt} = i(t)$$

Rearrangement of these equations gives the rates of change of capacitor voltage and inductor current.

$$\left.\begin{aligned}
\frac{de(t)}{dt} &= \frac{1}{C}i(t) \\
\frac{di(t)}{dt} &= -\frac{1}{L}e(t) - \frac{R}{L}i(t) + \frac{1}{L}e_i(t)
\end{aligned}\right\} \tag{2.1a}$$

The solution of these equations for given input $e_i(t)$ applied at $t = 0^+$, and given initial state $\{e(0), i(0)\}$ yields the state $\{e(t), i(t)\}$, $t > 0$. If $y(t)$ shown in Fig. 2.1 is the desired output information, we have the following algebraic relation to obtain $y(t)$:

$$y(t) = -e(t) - Ri(t) + e_i(t) \tag{2.1b}$$

Equations (2.1a) give the rates of change of state variables (capacitor voltage $e(t)$, and inductor current $i(t)$) in terms of the state variables and the input. These equations are called the *state equations*. Equation (2.1b) is an instantaneous relation, reading output $y(t)$ from the state variables $\{e(t), i(t)\}$ and the input $e_i(t)$. This equation is called the *output equation*.

It may be noted that the state of a system is not uniquely specified. For the network of Fig. 2.1, the charge $q(t)$ deposited on the capacitor is given by

$$q(t) = Ce(t)$$

Therefore, the variables $q(t)$ and $i(t)$ also qualify as state variables for this network.

In terms of these state variables, the state and output equations are given below:

$$\left.\begin{aligned}
\frac{dq(t)}{dt} &= i(t) \\
\frac{di(t)}{dt} &= -\frac{1}{LC}q(t) - \frac{R}{L}i(t) + \frac{1}{L}e_i(t)
\end{aligned}\right\} \tag{2.2a}$$

$$y(t) = -\frac{1}{C}q(t) - Ri(t) + e_i(t) \tag{2.2b}$$

In mass-spring-damper systems, we are usually interested in the displacements, velocities, and forces associated with various elements of the systems. Normally, an independent set of displacements and velocities of the masses, and displacements of the springs constitutes a set of state variables of the system. The values of these variables at time t describe the status of energy storage elements at that time, and also ensure that the desired output information can be 'read' from the state variables.

For the mass-spring-damper system of Fig. 2.2a, the displacement $x(t)$ and velocity $v(t)$ are state variables. A systematic way of setting up dynamical equations for mass-spring-damper systems is to draw a free-body diagram. In a free-body diagram, each mass is isolated from the rest of the system; forces acting on each free-body are due to the rest of the system, including external forces. The free-body mass moves under the action of the resultant force. By applying Newton's law of motion to each free-body, we get the force equations describing the dynamics of the system.

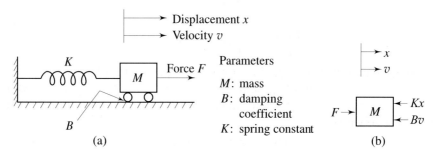

Fig. 2.2 *(a) A mass-spring-damper system*
(b) Free-body diagram

Figure 2.2b shows the free-body diagram of the system of Fig. 2.2a. Applying Newton's law of motion, the force equation can be written as

$$F(t) - Bv(t) - Kx(t) = M\frac{dv(t)}{dt}$$

Since $\qquad\qquad v(t) \overset{\Delta}{=} \dfrac{dx(t)}{dt}$, we have

$$M\frac{d^2x(t)}{dt^2} + B\frac{dx(t)}{dt} + Kx(t) = F(t)$$

Rearrangement of these equations gives the rates of change of displacement $x(t)$ and velocity $v(t)$:

$$\left.\begin{aligned}
\frac{dx(t)}{dt} &= v(t) \\[2mm]
\frac{dv(t)}{dt} &= -\frac{K}{M}x(t) - \frac{B}{M}v(t) + \frac{1}{M}F(t)
\end{aligned}\right\} \qquad (2.3a)$$

The solution of these equations for given input (force $F(t)$) applied at $t = 0^+$ and given initial state $\{x(0), v(0)\}$ yields the state $\{x(t), v(t)\}, t > 0$. If displacement of the mass is the desired output $y(t)$, we have the output equation

$$y(t) = x(t) \tag{2.3b}$$

Examples of hydraulic and thermal systems will appear later in this chapter.

Consider now the general SISO system shown in the block diagram of Fig. 2.3. We will denote the system *state* by n *state variables* $\{x_1(t), x_2(t), ..., x_n(t)\}$. In compact notation, this information may be represented by the *state vector*

$$\mathbf{x}(t) \triangleq \begin{bmatrix} x_1(t) \\ x_2(t) \\ \vdots \\ x_n(t) \end{bmatrix}$$

The dimension of the state vector defines the *order of the system*.

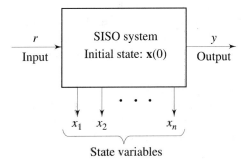

Fig. 2.3 *A SISO system*

The set of equations that describe the relationship among input, output, and the state variables, is called the *state variable model*. For nth order linear time-invariant system, the state variable model takes the form (refer Eqns (2.1), (2.2), (2.3)):

$$\dot{x}_1(t) \triangleq \frac{dx_1(t)}{dt} = a_{11}x_1(t) + a_{12}x_2(t) + \cdots + a_{1n}x_n(t) + b_1 r(t)$$

$$\dot{x}_2(t) \triangleq \frac{dx_2(t)}{dt} = a_{21}x_1(t) + a_{22}x_2(t) + \cdots + a_{2n}x_n(t) + b_2 r(t)$$

$$\vdots$$

$$\dot{x}_n(t) \triangleq \frac{dx_n(t)}{dt} = a_{n1}x_1(t) + a_{n2}x_2(t) + \cdots + a_{nn}x_n(t) + b_n r(t)$$

$$y(t) = c_1 x_1(t) + c_2 x_2(t) + \cdots + c_n x_n(t) + d\, r(t)$$

or in vector-matrix[1] form

$$\dot{\mathbf{x}}(t) = \mathbf{A}\mathbf{x}(t) + \mathbf{b}\, r(t) : \textit{state equation} \tag{2.4a}$$

$$y(t) = \mathbf{c}\mathbf{x}(t) + d\, r(t) : \textit{output equation} \tag{2.4b}$$

with

$$\mathbf{x}(t) = \begin{bmatrix} x_1(t) \\ x_2(t) \\ \vdots \\ x_n(t) \end{bmatrix}; \mathbf{A} = \begin{bmatrix} a_{11} & a_{12} & \cdots & a_{1n} \\ a_{21} & a_{22} & \cdots & a_{2n} \\ \vdots & \vdots & & \vdots \\ a_{n1} & a_{n2} & \cdots & a_{nn} \end{bmatrix}; \mathbf{b} = \begin{bmatrix} b_1 \\ b_2 \\ \vdots \\ b_n \end{bmatrix}$$

$$\mathbf{c} = \begin{bmatrix} c_1 & c_2 & \cdots & c_n \end{bmatrix}$$

where $\mathbf{x}(t)$, $r(t)$ and $y(t)$ are, respectively, the state, the input and the output of a system; $\mathbf{A}$ is $n \times n$ constant matrix; $\mathbf{b}$ is $n \times 1$ constant column vector; $\mathbf{c}$ is $1 \times n$ constant row vector; and d is a constant scalar representing direct coupling between input and output.

Equations (2.4a) are n first-order differential equations expressing time derivatives of each of the components of the state vector $\mathbf{x}(t)$ as a linear combination of system states and input. The solution of these equations for given input $r(t)$ applied at $t = 0^+$, and given initial state $\mathbf{x}(0)$ yields the system state $\mathbf{x}(t)$, $t > 0$. The output $y(t)$ (Eqn. (2.4b)) is a linear combination of system states and input.

Equations (2.4a) and (2.4b) together provide the input-output-state description of a dynamic system, represented diagrammatically in Fig. 2.4. Note that in this model structure, the dynamic evolution of system state in response to initial state $\mathbf{x}(0)$ and input $r(t)$ is obtained; desired output information $y(t)$ is then 'read' from $\mathbf{x}(t)$.

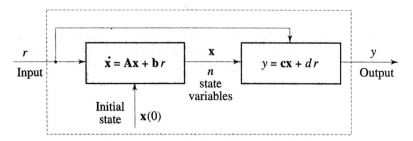

Fig. 2.4 *Input-output-state description*

The general MIMO system is shown in the block diagram of Fig. 2.5. Time functions, $r_1, r_2, \ldots, r_p$ are the input variables, and $y_1, y_2, \ldots, y_q$ are the output

---

1. We will use lower case bold letters to represent vectors, and upper case bold letters to represent matrices.

variables. The state, as in the case of SISO systems, is represented by the variables x_1, x_2, ..., x_n. For notational economy, the different variables may be represented by the input vector $\mathbf{r}(t)$, the output vector $\mathbf{y}(t)$, and the state vector $\mathbf{x}(t)$, where

$$\mathbf{r}(t) = \begin{bmatrix} r_1(t) \\ r_2(t) \\ \vdots \\ r_p(t) \end{bmatrix}; \ \mathbf{y}(t) = \begin{bmatrix} y_1(t) \\ y_2(t) \\ \vdots \\ y_q(t) \end{bmatrix}; \ \mathbf{x}(t) = \begin{bmatrix} x_1(t) \\ x_2(t) \\ \vdots \\ x_n(t) \end{bmatrix}$$

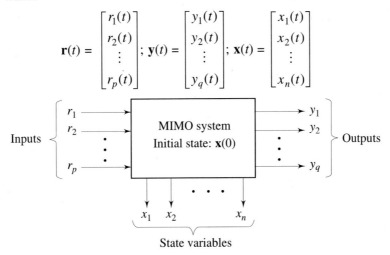

Fig. 2.5 *A MIMO system*

For MIMO systems, the derivative of each state variable becomes a linear combination of system states x_1, x_2, ..., x_n, and the inputs r_1, r_2, ..., r_p. Also, each output variable at time t is a linear combination of the states and the inputs at time t. The state variable model for MIMO systems takes the following form:

$$\dot{\mathbf{x}}(t) = \mathbf{A}\mathbf{x}(t) + \mathbf{B}\mathbf{r}(t) : \textit{state equation} \tag{2.5a}$$
$$\mathbf{y}(t) = \mathbf{C}\mathbf{x}(t) + \mathbf{D}\mathbf{r}(t) : \textit{output equation} \tag{2.5b}$$

with

$$\mathbf{A} = \begin{bmatrix} a_{11} & a_{12} & \cdots & a_{1n} \\ a_{21} & a_{22} & \cdots & a_{2n} \\ \vdots & \vdots & & \vdots \\ a_{n1} & a_{n2} & \cdots & a_{nn} \end{bmatrix}; \ \mathbf{B} = \begin{bmatrix} b_{11} & b_{12} & \cdots & b_{1p} \\ b_{21} & b_{22} & \cdots & b_{2p} \\ \vdots & \vdots & & \vdots \\ b_{n1} & b_{n2} & \cdots & b_{np} \end{bmatrix}$$

$$\mathbf{C} = \begin{bmatrix} c_{11} & c_{12} & \cdots & c_{1n} \\ c_{21} & c_{22} & \cdots & c_{2n} \\ \vdots & \vdots & & \vdots \\ c_{q1} & c_{q2} & \cdots & c_{qn} \end{bmatrix}; \ \mathbf{D} = \begin{bmatrix} d_{11} & d_{12} & \cdots & d_{1p} \\ d_{21} & d_{22} & \cdots & d_{2p} \\ \vdots & \vdots & & \vdots \\ d_{q1} & d_{q2} & \cdots & d_{qp} \end{bmatrix}$$

$\mathbf{A}$, $\mathbf{B}$, $\mathbf{C}$ and $\mathbf{D}$ are respectively. $n \times n$, $n \times p$, $q \times n$ and $q \times p$ constant matrices.

Since every real-world system has some nonlinearity, a mathematical model of the form (2.5) is always an approximation to reality. Many real-world nonlinearities involve a 'smooth' curvilinear relation between an independent variable x and a dependent variable y:

$$y = f(x) \tag{2.6a}$$

A linear approximation to the curve, accurate in the neighbourhood of selected operating point x_0, is the tangent line to the curve at that point. This approximation is given conveniently by the first two terms of the Taylor series expansion of $f(x)$:

$$y = f(x_0) + \left[\frac{df}{dx} \bigg|_{x = x_0} \right](x - x_0) + \left[\frac{d^2 f}{dx^2} \bigg|_{x = x_0} \right] \frac{(x - x_0)^2}{2!} + \cdots$$

The linear approximation is

$$y \cong f(x_0) + \left[\frac{df}{dx} \bigg|_{x = x_0} \right](x - x_0) \tag{2.6b}$$

When a dependent variable y is related nonlinearly to several independent variables x_1, x_2, x_3, etc., according to

$$y = f(x_1, x_2, x_3, \ldots) \tag{2.6c}$$

we may linearize using the multivariable form of the Taylor series:

$$y \cong f(x_{10}, x_{20}, \ldots) + \left[\frac{\partial f}{\partial x_1} \bigg|_{x_{10}, x_{20}, \ldots} \right](x_1 - x_{10})$$

$$+ \left[\frac{\partial f}{\partial x_2} \bigg|_{x_{10}, x_{20}, \ldots} \right](x_2 - x_{20}) + \cdots \tag{2.6d}$$

We will use the linearizing approximations in developing linear state variable models of the form (2.5) from nonlinear relationships of the form given below:

$$\left.
\begin{aligned}
\dot{x}_1(t) &= f_1(x_1(t), x_2(t), \ldots, x_n(t), r_1(t), \ldots, r_p(t)) \\
\dot{x}_2(t) &= f_2(x_1(t), x_2(t), \ldots, x_n(t), r_1(t), \ldots, r_p(t)) \\
&\vdots \\
\dot{x}_n(t) &= f_n(x_1(t), x_2(t), \ldots, x_n(t), r_1(t), \ldots, r_p(t))
\end{aligned}
\right\} \tag{2.7a}$$

$$\left.
\begin{aligned}
y_1(t) &= g_1(x_1(t), x_2(t), \ldots, x_n(t), r_1(t), \ldots, r_p(t)) \\
&\vdots \\
y_q(t) &= g_q(x_1(t), x_2(t), \ldots, x_n(t), r_1(t), \ldots, r_p(t))
\end{aligned}
\right\} \tag{2.7b}$$

where $f_i(\cdot)$, $i = 1, 2, \ldots, n$ are nonlinear functions describing state equations, and $g_j(\cdot)$, $j = 1, 2, \ldots, q$ are nonlinear functions describing output equations.

2.3 | IMPULSE RESPONSE MODELS

Consider the SISO system of Fig. 2.3. The system is excited by two types of inputs; the external input $r(t)$, and the initial state $\mathbf{x}(0)$ representing initial energy storage in the system. The response variables are the state variables $x_1(t)$, $x_2(t), \ldots, x_n(t)$, and the output variable $y(t)$.

In this section, we derive a mathematical model based on the following assumptions/requirements (Fig. 2.6):

   (i) Initial state $\mathbf{x}(0) = \mathbf{0}$, i.e., the output $y(t)$ is solely and uniquely excited by the input $r(t)$ for $t \geq 0$.

A system is said to be *relaxed*[2] at $t_0 = 0$, if $\mathbf{x}(0) = \mathbf{0}$.

(ii) We are interested only in the input–output relation; dynamic evolution of the state $\mathbf{x}(t)$ is not required.

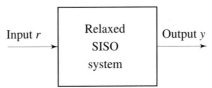

Fig. 2.6 *Input-output description*

The input $r(t)$ and the output $y(t)$ of any linear time-invariant system that is initially relaxed at $t_0 = 0$, can be described by an equation of the form

$$y(t) = \int_0^t g(t - \tau)\, r(\tau)\, d\tau = \int_0^t g(\tau)\, r(t - \tau)\, d\tau \tag{2.8}$$

This is called a *convolution integral*. The second integration is obtained from the first by substituting $\tau' = t - \tau$, and then changing the dummy variable τ' to τ. The function $g(t)$ is defined only for $t \geq 0$ and is called the *impulse response* of the system. In order to derive Eqn. (2.8) and give an interpretation of $g(t)$, we need the concept of impulse function.

A rectangular elementary *pulse function* is defined as

$$p_T(t) = \begin{bmatrix} 1 & \text{for } 0 < t < T \\ 0 & \text{otherwise} \end{bmatrix} \tag{2.9a}$$

Figure 2.7 gives the graphical representation of pulse functions.
$Ap_T(t - t_0)$ is a pulse of height A and duration T occurring at $t = t_0$:

$$Ap_T(t - t_0) = \begin{bmatrix} A & \text{for } 0 < (t - t_0) < T \\ 0 & \text{otherwise} \end{bmatrix} \tag{2.9b}$$

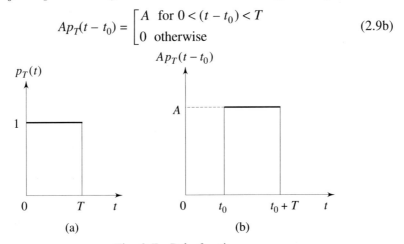

Fig. 2.7 *Pulse functions*

---

2. The case of zero initial conditions is common in control system design because the signals are usually defined as deviations from some initial steady-state. When this is done, the initial-value of the perturbation is, by definition, zero.

Control Systems: Principles and Design

Consider the *unit pulse function*

$$\delta_\Delta(t) = \frac{1}{\Delta} p_\Delta(t) \tag{2.10}$$

It is a pulse of height $\frac{1}{\Delta}$ and duration Δ (i.e., of unit 'area') occurring at $t = 0$.

The properties of $\delta_\Delta(t)$ are such that its height increases whenever its duration decreases, but in such a way that its 'area' thereby remains constant and is equal to unity.

As $\Delta \to 0$, we obtain the limiting 'function'

$$\delta(t) \triangleq \lim_{\Delta \to 0} \delta_\Delta(t) \tag{2.11}$$

which is called the *unit impulse function* or *δ-function*.

Properties of the δ-function are:

$$\delta(t) = \lim_{\Delta \to 0} \delta_\Delta(t) = \begin{bmatrix} 0 \text{ for } t \neq 0 \\ \infty \text{ for } t = 0 \end{bmatrix} \tag{2.12a}$$

$$\int_{-\infty}^{\infty} \delta(t)dt = \int_{-\infty}^{\infty} \lim_{\Delta \to 0} \delta_\Delta(t)dt = 1 \tag{2.12b}$$

From these properties it follows that $\delta(t)$ is not an ordinary function as we cannot assign a value to the dependent variable for each value of the independent variable. The quantitative characteristic of $\delta(t)$ does not lie in its amplitudes but is given solely by its 'area'. Consequently, $\delta(t)$ is not defined in the ordinary sense but $\int_{-\infty}^{\infty} \delta(t)dt$ is defined; $\delta(t)f(t)$ is not defined but $\int_{-\infty}^{\infty} \delta(t)f(t)dt$ is defined:

$$\int_{-\infty}^{\infty} \delta(t)f(t)dt = \int_{-\infty}^{\infty} \lim_{\Delta \to 0} \delta_\Delta(t)f(t)dt = \lim_{\Delta \to 0} \int_{-\infty}^{\infty} \frac{1}{\Delta} p_\Delta(t)f(t)dt$$

$$= \lim_{\Delta \to 0} \frac{1}{\Delta} \int_0^\Delta f(t)dt$$

$$= f(0), \text{ assuming } f(t) \text{ is continuous at } t = 0 \tag{2.13}$$

Figure 2.8 gives the graphical representation of impulse functions. The definition of impulse $\delta(t - t_0)$ occurring at $t = t_0$ is based on the following properties.

(i) $\int_{-\infty}^{\infty} \delta(t - t_0)dt = 1$

(ii) $\int_{-\infty}^{\infty} f(t)\delta(t - t_0)dt = f(t_0)$, for any $f(t)$ that is continuous at $t = t_0$

$$\left. \right\} (2.14)$$

$A\delta(t - t_0)$ is an impulse of 'area' A (strength A) occurring at $t = t_0$.

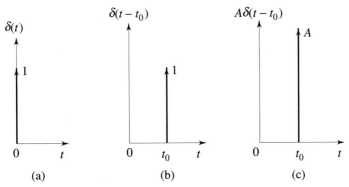

Fig. 2.8 *Impulse functions*

Example 2.1

Consider the situation shown in Fig. 2.9a where a mass M is acted upon by the force $F(t)$. The system is characterized by the second-order differential equation

$$F(t) = M\frac{d^2x(t)}{dt^2} \tag{2.15a}$$

The solution of this equation requires two initial conditions $\{x(0), \dot{x}(0) = v(0)\}$, and the input $F(t)$ applied at $t = 0^+$.

We will assume the system to be relaxed at $t = 0$, i.e.,

$$x(0) = v(0) = 0 \tag{2.15b}$$

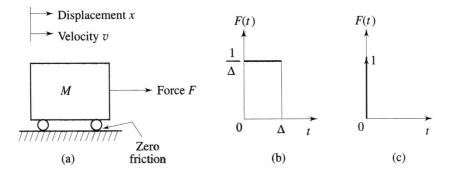

Fig. 2.9 *Approximating a pulse by an impulse*

It is intuitively obvious that the system state at time t can be described by state variables $x(t)$ and $v(t)$. The state equation for the mechanical system is given below:

$$\begin{bmatrix} \dot{x}(t) \\ \dot{v}(t) \end{bmatrix} = \begin{bmatrix} 0 & 1 \\ 0 & 0 \end{bmatrix} \begin{bmatrix} x(t) \\ v(t) \end{bmatrix} + \begin{bmatrix} 0 \\ 1/M \end{bmatrix} F(t) \qquad (2.16)$$

Equation (2.16) is of the form of general state equation (2.4a).

Let the force $F(t)$ be a pulse force of strength $1/\Delta$ and time duration Δ (Fig. 2.9b). For $t < \Delta$,

$$v(t) = \frac{1}{M} \int_0^t F(\tau)d\tau = \frac{t}{M\Delta}; \ x(t) = \int_0^t v(\tau)d\tau = \frac{t^2}{2M\Delta}$$

The mass moves a distance

$$x(\Delta) = \frac{\Delta}{2M}$$

before acquiring a steady velocity of

$$v(\Delta) = \frac{1}{M}$$

The energy transferred from the pulse source to the mass (in time Δ) is

$$KE = \frac{1}{2}Mv^2(\Delta) = \frac{1}{2M}$$

Consider now the situation shown in Fig. 2.9c. The force $F(t)$ is a unit impulse $\delta(t)$ occurring at $t = 0$. The velocity of the mass is given by

$$v(t) = \frac{1}{M} \int_0^t \delta(\tau)d\tau = \frac{1}{M}; \ t \geq 0$$

It is the same as the steady velocity $v(\Delta)$ for the pulse case except that it is acquired now in zero distance (and of course zero time). The energy acquired by the mass is the same in the two cases.

From Figs 2.9b and 2.9c, we see that there is practically no resemblance as far as the input function is concerned and it appears at first as if the approximation of a pulse by an impulse is in doubt. However, if our aim is to approximate the response of a linear system, the impulse approximation yields useful results provided pulse width Δ is small.

▲▲

We can now derive Eqn. (2.8). An input function $r(t)$ can easily be approximated by a train of pulses as shown in Fig. 2.10. It is convenient to take a uniform pulse width Δ for the pulse train. In the light of description of a pulse given by Eqns (2.9)–(2.10), we can express $r(t)$ as

$$r(t) \cong \sum_{i=0}^{\infty} r(i\Delta)\, p_\Delta(t - i\Delta) \cong \sum_{i=0}^{\infty} r(i\Delta)\, \delta_\Delta(t - i\Delta)\Delta \qquad (2.17)$$

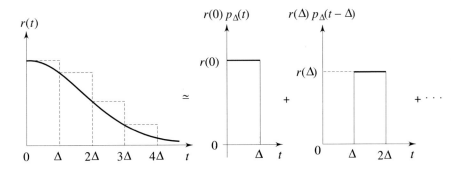

Fig. 2.10 *Resolution of a function*

Now if the output of the linear time-invariant system due to the input $\delta_\Delta(t)$ is denoted by $g_\Delta(t)$, then the properties of linearity and time-invariance imply that the output of the system due to $r(t)$ is given by

$$y(t) \cong \sum_{i=0}^{\infty} r(i\Delta)g_\Delta(t - i\Delta)\Delta \qquad (2.18)$$

As we allow $\Delta \to 0$, the pulse function becomes an impulse function, number of impulses grow so that $(i\Delta)$ becomes a continuous variable τ, and the sum in Eqn. (2.18) approaches an integral. The output $y(t)$ resulting from an input $r(t)$ is thus

$$y(t) = \int_0^{\infty} r(\tau)\,g(t - \tau)d\tau \qquad (2.19)$$

where
$$g(t) \overset{\Delta}{=} \lim_{\Delta \to 0} g_\Delta(t) \qquad (2.20a)$$

is the response of the system to unit impulse input applied at $t = 0$.

Hence the function $g(t)$ is called the *impulse response* of the system. Since $g(t - \tau)$ is the response due to an input applied at $t = \tau$, it is not defined for $t < \tau$;

$$g(t - \tau) = 0, \text{ for } t < \tau \qquad (2.20b)$$

On the basis of this property, Eqn. (2.19) reduces to

$$y(t) = \int_0^t g(t - \tau)r(\tau)d\tau$$

Equation (2.8) is thus proved.

▲▲

A very important property of the impulse response model is that it can be obtained from the input and output terminals of a system even if the system's internal structure is not known. If the system is known to be linear, time-invariant, and relaxed at $t = 0$, then by applying $\delta_\Delta(t)$ function at the input terminal, the response at the output terminal gives us immediately the impulse response (approximate one; goodness of approximation is dependent on Δ) of the system. If the impulse response is known, the output of the system due to any input can be computed from Eqn. (2.8).

▲▲

The application of Laplace transform to Eqn. (2.8) gives an extremely useful mathematical description of a linear time-invariant system. Fundamental definition for the Laplace transform[3] $F(s)$ of the time function $f(t)$ is (refer[4] Eqn. (A.28) in Appendix A)

$$\mathscr{L}[f(t)] \triangleq F(s) \triangleq \int_0^\infty f(t)e^{-st}\, dt; t > 0 \tag{2.21}$$

$$s = \text{a complex variable} = \sigma + j\omega$$

The application of Laplace transform to Eqn. (2.8) yields

$$Y(s) \triangleq \mathscr{L}[y(t)] = \int_0^\infty y(t)e^{-st}\, dt$$

$$= \int_0^\infty \left[\int_0^t g(t-\tau)r(\tau)d\tau\right]e^{-st}dt \tag{2.22}$$

Since $g(t - \tau) = 0$ for $\tau > t$ as implied by Eqn. (2.20b), the upper limit t of integration in Eqn. (2.22) can be set at ∞;

$$Y(s) = \int_0^\infty \left[\int_0^\infty g(t-\tau)r(\tau)d\tau\right]e^{-st}dt$$

Changing the order of integrations, gives

$$Y(s) = \int_0^\infty \left[\int_0^\infty g(t-\tau)e^{-st}dt\right]r(\tau)d\tau = \int_0^\infty \left[\int_0^\infty g(t-\tau)e^{-s(t-\tau)}dt\right]e^{-s\tau}r(\tau)d\tau$$

which, if we substitute $\theta = t - \tau$, can be expressed as

$$Y(s) = \int_0^\infty \left[\int_{-\tau}^\infty g(\theta)e^{-s\theta}d\theta\right]e^{-s\tau}r(\tau)d\tau$$

Using the fact that $g(\theta) = 0$ for $\theta < 0$ (refer Eqn. 2.20b)), we obtain

$$Y(s) = \int_0^\infty \left[\int_0^\infty g(\theta)e^{-s\theta}d\theta\right]e^{-s\tau}r(\tau)d\tau = \left[\int_0^\infty g(\theta)e^{-s\theta}d\theta\right]\left[\int_0^\infty r(\tau)e^{-s\tau}d\tau\right]$$

or

$$Y(s) = G(s)\,R(s) \tag{2.23}$$

---

3. It is conventional to use capital letters for s-functions and lower case for t-functions. Our notation mostly follows this convention.
4. We assume that the reader has had a previous introduction to the theory of Laplace transforms. Appendix A provides a very brief review of the Laplace transform techniques, adequate for the purposes of this text.

where $$R(s) \triangleq \mathscr{L}[r(t)]$$

and

$$G(s) \triangleq \mathscr{L}[g(t)]$$

We see that by applying the Laplace transform, a convolution integral is transformed into an algebraic equation. The function $G(s)$ is called the *transfer function* of the system. *The transfer function of a linear time-invariant system is, by definition, the Laplace transform of the impulse response of the system.*

The Laplace transform variable s in a transfer function $G(s)$, as will be seen later, can be associated with frequency. Hence the transfer function description of a system is often referred to as in *frequency-domain*, whereas the impulse response description is said to be in *time-domain*.

In this book, the major emphasis is on frequency-domain design methods. Providing more space for discussion on transfer functions will be in order here. The next section is exclusively devoted to transfer function models.

2.4 | TRANSFER FUNCTION MODELS

In the last section, we have defined the transfer function of a linear time-invariant system as the Laplace transform of the impulse response of the system.

The transfer function can also be defined as (refer Eqn. (2.23)),

$$G(s) = \frac{\mathscr{L}[y(t)]}{\mathscr{L}[r(t)]}\bigg|_{\substack{\text{system}\\\text{relaxed}\\\text{at } t_0 = 0}} = \frac{Y(s)}{R(s)}\bigg|_{\substack{\text{system}\\\text{relaxed}\\\text{at } t_0 = 0}} \qquad (2.24)$$

where $Y(s)$ = Laplace transform of the output variable $y(t)$,

$R(s)$ = Laplace transform of the input variable $r(t)$, and

$G(s)$ = transfer function of the system.

Thus the *transfer function of a time-invariant system is the ratio of the Laplace transforms of its output and input variables, assuming zero initial conditions.* Figure 2.11 gives a block diagram of a SISO system in transform domain.

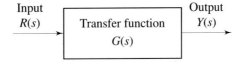

Fig. 2.11 *Description of a SISO system in transform domain*

Note that whenever a transfer function is used to describe a system, the system is always implicitly assumed to be linear, time-invariant, and relaxed at $t_0 = 0$.

There are two different ways in which transfer function models are usually obtained.

(i) For lumped linear time-invariant systems, mathematical model building based on physical laws normally results in a set of (first-order, and second-order) differential equations. Applying Laplace transform to the differential equations results in a transfer function model of the system.

We will be mostly concerned with this approach. A number of examples of mechanical, electrical, hydraulic and thermal systems will be taken to illustrate the modelling procedure. One important feature will clearly emerge from these examples—application of physical laws to a system results in a set of differential equations which directly provide us with the rates of change of state variables of the system. State variable formulation is thus a 'natural' representation of the system dynamics. We, in fact, first obtain the state variable formulation by applying physical laws and therefrom derive the transfer function model by Laplace transformation.

(ii) The transfer function model of a system can be identified from experimentally obtained input-output data. Generally the identification methods can be considered to be a type of curve-fitting, where the assumed transfer function is fitted to the available data in some optimal manner. The methods may be based on frequency response (sinusoidal input), step response (step input), impulse response (pulse input; pulse of small width approximating an impulse), or the response to more general inputs.[5]

Identification methods have not been covered in this book. Only simple methods based on step response and frequency response are given in later chapters.

Example 2.2_____

Consider the mass-spring-damper system shown in Fig. 2.2.

Application of Newton's law results in the following equation (refer Fig. 2.2b).

$$M\frac{dv(t)}{dt} = F(t) - Bv(t) - K\,x(t)$$

with   (2.25)

$$\frac{dx(t)}{dt} = v(t)$$

$x(t)$ is the displacement of the mass, $v(t)$ is the velocity, $F(t)$ is the applied force; M, B and K are the parameters of the system.

_____

5. In Chapter 12, methods of deriving *canonical* (special) state variable models from a given transfer function will be presented. This is called the *realization problem*.

Equations (2.25), as recognized earlier in Section 2.2, are in fact the state equations of the mechanical system. We can express these two first-order differential equations in terms of a single second-order differential equation:

$$M\frac{d^2x(t)}{dt^2} + B\frac{dx(t)}{dt} + K\,x(t) = F(t) \qquad (2.26)$$

Laplace transformation of either Eqns (2.25) or Eqn. (2.26) will give us the transfer function model of the system.

Laplace transformation of differential equations of the first and second-order, will require following results (refer Eqn. (A.31) in Appendix A):

$$\mathcal{L}\left[\frac{dx(t)}{dt}\right] = sX(s) - x(0);$$

$$\mathcal{L}\left[\frac{d^2x(t)}{dt^2}\right] = s^2X(s) - sx(0) - \frac{dx}{dt}(0)$$

Taking the Laplace transform of all the terms of Eqn. (2.26), under the assumption of zero initial conditions we obtain

$$M[s^2\,X(s)] + B[sX(s)] + KX(s) = F(s)$$

where $\qquad X(s) \overset{\Delta}{=} \mathcal{L}[x(t)]; \; F(s) \overset{\Delta}{=} \mathcal{L}[F(t)].$

Solving for $X(s)$:

$$X(s) = \frac{F(s)}{Ms^2 + Bs + K}$$

Therefore, the transfer function $G(s)$ of the mass-spring-damper system is

$$G(s) = \frac{X(s)}{F(s)} = \frac{1}{Ms^2 + Bs + K} \qquad (2.27)$$

The highest power of the complex variable s in the denominator polynomial of a transfer function determines the *order of the transfer function*. The mechanical system under consideration is thus described by the second-order transfer function given by Eqn. (2.27). Note that differential equation (2.26) or the state equation model (2.25), governing the behaviour of the mechanical system, is also of second-order.

Example 2.3

Consider the electrical network of Fig. 2.1. Application of Kirchhoff's voltage law results in the following equation.

$$L\frac{di(t)}{dt} + Ri(t) + e(t) = e_i(t)$$

with $\qquad\qquad\qquad\qquad\qquad\qquad\qquad\qquad\qquad\qquad$ (2.28)

$$C\frac{de(t)}{dt} = i(t)$$

$e(t)$ is the voltage across the capacitor, $i(t)$ is the current through the inductor, $e_i(t)$ is the voltage source and R, L, and C are the parameters of the system.

Equations (2.28), as recognized earlier in Section 2.2, are in fact state equations of the electrical network.

Taking the Laplace transform of all the terms of these equations, under the assumption of zero initial conditions, we obtain

$$C[sE(s)] = I(s); \; L[sI(s)] + R\,I(s) + E(s) = E_i(s)$$

where

$$E_i(s) \overset{\Delta}{=} \mathscr{L}[e_i(t)]$$

$$E(s) \overset{\Delta}{=} \mathscr{L}[e(t)]$$

$$I(s) \overset{\Delta}{=} \mathscr{L}[i(t)]$$

Eliminating $E(s)$ from these equations, we get

$$\left(R + sL + \frac{1}{sC}\right)I(s) = E_i(s) \tag{2.29a}$$

The output (refer Fig. 2.1)

$$y(t) = L\frac{di}{dt}$$

or under the assumption of zero initial conditions,

$$Y(s) = sL\,I(s) \tag{2.29b}$$

The transfer function $G(s)$ of the RLC network (obtained from Eqns (2.29a) and (2.29b)) is

$$G(s) = \frac{Y(s)}{E_i(s)} = \frac{s^2}{s^2 + \dfrac{R}{L}s + \dfrac{1}{LC}} \tag{2.30}$$

Since the highest power of s in the denominator polynomial of $G(s)$ is two, the transfer function model of the RLC network is of second-order. Note that state equation model of this network is also of second-order.

▲▲

Since $G(s)$ is a rational function of a complex variable, we use the terminology of the theory of complex variables (refer Section A.2 in Appendix A). Consider a general transfer function model

$$G(s) = \frac{X(s)}{R(s)} = \frac{b_0 s^m + b_1 s^{m-1} + \cdots + b_{m-1}s + b_m}{s^n + a_1 s^{n-1} + \cdots + a_{n-1}s + a_n}; \; m \le n \tag{2.31}$$

where a_i and b_j are constant parameters of the model of the system with input $r(t)$ and output $y(t)$. As seen from Eqns (2.27) and (2.30), a_i and b_j are given by physical parameters of the system.

$G(s)$ is a rational function of s, i.e., a quotient of two polynomials of s. For $m \le n$, $G(s)$ is a *proper rational function*, and for $m < n$, $G(s)$ is a *strictly proper rational function*.

We will represent the numerator polynomial of $G(s)$ by $N(s)$, and the denominator polynomial by $\Delta(s)$:

$$G(s) = \frac{N(s)}{\Delta(s)} \qquad (2.32)$$

where

$$N(s) = b_0 s^m + b_1 s^{m-1} + \cdots + b_{m-1}s + b_m$$
$$\Delta(s) = s^n + a_1 s^{n-1} + \cdots + a_{n-1}s + a_n$$

Note that there is no loss in generality to assume that the coefficient of s^n in the polynomial $\Delta(s)$ is unity (i.e., the denominator polynomial $\Delta(s)$ is assumed to be *monic*[6]).

The highest power of the complex variable s in the denominator polynomial $\Delta(s)$ of the transfer function $G(s)$ determines the *order of the transfer function model*. The denominator polynomial $\Delta(s)$ is called the *characteristic polynomial*.

The roots of the equation

$$\Delta(s) = 0 \qquad (2.33a)$$

are called the *poles* of the transfer function $G(s)$ and roots of the equation

$$N(s) = 0 \qquad (2.33b)$$

are called the *zeros*.

Equation (2.33a) is called the *characteristic equation*; the poles are the *characteristic roots*.

The transfer function $G(s)$ given by Eqn. (2.31) can be expressed in the *pole-zero form* as

$$G(s) = \frac{K(s + z_1)(s + z_2)\cdots(s + z_m)}{(s + p_1)(s + p_2)\cdots(s + p_n)}; \; m \le n \qquad (2.34a)$$

where K, p_i and z_j are constants; $K = b_0$ is the *gain constant* of the transfer function, $-p_1, -p_2, \ldots, -p_n$ are the n poles (real or complex) of the transfer function (n roots of the characteristic equation (2.33a)), and $-z_1, -z_2, \ldots, -z_m$ are the m finite zeros (real or complex) of the transfer function (m roots of Eqn. (2.33b)).

In the representation of $G(s)$ in pole-zero form given by Eqn. (2.34a), it has been assumed that the poles and zeros are *distinct* (*simple*). If a pole, say at $s = -p_1$, is *multiple* (repeated) with multiplicity v, the corresponding transfer function in pole-zero form becomes

$$G(s) = \frac{K(s + z_1)(s + z_2)\cdots(s + z_m)}{(s + p_1)^v (s + p_{v+1})\cdots(s + p_n)}; \; m \le n \qquad (2.34b)$$

Multiple zeros may also appear in a transfer function model.

---

6. A monic polynomial has a leading coefficient equal to unity.

We have so far considered SISO systems. Consider now the two-input, two-output system shown in the block diagram of Fig. 2.12. The terms $G_{11}(s)$ and $G_{21}(s)$ are the transfer functions of the input variable $R_1(s)$ on the two output variables $Y_1(s)$ and $Y_2(s)$ respectively; the terms $G_{12}(s)$ and $G_{22}(s)$ are the corresponding transfer functions for input variable $R_2(s)$. The mathematical model of the system is, therefore, 2×2 *transfer function matrix* defined below:

$$\begin{bmatrix} Y_1(s) \\ Y_2(s) \end{bmatrix} = \underbrace{\begin{bmatrix} G_{11}(s) & G_{12}(s) \\ G_{21}(s) & G_{22}(s) \end{bmatrix}}_{\text{Transfer function matrix}} \begin{bmatrix} R_1(s) \\ R_2(s) \end{bmatrix} \tag{2.35}$$

$$G_{11}(s) = \left. \frac{Y_1(s)}{R_1(s)} \right|_{R_2(s)=0} \; ; \; G_{12}(s) = \left. \frac{Y_1(s)}{R_2(s)} \right|_{R_1(s)=0}$$

$$G_{21}(s) = \left. \frac{Y_2(s)}{R_1(s)} \right|_{R_2(s)=0} \; ; \; G_{22}(s) = \left. \frac{Y_2(s)}{R_2(s)} \right|_{R_1(s)=0}$$

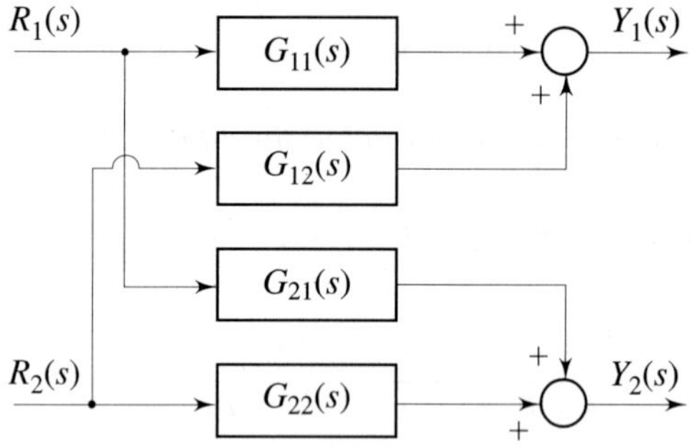

Fig. 2.12 *Description of a MIMO system in transform domain*

Extension of the model given by Eqn. (2.35) to the case of p-input, p-output system is obvious.

▲▲

In this book, the major emphasis is on frequency-domain design methods. Hence we mostly deal with transfer functions (Chapters 2–11).

The frequency-domain design methods have been greatly enhanced by the availability of low-cost computers for system analysis and simulation. The use of state variable formulation, introduced earlier in Section 2.2, has become widespread in CAD packages. In this introductory book, modest investment in state variable methods is therefore necessary. In Chapter 12, we give an adequate coverage of state variable representation and its relationship with transfer function representation.

2.5 | MODELS OF DISTURBANCES AND STANDARD TEST SIGNALS

To motivate the discussion in a control systems context, we revisit the generalized functional block diagram of Fig. 1.12. There are two inputs (external excitations) applied to a control system: a command input $y_r(t)$ (or reference input $r(t)$), and a disturbance input $w(t)$. We will first talk of disturbances.

Simple Models of Disturbances

External disturbances, $w(t)$, are typically the uncontrolled variations in the load on a control system. In systems controlling mechanical motions, load disturbances may represent forces, e.g., wind gusts on a stabilized antenna (refer to Example 1.5), variations in payload of a robot (refer to Example 1.10), etc. In voltage regulating systems, variations in electrical load are a major source of disturbances. In thermal systems, the load disturbances may be caused by variations in surrounding temperature (refer to Example 1.4). In fluidic systems, the load disturbances may result from variations in feedflow or variations in demanded flow (refer to Example 1.7).

Disturbances which are erratic, uncertain signals having no distinguishing waveform properties, are commonly referred to as *noise*. The accommodation of noise in a control problem is best handled by treating the noise as a *stochastic* or *random process*. The general theory of stochastic processes is quite complex, and is beyond the scope of this book.

In this book we consider load disturbances which typically vary slowly. Such disturbances are normally well behaved uncertain signals having distinguishing waveform properties. As we shall see in Chapter 4, the errors due to load disturbances tend to be corrected by proper design of feedback control.

In the following, we consider simple, yet effective, models that characterize commonly occurring disturbances.

Pulse and Impulse Functions

The pulse and the impulse are simple idealizations of sudden disturbances of short duration.

A *pulse function* (Fig. 2.13a) is defined as (refer Eqn. (2.9a)),

$$p_T(t) = \begin{cases} 1 \text{ for } 0 < t < T \\ 0 \text{ otherwise} \end{cases}$$

(2.36a)

Laplace transform of pulse function is (refer Eqn. (2.21)),

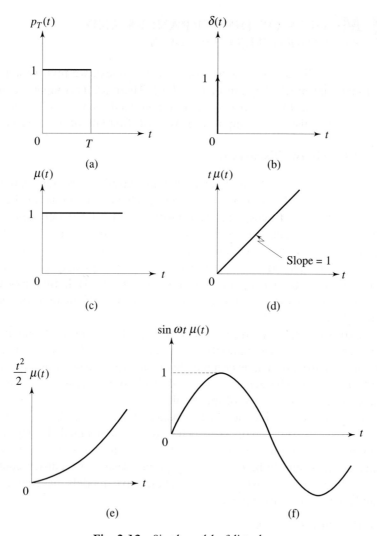

Fig. 2.13 *Simple models of disturbances*

$$\mathscr{L}[p_T(t)] = \int_0^\infty p_T(t)e^{-st}dt = \int_0^T e^{-st}dt = \frac{1}{s}(1-e^{-sT}) \qquad (2.36b)$$

A *unit impulse function* (Fig. 2.13b) is defined as (refer Eqns (2.12) and (2.13),

$$\delta(t) = \begin{bmatrix} 0 \text{ for } t \neq 0 \\ \infty \text{ for } t = 0 \end{bmatrix}$$

$$\int_{-\infty}^{\infty} \delta(t)dt = 1 \qquad\qquad\qquad (2.37a)$$

$$\int_{-\infty}^{\infty} \delta(t)f(t)dt = f(0)$$

Using Eqn. (2.36b), we can write

$$\mathscr{L}[\delta_\Delta(t)] = \frac{1}{s\Delta}(1 - e^{-s\Delta})$$

where $\quad \delta_\Delta(t) = \frac{1}{\Delta}p_\Delta(t)$ is a pulse of height $\frac{1}{\Delta}$ and duration Δ.

Applying L' Hospital's rule, we can write

$$\mathscr{L}[\delta(t)] = \lim_{\Delta \to 0} \frac{\dfrac{d}{d\Delta}(1 - e^{-s\Delta})}{\dfrac{d}{d\Delta}(s\Delta)} = \lim_{\Delta \to 0} \frac{se^{-s\Delta}}{s}$$

Therefore,

$$\mathscr{L}[\delta(t)] = 1 \qquad\qquad (2.37b)$$

Step Function

A step signal is another prototype for a disturbance. It is typically used to represent a sudden jump in the magnitude of otherwise constant (slowly varying) disturbances. A *unit step function*[7] (Fig. 2.13c),

$$\mu(t) = \begin{bmatrix} 1 \text{ for } t > 0 \\ 0 \text{ otherwise} \end{bmatrix} \qquad\qquad (2.38a)$$

$$\mathscr{L}[\mu(t)] = \frac{1}{s} \qquad\qquad (2.38b)$$

Ramp Function

A *unit ramp function* (Fig. 2.13d) is defined as

$$f(t) = \begin{bmatrix} t \text{ for } t > 0 \\ 0 \text{ otherwise} \end{bmatrix} \qquad\qquad (2.39a)$$

or simply,

$$f(t) = t\mu(t) \qquad\qquad (2.39b)$$

$$\mathscr{L}[f(t)] = \frac{1}{s^2} \qquad\qquad (2.39c)$$

A ramp function is used to represent disturbances that suddenly start to drift away. In practice, the disturbances are often bounded; however, the ramp is a useful idealization.

Parabolic Function

A parabolic function is one degree faster than the ramp function (in practice, we seldom find it necessary to use a signal faster than a parabolic function). A *unit parabolic function* (Fig. 2.13e) is defined as

---

7. Unit step function is generally denoted as $u(t)$ in system theory. However, in control theory, $u(t)$ is commonly used to represent control signal. In this book we will use $u(t)$ for control signal representation, and $\mu(t)$ for unit step function.

$$f(t) = \left[\begin{array}{ll} \dfrac{t^2}{2} & \text{for } t > 0 \\ 0 & \text{otherwise} \end{array} \right. \tag{2.40a}$$

or simply

$$f(t) = \frac{t^2}{2}\,\mu(t) \tag{2.40b}$$

$$\mathscr{L}[f(t)] = \frac{1}{s^3} \tag{2.40c}$$

Sinusoidal Function

The sine wave is a prototype for a periodic disturbance—for example, waves in ship control systems.

For a sine wave of unity amplitude and frequency ω (Fig. 2.13f), i.e.,

$$f(t) = \sin \omega t\,\mu(t), \tag{2.41a}$$

the Laplace transformation gives

$$\mathscr{L}[f(t)] = \frac{\omega}{s^2 + \omega^2} \tag{2.41b}$$

Standard Test Signals

In addition to disturbance input, the other excitation signal to a control system is the command input (Fig. 1.12). The command (or reference) signals of some control systems are known to the designer. The command signal of a residential heating system (Example 1.4) is a step function, whose magnitude is the desired temperature. If an antenna is used to track a communication satellite (refer Example 1.5), then the command signal is very close to a ramp function.

In many control systems, however, the command signals are not known fully ahead of time. For instance, in a radar tracking system for military applications (refer Example 1.5), the position and speed of the target to be tracked vary in an unpredictable manner; it is thus difficult to express the actual input signals mathematically by simple functions. The characteristics of actual signals which severely strain a control system are

  (i) a sudden shock (modelled by impulse function),

 (ii) a sudden change (modelled by step function),

(iii) a linear change with time (modelled by ramp function), and

(iv) faster changes with time (a parabolic function is one degree faster than a ramp function).

System dynamic behaviour can be adequately judged and compared under the application of standard test signals—an impulse input, a step input, a ramp input, and a parabolic input.

Another standard test signal of great importance is the sinusoidal signal. When the response of a linear time-invariant system is analysed in frequency domain, a sinusoidal function with variable frequency is used as input function. Input frequency is swept from zero to beyond the significant range of system characteristics; curves in terms of amplitude ratio and phase between input and output are drawn as functions of frequency. It is possible to predict the time-domain behaviour of the system from its frequency-domain characteristics. We will take up this aspect of control system analysis in Chapters 8 and 9.

2.6 | DYNAMIC RESPONSE

This section is concerned with the dynamic response of linear time-invariant systems to disturbance signals and standard test signals. We will study the response of a system from its transfer function model; therefore the system is implicitly assumed to be initially relaxed.

Basically four steps are involved in the computation of $y(t)$ from

$$Y(s) = G(s)\,R(s)$$

1. Find the Laplace transform of $r(t)$ using results of Section 2.5 or Table of transform pairs given in Appendix A.
2. Compute the poles of $G(s)\,R(s)$.
3. Expand $Y(s)$ into partial fractions (Eqns (A.3)–(A.14) of Appendix A give the required procedure).
4. Obtain $y(t)$ by taking inverse Laplace transform of $Y(s)$ using transform pairs listed in the Table of Appendix A.

In the following, we give examples to illustrate the procedure.

Example 2.4

Given the transfer function

$$G(s) = \frac{Y(s)}{R(s)} = \frac{1}{s^2 + 3s + 2};$$

find the response $y(t)$ to the input

(i) $r(t) = 5\,\mu(t)$, (ii) $r(t) = 5t\,\mu(t)$

Solution

(i) For the given step input, $R(s) = \dfrac{5}{s}$

Therefore,

$$Y(s) = \frac{1}{s^2 + 3s + 2}R(s) = \frac{1}{(s+1)(s+2)}\left(\frac{5}{s}\right)$$

Expanding $Y(s)$ into partial fractions, gives

$$Y(s) = \frac{5}{s(s+1)(s+2)} = \frac{A_1}{s} + \frac{A_2}{s+1} + \frac{A_3}{s+2}$$

$$A_1 = \lim_{s \to 0}\left[(s)\frac{5}{s(s+1)(s+2)} \right] = \frac{5}{2}$$

$$A_2 = \lim_{s \to -1}\left[(s+1)\frac{5}{s(s+1)(s+2)} \right] = -5$$

$$A_3 = \lim_{s \to -2}\left[(s+2)\frac{5}{s(s+1)(s+2)} \right] = \frac{5}{2}$$

or

$$Y(s) = \underbrace{\frac{5/2}{s}}_{\text{Excitation pole}} \underbrace{- \frac{5}{s+1} + \frac{5/2}{s+2}}_{\text{System poles}}$$

Inverting $Y(s)$, we obtain the time response

$$y(t) = \left[\underbrace{\frac{5}{2}}_{\text{Steady-state response}} \underbrace{-5e^{-t} + \frac{5}{2}e^{-2t}}_{\text{Transient response}} \right] \mu(t)$$

The transient response terms correspond to system poles excited by the input. These terms vanish as $t \to \infty$.

The second response term arises due to the excitation pole, and has the same nature as the input itself except for a modification in magnitude caused by the system's behaviour to the specified input. Since the input exists as $t \to \infty$, the second response term does not vanish and is called the *steady-state response* of the system. Figure 2.14a shows the response to the given step input.

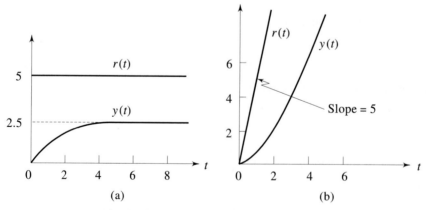

Fig. 2.14   *(a) Step response; (b) Ramp response*

The steady-state response can be quickly obtained without doing the complete inverse Laplace transform, by use of the *final value theorem* (Eqn. (A.35) of Appendix A):

$$\lim_{t \to \infty} y(t) = \lim_{s \to 0} sY(s) \tag{2.42}$$

if $s\,Y(s)$ has no poles on the imaginary axis and in the right half s-plane.

(ii) For the given ramp input, $R(s) = \dfrac{5}{s^2}$

Therefore, $\qquad Y(s) = \dfrac{5}{s^2(s+1)(s+2)}$

Expanding $Y(s)$ in partial fractions, gives

$$Y(s) = \frac{A_1}{s^2} + \frac{A_2}{s} + \frac{A_3}{s+1} + \frac{A_4}{s+2}$$

$$A_1 = \lim_{s \to 0}\left[(s^2)\frac{5}{s^2(s+1)(s+2)}\right] = \frac{5}{2}$$

$$A_2 = \lim_{s \to 0}\frac{d}{ds}\left[(s^2)\frac{5}{s^2(s+1)(s+2)}\right]$$

$$\quad = \lim_{s \to 0}\left[\frac{-5(2s+3)}{(s^2+3s+2)^2}\right] = \frac{-15}{4}$$

$$A_3 = \lim_{s \to -1}\left[(s+1)\frac{5}{s^2(s+1)(s+2)}\right] = 5$$

$$A_4 = \lim_{s \to -2}\left[(s+2)\frac{5}{s^2(s+1)(s+2)}\right] = \frac{-5}{4}$$

or $\qquad Y(s) = \dfrac{5/2}{s^2} - \dfrac{15/4}{s} + \dfrac{5}{s+1} - \dfrac{5/4}{s+2}$

Inverting $Y(s)$, we obtain the time response

$$y(t) = \left(\frac{-15}{4} + \frac{5}{2}t + 5e^{-t} - \frac{5}{4}e^{-2t}\right)\mu(t)$$

The ramp response is composed of three types of terms—constant, ramp, and exponentials. The exponentials (transient component) decay leaving behind the steady-state response

$$y_{ss}(t) = \frac{5}{2}t - \frac{15}{4}$$

Figure 2.14b shows the response to given ramp input.

Example 2.5————————————————————————

Given the transfer function

$$G(s) = \frac{Y(s)}{R(s)} = \frac{K}{s+a};$$

find the response $y(t)$ to the input $r(t) = R_0 \sin \omega t$; K, a and R_0 are constants, and ω is sinusoidal frequency.

Solution

For the given sinusoidal input, $R(s) = \dfrac{R_0\,\omega}{s^2 + \omega^2}$

Therefore,

$$Y(s) = \frac{KR_0\,\omega}{(s + a)(s^2 + \omega^2)}$$

$$= \frac{KR_0\,\omega}{(s + a)(s - j\omega)(s + j\omega)} ; j \triangleq \sqrt{-1}$$

Expanding $Y(s)$ in partial fractions, gives

$$Y(s) = \frac{A_1}{s + a} + \frac{A_2}{s - j\omega} + \frac{A_3}{s + j\omega}$$

$$A_1 = \lim_{s \to -a}\left[(s + a)\frac{KR_0\omega}{(s + a)(s^2 + \omega^2)}\right] = \frac{KR_0\omega}{\omega^2 + a^2}$$

$$A_2 = \lim_{s \to j\omega}\left[(s - j\omega)\frac{KR_0\omega}{(s + a)(s - j\omega)(s + j\omega)}\right]$$

$$= \frac{KR_0\omega}{j2\omega(a + j\omega)} = \frac{-KR_0(\omega + ja)}{2(\omega^2 + a^2)}$$

$A_3 = $ complex conjugate of A_2

$$= \frac{-KR_0(\omega - ja)}{2(\omega^2 + a^2)}$$

or $\qquad Y(s) = \dfrac{KR_0\,\omega}{\omega^2 + a^2}\left(\dfrac{1}{s + a}\right) - \dfrac{KR_0}{2(\omega^2 + a^2)}\left[\dfrac{\omega + ja}{s - j\omega} + \dfrac{\omega - ja}{s + j\omega}\right]$

$$= \frac{KR_0\,\omega}{\omega^2 + a^2}\left(\frac{1}{s + a}\right) - \frac{KR_0\,\omega}{\omega^2 + a^2}\left(\frac{s - a}{s^2 + \omega^2}\right)$$

Inverting $Y(s)$, we obtain the time response

$$y(t) = \frac{KR_0\,\omega}{\omega^2 + a^2}e^{-at} + \frac{KR_0\,\omega}{\omega^2 + a^2}\left(\frac{a}{\omega}\sin \omega t - \cos \omega t\right)$$

$$= \frac{KR_0\,\omega}{\omega^2 + a^2}e^{-at} + \frac{KR_0\,a}{\omega^2 + a^2}\left(\sin \omega t - \frac{\omega}{a}\cos \omega t\right)$$

Using the identity

$A \cos at + B \sin at = R \sin (at + \theta)$

where
$$R = \sqrt{A^2 + B^2}, \quad \theta = \tan^{-1}\left(\frac{A}{B}\right),$$

the $y(t)$ expression can be changed to

$$y(t) = \frac{KR_0\omega}{\omega^2 + a^2}e^{-at} + \frac{KR_0}{\sqrt{\omega^2 + a^2}}\sin\left[\omega t - \tan^{-1}\left(\frac{\omega}{a}\right)\right] \qquad (2.43)$$

Equation (2.43) shows that as time increases, the exponential term goes to zero; this is the transient term that dies out. When this happens, the output expression becomes

$$y(t)\Big|_{t \text{ very large}} = y_{ss}(t) = \frac{KR_0}{\sqrt{\omega^2 + a^2}}\sin\left[\omega t - \tan^{-1}\left(\frac{\omega}{a}\right)\right] \qquad (2.44)$$

which displays the sinusoidal behaviour of the output signal. The amplitude of this output is

$$Y_0 = \frac{KR_0}{\sqrt{\omega^2 + a^2}}$$

The output 'lags' the input signal by an amount $\theta = \tan^{-1}\left(\frac{\omega}{a}\right)$. All of this information is shown graphically in Fig. 2.15.

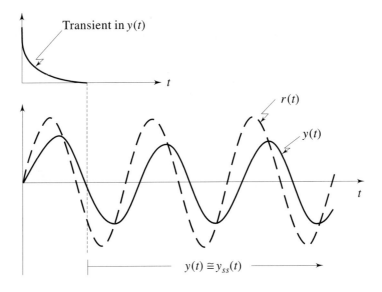

Fig. 2.15 *Sinusoidal response*

Sinusoidal Transfer Function

Consider the general model of transfer function given by

$$G(s) = \frac{K(s + z_1)(s + z_2)\cdots(s + z_m)}{(s + p_1)(s + p_2)\cdots(s + p_n)}; \; m \le n \tag{2.45}$$

When $r(t) = R_0 \sin \omega t$, the response $y(t)$ will consist of two components; the transient component and the steady-state component (refer Example 2.5). For a stable system, the transient component will always disappear as time goes by (this will be established quantitatively in Chapter 5).

The sinusoidal steady-state that results after the transient component dies out is, by definition, the *frequency response* of the system. The output is of the form $Y_0 \sin(\omega t + \theta)$; both the amplitude ratio Y_0/R_0, and the phase angle θ change when we use a different frequency ω, and our desired results are graphs of these two quantities against frequency, the so-called *frequency-response curves*.

For obtaining frequency response, one need not resort to a complete solution for a given sinusoidal input. *Sinusoidal transfer function* provides a much better method.

It can be shown that if we replace s by $j\omega$ $\left(j \overset{\Delta}{=} \sqrt{-1}; \omega \overset{\Delta}{=}\right.$ sinusoidal frequency, radian/time$\left.\right)$, in $G(s)$ to obtain $G(j\omega)$—the sinusoidal transfer function, we get a complex number $M \angle \theta$ where M will be the amplitude ratio Y_0/R_0 and θ will be the angle by which the output sine wave leads the input sine wave (negative θ means the output sine wave lags the input sine wave). For example, for the first-order system (refer Example 2.5)

$$\frac{Y(s)}{R(s)} = G(s) = \frac{K}{s + a},$$

the sinusoidal transfer function

$$G(j\omega) = \frac{K}{j\omega + a} = \frac{K}{\sqrt{\omega^2 + a^2}} \angle -\tan^{-1}(\omega/a) = M\angle\theta \tag{2.46}$$

For input $r(t) = R_0 \sin \omega t$, we have steady-state output $y_{ss}(t) = Y_0 \sin(\omega t + \theta)$, where $Y_0 = MR_0$.

Equation (2.46) allows us to plot frequency-response curves of Fig. 2.16.

Frequency-response curves form the basis of many important analysis and design methods for control systems. These methods will be discussed in later chapters of the book.

Computer Simulation

The Laplace transform approach of investigating the dynamics of a linear system results in *closed form response* (refer Examples 2.4 and 2.5)—the response

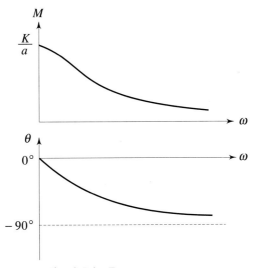

Fig. 2.16 *Frequency-response curves*

variable y is given by a mathematical expression in terms of independent variable t. The method works well if the system model is relatively of low-order, with relatively simple input functions[8]. If the model does not have these characteristics, we have to resort to numerical solution methods (*digital simulation*). The disadvantage of this type of solution is that generality is lost; the numerical values of the input functions, coefficients of the model, etc., must be specified [173-175, 177-178]. However, often there is no alternative.[9]

2.7 | CHARACTERISTIC PARAMETERS OF FIRST- AND SECOND-ORDER MODELS

In this book, we will frequently come across first- and second-order transfer function models. Special emphasis on the characteristics of these models is justified.

First-Order Models

As an example of a dynamic system represented by a first-order model, we consider here mechanical system of Fig. 2.17a involving fixed-axis rotation.

---

8. Most of the models used in the following chapters are of first-, second-, and third-order with simple input functions. Computer simulation is therefore not essential. However CAD facility, if available, can provide a better feel of how control system design is done in practice.

9. The analog computer simulation provides another way of investigating system dynamics. This method is rarely used now because of the advantages of digital simulation. However, it still provides an excellent means of developing control system prototypes (Section 2.9).

The free-body diagram is shown in Fig. 2.17b. It is assumed that the torque $T(t)$ is the input and angular velocity $\omega(t)$ is the output.

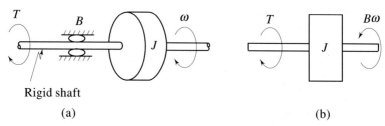

Rigid shaft

(a)   (b)

Fig. 2.17   *(a) An inertia-damper system*
(b) Free-body diagram

The torque equation obtained from the free-body diagram is

$$T(t) - B\omega(t) = J\frac{d\omega(t)}{dt}$$

or $$J\frac{d\omega(t)}{dt} + B\omega(t) = T(t) \qquad\qquad (2.47)$$

This is a linear constant-coefficient differential equation of first order.

Taking the Laplace transform of each term of this equation (assuming zero initial conditions), we obtain

$$Js\omega(s) + B\omega(s) = T(s)$$

where

$$\omega(s) \triangleq \mathscr{L}[\omega(t)]; \; T(s) \triangleq \mathscr{L}[T(t)]$$

Therefore, the transfer function of the system is

$$G(s) = \frac{\omega(s)}{T(s)} = \frac{1}{Js + B} = \frac{1/J}{s + B/J} \qquad\qquad (2.48)$$

J = moment of inertia, Newton-m/(rad/sec^2)
B = damping coefficient, Newton-m/(rad/sec)

Equation (2.48) gives a first-order transfer function of the mechanical system in pole-zero form; with pole at $s = -B/J$, no finite zero and gain constant = $1/J$.

A more common notation for first-order transfer functions is

$$G(s) = \frac{K}{\tau s + 1},$$

since the physical meaning can be given to both K and τ.

For the mechanical system under consideration,

$$\tau = J/B, \text{ and } K = 1/B \qquad\qquad (2.49a)$$

$$\frac{\omega(s)}{T(s)} = \frac{K}{\tau s + 1} \qquad\qquad (2.49b)$$

In the following, we obtain the time response from Eqns (2.49) to a step signal. From the characteristics of the time response, the physical meaning of the parameters K and τ will become clear,

For a unit-step input $T(t) = \mu(t)$, we have $T(s) = 1/s$.

Therefore,

$$\omega(s) = \frac{K}{s(s\tau + 1)} = K\left[\frac{1}{s} - \frac{\tau}{s\tau + 1}\right]$$

$$\omega(t) = K(1 - e^{-t/\tau}); \quad t \geq 0 \qquad (2.50)$$

This solution is now investigated in detail. The step response as given by Eqn. (2.50) is plotted in Fig. 2.18; the two components of the response are plotted separately along with the complete response. Note that the exponentially decaying term has an initial slope of K/τ, i.e.,

$$\frac{d}{dt}(-Ke^{-t/\tau})\bigg|_{t=0} = \frac{K}{\tau}e^{-t/\tau}\bigg|_{t=0} = \frac{K}{\tau}$$

Mathematically, the exponential term does not decay to zero in a finite length of time. However, if the term continued to decay at its initial rate, the term would reach a value of zero in time $t = \tau$. The parameter τ is called the system *time-constant*.

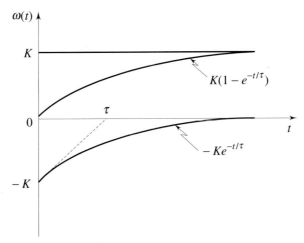

Fig. 2.18   *Step-response of a first-order system*

The decay of the exponential term is illustrated in Table 2.1 as a function of time-constant τ.

Table 2.1

t	$e^{-t/\tau}$	
τ	e^{-1}	$= 0.3679$
2τ	e^{-2}	$= 0.1353$
3τ	e^{-3}	$= 0.0498$
4τ	e^{-4}	$= 0.0183$
5τ	e^{-5}	$= 0.0067$

We observe that the exponential function has decayed to less than two per-cent of its initial value in four time-constants and to less than one per cent of its initial value in five time-constants. In a practical sense, we consider an exponential term to have decayed to zero in four to five time-constants.

Therefore, the time-constant is related to the speed of response of the system. The slower the system responds to an input, the larger the value of τ. The faster the system responds to an input, the smaller the value of τ. The unit of τ is seconds (this can be verified from Eqns (2.49a) using the units of the physical parameters given in Eqn. (2.48)).

Another important parameter encountered in Eqns (2.49) – (2.50) is K. Note that

$$\lim_{t \to \infty} \omega(t) = K$$

The parameter K is the *system gain*, which tells us how much the output variable will change at steady-state in response to a unit change in the input variable.

The gain K and time-constant τ are the two parameters which describe the 'personality' of the first-order system. These parameters may be obtained from the physical parameters of the system or experimentally by conducting the step-response test/sinusoidal-response test.

The transfer function

$$G(s) = \frac{K}{\tau s + 1} \tag{2.51}$$

is called the time-constant form for first-order transfer functions and will be encountered in all types of systems—electrical, mechanical, thermal, hydraulic, etc. A process described by this form of transfer function is called a *first-order lag* or a *simple lag*.

Second-Order Models

The study of second-order systems may be generalized by the introduction of certain parameters just as the study of first-order systems was facilitated by the use of time-constant.

As an example of a dynamic system represented by a second-order model, we consider here the mechanical system of Fig. 2.19(a) involving fixed-axis rotation. The shaft is assumed to behave like a torsional spring. The free-body diagram is shown in Fig. 2.19(b). It is assumed that the torque $T(t)$ is the input and angular displacement $\theta(t)$ is the output.

The torque equation obtained from the free-body diagram is

$$T(t) - B \frac{d\theta(t)}{dt} - k\,\theta(t) = J \frac{d^2\theta(t)}{dt^2}$$

or
$$J \frac{d^2\theta(t)}{dt^2} + B \frac{d\theta(t)}{dt} + k\theta(t) = T(t) \tag{2.52}$$

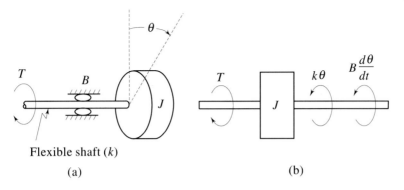

Flexible shaft (k)

(a)   (b)

Fig. 2.19   *(a) An inertia-spring-damper system*
(b) A free-body diagram

This is a linear constant-coefficient differential equation of second-order.

Taking the Laplace transform of each term of this equation (assuming zero initial conditions), we obtain

$$Js^2\,\theta(s) + Bs\,\theta(s) + k\theta(s) = T(s)$$

where $\quad\quad \theta(s) \triangleq \mathscr{L}[\theta(t)]; \ T(s) \triangleq \mathscr{L}[T(t)]$

Therefore, the transfer function of the system is

$$G(s) = \frac{\theta(s)}{T(s)} = \frac{1}{Js^2 + Bs + k} = \frac{1/J}{s^2 + \dfrac{B}{J}s + \dfrac{k}{J}} \quad\quad (2.53)$$

J = moment of inertia, Newton-m/(rad/sec^2)
B = damping coefficient, Newton-m/(rad/sec)
k = torsional spring constant, Newton-m/rad

Equation (2.53) gives a second-order transfer function of the mechanical system; the system has two poles—the roots of second-order characteristic polynomial with coefficients B/J and k/J, no finite zeros, and gain constant = $1/J$.

A more common notation for second-order transfer function is

$$G(s) = \frac{K}{\dfrac{1}{\omega_n^2}s^2 + \dfrac{2\zeta}{\omega_n}s + 1}$$

As we shall see shortly, physical meaning can be given to the three parameters K, ζ, and ω_n.

For the mechanical system under consideration,

$$K = \frac{1}{k}, \ \omega_n = \sqrt{\frac{k}{J}}, \ \zeta = \frac{1}{2}\frac{B}{\sqrt{kJ}} \quad\quad (2.54a)$$

$$\frac{\theta(s)}{T(s)} = \frac{K\omega_n^2}{s^2 + 2\zeta\omega_n s + \omega_n^2} \quad\quad (2.54b)$$

In the following, we investigate the time response to a step signal. From the characteristics of the time response, the physical meaning of the parameters K, ω_n, and ζ will become clear.

Physical parameters of the mechanical system—J, B, and k, can lead to the following four situations.

1. Undamped systems   ($\zeta = 0$)

For $B = 0$ (no damping), we have

$$\frac{\theta(s)}{T(s)} = \frac{1/J}{s^2 + k/J} = \frac{K\omega_n^2}{s^2 + \omega_n^2} \tag{2.55}$$

where K and ω_n are given by Eqns (2.54a). Note that this case corresponds to $\zeta = 0$.

For $T(t) = \mu(t)$ or $T(s) = 1/s$, we have

$$\theta(s) = \frac{K\omega_n^2}{s(s^2 + \omega_n^2)} = K\left[\frac{1}{s} - \frac{s}{s^2 + \omega_n^2}\right]$$

$$\theta(t) = K(1 - \cos\omega_n t); \; t \geq 0 \tag{2.56}$$

The curve corresponding to $\zeta = 0$ in Fig. 2.20 follows Eqn. (2.56). This curve provides the physical significance of the parameter ω_n, called the *undamped natural frequency* of the system. It is the frequency at which the system would oscillate if the damping were reduced to zero. It has the dimension of reciprocal time (this can be verified from Eqns (2.54a) using the units of the physical parameters given in Eqn. (2.53)), and its unit is rad/sec.

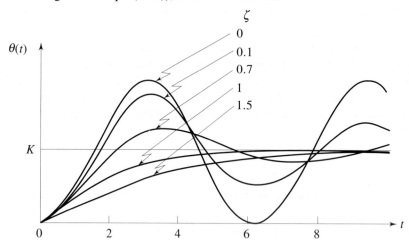

Fig. 2.20   *Step-response curves of a second-order system* ($\omega_n = 1$)

2. Underdamped systems ($0 < \zeta < 1$)

Let us now consider the damped case ($B \neq 0$) under the condition,

$$\frac{k}{J} > \left(\frac{B}{2J}\right)^2$$

In terms of the parameter ζ given in Eqns (2.54a), this condition corresponds to $0 < \zeta < 1$. The parameter ζ, called the *damping ratio*, is a dimensionless quantity (this can be verified from Eqns (2.54a) using the units of the physical parameters given in Eqn. (2.53)).

For $T(t) = \mu(t)$ or $T(s) = 1/s$, we have

$$\theta(s) = \frac{K\omega_n^2}{s(s^2 + 2\zeta\omega_n s + \omega_n^2)}$$

$$= K\left[\frac{1}{s} - \frac{s + \zeta\omega_n}{(s + \zeta\omega_n)^2 + \omega_d^2} - \frac{\zeta\omega_n}{(s + \zeta\omega_n)^2 + \omega_d^2}\right] \qquad (2.57a)$$

where
$$\omega_d = \omega_n\sqrt{1 - \zeta^2} \qquad (2.57b)$$

Using the Table of transform pairs given in Appendix A, we get

$$\theta(t) = K\left[1 - e^{-\zeta\omega_n t}\left(\cos\omega_d t + \frac{\zeta}{\sqrt{1 - \zeta^2}}\sin\omega_d t\right)\right]$$

$$= K\left[1 - \frac{e^{-\zeta\omega_n t}}{\sqrt{1 - \zeta^2}}\sin\left(\omega_d t + \tan^{-1}\frac{\sqrt{1 - \zeta^2}}{\zeta}\right)\right]; t \geq 0 \qquad (2.58)$$

The step response as given by Eqn. (2.58) is plotted in Fig. 2.20 for various values of $\zeta (0 < \zeta < 1)$, and fixed ω_n. These plots provide the physical significance of the parameter ζ. For $0 < \zeta < 1$, the system response exhibits decaying oscillations of frequency $\omega_d = \omega_n\sqrt{1 - \zeta^2}$. ω_d is called the *damped natural frequency*. With ζ approaching zero, ω_d approaches ω_n, and the system response exhibits continuous oscillations. With ζ approaching one, the system response approaches the final value without overshooting it and consequently there are no oscillations (this will be proved shortly). Systems with $0 < \zeta < 1$ are called underdamped systems.

The curves

$$K\left[1 \pm \frac{e^{-\zeta\omega_n t}}{\sqrt{1 - \zeta^2}}\right] \qquad (2.59a)$$

are the envelope curves for the step response. The response curve $\theta(t)$ always remains within this pair of envelope curves as shown in Fig. 2.21. The time-constant of these envelope curves is $1/\zeta\omega_n$. The speed of decay of the transient response depends on the value of the time-constant

$$\tau = \frac{1}{\zeta\omega_n} \qquad (2.59b)$$

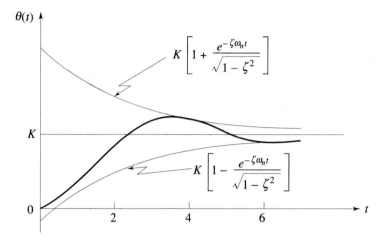

Fig. 2.21 *Envelope curves for the step response of a second-order system ($\omega_n = 1$, $\zeta = 0.7$)*

Therefore, the larger the product $\zeta\omega_n$, the greater is the rate of decay of the transient.

The steady-state value of the system response to unit step input is K; this parameter is thus the *system gain* parameter which gives us the change in the output variable at steady-state in response to a unit change in the input variable.

3. Critically damped systems   ($\zeta = 1$)

The damped case ($B \neq 0$) under the condition $\dfrac{k}{J} = \left(\dfrac{B}{2J}\right)^2$, corresponds to $\zeta = 1$.

For $T(t) = \mu(t)$ or $T(s) = 1/s$, we have

$$\theta(s) = \frac{K\omega_n^2}{s(s^2 + 2\omega_n s + \omega_n^2)} = K\left[\frac{1}{s} - \frac{\omega_n}{(s + \omega_n)^2} - \frac{1}{(s + \omega_n)}\right]$$

$$\theta(t) = K\left[1 - e^{-\omega_n t} - \omega_n t e^{-\omega_n t}\right]; \; t \geq 0 \qquad (2.60)$$

The curve corresponding to $\zeta = 1$ in Fig. 2.20 follows Eqn. (2.60). The response for $\zeta = 1$ approaches the final value without overshooting it, and consequently there are no oscillations. For $\zeta < 1$, the system response exhibits oscillations. Systems with $\zeta = 1$ are called critically damped systems.

4. Overdamped systems   ($\zeta > 1$)

The damped case ($B \neq 0$) under the condition $\dfrac{k}{J} < \left(\dfrac{B}{2J}\right)^2$, corresponds to $\zeta > 1$.

For this case, the system response to a step change of unit magnitude is obtained as follows:

$$\theta(s) = \frac{K\omega_n^2}{s(s^2 + 2\zeta\omega_n s + \omega_n^2)}$$

$$= \frac{K\omega_n^2}{s\left(s + \zeta\omega_n + \omega_n \sqrt{\zeta^2 - 1}\right)\left(s + \zeta\omega_n - \omega_n \sqrt{\zeta^2 - 1}\right)}$$

$$= K\left[\frac{1}{s} + \frac{1}{2\sqrt{\zeta^2 - 1}\left(\zeta + \sqrt{\zeta^2 - 1}\right)}\left(\frac{1}{s + \zeta\omega_n + \omega_n \sqrt{\zeta^2 - 1}}\right)\right.$$

$$\left. - \frac{1}{2\sqrt{\zeta^2 - 1}\left(\zeta - \sqrt{\zeta^2 - 1}\right)}\left(\frac{1}{s + \zeta\omega_n - \omega_n \sqrt{\zeta^2 - 1}}\right)\right]$$

$$\theta(t) = K\left[1 + \frac{1}{2\sqrt{\zeta^2 - 1}\left(\zeta + \sqrt{\zeta^2 - 1}\right)}e^{-\left(\zeta + \sqrt{\zeta^2 - 1}\right)\omega_n t}\right.$$

$$\left. - \frac{1}{2\sqrt{\zeta^2 - 1}\left(\zeta - \sqrt{\zeta^2 - 1}\right)}e^{-\left(\zeta - \sqrt{\zeta^2 - 1}\right)\omega_n t}\right] ; t \geq 0 \qquad (2.61)$$

Representative response curve for $\zeta > 1$ is shown in Fig. 2.20. The effect of increasing damping beyond its critical value is to make the response sluggish. Systems with $\zeta > 1$ are called overdamped systems.

▲▲

The parameters K, ζ, and ω_n describe the 'personality' of a second-order system. These parameters may be obtained from the physical parameters of a system or experimentally by conducting the sinusoidal response test.

The transfer function

$$G(s) = \frac{K}{\dfrac{1}{\omega_n^2}s^2 + \dfrac{2\zeta}{\omega_n}s + 1} \qquad (2.62)$$

is the standard form for second-order transfer functions, and will be encountered in all types of systems—electrical, mechanical, thermal, hydraulic, etc. It is called a *second-order lag* or *quadratic lag*. For $\zeta > 1$, the system no longer has a quadratic lag; it is then a cascade of two simple lags.

2.8 MODELS OF MECHANICAL SYSTEMS

The present and the next four sections are concerned with the modelling of simple physical systems. In these sections, the presentation of the basic material from the system dynamics area is, for reasons of space, limited to essentials. The reader interested in more detail is referred to other literature [37–43].

In the analysis of mechanical systems, it is convenient to make use of three idealized elements—the mass, the spring and the dashpot. These elements represent three essential phenomena which occur in various ways in mechanical systems.

Mechanics of Translation

The ideal mass element represents a particle of mass which is the lumped approximation of the mass of a body concentrated at the centre of the mass.

The concept of the elastic deformation of a body is symbolized by the ideal element shown as a helical spring.

Friction exists in physical systems whenever mechanical surfaces are operated in sliding contact. Friction encountered in physical systems may be of many types.

1. *Coulomb friction force*: It is the force of sliding friction between dry surfaces. This force is substantially constant.
2. *Viscous friction force*: It is the force of friction between moving surfaces separated by viscous fluid, or the force between a solid body and a fluid medium. This force is approximately linearly proportional to velocity over a certain limited velocity range.
3. *Stiction*: It is the force required to initiate motion between two contacting surfaces (which is obviously more than the force required to maintain them in relative motion).

In many situations of interest, viscous friction predominates. Our models of mechanical systems are based on this assumption. Refer [180] for situations where this approximation is not valid.

Sometimes it may even be necessary to introduce viscous friction intentionally to improve the dynamic response of a system. A *dashpot* is a device that provides viscous friction or damping. It consists of a piston and an oil-filled cylinder with a narrow annular passage between the piston and the cylinder (Fig. 2.22). Any relative motion between the piston and the cylinder is resisted by oil.

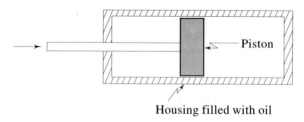

Housing filled with oil

Fig. 2.22 *Dashpot*

Mechanical translational systems consisting of the three parameters M, B, and K are components of many control systems. To cite an example, we revisit the hydraulic power steering mechanism for automobiles shown in Fig. 1.8. In this system, the rotation of the steering wheel is the command signal. This signal is amplified by the hydraulic power amplifier; the force signal $F(t)$ so generated causes the power ram to move which then rotates the wheels through a proper drive linkage.

The load on the power ram is the mass M of the power piston, wheels, and the drive linkage; tyre stiffness represented by spring constant K; and friction with coefficient B because of the motion of the power piston, drive linkage, etc., in the viscous medium. Constant sliding friction also exists at the tyre–road interface. This force depends on road conditions and is therefore an uncontrolled disturbance input to the system.

As another example, consider the system for machining a work piece on a lathe. Tool movement of such a system is shown in Fig 2.23a. The carriage is moved at a constant speed and the control of the tool position is in the direction of the cross slide. The load on the hydraulic actuator consists of mass M, and viscous friction with coefficient B. The disturbance acting on the actuator is the thrust force on the tool required to machine the work piece.

Yet another example of mass-spring-damper systems is shown in Fig. 2.23b. The system controls the thickness of the rolled steel in a steel mill. The rolls are driven at a constant speed by drive motors. The translational motion of the movable roll is controlled by the hydraulic actuator. The load on the hydraulic actuator consists of mass M, and viscous friction with coefficient B. The disturbance acting on the actuator is the upward force on the roll which is quite significant when the slabs enter the rolls or leave the rolls.

Feedback control schemes for the applications referred above will be discussed in the next chapter.

The mass-spring-damper system shown in Fig. 2.24a is thus a useful model of the load on a linear actuator in industrial control systems. The viscous friction has been indicated by a stylized dashpot and F_w represents the load disturbance. Let us obtain the transfer function model of this system. In order to obtain a linear model, we will assume that the friction force of the dashpot is proportional to $\dot{y}$ (true for small velocities). Also the spring is considered a linear device; the spring force is proportional to y (true for small displacements).

Figure 2.24b shows the free-body diagram of the system. Applying Newton's law of motion, the force equation can be written as

$$F(t) - F_w(t) - B\frac{dy(t)}{dt} - Ky(t) = M\frac{d^2y(t)}{dt^2}$$

or
$$M\frac{d^2y(t)}{dt^2} + B\frac{dy(t)}{dt} + Ky(t) = F(t) - F_w(t) \qquad (2.63)$$

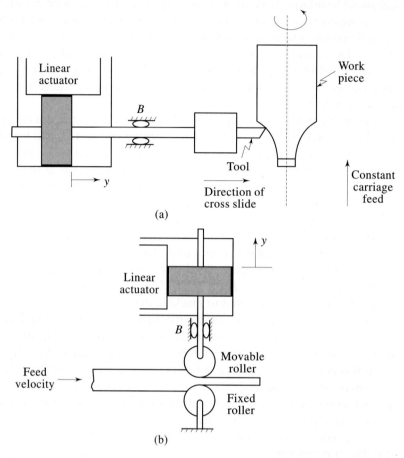

Fig. 2.23 *(a) Machining control system; (b) System for controlling the thickness of rolled steel*

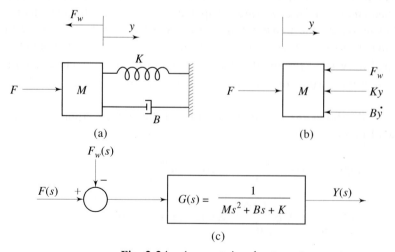

Fig. 2.24 *A mass-spring-damper system*

This is a linear, constant-coefficient differential equation of the second-order.

Taking the Laplace transform of each term of this equation (assuming zero initial conditions), we obtain

$$Ms^2Y(s) + BsY(s) + KY(s) = F(s) - F_w(s)$$

where

$$Y(s) \overset{\Delta}{=} \mathscr{L}[y(t)]; F(s) \overset{\Delta}{=} \mathscr{L}[F(t)]; F_w(s) \overset{\Delta}{=} \mathscr{L}[F_w(t)]$$

Therefore,

$$Y(s) = \frac{1}{Ms^2 + Bs + K} F(s) - \frac{1}{Ms^2 + Bs + K} F_w(s) \qquad (2.64a)$$

Figure 2.24c gives the block diagram representation of the system.

$$G(s) = \frac{1}{Ms^2 + Bs + K} = \frac{1/K}{\dfrac{M}{K}s^2 + \dfrac{B}{K}s + 1} = \frac{1/K}{\dfrac{1}{\omega_n^2}s^2 + \dfrac{2\zeta}{\omega_n}s + 1} \qquad (2.64b)$$

is a quadratic lag; the parameters of the standard form (2.62) of a quadratic lag can easily be obtained from the physical parameters M, B, and K.

The metric system of units for mechanical translational systems is given in Table 2.2.

Fixed-Axis Rotation

Mechanical systems involving fixed-axis rotation occur in the study of machinery of many types and are very important. The modelling procedure is very close to that used in translation. In these systems, the variables of interest are the torque and the angular velocity (or angular displacement). The three basic components for the rotational systems are moment of inertia, torsional spring, and viscous friction.

In low-power servos, the driving and driven shafts can be treated as having negligible elasticity; these rotational systems can therefore be modelled using two components: the moment of inertia J, and the viscous friction with coefficient B. High-power servos, however, may require three components: moment of inertia J, viscous friction with coefficient B, and torsional spring with spring constant K.

To cite an example of rotational load, we revisit the servomechanism for steering of the antenna, shown in Fig. 1.16a. A simple model of the load (antenna) is the moment of inertia–damper system shown in Fig. 1.16b. This model is resketched in Fig. 2.25a; J is the moment of inertia of the antenna, and B represents the viscous friction introduced by bearings and other sources. Torque $T(t)$ is the controlled input generated by the motor, angular displacement $\theta(t)$ of the antenna is the output, and $T_w(t)$ represents the uncontrolled load disturbance torque (due to wind, for example).

The free-body diagram is shown in Fig. 2.25b. The torque equation is

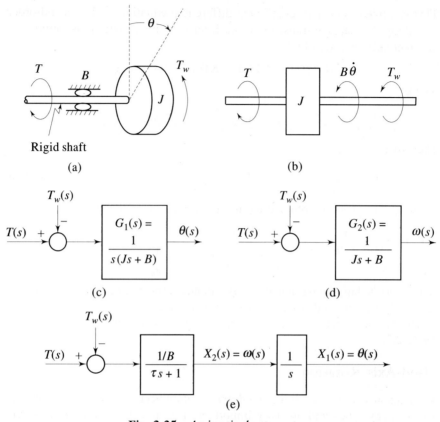

Fig. 2.25 *An inertia-damper system*

$$T(t) - B\frac{d\theta(t)}{dt} - T_w(t) = J\frac{d^2\theta(t)}{dt^2}$$

or

$$J\frac{d^2\theta(t)}{dt^2} + B\frac{d\theta(t)}{dt} = T(t) - T_w(t) \tag{2.65}$$

This is a linear, constant-coefficient differential equation of second-order.

Taking the Laplace transform of each term of this equation (assuming zero initial conditions), we obtain

$$Js^2\theta(s) + Bs\theta(s) = T(s) - T_w(s)$$

where $\quad \theta(s) \overset{\Delta}{=} \mathcal{L}[\theta(t)]; \ T(s)\overset{\Delta}{=}\mathcal{L}[T(t)]; \ T_w(s)\overset{\Delta}{=}\mathcal{L}[T_w(t)]$

Therefore, $\quad \theta(s) = \dfrac{1}{Js^2 + Bs} T(s) - \dfrac{1}{Js^2 + Bs} T_w(s) \tag{2.66a}$

Figure 2.25c gives the block diagram representation of the system.

$$G_1(s) = \frac{1}{s(Js + B)} = \frac{1/B}{s\left(\dfrac{J}{B}s + 1\right)} = \frac{1/B}{s(\tau s + 1)} \tag{2.66b}$$

where $\tau = J/B$.

If we assume that angular velocity $\omega(t) = \dfrac{d\theta(t)}{dt}$ is the output, then the differential equation of the system becomes

$$J \frac{d\omega(t)}{dt} + B\omega(t) = T(t) - T_w(t) \tag{2.67}$$

This is a linear constant-coefficient differential equation of the first-order.

The Laplace transformation of Eqn. (2.67) under the assumption of zero initial conditions, gives

$$(Js + B)\omega(s) = T(s) - T_w(s)$$

where

$$\omega(s) \stackrel{\Delta}{=} \mathscr{L}[\omega(t)].$$

Therefore, $\omega(s) = \dfrac{1}{Js + B} T(s) - \dfrac{1}{Js + B} T_w(s)$ $\tag{2.68a}$

Figure 2.25d shows the corresponding block diagram.

$$G_2(s) = \frac{1}{Js + B} = \frac{1/B}{\dfrac{J}{B}s + 1} = \frac{1/B}{\tau s + 1} \tag{2.68b}$$

where τ is the time-constant of the simple lag.

The differential equations obtained by applying physical laws to mechanical rotational systems are, in fact, the state equations[10] of the system. Only some rearrangement of these equations is required to obtain state variable model in the standard format given in Eqns (2.4).

A selection of the state variables and corresponding state equations are given below.

$$x_1(t) = \theta(t); \; x_2(t) = \omega(t) = \dot{\theta}(t)$$

$$\dot{x}_1(t) = x_2(t)$$

$$\dot{x}_2(t) = -\frac{B}{J} x_2(t) + \frac{1}{J}(T(t) - T_w(t))$$

Taking the Laplace transform on both sides of the state equations (assuming zero initial conditions), we obtain

$$sX_1(s) = X_2(s)$$

$$sX_2(s) = -\frac{B}{J} X_2(s) + \frac{1}{J}[T(s) - T_w(s)]$$

$$X_1(s) \stackrel{\Delta}{=} \mathscr{L}[x_1(t)]; X_2(s) \stackrel{\Delta}{=} \mathscr{L}[x_2(t)]$$

---

10. In mechanical rotational systems with inertia, torsional spring, and damper elements, normally an independent set of angular velocities and displacements associated with inertia elements, and angular displacements associated with torsional spring elements constitutes a state vector.

The corresponding block diagram representation is shown in Fig. 2.25e. It consists of two blocks; the first block is a simple lag with speed $\omega(s)$ as the output, and the second block is an integrator whose output is displacement $\theta(s)$.

The metric system of units for mechanical rotational systems is summarized in Table 2.2.

Table 2.2 *Mechanical symbols and units*

Quantity	Metric units	Quantity	Metric units
Force (F)	Newton or kg-m/sec^2	Torque (T)	Newton-m
Displacement (y)	Metres (m)	Angle (θ)	Radians (rad)
Velocity (v)	m/sec	Angular velocity (ω)	rad/sec
Acceleration ($\dot{v}$)	m/sec^2	Angular acceleration ($\dot{\omega}$)	rad/sec^2
Mass (M)	kg	Moment of inertia(J)	Newton-m/(rad/sec^2) or kg-m^2
Spring constant(K)	Newtons/m	Torsional spring constant (K)	Newton-m/rad
Damping coefficient (B)	Newtons/(m/sec)	Damping coefficient (B)	Newton-m/(rad/sec)

Example 2.6

Consider the mechanical system shown in Fig. 2.26a. This system is a simplified 'one-wheeled' model of an automobile suspension system with M_1: the mass of the automobile, B: the shock absorbers, K_1: the springs, M_2: the mass of the wheels, and K_2: the elastance of the tyres. The system objective is to reduce vibrations $y_1(t)$ due to disturbance force $F_w(t)$.

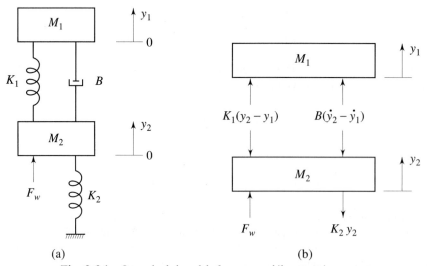

(a)   (b)

Fig. 2.26 *One-wheeled model of an automobile suspension system*

The displacements $y_1(t)$ and $y_2(t)$ are considered with respect to positions of the vehicle and the wheels on a level road under the loaded condition. The gravitational forces, therefore, do not appear in the model being formulated.

Figure 2.26b shows the free-body diagram for the system. From this figure, we have the following differential equations describing the dynamics of the system.

$$M_1 \ddot{y}_1(t) = K_1(y_2(t) - y_1(t)) + B(\dot{y}_2(t) - \dot{y}_1(t)) \tag{2.69a}$$

$$M_2 \ddot{y}_2(t) = F_w(t) - K_1(y_2(t) - y_1(t)) - B(\dot{y}_2(t) - \dot{y}_1(t)) - K_2 y_2(t) \tag{2.69b}$$

Taking the Laplace transform of these equations, assuming zero initial conditions, we obtain

$$M_1 s^2 Y_1(s) + B(sY_1(s) - sY_2(s)) + K_1(Y_1(s) - Y_2(s)) = 0 \tag{2.70a}$$

$$M_2 s^2 Y_2(s) + B(sY_2(s) - sY_1(s)) + K_1(Y_2(s) - Y_1(s)) + K_2 Y_2(s) = F_w(s) \tag{2.70b}$$

Suppose that a transfer function is desired between $F_w(s)$ and $Y_1(s)$, i.e., between the disturbance force applied to the wheels and the resulting displacement of the automobile. This transfer function can be found by eliminating $Y_2(s)$ in Eqns. (2.70). Solving Eqn. (2.70a) for $Y_1(s)$, we obtain

$$Y_1(s) = \frac{Bs + K_1}{M_1 s^2 + Bs + K_1} Y_2(s)$$

Now Eqn. (2.70b) can be solved for $Y_2(s)$:

$$Y_2(s) = \frac{1}{M_2 s^2 + Bs + K_1 + K_2} F_w(s) + \frac{Bs + K_1}{M_2 s^2 + Bs + K_1 + K_2} Y_1(s)$$

Eliminating $Y_2(s)$ from these equations, gives

$$G(s) = \frac{Y_1(s)}{F_w(s)}$$

$$= \frac{Bs + K_1}{\left[M_1 M_2 s^4 + B(M_1 + M_2)s^3 + (K_1 M_2 + K_1 M_1 + K_2 M_1)s^2 + K_2 Bs + K_1 K_2 \right]}$$

The dynamics of the mechanical system are completely described by the transfer function. Given the mass of the automobile, the mass of the wheels, and the elastance of the tyres, the smoothness of the ride is determined by the parameters of the shock absorber and the springs. These parameters are used to tune the system to give a good response. As a physical shock absorber deteriorates, the value of the parameter B changes, which changes the transfer function and the quality of the ride.

Rearrangement of Eqns (2.69) in the standard form given by Eqns (2.4) directly gives us the state variable formulation of the mechanical system.

Independent set of displacements and velocities of masses, and displacements of springs constitutes a state vector for the mass-spring-damper systems. In accordance with this choice, state variables for the system of Fig. 2.26 are

$$x_1(t) = y_1(t); \quad x_2(t) = y_2(t);$$
$$x_3(t) = \dot{y}_1(t); \quad x_4(t) = \dot{y}_2(t)$$

With these definitions of state variables, the two second-order differential equations (2.69a) and (2.69b) can be written in the form of state equations (first-order equations):

$$\dot{x}_1(t) = x_3(t)$$
$$\dot{x}_2(t) = x_4(t)$$

$$\dot{x}_3(t) = -\frac{K_1}{M_1}x_1(t) + \frac{K_1}{M_1}x_2(t) - \frac{B}{M_1}x_3(t) + \frac{B}{M_1}x_4(t)$$

$$\dot{x}_4(t) = \frac{K_1}{M_2}x_1(t) - \frac{(K_1 + K_2)}{M_2}x_2(t) + \frac{B}{M_2}x_3(t) - \frac{B}{M_2}x_4(t) + \frac{1}{M_2}F_w(t)$$

In the vector-matrix notation, these equations are written as

$$
\begin{bmatrix} \dot{x}_1(t) \\ \dot{x}_2(t) \\ \dot{x}_3(t) \\ \dot{x}_4(t) \end{bmatrix} =
\begin{bmatrix}
0 & 0 & 1 & 0 \\
0 & 0 & 0 & 1 \\
-\dfrac{K_1}{M_1} & \dfrac{K_1}{M_1} & -\dfrac{B}{M_1} & \dfrac{B}{M_1} \\
\dfrac{K_1}{M_2} & -\dfrac{(K_1 + K_2)}{M_2} & \dfrac{B}{M_2} & -\dfrac{B}{M_2}
\end{bmatrix}
\begin{bmatrix} x_1(t) \\ x_2(t) \\ x_3(t) \\ x_4(t) \end{bmatrix} +
\begin{bmatrix} 0 \\ 0 \\ 0 \\ 1/M_2 \end{bmatrix} F_w(t)
$$

Since $y_1(t)$ is the desired output, the output equation is

$$y(t) = y_1(t) = \begin{bmatrix} 1 & 0 & 0 & 0 \end{bmatrix} \begin{bmatrix} x_1(t) \\ x_2(t) \\ x_3(t) \\ x_4(t) \end{bmatrix}$$

Example 2.7

Many servomechanisms involve mechanical systems that can be modelled as in Fig. 2.27a. The inertia J_1 represents the rotating member of a motor that applies the torque T; whereas J_2 is the driven load. Twisting of the long shaft due to the application of the torque is represented by the torsional spring constant K. Damping B represents frictional losses in the shaft.

Figure 2.27b shows the free-body diagram for the system. From this figure, we have the following differential equations describing the dynamics of the system.

$$J_1\ddot{\theta}_1(t) = T(t) - B(\dot{\theta}_1(t) - \dot{\theta}_2(t)) - K(\theta_1(t) - \theta_2(t))$$
$$J_2\ddot{\theta}_2(t) = B(\dot{\theta}_1(t) - \dot{\theta}_2(t)) + K(\theta_1(t) - \theta_2(t))$$

Laplace transformation of these equations under the assumption of zero initial conditions, gives

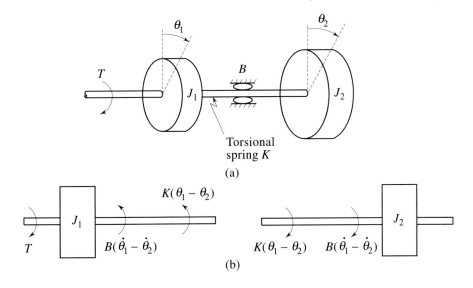

Fig. 2.27 *A motor-load system*

$$(J_1 s^2 + Bs + K)\theta_1(s) = (Bs + K)\theta_2(s) + T(s)$$

$$(J_2 s^2 + Bs + K)\theta_2(s) = (Bs + K)\theta_1(s)$$

Manipulation leads to

$$\frac{\theta_2(s)}{T(s)} = G(s) = \frac{\left[\dfrac{1}{J_1 + J_2}\right](\tau s + 1)}{s^2\left[\dfrac{1}{\omega_n^2}s^2 + \dfrac{2\zeta}{\omega_n}s + 1\right]} \tag{2.71}$$

where $\qquad \tau = \dfrac{B}{K}; \quad \omega_n = \sqrt{\dfrac{K(J_1 + J_2)}{J_1 J_2}}; \quad \zeta = \dfrac{B}{2\sqrt{KJ_1 J_2 / (J_1 + J_2)}}$

2.9 | MODELS OF ELECTRICAL CIRCUITS

In later chapters of this book, we will frequently use electric circuits to meet the functional requirements of the amplification of weak control/sensor signals, filtering of high frequency 'noise' (such as measurement noise), and to improve the performance of feedback control systems. Here the objective is to develop mathematical models of commonly used electric circuits.

Passive Circuits

The resistor, the inductor, and the capacitor are the three basic elements of passive (no internal power source) electric circuits. These circuits are analysed by the application of Kirchhoff's voltage and current laws.

Let us analyse the RLC circuit of Fig. 2.28 by using Kirchhoff's current law.

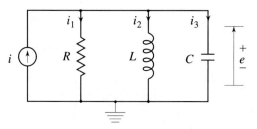

Fig. 2.28 *An RLC circuit*

The governing equations of the system are

$$i(t) = i_1(t) + i_2(t) + i_3(t) = \frac{e(t)}{R} + i_2(t) + C\frac{de(t)}{dt}$$

$$e(t) = L\frac{di_2(t)}{dt}$$

These equations may be rearranged to give state equations for the circuit:

$$\left.\begin{aligned}\frac{de(t)}{dt} &= -\frac{1}{RC}e(t) - \frac{1}{C}i_2(t) + \frac{1}{C}i(t)\\[2mm]\frac{di_2(t)}{dt} &= \frac{1}{L}e(t)\end{aligned}\right\} \qquad (2.72)$$

$e(t)$ and $i_2(t)$ are the state variables and $i(t)$ is the current source (input variable).

Analogous Systems

If two systems are described by dynamical equations of identical form, these are said to be *analogs* of each other. For example, the electric analog of the mechanical system of Fig. 2.2 is the RLC circuit shown in Fig. 2.28. This can be established as follows.

The mechanical system of Fig. 2.2 is governed by the differential equation (refer Eqn. (2.26))

$$M\frac{d^2x(t)}{dt^2} + B\frac{dx(t)}{dt} + K x(t) = F(t)$$

Rewriting this equation in terms of velocity variable $v(t) = \dot{x}(t)$ results in the following integro-differential equation.

$$M\frac{dv(t)}{dt} + B\,v(t) + K \int_{-\infty}^{t} v(\tau)d\tau = F(t) \qquad (2.73)$$

The electric circuit of Fig. 2.28 is governed by the state equations (2.72). Rewriting these equations in terms of voltage $e(t)$, results in the following integro-differential equation.

$$C \frac{de(t)}{dt} + \frac{1}{R} e(t) + \frac{1}{L} \int_{-\infty}^{t} e(\tau) d\tau = i(t)$$

Comparing this equation with Eqn. (2.73), we at once observe their mathematical similarity with respect to the following analogous pairs:

$$F(t) \leftrightarrow i(t); \ v(t) \leftrightarrow e(t)$$
$$M \leftrightarrow C; K \leftrightarrow 1/L; B \leftrightarrow 1/R \tag{2.74}$$

The commonly-used characterizing variables in an electrical system—the voltage and the current—are respectively called *across* and *through* variables of the system. By analogy, velocity and force are, respectively, the across and through variables of mechanical systems. The analogous variables and element pairs in (2.74) are appropriately called the *force-current analogy*.[11]

The variables and basic elements of mechanical rotational systems with their electrical analogs (*torque-current analogy*) are listed below.

$$T(t) \leftrightarrow i(t); \quad \omega(t) \leftrightarrow e(t)$$
$$J \leftrightarrow C; \quad K \leftrightarrow 1/L; \ B \leftrightarrow 1/R \tag{2.75}$$

▲▲

The concept of analogous systems is a useful technique for the study of various systems such as electrical, mechanical, thermal, liquid level, etc. Generally it is convenient to study a non-electrical system in terms of its electrical analog as electrical systems are more easily amenable to experimental study.

The principle of analogy is the basic principle behind the use of analog computers for investigating system behaviour—an analog to the physical system can be developed, as will be seen shortly, from the components of an analog computer.

The metric system of units for electrical systems is summarized in Table 2.3.

Table 2.3 *Electrical symbols and units*

Quantity	Metric units
Voltage (*e*)	Volts
Current (*i*)	Amperes
Inductance, (*L*)	Henrys
Capacitance (*C*)	Farads
Resistance (*R*)	Ohms

Example 2.8

Figure 2.29 shows five passive (no internal power source) circuits. In the following, we write describing equations (using Kirchhoff's voltage and cur-

11. Another possible analogy between mechanical and electrical systems is the *force-voltage analogy*. The corresponding analogous electrical system for the mechanical system of Fig. 2.2 will be an RLC series circuit excited by a voltage source.

rent laws) for each circuit. Transfer function models are then obtained by Laplace transformation.

For each circuit given in Fig. 2.29, capacitor voltages are the state variables. State equations can directly be 'read' from the describing equations given here.

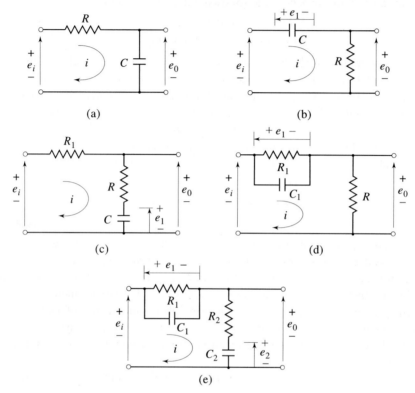

(a)   (b)

(c)   (d)

(e)

Fig. 2.29 *Commonly-used passive circuits*

Figure 2.29a

$$i(t) = C \frac{de_0(t)}{dt} \; ; \; R \, i(t) + e_0(t) = e_i(t)$$

$$G(s) = \frac{E_0(s)}{E_i(s)} = \frac{1}{\tau s + 1} \; ; \; \tau = RC \tag{2.76}$$

Figure 2.29b

$$e_1(t) = e_i(t) - e_0(t); \quad i(t) = C \frac{de_1(t)}{dt}; \; e_0(t) = Ri(t)$$

$$G(s) = \frac{E_0(s)}{E_i(s)} = \frac{\tau s}{\tau s + 1} \; ; \; \tau = RC \tag{2.77}$$

Figure 2.29c

$$e_1(t) = e_0(t) - Ri(t); \quad i(t) = C \frac{de_1(t)}{dt}; \quad (R + R_1) i(t) + e_1(t) = e_i(t)$$

$$G(s) = \frac{E_0(s)}{E_i(s)} = \frac{\tau s + 1}{(\tau/\alpha)s + 1}; \ \tau = RC, \ \alpha = \frac{R}{R_1 + R} \qquad (2.78)$$

Figure 2.29d

$$e_1(t) = e_i(t) - e_0(t); \quad i(t) = \frac{e_1(t)}{R_1} + C_1 \frac{de_1(t)}{dt}; \ e_0(t) = R\,i(t)$$

$$G(s) = \frac{E_0(s)}{E_i(s)} = \alpha \frac{\tau s + 1}{\alpha \tau s + 1}; \ \tau = R_1 C_1, \ \alpha = \frac{R}{R_1 + R} \qquad (2.79)$$

Figure 2.29e

$$e_1(t) = e_i(t) - e_0(t); \quad e_2(t) = e_0(t) - R_2\,i(t);$$

$$i(t) = \frac{e_1(t)}{R_1} + C_1 \frac{de_1(t)}{dt} = C_2 \frac{de_2(t)}{dt}$$

$$G(s) = \frac{E_0(s)}{E_i(s)} = \frac{(\tau_1 s + 1)(\tau_2 s + 1)}{\tau_1 \tau_2 s^2 + (\tau_1 + \tau_2 + \tau_{12})s + 1}; \qquad (2.80)$$

$$\tau_1 = R_1 C_1, \ \tau_2 = R_2 C_2, \ \tau_{12} = R_1 C_2$$

▲▲

As a final point on circuit analysis, we cover the technique that is called the *impedance approach*. This approach is useful for developing transfer function models of electric circuits.

Impedance $Z(s)$ of a passive circuit is the ratio of the Laplace transform of the voltage across the circuit to the Laplace transform of the current through the circuit under the assumption of zero initial conditions. For impedances in series, the equivalent impedence is equal to the sum of the individual impedances. For impedances in parallel, the reciprocal of the equivalent impedance is equal to the sum of the reciprocals of the individual impedances.

Figure 2.30a shows an RLC-series circuit.

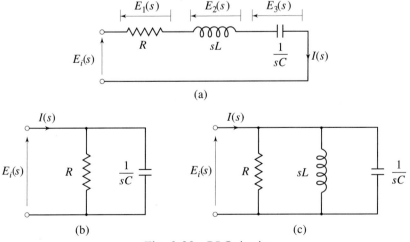

Fig. 2.30 *RLC circuits*

For the resistor,

$$e_1(t) = R\,i(t)\,; \quad Z_1(s) = \frac{E_1(s)}{I(s)} = R$$

For the inductor,

$$e_2(t) = L\,\frac{di(t)}{dt}\,; \; Z_2(s) = \frac{E_2(s)}{I(s)} = sL$$

For the capacitor,

$$i(t) = C\,\frac{de_3(t)}{dt}\,; \; Z_3(s) = \frac{E_3(s)}{I(s)} = \frac{1}{sC}$$

Total impedance of the circuit

$$Z(s) = Z_1(s) + Z_2(s) + Z_3(s) = R + sL + \frac{1}{sC}$$

The circuit obeys the relation

$$E_i(s) = Z(s)\,I(s)$$

For the RC-parallel circuit shown in Fig. 2.30b, total impedance $Z(s)$ is given by the relation

$$\frac{1}{Z(s)} = \frac{1}{R} + \frac{1}{1/sC}\,; \quad \text{or} \quad Z(s) = \frac{R(1/sC)}{R + 1/sC}$$

For the RLC-parallel circuit shown in Fig. 2.30c, total impedance $Z(s)$ is given by the relation

$$\frac{1}{Z(s)} = \frac{1}{R} + \frac{1}{sL} + \frac{1}{1/sC}$$

Example 2.9

Let us derive transfer functions for the circuits of Fig. 2.29 using the impedance approach.

Figure 2.29a

$$E_0(s) = \frac{1}{sC}\,I(s) = \frac{1}{sC}\left[\frac{E_i(s)}{R + 1/sC}\right]$$

Manipulation of this equation gives Eqn. (2.76).

Figure 2.29b

$$E_0(s) = R\,I(s) = R\left[\frac{E_i(s)}{R + 1/sC}\right]$$

Manipulation of this equation gives Eqn. (2.77).

Figure 2.29c

$$E_0(s) = \left(R + \frac{1}{sC} \right) I(s) = \left(R + \frac{1}{sC} \right) \left[\frac{E_i(s)}{R + R_1 + 1/sC} \right]$$

Manipulation of this equation gives Eqn. (2.78).

Figure 2.29d

$$E_0(s) = R I(s) = R \left[\frac{E_i(s)}{R + \dfrac{R_1(1/sC_1)}{R_1 + 1/sC_1}} \right]$$

Manipulation of this equation gives Eqn. (2.79).

Figure 2.29e

$$E_0(s) = \left(R_2 + \frac{1}{sC_2} \right) I(s) = \left(R_2 + \frac{1}{sC_2} \right) \left[\frac{E_i(s)}{R_2 + 1/sC_2 + \dfrac{R_1(1/sC_1)}{R_1 + 1/sC_1}} \right]$$

Manipulation of this equation gives Eqn. (2.80).

Op Amp Circuits

With the development of operational amplifiers (op amps), and the ever-increasing reliability of integrated circuits, electronic controllers are commonly used in industrial applications. In the process industry, electronic controllers have gradually replaced pneumatic controllers. The development is fast moving towards microprocessor-based controllers.

In the following, we give some simple and useful op amp circuit models. In later chapters, these circuits will be used as control logic elements.

The circuit symbol for an op amp is shown in Fig. 2.31a. Two input terminals marked '+' and '−' are shown. These polarity signs refer to the phase relationship between the individual input signals and the output signal; the output signal is in phase with the signal applied to the input pin marked '+', known as the *non-inverting input*, and is in antiphase to the signal applied to the pin marked '−', known as the *inverting input*. The power supply connections are labelled V^+ for the positive voltage and V^- for the negative voltage. The op amp is usually shown as in Fig. 2.31b, without the power supply connections.

Characteristics of an *ideal amplifier* are listed below.

1. Infinite input impedance; an ideal amplifier can be connected to any signal source with no loading effects.
2. Infinite gain.
3. Zero output impedance; an ideal amplifier is capable of driving any load.

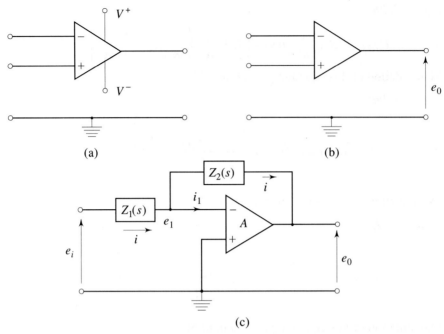

Fig. 2.31 (a) *Circuit symbol of op amp*
(b) *Simplified symbol*
(c) *Op amp circuit building block*

4. Infinite bandwidth; an ideal amplifier can amplify any signal frequency.

Op amps approach the first three characteristics closely. The 741 op amp has an input impedance of 6 MΩ, gain of the order of 10^5, and can supply at least 5 mA to a load of 2000 Ω.

The gain of 741 op amp is 10^5 at frequencies between zero (dc) and 10 Hz. Beyond this value of frequency, the gain reduces considerably. Therefore, the op amps approach the ideal amplifier for dc and low frequency signals.

Analysis of op amp circuits becomes simple under the assumption of ideal characteristics. Consider, for example, the circuit of Fig. 2.31c.

1. Since gain A is infinite and output e_0 is finite, the voltage e_1 is virtually zero.
2. Input impedance is infinite, therefore $i_1 = 0$.

For the circuit of Fig. 2.31c (under the second assumption),

$$I(s) = \frac{E_i(s) - E_1(s)}{Z_1(s)} = \frac{E_1(s) - E_0(s)}{Z_2(s)}$$

Since $E_1(s) = 0$ as per first assumption, we get

$$I(s) = \frac{E_i(s)}{Z_1(s)} = -\frac{E_0(s)}{Z_2(s)}$$

or
$$\frac{E_0(s)}{E_i(s)} = -\frac{Z_2(s)}{Z_1(s)} \tag{2.81}$$

where

$Z_1(s)$ = impedance connected to the input of the amplifier,
$Z_2(s)$ = impedance connected between output and input of the amplifier.

By choosing proper values of $Z_1(s)$ and $Z_2(s)$, operational amplifiers can be used for various purposes.

Example 2.10

Figure 2.32 shows seven simple op amp circuits. In the following, we derive transfer function for each circuit. From the transfer function models, it will become obvious that these circuits are used for amplification, integration, and differentiation of a given signal.

Figure 2.32a
$$\frac{E_0(s)}{E_i(s)} = \frac{-R_2}{R_1} \tag{2.82a}$$

The circuit is thus a constant gain amplifier. The gain can be made adjustable by using a potentiometer for one of the resistances.

Note the phase relationship between input and output; the circuit of Fig. 2.32a is called an *inverting amplifier*.

Figure 2.32b
A circuit with $R_1 = R_2$ is an *inverter*; it simply inverts the sign of the input voltage without changing its magnitude. It can be used in cascade with other elements to maintain proper sign relations, as shown in Fig. 2.32b. For this circuit,

$$\frac{E_0(s)}{E_i(s)} = \frac{R_2}{R_1} \tag{2.82b}$$

Figure 2.32c
$$\frac{E_0(s)}{E_i(s)} = -\frac{1/sC}{R} = -\frac{1}{RCs} \tag{2.83a}$$

The circuit is thus an integrator.

Equation (2.83a) is true if the initial voltage on the capacitor is zero. Inverse Laplace transformation of this equation gives

$$e_0(t) = -\frac{1}{RC} \int_0^t e_i(\tau)d\tau \tag{2.83b}$$

Figure 2.32d
$$\frac{E_0(s)}{E_i(s)} = -\frac{R_2 + 1/sC}{R_1} = -\frac{R_2}{R_1} - \frac{1}{R_1Cs} \tag{2.84a}$$

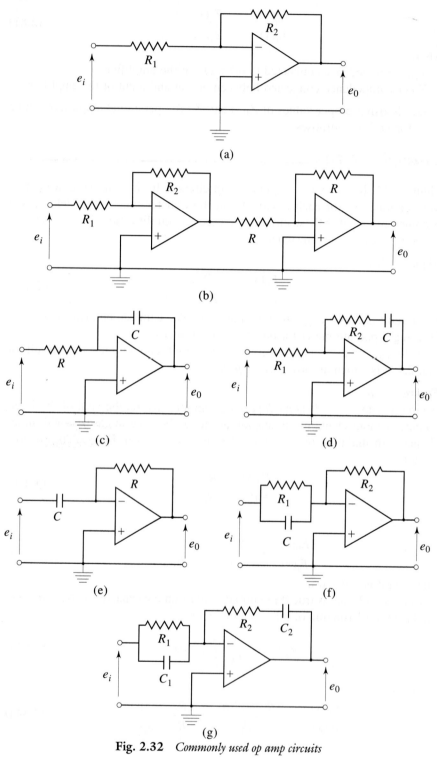

Fig. 2.32 *Commonly used op amp circuits*

$$e_0(t) = -\frac{R_2}{R_1}e_i(t) - \frac{1}{R_1 C}\int_0^t e_i(\tau)d\tau \tag{2.84b}$$

The circuit thus processes the input signal by 'proportional + integral' action.

Figure 2.32e

$$\frac{E_0(s)}{E_i(s)} = -\frac{R}{1/sC} = -RCs \tag{2.85a}$$

$$e_0(t) = -RC\frac{de_i(t)}{dt} \tag{2.85b}$$

The circuit is thus a differentiator.

Figure 2.32f

$$\frac{E_0(s)}{E_i(s)} = -\frac{R_2}{\dfrac{R_1(1/sC)}{R_1 + 1/sC}} = -\frac{R_2}{R_1}(R_1 Cs + 1) \tag{2.86a}$$

$$e_0(t) = -\frac{R_2}{R_1}e_i(t) - R_2 C\frac{de_i(t)}{dt} \tag{2.86b}$$

The circuit thus processes the input signal by 'proportional + derivative' action.

Figure 2.32g

$$\frac{E_0(s)}{E_i(s)} = -\frac{R_2 + 1/sC_2}{\dfrac{R_1(1/sC_1)}{R_1 + 1/sC_1}} = -\frac{(R_2 C_2 s + 1)(R_1 C_1 s + 1)}{R_1 C_2 s}$$

$$= -\left[\frac{R_2 C_2 R_1 C_1 s^2 + R_2 C_2 s + R_1 C_1 s + 1}{R_1 C_2 s}\right]$$

$$= -\left[\frac{R_1 C_1 + R_2 C_2}{R_1 C_2} + \frac{1}{R_1 C_2 s} + R_2 C_1 s\right] \tag{2.87a}$$

$$e_0(t) = -\frac{R_1 C_1 + R_2 C_2}{R_1 C_2}e_i(t) - \frac{1}{R_1 C_2}\int_0^t e_i(\tau)d\tau - R_2 C_1\frac{de_i(t)}{dt} \tag{2.87b}$$

The circuit thus processes the input signal by 'proportional + integral + derivative' action.

Simulation with an Analog Computer

Operational amplifiers can be used to solve the dynamic model of a physical system. The essence of the technique is to construct an op amp circuit whose governing equations are the same as those of the system under study except for magnitude and time-scale factors. The resulting circuit is said to be an *analog computer*.

Analog computation has lost some of its importance because of the increasing availability of digital computers. However, it still provides an excellent means of developing control system prototypes.

2.10 | MODELS OF THERMAL SYSTEMS

The basic requirement for the representation of thermal systems by lumped-parameter models is that the temperature of the medium be considered uniform. When the medium is small, this approximation is valid. Also when the medium consists of a body of air or liquid, the temperature can be considered uniform if there is perfect mixing of the fluid. When a single temperature does not accurately represent the thermal state of the entire medium, i.e., there is complex temperature distribution throughout the medium, the problem becomes one of the distributed parameters, requiring the use of partial differential equations. Here, however, in order to simplify the analysis, uniformity of temperature is assumed and thereby the systems are represented by lumped-parameter models.

Heat flow rate h (through variable; analogous to current), and temperature θ (across variable; analogous to voltage) are the commonly used characterizing variables of thermal systems for the purpose of modelling. Thermal resistance and capacitance are the two basic elements. The resistance that we have encountered so far has been an element that dissipates energy and converts it into heat (damper in mechanical systems, and resistor in electrical systems). Thermal resistance is not an element that dissipates energy; it is a consequence of the fact that a temperature difference is required to cause heat to flow. Thermal capacitance is an energy storage element; a parameter representing internal thermal energy (determined by molecular activity) of the substance.

Heat-Transfer Systems without Carrier Fluids

The flow of heat through a solid material occurs by conduction. The basic equation for one-dimensional heat conduction through a plane wall of surface area $A(m^2)$ and thickness $l(m)$ is

$$h = \sigma A\left(\frac{\theta_1 - \theta_2}{l}\right) \qquad (2.88)$$

where h = heat flow rate, Joules/sec;

$\Delta\theta = \theta_1 - \theta_2$ = temperature drop along the direction of heat flow, °C; and

σ = thermal conductivity of the material, Joules/(°C) (m) (sec).

Many solids interface with fluids. A simple model for convective heat transfer mechanism at solid–fluid interface is given by the relation

$$h = UA(\theta_S - \theta_F) \qquad (2.89)$$

where h = heat flow rate, Joules/sec (negative sign of h will indicate flow of heat from fluid to solid);

A = area of the surface (solid–fluid interface), m^2;

θ_S = temperature of the solid, °C;

θ_F = temperature of the fluid, °C; and

U = film coefficient of the solid–fluid interface, Joules/(m^2) (°C) (sec).

Using Eqns (2.88)–(2.89), we define *thermal resistance* as follows:

$$R_{CD} = \text{conductive thermal resistance} = \frac{l}{\sigma A}, \text{°C/(Joules/sec)} \qquad (2.90a)$$

$$R_{CV} = \text{convective thermal resistance} = \frac{1}{UA}, \text{°C/(Joules/sec)} \qquad (2.90b)$$

The rate of heat storage (in the form of internal energy) in a substance is governed by the relation

$$h_1 - h_2 = Mc\frac{d\theta}{dt} \qquad (2.91)$$

where h_1 = heat-input rate, Joules/sec;

h_2 = heat-output rate, Joules/sec;

M = mass of the substance, kg;

c = specific heat of the substance, Joules/(kg) (°C); and

θ = temperature of the substance, °C.

Using Eqn. (2.91), we define *thermal capacitance* as follows:

$$C = Mc, \text{Joules/°C} \qquad (2.92)$$

Heat-Transfer Systems with Carrier Fluids

When large quantities of heat are to be transported over considerable distances, it can be best done by the flowing fluid as a carrier of thermal energy. In such systems, there exist many energy storage effects, in addition to storage of energy in the form of internal thermal energy—storage in a gravity field, storage due to compressibility of the fluid, storage due to change in the volume of the container, storage due to inertia of the fluid flowing through a pipe, etc.

We first consider the case where the changes in internal thermal energies outweigh the changes in the mechanical energies associated with the fluid. The extreme opposite case will be taken up in the next section where it will be assumed that the changes in mechanical energies outweigh the changes in internal thermal energy. There are many important practical examples where none of these two approximations is sufficiently accurate for dynamic modelling. These are characterized by strong mechanical–thermal interactions. Fuel flow in turbines and rockets are specific examples. These areas are somewhat specialized; we shall give examples from only the two simple categories mentioned above.

In the following we define important parameters of heat-transfer systems with carrier fluids, under the assumption that the changes in the internal thermal energy outweigh the changes in mechanical energies.

Thermal capacitance of the carrier fluid is defined as follows:

$$C = V\rho c, \text{Joules/}°C \tag{2.93}$$

where

V = volume of the fluid chamber, m^3;
ρ = fluid density, kg/m^3; and
c = specific heat of the fluid, Joules/(kg) (°C).

Carrier fluid-flow into a chamber is a source of thermal-energy input. Also, the outflowing fluid takes away thermal energy from the chamber. Carrier flow heat-input rate and heat-output rate depend upon the temperatures of the inflowing and outflowing fluids, respectively.

Let θ_i (°C) be the temperature of the inflowing fluid into a chamber and θ_0(°C) be the temperature of the outflowing fluid. Flow rate $Q(m^3/\text{sec})$ and density ρ (kg/m^3) are assumed constant.

Heat-input rate, $h_1 = Q\rho c\theta_i$, Joules/sec

Heat-output rate, $h_2 = Q\rho c\theta_0$, Joules/sec

Net change in transportation of heat is given by

$$h_1 - h_2 = Q\rho c(\theta_i - \theta_0) \tag{2.94}$$

From this equation, we define the *thermal resistance* due to carrier fluid-flow as

$$R = \frac{1}{Q\rho c}, °C/(\text{Joules/sec}) \tag{2.95}$$

Table 2.4 summarizes the metric system of units for thermal systems.

Table 2.4   *Thermal symbols and units*

Quantity	Metric units
Rate of heat flow (h)	Joules/sec
Temperature (θ)	°C
Thermal capacitance (C)	Joules/°C
Thermal resistance (R)	°C/(Joules/sec)

Example 2.11

As an illustration of a heat-transfer system without carrier fluids, consider the room-heating system shown in Fig. 2.33. The heat released for heating the room is the latent heat of condensation.

To obtain a lumped-parameter model for the system, assume that the state of air in the room can be described by a single temperature. Definitions of system parameters and variables are as follows:

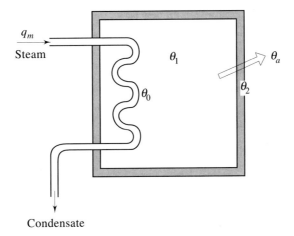

Fig. 2.33 *A room-heating system*

$\overline{Q}_m$ = steady-state steam flow rate, kg/sec

λ = latent heat of condensation, Joules/kg

C_0 = thermal capacitance of the radiator, Joules/°C

C_1 = thermal capacitance of air in the room, Joules/°C

C_2 = thermal capacitance of the room walls, Joules/°C

R_0 = convective thermal resistance for heat transfer at the solid–fluid interface between the radiator and the room-air, °C/(Joules/sec)

R_1 = $R_{CV} + R_{CD}$; R_{CV} is convective thermal resistance for heat transfer at the fluid–solid interface between the fluid and inside of the room walls; R_{CD} is conductive thermal resistance for conduction through the room walls, °C/(Joules/sec).

R_2 = convective thermal resistance for heat transfer between the outside of room walls and its surroundings, °C/(Joules/sec).

$\theta_0, \theta_1, \theta_2$: perturbations in temperatures of the radiator, the room-air, and the room-walls respectively from the nominal point of operation $\{\overline{\theta}_0, \overline{\theta}_1, \overline{\theta}_2, \}$, in response to perturbation $q_m(t)$ in the steam flow rate.

θ_a: perturbation in ambient temperature; it is uncontrolled and hence is the disturbance input for the process.

Heat-balance equation for the radiator is

$$C_0 \underbrace{\frac{d\theta_0(t)}{dt}}_{\substack{\text{Rate of heat} \\ \text{storage}}} = \underbrace{q_m(t)\lambda}_{\substack{\text{Rate of} \\ \text{heat input}}} - \underbrace{\frac{\theta_0(t) - \theta_1(t)}{R_0}}_{\substack{\text{Rate of heat} \\ \text{output}}} \qquad (2.96a)$$

Heat-balance equation for the room-air is

$$C_1 \frac{d\theta_1(t)}{dt} = \frac{\theta_0(t) - \theta_1(t)}{R_0} - \frac{\theta_1(t) - \theta_2(t)}{R_1} \qquad (2.96b)$$

Heat-balance equation for the room-walls is

$$C_2 \frac{d\theta_2(t)}{dt} = \frac{\theta_1(t) - \theta_2(t)}{R_1} - \frac{\theta_2(t) - \theta_a(t)}{R_2} \tag{2.96c}$$

Assuming the heat capacity of the radiator to be negligible compared to that of room-air, we can simplify Eqns (2.96) to the following:

$$C_1 \frac{d\theta_1(t)}{dt} = q_m(t)\lambda - \frac{\theta_1(t) - \theta_2(t)}{R_1} \tag{2.97a}$$

$$C_2 \frac{d\theta_2(t)}{dt} = \frac{\theta_1(t) - \theta_2(t)}{R_1} - \frac{\theta_2(t) - \theta_a(t)}{R_2} \tag{2.97b}$$

An independent set of temperatures associated with various energy-storing elements of a thermal system constitutes a state vector for the system.

For the thermal system under consideration, the state is defined by the variables θ_1 and θ_2; we can therefore choose these variables as state variables x_1 and x_2 respectively. Rearrangement of Eqns (2.97) directly gives the state equations of the system:

$$\dot{x}_1(t) = -\frac{1}{R_1 C_1} x_1(t) + \frac{1}{R_1 C_1} x_2(t) + \frac{\lambda}{C_1} q_m(t)$$

$$\dot{x}_2(t) = \frac{1}{R_1 C_2} x_1(t) - \left(\frac{1}{R_1} + \frac{1}{R_2}\right)\frac{1}{C_2} x_2(t) + \frac{1}{R_2 C_2} \theta_a(t)$$

where $q_m(t)$ and $\theta_a(t)$ are the input variables; $q_m(t)$ is the controllable input, and $\theta_a(t)$ is the uncontrollable disturbance.

$\theta_1(t)$ is the output variable of interest. We eliminate $\theta_2(t)$ from Eqns (2.97) to obtain the transfer function model.

Taking Laplace transform on both sides of Eqns (2.97), assuming zero initial conditions, we obtain

$$sC_1 \theta_1(s) = \lambda Q_m(s) - \frac{\theta_1(s) - \theta_2(s)}{R_1} \tag{2.98a}$$

$$sC_2 \theta_2(s) = \frac{\theta_1(s) - \theta_2(s)}{R_1} - \frac{\theta_2(s) - \theta_a(s)}{R_2} \tag{2.98b}$$

where

$$Q_m(s) \overset{\Delta}{=} \mathscr{L}[q_m(t)]; \; \theta_1(s) \overset{\Delta}{=} \mathscr{L}[\theta_1(t)]; \; \theta_2(s) \overset{\Delta}{=} \mathscr{L}[\theta_2(t)]; \; \theta_a(s) \overset{\Delta}{=} \mathscr{L}[\theta_a(t)]$$

Solving for $\theta_2(s)$ from Eqn. (2.98b), we get

$$\theta_2(s) = \left(\frac{1}{R_1 C_2 s + 1 + R_1/R_2}\right)\theta_1(s) + \frac{R_1/R_2}{R_1 C_2 s + 1 + R_1/R_2}\theta_a(s)$$

Substituting $\theta_2(s)$ in Eqn. (2.98a) and simplifying the expression, we obtain

$$\theta_1(s) = \frac{\lambda R_2 (R_1 C_2 s + 1 + R_1 / R_2)}{R_1 C_1 R_2 C_2 s^2 + (R_1 C_1 + R_2 C_2 + R_2 C_1)s + 1} Q_m(s)$$

$$+ \frac{1}{R_1 C_1 R_2 C_2 s^2 + (R_1 C_1 + R_2 C_2 + R_2 C_1)s + 1} \theta_a(s)$$

We now define the following parameters for the 'sluggish' thermal system (this corresponds to damping factor $\zeta > 1$):

$$\tau_1 \tau_2 = R_1 C_1 R_2 C_2$$
$$\tau_1 + \tau_2 = R_1 C_1 + R_2 C_2 + R_2 C_1 \qquad (2.99a)$$

$$\tau_3 = \left(\frac{R_2}{R_1 + R_2}\right) R_1 C_2; \; K = (R_1 + R_2)\lambda$$

In terms of these parameters,

$$\theta_1(s) = \left[\frac{K(\tau_3 s + 1)}{(\tau_1 s + 1)(\tau_2 s + 1)}\right] Q_m(s) + \left[\frac{1}{(\tau_1 s + 1)(\tau_2 s + 1)}\right] \theta_a(s) \quad (2.99b)$$

Figure 2.34 is the block diagram representation of the system.

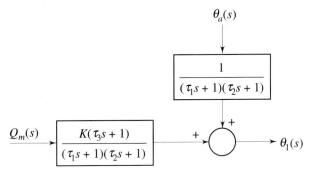

Fig. 2.34 *Block diagram representation of the system of Fig. 2.33*

Example 2.12

Continuously Stirred Tank Heater

The stirred tank sketched in Fig. 2.35 is used to heat a process stream so that its premixed components achieve a uniform composition. Temperature control is important because high temperature tends to decompose the product while a low temperature results in incomplete mixing. The tank is heated by a heater.

In the following we develop the model of the process. The temperature control problem will be studied later.

Definitions of system parameters and variables are as follows:

C_1 = thermal capacitance of the heater mass, Joules/°C
C_2 = thermal capacitance of the liquid in the tank, Joules/°C
R_1 = convective thermal resistance for heat transfer at the heater–liquid interface, °C/(Joules/sec)

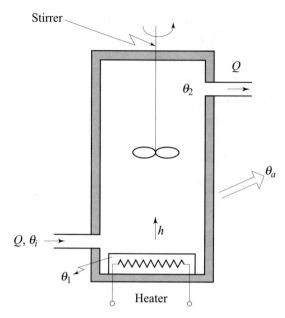

Stirrer

Q

θ_2

θ_a

h

Q, θ_i

θ_1

Heater

Fig. 2.35 *Continuously stirred tank heater*

R_2 = thermal resistance of the carrier fluid, °C/(Joules/sec)

R_3 = convective thermal resistance for heat transfer at the tank wall–air interface, °C/(Joules/sec)

Q = flow rate of liquid (constant), m³/sec

θ_1, θ_2 : perturbations in temperatures of heater-mass, and liquid in the tank respectively from the nominal point of operation, in response to perturbation h (Joules/sec) in the heat flow rate.

θ_i, θ_a : perturbations in inflowing liquid and ambient temperatures respectively. These perturbations are uncontrolled and hence are disturbance inputs for the process.

The following assumptions are made for simplified analysis.

1. The liquid inflow and outflow rates for the tank are equal so that the liquid level in the tank is maintained constant during the operation.

2. The tank is kept at a uniform temperature by perfect mixing with the help of a stirrer. Thus, a single temperature is used to describe the thermal state of the entire liquid. The temperature inside the tank = temperature of the outflowing liquid.

3. The heat storage capacity of the tank walls is negligible.

The heat balance equation for the heater:

$$C_1 \frac{d\theta_1(t)}{dt} = h(t) - \frac{\theta_1(t) - \theta_2(t)}{R_1} \qquad (2.100a)$$

The heat balance equation for the tank liquid:

$$C_2 \frac{d\theta_2(t)}{dt} = \frac{\theta_1(t) - \theta_2(t)}{R_1} + \frac{\theta_i(t) - \theta_2(t)}{R_2} - \frac{\theta_2(t) - \theta_a(t)}{R_3} \quad (2.100b)$$

Taking Laplace transform on both sides of Eqns (2.100) assuming zero initial conditions, we obtain

$$sC_1\theta_1(s) = H(s) - \frac{\theta_1(s) - \theta_2(s)}{R_1} \quad (2.101a)$$

$$sC_2\theta_2(s) = \frac{\theta_1(s) - \theta_2(s)}{R_1} + \frac{\theta_i(s) - \theta_2(s)}{R_2} - \frac{\theta_2(s) - \theta_a(s)}{R_3} \quad (2.101b)$$

where

$$H(s) \overset{\Delta}{=} \mathscr{L}[h(t)]; \quad \theta_1(s) \overset{\Delta}{=} \mathscr{L}[\theta_1(t)];$$

$$\theta_2(s) \overset{\Delta}{=} \mathscr{L}[\theta_2(t)]; \quad \theta_i(s) \overset{\Delta}{=} \mathscr{L}[\theta_i(t)]$$

$$\theta_a(s) \overset{\Delta}{=} \mathscr{L}[\theta_a(t)]$$

Solving for $\theta_1(s)$ from Eqn. (2.101a), we get

$$\theta_1(s) = \left[\frac{R_1}{sC_1R_1 + 1}\right] H(s) + \left[\frac{1}{sC_1R_1 + 1}\right] \theta_2(s)$$

Substituting $\theta_1(s)$ in Eqn. (2.101b) and simplifying the expression, we obtain

$$\left[\left(\frac{R_2R_3}{R_2 + R_3}\right)C_2R_1C_1s^2 + \left(\frac{R_2R_3}{R_2 + R_3}\right)\left\{R_1C_1\left(\frac{1}{R_1} + \frac{1}{R_2} + \frac{1}{R_3}\right) + C_2\right\}s + 1\right]\theta_2(s)$$

$$= \left(\frac{R_2R_3}{R_2 + R_3}\right)H(s) + \frac{R_3}{R_2 + R_3}(sR_1C_1 + 1)\theta_i(s) + \frac{R_2}{R_2 + R_3}(sR_1C_1 + 1)\theta_a(s)$$

For the 'sluggish' thermal system (this corresponds to the case of $\zeta > 1$), we define the following parameters:

$$\tau_3 \overset{\Delta}{=} R_1C_1; \quad \tau_1\tau_2 \overset{\Delta}{=} \left(\frac{R_2R_3}{R_2 + R_3}\right)C_2R_1C_1$$

$$\tau_1 + \tau_2 \overset{\Delta}{=} \left(\frac{R_2R_3}{R_2 + R_3}\right)\left\{\tau_3\left(\frac{1}{R_1} + \frac{1}{R_2} + \frac{1}{R_3}\right) + C_2\right\}$$

$$K \overset{\Delta}{=} \frac{R_2R_3}{R_2 + R_3}; \quad K_{D1} \overset{\Delta}{=} \frac{R_3}{R_2 + R_3}, \quad K_{D2} \overset{\Delta}{=} \frac{R_2}{R_2 + R_3}$$

$$(2.102a)$$

In terms of these parameters,

$$\theta_2(s) = \left[\frac{K}{(\tau_1 s + 1)(\tau_2 s + 1)}\right] H(s) + \left[\frac{K_{D1}(\tau_3 s + 1)}{(\tau_1 s + 1)(\tau_2 s + 1)}\right]\theta_i(s)$$

$$+ \left[\frac{K_{D2}(\tau_3 s + 1)}{(\tau_1 s + 1)(\tau_2 s + 1)}\right]\theta_a(s) \quad (2.102b)$$

Figure 2.36a is the block diagram representation of the system. $H(s)$ is the controlled input, and $\theta_i(s)$ and $\theta_a(s)$ are uncontrolled disturbances.

Figure 2.36b shows rearrangement of the block diagram of Fig. 2.36a.

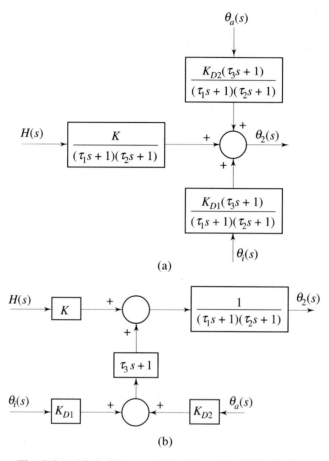

(a)

(b)

Fig. 2.36 *Block diagram models of the system of Fig. 2.35*

We have made three simplifying assumptions (stated earlier) to derive model (2.102). Before concluding this example, we study the effects of relaxing these assumptions.

1. Relaxing assumption 1 (inflow and outflow rates are different) will lead to a change in the level of the liquid in the tank. This amounts to a change in energy in the gravity field. We are considering only those cases where the change in energy is due to the change in internal thermal energy only. Modelling of mechanical–thermal energy interactions is not covered.

2. Relaxing assumption 2 (state of the tank cannot be described by a single temperature) will lead to distributed parameter system, requiring partial differential equations to describe the system.

3. Relaxing assumption 3 (heat capacity of the tank walls is not negligible)
   will add one more energy storage element; the order of the model will
   therefore increase by one.

2.11 MODELS OF HYDRAULIC SYSTEMS

The hydraulic systems of interest to control engineers may be classified into
two main types:

1. *Liquid-level systems* consisting of storage tanks and connecting pipes.
   Liquid height in tanks and flow rate in pipes are the variables to be
   controlled. The driving force is the relative difference in the liquid-heights
   in the tanks.
2. *Hydraulic devices* using an incompressible oil as their working medium.
   These devices are used for controlling the forces and motions. The
   driving force is the high pressure oil supplied by the hydraulic pumps.

Liquids are slightly compressible at high pressures. However, approximate
dynamic models based on the assumption of incompressibility of liquids are
usually sufficiently accurate. Simple models developed in this book use this
approximation.

Volumetric flow rate q (through variable; analogous to current) and pressure
p (across variable; analogous to voltage) are the commonly used characterizing
variables of hydraulic systems. The three basic elements of hydraulic systems
are the resistance, the capacitance, and the inertance. The inertance represents
fluid inertia and is derived from the inertia forces required to accelerate a fluid
in a pipe. It is an energy-storing element. Another energy-storing element is the
capacitance which, as we shall see, represents storage in gravity field. In most
applications of interest to us, energy storage due to the inertance element is
negligible compared to that due to the capacitance element.

The tank shown in Fig. 2.37 illustrates the concept of hydraulic capacitance.
A (m^2) is the surface area of the tank's bottom, and tank's sides are vertical.
If $\overline{Q}_i$ (m^3/sec) represents the steady-state inflow rate, $\overline{Q}$ (m^3/sec) represents
the steady-state outflow rate, and $\overline{H}$ (m) represents the steady-state height of
the liquid in the tank, then the volume-balance at steady-state gives

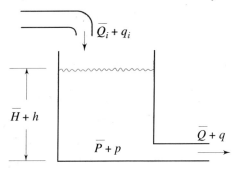

Fig. 2.37 *Capacitance of a storage tank*

$$\overline{Q}_i = \overline{Q} \; ; \; \overline{H} = \text{constant}$$

The hydrostatic pressure due to height $\overline{H}$ is

$$\overline{P} = \rho g \overline{H} , \text{ Newtons/m}^2$$

where ρ = density of the liquid, kg/m^3; and
g = acceleration due to gravity, m/sec^2.

The standard unit of pressure is *pascal* (Pa): 1 Pa of pressure is defined as the force of 1 Newton applied over an area of 1 m^2. Industrial pressures are often measured in pounds per square inch (psi). Pascals can be obtained by multiplying psi by 6.8948×10^3.

The atmospheric pressure is 14.70 psi (101 kPa) at sea level. *Gauge pressure* is referenced to atmospheric pressure, and *absolute pressure* is referenced to perfect vacuum. Gauge pressure can be obtained by subtracting the ambient atmospheric value from the absolute value. Likewise, absolute pressure can be found by adding the ambient pressure to the gauge pressure. Letters *g* or *a* may be suffixed to the pressure units to clearly denote gauge pressure or absolute pressure (e.g., psig, psia). The pressure variables in our discussion represent gauge pressures. The atmospheric pressure has been taken as zero gauge pressure.

In the system of Fig. 2.37, the disturbance $q_i(t)$ in the inflow rate will change the height of the liquid in the tank by $h(t)$, the pressure across the pipe by $p(t)$ and the outflow rate by $q(t)$. The volume-balance equation becomes

$$\overline{Q}_i + q_i(t) = A \frac{d}{dt}(\overline{H} + h(t)) + \overline{Q} + q(t)$$

Perturbation from steady-state is described by the equation

$$q_i(t) = A \frac{dh(t)}{dt} + q(t) \tag{2.103}$$

Since

$$p(t) = \rho g h(t), \tag{2.104}$$

it follows that

$$q_i(t) - q(t) = \frac{A}{\rho g} \frac{dp(t)}{dt} \tag{2.105}$$

The *hydraulic capacitance* due to storage in gravity field is defined as

$$C = \frac{A}{\rho g}, \text{ cub-m/(Newtons/m}^2) \tag{2.106}$$

In terms of hydraulic capacitance, Eqn. (2.105) may be written as

$$q_i(t) - q(t) = C \frac{dp(t)}{dt} \tag{2.107}$$

With reference to Fig. 2.37, the outflow $q(t)$ should obviously depend on $p(t)$ somehow. The greater the pressure $p(t)$, the greater the outflow rate. The concept of hydraulic resistance introduced below will help in establishing a relationship between $q(t)$ and $p(t)$.

Liquid trying to flow out of a container, as in Fig. 2.37, can meet with resistance in several ways. If the outlet is simply a hole, the liquid meets resistance merely because it cannot easily flow through the hole. This is known as *orifice flow*. If the outlet is a pipe, the friction between the liquid and the pipe walls produces resistance to flow. The presence of a component such as valve in the pipe increases the resistance. Components such as elbow bends, couplings of pipes of different diameters, etc., also resist the flow.

Symbolic representation of an obstruction to flow is shown in Fig. 2.38a. A controllable obstruction, such as a hydraulic valve with an adjustable opening, may be represented as in Fig. 2.38b. The upstream pressure is P_1 and the back pressure achieved downstream is P_2. The flow rate Q depends on the pressure difference $\Delta P = (P_1 - P_2)$. This relationship is usually nonlinear; it can be obtained either experimentally or analytically.

Suppose that an experimental curve relating the flow rate Q to the pressure drop ΔP is available for an obstruction. A typical curve is shown in Fig. 2.38c.

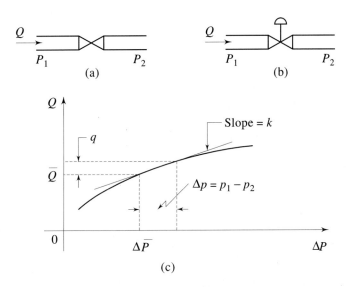

Fig. 2.38   (a) *Flow obstruction; (b) Adjustable obstruction;*
(c) *Steady-state operating point*

Let the slope of the curve at the equilibrium point $(\overline{Q}, \Delta\overline{P})$ be denoted by k. Then, for a small deviation from equilibrium, we obtain

$$q(t) = k\Delta p(t) \tag{2.108}$$

From this equation, *hydraulic resistance* is defined as

$$R = \frac{1}{k}, \left(\frac{\text{Newton}/\text{m}^2}{\text{m}^3/\text{sec}} \right) \tag{2.109}$$

The value of R depends on the steady-state condition chosen for linearization.

When an equation relating the flow to the pressure drop is available, the resistance can be obtained analytically. The following flow-pressure relationship models the orifice flow.

$$Q = C_0 A_0 \sqrt{\frac{2(P_1 - P_2)}{\rho}} \qquad (2.110)$$

where

A_0 = orifice area;

C_0 = the experimentally determined number, called the orifice coefficient;

ρ = density of the fluid;

$P_1 - P_2 = \Delta P$ = pressure difference across the orifice.

The orifice coefficient is dependent on the geometric configuration of the orifice and to some extent upon the flow velocity. For sharp-edged orifices, it normally ranges from 0.6 to 0.8.

For incompressible fluids, ρ is constant and therefore Q is a function of pressure difference ΔP:

$$Q = f(\Delta P) \qquad (2.111a)$$

This equation may be linearized about an equilibrium point using Taylor series expansion (refer Eqns (2.6)).

The flow rate through a valve with adjustable opening is a function of both the pressure difference ΔP across the valve and the adjustable area A_0, or equivalently the adjustable valve opening x_v:

$$Q = f(x_v, \Delta P) \qquad (2.111b)$$

Table 2.5 summarizes the metric system of units for hydraulic systems.

Table 2.5   *Hydraulic symbols and units*

Quantity	*Metric units*
Volume flow rate(q)	m^3/sec
Pressure (p)	$Newtons/m^2$
Hydraulic capacitance (C)	$m^3/(Newtons/m^2)$
Hydraulic resistance (R)	$\dfrac{Newtons/m^2}{m^3/sec}$

▲▲

The concepts of hydraulic capacitance and hydraulic resistance will now be used to develop models of hydraulic systems. In the following, we develop a complete model for a liquid-level system. Models of hydraulic devices for controlling forces and motions will be developed in the next chapter.

Example 2.13

Consider the process shown in Fig. 2.39. We are interested in knowing how the level of the liquid in the tank will respond to changes in the inlet valve opening.

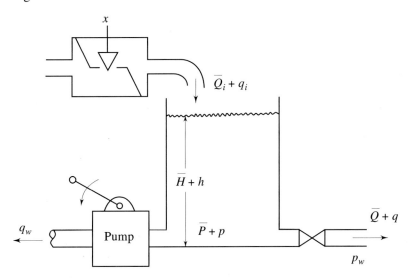

Fig. 2.39 *A liquid-level control system*

For steady-state equilibrium flow, steady-state inflow rate $\overline{Q}_i$ = steady-state outflow state $\overline{Q}$, and liquid-height $\overline{H}$ = constant.

Let $q_i(t)$, $q(t)$ and $h(t)$ be the deviations about this equilibrium. It is assumed that the liquid is incompressible and the tank walls are rigid. Hence the only capacitance effect is due to storage in the gravity field. From Eqn. (2.107) we obtain

$$C \frac{dp(t)}{dt} = q_i(t) - q(t) \tag{2.112a}$$

where $p(t) = \rho g h(t)$ is the change in pressure at the tank's bottom, and C is the hydraulic capacitance (refer Eqn. (2.106)), ρ = density of the liquid, and g = acceleration due to gravity.

Neglecting fluid inertance, the orifice equation is given by

$$p(t) = R q(t) \tag{2.112b}$$

where R is hydraulic resistance (refer Eqn. (2.109)).

Eliminating $q(t)$ from Eqns (2.112a) and (2.112b), we obtain

$$C \frac{dp(t)}{dt} + \frac{1}{R} p(t) = q_i(t)$$

Defining time-constant $\tau = RC$, we get

$$\tau \frac{dp(t)}{dt} + p(t) = R q_i(t)$$

Taking the Laplace transform on both sides of this equation (assuming zero initial conditions), we obtain

$$P(s) = \frac{RQ_i(s)}{\tau s + 1}$$

In developing this model, we have not considered disturbances in the process. Disturbances may enter in the model in the following ways:

1. Liquid may be drawn off from the tank (to be used elsewhere in the processing operation) by a variable displacement pump. $q_w(m^3/sec)$ is the disturbance flow rate.
2. If the tank of Fig. 2.39 is connected to another tank in the processing operation, there will be a variable back pressure $\{p_w(t)\}$ at the orifice outlet and the flow equation (2.112b) then gets modified to the following:

$$p(t) - p_w(t) = R q(t)$$

The volume-balance equation now becomes

$$C \frac{dp(t)}{dt} = q_i(t) - \frac{p(t) - p_w(t)}{R} - q_w(t)$$

or $(\tau s+1) P(s) = RQ_i(s) + P_w(s) - RQ_w(s)$

or $$P(s) = \frac{R}{\tau s + 1} Q_i(s) + \frac{1}{\tau s + 1} P_w(s) - \frac{R}{\tau s + 1} Q_w(s) \qquad (2.113)$$

The flow rate through the inlet valve is governed by a relation of the form (2.111b). Since the pressure drop across the inlet valve is constant, the flow rate $q_i(t)$ is directly proportional to the valve opening x (refer Eqn. (2.110)):

$$q_i(t) = K_v x(t) \qquad (2.114)$$

Substituting in Eqn. (2.113), we obtain

$$P(s) = \frac{R K_v}{\tau s + 1} X(s) + \frac{1}{\tau s + 1} P_w(s) - \frac{R}{\tau s + 1} Q_w(s)$$

or $$H(s) = \frac{RK_v/\rho g}{\tau s + 1} X(s) + \frac{1/\rho g}{\tau s + 1} P_w(s) - \frac{R/\rho g}{\tau s + 1} Q_w(s) \qquad (2.115)$$

Figure 2.40 shows the block diagram representation of the system.

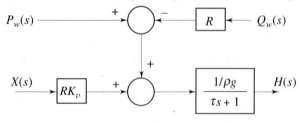

Fig. 2.40 *Block diagram model of the system of Fig. 2.39*

2.12 | OBTAINING MODELS FROM EXPERIMENTAL DATA

In the preceding sections, the laws of physics were used to obtain models of physical systems. The best of model building from application of physical laws is only an approximation of the reality. Sometimes, as in the case of an essentially rigid spacecraft, the model is extremely good, and sometimes, as in the case of many systems in the process industry such as a heat exchanger (Fig. 1.18), the model is very approximate. In every case, before final control design is done, it is important and prudent to verify the theoretical model obtained by application of physical laws, with experimental data.

In cases where our knowledge of the system under study is limited or the theoretical model turns out to be highly complex, the only reliable information on which to base the control design is the experimental data. Also the changes taking place in the parameters of a system during operation (e.g., the mass of a spacecraft varies over its life because of the consumption of fuel; time-constant of a heat exchanger changes with change in velocity of the process fluid), demand change in control parameters. In order to do this, it is necessary to have a model under the new conditions, and experimental data are often the most effective information available for this purpose.

A model may be obtained from the transient response data collected as part of special tests conducted on the system. The tests are designed so that the signal-to-noise ratio is sufficiently high. Computation of the model, such as poles and zeros, from the transient response data is complex in general; it is simple only in special cases. Zeigler and Nichols use step-response data in the design of certain classes of processes (see Chapter 11 for details).

As we shall see in Chapter 8, computation of the model from frequency response data is simple. Also, one of the most effective methods (Bode plot) of control system design is based on the frequency response of the controlled process; the control design can therefore immediately proceed once the frequency response data is experimentally obtained.

Normal operating records are an attractive basis for model building since they are non-disruptive and inexpensive to obtain. Unfortunately the quality of such data, sometimes, is not good; it is worst just when the control is the best, for then the upsets are minimal and some or even most of the system dynamics are hardly excited. The result is a model that represents only a part of the system. Model-building methods based on input-output data from the process impose certain conditions (sufficient richness or persistent excitation) on the input signal so that all the dynamic modes of the process are sufficiently excited. These methods, called *system identification* methods, are beyond the scope of this book [146,151–154].

2.13 | SYSTEMS WITH DEAD-TIME ELEMENTS

Consider the process shown in Fig. 2.41. This is essentially the same process (continuously stirred tank heater) as the one shown in Fig. 2.35. The difference is that in this case we have used a sensor (measuring device) to measure the output temperature $\theta(t)$. Any change in the inlet temperature θ_i and the surrounding temperature θ_a will change the outlet temperature θ, and this information is needed by control logic elements in a feedback control scheme to take suitable corrective action (feedback control scheme for the thermal process of Fig. 2.41 will be discussed in the next chapter). We have used thermocouple temperature sensor to measure $\theta(t)$.

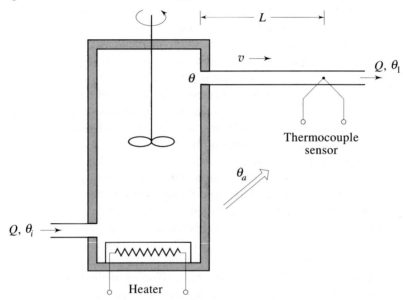

Fig. 2.41　*A thermal process with dead-time element*

Although, we generally prefer to measure the controlled variable (outlet temperature θ) as directly as possible, the location of the thermocouple temperature sensor (output is few millivolts) in the tank encounters problems of vibrations caused by tank stirrer; thus we locate it in the pipe line downstream of the tank. Under this situation, the measured response $\theta_1(t)$ to the disturbances $\theta_i(t)$ and $\theta_a(t)$ will be the same as actual response $\theta(t)$ except that it will be delayed by some amount of time. The time delay thus introduced is referred to as *dead-time* or *transportation lag* to distinguish it from the delay associated with the time-constant of a simple lag. We will see in later chapters that the presence of such delays tends to cause oscillations and makes the system less stable. Dead-time should be avoided to the extent possible.

Figure 2.42 defines the behaviour of the dead-time element (pipe). The input $\theta(t)$ and the output $\theta_1(t)$ are related by

$$\theta_1(t) = \theta(t - \tau_D) \; ; t > \tau_D \qquad (2.116a)$$

where τ_D = dead-time = $\dfrac{\text{distance}}{\text{velocity}} = \dfrac{L}{v} = \dfrac{L}{Q/A_p}$ sec;

L = length of pipe, m;
A_p = cross-sectional area of pipe, m^2; and
Q = flow rate, m^3/sec.

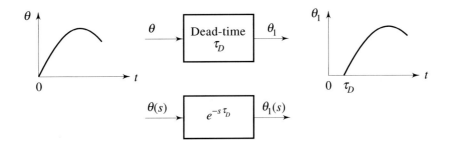

Fig. 2.42 *Behaviour of a dead-time element*

In terms of a delayed step function

$$\mu(t - \tau_D) = \begin{bmatrix} 1 & \text{for } t > \tau_D \\ 0 & \text{otherwise} \end{bmatrix}$$

we can write output $\theta_1(t)$ as

$$\theta_1(t) = \theta(t - \tau_D)\mu(t - \tau_D)$$

Laplace transform of $\theta_1(t)$ is

$$\theta_1(s) = \mathscr{L}[\theta_1(t)] = \int_0^\infty \theta(t - \tau_D)\mu(t - \tau_D)e^{-st}dt$$

$$= \int_{\tau_D}^\infty \theta(t - \tau_D)e^{-s(t - \tau_D)}e^{-s\tau_D}\,dt = e^{-s\tau_D}\int_0^\infty \theta(\tau)e^{-s\tau}d\tau = e^{-s\tau_D}\,\theta(s)$$

The transfer function of the dead-time element becomes

$$\frac{\theta_1(s)}{\theta(s)} = e^{-s\tau_D} \qquad (2.116b)$$

Dead-time Approximations

The simplest dead-time approximation can be developed by the graphical approach of Fig. 2.43, from which we see that

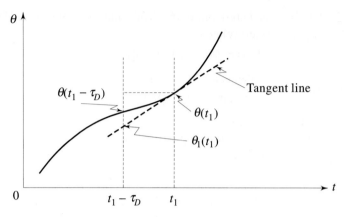

Fig. 2.43 *Dead-time approximation*

$$\theta_1(t) \cong \theta(t) - \tau_D \frac{d\theta(t)}{dt}$$

or
$$\theta_1(s) \cong (1 - \tau_D s)\theta(s)$$

With this approximation, the transfer function of dead-time element becomes

$$\frac{\theta_1(s)}{\theta(s)} = (1 - \tau_D s) \qquad (2.117)$$

The accuracy of this approximation depends on the dead-time being sufficiently small relative to the rate of change of the slope of θ. If θ were a ramp function (constant slope), the approximation would be perfect for any value of τ_D. When the slope of θ varies rapidly, only small τ_D will give a good approximation.

The Pade approximants [77] provide a family of approximations of increasing accuracy and complexity. These approximations are based on frequency-response comparisons; the simplest one being

$$\frac{\theta_1(s)}{\theta(s)} = \frac{1 - \frac{\tau_D}{2}s}{1 + \frac{\tau_D}{2}s} \qquad (2.118)$$

▲▲

In control systems, we frequently come across situations where there is unavoidable time delay in the signal flow between sub-systems or components. The delay usually results from the physical separation of the components and typically occurs as a delay between the change in the manipulated variable and its effect on the plant, or a delay in the measurement of the output. Dead-time elements are needed for accurate modelling of such systems. Digital computers in control systems also introduce the necessity of dead-time elements to model the computational delay inherent in these systems.

In the process-control field (control of pressure, flow, liquid-level, temperature, etc.) systems are relatively slow and complex, and in most cases, the time delay in signal flow between sub-systems results in dead-time effects. Even where a pure dead-time element is not present, the complexity of the process (which will typically contain several first-order lags) will often result in a response which has the appearance of a pure dead-time element. Modelling of such complex systems is a very difficult task. However, many years of experience has proved that the controllers based on approximate process models are quite versatile. The two most common models used to characterize a process are the following:

First-Order Plus Dead-time Model

$$G(s) = \frac{K e^{-s\tau_D}}{\tau s + 1} \tag{2.119}$$

K = the process steady-state gain;
τ_D = the effective process dead-time; and
τ = the effective process time-constant.

Second-Order Plus Dead-time Model

$$G(s) = \frac{K e^{-s\tau_D}}{(\tau_1 s + 1)(\tau_2 s + 1)} \tag{2.120}$$

τ_1, τ_2: the effective process time-constants.

The crudity of such models precludes the use of the sophisticated design techniques which have been formulated in recent years. These models are useful in the simple 'experimental design' approach called *controller tuning* where a controller based on approximate process characterization is first installed, and then controller parameters are tuned by experiment.

Most of the controller tuning formulae are based on first-order plus dead-time process model. This model characterizes the process by three parameters; the gain K, the dead-time τ_D, and the time-constant τ. These parameters can be experimentally determined by performing a step test. We will study controller tuning and step testing methods in Chapter 11.

2.14 | LOADING EFFECTS IN INTERCONNECTED SYSTEMS

We consider here the two-tank system shown in Fig. 2.44. $q_i(t)$ is the input and $h_1(t)$ is the output of tank 1, and $q_1(t)$ is the input and $h_2(t)$ is the output of tank 2.

The flow-balance equation for tank 1 is

$$q_i(t) = C_1 \frac{dp_1(t)}{dt} + q_1(t); \ p_1(t) = \rho g h_1(t) \tag{2.121a}$$

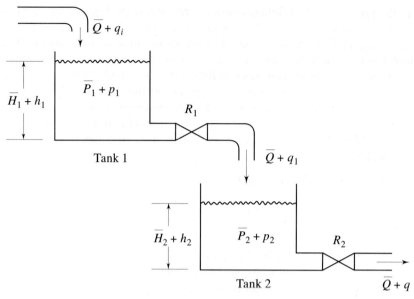

Fig. 2.44 *A non-loading two-tank system*

The flow $q_1(t)$ through resistance R_1 is given by

$$q_1(t) = \frac{p_1(t)}{R_1} \qquad (2.121b)$$

Definitions of various parameters and variables of the hydraulic system are obvious.

Transfer function model of tank 1, obtained from Eqns (2.121) is

$$\frac{H_1(s)}{Q_i(s)} = \frac{R_1/\rho g}{\tau_1 s + 1}; \ \tau_1 = R_1 C_1 \qquad (2.122)$$

Similarly, the transfer function model of tank 2 is given by

$$\frac{H_2(s)}{Q_1(s)} = \frac{R_2/\rho g}{\tau_2 s + 1}; \ \tau_2 = R_2 C_2$$

Substituting for $Q_1(s)$ from Eqns (2.121), we obtain

$$\frac{H_2(s)}{H_1(s)} = \frac{R_2/R_1}{\tau_2 s + 1} \qquad (2.123)$$

The block diagram of Fig. 2.45a is developed by 'chaining' Eqns (2.122) and (2.123). This diagram shows that the inlet flow $q_i(t)$ initially affects the level $h_1(t)$ in tank 1. A change in this level then affects the level $h_2(t)$ in tank 2. The level of the first tank affects the level of the second tank, but this level does not in turn affect the level of the first tank. The overall transfer function in such cases where there is no loading due to sub-system interconnection, is obtained by multiplying together the individual transfer functions. The block diagram of Fig. 2.45a can be reduced to that of Fig. 2.45b. The overall transfer function of the two-tank system of Fig. 2.44 is given by

$$\frac{H_2(s)}{Q_i(s)} = \frac{R_2/\rho g}{\tau_1\tau_2 s^2 + (\tau_1 + \tau_2)s + 1} \tag{2.124}$$

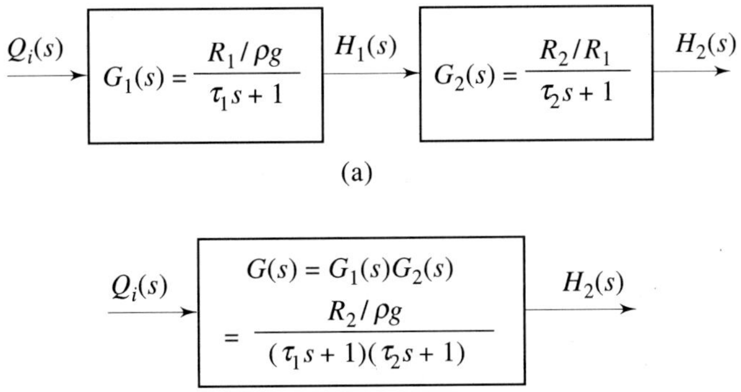

$$Q_i(s) \longrightarrow \boxed{G_1(s) = \frac{R_1/\rho g}{\tau_1 s + 1}} \xrightarrow{H_1(s)} \boxed{G_2(s) = \frac{R_2/R_1}{\tau_2 s + 1}} \xrightarrow{H_2(s)}$$

(a)

$$Q_i(s) \longrightarrow \boxed{\begin{array}{c} G(s) = G_1(s)G_2(s) \\[2mm] = \dfrac{R_2/\rho g}{(\tau_1 s + 1)(\tau_2 s + 1)} \end{array}} \xrightarrow{H_2(s)}$$

(b)

Fig. 2.45 *Block diagram models of the system of Fig. 2.44*

We now connect the two tanks as shown in Fig. 2.46. Loading is now present and Eqn. (2.124) is not a valid transfer function model for this system as explained below.

The flow-balance equation for tank 1 is

$$q_i(t) = C_1\frac{dp_1(t)}{dt} + q_1(t)$$

Similarly, for tank 2

$$q_1(t) = C_2\frac{dp_2(t)}{dt} + q(t)$$

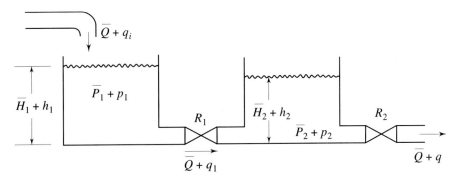

Fig. 2.46 *Loading effect in a two-tank system*

The flow $q_1(t)$ through resistance R_1 is governed by the equation

$$q_1(t) = \frac{p_1(t) - p_2(t)}{R_1}$$

and the flow $q(t)$ through resistance R_2 is given by

$$q(t) = \frac{p_2(t)}{R_2}$$

If $h_2(t)$ is considered the output and $q_i(t)$ the input, the transfer function of the system becomes

$$\frac{H_2(s)}{Q_i(s)} = \frac{R_2/\rho g}{\tau_1\tau_2 s^2 + \left(\tau_1 + \tau_2 + \dfrac{R_2}{R_1}\tau_1\right)s + 1} \tag{2.125}$$

Note that the transfer function is not equal to that given by Eqn. (2.124). The difference is due to the presence of the loading effect; the level $h_2(t)$ of tank 2 now affects the level $h_1(t)$ of tank 1. The degree to which the overall transfer function is modified from the product of the individual transfer functions depends upon the amount of loading.

▲▲

In general, loading effects occur because while analysing an isolated sub-system, we assume that no power is being withdrawn at its output location. When we later decide to attach another sub-system to the output of the first, this second sub-system does withdraw some power violating our earlier assumption and thereby invalidating the analysis based on this assumption.

One way to reduce loading effects to negligible proportions is to interpose *buffer amplifiers* between the sub-systems. These devices, which may be electrical, hydraulic, pneumatic, or the like, to suit the physical nature of the connected sub-systems, have their own internal power supplies and can thus supply power to a 'downstream' sub-system without withdrawing their power from the 'upstream' sub-system. That is, such amplifiers have high input impedance and low output impedance (op amp is one example).

When we model chains of sub-systems by simple multiplication of their individual transfer functions later in the text, the assumption will always be that the interconnection of various sub-systems is non-loading; loading effects are either not present, have been proven negligible, or have been made negligible by use of buffer amplifiers.

Review Examples

*Review Example 2.1*_____

Consider a first-order system described by the transfer function

$$\frac{Y(s)}{R(s)} = \frac{K}{\tau s + 1}$$

where τ is the time-constant of the system.

For a unit ramp input $r(t) = t\mu(t)$, we have

$$R(s) = \frac{1}{s^2}$$

Therefore, the unit ramp response is

$$Y(s) = \frac{K}{s^2(\tau s + 1)} = K\left[\frac{1}{s^2} - \frac{\tau}{s} + \frac{\tau^2}{\tau s + 1}\right]$$

$$y(t) = K(t - \tau + \tau e^{-t/\tau})$$

The term $K\tau e^{-t/\tau}$ is the transient response term which decays to zero with increasing time. Its rate of decay is dictated by the time-constant τ. The steady-state component of the response to unit ramp input $r(t) = t$ is

$$y_{ss} = K(t - \tau),$$

which is also a ramp function.

Note that the steady-state ramp output is nothing but Kt delayed by τ as shown in Fig. 2.47a. This phenomenon of steady-state lag in ramp response gives another interpretation of the time-constant of first-order system.

For $K = 1$, the steady-state error (Fig. 2.47b)

$$e_{ss} = r(t) - y_{ss} = \tau$$

If K does not equal 1, the response diverges from the unit ramp input as t increases.

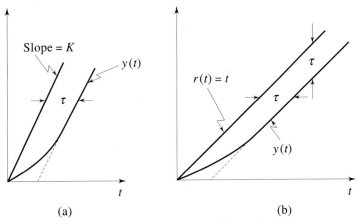

(a)　　　　　　　　　　　(b)

Fig. 2.47 *Ramp response of first-order systems*

Review Example 2.2

Consider a second-order system described by the transfer function

$$\frac{Y(s)}{R(s)} = \frac{K}{\dfrac{1}{\omega_n^2}s^2 + \dfrac{2\zeta}{\omega_n}s + 1}$$

where ω_n = undamped natural frequency

ζ = damping ratio

For an underdamped system, $0 < \zeta < 1$.

Assume that this system is excited by a unit ramp input

$$R(s) = \frac{1}{s^2}$$

This gives

$$Y(s) = \frac{K\omega_n^2}{s^2\left(s^2 + 2\zeta\omega_n s + \omega_n^2\right)}$$

$$= K\left[\frac{1}{s^2} - \frac{2\zeta/\omega_n}{s} + \frac{2\zeta}{\omega_n}\frac{s + \zeta\omega_n}{(s + \zeta\omega_n)^2 + \omega_d^2} + \frac{2\zeta^2 - 1}{(s + \zeta\omega_n)^2 + \omega_d^2}\right]$$

where $\omega_d = \omega_n\sqrt{1 - \zeta^2}$

Using the table of transform pairs given in Appendix A, we get

$$y(t) = K\left[t - \frac{2\zeta}{\omega_n} + \frac{2\zeta}{\omega_n}e^{-\zeta\omega_n t}\cos\omega_d t + \frac{(2\zeta^2 - 1)}{\omega_d}e^{-\zeta\omega_n t}\sin\omega_d t\right]$$

$$= K\left[t - \frac{2\zeta}{\omega_n} + \frac{e^{-\zeta\omega_n t}}{\omega_d}\left\{2\zeta\sqrt{1 - \zeta^2}\cos\omega_d t + (2\zeta^2 - 1)\sin\omega_d t\right\}\right]$$

$$= Kt - \frac{2\zeta}{\omega_n}K + \frac{Ke^{-\zeta\omega_n t}}{\omega_n\sqrt{1 - \zeta^2}}\sin\left(\omega_d t + 2\tan^{-1}\frac{\sqrt{1 - \zeta^2}}{\zeta}\right) \qquad (2.126)$$

The last term in this expression is the transient response term, which decays to zero with increasing time. Its rate of decay is dictated by the time-constant $1/\zeta\omega_n$. The steady-state component of the response to unit ramp input $r(t) = t$ is

$$y_{ss} = K\left(t - \frac{2\zeta}{\omega_n}\right) \qquad (2.127)$$

which is also a ramp function.

Note that the steady-state ramp output is nothing but Kt delayed by $2\zeta/\omega_n$ as shown in Fig. 2.48a. The damped oscillations contributed by the transient component of the response are centred on the ramp.

For $K = 1$, the steady-state error (Fig. 2.48b)

$$e_{ss} = r(t) - y_{ss} = \frac{2\zeta}{\omega_n} \qquad (2.128)$$

If K does not equal 1, the response diverges from the unit ramp input as t increases.

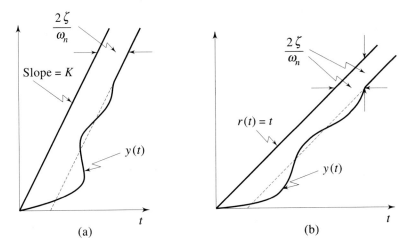

Fig. 2.48 *Ramp response of second-order underdamped systems*

By similar analysis, it can easily be established that the critically damped and overdamped responses ($\zeta \geq 1$) are characterized by the exponential rise toward the steady-state ramp output $K\left(t - \dfrac{2\zeta}{\omega_n}\right)$.

Review Example 2.3

A common cause of sinusoidal forcing in machines is the imbalance that exists to some extent in every rotating machine. The imbalance is caused by the fact that the centre of mass of the rotating part does not coincide with the centre of rotation. Figure 2.49 shows a situation where the main mass of a machine is constrained to have only vertical motion. The rotating mass m is lumped at its

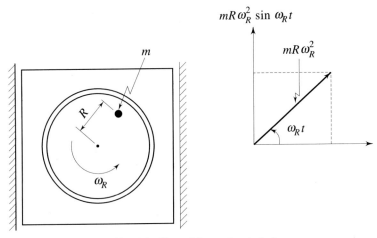

Fig. 2.49 *Machine with rotating imbalance*

centre of mass, a distance R from the centre of rotation. For a constant speed of rotation ω_R, a radial acceleration of m equal to $R\omega_R^2$ is produced. This causes a force to be exerted on the bearings at the centre of rotation. This force has a magnitude of $mR\omega_R^2$, and is directed radially outward. The vertical component of this imbalance force is $mR\omega_R^2 \sin \omega_R t$.

Consider the system of Fig. 2.50a, where an ac motor designed to run at a constant speed is mounted on a steel cantilever beam. The rotating part of the motor has an eccentricity; this gives rise to an exciting force of frequency, say ω_F: $F(t) = A \sin \omega_F t$.

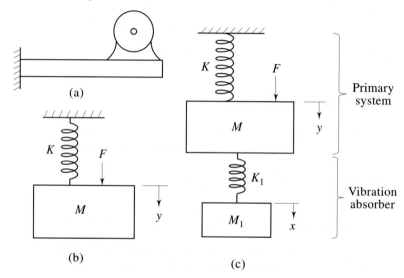

Fig. 2.50 *Motor vibration problem*

A lumped-parameter model for the system of Fig. 2.50a is of the form shown in Fig. 2.50b [31]. For this model, the governing equation is

$$F(t) - K y(t) = M \ddot{y}(t)$$

or $\qquad M \ddot{y}(t) + K y(t) = F(t)$ \hfill (2.129)

The zero position of y is taken to be at the point where the spring and the mass are in static equilibrium. The gravitational effect is eliminated by this choice of the zero position.

From Eqn. (2.129), we obtain

$$G(s) = \frac{Y(s)}{F(s)} = \frac{1}{Ms^2 + K} = \frac{1/K}{\dfrac{M}{K}s^2 + 1}$$

The sinusoidal transfer function

$$G(j\omega) = \frac{1/K}{1 - \left(\dfrac{\omega}{\omega_n}\right)^2} \; ; \; \omega_n = \sqrt{\frac{K}{M}}$$

The steady-state response to an input $A \sin \omega_F t$ is given by

$$y_{ss} = A| G(j\omega_F) |\sin(\omega_F t + \phi); \phi = \angle G(j\omega_F)$$

The machine thus vibrates with an amplitude $A|G(j\omega_F)|$. The vibrations become violent as the forcing frequency ω_F approaches ω_n—the natural frequency of the system, resulting in high dynamic stresses on the beam. This violent resonance condition can be controlled by adding a small mass to the system to shift ω_n.

Consider the model of Fig. 2.50c, where K and M are the parameters of the primary system when vibrating in the troublesome mode. A *vibration absorber* represented by the parameters K_1 and M_1 has been added to the primary system. The equations of motion now become

$$F(t) - Ky(t) - K_1(y(t) - x(t)) = M\ddot{y}(t); \quad K_1(y(t) - x(t)) = M_1\ddot{x}(t)$$

The transfer function

$$G(s) = \frac{Y(s)}{F(s)} = \frac{M_1 s^2 + K_1}{MM_1 s^4 + (MK_1 + M_1 K + M_1 K_1)s^2 + KK_1}$$

The sinusoidal transfer function

$$G(j\omega) = \frac{\dfrac{1}{K}\left[1 - \left(\dfrac{\omega}{\omega_0}\right)^2\right]}{\left[1 - \left(\dfrac{\omega}{\omega_{n1}}\right)^2\right]\left[1 - \left(\dfrac{\omega}{\omega_{n2}}\right)^2\right]}$$

where

$$\omega_0 = \sqrt{\frac{K_1}{M_1}};$$ ω_{n1} and ω_{n2} are given by the parameters M, K, M_1 and K_1.

It is seen that the system now possesses two natural frequencies: ω_{n1} and ω_{n2}. The separation between the forcing frequency ω_F and the natural frequencies ω_{n1}, and ω_{n2} can be controlled by changing the parameters M_1 and K_1.

Note that when $\omega_0 = \omega_F$, the motor vibration becomes zero. The vibration of the primary system (without vibration absorber) was violent when $\omega_F = \omega_n = \sqrt{K/M}$. This violent vibration can be made zero by adding a vibration absorber with $\sqrt{K_1/M_1} = \sqrt{K/M}$.

Figure 2.51 shows the amplitude of vibrations as a function of forcing frequency. ω_{n1} and ω_{n2} are the resonance frequencies and ω_0 is the anti-resonance frequency.

Resonances arise in control engineering practice, for example, in servomechanisms where the mechanical drive train has vibration problems, or in aircrafts and missiles where the structure bending vibration is coupled into

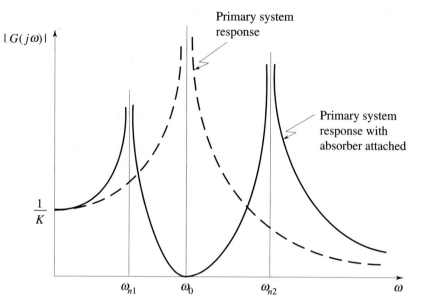

Fig. 2.51 *Amplitude-frequency response for a system with and without absorber*

the control system. The separation between the vibration frequencies and the natural frequencies of the systems can be controlled by the appropriate design of the controller. Controller design methods will be developed in later chapters.

Review Example 2.4

Consider the mechanical system shown in Fig. 2.52a. A force $F(t)$ is applied to mass M_2. The free-body diagrams for the two masses are shown in Fig. 2.52b. From this figure, we have the following differential equations describing the dynamics of the system.

$$M_1 \ddot{y}_1 = K_2(y_2 - y_1) + B_2(\dot{y}_2 - \dot{y}_1) - K_1 y_1 - B_1 \dot{y}_1$$
$$M_2 \ddot{y}_2 = F(t) - K_2(y_2 - y_1) - B_2(\dot{y}_2 - \dot{y}_1)$$

Rearranging, we get

$$M_1 \ddot{y}_1 + B_1 \dot{y}_1 - B_2(\dot{y}_2 - \dot{y}_1) + K_1 y_1 - K_2(y_2 - y_1) = 0$$
$$M_2 \ddot{y}_2 + B_2(\dot{y}_2 - \dot{y}_1) + K_2(y_2 - y_1) = F(t)$$

These are two simultaneous second-order linear differential equations. Manipulation of these equations will result in a single differential equation (fourth-order) relating the response y_2 (or y_1) to input $F(t)$.

A spring-mass-damper system may be schematically represented as a network by showing the mass as a two-terminal component; one terminal is free and has associated with it the motional variable v, and the other terminal represents a reference (commonly earth) with respect to which the motional variable of the free terminal is measured. As an example, the mechanical system of Fig. 2.52a is redrawn in Fig. 2.52c which may be referred to as the *mechanical network*.

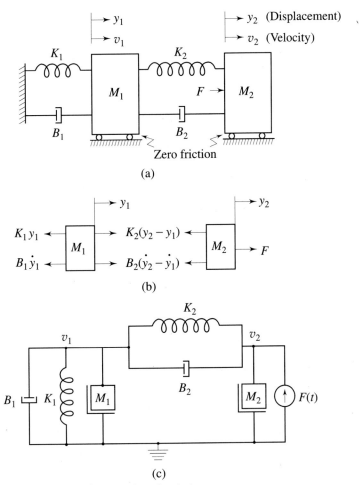

Fig. 2.52   *(a) A mechanical system*
(b) Free-body diagram
(c) Mechanical network

The dynamical equations of the system of Fig. 2.52a could also be obtained by writing nodal equations for the mechanical network of Fig. 2.52c (with force and velocity analogous to current and voltage, respectively; the algebraic sum of all the forces at a node is zero). The result is

$$B_1 v_1 + K_1 \int_{-\infty}^{t} v_1 dt + M_1 \dot{v}_1 + K_2 \int_{-\infty}^{t} (v_1 - v_2) dt + B_2 (v_1 - v_2) = 0$$

$$M_2 \dot{v}_2 + K_2 \int_{-\infty}^{t} (v_2 - v_1) dt + B_2 (v_2 - v_1) = F(t)$$

Since $\int_{-\infty}^{t} v\,dt = y$, we can write these equations as

$$B_1 v_1 + K_1 y_1 + M_1 \dot{v}_1 + K_2(y_1 - y_2) + B_2(v_1 - v_2) = 0$$
$$M_2 \dot{v}_2 + K_2(y_2 - y_1) + B_2(v_2 - v_1) = F(t)$$

The result is same as obtained earlier using the free-body diagram approach.

Review Example 2.5

A large number of process systems, used to control temperature, liquid level, composition and the like, use some sort of valve as the control actuator. The flow rate through a valve with adjustable opening is a function of both the pressure difference ΔP across the valve and the valve opening x_v:

$$Q = f(x_v, \Delta P) \qquad (2.130a)$$

In many applications, there is a fairly constant pressure drop across the control valves; therefore the flow through a control valve is directly related to valve opening. If all components (including the process) in a feedback control system are essentially linear, then the valve characteristic—relation between the valve flow rate and valve opening when valve pressure drop is kept constant— is designed to be *linear*, since then the system performance (stability, response speed, etc.) will be uniform over all operating conditions. The linear characteristic of a valve is described by the relation

$$q(t) = K_v\, x_v(t) \qquad (2.130b)$$

where K_v is the *valve gain*.

Let us consider a simple *composition control process* using a valve with linear characteristic as control actuator. In the scheme of Fig. 2.53a, a concentrated solution of salt is continuously mixed with pure water in a mixing valve. The valve characteristic is such that the total flow rate Q through it is maintained constant. When the inflow of the salt solution is varied by q_i from its initial equilibrium value $\overline{Q}_i$, the water inflow is automatically adjusted to the value $(Q - \overline{Q}_i - q_i)$. The inflow q_i may be linearly varied by controlling valve stem position x_v. The outflow rate from the salt-mixing tank is the same as the flow rate into it from the mixing valve, such that the level of the dilute salt solution in the tank is maintained constant. We assume that $\overline{C}_i$ (moles[12] of salt/ m^3 of solution) is the concentration of the salt in the inflow stream at the initial equilibrium operating point; $c_i(t)$ represents the uncontrolled disturbance in the inlet concentration. The outlet stream has a concentration $\overline{C}$ at the equilibrium operating point; $c(t)$ represents perturbations in concentration due to $q_i(t)$ and/ or $c_i(t)$.

---

12. A mole of a substance is defined as the amount of substance whose mass numerically equals its molecular weight. For example, a gram-mole of helium would have mass of 4.003 g (molecular weight of helium = 4.003).

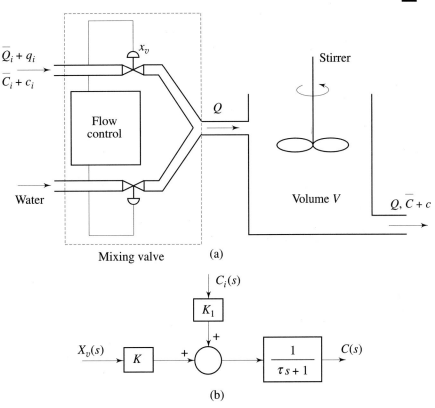

Fig. 2.53 *A salt-mixing tank*

We assume that stirring causes perfect mixing so that composition of the liquid in the tank is uniform throughout.

The rate of salt inflow in the tank

$$= [\overline{Q}_i + q_i(t)][\overline{C}_i + c_i(t)] \left(\frac{m^3}{sec} \frac{moles}{m^3} = moles/sec \right)$$

The rate of salt outflow from the tank

$$= Q(\overline{C} + c(t)) \ moles/sec$$

The rate of salt accumulation in the tank

$$= \frac{d}{dt}[V(\overline{C} + c(t))] = V \frac{dc(t)}{dt}$$

From the law of conservation of mass, we have

$$V \frac{dc(t)}{dt} = [\overline{Q}_i + q_i(t)][\overline{C}_i + c_i(t)] - Q(\overline{C} + c(t))$$

Under steady-state,

$$0 = \overline{Q}_i \overline{C}_i - Q\overline{C}$$

Perturbations about the steady-state are described by the equation

$$V \frac{dc(t)}{dt} = -Qc(t) + \overline{C}_i q_i(t) + \overline{Q}_i c_i(t) \qquad (2.131)$$

on the assumption that $q_i(t)c_i(t)$, the second-order term in perturbation variables, can be neglected.

Equation (2.131) may be rearranged as

$$\tau \frac{dc(t)}{dt} + c(t) = \frac{\overline{C}_i}{Q} q_i(t) + \frac{\overline{Q}_i}{Q} c_i(t)$$

where $\tau = V/Q = $ *holding time* for the tank. The holding time is equivalent to the time required to withdraw a volume V at a rate Q from the tank.

If $q_i(t) = K_v x_v(t)$, we obtain the following equation describing the dynamics of the system.

$$\tau \frac{dc(t)}{dt} + c(t) = Kx_v(t) + K_1 c_i(t)$$

where

$$K = \frac{\overline{C}_i K_v}{Q}, \; K_1 = \frac{\overline{Q}_i}{Q}$$

In terms of Laplace variable s,

$$(\tau s + 1)C(s) = KX_v(s) + K_1 C_i(s)$$

Figure 2.53b gives block diagram representation of this equation.

Review Questions

2.1 (a) Write an expression for the final value theorem of the Laplace transform. What is the condition under which the theorem is valid? (Help: p 859)

(b) We have used one-sided Laplace transform (and not two-sided Laplace transform) for all the control system analysis and design problems. Why? (Help: pp 855-856)

2.2 (a) Define a linear time-invariant system. Give input-output relation of such a system in terms of impulse response. In this relation, how do you account for the initial state representing initial energy storage in the system?

(b) Define the transfer function of a linear time-invariant system in terms of its impulse response.

(c) Define the transfer function of a linear time-invariant system in terms of its differential-equation model. What is the characteristic equation of the system?

2.3 (a) Dynamic behaviour of control systems can be adequately judged and compared under application of standard test signals. Describe various standard test signals commonly used in control system design. Give time-domain and *s*-domain representations of the signals.

(b) Impulse response of a system can be experimentally determined by approximating impulse by a short duration pulse. Justify the experimental procedure when we know that impulse and pulse look so different. (Help: Example 2.1)

2.4 (a) Analog simulation has lost much of its importance because of the increasing availability of digital computers. What is the current role of analog computers in Control Systems field? (Help: pp 97-98)

(b) Explain the reasons for dead-time element in process control loops. Show that dead-time can be represented by the transfer function $e^{-s\tau_D}$. How do you approximate this transfer function by a rational function? (Help: pp 116-117)

Problems

2.1 The transfer function of a first-order process is given by

$$\frac{Y(s)}{R(s)} = G(s) = \frac{K}{\tau s + 1}$$

(a) Find the impulse response to an impulse of strength A.
(b) Find the step response to a step of strength A.
(c) Find the ramp response to a ramp function with slope A.
(d) Find the response to sinusoidal input $A \sin \omega t$.

Identify the steady-state and transient components of the response in each case.

2.2 Consider a second-order model

$$\frac{Y(s)}{R(s)} = G(s) = \frac{\omega_n^2}{s^2 + 2\zeta\omega_n s + \omega_n^2}; 0 < \zeta < 1$$

Find the response $y(t)$ to the input

(a) $r(t) = \mu(t)$, a unit step function
(b) $r(t) = t\mu(t)$, a unit ramp function

Find the steady-state component y_{ss} of $y(t)$ in each case.
Will the final value theorem give the correct value of y_{ss} in each case? Why?

2.3 If the input to the system in Fig. P2.3 is $e_i(t) = 10t\,\mu(t)$, calculate the values of R and C such that the response is able to track the input with a steady-state delay of 100 μsec. What is the value of steady-state error:

$$\lim_{t\to\infty}(e_i(t) - e_0(t))\,?$$

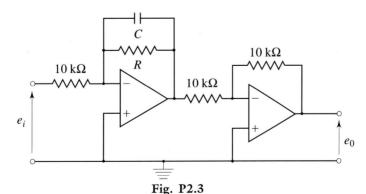

Fig. P2.3

2.4 A second-order transfer function model is given by

$$\frac{Y(s)}{R(s)} = \frac{10000}{s^2 + 600s + 10000}$$

and the input is $r(t) = 25t\,\mu(t)$.

Show that the response is able to track the input with a steady-state delay of 60 msec. What is the value of steady-state error: $\lim\limits_{t\to\infty}(r(t) - y(t))$?

2.5 The parameters of the mechanical system of Fig. P2.5 are

$M = 1{,}000$ kg
$B = 10{,}000$ N/(m/sec)
$K = 100{,}000$ N/m

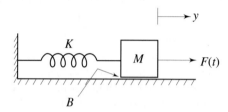

Fig. P2.5

A step force of 1000 Newton is applied to the mass at $t = 0$. The initial conditions are $y(0) = \dot{y}(0) = 0$.

From the physical parameters of the system, obtain the parameters: damping ratio ζ, undamped natural frequency ω_n, and damped natural frequency ω_d, which describe the dynamical behaviour of the system. Also obtain the step response.

2.6 A system is described by the differential equation

$$\ddot{y}(t) + 7\dot{y}(t) + 6y(t) = 6r(t);\ y(0) = \dot{y}(0) = 0$$

Find the steady-state response of the system to an input $r(t) = \sin 2t\,\mu(t)$.

2.7 Consider a system described by the differential equation

$$\ddot{y}(t) + 7\dot{y}(t) + 10y(t) = \dot{r}(t) + 3r(t)$$

(a) Find the system response to an input $e^{-t}\mu(t)$ assuming zero initial conditions.

(b) Find the system response to an input $e^{-t}\mu(t)$ when the initial conditions are $y(0) = 1$, $\dot{y}(0) = 1/2$.

2.8 Figure P2.8a shows the schematic diagram of a system for the magnetic lavitation of a ball. The equation of motion for the ball is

$$M\ddot{X} = F(X, I) - Mg$$

where the force $F(X, I)$, caused by the field of the electromagnet, is described by the experimental curves of Fig. P2.8b for a ball of mass $M = 8.4$ grams. The objective of the control is to keep the ball suspended at an equilibrium position by controlling the current in the magnet.

(a) Find the current $\bar{I}$ and displacement $\bar{X}$ corresponding to an equilibrium position.

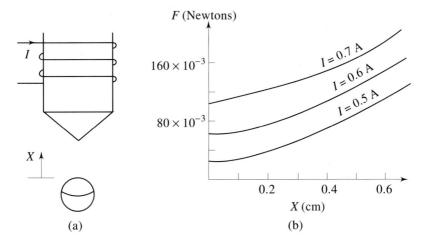

Fig. P2.8

(b) Let x and i represent perturbations in X and I from the equilibrium point
$(\bar{X}, \bar{I})$. Find the transfer function model for the perturbation dynamics
of the system.

2.9 Measurements made on vehicles travelling on typical roads have shown that
some construction techniques result in sinusoidal wave patterns in the road
surface; a representative wavelength λ is 15 m, and a representative road-
surface peak amplitude is 7.5 cm. The forcing frequency of road patterns on a
vehicle travelling with a speed of v m/sec is $\omega = 2\pi v/\lambda$ rad/sec.

A simplified representation of a vehicle's front wheel system consisting of
a tyre of mass M and a shock absorber of damping coefficient B is shown in
Fig. P2.9. Spring K_1 represents the elasticity of the tyre, while K represents
that of shock absorber. We assume that the inertia of the car body is so large
that the body can be considered as a fixed support.
Determine the transfer function $X(s)/Y(s)$ and therefrom obtain the peak
amplitude of the tyre displacement x when the car speed is 100 km/hr.
Given: $M = 15$ kg, $B = 5.25$ kN/(m/sec), $K_1 = 175$ kN/m, and
$K = 35$ kN/m.

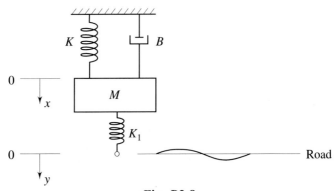

Fig. P2.9

2.10 Figure P2.10a shows a machine of mass M mounted on a foundation using a
spring of stiffness K with a damper of coefficient B in parallel.
   (a) The machine generates a disturbing force $F(t) = A \sin \omega t$. Find the force
       transmitted to the foundation at steady-state.
   (b) With reference to Fig. P2.10b, determine the machine vibration $x(t)$ due
       to the foundation vibration $y(t) = A \sin \gamma t$.

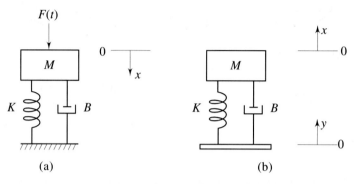

(a)   (b)

Fig. P2.10

2.11 A dynamic absorber is shown in Fig. P2.11. This system is representative of
many situations involving the vibration of machines containing unbalanced
components. The parameters M_2, K_2 and B_2 may be chosen so that the main
mass M_1 does not vibrate in response to foundation vibration. Obtain a set of
differential equations describing the dynamics of the system.

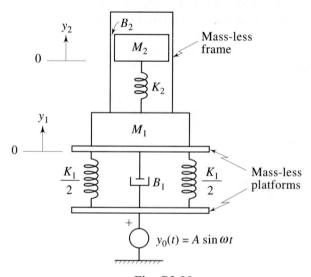

Fig. P2.11

2.12 Find the transfer function models for the two bridged-T networks shown in
Fig. P2.12.

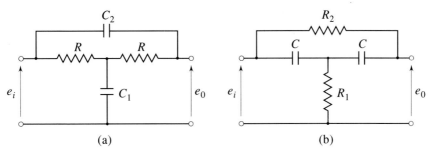

Fig. P2.12

2.13 Consider the op amp circuit shown in Fig. P2.13; $r(t)$ and $y(t)$ are the inputs and $e(t)$ is the output. Neglecting the loading effect on the potentiometer R_2, prove that

$$E(s) = \frac{R_2}{R_2'}\left(1 + \frac{1}{R_3 C s}\right)[R(s) - Y(s)]$$

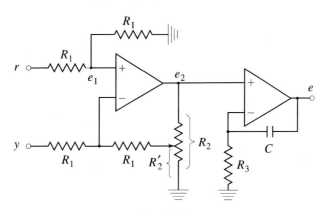

Fig. P2.13

2.14 Consider the op amp circuit shown in Fig. P2.14, $r(t)$ and $y(t)$ are the inputs and $e(t)$ is the output. Prove that

$$E(s) = R_2 C s\,[R(s) - Y(s)]$$

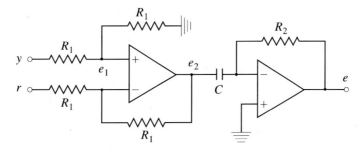

Fig. P2.14

2.15 Consider the inverted pendulum shown in Fig. P2.15. The pivot of the pendulum is mounted on a carriage which can move in a horizontal direction. The carriage is driven by a small motor that at time t exerts a force $F(t)$ on the carriage. This force is the input variable for the system. This somewhat artificial system represents a dynamic model of a space booster on take-off— the booster is balanced on top of the rocket engine thrust vector.

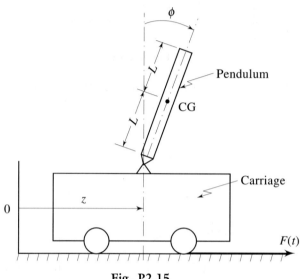

Fig. P2.15

Taking the carriage position z, carriage velocity $\dot{z}$, angular position ϕ of the pendulum, and angular velocity $\dot{\phi}$ of the pendulum as state variables, derive a state variable model of the system for small deviations in ϕ ($\sin \phi \cong \phi$).

Given: M = mass of the carriage = 1 kg; m = mass of the pendulum = 0.15 kg;

$2L$ = length of the pendulum = 2 m; $J = \dfrac{4}{3} mL^2$ = moment of inertia of the pendulum with respect to centre of gravity.

2.16 The scheme of Fig. P2.16 produces a steady steam flow of fluid with controlled temperature θ. A stream of hot fluid at constant temperature θ_H is continuously mixed with a stream of cold fluid at constant temperature θ_C, in a mixing valve. The valve characteristic is such that the total flow rate Q (m³/sec) through it is maintained constant but the inflow $q_i(t)$((m³/sec) of hot fluid may be linearly varied by controlling valve stem position $x (q_i = K_v x)$.

The valve stem position x thus controls the temperature θ_i(°C) of the outflow from the mixing valve.

Due to the distance between the valve and the point of discharge into the tank of volume V(m³), there is a time delay of τ_D sec between the change in θ_i and the discharge of the flow with the changed temperature into the tank. Derive a transfer function model $\theta(s)/\theta_i(s)$, and a linear relationship between θ_i and x for small perturbations about the equilibrium operating point.

Given: $\dfrac{Q}{V} = 1, \ \tau_D = 1.5, K_v = 0.5$

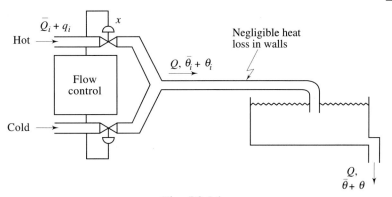

Fig. P2.16

2.17 The stirred tank sketched in Fig. P2.17 is used to heat a process stream by steam condensing inside a coil.

Given:

λ = latent heat of condensation of saturated steam

= 2247×10^3 Joules/kg

C_1 = thermal capacitance of the coil mass = 503×10^3 J/°C

U = overall convective heat transfer coefficient at the coil-liquid interface

= 42.97×10^3 J/(min)(m²)(°C)

A = heat transfer area = 22.57 m²

Q = feed flow rate = 0.425 m³/min

ρ = density of the feed = 1090 kg/m³

c = heat capacity of the feed = 3350 J/(kg)(°C)

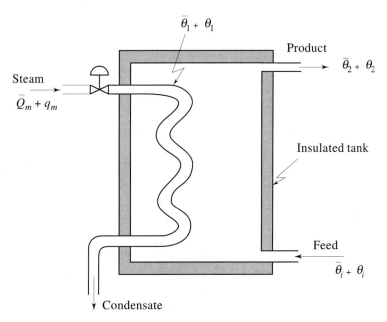

Fig. P2.17

$V =$ volume of the liquid in the tank $= 3.4 \text{ m}^3$

θ_1, θ_2 : perturbations (°C) of the temperature of coil mass and liquid in the tank respectively, in response to perturbation q_m (kg/min) in the steam flow rate.

$\theta_i =$ perturbation of the temperature of the feed (disturbance input)

Derive a state variable model with θ_1 and θ_2 as state variables, and q_m and θ_i as input variables.

2.18 Reconsider the stirred tank of Problem 2.17 (Fig. P2.17). At steady-state, the temperature of the feed is $\bar{\theta}_i = 55°\text{C}$, and the temperature of the liquid in the tank is $\bar{\theta}_2 = = 80°\text{C}$. Find the steady-state mass flow rate $\bar{Q}_m$ of steam through the control valve.

2.19 Consider the unit shown in Fig. P2.19. The objective of this unit is to cool a hot process fluid with constant inlet temperature θ_{i2}, constant inflow rate Q_2, density ρ_2, and heat capacity c_2. The cooling medium (water) with constant inlet temperature θ_{i1}, density ρ_1, and heat capacity c_1 is circulated through the jacket at the rate $(\bar{Q}_1 + q_1)$, where $\bar{Q}_1$ is the steady-state value. It is assumed that the jacketed tank is well insulated.

Write the unsteady-state energy balance equations on the process fluid with temperature $(\bar{\theta}_2 + \theta_2)$, and on the cooling water with temperature $(\bar{\theta}_1 + \theta_1)$. Linearize these equations about the operating point $\{Q_2, \theta_{i1}, \theta_{i2}, \bar{Q}_1, \bar{\theta}_1, \bar{\theta}_2\}$ and therefrom obtain the transfer function $\theta_2(s)/Q_1(s)$.

Given: $\theta_{i2} = 66°\text{C}, Q_2 = 7.5 \times 10^{-3} \text{m}^3/\text{sec}, \bar{\theta}_2 = 55°\text{C}$

$\rho_2 = 19.2 \text{ kg mole/m}^3, c_2 = 1.815 \times 10^5 \text{ J/(kg)(mole)}(°\text{C})$

$\theta_{i1} = 27°\text{C}, \rho_1 = 1000 \text{ kg/m}^3$

$c_1 = 4184 \text{ J/(kg)}(°\text{C})$

$V_2 =$ volume of the tank $= 7.08 \text{ m}^3$

$A =$ heat transfer area $= 5.4 \text{ m}^2$

$U =$ average convective heat transfer coefficient
$= 3550 \text{ J/(sec)(m}^2) (°\text{C})$

$V_1 =$ volume of the jacket $= 1.82 \text{ m}^3$

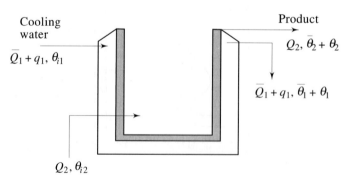

Fig. P2.19

2.20 Figure P2.20 shows a process consisting of two interconnected tanks with surface areas A_1 and A_2. h_1 and h_2 are the deviations in tank levels from equilibrium values. q_1 and q_2 are the deviations in inflow rates from equilibrium values, and R_0, R_1 and R_2 are linearized valve resistance values (R = incremental change in pressure across the valve/incremental change in flow through the valve). The flow rates q_1 and q_2 into the tanks are controlled by the signals r_1 and r_2 via valves and actuators, and are modelled by the linear equations

$$q_1 = K_1 r_1 \; ; \; q_2 = K_2 r_2$$

We are interested in knowing how the tank levels will respond to changes in r_1 and r_2. Develop a state variable model for the system.

Given:
$$A_1 = 1, A_2 = 0.5, K_1 = 1, K_2 = 0.5$$
$$R_0/\rho g = 1, R_1/\rho g = 0.5, R_2/\rho g = 2$$
$$\rho = \text{density of the liquid}$$
$$g = \text{acceleration due to gravity}$$

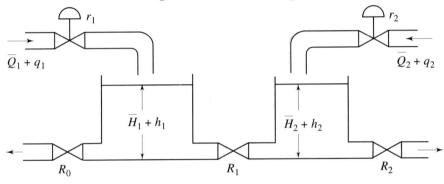

Fig. P2.20

2.21 The scheme of Fig. P2.21 describes a simple concentration control process. Two concentrated solutions of some chemical with constant concentrations C_1 and C_2 are fed with flow rates $Q_1(t) = \overline{Q}_1 + q_1(t)$, and $Q_2(t) = \overline{Q}_2 + q_2(t)$ respectively and are continuously mixed in the tank. The outflow from the mixing tank is at a rate $Q(t) = \overline{Q} + q(t)$ with concentration $C(t) = \overline{C} + c(t)$. The flow $Q(t)$ is characterized by the turbulent flow relation

$$Q(t) = K\sqrt{H(t)}$$

where $H(t) = \overline{H} + h(t)$ is the head of the liquid in the tank, A is the cross-sectional area of the tank and K is a constant. Values of various parameters at the equilibrium operating point are:

$$\overline{Q}_1 = 10 \text{ litres/sec};$$
$$\overline{Q}_2 = 20 \text{ litres/sec};$$
$$C_1 = 9 \text{ g-moles/litre};$$
$$C_2 = 18 \text{ g-moles/litre; and}$$
$$\overline{H} = 200 \text{ cm}$$

The area $A = 7500 \text{ cm}^2$

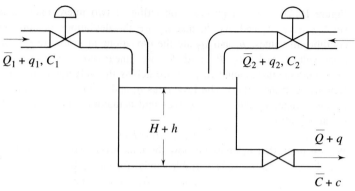

Fig. P2.21

(i) Assuming small perturbations about the equilibrium operating point, obtain a linear relationship between $q(t)$ and $h(t)$.

(ii) Derive a state variable model of the system with $h(t)$ and $c(t)$ as state variables.

2.22 The transfer function of a dead-time element $e^{-\tau_D s}$ may be approximated by a rational function. Two often-used approximations are given below:

(i) $e^{-\tau_D s} = \dfrac{1 - \tau_D s/2}{1 + \tau_D s/2}$

(ii) $e^{-\tau_D s} = \dfrac{1 - \tau_D s/2 + \tau_D^2 s^2/12}{1 + \tau_D s/2 + \tau_D^2 s^2/12}$

Prove that the first approximation is correct through the first three terms, and the second approximation is correct through the first five terms of the Taylor series expansion of $e^{-\tau_D s}$.

chapter 3

Models of Industrial Control Devices and Systems

3.1 | INTRODUCTION

Control systems are generally built by the interconnection of various components. These components can be mechanical, electrical, hydraulic, pneumatic, or other devices. In this chapter, some of the most commonly used devices and some typical control systems will be introduced.

The design of control systems can be divided into two categories. One concerns the design of better components for control systems; the other involves the design of overall systems by utilizing existing devices. We shall be mainly concerned with the design of overall systems, and hence the detailed structures of control components will not be studied. We shall instead study only the functions of the devices. Simple mathematical models will be derived for the devices; the limitations of the models will also be discussed.

We shall not attempt to discuss all existing devices. Also all existing industrial control systems cannot be introduced. Our discussion will be limited to the widely used control devices and systems for control of speed or position of an inertia load, and for control of temperature, pressure, or composition of a process fluid. The objective is to show the reader how the mathematical models that we shall be dealing with in the remainder of the book arise from physical systems.

Control configurations and control laws employed in our examples represent only the conceptual designs of control systems for given control problems. In most of our examples, we have used a simple proportional control law realized by an amplifier. It should be understood that these conceptual designs may not be the final designs to be adopted. It may be necessary to modify a conceptual design after completing a detailed analysis of its mathematical model, and in some cases the entire conceptual design may have to be discarded as unsuitable in favour of another design. This chapter meets the limited objective of deriving a mathematical model of a control system for a given conceptual design. Several of the examples given in this chapter will be reconsidered later for detailed analysis and design.

3.2 | GENERALIZED BLOCK DIAGRAM OF A FEEDBACK SYSTEM

We have already used block diagrams to represent the input–output behaviour of a linear system; the signal into the *block* represents the input, the signal out of the block represents the output, while the block itself stands for the transfer function of the linear system (Fig. 3.1a). The flow of information (signal) is unidirectional from the input to the output, with the output being equal to the input multiplied by the transfer function of the block. A complex system comprising of several non-loading elements is represented by the interconnection of the blocks for the individual elements. The blocks are connected by lines and arrows indicating the unidirectional flow of information from the output of one block to the input of the other (Fig. 3.1b). In addition to this, a *summing junction* (Fig. 3.1c) in a block diagram represents the dynamic summation of signals, and a *branch point* (Fig. 3.1d) is a take-off point at which the information branches out and goes concurrently to other blocks or summing junctions.

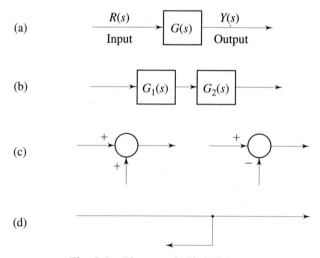

Fig. 3.1 *Elements of a block diagram*

Various feedback control configurations were described in Chapter 1 using block diagrams of general functional nature. With the transfer function concept introduced in Chapter 2, we are now equipped to consider *operational block diagrams* necessary for design and analysis. We begin with the block diagram shown in Fig. 3.2. It represents the basic structure of feedback control systems (refer Fig. 1.12). Not all systems can be forced into this format, but it serves as a reference for discussion.

In Fig. 3.2, the variable $y(t)$ is the *controlled variable* of the system. The desired value of the controlled variable is $y_r(t)$, the *command input*. $y_r(t)$ and $y(t)$ have the same units. In this chapter, we will discuss many motion control systems with speed or position of an inertia load as controlled variable. Process control examples with temperature, pressure, or composition of a process fluid as controlled variable will also appear.

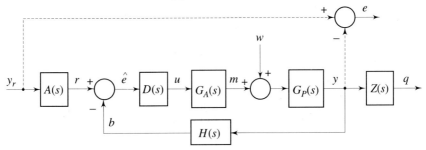

Fig. 3.2 *Generalized operational block diagram of a feedback system*

The *feedback elements* with transfer function $H(s)$ are system components that act on the controlled variable $y(t)$ to produce the *feedback signal* $b(t)$. $H(s)$ typically represents the sensor action to convert the controlled variable $y(t)$ to an electrical sensor output signal $b(t)$.

The *reference input elements* with transfer function $A(s)$ convert the command signal $y_r(t)$ into a form compatible with the feedback signal $b(t)$. The transformed command signal is the actual physical input to the system. This actual signal input is defined as the *reference input*.

The comparison device (*error detector*) of the system compares the reference input $r(t)$ with the feedback signal $b(t)$ and generates the *actuating error signal* $\hat{e}(t)$. The signals $r(t), b(t)$ and $\hat{e}(t)$ have the same units. The *controller* with transfer function $D(s)$ acts on the actuating error signal to produce the *control signal* $u(t)$.

The control signal $u(t)$ has the knowledge about the desired control action. The power level of this signal is relatively low. The *actuator elements* with transfer function $G_A(s)$ are the system components that act on the control signal $u(t)$ and develop enough torque, pressure, heat, etc. (*manipulated variable $m(t)$*), to influence the *controlled system*. $G_P(s)$ is the transfer function of the controlled system.

The *disturbance $w(t)$* represents the undesired signals that tend to affect the controlled system. The disturbances may be introduced into the system at more than one location.

There are situations where the variable $q(t)$ which we really wish to control is not used to generate a feedback signal. The transfer function $Z(s)$ in Fig. 3.2 is the transfer function of the *indirectly controlled system elements*; it relates the *indirectly controlled variable* $q(t)$ to the controlled variable $y(t)$. Note that $Z(s)$ is outside the feedback loop.

The dashed-line portion of Fig. 3.2 shows the *system error* $e(t) = y_r(t) - y(t)$. Note that the actuating error signal $\hat{e}(t)$ and the system error $e(t)$ are two different variables.

Figure 3.2 defines the basic types of signals and components necessary for description of any feedback control system; however it must be adopted to the needs of each specific design. A large number of motion and process control examples given later in this chapter will (surely) help in better appreciation of what has been said in this section.

3.3 | BLOCK DIAGRAM MANIPULATIONS

The basic feedback system block diagram of Fig. 3.2 is shown in abridged form in Fig. 3.3. The output $Y(s)$ is influenced by the control signal $U(s)$ and the disturbance signal $W(s)$ as per the following relation:

$$Y(s) = G_P(s)G_A(s)U(s) + G_P(s)W(s) \tag{3.1a}$$

$$= G(s)U(s) + N(s)W(s) \tag{3.1b}$$

where $G(s)$ is the transfer function from the control signal $U(s)$ to the output $Y(s)$, and $N(s)$ is the transfer function from the disturbance input $W(s)$ to the output $Y(s)$. Using Eqns (3.1), we can modify the block diagram of Fig. 3.3 to the form shown in Fig. 3.4. Note that in the block diagram model of Fig. 3.4, the plant includes the actuator elements.

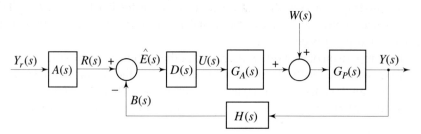

Fig. 3.3   *A general linear feedback system*

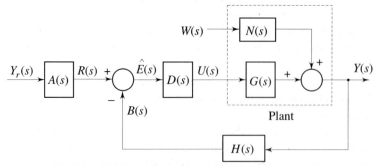

Fig. 3.4   *Equivalent representation of the block diagram of Fig. 3.3*

The actuating error signal

$$\hat{E}(s) = R(s) - B(s) = A(s)Y_r(s) - H(s)Y(s)$$

The control signal

$$U(s) = D(s)A(s)Y_r(s) - D(s)H(s)Y(s) \tag{3.2a}$$

$$= D(s)H(s)\left[\frac{A(s)}{H(s)}Y_r(s) - Y(s)\right] \tag{3.2b}$$

Using Eqns (3.2), we can simplify Fig. 3.4 to obtain the structure shown in Fig. 3.5.

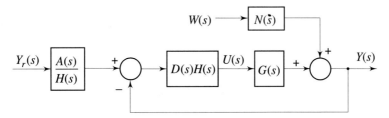

Fig. 3.5 *Simplification of the block diagram of Fig. 3.4*

A further simplification of Fig. 3.5 is possible if $H = A$. In this case, which is quite common, we can model the system as the *unity feedback system* as shown in Fig. 3.6, and take advantage of the fact that now the actuating signal is the system error $e(t)$.

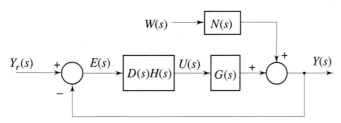

Fig. 3.6 *Unity feedback system*

The block diagrams in Figs 3.4–3.6, as we shall see later, are very useful for the purpose of system design. However, it should be clear that these block diagrams have lost the physical significance. For example, the block in Fig. 3.5 with transfer function $A(s)/H(s)$, does not refer to any physical portion of the original system. Rather, it represents the result of manipulating Eqn. (3.2a) into the form given by Eqn. (3.2b).

Thus the reader is advised to think in terms of the *equations* that the block diagrams represent, rather than to attach any special significance to block diagrams themselves. The only role played by a block diagram is that it is a convenient means of representing the various system equations, rather than writing them out explicitly. *Block diagram manipulation* is nothing more than the manipulation of a set of algebraic transform equations.

▲▲

For the analysis of a feedback system, we require the transfer function between the input—either reference or disturbance—and the output. We can use block diagram manipulations to eliminate all the signals except the input and the output. The reduced block diagram leads to the desired result.

Consider the block diagram of Fig. 3.7. This feedback system has two inputs. We shall use superposition to treat each input separately.

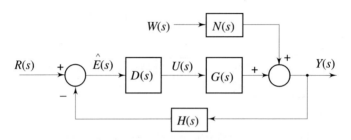

Fig. 3.7 *A typical feedback system with two inputs*

When disturbance input is set to zero, the single-input system of Fig. 3.8 results. The transfer function between the input $R(s)$ and the output $Y(s)$ is referred to as the *reference transfer function* and will be denoted by $M(s)$. To solve for $M(s)$, we write the pair of transform equations

$$\hat{E}(s) = R(s) - H(s)Y(s); \; Y(s) = G(s)U(s) = G(s)D(s)\hat{E}(s)$$

and then eliminate $\hat{E}(s)$ to obtain

$$[1 + D(s)G(s)H(s)]Y(s) = D(s)G(s)R(s)$$

which leads to the desired result:

$$M(s) = \left.\frac{Y(s)}{R(s)}\right|_{W(s)=0} = \frac{D(s)G(s)}{1 + D(s)G(s)H(s)} \tag{3.3}$$

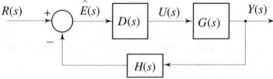

Fig. 3.8 *Block diagram without disturbance input*

Similarly we obtain the *disturbance transfer function* $M_w(s)$ by setting the reference input to zero in Fig. 3.7 yielding Fig. 3.9, and then solving for $Y(s)/W(s)$. From the revised block diagram,

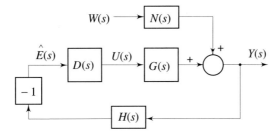

Fig. 3.9 *Block diagram without reference input*

$$\hat{E}(s) = - H(s)Y(s)$$
$$Y(s) = G(s)D(s)\hat{E}(s) + N(s)W(s)$$

from which $\hat{E}(s)$ can be eliminated to give

$$M_w(s) = \frac{Y(s)}{W(s)}\bigg|_{R(s)=0} = \frac{N(s)}{1 + D(s)G(s)H(s)} \qquad (3.4)$$

The response to the simultaneous application of $R(s)$ and $W(s)$ is given by

$$Y(s) = M(s)R(s) + M_w(s)W(s) \qquad (3.5)$$

Figure 3.10 shows the reduced block diagram model of the given feedback system.

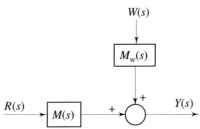

Fig. 3.10 *Reduced block diagram model for system of Fig. 3.7*

The transfer functions given by Eqns (3.3) and (3.4) are referred to as *closed-loop* transfer functions. Looking at Eqn. (3.3), we notice that the numerator is the multiplication of the transfer functions in the *forward path* between the two variables $R(s)$ and $Y(s)$. The denominator of this equation has the term $D(s)G(s)H(s)$ which is the multiplication of all the transfer functions in the *feedback loop*. An inspection of Eqn. (3.4) shows that the numerator is again the multiplication of the transfer functions in the forward path between $W(s)$ and $Y(s)$. The denominator is the same as in the case of Eqn. (3.3).

From the examples of block diagram manipulations given above, we observe that there are two different objectives which may motivate one to manipulate a block diagram. The most obvious is to obtain the overall transfer function for the purpose of analysis (the block diagram of Fig. 3.7 was manipulated to obtain the one given in Fig. 3.10). The other objective is to manipulate a block diagram into a simpler form which is more convenient in the design process (the block diagram of Fig. 3.3 was manipulated to obtain the one given in Fig. 3.6).

The process by which we have manipulated the block diagrams is nothing more than the manipulation of a set of algebraic transform equations. We can, in fact, manipulate a complex block diagram directly by using the simple rules of block diagram reduction. The most commonly encountered block diagram operations are summarized in Table 3.1.

Table 3.1   *Rules of block diagram algebra*

Rule	Original diagram	Equivalent diagram
1	X_1, $X_1 - X_2$, X_2, X_3 → $X_1 - X_2 + X_3$	X_1, $X_1 + X_3$, X_3, X_2 → $X_1 + X_3 - X_2$
2	X_1, X_3, X_2 → $X_1 - X_2 + X_3$	X_1, $X_1 - X_2$, X_2, X_3 → $X_1 - X_2 + X_3$
3	X → G_1 (XG_1), G_2 (XG_2) → $XG_1 + XG_2$	X → $G_1 + G_2$ → $X(G_1 + G_2)$
4	X → G_1 (XG_1) → G_2 → XG_1G_2	X → G_1G_2 → XG_1G_2
5	X_1 → G (X_1G) → $X_1G - X_2$, X_2	X_1 → G → $X_1G - X_2$; $X_1 - X_2/G$; $\dfrac{X_2}{G}$ → $\dfrac{1}{G}$ ← X_2
6	X_1, $X_1 - X_2$, X_2 → G → $(X_1 - X_2)G$	X_1 → G (X_1G) → $X_1G - X_2G$; X_2G → G ← X_2
7	X → G → XG ; XG ←	X → G → XG ; XG ← G ←

(Contd)

Table 3.1 (*Contd*)

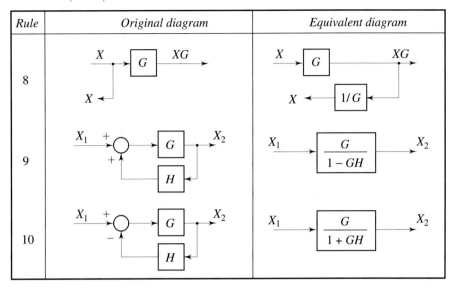

Rule	Original diagram	Equivalent diagram
8		
9		
10		

Example 3.1

As we shall see later in this chapter, often a feedback system will have more than one feedback path resulting in a multiple-loop configuration. The block diagram of a typical multiple-loop feedback control system is shown in Fig. 3.11 (Note that the loop $G_3(s)G_4(s)H_1(s)$ is a positive feedback loop). Let us obtain the closed-loop transfer function of this system using block diagram manipulation rules given in Table 3.1.

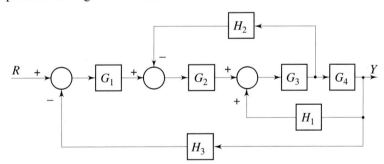

Fig. 3.11 *A multiple-loop feedback control system*

The block diagram reduction procedure is based on the utilization of rules 9 and 10, which eliminate feedback loops. The other rules are used to transform the diagram to the form ready for eliminating feedback loops. First, in order to eliminate the loop $G_3G_4H_1$, we move H_2 behind block G_4 by using rules 8 and 4 and obtain Fig. 3.12a. Eliminating the loop $G_3G_4H_1$ by rules 4 and 9, we obtain Fig. 3.12b. Then eliminating the inner loop containing H_2/G_4 by rules 4 and 10, we obtain Fig. 3.12c. Finally, by reducing the loop containing H_3, we obtain the closed-loop transfer function as shown in Fig. 3.12d.

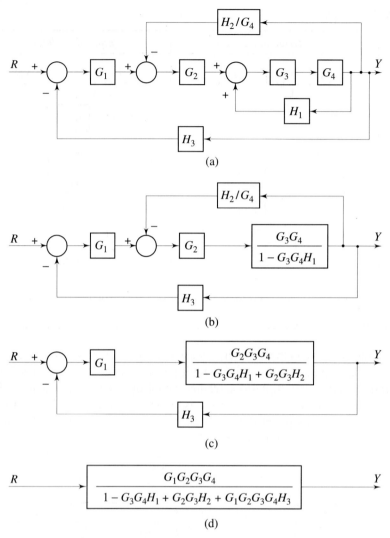

Fig. 3.12 *Block diagram reduction of the system of Fig. 3.11*

An alternate approach is to move the summing point of the positive feedback loop containing H_1, outside the negative feedback loop containing H_2. Application of rules 5, 4 and 1 results in Fig. 3.13a. Eliminating the feedback loop containing H_2, we get Fig. 3.13b. Then, the elimination of loop containing H_1/G_2 gives Fig. 3.13c. Finally, eliminating the loop containing H_3 results in Fig. 3.13d.

3.4 │ SIGNAL FLOW GRAPHS AND THE MASON'S GAIN RULE

Block diagrams are adequate for the representation of the inter-relationships of the variables of a control system. However for a system with reasonably com-

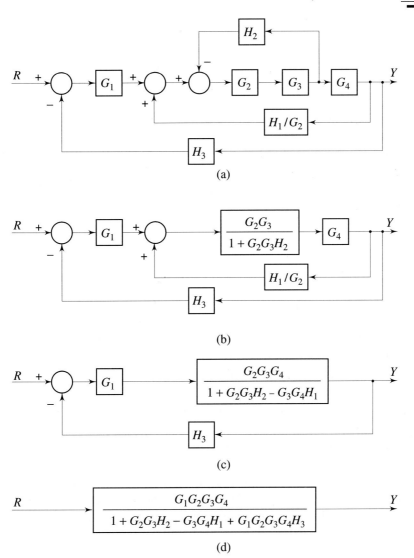

Fig. 3.13 *Block diagram reduction of the system of Fig. 3.11*

plex inter-relationships, the block diagram reduction procedure is cumbersome and often quite difficult to complete. An alternative method for determining the relationship between system variables, called the *signal flow graph* method, is based on a representation of the system by line segments. The advantage of this method is the availability of a *gain rule*, which provides the relation between system variables without requiring any reduction procedure or manipulation of the signal flow graph.

Signal Flow Graph Terminology

The basic element of a signal flow graph is a unidirectional line segment called a *branch*, which relates the dependency of an input and an output variable in a manner equivalent to a block of a block diagram. The input and output points of the branch, called *nodes*, represent the input and output variables; the branch transmits the input-node signal to the output node through a gain, called the *transmittance* of the branch.

In the signal flow graph of Fig. 3.14, the branch is directed from node X_1 to node X_2, representing the dependence of the variable X_2 upon X_1. The signal X_1 travelling from the node X_1 along the branch is multiplied by the transmittance G of the branch so that a signal GX_1 is delivered at node X_2, $X_2 = GX_1$.

Fig. 3.14   *Signal flow graph of $X_2 = GX_1$*

In a signal flow graph with several nodes and branches, each node variable is the algebraic sum of all incoming signals; and all outgoing signals from any node equal the node variable and do not affect it. As an illustrative example, consider a system described by the following set of algebraic equations:

$$X_2 = G_{12}X_1 + G_{32}X_3 + G_{42}X_4 + G_{52}X_5; \quad X_3 = G_{23}X_2;$$
$$X_4 = G_{34}X_3 + G_{44}X_4; \quad X_5 = G_{35}X_3 + G_{45}X_4 \tag{3.6}$$

where X_1 is the input variable and X_5 is the output variable.

The signal flow graph for this system is constructed as shown in Fig. 3.15, although the indicated sequence of steps is not unique.

The nodes representing the variables X_1, X_2, X_3, X_4 and X_5 are located in order from left to right (Fig. 3.15a). The first equation in the set (3.6) states that X_2 depends upon four signals; its signal flow graph is shown in Fig. 3.15b. Similarly, the signal flow graphs of the remaining three equations in the set (3.6) are shown in Figs 3.15c, 3.15d, and 3.15e respectively giving the complete signal flow graph of Fig. 3.15f.

Let us now precisely define the various terms used in connection with signal flow graphs.

(i) *Node*: It represents a system variable which is equal to the sum of all incoming signals at the node. All outgoing signals from the node are equal to the node variable and do not affect the value of the node variable.

For example, X_1, X_2, X_3, X_4 and X_5 are nodes of Fig. 3.15f.

(ii) *Branch*: A signal travels along a branch from one node to another in the direction indicated by the branch arrow and in the process gets multiplied by the gain or transmittance of the branch. The branch operator (gain/transmittance) is written on the signal flow graph near the branch arrow.

For example, in Fig. 3.15f, the signal reaching node X_3 from node X_2 is given by $G_{23}X_2$ where G_{23} is the transmittance from node X_2 to node X_3.

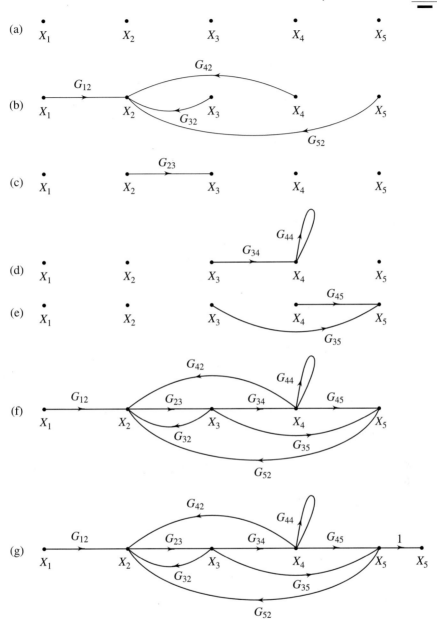

Fig. 3.15 *Construction of signal flow graph for Eqns (3.6)*

(iii) *Input node or source*: It is a node with only outgoing branches (X_1 in Fig. 3.15f).

(iv) *Output node or sink*: It is a node with only incoming branches.

Node X_5 in Fig. 3.15f has an outgoing branch, but after introducing an additional branch with unit transmittance as shown in Fig. 3.15g, the added node becomes an output node. This operation is equivalent to adding an equation

$$X_5 = X_5$$

in the set (3.6).

However, we cannot convert a non-input node into an input node by a similar operation.

(v) *Path*: It is the traversal of connected branches in the direction of the branch arrows such that no node is traversed more than once.

(vi) *Forward path*: It is a path from the input node to the output node.

For the signal flow graph of Fig. 3.15g, there are two forward paths shown in Figs 3.16a and 3.16b.

(vii) *Loop*: It is a path which originates and terminates at the same node. The flow graph of Fig. 3.15g has five loops shown in Figs 3.16c to 3.16g.

(viii) *Nontouching loops*: Loops are said to be nontouching if they do not possess any common node.

The flow graph of Fig. 3.15g has two possible combinations of two nontouching loops. These are shown in Figs 3.16h and 3.16i. This flow graph does not have combinations of more than two nontouching loops.

(ix) *Forward path gain*: It is the product of the branch gain encountered in traversing a forward path.

The two forward paths of Figs 3.16a and 3.16b have the path gains $(G_{12}G_{23}G_{34}G_{45})$ and $(G_{12}G_{23}G_{35})$ respectively.

(x) *Loop gain*: It is the product of the branch gains encountered in traversing a loop.

The five individual loops of Figs 3.16c to 3.16g have loop gains $(G_{23}G_{32})$, $(G_{23}G_{34}G_{42})$, G_{44}, $(G_{23}G_{34}G_{45}G_{52})$; and $(G_{23}G_{35}G_{52})$ respectively.

The Mason's Gain Rule

The relationship between an input variable and an output variable of a signal flow graph is given by the net gain between the input and the output nodes and is known as the overall gain of the system. Mason's gain rule[1] for the determination of the overall system gain is given below.

$$M = \frac{1}{\Delta} \sum_{k=1}^{N} P_k \Delta_k = \frac{X_{\text{out}}}{X_{\text{in}}} \tag{3.7a}$$

where M = gain between X_{in} and X_{out}

X_{out} = output node variable

X_{in} = input node variable

N = total number of forward paths

P_k = path gain of the kth forward path

Δ = 1–(sum of loop gains of all individual loops) + (sum of gain products of all possible combinations of two nontouching loops)– (sum of gain products of all possible combinations of three nontouching loops) + $\cdots$

---

1. For the derivation, based on Cramer's rule for solving linear equations by determinants, the papers of Mason [44, 45] should be consulted.

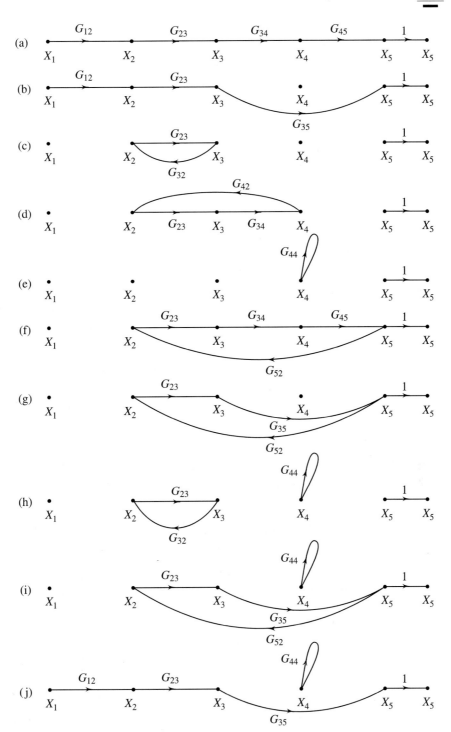

Fig. 3.16 *Application of Mason's gain rule to the signal flow graph of Fig. 3.15g*

$$= 1 - \sum_m P_{m1} + \sum_m P_{m2} - \sum_m P_{m3} + \cdots \qquad (3.7b)$$

P_{mr} = gain product of the mth possible combination of r nontouching loops.
Δ_k = the value of Δ for that part of the graph not touching the kth forward path.

Let us illustrate the use of Mason's gain rule by finding the overall gain of the signal flow graph shown in Fig. 3.15g. The following conclusions are drawn by inspection of this signal flow graph.

(i) There are two forward paths with path gains

$$P_1 = G_{12}G_{23}G_{34}G_{45} \qquad \text{(Fig. 3.16a)}$$
$$P_2 = G_{12}G_{23}G_{35} \qquad \text{(Fig. 3.16b)}$$

(ii) There are five individual loops with loop gains

$$P_{11} = G_{23}G_{32} \qquad \text{(Fig. 3.16c)}$$
$$P_{21} = G_{23}G_{34}G_{42} \qquad \text{(Fig. 3.16d)}$$
$$P_{31} = G_{44} \qquad \text{(Fig. 3.16e)}$$
$$P_{41} = G_{23}G_{34}G_{45}G_{52} \qquad \text{(Fig. 3.16f)}$$
$$P_{51} = G_{23}G_{35}G_{52} \qquad \text{(Fig. 3.16g)}$$

(iii) There are two possible combinations of two nontouching loops with loop gain products

$$P_{12} = G_{23}G_{32}G_{44} \qquad \text{(Fig. 3.16h)}$$
$$P_{22} = G_{23}G_{35}G_{52}G_{44} \qquad \text{(Fig. 3.16i)}$$

(iv) There are no combinations of three nontouching loops, four nontouching loops, etc. Therefore

$$P_{m3} = P_{m4} = \cdots = 0$$

Hence from Eqn. (3.7b),

$$\Delta = 1 - (G_{23}G_{32} + G_{23}G_{34}G_{42} + G_{44} + G_{23}G_{34}G_{45}G_{52} + G_{23}G_{35}G_{52})$$
$$+ (G_{23}G_{32}G_{44} + G_{23}G_{35}G_{52}G_{44})$$

(v) The first forward path is in touch with all the loops. Therefore $\Delta_1 = 1$. The second forward path is not in touch with one loop (Fig. 3.16j). Therefore, $\Delta_2 = 1 - G_{44}$.

From Eqn. (3.7a), the overall gain is

$$M = \frac{X_5}{X_1} = \frac{P_1\Delta_1 + P_2\Delta_2}{\Delta}$$

$$= \frac{G_{12}G_{23}G_{34}G_{45} + G_{12}G_{23}G_{35}(1 - G_{44})}{\left[\begin{array}{l}1 - (G_{23}G_{32} + G_{23}G_{34}G_{42} + G_{44} + G_{23}G_{34}G_{45}G_{52} + G_{23}G_{35}G_{52}) \\ \qquad + G_{23}G_{32}G_{44} + G_{23}G_{35}G_{52}G_{44}\end{array}\right]}$$

Block Diagram Reduction Using The Mason's Gain Rule

Due to the similarity between block diagrams and signal flow graphs, the Mason's gain rule can be used to determine the input-output relationships of either. In general, given a block diagram of a linear system, we apply the gain rule directly to it. However, in order to be able to identify all the loops and non-touching parts clearly, it may sometimes be helpful if an equivalent signal flow graph for the given block diagram is drawn before applying the gain rule.

*Example 3.2*_____·_____

Consider the block diagram shown in Fig. 3.17a. The equivalent signal flow graph is drawn in Fig. 3.17b. Note that since a node on the signal flow graph is interpreted as a summing point of all incoming signals to the node, the negative feedbacks on the block diagram are represented by assigning negative gains to the feedback paths on the signal flow graph.

There are two forward paths with path gains

$$P_1 = G_1 G_2 G_3; \; P_2 = G_4$$

There are four individual loops with loop gains

$$P_{11} = -G_1 H_1; \; P_{21} = -G_2 H_2; \; P_{31} = -G_3 H_3; \; P_{41} = -G_4 H_3 H_2 H_1$$

There is one combination of two nontouching loops with loop gain product

$$P_{12} = G_1 H_1 G_3 H_3$$

There are no combinations of more than two nontouching loops.

Hence from Eqn. (3.7b),

$$\Delta = 1 - (-G_1 H_1 - G_2 H_2 - G_3 H_3 - G_4 H_3 H_2 H_1) + G_1 H_1 G_3 H_3$$

The first forward path is in touch with all the loops. Therefore $\Delta_1 = 1$. The second forward path is not in touch with one loop (Fig. 3.17b). Therefore $\Delta_2 = 1 - (-G_2 H_2)$.

From Eqn. (3.7a), the overall gain is

$$M = \frac{Y}{R} = \frac{P_1 \Delta_1 + P_2 \Delta_2}{\Delta}$$

$$= \frac{G_1 G_2 G_3 + G_4 + G_4 G_2 H_2}{1 + G_1 H_1 + G_2 H_2 + G_3 H_3 + G_4 H_3 H_2 H_1 + G_1 H_1 G_3 H_3}$$

*Example 3.3*_____

Consider another typical block diagram shown in Fig. 3.18. This feedback system has two inputs. We shall use the superposition to treat each input separately. The Mason's gain rule may be applied directly to the block diagram without transforming it into an equivalent signal flow graph.

When the disturbance input $W(s)$ is zero, the resulting block diagram has one forward path and two loops. The two loops touch each other and the forward path touches both the loops. By Mason's gain rule (Eqns (3.7))

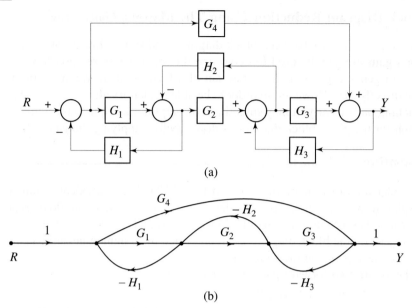

(a)

(b)

Fig. 3.17 (a) *Block diagram of a control system*
(b) *Equivalent signal flow graph*

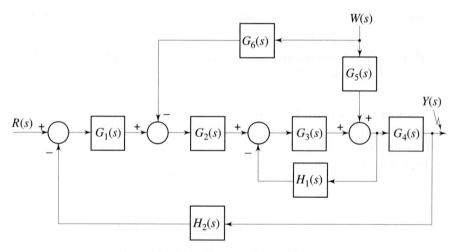

Fig. 3.18 *Block diagram of a control system*

$$M(s) = \left.\frac{Y(s)}{R(s)}\right|_{W(s)=0} = \frac{G_1(s)G_2(s)G_3(s)G_4(s)}{1 + G_3(s)H_1(s) + G_1(s)G_2(s)G_3(s)G_4(s)H_2(s)}$$

With $R(s) = 0$, the block diagram has two forward paths and two loops. The two loops touch each other and both the forward paths touch both the loops. By Mason's gain rule,

$$M_w(s) = \left. \frac{Y(s)}{W(s)} \right|_{R(s)=0} = \frac{G_5(s)G_4(s) - G_6(s)G_2(s)G_3(s)G_4(s)}{1 + G_3(s)H_1(s) + G_1(s)G_2(s)G_3(s)G_4(s)H_2(s)}$$

The response to the simultaneous application of $R(s)$ and $W(s)$ is given by

$$Y(s) = M(s)R(s) + M_w(s)W(s)$$

3.5 | DC AND AC MOTORS IN CONTROL SYSTEMS

One of the most common uses of feedback control is to position an inertia load. The inertia load may consist of a very large, massive object such as a radar antenna or a small object such as a precision instrument. An important aspect of the control system design is the selection of a suitable actuator, capable of achieving the desired dynamic response and suited to the objectives in cost, size, weight, etc. Electric motors (both dc and ac), hydraulic motors and linear actuators, and pneumatic linear actuators are the commonly used positioning devices in servo systems. Electric and hydraulic motors are also the most widely used actuators in servo systems requiring speed control of inertia loads.

Electric power is more readily available, cleaner and quieter, and easier to transmit; these are some of the factors that lead to the choice of electric motors as actuators (Hydraulic/pneumatic actuation is preferable in certain circumstances, as we shall see later).

The ac servomotors possess many virtues in comparison to dc servomotors. These include significantly lower costs, weight, and inertia, higher efficiency, and fewer maintenance requirements because of no commutator and brushes. However, as we shall see later, the characteristics of ac motors are quite nonlinear and these motors are more difficult to control, especially for positioning applications. The ac motors are best suited for low-power applications such as in instrument servos (e.g., control of pen in X-Y recorders) and computer-related equipment (e.g., disk drives, tape drives, printers, etc).

The dc motors are expensive because of brushes and commutators. These motors have relatively lower torque-to-volume, and torque-to-inertia ratios. However the characteristics of dc motors are quite linear and these motors are easier to control. The dc motors have been generally used for large-power applications such as in machine tools and robotics.

Developments in technology are opening new applications for both ac and dc motors. Today, with the development of the rare-earth magnet, dc motors with very high torque-to-volume ratio at reasonable costs have become possible. Furthermore, the advances made in brush-and-commutator technology have made these wearable parts practically maintenance-free. The advancements made in power electronics have made brushless dc motors quite popular in high-performance control systems [50]. Advanced manufacturing techniques have also produced dc motors with rotors of very low inertia, thus achieving very high torque-to-inertia ratios. These properties have made it possible to use dc motors in many low-power control applications that formerly used ac motors. On the other hand, three-phase induction motors with pulse-width modulated power amplifiers are currently gaining popularity in high-power control applications.

In the following, we describe basic characteristics of dc and ac motors and develop linear mathematical models for these devices.

DC Servomotors

A sketch of the basic components of a dc motor is given in Fig. 3.19. The nonturning part (called the *stator*) has magnets which establish a field across the turning part (called the *rotor*). The magnets may be electromagnets or, for small motors, permanent magnets. In an electromagnet motor, the stator is wound with wire and current is forced through this winding (called the *field winding*). For a constant field current i_f, the magnetic flux ϕ is constant; the magnetic flux may be varied by varying the field current.

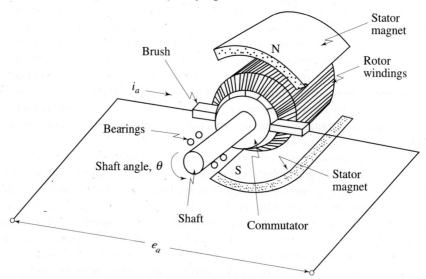

Fig. 3.19 *Sketch of a dc motor*

The rotor is wound with wire and through this winding (called the *armature winding*) a current i_a is forced through the (stationary) brushes and the (rotating) commutator. The reaction of the magnetic flux ϕ with the armature current i_a produces a torque T_M that forces the armature to rotate. The relationship among the developed torque T_M (newton-m), flux ϕ (webers) and current i_a (amps) is

$$T_M = K_{M1}\, \phi\, i_a \tag{3.8a}$$

where K_{M1} is a constant.

In servo applications, a wound-field dc motor is generally used in the linear range of magnetization; the flux ϕ is therefore proportional to field current i_f and

$$T_M = K_{M2}\, i_f\, i_a \tag{3.8b}$$

where K_{M2} is a constant.

As the armature rotates in the magnetic field, a voltage is induced into the armature winding. This voltage is 180° out of phase with the applied armature voltage and is therefore called back emf. The relationship among the back emf e_b (volts), rotor velocity ω (rad/sec) and flux ϕ (webers) is

$$e_b = K_{m1} \phi \omega \qquad (3.9a)$$

where K_{m1} is a constant
For the wound-field motor,

$$e_b = K_{m2} i_f \omega \qquad (3.9b)$$

where K_{m2} is a constant.

Equations (3.8) and (3.9) form the basis of dc motor operation.

In a permanent-magnet (PM) motor, the flux ϕ is constant; the torque T_M exerted on the motor rotor can therefore be controlled by varying the armature current (refer Eqn. (3.8a)). If the direction of the armature current is reversed, the direction of the torque is reversed.

In a wound-field motor, the torque may be controlled by varying the armature current and/or the field current (refer Eqn. (3.8b)). Generally, one of these is varied to control the torque while the other is held constant. In the *armature control* mode of operation, the field current is held constant and armature current is varied to control the torque. In the *field-control* mode, the armature current is maintained constant and field current controls the torque; a reversal in the direction of field current reverses the direction of the torque.

In servo applications, a dc motor is required to produce rapid accelerations from standstill. Therefore, the physical requirements of such a motor are low inertia and high starting torque. Low inertia is attained with reduced armature diameter, with a consequent increase in armature length such that the desired power output is achieved. Thus, except for minor differences in constructional features, a dc servomotor is essentially an ordinary dc motor.

Armature-Controlled dc Motor

The symbolic representation of armature-controlled dc motor as a control system component is shown in Fig. 3.20. Under consideration is a wound-field motor. An external dc source supplies a constant current i_f to the field winding. The armature circuit consists of the armature resistance R_a and the armature

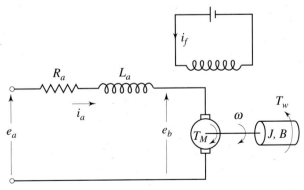

Fig. 3.20 *Armature-controlled dc motor with load*

inductance L_a; both are due to the total armature winding which makes an electrical contact with the brushes of the commutator, e_a is the applied armature voltage which controls the motor operation, and e_b is the back emf.

On the mechanical side, the motor rotor and the attached load can be treated as inertia and viscous friction; J and B are the corresponding parameters. T_w is the disturbance load torque. The torque T_M developed by the motor drives the load with angular velocity ω.

Let us summarize the variables and parameters in the dc motor model of Fig. 3.20:

R_a = armature winding resistance (ohms);
L_a = armature winding inductance (henrys);
i_a = armature current (amps);
i_f = field current (amps) = a constant;
e_a = applied armature voltage (volts);
e_b = back emf (volts);
ω = angular velocity of the motor rotor (rad/sec);
θ = angular displacement of the motor rotor (rad);
T_M = torque developed by the motor (newton-m);
J = moment of inertia of the motor rotor with attached mechanical load (kg-m^2 or (newton-m)/(rad/sec^2));
B = viscous-friction coefficient of the motor rotor with attached mechanical load ((newton-m)/(rad/sec)); and
T_w = disturbance load torque (newton-m).

Since the field current is kept constant in the armature-control mode of operation, Eqns (3.8b) and (3.9b) become

$$T_M = K_T i_a \tag{3.10a}$$
$$e_b = K_b \omega \tag{3.10b}$$

where

$$K_T \overset{\Delta}{=} \text{torque constant}; \quad K_b \overset{\Delta}{=} \text{back emf constant}$$

The differential equation of the armature circuit is

$$L_a \frac{di_a}{dt} + R_a i_a + e_b = e_a \tag{3.11}$$

The torque equation is

$$J \frac{d\omega}{dt} + B\omega + T_w = T_M \tag{3.12}$$

Taking the Laplace transform of Eqns (3.10)–(3.12), assuming zero initial conditions, we get

$$T_M(s) = K_T I_a(s) \tag{3.13a}$$
$$E_b(s) = K_b \omega(s) \tag{3.13b}$$
$$(L_a s + R_a) I_a(s) = E_a(s) - E_b(s) \tag{3.13c}$$

$$(Js + B)\, \omega(s) = T_M(s) - T_w(s) \tag{3.13d}$$

Figure 3.21 shows a block diagram representation of the dc motor system. The block diagram gives a clear picture of the cause and effect relationships in the physical system of Fig. 3.20. The voltage applied to the armature circuit is $E_a(s)$ which is opposed by the back emf $E_b(s)$. The net voltage $(E_a(s) - E_b(s))$ acts on a linear circuit comprised of resistance and inductance in series, having the transfer function $1/(sL_a + R_a)$. The result is an armature current $I_a(s)$. For the fixed field, the torque developed by the motor is $K_T I_a(s)$. The torque rotates the load at a speed $\omega(s)$ against the disturbance $T_w(s)$; the load having moment of inertia J and viscous friction with coefficient B has the transfer function $1/(Js + B)$. The back emf signal $E_b(s) = K_b \omega(s)$ is taken off from the shaft speed and fedback negatively to the summing point. Note that although a dc motor by itself is basically an open-loop system, it has a 'built in' feedback loop caused by the back emf.

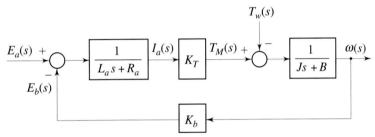

Fig. 3.21   *Block diagram of a dc motor (armature-controlled) system*

The transfer function between the motor velocity $\omega(s)$ and the input voltage $E_a(s)$, obtained from the block diagram, is

$$\frac{\omega(s)}{E_a(s)} = \frac{K_T}{(L_a s + R_a)(Js + B) + K_T K_b} \tag{3.14}$$

The inductance L_a in the armature circuit is usually small and may be neglected. If L_a is neglected, then the transfer function given by Eqn. (3.14) reduces to

$$\frac{\omega(s)}{E_a(s)} = \frac{K_T / R_a}{Js + B + K_T K_b / R_a} \tag{3.15}$$

The back emf constant K_b represents an added term to the viscous friction coefficient B. Therefore, the back emf effect is equivalent to an 'electric friction' which tends to improve the stability of the dc motor system.

The transfer function given by Eqn. (3.15) may be written in the form given below.

$$\frac{\omega(s)}{E_a(s)} = \frac{K_m}{\tau_m s + 1} \tag{3.16}$$

where $$K_m = \frac{K_T}{R_a B + K_T K_b} = \text{motor gain constant}$$

and $$\tau_m = \frac{R_a J}{R_a B + K_T K_b} = \text{motor time-constant}$$

When the motor is used to control shaft position θ, rather than the speed ω, we get the block diagram model shown in Fig. 3.22. The transfer function between the shaft position $\theta(s)$ and the input voltage $E_a(s)$ becomes

$$\frac{\theta(s)}{E_a(s)} = \frac{K_m}{s(\tau_m s + 1)} \tag{3.17}$$

The significance of this transfer function is that the dc motor is essentially an integrating device between the input voltage and the shaft position. This is expected since if e_a is a constant input, the motor displacement will behave as the output of an integrator; that is, it will increase linearly with time. We shall see later that the integrating effect $1/s$ in Eqn. (3.17) gives a feedback position control system better steady-state behaviour than the corresponding speed control system.

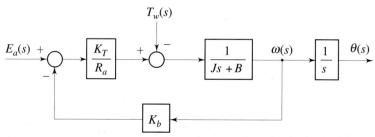

Fig. 3.22   *The dc motor (armature-controlled) model with displacement as output*

The motor torque and back emf constants are inter-related. Their relationship is deduced below.

Power developed in the armature is

$$P = e_b(t)\, i_a(t) \ [(\text{volts})\,(\text{amps}) = \text{watts}]$$

$$= K_b\, \omega(t)\, i_a(t) \left[\left(\frac{\text{volts}}{\text{rad/sec}} \right)(\text{rad/sec})(\text{amp}) \right]$$

In terms of torque and angular velocity,

$$P = T_M(t)\omega(t) \ [(\text{newton-m})\,(\text{rad/sec}) = \text{watts}]$$

$$= K_T\, i_a(t)\omega(t) \left[\left(\frac{(\text{newton-m})}{\text{amp}} \right)(\text{amp})(\text{rad/sec}) \right]$$

Therefore,

$$K_b(\text{volts}/(\text{rad/sec})) = K_T\ (\text{newton-m/amp}) \tag{3.18}$$

This result can be used to advantage in practice as K_b can be measured more easily and with greater accuracy than K_T.

In a PM motor, the field winding is absent and a constant magnetic flux is provided by the permanent magnet. Since in the preceding development, the magnetic flux is a constant, Eqns (3.14)–(3.18) are also valid for a PM motor.

Torque Speed Curves

The torque-speed curves of a dc motor describe the static torque-producing capability of the motor with respect to the applied voltage and motor speed. With reference to Fig. 3.21, in the steady-state the effect of the inductance is zero, and the torque equation of the motor is

$$T_M = \frac{K_T}{R_a}(E_a - K_b\omega) = -\frac{K_T K_b}{R_a}\omega + \frac{K_T}{R_a}E_a$$

where T_M, E_a, and ω represent the steady-state values of the motor torque, applied voltage and speed, respectively.

Figure 3.23 shows a typical set of torque-speed curves (experimentally obtained/supplied by the manufacturer) of a dc motor for various constant armature voltages.

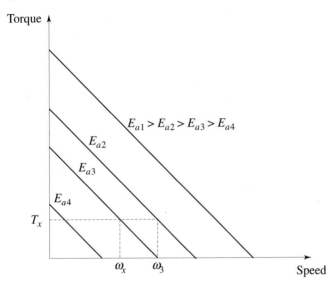

Fig. 3.23 *Typical torque-speed curves of an armature-controlled dc motor*

The no-load point on the torque-speed characteristic corresponding to armature voltage E_{a3} is defined by the coordinates $(\omega_3, 0)$ in Fig. 3.23. If a load T_x is applied to the motor shaft, the operating point of the motor shifts from the point $(\omega_3, 0)$ to the point (ω_x, T_x) as shown in the figure.

Thus, the applied torque reduces the motor speed. The reduction in speed results in a lower back emf and, for a constant armature voltage E_{a3}, reduction in back emf causes an increase in armature current. The increase in armature current is responsible for an increase in motor-generated torque to accommodate the applied load T_x. If the new steady-state speed ω_x is too low and the original speed ω_3 must be restored, the armature voltage must be increased. This is illustrated in Fig. 3.23; the increase in armature voltage from E_{a3} to E_{a2} restores the original no-load speed ω_3 with the load T_x applied.

▲▲

In a dc motor system, there may be a significant nonlinear friction due to the rubbing contact between the brushes and the commutator. Also, torque saturation may occur because of limitation of the maximum current that the motor can handle due to the heat-dissipation rating of the motor. Refer [180] for methods for analysis of control systems with nonlinearities in the closed loop.

Field-Controlled dc Motor

The schematic diagram of a field-controlled dc motor is shown in Fig. 3.24. In this system,

R_f = field winding resistance (ohms);
L_f = field winding inductance (henrys);
i_f = field current (amps);
i_a = armature current (amps) = a constant;
e_f = applied field voltage (volts);
ω = angular velocity of the motor rotor (rad/sec);
θ = angular displacement of the motor rotor (rad);
T_M = torque developed by the motor (newton-m);
J = moment of inertia of the motor rotor with attached mechanical load (kg-m^2 or (newton-m)/(rad/sec^2));
B = viscous-friction coefficient of the motor rotor with attached mechanical load ((newton-m)/(rad/sec)); and
T_w = disturbance load torque (newton-m).

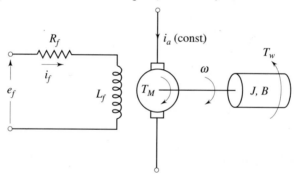

Fig. 3.24 *Field-controlled dc motor with load*

The following assumptions are made in the derivation of the transfer function of field-controlled motor:

(a) a constant current i_a is fed into the armature;
(b) the air gap flux ϕ is proportional to field current i_f; and
(c) the torque developed by the motor is proportional to field current;

$$T_M = K'_T i_f; \; K'_T \triangleq \text{torque constant.}$$

The voltage applied to the field circuit is $E_f(s)$ which acts on a linear circuit comprising of resistance and inductance in series, having the transfer function $1/(L_f s + R_f)$. The result is a field current $I_f(s)$. For fixed armature current, the torque developed by the motor is $K'_T I_f(s)$. This torque rotates the load at a speed $\omega(s)$ against the disturbance $T_w(s)$; the load having moment of inertia J and viscous-friction coefficient B has the transfer function $1/(Js + B)$. These cause and effect relationships are described by the block diagram of Fig. 3.25. The transfer function between the motor displacement $\theta(s)$ and the input voltage $E_f(s)$, obtained from the block diagram, is

$$\frac{\theta(s)}{E_f(s)} = \frac{K'_T}{s(L_f s + R_f)(Js + B)} = \frac{K'_m}{s(\tau_f s + 1)(\tau_m s + 1)} \qquad (3.19)$$

where

$K'_m = K'_T/(R_f B) =$ motor gain constant;

$\tau_f = L_f/R_f =$ time-constant of the field circuit; and

$\tau_m = J/B =$ mechanical time-constant.

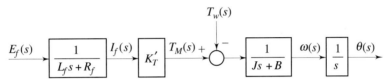

Fig. 3.25   *Block diagram of a field-controlled dc motor*

▲▲

Split-field motors are used to provide a smooth control of motor speed (or position) in low-power systems. The general arrangement is shown in Fig. 3.26, the armature current being kept substantially constant by using a high voltage E and a high value of resistance R. Providing that the back emf of the motor at its maximum speed is small compared with E, the armature current is approximately E/R. The field is energized by a balanced amplifier which has the input e_f. When this input is zero, the currents i_1 and i_2 are equal. Since they flow in opposite directions, the net flux is zero; thus the torque is zero and the motor is stationary. If e_f is not zero, one of the currents increases and the other decreases in proportion to the magnitude of e_f. The resulting flux is proportional to the magnitude of e_f, and its direction depends on the polarity of e_f. The size and direction of the generated torque and the resulting speed therefore respond to the magnitude and polarity of the input e_f.

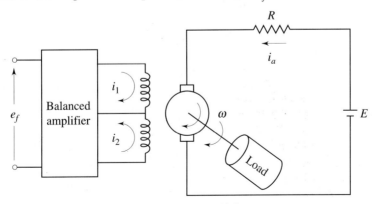

Fig. 3.26   *A split-field dc motor*

For small-size motors, field control is advantageous because only a low power servo amplifier is required while the constant armature current, which is not large, can be supplied from an inexpensive constant voltage source. This control scheme poses great practical difficulties in medium- and large-size motors; because of large back emf of the motor, the armature current cannot be kept constant by supplying a constant voltage to the armature. The assumption of constant armature current leads to the linear equations representing the operation of the motor. However, if instead, a constant voltage source is applied to the armature, the equation of the motor becomes nonlinear and cannot be handled by linear analysis methods. For this reason, it is normal practice to have a fixed excitation and control the armature current.

AC Servomotors

An ac servomotor is basically a two-phase induction motor except for certain special design features. A brief description of constructional and operational features of induction motors will be helpful in developing a mathematical model of an ac servomotor.

The two inputs required for motor action are a magnetic field and current-carrying conductors. In the dc motor, current for the conductors is supplied conductively by connection to a voltage source. In the ac induction motor, current for the conductors is supplied inductively by the change in the flux linkages of the conductors with the alternating magnetic field, supplied by an electromagnetic field structure excited by alternating current. The field windings are on the stationary part of the motor (stator) and the current carry-ing conductors are on the rotating part (rotor).

Figure 3.27a shows the physical arrangement of a two-phase field. This consists of two identical pole pairs A–B and C–D oriented 90° away from each other in space (space quadrature). The two currents used to excite the two pole pairs are 90° out of phase (time quadrature).

The simplest form of rotor construction is shown in Fig. 3.27b, comprising copper or aluminium conductors connected by stout end-rings formed into a cylindrical cage-like structure (squirrel-cage construction). The conductors pass through the laminated iron rotor core. Since no external connections are made to the rotor circuit, the motor can be made very robust and requires little maintenance. The machine characteristics can be modified by altering the rotor conductor resistance, and by having two or three sets of rotor bars set at different depths in the rotor.

The principle of operation of the induction motor is as follows. Voltages of equal rms magnitude and 90° phase difference are applied to the two field windings. This results in field currents i_1 and i_2 that are phase displaced by 90° and have equal rms values. These currents give rise to a rotating magnetic field of constant magnitude. The direction of rotation depends on the phase rela-tionship of the two currents (or voltages). Assuming that the two currents shown in Fig. 3.27a result in CW rotation, then a phase shift of 180° in i_1 will cause rotation in CCW direction.

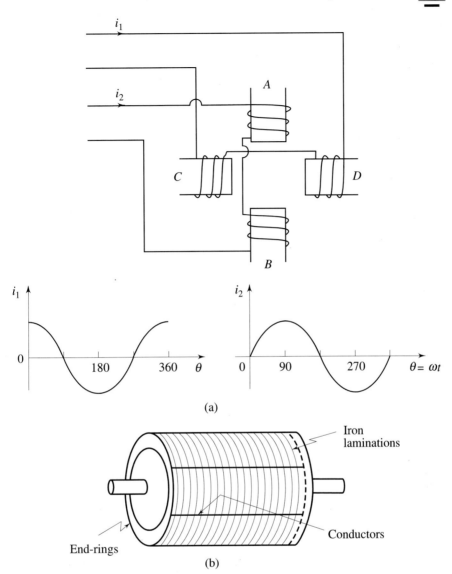

(a)

(b)

Fig. 3.27 *Constructional features of induction motor*

As the moving field sweeps over the rotor, voltages are induced in the rotor conductors, producing currents in the short-circuited paths. The rotating field interacts with these currents producing a torque on the rotor in the direction of field rotation. This torque causes the rotor to turn so that it chases the rotating magnetic field.

Elementary analysis of the ac motor is more complex than is that of the dc motor. So, rather than give the details of production of rotating magnetic field, and derivation of motor-torque equation, we present the experimental facts in the form of set of curves of speed versus torque. A typical set appears in

Fig. 3.28. For an induction motor used in power applications, the rotor resistance is low in order to obtain high maximum torque (Curve *A*, Fig. 3.28). However, this type of characteristic is not suitable for feedback control systems, mainly because of the positive slope on part of the curve. We will shortly see that a negative slope on the torque-speed curve is essential for stability (The dc motors inherently exhibit the desired torque-speed characteristic, Fig. 3.23). In order to obtain the desired type of characteristic, induction motors for servo applications are designed to have high rotor resistance (Curve *B*, Fig. 3.28). It should be noted that the required characteristic is purchased at a price of power which is dissipated as heat in the high rotor resistance. This decreases the efficiency of the motor and also limits its maximum power rating since the temperature rise in the motor becomes excessive for motors with high power rating.

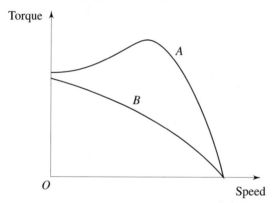

Fig. 3.28 *Torque-speed characteristics of ac motors*

In servo applications, an induction motor is required to produce rapid accelerations from standstill. Therefore, low inertia is a physical requirement of a servomotor. In a squirrel-cage construction, low inertia is attained with reduced rotor diameter (drag-cup construction is used for very low inertia applications [57]). Thus, except for minor differences in constructional features (rotor has high resistance and low inertia), an ac servomotor is essentially a two-phase induction motor.

The symbolic representation of an ac servomotor as a control system component is shown in Fig. 3.29. One phase, designated as the *reference phase*, is excited by a constant voltage source, the frequency of which is usually 50/60, 400, or 1000 Hz. By using frequencies of 400 Hz or higher, the system can be made less susceptible to low-frequency noise. Due to this feature, ac devices are extensively used in aircraft and missile control systems in which noise and disturbance often create problems.

The second phase of the servomotor, designated as the *control phase*, is excited by a voltage of variable magnitude and polarity. The control signal of the servo loop dictates the magnitude and polarity of this voltage.

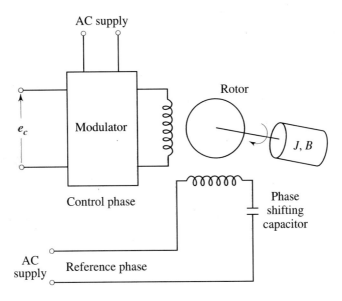

Fig. 3.29 *Symbolic representation of an ac servomotor*

The control signals in a servo loop are usually of low frequency, in the range of 0 to 20 Hz. For production of rotating magnetic field, the control-phase voltage must be of the same frequency as the reference-phase voltage, and in addition, the two voltages must be in time quadrature. The arrangement shown in Fig. 3.29 meets these requirements. The input signal $e_c(t)$ is applied to the control phase after modulation; the carrier frequency of the modulation process is equal to the frequency of the reference-phase supply. The 90° phase difference between the control-phase and reference-phase voltages is obtained by the insertion of a capacitor. (Note that a single-phase power supply is required to run the motor).

Figure 3.30 shows the waveforms of a typical input signal $e_c(t)$, the carrier signal $\cos \omega_c t$ and the *suppressed-carrier modulated signal* $e_{cm}(t) = e_c(t) \cos \omega_c t$. Note that the envelope of the modulated signal e_{cm} is identical to the low-frequency signal e_c. The polarity of e_c dictates the phase of e_{cm} with respect to that of $\cos \omega_c t$. If e_c is positive, then e_{cm} and $\cos \omega_c t$ have the same phase; otherwise they have 180° phase difference:

$$e_{cm}(t) = |e_c(t)| \cos \omega_c t \qquad \text{for } e_c(t) > 0$$
$$= |e_c(t)| \cos(\omega_c t + \pi) \qquad \text{for } e_c(t) < 0 \qquad (3.20)$$

This means that a reversal in phase of e_{cm} occurs whenever the signal e_c crosses the zero-magnitude axis. This reversal in phase causes a reversal in the direction of rotation of the magnetic field and hence a reversal in the direction of rotation of the motor shaft.

The modulator in Fig. 3.29 transforms the signal e_c into the signal e_{cm}. If we consider e_c as the input and e_{cm} in Eqn. (3.20) as the output, then the math-

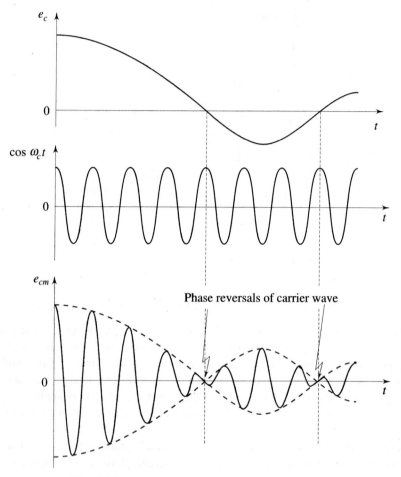

Fig. 3.30 *Input–output waveforms of a modulator*

ematical description of the modulator will be rather complicated. Recall that the reason for the introduction of e_{cm} is to match the operational frequency ranges; therefore the information is not stored in e_{cm}, but rather in its envelope. Hence, we should consider e_c as the input and the envelope of e_{cm} as the output of the modulator. Therefore, the transfer function of the modulator is just equal to 1, for the envelope of e_{cm} is identical to e_c.

The torque-speed curves of typical ac servomotor plotted for fixed reference-phase voltage $E_r\cos \omega_c t$ and different values of constant input voltages $e_c \leq E_r$ are shown in Fig. 3.31. All these curves have negative slope. Note that the curve for $e_c = 0$ goes through the origin; this means that when the control-phase voltage becomes zero, the motor develops a decelerating torque, causing it to stop. The curves show a large torque at zero speed. This is a requirement for a servomotor in order to provide rapid acceleration.

It is seen that the torque-speed curves of ac servomotor are nonlinear except in the low-speed region. In order to derive a transfer function for the motor, some linearizing approximations are necessary. A servomotor seldom operates

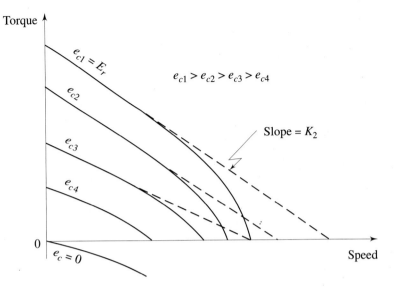

Fig. 3.31 *Torque-speed curves of an ac servomotor*

at high speeds; therefore, the linear portions of the torque-speed curves can be extended out to the high speed region, as shown in Fig. 3.31 by use of dashed lines. But even with this approximation, the resultant curves are still not parallel to each other. This means that for constant speeds, except near-zero speed, the torque does not vary linearly with respect to input voltage e_c. The curves in Fig. 3.32 illustrate this effect.

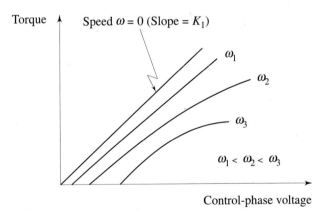

Fig. 3.32 *Torque vs control voltage curves of an ac servomotor*

For speeds near zero, all the curves are straight lines parallel to the characteristic at rated input voltage ($e_c = E_r$), and are equally spaced for equal increments of the input voltage. Under this assumption, the torque T_M generated by the motor is represented by the equation

$$T_M = K_1 e_c - K_2 \dot{\theta} \tag{3.21}$$

where K_1 and K_2 are the slopes defined in Figs 3.31 and 3.32. Note that both K_1 and K_2 are positive numbers.

If we consider that the moment of inertia of the motor rotor with attached mechanical load is J, the viscous-friction coefficient of the motor rotor with attached mechanical load is B, and the disturbance load torque is T_w, then we have

$$T_M = K_1 e_c - K_2 \dot{\theta} = J\ddot{\theta} + B\dot{\theta} + T_w \tag{3.22}$$

Figure 3.33 shows a block diagram representation of the ac motor system. The transfer function between the shaft position $\theta(s)$ and the input voltage $E_c(s)$, obtained from the block diagram, is

$$\frac{\theta(s)}{E_c(s)} = \frac{K_1}{s(Js + B + K_2)} = \frac{K_m}{s(\tau_m s + 1)} \tag{3.23}$$

where $\quad K_m = \dfrac{K_1}{B + K_2} =$ motor gain constant

$\qquad \tau_m = \dfrac{J}{B + K_2} =$ motor time-constant

Since K_2 is a positive number, the above equations show that the effect of the slope of the torque-speed curve is to add more friction to the motor, which does improve the damping of the motor. However, if K_2 is a negative number, for $|K_2| > B$, negative damping occurs and the motor becomes unstable. This verifies the statement made previously that the conventional induction motors are not suitable for servo applications.

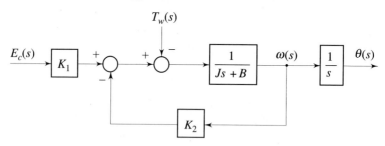

Fig. 3.33 *Block diagram of an ac motor system*

It must be noted that the modulation process for running the ac servomotor is not necessary if the control signal in the servo loop is an ac signal of frequency equal to that of reference phase supply. The transfer function model given by Eqn. (3.23) is applicable in these situations also, with the only difference that the input variable for the model is not the control-phase voltage itself but rather its envelope. This is in order as the information about the required control action is stored in the envelope of the control-phase voltage; the frequency of the voltage is governed only by the operational frequency range of the servomotor.

3.6 | MOTION CONTROL SYSTEMS

This section is concerned with speed and position control systems, and the components that make up these systems. We begin with the discussion of the commonly used components. Here, our discussion is restricted to devices used in analog control systems. The devices commonly used in digital control systems are covered later in Chapter 11.

Geared Drives

Electrical motors generally produce their maximum power at high speed. In other words, generally electrical motors exert rather small torques while rotating at high speeds (power = torque × angular velocity). In consequence, appropriate gearing is necessary for the electrical motors in order for these systems to drive large loads (requiring large torques) at low speeds. For example, robot arms are usually moved at low speeds, less than 1 revolution/sec, while required maximum torques range from a few newton-m to several hundred newton-m. A large gear reduction is typically required for standard servomotors.

Figure 3.34 shows a motor driving a load through a gear train which consists of two gears coupled together. The gear with N_1 teeth is called the primary gear and the gear with N_2 teeth is called the secondary gear. Angular displacements of shafts 1 and 2 are denoted by θ_1 and θ_2 respectively with their positive directions as indicated in the figure. The moment of inertia and viscous friction of motor and gear 1 are denoted by J_1 and B_1 respectively, and those of gear 2 and load are denoted by J_2 and B_2 respectively. T_M is the torque developed by the motor and T_w is the disturbance torque on the load. Elasticity of the gear teeth and shafts is assumed negligible.

A free-body diagram is shown in Fig. 3.35. T_{12} is the torque exerted on gear 1 by gear 2, and T_{21} is the torque transmitted to gear 2 through gear 1. For the motor shaft, the differential equation is

$$J_1 \ddot{\theta}_1 + B_1 \dot{\theta}_1 + T_{12} = T_M \qquad (3.24)$$

For the load shaft,

$$J_2 \ddot{\theta}_2 + B_2 \dot{\theta}_2 + T_w = T_{21} \qquad (3.25)$$

Idealized characteristic of the gear train is given by the relationship $\theta_2 = (N_1/N_2)\,\theta_1$. In reality, there is always a certain amount of backlash (free play) between coupled gears. Keeping the backlash small will inevitably increase the friction between the teeth, and wear out the teeth faster. On the other hand, an excessive amount of backlash may cause sustained oscillations or chattering phenomenon in control systems (refer [180]). The assumption of zero backlash is reasonable for high quality, well-adjusted gear boxes.

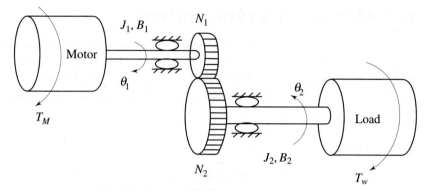

Fig. 3.34 *Motor driving a load through gearing*

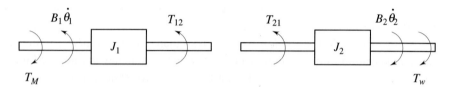

Fig. 3.35 *Free-body diagram for system of Fig. 3.34*

Let r_1 be the radius of gear 1 and r_2 be the radius of gear 2. Since the linear distance travelled along the surface of each gear is the same, $\theta_1 r_1 = \theta_2 r_2$. The number of teeth on a gear surface being proportional to gear radius, we have $(N_1/r_1) = (N_2/r_2)$. The linear forces developed at the contact point of both the gears are equal, hence $(T_{12}/r_1) = (T_{21}/r_2)$. By combining these equalities, we obtain

$$\frac{T_{12}}{T_{21}} = \frac{N_1}{N_2} = \frac{\theta_2}{\theta_1} \tag{3.26}$$

Differentiating this equation twice, we have the following relation for speed and acceleration:

$$\frac{\ddot{\theta}_2}{\ddot{\theta}_1} = \frac{\dot{\theta}_2}{\dot{\theta}_1} = \frac{N_1}{N_2} \tag{3.27}$$

From Eqns (3.26) and (3.27), it is observed that with $(N_1/N_2) < 1$, the gear train provides torque magnification and speed reduction. By proper selection of N_1/N_2, gear trains can be used to attain mechanical matching of motor to load: a servomotor operating at high speed and generating low torque is matched to a load to be moved at low speed but requiring high torque.

Eliminating T_{12} and T_{21} from Eqns (3.24) and (3.25) with the help of Eqn. (3.26), we obtain

$$J_1 \ddot{\theta}_1 + B_1 \dot{\theta}_1 + \frac{N_1}{N_2}(J_2 \ddot{\theta}_2 + B_2 \dot{\theta}_2 + T_w) = T_M \tag{3.28}$$

Elimination of θ_2 from Eqn. (3.28) with the help of Eqn. (3.27), yields

$$\left[J_1 + \left(\frac{N_1}{N_2} \right)^2 J_2 \right] \ddot{\theta}_1 + \left[B_1 + \left(\frac{N_1}{N_2} \right)^2 B_2 \right] \dot{\theta}_1 + \frac{N_1}{N_2} T_w = T_M \qquad (3.29)$$

Note that the load inertia J_2 is reflected on the motor shaft as $(N_1/N_2)^2 J_2$, load viscous-friction B_2 is reflected on the motor shaft as $(N_1/N_2)^2 B_2$, and the load disturbance T_w is reflected on the motor shaft as $(N_1/N_2) T_w$.

Equation (3.29) suggests that the geared system of Fig. 3.34 is equivalent to non-geared (direct drive) system of Fig. 3.36 with equivalent moment of inertia

$$J_{1eq} = J_1 + \left(\frac{N_1}{N_2} \right)^2 J_2, \qquad (3.30a)$$

equivalent friction

$$B_{1eq} = B_1 + \left(\frac{N_1}{N_2} \right)^2 B_2 \qquad (3.30b)$$

and equivalent disturbance torque

$$T_{weq} = \left(\frac{N_1}{N_2} \right) T_w \qquad (3.30c)$$

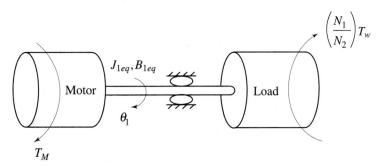

Fig. 3.36 *Equivalent direct-drive system for the geared system of Fig. 3.34*

▲▲

The problems that the mechanical gearing unavoidably possesses (backlash, friction, etc.), can be solved completely using the *direct-drive technology*. An order of magnitude larger torque must be generated by direct-drive motors in a compact and light-weight body. The dc torque motors are capable of exerting much larger torque compared with regular dc motors. These motors are designed in such a way that the output torque rather than power is maximized (refer [22] for details).

Electronic Amplifiers

Broadly speaking, there are two types of electronic amplifiers used in control systems:

    (a) A *small signal amplifier* is one which linearly amplifies a small signal (usually voltage) and is suitable for sensor circuits to amplify weak measured signals. The operational amplifier (usually called the op amp) is in common use.

From the block diagram of Fig. 3.2, we see that a control signal in a feedback loop is a function of the error signal. The functional dependence is given by the controller transfer function $D(s)$. Mechanization of $D(s)$, as we shall see in the next chapter, usually requires amplification of the error signal, and generation of the derivative and the integral of the error signal. Op amp circuits are now commonly used for mechanization of the controller transfer function $D(s)$.

    (b) A *power amplifier* is one which controls a large amount of power, and is therefore suitable for actuating devices.

Power amplifiers are available in three major types: the smooth transistor, the switching transistor (pulse-width modulated (PWM)), and the silicon control rectifier (SCR). Smooth transistor amplifiers use the transistors in a smooth modulating fashion and produce an output voltage that is high-power copy of the input. These amplifiers are used mainly below 1 kW applications. Switching (PWM) amplifiers use the transistors as on–off switches; the output voltage is a constant-frequency, fixed-amplitude waveform whose duty cycle is smoothly varied with input voltage. Switching amplifiers are economical in the 25 W to 5 kW range. In SCR amplifiers, the input voltage smoothly modulates the point in each power-line cycle at which the SCR (this term arises from the device as controlled rectifier constructed from silicon), also known as the *thyristor*, is made to conduct. These amplifiers are often used in high power applications.

To be precise, the transfer function of an electronic amplifier is of the form

$$G(s) = \frac{K_A}{\tau_A s + 1} \tag{3.31}$$

However, usually the time constant τ_A is negligibly small compared to the dynamics of the plant; the transfer function can therefore be approximated as

$$G(s) = K_A \tag{3.32}$$

where K_A is the proportional gain of the amplifier.

In addition to neglecting 'fast' dynamics, the model (3.32) of the amplifier further differs from reality because of its perfect linearity which assumes no limit on the magnitude of the input signal. Actually the amplifier, like other devices, exhibits saturation, limiting its output when input becomes too large (refer [180]).

Discussion on hardware aspects of various types of electronic amplifiers is beyond the scope of this book [49].

Tachogenerators

A tachogenerator (tachometer) is an electromechanical device which produces an output voltage that is proportional to its shaft speed. Two of the most commonly used tachogenerators, a dc and an ac tachogenerator, are shown in Fig. 3.37.

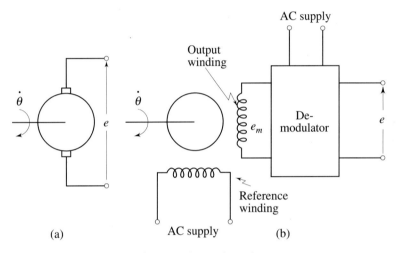

Fig. 3.37 *Schematic diagram of (a) a dc, and (b) an ac tachogenerator*

The dc tachogenerator resembles a small dc motor in that it comprises a stator with a permanent-magnet field, a rotating armature circuit, and a commutator and brush assembly. The rotor is connected to the shaft to be measured. The output voltage of the tachogenerator is proportional to the angular velocity of the shaft. The polarity of the output voltage is dependent on the direction of rotation of the shaft.

Dynamics of a dc tachogenerator can be represented by the equation

$$e(t) = K_t \frac{d\theta(t)}{dt} = K_t \dot{\theta}(t) \tag{3.33}$$

where e is the output voltage (volts), θ is the rotor displacement (rad), and K_t is the sensitivity of the tachogenerator (volts per rad/sec).

A problem associated with dc tachogenerators is the high-frequency ripple generated by the commutator and brushes. They also suffer from maintenance problems.

The ac tachogenerator resembles a two-phase induction motor in that it comprises two stator windings arranged in space quadrature, and a rotor which is not conductively connected to any external circuit. A sinusoidal voltage

$$e_r(t) = E_r \sin \omega_c t$$

is applied to the *excitation (reference) winding* (refer Fig. 3.37b). When the rotor is stationary ($\dot{\theta} = 0$), no emf is induced in the *output winding* and therefore the output voltage will be zero. When the motor turns, a voltage at the reference frequency ω_c is induced in the output winding. The magnitude of the output voltage is proportional to the rotational speed. A change in the direction of shaft rotation causes a 180° phase shift in the output voltage. When the output voltage is in phase with the reference, the direction of rotation is said to be *positive*, and when the output voltage is 180° out of phase, the direction is said to be *negative*.

The output voltage of an ac tachogenerator is, thus, in modulated form. A typical waveform of the output voltage $e_m(t)$ is shown in Fig. 3.38. It can be mathematically represented as

$$e_m(t) = e(t) \sin \omega_c t$$

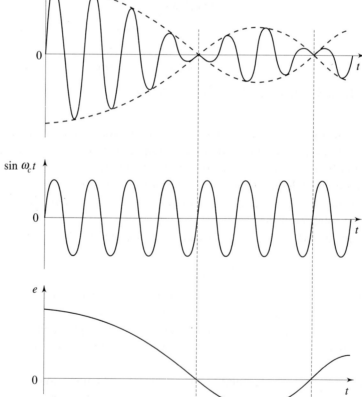

Fig. 3.38 *Waveforms illustrating the operation of a demodulator*

In the measurement system shown in Fig. 3.37, we have used a *demodulator* for signal conditioning. The input to the demodulator is $e_m(t)$ and its output is $e(t)$. Since the information about shaft speed is stored not in $e_m(t)$ itself but rather in its envelope, we should consider the envelope of $e_m(t)$ as the input of the demodulator. Therefore, the transfer function of the demodulator is just equal to 1, for the envelope of $e_m(t)$ is identical to the output $e(t)$. The output voltage of an ac tachogenerator (with signal conditioning) is therefore of the same form as that for a dc tachogenerator, i.e.,

$$e(t) = K_t \frac{d\theta(t)}{dt} \tag{3.34a}$$

The transfer function from $\theta(t)$ to $e(t)$ of an ac or a dc tachogenerator is of the form

$$\frac{E(s)}{\theta(s)} = s\,K_t \tag{3.34b}$$

Example 3.4

A conceptual design of a speed control system is shown in the schematic diagram of Fig. 3.39a. An application of such a system is for the speed control of electric locomotives. The locomotive is powered by dc motors, located on each of the axles. In Fig. 3.39a, only one motor is shown for convenience.

The operation of the system is as follows. The feedback voltage e_t from the tachogenerator of sensitivity K_t volts/(rad/sec) represents the actual speed ω of the motor. The reference-input voltage e_r represents the desired motor speed ω_r. An op amp circuit amplifies the error $(e_r - e_t)$ between the reference and feedback voltage signals and supplies a voltage u to a power amplifier (the old approach is to use a dc generator as a power amplifier, but in modern drives SCR amplifiers are used (refer Review Example 3.3). The output e_a of the power amplifier drives the armature-controlled dc motor which rotates in the direction to reduce the error $(e_r - e_t)$ as a consequence of the negative feedback. Reduction in $(e_r - e_t)$ results in reduction in the difference between the desired motor speed and actual motor speed. Reversal in the polarity of e_r reverses the direction of rotation of the motor.

A block diagram of the system is shown in Fig. 3.39b (refer Eqns (3.10)–(3.13), and Fig. 3.22). Here K_b is the back emf constant of the motor, R_a is the armature resistance (armature inductance is assumed negligible), K_T is the torque constant of the motor, J and B are, respectively, moment of inertia and viscous-friction coefficient on motor shaft, and T_w is the disturbance torque on motor shaft.

It is seen that the control law is

$$u = \frac{R_f}{R}(e_r - e_t)$$

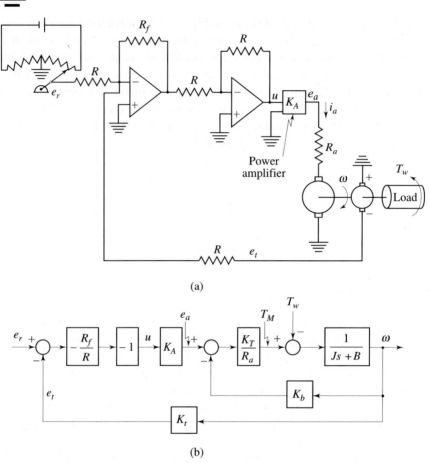

(a)

(b)

Fig. 3.39 *Closed-loop speed control system (a) schematic diagram (b) block diagram*

i.e., the control signal is proportional to the error. It will be seen in the next chapter that the speed control system of Fig. 3.39 has poor disturbance-rejection property with a proportional control law. The performance of the control system can be improved by introducing an appropriately designed controller $D(s)$ in the forward path of the system. We will talk about $D(s)$ in the next chapter[2].

Example 3.5

A conceptual design of a position control system is shown in the schematic diagram of Fig. 3.40a. An application of such a system is in the area of robotics

---

2. The objective set for this chapter is the control hardware familiarity. In almost all the control system examples in this chapter, we will use an amplifier (proportional control law) as a controller, knowing very well that it may not satisfy the control requirements. The problem of design of controllers will be discussed in the next and later chapters.

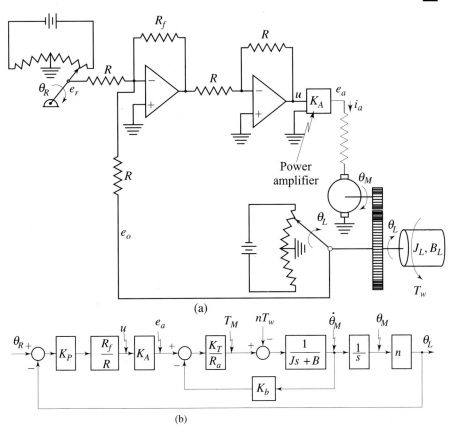

Fig. 3.40 *Closed-loop position control system (a) Schematic diagram*
(b) block diagram

for the position control of arms. Usually each degree of freedom employs its own actuator and this example has relevance to the control of a single axis (see Fig. 1.28).

The operation of the system is as follows. The load with an inertia J_L and viscous friction with coefficient B_L is to be positioned at some desired angle θ_R (T_w represents the load torque disturbance). The desired angle θ_R may be set, as shown in Fig. 3.40a, on an input potentiometer which provides the reference voltage e_r. The feedback potentiometer, whose wiper arm is mechanically coupled to the load shaft, produces a voltage e_o which represents the actual load position θ_L. The error voltage $(e_r - e_o)$ is amplified by an op amp circuit that supplies a voltage u to a power amplifier. The output e_a of the power amplifier drives the armature-controlled dc motor (reversal in the polarity of e_r reverses the direction of rotation of the motor). The torque developed by the motor is transmitted to the load shaft through a gear train. The transmitted torque rotates the load shaft in the direction to reduce the error $(e_r - e_o)$ as a consequence of the negative feedback. When $e_r = e_o$, the motor stops, as its drive is cut off. This must necessarily occur when $\theta_R = \theta_L$ because both the potentiometers have the same sensitivity K_P:

$$e = K_P\theta \qquad (3.35)$$

where K_P = sensitivity of the potentiometer is volts/deg.

A change in the load position caused by disturbances in the system (internal or external) causes the error signal $(e_r - e_o)$ to reappear, which after amplification acts on the motor; the motor torque transmitted to the load shaft forces the load to return to its original position.

A block diagram of the system is shown in Fig. 3.40b (refer Eqns (3.10)–(3.13), (3.30), and Fig. 3.22). Here K_b is the back emf constant of the motor, R_a is the armature resistance (armature inductance is assumed negligible), K_T is the torque constant of the motor, n is the gear ratio (n = load shaft speed $\dot\theta_L$/ motor shaft speed $\dot\theta_M$), J and B are, respectively, equivalent moment of inertia and viscous-friction coefficient on motor shaft, and nT_w is the equivalent disturbance torque on motor shaft.

It will be seen in the next chapter that the performance of position control system of Fig. 3.40 can be improved by introducing minor-loop feedback (refer Figs 1.15 and 1.16). A signal proportional to motor/load angular velocity, generated by a tachometer, is fedback. Since tachometers tend to be noisy at low speeds, in a geared system one usually puts the tacho on the motor, rather than the load.

Potentiometers, LVDT and Synchros

Potentiometers

For conversion of a linear or an angular displacement into voltage, a potentiometer (refer Figs 3.39a and 3.40a) is probably the simplest device. Potentiometric transducers are relatively inexpensive and easy to apply. However, they have some limitations. The resolution (minimum change in output voltage obtained by moving the wiper, expressed as a percentage of the total applied voltage) of precision wire-wound potentiometers (constructed by winding resistance wire on a form) ranges from 0.001 to 0.5 percent. This discontinuous output voltage contributes to servo inaccuracy. Potentiometers are temperature-sensitive, a characteristic that affects their accuracy. The wiper contact is another limiting factor, being subject to wear and dirt and potentially producing electrical noise.

In a large number of control systems, the low-amplitude high-frequency noise generated by the potentiometer does not create problems. This is because the plant usually acts as a low-pass filter. However, if the potentiometer output is differentiated to obtain a measure of velocity, the resulting signal will be completely useless.[3]

---

3. Differentiation of the signal $\sin t$ contaminated by low-magnitude high-frequency noise $0.01 \sin 10^3 t$ gives $(\cos t + 10 \cos 10^3 t)$; noise becomes the dominant term after differentiation.

A non-wire potentiometer (constructed by depositing conductive plastic re-sistance material on a form) is stepless and therefore resolution is better. How-ever, values less than 1000 Ω are hard to obtain with non-wire type of potentiometers, while wire-wound potentiometers can be made with very low values.

The applied voltage of a potentiometer can be either a dc or an ac source. In case of an ac source, the information is transmitted in the envelope of the output voltage signal.

In addition to the potentiometer, displacement can also be measured electri-cally with a *linear variable differential transformer* (LVDT) or a *synchro*. An LVDT measures a linear displacement, and a synchro measures an angular displacement. These devices are more costly but outperform the potentiometric transducers.

Linear Variable Differential Transformer

The schematic diagram of an LVDT is shown in Fig. 3.41. A primary coil is wound between two secondary coils on a hollow cylindrical form. A movable core is positioned inside the coil form. The primary is excited by an ac source. When the core is in its exact centre position ($y = 0$), the two secondaries are linked by an equal number of flux lines; the emf induced in secondary 1 will be the same as the emf induced in secondary 2. The two secondaries are so con-nected that their induced voltages oppose each other, and the output voltage

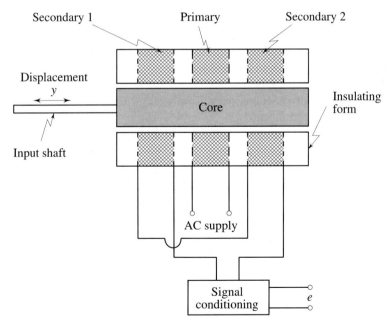

Fig. 3.41 *Linear variable differential transformer (LVDT)*

will be zero corresponding to $y = 0$. When the core is moved to the right, fewer lines of flux link secondary 1 than secondary 2. Thus a greater emf is induced in secondary 2 than in secondary 1 and a net voltage appears at the output. When the core is moved to the left, a net voltage will again appear at the output, but it is in anti-phase to that for an equivalent displacement to the right.

The output voltage of LVDT is in a modulated form, i.e.,

$$e_m(t) = K y(t) \sin \omega_c t$$

where ω_c, the carrier frequency, is the same as the frequency of ac supply. The magnitude of the modulated carrier wave is proportional to the core displacement $y(t)$ with K as the constant of proportionality, and the phase reversals of the modulated carrier wave depend on the sign of $y(t)$ (refer Fig. 3.38).

Signal conditioning by a demodulator and an amplifier gives an output voltage

$$e(t) = K_s \, y(t) \tag{3.36}$$

where K_s = sensitivity of the displacement transducer in volts/mm.

Synchros

The term *synchro* is a generic name for a family of inductive devices which can be connected in various ways to form shaft angle measurements. All of these devices work on essentially the same principle, which is that of a rotating transformer.

A synchro system formed by interconnection of the devices called the *synchro transmitter* and the *synchro control transformer*, is perhaps the most widely used error detector in feedback control systems. It measures and compares two angular displacements and its output voltage is approximately linear with angular difference. Our discussion on synchro devices will be limited to the basic features of the synchro transmitter and the synchro control transformer.

The constructional features, electrical circuit, and a schematic symbol of a synchro transmitter are shown in Fig. 3.42. The stationary part of the machine (stator) is of laminated silicon steel and is slotted to accommodate three Y connected coils wound with their axes 120° apart. The stator windings are not directly connected to the ac power source. Their excitation is supplied by the ac magnetic field produced by the rotating part of the machine (rotor).

The rotor is of dumb-bell construction with a single winding. A single-phase excitation voltage is applied to the rotor through two slip rings. The resultant current produces a magnetic field and by transformer action induces voltages

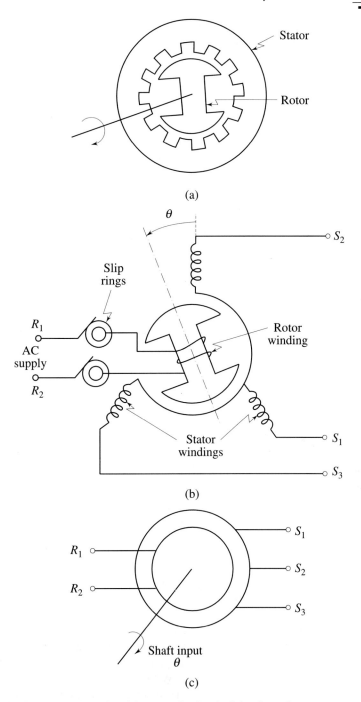

Fig. 3.42 *(a) Constructional features, (b) electrical circuit, and*
(c) schematic symbol of a synchro transmitter

in the stator coils. The effective voltage induced in any stator coil depends upon the angular position of the coil's axis with respect to rotor axis.

Let the ac voltage applied to the rotor be

$$e_r(t) = E_r \sin \omega_c t \tag{3.37}$$

When the rotor is in the position corresponding to $\theta = 0$ in Fig. 3.44b, the voltage induced across the stator winding S_2 and the neutral is maximum and is written as

$$e_{S_2n} = KE_r \sin \omega_c t$$

where K is a proportional constant.

When the rotor is in position corresponding to $\theta = 90°$ in Fig. 3.42b, the voltage e_{S_2n} is zero. Therefore when $\theta = 0$, the coupling coefficient between the rotor winding and the stator winding S_2 is 1, and when $\theta = 90°$, the coupling coefficient equals 0. In fact, in general, the coupling coefficient between S_2 winding and rotor winding is equal to $\cos \theta$ for any position of the rotor:

$$e_{S_2n} = KE_r \cos \theta \sin \omega_c t$$

When the rotor is at $0°$ position with respect to the S_2 winding, it is at $-120°$ position with respect to the S_3 winding; that is, positive (counter clockwise) rotation of $120°$ is required to move the rotor from the first position to the second position. Thus, if S_2 winding is taken as a reference,

$$e_{S_3n} = KE_r \cos(\theta - 120) \sin \omega_c t$$

In the same way,

$$e_{S_1n} = KE_r \cos(\theta - 240) \sin \omega_c t$$

The three terminal voltages of the stator are

$$e_{S_1S_2} = e_{S_1n} + e_{nS_2} = \sqrt{3} KE_r \sin(\theta + 240) \sin\omega_c t \tag{3.38a}$$

$$e_{S_2S_3} = e_{S_2n} + e_{nS_3} = \sqrt{3} KE_r \sin(\theta + 120) \sin\omega_c t \tag{3.38b}$$

$$e_{S_3S_1} = e_{S_3n} + e_{nS_1} = \sqrt{3} KE_r \sin\theta \sin\omega_c t \tag{3.38c}$$

When $\theta = 0°$, maximum voltage is induced in winding S_2, and it follows from Eqn. (3.38c) that the terminal voltage $e_{S_3S_1}$ is zero. This position of the rotor is defined as the *electrical zero* of the transmitter and is used as reference for specifying the angular position of the rotor.

It should be noted that the synchro is not a three-phase machine. In a three-phase machine, there are three voltages equal in magnitude, displaced from each other by 120 electrical degrees. With the synchro, which is a single-phase device, the three stator voltages vary in magnitude, and one stator coil is in phase or 180° out of phase with another coil.

It is seen that the input to the synchro transmitter is the angular position of its rotor shaft and the output is a set of three stator coil-to-coil voltages (common connection between the stator coils is not accessible) given by Eqns (3.38). By measuring and identifying the set of voltages at the stator terminals, it is possible to identify the angular position of the rotor.[4]

Our interest here is in synchro error detector formed by interconnection of two synchro devices— the transmitter and the control transformer. A typical arrangement of a synchro error detector in servo applications is to connect the stator leads of the transmitter to the stator leads of the control transformer. A servo loop using the synchro error detector is shown in Fig. 3.43. Basically, the principle of operation of a synchro control transformer is identical to that of the synchro transmitter, except that the rotor is cylindrically shaped so that the air-gap flux is uniformly distributed around the rotor. This feature of the control transformer minimizes the change in the rotor impedance with the rotation of the shaft; the signal conditioning circuit, therefore, sees a constant impedance.

Referring to the arrangement shown in Fig. 3.43, the voltages given in Eqns (3.38a)–(3.38c) are impressed across the corresponding stator terminals of the control transformer. Due to the similarity in the magnetic construction, the flux patterns produced in the two synchros will be the same if all losses are

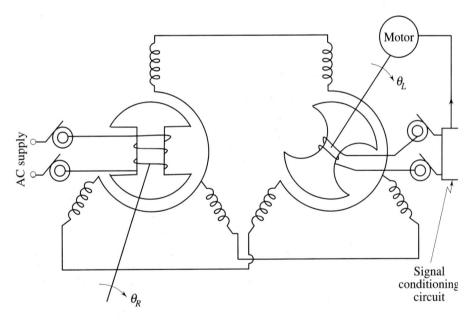

Fig. 3.43 *Servo loop using synchro error detector*

---

4. A synchro/digital (S/D) converter accepts the three ac voltages from the synchro as input and gives out a digital output which is a measure of the magnitude and direction of rotor movement (refer [74] for details).

neglected. For example, if the rotor of the transmitter is in its electrical zero position, the fluxes produced in the transmitter and in the control transformer are as shown in Fig. 3.44. When the rotor of the control transformer is in the position shown in the figure, the induced voltage at its rotor winding terminals is zero; the shafts of the two synchros are considered to be in alignment, and the control transformer is said to be in *null position*. Thus the null position of a control transformer in a servo loop is that position of its rotor for which the output voltage on the rotor winding is zero with the transmitter in its electrical zero position.

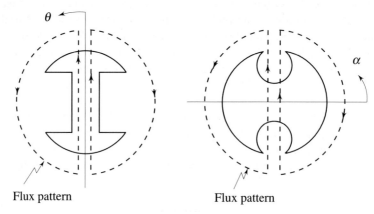

Flux pattern   Flux pattern

Fig. 3.44   *Rotor positions and flux patterns*

Let the rotor of the transmitter rotate through an angle θ from its electrical zero position, and let the rotor of the control transformer rotate in the same direction through an angle α from its null position (refer Fig. 3.44); the net angular separation of the two rotors is then $(90 - \theta + \alpha)$ and the voltage induced in the control transformer is proportional to the cosine of this angle:

$$e_m(t) = K'E_r \cos(90 - \theta + \alpha)\sin\omega_c t = K'E_r \sin(\theta - \alpha)\sin\omega_c t$$

where K' is a proportional constant.

For small values of $\quad\quad\quad \phi(t) = \theta(t) - \alpha(t),$

$$e_m(t) = K'E_r\phi(t)\sin\omega_c t$$

The output voltage of the synchro error detector is thus a modulated signal with the carrier frequency ω_c equal to the frequency of the ac supply to the rotor winding of the synchro transmitter. The magnitude of the modulated carrier wave is proportional to $\phi(t) = \theta(t) - \alpha(t)$, and the phase reversals of the modulated wave depend on the sign of $\phi(t)$ (refer Fig. 3.38).

Signal conditioning of the modulated output of the synchro error detector by an amplifier and a demodulator gives an output voltage

$$e(t) = K_s \,\phi(t) \tag{3.39}$$

where K_s = sensitivity of the synchro error detector in volts/deg.

The transfer function of the synchro error detector is, therefore, of the form

$$\frac{E(s)}{\phi(s)} = K_s \qquad (3.40)$$

It must be noted that the signal-conditioning circuit will not include the demodulation process if the synchro-output signal is connected to an ac device (e.g., ac servomotor). The transfer function model given by Eqn. (3.40) is applicable in these situations also, with the only difference that the output variable of the model is not the synchro-output voltage itself but rather its envelope. This is in order as the information about the angular separation of the two shafts is stored in the envelope of the synchro-output voltage; the frequency of the voltage is governed only by the operational frequency range of the synchro device.

Example 3.6

A heavy telephoto camera can be controlled by the system shown in Fig. 3.45a. The camera is driven by an ac motor through a gear train and is designed to follow the movement of the spotting scope. This system employs ac components and all the signals other than the input and output shaft positions are suppressed-carrier modulated signals. Such systems are known as *carrier control systems* and are designed so that the signal cut-off frequency is much less than the carrier frequency. It is then sufficiently accurate to analyze these systems on the basis of modulating signals only.

In the system of Fig. 3.45a, a pair of synchros with sensitivity K_s is used as an error detector to generate the error signal $e = K_s(\theta_R - \theta_L)$. An ac amplifier of gain K_A is used to amplify this signal. The output e_c of the amplifier drives the ac servomotor. The torque developed by the motor is transmitted to the load shaft through a gear train with gear ratio n ($n = N_1/N_2$ = load shaft speed $\dot{\theta}_L$/motor shaft speed $\dot{\theta}_M$).

The two-phase motor develops a torque in accordance with the equation (refer Eqn. (3.21))

$$T_M = K_1 e_c - K_2 \dot{\theta}_M$$

where the constants K_1 and K_2 are given by torque-speed characteristics of the motor.

This torque drives the load (camera) of moment of inertia J_L and viscous-friction with coefficient B_L, against the disturbance load torque T_w. Assume that the moment of inertia and viscous-friction of the motor are represented by J_M and B_M, respectively. The equivalent moment of inertia of the motor-load combination reflected on the motor shaft is given by (refer Eqns (3.30))

$$J = J_M + n^2 J_L$$

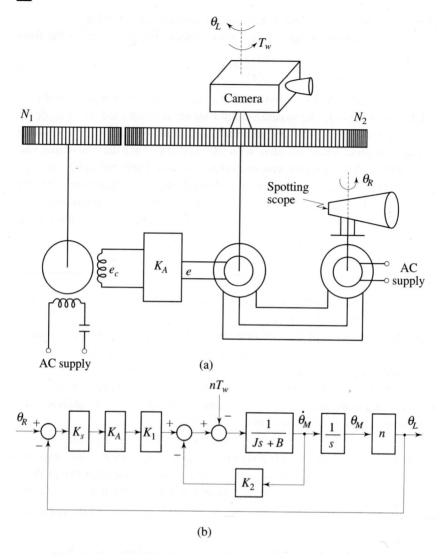

Fig. 3.45 *An ac (carrier) control system (a) schematic diagram (b) block diagram*

and the equivalent viscous-friction coefficient

$$B = B_M + n^2 B_L$$

nT_w is the equivalent disturbance torque on the motor shaft.

In terms of these parameters, the torque equation of the system becomes

$$T_M = J\ddot{\theta}_M + B\dot{\theta}_M + nT_w$$

A block diagram of the system is shown in Fig. 3.45b.

In the electromechanical servo of Fig. 3.40, angle measurement and comparison is by means of a synchro pair. Compared with potentiometers, the synchros offer higher sensitivity, longer life, ruggedness, and continuous rotation capability.

The output of the synchro error detector is a carrier-modulated signal. The information about the misalignment of the two shaft positions is carried by the envelope of this signal. As we shall see in the next chapter, generation of the control signal requires processing on the information signal, i.e., the envelope of the synchro-output signal. For example, we may require derivative and/or integration of the information signals in addition to amplification. A demodulator provides the necessary interface between the synchro error detector and the op amp circuit for generating the control signal. The low-frequency control signal can drive a dc motor after power amplification. Alternatively, the control signal may be modulated to drive an ac motor.

3.7 HYDRAULIC DEVICES FOR MOTION CONTROL

Hydraulically operated devices are frequently used in control systems. In these devices, power is transmitted through fluid flow under pressure. The fluid used is relatively incompressible such as petroleum-based oils or certain non-inflammable synthetic oils.

There are certain advantages and disadvantages in using hydraulic systems. The important ones are listed below.

1. A comparatively small-size hydraulic actuator using high-pressure fluid can develop very large forces or torques to provide rapid acceleration or deceleration of heavy loads. Hence, for the same horse power, hydraulic actuators are lighter than electric motors and considerable reduction in size and weight can be achieved.
2. Hydraulic components are more rugged and more resistant to vibrations and shocks than electrical components.
3. Availability of both the hydraulic linear actuators and rotary motors makes the design versatile.
4. Electrical power is readily available; for hydraulic systems, a source of pressurized hydraulic fluid with supply and return lines is required.
5. It has to be ensured that dirt does not contaminate the hydraulic fluid; this may lead to the failure of the components.
6. Leaks can be a problem and cause fire hazards unless fire-resistant hydraulic fluids are used.
7. The cost of a hydraulic system may be higher than a comparable electrical system performing a similar function.

When both high speed and high power are required, hydraulic systems may be mandatory or desirable. Common hydraulic control applications are power steering and brakes in automobiles, steering mechanism of ships, aircraft control surface actuators, control of large machine tools, servo systems for cranes and hoists, robots, and rolling mills, etc.

Some of the important hydraulic devices are discussed in this section.

Hydraulic Actuators

The hydraulic output devices used in control systems are generally of two types— those intended to produce rotary motion and those whose output is translational. The first type is known as the hydraulic motors and the second ones known as the hydraulic linear actuators.

The hydraulic linear actuator shown in Fig. 3.46 consists of a pilot valve and a power cylinder. The piston inside the power cylinder divides the cylinder into two chambers. The pilot valve— known as *spool valve* because of its shape— controls the flow rate of the hydraulic fluid to the power cylinder. It is a four-port valve: one port is connected to the hydraulic fluid supply at constant pressure, two control ports are connected to each chamber of the cylinder, and the drain port (the two drain ports are joined) is connected to the reservoir. The valve spool has two lands.

When the spool is in the neutral position ($x = 0$), the fluid flow in the power cylinder is blocked completely and the position of the piston, which moves the load, is $y = 0$. As the spool is moved to the right (x positive), the right-chamber port of the power cylinder is opened to the supply pressure P_s whereas the left-

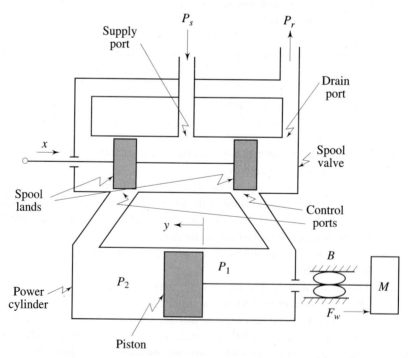

Fig. 3.46 *Hydraulic linear actuator with a load*

chamber port is opened to pressure P_r, which is slightly above the atmospheric pressure but we approximate it as zero gauge pressure in our model. Right-chamber pressure P_1 thus rises (while left-chamber pressure P_2 falls), producing an accelerating force on the load that moves to the left (y positive). If the spool is moved to the left (x negative), the left-chamber port of the power cylinder is opened to the supply pressure P_s, whereas the right-chamber port is opened to P_r. The direction of the fluid flow in the cylinder and hence the direction of displacement y of the load is reversed. This hydromechanical system acts as a power amplifier since the power (force $\times$ velocity) applied to position the valve is much smaller than that developed at the load.

Note that when the valve spool is in its neutral position, the flow area of the control ports is not in general zero. This is because spool lands and ports cannot be manufactured with perfectly sharp edges. Thus, a real valve will either be underlapped or overlapped (Fig. 3.47). Since an overlapped valve causes a dead zone for small spool motions (which is undesirable in control systems [180]), underlapped valves are often preferred.

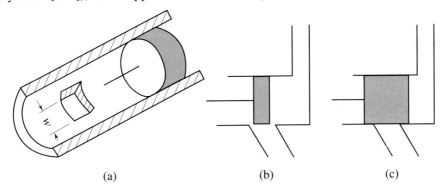

(a)   (b)   (c)

Fig. 3.47 (a) Spool valve construction (b) underlapped valve
(c) overlapped valve

With an underlapped valve in the neutral position, the cylinder pressures P_1 and P_2 will approach one half the supply pressure P_s. This can be explained as follows.

The fluid flow through the valve ports is similar to the flow through an orifice; the orifice flow relation (2.110) can therefore be applied. Let ΔP_v be the pressure drop across a valve port. Then

$$q = C_o A_o \sqrt{\frac{2(\Delta P_v)}{\rho}} \tag{3.41}$$

where

$q =$ volume flow rate through the port;
$A_o =$ uncovered area of the port;
$C_o =$ discharge coefficient; and
$\rho =$ density of the fluid.

The area A_o is equal to $w \times x$, where w is the width of the port (refer Fig. 3.47a). Since C_o, ρ (compressibility assumed negligible), and w are constant, the flow q is a function of x and ΔP_v.

Let us now examine the neutral position of the spool valve. In this position, the fluid leakage into the right chamber of the cylinder is at the rate proportional to $(P_s - P_1)^{1/2}$, and the leakage out of the right chamber is at the rate proportional to $(P_1 - P_r)^{1/2}$. Equilibrium of leakage in and out of the right chamber of the cylinder will be achieved when $P_1 = P_s/2$. Similarly, equilibrium of leakage in and out of the left chamber will be achieved when $P_2 = P_s/2$. This situation will be taken as the equilibrium point.

The movement of the spool from its neutral position and the load-induced pressure on the power piston will disturb the system from its equilibrium position. Assume that the load changes the right-chamber pressure to $P_1 = (P_s/2) + p_1$, and the left-chamber pressure to $P_2 = (P_s/2) + p_2$; the load-induced pressure

$$\Delta p = P_1 - P_2 = p_1 - p_2$$

The pressure drop from the supply to the reservoir, $P_s - P_r$, must equal the sum of the drops across both the control ports and the power piston. That is

$$P_s - P_r = 2\Delta P_v + \Delta p$$

where the drop across a control port is $\Delta P_v = P_s - P_1 = P_2 - P_r$ and the drop across the piston is

$$\Delta p = P_1 - P_2$$

Therefore,

$$\Delta P_v = \frac{1}{2}[P_s - P_r - \Delta p]$$

Since P_s = constant and $P_r = 0$, we see that ΔP_v varies only if Δp changes. Thus the variables x and Δp determine the volume flow rate:

$$q = f(x, \Delta p) \tag{3.42}$$

This relation is nonlinear. Linearization about the equilibrium point ($x = 0$, $\Delta p = 0$, $q = 0$) gives

$$q = K_1 x - K_2 \Delta p \tag{3.43}$$

where $\qquad K_1 \triangleq \left.\dfrac{\partial f}{\partial x}\right|_{x = \Delta p = 0} > 0$ is the flow gain; and

$\qquad K_2 \triangleq \left.\dfrac{\partial f}{\partial \Delta P}\right|_{x = \Delta p = 0} > 0$ is the pressure coefficient.

Figure 3.48 shows this linearized relationship among q, x, and Δp. The straight lines shown are the linearized characteristic curves of hydraulic actuator. Note that the region near the origin is most important because system operation usually occurs near this point. The flow gain K_1 and the pressure coefficient K_2 can be estimated theoretically from Eqn. (3.41), or more accurately from the experimental tests once the valve has been built.

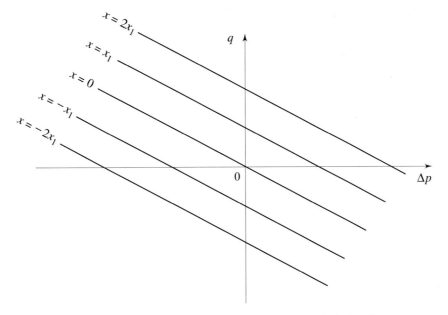

Fig. 3.48 *Linearized characteristic curves of a hydraulic*

Referring to Fig. 3.46 we see that the rate of fluid flow into the power cylinder is proportional to the rate at which the piston moves, i.e.,

$$K_1 x - K_2 \Delta p = A \dot{y} \qquad (3.44)$$

where A is the area of the piston.

Notice that because of high force levels and pressure differentials, there may be leakage from one chamber of the power cylinder to the other. However, translational actuators usually have piston rings that are essentially leak free. Equation (3.44) is true under the assumption of zero leakage around the piston.

The force developed by the power piston is equal to the pressure difference Δp times the piston area A. Assume that the power piston moves a load consisting of a mass M, and viscous friction with coefficient B. Then

$$A \Delta p = M \ddot{y} + B \dot{y} + F_w \qquad (3.45)$$

where F_w represents the load disturbance.

Figure 3.49 shows a block diagram representation of the hydraulic system. The transfer function between the load displacement y and the spool displacement x, obtained from the block diagram,

$$\text{is } \frac{Y(s)}{X(s)} = \frac{K}{s(\tau s + 1)} \qquad (3.46)$$

where $\qquad K = \dfrac{AK_1}{BK_2 + A^2}$ = gain constant of the actuator,

$$\tau = \dfrac{MK_2}{BK_2 + A^2}$$ = time-constant of the actuator.

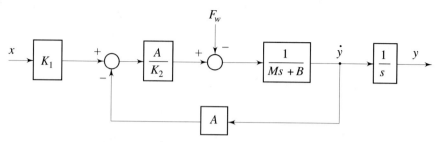

Fig. 3.49 *Block diagram of the hydraulic system of Fig. 3.46*

The controlled fluid power from a spool valve can be converted into rotating mechanical power by a hydrualic motor (refer [48, 57]).

Electrohydraulic Servovalves

The key to harnessing the power developed by hydraulic actuators and controlling them with analog electronic devices/digital computers, is the electrohydraulic servovalve. In its simplest form, an electrohydrualic servovalve is a spool valve with a spool positioned by solenoid-type magnetic actuators. These valves are called *single-stage valves*.

For a large flow rating, the forces required to rapidly and accurately position the spool are beyond the capabilities of solenoid-type electromagnetic positioners. Miniature hydromechanical actuators, internal to the servovalve perform this function. Large electrohydraulic servovalves will thus have an electromechanical first stage and a hydromechanical second stage.

Electrohydraulic valves of different sizes and constructional features are commercially available. The basic principle of operation of these valves is illustrated by the schematic diagram in Fig. 3.50. A magnetic torque motor activates this *two-stage valve*. The armature of the torque motor, which acts as a flapper, extends into the airgaps of the magnetic flux provided by a permanent magnet. The armature (flapper) is pivoted and its one end is positioned between two nozzles.

The armature winding is energized by a balanced amplifier which has the input e. When the input is zero, the currents i_1 and i_2 are equal. Since they flow in opposite directions, the net flux is zero, thus the torque is zero and the flapper is stationary at its central position between the two nozzles. If e is not zero, one of the currents increases and the other decreases in proportion to the magnitude of e. The resulting flux is proportional to the magnitude of e and its direction depends on the polarity of e. The size and direction of the generated torque therefore respond to the magnitude and polarity of e.

The developed torque, balanced by the torsional spring at the pivot, moves the flapper to the right or left. If the flapper moves to the right, the back pressure of the right-hand nozzle rises while that of the left-hand nozzle falls. A differential pressure between the nozzles is created which produces a force on

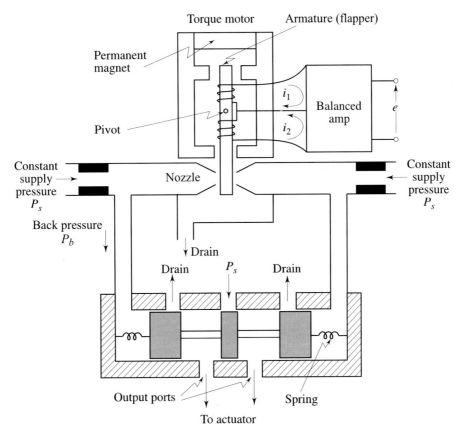

Fig. 3.50 *An electrohydraulic*

the spool. This force, balanced by springs, results in spool displacement to the left.

A servovalve model is given by the equation

$$x = Ke \qquad (3.47)$$

where x = spool displacement;
       e = input voltage; and
       K = valve gain.

This approximate model is adequate since the dynamics relating x to e is generally quite fast relative to the time-constants of the hydraulic actuator interfaced to the servovalve.

Example 3.7

The hydraulic servomechanism shown in Fig. 3.51a is one of the simplest types used. The system comprises a spool valve and a power cylinder, with the spool and the power ram interconnected by a feedback lever.

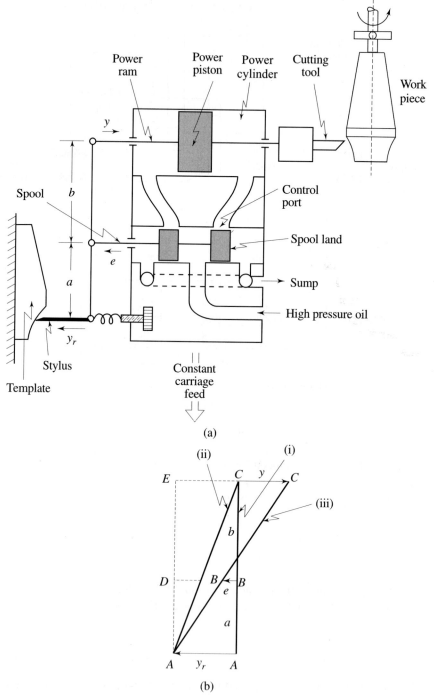

Fig. 3.51 *(a) A simple position control system using mechanical feedback (b) Geometry of feedback linkage for small values of y_r*

The operation of the system is as follows. Assume that the displacements y_r, y, and e are measured from an equilibrium position corresponding to some rest position of the load (the spool lands completely cover the control ports). This is shown in Fig. 3.51b as lever position (i). For a reference displacement y_r to the left from the equilibrium position, the upper end of the lever acts as a pivot, because the inertia and friction of the power piston are greater than those of the spool (lever position (ii) in Fig. 3.51b). This motion moves the spool to the left, admitting high pressure fluid to the left chamber of the power cylinder and thereby causing the power piston to move to the right. The lever now pivots about the lower end, which is held fixed by the mechanism that produces the reference displacement (lever position (iii) in Fig. 3.51b). This motion moves the spool to the right until the flow is shut off and the load comes to rest at a new position.

For small movements, y_r, y, and e can be regarded as linear. From the link geometry in Fig. 3.51b,

$$\frac{C'E}{A'E} = \frac{B'D}{A'D}$$

or

$$\frac{y + y_r}{a+b} = \frac{y_r - e}{a}$$

or

$$e = \frac{b}{a+b} y_r - \frac{a}{a+b} y \qquad (3.48)$$

In the system of Fig. 3.51a, the servomechanism has been used as a hydraulic shaper. A spring-loaded stylus traces over the template; the cutting tool is powerfully positioned by the hydraulic cylinder fed by the spool valve. The load on the power piston may be assumed to consist of mass M and viscous friction with coefficient B. The disturbance acting on the power piston is the thrust force F_w on the tool.

A block diagram of the system is shown in Fig. 3.52 (refer Eqns (3.42)—(3.46), and Fig. 3.49). Here K_1 and K_2 are given by the linearized characteristic curves of the hydraulic actuator, and A is the area of the power piston.

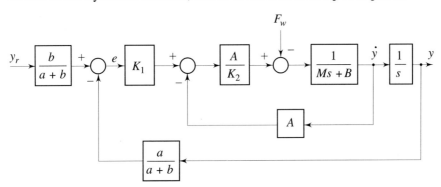

Fig. 3.52 *Block diagram of the hydraulic shaper shown in Fig. 3.51*

Example 3.8

Figure 3.53 shows the conceptual design of an electrohydraulic servomecha-nism used to position an aerodynamic control surface, such as aileron (refer Fig. 1.26), to the commands of the control stick. Very little power should be required to move the control stick so that it can be moved quickly and accu-rately by the pilot. However, large forces are required to move the control surface against the wind pressure. The servomechanism shown provides the necessary power boost.

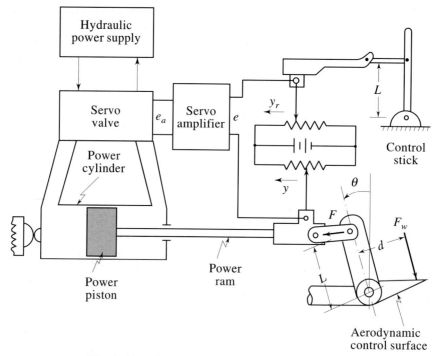

Fig. 3.53 *Electrohydraulic servomechanism*

The operation of the system is as follows. The command θ_r from the pilot moves the wiper on the input potentiometer by $y_r = L\theta_r$. The controlled position θ is sensed by the output potentiometer; the movement y of the wiper of the output potentiometer is related to θ as $y = L\theta$. The servo amplifier amplifies the error voltage $e = K_P(y_r - y)$ and generates a signal $e_a = K_A e$. The polarity of this voltage depends on the direction the stick is moved, and the magnitude of the voltage is proportional to the difference in commanded position θ_r and actual position θ of the control surface. The servovalve admits hydraulic fluid to one of the chambers of the power cylinder, depending on the polarity of e_a. The power piston positions the load; power piston displacement y follows the refer-ence y_r.

A linear mathematical model of this control system is now obtained in the following. Spool displacement x of the servovalve is related to the voltage e_a as (refer Eqn. (3.47))

$$x = K_v e_a$$

where K_v = valve gain.

Rate of fluid flow into the power cylinder is given by (refer Eqn. (3.43))

$$q = K_1 x - K_2 \Delta p$$

where Δp is the pressure drop across the piston, and K_1 and K_2 are constants obtained from linearized characteristic curves of the hydraulic actuator.

The rate of fluid flow into the power cylinder is proportional to the rate at which the piston moves (refer Eqn. (3.44)), i.e.,

$$K_1 x - K_2 \Delta p = A \dot{y}$$

where A = area of the piston.

The force balance on the power piston yields,

$$A \Delta p - F = M \ddot{y}$$

where M is the mass of the power piston and power ram, and F is the force applied by the power ram to the control surface attachment point. Furthermore, the control surface moment balance yields

$$J \ddot{\theta} = FL - F_w d$$

where J is the moment of inertia of the control surface and attachment about the hinge, and F_w is the applied aerodynamic load.

Compared to the inertial force $J \ddot{\theta}$, the inertial force $M \ddot{y}$ may be neglected. The block diagram of Fig. 3.54 is based on this assumption.

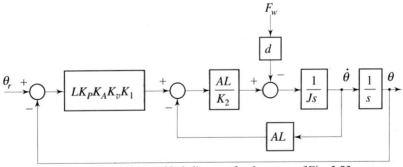

Fig. 3.54 *A block diagram for the system of Fig. 3.53*

3.8 | PNEUMATIC DEVICES FOR PROCESS CONTROL

While hydraulic devices use an incompressible fluid (oil), the working medium in a pneumatic device is a compressible fluid, generally air. It is primarily the different properties of the fluids involved that characterize the differences between the two types of devices. These differences can be listed as follows.

1. The air as a working medium is an advantage for pneumatic devices because it may be exhausted to the atmosphere at the end of the device's work cycle, thus eliminating the need for return lines.
2. The air medium has the advantage of being non-inflammable.
3. Air has almost negligible viscosity compared to the high viscosity of oils, which varies considerably with temperature. Pneumatic systems are thus insensitive to temperature changes in contrast to hydraulic systems where fluid friction due to viscosity depends greatly on temperature.
4. High incompressibility of the hydraulic fluid causes the force wave to travel faster and therefore hydraulic systems have shorter response time; while in pneumatic systems there is a considerable amount of compressibility flow so that such systems are characterized by longer time delays.
5. Air lacks lubricating property and always contains water vapour. Oil functions as a hydraulic fluid as well as a lubricator.
6. The normal operating pressure of pneumatic systems is much less than that of hydraulic systems, and consequently the output power is also less for the same size.

Many additional factors bear on the electric/hydraulic/pneumatic decision for those applications where all are technically feasible. Some of these factors are initial cost, maintenance, the nonlinear and other complex characteristics involved, etc.

Pneumatic devices are widely used in process systems used to control temperature, pressure, flow rate, liquid level, and the like. These systems have long time-constants; the response time of pneumatic devices is adequate for their control. Some of the important devices used in process control systems are discussed in this section.

Flow Control Valve

In a large number of process control systems, the final actuator controls the flow of some fluid—liquid, gas, or steam—using flow control valves. All control valves operate by inserting a variable restriction in the flow path. The plug valve (Fig. 3.55) operates by moving a tapered plug, thereby varying the gap between the plug and the valve seat. The flow is controlled by the linear movement of the valve stem.

Pneumatic actuation of the control valves is most common in the process industries. When a valve is supplied by a manufacturer; the pneumatic actuator and the valve are usually attached to each other to form one unit. Figure 3.55 shows a unit where the pneumatic device controls the reciprocating stem of the

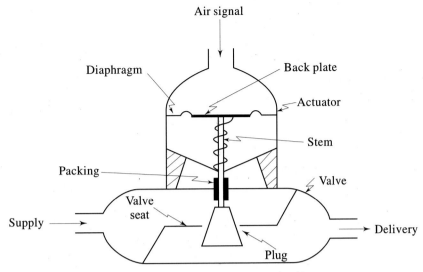

Fig. 3.55 *A pneumatic control valve*

valve as the pressure on the spring-loaded diaphragm changes[5]. The stem positions a plug in the orifice of the valve body.

An increase in the signal pressure above the diaphragm exerts a force on the diaphragm and the back plate which causes the stem to move down 'until the force from the now more compressed spring balances the force on the stem. This results in an increase in the cross-sectional area for flow between the plug and the seat, thereby increasing the flow.[6]

In general, the flow rate of fluid through the valve depends upon the upstream and downstream fluid pressures and the size of the opening through the valve. If all components (including the process) in a feedback control system are essentially linear, then the control valve flow characteristic (relationship between flow through the valve and valve stem position) should also be linear, since then system performance (stability, speed of response, etc.) will be uniform over all system operating conditions. If other system components (usually the process) exhibit significant nonlinearities, then we can choose a valve characteristic that is the inverse of the process nonlinearity, thereby linearizing the overall system and gaining the benefits of uniform performance [48].

---

5. Electromechanical actuation of a control valve having rotating stem is another popular choice. A dc motor is configured as the position control actuator. The shaft of the motor is coupled to the rotating stem of the valve through gearing. The motor and the reduction gears provide an incremental control of fluid flow.

6. The reverse action—reduction in flow with increase in the signal pressure—can be accomplished by inverting the plug on the valve stem. Refer Chapter 11 for details.

Control valves with linear flow characteristics are commonly used in processes where the pressure drop across the valve is fairly constant. In our process control examples, we will use control valves with the following characteristics:

(i) the flow through the valve is proportional to valve stem position; and
(ii) the valve stem position is proportional to input signal pressure.

Electropneumatic Transducer

The key to harnessing the power developed by pneumatic actuators and controlling them with analog electronic devices/digital computers, is the electropneumatic transducer. It receives an electrical signal and transmits a proportional output pressure.

Electropneumatic transducers of different sizes and constructional features are commercially available. The basic principle of operation of these devices is illustrated by the schematic diagram in Fig. 3.56. A magnetic torque motor

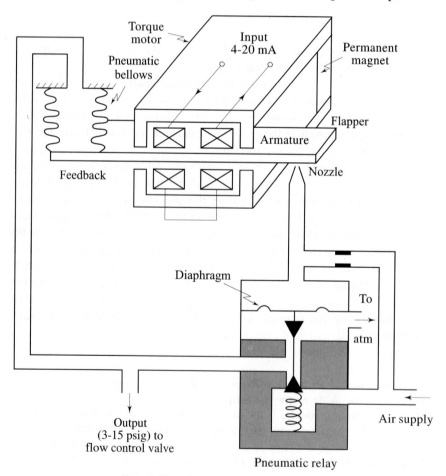

Fig. 3.56 *Current to pressure converter*

activates the transducer. The armature of the torque motor, which acts as a flapper, extends into the airgaps of magnetic flux provided by a permanent magnet. The signal current is passed through four coils, wired as shown, and causes a rotary torque on the armature (flapper arm). The torque is proportional to the signal current and causes a change in the flapper/nozzle gap.

Assume that an increase in signal current develops a torque that moves the flapper downwards at the nozzle end. The resulting restriction produces an increased pressure in the nozzle and in the upper chamber of the pneumatic relay. The relay responds to the increase in pressure by closing the exhaust port and opening the supply port, thereby increasing the output pressure to the control valve.

When a decreasing signal current is received, the armature rotates to uncover the nozzle, resulting in a decrease in the pressure in the nozzle and the relay. The relay diaphragm moves upward and the exhaust port opens to bleed the output pressure to atmosphere, thereby reducing the pressure applied to the control valve.

Figure 3.56 shows that the electropneumatic transducer is also itself a complete feedback system; thus it must be properly designed for stability and accuracy. If we are users (rather than designers) of such a device, we are concerned only with its overall dynamics from input current i to output pressure p. The dynamics relating p to i is generally quite fast compared to other time-constants in the process control loop; so we model the electropneumatic transducer as a zero-order system with p proportional to i.

Example 3.9

The stirred tank in Fig. 3.57 is used to heat a process stream so that its pre-mixed components achieve a uniform composition. Temperature control is important because a high temperature tends to decompose the product while a low temperature results in incomplete mixing. The tank is heated by the steam condensing inside a coil. The temperature in the tank is controlled by manipulating the steam valve position.

The control hardware required to control the temperature of a process stream leaving a continuously stirred tank reactor (CSTR) is shown in Fig. 3.57. This hardware, available from manufacturers of process-control equipment, consists of the components listed below along with their respective conversions:
- sensor (temperature to current);
- controller (current to current);
- transducer (current to pressure); and
- control valve (pressure to flow rate).

A thermocouple is used to measure the temperature; the signal from the thermocouple is sent to the signal-conditioning circuit, which produces an output in the range of 4-20 mA, which is a linear function of the input. The output

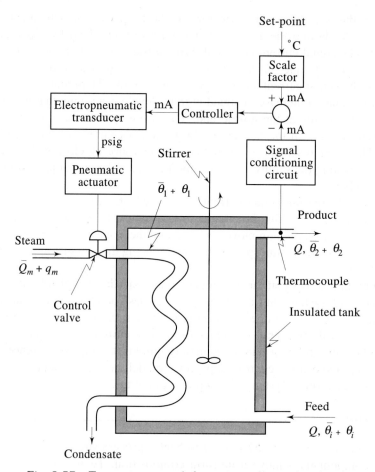

Fig. 3.57 *Temperature control of a continuously stirred tank reactor*

of the sensor is compared with the set-point to produce an error signal. The controller converts the error to an output in the range of 4-20 mA according to the control law. The only control law we have considered so far has been proportional. In the next chapter, other control laws will be described. The output of the controller enters the electropneumatic transducer, which produces an output in the range of 3-15 psig, which is a linear function of the input. Finally, the output of the electropneumatic transducer is sent to the top of the pneumatic control valve, which adjusts the flow of the steam to the coil in the stirred tank. We will assume that the valve is linear.

Simplifying assumptions:

1. The liquid inflow and outflow rates for the tank are equal so that the liquid level in the tank is maintained constant during the operation.
2. The liquid in the tank is well-stirred so that its state can be described by the temperature of the outflowing liquid.
3. The tank is well-insulated so that the heat loss through its walls is negligible. Also, the heat storage capacity of the tank walls is negligible.

We consider here a CSTR where the process feed has a density ρ of 1090 kg/m^3 and a heat capacity c of 3350 Joules/kg-°C. The volume V of the liquid in the reactor is maintained constant at 3.4 m^3 by a constant feed rate Q of 0.425 m^3/min. Thermal capacitance C_1 of the coil mass is 503×10^3 Joules/°C. The heat transfer area A is 22.57 m^2 and the heat transfer coefficient U is 42.97×10^3 Joules/min-m^2-°C. The steam available is saturated; it can be assumed that its latent heat of condensation λ is constant at 2247×10^3 Joules/kg.

At steady state, the temperature of the feed $\bar{\theta}_i$ is 55 °C. Assume that the design requirement is to maintain the tank liquid at a temperature $\bar{\theta}_2$ of 80 °C. Possible perturbations from the steady state are caused by the desired change θ_r in the temperature of the tank liquid, and the change θ_i in the feed temperature (a disturbance). These perturbation signals give rise to perturbations θ_1 and θ_2 in the temperatures of the coil mass and the tank liquid, respectively, from their steady-state values $\bar{\theta}_1$ and $\bar{\theta}_2$.

The heat balance for the coil mass:

$$C_1 \frac{d}{dt}(\bar{\theta}_1 + \theta_1) = (\bar{Q}_m + q_m)\lambda - UA\,[\bar{\theta}_1 + \theta_1 - (\bar{\theta}_2 + \theta_2)] \tag{3.49}$$

where

$\bar{Q}_m$ = steam flow rate (kg/min) at steady state, and

q_m = manipulation of the steam flow rate.

The heat balance for the tank liquid:

$$V\rho c \frac{d}{dt}(\bar{\theta}_2 + \theta_2) = Q\rho c\,[\bar{\theta}_i + \theta_i] + UA\,[\bar{\theta}_1 + \theta_1 - (\bar{\theta}_2 + \theta_2)]$$
$$- Q\rho c\,[\bar{\theta}_2 + \theta_2] \tag{3.50}$$

The process steady state is described by the following equations:

$$\bar{Q}_m\,\lambda - UA(\bar{\theta}_1 - \bar{\theta}_2) = 0$$

$$Q\rho c\bar{\theta}_i + UA(\bar{\theta}_1 - \bar{\theta}_2) - Q\rho c\,\bar{\theta}_2 = 0$$

This gives
$$Q\rho c(\bar{\theta}_i - \bar{\theta}_2) + \bar{Q}_m\,\lambda = 0$$

Since $\bar{\theta}_i = 55\,°\text{C}$ and $\bar{\theta}_2 = 80\,°\text{C}$, the steady-state mass flow rate of steam through the coil is

$$\bar{Q}_m = \frac{0.425 \times 1090 \times 3350 \times (80 - 55)}{2247 \times 10^3}$$

$$= 17.27 \text{ kg/min}$$

At steady state, the error signal in the control configuration of Fig. 3.57 is zero. The necessary steam flow rate $\bar{Q}_m$ can be achieved with the zero error signal because the electropneumatic transducer has a zero adjustment which allows pressure to be at the middle (9 psig) of its 3–15 psig range when the input to the transducer is zero, and the valve actuator has a zero adjustment which allows the valve opening to be put anywhere desired with its input pressure at 9 psig.

Let us now derive the process model that describes perturbation dynamics about the steady state.

From Eqns (3.49) and (3.50) we obtain

$$C_1 \frac{d\theta_1}{dt} = q_m \lambda - UA(\theta_1 - \theta_2)$$

$$V\rho c \frac{d\theta_2}{dt} = Q\rho c(\theta_i - \theta_2) + UA(\theta_1 - \theta_2)$$

By Laplace transformation and manipulation of these equations, we obtain

$$(\tau_1 s + 1)\, \theta_1(s) = \theta_2(s) + K_1 Q_m(s)$$
$$(\tau_2 s + 1)\, \theta_2(s) = K_2 \theta_1(s) + K_3 \theta_i(s)$$

where

$$\tau_1 = \frac{C_1}{UA}; \; \tau_2 = \frac{V\rho c}{UA + Q\rho c}; K_1 = \frac{\lambda}{UA};$$

$$K_2 = \frac{UA}{UA + Q\rho c}; K_3 = \frac{Q\rho c}{UA + Q\rho c}$$

Block-diagram representation of these equations in shown in Fig. 3.58a.

Substituting the numerical values of various parameters, we obtain

$$\tau_1 = 0.52 \text{ min}, \; \tau_2 = 4.92 \text{ min}, K_1 = 2.32 \text{ °C/kg-min}$$
$$K_2 = 0.385 \text{ °C/°C}, K_3 = 0.615 \text{ °C/°C}$$

Manipulation of the block diagram of Fig. 3.58a with the above numerical values for various parameters, gives

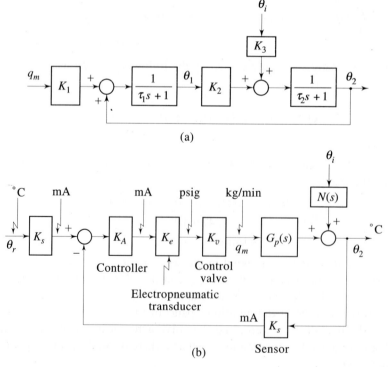

(a)

(b)   Sensor

Fig. 3.58 *Block diagrams for the system of Fig. 3.57*

$$\theta_2(s) = G_p(s)\, Q_m(s) + N(s)\theta_i(s)$$

where

$$G_p(s) = \frac{0.35}{s^2 + 2.13s + 0.24}\; ; N(s) = \frac{0.24(0.52s + 1)}{s^2 + 2.13s + 0.24}$$

The dynamics of the other components of the feedback system—the temperature sensor, the controller (amplifier), the electropneumatic transducer and the pneumatic control valve—are negligible relative to the process time-constants. All these components are fast enough to be treated as zero-order systems. Fig. 3.58b shows a block-diagram representation of the temperature control loop.

Review Examples

Review Example 3.1 ——————————————————————————

Consider the temperature control system of Fig. 3.59 which is set up to produce a steady process stream at a controlled temperature. The temperature $\theta(°C)$ of the outflowing liquid is measured by a thermocouple which produces an output voltage e_t(volts) proportional to $\theta(e_t = K_t\theta)$. This voltage is subtracted from the reference voltage e_r to generate the error signal $e = (e_r - e_t)$ which in turn regulates the heating rate h by means of an SCR amplifier [3]. Basically a solid state switch, the SCR amplifier controls the heating rate by varying the point in the ac power cycle at which the heater is connected to (or disconnected from) the power line (see Fig. 3.60). As the line frequency (50 Hz) is very high relative to the thermal system frequency response, we take h to

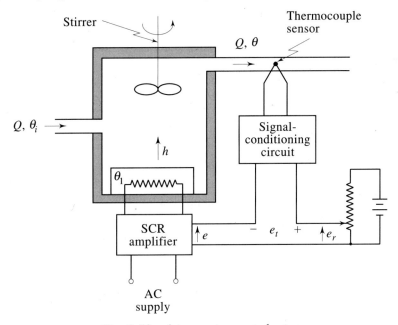

Fig. 3.59 *A temperature control system*

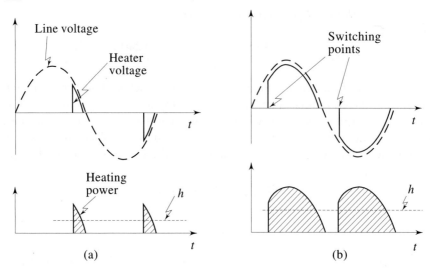

Fig. 3.60 *SCR control of heating rate; (a) low heating rate (b) high heating rate*

mean the *average* power over the cycle, rather than the instantaneous electrical power and assume that h follows the amplifier input voltage e instantly. The nonlinear steady-state relation (static calibration curve) between e and h can be linearized at any chosen operating point, giving heater gain K_h; $h = K_h e$ watts. Simplifying assumptions:

1. The liquid inflow and outflow rates for the tank are equal (Q m³/sec) so that the liquid level in the tank is maintained constant (volume V m³ of the liquid in the tank is therefore constant).
2. The liquid in the tank is well stirred so that its state can be described by the temperature θ of the outflowing liquid.
3. The tank is well insulated so that the heat loss through its walls is negligible. Also the heat storage capacity of the tank walls is negligible.
4. The heat storage capacity of the heater mass is negligible.

Assuming an initial equilibrium point and taking all the variables as perturbations, we obtain the following heat-balance equation.

$$V\rho c\,\frac{d\theta}{dt} = h + Q\rho c\,\theta_i - Q\rho c\,\theta \qquad (3.51)$$

where $\rho =$ density of the liquid;
      $c =$ specific heat of the liquid; and
      $\theta_i =$ perturbation in the temperature of the inflowing stream; this will be treated as a disturbance in our model.

Taking the Laplace transform of Eqn. (3.51) and reorganizing, we get

$$(s\tau + 1)\,\theta(s) = \frac{1}{Q\rho c}H(s) + \theta_i(s) \qquad (3.52)$$

where $\tau = \dfrac{V}{Q}$ = process time-constant.

Although we generally prefer to measure the controlled variable as directly as possible, location of the thermocouple (which has an output of a few millivolts) in the tank encounters problems of electrical noise due to high-power SCR switching, and vibration caused by the tank stirrer. Thus, we locate it in the pipeline downstream of the tank causing a deadtime τ_D between θ and its measurement θ_o:

$$\frac{\theta_o(s)}{\theta(s)} = e^{-s\tau_D} \tag{3.53}$$

Using Eqns (3.52) and (3.53), we can draw the block diagram of the system as shown in Fig. 3.61.

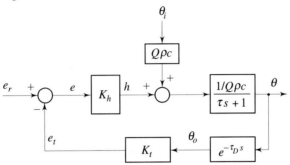

Fig. 3.61 *A block diagram for the system of Fig. 3.59*

Review Example 3.2 _____

Let us reconsider the toilet-tank control system of Fig. 1.5. A change in the liquid level is sensed by a float which is connected by a mechanical lever to a control valve. At steady state, the upward-acting buoyant force due to the liquid displaced by the float is just balanced by its weight. The control valve is closed in this state. Assume now that due to disturbance flow q_w, the liquid level goes down by h. This will decrease the buoyant force, and the float will start moving down. We denote the downward movement of the float by x.

Due to unavoidable friction effects, x and h will be related by

$$X(s) = \frac{1}{\tau_f s + 1} H(s)$$

where τ_f is the time-constant of the float dynamics. However τ_f is normally quite small compared to the process dynamics and an be neglected.

The downward movement of the float by x will cause a downward movement of the control valve stem by z:

$$z = \frac{l_1}{l_1 + l_2} x$$

This will give rise to liquid inflow at the rate $q_i(t)$: $q_i(t) = K_v z(t)$; K_v = valve gain.

The tank process dynamics is found by applying conservation of volume:

$$A\frac{dh}{dt} = q_i - q_w$$

where A = tank cross-sectional area.

The block diagrams of Fig. 3.62 corresponds to perturbation dynamics of the system about the steady-state level $\overline{H}$. Since the desired change in the level $\overline{H}$ is zero, the reference input in the perturbation model of Fig. 3.62 has been taken as zero.

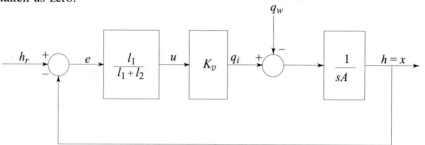

Fig. 3.62   *A block diagram model of system of Fig. 1.5*

Review Example 3.3

In a steel or paper mill, the products are moved by rollers, as shown in Fig. 3.63a. In order to maintain a prescribed uniform tension, the roller speeds are kept constant and equal to each other. This can be achieved by using the control system shown in Fig. 3.63b. Each roller is driven by an armature-controlled dc motor.

The motor speed is measured by the dc tachometer coupled to the motor shaft. The tachometer output is K_t volts/(rad/sec). This voltage is compared with the reference voltage e_r which represents the desired motor speed. The difference in voltage is amplified by a pre-amplifier of gain K_A, and then power-amplified by a power amplifier. The old approach was to use a motor-generator set. The generator, which is essentially a power amplifier, is run at a constant speed by a prime-mover such as a synchronous motor. However, in modern drives, the classical motor-generator set is replaced by a thyristorized dc drive, which has the advantages of high efficiency, small size, fast response, and lower cost.

In the thyristor-driven speed control system of Fig. 3.63b, the output voltage e_c of the pre-amplifier is fed to the driver of the thyristor rectifier (refer Fig. 1.17). The driver produces time gate pulses that control the conduction of the thyristors in the rectifier module. The rectified output voltage e_a depends on the firing angle of the pulses relative to the ac supply waveform [3]. A linear relationship between the input voltage e_c and output voltage e_a can be obtained when a proper firing control scheme is used. The time-constants associated with the rectifier are negligibly small. Neglecting the dynamics of the rectifier, we get

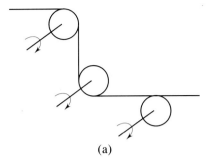

(a)

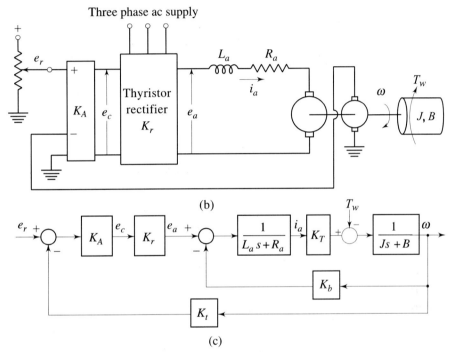

(b)

(c)

Fig. 3.63 *Speed control of rollers*

$$e_a = K_r e_c \qquad (3.54\text{a})$$

where K_r is the gain of the rectifier.

The motor is separately excited with a constant field current and has a counter emf of K_b volts/(rad/sec). It produces a torque of K_T newton-m/amp of armature current. It drives a load of moment of inertia J newton-m/(rad/sec^2) and viscous friction with coefficient B newton-m/(rad/sec), against the load-torque disturbance T_w newton-m.

The functional block diagram of the speed control system is shown in Fig. 3.63c.

The thyristorized drives are usually provided with current-limiting features to prevent damage to the thyristors. A current limit can be implemented by constructing a current-control loop as shown in Fig. 3.64. A resistance R is inserted in the armature circuit to generate a voltage proportional to the armature current. An isolating amplifier is used to take care of the loading effect.

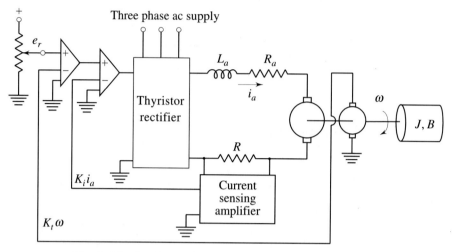

Fig. 3.64 *Speed control system with inner current-control loop*

*Review Example 3.4*_____

Let us reconsider the hydraulic power steering mechanism discussed earlier in Example 1.3. A simplified schematic diagram of the system is shown in Fig. 1.8. The input to the system is rotation (θ_r) of the steering wheel by the driver, and the output is position (θ) of the tyre wheels of the vehicle.

When the steering wheel is in the zero position, i.e., the cross bar is horizontal, the tyre wheels are directed parallel to the longitudinal axis of the vehicle. For this condition, the spool is in the neutral position ($x = 0$) and the oil supply to the power cylinder is cut-off. When the steering wheel is turned anticlockwise through an angle θ_r, the spool is made to move towards right by an amount x with the help of the gear mechanism. The high-pressure oil enters on the left-hand side of the power cylinder causing the power piston and hence the power ram to move towards right by an amount y. Through a proper drive linkage, a torque is applied to the wheels causing a displacement θ of wheels.

A rigid linkage bar connects the power ram and the movable housing. Movement y of the power ram towards right causes a movement z of the valve housing in such a direction as to seal off the high pressure line.

The geometry of the linkage is shown in Fig. 3.65, from which we obtain for small movements.

$$\frac{AA'}{AC} = \frac{AA'}{AB + BC} = \frac{BB'}{BC}$$

or

$$\frac{y}{a + b} = \frac{z}{a}$$

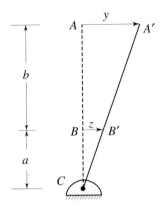

Fig. 3.65 *Geometry of the feedback linkage in the system in Fig. 1.8*

Therefore
$$z = \frac{a}{a+b}\, y \tag{3.55}$$

The flow rate of the oil into power cylinder due to spool movement is given by (refer Eqn. (3.43))

$$q = K_1 e - K_2 \Delta p, \quad K_1 \text{ and } K_2 \text{ are constants;}$$

where $e = (x - z)$ is the net displacement of the spool relative to the valve housing, and Δp is the differential pressure across the piston.

The flow rate of the oil into the power cylinder is proportional to the rate at which the piston moves (refer Eqn. (3.44)), i.e.,

$$K_1 e - K_2 \Delta p = A\,\dot{y} \tag{3.56}$$

where A is the area of the piston.

Assuming the load on the power piston to consist of mass M, tyre stiffness K and viscous friction coefficient B, the force equation is given by (refer Eqn. (3.45))

$$A\Delta p = M\,\ddot{y} + B\,\dot{y} + Ky \tag{3.57}$$

A block diagram of the power steering mechanism obtained from Eqns (3.55) – (3.57) is shown in Fig. 3.66.

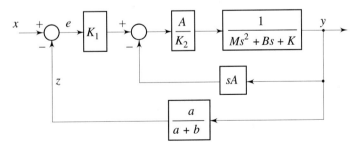

Fig. 3.66 *A block diagram of the system in Fig. 1.8*

Review Example 3.5 _____

The dynamic behaviour of certain processes deviates drastically from what we have seen so far. Consider the simple drum boiler shown in Fig. 3.67a. Feedwater enters the boiler with a mass flow rate $\overline{Q}_{mf} + q_{mf}$, at a constant temperature. It is heated by a constant amount of heat supplied by burned fuel. The generated steam flows out from the top of the boiler with a mass flow rate $\overline{Q}_{ms} + q_{ms}$, at a constant pressure. A simple feedback control system has been installed to keep the level of the water in the drum boiler constant by manipulating the flow rate q_{mf} of the feedwater stream. Variations in steam flow q_{ms} are the main disturbances affecting the system.

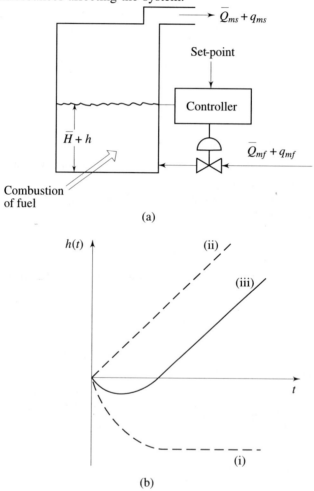

(a)

(b)

Fig. 3.67   *Liquid-level control in a boiler system*

If the flow rate of the cold feedwater is increased by step,thetotal volume of the boiling water and consequently the liquid level will be decreased for a short period and then it will start increasing asshown by the response in Fig. 3.67b. Such a behaviour is the net result of two opposing effects and can be explained as follows.

  (i) The cold feedwater causes a temperature drop which decreases the volume of the entrained vapour bubbles. This leads to a decrease in the liquid level of the boiling water, following first-order behaviour (curve (i) in Fig. 3.67b), i.e., $-K_1/(\tau_1 s + 1)$.

 (ii) With constant heat supply, the steam production remains constant and consequently the liquid level of the boiling water will start increasing in an integral form (curve (ii) in Fig. 3.67b), i.e., K_2/s.

(iii) The two opposing effects give rise to the response represented by curve (iii) in Fig. 3.67b.

Figure 3.68 shows block diagram of a feedback control scheme; K_v is the gain of the flow control valve, and K_c is the gain of the controller. The plant model is given by

$$G(s) = \frac{K_2}{s} - \frac{K_1}{\tau_1 s + 1} = \frac{(K_2 \tau_1 - K_1)s + K_2}{s(\tau_1 s + 1)}$$

(3.58)

When $K_2 \tau_1 < K_1$, then from Eqn. (3.58) we notice that the transfer function has a zero in the right-half s-plane at the point $s = -K_2/(K_2\tau_1 - K_1) > 0$.

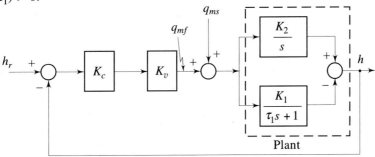

Fig. 3.68 *Block diagram of the system in Fig. 3.67*

Systems with zeros in the right-half s-plane are particularly difficult to control and require special attention.

Review Questions

3.1 (a) X_{in} is the input-node variable and X_{out} is the output node variable of a signal flow graph with N forward paths. Describe the Mason's gain rule for the determination of the overall gain X_{out}/X_{in} of the signal flow graph.

    (b) Unity-feedback block diagram model can be obtained only for control systems with sensor gain of unity. Do you agree with this statement? Justify your answer. (Help: p145)

3.2 In an armature-controlled dc motor, a voltage e_a is applied to the armature through an amplifier of gain K_A. Other parameters and variables of the system are:

R_a = armature winding resistance
L_a = armature winding inductance
K_b = back emf constant
K_T = motor torque constant
J = moment of inertia of the motor rotor with attached mechanical load
B = viscous-friction coefficient of the motor rotor with attached mechanical load
θ = angular displacement of the motor rotor

Derive the transfer function $\theta(s)/E_a(s)$ of the motor. Clearly state the assumptions made.

How is the torque constant K_T of the motor related to the back emf constant K_b? (Help: p164)

3.3 (a) For a field-controlled dc motor,

      R_f = field winding resistance
      L_f = field winding inductance
      e_f = applied field voltage
      θ = angular displacement of the motor rotor
      J = moment of inertia of the motor rotor with attached mechanical load
      B = viscous-friction coefficient of the motor rotor with attached mechanical load.

      Derive the transfer function $\theta(s)/E_f(s)$ of the motor. State the assumptions made.

    (b) List the advantages and disadvantages of the field control compared to the armature control of a dc motor. (Help: p168)

3.4 (a) Describe the construction and working of a two-phase motor suitable for use in ac servo systems. Give the torque-speed characteristics of the motor and derive the transfer function model based on the linearized characteristics. Justify the use of linear model. Appropriate symbols for variables and parameters may be used in your derivation.

      What will happen if induction motor is used for servo applications? Can we use servomotor for applications where induction motor is normally used? (Help: p170, p174)

    (b) Compare and contrast the usefulness of ac and dc servomotors in motion control systems. (Help: p159, p170)

3.5 Given a two-gear system with angular displacements θ_1 and θ_2, number of teeth N_1 and N_2, and torques T_{12} (exerted on gear 1 by gear 2) and T_{21} (transmitted to gear 2 by gear 1). Develop the mathematical relations between these variables and parameters. Clearly state the assumptions made.

3.6 Explain using labelled diagrams, the construction and operation of the following transducers:
    (a) AC tachogenerator
    (b) DC tachogenerator

Describe briefly using suitable block diagrams, an application of each in motion control systems. (Help: Fig. P3.10, Fig. 3.64)

3.7 Explain with the aid of a sketch, the construction and operation of a linear variable differential transformer (LVDT). Describe briefly using appropriate diagrams, an application of LVDT in motion control systems. (Help: Fig. P3.15)

3.8 (a) Explain with the aid of appropriate diagrams, the construction and operation of
   (i) synchro transmitter; and
   (ii) synchro control transformer
   Give a schematic diagram showing how the synchro pair (transmitter and control transformer) would be embodied in an ac position control system. (Help: Fig. 3.45)
   (b) Rotor of synchro transmitter is of dumb-bell type while that of control transformer is cylindrical. Why? (Help: p189)
   (c) Is synchro a three phase machine? Justify your answer. (Help: p188)

3.9 (a) Compare the advantages and disadvantages of the following transducers when used as error-forming devices in servosystems:
   (a) a pair of rotary potentiometers; and
   (b) a synchro pair.
   Give a schematic diagram showing how each would be embodied in a position control system. (Help: p184, p186, Fig. 3.40; Fig. 3.45)
   (b) Why are ac devices (servomotor, synchro) normally operated at higher frequencies (400 Hz, for example) and not at 50 Hz? (Help: p170)

3.10 Draw an electromechanical schematic diagram of a dc position control servosystem incorporating tachogenerator damping. Describe the operation of the main components used, explaining clearly how the error signal is formed. (Help: Figs 1.15 and 1.16)
   Why do we put tacho on the motor shaft rather than the load shaft? (Help: Problem 3.9)

3.11 (a) Armature control of a dc motor is used in a closed-loop speed control system. Draw a schematic layout for the system. Describe the operation of main components used, explaining clearly how the error signal is formed. (Help: Review Example 3.3)
   (b) The classical approach of variable speed drives was motor-generator set; generator used as a power amplifier. What is the modern approach? (Help: p 214)

3.12 (a) Sketch an op amp circuit capable of providing an output which approximates to proportional plus integral plus derivative of the input.
   Explain using a block diagram how this unit can be connected into a position control system which has been constructed using synchro error detector, ac servomotor, gear box, and other relevant components. (Help: Example 2.10; p193)
   (b) Modify the block diagram to include an ac tachogenerator to provide damping, with the op amp circuit providing proportional plus integral plus derivative actions.

3.13 Hydraulically operated devices are frequently used in control systems. List the advantages and disadvantages in using hydraulic systems. (Help: p193) Using appropriate diagrams, give the constructional and operational features of a hydraulic linear actuator. Derive the transfer function model of the actuator. Use appropriate symbols for variables and parameters. Clearly state the assumptions made.

3.14 Draw a schematic diagram of position control system for controlling the linear displacement of a load mass. Use potentiometers for formation of error and hydraulic linear actuator for moving the mass. Give a brief description of the equipment used in the system. (Help: Fig. 3.53)

3.15 Pneumatic devices are widely used in process control systems. In a thermal system, the following hardware has been used to control the temperature of the process stream leaving a CSTR (Continuously Stirred Tank Reactor):
Sensor (temperature to current)
Controller (current to current)
Transducer (current to pressure)
Control valve (pressure to flow rate)
Select appropriate control hardware and draw a schematic diagram describing the complete temperature control system. Explain the constructional and operational features of the selected hardware. (Help: Fig. 3.57)

3.16 Give an example of a feedback system with closed-loop transfer function of the form

$$\frac{Y(s)}{R(s)} = \frac{K}{\tau s + 1}$$

Find the response of the system to unit-step input and discuss the effects of variations in parameters K and τ on transient behaviour. What is the effect of variations in these parameters on steady-state response to step and ramp inputs? (Help: Fig. 3.39, pp 69-71, Review Example 2.1)

3.17 Give an example of a feedback system into closed-loop transfer function of the form

$$\frac{Y(s)}{R(s)} = \frac{K\omega_n^2}{s^2 + 2\zeta\omega_n s + \omega_n^2}$$

Find the response of the system to unit-step input and discuss the effects of variations in parameters K, ζ, and ω_n, on transient behaviour. What are the effects of variations in these parameters on steady-state response to step and ramp inputs? (Help: Fig. 3.40, pp 72-77, Review Example 2.2)

Problems

3.1 A linear feedback control system has the block diagram shown in Fig. P3.1. Using block diagram reduction rules, obtain the closed-loop transfer function $Y(s)/R(s)$.

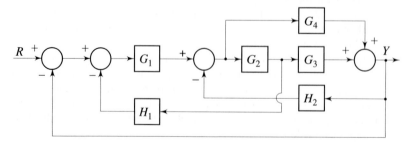

Fig. P3.1

3.2 Using block diagram reduction rules, convert the block diagram of Fig. P3.2 to a simple loop.

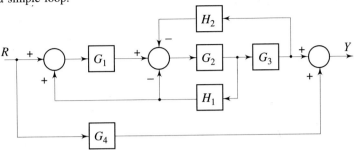

Fig. P3.2

3.3 Convert the block diagram of Fig. P3.3 to a signal flow graph, and therefrom obtain the input–output transfer function using Mason's gain rule.

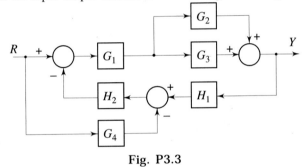

Fig. P3.3

3.4 The block diagram of a feedback control system is shown in Fig. P3.4. The output

$$Y(s) = M(s)R(s) + M_w(s)W(s)$$

Find the transfer functions $M(s)$ and $M_w(s)$.

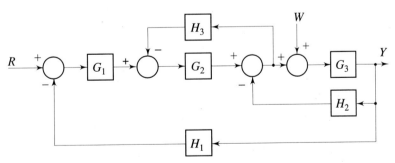

Fig. P3.4

3.5 The block diagram of a feedback control system is shown in Fig. P3.5. The input-output relation is of the form

$$\mathbf{Y}(s) = \mathbf{G}(s)\,\mathbf{R}(s)$$

where $\mathbf{Y}(s) = \begin{bmatrix} Y_1(s) \\ Y_2(s) \end{bmatrix}; \mathbf{R}(s) = \begin{bmatrix} R_1(s) \\ R_2(s) \end{bmatrix}$

Find the transfer function matrix $\mathbf{G}(s)$ using Mason's gain rule.

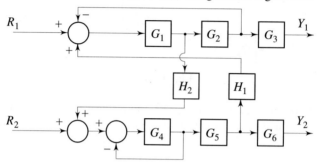

Fig. P3.5

3.6 In the speed control system shown in Fig. P3.6, the generator field time-constant is negligible. It is driven at constant speed giving a generated voltage of K_g volts/field amp. The separately excited motor has a back emf of K_b volts/(rad/sec). It produces a torque of K_T N-m/amp. The motor and its load have a combined moment of inertia J kg-m^2 and negligible friction. The tachometer gives K_t volts/(rad/sec) and the amplifier gain is K_A amps/volts.

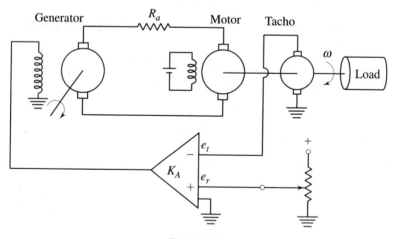

Fig. P3.6

Draw a block diagram of the system and determine therefrom the transfer function $\omega(s)/E_r(s)$, where ω is the load speed and e_r is the reference signal which corresponds to the desired speed.

With the system initially at rest, $e_r = 100$ volts is suddenly applied.

Determine how the load speed will change with time.

Given: $K_A = 4$ amps/volts; $K_T = 1.5$ N-m/amp;

$K_g = 50$ volts/amp; $K_t = 0.2$ volts/(rad/sec);

$R_a = 1\Omega$; $J = 6$ kg-m^2

3.7 Consider the positional servomechanism shown in Fig. P3.7. Assume that the input to the system is reference shaft position θ_R and the system output is the load shaft position θ_L. Draw a block diagram of the system indicating the transfer function of each block. Simplify the block diagram to obtain $\theta_L(s)/\theta_R(s)$. The parameters of the system are given below.

Sensitivity of error detector	$K_P = 10$ volts/rad
Amplifier gain	$K_A = 50$ volts/volt
Motor field resistance	$R_f = 100$ ohms
Motor field inductance	$L_f = 20$ henrys
Motor torque constant	$K_T = 10$ Newton-m/amp
Moment of inertia of load	$J_L = 250$ kg-m^2
Coefficient of viscous friction of load	$B_L = 2500$ Newton-m/(rad/sec)
Motor to load gear ratio	$\dot{\theta}_L/\dot{\theta}_M = 1/50$
Load to potentiometer gear ratio	$\dot{\theta}_P/\dot{\theta}_L = 1$

Motor inertia and friction are negligible.

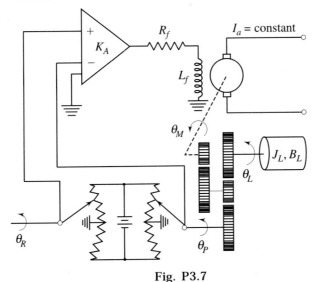

Fig. P3.7

3.8 Consider the system shown in Fig. P3.8a. The characteristic of ac motor is shown in Fig. P3.8b. The moment of inertia of the motor is $J_M = 0.003$ N-m/(rad/sec^2). The motor drives a load through a gear train. N_1, N_2, N_3, and N_4 are the number of teeth with $N_1/N_2 = 1/2$ and $N_3/N_4 = 1/5$. The moment of inertia of the load is $J_L = 0.02$ N-m/(rad/sec^2), and coefficient of viscous friction of the load is $B_L = 0.001$ N-m/(rad/sec). Find the transfer function $\theta_L(s)/E_c(s)$.

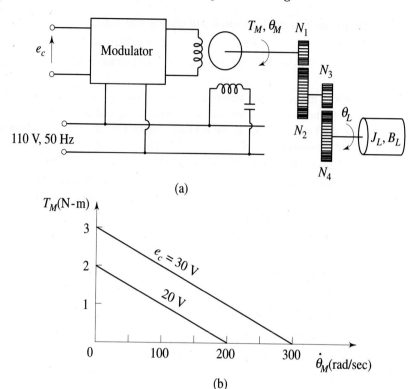

(a)

(b)

Fig. P3.8

3.9 Consider the system shown in Fig. P3.9 with R_a = 10 Ω, L_a = 0.1H, K_b = 1 volt/(rad/sec), $\dot{\theta}_L/\dot{\theta}_M$ = 1/2, K_t = 0.8 volt/(rad/sec), K_P = 1.5 volt/rad. Moment of inertia of load, J_L = 2 N-m/(rad/sec^2).
Moment of inertia of motor shaft, J_M = 0.1 N-m/(rad/sec^2).
Coefficient of viscous friction of load, B_L = 0.02 N-m/(rad/sec).
Coefficient of viscous friction on motor shaft, B_M = 0.01 N-m/(rad/sec)

 (i) Find the transfer function $\theta_M(s)/E_a(s)$
 (ii) A multi-loop (consisting of a speed-feedback loop and a position-feedback loop) feedback control system built around the system of Fig. P3.9 with suitable additional hardware drives the load to the commanded position θ_R inspite of load torque disturbances.
     Make a sketch of the feedback control system showing how the hardware is connected.
 (iii) What will be the effect of opening the position feedback loop on the performance of the control system?
 (iv) What will be the effect of opening the speed feedback loop on the performance of the control system?

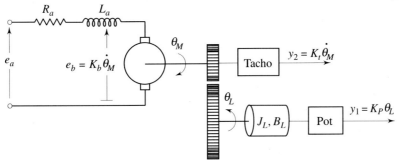

Fig. P3.9

(Since tachometers tend to be noisy at low speeds, in a geared system one usually puts the tacho on the motor, rather than the load)

3.10 The schematic diagram of a servo system is shown in Fig. P3.10. The two-phase servomotor develops a torque in accordance with the equation

$$T_M = K_1 e_c - K_2 \dot{\theta}_M$$

where

$$K_1 = 1 \times 10^{-5} \text{ N-m/volt}; \quad K_2 = 0.25 \times 10^{-5} \text{ N-m/(rad/sec)}$$

The other parameters of the system are:

Synchro sensitivity $K_s = 1$ volt/rad
Amplifier gain $K_A = 20$ volt/volt
Tachometer constant $K_t = 0.2$ volt/(rad/sec)
Load inertia $J_L = 1.5 \times 10^{-5}$ kg-m^2
Viscous friction $B_L = 1 \times 10^{-5}$ N-m/(rad/sec)

$$\dot{\theta}_M / \dot{\theta}_S = 1; \quad \dot{\theta}_M / \dot{\theta}_T = 1$$

Motor inertia and friction are negligible.

Draw the block diagram of the system and therefrom obtain the transfer function $\theta_M(s) / \theta_R(s)$.

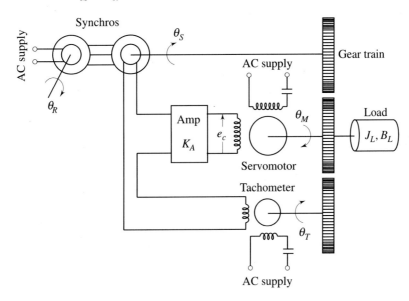

Fig. P3.10

3.11 An ac-dc servo system is shown in Fig. P3.11. The sensitivity of the synchro
error detector is K_s volt/rad, and the gain of the generator is K_g volts/field amp.
The dc motor is separately excited and has a back emf of K_b volts/(rad/sec) and
a torque constant of K_T N-m/amp. Motor inertia and friction are negligible.
Draw the block diagram of the system indicating the transfer function of each
block. Obtain $\theta_L(s)/\theta_R(s)$.

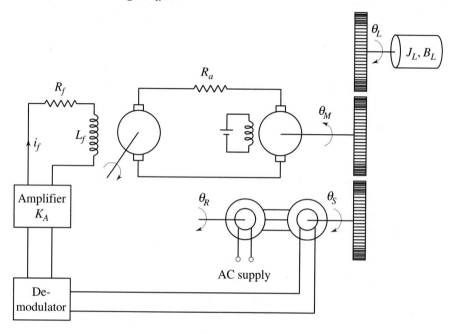

Fig. P3.11

The system parameters are given below:

K_s = 30 volts/rad;	K_A = 5 volts/volt;	R_f = 100 ohms;
L_f = 2 henrys;	K_g = 100 volts/field amp;	R_a = 1 ohm;
K_b = 1 volt/(rad/sec);	J_L = 0.5 kg-m^2	B_L = 1 N-m/(rad/sec);

$\dot\theta_L/\dot\theta_M = \dot\theta_S/\dot\theta_M = 1$

3.12 Figure P3.12 shows a closed-loop drive system. The desired speed ω_r is set
on a potentiometer which provides the reference voltage e_r. The parameters
describing the system are given below:

$$R_a = 6\,\Omega, \qquad\qquad L_a = 46\,\text{mH}$$
$$J = 0.093\,\text{kg-m}^2, \qquad B = 0.008\,\text{N-m/(rad/sec)}$$

Motor torque constant $\qquad\qquad K_T$ = 0.55 N-m/amp
Thyristor rectifier gain constant $\quad K_r$ = 25
Amplifier gain $\qquad\qquad\qquad\quad K_A$ = 20
Tachometer sensitivity $\qquad\qquad K_t$ = 0.057 volts/(rad/sec)

(a) Draw a block diagram of the system that includes transfer functions of
all the sub-systems, and therefrom obtain $\omega(s)/E_r(s)$.

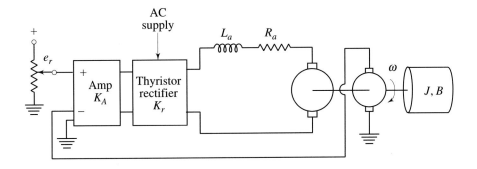

Fig. P3.12

(b) The thyristorized drives are usually provided with a current-limiting feature to prevent damage to the thyristors. Modify the drive system of Fig. P3.12 to implement the current limit. Draw a block diagram of the proposed system.

3.13 A dc position control servomechanism comprises of a split-field dc servomotor with constant armature current, potentiometer error detector with sensitivity K_P volts/rad, and a dc amplifier of gain K_A amps/volts. The motor produces a torque of K_T N-m/amp. Separate motor and load inertias J_M (kg-m^2) and J_L (kg-m^2) are identified, and the connecting structure is modelled by a shaft with spring constant K (N-m/rad) and damping coefficient B (N-m per rad/sec). A load disturbance T_w (N-m) acts on J_L opposite the developed motor torque T_M (N-m). T_M accelerates J_M and supplies the torque transmitted by the shaft. This shaft torque, in turn, accelerates J_L and supplies T_w.

Motor field time-constant is assumed to be negligible.

(a) Make a sketch of the system showing how the hardware is connected.
(b) Determine the transfer functions $\theta_L(s)/\theta_R(s)$ and $\theta_L(s)/T_w(s)$, where θ_L (rad) and θ_R (rad) are, respectively, the actual and commanded load positions.

3.14 The electrohydraulic position control system shown in Fig. P3.14 positions a mass M with negligible friction. Assume that rate of oil flow in the power cylinder is $q = K_1 x - K_2 \Delta p$ where x is the displacement of the spool and Δp is the differential pressure across the power piston. Draw a block diagram of the system and obtain therefrom the transfer function $Y(s)/R(s)$.

The system constants are given below.

Mass $M = 1000\,\text{kg}$

Constants of the hydraulic actuator:

$K_1 = 200\ \text{cm}^2/\text{sec per cm of spool displacement}$

$K_2 = 0.5\ \text{cm}^2/\text{sec per gm-wt/cm}^2$

Potentiometer sensitivity $K_P = 1\ \text{volt/cm}$

Power amplifier gain $K_A = 500\ \text{mA/volt}$

Linear transducer constant $K = 0.1\ \text{cm/mA}$

Piston area $A = 100\ \text{cm}^2$

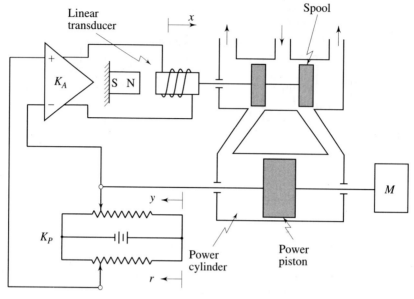

Fig. P3.14

3.15 The conceptual design of a hydraulic control system for machining a workpiece on a lathe is shown in the schematic diagram of Fig. P3.15. The control system is a servomechanism, where the actual tool position $y(t)$ is required to follow a time-varying command input position $y_r(t)$. The command input $y_r(t)$ may be generated by a punched-tape reader. The input device produces a voltage $e_r = K_r\,y_r$. The carriage is moved at a constant speed and the control of the tool position is in the direction of the cross slide.

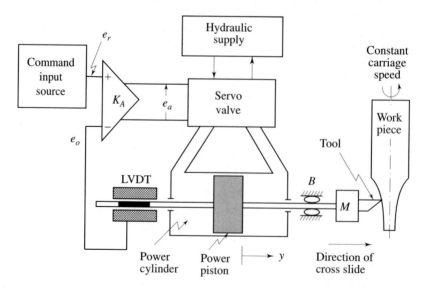

Fig. P3.15

The LVDT provides a feedback voltage $e_o(t)$ proportional to the actual tool position ($e_o(t) = K_s y(t)$, K_s is a constant). The error ($e_r - e_o$) is amplified by an amplifier of gain K_A volts/volt. The servovalve regulates the spool displacement and hence controls port opening x; $x = K_v e_a$, where K_v is the valve gain. The rate of oil flow in the power cylinder is $q = K_1 x - K_2 \Delta p$, where Δp is the differential pressure across the piston of area A, and K_1 and K_2 are constants.

The load on the piston consists of mass M and viscous friction with coefficient B. Treat the reactive force F_w of the cutting tool as a disturbance. Assuming all the variables to be deviations from an equilibrium position, draw a functional block diagram that describes perturbation dynamics of the system. Derive the transfer function $Y(s)/E_r(s)$.

3.16 A hydraulic servo system used to control the transverse feed of a machine tool is shown in Fig. P3.16. Each angular position of the cam corresponds to a desired reference position y_r such that $x = K_r y_r$. The load on the piston is that due to tool reactive force and may be assumed to consist of mass M, friction B and spring with constant K. Draw a block diagram and obtain therefrom the transfer function $Y(s)/Y_r(s)$, assuming that rate of oil flow in the power cylinder is $q = K_1 e - K_2 \Delta p$, where K_1 and K_2 are constants and Δp is the differential pressure across the power piston of area A.

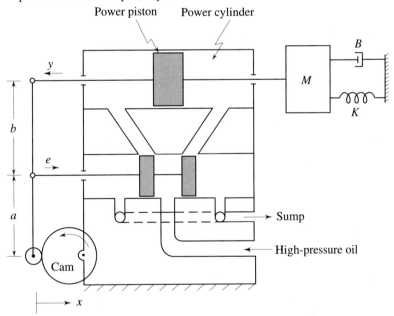

Fig. P3.16

3.17 The schematic diagram of a steel-rolling process is shown in Fig. P3.17. The steel plate is fed through rollers at a constant speed of v cm/sec. The distance between the rollers and the point where the thickness is measured is d cm. The thickness gauge provides a feedback voltage $e_o(t)$ proportional to the actual thickness $y(t)$ of the plate ($e_o(t) = K_s\, y(t)$; K_s is a constant). A voltage e_r corresponding to the desired thickness is the reference input to the system. The error ($e_r - e_o$) is amplified by an amplifier of gain K_A amps/volt. The servo valve regulates the spool displacement and hence controls port opening x; $x = K_v i$, where K_v is the valve gain. The rate of oil flow in the power cylinder is $q = K_1 x - K_2 \Delta p$ where Δp is the differential pressure across the piston of area A, and K_1 and K_2 are constants.

The load on the piston is that of the roller mass M and viscous friction with coefficient B. Normal force F_w on the roller is a load disturbance.

Assuming all the variables to be deviations from an equilibrium position, draw a functional block diagram that describes perturbation dynamics of the system. Derive the transfer function $Y(s)/E_r(s)$.

3.18 Consider the two-tank system shown in Fig. P3.18. The height h_2 in the second tank is to be controlled by adjusting the flow rate q_1 into the first tank. The system disturbance is the flow rate q_w drawn off from the first tank (to be used elsewhere in the processing operation) by a variable displacement pump.

The command signal h_r for the desired height in tank 2 is set on a pot whose output is $e_r = K_s h_r$. The sensor output is $e_o = K_s h_2$. The differential amplifier has a gain K_a, the electropneumatic transducer has a gain K_e, and the pneumatic control valve (pneumatic actuator + flow control valve) has a gain K_v. At the initial equilibrium point, the inflow rate exactly matches the outflow rates, and the heights in the two tanks are $\overline{H}_1$ and $\overline{H}_2$ with $h_2 = h_r = 0$. A_1 is the surface area of tank 1, and R_1 is the resistance to flow offered by the valve in the outflow path (R = incremental change in pressure across the valve/ incremental change in flow through the valve). A_2 and R_2 are the corresponding values for tank 2.

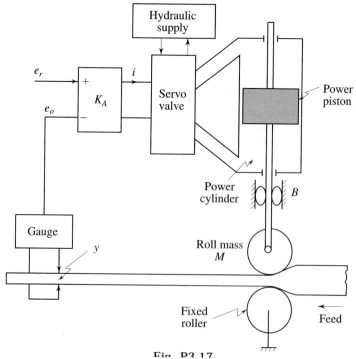

Fig. P3.17

Draw a functional block diagram of the system and therefrom derive the transfer function between h_2 and h_r.

3.19 A system to control the temperature of an oven chamber is shown in Fig. P3.19. The temperature θ is sensed by a thermocouple whose output is $K_t\theta_2$. The desired temperature θ_r is set on a pot whose output is e_r. The differential amplifier generates a signal e_A which controls the electrical resistance heater through an SCR amplifier and gives rise to heat flow at the rate $h = K_h e_A$ to the oven chamber. Heat also flows out of the oven due to imperfect insulation of its walls. The temperature of the ambient air is θ_a. Thermal capacitance of the medium inside the chamber is C_t and thermal resistance of the wall material is R_t. Thermal capacitances of the heater and wall are negligible.

Assuming all the variables are deviations from the equilibrium, obtain a block diagram model of the system that includes the transfer functions of all the sub-systems. Derive the transfer function $\theta(s)/E_r(s)$.

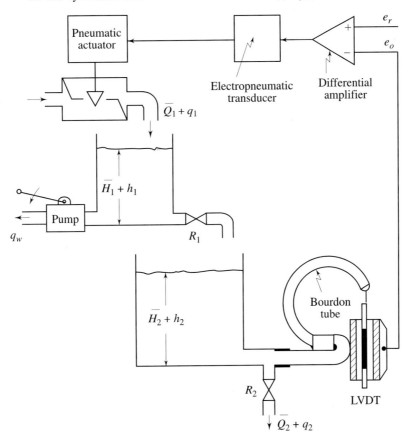

Fig. P3.18

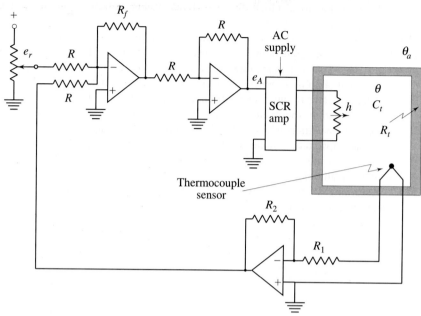

Fig. P3.19

3.20 In a heating system, air flows at constant volumetric flow rate Q into and out of a chamber of volume V. The density of the inflowing air is ρ, specific heat c, and temperature θ_i.

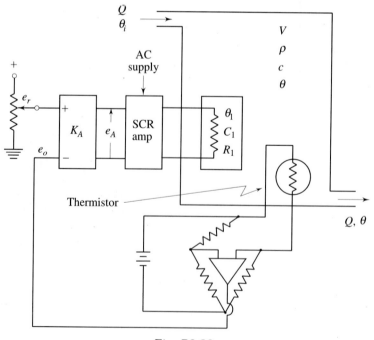

Fig. P3.20

A system to control the outflow temperature is shown in Fig. P3.20. The temperature θ is sensed by a thermistor with a Wheatstone bridge whose output $e_o = K_2\theta$. The desired temperature θ_r is set on a pot whose output $e_r = K_P\theta_r$. The differential amplifier generates a signal e_A which controls electrical resistance heater through an SCR amplifier and gives rise to heat flow at the rate $h = K_h e_A$. The heater has temperature θ_1, thermal capacitance C_1, and thermal resistance R_1. The walls of the chamber are perfectly insulated and have negligible thermal capacitance.

Assume that the variables $\{\theta_r, \theta, \theta_1, \theta_i\}$ are deviations from the equilibrium position. Considering θ_i as the disturbance, draw a functional block diagram of the system that includes the transfer functions of all the sub-systems. Derive the transfer functions $\theta(s)/\theta_r(s)$, and $\theta(s)/\theta_i(s)$.

3.21 Consider the unit shown in Fig. P3.21. The objective of this unit is to cool a hot process fluid of density ρ_2 and heat capacity c_2, flowing at a rate Q_2; the temperature of the inflowing process fluid is $\overline{\theta}_{i2} + \theta_{i2}$

The cooling medium (water) having density ρ_1 and heat capacity c_1 is circulated through the jacket at the rate $(\overline{Q}_1 + q_1)$, the temperature of the inflowing cooling water is $\overline{\theta}_{i1} + \theta_{i1}$. It is assumed that the jacketed tank is well-insulated.

Write the unsteady-state energy balance equations on the process fluid with temperature $(\overline{\theta}_2 + \theta_2)$, and on the cooling water with temperature $(\overline{\theta}_1 + \theta_1)$. Linearize these equations about the operating point $\{\overline{Q}_2, \overline{\theta}_{i2}, \overline{\theta}_{i1}, \overline{Q}_1, \overline{\theta}_1, \overline{\theta}_2\}$.

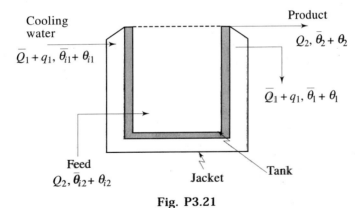

Fig. P3.21

The control hardware required to control the temperature of the process stream consists of the following components:

        Sensor (temperature to voltage): gain K_1
        Reference signal generator (temperature to voltage): gain K_1
        Amplifier (voltage to voltage): gain K_2
        Converter (voltage to pressure): gain K_3
        Control valve (pressure to flow rate): gain K_4
q_1 is the manipulated variable, θ_{i1} and θ_{i2} are the disturbance variables, θ_2 is

the output variable, and θ_r represents the desired change in the initial setting of the output variable.

   (i) Suggest suitable hardware and make a sketch of the system showing how the hardware is connected.

  (ii) Draw a functional block diagram of the system that includes the transfer functions of all the sub-systems.

 (iii) Derive the transfer function $\theta_2(s)/\theta_r(s)$.

Given: $\rho_2 = 19.2$ kg-mole/m^3; $c_2 = 1.815 \times 10^5$ J/kg-moles-°C;

         $\rho_1 = 1000$ kg/m^3; $c_1 = 4184$ J/kg-°C

         $V_2 = $ volume of the tank $= 7.08$ m^3

         $A = $ heat transfer area $= 5.4$ m^2

         $U = $ average convective heat transfer coefficient

          $= 3550$ J/sec-m^2-°C

         $V_1 = $ volume of the jacket $= 1.82$ m^3

Design conditions:

         $Q_2 = 7.5 \times 10^{-3}$ m^3/sec;

         $\bar{\theta}_{i2} = 66$ °C; $\bar{\theta}_2 = 55$ °C;

         $\bar{\theta}_{i1} = 27$ °C

3.22 Reconsider the system of Fig. P3.21. The simplest control strategy to handle disturbances satisfactorily is to measure the tank temperature, compare it with the reference value and adjust the control valve on the cooling water inlet stream to eliminate the error.

    For fast control action, a feedback controller for the jacket temperature with its set-point determined by the feedback controller for the tank temperature could be added to provide cascade control. The two feedback control loops are nested, with the jacket-temperature control loop (secondary control loop) located inside the tank-temperature control loop (primary control loop). Suggest suitable hardware and make a sketch showing how the hardware is connected to implement the cascade control scheme.

chapter 4

Basic Principles of Feedback Control

4.1 ## INTRODUCTION

Although a detailed exploration of the possibilities and problems of feedback control will mostly occupy the rest of this text, some essential characteristics can be illustrated quite easily to give a helpful preview of the forthcoming developments.

Recall the basic feedback system block diagram defined in Chapter 3 and shown in abridged form as Fig. 4.1a. When we speak of a controller $D(s)$, our concern is mainly with the *information handling devices*; the sources of information are the reference input $r(t)$ which is derived from the command $y_r(t)$, and the feedback signal $b(t)$ which is produced by the feedback path elements $H(s)$ from the controlled output $y(t)$. The *power handling devices*—actuators and the controlled process itself—are represented by $G(s)$ in the block diagram of Fig. 4.1a. $N(s)$ is the plant transfer function from the disturbance input $w(t)$ to the output $y(t)$.

The controller $D(s)$ is designed to act on the actuating error signal $\hat{e}(t) = r(t) - b(t)$ to produce the control signal $u(t)$. The control logic that is physically implemented for this purpose is the *control law* or *control action*.

A non-zero system error $e(t) = y_r(t) - y(t)$ results from either a change in command or a disturbance. The general function of the controller is to keep the controlled variable near its desired value. Since we never know the numerical values of the parameters of the controlled process with true certainty, and some controller designs can be more sensitive to such parameter variations than others, a parameter sensitivity specification might also be included. In this chapter, we will demonstrate that by using feedback control configuration of the form shown in Fig. 4.1a, we can meet these control requirements.

A special case of feedback systems which is of particular interest arises when $H(s) = 1$ (Fig. 4.1b) and is often referred to as a *unity-feedback system*. The reference input $r(t)$, in this case, is equal to the commanded value of the controlled output. It may be noted that a system's block diagram may not appear to be of unity-feedback form when initially derived. It is often possible and convenient to manipulate the block diagram into a unity-feedback model where the system error appears explicitly as the actuating signal.

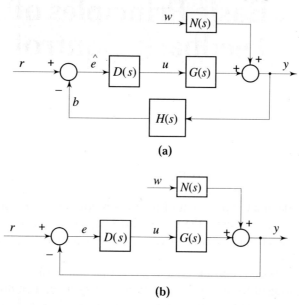

(a)

(b)

Fig. 4.1   *(a) A nonunity feedback system (b) A unity feedback system*

An important aspect of feedback control covered in this chapter is the characteristics of various commonly used modes of control. By *mode of control* we mean the nature of behaviour of the controller $D(s)$ in the general system diagrams of Fig. 4.1. The basic modes of control are:

   (i) on-off control;
  (ii) proportional control;
 (iii) integral control; and
 (iv) derivative control.

In the control system field, on–off controls are generally the simplest possible from a hardware point of view. This class of controllers have only two fixed states rather than a continuous output; the fixed states are, in many cases, simply on and off. In its wider application, the states of an on-off controller may not be simply on and off however, but could represent any two values of a control variable. Figure 4.2 shows a unity-feedback system with an on-off controller (refer Example 1.4). Oscillatory behaviour is a typical response characteristic of a system under two-portion control. Refer [180] for details.

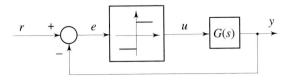

Fig. 4.2 *An on-off controller in a control loop*

For a controller with proportional control mode, the relationship between the control variable $u(t)$ and the error signal $e(t)$ is

$$u(t) = K_c\, e(t) \tag{4.1a}$$

or $\qquad U(s) = K_c\, E(s) \tag{4.1b}$

where K_c is the *controller gain*.

Whatever the actual mechanism may be and whatever the form of operating power, the proportional controller is essentially an amplifier with an adjustable gain. A block diagram of such a controller is shown in Fig. 4.3a.

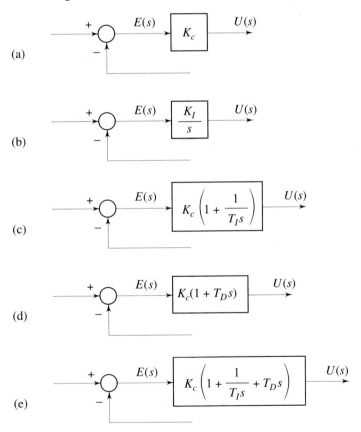

Fig. 4.3 *(a) Proportional control (b) Integral control (c) PI control (d) PD control (e) PID control*

In the integral control mode, also called the *reset control*, the change in the control signal is proportional to the integral of the error:

$$u(t) = K_I \int_0^t e(t)dt \qquad (4.2a)$$

or

$$U(s) = \frac{K_I}{s} E(s) \qquad (4.2b)$$

where K_I is the *integral gain*.

Figure 4.3b shows the block diagram of such a controller.

Integral control can be used by itself or in combination with other control modes; indeed *proportional plus integral* (PI) control is the most common mode. The control action of a PI controller is defined by the following equations:

$$U(s) = K_c E(s) + \frac{K_I}{s} E(s)$$

$$= K_c \left(1 + \frac{1}{T_I s} \right) E(s) \qquad (4.3a)$$

$$u(t) = K_c \left[e(t) + \frac{1}{T_I} \int_0^t e(t)dt \right] \qquad (4.3b)$$

where T_I is the *integral* or *reset time*.

Figure 4.3c shows the block diagram of a PI controller.

The derivative control mode, also called the *rate control*, is described by the following equations:

$$u(t) = K_D \frac{d}{dt} e(t) \qquad (4.4a)$$

or

$$U(s) = K_D s E(s) \qquad (4.4b)$$

where K_D is the *derivative gain*.

Derivative control mode is normally not used alone; this is because the control produces no corrective effort for any constant error and would therefore allow uncontrolled steady-state errors. A combination of proportional and derivative controls is a practical mode of control for industrial processes. The control action of a *proportional plus derivative* (PD) controller is defined by the following equations:

$$U(s) = K_c E(s) + K_D s E(s)$$
$$= K_c (1 + T_D s) E(s) \qquad (4.5a)$$

$$u(t) = K_c \left[e(t) + T_D \frac{de(t)}{dt} \right] \qquad (4.5b)$$

where T_D is the *derivative* or *rate time*.

Figure 4.3d shows the block diagram of a PD controller.

A combination of the three basic modes—proportional, integral and derivative—results in a *proportional plus integral plus derivative* (PID) controller described by the following equations:

$$U(s) = K_c\left(1 + \frac{1}{T_I s} + T_D s\right)E(s) \tag{4.6a}$$

$$u(t) = K_c\left[e(t) + \frac{1}{T_I}\int_0^t e(t)dt + T_D\frac{de(t)}{dt}\right] \tag{4.6b}$$

Figure 4.3e shows the block diagram of such a controller.

In the block diagrams of Fig. 4.3, the controller is in the forward path and therefore the control actions are based on the error signal. This, however, is not a restriction. The PID control actions may be taken on controlled output variable/state variables; many a times to advantage , as we shall see in this chapter. The resulting *multiloop* (loop within a loop) *control configuration* is known in the literature as *cascade control/state variable feedback control*.

In this chapter, we will also study the basic characteristics of feedforward-feedback control configurations, and the control of multivariable systems.

4.2 THE CONTROL OBJECTIVES

In this section, we describe a control problem in general terms. Given a plant, which cannot be altered by the designer, with the following variables associated with it (Fig. 4.4):

1. A controlled variable $y(t)$, which is the variable we wish to control.
2. A command variable $y_r(t)$ which represents the prescribed value of the controlled variable.
3. An observed variable $y_s(t)$ which is measured by means of a sensor and which is used to obtain information about the plant during operation; the observed variable is usually contaminated with observation noise $v(t)$.
4. A disturbance variable $w(t)$ which influences the plant but which cannot be manipulated.
5. A control variable $u(t)$ which influences the plant and which can be manipulated.

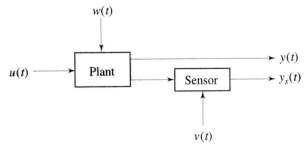

Fig. 4.4 *The plant of a control system*

The *control problem* is roughly described below.

For a given command variable, find an appropriate input $u(t)$ so that the controlled variable follows the command variable:

$$y(t) \cong y_r(t); \; t \geq t_0$$

where t_0 is the time at which the control starts.

An important class of control problems consists of those problems where the command variable is constant over long periods of time; the control objective is to force the controlled variable to reach the commanded value quickly and to maintain the controlled variable at that value thereafter. The duration of the transient period of control, which starts at the beginning of the control process and terminates when the controlled variable approximately reaches its prescribed value, will be referred to as the *settling time*. The lower the settling time, the higher the *speed of response* of the process. The *steady-state accuracy* (negligible error between the controlled output and command input during steady-state period of control) is of critical importance in control systems.

In designing control systems, the following aspects must be taken into account.

1. Stability   Roughly speaking, stability in a system implies that small changes in reference inputs, disturbance inputs, and/or initial conditions do not result in large changes in the system output. Stability is a very important property of control systems. Almost every working system is designed to be stable; we seek to improve the speed of response, steady-state accuracy, and other aspects of system performance within the constraints imposed by stability considerations. Analytical study of stability will be taken up in Chapter 5.

Feedback control systems are prone to instability. For a stable plant, the closed-loop system may not be always stable. Feedback control system design may therefore demand a trade off between the accuracy in realizing control objectives and the stability.

2. Input Amplitude Constraints   For a control system designed according to linear theory and methods, it is essential that the devices used in the system operate in linear fashion under various operating conditions. If under certain circumstances, the devices are driven into the region of nonlinear characteristics, linear design theory may describe only approximately, or quite often may give a completely erroneous prediction of the system performance. Excessive large magnitudes of signals at various levels in a control system can drive the devices into the nonlinear region of operation. Some examples are: torque-speed curves of motors, synchro error detectors, process control valves, hydraulic servovalves, amplifiers, gears, dampers, etc. The requirement of linear operation of devices under various operating conditions imposes a constraint on the range of values over which the plant input $u(t)$ is allowed to vary. As will be seen, this constraint is of major importance and prevents us from obtaining perfect command-following systems.

3. Disturbance Rejection   External disturbances $w(t)$ influence the plant in an unpredictable way. They are typically the uncontrolled variations in the load on a system. In systems controlling mechanical motions, load disturbances may represent forces, e.g., wind gusts on a stabilized antenna, waves on a ship, variations in payload of a robot manipulator, etc. In voltage regulating systems, variations in electrical load is a major source of disturbances. In thermal systems, the load disturbances may be caused by variations in surrounding temperature. In fluid systems, the load disturbances may result from variations in feed flow or variations in demanded flow.

Load disturbances typically vary slowly. As we shall see later in this chapter, the errors due to load disturbances tend to be corrected by proper design of feedback control.

4. Noise Filtering   Excitation of the plant by high-frequency measurement-error signals (observation noise) $v(t)$, entering through the sensors of the controlled variable, influences the plant in an unpredictable way. In systems controlling mechanical motions, mechanical vibrations may lead to high-frequency components in the output signals of position and speed sensors. Continuous stirring of fluid in tank reactors gives rise to noise in output signals of thermocouple or other temperature sensors.

Feedback control depends virtually on accurate measurement of controlled variables, because the feedback action has little correcting effect for the wrong information given by the sensors. The character of the measurement errors often depends on filtering in the instruments. Effects of measurement errors on control system performance can therefore be reduced by examining the instrument and modifying the filtering so that it satisfies the requirements of the particular control problem.

5. Sensitivity and Robustness   Robustness is an important concern in control system design. We will briefly discuss two aspects of the robustness problem.

The first aspect arises because every control system is designed on the basis of necessarily approximate model of the plant. Since the success of the analytical approach of design is heavily dependent on the simplicity of the mathematical model, many idealizing assumptions are usually made which lead to uncertainties not only in the parameters of the model but also in the model structure—using a linear model for an intrinsically nonlinear process is an example of deviation in model structure; omitting certain time lags in order to obtain a reduced-order model is another example. The question arises: will the physical system have a performance that is sufficiently close to the performance predicted by the idealized model? For example, if the linear model is stable, will the physical system, which in fact is a small perturbation (possibly nonlinear) from the linear model, still be stable?

The second aspect of the robustness appears in the following manner: the design is based on the (idealized) model which characterizes a number of nominal properties of the plant. Once the controller is implemented and the controlled plant is operating in the field, the properties of the physical system differ from the nominal properties because of environment effects, wear, aging, and other natural factors. So the question is: what is the effect of all such time dependent deviations from nominal values on the performance of the physical system in the field? Such questions can be studied by calculating the effect on the system performance due to changes in design parameters and exogenous disturbances. It is a fact that some designs, which perform nominally per- fectly, are totally inadequate in the field because they are too sensitive to small perturbations in some of their parameters.

In the course of this text, we will discuss from time to time these questions of *robustness*.

The effect of differentially small deviations in the parameters of a model of known structure can be studied using *sensitivity* analysis. The motivation for sensitivity analysis is given by the practical experience that parameters often drift during the operation of the system in the field, but they typically remain in the vicinity of their nominal values. It is interesting to know whether such parameter variations cause severe changes of the system behaviour or have merely a minor influence on the important system properties.

For the analysis, the system behaviour is characterized by some specific measure, e.g., speed of response; or even by some characteristic function such as the frequency response of the closed-loop system. For the sake of simplicity of representation, we take J as the performance measure characterizing the system behaviour, which depends on parameter θ in addition to other param- eters. Consider perturbation only in the parameter θ. For the nominal parameter θ_n, we get the nominal value of the performance measure as $J_n = J(\theta_n)$.

Parameter changes $\Delta\theta$ induce changes ΔJ in the performance measure. Hence, instead of J_n, we get the new value $J_n + \Delta J = J(\theta_n + \Delta\theta)$.

Taylor's series expansion of $J(\theta)$ about the nominal point θ_n yields (assuming that the function is differentiable):

$$J(\theta_n + \Delta\theta) = J(\theta_n) + \left.\frac{\partial J(\theta)}{\partial \theta}\right|_{\theta = \theta_n} \Delta\theta + \cdots$$

If we restrict our attention to terms of atmost first order, we get

$$\Delta J = \left.\frac{\partial J(\theta)}{\partial \theta}\right|_{\theta = \theta_n} \Delta\theta$$

Expressing deviations in terms of relative changes, we obtain

$$\frac{\Delta J}{J_n} = \frac{\Delta\theta}{\theta_n}\left[\left(\left.\frac{\partial J(\theta)}{\partial \theta}\right|_{\theta = \theta_n}\right)\frac{\theta_n}{J_n}\right]$$

System sensitivity to parameter θ is defined as the ratio of the percentage change in the system performance measure J from its nominal value to the percentage change in the parameter. S_θ^J denotes the sensitivity of J with respect to θ and is given by

$$S_\theta^J = \frac{\Delta J / J_n}{\Delta \theta / \theta_n} = \left[\frac{\partial J(\theta)}{\partial \theta} \bigg|_{\theta = \theta_n} \right] \frac{\theta_n}{J_n} \qquad (4.7)$$

If $S_\theta^J = 0$, then the measure J is insensitive to the parameter θ at the nominal point θ_n. If $S_\theta^J \neq 0$, then J is sensitive and the value of S_θ^J is a measure of the degree of dependence of J on θ.

A plausible interpretation of the sensitivity function is shown in Fig. 4.5. Here we treat the relative change in the parameter θ, $\Delta\theta/\theta_n$, as an input to the process modelled by the sensitivity function with the output being the relative change in the system performance measure, $\Delta J/J_n$.

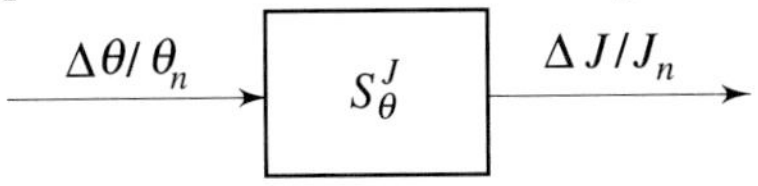

Fig. 4.5   *Interpretation of sensitivity function as a gain function*

Note that sensitivity function deals with infinitesimally small parameter perturbations near a given nominal parameter value and does not refer to the amount of perturbation. Experience on use of such functions, however, shows that sensitivity function is a reasonable characteristic of the effects of small rather than infinitesimally small perturbations.

As we shall see later in this chapter, the errors due to parameter variations tend to be corrected by the proper design of feedback control.   ▲▲

The next section will demonstrate that feedback control can

(i)   force the controlled variable to accurately follow its prescribed value in steady-state;

(ii) shape the dynamics of the controlled variable;

(iii) greatly reduce the effect on the controlled variable of all external disturbances except those associated with the sensor; and

(iv) make the system tolerant of variations in hardware parameters other than those of the sensor.

The use of feedback is motivated by the presence of external disturbances and model uncertainties. More strictly, the use of feedback can be regarded as unreasonable if there is no uncertainty in the system because, for the unperturbed system, open-loop control may produce the same or probably better result.

*Example 4.1*_____

In the following, we review the control objectives of heat-exchanger control system discussed in Chapter 1 (Fig. 1.18). A sketch of the exchanger is given in Fig. 4.6a.

The objective is to maintain the outlet temperature of the process fluid, $\theta(t)$ °C, at its desired value or set point, θ_r°C, in the presence of disturbances in the process fluid flow, $q_m(t)$ kg/sec ($= Q\rho$; Q m³/sec is the volumetric fluid flow and ρ kg/m³ is the fluid density), flowing inside the tubes of the heat exchanger, and inlet temperature $\theta_i(t)$ °C. The steam flow, $q_{ms}(t)$ kg/sec, con-

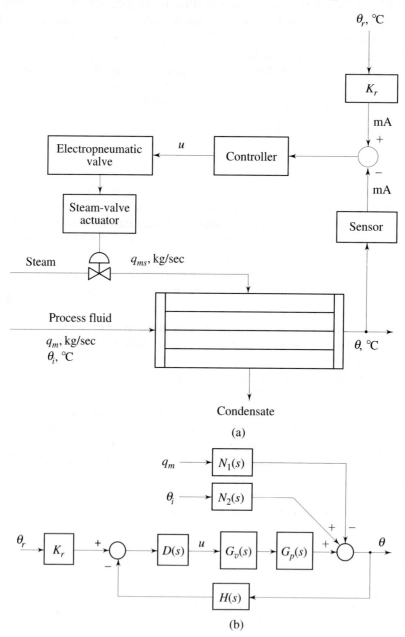

Fig. 4.6   *Heat exchanger control loop*

densing on the outside of the tubes, is the variable that can be adjusted to control the outlet temperature as it determines the amount of energy supplied to the process fluid. In addition to counteracting the effects of disturbances, the control system will be called upon to follow the commands for change in the outlet temperature of the process fluid.

The first step in the design is the selection of the temperature sensor and steam-valve actuator. For temperature measurement, we select an intelligent sensor which has, in addition to the basic device such as thermocouple, a signal processing circuit which takes the output from the thermocouple and converts it to a current signal that is proportional to the temperature. The signal processing circuit includes an amplifier and a filter. For steam valve adjustments, we select a pneumatic actuator which can provide large output power. Since the valve actuator must be operated by air pressure and the sensor generates electric current signals, a current to pressure transducer is also required in the feedback loop.

The feedback control scheme works as follows: the measured controlled variable is compared with the set-point; K_r in Fig. 4.6a represents the conversion of set-point scale. The controller generates a control signal, $u(t)$, on the basis of the difference between the measurement and set-point. The control signal is then connected to the pneumatic actuator of the steam valve through an electropneumatic device—a current to pressure transducer. The function of the valve actuator is to position the valve in proportion to the control signal. The steam flow is then a function of the valve position.

Once the hardware is chosen, the remainder of the design is concerned with trying to make the best use of the process. If the design is to be carried out analytically, a transfer function description of the feedback system must be found. Figure 4.6b shows the block diagram of the entire feedback loop. We now find the transfer function model of each block. Let us start with the heat exchanger.

As shown in Fig. 4.6b, the heat exchanger consists of three blocks, one for each of its three inputs. $G_p(s)$ is the process transfer function relating the outlet temperature to the steam flow, $N_1(s)$ is the process transfer function relating the outlet temperature to disturbance in process fluid flow and $N_2(s)$ is the process transfer function to disturbance in inlet temperature.

The following experimentally obtained parameters will be used in developing a model of the feedback system.

The exchanger response to the steam flow has a gain of 50 °C/(kg/sec), and a time-constant of 30 sec. The exchanger response to the process fluid flow has a gain of 3 °C/(kg/sec), and to inlet temperature the gain is 1°C/ °C. Therefore

$$G_p(s) = \frac{50}{30s + 1} \; ; N_1(s) = \frac{3}{30s + 1} \; ; N_2(s) = \frac{1}{30s + 1}$$

The time-constant of the process depends on the residence time (tube volume/volumetric flow rate) of the fluid in the tubes. As a consequence, the time-constant may vary because of flow-rate fluctuations and fouling. Therefore, we should ascertain how sensitive the performance of the final system design will be to changes in the time-constant of the process.

The control valve has a maximum capacity of 1.6 kg/sec of steam, linear characteristics, and a time-constant of 3 sec. The nominal pressure range of the valve is 3 to 15 psig.

$$\text{Valve gain} = \frac{1.6(\text{kg/sec})}{(15-3)\text{psi}} = \frac{1.6}{12}(\text{kg/sec})/\text{psi}$$

The electropneumatic valve has a constant gain

$$\frac{\Delta P}{\Delta I} = \frac{(15-3)\text{psi}}{(20-4)\text{mA}} = \frac{12}{16}\text{psi/mA}$$

Including the constant gain of the current-to-pressure transducer in the control-valve transfer function, $G_v(s)$, we obtain

$$G_v(s) = \frac{0.1}{3s+1}$$

The sensor has a calibrated range of 50 to 150°C and a time-constant of 10 sec.

$$\text{Sensor gain} = \frac{16\,\text{mA}}{(150-50)°\text{C}} = 0.16\,\text{mA/°C}$$

The transfer function of the sensor is given by

$$H(s) = \frac{0.16}{10s+1}$$

The set-point scale factor

$$K_r = 0.16\ \text{mA/°C}$$

The block diagram of the temperature control loop, as initially proposed, is shown in Fig. 4.7. θ_r is the change in the set-point value from the initial setting

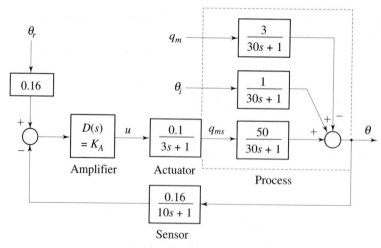

Fig. 4.7   *A model of a heat exachanger control loop*

$\overline{\theta}_r$, θ_i is the deviation in the process fluid temperature from the nominal value $\overline{\theta}_i$, q_m is the deviation in the process fluid flow from the nominal value $\overline{Q}_m$, θ is the deviation in the outlet temperature from the nominal value $\overline{\theta}$, and q_{ms} is the deviation in the steam flow rate from the nominal value $\overline{Q}_{ms}$ (refer to Review Example 4.2).

Example 4.2

Consider the problem of designing an attitude control system for a rigid satellite. Satellites usually require attitude control so that antennas, sensors, and solar panels are properly oriented. For example, antennas are usually pointed toward a particular location on earth, while solar panels need to be oriented toward the sun for maximum power generation.

The satellite will be subjected to a variety of disturbance torques from such sources as aerodynamic drag, solar pressure, gravity gradient torques, and the rotation of various satellite components, e.g., pumps, motors and antennas. It will be assumed that the vehicle has initially been aligned to the desired attitude. Due to the above mentioned disturbance torques, it will be necessary to provide a feedback control system in order to maintain the satellite very close to the desired attitude. In addition to counteracting the effects of the disturbance torques acting on the vehicle, the control system will be called upon to change the attitude, subject to commands received from ground stations.

In this example, we shall highlight the important physical aspects of the system, taking a number of liberties with the practical aspects so as to avoid undue complication which should tend to obscure our main objectives.

So long as the angular velocity and the error angles of the vehicle are small, angular motions about the three axes are essentially *uncoupled* and may be controlled independently. Thus, we may design each of the three attitude-control loops independently, which is an important simplification. Figure 4.8 depicts single-axis attitude control schematic, where motion is only allowed about the axis perpendicular to the page. The angle θ that describes the satellite orientation must be measured with respect to an 'inertial' reference, that is, a reference that has no angular acceleration. The control signal comes from the gas jets that produce a torque $T(t)(= F \times d)$ about the mass centre.

A block diagram of the control system, as initially proposed, is given in Fig. 4.9. The command signal θ_r rad, transmitted from earth, is converted to electrical form ($e_r = K_P \theta_r(t)$ volts) in the satellite. A sensor on the satellite measures the deviation θ rad; its output is a voltage equal to $K_P \theta(t)$. A difference amplifier provides the voltage $u(t)$ proportional to $\hat{e}(t)$: the difference of the voltages corresponding to the command signal and measured signal. The amplifier must provide sufficient power to actuate the gas jets. The gas jets exert a torque $T(t) = K_T u(t)$ about the mass centre. We have neglected the dynamics of the gas jets, assuming that the opening time is short compared to the important time-constants of the system.

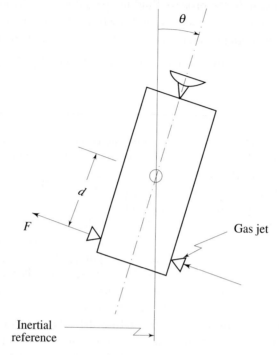

Fig. 4.8 *Satellite control schematic*

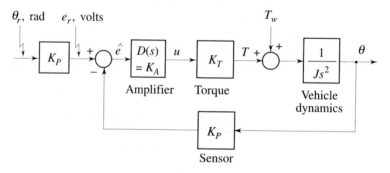

Fig. 4.9 *A model of a satellite attitude control system*

The vehicle dynamics are governed by the differential equation (assuming frictionless environment)

$$J\ddot{\theta} = T(t) + T_w(t)$$

where J is the moment of inertia about the axis of rotation, and the total torque is the sum of control torque and the disturbance torque. Although the moment of inertia will vary over the life of the satellite because of the consumption of fuel, it presumably changes very slowly compared with the response of the vehicle. Thus, we are justified in treating it as a constant but should ascertain how sensitive the performance of the final system design is to anticipated changes in *J*.

4.3 FEEDBACK CONTROL SYSTEM CHARACTERISTICS

Feedback systems play an important role in control engineering practice because the use of feedback can accomplish certain desirable results that would not be readily possible with an open-loop system. Some of the potential benefits (and liabilities) of feedback will be discussed in this section. Generally, the material presented here is applicable to any system whose mathematical model takes the form of a fixed linear feedback configuration. These occur not only in automatic control systems and electronic circuits, where the feedback is introduced by design, but also in much diverse fields as physiology, economics, ecology, etc., where feedback is inherent in the natural laws governing the process. However, consistent with the major thrust of this book, our terminology, convention, and illustrations will be taken in the context of control engineering.

System Sensitivity

A process represented by the transfer function $G(s)$, whatever its nature, is subject to modelling errors, changing environment, aging, and other natural factors that affect the control system performance. Consider the open-loop control system of Fig. 4.10. Assume that the controller $D_o(s)$ has been designed using a given transfer function model of the process, and it meets the specifications on the system output $y(t)$. Obviously, the output will approach the desired value only if the dynamical behaviour of the real process approaches that of its model. The modelling approximations and the process-behaviour changes with time during operation result in an inaccurate output. There is no provision within the system for supervision of the output and no mechanism is provided to correct the output. Consider now the closed-loop control system of Fig. 4.11. This system senses the change in the output through the feedback signal and attempts to correct the output. The feedback signal gives this system the capability to act as a self-correcting mechanism.

For simplicity, we assume that the structure and order of the process model are chosen exactly and they do not change with time. Then the differences

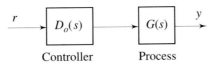

Fig. 4.10   *An open-loop control system*

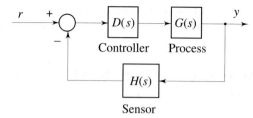

Fig. 4.11   *A closed-loop control system*

between the process model and the real process behaviour are manifested as *parameter errors*. Let θ_1, θ_2, ... be the parameters of the process model $G(s)$ which are subject to change. If θ_{n1}, θ_{n2}, ... are the nominal values of the parameters, then the process model corresponding to the nominal working point may be expressed as $G(\theta_n, s)$, where θ_n is the nominal parameter vector. We assume that $H(s)$ is not subject to parameter variations.

The closed-loop input/output behaviour corresponding to the nominal working point is described by (Fig. 4.11)

$$M(\theta_n,\, s) = \frac{Y(s)}{R(s)} = \frac{D(s)G(\theta_n,\, s)}{1 + D(s)G(\theta_n,\, s)H(s)} \tag{4.8}$$

The process parameter vector now changes by an infinitesimal value $d\theta$. For the closed loop, it follows that

$$\left.\frac{\partial M(\theta,\, s)}{\partial \theta}\right|_{\theta = \theta_n} = \frac{D(s)}{[1 + D(s)G(\theta_n,\, s)H(s)]^2}\left(\frac{\partial G(\theta,\, s)}{\partial \theta}\right)\Bigg|_{\theta = \theta_n} \tag{4.9}$$

From Eqns (4.7)–(4.9), it follows that

$$\frac{d M(\theta_n,\, s)}{M(\theta_n,\, s)} = S(\theta_n,\, s)\frac{dG(\theta_n, s)}{G(\theta_n,\, s)} \tag{4.10a}$$

with the *sensitivity function* of the feedback control given as

$$S_G^M = S(\theta_n,\, s) = \frac{1}{1 + D(s)G(\theta_n,\, s)H(s)} \tag{4.10b}$$

Consider perturbation only in θ_i. Sensitivity of M with respect to θ_i is given by

$$S_{\theta_i}^M = \frac{d M(\theta_n,\, s)/M(\theta_n,\, s)}{d\theta_{in}/\theta_{in}} \tag{4.11a}$$

$$= \frac{d M/M}{dG/G}\left(\frac{dG/G}{d\theta_{in}/\theta_{in}}\right)$$

$$= S(\theta_n,\, s)\left[\frac{\theta_{in}}{G(\theta_n,\, s)}\right]\left[\frac{\partial G(\theta_n,\, s)}{\partial \theta_i}\right]\Bigg|_{\theta_i = \theta_{in}} \tag{4.11b}$$

The sensitivity function given by Eqns (4.10) shows how relative changes in the input/output behaviour of the closed-loop system depend on the changes in the process transfer function. In general, the sensitivity function is a function of the Laplace transform variable s, which makes sensitivity very difficult to interpret. However, if we replace s in Eqn. (4.10b) by $j\omega$, we get the sensitivity as a frequency response. Then we can assign meaning to the sensitivity for frequencies within the bandwidth[1] of the system. Since the system will not transmit frequencies outside its bandwidth (an approximation), the sensitivity for frequencies much greater than the system bandwidth is of little interest.

Evaluating the sensitivity in Eqn. (4.10b) as a function of frequency, yields

$$S_G^M = S(\theta_n, j\omega) = \frac{1}{1 + D(j\omega)G(\theta_n, j\omega)H(j\omega)} \qquad (4.12)$$

The term DGH evaluated at a specific frequency is called the *loop gain* at that frequency. At frequencies within the system bandwidth, we would like the loop gain to be as large as possible to reduce the sensitivity of the closed-loop behaviour to the process parameters. Generally, one of the purposes of the controller $D(s)$ is to allow the loop gain to be increased without destabilizing the system.

Assume now that we are dealing with an open-loop system such as the one depicted in Fig. 4.10. It is clear that for this system we can apply the result given by Eqns (4.10) with $H(s) = 0$. Thus

$$S_G^M = 1, \text{ where } M(\theta_n, s) = D_o(s)G(\theta_n, s) \qquad (4.13)$$

It can readily be seen that feedback reduces the system sensitivity to changes in process parameters.

Next we derive the sensitivity of the closed-loop transfer function to parameter changes in the sensor $H(s)$. Assume that the parameter vector θ_n is a part of $H(s)$, and the process transfer function $G(s)$ is not subject to parameter variations. For this case, the closed-loop transfer function becomes

$$M(\theta_n, s) = \frac{Y(s)}{R(s)} = \frac{D(s)G(s)}{1 + D(s)G(s)H(\theta_n, s)} \qquad (4.14)$$

For an infinitesimal change $d\theta$ in the nominal parameter vector, θ_n, we obtain

$$\left. \frac{\partial M(\theta, s)}{\partial \theta} \right|_{\theta = \theta_n} = -\left[\frac{D(s)G(s)}{1 + D(s)G(s)H(\theta_n, s)} \right]^2 \left. \frac{\partial H(\theta, s)}{\partial \theta} \right|_{\theta = \theta_n} \qquad (4.15)$$

From Eqns (4.14) and (4.15), it follows that

$$\frac{dM(\theta_n, s)}{M(\theta_n, s)} = S_H^M \frac{dH(\theta_n, s)}{H(\theta_n, s)} \qquad (4.16a)$$

---

1. It gives the significant frequency range of the closed-loop system. Chapter 9 on frequency response analysis will describe this important parameter of control system performance.

where

$$S_H^M = \frac{-D(s)G(s)H(\theta_n, s)}{1 + D(s)G(s)H(\theta_n, s)} \qquad (4.16b)$$

This equation shows that for large values of loop gain DGH, sensitivity of the feedback system with respect to H approaches unity. Thus, we see that the changes in H directly affect the system output. To solve this problem, we generally can use high-quality stable components for the sensor.

The use of feedback in reducing sensitivity to parameter variations is an important advantage of the feedback control systems. To have a highly accurate open-loop system, the components of the process plant must be carefully selected so that the parameters of the physical system are close to that of $G(s)$—the model used in design, under all operating conditions. On the other hand, a closed-loop system allows $G(s)$ to be less accurately specified, since the effects of parameter variations are mitigated by the use of feedback. However, a closed-loop system requires careful selection of the components of the feedback sensor. Since the plant is made up of power elements and the sensor is made up of measuring elements which operate at low power levels, the selection of accurate $H(s)$ is far less costly than that of $G(s)$ to meet the exact specifications.

Many plants, by their very nature, have parameters that vary extensively during operation. An example is an aircraft whose parameters vary over very wide ranges with speed, altitude, and so on. Hence, aircraft autopilot design must satisfy a rigorous specification on sensitivity to plant parameter variations. Feedback control is the only solution.

The price for improvement in sensitivity by use of feedback is paid in terms of *loss of system gain*. The gain of the closed-loop system shown in Fig. 4.11 is $D(s)G(s)/[1 + D(s)G(s)H(s)]$ while with $H(s) = 0$, the gain becomes $D(s)G(s)$. Hence, by use of feedback, the system gain is reduced by the same factor as by which the sensitivity of the system to parameter variations is reduced. Sufficient open-loop gain can, however, be built into a system so that we can afford to lose some gain to achieve improvement in sensitivity. We should not place a gain outside the feedback loop; the overall system will be quite sensitive to elements outside the loop.

Example 4.3

Several important speed control systems are used in steel mills for rolling the steel sheets and moving the steel through the mill (Fig. 4.12). We consider here a speed control system employing an armature-controlled dc motor with negligible armature inductance, as the actuator. Figure 4.13 gives the schematic of the speed control system and Fig. 4.14 gives the operational block diagram:

$e_a(t)$ = armature applied voltage
R_a = armature resistance
K_b = motor back-emf constant
K_T = motor torque constant

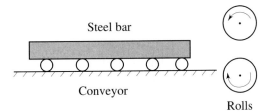

Fig. 4.12

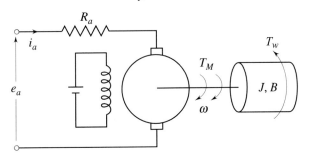

Fig. 4.13

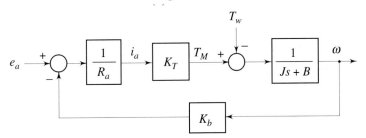

Fig. 4.14 *Open-loop speed control system*

J = moment of inertia of motor and load

B = viscous-friction coefficient of motor and load

$T_w(t)$ = disturbance torque representing loading effect on the rolls when the steel bar engages in the rolls

$\omega(t)$ = motor velocity

The transfer function of the open-loop speed control system obtained from Fig. 4.14, is

$$M_o(s) = \frac{\omega(s)}{E_a(s)} = \frac{K}{\tau s + 1} \tag{4.17}$$

where $\quad K = \dfrac{K_T}{B R_a + K_T K_b} \; ; \tau = \dfrac{J R_a}{B R_a + K_T K_b}$

The sensitivity of the open-loop mode of operation to variation in the constant K is

$$S_K^{M_o} = \frac{\partial M_o}{\partial K}\left(\frac{K}{M_o}\right) = 1 \tag{4.18}$$

A closed-loop speed control system is easily obtained by utilizing a tachometer to generate a voltage proportional to speed as shown in Fig. 4.15. This voltage is subtracted from the reference voltage representing the desired speed, and amplified. The closed-loop transfer function is

$$\frac{\omega(s)}{\omega_r(s)} = M(s) = \frac{KK_AK_t}{\tau s + 1 + KK_AK_t} \tag{4.19}$$

where K_t = tachometer constant; and
K_A = amplifier gain.

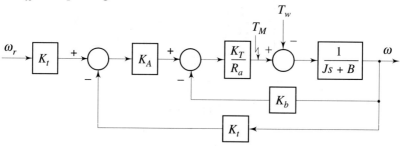

Fig. 4.15   *Closed-loop speed control system*

The sensitivity of the closed-loop system to variation in K is

$$S_K^M = \frac{\partial M}{\partial K}\left(\frac{K}{M}\right)$$

$$= \frac{\tau s + 1}{\tau s + 1 + KK_AK_t} \tag{4.20}$$

For a typical application, we might have $1/\tau = 0.1$ and $(1 + KK_AK_t)/\tau = 10$. Therefore, from Eqn. (4.20) we obtain

$$S_K^M = \frac{s + 0.1}{s + 10}$$

We find that the sensitivity is a function of s and must be evaluated for various values of frequency. This type of frequency analysis is straightforward but will be deferred until a later chapter. However, it is clearly seen that at a specific frequency, for example, $s = j\omega = j1$, the magnitude of the sensitivity of the closed-loop system is

$$\left|S_K^M\right| \cong 0.1$$

Thus, compared to that of the open-loop case, the sensitivity of the closed-loop speed control system at $\omega = 1$ is reduced by a factor of ten.

It should be noted that in order to reduce sensitivity of the closed-loop system to parameter variations, the amplifier gain K_A must be reasonably large (refer Eqn. (4.20)). The armature voltage signal and its associated torque signal will be larger for the closed-loop than for the open-loop operation. Therefore a large motor will be required in order to avoid saturation of the motor.

Disturbance Rejection

The second most important effect of feedback in a control system is the control and partial elimination of the effects of disturbance signals. A feedback control system with a disturbance input is shown in Fig. 4.1a. By superposition, the system output is

$$Y(s) = \frac{D(s)G(s)}{1 + D(s)G(s)H(s)} R(s) + \frac{N(s)}{1 + D(s)G(s)H(s)} W(s) \qquad (4.21)$$

With $R(s) = 0$, the system output becomes

$$Y(s) = \frac{N(s)}{1 + D(s)G(s)H(s)} W(s) \qquad (4.22)$$

For the open-loop system,

$$Y(s) = N(s)W(s) \qquad (4.23)$$

It can readily be seen that feedback reduces the effect of disturbances on the controlled output.

We use frequency-response approach to investigate disturbance-rejection property of feedback control systems. Replacing s in Eqn. (4.22) by $j\omega$, we get

$$\frac{Y(j\omega)}{W(j\omega)} = \frac{N(j\omega)}{1 + D(j\omega)G(j\omega)H(j\omega)}$$

$$= S(j\omega)N(j\omega)$$

where

$$S(j\omega) = \frac{1}{1 + D(j\omega)G(j\omega)H(j\omega)}$$

is the sensitivity function of the control system defined in Eqn. (4.10b). Recall from the preceding sub-section that the loop gain $D(j\omega)G(j\omega)H(j\omega)$ must be made large to reduce sensitivity to variations in plant parameters. This condition also meets the requirement of reducing the effects of disturbance input on the controlled output of the system.

For the case that loop gain is large ($DGH \gg 1$), the disturbance transfer function

$$\frac{Y(j\omega)}{W(j\omega)} \cong \frac{N(j\omega)}{D(j\omega)G(j\omega)H(j\omega)}$$

An obvious way to accomplish disturbance rejection is to make $N(j\omega)$ small. Since $N(j\omega)$ is a function of the plant parameters, it cannot be modified. Alternatively, we may increase the loop gain by increasing the gain of $D(j\omega)$. Note that increasing the plant gain (if possible) will also increase the loop gain, but increasing the plant gain may also increase the gain of $N(j\omega)$. Hence, in this case disturbance rejection may not be improved. Thus, to reject disturbances, the loop gain must be increased in such a manner that the gain from the disturbance input to the system output is not increased.

Figure 4.16 gives a block diagram of the situation wherein measurement noise $V(s)$ enters the system through the feedback link. The closed-loop transfer function for this disturbance is

$$\frac{Y(s)}{V(s)} = -\frac{D(s)G(s)}{1 + D(s)G(s)}$$

Thus, the measurement noise is transferred to the output whenever loop gain $|D(j\omega)G(j\omega)| > 1$. Hence, large loop gain will lead to large output error due to measurement noise. This is in conflict with the disturbance-rejection property with respect to the configuration of Fig. 4.1a. To solve this problem, we generally can examine the measuring instrument and modify the filtering so that it satisfies the requirements of a particular control system.

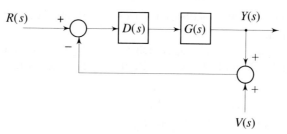

Fig. 4.16 *Closed-loop system with measurement noise*

Example 4.4

As a specific example of a system with an unwanted disturbance, let us reconsider the speed control system for a steel rolling mill (Figs 4.12–4.15). Rolls passing steel through are subject to large load changes or disturbances. As a steel bar approaches the rolls, the rolls turn unloaded. However, when the bar engages in the rolls, the load on the rolls increases immediately to a large value. This loading effect can be approximated by a step change of disturbance torque $T_w(s)$.

Let us study the effect of load torque $T_w(s) = A/s$ in the open-loop speed control system of Fig. 4.14 and the closed-loop speed control system of Fig. 4.15.

In the open-loop case, the change in speed due to load disturbance (obtained by manipulation of the block diagram of Fig. 4.14) is,

$$\omega(s) = \left(\frac{-1}{Js + B + K_T K_b / R_a} \right) T_w(s)$$

The steady-state error in speed due to $T_w(s) = A/s$ is found by using the final value theorem:

$$\lim_{t \to \infty} \omega(t) = \lim_{s \to 0} s\omega(s) = \lim_{s \to 0} s\left[\frac{-1}{Js + B + K_T K_b/R_a}\right]\frac{A}{s}$$

$$= \frac{-A}{B + K_T K_b/R_a}$$

Manipulation of the block diagram of Fig. 4.15 gives the following relation between output speed and load disturbance (alternatively, draw a signal flow graph and use Mason's gain rule) for the closed-loop speed control system:

$$\omega(s) = \frac{-1}{Js + B + (K_T/R_a)[K_b + K_A K_t]}T_w(s)$$

Again the steady-state output is obtained by utilizing the final value theorem, and we have

$$\lim_{t \to \infty} \omega(t) = \lim_{s \to 0} s\omega(s)$$

$$= \frac{-A}{B + (K_T/R_a)[K_b + K_A K_t]}$$

The ratio of the closed-loop to open-loop steady-state speed output due to an undesirable disturbance is

$$\frac{\omega_{ss}(CL)}{\omega_{ss}(OL)} = \frac{BR_a + K_T K_b}{BR_a + K_T(K_b + K_A K_t)}$$

and is usually less than 0.02.

Shaping the Dynamic Response

Consider the feedback control system of Fig. 4.1a. The output with $W(s) = 0$ is given by

$$Y(s) = \frac{D(s)G(s)}{1 + D(s)G(s)H(s)}R(s) \qquad (4.24a)$$

$$= M(s)R(s) \qquad (4.24b)$$

By finding the poles and zeros of $M(s)$, we can characterize the behaviour of the closed-loop system's response to a reference input.

Assume that $D(s)$, $G(s)$ and $H(s)$ are rational functions of s; they can each be expressed as ratios of their numerator and denominator polynomials of the form

$$\frac{D_1(s)}{D_2(s)} \triangleq D(s) \qquad (4.25a)$$

$$\frac{G_1(s)}{G_2(s)} \triangleq G(s) \qquad (4.25b)$$

and
$$\frac{H_1(s)}{H_2(s)} \triangleq H(s) \tag{4.25c}$$

Substituting $D(s)$, $G(s)$ and $H(s)$ from Eqns (4.25) into Eqns (4.24), we obtain

$$M(s) = \frac{D_1(s)\,G_1(s)/D_2(s)\,G_2(s)}{1 + D_1(s)\,G_1(s)H_1(s)/D_2(s)\,G_2(s)H_2(s)}$$

which reduces to

$$M(s) = \frac{D_1(s)G_1(s)H_2(s)}{D_2(s)G_2(s)H_2(s) + D_1(s)G_1(s)H_1(s)} \tag{4.26}$$

Having obtained the closed-loop transfer function in rational form, we are ready to make two rather important observations.

First, the finite *zeros* of $M(s)$ are given by the zeros of the plant transfer function $G(s)$, the poles of the feedback block $H(s)$, and the zeros of the controller transfer function $D(s)$. Second, the *poles* of $M(s)$ are the roots of the equation

$$D_2(s)G_2(s)H_2(s) + D_1(s)G_1(s)H_1(s) = 0 \tag{4.27}$$

which, because its left-hand side is the denominator polynomial of the transfer function, must be the *characteristic equation* of the closed-loop system.

We will see in the next chapter that the poles of $M(s)$ determine the modes of closed-loop system's response; poles in the left-half of the complex plane give rise to decaying modes (a requirement for system stability) and the poles in the right-half of the complex plane give rise to growing modes (making the system unstable). The zeros of $M(s)$ control the magnitude of each mode and, hence, the contribution of each mode in the total response. Thus, we can shape the dynamic response of the closed-loop system by controlling the locations of poles and zeros of $M(s)$ through the controller $D(s)$.

We see from Eqn. (4.26) that the poles of a feedback system do not have a direct relationship to the open-loop poles and zeros; this tends to complicate the analysis. However, it does mean that the designer has the capability of making the closed-loop system behave quite differently from the open-loop system. In order to make effective use of this ability, it is necessary to have methods for analyzing the effects of changes in parameters of the controller $D(s)$ without having to solve Eqn. (4.26) for $M(s)$ or Eqn. (4.27) for the closed-loop poles each time a parameter is changed. Much of our subsequent work will be directed toward developing analytical tools that will allow us to take advantage of this unusual property of feedback systems.

Consider now the total response of the closed-loop system of Fig. 4.1a to both the reference and the disturbance inputs (refer Eqn. (4.21)):

$$Y(s) = \frac{D(s)G(s)}{1 + D(s)G(s)H(s)} R(s) + \frac{N(s)}{1 + D(s)G(s)H(s)} W(s)$$

$$= M(s)R(s) + M_w(s)W(s)$$

The denominators of $M(s)$ and $M_w(s)$ are identical, implying that both the transfer functions have precisely the same poles. This situation is a consequence of the fact that the characteristic equation is a property of the closed-loop configuration and not of the particular variables that happen to be designated as the input and output.

The zeros of $M(s)$ and $M_w(s)$ are different. In fact, it would be rather unfortunate if this difference did not exist because we certainly do not want the output to respond to disturbance inputs in the same way that it responds to reference inputs—generally we would prefer $M(s)$ to be unity, so that the output follows the reference input exactly, and $M_w(s)$ to be zero, so that the output would be unaffected by disturbances.

Upon examination of Fig. 4.10, one notes that the open-loop control system can easily shape the dynamics of the controlled output: the output y follows the input r exactly if

$$D_o(s) = \frac{1}{G(s)}$$

If $D_o(s)$ is realizable (i.e., a physical system with transfer function $D_o(s)$ can be constructed), it can cancel the process dynamics completely since it has the reciprocal transfer function behaviour. Therefore, one may logically ask, what is the advantage of the closed-loop system in this case? Again, we return to the concepts of the sensitivity of the system to parameter changes and effects of disturbances as our answer to this question. In the open-loop control configuration of Fig. 4.10, one may implement $D_o(s)$ so that it is equal to the inverse of the nominal transfer function $G(s)$, but $G(s)$ is usually an approximate model of the process, and during the operation of the system it is inevitable that the parameters of $G(s)$ will change due to environmental changes and $D_o(s)G(s)$ will no longer be equal to unity. Also, because of the disturbances acting on the process $G(s)$ but not on the controller $D_o(s)$, the output $y(t)$ will deviate from the input $r(t)$. By contrast, a closed-loop system continually monitors the output $y(t)$, and provides an actuating signal in order to reduce the effects of parameter variations and disturbances. Thus, we find that the properties of insensitivity to model uncertainties, parameter variations, and disturbance rejection encourage the introduction of feedback.

Example 4.5

Figure 4.7 gives the block diagram description of a heat-exchanger control system (refer Example 4.1). Assume that the actuator and the sensor devices have zero dynamic lags, i.e., the transfer function of the actuator is 0.1, and that of the sensor is 0.16. Under this assumption,

$$\frac{\theta(s)}{\theta_r(s)} = \frac{D(s)G(s)}{1 + D(s)G(s)}$$

where
$$G(s) = \frac{0.8}{30s + 1}.$$

If the controller $D(s)$ is an amplifier of gain K_A with negligible dynamic lag, we get

$$\frac{\theta(s)}{\theta_r(s)} = \frac{0.8\,K_A}{30s + 1 + 0.8\,K_A}$$

For positive values of K_A, the effect of the feedback is to shift the pole negatively from the open-loop location $s = -1/30$ to the location $s = -(1 + 0.8K_A)/30$; the time-constant reduces from 30 to $30/(1 + 0.8K_A)$. This implies that as K_A (and hence the loop gain) increases, the system dynamics continuously becomes faster, i.e., the transient response decays more quickly. Thus, the *relative stability* (which is a quantitative measure of how fast the transients die out in the system) improves with an increase in loop gain.

Consider now the situation which is more closer to the real world: the actuator and the sensor devices in heat-exchanger control system have dynamic lags as shown in Fig. 4.7. Excessive loop gain may result in the instability of the feedback system. The instability phenomenon may be qualitatively described as follows (quantitative discussion will appear in the next chapter).

Consider the feedback system of Fig. 4.7 with a fixed desired value θ_r and in equilibrium with the controlled variable θ at the desired value. If a process disturbance occurs, the ensuing deviation of the controlled variable will cause a correction to be applied but it will be delayed by the cumulative lags of the sensor, actuator, and process. Eventually, however, the trend of the controlled variable caused by the disturbance will be reversed by the opposition of the process manipulated input q_{ms}, returning the controlled variable toward the desired value. Now if the loop gain is high, a *strong* correction is applied and the controlled variable overshoots the desired value, causing a reversal in the algebraic sign of the system error (difference between desired value and controlled variable). Unfortunately, because of the system lags, a reversal of the correction does not occur immediately, and the process manipulated input (acting on 'old' information) is now actually driving the controlled variable in the same direction as it was already going, rather than opposing its excursions, leading to a larger deviation. If the loop gain is not too large and/or system lag is not too large, it may be possible to bring the controlled variable back to its desired value. The combination of excessive loop gain with excessive lags always results in feedback system instability.

Steady-State Accuracy

A feedback control system is valuable because the sensitivity of the system to parameter variations, and effect of disturbances can be reduced significantly. In addition, as we have seen, it provides us with the ability to adjust the transient response. However, as a further requirement, one must examine and compare the final steady-state error for an open-loop and a closed-loop system.

The error of the closed-loop system shown in Fig. 4.1b with $W(s) = 0$ is given by

$$E(s) = \frac{1}{1 + D(s)G(s)} R(s)$$

In order to calculate the steady-state error, we utilize the final value theorem:

$$\lim_{t \to \infty} e(t) = e_{ss} = \lim_{s \to 0} sE(s)$$

For a unit step input, $R(s) = \dfrac{1}{s}$,

the steady-state error is given by

$$e_{ss} = \lim_{t \to \infty} [r(t) - y(t)] = \lim_{s \to 0} sE(s)$$

$$= \lim_{s \to 0} s \left[\frac{1}{1 + D(s)G(s)} \right] \frac{1}{s}$$

$$= \frac{1}{1 + D(0)G(0)} \tag{4.28}$$

The value of $D(s)G(s)$ when $s = 0$ is often called the dc loop gain. Therefore, a closed-loop system with a reasonably large dc loop gain will have a small steady-state error.

Consider now the open-loop control system shown in Fig. 4.10. The error

$$E(s) = R(s) - Y(s) = [1 - D_o(s)G(s)] R(s)$$

For a unit step input, the steady-state error is given by

$$e_{ss} = \lim_{s \to 0} sE(s) = 1 - D_o(0)G(0) \tag{4.29}$$

Upon examination of Eqn. (4.29), one notes that the open-loop control system can possess a zero steady-state error by simply adjusting the dc loop gain so that $D_o(0)G(0) = 1$. However, during the operation of the system, it is inevitable that the parameters of $G(s)$ will change and dc loop gain of the system will no longer be equal to unity. The steady-state error will continue to be other than zero until the system is recalibrated. By contrast, the feedback system of Fig. 4.1b continually monitors the steady-state error and provides an actuating signal in order to reduce the steady-state error.

The Case for High-Gain Feedback

Summarizing the benefits of negative feedback in systems with high loop gain, we can state that such systems result in:
  (i)   good steady-state tracking accuracy;
  (ii) good disturbance signal rejection;
  (iii) low sensitivity to process parameter variations; and
  (iv) good relative stability, i.e., rate of decay of transients.
There are, however factors limiting the gain:
  (i)   High gain may result in instability problems.
  (ii) Input amplitudes limit the gain; excessively large amplitudes of control signals will drive the process to the saturation region of its operation, and

the control system design based on linear model of the plant will no longer give satisfactory performance.

(iii) Measurement noise limits the gain; with high gain feedback, measurement noise appears unattenuated in the controlled output.

Therefore, in design we are faced with trade offs.

4.4 PROPORTIONAL MODE OF FEEDBACK CONTROL

We use a temperature control system to develop an understanding of proportional control characteristics.

The system shown in Fig. 4.17 is designed to maintain the chamber temperature θ at desired value θ_r in the face of disturbances in outdoor temperature. We will assume an initial equilibrium operating point (all variables steady) at which steam inflow $\overline{Q}_m$ kg/sec exactly matches the heat loss to the surroundings with chamber temperature $\overline{\theta}$ = set-point value $\overline{\theta}_r$. The necessary steam flow rate $\overline{Q}_m$ can be achieved because the electropneumatic transducer has a zero adjustment which allows pressure $\overline{P}$ to be set at the middle (9 psig)

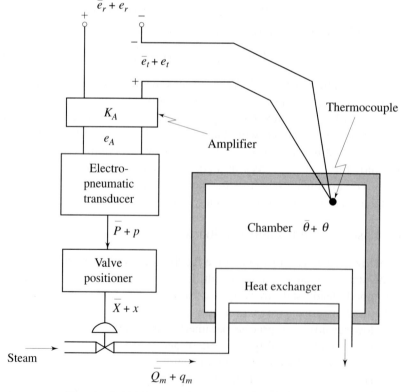

Fig. 4.17 *Heating system with proportional control*

of its 3-to-15 psig range when $e_A = 0$, and the valve positioner has a zero adjustment which allows the valve opening to be put anywhere desired, with the pressure $\overline{P}$ at 9 psig. With these initial 'trimming' adjustments made, all the variables named in Fig. 4.18 are considered as small perturbations away from the initial steady state.

The thermocouple output is $e_t = K_t\theta$. This simple model is justifiable if the dynamics of the sensor are negligible relative to the process time-constant τ_p. The electronic amplifier is obviously fast enough to be treated as zero-order system. The dynamics of the electropneumatic transducer and valve positioner have been neglected in the block diagram of Fig. 4.18, assuming their response to be very fast relative to τ_p. Also the relation between q_m and x is assumed statically linear and dynamically instantaneous.

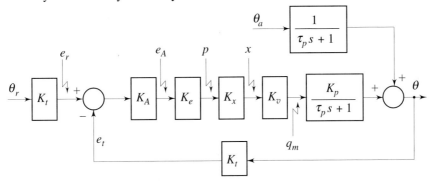

Fig. 4.18   *A block diagram for the system of Fig. 4.17*

Having justified the block diagram of Fig. 4.18, we now use it directly to obtain the transfer function of the closed-loop system, relating θ to θ_r and θ_a:

$$[(K_t\theta_r(s) - K_t\theta(s))K_A K_e K_x K_v] \frac{K_p}{\tau_p s + 1} + \left(\frac{1}{\tau_p s + 1}\right)\theta_a(s) = \theta(s)$$

or $(\tau_p s + 1)\theta(s) + K_t K_A K_e K_x K_v K_p \theta(s) = K_t K_A K_e K_x K_v K_p \theta_r(s) + \theta_a(s)$

or $$(\tau s + 1)\theta(s) = \frac{K}{1 + K}\theta_r(s) + \frac{1}{1 + K}\theta_a(s) \qquad (4.30)$$

where $\tau \triangleq$ closed-loop system time-constant $= \dfrac{\tau_p}{1 + K}$;

$K \triangleq$ system loop gain $= K_t K_A K_e K_x K_v K_p$

For the linear model of Eqn. (4.30), superposition holds and we can investigate the effects of command θ_r and disturbance θ_a separately. For θ_r, a step input of size unity (perturbation θ_a is held at zero), we get

$$\theta(t) = \frac{K}{1 + K}(1 - e^{-t/\tau}) \qquad (4.31)$$

Figure 4.19 shows the first-order system response with speed determined by τ and the steady-state error given by

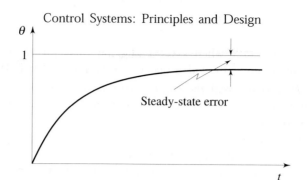

Fig. 4.19   *System response to step command*

$$e_{ss} = 1 - \theta_{ss} = \frac{100}{K+1}\,\%$$

Since $\tau = \tau_p/(K+1)$, we see that both the speed of response and the steady-state error are improved if we increase loop gain K. For step disturbance input $\theta_a(s) = 1/s$ $(\theta_r = 0)$, we get

$$\theta(t) = \frac{1}{(K+1)}(1 - e^{-t/\tau}) \tag{4.32}$$

and again increasing K improves both the speed of response and the steady-state error.

The steady-state errors discovered in the present example are in fact characteristic of the proportional control in general. The basic reason for this behaviour can be explained as follows. For the initial equilibrium point assumed, we are able to get zero steady-state error because the zero adjustments on various devices allow us to open the valve exactly the right amount to supply the steam with $e = \theta_r - \theta = 0$. When we then ask θ_r to change by a unit step, a different valve opening is required to reach equilibrium at the new θ_r because the required rate of steam flow will be larger than that for the initial equilibrium state. When flow rate q_m is proportional to e, a new q_m can only be achieved if e is different from zero; thus there must be a steady-state error. Similar reasoning holds for step changes in disturbances. Thus for any initial equilibrium condition, we can 'trim' the system for zero error but subsequent steady commands and/or disturbances must cause steady-state errors.

The steady-state error due to step commands can theoretically be eliminated from proportional control systems by intentionally 'misadjusting' θ_r. For example, for a step input θ_r of size $(1 + K)/K$ with $\theta_a = 0$, we get from Eqn. (4.30):

$$\theta(t) = 1 - e^{-t/\tau}\,;\ \theta_{ss} = \text{steady-state value of } \theta(t) = 1$$

Thus, if we want θ to change by a unit step, we ask for a step input of size $(1 + K)/K$.

This trick does in fact work, but depends upon our knowledge about K. If K is not accurately known or varies, then the trick is not 100% effective. Also the trick does not help in reducing steady-state errors caused by disturbances. In the next section we will see that the *integral mode* of feedback control removes steady-state errors due to both commands and disturbances and does not depend on the knowledge of specific numerical values for system parameters.

Equations (4.30)–(4.32) indicate that the following aspects of systems behaviour are improved by increasing loop gain:

(i) steady-state tracking accuracy;

(ii) disturbance signal rejection; and

(iii) relative stability, i.e., rate of decay of the transients.

In addition, it can easily be established that increase in loop gain decreases the sensitivity of the system to parameter variations. Thus all aspects of system behaviour are improved by high-gain proportional control. This is, however, true up to a point but connot be carried to extremes because the system will go unstable. Note that the model of Fig. 4.18 gives no warning of instability[2]. This defect in our model is caused by our neglect of dynamics in some of the system components. We originally neglected these dynamics relative to τ_p, but in the closed-loop system, response speed is determined by τ and not τ_p. Equation (4.30) shows that τ decreases as K is increased and therefore at some point the initially neglected dynamics are no longer negligible. Thus, the model of Fig. 4.18 correctly predicts system behaviour, as long as loop gain is not made 'too large'; it is not valid for stability predictions. If we want to make valid stability predictions, we must include enough dynamics in our system model. The next chapter will show that instability will occur for large values of loop gain when the closed-loop system is of order 3 or more.

In addition to neglecting some 'fast' dynamics, the model of Fig. 4.18 further differs from reality because of its perfect linearity, which assumes no limit on the magnitude of corrective control action that can be applied by the system. Actually the amplifier, the electropneumatic transducer, and valve positioner all exhibit saturation, limiting their output when input becomes too large. All aspects of closed-loop system behaviour suffer from saturation.

4.5 | INTEGRAL MODE OF FEEDBACK CONTROL

Consider the closed-loop system of Fig. 4.20a. Assume that initial 'trimming' (zero adjustments) of the control system has been done to obtain $y = r$, with $e = u = 0$. In response to a change in the set-point, the controller must change the flow of energy and/or material to the process in order to achieve equilibrium at the new operating conditions. If the controller is based on proportional logic, then in the new steady-state, a non-zero error e_{ss} must exist to get a non-zero value of control signal u_{ss} (Fig. 4.20b). The new set-point is, say, 10. It will result in a response y_{ss} of less value, say 9.9. The steady-state error is 0.1 and the steady value of the control signal is $0.1K_c$ where K_c is controller gain. The operator must then 'reset' the set-point to bring the output to the desired value of 10.

---

2. The characteristic equation of the system is (refer Eqn. (4.30))

$$\tau_p s + 1 + K = 0$$

The characteristic root (closed-loop pole) is always in the left half of complex plane.

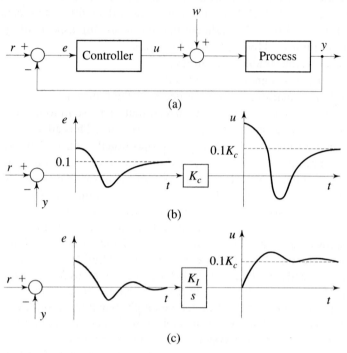

Fig. 4.20 *Comparison of proportional and integral control*

We need a controller that automatically brings the output to 10 with a set-point of 10, i.e., it gives a steady control signal of value $0.1K_c$ with system error $e_{ss} = 0$. An integrator is capable of exactly this type of behaviour (Fig. 4.20c). Integral control is thus a means of removing steady-state errors without the need for manual reset and, in fact, it is sometimes called *automatic reset*. We shall see that integral control can be used by itself or in combination with other control modes; indeed, PI control is the most common mode (refer Eqns (4.3)):

$$u(t) = K_c \left[e(t) + \frac{1}{T_I} \int_0^t e(t)dt \right] \tag{4.33a}$$

or

$$U(s) = K_c \left(1 + \frac{1}{T_I s} \right) E(s) \tag{4.33b}$$

where T_I is the integral or reset time.

Although integral control is very useful for removing or reducing steady-state errors, it has the undesirable side-effects of degrading stability. Conversion of the proportional control system of Fig. 4.18 to integral control will bring out some general results about integral mode. Suppose we replace the amplifier block K_A by K_I/s. The closed-loop system is then described by the equation

$$\left[(K_t\theta_r(s) - K_t\theta(s))\frac{K_I}{s}K_eK_xK_v \right]\frac{K_p}{\tau_p s + 1} + \frac{1}{\tau_p s + 1}\theta_a(s) = \theta(s)$$

or $(\tau_p s + 1)\theta(s) + \dfrac{K_t K_I K_e K_x K_v K_p}{s}\theta(s) = \dfrac{K_t K_I K_e K_x K_v K_p}{s}\theta_r(s) + \theta_a(s)$

or $\qquad (\tau_p s^2 + s + K)\theta(s) = K\theta_r(s) + s\theta_a(s)$ $\qquad$ (4.34)

where $\qquad K \triangleq$ loop gain $= K_t K_I K_e K_x K_v K_p$

For θ_r, step input of size unity (perturbation θ_a held at zero), we get

$$\theta(s) = \left(\frac{K}{\tau_p s^2 + s + K} \right)\frac{1}{s}$$

By final-value theorem, the steady-value of the output is unity, and therefore steady-state error is zero. For step disturbance input $\theta_a(s) = 1/s$ ($\theta_r = 0$), we get

$$\theta(s) = \left(\frac{s}{\tau_p s^2 + s + K} \right)\frac{1}{s}; \ \theta_{ss} = \text{ steady-state value of output} = 0$$

Thus, step changes of θ_r and θ_a give zero steady-state errors regardless of the value of loop gain K. The steady-state performance of the system with constant inputs is thus insensitive to parameter variations.

We need to consider what integral control does to the dynamic response. For this we need to look at the characteristic equation corresponding to Eqn. (4.34), which is

$$\tau_p s^2 + s + K = 0.$$

The roots of this equation, which are readily computed, vary as gain K is varied. In fact, it is informative to compute these and plot them as a function of K. By quadratic formula of algebra, the roots are

$$s = \frac{-1 \pm \sqrt{1 - 4K\tau_p}}{2\tau_p}$$

and are plotted in Fig. 4.21b for changing values of the gain K. When the gain is zero, the roots are at $-1/\tau_p$ and at 0. As the gain is raised, the roots move closer until there is a double root at $-1/2\tau_p$, and then for higher gains, the roots become complex conjugate.

Recall the case of proportional control; from Eqn. (4.30), we obtain the following characteristic equation:

$$\frac{\tau_p}{1 + K}s + 1 = 0$$

The root of this equation, $s = -\dfrac{1 + K}{\tau_p}$, moves increasingly to the left in the complex plane for increasing values of K (Fig. 4.21a) which implies a decreasing time-constant for the closed-loop system; the larger the loop gain, faster is the rate of decay of transients. With integral control, the rate of decay of transients is dictated by the real root closer to the imaginary axis or real part of the pair of complex conjugate roots. There is obviously a limit on the speed of response; also the response will be oscillatory for large values of K rather than exponential as with proportional control. Due to our too-simple dynamic modelling, instability for large values of loop gain is not predicted.

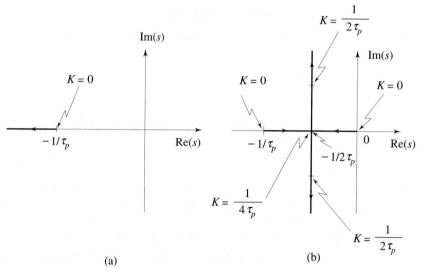

(a)   (b)

Fig. 4.21 *Destabilizing effect of integral control*

Example 4.6

Figure 4.22 shows an electromechanical servo wherein motor torque T_M controls position θ of inertia J which is subject to torque disturbance T_w. The field

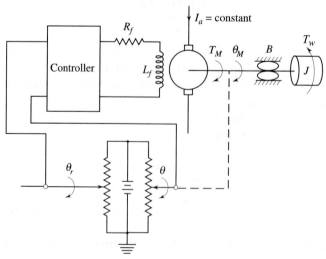

Fig. 4.22 *An electromechanical servo*

time-constant $\tau_f = L_f/R_f$ is negligibly small; K_T is the motor torque constant and K_P is the potentiometer sensitivity.

Notice that integrating effect naturally appears in the system plant. Let us examine whether we need integral control for such a plant. The block diagram in Fig. 4.23 shows the integrating plant with proportional control. The following equation easily follows from this block diagram:

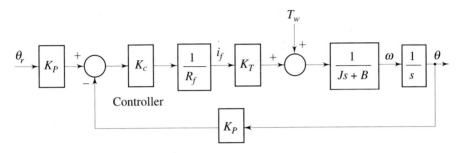

Fig. 4.23 *A block diagram of the system in Fig. 4.22*

$$[(\theta_r(s)K_P - \theta(s)K_P)K_c(K_T/R_f) + T_w(s)]\frac{1}{Js^2 + Bs} = \theta(s)$$

or
$$(Js^2 + Bs + K)\theta(s) = K\theta_r(s) + T_w(s) \qquad (4.35)$$

where

$$K \triangleq \frac{K_P K_c K_T}{R_f} = \text{loop gain}$$

For a unit step command input with $T_w = 0$, we have

$$\theta(s) = \left(\frac{K}{Js^2 + Bs + K}\right)\frac{1}{s}$$

By final-value theorem, the steady-state value of the output is given by

$$\theta_{ss} = \lim_{s \to 0} s \left(\frac{K}{Js^2 + Bs + K}\right)\frac{1}{s} = 1$$

and therefore, the steady-state error, $e_{ss} = \theta_r - \theta_{ss}$, is zero.

For a unit step disturbance with $\theta_r = 0$, have

$$\theta(s) = \left(\frac{1}{Js^2 + Bs + K}\right)\frac{1}{s}$$

and the steady-state value of the output is $\theta_{ss} = \dfrac{1}{K}$.

The plant integrator, thus, gives zero steady-state error for a step command but not for a step disturbance. If we replace the controller gain K_c by

$K_c \left(1 + \dfrac{1}{T_I s} \right)$, and examine the system for steady-state accuracy, we find that the steady-state errors to step commands as well as to step disturbances are zero. Therefore, the location of the integrator relative to disturbance injection points determines its effectiveness in removing steady-state errors. The integrator must be located before the disturbance enters the system if it is to be effective in removing steady-state error due to disturbance; however, location is not significant for steady-state errors caused by commands.

Let us study the effect of the integrator on the stability of the system of Fig. 4.23. With proportional control, the characteristic equation of the system is (refer Eqn. (4.35))

$$Js^2 + Bs + \dot{K} = 0$$

which has roots in the left-half of the complex plane for all values of K; hence the system is stable for all values of loop gain.

Replacing K_c by $K_c \left(1 + \dfrac{1}{T_I s} \right)$, we get the following characteristic equation:

$$Js^3 + Bs^2 + Ks + K/T_I = 0$$

It is a third-order characteristic equation and, as we shall see in the next chapter, large values of loop gain K lead to instability.

▲▲

A controller with integral action can exhibit the phenomenon called *integral windup* (*reset windup*) when overdriven, if it is not properly designed. Chapter 11 gives the details.

Although controllers with a single integrator are most common, double (and occasionally triple)integrators are useful for the more difficult steady-state error problems; however they require careful stability augmentation. Conventionally, the number of integrators in the forward path has been called the system *type number*; type 0 systems have no integrators, type 1 have one, and so forth. In addition to the number of integrators, their location (relative to disturbance injection points) determines their effectiveness in removing steady-state errors. Detailed treatment of steady-state error analysis will appear in Chapter 6.

4.6 | DERIVATIVE MODE OF FEEDBACK CONTROL

Consider the closed-loop system shown in Fig. 4.24. The controller is given the information on system error $e(t)$ and has the task of changing control variable $u(t)$ so as to keep $e(t)$ close to zero. If the control logic is a proportional control action, then the value of u at time t_1 will be same as that at t_2. However, a stronger corrective effort seems appropriate at t_1 and lesser one at t_2, since at t_1 the error is e_{12} and *increasing*, whereas at t_2 it is again e_{12} but *decreasing*. That

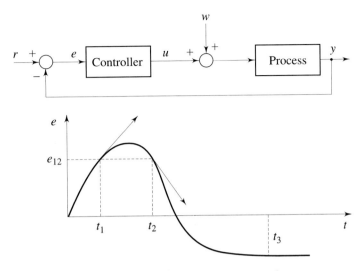

Fig. 4.24   *Genesis of derivative control*

is, the controller must sense not only the ordinate of the error curve but also its trend or slope. Slope is clearly *de/dt*; so to mechanize this desirable control logic, we need a controller sensitive to error derivative. Such a controller can, however, not be used alone since it acts as open circuit for *steady* errors of any size, as at t_3; thus a combination of proportional plus derivative (PD), for example, makes sense (refer Eqns (4.5)):

$$u(t) = K_c \left[e(t) + T_D \frac{de(t)}{dt} \right] \qquad (4.36a)$$

or $\qquad\qquad U(s) = K_c (1 + T_D s)E(s) \qquad (4.36b)$

where K_c is the controller gain and T_D is the derivative or rate time.

The noise-accentuating characteristics of derivative operations may often require use of approximate (low-pass filtered) derivative signals. This prevents realization of ideal performance but significant system improvement is still often possible. Here we will explore idealized versions of derivative controls in order to make clear their basic characteristics. Later chapters will develop their practical implementation in a more comprehensive way.

Figure 4.22 shows an electromechanical servo where motor torque T_M controls position θ of inertia J which is subject to torque disturbance T_w. The damper torque on J, due to viscous friction with coefficient B, behaves exactly like a derivative control mode in that it always opposes velocity $d\theta/dt$ with a strength proportional to $d\theta/dt$, making motion less oscillatory. We can therefore, by careful mechanical design, reduce the real friction B to nearly zero and obtain desired damping electronically by introducing derivative control as shown in Fig. 4.25a. The field time-constant $\tau_f = L_f/R_f$ has been assumed to be negligibly small; K_T is the motor torque constant and K_P is the potentiometer sensitivity. The closed-loop system is described by the following equation:

$$[(\theta_r(s)K_P - \theta(s)K_P)K_c(1 + T_D s)(K_T/R_f) + T_w(s)]\frac{1}{Js^2} = \theta(s)$$

or $\left(s^2 + \dfrac{KT_D}{J}s + \dfrac{K}{J}\right)\theta(s) = \dfrac{K}{J}(1 + T_D s)\theta_r(s) + \dfrac{1}{J}T_w(s)$ (4.37)

where $K \triangleq \dfrac{K_P K_c K_T}{R_f}$ = loop gain.

The second-order characteristic equation is

$$s^2 + 2\zeta\omega_n s + \omega_n^2 = s^2 + \frac{KT_D}{J}s + \frac{K}{J} = 0$$

Therefore

$$\omega_n = \sqrt{\frac{K}{J}} \; ; \; \zeta = \frac{T_D}{2}\sqrt{\frac{K}{J}}$$

If T_D is positive, motor torque is felt by the load in exactly the same way as a mechanical viscous damping torque; the load cannot distinguish between them. The derivative control may therefore be interpreted as pseudo-friction effect.

We now change the system of Fig. 4.25a by using a proportional controller in the forward path and adding derivative mode at the controlled variable θ (Fig. 4.25b). Derivative modes of angular position are extremely common in all kinds of servomechanisms and are usually implemented using a tachogenerator to get a voltage proportional to shaft speed (Fig. 4.25c).

From the block diagram of Fig. 4.25b, we obtain

$$\left[[(\theta_r(s) - \theta(s))K_P K_1 - K_2 s\theta(s)]\frac{K_T}{R_f} + T_w(s)\right]\frac{1}{Js^2} = \theta(s)$$

or $\left(s^2 + \dfrac{K_2 K_T}{JR_f}s + \dfrac{K_P K_1 K_T}{JR_f}\right)\theta(s) = \dfrac{K_P K_1 K_T}{JR_f}\theta_r(s) + \dfrac{1}{J}T_w(s)$ (4.38)

In comparing derivative control applied to system error with that applied to the controlled variable, we see that the effects on the characteristic equation are identical. Error-derivative control, however, has a more violent response to sudden command changes (such as steps) because of the presence of derivative term of θ_r (refer Eqn. (4.37)).

Let us now study the effect of derivative control on steady-state errors. For a unit step disturbance with $\theta_r = 0$, the steady-state value of the output, obtained from Eqn. (4.38), is given below.

$$\theta_{ss} = \lim_{s \to 0} s\left[\frac{1/J}{s^2 + (K_2 K_T/JR_f)s + K_P K_1 K_T/JR_f}\right]\frac{1}{s} = \frac{R_f}{K_P K_1 K_T}$$

This constant steady-state error for a step disturbance does not depend on K_2; so this feature of performance is unaffected by the derivative control mode. However, there is an indirect method for possibly gaining some improvement in steady-state accuracy using a PD controller: improvement of relative stability by proper choice of K_2 (derivative mode) allows the use of higher values of K_1 (proportional gain), thereby improving the steady-state accuracy. The benefit obtained this way will however be limited because saturation will prevent the use of large values of K_1.

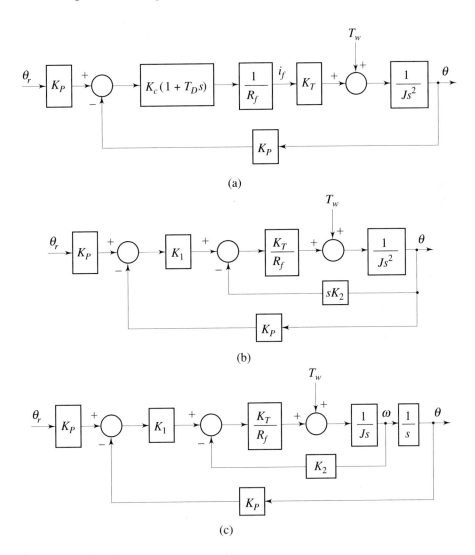

Fig. 4.25   *PD control of the system in Fig. 4.22*

A suitable combination of the three basic modes—proportional, integral, and derivative (PID)—can improve 'all' aspects (stability, speed of response, and steady-state errors) of system performance and is the most complex method available as an off-the-shelf, general-purpose controller. The 'staying power' of PID control over the years is testimony to the basic soundness of these fundamental control actions.

In the preceding sections, we have introduced the basic control modes. Each of these has its own advantages and drawbacks; thus it should not be surprising that many practical applications are best served by some combinations of the basic modes. In fact, we have already encountered some examples of this. We have considered the idealized versions of the modes so that their essential features could be brought out most clearly without confusing side issues. Practical versions of some controllers are not able to faithfully realize the idealised behaviour. Also, sometimes a non-ideal controller can meet specifications with simpler hardware. Combined and approximate control modes— *lag compensator, lead compensator* etc.—will appear in later chapters. Hardware and software implementation of the control modes will appear in Chapter 11.

4.7 ALTERNATIVE CONTROL CONFIGURATIONS

The configuration shown in Fig. 4.1a is that of a basic feedback control system, but it is not the only configuration used. In many systems it is possible and profitable to improve the performance attained with feedback control by using other control configurations. The purpose of this section is to present some of the control structures that have been developed, and often used, to improve on the control performance provided by feedback control.

Disturbance Feedforward

The basic feedback control structure of Fig. 4.1a counteracts disturbances by using measurements of the output. One difficulty with this approach is that the effects of the disturbance must show up in the output of the plant before the controller can begin to take action. On the other hand, if we can measure the disturbance, the performance of the controller can be improved by using the measurement to augment the control signal sent from the controller to the plant. This is the essence of feedforward disturbance rejection.

Feedforward disturbance rejection is illustrated in Fig. 4.26. In this system, the disturbance $W(s)$ is measured and transmitted to the summing junction through the transfer function $D_2(s)$. The addition of $D_2(s)$ does not affect the transfer function from the reference input $R(s)$ to the output. However, the transfer function from the disturbance input to the output now becomes

$$\frac{Y(s)}{W(s)} = \frac{N(s) - D_1(s) D_2(s) G(s)}{1 + D_1(s) G(s) H(s)} \tag{4.39}$$

If the product $D_1(s)D_2(s)$ can be chosen such that the numerator is small, then good disturbance rejection will occur. If the numerator can be made equal to zero, that is, if

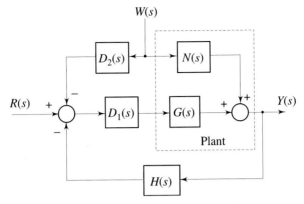

Fig. 4.26 *A system with disturbance feedforward*

$$N(s) - D_1(s)D_2(s)G(s) = 0$$

or if
$$D_1(s)D_2(s) = \frac{N(s)}{G(s)}, \tag{4.40}$$

the disturbance will be rejected completely. If Eqn. (4.40) cannot be satisfied exactly for all frequencies, good disturbance rejection will occur over the frequency band for which it is approximately satisfied. However, remember that a transfer function is only an approximate model of a physical system. Hence if Eqn. (4.40) is satisfied exactly, the quality of the disturbance rejection in the physical system will depend on the accuracy of the models $G(s)$ and $N(s)$. Uncertainties in these models are taken care of by the self-correcting action of the feedback control loop.

For a complex system represented by high-order models $G(s)$ and $N(s)$, the resulting feedforward controller given by Eqn. (4.40) will be quite complex. The instrumentation and engineering efforts required may not justify the feedforward disturbance rejection using such a controller. A common practice is to install a first-order controller of the type

$$D_2(s) = \frac{K(\tau_1 s + 1)}{\tau_2 s + 1}$$

in the forward control path and adjust the values of K, τ_1 and τ_2 by trial and error to shape the dynamics of the controlled variable in response to disturbance input.

Many control systems in process industries are working satisfactorily with feedforward disturbance rejection only in steady-state (refer Review Example 4.2).

Command Feedforward

The main objective in control system design is to make the controlled variable y follow the command y_r as closely as possible. If the model $G(s)$ of the stable process is known exactly and if there is no other disturbance, this problem could be solved by using a feedforward control system shown in Fig. 4.27a. Ideally, one could require that the output y follows the command y_r exactly. This would be the case if

$$D_o(s) = \frac{1}{G(s)}$$

This is the design principle of command feedforward control. As usual, the perfection implied by $y \equiv y_r$ is in practice unattainable; however significant improvements in control can often be achieved. The difficulty here is that the process dynamics $G(s)$ are often the 'lagging' type, such as $K/(\tau s + 1)$, which means that for perfect control we need $D(s) = (\tau s + 1)/K$ which is not physically realizable. A practical goal for the controller design would be

$$D_o(s) = G_1(s)/G(s)$$

giving
$$\frac{Y(s)}{R(s)} = G_1(s)$$

The dynamics $G_1(s)$ can easily be made to have a steady-state gain of 1.0 and can often be made to yield faster response than did $G(s)$, thus giving improved control. For our earlier example where $G(s) = K/(\tau s + 1)$ we could use

$$D_o(s) = (\tau s + 1)/K(\tau_1 s + 1),$$

giving
$$\frac{Y(s)}{R(s)} = \frac{\tau s + 1}{K(\tau_1 s + 1)}\left[\frac{K}{\tau s + 1}\right] = \frac{1}{\tau_1 s + 1}$$

We can make τ_1 significantly less than τ.

The command feedforward controller alone cannot be implemented in practice because the assumptions made for its design do not hold, i.e., the process model is not known exactly, and the disturbances arise. The feed-forward–feedback structure of Fig. 4.27b takes care of the uncertainties in process model and disturbances (refer Review Example 4.3).

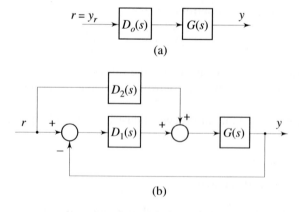

(a)

(b)

Fig. 4.27 *A system with command feedforward*

Minor-loop Feedback

Useful control effects can be realized by feeding back in addition to the controlled variable, other significant variables of the process. Fig. 4.28 is an illustration of such a control strategy. We have already encountered an example; both the position (controlled variable) and velocity (other significant variable) are feedback in the control scheme shown in Fig. 4.25c.

The difference between the control structure of Fig. 4.28 and the basic feedback structure shown earlier in Fig. 4.1a, is that instead of one feedback loop we now have two loops: a minor loop within the primary loop. More minor loops may be added to improve the control performance.[3]

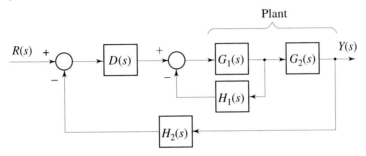

Fig. 4.28   *A system with minor-loop feedback*

Minor-loop feedback exists in disguise in many systems because the final control elements usually include feedback loops to improve their performance. For example a power amplifier has a feedback loop to regulate voltage level while supplying current to the load. An armature-controlled dc motor has a feedback loop through back emf of the motor, which effectively increases system damping.

State Variable Feedback

One of the design techniques developed in 'modern control theory', called state variable feedback, suggests that *all* the state variables of a system be measured and fedback, each through its own adjustable gain. If we do this we find that the coefficient of each power of s in the closed-loop system characteristic equation includes one or more of the state variable feedback gains in such a way that we have complete freedom to design the numerical value of each coefficient. We can thus specify the closed-loop response in terms of roots of the characteristic equation and then adjust the various feedback gains until we get it. Refer [180] for detailed study of control systems with state variable feedback.

---

3. The basic design principle of   *cascade control,* commonly used in process industry, is to use the multiloop control configuration with a separate controller (PID type) in each loop.

Positive Feedback

Positive feedback is an operation which augments an imbalance, thereby pre-
cluding stability. If a temperature controller with positive feedback were used
to heat a room, it would increase the heat when the temperature was above the
set-point, and turn it off when it was below. Obviously, this property is not
conducive to regulations. Sometimes positive feedback is used in minor loops
of feedback control configurations; the stability and regulation of the controlled
variable is provided by the primary feedback loop. Figure 4.29a shows a feedback system with the minor loop having positive feedback. The equivalent
single-loop block diagram is shown in Fig. 4.29b. If $G_m(s)$ is selected to be
nearly unity, the loop gain becomes very high and the closed-loop transfer
function approximates to

$$\frac{Y(s)}{R(s)} = \frac{G(s)}{1 - G_m(s) + G(s)} \cong 1$$

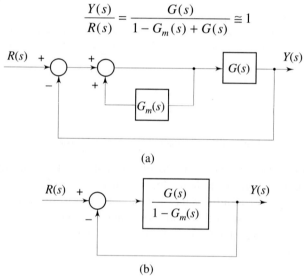

(a)

(b)

Fig. 4.29 *A system with positive feedback in minor loop*

Thus, due to the high loop gain provided by the minor positive feedback loop,
the closed-loop transfer function becomes insensitive to $G(s)$.

4.8   MULTIVARIABLE CONTROL SYSTEMS

Complex processes and machines often have several variables (outputs) that
we wish to control, and several manipulated inputs to provide this control.
Consider a plant with m output variables $y_1, y_2, \ldots, y_m$, and m control variables,
$u_1, u_2, \ldots, u_m$. A mathematical model of this system is therefore an $m \times m$
transfer function matrix defined below (refer Eqn. (2.35)):

$$\underset{m \times 1}{\mathbf{Y}(s)} = \underset{m \times m}{\mathbf{G}(s)} \quad \underset{m \times 1}{\mathbf{U}(s)}$$

or
$$\begin{bmatrix} Y_1(s) \\ Y_2(s) \\ \vdots \\ Y_m(s) \end{bmatrix} = \begin{bmatrix} G_{11}(s) & G_{12}(s) & \cdots & G_{1m}(s) \\ G_{21}(s) & G_{22}(s) & \cdots & G_{2m}(s) \\ \vdots & \vdots & & \vdots \\ G_{m1}(s) & G_{m2}(s) & \cdots & G_{mm}(s) \end{bmatrix} \begin{bmatrix} U_1(s) \\ U_2(s) \\ \vdots \\ U_m(s) \end{bmatrix} \qquad (4.41)$$

An important general property of such systems (and a major source of design difficulties) is *interaction* (or *coupling*) between inputs u_i and outputs y_j in the sense that any input u_i ; $1 \le i \le m$, will have a dynamic effect on all the outputs y_j ; $1 \le j \le m$. If each input u_i has a dynamic effect only on y_i, the system is said to be *non-interacting* (or *decoupled*). The following very important result concerning system interaction follows immediately:

The system (4.41) is non-interacting if, and only if, the $m \times m$ transfer function matrix $\mathbf{G}(s)$ is diagonal for all s:

$$\mathbf{G}(s) = \begin{bmatrix} G_1(s) & 0 & \cdots & 0 \\ 0 & G_2(s) & \cdots & 0 \\ \vdots & \vdots & & \vdots \\ 0 & 0 & \cdots & G_m(s) \end{bmatrix} \qquad (4.42)$$

By considering the relation $\mathbf{Y}(s) = \mathbf{G}(s)\mathbf{U}(s)$, it is clear that $Y_i(s) = G_i(s)U_i(s)$, $1 \le i \le m$, and hence that our 'multivariable' system consists of m independent SISO systems. It is also self-evident that each of these systems can be individually controlled by SISO feedback loops, as shown in Fig. 4.30, with transfer function

$$M_i(s) = \frac{D_i(s)\,G_i(s)}{1 + D_i(s)\,G_i(s)}$$

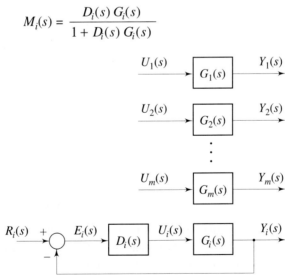

Fig. 4.30 *A non-interacting multivariable system*

In the multivariable systems language, the controller $\mathbf{D}(s)$ for a non-interacting plant $\mathbf{G}(s)$ is given by (refer Fig. 4.31)

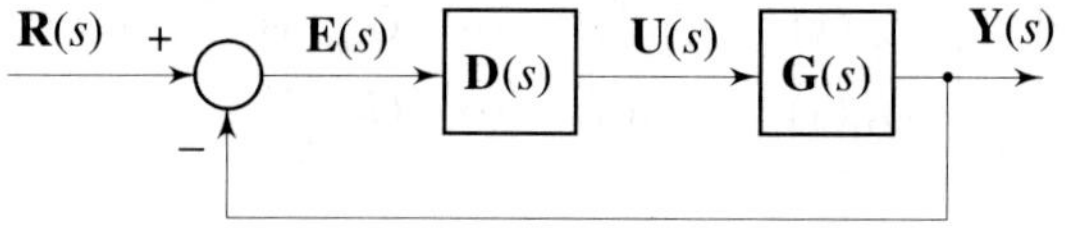

Fig. 4.31 *A multivariable control system*

$$\mathbf{D}(s) = \begin{bmatrix} D_1(s) & 0 & \cdots & 0 \\ 0 & D_2(s) & \cdots & 0 \\ \vdots & \vdots & & \vdots \\ 0 & 0 & \cdots & D_m(s) \end{bmatrix}$$

If the plant possesses interaction effects (reflected by the presence of off-diagonal terms in $\mathbf{G}(s)$), then the above analysis fails and there is a consequent increase in the complexity of the design exercise. It is, however, tempting to choose our controller $\mathbf{D}(s)$ in such a way that similar design principles may apply. Figure 4.32 illustrates a method to realize this objective. The controller $\mathbf{D}(s)$ is viewed as two sub-systems $\mathbf{D}_c(s)$ and $\mathbf{D}_p(s)$ in series. The sub-system $\mathbf{D}_p(s)$ is chosen so that the 'plant' seen by $\mathbf{D}_c(s)$ is diagonal:

$$\mathbf{Y}(s) = \mathbf{G}(s)\mathbf{U}(s) = \mathbf{G}(s)\mathbf{D}_p(s)\mathbf{V}(s)$$

$$\mathbf{G}(s)\mathbf{D}_p(s) = \begin{bmatrix} \hat{G}_1(s) & 0 & \cdots & 0 \\ 0 & \hat{G}_2(s) & \cdots & 0 \\ \vdots & \vdots & & \vdots \\ 0 & 0 & \cdots & \hat{G}_m(s) \end{bmatrix}$$

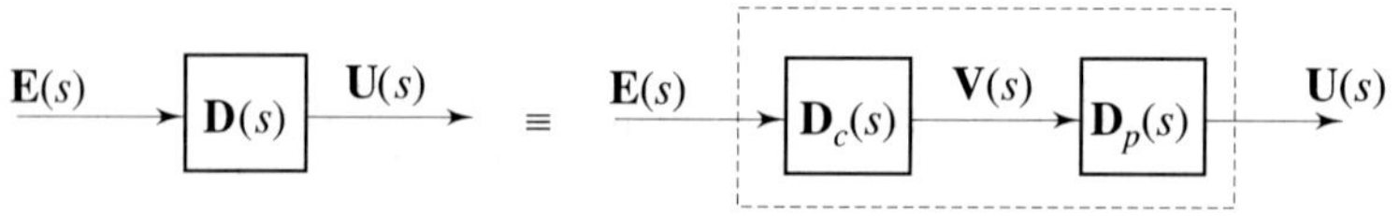

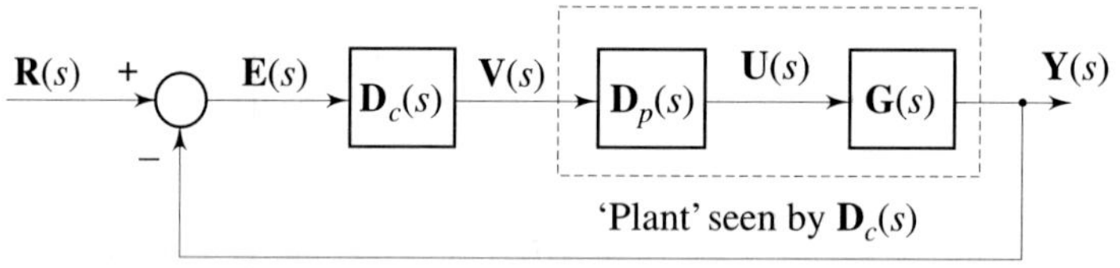

Fig. 4.32 *Extension of SISO design methods to multivariable systems*

The design of $\mathbf{D}_c(s)$ is then carried out by considering the 'plant' $\mathbf{G}(s)\mathbf{D}_p(s)$ as a set of m decoupled systems. This principle of control design is, in fact, the basis of extension of 'classical' methods of design of SISO systems to multivariable systems. For example, the important Nyquist array design techniques originated by Rosenbrock are based on the principle of *diagonal dominance* which represents a condition under which interaction has been reduced sufficiently that the overall control can be obtained by independent SISO design of diagonal loops [129–134].

As the demands on technology become more severe for safety, environmental, and efficiency considerations, multivariable control designs are required to include the interaction effects. Optimal control theory has an answer to this problem. The interactive multivariable plant is considered as a single unit, and a controller, which manipulates all the plant input variables simultaneously, is designed to force all the output variables to behave in a prescribed way[4].

This book is mostly concerned with the design of multivariable systems with weak interactions. We will neglect the interactions and design the controller for each loop as if it were a separate system. The interactions will be viewed as disturbances on the independent control loops.

Review Examples

Review Example 4.1

Figure 4.9 shows the block diagram model of satellite attitude system with proportional control. The closed-loop system is described by the equation

$$[(K_P\theta_r(s) - K_P\theta(s))K_AK_T + T_w(s)]\frac{1}{Js^2} = \theta(s)$$

or
$$(Js^2 + K_PK_AK_T)\theta(s) = K_PK_AK_T\,\theta_r(s) + T_w(s) \tag{4.43}$$

Let us first set the disturbance torque equal to zero and investigate the effects of changes in command θ_r. The closed-loop reference transfer function, obtained from (4.43), is

$$M(s) = \frac{\theta(s)}{\theta_r(s)} = \frac{\omega_n^2}{s^2 + \omega_n^2}; \; \omega_n \triangleq (K_PK_AK_T/J)^{1/2} \tag{4.44}$$

The response to a unit step change in θ_r is

$$\theta(t) = 1 - \cos\omega_n t$$

It is obvious that the control system of Fig. 4.9 does not provide a satisfactory response because the oscillations following a change in θ_r do not decay with time. One way of approaching a solution to this problem is to replace the amplifier block K_A by $K_c(1 + T_Ds)$. This, as we know, is the transfer function of a PD controller with controller gain K_c and derivative time T_D. The closed-loop system with the PD controller is described by the equation

$$[(K_P\theta_r(s) - K_P\theta(s))K_c(1 + T_Ds)K_T + T_w(s)]\frac{1}{Js^2} = \theta(s)$$

or
$$(Js^2 + K_PK_cT_DK_Ts + K_PK_cK_T)\theta(s)$$
$$= K_PK_cK_T(1 + T_Ds)\theta_r(s) + T_w(s) \tag{4.45}$$

The closed-loop reference transfer function is found to be

---

4. Chapter 9 of reference [180].

$$M(s) = \frac{\theta(s)}{\theta_r(s)} = \frac{\omega_n^2(1 + T_D s)}{s^2 + T_D \omega_n^2 s + \omega_n^2}; \ \omega_n = (K_P K_c K_T / J)^{1/2} \qquad (4.46)$$

A comparison of Eqn. (4.46) with Eqn. (4.44) reveals two major changes in the reference transfer function of the closed-loop system due to the inclusion of the derivative term. The most important change is that the denominator of Eqn. (4.46) contains a term proportional to s, which means that for $T_D > 0$, the oscillations will be damped out. An increase in value of T_D results in increased damping.

The other difference in the two cases is that $M(s)$ now has closed-loop zero at $s = -1/T_D$ whereas the previous version has no zeros in the finite s-plane. A large value of T_D will result in a violent response to sudden command changes (such as steps) because of the differentiating action of the PD controller. Thus, although the basic ingredients of the derivative control are favourable for increased damping and reduction of overshoots, the designer still has to design the PD controller properly, otherwise a negative effect could very well result. We will deal with the design problem in later chapters of the book.

Thus far our attention has been directed towards the control system's ability to make the satellite follow the reference pointing angle θ_r. An equally important task for the system is that of reducing the effects of disturbance torque upon the vehicle's orientation. From Eqn. (4.45), we get the following disturbance transfer function:

$$\frac{\theta(s)}{T_w(s)} = \frac{1/J}{s^2 + T_D \omega_n^2 s + \omega_n^2}; \ \omega_n \triangleq (K_P K_c K_T / J)^{1/2}$$

Let us examine the steady-state response to a constant disturbance torque. Letting $T_w(s) = A/s$, it follows that

$$\theta(s) = \frac{A/J}{s(s^2 + T_D \omega_n^2 s + \omega_n^2)}$$

Provided that $T_D > 0$, the final-value theorem may be applied to $\theta(s)$ in order to find the steady-state component of the pointing angle; the result is

$$\theta_{ss} = \frac{A}{J \omega_n^2} = \frac{A}{K_P K_c K_T}$$

The magnitude of the steady-state offset angle is proportional to the magnitude of the disturbance torque and inversely proportional to the loop gain.

Thus, if the satellite specifications require that it be capable of having no pointing error while subjected to a constant or very low frequency disturbance torque, it is not possible to meet this objective with a PD controller because the loop gain must certainly remain finite. The obvious conclusion is that the structure of the control system must be modified.

One way of approaching a solution to this problem is to replace the PD controller $K_c(1 + T_D s)$ by a PID controller $K_c\left(1 + T_D s + \dfrac{1}{T_I s}\right)$, where T_I is the integral time. With the PID controller, the closed-loop system of Fig. 4.9 is described by the equation

$$\left[(K_P \theta_r(s) - K_P \theta(s)) K_c \left(1 + T_D s + \frac{1}{T_I s} \right) K_T + T_w(s) \right] \frac{1}{Js^2} = \theta(s)$$

or $\quad (Js^3 + K_P K_c K_T T_D s^2 + K_P K_c K_T s + K_P K_c K_T / T_I) \theta(s)$

$$= K_P K_c K_T (T_D s^2 + s + 1/T_I) \theta_r(s) + s T_w(s)$$

or $\quad \left(s^3 + T_D \omega_n^2 s^2 + \omega_n^2 s + \frac{1}{T_I} \omega_n^2 \right) \theta(s)$

$$= \omega_n^2 (T_D s^2 + s + 1/T_I) \theta_r(s) + \frac{1}{J} s T_w(s); \ \omega_n \triangleq (K_P K_c K_T / J)^{1/2}$$

The disturbance transfer function is

$$\frac{\theta(s)}{T_w(s)} = \frac{s/J}{s^3 + T_D \omega_n^2 s^2 + \omega_n^2 s + \frac{1}{T_I} \omega_n^2}$$

For $\quad T_w(s) = A/s,$

$$\theta_{ss} = \lim_{s \to 0} s \left[\frac{s/J}{s^3 + T_D \omega_n^2 s^2 + \omega_n^2 s + \frac{1}{T_I} \omega_n^2} \right] \frac{A}{s} = 0$$

provided that the transients decay.

Before we can attain the improved steady-state response, we must be assured that the transients will indeed decay, which is to say that the roots of the characteristic equation must lie in the left half of the complex plane. Inspection of the characteristic equation

$$s^3 + T_D \omega_n^2 s^2 + \omega_n^2 s + \frac{1}{T_I} \omega_n^2 = 0$$

reveals that it is possible to meet this requirement by adjusting the parameters T_D, ω_n, and T_I.

The task of ascertaining a combination of T_D, T_I and ω_n which, in addition to meeting the stability requirement, results in an acceptable transient response, is not likely to be a simple one. We will deal with this problem in later chapters of this book.

Review Example 4.2

Heat exchangers such as that in Fig. 4.6, often use feedforward control for disturbance rejection to achieve better control of process fluid outlet temperature θ by measuring and correcting for two major disturbances in process fluid: mass flow rate q_m and inlet temperature θ_i. In this example, we design a feedforward controller for the heat exchanger process with the objective of complete rejection of disturbances in steady state. The design easily follows from the steady-state mathematical model of the process. A steady-state energy balance for the heat exchanger gives

$$\overline{Q}_m c(\overline{\theta} - \overline{\theta}_i) = \overline{Q}_{ms} \lambda$$

where

$\overline{Q}_m$ = steady-state flow rate of process fluid (kg/sec)

$\overline{Q}_{ms}$ = steady-state flow rate of steam(kg/sec)

$\overline{\theta}$ = steady-state value of outlet temperature of process fluid (°C)

$\overline{\theta}_i$ = steady-state value of inlet temperature of process fluid (°C)

c = specific heat of the fluid [Joules/(kg)(°C)] = 3750

λ = latent heat of condensation, (Joules/kg) = 2.25×10^6

With $\overline{Q}_m = 12$, $\overline{\theta}_i = 40$ °C, $\overline{\theta}$ = the set-point value = 90 °C, the steady-state value of steam flow rate is

$$\overline{Q}_{ms} = \frac{12 \times 3750(90 - 40)}{2.25 \times 10^6} = 0.8 \text{ kg/sec}$$

With this flow rate, the steady-state balance will be maintained in absence of disturbances.

Assume now that perturbations q_m and θ_i occur in the steady-state values of process fluid flow rate and inlet temperature respectively. The steam flow rate required to maintain steady-state balance under these perturbed conditions is given by

$$\overline{Q}_{ms} + q_{ms} = \frac{(\overline{Q}_m + q_m)c(\overline{\theta} - (\overline{\theta}_i + \theta_i))}{\lambda} \tag{4.47}$$

Assuming $\overline{\theta}$ (= set-point value of θ), c and λ known, measurement of $\overline{Q}_m + q_m$ and $\overline{\theta}_i + \theta_i$ allows calculation of needed $\overline{Q}_{ms} + q_{ms}$, which becomes the set-point of a steam flow controller (Fig. 4.33).

As usual, modelling inaccuracies in Eqn. (4.47) prevent perfect control of θ. If specifications cannot be met, we can augment the feedforward control mode with feedback.

Review Example 4.3

In this example, we will investigate the linear position control of a single-link robot manipulator.

A single-link manipulator consists of a single rigid link attached to a joint. The joint can move the link and the gripper in two-dimensional space (Fig. 4.34). The manipulator is driven by an armature-controlled dc motor through a gear train.

We model the manipulator link and its payload (the object picked up by the gripper) as a lumped parameter system with moment of inertia J_L and viscous

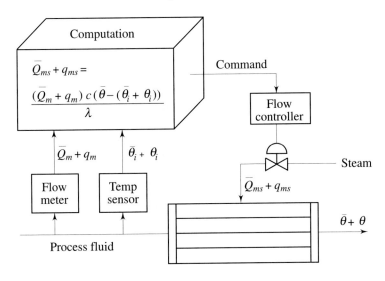

Fig. 4.33 *Heat exchanger control using disturbance compensation only*

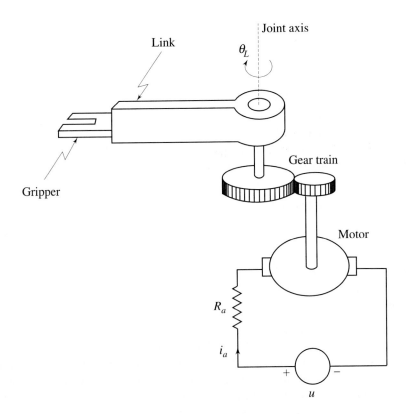

Fig. 4.34 *A single-link robot manipulator*

damping factor B_L. In response to motor torque T_M, the link will rotate; the angular position of the link is designated by θ_L. It may be noted that the moment of inertia will not necessarily be constant because during the course of an operation, the robot may pick up different objects with its gripper. The variation in the payload will change the effective moment of inertia of the link. In robotic applications, J_L is usually constant during each task; however it may vary from task to task.

The objectives set for the design of a robot control system are:

(i) perfect command tracking, i.e., the output (position of the gripper) must track the time-varying trajectory $\theta_R(t)$; and

(ii) robustness in command tracking with respect to variations in payload.

The plant of the robot control system is described by the equations:

$$u(t) = R_a\, i_a(t) + K_b \frac{d\theta_M(t)}{dt}$$

$$K_T i_a(t) = J \frac{d^2\theta_M(t)}{dt^2} + B \frac{d\theta_M(t)}{dt} + T_w(t) \qquad (4.47)$$

$$\theta_L(t) = n\theta_M(t)$$

where

u = applied armature voltage
R_a = armature resistance
i_a = armature current
θ_M = angular position of the motor shaft
θ_L = angular position of the load shaft
n = gear ratio
K_b = back emf constant
J = moment of inertia referred to the motor shaft
B = viscous friction coefficient referred to the motor shaft
T_w = disturbance torque

Manipulation of Eqns (4.47) yields

$$u(t) - \frac{R_a}{K_T} T_w(t) = M\ddot{\theta}_L(t) + N\dot{\theta}_L(t) \qquad (4.48)$$

where
$$M = \frac{JR_a}{nK_T};\ N = \frac{BR_a + K_b K_T}{nK_T}$$

The transfer function of the plant is ($T_w = 0$)

$$G(s) = \frac{\theta_L(s)}{U(s)} = \frac{1}{Ms^2 + Ns} \qquad (4.49)$$

The proposed control scheme utilizes manipular 'inverse' as a feedforward controller to provide the ability for the output position to track the command input $\theta_R(t)$. From Fig. 4.35a, we find that for

$$D_o(s) = Ms^2 + Ns,$$

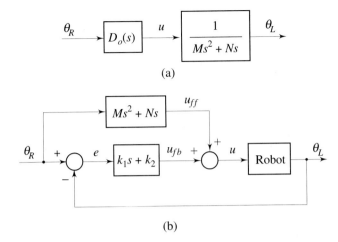

Fig. 4.35 *Feedforward plus feedback control scheme for robot manipulator*

$$\theta_L(t) = \theta_R(t)$$

It is observed that the feedforward controller is not physically realizable. However if θ_R, $\dot{\theta}_R$ and $\ddot{\theta}_R$ are known functions, then the output of the feedforward controller may be constructed using the following relation:

$$u(t) = M\ddot{\theta}_R(t) + N\dot{\theta}_R(t)$$

The command tracking provided by the feedforward controller cannot be perfect since we cannot exactly estimate the system parameters. Also, the deviations in nominal values of system parameters (due to payload variations), and disturbances $T_w(t)$ will destabilize the system if only feedforward control is used. Robustness with respect to variations in system parameters and disturbances may be provided by a simple feedback control scheme shown in Fig. 4.35b. The total control input is given by the sum of the two components: u_{ff} for command tracking and u_{fb} for system stabilization.

$$u(t) = u_{ff}(t) + u_{fb}(t)$$
$$= M\ddot{\theta}_R(t) + N\dot{\theta}_R(t) + k_1\dot{e}(t) + k_2e(t) \qquad (4.50)$$

where $\qquad e(t) = \theta_R(t) - \theta_L(t)$

The closed-loop dynamics can be expressed as (refer Eqns (4.48) and (4.50))

$$M\ddot{\theta}_L + N\dot{\theta}_L = M\ddot{\theta}_R + N\dot{\theta}_R + k_1\dot{e} + k_2e$$

or $\qquad\qquad M\ddot{e} + N\dot{e} + k_1\dot{e} + k_2e = 0$

The characteristic equation of the closed-loop system becomes

$$Ms^2 + (N + k_1)\, s + k_2 = 0$$

or
$$s^2 + \frac{N + k_1}{M} s + \frac{k_2}{M} = 0 \qquad (4.51)$$

Matching the characteristic equation of the closed-loop system with the standard damped oscillator equation, we obtain

$$s^2 + \frac{N + k_1}{M} s + \frac{k_2}{M} = s^2 + 2\zeta\omega_n s + \omega_n^2$$

On equating like terms, the expressions for the damping ratio and natural frequency are found as follows:

$$\omega_n = \sqrt{\frac{nK_T k_2}{JR_a}} ; \; \zeta = \frac{BR_a + K_b K_T + nK_T k_1}{2\sqrt{nK_T k_2 JR_a}} \qquad (4.52)$$

The robot manipulator should not be an underdamped system because any overshoot in the system response could cause the manipulator to collide with a solid object. Consequently, the damping ratio should be greater than or equal to unity.

Once the designer specifies numerical values for ζ and ω_n, the required controller gains can be obtained from Eqns (4.52). For given $\{\theta_R, \dot{\theta}_R, \ddot{\theta}_R\}$ the control law (4.50) will force $\theta_L(t)$ to follow $\theta_R(t)$; the tracking will be robust in the presence of 'small' modelling errors and variations in payload.

Review Questions

4.1 (a) Open-loop control action on a stable plant does not run the risk of instability, but negative feedback control action may result in instability problems. Inspite of this fact, most of the industrial control schemes are based on negative feedback concept. Why? (Help: pp 13-16, pp 242-245, p 261, p 263)

(b) Comment on the role of positive feedback in closed-loop control configurations. (Help: p 280)

4.2 In designing control systems, the following aspects must be taken into account.
(a) Stability
(b) Input amplitude constraints
(c) Disturbance rejection
(d) Noise filtering
(e) Sensitivity and robustness
Explain the significance of each.

4.3 The use of feedback in control systems is motivated by the presence of external disturbance uncertainties and model uncertainties. The use of feedback can be regarded as unreasonable if there is no uncertainty in the system. Show that feedback control can
(a) greatly reduce the effect on the controlled variable of all external disturbances except those associated with the sensor (measurement system); and

(b) make the system tolerant of variations in hardware parameters other than those of the sensor.

How can we reduce the effects of measurement errors on control system performance? (Help: p 243, pp 257-258)

4.4 Show that high loop gain in feedback systems results in

(i) good steady-state tracking accuracy;

(ii) good disturbance signal rejection;

(iii) low sensitivity to process parameter variations; and

(iv) good relative stability, i.e., rate of decay of transients.

What are the factors limiting the gain? (Help: p 263)

4.5 (a) Differentiate between theterms'servo system'and'regulator'.(Help: pp 2-3)

(b) A multivariable system can be considered as consisting of an appropriate number of separate single-input, single-output systems if the interactions are weak. Explain. (Help: pp 25-33, Section 4.8)

4.6 The configuration shown in Fig. 4.1 is that of a basic feedback control system, but it is not the only configuration used. In many systems it is possible and profitable to improve the performance attained with feedback control by using other control configurations. Discuss the use of feedforward-feedback, and minor-loop feedback control structures for performance improvement. (Help: Fig. 1.15, pp 21-25, pp 276-279)

4.7 A position control system has a two-loop configuration. The minor-loop is a velocity feedback loop realized through tachometer mounted on the motor shaft. The major loop is a position-feedback loop realized through gears and potentiometer.

Comment on the effects of the following on the general performance characteristics of the system (Help: Fig. 1.15):

(a) Minor loop is broken

(b) Major loop is broken

4.8 (a) An open-loop controller $D(s) = 1/G(s)$ in cascade with process $G(s)$ will provide perfect tracking of the input. Why do we need feedback schemes? (Help: p 261, Review Example 4.3)

(b) Consider the speed control system of Fig. 4.15. When $\omega = \omega_r$, the error signal is zero. How is the torque generated to maintain the motor at the speed $\omega = \omega_r$ when the error is zero?

4.9 (a) The steady-state error due to step commands can be eliminated from proportional control systems with type-0 plants, by

(i) intentionally 'misadjusting' reference input,

(ii) introducing integral mode in the controller

The second approach increases the order of the closed-loop system, making relative stability poorer. Show that these statements are correct. Are there any limitations of the first approach? (Help: pp 266-272)

(b) Consider a position control system. Show that the integrating effect naturally appears in the system plant.

Do you require integral control for such a plant for zero steady-state errors to step commands/disturbances? Why? (Help: Example 4.6)

4.10 (a) Show with the help of examples that introduction of derivative mode of control in a feedback system with proportional control makes the system response less oscillatory. What is its effect on steady-state accuracy? (Help: Section 4.6)

(b) Derivative control may be applied to the system error or the controlled variable. Which scheme do you prefer? Why? (Help: pp 274-275)

(c) When do we introduce integral mode in a feedback system with proportional-derivative control? (Help: Review Example 4.1)

Problems

4.1 The block diagram of a position control system is shown in Fig. P4.1. Determine the sensitivity of the closed-loop transfer function $M(s)$ with respect to G and H, the forward path, and feedback path transfer functions respectively, for $s = j\omega = j1$.

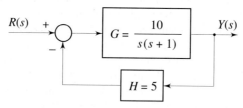

Fig. P4.1

4.2 A servo system is represented by the signal flow graph shown in Fig. P4.2. The nominal values of the parameters are $K_1 = 1$, $K_2 = 5$ and $K_3 = 5$. Determine the overall transmission $Y(s)/R(s)$, and its sensitivity to changes in K_1 under steady dc conditions, i.e., $s = 0$.

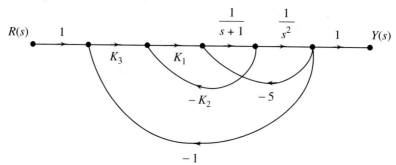

Fig. P4.2

4.3 A unity feedback system has forward path transfer function $G(s) = 20/(s + 1)$. Determine the response of open- and closed-loop systems for unit-step input.

Suppose now that parameter variations occurring during operating conditions cause $G(s)$ to modify to $G'(s) = 20/(s + 0.4)$. What will be the effect on unit-step response of open- and closed-loop systems? Comment upon the sensitivity of the two systems to parameter variations.

4.4 Consider the two control systems shown in Fig. P4.4. In the open-loop control system, gain K_c is calibrated so that $K_c = 1/10$. In the closed-loop control system, gain K_p of the controller is set so that $K_p = 10$. Find the steady-state error to unit-step input in both the cases.

Suppose now that parameter variations occurring during operating conditions cause $G(s)$ to modify to $G'(s) = 11/(\tau s + 1)$. What will be the effect on the steady-state error of open- and closed-loop systems? Comment upon the sensitivity of the two systems to parameter variations.

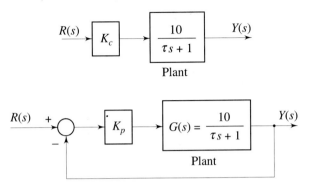

Fig. P4.4

4.5 The field of a dc servomotor is separately excited by means of an amplifier of gain $K_A = 90$ (see Fig. P4.5). The field has an inductance of 2 henrys and a resistance of 50 ohms. Calculate the field time-constant.

A voltage proportional to the field current is now fedback negatively to the amplifier input. Determine the value of the feedback constant K to reduce the field time-constant to 4 milliseconds.

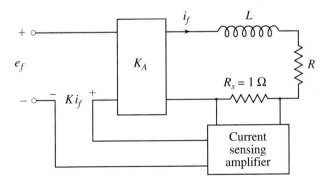

Fig. P4.5

4.6 Consider the system shown in Fig. P4.6, where $w(t)$ is a unit-step disturbance. Calculate K such that the steady-state error in $y(t)$ due to $w(t)$ is less than one percent of $w(t)$.

4.7 The two control configurations shown in Fig. P4.7 have identical plants; however, external disturbances enter the two systems at different points along the forward path. Find the steady-state error in the two cases in response to step disturbance of unit magnitude. If in any of the two cases the steady-state error is non-zero, suggest a suitable control scheme to eliminate this error.

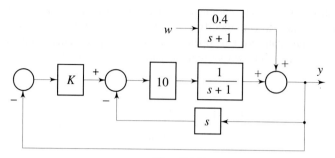

Fig. P4.6

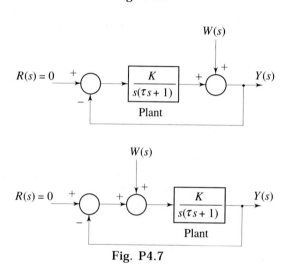

Fig. P4.7

4.8 A temperature control system has the block diagram given in Fig. P4.8. The input signal is a voltage and represents the desired temperature θ_r. Find the steady-state error of the system when θ_r is a unit step function and (i) $D(s) = 1$, (ii) $D(s) = 1 + \dfrac{0.1}{s}$, (iii) $D(s) = 1 + 0.3s$. What is the effect of the integral term in the PI controller, and derivative term in the PD controller on the steady-state error ?

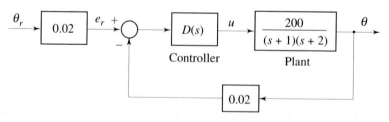

Fig. P4.8

4.9 Consider the closed-loop system of Fig. P4.9. Compute the characteristic equation and therefrom determine the stability of the system when

(i) $D(s) = 1$, (ii) $D(s) = 1 + 2s$, and (iii) $D(s) = 1 + \dfrac{2}{s}$.

What is the effect of derivative term in the PD controller, and integral term in the PI controller on system stability?

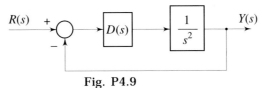

Fig. P4.9

4.10 An automobile speed control system will be necessary for passenger cars travelling on the automatic highways of the future. A model of a feedback control system for a standard vehicle is shown in Fig. P4.10. The load disturbance due to a percent gradient, w, of the highway is also shown. The engine constant $K_e = 500$.

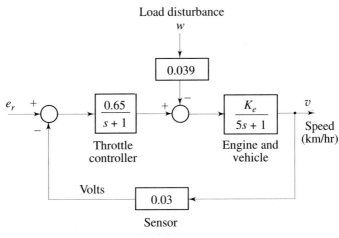

Fig. P4.10

(a) If the desired speed is $v_r = 50$ km/hr, find the constant input voltage e_r that should be applied.

(b) Determine the sensitivity of $V(s)/E_r(s)$ to changes in engine constant K_e.

(c) Determine the constant percent gradient for which the engine stalls; the speed setting is 50 km/hr.

4.11 A simple voltage regulator is shown in Fig. P4.11. A potentiometer is used at the output terminals of the generator to give feedback voltage Ke_0 where K is a constant ($K \leq 1$). The potentiometer resistance is high enough that it may be assumed to draw negligible current. The amplifier has a gain of 20 volts/volt. The generator gain is 50 volts/field amp. Reference voltage $e_r = 50$ volts.

(a) Draw a block diagram of the system when the generator is supplying a load current.

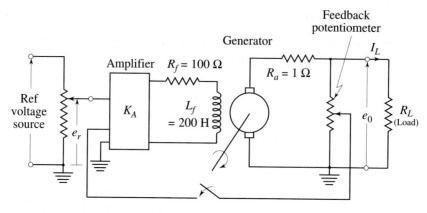

Fig. P4.11

(b) The system is operated closed loop (switch closed). Determine the value of K in order to give a steady no-load terminal voltage of 250 volts. What is the change in terminal voltage caused by a steady load current of 30 amps? What reference voltage would be required to restore the generator terminal voltage of 250 V?

(c) The system is operated open loop (switch open). Determine the reference voltage needed to obtain a steady no-load voltage of 250 V. What would be the change in terminal voltage for a load of 30 amps ?

(d) Compare the changes in terminal voltage in parts (b) and (c) and comment upon the effect of feedback in countering the changes in terminal voltage caused by load current.

4.12 For the speed control system shown in Fig. P4.12, assume that

 (i) generator field time-constant is negligible and its generated voltage is K_g volts/amp;

 (ii) friction of the motor and mechanical load is negligible.

  (a) Find the time variation of output speed (ω_o) for a sudden command input (ω_r) of 10 rad/sec. Find also the steady-state output speed.

  (b) If the feedback loop is opened and gain K_A adjusted to give the same steady-state speed as in the case of closed loop, determine how the output speed varies with time, and compare the speed of response in the two cases.

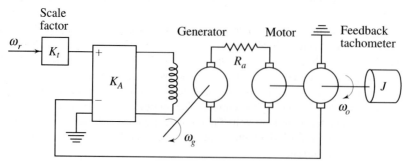

Fig. P4.12

(c) Compare the sensitivity of $\omega_o(s)/\omega_r(s)$ to changes in amplifier gain K_A and generator speed ω_g with and without feedback.

The system parameters are given below:

Moment of inertia of motor and load $J = 5$ kg-m^2

Motor back emf constant $K_b = 5$ volts per rad/sec

Total armature resistance of motor
and generator $R_a = 1$ ohm

Generator gain constant $K_g = 50$ volts/amp

Amplifier gain $K_A = 5$ amps/volt

Tachometer constant $K_t = 0.5$ volts per rad/sec

4.13 Figure P4.13 shows a control scheme for controlling the azimuth angle of a rotating antenna. The plant consists of an armature-controlled dc motor with dc generator used as an amplifier. The parameters of the plant are given below:

Motor torque constant	$K_T =$	1 N-m/amp
Motor back emf constant	$K_b =$	1 volt/(rad/sec)
Generator gain constant	$K_g =$	100 volt/amp
Potentiometer sensitivity	$K_P =$	1 volt/rad
Amplifier gain	$K_A =$	50 volt/volt
Moment of inertia of load	$J_L =$	4 N-m/(rad/sec^2)

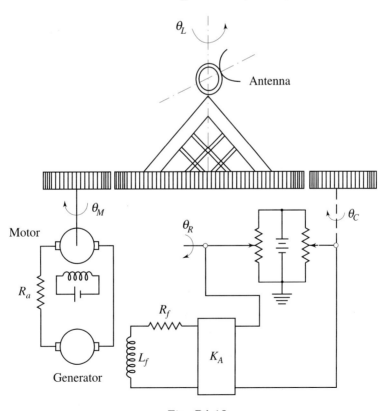

Fig. P4.13

$$\dot{\theta}_L / \dot{\theta}_M = \dot{\theta}_L / \dot{\theta}_C = 1/2$$
$$R_f = 20\ \Omega,\ L_f = 5\text{H},\ R_a = 1\Omega$$

Load friction, and motor inertia and friction are negligible.

The antenna is subject to wind gust torque T_w. Experiments on the antenna show that wind exerts a maximum disturbance of 100 N-m at the antenna.

(a) Draw a block diagram of the system showing the variables θ_R, θ_C, θ_M, θ_L, and T_w. Give the transfer function of each block.

(b) Determine the sensitivity of $\theta_L(s)/\theta_R(s)$ to changes in generator gain K_g for $s = j\omega = j0.1$.

(c) Determine the steady-state error in θ_L when the antenna is subjected to a constant wind gust torque of 100 N-m, with the reference position $\theta_R = 0$.

(d) The antenna is required to have steady-state error of less than $0.2°$. Propose a control scheme to meet this objective.

4.14 Aircraft transfer function relating pitch angle θ to the elevator angle δ is of the form

$$\frac{\theta(s)}{\delta(s)} = \frac{K(\tau s + 1)}{s\left(\dfrac{s^2}{\omega_n^2} + \dfrac{2\zeta}{\omega_n}s + 1\right)}$$

For a given vehicle, the numerical values of the parameters K, τ, ζ and ω_n vary with altitude and Mach number. For a vehicle flying at four times the speed of sound (Mach 4) at an altitude of 30,000 m, the parameters are

$$\tau = 25,\ K = 0.02,\ \omega_n = 2,\ \zeta = 0.02$$

A basic pitch-command control system is shown in Fig. P4.14. θ_r is the pilot's control stick rotation. The elevator is controlled by an electrohydraulic servo. The transfer function of the servo compared with the dynamics of the aircraft, may be simplified as a constant K_e.

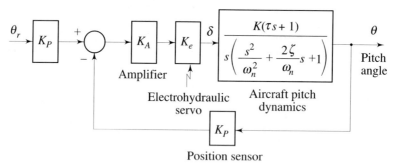

Fig. P4.14

(a) Compare the open-loop and closed-loop systems for sensitivity to changes in the parameter K.

(b) Assume that both the pitch angle θ and its rate of change $\dot{\theta}$ are available for feedback. Suggest a feedback control scheme for increasing the aircraft damping.

4.15 Figure P4.15a shows a two-axis (r, θ) robot whose task is to position a payload at any commanded position in a single vertical plane. The elastic deflection due to gravity causes the payload position to be in error. Another problem that leads to an error in payload position is the variable inertia J of the robot arm. A servo system for positioning the θ-axis of the two-axis robot is given in Fig. P4.15b. K_A is the amplifier gain, K_T, K_b and R_a are the parameters of the armature-controlled dc motor, and J and B are the parameters of the load on the motor.

(a) What is the effect of constant disturbance torque $T_w(s) = K_w/s$ on the steady-state value of $\theta(s)$? Assume $\theta_r = 0$ at the index position.

(b) Determine the sensitivity of the closed-loop system to variations in J.

(c) Show that as $K_A \rightarrow \infty$, the steady-state error in θ due to constant disturbance, and sensitivity of the system to variations in J reduces to zero. What are the constraints on the use of large values of K_A?

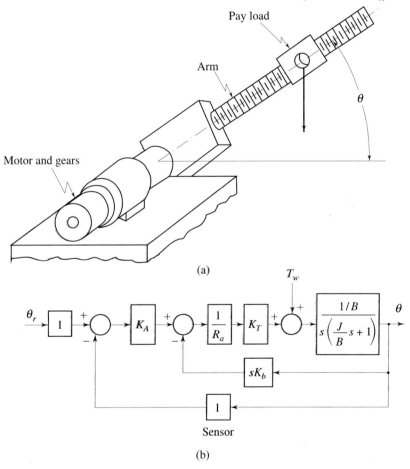

(a)

(b)

Fig. P4.15

4.16 In the system shown in Fig. P4.16, $h(t)$ represents deviation of liquid head from the steady-state value $\overline{H}$ and $q(t)$ represents the deviation of liquid outflow

rate from the steady-state value $\bar{Q}$. The pump controls the liquid head/
outflow rate by supplying liquid at a rate $\bar{Q}_i + q_i(t)$; $q_i(t) = -K[h(t) - h_r(t)]$,
where K is a constant and $h_r(t)$ is the desired change in the initial set-point
value.

(a) Prove that the following equation represents perturbation dynamics:

$$RC\frac{dh(t)}{dt} + h(t) = R\,q_i(t)$$

where R is a constant so that $q(t) = h(t)/R$, and C = cross-sectional area
of the tank.

(b) Draw a block diagram of the closed-loop system showing the variables
h_r, q_i, h and q.

(c) Determine the sensitivity of the closed-loop transfer function $H(s)/H_r(s)$
to changes in the parameter R under steady dc conditions, i.e., $s = 0$.

(d) Determine the steady-state error for a unit step command $h_r(t)$. Explain
what modification could be made in the system to eliminate the steady-
state error to step input. What is the effect of the proposed modification
on system sensitivity to changes in R under steady dc conditions?

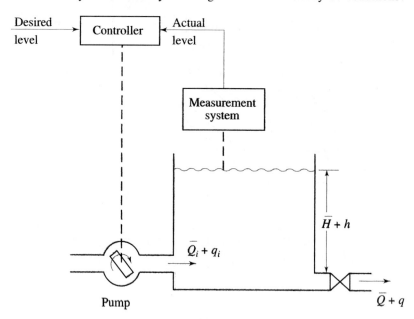

Fig. P4.16

4.17 In the scheme of Fig. P4.17, a concentrated solution of salt is continuously
mixed with pure water in a mixing valve. The valve characteristic is such that
the total flow rate Q through it is maintained constant. $\bar{Q}_i$ is the steady-state
value of inflow rate of salt solution with salt concentration $\bar{C}_i$, and $\bar{C}$ is the
steady-state value of the salt concentration in the outflowing stream. $q_i(t)$,

$c_i(t)$ and $c(t)$ represent perturbations in these variables. Prove that the following equation represents the perturbation dynamics:

$$V \frac{dc(t)}{dt} + Q c(t) = \overline{C}_i q_i(t) + \overline{Q}_i c_i(t)$$

To reduce the effect of uncontrolled disturbance $c_i(t)$, the valve is controlled so that $q_i(t) = -Kc(t)$ where K is a constant. Draw a block diagram of the closed-loop system. Assuming a step disturbance of magnitude A, determine the steady-state error. What is the steady-state error if the valve is controlled so that

$$q_i(t) = -K \int_0^t c(t) dt \ ?$$

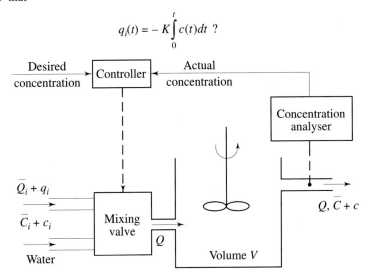

Fig. P4.17

4.18 The temperature control system of Fig. P4.18 is set up to produce a steady stream of hot liquid at a controlled temperature. The liquid enters at a constant flow rate Q and variable temperature $\overline{\theta}_i + \theta_i$, and leaves at constant flow rate Q with temperature $\overline{\theta} + \theta$. The temperature of the outflowing liquid is measured by means of a thermocouple which produces an output voltage proportional to the temperature of the outflowing liquid ($e_t = K_t \theta$). This voltage is subtracted from the reference voltage to generate an error signal which in turn regulates the heating rate produced by electrical resistance heater controlled by an SCR amplifier.

The perturbation dynamics of the temperature control system is described by the equation

$$K(e_r - e_t) = C \frac{d\theta}{dt} + \frac{\theta - \theta_i}{R_1}$$

where

C = thermal capacitance of the liquid in the tank; (Joules/ °C)

R_1 = thermal resistance of the carrier fluid; (°C/(Joules/sec))

$K =$ gain of the SCR amplifier-heater circuit; ((Joules/sec)/volt).

(a) Draw a block diagram of the closed-loop system showing reference voltage, e_r, disturbance in temperature, θ_i, and the controlled temperature, θ.

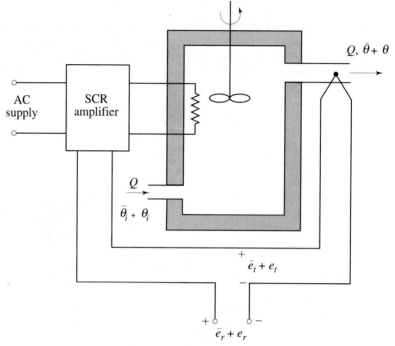

Fig. P4.18

(b) Compare the open-loop ($K_t = 0$) and the closed-loop systems for (i) sensitivity to changes in parameter K, (ii) the ability to reduce the effects of step disturbance θ_i, and (iii) the system time-constants in the two cases.

(c) Modify the block diagram of part (a) to include the effect of the disturbance signal θ_a caused by changes in the ambient temperature. Find the steady change in the temperature of the outflowing liquid for open- and closed-loop cases due to a unit step disturbance θ_a. The surface area of the tank is A m^2, and the heat transfer coefficient of the tank-air interface is U Joules/(m^2)(°C) (sec).

4.19 A system with feedforward-feedback control structure is shown in Fig. P4.19.

(a) Find the steady-state error to unit step disturbance when $K_f = 0$, and the feedback controller is a proportional controller with $K_c = 1.25$.

(b) Show that the steady-state error of part (a) can be reduced to zero if the proportional controller is modified to PI controller.

(c) Alternatively, the steady-state error of part (a) may be reduced to zero by including feedforward control. Find the feedforward gain K_f which realizes this objective.

Compare the usefulness of schemes (b) and (c) for control system design.

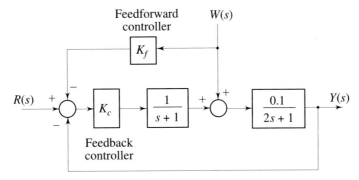

Fig. P4.19

4.20 Figure P4.20 shows a field controlled dc motor with a dc amplifier. The parameters of the system are given below:

Amplifier gain $K_A = 50$ volt/volt

Motor field resistance $R_f = 99\,\Omega$

Motor field inductance $L_f = 20\,\mathrm{H}$

Motor torque constant $K_T = 10$ N-m/amp

Moment of inertia of load, $J = 0.5$ N-m/(rad/sec^2)

Coefficient of viscous friction of load, $B = 0.5$ N-m/(rad/sec)

Motor inertia and friction are negligible.

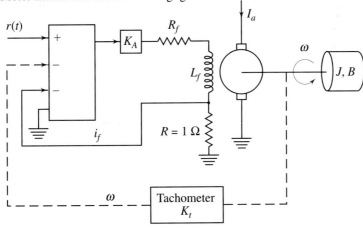

Fig. P4.20

(a) The time-constant of devices with high inductance, such as the field-controlled dc motor, is too long for design requirements. Current feedback may be used to decrease the time-constant. For the system of Fig. P4.20, determine the time-constant of the field circuit with and without current feedback.

(b) Now add a speed-feedback loop (shown dotted in Fig. P4.20) around the current-feedback loop and obtain the closed-loop transfer function of the system.

(c) Modify the system of part (b) to convert it into a position control system. Use both the current-feedback and the speed-feedback loops in the modified scheme.

4.21 Figure P4.21 shows a position control system.

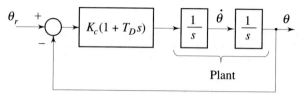

Fig. P4.21

(a) Compute the values of K_c and T_D so that the characteristic equation of the closed-loop system will have roots at $-1 \pm j1.732$.

(b) We know that it is advantageous to avoid derivative action on the error signal if it is possible to obtain equivalent effect with an alternative control configuration. Suggest an alternative control scheme that results in the same characteristic roots of closed-loop system as in part (a) and avoids derivative action on the error signal.

4.22 Figure P4.22a shows the block diagram of a dc servomechanism. Determine the sensitivity of the closed-loop transfer function $M(s)$ to the variations in K at $\omega = 5$ rad/sec. The nominal value of $K = 1$.

Change the control configuration of the system to two-loop configuration with feedback of θ and $\dot{\theta}$ (see Fig. P4.22b); the closed-loop transfer function of the two-loop configuration must be equal to that of the system shown in Fig. P4.22a. Obtain sensitivity of $M(s)$ to variations in K at $\omega = 5$ for the new configuration. Comment on the result.

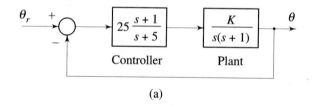

(a)

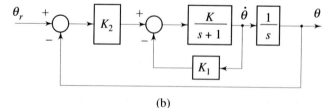

(b)

Fig. P4.22

chapter 5

Concepts of Stability and the Routh Stability Criterion

INTRODUCTION

Roughly speaking, stability in a system implies that small changes to the system stimulus do not result in large effects on system response. Stability is a very important characteristic of the transient performance of a system. Almost every working system is designed to be stable. Within the boundaries of parameter variations permitted by stability considerations, we can then seek to improve the system performance.

In testing the stability of a dynamic system we must carefully define the terms 'response', 'stimulus', 'small change', and 'large effect'. For example, it is possible for a system to have a well-behaved output while an internal variable (state variable) is growing without bound. If we consider only the output as the 'response', we might call such a system stable. However, if we consider the state variables to be the response, we might just as reasonably call this system unstable. The stimulus might be a signal persisting for all time, or it might be only a set of initial conditions. Finally, we might require that the response not grow if the stimulus is removed, or we might require that the response go to zero if the stimulus is removed. For systems that are nonlinear or time-varying, the number of definitions of stability is large, and some of the definitions can be quite complicated in order to account for the varieties of the responses the systems can display. We will describe a few elementary results, particularly those useful in the study of linear time-invariant systems.

Consider an n-dimensional linear time-invariant system described by a state variable model of the form (refer Eqns (2.4))

$$\dot{\mathbf{x}}(t) = \mathbf{A}\mathbf{x}(t) + \mathbf{b}r(t); \ \mathbf{x}(t = 0) \overset{\Delta}{=} \mathbf{x}^0$$
$$y(t) = \mathbf{c}\mathbf{x}(t) + du(t)$$

(5.1)

where $\mathbf{x}$ is the $n \times 1$ state vector, r is the scalar input, y is the scalar output, $\mathbf{A}$ is $n \times n$ real constant matrix, $\mathbf{b}$ and $\mathbf{c}$ are, respectively, $n \times 1$ and $1 \times n$ real constant vectors, and d is a constant scalar.

The system (5.1) has two sources of excitation:

  (i) the initial state $\mathbf{x}^0$ representing initial internal energy storage; and

  (ii) external input $r(t)$; $t \geq 0$.

In the stability study, we are generally concerned with the following questions:

1. If the system is relaxed ($\mathbf{x}^0 = \mathbf{0}$), will a bounded input $r(t)$; $t \geq 0$, produce a bounded output $y(t)$ for all t (regardless of what goes on inside the system) ?

2. A relaxed system ($\mathbf{x}^0 = \mathbf{0}$) with input $r(t) = 0$; $t \geq 0$, will continue to be in the zero state for all time. This condition can be viewed as the *equilibrium state* of the system: the system is said to be in equilibrium state $\mathbf{x}^e = \mathbf{0}$ when both the initial internal energy storage and the external input are zero.

    Taking changes in initial conditions as the stimulus and system state $\mathbf{x}(t)$ as the response, we pose the following question:

    If the system with zero input ($r(t) = 0$; $t \geq 0$) is perturbed from its equilibrium state $\mathbf{x}^e = \mathbf{0}$ at $t = 0$, will the state $\mathbf{x}(t)$ return to $\mathbf{x}^e$, remain 'close' to $\mathbf{x}^e$, or diverge from $\mathbf{x}^e$?

The first notion of stability is concerned with the boundedness of the output of a relaxed system in response to bounded input, and is called *bounded-input, bounded-output* (BIBO) *stability*. Clearly, if a system is subjected to an unbounded input and produces an unbounded response, nothing can be said about its stability. However, if it is subjected to a bounded input and produces an unbounded response, it is, by definition, unstable. Actually the output of an unstable system may increase to a certain extent and then the system may break down or become nonlinear after the output exceeds a certain magnitude, so that the linear mathematical model no longer applies.

The second notion of stability is concerned with the boundedness of the state of free (unforced) system in response to arbitrary initial state, and is called *zero-input stability*.

As we shall see in this chapter, the two notions of stability defined above are essentially equivalent in linear time-invariant systems. Simple and powerful tools are available to determine the stability of such systems.

In nonlinear systems, there is no definite correspondence between the two notions. For a free stable nonlinear system, there is no guarantee that the output will be bounded whenever input is bounded. Also, if the output is bounded for a particular input, it may not be bounded for other inputs. Most of the important results obtained thus far concern the stability of nonlinear systems in the sense of the second notion above, i.e., when the system has no input. It may be noted that even for this class of nonlinear systems, the concept of stability is not clear cut. System behaviour for small deviations about the equilibrium point may be different from that for large deviations. Also because of possible existence of multiple equilibrium states in nonlinear systems, the system may move away from one equilibrium state to the other as time progresses.

Another important point to be kept in mind is that when oscillations occur in free linear time-invariant systems, the amplitude of the oscillations is not fixed; it changes with the size of the initial conditions. Slight changes in system parameters will destroy the oscillations. In nonlinear systems, on the other hand, there can be oscillations that are independent of the size of initial conditions and these oscillations (*limit cycles*) are usually much less sensitive to parameter variations. Limit cycles of fixed amplitude and period can be sustained over a finite range of system parameters.

Treatment of nonlinear systems is beyond the scope of this book. Reference [180] highlights the problems associated with nonlinear control systems, and presents commonly used analysis tools. In this chapter, we concern ourselves exclusively with the stability of linear time-invariant systems.

5.2 | BOUNDED-INPUT BOUNDED-OUTPUT STABILITY

A linear relaxed system (initial conditions zero) is said to have BIBO stability if every bounded input results in a bounded[1] output. A test for this property is readily found using convolution (refer Section 2.3). If the system has input $r(t)$, output $y(t)$, and impulse response $g(t)$, then

$$y(t) = \int_0^\infty g(\tau) r(t - \tau) d\tau \tag{5.2}$$

If $r(t)$ is bounded, there exists a constant M such that $|r(t)| \le M < \infty$, and the output is bounded by

$$|y(t)| = \left| \int_0^\infty g(\tau) r(t - \tau) d\tau \right| \tag{5.3}$$

Since the absolute value of an integral is not greater than the integral of the absolute value of the integrand, Eqn. (5.3) may be written as

$$|y(t)| \le \int_0^\infty |g(\tau) r(t - \tau)| d\tau \le \int_0^\infty |g(\tau)| |r(t - \tau)| d\tau \le M \int_0^\infty |g(\tau)| d\tau$$

Therefore, the output will be bounded if

$$\int_0^\infty |g(\tau)| d\tau < \infty \tag{5.4}$$

The condition given by (5.4) is *sufficient* to guarantee BIBO stability. This condition is also *necessary*, for if we consider the bounded input

---

1. A function $f(t)$ is said to be bounded if its magnitude does not go to infinity in the time interval $[0, \infty)$, or equivalently there exists a real constant M such that $|f(t)| \le M < \infty$ for all t in $[0, \infty)$.

$$r(t - \tau) = \begin{bmatrix} +1 & \text{if} & g(\tau) > 0 \\ 0 & \text{if} & g(\tau) = 0 \\ -1 & \text{if} & g(\tau) < 0 \end{bmatrix}$$

then the output at any fixed value of t is given by

$$|y(t)| = \left| \int_0^\infty g(\tau) r(t - \tau) d\tau \right| = \int_0^\infty |g(\tau)| d\tau$$

Thus, unless the condition given by (5.4) is true, the system is not BIBO stable.

We, therefore, conclude that a system with impulse response $g(t)$ is BIBO stable if and only if the impulse response is absolutely integrable, i.e., $\int_0^\infty |g(\tau)| d\tau$ is finite (area under the absolute-value curve of the impulse response $g(t)$ evaluated from $t = 0$ to $t = \infty$ must be finite).

We shall now show that the requirement (5.4) on the impulse response for BIBO stability can be linked to the restrictions on the poles of the transfer function $G(s)$, given by

$$G(s) = \frac{Y(s)}{R(s)} = \frac{b_0 s^m + b_1 s^{m-1} + \cdots + b_{m-1} s + b_m}{a_0 s^n + a_1 s^{n-1} + \cdots + a_{n-1} s + a_n}; \; m \le n \qquad (5.5)$$

The nature of $g(t) = \mathscr{L}^{-1}[G(s)]$ is dependent on the roots of the characteristic equation

$$\Delta(s) = a_0 s^n + a_1 s^{n-1} + \cdots + a_{n-1} s + a_n = 0 \qquad (5.6)$$

i.e., the poles of the transfer function $G(s)$. These poles may be both real and complex-conjugate, and may have multiplicity of various orders.

Consider a second-order system

$$\frac{Y(s)}{R(s)} = G(s) = \frac{1}{s^2 + a_1 s + a_2}$$

For impulse input, $R(s) = 1$. Therefore, response transform

$$Y(s) = \frac{1}{s^2 + a_1 s + a_2}$$

The impulse response of the system is given by

$$y(t) = g(t) = \mathscr{L}^{-1} \left[\frac{1}{s^2 + a_1 s + a_2} \right]$$

Assume that the poles of the response transform $Y(s)$ are real and distinct:

$$s^2 + a_1 s + a_2 = (s - \alpha_1)(s - \alpha_2)$$

Partial fraction expansion of $Y(s)$ is then of the form

$$Y(s) = \frac{A_1}{s - \alpha_1} + \frac{A_2}{s - \alpha_2}$$

where A_1 and A_2 are real constants.
This gives

$$y(t) = a_1 e^{\alpha_1 t} + a_2 e^{\alpha_2 t}$$

The time functions $e^{\alpha_1 t}$ and $e^{\alpha_2 t}$ are the response functions contributed by the system poles at $s = \alpha_1$ and $s = \alpha_2$, respectively. These time functions dictate the qualitative nature of the impulse response of the system. A time function $e^{\alpha t}$ is either a constant or a growing or decaying exponential depending on whether $\alpha = 0$, $\alpha > 0$, or $\alpha < 0$, respectively, as sketched in Fig. 5.1.

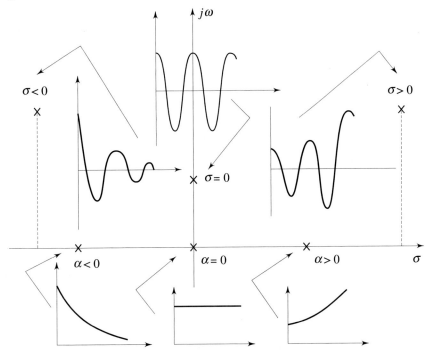

Fig. 5.1 *Time functions associated with poles in the s-plane*

For complex-conjugate pole pair at $s = p = \sigma + j\omega$ and $s = p^* = \sigma - j\omega$ of $Y(s)$, the response $y(t)$ is obtained as follows:

$$Y(s) = \frac{A}{s - p} + \frac{A^*}{s - p^*}$$

where $A = |A|\angle\phi$, and A^* is complex-conjugate of A.

$$y(t) = Ae^{pt} + A^* e^{p^* t} = Ae^{pt} + (Ae^{pt})^* = 2\,\text{Re}[Ae^{pt}]$$

$$= 2\,\text{Re}[|A|\,e^{j\phi} e^{\sigma t} e^{j\omega t}] = 2\,|A|e^{\sigma t}\text{Re}[e^{j(\omega t + \phi)}]$$

$$= 2\,|A|e^{\sigma t}\cos(\omega t + \phi) \qquad (5.7)$$

Therefore, the complex-conjugate pair of poles of the response transform $Y(s)$ gives rise to a sinusoidal or oscillatory response whose envelope $2|A|e^{\sigma t}$

can be constant, growing or decaying depending on whether $\sigma = 0$, $\sigma > 0$, or $\sigma < 0$, respectively, as sketched in Fig. 5.1.

For an nth-order linear system, the response transform $Y(s)$ has an nth-order characteristic polynominal. Assume that $Y(s)$ has real pole at $s = \alpha$ of multiplicity m, and partial fraction expansion of $Y(s)$ is of the form

$$Y(s) = \frac{A_{1(m)}}{(s-\alpha)^m} + \frac{A_{1(m-1)}}{(s-\alpha)^{m-1}} + \cdots + \frac{A_{12}}{(s-\alpha)^2} + \frac{A_{11}}{(s-\alpha)} + \cdots$$

where $A_{1(m)}$, ..., A_{12}, A_{11} are real constants.

Response function contributed by the real pole of multiplicity m can be evaluated as follows:

Consider the transform pair

$$\frac{1}{s-\alpha} \leftrightarrow e^{\alpha t}$$

Using Eqn. (A.30) of Appendix A,

$$-\frac{d}{ds}\left(\frac{1}{s-\alpha}\right) \leftrightarrow te^{\alpha t} \quad \text{or} \quad \frac{1}{(s-\alpha)^2} \leftrightarrow te^{\alpha t}$$

Performing differentiation once again,

$$\frac{1}{(s-\alpha)^3} \leftrightarrow \frac{1}{2!}t^2 e^{\alpha t}$$

In general,

$$\frac{1}{(s-\alpha)^m} \leftrightarrow \frac{1}{(m-1)!}t^{m-1}e^{\alpha t}$$

It can easily be established using final-value theorem (Eqn. (A.35) of Appendix A) that the response function $[1/(m-1)!]t^{m-1}e^{\alpha t}$ equals zero as $t \to \infty$ if $\alpha < 0$. However, the response function grows without bound for $\alpha \geq 0$.

Similar conclusions can be derived in case of response functions corresponding to complex-conjugate pair of poles $(\sigma \pm j\omega)$ of multiplicity m. The limit of each response function as $t \to \infty$ equals zero if $\sigma < 0$. The case of $\sigma \geq 0$ contributes growing response functions.

From the foregoing discussion it follows that the nature of response terms contributed by the system poles (i.e., the poles of the transfer function $G(s)$) gives the nature of the impulse response $g(t) = \mathcal{L}^{-1}[G(s)]$ of the system, and hence answers the question of BIBO stability through condition (5.4) which says that for a system with transfer function $G(s)$ to be BIBO stable, it is

necessary and sufficient that $\int_{0}^{\infty}|g(\tau)|\,d\tau < \infty$.

Table 5.1 summarizes the nature of response terms contributed by various types of poles of $G(s)$ given by Eqn. (5.5), i.e., the roots of the characteristic equation (5.6). Certain observations are easily made from the study of this table. All the roots which have non-zero real parts [cases (i), (ii), (iii), and iv)] contribute response terms with a multiplying factor of $e^{\sigma t}$. If $\sigma < 0$ (i.e., the roots have negative real parts), the response terms vanish as $t \to \infty$, and if $\sigma > 0$ (i.e., the roots have positive real parts), the response terms increase without bound. Roots on the $j\omega$-axis with multiplicity two or higher [cases (vi) and (viii)] also contribute terms which increase without bound as $t \to \infty$. Single root at the origin [case (v)] or non-multiple root pairs on the $j\omega$-axis [case (vii)] contribute terms which are constant amplitude or constant amplitude oscillation. These observations lead us to the following general conclusions on BIBO stability.

1. If all the roots of the characteristic equation lie in the left half of the s-plane, then the impulse response is bounded and eventually decays to zero. Therefore $\int_0^\infty |g(\tau)| \, d\tau$ is finite and the system is BIBO stable.

Table 5.1   *Response terms contributed by various types of roots*

Type of roots	Nature of response terms
(i) Single root at $s = \sigma$	$Ae^{\sigma t}$
(ii) Roots of multiplicity m at $s = \sigma$	$\left[A_1 + A_2 t + \dfrac{A_3}{2!} t^2 + \cdots + \dfrac{A_m}{(m-1)!} t^{m-1} \right] e^{\sigma t}$
(iii) Complex-conjugate root pair at $s = \sigma \pm j\omega$	$A \cos(\omega t + \phi) \, e^{\sigma t}$
(iv) Complex-conjugate root pairs of multiplicity m at $s = \sigma \pm j\omega$	$[A_1 \cos(\omega t + \phi_1) + A_2 t \cos(\omega t + \phi_2) + \cdots$ $+ \dfrac{A_m}{(m-1)!} t^{m-1} \cos(\omega t + \phi_m)] e^{\sigma t}$
(v) Single root at the origin, i.e., $s = 0$	A
(vi) Roots of multiplicity m at the origin	$\left[A_1 + A_2 t + \cdots + \dfrac{A_m}{(m-1)!} t^{m-1} \right]$
(vii) Single complex-conjugate root pair on the $j\omega$-axis, i.e., $s = \pm j\omega$	$A \cos(\omega t + \phi)$
(viii) Complex-conjugate root pair of multiplicity m on the $j\omega$-axis	$[A_1 \cos(\omega t + \phi_1) + A_2 t \cos(\omega t + \phi_2) + \cdots$ $+ \dfrac{A_m}{(m-1)!} t^{m-1} \cos(\omega t + \phi_m)]$

2. If any root of the characteristic equation lies in the right half of the s-plane, $g(t)$ grows without bound and $\int_0^\infty |g(\tau)| d\tau$ is infinite. The system is therefore unstable.

3. If the characteristic equation has repeated roots on the $j\omega$-axis in the s-plane, $g(t)$ grows without bound and $\int_0^\infty |g(\tau)| d\tau$ is infinite. The system is therefore unstable.

4. If one or more non-repeated roots of the characteristic equation are on the $j\omega$-axis in the s-plane, then $g(t)$ is bounded but $\int_0^\infty |g(\tau)| d\tau$ is infinite. The system is therefore unstable.

An exception to the definition of BIBO stability is brought out by the following observations.

Consider a system with transfer function

$$G(s) = \frac{N(s)}{s(s - j\omega)(s + j\omega)}$$

The system has non-repeated poles on the $j\omega$-axis in the s-plane. The response functions contributed by the poles at $s = 0$, and $s = \pm j\omega$ are, respectively, A_1, and $A_2 \cos(\omega t + \phi)$, where A_1 and A_2 are real constants. The terms A_1 and $A_2 \cos(\omega t + \phi)$ are bounded, $\int_0^\infty |g(\tau)| d\tau$ is infinite and the system is unstable in the sense of our definition of BIBO stability.

Careful examination of the input–output relation

$$Y(s) = G(s)R(s) = \frac{N(s)}{s(s - j\omega)(s + j\omega)} R(s)$$

shows that $y(t)$ is bounded for all bounded $r(t)$ unless the input has a pole matching one of the system poles on the $j\omega$-axis. For example, for a unit step input $r(t) = \mu(t)$,

$$R(s) = \frac{1}{s}, \quad \text{and} \quad Y(s) = \frac{N(s)}{s^2(s - j\omega)(s + j\omega)}$$

The response $y(t)$ is a linear combination of the terms A_3, $A_4 t$ and $A_5 \cos(\omega t + \phi)$, and therefore $y(t) \to \infty$ as $t \to \infty$. Such a system which has bounded output for all bounded inputs except for the inputs having poles matching the system poles, may be treated as acceptable or non-acceptable. We will bring the situations where the system has non-repeated poles on the $j\omega$-axis under the class of *marginally stable systems*.

5.3 | ZERO-INPUT STABILITY

This concept of stability is based on the dynamic evolution of the system state in response to the arbitrary initial state representing initial internal energy storage. State variable model[2] (refer Eqns (5.1))

$$\dot{\mathbf{x}}(t) = \mathbf{A}\mathbf{x}(t); \mathbf{x}(t = 0) \triangleq \mathbf{x}^0 \tag{5.8}$$

is most appropriate to study dynamic evolution of the state $\mathbf{x}(t)$ is response to the initial state $\mathbf{x}(0)$.

We may classify stability as follows:

1. *Unstable*: There is at least one finite initial state $\mathbf{x}(0)$ such that $\mathbf{x}(t)$ grows thereafter without bound as $t \to \infty$.

2. *Asymptotically stable:* For all possible initial states $\mathbf{x}(0)$, $\mathbf{x}(t)$ eventually decays to zero as $t \to \infty$.

3. *Marginally stable:* For all initial states $\mathbf{x}(0)$, $\mathbf{x}(t)$ remains thereafter within finite bounds for $t > 0$.

Taking Laplace transform on both the sides of Eqn. (5.8), yields

$$s\mathbf{X}(s) - \mathbf{x}(0) = \mathbf{A}\mathbf{X}(s)$$

where $$\mathbf{X}(s) \triangleq \mathscr{L}[\mathbf{x}(t)].$$

Solving for $\mathbf{X}(s)$, we get

$$\mathbf{X}(s) = (s\mathbf{I} - \mathbf{A})^{-1}\mathbf{x}(0) = \phi(s)\mathbf{x}(0)$$

where $$\phi(s) = (s\mathbf{I} - \mathbf{A})^{-1} = \frac{(s\mathbf{I} - \mathbf{A})^+}{|s\mathbf{I} - \mathbf{A}|} = \frac{adj(s\mathbf{I} - \mathbf{A})}{det(s\mathbf{I} - \mathbf{A})}$$

The state vector $\mathbf{x}(t)$ can be obtained by inverse transforming $\mathbf{X}(s)$:

$$\mathbf{x}(t) = \mathscr{L}^{-1}[\phi(s)\mathbf{x}(0)]$$

Note that for an $n \times n$ matrix $\mathbf{A}$, $|s\mathbf{I} - \mathbf{A}|$ is an nth-order polynomial in s. Also, each element of the adjoint matrix $(s\mathbf{I} - \mathbf{A})^+$ is a polynomial in s of order less than or equal to $(n - 1)$. Therefore, each element of $\phi(s)$ is a strictly proper rational function, and can be expanded in a partial fraction expansion. Using the time-response analysis given in the earlier section, it is easy to establish that

$$\lim_{t \to \infty} \mathbf{x}(t) \to 0$$

if all the roots of the characteristic polynomial $|s\mathbf{I} - \mathbf{A}|$ lie strictly in the left half of the complex plane. In Chapter 12 we will see that under mildly restrictive conditions (namely, the system must be both controllable and observable), the roots of the characteristic polynomial $|s\mathbf{I} - \mathbf{A}|$ are same as the poles of the corresponding transfer function, and asymptotic stability ensures BIBO stability and *vice versa*. This implies that stability analysis can be carried out using only the BIBO stability test (or only the asymptotic stability test).

---

2. This, in fact, is the model of a linear *autonomous system*. An autonomous system is one that is both free (zero input) and time-invariant.

We will use the following terminology and tests for stability analysis of linear time-invariant systems described by the transfer function $G(s) = N(s)/\Delta(s)$, with the characteristic equation $\Delta(s) = 0$.

1. If all the roots of the characteristic equation lie in the left half of the s-plane, the system is *stable*.
2. If any root of the characteristic equation lies in the right half of the s-plane, the system is *unstable*.
3. If condition 1 is satisfied except for the presence of one or more non-repeated roots on the $j\omega$-axis in the s-plane, the system is *marginally stable*.

It follows from the above discussion that stability of a linear time-invariant system can be determined by finding the roots of its characteristic polynomial. For first- and second-order polynomials, this is trivial. Algebraic methods are available for third-order polynomials, but are somewhat difficult to apply. For polynomials of order higher than three, numerical procedures are usually required. Computer Programs are available [176–179] that can be used to find the roots of a polynomial. A disadvantage of using numerical techniques is that all parameters in the system must be assigned numerical values. Finding the range of a certain parameter that results in a stable system becomes difficult when a numerical technique is used to determine the stability. From the point of view of control system design, information on range of system parameters for stability is important.

The Routh stability criterion, which is an analytical procedure of stability study, is well suited for finding the range of a parameter for stability.

5.4 | THE ROUTH STABILITY CRITERION

The Routh stability criterion is an analytical procedure for determining if all the roots of a polynomial have negative real parts, and is used in the stability analysis of linear time-invariant systems. The characteristic equation for a linear time-invariant system is a polynomial equation, except for the case that the system contains dead-time elements. For this special class, the Routh stability criterion cannot be employed (the Nyquist stability criterion, which is covered later, can be employed). However, with dead-time approximations (refer Eqns (2.117)–(2.118)), the characteristic equation reduces to a polynomial equation and the Routh stability criterion becomes applicable.

Characteristic equation of linear time-invariant systems is of the form

$$\Delta(s) = a_0 s^n + a_1 s^{n-1} + \cdots + a_{n-1} s^1 + a_n s^0 = 0 \qquad (5.9)$$

where the coefficients a_i are real numbers.

One can assume with no loss of generality that a_n, the coefficient of s^0, is not zero. Otherwise, the characteristic polynomial $\Delta(s)$ can be expressed as a power of s times a polynomial in which the coefficient of s^0 is non-zero. The power of s indicates roots at the origin of the s-plane, the number of which is evident; hence only the latter polynomial need be investigated using the Routh stability criterion. We assume in the following development that the coefficient of s^0 is not zero.

We will also assume with no loss of generality that $a_0 > 0$. In case $a_0 < 0$, it can be made positive by multiplying the characteristic equation by -1 throughout.

In order to ascertain the stability of a linear time-invariant system, it is necessary to determine if any of the roots of its characteristic equation lie in the right half of the s-plane. Assume that the roots of nth-order characteristic equation (5.9) are given by $s = r_1, r_2, \ldots, r_n$. These roots are functions of the coefficients $a_0, a_1, \ldots, a_{n-1}, a_n$.

A second-order polynomial

$$a_0 s^2 + a_1 s + a_2 = a_0(s - r_1)(s - r_2)$$
$$= a_0 s^2 - a_0(r_1 + r_2)s + a_0 r_1 r_2 \tag{5.10}$$

A third-order polynomial

$$a_0 s^3 + a_1 s^2 + a_2 s + a_3 = a_0(s - r_1)(s - r_2)(s - r_3)$$
$$= a_0 s^3 - a_0(r_1 + r_2 + r_3)s^2 + a_0(r_1 r_2 + r_1 r_3 + r_2 r_3)s - a_0 r_1 r_2 r_3 \tag{5.11}$$

Extending this expansion to the nth-order polynomial, we get

$$\Delta(s) = a_0 s^n + a_1 s^{n-1} + \cdots + a_{n-1}s + a_n$$
$$= a_0 s^n - a_0 \text{ (sum of all the roots)} s^{n-1}$$
$$+ a_0 (\text{sum of the products of the roots taken 2 at a time}) s^{n-2}$$
$$- a_0 (\text{sum of the products of the roots taken 3 at a time}) s^{n-3}$$
$$+ \cdots + a_0(-1)^n (\text{product of all the } n \text{ roots}) \tag{5.12}$$

Suppose that all the roots of a polynomial are real and in the left half plane. Then all r_i in Eqns (5.10) and (5.11) are real and negative. Therefore, all polynomial coefficients are positive. This characteristic also applies to the general case of Eqn. (5.12). The only case for which a coefficient can be negative is that there be at least one root in the right half plane. Note also that if all the roots are in the left half plane, no coefficient can be zero.

If any roots of the polynomials above are complex, the roots must appear in complex-conjugate pairs, since the polynomial coefficients are assumed real. Then, as per the rules given for forming the polynomial coefficients, all imaginary parts of roots/products of roots will cancel. Therefore, if all roots occur in the left half plane, all coefficients of the general polynomial of Eqn. (5.12) will be positive. Presence of a negative coefficient implies that there is at least one root in the right half plane. A zero coefficient indicates presence of complex-conjugate roots on the $j\omega$-axis and/or one or more roots in the right half plane.

In summary, given a polynomial as in Eqn. (5.12):

(i) if any coefficient a_i is equal to zero, then *not all* the roots are in the left half plane; and

(ii) if any coefficient a_i is negative, then *at least one root* is in the right half plane.

We therefore conclude that the absence or negativeness of any of the coefficients of a characteristic polynomial indicates that the system is either unstable or at most marginally stable. Thus, it is necessary for a stable system that all the coefficients of its characteristic polynomial be positive. If any coefficient is zero/negative, we immediately know that the system is not stable. The converse is, however, not true: when all the coefficients are positive, the system is not necessarily stable; there may still be roots in the right half plane and/or on the imaginary axis. In order for all the roots to have negative real parts, it is *necessary but not sufficient* that all of the coefficients of the characteristic equation be positive. For example, when the characteristic equation is

$$\Delta(s) = (s + 2)\left(s - \frac{1}{2} - j\frac{\sqrt{15}}{2}\right)\left(s - \frac{1}{2} + j\frac{\sqrt{15}}{2}\right) = s^3 + s^2 + 2s + 8 = 0,$$

the system is unstable, and yet the polynomial possesses all positive coefficients.

The first step in analysing the stability of a system is to examine its characteristic equation. If some of the coefficients are zero or negative, it can be concluded that the system is not stable. On the other hand, if all the coefficients of the characteristic equation are positive, the possibility of the stability of the system exists and one should proceed further to examine the sufficient conditions of stability.

A. Hurwitz and E. J. Routh independently published the method of investigating the sufficient conditions of stability of a system. The Hurwitz criterion is in terms of determinants and the Routh criterion is in terms of array formulation, which is more convenient to handle. We present here the Routh stability criterion[3].

The Routh stability criterion is based on ordering the coefficients of the characteristic equation

$$\Delta(s) = a_0 s^n + a_1 s^{n-1} + a_2 s^{n-2} + \cdots + a_{n-1}s + a_n = 0; \, a_0 > 0 \qquad (5.13)$$

into a schedule, called the *Routh array*.

A necessary and sufficient condition for stability is that all of the elements in the first column of the Routh array be positive. If this condition is not met, the system is unstable, and the number of sign changes in the elements of the first column of the Routh array corresponds to the number of roots of the characteristic equation in the right half of the s-plane.

To determine the Routh array, coefficients of the characteristic equation are arranged in two rows, beginning with the coefficients of s^n and s^{n-1}, respectively, and followed by even-numbered and odd-numbered coefficients as follows:

$$s^n \quad : \quad a_0 \quad a_2 \quad a_4 \quad \cdots$$
$$s^{n-1} : \quad a_1 \quad a_3 \quad a_5 \quad \cdots$$

3. Proof of the Routh stability criterion involves delicate algebra and is omitted here. This algebraic criterion is derived in textbooks, such as Schwarz and Friedland [43], on linear systems.

The following rows are subsequently added to complete the Routh array:

$$
\begin{array}{llllll}
\text{row } n & : s^n & a_0 & a_2 & a_4 & \cdots \\
\text{row}(n-1) & : s^{n-1} & a_1 & a_3 & a_5 & \cdots \\
\text{row}(n-2) & : s^{n-2} & b_1 & b_2 & b_3 & \cdots \\
\text{row}(n-3) & : s^{n-3} & c_1 & c_2 & c_3 & \cdots \\
& \vdots & & & & \\
\text{row } 2 & : s^2 & * & a_n & & \\
\text{row } 1 & : s^1 & * & & & \\
\text{row } 0 & : s^0 & a_n & & &
\end{array}
$$

$$(5.14)$$

where the elements from $(n-2)$th row on are computed as follows (the column with the powers of s is included as a convenient accounting method for rows).

$$
b_1 = \frac{-\det\begin{bmatrix} a_0 & a_2 \\ a_1 & a_3 \end{bmatrix}}{a_1} = (a_1 a_2 - a_0 a_3)/a_1
$$

$$
b_2 = \frac{-\det\begin{bmatrix} a_0 & a_4 \\ a_1 & a_5 \end{bmatrix}}{a_1} = (a_1 a_4 - a_0 a_5)/a_1
$$

$$(5.15)$$

$$\vdots$$

Note that the elements b_i of the s^{n-2}-row are formed from the elements of the two previous rows, s^n-row and s^{n-1}-row, using determinants with the two elements in the first column and other elements in the successive columns. This pattern is continued until the rest of the b_i's are all equal to zero.

Elements of s^{n-3}-row are formed from the elements of the two previous rows, s^{n-1}-row and s^{n-2}-row, as follows:

$$
c_1 = \frac{-\det\begin{bmatrix} a_1 & a_3 \\ b_1 & b_2 \end{bmatrix}}{b_1} = (b_1 a_3 - a_1 b_2)/b_1
$$

$$
c_2 = \frac{-\det\begin{bmatrix} a_1 & a_5 \\ b_1 & b_3 \end{bmatrix}}{b_1} = (b_1 a_5 - a_1 b_3)/b_1
$$

$$(5.16)$$

$$\vdots$$

This is continued until no more c_i elements are present. The rest of the rows are formed in this way down to the s^0-row. The complete array is triangular. Notice that the s^1-row and s^0-row contain one term each.

The elements of the first column of the Routh array must all be positive if all the roots of the characteristic equation are in the left half of s-plane. However, if the elements of the first column are not all positive, the number of roots in the right half of s-plane equals the number of sign changes in the first column. A pattern of $+, -, +$ is counted as *two* sign changes, one going from $+$ to $-$ and the other from $-$ to $+$.

It is to be noted here that in the process of generating the Routh array, the missing terms are regarded as zeros. Also, all the elements of any row can be multiplied or divided by a positive constant during the process to simplify the computational work; this modification does not change the signs of the elements of first column.

Example 5.1

Consider a fourth-order system with the characteristic equation

$$s^4 + 8s^3 + 18s^2 + 16s + 5 = 0$$

Since the equation has no missing terms and the coefficients are all positive, it satisfies the necessary condition for stability. However, the sufficient condition must still be checked. Routh array is made as follows:

s^4	1	18	5
s^3	8	16	0 (for the missing term)
s^2	$16 = \dfrac{(8)(18) - (1)(16)}{8}$	$5 = \dfrac{(8)(5) - (1)(0)}{8}$	
s^1	$\dfrac{27}{2} = \dfrac{(16)(16) - (8)(5)}{16}$	0	
s^0	5		

The elements of the first column are all positive, and hence the system is stable.

Example 5.2

Consider the characteristic equation

$$3s^4 + 10s^3 + 5s^2 + 5s + 2 = 0$$

which satisfies the necessary condition for stability since all the coefficients are positive and non-zero. The Routh array for this equation is

s^4	3	5	2
s^3	~~10~~	~~5~~	~~0~~ ←divide by 5
	2	1	0
s^2	$\dfrac{7}{2} = \dfrac{(2)(5) - (3)(1)}{2}$	$2 = \dfrac{(2)(2) - (3)(0)}{2}$	
s^1	$-\dfrac{1}{7} = \dfrac{(7/2)(1) - (2)(2)}{(7/2)}$		
s^0	2		

It may be noted that in order to simplify computational work, the s^3-row in the formation of the Routh array has been modified by dividing it by 5 throughout. The modified s^3-row is then used to complete the process of array formation.

Examining the first column of the Routh array, it is found that there are two changes in sign $\left(\text{from } \dfrac{7}{2} \text{ to } -\dfrac{1}{7} \text{ and from } -\dfrac{1}{7} \text{ to } 2\right)$. Therefore the system under consideration is unstable with two poles in the right half of s-plane.

The Routh stability criterion gives only the number of roots in the right half of s-plane. It gives no information as regards the values of the roots, and also does not distinguish between real and complex roots.

Example 5.3

Consider the polynomial
$$\Delta(s) = s^6 + 4s^5 + 3s^4 + 2s^3 + s^2 + 4s + 4$$
which satisfies the necessary condition for stability since all the $\{a_i\}$'s are positive and non-zero. The Routh array for this polynomial is

s^6	1	3	1	4
s^5	$\cancel{4}$	$\cancel{2}$	$\cancel{4}$	$\cancel{0}$ ←divide by 2
	2	1	2	0
s^4	$\dfrac{5}{2}$	0	4	
s^3	1	$-\dfrac{6}{5}$	0	
s^2	3	4		
s^1	$-\dfrac{38}{15}$			
s^0	4			

It is seen that the polynomial has right-half plane roots, since the elements of the first column are not all positive. In fact, there are two roots in the right-half plane since there are two sign changes.

Special Cases

Formation of Routh array for the polynomials of Examples 5.1– 5.3 could easily be carried out using the standard procedure given in Eqns (5.15) – (5.16). However, the standard procedure fails if we encounter any of the following situations on our way to formation of the array.

I. A row of all zeros appears.

II. *Pivot element* (first element of a row, appearing in first column of the array) of a row is zero, but the entire row is not all zeros.

For these special situations, we have to use special techniques to complete the process of array formation.

Case I: A row of all zeros

When we encounter a row with all zero elements (or with single element which is zero) on our way to formation of Routh array, the process of array formation terminates prematurely because all the terms in the row next to the all-zero row become infinite.

An all-zero row indicates the existence of an even polynomial as a factor of the given characteristic polynomial. An even polynomial is one in which the exponents of s are even integers or zero only. This even-polynomial factor is called the *auxiliary polynomial*. The coefficients of the auxiliary polynomial will always be the elements in the row directly above the row of zeros in the array. The exponent of the highest power in the auxiliary polynomial is the exponent that denotes the row containing its coefficients.

The roots of an even polynomial occur in pairs that are equal in magnitude and opposite in sign. Hence, these roots can be purely imaginary (Fig. 5.2a), purely real (Fig. 5.2b) or complex (Fig. 5.2c). Since complex roots must occur in conjugate pairs, any complex roots of an even polynomial must occur in groups of four, which is apparent in Fig. 5.2c. Such roots have quadrantal symmetry, that is, the roots are symmetrical with respect to both the real and the imaginary axes.

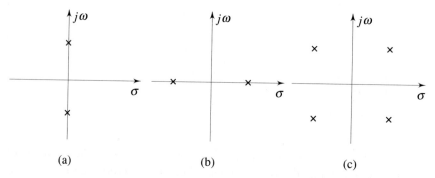

    (a)   (b)   (c)

Fig. 5.2 *The roots of an even polynomial*

The *Case I* polynomial may be analyzed in either of the two ways:

(i) Once the auxiliary polynomial $A(s)$ is found, it is factored from the characteristic equation, leaving a second factor which may be analyzed by applying the Routh stability criterion. The auxiliary polynomial may be factored algebraically to give the roots.

(ii) Once the auxiliary polynomial $A(s)$ is found, it is differentiated with respect to s, and the row of zeros is replaced with the coefficients of $dA(s)/ds$. The construction of the array then continues in the usual manner, and the array is interpreted in the usual way. However, the roots of the auxiliary polynomial are also roots of the given characteristic equation, and these must be tested separately.

Example 5.4

Consider a fifth-order system with the characteristic equation

$$\Delta(s) = s^5 + s^4 + 4s^3 + 24s^2 + 3s + 63 = 0$$

for which the Routh array is constructed as

s^5	1	4	3	
s^4	1	24	63	
s^3	~~-20~~	~~-60~~	~~0~~	←divide by 20
	-1	-3	0	
s^2	~~21~~	~~63~~		← divide by 21
	1	3		
s^1	0	0		

Since a row of zeros appears prematurely, we form the auxiliary polynomial using the coefficients of the s^2-row.

$$A(s) = s^2 + 3$$

Solving the auxiliary equation

$$A(s) = s^2 + 3 = 0,$$

we get the roots at $s = \pm j\sqrt{3}$.

In order to examine the remaining roots, we divide $\Delta(s)$ by $A(s)$ to obtain

$$\frac{\Delta(s)}{A(s)} = s^3 + s^2 + s + 21$$

Establishing Routh array for this factor, we have

s^3	1	1
s^2	1	21
s^1	-20	0
s^0	21	

The two changes in sign in the first column indicate the presence of two roots in the right-half plane, and the system is unstable.

Example 5.5

Consider a sixth-order system with the characteristic equation

$$\Delta(s) = s^6 + 2s^5 + 8s^4 + 12s^3 + 20s^2 + 16s + 16 = 0$$

for which the Routh array is constructed as

s^6	1	8	20	16	
s^5	~~2~~	~~12~~	~~16~~	~~0~~	←divide by 2
	1	6	8	0	
s^4	~~2~~	~~12~~	~~16~~		←divide by 2
	1	6	8		
s^3	0	0			

The auxiliary polynomial

$$A(s) = s^4 + 6s^2 + 8$$

The derivative of the polynomial with respect to s is

$$\frac{dA(s)}{ds} = 4s^3 + 12$$

The zeros in the s^3-row are now replaced by the coefficients 4 and 12. The Routh array then becomes

s^6	1	8	12	16	
s^5	~~2~~	~~12~~	~~16~~	0	←divide by 2
	1	6	8	0	
s^4	~~2~~	~~12~~	~~16~~		←divide by 2
	1	6	8		
s^3	0	0			$\leftarrow \dfrac{dA(s)}{ds} = 4s^3 + 12$
	~~4~~	~~12~~			←divide by 4
	1	3			
s^2	3	8			
s^1	$\dfrac{1}{3}$				
s^0	8				

Since there are no sign changes in the first column of the Routh array, the polynomial $\Delta(s)$ does not have any root in the right half of s-plane. Solving the auxiliary equation

$$A(s) = s^4 + 6s^2 + 8 = 0$$

we get the roots at $s = \pm j\sqrt{2}$, and $s = \pm j2$, which are also the roots of $\Delta(s)$. Therefore the system under consideration is marginally stable. The oscillation frequencies are $\sqrt{2}$ rad/sec, and 2 rad/sec.

Case II: A zero Pivot Element, but the Entire Row is not all Zero

Consider now a situation wherein we encounter a row with zero pivot element while at least one element of the row is non-zero. Because of the zero pivot element, the terms in the next row all become infinite and the array formation cannot continue.

To remedy this situation, we replace the zero pivot element by an arbitrary small number ε and then proceed with the construction of the array. The limit $\varepsilon \rightarrow 0$ is then taken to determine the changes in algebraic signs of the first column terms, yielding the information regarding the number of right-half plane roots.

Let us examine the rationale of the method. If the polynomial under test had slightly different coefficients, the troublesome zero pivot element would instead be some small non-zero number. As long as the polynomial has no roots on the imaginary axis, sufficiently small perturbations of its coefficients will not alter the number of right-half plane roots. Rather than to actually perturb the polynomial coefficients, the effect of such perturbations is indicated by replacing the zero term with ε. Therefore, for a polynomial with no imaginary-axis roots, $\varepsilon \rightarrow 0$ from positive or negative side would give identical results. ε is generally taken to be positive for convenience.

Example 5.6

Consider the polynomial

$$\Delta(s) = s^5 + 3s^4 + 2s^3 + 6s^2 + 6s + 9$$

for which the Routh array is

s^5	1	2	6		
s^4	~~3~~	~~6~~	~~9~~	$\leftarrow$ divide by 3	
	1	2	3		
s^3	~~0~~	~~3~~		$\leftarrow$ replace 0 by ε	
	ε	3			
s^2	$\dfrac{2\varepsilon - 3}{\varepsilon}$	3			
s^1	$3 - \dfrac{3\varepsilon^2}{2\varepsilon - 3}$				
s^0	3				

The first element in the s^2-row is $(2\varepsilon - 3)/\varepsilon$ which has a negative sign as $\varepsilon \rightarrow 0$ (in the Routh stability criterion, we are interested only in the signs of terms in the first column and not in their magnitudes). The first term of s^1-row is $[3 - 3\varepsilon^2/(2\varepsilon - 3)]$ which has a limiting value of +3 as $\varepsilon \rightarrow 0$. Examining the terms in the first column of the Routh array, it is found that there are two changes in sign, which implies that there are two poles in the right-half plane.

▲▲

For the case where the characteristic equation has imaginary-axis roots, replacement of the zero pivot element by ε would cause the imaginary-axis roots to move into either left or right half of the s-plane, with the result that the roots of the characteristic polynomial in the right-half s-plane cannot be correctly determined. Therefore, to apply the ε-limiting method for a characteristic polynomial with the imaginary-axis roots, one must first extract these roots and then apply the test on the remainder polynomial with no imaginary-axis roots.

*Example 5.7*_____

Consider the polynomial
$$\Delta(s) = s^6 + s^5 + 3s^4 + 3s^3 + 3s^2 + 2s + 1$$

The Routh array is

s^6	1	3	3	1
s^5	1	3	2	
s^4	$\cancel{0}$	$\cancel{1}$	$\cancel{1}$	$\leftarrow$ replace 0 by ε
s^3	$\dfrac{3\varepsilon - 1}{\varepsilon}$	$\dfrac{2\varepsilon - 1}{\varepsilon}$		
s^2	$\dfrac{-2\varepsilon^2 + 4\varepsilon - 1}{3\varepsilon - 1}$	1		
s^1	$\dfrac{4\varepsilon^2 - \varepsilon}{2\varepsilon^2 - 4\varepsilon + 1}$			
s^0	1			

As $\varepsilon \to 0$, the elements of s^1-row tend to zero. This indicates the possibility of existence of imaginary-axis roots in the s-plane. We therefore need to examine the auxiliary polynomial. If the imaginary-axis roots do not exist, the usual procedure of replacing the all-zero row by coefficients of the derivative of the auxiliary polynomial is adopted. If the imaginary-axis roots are found to exist, the original polynomial is divided out by the auxiliary polynomial and the test is performed on the remainder polynomial.

For the example under consideration, the auxiliary polynomial is (let $\varepsilon \to 0$ in s^2-row):
$$A(s) = s^2 + 1 = 0$$

yielding two roots on the imaginary axis. Dividing the original polynomial $\Delta(s)$ by $A(s)$, we get
$$\frac{\Delta(s)}{A(s)} = s^4 + s^3 + 2s^2 + 2s + 1$$

The Routh array for this polynomial is

s^4	1	2	1	
s^3	1	2		
s^2	~~0~~	~~2~~		← replace 0 by ε
	ε	1		
s^1	$\dfrac{2\varepsilon - 1}{\varepsilon}$			
s^0	1			

As $\varepsilon \to 0$, there are two sign changes in the first column of the array. This indicates that there are two roots in the right half s-plane. The original polynomial $\Delta(s)$, therefore, has two roots in the right-half plane and two roots on the imaginary axis.

Relative Stability (Shifting the Origin)

The Routh stability criterion ascertains *absolute stability* of a system by determining if all the roots of the characteristic equation lie in the left half of s-plane. Once a system is found to be absolutely stable (all characteristic roots in left half of s-plane), it is desirable to determine its *relative stability,* which is concerned with the attributes of transient behaviour of the system. We shall see in the next chapter that parameters such as overshoot, settling time, etc., are used to capture important attributes of transient response of a stable system; these parameters are therefore quantitative measures of relative stability. Stability margins (gain margin, phase margin) are commonly used as frequency-domain measures of relative stability. Frequency-domain analysis will appear in Chapter 8.

In the following, we show that the Routh stability criterion can be extended for a preliminary relative-stability analysis. We know that for a real root or a complex-conjugate pair of roots on the vertical line in the s-plane defined by $s = -\sigma$, $\sigma > 0$ (refer Fig. 5.3), the time-constant $\tau = 1/\sigma$. The transient response modes corresponding to smaller time-constants decay faster, and therefore the dynamic behaviour of a system is dominated by the roots with larger time-constants. The largest time-constant associated with a system can be obtained by determining the minimum distance of the characteristic roots from the imaginary axis.

We substitute

$$s = \hat{s} - \sigma \qquad (5.17)$$

into the characteristic equation, write a polynomial in terms of $\hat{s}$, and apply Routh stability criterion to the new polynomial in $\hat{s}$. If there are no changes of sign in the first column of the array developed for the polynomial in $\hat{s}$, it implies that all the roots of the original characteristic equation are more negative than $-\sigma$. Shifting the vertical axis on a trial-and-error basis, we can find the minimum distance of the roots from the imaginary axis, and hence the largest time-constant associated with the system.

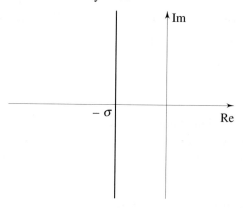

Fig. 5.3 *Shifting of the origin in the s-plane*

Example 5.8_____

Consider a third-order system with the characteristic equation

$$s^3 + 7s^2 + 25s + 39 = 0$$

which, by the Routh stability criterion, can be shown to have all its roots in the left half of the s-plane. Let us check if all the roots of this equation have real parts more negative than -1.

The substitution

$$s = \hat{s} - 1$$

results in the following polynomial in $\hat{s}$:

$$f(\hat{s}) = \hat{s}^3 + 4\hat{s}^2 + 14\hat{s} + 20$$

Forming the Routh array, we get

$\hat{s}^3$	1	14	
$\hat{s}^2$	~~4~~	~~20~~	← divide by 4
	1	5	
$\hat{s}^1$	9		
$\hat{s}^0$	5		

As the signs of all the elements of the first column of the Routh array are positive, all the roots of the original characteristic polynomial are more negative than -1.

5.5 | STABILITY RANGE FOR A PARAMETER

Our discussion so far has centred on determining whether or not a given characteristic equation has roots in the right half of the s-plane, using the Routh stability criterion. Since even pocket calculators can find roots of polynomials these days, the real value of the Routh test is in design of control systems where ranges of certain parameters have to be obtained ensuring a stable operation. We illustrate the concepts involved using a couple of examples.

Example 5.9

Consider the closed-loop system shown in Fig. 5.4. Let us determine the range of K for which the system is stable.

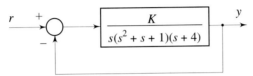

Fig. 5.4 *A feedback system*

The closed-loop transfer function of the system is

$$\frac{Y(s)}{R(s)} = \frac{K}{s\left(s^2 + s + 1\right)(s+4) + K}$$

Therefore, the characteristic equation is

$$s(s^2 + s + 1)(s + 4) + K = 0$$

or

$$s^4 + 5s^3 + 5s^2 + 4s + K = 0$$

The Routh array for this equation is

s^4	1	5	K
s^3	5	4	
s^2	21/5	K	
s^1	$\left(\dfrac{84}{5} - 5K\right)\Big/\left(\dfrac{21}{5}\right)$		
s^0	K		

Since for a stable system, the signs of elements of the first column of the Routh array should be all positive, the condition of system stability requires that

$$K > 0$$

and

$$\left(\frac{84}{5} - 5K\right) > 0$$

Therefore for stability, K should lie in the range

$$\frac{84}{25} > K > 0$$

If we let $K = \dfrac{84}{25}$, the s^1-row of the Routh array becomes an all-zero row, resulting in the auxiliary equation

$$\frac{21}{5}s^2 + \frac{84}{25} = 0$$

which has roots at $s = \pm j\sqrt{(4/5)} = \pm j\omega_0$. Therefore, $K = \dfrac{84}{25}$ will cause substained oscillations of frequency $\omega_0 = \sqrt{(4/5)}$ rad/sec.

Example 5.10

Consider the closed-loop system shown in Fig. 5.5. A PI controller controls a second-order plant. Let us determine the range of K_c for which the closed-loop poles satisfy $\text{Re}(s) < -2$.

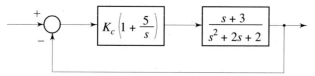

Fig. 5.5 *A feedback system*

The characteristic equation of the system is

$$s^2 + 2s + 2 + K_c\left(1 + \frac{5}{s}\right)(s + 3) = 0$$

or $\qquad s^3 + (2 + K_c)s^2 + (2 + 8K_c)s + 15K_c = 0$

Letting $s = \hat{s} - 2$, we have

$$(\hat{s} - 2)^3 + (2 + K_c)(\hat{s} - 2)^2 + (2 + 8K_c)(\hat{s} - 2) + 15K_c = 0$$

or $\qquad \hat{s}^3 + (K_c - 4)\hat{s}^2 + (4K_c + 6)\hat{s} + (3K_c - 4) = 0$

Applying the Routh's test yields the array

$\hat{s}^3$	1	$4K_c + 6$
$\hat{s}^2$	$K_c - 4$	$3K_c - 4$
$\hat{s}^1$	$\dfrac{4K_c^2 - 13K_c - 20}{K_c - 4}$	
$\hat{s}^0$	$3K_c - 4$	

If there are no sign changes in the first column of the array, then all roots satisfy $\text{Re}(\hat{s}) < 0$, that is, the roots of the original characteristic equation satisfy Re $(s) < -2$. Thus, we require that K_c satisfy all the following conditions:

$$K_c > 4; \ K_c > 4.3892 \quad \text{or} \quad K_c < -1.1392; \ K_c > \frac{4}{3}$$

The requirement $K_c < -1.1392$ is disregarded since K_c cannot be negative. Therefore, we have $\text{Re}(s) < -2$ for all closed-loop poles provided that $K_c > 4.3892$.

Review Examples

Review Example 5.1

Consider the polynomial
$$\Delta(s) = s^5 + 2s^4 + 2s^3 + 4s^2 + 11s + 10$$
The Routh array is calculated as

s^5	1	2	11	
s^4	2̶	4̶	1̶0̶	← divide by 2
	1	2	5	
s^3	0̶	6̶		← replace 0 by ε
	ε	6		
s^2	$-\dfrac{6}{\varepsilon}$	5		
s^1	6			
s^0	5			

In array formation, the limits were taken as $\varepsilon \to 0$ at convenient points in the calculations rather than waiting until the array was complete. This procedure simplifies the calculations and the final form of the array.

From the array we see that there are two sign changes in the first column; the polynomial $\Delta(s)$, by Routh stability criterion, has two roots in the right half s-plane.

Review Example 5.2

A feedback control system is shown in Fig. 5.6. The process transfer function is

$$G(s) = \frac{K(s + 40)}{s(s + 10)}$$

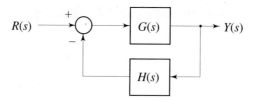

Fig. 5.6   *A feedback control system*

and the sensor transfer function is

$$H(s) = \frac{1}{s + 20}$$

(a) Find the gain K that results in marginal stability. Determine the oscillation frequency.

(b) Reduce the gain to half the value found in (a) and study the relative stability of the system.

Solution

The characteristic equation of the system is

$$1 + G(s)H(s) = 0$$

This gives $s(s + 10)(s + 20) + K(s + 40) = 0$

or

$$s^3 + 30s^2 + (K + 200)s + 40K = 0$$

for which the Routh array is

s^3	1	$K + 200$	
s^2	~~30~~	~~40 K~~	←divide by 10
	3	$4K$	
s^1	$\dfrac{600 - K}{3}$		
s^0	$4K$		

(a) $K = 600$ results in an all-zero row in the array. The auxiliary equation, for this value of K, is

$$3s^2 + 2400 = 0$$

which has the roots $s = \pm j\sqrt{800}$.

Therefore, $K = 600$ results in marginal stability; the oscillation frequency is $\sqrt{800}$ rad/sec.

(b) The characteristic polynomial of the system for $K = 300$ is

$$\Delta(s) = s^3 + 30s^2 + 500s + 12000$$

The substitution $s = \hat{s} - 1$ results in the following polynomial in $\hat{s}$:

$$f(\hat{s}) = \hat{s}^3 + 27\hat{s}^2 + 443\hat{s} + 11529$$

Forming the Routh array, we get

$\hat{s}^3$	1	443	
$\hat{s}^2$	~~27~~	~~11529~~	← divide by 27
	1	427	
$\hat{s}^1$	16		
$\hat{s}^0$	427		

As the signs of all the elements of the first column of the Routh array are positive, all the roots of the original characteristic polynomial $\Delta(s)$ are more negative then -1.

The substitution $s = \bar{s} - 2$ in $\Delta(s)$, results in the following polynomial:

$$g(\bar{s}) = \bar{s}^3 + 24\bar{s}^2 + 392\bar{s} + 11112$$

Forming the Routh array, we get

$\bar{s}^3$	1	392	
$\bar{s}^2$	~~24~~	~~11112~~	← divide by 24
	1	463	
$\bar{s}^1$	-71		
$\bar{s}^0$	463		

There are two sign changes in the first column of the Routh array; there are, therefore, two roots of the original characteristic polynomial that satisfy $\text{Re}(s) > -2$.

The largest time-constant of the closed-loop system is greater than 0.5 and less than 1.

Review Example 5.3

Consider the feedback system shown in Fig. 5.6. The process transfer function

$$G(s) = \frac{K}{s(s+1)}$$

and the feedback transfer function is a first-order Pade approximation (refer Eqn. (2.118)) for the transducer delay:

$$H(s) = \frac{1 - \dfrac{\tau_D}{2}s}{1 + \dfrac{\tau_D}{2}s} = \frac{1 - Ts}{1 + Ts}; \tau_D = 2T$$

The question to be studied is: what are the combinations of K and T for which the system is stable ?

The characteristic polynomial of the system is

$$\Delta(s) = Ts^3 + (1 + T)s^2 + (1 - KT)\, s + K$$

The Routh array is

s^3	T	$1 - KT$
s^2	$1 + T$	K
s^1	$\dfrac{1 + T - 2KT - KT^2}{1 + T}$	
s^0	K	

The stability boundary is given by the condition

$$1 + T - KT(2 + T) = 0$$

or

$$KT = \frac{1 + T}{2 + T}$$

The relationship between the maximum allowable gain K_{max} and the delay T is sketched in Fig. 5.7.

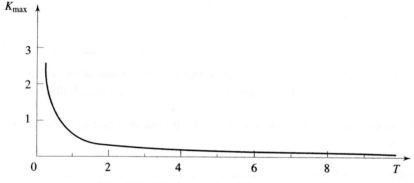

Fig. 5.7 *Maximum allowable gain versus delay*

Review Questions

5.1 Define the terms:
    (a) bounded-input, bounded-output (BIBO) stability; and
    (b) asymptotic stability
    State the conditions under which asymptotic stability of a linear time-invariant system ensures BIBO stability and vice versa. (Help: p 306, p 313)

5.2 (a) Define the terms : absolute stability, and relative stability. (Help: p 325)
    (b) Derive conditions for absolute stability of a linear time-invariant system described by the transfer function

$$G(s) = \frac{b_0 s^m + b_1 s^{m-1} + \cdots + b_{m-1} s + b_m}{a_0 s^n + a_1 s^{n-1} + \cdots + a_{n-1} s + a_n} \, ; \, m \le n$$

    Comment upon the stability property of the system when $G(s)$ has non-repeated poles on the imaginary axis in the s-plane. (Help: p 312)

5.3 Stability of a linear time-invariant system can easily be determined by finding roots of its characteristic polynomial using commercially available CAD software tools. What, then, is the use of Routh stability criterion? (Help: p 314) Demonstrate, through an example, the application of the criterion in control systems field. (Help: Review Example 5.3)

Problems

5.1 Use the Routh stability criterion to determine the number of roots in the left-half plane, the right-half plane, and on the imaginary axis for the given characteristic equation:

(a) $s^4 + 2s^3 + 8s^2 + 4s + 3 = 0$
(b) $s^6 + 3s^5 + 2s^4 + 9s^3 + 5s^2 + 12s + 20 = 0$
(c) $s^5 + s^4 + 2s^3 + 2s^2 + 3s + 5 = 0$
(d) $s^5 + 4s^4 + 8s^3 + 8s^2 + 7s + 4 = 0$
(e) $s^4 + 9s^3 + 4s^2 - 36s - 32 = 0$
(f) $s^7 + 5s^6 + 9s^5 + 9s^4 + 4s^3 + 20s^2 + 36s + 36 = 0$

5.2 Obtain the roots of the given characteristic polynomial on the basis of the Routh array:

(a) $s^4 + 2s^3 + 11s^2 + 18s + 18 = 0$
(b) $s^5 + 2s^4 + 24s^3 + 48s^2 - 25s - 50 = 0$
(c) $s^6 + 3s^5 + 5s^4 + 9s^3 + 8s^2 + 6s + 4 = 0$

5.3 Determine whether the largest time-constant of the roots of the characteristic equation given below is greater than, less than or equal to 1.0 sec.

$$s^3 + 4s^2 + 6s + 4 = 0$$

5.4 The characteristic equations for certain feedback control systems are given below. In each case, determine the range of values of K ($K > 0$) for which the system is stable.

(a) $s^4 + s^3 + s^2 + s + K = 0$
(b) $s^4 + Ks^3 + s^2 + s + 1 = 0$
(c) $s^4 + 3s^3 + 3s^2 + 2s + K = 0$
(d) $s^3 + 3Ks^2 + (K + 2)s + 4 = 0$

5.5 Determine the range of values of K ($K > 0$) such that the characteristic equation

$$s^3 + 3(K + 1)s^2 + (7K + 5)s + (4K + 7) = 0$$

has roots more negative than $s = -1$.

5.6 The block diagram of a feedback control system is shown in Fig. P5.6. Determine the values of K ($K > 0$) that result in a stable closed-loop system.

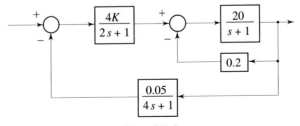

Fig. P5.6

5.7 A feedback system has open-loop transfer function

$$G(s)H(s) = \frac{Ke^{-\tau_D s}}{s(s^2 + 5s + 9)}$$

Determine the range of K ($K > 0$) for which the system is stable when

(i) dead-time $\tau_D = 0$,

(ii) dead-time $\tau_D = 1$, and $e^{-\tau_D s}$ is approximated by $(1 - \tau_D s)$, and

(iii) dead-time $\tau_D = 1$, and $e^{-\tau_D s}$ is approximated by a first-order Pade approximation:

$$e^{-\tau_D s} = \frac{1 - \dfrac{\tau_D}{2} s}{1 + \dfrac{\tau_D}{2} s}$$

5.8 Open-loop transfer functions of certain unity-feedback systems are given below. In each case, determine

(i) the range of values of K ($K > 0$) for which the system is stable,

(ii) the value of K that will result in the system being marginally stable, and

(iii) the location of the roots of the characteristic equation for the value of K found in (ii).

(a) $G(s) = \dfrac{K(s + 13)}{s(s + 3)(s + 7)}$

(b) $G(s) = \dfrac{K(s + 1)}{s(s - 1)(s + 6)}$

(c) $G(s) = \dfrac{K(s + 2)}{s(s + 5)(s^2 + 2s + 5)}$

5.9 The open-loop transfer functions of certain unity-feedback control systems are given below. In each case, discuss the stability of the closed-loop system as a function of $K > 0$. Determine the values of K which will cause sustained oscillations in the closed-loop system. What are the corresponding oscillation frequencies ?

(a) $G(s) = \dfrac{K}{(s + 2)(s + 4)(s^2 + 6s + 25)}$

(b) $G(s) = \dfrac{K(s + 1)}{s(s - 1)(s^2 + 4s + 16)}$

5.10 Determine the values of $K > 0$ and $a > 0$, so that the system shown in Fig. P5.10 oscillates at a frequency 2 rad/sec.

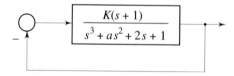

Fig. P5.10

5.11 A feedback control system is shown in Fig. P5.11. The process transfer function is

$$G(s) = \frac{K}{s(0 \cdot 2s + 1)}$$

and the sensor transfer function is $H(s) = 1/(0.1s + 1)$.

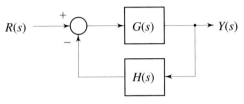

Fig. P5.11

(a) Determine the limiting value of gain $K > 0$ for a stable system.
(b) For the gain that results in marginal stability, determine the oscillation frequency.
(c) Reduce the gain to half the value found in (b) and study the relative stability of the system by shifting the axis and using the Routh stability criterion.

5.12 A unity-feedback control system has the open-loop transfer function

$$G(s) = \frac{K_c(1 + T_D s)}{s^2(\tau s + 1)}$$

Determine the stability limits on the controller parameters $K_c > 0$ and T_D for the following cases:

(a) proportional-only control ($T_D = 0$); and
(b) proportional-derivative control ($T_D > 0$).

5.13 Shown in Fig. P5.13 is a closed-loop control system.

(a) Find the range of gain K ($K > 0$), for which the system is stable.

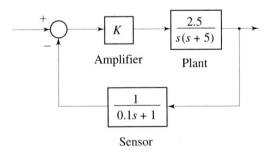

Fig. P5.13

(b) Suppose that the gain K is set to a value of 20. In addition, suppose that the sensor has a general time-constant of τ, rather than 0.1 sec given value. The transfer function of the sensor is then $1/(\tau s + 1)$. Find the allowable range for time-constant $\tau > 0$ such that the system is stable.

(c) Suppose that in (b), the gain K is also variable. Find the range of gain K

as a function of the sensor time-constant τ such that the system is stable.

The parameters K and τ may be represented in a plane with τ as the horizontal axis and K as the vertical axis. Determine the regions in the K-vs-τ plane in which the closed-loop system is stable, and unstable. Indicate the boundary on which the system is marginally stable.

5.14 Figure P5.14 shows a closed-loop system with a proportional-integral controller. Find the range of gain $K_c > 0$ as a function of integral time $T_I > 0$ such that the system is stable. Comment on the effect of decreasing T_I on the limit on gain K_c for stability.

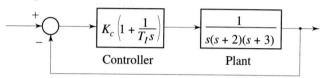

Fig. P5.14

5.15 The block diagram of a motor-control system with tachometer feedback is shown in Fig. P5.15. Find the range of $K > 0$ as a function of $K_t > 0$ such that the system is stable. Comment on the effect of increasing K_t on the limit on gain K for stability.

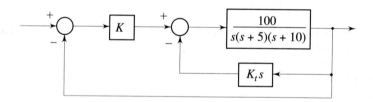

Fig. P5.15

chapter 6

The Performance of
Feedback Systems

6.1 | INTRODUCTION

Recall the basic feedback system block diagram defined in Chapter 3; shown as Fig. 6.1 in a form convenient for analysis. The control system objectives are that output y follow input r, and ignore disturbance w. Performance criteria must have to do with how well these two objectives are attained.

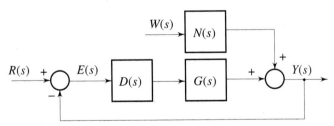

Fig. 6.1 *Block diagram representation of a feedback system*

Clearly, the performance depends both on the system characteristics and on the nature of r and w. Precise mathematical functions for r and w will not generally be known in practice. For example, in a residential heating system (Example 1.4), we may be quite clear that r will be constant (say, 20 °C) but we cannot predict the variation of the main disturbance—outdoor temperature. In a contouring machine control (Example 3.7), we don't know at the design stage all the different shapes of parts that the machine will need to produce during its lifetime. In a radar tracking system (Example 1.5), the position and speed of the target to be tracked may vary in a random fashion. The uncertain nature of many practical commands and disturbances makes the development of performance criteria, based on the actual r and w experienced by the real system, difficult. It is common to base performance evaluation on system response to simple 'standard' test signals such as impulse, pulse, step, ramp, parabola, and sine wave (refer Section 2.2). This approach has been successful for a number of reasons.

1. The characteristics of actual signals which severely strain a control system are a sudden shock (impulse), a sudden change (step), constant velocity (ramp), and constant acceleration (parabola). Experience with the actual performance of various classes of control systems has established a good correlation between the response of systems to standard inputs and the capability of the systems to accomplish their required tasks.

2. Design is much concerned with the comparison of competitive systems. This comparison can often be made nearly as well in terms of standard inputs as for real inputs.

3. The simplicity of the form of standard inputs facilitates mathematical analysis and experimental verification.

4. For linear time-invariant systems, frequency-response curves (Chapter 9) are a complete description of the system's dynamic behaviour and allow one to compute the response to any input, not just sine waves.

The standard performance criteria in common use may be classified as falling into the *time domain* or the *frequency domain*. Time-domain specifications have to do with the response to steps, ramps, parabolas, and the like; while frequency-domain specifications are concerned with certain characteristics of the system's frequency response. Both types of specifications are often applied for the same system to ensure that certain behaviour characteristics will be obtained. It may be noted that all performance specifications are meaningless unless the system is absolutely stable.

The majority of analysis and design tools for feedback systems presuppose that a sufficiently accurate model of the process to be controlled has been set up. Using this model, the design is carried out to meet the time-domain and/or frequency-domain performance specifications. The analysis tools that verify the design also use the same model. This design is bound to be a disappointing one when the control system is put to real-life use. This is because in a reasonably complex system, there are always discrepancies between the model and the real process. Design methods that enable us to explicitly consider these discrepancies, i.e., designing a controller without having a precise mathematical model at hand, have yet to mature [158–168]. We need the design that is not only valid for the approximate model but does hold with certainty for a class of plant models and hence for the real process. Good robustness against modelling errors and against variations in parameters of the model due to environmental and other effects, is an important design requirement.

We will not include the robustness/insensitivity requirements in our performance specifications for design. Our design is based on the assumption that the model is fixed once the model structure and parameters are given. The design is then analysed to study its robustness properties. Qualitative guidelines will be given to improve robustness.

6.2 | THE PERFORMANCE SPECIFICATIONS

The study of a control system in time domain essentially involves the evaluation of transient and steady-state responses of the system. The nature of transient response of a linear control system is revealed by any of the standard test signals—impulse, step, ramp, parabola—as this nature is dependent upon system poles only and not on the type of the input. It is therefore sufficient to analyse the transient response to one of the standard test signals; a step is generally used for this purpose. Steady-state response depends on both the system and the type of input. From the steady-state viewpoint, the 'easiest' input is generally a step since it requires only maintaining the output at a constant value once the transient is over. A more difficult problem is the tracking of a ramp input. Tracking of a parabola is even more difficult since a parabolic function is one degree faster than the ramp function. In practice, we seldom find it necessary to use a signal faster than a parabolic function; characteristics of actual signals, which the control systems encounter, are adequately represented by step, ramp, and parabolic functions.

The superposition principle allows us to consider response to commands apart from response to disturbances. If both occur simultaneously, the total response is just the superposition of the two individual responses.

Transient Response

The transient response of a practical control system often exhibits damped oscillations before reaching steady state. In specifying the transient-response characteristics of a control system to a unit-step input, it is common to specify the following:

(i) rise time, t_r;
(ii) peak time, t_p;
(iii) peak overshoot, M_p; and
(iv) settling time, t_s.

These specifications are defined below and are shown graphically in Fig. 6.2.

Rise Time, t_r

For underdamped systems, the rise time is normally defined as the time required for the step response to rise from 0 to 100% of its final value. For overdamped systems, the 10 to 90% rise time is commonly used.

Peak Time, t_p

It is the time required for the response to reach the first peak of the overshoot.

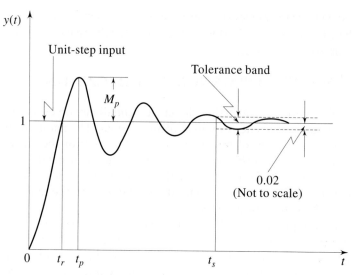

Fig. 6.2 *Typical unit-step response of a control system*

Peak Overshoot, M_p

It is the peak value of the response curve measured from unity. If the final steady-state value of the response differs from unity, then it is common to use *per cent peak overshoot*. It is defined by

$$\text{Per cent peak overshoot} = \frac{y(t_p) - y(\infty)}{y(\infty)} \times 100\% \qquad (6.1)$$

Settling Time, t_s

The time required for the response to damp out all transients is commonly called the setting time. Theoretically, the time taken to damp out all transients may be infinity. In practice, however, the transient is assumed to be over when the error is reduced below some acceptable value. Typically, the acceptable level is set at two or five per cent of the final value. Figure 6.2 shows a *tolerance band* of $\pm$ 2%.

▲▲

Rise time and peak time are intended as speed of response criteria. Clearly, the smaller these values, the faster the system response. Peak overshoot is used mainly for relative stability. Values in excess of about 40% may indicate that the system is dangerously close to absolute instability. Settling time combines stability and speed of response aspects and is widely used. Note in Fig. 6.3 that system *A* (which has a much shorter rise time than system *B*) is, in a sense, not really faster than *B* since it does not settle in the neighbourhood of the desired value until a later time because of the undesirable feature of overshooting (or undershooting) the final value and then having to come back in the opposite direction.

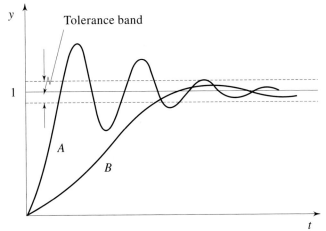

Fig. 6.3 *Significance of settling time*

Steady-State Response

Steady-state error, e_{ss}, is an index of steady-state response of a system to a specified input. It indicates the error between the actual output and the desired output as time t tends to infinity. With reference to the block diagram of Fig. 6.1, the steady-state error is defined as

$$e_{ss} = \lim_{t\to\infty}[r(t) - y(t)] \qquad (6.2)$$

In specifying the steady-state response characteristics of a system, it is common to specify the steady-state error of the system to one or more of the standard test signals—step, ramp, parabola. We will discover later a certain pattern of behaviour as the input is made more difficult from the steady-state viewpoint. Figure 6.4 is a typical illustration of the effect of input severity on steady-state error. The steady-state error to step inputs is zero, as in Fig. 6.4a. The very same system subjected to a ramp input has constant e_{ss}, as shown in Fig. 6.4b. The parabolic input of Fig. 6.4c causes an error that increases linearly with respect to time.

▲▲

When the system input is a disturbance $w(r \equiv 0)$, some of the performance criteria given above can still be used, although others cannot. It is still possible to define a peak time t_p (Fig. 6.5). However, t_r, t_s, and M_p are all referenced to the desired step size, which is now zero; thus these indices cannot be used.

Decay ratio, the ratio of the second overshoot divided by the first, is a transient performance criterion often used in process control systems, the most common design value being 1/4. We could also use the number of cycles to damp the amplitude to, say, 10% of M_{wp}—the peak value of the response to disturbance input. The smaller the number of cycles, the better is the speed of response and relative stability.

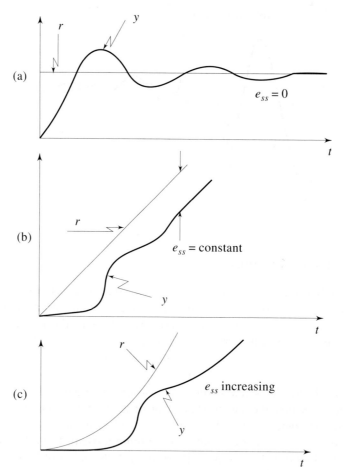

Fig. 6.4   *Effect of input severity on steady-state error*

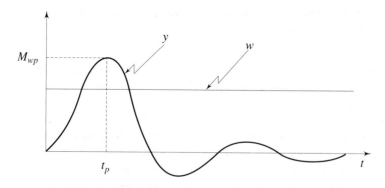

Fig. 6.5   *Time-domain specifications for disturbance input*

When the system input is a disturbance w, the definition of steady-state error still applies and we would expect the trend of worsening error as w is changed from step to ramp to parabola, similar to the behaviour of Fig. 6.4.

6.3 RESPONSE OF A STANDARD SECOND-ORDER SYSTEM

Although true second-order control systems are rare in practice, their analysis generally helps to form a basis for the understanding of analysis and design of higher-order systems.

Figure 6.6 shows the block diagram of a standard second-order control system (refer Section 2.7). The closed-loop transfer function of the system is

$$\frac{Y(s)}{R(s)} = \frac{\omega_n^2}{s^2 + 2\zeta\omega_n s + \omega_n^2} \tag{6.3}$$

where ζ and ω_n are, respectively, the *damping ratio* and the *undamped natural frequency* of the system; $\zeta = 0$ for an *undamped* system, $0 < \zeta < 1$ for an *underdamped* system, $\zeta = 1$ for a *critically damped* system, and $\zeta > 1$ for an *overdamped* system.

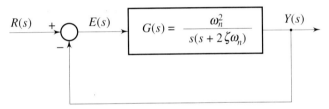

Fig. 6.6 *A standard second-order control system*

The characteristic equation of the closed-loop system is

$$\Delta(s) = s^2 + 2\zeta\omega_n s + \omega_n^2 = 0 \tag{6.4a}$$

The characteristic roots

$$s_{1,2} = -\zeta\omega_n \pm j\omega_n\sqrt{1 - \zeta^2} \tag{6.4b}$$

are the closed-loop poles of the system.

Figure 6.7 shows the locus of the poles of second-order system with ω_n held constant and ζ varying. For $\zeta = 0$, the poles are on the imaginary axis. As ζ increases, the poles move away from the imaginary axis along a circular path of radius ω_n meeting at the point $s = -\omega_n$, and then separating and travelling along the real axis, one towards zero and the other towards infinity. For $0 < \zeta < 1$, the poles are complex conjugate pair making an angle

$$\theta = \cos^{-1}\zeta \tag{6.5}$$

with the negative real axis; θ may be referred to as *damping angle*. For $\zeta = 1$, both the poles are on the negative real axis, repeated, and for $\zeta > 1$, the two poles are on the negative real axis, distinct.

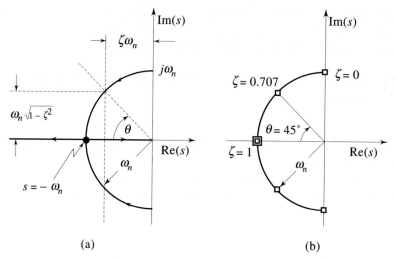

Fig. 6.7 *Pole locations for the standard second-order system*

We now study the transient response of the second-order system to unit-step input. The unit-step response has the Laplace transform (refer Eqn. (6.3))

$$Y(s) = \frac{\omega_n^2}{s(s^2 + 2\zeta\omega_n s + \omega_n^2)} \tag{6.6}$$

For $0 < \zeta < 1$, the inverse Laplace transformation gives (refer Eqn. (2.58))

$$y(t) = 1 - \frac{e^{-\zeta\omega_n t}}{\sqrt{1 - \zeta^2}} \sin\left(\omega_n \sqrt{1 - \zeta^2}\ t + \theta\right) \tag{6.7}$$

where $\theta = \cos^{-1}\zeta$

The characteristic features of this response are shown in Fig. 6.8. The response exhibits decaying oscillations of frequency $\omega_d = \omega_n\sqrt{1 - \zeta^2}$; ω_d is called the *damped natural frequency*. The curves

$$\left[1 \pm \frac{e^{-\zeta\omega_n t}}{\sqrt{1 - \zeta^2}} \right]$$

are the envelope curves for the step response. The response curve $y(t)$ always remains within this pair of envelope curves. The time-constant of these envelope curves is $1/\zeta\omega_n$. The speed of decay of the transient response depends on the value of the *time-constant*

$$\tau = \frac{1}{\zeta\omega_n} \tag{6.8}$$

Therefore, the larger the product $\zeta\omega_n$, the greater is the decay of the transient.

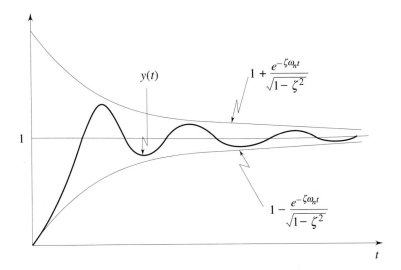

Fig. 6.8   *Typical unit-step response of underdamped standard second-order system*

The time response curves for various values of ζ plotted against normalized time $\omega_n t$ are shown in Fig. 6.9. For $\zeta = 0$, the system response exhibits continuous oscillations (refer Eqn. (2.56)). As ζ is increased, the response becomes progressively less oscillatory till it becomes critically damped (just non-oscillatory) for $\zeta = 1$ (refer Eqn. (2.60)), and overdamped for $\zeta > 1$ (refer Eqn. (2.61)).

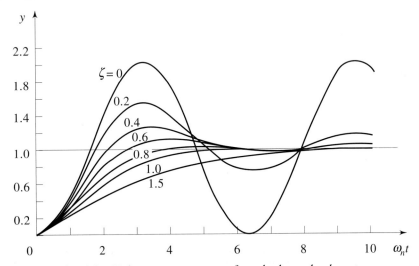

Fig. 6.9   *Unit-step response curves of standard second-order system*

Larger values of ζ give smaller values of peak overshoot but a slower rise of response. No overshoot at all is sometimes desirable; but usually this needlessly penalizes speed of response. Many systems are designed for 5 to 25% peak overshoot. For designs with peak overshoot less than five per cent, the price is paid in terms of speed of response, and the designs with peak overshoot more than 25% run the risk of being close to absolute instability.

Let us obtain the expressions for rise time, peak time, peak overshoot, settling time, and steady-state error, for a second-order system whose block diagram is shown in Fig. 6.6 and whose dynamics for the underdamped case are described by Eqn. (6.7).

Rise Time, t_r

Of the various definitions for rise time, the $0 - 100\%$ rise time is meaningful for the underdamped response and easy to find. Referring to Eqn. (6.7), we observe that $y(t)$ crosses the final value of unity where the sine function is zero. The first crossing will occur when the argument is equal to π. Therefore, the rise time is

$$t_r = \frac{\pi - \theta}{\omega_n \sqrt{1 - \zeta^2}}; \ \theta = \cos^{-1} \zeta \tag{6.9}$$

It can be seen that the value of θ lies between $\pi/2$ and 0 for $0 < \zeta < 1$. For moderate overshoots of 5–25%, the damping ratio ζ is in the range 0.4–0.7 (this we will prove shortly) and the normalized rise time $\omega_n t_r$ is approximately the same over this range, as is seen from Fig. 6.10. Thus, for a small value of t_r, ω_n must be large.

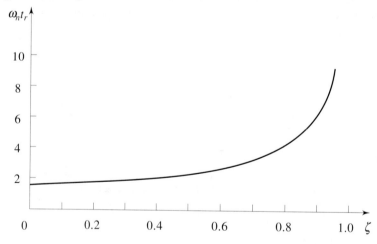

Fig. 6.10 *Normalized rise time versus damping ratio*

In frequency domain, the speed of response of a system is characterized by its *bandwidth*. Precise definition of bandwidth and its relationship to speed of response will be given in Chapter 9. Here we rely on the intuitive notion of bandwidth by reasoning as follows: Every input can be regarded as comprising components at various frequencies; a rapidly changing input means that it has a large high-frequency content, while a smooth, slow varying input has a relatively smaller high-frequency content. Thus, if the control system is to faithfully reproduce an input that is changing rapidly, it must be capable of faithfully reproducing inputs at high frequencies, i.e., have a large bandwidth. A step change (i.e., a discontinuity) in the input has a large amount of high-frequency content: to reproduce it faithfully (with a short rise time) requires a high bandwidth.

In a control system, the input signal may contain spurious noise signals in addition to the true signal input, or there may be sources of noise within the closed-loop system. This noise is generally in a band of frequencies above the dominant frequency band of the true signal. Thus, in order to reproduce the true signal and attenuate the noise, feedback control systems are designed to have a moderate bandwidth. This imposes a limit on reducing rise time and increasing ω_n. Large ω_n has a large bandwidth and will therefore allow the high-frequency noise signals to affect the performance.

Peak time, t_p

Equating the derivative of $y(t)$ in Eqn. (6.7) to zero to determine the extrema of the response, easily yields the equation

$$\frac{\zeta \omega_n}{\sqrt{1-\zeta^2}} e^{-\zeta \omega_n t} \sin\left(\omega_n \sqrt{1-\zeta^2}\, t + \theta\right)$$

$$-\frac{e^{-\zeta \omega_n t}}{\sqrt{1-\zeta^2}}\, \omega_n \sqrt{1-\zeta^2}\, \cos\left(\omega_n \sqrt{1-\zeta^2}\, t + \theta\right) = 0$$

or

$$\frac{\omega_n e^{-\zeta \omega_n t}}{\sqrt{1-\zeta^2}}\left[\zeta \sin\left(\omega_n \sqrt{1-\zeta^2}\, t + \theta\right) - \sqrt{1-\zeta^2}\, \cos\left(\omega_n \sqrt{1-\zeta^2}\, t + \theta\right)\right] = 0$$

$$(6.10)$$

From Fig. 6.7a, we observe that $\zeta = \cos\theta$, and $\sqrt{1-\zeta^2} = \sin\theta$. Therefore, the quantity inside the brackets in Eqn. (6.10) can be expressed as

$$\sin\left(\omega_n \sqrt{1-\zeta^2}\, t + \theta\right) \cos\theta - \cos\left(\omega_n \sqrt{1-\zeta^2}\, t + \theta\right) \sin\theta = 0$$

which gives
$$\sin\left(\omega_n \sqrt{1-\zeta^2}\, t\right) = 0$$

This implies that at the extrema of the response,

$$\omega_n \sqrt{1-\zeta^2}\, t = m\pi; \ m = 0, 1, 2, \ldots \tag{6.11}$$

Since the peak time corresponds to first overshoot,

$$t_p = \frac{\pi}{\omega_n \sqrt{1-\zeta^2}} \tag{6.12}$$

The first undershoot will occur at $t = 2\pi\big/\left[\omega_n \sqrt{1 - \zeta^2}\,\right]$, the second overshoot

at $t = 3\pi\big/\left[\omega_n \sqrt{1 - \zeta^2}\,\right]$, and so on. A plot of normalized peak time $\omega_n t_p$ vs ζ is given in Fig. 6.11.

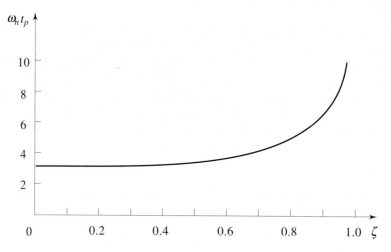

Fig. 6.11   *Normalized peak time versus damping ratio*

Peak overshoot, M_p

From Eqns (6.7) and (6.12) , we obtain

$$M_p = y(t_p) - 1 = -\frac{e^{-\zeta\omega_n t_p}}{\sqrt{1 - \zeta^2}} \sin\left(\omega_n \sqrt{1 - \zeta^2}\; t_p + \theta\right)$$

which gives $M_p = e^{-\pi\zeta/\sqrt{1 - \zeta^2}}$ (6.13)

Therefore, the per cent peak overshoot

$$= 100\; e^{-\pi\zeta/\sqrt{1 - \zeta^2}}\;\% \tag{6.14}$$

Solving for ζ from Eqn. (6.13), we get

$$\zeta^2 = \frac{\left[\ln\left(M_p\right)\right]^2}{\left[\ln\left(M_p\right)\right]^2 + \pi^2} \tag{6.15}$$

As seen from Fig. 6.12, the peak overshoot is a monotonically decreasing function of damping ζ and is independent of ω_n. It is therefore an excellent measure of system damping.

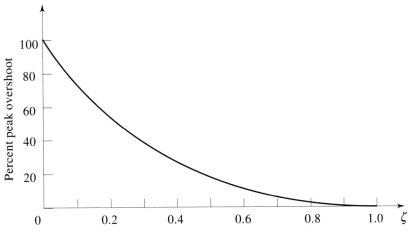

Fig. 6.12 *Per cent peak overshoot versus damping ratio*

Settling time t_s

In the following discussion, the product of undamped natural frequency and settling time will be called the *normalized settling time*, and the product of undamped natural frequency and time is called *normalized time*. For a five per cent tolerance band, the normalized settling time *versus* damping ratio curve is shown in Fig. 6.13a. This curve can be understood by examining Fig. 6.13b which has an exaggerated scale to facilitate the discussion. If the damping ratio is 1, the response enters the tolerance band when the normalized time is 4.7 and stays within the band thereafter. This result has been obtained from Eqn. (2.60):

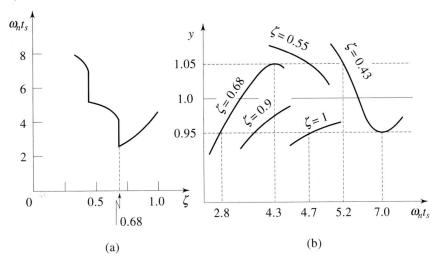

(a) (b)

Fig. 6.13 *Normalized settling time versus damping ratio*

For a critically damped system, the response

$$y(t) = 1 - e^{-\omega_n t} - \omega_n t\, e^{-\omega_n t}$$

The equation $1 - e^{-\eta} - \eta\, e^{-\eta} = 0.95$

gives $\eta = \omega_n t = 4.7$

As the damping ratio is reduced, $\omega_n t_s$ reduces. A damping ratio of 0.68 has the smallest $\omega_n t_s$ since the response curve crosses the lower limit of the band at $\omega_n t_1 = 2.8$ and overshoots five per cent reaching the upper limit at $\omega_n t_2 = 4.3$; a small decrease in ζ from the value 0.68 will result in a jump in $\omega_n t_s$ from 2.8 to 4.3. These results have been obtained from the following equations.

$$t_2 = \frac{\pi}{\omega_n \sqrt{1 - \zeta^2}}$$

$$y(t) = 1 - \frac{e^{-\zeta \omega_n t}}{\sqrt{1 - \zeta^2}} \sin\left(\omega_n \sqrt{1 - \zeta^2}\, t + \cos^{-1} \zeta\right)$$

When $\zeta = 0.68$, $\omega_n t_2 = 4.3$ and $y(t_2) = 1.05$. Also, when $\zeta = 0.68$, the equation $y(t_1) = 0.95$ gives $\omega_n t_1 = 2.8$. The normalized settling time increases from the value 4.3 as ζ is reduced. At a damping ratio of 0.43, the response curve crosses the upper limit of the band at $\omega_n t = 5.2$ and undershoots five per cent reaching the lower limit at $\omega_n t = 7$. Therefore, there is a jump in normalized settling time at $\zeta = 0.43$. Extending this logic, we can get the $\omega_n t_s$ vs ζ curve.

We observe that normalized settling time is minimum for $\zeta = 0.68$. This fact justifies why control systems are normally designed to be underdamped.

Analytical expression for the $\omega_n t_s$ vs ζ curve of Fig. 6.13a is difficult to obtain. We can use an approximation for the range $0 < \zeta < 0.68$ by using the envelope of the damped sinusoid shown in Fig. 6.8. Setting the time at which the lower envelope of $y(t)$ equals the value of 0.95 as the settling time t_s, we get

$$1 - \frac{e^{-\zeta \omega_n t_s}}{\sqrt{1 - \zeta^2}} = 0.95$$

Solving for t_s, we obtain

$$t_s = -\frac{1}{\zeta \omega_n} \ln\left(0.05 \sqrt{1 - \zeta^2}\right) \tag{6.16}$$

The value of $\ln\left(0.05 \sqrt{1 - \zeta^2}\right)$ varies between -3.0 and -3.3 as ζ varies from 0 to 0.68. A common design practice is to approximate settling time to three time-constants of the envelope of the damped sinusoidal oscillations (refer Eqn. (6.8)):

$$t_s \ (5\% \text{ tolerance}) \cong \frac{3}{\zeta \omega_n}; \ 0 < \zeta < 0.68 \tag{6.17}$$

On similar lines, it can be established that for a two per sent tolerance band, normalized settling time is minimum at $\zeta = 0.8$. For $0 < \zeta < 0.8$, the settling time

$$t_s = -\frac{1}{\zeta\omega_n} \ln\left(0.02\sqrt{1-\zeta^2}\right) \tag{6.18}$$

The value of $\ln\left(0.02\sqrt{1-\zeta^2}\right)$ varies between -3.91 and -4.42 as ζ varies from 0 to 0.8. A common design practice is to approximate settling time to four time-constants of the envelope of the damped sinusoidal oscillation (refer Eqn. (6.8)):

$$t_s \text{ (2\% tolerance)} \cong \frac{4}{\zeta\omega_n};\ 0 < \zeta < 0.8 \tag{6.19}$$

Unless otherwise specified, we will use two per cent tolerance band for settling-time calculations.

Steady-state Error, e_{ss}

From Eqn. (6.7), we obtain

$$e_{ss}\big|_{\text{unit step}} = \lim_{t\to\infty}[1 - y(t)] = 0$$

Thus, the standard second-order system has zero steady-state error to step inputs.

We now study the response of the standard second-order system to unit-ramp input $R(s) = 1/s^2$. The unit-ramp response has the Laplace transform (refer Eqn. (6.3))

$$Y(s) = \frac{\omega_n^2}{s^2(s^2 + 2\zeta\omega_n s + \omega_n^2)} \tag{6.20}$$

For $0 < \zeta < 1$, the inverse Laplace transformation gives (refer Eqn. (2.126))

$$y(t) = t - \frac{2\zeta}{\omega_n} + \frac{e^{-\zeta\omega_n t}}{\omega_n\sqrt{1-\zeta^2}}\sin(\omega_d t + 2\theta) \tag{6.21}$$

where $\quad\quad\quad\quad \theta = \cos^{-1}\zeta$

The response $y(t)$ for a typical value of ζ is plotted in Fig. 6.14. The steady-state error for unit-ramp input is given by

$$e_{ss}\big|_{\text{unit ramp}} = \lim_{t\to\infty}[t - y(t)] = \frac{2\zeta}{\omega_n} \tag{6.22}$$

From Fig. 6.14 it is observed that the nature of transient response to ramp input is similar to that to step input (damped oscillatory) and yields no new information about the transient behaviour of the system. As pointed out earlier, it is sufficient to investigate the transient response of a system to a step input only. Ramp-input response, of course, gives new information about the steady-state behaviour, which may be evaluated directly by the final-value theorem (Eqn. (A.35) in Appendix A).

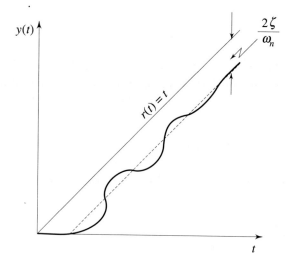

Fig. 6.14 *Typical unit-ramp response of an underdamped standard second-order system*

From the block diagram of Fig. 6.6, we have

$$E(s) = \frac{1}{1 + G(s)} R(s) = \frac{s(s + 2\zeta\omega_n)}{s^2 + 2\zeta\omega_n s + \omega_n^2} R(s) \qquad (6.23)$$

For a unit-ramp input, $R(s) = 1/s^2$ and

$$E(s) = \frac{s + 2\zeta\omega_n}{s(s^2 + 2\zeta\omega_n s + \omega_n^2)}$$

$$e_{ss}\big|_{\text{unit ramp}} = \lim_{s \to 0} s E(s) = \frac{2\zeta}{\omega_n} \qquad (6.24)$$

To investigate the steady-state behaviour of the standard second-order system to unit-parabolic input, we substitute $R(s) = 1/s^3$ in Eqn. (6.23):

$$E(s) = \frac{s + 2\zeta\omega_n}{s^2(s^2 + 2\zeta\omega_n s + \omega_n^2)}$$

Since $E(s)$ has repeated pole at $s = 0$, the error response $e(t)$ will be unbounded, and therefore

$$\lim_{t \to \infty} e(t) = \infty = e_{ss}\big|_{\text{unit parabola}} \qquad (6.25)$$

Therefore, in control systems represented by standard second-order model, the steady-state error will be finite only if the actual signals which the control systems encounter are not faster than a ramp function.

▲▲

From Eqns (6.9), (6.12), (6.13), (6.19) and (6.24), we observe that rise time, peak time, peak overshoot, settling time and steady-state error measures of the performance of a standard second-order system are mutually dependent, and therefore must be specified in a consistent manner.

What is the Best Damping Ratio to Use?

A very important question to answer before leaving this section is the best value of damping ratio ζ to choose for a control system.

Selection of damping ratio for industrial control applications requires a trade-off between relative stability and speed of response. A smaller damping ratio decreases normalized rise time (refer Fig. 6.10), but it increases the peak overshoot (refer Fig. 6.12). The final choice of the damping ratio is subjective. Many systems are designed for damping ratio in the range $0.4 - 0.7$ (this corresponds to peak overshoot in the range $5 - 25\%$). If allowed by rise-time considerations, ζ close to 0.7 is the most obvious choice because it results in minimum normalized settling time (refer Fig. 6.13a).

If the requirement is to design an extremely accurate control system whose steady-state errors to position and velocity inputs are extremely small (e.g., to be used for navigation purposes), the transient response is not the primary performance criterion to optimize; minimum steady-state error is the major objective. With reference to Eqn. (6.24) we observe that the damping ratio ζ should be as small as possible because the steady-state error is proportional to ζ. Values close to 0.1 are not unreasonable for such applications; the disadvantage of relatively long settling time must be tolerated.

There are situations (e.g., in some robot-manipulator applications) where the overshoot cannot be tolerated. A good compromise between rise time and overshoot is $\zeta = 1$.

Example 6.1

In this example, we study the time-domain performance of a control system whose objective is to control the position of a mechanical load. Figure 6.15 shows transfer-function block diagram of the system. The two potentiometers having sensitivity K_P convert the input and output positions into proportional electrical signals, which are in turn compared and the error signal, amplified by a factor K_A, is applied to the armature circuit of a dc motor whose field winding is excited with a constant voltage. The motor is coupled to the load through a gear train of ratio n. The block diagram also shows a minor feedback loop which corresponds to a tachogenerator connected in the system to improve damping.

When switch S is open (tachogenerator disconnected), the block diagram of Fig. 6.15 reduces to that given in Fig. 6.16. The open-loop transfer function

$$D(s)G(s) = \frac{4500K_A}{s(s + 361.2)} \tag{6.26}$$

The characteristic equation of the unity-feedback system is

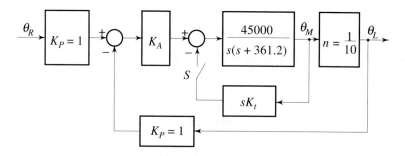

Fig. 6.15 *Block diagram of a position control system*

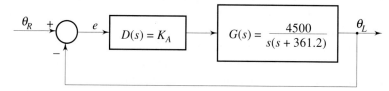

Fig. 6.16 *Simplified block diagram of the system in Fig. 6.15 with $K_t = 0$*

$$s^2 + 361.2\,s + 4500K_A = s^2 + 2\zeta\omega_n\,s + \omega_n^2 = 0 \qquad (6.27a)$$

Natural frequency $\qquad\qquad \omega_n = \sqrt{4500K_A} \qquad\qquad\qquad\qquad (6.27b)$

Damping ratio $\qquad\qquad \zeta = \dfrac{361.2}{2\sqrt{4500K_A}} = \dfrac{2.692}{\sqrt{K_A}} \qquad (6.27c)$

The closed-loop poles are

$$s_{1,\,2} = -\,180.6 \pm \sqrt{32,\,616.36 - 4500K_A} \qquad (6.28)$$

From the block diagram of Fig. 6.16, we obtain

$$\frac{E(s)}{R(s)} = \frac{1}{1 + D(s)G(s)} = \frac{1}{1 + \dfrac{4500K_A}{s(s + 361.2)}} = \frac{s(s + 361.2)}{s(s + 361.2) + 4500K_A}$$

The steady-state error of the system due to a ramp input $R(s) = 1/s^2$ is given by

$$e_{ss}\big|_{\text{unit ramp}} = \lim_{s \to 0} s\,E(s) = \frac{361.2}{4500K_A} = \frac{0.0803}{K_A} \qquad (6.29)$$

(i) *System with critical damping*

For $K_A = 7.247$, the damping ratio $\zeta = 1$, the natural frequency $\omega_n = 180.6$, and both the closed-loop poles are located at -180.6. From Fig. 6.13a, we observe that normalized settling time (five per cent tolerance) corresponding to $\zeta = 1$ is 4.7. Therefore

$$t_s\ (5\%\ \text{tolerance}) = \frac{4.7}{180.6} = 0.026\ \text{sec}$$

The steady-state error (Eqn. (6.29))

$$e_{ss}\big|_{\text{unit ramp}} = 0.011 \text{ rad}$$

(ii) *System with moderate damping*

For $K_A = 14.5$, the damping ratio $\zeta = 0.707$, the natural frequency $\omega_n = 255.44$ rad/sec, and the closed-loop poles are located at $-180.6 \pm j\,180.6$. The damped natural frequency is $\omega_d = \omega_n\sqrt{1-\zeta^2} = 180.6$ rad/sec.

Rise time
$$t_r = \frac{\pi - \cos^{-1}\zeta}{\omega_d} = \frac{\pi - 45\left(\dfrac{\pi}{180}\right)}{180.6} = 0.013 \text{ sec}$$

Peak time
$$t_p = \frac{\pi}{\omega_d} = 0.0174 \text{ sec}$$

Peak overshoot
$$M_p = e^{-\pi\zeta/\sqrt{1-\zeta^2}} \times 100 = 4.3\%$$

From Fig. 6.13a, we observe that normalized settling time corresponding to $\zeta = 0.707$ is 3. Therefore t_s (five per cent tolerance) $= \dfrac{3}{255.44} = 0.0117\,\text{sec}$.

The steady-state error
$$e_{ss}\big|_{\text{unit ramp}} = 0.0055 \text{ rad}$$

Therefore, the increase in amplifier gain K_A from the value 7.247 to 14.5 has resulted in a decrease in damping from $\zeta = 1$ to $\zeta = 0.707$, decrease in settling time from 0.026 sec to 0.0117 sec, and decrease in steady-state error from 0.011 to 0.0055 rad. The price has been paid in terms of overshoot. Since 4.3 % peak overshoot is acceptable in many industrial control applications, moderate value of ζ results in better system performance compared to the critical value $\zeta = 1$.

(iii) *System with low damping*

For larger values of K_A, the damping ratio ζ reduces, natural frequency ω_n increases, and the real part of the poles is constant at -180.6, i.e., $\zeta\omega_n = 180.6$. As given by the approximate expression (6.17), the settling time does not change appreciably for $K_A > 14.5$. However, increase in K_A will result in reduced steady-state error to ramp input. Also, it will result in reduced rise time and hence better speed of response. The price is paid in terms of increased peak overshoot and hence poor relative stability. This means K_A can be increased at the most to a value for which the step-response overshoot is acceptable.

If 25% peak overshoot is considered acceptable, we have from Eqn. (6.15), $\zeta = 0.4$. $K_A = 45.3$ gives this value of damping. The other performance measures are:

$$\omega_n = 451.5 \text{ rad/sec}, \quad \omega_d = 413.8 \text{ rad/sec}$$
$$t_r = 0.0048 \text{ sec}, \quad t_p = 0.0076 \text{ sec},$$
$$e_{ss}\big|_{\text{unit ramp}} = 0.0018 \text{ rad}.$$

6.4 | EFFECTS OF AN ADDITIONAL ZERO AND AN ADDITIONAL POLE

The expressions for features of the step response of a system—rise time, peak time, peak overshoot, settling time—derived in the last section are valid only for the standard second-order system with closed-loop transfer function

$$M(s) = \frac{Y(s)}{R(s)} = \frac{\omega_n^2}{s^2 + 2\zeta\omega_n s + \omega_n^2} \tag{6.30}$$

The transfer function $M(s)$ has two poles and no zeros. For many practical systems, the closed-loop transfer function has more than two poles and/or finite zeros. In this section, we study the effects of adding poles and zeros to the standard second-order model.

Let a zero be added to $M(s)$ of Eqn. (6.30). Then we have

$$M_1(s) = \frac{Y_1(s)}{R(s)} = \frac{(s + \alpha)(\omega_n^2/\alpha)}{s^2 + 2\zeta\omega_n s + \omega_n^2} \tag{6.31}$$

The transfer function $M_1(s)$ has been normalized to have the gain at $s = 0$ equal to unity. This makes the final value of the unit-step response also 1, and thus the transfer function has been adjusted so that the system will track a step with zero steady-state error. The unit-step response of the one-zero, two-pole system may be determined from

$$Y_1(s) = \frac{(s + \alpha)(\omega_n^2/\alpha)}{s(s^2 + 2\zeta\omega_n s + \omega_n^2)} \tag{6.32}$$

$$= \frac{\omega_n^2}{s(s^2 + 2\zeta\omega_n s + \omega_n^2)} + \frac{s}{\alpha}\frac{\omega_n^2}{s(s^2 + 2\zeta\omega_n s + \omega_n^2)}$$

$$= Y(s) + \frac{s}{\alpha}Y(s) \tag{6.33a}$$

where $Y(s)$ is the unit-step response of standard second-order system (6.30).

From Eqn. (6.33a), we obtain

$$y_1(t) = y(t) + \frac{1}{\alpha}\frac{dy(t)}{dt} \tag{6.33b}$$

The effect of the added derivative term may be seen by examining Fig. 6.17a, where a case for a typical value of ζ is considered. We see from the figure that the effect of the zero is to contribute a pronounced early peak to the system's response whereby the peak overshoot may increase appreciably. From Fig. 6.17b, it is seen that the smaller the value of α, i.e., the closer the zero to the origin, the more pronounced is the peaking phenomenon. On account of this fact, *the zeros on the real axis near the origin are generally avoided in design.* However, in a sluggish system, the artful introduction of zero at the proper position can improve the transient response.

We further observe from Eqn. (6.33b) that as α increases, i.e., the zero moves farther into the left half of the s-plane, its effect becomes less pro-

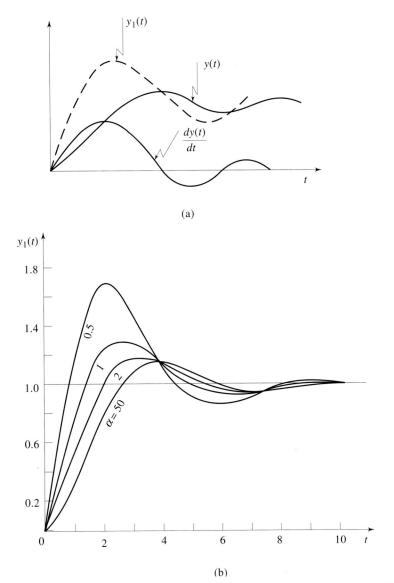

Fig. 6.17 (a) Unit-step response of a standard second-order system with an additional zero
         (b) Response for several zero locations with $\zeta = 0.5$, $\omega_n = 1$

nounced. For sufficiently large values of α, the effect of zero on transient response may become negligible.

The transient analysis given by Eqn. (6.33b) is very informative in case the zero is in the right-half plane. In this case, α is negative and the derivative term is subtracted rather than added. A typical case is sketched in Fig. 6.18.

For a quantitative transient analysis of the standard second-order system with a finite zero, we obtain $y_1(t)$ from $Y_1(s)$ of Eqn. (6.32). Partial-fraction expansion of $Y_1(s)$ gives

$$Y_1(s) = \frac{1}{s} + \frac{A}{s + \zeta\omega_n - j\omega_n\sqrt{1-\zeta^2}} + \frac{A^*}{s + \zeta\omega_n + j\omega_n\sqrt{1-\zeta^2}}$$

where A^* is complex-conjugate of A.

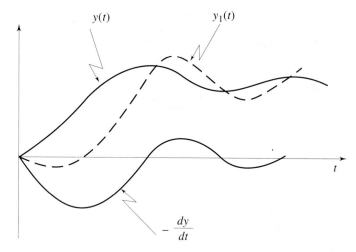

Fig. 6.18   *Unit-step response of a standard second-order system with a zero in the right-half plane*

The pole-zero pattern of $Y_1(s)$ is shown in Fig. 6.19. From the geometry of this figure, we obtain

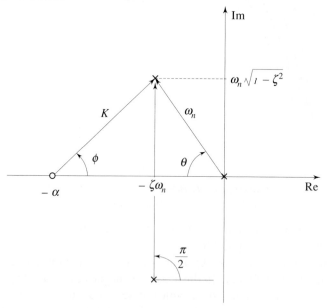

Fig. 6.19   *Pole-zero pattern of $Y_1(s)$ in Eqn. (6.32)*

$$A = \frac{\omega_n^2}{\alpha} \left. \frac{s + \alpha}{s\left(s + \zeta\omega_n + j\omega_n\sqrt{1-\zeta^2}\right)}\right|_{s=-\zeta\omega_n+j\omega_n\sqrt{1-\zeta^2}}$$

$$= \frac{\omega_n^2}{\alpha} \frac{K e^{j\phi}}{\left[\omega_n e^{j(\pi-\theta)}\right]\left[2\omega_n\sqrt{1-\zeta^2}\, e^{j\pi/2}\right]} = \frac{K}{2\alpha\sqrt{1-\zeta^2}} e^{j\left(\phi+\theta+\frac{\pi}{2}\right)}$$

The response $y_1(t)$ is obtained as follows (refer Eqn. (5.7)):

$$y_1(t) = 1 + 2\frac{K}{2\alpha\sqrt{1-\zeta^2}} e^{-\zeta\omega_n t} \cos\left(\omega_n\sqrt{1-\zeta^2}\, t + \phi + \theta + \frac{\pi}{2}\right)$$

$$= 1 + \frac{K}{\alpha\sqrt{1-\zeta^2}} e^{-\zeta\omega_n t} \cos\left(\omega_n\sqrt{1-\zeta^2}\, t + \phi + \theta + \frac{\pi}{2}\right) \qquad (6.34)$$

Figure 6.20 shows the effect of the zero on peak overshoot of the step response $y_1(t)$ when $\zeta = 0.5$ and $\omega_n = 1$. The parameter η in the figure represents normalized zero location: $\alpha = \eta\zeta\omega_n$. When η is large, the zero is far removed from the poles and will have little effect on the response. If $\eta = 1$, the zero is at the value of the real part of the poles and has a substantial influence on the response. $\eta < 1$ results in the highly pronounced peaking phenomenon.

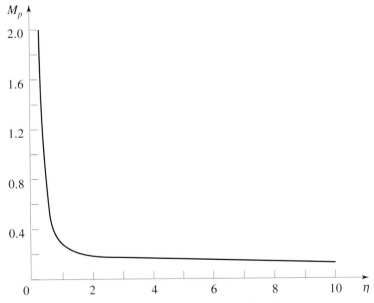

Fig. 6.20 *Plot of peak overshoot for several locations of an additional zero ($\zeta = 0.5$, $\omega_n = 1$)*

Now let us consider the effect of an additional pole on the response of a standard second-order system (6.30). To this end we consider a transfer function of the form

$$M_2(s) = \frac{Y_2(s)}{R(s)} = \frac{\omega_n^2 \alpha}{(s + \alpha)(s^2 + 2\zeta\omega_n s + \omega_n^2)} \tag{6.35}$$

The transfer function $M_2(s)$ has been normalized to have the gain at $s = 0$ equal to unity. The unit-step response of this no-zero, three-pole system may be determined from

$$
\begin{aligned}
Y_2(s) &= \frac{\omega_n^2 \alpha}{s(s + \alpha)(s^2 + 2\zeta\omega_n s + \omega_n^2)} \\
&= \frac{1}{s} + \frac{A_1}{s + \alpha} + \frac{A_2}{s + \zeta\omega_n - j\omega_n\sqrt{1-\zeta^2}} + \frac{A_2^*}{s + \zeta\omega_n + j\omega_n\sqrt{1-\zeta^2}}
\end{aligned}
$$

From the geometry of Fig. 6.21a, we obtain

$$A_1 = \frac{\omega_n^2 \alpha}{\alpha e^{j\pi} K e^{j(\pi+\phi)} K e^{j(\pi-\phi)}} = \frac{\omega_n^2}{K^2 e^{j\pi}} = \frac{-\omega_n^2}{K^2} \tag{6.36a}$$

From the geometry of Fig. 6.21b, we obtain

$$A_2 = \frac{\omega_n^2 \alpha}{\omega_n e^{j(\pi-\theta)} \left(2\omega_n\sqrt{1-\zeta^2} e^{j\pi/2}\right) K e^{j\phi}}$$

$$= \frac{\alpha}{2 K\sqrt{1-\zeta^2} e^{j\left(\pi-\theta+\frac{\pi}{2}+\phi\right)}} = \frac{\alpha e^{j\left(\frac{\pi}{2}+\theta-\phi\right)}}{2 K\sqrt{1-\zeta^2}} \tag{6.36b}$$

The response

$$y_2(t) = 1 - \frac{\omega_n^2}{K^2} e^{-\alpha t} + \frac{\alpha}{K\sqrt{1-\zeta^2}} e^{-\zeta\omega_n t} \cos\left(\omega_n\sqrt{1-\zeta^2}\, t + \theta + \frac{\pi}{2} - \phi\right) \tag{6.37}$$

From Fig. 6.21 and Eqns (6.36), it can be seen that

$$\lim_{\alpha \to 0} |A_1| = 1; \quad \lim_{\alpha \to 0} |A_2| = 0$$

from which we deduce that as $\alpha \to 0$, the effect of the two complex poles at $-\zeta\omega_n \pm j\omega_n\sqrt{1-\zeta^2}$ diminishes and the transient response becomes dominated by the pole at $-\alpha$, i.e., the term $e^{-\alpha t}$ of Eqn. (6.37). This means that a pole on the negative real axis near the origin will dominate the response of the system. This domination is enhanced by the fact that if $\alpha \ll \zeta\omega_n$, the effect of the term $e^{-\alpha t}$ will last much longer than that of the term $e^{-\zeta\omega_n t}$.

Now let us see what happens as α becomes large. A simple calculation shows that

$$\lim_{\alpha \to \infty} |A_1| = 0; \quad \lim_{\alpha \to \infty} |A_2| = \frac{1}{2\sqrt{1-\zeta^2}}$$

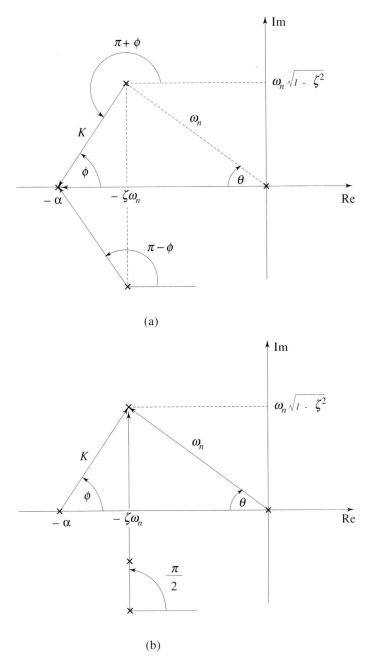

(a)

(b)

Fig. 6.21 *Pole-zero pattern of $Y_2(s)$ in Eqn. (6.35)*

from which we see that as α increases, an opposite effect is observed. The complex poles at $-\zeta\omega_n \pm j\omega_n\sqrt{1-\zeta^2}$ now dominate the response, while the contribution of the pole at $-\alpha$ diminishes in significance. Further, if $\zeta\omega_n \ll$

α, the effect of the term $e^{-\alpha t}$ will be over much more quickly than the term whose magnitude decreases as $e^{-\zeta \omega_n t}$. All the preceding effects may be seen quite clearly in Fig. 6.22. Figure 6.23 shows the effect of the third pole at $s = - \alpha = - \eta \zeta \omega_n$ on rise time of the step response. When η is large, the real pole is far removed from complex poles and will have little effect on the response. If $\eta = 1$, the real pole is at the value of the real part of the complex pole pair and has a substantial effect on the response. $\eta < 1$ makes the system very sluggish.

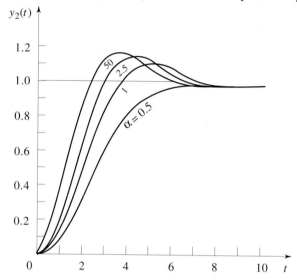

Fig. 6.22 *Unit-step response of a standard second-order system ($\zeta = 0.5$, $\omega_n = 1$) for several locations of an additional pole*

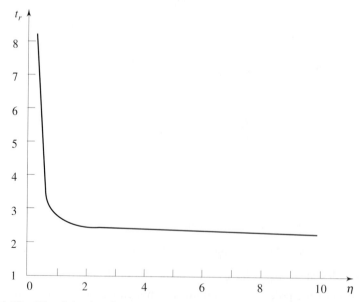

Fig. 6.23 *Plot of rise time for several locations of an additional pole ($\zeta = 0.5$, $\omega_n = 1$)*

6.5 | DESIRED CLOSED-LOOP POLE LOCATIONS AND THE DOMINANCE CONDITION

From the discussions given in the preceding sections, it becomes apparent that for second-order feedback control systems with no finite zeros, the transient performance specifications can be translated into the desired locations for the two closed-loop poles. Acceptable values of damping ratio ζ and undamped natural frequency ω_n are first obtained from the consistent set of specifications on rise time, peak time, peak overshoot, and settling time using the second-order correlations given below (refer Eqns (6.9), (6.12), (6.13) and (6.19)):

Rise time:
$$t_r = \frac{\pi - \cos^{-1}\zeta}{\omega_n\sqrt{1 - \zeta^2}}$$
(6.38a)

Peak time:
$$t_p = \frac{\pi}{\omega_n\sqrt{1 - \zeta^2}}$$
(6.38b)

Peak overshoot:
$$M_p = e^{-\pi\zeta/\sqrt{1-\zeta^2}}$$
(6.38c)

Settling time:
$$t_s = \frac{4}{\zeta\omega_n}$$
(6.38d)

The desired locations of the closed-loop poles are then obtained as

$$s_{1,2} = -\zeta\omega_n \pm j\omega_n\sqrt{1 - \zeta^2}$$
(6.39)

We know that a large ω_n is desirable because it results in high speed of response. However, measurement noise considerations impose a limit on ω_n; a system with large ω_n has a large bandwidth and will therefore allow the high-frequency noise signals to affect the performance. We also know that damping ratio in the range of 0.4 to 0.7 is desirable from relative stability and speed of response considerations. Therefore, the desired closed-loop poles should most likely be located in the shaded regions in Fig. 6.24. We have intentionally not assigned numerical values to ω_{n1} and ω_{n2}, since these are relative to a given system. A large value of ω_{n1} is desirable from the speed of response considerations; ω_{n2} represents the limit imposed by noise considerations. The design problem is to force the closed-loop poles of the controlled system to the desired locations.

The second-order correlations (6.38)–(6.39) derived for the standard second-order system can be used for a second-order system with a finite zero by appropriately accommodating the effect of the zero on the transient response. The effect of a zero in the left half s-plane is to contribute a pronounced early peak to the system's response whereby the peak overshoot may increase appreciably. The closer the zero to the origin, the more pronounced is the peaking phenomenon. If the zero moves farther into the left half s-plane, its effect

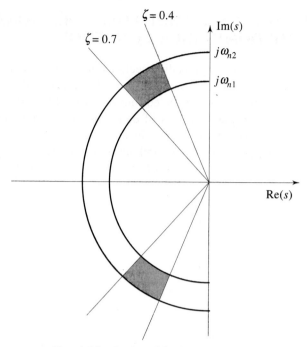

Fig. 6.24   *Region of dominant poles in the s-plane*

becomes less pronounced. *If the magnitude of the zero is more than five times the magnitude of the real part of the complex-conjugate poles of the second-order system, then the zero may be regarded as insignificant insofar as the transient response is concerned* (Fig. 6.25). However, if it is not possible to avoid a zero in the region of significant effect on the transient response, we may design the system for a higher value of ζ than the one that is acceptable, to account for the effect of increase in overshoot due to the presence of zero. A simulation study is carried out to see whether the design is acceptable. If not, one has to re-enter the design cycle with a different and more appropriate choice of ζ.

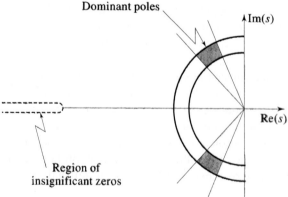

Fig. 6.25   *Regions of dominant poles and insignificant zeros in the s-plane*

When a system is higher than second-order, strictly we can no longer characterize its dynamics by damping ratio ζ and undamped natural frequency ω_n, which are defined for standard second-order systems. However, by a proper design, it may be possible to force the closed-loop poles of a higher-order system to the two regions shown in Fig. 6.26; a complex-conjugate pole pair in region I and all other poles in region II. It has been recognized in practice that *if the magnitudes of the real parts of all the poles in region* II *are more than five times that of poles in region* I, *then the poles of region* II *may be regarded as insignificant insofar as the transient response is concerned.* The pair of complex-conjugate poles in region I has a dominant effect on transient response; we will refer to these poles as *dominant poles* of the higher-order system. The parameters (ζ, ω_n), associated with the dominant poles, characterize the dynamics of the higher-order system.

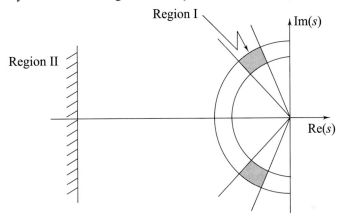

Fig. 6.26 *Regions of dominant and insignificant poles in the s-plane*

The design procedure for the higher-order systems is as follows. The specifications of relative stability and speed of response are translated into a pair of dominant closed-loop poles using the correlations (6.38)–(6.39). The design requirement is to force two of the closed-loop poles at the specified dominant positions and all other poles in the insignificant region. If the dominance condition is not satisfied, nothing can be said about the usefulness of design. A simulation study is carried out to see whether the design is acceptable. If not, one has to re-enter the design cycle to get a different distribution of closed-loop poles.

When a system is higher than second-order and has finite zeros, the dominance condition is satisfied only when the contributions to the transient response of the zeros and all the poles other than the pair corresponding to specified ζ and ω_n, is insignificant. An artful placement of a zero can cancel the dynamics contributed by a pole; this technique of *pole-zero cancellation* may be utilized to meet the dominance condition. To illustrate this concept, we consider the following two transfer functions, which have the same poles but differ in the locations of their zeros. They are normalized to have the same gain at $s = 0$.

$$G_1(s) = \frac{2}{(s+1)(s+2)} = \frac{2}{(s+1)} - \frac{2}{(s+2)}$$

$$G_2(s) = \frac{2(s+1.1)}{1.1(s+1)(s+2)} = \frac{2}{1.1}\left(\frac{0.1}{s+1} + \frac{0.9}{s+2}\right)$$

$$= \frac{0.18}{s+1} + \frac{1.64}{s+2}$$

Notice that the coefficient of the $(s+1)$ term has been modified from 2 in $G_1(s)$ to 0.18 in $G_2(s)$. This dramatic reduction is brought out by the zero at $s = -1.1$ in $G_2(s)$, which almost cancels the poles at $s = -1$. Of course, if we place the zero exactly at $s = -1$, this term will vanish completely.

The following remarks generalize the implications of this example for the significance of zeros in the system pole-zero pattern.

1. The residue A_i at pole $s = -\alpha_i$ corresponds to the transient term $A_i e^{-\alpha_i t}$; the significance of the residue is that its magnitude is the initial size of the transient corresponding to the pole.
2. If a zero is close to a pole, the residue at the pole tends to be small, and the corresponding transient becomes small.
3. If the zero coincides the pole, it cancels it and the corresponding transient term is zero.

Thus, the significance of zeros is that they affect the residues at the poles, and hence the sizes of the corresponding transients. Any pole outside the insignificant region (region II in Fig. 6.26) is acceptable if the nearby zero makes the corresponding transient small. Therefore, for the dominance condition to be satisfied, all the closed-loop poles other than the two corresponding to specified ζ and ω_n, should either lie in the insignificant region or have zeros nearby.

6.6   STEADY-STATE ERROR CONSTANTS AND SYSTEM-TYPE NUMBER

Steady-state error is a measure of system accuracy when a specific type of input is applied to a control system. The designer always strives to design the system to minimize the error for a certain anticipated class of inputs. This section considers the techniques that are available for determining the system accuracy.

Theoretically, it is desirable for a control system to have the capability of responding with zero error to all the polynomial inputs

$$r(t) = (t^k/k!)\,\mu(t) \tag{6.40}$$

of degree k. If $k = 0$, the input is a step of unit magnitude; if $k = 1$, the input is a ramp with unit slope; if $k = 2$, the input is a parabola with unit second derivative; $k = 3$ corresponds to an input one degree faster than parabola, and so on. From the common problems of mechanical motion control, the *step, ramp,* and *parabolic* inputs are called, respectively, *position, velocity* and *acceleration* inputs.

The specification of the zero-error response to all the polynomial inputs is very impractical and unrealistic. Fortunately, the requirements of practical systems are much less stringent. For example, consider the position control system for a robot manipulator. For a typical application, it would be desirable for this system to respond well to inputs of position and velocity, but not necessarily to those of acceleration. In addition, it would be desirable for this system to respond with zero error for positional-type inputs. However, a finite error could probably be tolerated for inputs of velocity.

For quantitative analysis, we consider the unity-feedback system shown in Fig. 6.27. The input is $R(s)$, the output $Y(s)$, and the difference between the input and the output is the error $E(s)$. For a stable system, the *transient component* of the error response $e(t)$ will eventually die away, leaving only the *steady-state component* $e_s(t)$ whose form is dictated directly by the forcing input.

The steady-state error

$$e_{ss} = \lim_{t \to \infty} e_s(t) = \lim_{t \to \infty} e(t) = \lim_{t \to \infty} [r(t) - y(t)] \tag{6.41a}$$

By the final-value theorem (Eqn. (A.35) in Appendix A),

$$e_{ss} = \lim_{s \to 0} sE(s) \tag{6.41b}$$

provided that $sE(s)$ has no poles on the $j\omega$-axis and in the right half plane.

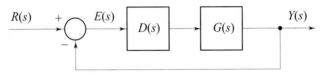

Fig. 6.27 *A unity-feedback system*

For the system shown in Fig. 6.27,

$$E(s) = R(s) - Y(s) = \left[1 - \frac{Y(s)}{R(s)} \right] R(s) = \frac{1}{1 + D(s)\,G(s)}\, R(s) \tag{6.42}$$

Substituting Eqn. (6.42) into Eqn. (6.41b), we obtain

$$e_{ss} = \lim_{s \to 0} \frac{s\,R(s)}{1 + D(s)\,G(s)} \tag{6.43}$$

Thus, the steady-state of a system with unity feedback depends on the input signal $R(s)$ and the open-loop transfer function $D(s)G(s)$. By the nature of the limit in Eqn. (6.43), we see that the result of the limit can be zero, can be a constant different from zero, or the limit may not exist in which case the final-value theorem does not apply; but it is easy to see from the basic definition (6.41a) that $e_{ss} = \infty$ in this case anyway because $E(s)$ will have a pole at $s = 0$ that is of order higher than one. Systems having a finite non-zero steady-state error when the reference input is a zero-order polynomial input (a step) are labelled "type-0". Similarly, a system that has finite non-zero steady-state error to a first-order polynomial input (a ramp) is called a "type-1" system; a system with finite non-zero steady-state error to a second-order polynomial input (a parabola) is called a "type-2" system, and so on.

The control engineer is usually interested in step (position), ramp (velocity), and parabola (acceleration) inputs. For a step input $r(t) = \mu(t)$, the steady-state error may be obtained by substituting $R(s) = 1/s$ into Eqn. (6.43):

$$e_{ss} = \lim_{s \to 0} \frac{1}{1 + D(s)\, G(s)} = \frac{1}{1 + \lim_{s \to 0} D(s)\, G(s)}$$

The quantity $\lim_{s \to 0} D(s)G(s)$ is defined as the *position error constant* and is denoted by K_p:

$$K_p = \lim_{s \to 0} D(s)G(s) \tag{6.44a}$$

Therefore, steady-state error in terms of K_p is given by

$$e_{ss} = \frac{1}{1 + K_p} \tag{6.44b}$$

The steady-state error to a velocity input $r(t) = t\mu(t)$ can be obtained by substituting $R(s) = 1/s^2$ into Eqn. (6.43):

$$e_{ss} = \lim_{s \to 0} \frac{1}{s\big(1 + D(s)\, G(s)\big)} = \frac{1}{\lim_{s \to 0} s\, D(s)\, G(s)}$$

The quantity $\lim_{s \to 0} sD(s)G(s)$ is defined as the *velocity error constant* and is denoted by K_v:

$$K_v = \lim_{s \to 0} sD(s)G(s) \tag{6.45a}$$

Therefore, the steady-state error in terms of K_v is given by

$$e_{ss} = 1/K_v \tag{6.45b}$$

An expression for steady-state error due to acceleration input $r(t) = \frac{1}{2} t^2 \mu(t)$ can be obtained by substituting $R(s) = 1/s^3$ into Eqn. (6.43):

$$e_{ss} = \lim_{s \to 0} \frac{1}{s^2 \big(1 + D(s)\, G(s)\big)} \lim_{s \to 0} \frac{1}{s^2\, D(s)\, G(s)}$$

The quantity $\lim_{s \to 0} s^2 D(s)G(s)$ is defined as the *acceleration error constant* and is denoted by K_a:

$$K_a = \lim_{s \to 0} s^2 D(s)G(s) \tag{6.46a}$$

Therefore, the steady-state error in terms of K_a is

$$e_{ss} = 1/K_a \tag{6.46b}$$

▲▲

As said earlier, feedback systems can be classified on the basis of their steady-state response to polynomial inputs. We can always express the open-loop transfer function $D(s)G(s)$ as

$$D(s)G(s) = \frac{K \prod\limits_{i}(s + z_i)}{s^N \prod\limits_{j}(s + p_j)}; \; z_i \neq 0, \, p_j \neq 0 \tag{6.47}$$

The term $1/s^N$ corresponds to N number of pure integrations in $D(s)G(s)$. As $s \to 0$, this term dominates in determining the steady-state error. Feedback systems are therefore classified in accordance with the number of pure integrators in the open-loop transfer function $D(s)G(s)$, as described below:

Type-0 System

If $N = 0$, the steady-state error to various standard inputs obtained from Eqns (6.44)–(6.46) are

$$e_{ss} = \begin{cases} \dfrac{1}{1 + K_p} & \text{in response to unit-step input; } K_p = \left. \dfrac{K \prod_i (s + z_i)}{K \prod_j (s + p_j)} \right|_{s=0} \\[4mm] \infty & \text{in response to unit-ramp input} \\[2mm] \infty & \text{in response to unit-parabolic input} \end{cases} \tag{6.48}$$

Thus, a system with $N = 0$ (i.e., with no integrator in $D(s)G(s)$) has a finite non-zero position error, infinite velocity and acceleration errors at steady state.

Type-1 System

If $N = 1$, the steady-state errors to various standard inputs are

$$e_{ss} = \begin{cases} 0 & \text{in response to unit-step input} \\[2mm] \dfrac{1}{K_v} & \text{in response to unit-ramp input; } K_v = \left. \dfrac{K \prod_i (s + z_i)}{\prod_j (s + p_j)} \right|_{s=0} \\[4mm] \infty & \text{in response to unit-parabolic input} \end{cases} \tag{6.49}$$

Thus, a system with $N = 1$ (i.e., with one integrator in $D(s)G(s)$) has zero position error, a finite non-zero velocity error, and infinite acceleration error at steady state.

Type-2 System

If $N = 2$, the steady-state errors to various standard inputs are

$$e_{ss} = \begin{cases} 0 & \text{in response to unit-step input} \\[1mm] 0 & \text{in response to unit-ramp input} \\[2mm] \dfrac{1}{K_a} & \text{in response to unit parabolic input; } K_a = \dfrac{K \prod_i (s + z_i)}{\prod_j (s + p_j)} \end{cases} \tag{6.50}$$

Thus, a system with $N = 2$ (i.e., with two integrators in $D(s)G(s)$) has zero position and velocity errors and a finite non-zero acceleration error at steady state.

Steady-state errors for various inputs and systems are summarized in Table 6.1.

Table 6.1 *Steady-state errors for various inputs and systems*

Type of input	Steady-state error		
	Type-0 system	Type-1 system	Type-2 system
Unit-step	$\dfrac{1}{1 + K_p}$	0	0
Unit-ramp	∞	$\dfrac{1}{K_v}$	0
Unit-parabolic	∞	∞	$\dfrac{1}{K_a}$
	$K_p = \lim\limits_{s \to 0} D(s)G(s)$	$K_v = \lim\limits_{s \to 0} sD(s)G(s)$	$K_a = \lim\limits_{s \to 0} s^2 D(s)G(S)$

The development above indicates that, in general, increased system gain K and/or addition of an integration in $D(s)G(s)$ tend to decrease steady-state errors. However, as we have seen earlier in Chapters 4 and 5, both large system gain and the integrator in $D(s)G(s)$ have destabilizing effects on the system. Thus, a control system design is usually a trade-off between steady-state accuracy and acceptable relative stability

▲▲

For nonunity feedback system (Fig. 6.28), the difference between the input signal $R(s)$ and the feedback signal $B(s)$ is the actuating error signal $\hat{E}(s)$ which is given by

$$\hat{E}(s) = \frac{1}{1 + D(s)\,G(s)\,H(s)}\,R(s) \qquad (6.51)$$

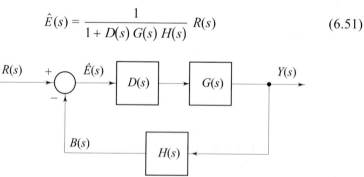

Fig. 6.28 *A nonunity feedback system*

Therefore, the steady-state actuating error is

$$\hat{e}_{ss} = \lim_{s \to 0} \frac{s R(s)}{1 + D(s) G(s) H(s)} \tag{6.52}$$

The error constants for nonunity feedback systems may be obtained from Table 6.1 by replacing $D(s)G(s)$ by $D(s)G(s)H(s)$.

6.7 INTRODUCTION TO DESIGN AND COMPENSATION

Just as far any other engineered product or service, the overall design of feedback control systems proceeds in systematic fashion through a sequence of steps. Control design begins with a proposed product or process whose satisfactory dynamic performance depends upon feedback for stability, disturbance regulation, and reduction of the effects of parameter variations. The first step in the design cycle is to understand the process and the dynamic performance requirements. The importance of understanding the process, what it is intended to do, how much system error is permissible, how to describe the class of command and disturbance signals to be expected, and what the physical capabilities and limitations are; all of these can hardly be overemphasized. Based on this information, the designer must conceive a system configuration. New systems generally utilize combinations and/or variations of well-known principles; thus familiarity with basic principles is essential. Practical designers must also maintain up-to-date knowledge of available hardware in their field of application. Although new hardware is being developed continually, there are many classes of equipment that have been in wide use for decades and that show no signs of disappearing. Hardware of such enduring nature was discussed at reasonable length in Chapter 3, and the basic principles of feedback control were presented in Chapter 4.

Once a tentative system configuration has been developed, components must be 'sized' to meet the needs of specific application. The *power-handling* devices that comprise the actuator and the controlled process itself must be properly sized to accommodate the maximum energy, force, and the like, demands of system operation. Sizing of *information-handling* hardware found in reference-input signal generation, sensing and error-detecting sections of the system is usually a straightforward process of choosing suitable full-scale range, resolutions, and so forth.

After component-sizing phase is completed, the equilibrium point of interest is identified and a small-signal dynamic model is constructed. The model is validated with experimental data where possible. One parameter of the model— the loop gain—is left open to choice. The 'proper' value of the loop gain is the one that meets the system accuracy requirements while maintaining adequate stability margins. Some components of the chosen configuration may be easily replaced to meet the gain requirements, e.g., if an electronic amplifier is a component in the control system, its replacement is not a big problem because of the low costs and the wide range of availability of such amplifiers.

Merely by gain adjustment, it may be possible to meet the given specifications of simple control systems. Gain setting has, in fact, been used at several places in the preceding chapters to improve system performance. Classical control theory provides systematic methods for solving this most basic design problem. The two most successful practical methods, the *root locus* and the *frequency response*, will be explained in Chapters 7–10.

However, in most practical cases, the gain adjustment does not provide the desired result. As is usually the case, increasing the gain reduces the steady-state error but results in oscillatory transient response or even instability. Under such circumstances, it is usually possible to introduce some kind of corrective sub-systems to force the chosen plant to meet the given specifications. These sub-systems are known as *compensators* and their job is to compensate for the deficiency in the performance. Some of the well-known compensators are the PID controllers. These devices may be inserted into the system either in cascade with the forward portion of the loop or as part of a minor feedback loop. We have discussed these and other compensation schemes in Chapter 4.

Most of the conventional design methods in control systems rely on the so-called fixed-configuration design in that the designer at the outset decides the basic configuration of the overall system and the place where the controller (compensator) is to be positioned relative to the controlled process. The problem then involves the design of the elements of the controller. The root locus and the frequency response methods, discussed later in Chapters 7–10, are the two commonly used methods for compensator design.

There is no guarantee that a compensator for the *initial* choice of components will meet all system specifications. When the failure occurs, changes other than compensation must be tried. These include the use of components with improved dynamics and/or totally new system concepts (change from electric drive to hydraulic drive, for example). The modified system must then again have its gain set, and compensator design; it is hoped that sufficient iterations of this 'modify/gain set/compensator design/evaluate performance' procedure lead to an acceptable solution.

In the following, we discuss basic features of the well-known compensation[1] schemes. The next four chapters are primarily concerned with the compensator design problem.

Derivative Error Compensation

A system is said to possess derivative error compensation when the generation of its output depends in some way on the rate of change of actuating signal. In the feedback control system of Fig. 6.29, this type of compensation has been introduced by using a PD controller. The plant transfer function is

---

1. The term 'compensation' is usually used to indicate the process of increasing accuracy and speeding up the response. The gain adjustment which is a simple proportional control, is therefore viewed as a compensation scheme. We use the term 'design' to incompass the entire process of basic system selection and modification; compensation is an important aspect of overall control system design.

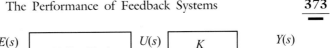

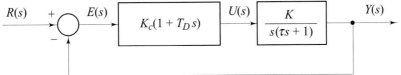

Fig. 6.29 *Derivative error compensation scheme*

$$G(s) = \frac{K}{s(\tau s + 1)} \tag{6.53}$$

The controller transfer function is

$$D(s) = K_c(1 + T_D s)$$

$$= K_c + K_c T_D s = K_c + K_D s \tag{6.54}$$

The control signal is

$$u(t) = K_c e(t) + K_D \frac{de(t)}{dt} \tag{6.55}$$

The open-loop transfer function of the overall system is

$$D(s)G(s) = \frac{K(K_c + K_D s)}{s(\tau s + 1)} \tag{6.56}$$

which shows that the PD control is equivalent to adding a simple zero at $s = -K_c/K_D$ to the open-loop transfer function.

The proper selection of performance specifications is the most important step in control system design. The desired behaviour is specified in terms of transient response measures and steady-state error. The steady-state error is usually specified in terms of error constants for specific inputs while the transient response is specified by measures of relative stability and speed of response; the relative stability is measured in terms of damping ζ or peak overshoot M_p, while the speed of response is measured in terms of rise time, settling time or natural frequency.

For the system under consideration, velocity error constant

$$K_v = \lim_{s \to 0} sD(s)G(s) = KK_c \tag{6.57a}$$

Therefore, the steady-state error to velocity input

$$e_{ss} = \frac{1}{K_v} = \frac{1}{KK_c} \tag{6.57b}$$

The characteristic equation of the system is

$$\tau s^2 + (1 + KK_D)s + KK_c = 0$$

or

$$s^2 + \left(\frac{1 + KK_D}{\tau}\right)s + \frac{KK_c}{\tau} = 0 \tag{6.58}$$

The natural frequency and damping of the compensated system are given by

$$\omega_n = \sqrt{\frac{KK_c}{\tau}} \tag{6.59a}$$

$$\zeta = \frac{1}{2}\left[\frac{1 + KK_D}{\sqrt{KK_c\tau}}\right] \tag{6.59b}$$

It is obvious from the above equations that only two of the three specifications, i.e., K_v, ζ and ω_n, can be met exactly by a suitable choice of K_c and K_D. For a specified K_v, the proportional gain K_c of the PD controller gets fixed (refer Eqn. (6.57a)). The closed-loop damping can now be raised to the desired level by a suitable choice of K_D (refer Eqn. (6.59b)) which is the gain of derivative term of the PD controller. These values of K_c and K_D may not satisfy the requirement on speed of response, specified in terms of ω_n (refer Eqn. (6.59a)) or settling time $t_s = 4/(\zeta\omega_n)$. Practically, most control systems require a trial and error parameter adjustment to achieve at least an acceptable performance if it is not possible to satisfy exactly all the performance specifications. Two commonly used trial and error procedures—the root-locus method and the frequency-response method—will be presented in Chapters 7–10.

We should point out here that since Eqn. (6.56) no longer represents a standard second-order system, the transient response is also affected by the zero of the transfer function at $s = -K_c/K_D$. In general, if the value of K_D is very large, the zero will be very close to the origin in the s-plane, the overshoot could be increased substantially, and the damping ratio ζ is then no longer an accurate estimate on the maximum overshoot of the output. Simulation of the compensated system is necessary to check the design. If the transient response is not acceptable, we have to re-enter the design cycle to make necessary changes in design.

Example 6.2

Reconsider the design problem of Example 6.1. The position control system of Fig. 6.16 has open-loop transfer function

$$D(s)G(s) = \frac{4500\,K_A}{s(s + 361.2)}$$

Let us consider an application wherein static accuracy requirement is very high; steady-state error to unit-ramp input is required to be less than 0.025 deg (0.000436 rad).

Required $K_v = \dfrac{1}{0.000436} = 2293.6$

This requirement is satisfied if

$$K_A = \frac{2293.6 \times 361.2}{4500} = 184.1$$

For this value of K_A, the characteristic equation of the system becomes

$$s^2 + 361.2\, s + 828450 = 0$$

Therefore

$$\omega_n = \sqrt{828450} = 910.2$$

$$\zeta = \frac{361.2}{2 \times 910.2} = 0.198$$

$$M_p = e^{-\pi\zeta/\sqrt{1-\zeta^2}} \times 100 = 53\%$$

Relative stability is obviously very poor. To improve damping and peak over-shoot while maintaining K_v at 2293.6, we propose the replacement of amplifier with gain K_A by a PD controller (refer Fig. 6.16)

$$D(s) = K_c + K_D s$$

With the PD controller, the open-loop transfer function becomes

$$D(s)G(s) = \frac{4500\left(K_c + K_D s\right)}{s(s + 361.2)} \tag{6.60}$$

The closed-loop transfer function

$$\frac{\theta_L(s)}{\theta_R(s)} = \frac{4500\left(K_c + K_D s\right)}{s^2 + \left(361.2 + 4500\,K_D\right)s + 4500\,K_c} \tag{6.61}$$

Velocity error constant

$$K_v = \frac{4500\,K_c}{361.2} = 2293.6$$

when $K_c = 184.1$

For this value of K_c, the characteristic equation of the system becomes

$$s^2 + (361.2 + 4500\,K_D)s + 828450 = 0$$

Therefore

$$\omega_n = \sqrt{828450} = 910.2$$

$$\zeta = \frac{361.2 + 4500\,K_D}{2 \times 910.2} = 0.198 + 2.472\,K_D$$

This clearly shows the positive effect of K_D on damping. For critical damping,

$$K_D = \frac{1 - 0.198}{2.472} = 0.324$$

We should point out here that Eqn. (6.61) no longer represents a standard second-order system; the transient response is also affected by the zero of the transfer function at $s = -K_c/K_D$. In general, if K_D is large, zero will be close to the origin in the s-plane, the overshoot will be increased substantially and damping ratio ζ no longer gives an accurate estimate on the peak overshoot of the output. In the present case, the increase in the overshoot is acceptable as seen from the unit-step response curves in Fig. 6.30. Without the PD controller, the response has a peak overshoot of 53%. With the PD controller, the peak overshoot is about four per cent. Although K_D was chosen for critical damping, the overshoot is due to the zero at $s = -K_c/K_D = -568.2$ (the two closed-loop poles are located at $s = -\omega_n = -910.2$ when $\zeta = 1$).

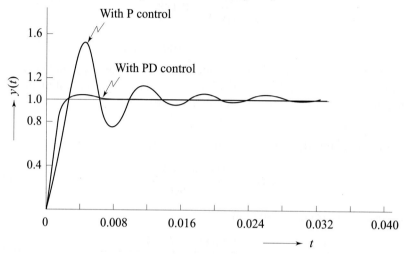

Fig. 6.30   *Unit-step responses for system of Example 6.2*

Derivative Output Compensation

The philosophy of using the derivative of the actuating error signal to improve the damping of a system can also be extended to the output signal. Figure 6.31 shows the block diagram of a second-order system with a secondary path feeding back the derivative of the output.

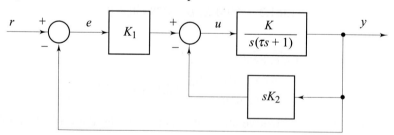

Fig. 6.31   *Derivative output compensation scheme*

Eliminating the minor feedback loop, we obtain the following forward-path transfer function.

$$G(s) = \frac{K K_1}{s(\tau s + 1 + K K_2)} \tag{6.62}$$

The velocity error constant

$$K_v = \lim_{s \to 0} sG(s) = \frac{K K_1}{1 + K K_2} \tag{6.63}$$

The closed-loop transfer function is given by

$$\frac{Y(s)}{R(s)} = \frac{K K_1}{\tau s^2 + (1 + K K_2)s + K K_1} \tag{6.64}$$

and the characteristic equation is

$$s^2 + \frac{(1 + K K_2)}{\tau} s + \frac{K K_1}{\tau} = 0 \tag{6.65}$$

The natural frequency and damping of the compensated system are given by

$$\omega_n = \sqrt{\frac{K K_1}{\tau}} \tag{6.66a}$$

$$\zeta = \frac{1}{2} \left[\frac{1 + K K_2}{\sqrt{K K_1 \tau}} \right] \tag{6.66b}$$

For a specified K_v and ζ, we can write from Eqns (6.63) and (6.66b),

$$\zeta K_v = \frac{1}{2} \left[\sqrt{\frac{K K_1}{\tau}} \right] \tag{6.67}$$

from which K_1 can be determined. Using this value of K_1, K_2 is obtained from Eqn. (6.63). Thus, we notice that by a suitable choice of K_1 and K_2, we can simultaneously meet the specifications on K_v and ζ. We will have to resort to trial and error methods of compensator design if the resulting speed of response is not acceptable.

Example 6.3

Consider the position control system of Fig. 6.15. When switch 'S' is open (tachogenerator disconnected), the forward-path transfer function of the system becomes

$$G(s) = \frac{4500 K_A}{s(s + 361.2)}$$

Assume that the steady-state error to unit-ramp input is required to be less than 0.025 deg (0.000436 rad).

Required $K_v = \dfrac{1}{0.000436} = 2293.6$

This requirement is satisfied if

$$K_A = \frac{2293.6 \times 361.2}{4500} = 184.1$$

For this value of K_A, the characteristic equation of the system becomes
$$s^2 + 361.2s + 828450 = 0$$

This gives
$$\omega_n = 910.2, \quad \zeta = 0.198$$

Relative stability is obviously very poor.

Closing the switch 'S' will result in a minor feedback loop which represents the feeding back of the derivative of the output signal using a tachogenerator. Eliminating the minor feedback loop, we obtain the following forward-path transfer function:

$$G(s) = \frac{4500\,K_A}{s\left(s + 361.2 + 45000\,K_t\right)} \tag{6.68}$$

The closed-loop transfer function

$$\frac{\theta_L(s)}{\theta_R(s)} = \frac{4500\,K_A}{s^2 + \left(361.2 + 45000\,K_t\right)s + 4500\,K_A} \tag{6.69}$$

Velocity error constant

$$K_v = \frac{4500\,K_A}{361.2 + 45000\,K_t} \tag{6.70}$$

The characteristic equation of the system is
$$s^2 + \left(361.2 + 45000K_t\right)s + 4500K_A = 0 \tag{6.71a}$$

from which we obtain

$$\omega_n = \sqrt{4500\,K_A} \tag{6.71b}$$

$$\zeta = \frac{361.2 + 45000\,K_t}{2\sqrt{4500\,K_A}} \tag{6.71c}$$

From these equations, it is apparent that the tachogenerator feedback increases the damping of the system; it, however, reduces the system K_v.

With $K_A = 184.1$, we get critical damping when $K_t = 0.0324$. For these values of K_A and K_t, we obtain from Eqn. (6.70):

$$K_v = 455.4$$

Therefore
$$e_{ss}|_{\text{unit ramp}} = 0.0022 \text{ rad} = 0.126 \text{ deg.}$$

With the amplifier gain K_A set at the value 184.1, the tachogenerator feedback ($K_t = 0.0324$) increases the damping ratio from 0.198 to 1; it also increases the steady-state error to unit-ramp input from 0.025 deg to 0.126 deg.

Equations (6.70) and (6.71c) show that specified values of K_v and ζ can be realized by appropriate choice of K_A and K_t. For example, $K_v = 2293.6$ (steady-state error to unit-ramp input = 0.025 deg) and $\zeta = 1$ are realized by
$$K_A = 4676.4 \text{ and } K_t = 0.196$$

This choice of K_A gives $\omega_n = 4587.35$ rad/sec. Hardware considerations (e.g., amplifier saturation) and bandwidth considerations (large ω_n corresponds to large bandwidth) impose a limit on K_A which in turn imposes a limit on achievable accuracy/relative stability.

Integral Error Compensation

In an integral error compensation scheme, the output response depends in some manner upon the integral of the actuating signal. In the feedback control system of Fig. 6.32, this type of compensation has been introduced by using a PI controller. The plant transfer function is

$$G(s) = \frac{K}{s(\tau s + 1)} \qquad (6.72a)$$

The controller transfer function is

$$D(s) = K_c\left(1 + \frac{1}{T_I s}\right)$$

$$= K_c + \frac{K_c}{T_I s} = K_c + \frac{K_I}{s} \qquad (6.72b)$$

The control signal is

$$u(t) = K_c e(t) + K_I \int_0^t e(\tau)\, d\tau$$

The open-loop transfer function of the overall system is

$$D(s)G(s) = \frac{K(K_c s + K_I)}{s^2(\tau s + 1)} \qquad (6.73)$$

Clearly, the PI control adds a zero at $s = -K_I/K_c$, and a pole at $s = 0$ to the open-loop transfer function. One obvious effect of the integral control is that it increases the order of the system by one; it may therefore be less stable than the original second-order system or even become unstable if the parameters K_c and K_I are not properly chosen.

Integral control increases the *type* of the system by one. The PI controller in Fig. 6.32 converts a type-1 system to type-2. Therefore, the steady-state error of the compensated system is always zero for velocity input. The problem is to

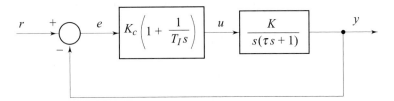

Fig. 6.32 *Integral error compensation scheme*

choose a proper combination of K_c and K_I so that the transient response is satisfactory.

The characteristic equation of the closed-loop system is

$$\tau s^3 + s^2 + KK_c s + KK_I = 0 \tag{6.74}$$

Applying Routh's test to this equation yields the result that the system is stable for $0 < K_I < K_c/\tau$. This means that the system zero at $s = - K_I/K_c$ cannot be placed too far to the left in the left half of s-plane, or the system would be unstable.

A viable method of designing a PI controller is to determine the ranges of parameters K_c and K_I that result in a pair of complex-conjugate closed-loop poles and a real closed-loop pole. The zero at $s = - K_I/K_c$ is then selected so that it is relatively close to the real closed-loop pole. We know that if the zero is close to a pole, the residue at the pole tends to be small so that the corresponding transient is small. The dynamics of the system is then dominated by only the complex-conjugate pair of closed-loop poles. By trial and error parameter adjustments, it is possible to almost cancel a closed-loop pole with a zero, and simultaneously achieve the desired transient performance. Trial and error procedures of parameter adjustment are given in Chapters 7–10.

Example 6.4

Reconsider the design problem of Example 6.1. Assume that we require zero steady-state error to ramp inputs. To realize this objective, we replace the amplifier with gain K_A (refer Fig. 6.16) by a PI controller

$$D(s) = K_c + \frac{K_I}{s}$$

With the PI controller, the open-loop transfer function becomes

$$D(s)G(s) = \frac{4500 \left(K_c s + K_I\right)}{s^2 \left(s + 361.2\right)} \tag{6.75}$$

The closed-loop transfer function

$$\frac{\theta_L(s)}{\theta_R(s)} = \frac{4500 \left(K_c s + K_I\right)}{s^3 + 361.2\, s^2 + 4500\, K_c s + 4500\, K_I} \tag{6.76}$$

From Eqn. (6.75), we see that with the PI controller, the system has become a type-2 system; therefore the steady-state error to ramp inputs is zero. To study the effect of PI controller on transient response, we consider the characteristic equation

$$s^3 + 361.2\, s^2 + 4500 K_c s + 4500 K_I = 0 \tag{6.77}$$

Applying Routh's test to this equation yields the result that the system is stable for $0 < K_I < 361.2\, K_c$. This means that the system zero at $s = - K_I/K_c$ cannot be placed too far to the left in the left half of s-plane.

Design to determine suitable values of K_c and K_I can be carried out using the root-locus and frequency-response methods discussed in the following chapters. Here we analyse the performance of the system for a typical design:

$$K_c = 14.728; \; K_I = 147.28$$

For these values of K_c and K_I, the characteristic equation becomes

$$s^3 + 361.2 \, s^2 + 66276 \, s + 662760 = 0$$

or $(s + 10.59)(s + 175.30 + j178.41)(s + 175.30 - j178.41) = 0$

The pole at $s = -10.59$ is insignificant as far as the transient response is concerned, because the zero at $s = -K_I/K_c = -10$ is close to this pole. The transient response is therefore dominated by the quadratic factor

$$(s + 175.30 + j \, 178.41)(s + 175.30 - j \, 178.41) = 0$$

or $s^2 + 350.6 \, s + 62560.22 = 0$

The unit-step response of the third-order system, therefore, resembles a second-order system with

$$\omega_n = \sqrt{62560.22} = 250.12 \text{ rad/sec}$$

and $$\zeta = \frac{350.6}{2 \times 250.12} = 0.7$$

The unit-step response of the PI-compensated system with $K_c = 14.728$ and $K_I = 147.28$ is shown in Fig. 6.33. Notice that although the damping is adequate, the integral control causes the step response to have long rise and settling times.

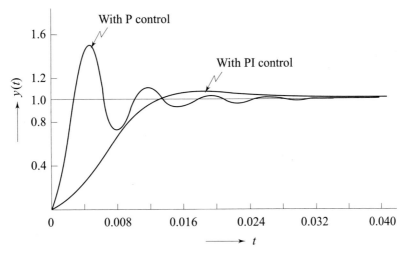

Fig. 6.33 *Unit-step responses for the system of Example 6.4*

Review Examples

Review Example 6.1

The open-loop transfer function of a unity-feedback system is given by

$$G(s) = \frac{K}{s(\tau s + 1)}; \ K > 0, \ \tau > 0$$

By what factor should the gain K be reduced so that the peak overshoot of unit-step response of the system is reduced from 75 to 25%?

Solution

The characteristic equation of the system is

$$s^2 + \frac{1}{\tau}s + \frac{K}{\tau} = 0 \tag{6.78}$$

Assume that corresponding to 75% overshoot, the gain is K_1 and damping ratio is ζ_1, and for 25% overshoot, the gain is K_2 and damping ratio is ζ_2. From the characteristic equation, we obtain

$$2\zeta_1 = \frac{1/\tau}{\sqrt{K_1/\tau}} = \frac{1}{\sqrt{K_1\tau}}; \ \ 2\zeta_2 = \frac{1}{\sqrt{K_2\tau}}$$

Therefore $\qquad \left(\dfrac{\zeta_2}{\zeta_1}\right)^2 = \dfrac{K_1}{K_2}$ $\hfill (6.79)$

Since $\qquad e^{-\pi\zeta/\sqrt{1-\zeta^2}} = M_p$

we have $\qquad \dfrac{\pi\zeta_1}{\sqrt{1-\zeta_1^2}} = -\ln(0.75) = 0.29 = \dfrac{\pi}{\sqrt{\dfrac{1}{\zeta_1^2} - 1}}$ $\hfill (6.80)$

and $\qquad \dfrac{\pi\zeta_2}{\sqrt{1-\zeta_2^2}} = -\ln(0.25) = 1.4 = \dfrac{\pi}{\sqrt{\dfrac{1}{\zeta_2^2} - 1}}$ $\hfill (6.81)$

Dividing, squaring and rearranging we get $\dfrac{\zeta_2^2}{\zeta_1^2} = 20 = \dfrac{K_1}{K_2}$.

Therefore the gain K should be reduced by a factor of 20 so that the peak overshoot of unit-step response of the system is reduced from 75 to 25%.

Review Example 6.2

A unity-feedback system is characterized by the open-loop transfer function

$$G(s) = \frac{1}{s(0.5s + 1)(0.2s + 1)}$$

(a) Determine the steady-state errors to unit-step, unit-ramp, and unit-parabolic inputs.

(b) Determine rise time, peak time, peak overshoot, and settling time of the unit-step response of the system.

Solution

(a) The given system is a type-1 system. The error constants are obtained as follows:

$$K_p = \lim_{s \to 0} G(s) = \infty; \ K_v = \lim_{s \to 0} sG(s) = 1; \ K_a = \lim_{s \to 0} s^2 G(s) = 0$$

Therefore

$$e_{ss}|_{\text{unit step}} = \frac{1}{1 + K_p} = 0; \ e_{ss}|_{\text{unit ramp}} = \frac{1}{K_v} = 1; \ e_{ss}|_{\text{unit parabola}} = \frac{1}{K_a} = \infty$$

(b) Since the system is of third order, we can no longer use the correlations (6.38) for rise time, peak time, peak overshoot, and settling time. These correlations were derived for a standard second-order system. For the transient analysis of the given system, we may determine the unit-step response (Eqn. (6.37)) and therefrom compute rise time, peak time, peak overshoot, and settling time.

However, if the system dynamics can be accurately represented by a pair of dominant poles, then the correlations (6.38) may be used. The characteristic equation of the given system is

$$s(0.5\ s + 1)(0.2\ s + 1) + 1 = 0$$

or

$$s^3 + 7s^2 + 10\ s + 10 = 0$$

Factorizing the characteristic equation, we obtain

$$(s + 5.5157)(s^2 + 1.4844\ s + 1.8131) = 0$$

The magnitude of the real root is more than 7 times the magnitude of the real part of the complex roots. Therefore, the complex-conjugate root pair gives the dominant closed-loop poles with

$$\omega_n = \sqrt{1.8131} = 1.3465 \text{ rad/sec}; \ \zeta = \frac{1.4844}{2 \times 1.3465} = 0.55$$

$$\omega_d = \omega_n \sqrt{1 - \zeta^2} = 1.1245$$

$$t_r = \frac{\pi - \cos^{-1} \zeta}{\omega_d} = \frac{\pi - 56.63 \times \dfrac{\pi}{180}}{1.1245} = 1.91 \text{ sec}$$

$$t_p = \frac{\pi}{\omega_d} = 2.79 \text{ sec}; \ M_p = e^{-\pi\zeta/\sqrt{1 - \zeta^2}} = 0.1265; \ t_s = \frac{4}{\zeta \omega_n}$$

$$= 5.4 \text{ sec}$$

Review Example 6.3

A servomechanism controls the angular position θ_L of a mass through a command signal θ_R. The moment of inertia of the moving parts referred to the load shaft is 200 kg-m^2 and the motor torque at the load is 6.88×10^4 Newton-m per rad of error. The damping torque coefficient referred to the load shaft is 5×10^3 N-m per rad/sec.

(a) Determine the frequency of transient oscillation, the peak overshoot, the time to peak, and the steady-state error resulting from the application of a step input of 1 rad.

(b) Determine the steady-state error when the command signal is a constant angular velocity of 1 rev/min.

(c) Determine the steady-state error which exists when a steady torque of 1200 N-m is applied at the load shaft.

Solution

Since the torque applied to the load must equal the reaction torque, we have

$$(200 \ \ddot{\theta}_L + 5 \times 10^3 \ \dot{\theta}_L) = 6.88 \times 10^4 (\theta_R - \theta_L) - T_w \qquad (6.82)$$

Figure 6.34 gives a block-diagram representation of this differential equation.

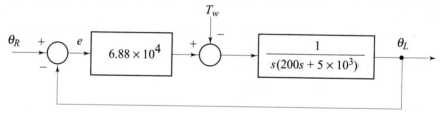

Fig. 6.34 *Block diagram representation of Eqn. (6.82)*

From the block diagram, we obtain

$$\frac{\theta_L(s)}{\theta_R(s)} = \frac{6.88 \times 10^4}{200 s^2 + 5 \times 10^3 s + 6.88 \times 10^4}$$

$$= \frac{344}{s^2 + 25s + 344}$$

$$\frac{\theta_L(s)}{T_w(s)} = \frac{-1}{200 s^2 + 5 \times 10^3 s + 6.88 \times 10^4} \qquad (6.83)$$

(a) The characteristic equation of the system is

$$s^2 + 25 \ s + 344 = 0$$

Comparing with the standard characteristic equation

$$s^2 + 2\zeta\omega_n s + \omega_n^2 = 0$$

we obtain $\omega_n = \sqrt{344} = 18.547$; $\zeta = \dfrac{25}{2 \times 18.547} = 0.674$

Frequency of transient oscillation, $\omega_d = \omega_n\sqrt{1-\zeta^2} = 13.7$ rad/sec

Peak overshoot, $M_p = e^{-\pi\zeta/\sqrt{1-\zeta^2}} \times 100 = 5.69\%$

Time to peak, $t_p = \pi/\omega_d = 0.229$ sec

Steady-state error, $e_{ss}|_{\text{step input}} = 0$

(b) Input = 1 rpm = $2\pi/60$ rad/sec; $\theta_R(t) = \dfrac{2\pi}{60}t$

$$e_{ss}|_{\text{unit ramp}} = \frac{2\zeta}{\omega_n} = 0.07268$$

For a ramp input of slope $2\pi/60$,

steady-state error $= 0.07268 \times \dfrac{2\pi}{60} = 0.0076$ rad $= 0.436$ deg.

(c) Steady-state output in response to load torque of 1200 N-m is given by (refer Eqn. (6.83))

$$\theta_{Lss} = \lim_{s \to 0} s\theta_L(s)$$

$$= \lim_{s \to 0} s\left[\frac{-1}{200\,s^2 + 5\times10^3 s + 6.88\times10^4}\right]\frac{1200}{s}$$

$$= \frac{-1200}{6.88\times10^4}\ \text{rad} = -1\ \text{deg}$$

Therefore, the steady-state error for a disturbance torque of 1200 N-m is 1 deg.

Review Example 6.4

Consider the unity-feedback system shown in Fig. 6.35. Assume that the controller is a proportional gain. With $D(s) = K$, the open-loop transfer function

$$D(s)G(s) = \frac{K}{(s+1)(0.5s+1)}$$

It is a type-0 system. The position error constant $K_p = K$, and

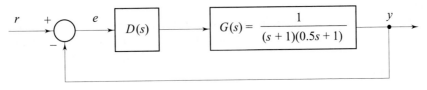

Fig. 6.35 *A unity-feedback system*

$$e_{ss}\big|_{\text{unitstep}} = \frac{1}{1+K}$$

Improvement in steady-state accuracy with higher gain is evident. Relative stability considerations, however, impose a limit on the gain K. Large values of gain give rise to large overshoots.

The closed-loop transfer function of the system is

$$\frac{Y(s)}{R(s)} = \frac{2K}{s^2 + 3s + 2 + 2K}$$

The characteristic equation is

$$s^2 + 3s + 2 + 2K = s^2 + 2\zeta\omega_n s + \omega_n^2 = 0$$

$\zeta = 0.5$ corresponds to peak overshoot $M_p = 16.3\%$. The limiting value of K for $M_p \leq 16.3\%$ is obtained from the following equations:

$$\omega_n = \sqrt{2 + 2K}\,; \; 2 \times 0.5 \times \omega_n = 3$$

Solving for K, we get $K = 3.5$

The steady-state error for this value of K is

$$e_{ss}\big|_{\text{unit step}} = \frac{1}{1+3.5} = 0.2222 = 22.22\%$$

An error of 22.22% is too large. We can reduce the error by increasing K, but this will result in an overshoot more than 16.3%. The objective of reducing the steady-state error without increasing overshoot can be realized using a PD controller:

$$D(s) = K_c + K_D s$$

With the PD controller, the open-loop transfer function becomes

$$D(s)G(s) = \frac{K_c + K_D s}{(s+1)(0.5s+1)}$$

The closed-loop transfer function

$$\frac{Y(s)}{R(s)} = \frac{2(K_c + K_D s)}{s^2 + (3 + 2K_D)s + 2 + 2K_c}$$

For $K_D = 0$, the characteristic equation is

$$s^2 + 3s + 2 + 2K_c = 0 = s^2 + 2\zeta\omega_n s + \omega_n^2$$

To achieve $\zeta = 0.5$, we require $K_c = 3.5$. The steady-state error for unit-step input is $1/(1 + K_c) = 0.2222$ or 22.22%.

If the specifications permit an error of 10%, $K_c = 9$ is required. Then for $K_D = 0$, the damping ratio ζ is 0.335 which is inadequate. With derivative control, the damping can be increased to 0.5 without affecting the value of e_{ss} as is seen below.

$$\omega_n = \sqrt{2 + 2K_c}\,, \; 2\zeta\omega_n = 3 + 2K_D$$

With $K_c = 9$, $\zeta = 0.5$ is obtained when K_D statisfies the following relations:

$$\omega_n = \sqrt{2 + 18} = = 4.47$$

$$3 + 2K_D = 2 \times 0.5 \times \omega_n$$

This gives $\qquad K_D = 0.736$

The zero of the closed-loop transfer function is at $s = - K_c/K_D = - 9/0.736 = - 12.23$. The magnitude of the zero is about 5.5 times the magnitude of the real part of the poles ($\zeta\omega_n = 2.235$). So the unit-step response of the system with the PD controller should closely resemble the response of a standard second-order system with $\zeta = 0.5$ and $\omega_n = 4.47$.

If static accuracy demand is very high, PI control would probably be necessary. With $D(s) = K_c + K_I/s$, the open-loop transfer function becomes

$$D(s)G(s) = \frac{s K_c + K_I}{s(s + 1)(0.5s + 1)}$$

The system has become a type-1 system and the steady-state error to step inputs is zero.

The velocity error constant $K_v = K_I$, and

$$e_{ss}|_{unit\ ramp} = \frac{1}{K_I}$$

Thus, the steady-state error to ramp inputs reduces as the integral gain factor K_I is increased (note that the steady-state error to ramp inputs is infinity for the system with only proportional control or PD control). As one would expect, this improvement in static accuracy is limited by considerations of relative stability. The closed-loop transfer function

$$\frac{Y(s)}{R(s)} = \frac{s K_c + K_I}{0.5s^3 + 15s^3 + (1 + K_c)s + K_I}$$

shows a third-order characteristic equation. Design to determine suitable values of K_c and K_I can be carried out using the root-locus and frequency-response methods discussed in the following chapters. This will show that careful design is necessary to avoid oscillatory or slow system dynamic behaviour.

Review Example 6.5

The system shown in Fig. 6.36 is a unity-feedback control system with a minor rate-feedback loop.

(a) In the absence of rate feedback ($\alpha = 0$), determine the peak overshoot of the system to unit-step input, and the steady-state error resulting from a unit-ramp input.

(b) Determine the rate-feedback constant α which will decrease the peak overshoot of the system to unit-step input to 1.5%. What is steady-state error to unit-ramp input with this setting of the rate-feedback constant?

(c) Illustrate how in the system with rate feedback, the steady-state error to

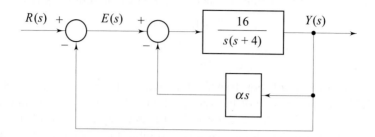

Fig. 6.36 *A unity-feedback system with a minor rate-feedback loop*

unit-ramp input can be reduced to the same level as in part (a), while the peak overshoot to unit-step input is maintained at 1.5%.

Solution

(a) With $\alpha = 0$, the forward-path transfer function

$$G(s) = \frac{16}{s(s + 4)}$$

Velocity error constant $K_v = \lim_{s \to 0} sG(s) = 4$

$$e_{ss}|_{\text{unit ramp}} = \frac{1}{K_v} = 0.25$$

The characteristic equation of the system is

$$s^2 + 4s + 16 = 0$$

Comparison with the standard characteristic equation

$$s^2 + 2\zeta\omega_n s + \omega^2_n = 0$$

gives $\omega_n = 4$, and $\zeta = 0.5$

Therefore $M_p = e^{-\pi\zeta/\sqrt{1-\zeta^2}} \times 100 = 16.3\%$

(b) With rate feedback, the forward-path transfer function is obtained by eliminating the inner loop:

$$G(s) = \frac{\dfrac{16}{s(s + 4)}}{1 + \dfrac{16\alpha s}{s(s + 4)}} = \frac{16}{s(s + 4 + 16\alpha)} \tag{6.84}$$

$$K_v = \frac{16}{4 + 16\alpha} = \frac{4}{1 + 4\alpha}$$

The characteristic equation now takes the form

$$s^2 + (4 + 16\alpha)s + 16 = 0 \tag{6.85}$$

Corresponding to 1.5% overshoot, the damping ratio ζ is given by

$$\zeta^2 = \frac{[\ln(0.015)]^2}{[\ln(0.015)]^2 + \pi^2}$$

Solving, we get $\zeta = 0.8$.

The value of α that results in $\zeta = 0.8$ is given by the following equation (refer Eqn. (6.85)):

$$2 \times 0.8 \times 4 = 4 + 16\alpha$$

Solving, we get $\alpha = 0.15$.

For this value of α, $e_{ss}|_{\text{unit ramp}} = \dfrac{1}{K_v} = \dfrac{1 + 4\alpha}{4} = 0.4$

(c) The system of Fig. 6.36 may be extended by including an amplifier K_A as shown in Fig. 6.37. The forward-path transfer function now becomes

$$G(s) = \frac{16\,K_A}{s(s + 4 + 16\alpha)} \tag{6.86}$$

$$K_v = \frac{16\,K_A}{4 + 16\alpha} = \frac{4\,K_A}{1 + 4\alpha}$$

The required $K_v = 4$. Therefore

$$\frac{4\,K_A}{1 + 4\alpha} = 4 \tag{6.87}$$

The characteristic equation of the extended system is

$$s^2 + (4 + 16\alpha)\,s + 16K_A = 0 \tag{6.88}$$

The requirement of $\zeta = 0.8$ gives rise to the following equation:

$$2 \times 0.8 \times \sqrt{16\,K_A} = 4 + 16\alpha \tag{6.89}$$

From Eqns (6.87) and (6.89), we obtain

$$K_A = 2.56; \quad \alpha = 0.39$$

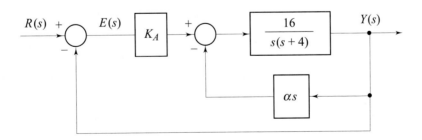

Fig. 6.37 *Amplifier added to the system shown in Fig. 6.36*

Review Questions

6.1 Describe a set of performance specifications characterizing desired time response, that are frequently used in the design of linear control systems using root-locus plots.

6.2 Given the following measures of step response of a unity-feedback system with open-loop transfer function

$$G(s) = \frac{\omega_n^2}{s(s + 2\zeta\omega_n)} :$$

(i)   rise time, t_r;
(ii) peak time, t_p;
(iii) peak overshoot; M_p;
(iv) settling time, t_s.

Through graphical plots, explain the correlations of these measures with ζ and ω_n.

6.3 (a) Many systems are designed for damping ratio in the range 0.4–0.7 (peak overshoot in the range 5-25%). Why? (Help: pp345-346, p353, Example 6.1)

(b) The natural frequency ω_n must be large for good performance; however bandwidth considerations impose a limit on increasing ω_n. Why?
(Help: pp 346-347, pp 594-595, pp 607-608)

(c) Show that rise time, peak time, and settling time measures of performance of a standard second-order system are mutually dependent, and therefore must be specified in a consistent manner. (Help: Eqns (6.9), (6.12), (6.19))

6.4 A feedback system is higher than second-order and has finite zeros.

(i)   Determine the region in the s-plane which is feasible for the system's dominant poles corresponding to a percentage overshoot $5\% \leq M_p \leq 10\%$, and a settling time $3 \leq t_s \leq 5$ seconds. (Help: p 363-364)

(ii) Define the regions of dominant and insignificant poles; and dominant poles and insignificant zeros in the s-plane. (Help: pp 363-365)

(iii) Show that pole-zero cancellation may be utilized to meet the dominance condition when non-dominant poles, and zeros do not lie in insignificant regions. (Help: pp 365-366)

6.5 (a) What is system-type number? Explain the practical significance of this number. (Help: p 272, p 367, p 369, pp 749-752)

(b) Define the error constants K_p, K_v, and K_a. (Help: p 368, 369)

(c) A unity feedback system has open-loop transfer function $G(s) = 1/s^2$. The system possesses satisfactory steady-state error to both step and ramp input signals. Comment. (Help: p 657)

6.6 We know that control system design is usually a trade-off between steady-state accuracy and acceptable relative stability.

Consider a unity feedback system with forward-path transfer function $D(s)G(s)$, where $G(s)$ is the transfer function of the plant and $D(s)$ corresponds to controller. Show that, in general, increased system gain and/ or addition of an integrator in $D(s)G(s)$ tend to decrease steady-state errors; however, both large system gain and the integrator in $D(s)G(s)$ have destabilizing effects on the system (Help: Sections 4.4-4.5, pp 451-453)

6.7 A unity feedback system has a plant

$$G(s) = \frac{K}{s(\tau s + 1)}$$

with a cascade controller

$$D(s) = K_c(1 + T_D s)$$

Describe the effects of K_c and T_D on steady-state error, settling time, and peak overshoot of the system response. (Help: pp 372-374, pp 445-448)

6.8 A unity feedback system has a plant

$$G(s) = \frac{K}{s(\tau s + 1)}$$

with a cascade controller

$$D(s) = K_c \left(1 + \frac{1}{T_I s}\right)$$

Describe the effects of K_c and T_I on steady-state error, settling time, and peak overshoot of the system response. (Help: pp 379-380, pp 451-453)

6.9 A unity feedback servosystem has the plant

$$G(s) = \frac{K}{s(\tau s + 1)}$$

Show how a cascade PD controller could be used to achieve acceptable performance. Compare the cascade PD compensation with that of minor-loop feedback compensation using a tachogenerator.(Help: Section 4.6, pp 376-377, pp 472-475)

6.10 (a) Desired dominant closed-loop poles are usually a complex-conjugate pair. Why? (Help: p 353)

 (b) Transient performance is usually judged by only one test signal—step, while the steady-state performance is usually judged by more than one test signal—step, ramp, parabola. Why? (Help: pp 337-339, pp 341-343, p 351)

 (c) The test signals are step, ramp and parabola. Actual control system will have different input. How is control system study using test signals useful? (Help: pp 337-339, p 341-343, p 351)

 (d) The formulas for t_r, t_p, M_p, t_s, etc., have been derived for second-order feedback system with plant transfer function of the form $G(s) = \omega_n^2/(s^2 + 2\zeta\omega_n s)$. However, we also apply these formulas for designing controllers when a plant is higher than second-order and/or has finite zeros. Justify. (Help: pp 364-365, pp 459-460)

 (e) We know that K_p, K_v, and K_a are defined for unity-feedback systems. How do you describe steady-state performance of a non-unity feedback system? (Help: pp 370-371)

6.11 (a) A feedback system has a PD compensator in the forward path. What will happen if the proportional term of the PD compensator becomes zero?

(Help: p 273, p 472)

(b) In many practical situations, derivative action of a PD compensator is implemented by means of minor-loop feedback employing a tachometer; and not with a derivative term in the forward path. Why? (Help: Section 4.6, pp 376-377, Section 7.9)

(c) In applications where tachometer cannot be employed, the derivative action of a PD compensator can be implemented by means of a network with transfer function $H_D(s) = \dfrac{K_D s}{\tau_D s + 1}$ in the minor loop. Suggest suitable active R filter that realizes $H_D(s)$. (Help: p 472, p 732, Problem 11.1)

(d) Can we place $H_D(s)$ in the forward path of the feedback system? Why?(Help: p 472)

6.12 Give an example of a feedback system with a pair of complex-conjugate poles and a finite zero. Discuss the effects of variation of the location of the zero relative to the poles. (Help: Section 4.6, Section 6.4)

6.13 Give an example of a third-order feedback system with a pair of complex-conjugate poles. Discuss the effects of variation of the real pole relative to the complex-conjugate poles. (Help: Example 4.6, Section 6.4)

Problems

6.1 (a) A unity-feedback system has open-loop transfer function

$$G(s) = \frac{\omega_n^2}{s(s + 2\zeta\omega_n)}; \zeta < 1$$

Derive expressions for peak overshoot M_p and peak time t_p of the time response of the given system to unit-step input.

(b) The feedback configuration of Fig. P6.1 is used to position a device in response to an input. The motor selected for this application has a gain constant $K_m = 0.5$ and a time-constant $\tau_m = 0.1$. For an amplifier gain $K_A = 20$, determine the following:

(i) Undamped natural frequency, damping ratio, and damped natural frequency.

(ii) Rise time, peak time, peak overshoot, and settling time.

(iii) Position, velocity and acceleration error constants K_p, K_v, and K_a.

(iv) Steady-state error resulting from the application of (a) unit-step input, (b) unit-ramp input, and (c) unit-parabolic input.

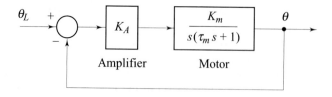

Fig. P6.1

6.2 Assume that control of one of the axes of a robot can be represented by the block diagram of Fig. P6.2.

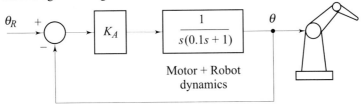

Fig. P6.2

(a) Determine the amplifier gain K_A so that the robot reaches steady-state in this axis in minimum time with no overshoot.
(b) Determine the steady-state error for an input command signal of $\theta_R = (5 + t)\mu(t)$,
with the value of K_A obtained in part (a).

6.3 A ground-based tracking radar is used to track aircraft targets. Assume that azimuth axis position control loop of the tracking radar can be represented by the block diagram of Fig. P6.3a.

(a) Determine the steady-state errors of the tracker for the following inputs caused by the aircraft motion.
   (i) $\theta_R = 10t$ (ii) $\theta_R = 10t + 0.1t^2$
(b) Compare the steady-state performance of system of Fig. P6.3b with that of Fig. P6.3a.

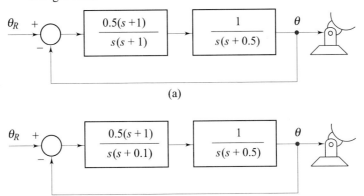

Fig. P6.3

6.4 The system of Fig. P6.4 has a constant reference input $r = 10$ and a constant disturbance input $w = 4$. Find the steady-state error.

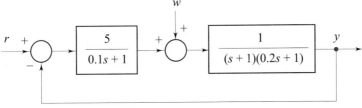

Fig. P6.4

6.5 Consider the heat-exchanger temperature control loop shown in Fig. P6.5.

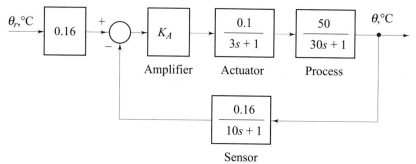

Fig. P6.5

(a) Find the range of values of $K_A > 0$ for which the system is stable.
(b) The acceptable value of stady-state error is 1°C for the step input of 10°C. Find the value of K_A that meets this specification on static accuracy.

6.6 Consider the control system in Fig. P6.6 in which a proportional compensator is employed. A specification on the control system is that the steady-state error must be less than two per cent for constant inputs.

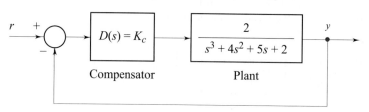

Fig. P6.6

(a) Find K_c that satisfies this specification.
(b) If the steady-state criterion cannot be met with a proportional compensator, use a dynamic compensator $D(s) = 3 + \dfrac{K_I}{s}$. Find the range of K_I that satisfies the requirement on steady-state error.

6.7 A control system with a PD controller is shown in Fig. P6.7.

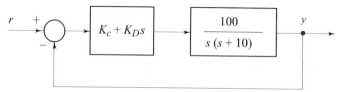

Fig. P6.7

(a) Find the values of K_c and K_D so that the velocity error constant K_v is 1000, the damping ratio is 0.5.
(b) Is damping ratio ζ a reasonably accurate estimate of peak overshoot of

the unit-step response? If not, why?

6.8 A control system with a type-0 process and a PI controller is shown in Fig.

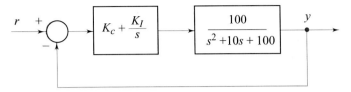

Fig. P6.8

(a) Find the value of K_I so that the velocity error K_v is 10.
(b) With the value of K_I found is part (a), determine the value of K_c so that the real part of the conjugate pair of complex roots of the characteristic equation of the closed-loop system is -1.
(c) Find the conjugate pair of complex roots and therefrom obtain the value of ζ.
(d) Is ζ a reasonably accurate estimate on peak overshoot of the unit-step response? Give reasons.

6.9 A three-term controller with transfer function

$$D(s) = 20\left[1 + \frac{1}{T_I s} + T_D s\right]$$

is used to control a process with transfer function

$$G(s) = \frac{4}{s^2 + 8s + 80}$$

The closed-loop system is a unity-feedback structure with $D(s)$ and $G(s)$ in cascade.

(a) If integral action is not employed, find the derivative time T_D required to make the closed-loop damping ratio unity.
(b) A simulation study on your design in part (a) shows overshoot in unit-step response. Give reasons.
(c) If the value of derivative time is maintained as in part (a), determine the minimum value of reset time T_I that can be used without instability arising.

6.10 (a) For the motor position servo shown in Fig. P6.10a without the rate feedback ($K_t = 0$), show that $K = 10$ will give a steady-state unit-ramp following error of 0.1. What is the corresponding damping ratio?
(b) With $K = 10$, what value of K_t will give a system damping ratio of 0.5? How does the steady-state error compare with that in part (a)?
(c) The system of Fig. P6.10a with $K = 10$ has been extended by including the amplifier K_A as shown in Fig. P6.10b. Determine whether it is now possible to achieve both the steady-state error of 0.1 and damping ratio of 0.5. If so, find the values of K_t and K_A required.

6.11 The block diagram of a control system is shown in Fig. P6.11.
(a) Find the values of K_1 and K_2 so that peak overshoot is 10% and settling time is 0.05 sec.
(b) For the values of K_1 and K_2 obtained in part (a), find the step, ramp and

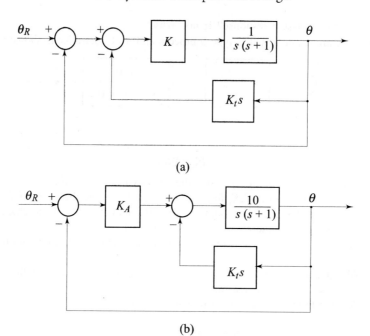

(a)

(b)

Fig. P6.10

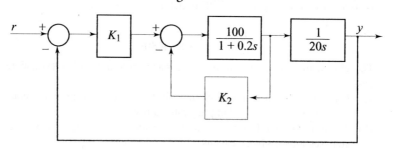

Fig. P6.11

parabolic error constants.

6.12 The block diagram of a motor position servo with a load disturbance torque T_w is shown in Fig. P6.12. Find K and K_t to obtain a system damping ratio 0.5 and 5% steady-state error for step input T_w.

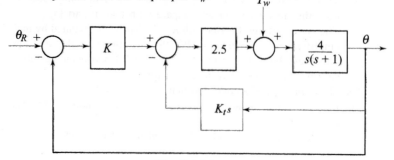

Fig. P6.12

6.13 Figure P6.13a shows a mechanical vibrating system. When 9 Newton of force is applied to the system, the mass oscillates as shown in Fig. P6.13b. Determine the parameters M, B, and K of the system from the response.

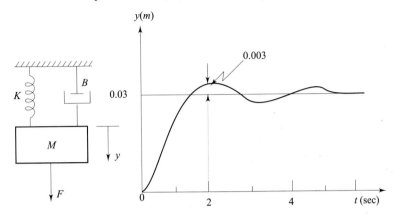

Fig. P6.13

6.14 A servomechanism controls the angular position θ of a mass through a command signal θ_R. The moment of inertia of the moving parts referred to the load shaft is J kg-m^2 and the motor torque at the load is K_T N-m per rad of error. The damping torque coefficient referred to the load shaft is B N-m per rad/sec. The following tests were conducted on the position control system

   (i)   Unit-step response was recorded and peak overshoot measured therefrom has a volume of 25%.

  (ii)   A constant velocity input of 1 rad/sec produced a steady-state error of 0.04 rad.

 (iii)   With the command θ_R held fixed, a torque of 10 N-m applied at the load shaft produced a steady-state error of 0.01 rad.

From the above data, determine the parameters J, B and K_T of the system.

6.15 The speed of a flywheel, driven by an electric motor, is to be controlled from the setting of an input potentiometer using a closed-loop control system. The moment of inertia of the flywheel and the motor is 100 kg-m^2 and the motor torque at the flywheel is 45 N-m for a speed error of 1 rad/sec. Frictional torque is 5 N-m when the flywheel velocity is 1 rad/sec.

With the system at rest, the input pot setting is suddenly increased from zero to 50 rev/min. Determine an expression for the subsequent flywheel angular velocity as a function of time and calculate steady-state velocity error of the flywheel.

Explain what modification could be made to the system to eliminate the steady-state error.

6.16 A flywheel driven by an electric motor is automatically controlled to follow the movement of a handwheel. The moment of inertia of the flywheel and the motor is 150 kg-m^2 and the motor torque applied to the flywheel is 2400 N-m per radian of misalignment between the flywheel and the handwheel. The viscous friction is equivalent to a torque of 600 N-m per rad/sec.

If the handwheel is suddenly turned through 60° when the system is at rest, determine an expression for the subsequent angular position of the flywheel as a function of time and calculate the peak overshoot of the response.

Explain what modification could be made to the system to eliminate the overshoot.

6.17 The schematic of a servo system is shown in Fig. P6.17. The two-phase servomotor develops a torque in accordance with the equation

$$T_M = K_1 e_c - K_2 \, \dot{\theta}_M$$

where $K_1 = 2 \times 10^{-3}$ N-m/volt, and $K_2 = 0.5 \times 10^{-3}$ N-m per rad/sec

The other parameters of the system are: load inertia, $J_L = 2.5$ kg-m²; coefficient of load friction, $B_L = 250$ N-m per rad/sec; motor to load gear ratio, $\left(\dot{\theta}_L / \dot{\theta}_M \right)$ = 1/50; motor to synchro gear ratio, $\left(\dot{\theta}_S / \dot{\theta}_M \right) = 1/1$, and sensitivity of synchro error detector, $K_s = 100$ volts/rad. The motor inertia and friction are negligible.

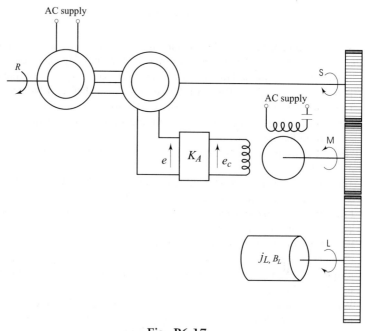

Fig. P6.17

(a) Draw a block diagram of the system indicating the transfer function of each block.

(b) If the input shaft is driven at a constant speed of π rad/sec, determine the value of the amplifier gain K_A such that the steady-state deviation between input and output positions is less than five degrees. For this value of amplifier gain, determine the peak overshoot and settling time of the system.

(c) The amplifier is now replaced by another which gives an output voltage of

$$e_c(t) = K_A e(t) + K_A \int e(t) dt$$

where the value of K_A is same as that obtained in part (b). Compare the steady-state behaviour of the system with that of part (b).

(d) A simulation study on the system of part (c) shows that the transient behaviour of the third-order system resembles that of the standard second-order system with characteristic equation

$$s^2 + 99.4508\,s + 3514.6322 = 0$$

Give reasons. Also determine the peak overshoot and settling time of the system.

6.18 In a dc position control servomechanism, the load is driven by a motor, supplied with constant armature current. The motor field current is supplied from a dc amplifier, the input to which is the difference between the voltages obtained from input and output potentiometers. A tachogenerator is coupled to the motor shaft and a fraction K of tachogenerator output is fed back to produce a stabilizing effect. The following particulars refer to the system: moment of inertia of motor, $J_M = 2 \times 10^{-3}$ kg-m^2; moment of inertia of load, $J_L = 5$ kg-m^2; motor to load gear ratio, $(\dot{\theta}_L/\dot{\theta}_M) = 1/50$; load to potentiometer gear ratio, $\dot{\theta}_P/\dot{\theta}_L = 1/1$; motor torque constant, $K_T = 2$ N-m/amp; tacho-generator constant, $K_t = 0.2$ volt per rad/sec; sensitivity of error detector, $K_P = 0.6$ volt/rad, and amplifier gain $= K_A$ amps/volt.

(a) Make a sketch of the system showing how the hardware is connected.
(b) Draw a block diagram of the system indicating the transfer function of each block.
(c) Determine the amplifier gain required and a fraction of the tachogenerator voltage fed back to give an undamped natural frequency of 4 rad/sec and damping ratio of 0.8.

6.19 The schematic diagram of a servomechanism is given in Fig. P6.19. The system constants are given below.
Sensitivity of error detector, $K_P = 1$ volt/rad; gain of dc amplifier $= K_A$ volts/volt; resistance of armature of motor, $R_a = 5$ ohms; equivalent inertia at the motor shaft $J = 4 \times 10^{-3}$ kg-m^2; equivalent friction at the motor shaft, $B = 2 \times 10^{-3}$ N-m per rad/sec; torque constant of motor, $K_T = 1$ N-m/amp; and gear ratio $(\dot{\theta}_L/\dot{\theta}_M)$, $n = 1/10$.

(a) Draw a block diagram of the system indicating the transfer function of each block.
(b) Find amplifier gain K_A so that the steady-state error to unit-ramp input is less than 0.01 rad. For this value of amplifier gain, determine the damping ratio, and peak overshoot to unit-step input.
(c) To improve the system damping, the amplifier is modified by introducing an additional derivative term such that its output is given by

$$e_a(t) = K_A e(t) + K_D \frac{de(t)}{dt}$$

where the value of K_A is same as that obtained in part (b). Does this modification affect the steady-state error as in part (b)?

Determine the value of K_D such that the damping ratio is improved to 0.6. Also calculate peak overshoot corresponding to this damping ratio using correlation for standard second-order systems.

(d) A simulation study of your design in part (c) shows a different value of peak overshoot. Give reasons.

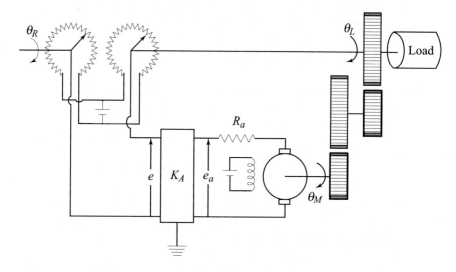

Fig. P6.19

6.20 Hydraulic actuators are used to drive cutting tools in machining applications (Fig. P6.20a). The command input e_r is a voltage representing the desired position y_r of the cutting tool as function of time. It can be generated by a cam drive, a punched paper tape, or a computer program. A model of a feedback control system is shown in Fig. P6.20b. The load disturbance due to reactive force F_w of the cutting tool is also shown.

(a) When $F_w = 0$, determine the steady-state tracking error for a constant velocity input of 0.03 mm/sec as a function of K_A.

(b) Determine the steady-state error in $y(t)$ introduced by a unit-step disturbance as a function of K_A.

(c) Find the minimum values of error in part (a) and that in part (b) which can be obtained by the control configuration of Fig. P6.20b.

6.21 An elementary magnetic suspension scheme is sketched in Fig. P6.21. For small motions near the equilibrium position, the voltage e is proportional to ball displacement x (in metres) such that $e = 100x$. The power amplifier is a voltage-to-current device so that $i = u$ amps. The transfer function of the open-loop unstable process is given by (refer Problem 2.9)

$$\frac{X(s)}{I(s)} = \frac{47.6}{(s + 4.083)(s - 4.083)}$$

(a) Show that the process cannot be made closed-loop stable by using a proportional feedback controller $u = -K_c e$.

(b) Show that closed-loop stability can be achieved using a PD controller $u = -K_c(e + T_D \dot{e})$. Find the restrictions on K_c and T_D for stability.

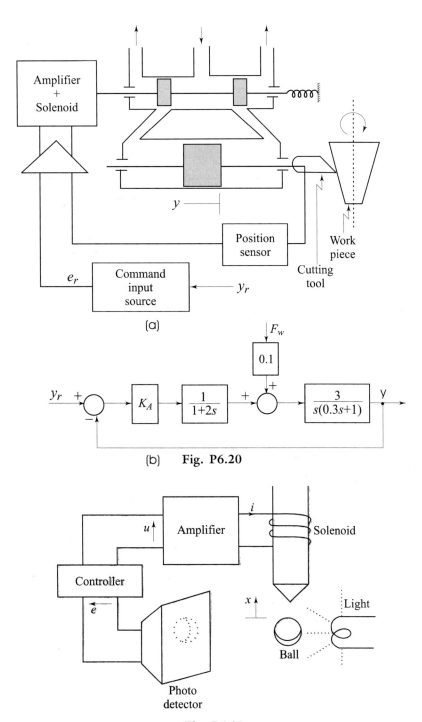

(a)

(b)   **Fig. P6.20**

Fig. P6.21

(c) Design a PD controller to meet the following specifications: $t_s \leq 0.4$ sec; peak overshoot $\leq 20\%$.

6.22 A tank-level control system is shown in Fig. P6.22a. If the level is not correct, an error voltage e is developed and a signal $K_c e + K_D \dot{e}$ is applied to a servomotor. This in turn adjusts a valve through appropriate gearing and thereby restores balance by adjusting the inlet flow rate. A model of the feedback control system is shown in Fig. P6.22b.
   (a) What is the system type number?
   (b) Find the ranges of values of K_c and K_D for which the steady-state error to unit-ramp disturbance is less than 0.1.

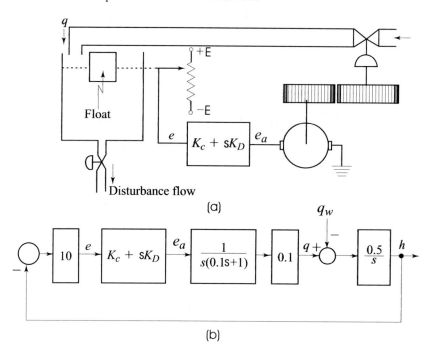

(a)

(b)

Fig. P6.22

6.23 Figure P6.23 shows a thermal system in which hot air is circulated to keep the temperature of a chamber constant. The transfer function of the plant can be adequately represented by

$$\frac{\theta(s)}{U(s)} = \frac{1}{s+1}$$

Determine the values of K_1 and K_2 which meet the following specifications on the feedback system:

$$M_p \leq 20\%, \; t_s \leq 2 \text{ sec}$$

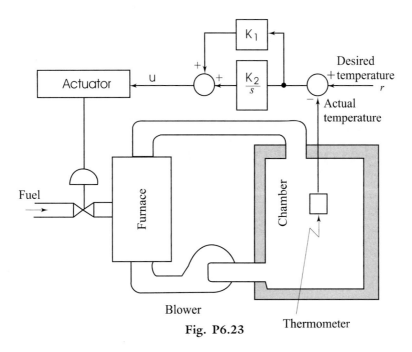

Blower

Fig. P6.23

Thermometer

chapter 7

Compensator Design
Using Root Locus Plots

7.1 INTRODUCTION

Proper selection of performance specifications is the most important step in control system design. The desired behaviour is specified in terms of transient response measures and steady-state error. The steady-state error is usually specified in terms of error constants for standard inputs, while the transient response is specified in terms of peak overshoot, settling time, rise time, etc., for a step input.

The transient-response specifications can be translated into desired locations for dominant closed-loop poles. In some control systems, simple gain adjustment moves the closed-loop poles to desired locations and, in addition, meets the steady-state accuracy demand. However, in most practical cases, we have to introduce a compensator and obtain its parameters that satisfy the selected specifications in the best possible manner. Parametric search is of course restricted to the feasible domain. Practically, most control systems require a trial-and-error parameter adjustment to achieve at least an acceptable performance if it is not possible to satisfy exactly all the performance specifications.

For adjusting one or more system parameters in order to obtain suitable closed-loop pole locations, it is worthwhile to determine how closed-loop poles (roots of the characteristic equation) of a given system migrate in the s-plane as the parameters are varied. The *root locus method* provides this information graphically. A *root locus plot* is a plot in the s-plane of all possible locations that the roots of a closed-loop system's characteristic equation can have as a specific parameter is varied, usually from zero to infinity. The root locus technique was introduced by Evans in 1948, and has been developed and utilized extensively in control engineering practice.

This chapter first introduces the basic concept of the root locus method and presents useful rules for graphically constructing the root loci. The use of the technique for gain adjustment and compensator design problems is then considered.

7.2 THE ROOT LOCUS CONCEPT

We introduce the root locus concept through an example. Consider the second-order system shown in Fig. 7.1, which represents a typical position control system. The plant consists of servomotor and load, driven by a power amplifier with gain K. The open-loop transfer function of the system is

$$G(s) = \frac{K}{s(s+2)} \tag{7.1}$$

The open-loop poles, marked $\times$ in Fig. 7.2, are at $s = 0$ and $s = -2$. The closed-loop transfer function of the system is

$$M(s) = \frac{G(s)}{1 + G(s)} = \frac{K}{s^2 + 2s + K} \tag{7.2}$$

The characteristic equation is

$$\Delta(s) = s^2 + 2s + K = 0 \tag{7.3}$$

The second-order system under consideration is always stable for positive values of K. The relative stability of the system depends on the location of the characteristic roots (closed-loop poles)

$$s_{1,2} = -1 \pm \sqrt{1 - K} \tag{7.4}$$

and hence on the choice of the parameter K. As K is varied from zero to infinity, the characteristic roots move in the s-plane as shown in Fig. 7.2. At $K = 0$, the root s_1 is equal to the open-loop pole at $s = 0$, and the root s_2 is equal to the open-loop pole at $s = -2$. As K increases, the roots move toward each other. The two roots meet at $s = -1$ for $K = 1$. As K is increased further, the roots break away from the real axis, become complex conjugate, and since the real part of both the roots remains fixed at $s = -1$, the roots move along the line $\sigma = -1$.

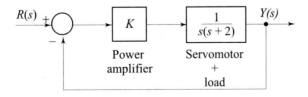

Fig. 7.1 *A position control system*

A root locus of a system is a plot of the roots of the system characteristic equation (poles of the closed-loop transfer function) as some parameters of the system are varied.

The two branches[1] *A-C-E* and *B-C-D* of the plot of Fig. 7.2 are thus two *root loci* of the system of Fig. 7.1. Each root locus starts at an open-loop pole with $K = 0$ and terminates at infinity as $K \to \infty$. Each root locus gives one characteristic root (closed-loop pole) for a specific value of K.

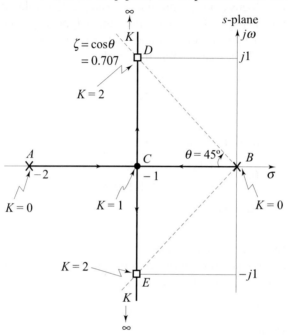

Fig. 7.2   *Root locus plot for Eqn. (7.3)*

The root locus plot gives us a great deal of information concerning the transient behaviour of the system as the gain K is varied. We can see from the plot that for $0 < K < 1$, the roots are real and distinct and the system is overdamped. For $K = 1$, the roots are real and repeated and the system is critically damped. For $K > 1$, the roots are complex conjugate and the system is underdamped with the value of ζ decreasing as K increases. From the viewpoint of design, we see that by choice of gain K, we can cause a characteristic root at any point on the root locus. For example, suppose that a system specification requires damping ζ equal to 0.707. The dashed lines in Fig. 7.2 correspond to $\zeta = 0.707$. The points when the root loci cross the dashed lines have been marked □. These points correspond to characteristic roots for $K = 2$. We could easily compute K in this case because we know that if $\zeta = 0.707$, the magnitude of the imaginary part of the root

---

1. Treating the two branches *A-C-D* and *B-C-E* as two root loci will give identical results.

$$\left| \sqrt{1-K} \right| = 1$$

which is true if $K = 2$.

Consider now the second-order system shown in Fig. 7.3 which represents a typical position control system with velocity feedback. It is a multi-loop system with closed-loop transfer function

$$M(s) = \frac{K}{s^2 + (0.2K + 2)s + K} \tag{7.5}$$

The characteristic equation is

$$\Delta(s) = s^2 + (0.2K + 2)s + K = 0 \tag{7.6}$$

which can be rearranged as

$$s^2 + 2s + K(0.2s + 1) = 0$$

or

$$1 + \frac{0.2K(s+5)}{s(s+2)} = 0 \tag{7.7}$$

Note that Eqn. (7.7) is also the characteristic equation of a unity feedback system with (open-loop) transfer function

$$F(s) = \frac{K'(s+5)}{s(s+2)} ; \, K' = 0.2K \tag{7.8}$$

which has two poles at $s = 0$ and $s = -2$, and a zero at $s = -5$. In Fig. 7.4, the open-loop poles (poles of $F(s)$) are indicated by $\times$ and the open-loop zero (zero of $F(s)$) is indicated by $\circ$.

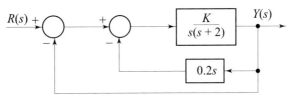

Fig. 7.3 *A position control system with velocity feedback*

Let us examine the nature of characteristic roots

$$s_{1,2} = -(0.1K + 1) \pm \sqrt{(0.1K + 1)^2 - K} \tag{7.9}$$

As K is varied from zero to infinity, the characteristic roots move in the s-plane as shown in Fig. 7.4. At $K = 0$, the root s_1 is equal to the open-loop pole at $s = 0$ and the root s_2 is equal to the open-loop pole at $s = -2$. As K increases, the roots move towards each other. The two roots meet at $s = -1.127$ for $K = 1.27$. As K is increased further, the roots break away from the real axis and become complex conjugate. It turns out that the complex roots move along a circle[2] of radius $\sqrt{15}$ with centre at $s = -5$.

---

2. This can easily be proved as we shall see later in Example 7.1.

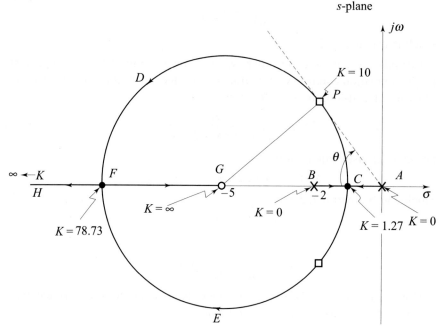

Fig. 7.4 *Root locus plot for Eqn. (7.6)*

The two complex-conjugate roots meet at $s = -8.873$ for $K = 78.73$. As K is increased further, the roots break away and depart in opposite directions along the real axis.

From Eqn. (7.9), we obtain

$$s_{1,2} = -(0.1K + 1) \pm (0.01K^2 - 0.8K + 1)^{1/2}$$

$$= -(0.1K + 1) \pm 0.1K \left(1 - \frac{80}{K} + \frac{100}{K^2}\right)^{\frac{1}{2}}$$

For large K,

$$s_{1,2} \cong -(0.1K + 1) \pm 0.1K \left(1 - \frac{40}{K} + \frac{50}{K^2}\right)$$

$$\cong -0.1K - 1 \pm 0.1K \mp 4$$

Therefore as $K \to \infty$, $s_1 \to -5$ and $s_2 \to -\infty$.

Figure 7.4 shows the two root loci: *A-C-D-F-G* and *B-C-E-F-H*.

As with the earlier example of Fig. 7.2, valuable information can be obtained from the root locus plot of Fig. 7.4. As K increases, the root loci move away from imaginary axis and the system becomes more stable. The least damped complex-conjugate poles are obtained by drawing straight line *AP* tangential to the circular locus as shown in Fig. 7.4.

By geometry,

$$\zeta_{\min} = \cos \theta = \frac{AP}{AG} = \frac{\sqrt{(AG)^2 - (GP)^2}}{AG}$$

$$= \frac{\sqrt{25-15}}{5} = \frac{\sqrt{10}}{5} = 0.632$$

The least damped complex-conjugate closed-loop poles, marked □ in Fig. 7.4, are

$$s_1 = -(0.1K + 1) + \sqrt{(0.1K+1)^2 - K} = -\sqrt{10} \cos \theta + j\sqrt{10} \sin \theta$$
$$= -2 + j2.45 \quad (7.10)$$

$$s_2 = -(0.1K + 1) - \sqrt{(0.1K+1)^2 - K} = -\sqrt{10} \cos \theta - j\sqrt{10} \sin \theta$$
$$= -2 - j2.45 \quad (7.11)$$

From Eqns (7.10)–(7.11), we find that corresponding to $\zeta = 0.632$,

$$0.1K + 1 = 2$$

which is true if $K = 10$. Therefore, $K = 10$ results in the least damping.

The two root locus plots we have presented, illustrate a number of properties which will be derived and discussed in the next section. First, a root locus plot is always symmetrical with respect to the real axis. This is so because the roots must always be complex conjugate. Second, a root locus plot is made of as many branches as there are poles in the open-loop transfer function, and each branch starts from one of the open-loop poles. The branches either go off to infinity or end on an open-loop zero.

The two cases we have discussed involved only a modest amount of analysis. The effort rapidly grows with the order of the system. The sketching rules given in the next section serve the purpose of avoiding direct solution for the roots. As one can imagine, repeated formation of the characteristic polynomial and factoring by hand calculator is a tedious job. Programs are now available [176–179] to generate the root locus plots; some of them based on repeated factoring and some that mechanize the sketching rules. Whatever the package available to us does, it will be useful to know its basis and its limitations. The hand-sketching process trains our intuition and helps us to avoid buying computer-generated trash results.

A graphical procedure for sketching root locus plots was developed by W.R. Evans in 1948. In the following, we present the locus equations which form the basis of the Evans method; guidelines for sketching root loci will be given in the next section.

The Locus Equations

Most control systems can be expressed in the form of Fig. 7.5a, where the closed-loop transfer function is

$$M(s) = \frac{Y(s)}{R(s)} = \frac{G(s)}{1 + G(s) H(s)} \quad (7.12)$$

In Fig. 7.5b, the feedback loop is broken at the feedback variable $B(s)$. The transfer function relating $B(s)$ to $R(s)$ is the open-loop transfer function $G(s)H(s)$. The characteristic equation of the system is

$$1 + G(s)H(s) = 0 \qquad (7.13)$$

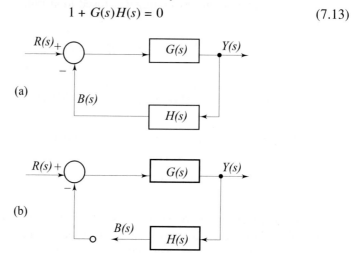

Fig. 7.5   *A feedback system*

The open-loop transfer function $G(s)H(s)$ is generally known in the factored form as it is obtained by modelling the transfer function of individual components comprising the system. Therefore $G(s)H(s)$ can generally be expressed in either of the factored forms given below:

Pole-zero form

$$G(s)H(s) = \frac{K \prod\limits_{i=1}^{m}(s + z_i)}{\prod\limits_{j=1}^{n}(s + p_j)} ; \, m \le n, K \ge 0 \qquad (7.14)$$

Time-constant form

$$G(s)H(s) = \frac{K' \prod\limits_{i=1}^{m}(\tau_{zi} s + 1)}{\prod\limits_{j=1}^{n}(\tau_{pj}s + 1)} ; \, m \le n, K \ge 0 \qquad (7.15)$$

These forms are interrelated by the following expressions.

$$-z_i = -\frac{1}{\tau_{zi}}; \, i = 1, 2, \ldots, m$$

$$-p_j = -\frac{1}{\tau_{pj}}; \, j = 1, 2, \ldots, n \qquad (7.16)$$

$$K = \frac{K' \prod\limits_{j=1}^{n} p_j}{\prod\limits_{i=1}^{m} z_i}$$

K' is the open-loop gain in time-constant form, K is the open-loop gain in pole-zero form, $-z_i$ are m open-loop zeros, and $-p_j$ are n open-loop poles. In all physically realizable systems, $n \geq m$.

The pole-zero form of Eqn. (7.14) is more convenient for drawing root locus and will be used throughout this chapter. The open-loop gain K is considered variable for drawing the root locus of the system.

Substituting Eqn. (7.14) into Eqn. (7.13), we obtain the characteristic equation

$$1 + \frac{K \prod\limits_{i=1}^{m}(s + z_i)}{\prod\limits_{j=1}^{n}(s + p_j)} = 0 \qquad (7.17)$$

or $$\prod\limits_{j=1}^{n}(s + p_j) + K \prod\limits_{i=1}^{m}(s + z_i) = 0 \qquad (7.18)$$

The characteristic equation given in (7.18) is in conventional polynomial form. The characteristic equation given in (7.17) is not in conventional form; however, the values of s for which it is satisfied will be same as those for which Eqn. (7.18) is satisfied provided that the numerator and denominator polynomials in Eqn. (7.17) have no common factors.

If the variable parameter is other than open-loop gain, the characteristic equation can be rearranged to obtain the form (7.17) with the parameter of interest appearing as the multiplying factor. The characteristic equation of a multi-loop control configuration can also be brought to the form (7.17) by block diagram manipulation rules or by Mason's gain formula. In our study of the root locus technique, we therefore consider a general characteristic equation:

$$1 + F(s) = 0 \qquad (7.19a)$$

with $$F(s) = \frac{K \prod\limits_{i=1}^{m}(s + z_i)}{\prod\limits_{j=1}^{n}(s + p_j)} \; ; \; m \leq n \qquad (7.19b)$$

where $K \geq 0$ is the *root locus gain*.

From Eqns (7.19) it is seen that the roots of the characteristic equation occur only for those values of s where

$$F(s) = \frac{K \prod_{i=1}^{m}(s + z_i)}{\prod_{j=1}^{n}(s + p_j)} = -1 \qquad (7.20)$$

Since s is a complex variable, Eqn. (7.20) is converted into two Evans conditions given below:

Magnitude criterion

$$|F(s)| = \frac{K \prod_{i=1}^{m}|s + z_i|}{\prod_{j=1}^{n}|s + p_j|} = 1 \qquad (7.21a)$$

Angle criterion

$$\angle F(s) = \sum_{i=1}^{m} \angle s + z_i - \sum_{j=1}^{n} \angle s + p_j = \pm 180° (2q + 1); \; q = 0, 1, 2, \dots$$

$$(7.21b)$$

Equations (7.21) imply that the roots of $1 + F(s) = 0$ are those values of s at which the magnitude of $F(s)$ equals 1 and the angle of $F(s)$ equals an odd multiple of 180°. Figure 7.6 illustrates graphical evaluation of $|s_0 + p_j|$, $|s_0 + z_i|$, $\angle s_0 + p_j$ and $\angle s_0 + z_i$ at a point s_0 in the s-plane.

It should be appreciated that not all values of s that satisfy Eqn. (7.21a) also satisfy Eqn. (7.21b), while for every s that satisfies Eqn. (7.21b), there exists a K satisfying Eqn. (7.21a). The root locus, thus, is a plot of the points in the complex plane where the angle criterion (7.21b) is satisfied. The value of gain corresponding to a root, i.e., a point on the root locus, can be obtained from the magnitude criterion (7.21a).

Example 7.1

Consider the second-order characteristic equation

$$1 + F(s) = 0$$

with

$$F(s) = \frac{K(s + b)}{(s + a_1)(s + a_2)}; \; K \geq 0$$

having pole-zero configuration shown in Fig. 7.7a.

We will search for all the points in the s-plane for which the angle criterion (7.21b) is satisfied. A plot of these points is the root locus of the given characteristic equation.

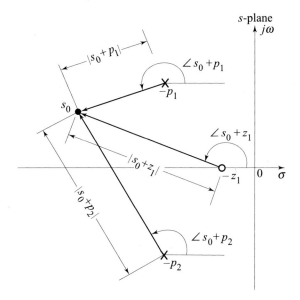

Fig. 7.6 *Evaluation of $|F(s)|$ and $\angle F(s)$*

We begin our search process with the real axis of the s-plane. Let us examine any point s_0 in between the two poles (refer Fig. 7.7a). As this point is joined by phasors to the poles at $s = -a_1$ and $s = -a_2$, and the zero at $s = -b$, it is easily seen that

(i) the pole at $s = -a_1$ contributes an angle of $180°$,

(ii) the pole at $s = -a_2$ contributes an angle of $0°$, and

(iii) the zero at $s = -b$ contributes an angle of $0°$.

Therefore, the angle criterion (7.21b) is satisfied and the point s_0 is on the root locus. Scanning all the points on the real axis, yields the real-axis root locus segments shown in Fig. 7.7b by dark lines.

To examine s-plane points not on the real axis, we consider a representative point $s = \sigma + j\omega$. At this point

$$F(s) = \frac{K(\sigma + j\omega + b)}{(\sigma + j\omega + a_1)(\sigma + j\omega + a_2)}$$

$$= \frac{K(\sigma + b + j\omega)}{(\sigma + a_1)(\sigma + a_2) + j\omega(\sigma + a_1 + \sigma + a_2) - \omega^2}$$

$$= \frac{K(\sigma + b + j\omega)}{(\sigma + a_1)(\sigma + a_2) - \omega^2 + j\omega(2\sigma + a_1 + a_2)}$$

$$\angle F(s) = \tan^{-1} \frac{\omega}{\sigma + b} - \tan^{-1} \frac{\omega(2\sigma + a_1 + a_2)}{(\sigma + a_1)(\sigma + a_2) - \omega^2}$$

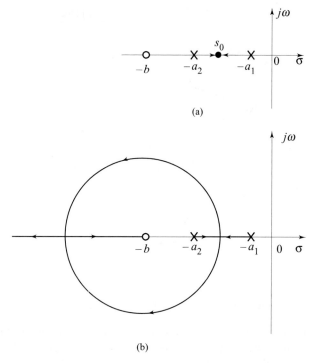

Fig. 7.7 *Search for points on root loci*

$$= \tan^{-1}\left\{\dfrac{\dfrac{\omega}{\sigma+b} - \dfrac{\omega(2\sigma+a_1+a_2)}{(\sigma+a_1)(\sigma+a_2)-\omega^2}}{1+\dfrac{\omega}{\sigma+b}\left[\dfrac{\omega(2\sigma+a_1+a_2)}{(\sigma+a_1)(\sigma+a_2)-\omega^2}\right]}\right\}$$

$\angle F(s)$ is a multiple of 180° if

$$\dfrac{\dfrac{\omega}{\sigma+b} - \dfrac{\omega(2\sigma+a_1+a_2)}{(\sigma+a_1)(\sigma+a_2)-\omega^2}}{1+\dfrac{\omega}{\sigma+b}\left[\dfrac{\omega(2\sigma+a_1+a_2)}{(\sigma+a_1)(\sigma+a_2)-\omega^2}\right]} = 0$$

Manipulation of this equation gives

$$(\sigma+b)^2 + \omega^2 = (b-a_1)(b-a_2)$$

This is the equation of a circle with centre at $(-b, 0)$ and radius $= \sqrt{(b-a_1)(b-a_2)}$. It can easily be verified that at every point on this circle in the s-plane, $\angle F(s)$ is $\pm 180°$. Every point on the circle, therefore, satisfies the angle criterion (7.21b).

Let us assume the following numerical values for open-loop poles and zeros.

$$a_1 = 1,\ a_2 = 2,\ b = 5$$

The root locus plot for this case is shown in Fig. 7.8. The two root loci are A-C-D-F-G and B-C-E-F-H; the locus A-C-D-F-G starts at open-loop pole $s = -2$ with $K = 0$ and terminates at open-loop zero $s = -5$ with $K = \infty$; and the locus B-C-E-F-H starts at open-loop pole $s = -1$ with $K = 0$ and goes off to infinity along the negative real axis as $K \to \infty$.

The value of K corresponding to least damping may be obtained by applying the magnitude criterion (7.21a) at the point P where OP is a straight line tangential to the circular locus.

$$K = \frac{\text{length of the vector } AP \times \text{length of the vector } BP}{\text{length of the vector } GP}$$

$$= \frac{2.6 \times 2.9}{3.45} \cong 2.2; \; \zeta_{min} = \cos \theta = 0.72$$

The closed-loop poles corresponding to this value of damping are (read from Fig. 7.8): $s_{1,2} = -2.6 \pm j2.5$.

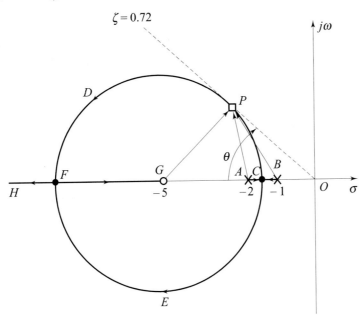

Fig. 7.8 *A root locus plot (Example 7.1)*

Example 7.2

Consider the second-order characteristics equation

$$1 + F(s) = 0$$

with

$$F(s) = \frac{K(s+b)}{(s+\alpha+j\beta)(s+\alpha-j\beta)}; \; K \geq 0$$

having pole-zero configuration shown in Fig. 7.9.

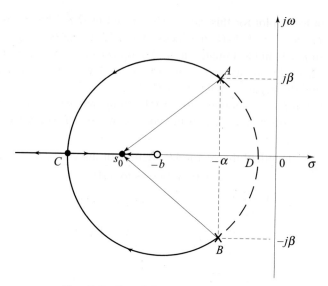

Fig. 7.9 *Search for points on root loci*

Let us examine any point s_0 on the negative real axis to the left of the zero at $s = -b$. As this point is joined by phasors to the two poles at $s = -\alpha \pm j\beta$ and the zero at $s = -b$, it is easily seen that (i) the zero contributes an angle of $180°$, and (ii) the net angle contribution of complex-conjugate pole pair is zero. Therefore, angle criterion (7.21b) is satisfied for all the points on the negative real axis to the left of the zero at $s = -b$. It can easily be verified that the angle criterion is not satisfied for all the points on the real axis to the right of the zero at $s = -b$.

To examine s-plane points not on the real axis, we consider a representative point $s = \sigma + j\omega$. At this point,

$$F(s) = \frac{K(\sigma + j\omega + b)}{(\sigma + j\omega + \alpha + j\beta)(\sigma + j\omega + \alpha - j\beta)}$$

$$= \frac{K(\sigma + b + j\omega)}{\left(\sigma^2 + \alpha^2 + 2\sigma\alpha - \omega^2 + \beta^2\right) + j2\omega(\sigma + \alpha)}$$

$$\angle F(s) = \tan^{-1}\frac{\omega}{\sigma + b} - \tan^{-1}\frac{2\omega(\sigma + \alpha)}{\left(\sigma^2 + \alpha^2 + 2\sigma\alpha - \omega^2 + \beta^2\right)}$$

$$= \tan^{-1}\left\{\frac{\dfrac{\omega}{\sigma + b} - \dfrac{2\omega(\sigma + \alpha)}{\sigma^2 + \alpha^2 + 2\sigma\alpha - \omega^2 + \beta^2}}{1 + \dfrac{\omega}{\sigma + b}\left[\dfrac{2\omega(\sigma + \alpha)}{\sigma^2 + \alpha^2 + 2\sigma\alpha - \omega^2 + \beta^2}\right]}\right\}$$

$\angle F(s)$ is a multiple of $180°$ if

$$\frac{\dfrac{\omega}{\sigma+b} - \dfrac{2\omega(\sigma+\alpha)}{\sigma^2+\alpha^2+2\sigma\alpha-\omega^2+\beta^2}}{1+\dfrac{\omega}{\sigma+b}\left[\dfrac{2\omega(\sigma+\alpha)}{\sigma^2+\alpha^2+2\sigma\alpha-\omega^2+\beta^2}\right]} = 0$$

Manipulation of this equation gives

$$(\sigma+b)^2 + \omega^2 = (\alpha-b)^2 + \beta^2$$

This is the equation of a circle with centre at $(-b,\ 0)$ and radius $= \sqrt{(\alpha-b)^2+\beta^2}$. It can easily be verified that at every point of the *A-C-B* section of the circle, $\angle F(s)$ is $\pm 180°$; and at every point of the *A-D-B* section of the circle, $\angle F(s) = 0°$. Every point of the *A-C-B* section, therefore, satisfies the angle criterion (7.21b). As we shall see later in this chapter, the *A-D-B* section of the circle corresponds to the root locus for $K < 0$.

Let us assume the following numerical values for the open-loop poles and zeros:

$$\alpha = 1,\ \beta = \sqrt{2},\ b = 2$$

The root locus plot for this case is shown in Fig. 7.10. The two root loci are *A-C-E* and *B-C-F*; the locus *A-C-E* starts at open-loop pole at $s = -1 + j\sqrt{2}$ with $K = 0$ and terminates at open-loop zero at $s = -2$ with $K = \infty$, and the locus *B-C-F* starts at open-loop pole at $s = -1 - j\sqrt{2}$ with $K = 0$ and goes off to infinity along the negative real axis as $K \to \infty$.

The value of K corresponding to a damping ratio of 0.7 may be obtained by applying the magnitude criterion (7.21a) at the point P in Fig. 7.10.

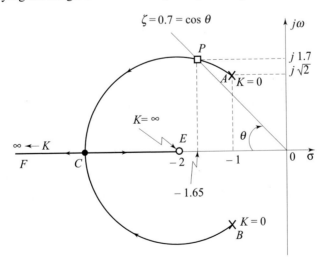

Fig. 7.10 *A root locus plot (Example 7.2)*

$$K = \frac{\text{length of the vector } AP \times \text{length of the vector } BP}{\text{length of the vector } EP}$$

$$= \frac{0.7 \times 3.2}{1.73} \cong 1.3$$

The closed-loop poles corresponding to this value of K are (read from Fig. 7.10): $s_{1,2} = -1.65 \pm j1.7$.

▲▲

In systems of Examples 7.1 and 7.2, the root loci in the complex plane are a part of a circle. Circular root loci may occur in systems that involve two poles and one zero, two poles and two zeros, or one pole and two zeros. Even in such systems, whether or not circular root loci occur depends on the locations of poles and zeros involved.

It is important to note that easily interpretable equations for the root locus can be derived for simple systems only. For complicated systems having many poles and zeros, any attempt to derive equations for the root loci is discouraged. Such derived equations are very complicated and their configuration in the complex plane is difficult to visualize. The next section provides a solution to this problem.

7.3 | GUIDELINES FOR SKETCHING ROOT LOCI

The purpose of the root locus is to show in graphical form the general trend of the roots of the characteristic equation

$$1 + F(s) = 0 \tag{7.22a}$$

where

$$F(s) = \frac{K \prod_{i=1}^{m} (s + z_i)}{\prod_{j=1}^{n} (s + p_j)} ; \; m \le n \tag{7.22b}$$

as the parameter K is varied from zero to infinity. Every point $s = \sigma + j\omega$ in the complex plane that satisfies the *angle criterion* (refer Eqn. (7.21b))

$$\angle F(s) = \sum_{i=1}^{m} \angle s + z_i - \sum_{j=1}^{n} \angle s + p_j = \pm 180° (2q + 1); \; q = 0, 1, 2, \ldots \tag{7.23a}$$

is on the root locus. The value of the parameter K (*root locus gain*) corresponding to a point on the root locus can be obtained from the *magnitude criterion* (refer Eqn. (7.21a))

$$|F(s)| = \frac{K \prod_{i=1}^{m} |s + z_i|}{\prod_{j=1}^{n} |s + p_j|} \tag{7.23b}$$

We can, in principle, sketch a root locus for a given $F(s)$ by measuring $\angle F(s)$ at all the points of the complex plane and marking down those places where we find $\angle F(s)$ equal to an odd multiple of $180°$. This trial-and-error procedure of sketching the root locus is illustrated in Fig. 7.6. The poles and zeros of $F(s)$ are located on the s-plane on a graph sheet and a trial point s_0 is selected. The lines joining each of the poles $(-p_j)$ and zeros $(-z_i)$ to s_0 represent the phasors $(s_0 + p_j)$ and $(s_0 + z_i)$ respectively, as shown in Fig. 7.6. The angles of these phasors can be measured by placing a protector or *spirule*[3] at the pole and zero locations, and the angle values are substituted in the angle criterion given by Eqn. (7.23a). The trial point s_0 is suitably shifted till the angle criterion is satisfied to a desired degree of accuracy. A number of points on the s-plane are determined in this manner and a smooth curve drawn through these points gives the root locus with variable K.

The value of K for a particular root location s_0 can be obtained from the magnitude criterion given by Eqn. (7.23b) by substituting the phasor magnitudes read to scale. It is to be noted that the same scale must be employed for both the real and imaginary axes of the complex plane.

From the magnitude criterion of Eqn. (7.23b),

$$K = \frac{\prod_{j=1}^{n} \left| s_0 + p_j \right|}{\prod_{i=1}^{m} \left| s_0 + z_i \right|} \tag{7.24a}$$

With reference to Fig. 7.6, we can write

$$K = \frac{\left[\begin{array}{l}\text{Product of phasor lengths (read to scale)}\\ \text{from } s_0 \text{ to pole of } F(s)\end{array}\right]}{\left[\begin{array}{l}\text{Product of phasor lengths (read to scale)}\\ \text{from } s_0 \text{ to zeros of } F(s)\end{array}\right]} \tag{7.24b}$$

If we were to use the trial-and-error method just described, the search for all the root locus points in the s-plane that satisfy the angle criterion (7.23a) would in general be a very tedious task. In order to help reduce the tedium of the trial-and-error procedure, certain rules have been developed for making a quick approximate sketch of the root locus. This approximate sketch provides a guide for the selection of trial points such that a more accurate root locus can be obtained by a few trials. Further, the approximate root locus sketch is very

---

3. The spirule is a device invented by W.R. Evans to graphically determine

$$\sum_{i=1}^{m} \angle s + z_i - \sum_{j=1}^{n} \angle s + p_j \quad \text{and} \quad \frac{K \prod_{j=1}^{n} \left| s + p_j \right|}{\prod_{i=1}^{m} \left| s + z_i \right|}$$

for any point in the s-plane, given a pole-zero plot of poles at $s = -p_j$ and zeros at $s = -z_i$.

useful in vizualizing the effects of variation of system parameter K, the effects of shifting pole-zero locations and of bringing in a new set of poles and zeros.

With the availability of digital computers and efficient root-finding techniques, the spirule and the trial-and-error method have become obsolete. Nevertheless, the analyst should still have an understanding of the properties of the root loci in order to interpret the computer results correctly and apply the root locus techniques for the design of linear control systems. Presentation of guidelines for hand-sketching an approximate root locus plot is, therefore, in order.

Rules for Constructing Root Loci

To help in the rough drafting of the general form of a root locus, construction rules have been devised. We shall discuss several of them, first stating the rule, then giving a justification for its validity, and finally citing an example if appropriate. We assume that $F(s)$ for which the root locus is desired, is of the form given by Eqn. (7.22b), i.e., with m zeros at $s = -z_i$, and n poles at $s = -p_j$; $m \leq n$. The m zeros and n poles of $F(s)$ will be referred to as open-loop zeros and open-loop poles, respectively[4].

Rule 1   Number of Root Loci

The root locus plot consists of n root loci as K varies from 0 to ∞. The loci are symmetric with respect to the real axis.

The characteristic equation (7.22a) can be written as

$$\prod_{j=1}^{n}\left(s + p_j\right) + K \prod_{i=1}^{m}\left(s + z_i\right) = 0$$

This equation has degree n. Thus for each real K, there are n roots. As the roots of this equation are continuous functions of its coefficients, the n roots form n continuous loci as K varies from 0 to ∞.

Since the complex roots of the characteristic equation always occur in conjugate pairs, the n root loci, must be symmetrical about the real axis.

Rule 2   Starting and Terminal Points of Root Loci

As K increases from zero to infinity, each root locus originates from an open-loop pole with K = 0 and terminates either on an open-loop zero or on infinity with K = ∞. The number of loci terminating on infinity equals the number of open-loop poles minus zeros.

The characteristic equation (7.22a) can be written as

$$\prod_{j=1}^{n}\left(s + p_j\right) + K \prod_{i=1}^{m}\left(s + z_j\right) = 0 \tag{7.25}$$

---

4. The equation $1 + F(s) = 0$ can be interpreted as the characteristic equation of a unity-feedback system with open-loop transfer function equal to $F(s)$.

When $K = 0$, this equation has roots at $-p_j$ ($j = 1, 2, ..., n$), which are the open-loop poles. The root loci, therefore, start at the open-loop poles.

The characteristic equation (7.25) can be rearranged as

$$\frac{1}{K} \prod_{j=1}^{n} (s + p_j) + \prod_{i=1}^{m} (s + z_i) = 0$$

When $K = \infty$, this equation has roots at $-z_i$ ($i = 1, 2, ..., m$), which are the open-loop zeros. Therefore, m root loci terminate on the open-loop zeros.

In case $m < n$, the open-loop transfer function has $(n - m)$ zeros at infinity. Examining the magnitude criterion (7.23b) in the form

$$\frac{\displaystyle\prod_{i=1}^{m} |s + z_i|}{\displaystyle\prod_{j=1}^{n} |s + p_j|} = \frac{1}{K}$$

we find that this is satisfied by $s \to \infty \, e^{j\phi}$ as $K \to \infty$. Therefore, $(n - m)$ root loci terminate on infinity.

Rule 3   Asymptotes to Root Loci

The $(n - m)$ root loci which tend to infinity do so along straight line asymptotes radiating out from a single point $s = -\sigma_A$ on the real axis (called the centroid), where

$$-\sigma_A = \frac{\sum (\text{real parts of open-loop poles}) - \sum (\text{real parts of open-loop zeros})}{n - m} \qquad (7.26a)$$

These $(n - m)$ asymptotes have angles

$$\phi_A = \frac{(2q + 1)\,180°}{n - m}; \quad q = 0, 1, ..., (n - m - 1) \qquad (7.26b)$$

We justify the rule by using the pole-zero pattern shown in Fig. 7.11a. For a point s_0 far away from the origin, the poles and zeros can be considered to cluster at the same point, say $-\sigma_A$, as shown in Fig. 7.11b.

Consequently, the characteristic equation in (7.22a) can be approximated by

$$1 + \frac{K \displaystyle\prod_{i=1}^{m} (s + z_i)}{\displaystyle\prod_{j=1}^{n} (s + p_j)} \cong 1 + \frac{K}{(s + \sigma_A)^{n-m}} = 0 \qquad (7.27)$$

In other words, all m zeros are cancelled by poles, and only $(n - m)$ poles are left at $-\sigma_A$. Now we compute the relationship among z_i, p_j, and $-\sigma_A$. From Eqn. (7.27), we obtain

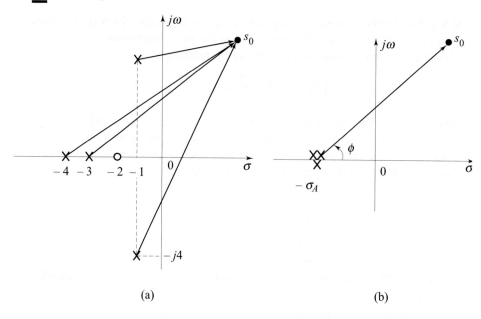

(a)   (b)

Fig. 7.11 *Asymptotes to root loci*

$$\frac{\prod\limits_{j=1}^{n}(s+p_j)}{\prod\limits_{i=1}^{m}(s+z_i)} \cong (s+\sigma_A)^{n-m}$$

or

$$\frac{s^n + \left(\sum\limits_{j=1}^{n} p_j\right) s^{n-1} + \cdots + \prod\limits_{j=1}^{n} p_j}{s^m + \left(\sum\limits_{i=1}^{m} z_i\right) s^{m-1} + \cdots + \prod\limits_{i=1}^{m} z_i} \cong (s+\sigma_A)^{n-m}$$

which implies, by direct division and expansion,

$$s^{n-m} + \left(\sum\limits_{j=1}^{n} p_j - \sum\limits_{i=1}^{m} z_j\right) s^{n-m-1} + \cdots$$

$$\cong s^{n-m} + (n-m)\sigma_A \, s^{n-m-1} + \cdots$$

Equating the coefficients of s^{n-m-1} yields

$$(n-m)\sigma_A = \sum\limits_{j=1}^{n} p_j - \sum\limits_{i=1}^{m} z_i$$

or

$$-\sigma_A = \frac{\sum\limits_{j=1}^{n}(-p_j) - \sum\limits_{i=1}^{m}(-z_i)}{n-m}$$

This establishes Eqn. (7.26a).

For the point s_0 in Fig. 7.11b to be on the root locus,

$$- (n - m)\phi = - (2q + 1)\ 180°;\ q = 0, 1, \ldots$$

or

$$\phi = \frac{(2q + 1)\ 180°}{n - m};\ q = 0, 1, \ldots$$

The $(n - m)$ angles given by this equation divide $360°$ equally and are symmetric with respect to real axis. The $(n - m)$ root loci, therefore, tend to infinity along $(n - m)$ asymptotes radiating out from $s = - \sigma_A$ given by Eqn. (7.26a) at angles ϕ_A given by Eqn. (7.26b).

The pole-zero map of Fig. 7.11a corresponds to

$$F(s) = \frac{K(s + 2)}{(s + 1 + j4)\ (s + 1 - j4)\ (s + 3)\ (s + 4)} \tag{7.28a}$$

The root locus plot of

$$1 + F(s) = 0 \tag{7.28b}$$

will consist of four root loci, each starting from an open-loop pole with $K = 0$. One root locus will terminate on open-loop zero with $K = \infty$. The other three loci will terminate on infinity as $K \to \infty$ along the asymptotes radiating out from $s = - \sigma_A$

where

$$- \sigma_A = \frac{-1 - 1 - 3 - 4 - (-2)}{4 - 1} = - 7/3$$

at angles $60°$, $180°$, and $300°$ respectively. Figure 7.12 shows the asymptotes. Note that asymptotes are developed for large s; thus the root loci will *approach* them for large s or large K.

Rule 4 *On-Locus Segments of the Real Axis*

A point on the real axis lies on the locus if the number of open-loop poles plus zeros on the real axis to the right of this point is odd.

For the fourth-order example under consideration (refer Eqns (7.28)), open-loop pole-zero configuration is shown in Fig. 7.13a. Let us examine any point s_0 on the real axis. As this point is joined by phasors to all the open-loop poles and zeros, it is easily seen that (i) the poles and zeros on the real axis to the right of this point contribute an angle of $180°$ each, (ii) the poles and zeros on the real axis to the left of this point contribute an angle of $0°$ each, and (iii) the net angle contribution of a complex conjugate pole or zero pair is always zero. Therefore,

$$\angle F(s) = (m_r - n_r)180° = \pm (2q + 1)180°,\ q = 0, 1, 2, \ldots$$

where

m_r = number of open-loop zeros on the real axis to the right of s_0; and
n_r = number of open-loop poles on the real axis to the right of s_0.

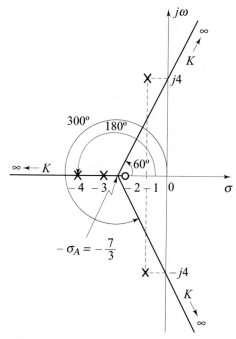

Fig. 7.12 *Asymptotes for the characteristic equation (7.28)*

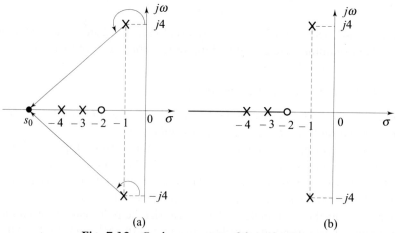

Fig. 7.13 *On-locus segments of the real axis*

We therefore see that for a point on the real axis, the angle criterion is met only if $(n_r - m_r)$ or $(n_r + m_r)$ is odd and hence the rule. If this rule is satisfied at any point on the real axis, it continues to be satisfied as the point is moved on either side unless the point crosses a real axis pole or zero. By use of this additional fact, the real axis can be divided into segments *on-locus* and *not-on-locus*; the dividing points being the real open-loop poles and zeros. The on-locus segments of the real axis alternate as shown in Fig. 7.13b.

Rule 5   On-Locus Points of the Imaginary Axis

The intersections (if any) of root loci with the imaginary axis can be determined by use of the Routh criterion.

Segments of root loci can exist in the right half of s-plane. This signifies instability. The points at which the root loci cross the imaginary axis define the stability limits. Basic application of the Routh array (Chapter 5) determines the gains at the stability limit. By substituting this value of gain in the auxiliary equation, the value of $s = j\omega_0$ at the stability limit is evaluated.

For the fourth-order example under consideration (refer Eqn. (7.28)), the characteristic equation is

$$1 + \frac{K(s+2)}{(s+1+j4)(s+1-j4)(s+3)(s+4)} = 0.$$

which is equivalent to

$$s^4 + 9s^3 + 43s^2 + (143 + K)s + 204 + 2K = 0 \qquad (7.29)$$

The Routh array for the characteristic polynomial is

s^4	1	43	$204 + 2K$
s^3	9	$143 + K$	
s^2	$\dfrac{244 - K}{9}$	$204 + 2K$	
s^1	$\dfrac{18368 - 61K - K^2}{244 - K}$		
s^0	$204 + K$		

For Eqn. (7.29) to have no roots on $j\omega$-axis or in the right-half s-plane, the elements in the first column of Routh array must all be of the same sign. Therefore, the following inequalities must be satisfied:

$$244 - K > 0$$
$$18368 - 61K - K^2 > 0$$
$$204 + K > 0$$

These inequalities are satisfied if K is less than 108.4, which means that the critical value of K which corresponds to the roots on the $j\omega$-axis is 108.4.

The value of $K = 108.4$ makes all the coefficients of s^1-row of the Routh array zero. For this value of K, the auxiliary equation formed from the coefficient of the s^2-row, is given by

$$\left(\frac{244 - K}{9}\right) s^2 + (204 + 2K) = 0$$

For $K = 108.4$, the roots of the above equation lie on the $j\omega$-axis and are given by

$$s = \pm j5.28$$

Thus the root loci intersect the $j\omega$-axis at $s = \pm j5.28$ and the value of K corresponding to these roots is 108.4.

Rule 6   Angle of Departure from Complex Poles

The angle to departure, ϕ_p, of a locus from a complex open-loop pole is given by

$$\phi_p = 180° + \phi \tag{7.30}$$

where ϕ is the net angle contribution at this pole of all other open-loop poles and zeros.

For the fourth-order example under consideration (refer Eqn. (7.28)), the characteristic equation is

$$1 + F(s) = 1 + \frac{K(s+2)}{(s+1+j4)\,(s+1-j4)\,(s+3)\,(s+4)} = 0$$

The pole-zero map of $F(s)$ is shown in Fig. 7.14. Let s_0 be an arbitrary point on the root locus starting from the pole at $s = -1 + j4$. Let the phase from this

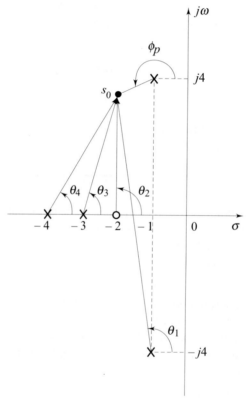

Fig. 7.14   *Angle of departure from complex poles*

pole to s_0 be denoted by ϕ_p. The net angle contribution of all other open-loop poles and zeros at the point s_0 is

$$\phi = \theta_2 - (\theta_1 + \theta_3 + \theta_4)$$

Therefore the total phase of $F(s)$ at s_0 is $\phi - \phi_p$. In order for s_0 to be on the root locus, the total phase must be $\pm 180°$. Thus we have $\phi_p = 180° + \phi$. This is the angle of departure from the complex open-loop pole.

If the point s_0 is very close to the pole at $-1 + j4$, then the vectors drawn from the zero and all other open-loop poles to s_0 can be approximated by the vectors drawn to the pole at $-1 + j4$, i.e., we consider the point s_0 to be at $-1 + j4$ for measurement of angles θ_1, θ_2, θ_3, and θ_4. Under this approximation, $\theta_1 = 90°$, $\theta_2 = 76°$, $\theta_3 = 63°$, and $\theta_4 = 53°$. Therefore

$$\phi = \theta_2 - (\theta_1 + \theta_3 + \theta_4) = -130°; \; \phi_p = 180° + \phi = 50°$$

We can now sketch a rough root locus plot for the fourth-order example under consideration. The plot is shown in Fig. 7.15. The information given in Figs 7.12–7.14 has been used to construct this plot.

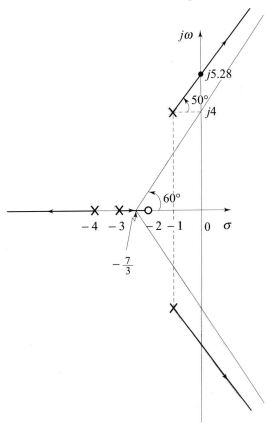

Fig. 7.15 *Root locus plot for the characteristic equation (7.28)*

There are four open-loop poles; so there are four loci. One locus departs from the real pole at -3 and terminates on the zero at -2 along the real axis. The second locus departs from another real pole at -4 and moves along the asymptote on the negative real axis. The third locus departs from the complex pole at $-1 + j4$ with a departure angle of $\phi_p = 50°$, and moves toward the asymptote radiating out from $-\sigma_A = -7/3$ at an angle $+60°$; it crosses the imaginary axis at $j\omega_0 = j5.28$. Using the symmetry property, the fourth locus is obtained immediately by reflection about the real axis.

Rule 7   *Angle of Arrival at Complex Zeros*

The angle of arrival, ϕ_z, of a locus at a complex zero is given by

$$\phi_z = 180° - \phi \qquad (7.31)$$

where ϕ is the net angle contribution at this zero of all other open-loop poles and zeros.

Consider the characteristic equation

$$1 + F(s) = 1 + \frac{K(s^2 + 1)}{s(s+2)} = 0 \qquad (7.32)$$

The pole-zero map of $F(s)$ is shown in Fig. 7.16. The open-loop poles are located at $s = 0$ and $s = -2$ and the open-loop zeros are located at $s = \pm j1$. Let s_0 be an arbitrary point on the root locus terminating on the zero at $s = j1$. Let the phase from this zero to s_0 be denoted by ϕ_z (refer Fig. 7.16a).

If the point s_0 is very close to the zero at $j1$, then the vectors drawn from the other zero at $-j1$ and open-loop poles at 0 and -2 to s_0 can be approximated by vectors drawn to the zero at $j1$. Under this approximation, the net angle contribution at s_0 of the zero at $-j1$ and open-loop poles at 0 and -2 is given by (refer Fig. 7.16b)

$$\phi = 90° - 90° - 26.5° = -26.5°$$

In order for s_0 to be on the root locus, the total phase must be $\pm 180°$. Thus we have $\phi_z = 180° - \phi = 206.5°$.

The complete root locus plot for roots of Eqn. (7.32) is shown in Fig. 7.16; it can easily be proved (refer Example 7.2) that the complex root branches lie on a circle with centre at $(1/2, 0)$ and radius equal to $\sqrt{5}/2$.

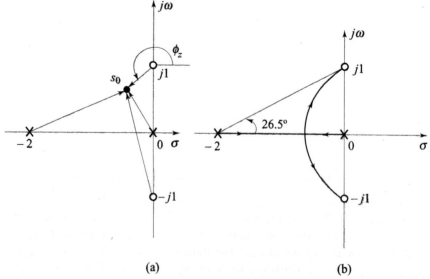

(a)   (b)

Fig. 7.16   *Angle of arrival at complex zeros*

Rule 8   Locations of Multiple Roots

Points at which multiple roots of the characteristic equation occur (breakaway points of root loci) are the solutions of

$$\frac{dK}{ds} = 0 \tag{7.33a}$$

where
$$K = - \frac{\prod\limits_{j=1}^{n}(s + p_j)}{\prod\limits_{i=1}^{m}(s + z_i)} \tag{7.33b}$$

Assume that the characteristic equation (7.22a) has a multiple root at $s = s_0$ of multiplicity r.

Then
$$1 + F(s) = (s - s_0)^r M(s) \tag{7.34}$$

where $M(s)$ does not contain the factor $(s - s_0)$.

Differentiating Eqn. (7.34) with respect to s, we have

$$\frac{dF(s)}{ds} = (s - s_0)^{r-1} [rM(s) + (s - s_0)M'(s)] \tag{7.35}$$

where $M'(s)$ represents the derivative of $M(s)$.

At $s = s_0$, the right hand side of this equation is zero because it has a factor $(s - s_0)^{r-1}$ and $r \geq 2$. Therefore, at $s = s_0$,

$$\frac{dF(s)}{ds} = 0$$

In pole-zero form, the characteristic equation may be written as

$$1 + F(s) = 1 + \frac{K \prod\limits_{i=1}^{m}(s + z_i)}{\prod\limits_{j=1}^{n}(s + p_j)} = 1 + \frac{KB(s)}{A(s)} = 0 \tag{7.36a}$$

Taking the derivative of this equation with respect to s, we get

$$\frac{dF(s)}{ds} = K\frac{A(s)B'(s) - A'(s)B(s)}{[A(s)]^2} = 0$$

Therefore, the breakaway points are given by the roots of

$$A(s)B'(s) - A'(s)B(s) = 0 \tag{7.36b}$$

This equation can equivalently be represented as

$$\frac{dK}{ds} = 0 \qquad (7.36c)$$

where
$$K = \frac{A(s)}{B(s)} = -\frac{\displaystyle\prod_{j=1}^{n}(s + p_j)}{\displaystyle\prod_{i=1}^{m}(s + z_i)}$$

Consider the characteristic equation

$$1 + \frac{K(s+2)(s+3)}{s(s+1)} = 1 + \frac{KB(s)}{A(s)} = 0 \qquad (7.37)$$

Figure 7.17 shows open-loop poles and zeros on the complex plane. Root loci segments exist on the negative real axis between 0 and -1 and between -2 and -3. At $K = 0$, the roots are at $s = 0$ and $s = -1$. As K increases, the two real roots move away from poles $s = 0$ and $s = -1$ toward each other inside the real-axis segment $[-1, 0]$. As K continues to increase, the two real roots will eventually coalesce into a repeated real root and then break away from the real axis into two complex conjugate roots. Such a point is called a *breakaway point*.

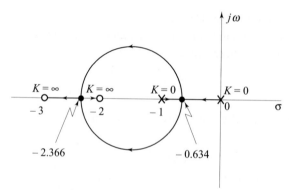

Fig. 7.17   *Root locus plot for characteristic equation (7.37)*

Similarly, as K approaches infinity, one root will approach zero at $s = -2$ along the negative real axis and another will approach zero at $s = -3$ along the negative real axis. As the root loci are continuous, the two complex-conjugate roots will approach the real axis somewhere inside the segment $[-3, -2]$ and then depart in opposite directions along the real axis. Such a point is also called a *breakaway point*.

From Eqns (7.36)–(7.37), we have

$$B(s) = (s + 2)(s + 3) = s^2 + 5s + 6; \; B'(s) = 2s + 5$$
$$A(s) = s(s + 1) = s^2 + s; \; A'(s) = 2s + 1$$

and $A(s)B'(s) - A'(s)B(s) = (s^2 + s)(2s + 5) - (2s + 1)(s^2 + 5s + 6)$
$$= -3s^2 - 12s - 6 = 0$$

Its roots are -0.634 and -2.366. Thus the root locus plot has two break-away points: $s = -0.634$ and $s = -2.366$.

The complete root locus plot for roots of Eqn. (7.37) is shown in Fig. 7.17; it can easily be proved (refer to Example 7.1) that the complex root branches lie on a circle with centre at $(-1.5, 0)$ that passes through the breakaway points.

It is important to note that the condition for the breakaway point given by Eqns (7.33) is *necessary* but not *sufficient*. In other words, all breakaway points on the root locus must satisfy Eqns (7.33) but not all solutions of Eqns (7.33) are breakaway points. To be a breakaway point, the solution of Eqns (7.33) must satisfy the characteristic equation (7.22) for some real K. This and many other important aspects of breakaway points will be illustrated through examples in the next section.

▲▲

Except for extremely complex cases, the rules described above should be adequate for making a reasonably accurate sketch of the root locus plot. For quick reference, these rules are summarized in Table 7.1.

Table 7.1 *Rules for construction of Root Locus Plot of*

$$1 + F(s) = 0; \quad F(s) = \frac{K \prod\limits_{i=1}^{m}(s + z_i)}{\prod\limits_{j=1}^{n}(s + p_j)}; \quad K \geq 0, n \geq m$$

z_i: m open-loop zeros; p_j: n open-loop poles

Rules
(i) The root locus plot consists of n root loci as K varies from 0 to ∞. The loci are symmetric with respect to the real axis.
(ii) As K increases from zero to infinity, each root locus originates from an open-loop pole with $K = 0$ and terminates either on an open-loop zero or on infinity with $K = \infty$. The number of loci terminating on infinity equals the number of open-loop poles minus zeros.
(iii) The $(n - m)$ root loci which tend to infinity, do so along straight-line asymptotes radiating out from a single point $s = -\sigma_A$ on the real axis (called the centroid), where $$-\sigma_A = \frac{\sum(\text{real parts of open-loop poles}) - \sum(\text{real parts of open-loop zeros})}{n - m}$$ These $(n - m)$ asymptotes have angles $$\phi_A = \frac{(2q + 1)180°}{n - m}; \quad q = 0, 1, \ldots, (n - m - 1)$$
(iv) A point on the real axis lies on the locus if the number of open-loop poles plus zeros on the real axis to the right of this point is odd. By use of this fact,

the real axis can be divided into segments *on-locus* and *not-on-locus*; the dividing points being the real open-loop poles and zeros.

(v) The intersections (if any) of root loci with the imaginary axis can be determined by use of the Routh criterion.

(vi) The angle of departure, ϕ_p, of a root locus from a complex open-loop pole is given by

$$\phi_p = 180° + \phi$$

where ϕ is the net angle contribution at this pole of all other open-loop poles and zeros.

(vii) The angle of arrival, ϕ_z, of a locus at a complex zero is given by

$$\phi_z = 180° - \phi$$

where ϕ is the net angle contribution at this zero of all other open-loop poles and zeros.

(viii) Points at which multiple roots of the characteristic equation occur (breakaway points of root loci) are the solutions of $\dfrac{dK}{ds} = 0$

where $K = -\dfrac{\prod\limits_{j=1}^{n}(s + p_j)}{\prod\limits_{i=1}^{m}(s + z_i)}$

(ix) The gain K at any point s_0 on a root locus is given by

$$K = \frac{\prod\limits_{j=1}^{n}|s_0 + p_j|}{\prod\limits_{i=1}^{m}|s_0 + z_i|} = \frac{\text{[Product of phasor lengths (read to scale)}}{\text{[Product of phasor lengths (read to scale)}}$$

[Product of phasor lengths (read to scale) from s_0 to poles of $F(s)$]

[Product of phasor lengths (read to scale) from s_0 to zeros of $F(s)$]

7.4 SELECTED ILLUSTRATIVE ROOT LOCI

The root locus concept was introduced in Section 7.2 and locus equations were derived in Examples 7.1 and 7.2 for two simple characteristic equations. Since for complex cases, it is not possible to derive easily interpretable locus equations, point-by-point plotting of the root loci becomes necessary. In Section 7.3, we presented some construction rules which help in making a quick rough sketch of the root locus plot.

In order to gain experience with the root-locus method, it is helpful to sketch a number of locus plots and visualize the various alternative shapes a locus of a given complexity can take. In this section, we will go through the construction rules for several cases selected to illustrate important features of root loci.

*Example 7.3*_____

Consider a feedback system with the characteristic equation

$$1 + \frac{K}{s(s+1)(s+2)} = 0; \; K \geq 0 \tag{7.38}$$

The open-loop poles are located at $s = 0, -1$ and -2, while there are no finite open-loop zeros. The pole-zero configuration is shown in Fig. 7.18.

Rule (i) (refer Table 7.1) tells us that the root locus plot consists of three root loci as K is varied from 0 to ∞.

Rule (ii) tells us that the three root loci originate from the three open-loop poles with $K = 0$ and terminate on infinity with $K = \infty$.

Rule (iii) tells us that the three root loci tend to infinity along asymptotes radiating out from

$$s = -\sigma_A = \frac{\sum \text{real parts of poles} \ - \ \sum \text{real parts of zeros}}{\text{number of poles} \ - \ \text{number of zeros}} = \frac{-2-1}{3} = -1$$

with angles
$$\phi_A = \frac{(2q+1)\,180°}{\text{number of poles} - \text{number of zeros}}; q = 0, 1, \dots$$

$$= \frac{(2q+1)\,180°}{3}; q = 0, 1, 2$$

$$= 60°, 180°, 300°$$

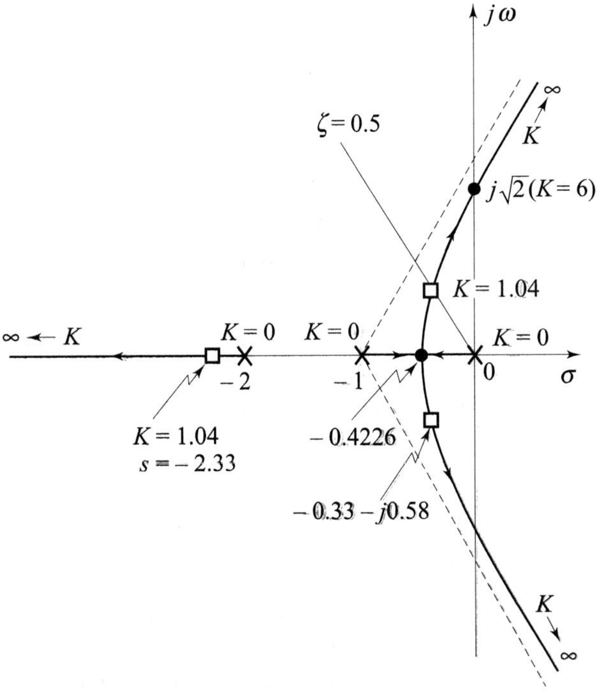

Fig. 7.18 *Root locus plot for the characteristic equation (7.38)*

The asymptotes are shown by dotted lines in Fig. 7.18.

Rule (iv) tells us that the segments of the real axis between 0 and -1, and between -2 and $-\infty$ lie on the root locus. On-locus segments of the real axis are shown by thick lines in Fig. 7.18.

From Fig. 7.18, it is seen that out of the three loci, one is a real-root locus which originates from $s = -2$ and terminates on $-\infty$. The other two loci originate from $s = 0$ and $s = -1$, and move on the real axis approaching each other as K is increased. These two loci must therefore meet on the real axis. The characteristic equation has a double root at such a point. As the gain K is further increased, the root loci breakaway from the real axis to give a complex conjugate pair of roots.

Rule (v) tells us to check by use of the Routh criterion if the two root loci breaking away from the real axis will intersect the imaginary axis. The system characteristics equation is

$$s(s + 1)(s + 2) + K = 0$$

or

$$s^3 + 3s^2 + 2s + K = 0$$

The Routh array becomes

s^3	1	2
s^2	3	K
s^1	$(6 - K)/3$	
s^0	K	

For all the roots of the characteristic equation to lie to the left of the imaginary axis, the following conditions must be satisfied:

$$K > 0; \ (6 - K)/3 > 0$$

Therefore the critical value of K which corresponds to the location of roots on the $j\omega$-axis is 6. This value of K makes all the coefficients of s^1-row of Routh array zero. The auxiliary equation formed from the coefficients of the s^2-row is given by

$$3s^2 + K = 3s^2 + 6 = 0$$

The roots of this equation lie on the $j\omega$-axis and are given by

$$s = \pm j\sqrt{2}$$

Thus the complex-root branches intersect the $j\omega$-axis at $s = \pm j\sqrt{2}$, and the value of K corresponding to these roots is 6.

The characteristic equation under consideration does not require application of rules (vi) and (vii).

Rule (viii) is used below to determine the breakaway points.

From the characteristic equation of the system,

$$K = -s(s + 1)(s + 2) = -(s^3 + 3s^2 + 2s)$$

Differentiating this equation, we get

$$\frac{dK}{ds} = -(3s^2 + 6s + 2)$$

The roots of the equation $dK/ds = 0$, are $s_{1,2} = -0.4226, -1.5774$

From Fig. 7.18, we see that the breakaway point must lie between 0 and -1. Therefore $s = -0.4226$ corresponds to the breakaway point. The other solution of the equation $dK/ds = 0$ is $s = -1.5774$. This solution is not on the root locus (it does not satisfy Eqn. (7.38) for any $K \geq 0$) and therefore does not represent a breakaway point. The derivative condition $dK/ds = 0$ is therefore necessary but not sufficient to indicate a breakaway, or multiple-root situation.

If two loci breakaway from a breakaway point, then their tangents will be 180° apart. In general, as we shall see in other illustrative examples, if r loci breakaway from a breakaway point, then their tangents will be 360°/r apart, i.e., the tangents will equally divide 360°.

With the information obtained through the use of these rules, the root locus is sketched in Fig. 7.18 from where it is seen that for $K > 6$, the system has two closed-loop poles in the right half of the s-plane and is thus unstable.

It is important to note that the root locus plot given in Fig. 7.18 is only a rough sketch; it gives qualitative information about the behaviour of the closed-loop system when the parameter K is varied. For quantitative analysis, the loci or specific segments of the loci need be constructed with sufficient accuracy.

Suppose it is required to determine dominant closed-loop poles with damping ratio $\zeta = 0.5$. A closed-loop pole with $\zeta = 0.5$ lies on a line passing through the origin and making an angle $\cos^{-1} \zeta = \cos^{-1} 0.5 = 60°$ with the negative real axis. The point of intersection of the ζ-line with the rough sketch of the root locus plot gives the first guess. In the region where the rough root locus sketch intersects the ζ-line, a trial-and-error procedure is adapted along the ζ-line by applying the angle criterion to determine the point of intersection accurately. From Fig. 7.18, we see that the point $-0.33 + j0.58$, which lies on the ζ-line, satisfies the angle criterion. Therefore the dominant closed-loop poles of the system are $s_{1,2} = -0.33 \pm j0.58$.

The value of K that yields these poles is found from the magnitude criterion as follows:

$$K = \{|s| \, |s + 1| \, |s + 2|\}_{s = -0.33 + j0.58}$$

= Product of the distances from the open-loop poles to the point $-0.33 + j0.58$

$$= 0.667 \times 0.886 \times 1.768 = 1.04$$

The third closed-loop pole will lie on the third locus which is along the negative real axis. We need to guess a test point, compute a trial gain, and correct the guess until we found the point where $K = 1.04$. Using this trial-and-error procedure, we find from Fig. 7.18 that the point $s = -2.33$ corresponds to $K = 1.04$. Therefore, the third closed-loop pole is at $s = -2.33$.

The closed-loop transfer function of the system under consideration is

$$M(s) = \frac{1.04}{(s + 0.33 - j0.58)\,(s + 0.33 + j0.58)\,(s + 2.33)}$$

Example 7.4

Consider a feedback system with the characteristic equation

$$1 + \frac{K}{s(s + 3)\left(s^2 + 2s + 2\right)} = 0; \; K \geq 0 \tag{7.39}$$

The open-loop poles are located at $s = 0, -3, -1 + j1$ and $-1 - j1$, while there are no finite open-loop zeros. The pole-zero configuration is shown in Fig. 7.19.

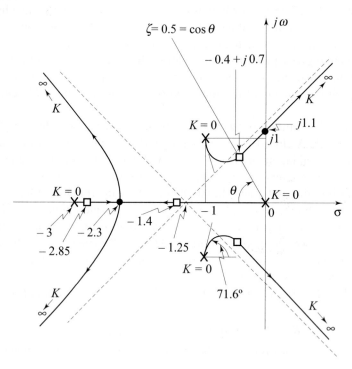

Fig. 7.19 *Root locus plot for the characteristics equation (7.39)*

Rule (i) tells us that the root locus plot consists of four root loci as K is varied from 0 to ∞.

Rule (ii) tells us that the four root loci originate from the four open-loop poles with $K = 0$ and terminate on infinity with $K = \infty$.

Rule (iii) tells us that the four root loci tend to infinity along asymptotes radiating out from

$$s = -\sigma_A = \frac{-3-1-1}{4} = -1.25$$

with angles

$$\phi_A = \frac{(2q+1)180°}{4}; \quad q = 0, 1, 2, 3$$

$$= 45°, 135°, 225°, 315°$$

The asymptotes are shown by dotted lines in Fig. 7.19.

Rule (iv) tells us that root loci exist on the real axis for $-3 \le s \le 0$; shown by thick line on the real axis in Fig. 7.19.

Rule (v) tells us to check by use of the Routh criterion if the root loci will intersect the imaginary axis. The system characteristic equation is

$$s(s + 3)(s^2 + 2s + 2) + K = 0$$

or

$$s^4 + 5s^3 + 8s^2 + 6s + K = 0$$

The Routh array becomes

s^4	1	8	K
s^3	5	6	
s^2	34/5	K	
s^1	$\dfrac{\{(204/5) - 5K\}}{34/5}$		
s^0	K		

Examination of the elements in the first column of the Routh array reveals that the root loci will intersect the imaginary axis at a value of K given by

$$(204/5) - 5K = 0$$

from which $K = 8.16$.

The auxiliary equation, formed from the coefficients of the s^2-row when $K = 8.16$, is

$$(34/5)s^2 + 8.16 = 0$$

from which $s = \pm j1.1$.

Therefore, purely imaginary closed-loop poles of the system are located at $s = \pm j1.1$ as shown in Fig. 7.19; the value of K corresponding to these poles is 8.16.

Rule (vi) tells us that a root locus leaves the pole at $s = -1 + j1$ at angle ϕ_p, given by (refer Fig. 7.19)

$$\phi_p = 180° + [-135° - 90° - 26.6°] = -71.6°$$

The characteristic equation under consideration does not require application of rule (vii).

Rule (viii) is used below to determine the breakaway points.

From the characteristic equation of the system,

$$K = -s(s + 3)(s^2 + 2s + 2)$$
$$= -(s^4 + 5s^3 + 8s^2 + 6s)$$

Differentiating this equation, we get

$$\frac{dK}{ds} = -4(s^3 + 3.75s^2 + 4s + 1.5)$$

The solutions to the cubic

$$s^3 + 3.75s^2 + 4s + 1.5 = 0 \qquad (7.40)$$

are the possible breakaway points.

From Fig. 7.19, we see that a breakaway point must lie between 0 and -3 on the real axis. By trial-and-error procedure, we find that $s = -2.3$ satisfies Eqn. (7.40) to a reasonable accuracy (when $dK/ds = 0$ is of order higher than 2, root solving software may be used to obtain the solutions of $dK/ds = 0$). The other two solutions of Eqn. (7.40) are $s_{1,2} = -0.725 \pm j0.365$.

It can easily be checked that $-0.725 \pm j0.365$ are not the root locus points as the angle criterion is not met at these points.

The root locus plot, therefore, has only one breakaway point at $s = -2.3$. Tangents to the two loci breaking away from this point will be 180° part.

With the information obtained through the use of these rules, the root locus plot is sketched in Fig. 7.19 from where it is seen that for $K > 8.16$, the system has two closed-loop poles in the right half of s-plane and is thus unstable.

Dominant roots of the characteristic equation with damping $\zeta = 0.5$ are determined as follows.

A ζ-line is drawn in the second quadrant at an angle of $\theta = \cos^{-1}0.5 = 60°$ with the negative real axis. By trial-and-error procedure, it is found that the point $s = -0.4 + j0.7$ which lies on the ζ-line, satisfies the angle criterion. Therefore the dominant roots of the characteristic equation are $s_{1,2} = -0.4 \pm j0.7$. The value of gain K at the dominant root is

$K =$ Product of distances from open-loop poles to the point $-0.4 + j0.7$
$= 0.84 \times 1.86 \times 2.74 \times 0.68 = 2.91$

The other two roots of the characteristic equation are obtained from the loci originating from the poles at $s = 0$ and $s = -3$. From Fig. 7.19, it is seen that at the double-root location $s = -2.3$, the value of K is 4.33:

$$K = \{|s||s + 3| |s + 1 + j1| |s + 1 - j1|\}_{s = -2.3}$$
$$= 2.3 \times 0.7 \times 1.64 \times 1.64 = 4.33$$

Therefore, the points corresponding to $K = 2.91$ must lie on the real-root segments of these loci. Using the trial-and-error procedure, it is found that the points $s = -1.4$ and $s = -2.85$ have gain $K = 2.91$. Thus the closed-loop transfer function of the system under consideration is

$$M(s) = \frac{2.91}{(s+0.4+j0.7)(s+0.4-j0.7)(s+1.4)(s+2.85)}$$

*Example 7.5*_____

In this example, we illustrate multiple roots of multiplicity more than two. Consider the root locus of $1 + F(s)$,

where
$$F(s) = \frac{K(s+1)}{s^2(s+9)}; \ K \geq 0$$

The pole-zero configuration is shown in Fig. 7.20.

Rule (i) tells us that the root locus plot consists of three root loci as K is varied from 0 to ∞.

Rule (ii) tells us that the three root loci originate from open-loop poles with $K = 0$; one of these terminates on the zero at $s = -1$ with $K = \infty$, and the other two terminate on infinity with $K = \infty$.

Rule (iii) tells us that the two root loci tend to infinity along asymptotes radiating out from

$$s = -\sigma_A = \frac{-9-0-(-1)}{3-1} = -4$$

with angles

$$\phi_A = \frac{(2q+1)180°}{3-1}; \ q = 0, 1$$
$$= 90°, 270°$$

The asymptotes are shown by dotted lines in Fig. 7.20.

Rule (iv) tells us that root loci exist on the real axis for $-9 \leq s \leq -1$; shown by thick line on the real axis in Fig. 7.20.

Rule (v) tells us to check by use of the Routh criterion if the root loci will intersect the imaginary axis. It is found that the root loci do not cross the imaginary axis.

The characteristics equation under consideration does not require application of rules (vi) and (vii).

Rule (viii) is used below to determine the breakaway points.

From the characteristic equation of the system,

$$K = -\frac{s^2(s+9)}{s+1} = -\frac{s^3+9s^2}{s+1}$$

Differentiating this equation, we get

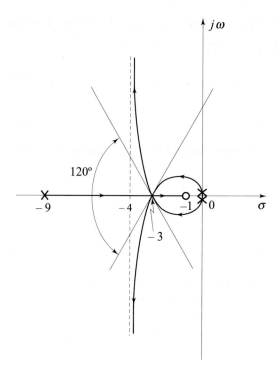

Fig. 7.20 *Root locus plot (Example 7.5)*

$$\frac{dK}{ds} = \frac{\left(s^3 + 9s^2\right) - (s+1)\left(3s^2 + 18s\right)}{(s+1)^2} = \frac{-2s(s+3)^2}{(s+1)^2}$$

Possible points of multiple roots are at $s = 0, -3, -3$, which are on the locus as seen in Fig. 7.20.

One feature of the breakaway point at $s = -3$ needs special attention. At $s = -3$, we have double root in the derivative dK/ds; which means that not only $dK/ds = 0$ at this point but d^2K/ds^2 is also zero. This equivalently means that (refer Eqns (7.36)) $d^2F(s)/ds^2 = 0$ at $s = -3$ which is possible only if $1 + F(s)$ has a root of multiplicity three at $s = -3$ (refer Eqn. (7.34)). Therefore the characteristic equation has three roots at $s = -3$; the three loci originating from the open-loop poles will approach this point and then break away. Tangents to the three loci breaking away from $s = -3$ will be $360°/3 = 120°$ apart.

Tangents to the two loci originating from $s = 0$ will be $180°$ apart.

With the information obtained through the use of these rules, the root locus is sketched in Fig. 7.20.

Example 7.6

In this example, we illustrate multiple roots off the real axis. Consider the root locus of $1 + F(s)$,

where $$F(s) = \frac{K}{s(s+2)\left(s^2 + 2s + 5\right)}; \; K \geq 0$$

The pole-zero configuration is shown in Fig. 7.21.

Rule (i) tells us that the root locus plot consists of four root loci as K is varied from 0 to ∞.

Rule (ii) tells us that the four loci originate from open-loop poles with $K = 0$ and terminate on infinity with $K = \infty$.

Rule (iii) tells us that the four loci tend to infinity along asymptotes radiating out from

$$s = -\sigma_A = \frac{-1-1-2}{4} = -1$$

with angles $$\phi_A = \frac{(2q+1)180°}{4}; \; q = 0, 1, 2, 3$$
$$= 45°, 135°, 225°, 315°$$

The asymptotes are shown by dotted lines in Fig. 7.21.

Rule (iv) tells us that root loci exist on the real axis for $-2 \leq s \leq 0$; shown by thick line on the real axis in Fig. 7.21.

Rule (v) tells us to check, by using the Routh criterion, if the root loci will intersect the imaginary axis.

The characteristic equation is

$$s(s+2)(s^2 + 2s + 5) + K = 0$$
or $$s^4 + 4s^3 + 9s^2 + 10s + K = 0$$

The Routh array becomes

s^4	1	9	K
s^3	4	10	
s^2	26/4	K	
s^1	$\dfrac{\{(260/4) - 4K\}}{26/4}$		
s^0	K		

Examination of the elements in the first column of the Routh array reveals that the root loci will intersect the imaginary axis at a value of K given by

$$(260/4) - 4K = 0$$

from which $K = 16.25$.

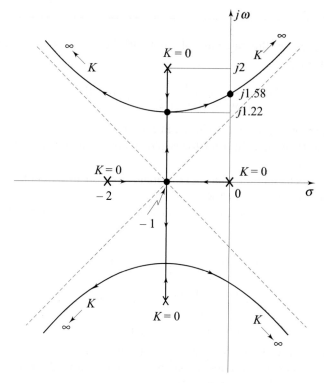

Fig. 7.21   *Root locus plot (Example 7.6)*

The auxiliary equation formed from the elements of s^2-row when $K = 16.25$, is

$$(26/4)s^2 + 16.25 = 0$$

from which $s = \pm\, j1.58$.

Therefore the root loci cross the imaginary axis at $s = \pm\, j1.58$; the value of K corresponding to these roots is 16.25.

Rule (vi) tells us that a root locus leaves the pole at $s = -1 + j2$ at angle ϕ_p, given by (refer Fig. 7.21)

$$\phi_p = 180° + [-116.6° - 90° - 63.4°] = -90°$$

In fact, we can observe at once that along the line $s = -1 + j\omega$, the angles contributed by the poles at $s = 0$ and $s = -2$ always add to 180°, and the angles contributed by the poles at $s = -1 + j2$ and $s = -1 - j2$ are respectively, $-90°$ and 90°; so the entire line from one complex pole to the other is on the locus *in this special case*.

The characteristic equation under consideration does not require application of rule (vii).

Rule (viii) is used below to determine the breakaway points.

From the characteristics equation of the system,

$$K = -s(s + 2)(s^2 + 2s + 5) = -(s^4 + 4s^3 + 9s^2 + 10s)$$

Differentiating this equation, we get

$$\frac{dK}{ds} = -4(s^3 + 3s^2 + 4.5s + 2.5)$$

We could find solutions to the cubic

$$s^3 + 3s^2 + 4.5s + 2.5 = 0,$$

but from the application of rule (vi) we know that the entire line $s = -1 + j\omega$ is on the locus; so there must be a breakaway at $s = -1$. Therefore $(s + 1)$ is one of the factors of the cubic. We can now easily show that

$$(s^3 + 3s^2 + 4.5s + 2.5) = (s + 1)(s + 1 + j1.22)(s + 1 - j1.22)$$

Since the solutions $-1 \pm j1.22$ are on the line between the complex poles, they are true points of multiple roots on the locus.

The complete root locus plot is sketched in Fig. 7.21. Notice that here we have complex multiple roots of multiplicity 2. Segments of the root loci come together at $-1 \pm j1.22$ and break away; tangents to the loci breaking away will be 180° apart.

7.5 | RESHAPING THE ROOT LOCUS

A simple control-system configuration of Fig. 7.22 is created by providing feedback around the plant $G_p(s)$ and adding an error signal amplifier with gain K_c. The amplifier gain is adjusted to provide acceptable performance, if possible. The system of Fig. 7.22 is often referred to as having *proportional compensation*.

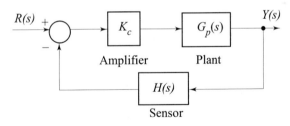

Fig. 7.22 *A simple control system configuration*

If the plant dynamics are of such a nature that a satisfactory design *cannot* be obtained by a gain adjustment alone, some dynamic compensation for the plant dynamics is required. A simple control-system configuration that includes dynamic compensation is shown in Fig. 7.23; the compensator $D_c(s)$ is placed in cascade with the forward-path transfer function $G_p(s)$. The system of Fig. 7.23 is often referred to as having *cascade compensation.*[5]

---

5. The term 'cascade compensation' used in Chapters 7–10 refers to the use of compensator (controller) in cascade (series) with the forward-path transfer function. It may be pointed out here that in process field, the term 'cascade control' is frequently used for feedback configurations having 'loop within a loop'.

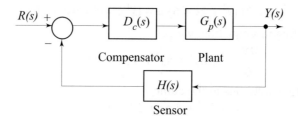

Fig. 7.23 *A control system with dynamic compensation*

The dynamic compensator will generally also have a gain K that has to be adjusted to improve steady-state accuracy, i.e., the transfer function $D_c(s)$ is typically of the form

$$\frac{K \prod_{i=1}^{m}(s + z_i)}{\prod_{j=1}^{n}(s + p_j)} \tag{7.41a}$$

$$= KD(s) \tag{7.41b}$$

For the purpose of simplifying the design procedure, we normally associate the adjustable gain parameter K with the plant transfer function and then design the dynamic compensator $D(s)$ given by Eqns (7.41) based on the new plant transfer function $KG_p(s)$. At the implementation stage, the gain K is associated with the compensator and the transfer function $D_c(s)$ is realized.

The configuration of Fig. 7.24a will accordingly be referred to as the *uncompensated system* and that of Fig. 7.24b as *compensated system*.

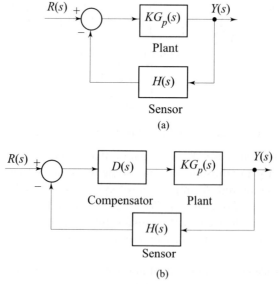

Fig. 7.24 *(a) Uncompensated system (b) Compensated system*

We introduce root-locus design through selected illustrative examples.

Design Problem 1

Consider the system of Fig. 7.25 which has an open-loop transfer function

$$G(s) = \frac{K_A}{s(s+1)\left(\frac{1}{5}s+1\right)}$$ (7.42)

From Eqn. (7.42), we have

$$G(s) = \frac{5K_A}{s(s+1)(s+5)} = \frac{K}{s(s+1)(s+5)}$$ (7.43)

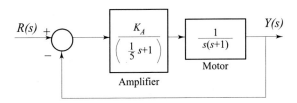

Fig. 7.25 *A position control system*

The root locus plot of the uncompensated system appears in Fig. 7.26.

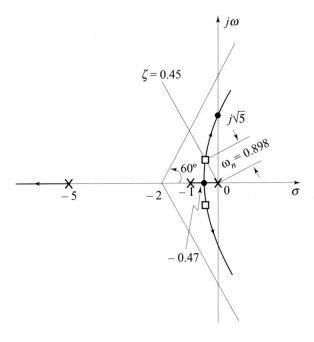

Fig. 7.26 *Root locus plot of* $1 + \dfrac{K}{s(s+1)(s+5)}$

Assume that the relative stability specification calls for a damping ratio $\zeta = 0.45$ (peak overshoot $\cong 20\%$). The ζ-line intersects the root locus at $s = -0.404 + j0.802$. For the dominant root pair, the undamped natural frequency ω_n is 0.898 rad/sec. The settling time ($= 4/\zeta\omega_n$) for the response is about 9.9 sec. The uncompensated system, therefore, has sluggish transient response.

In order to improve the speed of response, the root locus must be reshaped so that it is moved farther to the left, away from the imaginary axis. To accomplish this goal, let us consider the proposition of adding a compensating zero. Figure 7.27 shows the root locus plot of the system with the compensating zero placed at $s = -1.5$. Notice that the effect of the zero is to move the locus to the left, toward the more stable part of the plane. The $\zeta(= 0.45)$ line intersects the root locus at $-2.2 + j4.3$. For the dominant root pair, the undamped natural frequency ω_n is 4.85 rad/sec. The settling time for the response is therefore about 1.7 sec. Thus, the addition of a compensating zero helps to improve the speed of response for $\zeta = 0.45$.

A further observation about the effect of adding a compensating zero is made from Figs 7.26 and 7.27. Without the compensating zero, the real root in

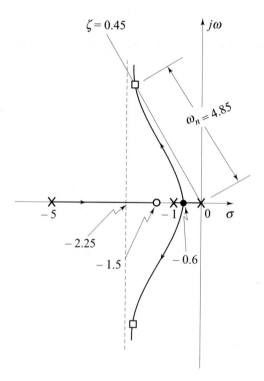

Fig. 7.27 *Root locus plot of* $1 + \dfrac{K(s + 1.5)}{s(s + 1)(s + 5)}$

addition to the dominant complex-root pair is always located to the left of the open-loop ploe at $s = -5$. On the other hand, in the presence of compensating zero, this root moves over to the right of $s = -5$ and the dominance condition is therefore weakend. Since the real root (which is the closed-loop pole) will be located close to the compensating zero, the amplitude of the response term due to this root will be small. Also, the time-constant of the real root will be comparable to that of complex dominant root-pair; therefore, its effect on settling time may be tolerable.

An acceptable transient response can generally be obtained by trial-and-error adjustments of the compensating zero on the real axis. It can easily be verified that if we place the compensating zero too far to the left (say, near the open-loop pole at $s = -5$), the dominance condition is improved but complex branches of the root locus are pressed toward the right and the dynamic response becomes poor. If, on the other hand, the zero is placed close to the origin (say, to the right of the open-loop pole at $s = -1$), the complex branches are advantageously far into the left, but a real root close to the origin appears. This root will also be close to the compensating zero; therefore amplitude of the response term due to this root may be small. However, since the real root will have a large time-constant compared to that of dominant complex root pair, its effect on settling time may be appreciable.

No general rule can be laid down for selecting the location of compensating zero that satisfactorily meets all the design requirements. Trial-and-error procedure is the best tool in hand. However, the following *guidelines* can be of considerable help.

Place the compensating zero on the real axis in the region below the desired closed-loop pole location such that it lies close to the left of any open-loop pole in this region. This technique ensures that the closed-loop pole on the real axis caused by the introduction of the compensating zero will be located close to it with a time-constant comparable to that of desired dominant closed-loop pole-pair, and would therefore make a negligible contribution to system dynamics. In case the uncompensated system does not have any open-loop pole in the region below the desired closed-loop poles, the dominance condition must be checked by locating the real-axis closed-loop pole created by the compensating zero.

The addition of a zero in the open-loop transfer function can be achieved by placing a compensator

$$D(s) = s + z = s + 1/\tau \tag{7.44}$$

in cascade with the forward path transfer function.

It is seen that the compensator given by Eqn. (7.44) is a form of proportional plus derivative (PD) controller

$$D(s) = K_c(1 + T_D s) = K_c T_D (s + 1/T_D) = K_c T_D (s + z)$$

The problem with PD compensation is that the inevitable high-frequency noise present at the input to the $D(s)$ will be greatly amplified. The usual method for overcoming this problem is to add a pole to the compensator transfer function which limits the high-frequency gain. The pole must of course be added such that it has relatively negligible effect on the root locus in the region where the two dominant closed-loop poles are to occur.

Figure 7.28 shows the root locus plot in the presence of both a compensating zero and a pole. The root locus near the dominant closed-loop poles gets somewhat modified by the presence of the compensating pole. The effect on the transient response of the system is not very pronounced. The $\zeta(= 0.45)$ line intersects the root locus at $s = -1.531 + j3.039$. For the dominant root-pair, the undamped natural frequency ω_n is 3.4 rad/sec. The settling time for the response is about 2.6 sec.

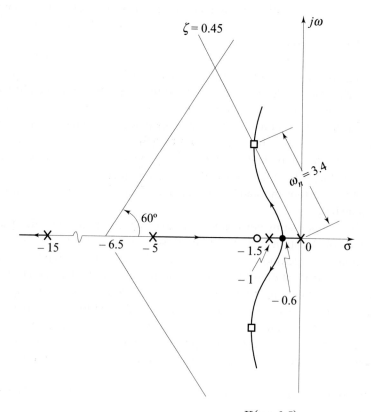

Fig. 7.28 *Root locus plot of* $1 + \dfrac{K(s + 1.5)}{s(s + 1)(s + 5)(s + 15)}$

As can be easily seen from Figs 7.27 and 7.28, the effect of the compensator pole is to press the locus toward the right. However, if the pole is added far away from the $j\omega$-axis, it has relatively negligible effect on the root locus in the region where the two dominant closed-loop poles are to occur.

The choice of the compensator pole location is a compromise between the conflicting effects of noise suppression and compensator effectiveness. In general, if the pole is too close to the zero, then the root locus moves back too far toward its uncompensated shape, and the zero is not successful in doing its job. On the other hand, if the pole is too far to the left, the magnification of noise at the output of $D(s)$ is too great and the motor or other actuator of the process will be overheated by noise energy. In many cases, a pole located at a distance from 3 to 10 times the value of the zero location resolves the conflict.

We see from the above discussion that the compensating pole must be located to the left of the compensating zero; both the pole and the zero confined to the left half of the s-plane. The transfer function of such a first-order compensator then becomes

$$D(s) = \frac{s + z}{s + p} = \frac{s + 1/\tau}{s + 1/\alpha\tau}; \ \alpha = \frac{z}{p} < 1, \ \tau > 0 \qquad (7.45)$$

Note that $\alpha < 1$ ensures that the pole is located to the left of the zero. The contribution of $D(s)$ to the angle criterion of the root locus is always positive. This type of compensator is called *lead compensator*. The name 'lead compensator' has a clearer meaning with respect to frequency-domain design, which is covered later in Chapter 10.

The physical realization of a lead compensator can be accomplished in many ways. Hardware and software implementation schemes commonly used in industrial practice are given in Chapter 11.

Concluding Comments

The system of Fig. 7.25 has an open-loop transfer function

$$G(s) = \frac{K}{s(s + 1)(s + 5)}$$

The root locus plot of this uncompensated system is shown in Fig. 7.26. A damping ratio $\zeta = 0.45$ yields the following pertinent data.

Dominant roots: $s_{1,2} = -0.404 \pm j0.802$

Root locus gain at s_1: $K = |s_1| |s_1 + 1| |s_1 + 5| = 4.188$

Velocity error constant: $K_v = \lim_{s \to 0} sG(s) = \dfrac{K}{5} = 0.838$

Undamped natural frequency: $\omega_n = 0.898$ rad/sec

Settling time (= $4/\zeta\omega_n$): $t_s = 9.9$ sec

Figure 7.28 is the root locus of lead-compensated system with open-loop transfer function

$$D(s)G(s) = \frac{K(s + 1.5)}{s(s + 1)(s + 5)(s + 15)}$$

A damping ratio $\zeta = 0.45$ yields the following pertinent data.

Dominant roots: $s_{1,2} = -1.531 \pm j3.039$

Root locus gain at s_1: $K = \dfrac{|s_1||s_1 + 1||s_1 + 5||s_1 + 15|}{|s_1 + 1.5|} = 220$

Velocity error constant: $K_v = \lim_{s \to 0} sD(s)G(s) = \dfrac{K(1.5)}{5 \times 15} = 4.4$

Undamped natural frequency: $\omega_n = 3.4$ rad/sec

Settling time: $t_s = 2.6$ sec

The positive angle contributed by the lead compensator shifts the root locus towards the left in the s-plane; this results in improvement in the dynamic response of the system. The lead compensator also helps to increase system error constant though to a limited extent.

In case of high demand on steady-state accuracy in addition to high demand on speed of response and margin of stability, it may not be possible to meet the objectives by lead compensation alone. In such cases, we design a lead compensator to meet the demand on the speed of response and the margin of stability, and look for an additional compensator that meets the steady-state accuracy demand without affecting the transient response of lead-compensated system. In the next design problem, we introduce such a compensation.

Design Problem 2

Consider the system of Fig. 7.25 which has an open-loop transfer function

$$G(s) = \frac{5K_A}{s(s + 1)(s + 5)} = \frac{K}{s(s + 1)(s + 5)} \tag{7.46}$$

The root locus plot of the uncompensated system appears in Fig. 7.26. Suppose that the relative stability specification calls for a damping ratio $\zeta = 0.45$. The ζ-line intersects the root locus at $s = -0.404 + j0.802$ for a value of $K = 4.188$. Therefore, the undamped natural frequency ω_n of the closed-loop system is 0.898 rad/sec, and the settling time ($= 4/\zeta\omega_n$) for the response is 9.9 sec. We assume that the dynamic response of the uncompensated system with $K = 4.188$ is satisfactory.

For the uncompensated system with $K = 4.188$, the velocity error constant

$$K_v = \lim_{s \to 0} sG(s) = \lim_{s \to 0} s\left\{ \frac{K}{s(s + 1)(s + 5)} \right\} = \frac{K}{5} = 0.898$$

and thus with a unit-ramp input (1 rad/sec), the steady-state error

$$e_{ss} = \frac{1}{K_v} = 1.114 \text{ rad}$$

which is too large. It is therefore required to raise the system K_v. To accomplish this, consider the proposition of adding a proportional plus integral (PI) controller in cascade with the plant transfer function in the forward path. A PI controller has transfer function of the form

$$D(s) = K_c \left(1 + \frac{1}{T_1 s}\right) = K_c \left(\frac{s + 1/T_I}{s}\right) = K_c \frac{(s + z)}{s} \qquad (7.47)$$

The PI controller, thus, adds a pole at $s = 0$ and a zero at $s = -z$ to the open-loop transfer function. System type increases by one because of the added open-loop pole at the origin. Hence, for stable design, the corresponding error constant is infinity and steady-state error is zero.

Let us now investigate the effects of the pole-zero pair of the PI controller on transient response of the system. It can easily be verified that the pole alone would move the root locus to the right, thereby making the system unstable. The zero must be near the pole in order to minimize the effect on the transient response. Figure 7.29 shows the root locus plot of the system with the compensating zero placed at $s = -0.01$; the compensating pole being at the origin. Notice that the angle contribution of the compensating pole-zero pair at the desired closed-loop pole $-0.404 \pm j0.802$ is negligibly small, and therefore the root locus in the vicinity of this point is not appreciably disturbed.

A further observation about the effect of adding pole-zero pair is made from Figs 7.26 and 7.29. Without the compensating pole-zero pair, the root locus has a real root in addition to the desired dominant complex root-pair $-0.404 \pm j0.802$. The real root is always located to the left of the open-loop pole at $s = -5$, and therefore its effect on transient response of the system will be negligible. On the other hand, in the presence of compensating pole-zero pair, there are two real roots in addition to the desired complex root-pair; one to the left of open-loop pole at $s = -5$ and the other on the real-axis segment between -0.02 and -0.01. The additional real root contributed by the compensating pole-zero pair is too close to the origin and therefore will have a very large time-constant, affecting the settling time appreciably. There is however a zero very close to this real root, and therefore the magnitude of the response term contributed by this root will be negligibly small. The closed-loop pole-zero *dipole* introduced by PI controller will not contribute significantly to the response of the closed-loop system.

It is desirable to place the compensating pole-zero combination as far to the left as possible without causing major shifts in the dominant root locations and giving required improvement in the steady-state response. The compensating pole-zero pair near the origin (the pole not necessarily at the origin) will give rise to a closed-loop pole-zero dipole shifted relatively to the left compared to the case of PI controller; therefore, the time-constant of the additional root will be relatively less resulting in a smaller effect on the settling time of the system. In system response, a long tail of small amplitude introduced by closed-loop dipole will decay relatively faster.

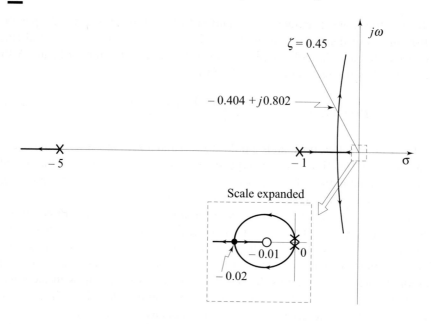

Fig. 7.29 *Root locus plot of* $1 + \dfrac{K(s+0.01)}{s^2(s+1)(s+5)}$

It can easily be verified that if the compensating pole-zero pair is placed too far to the left (say, on the real-axis segment to the left of desired dominant complex closed-loop poles), no significant improvement in the steady-state response is possible.

Figure 7.30 shows the root locus plot in the presence of compensating pole at $s = -0.005$ and the compensating zero at $s = -0.05$. The angle contributed by the compensator pole-zero pair at $s = -0.404 + j0.802$, which is the desired dominant root, is about 2.6° and is therefore acceptable. For the damping ratio $\zeta = 0.45$, the new locus is close to the locus of uncompensated system. The new dominant roots are $s_{1,2} = -0.384 \pm j0.763$; thus the roots are essentially unchanged.

For the compensated system adjusted to a damping ratio of 0.45, the following results are obtained.

Dominant roots: $s_{1,2} = -0.384 \pm j0.763$

Root locus gain at s_1: $K = \dfrac{|s_1||s_1+1||s_1+5||s_1+0.005|}{|s_1+0.05|} = 4.01$

Velocity error constant: $K_v = \lim\limits_{s \to 0} s \left\{ \dfrac{K(s+0.05)}{s(s+1)(s+5)(s+0.005)} \right\}$

$$= \frac{K(0.05)}{5 \times 0.005} = 8.02$$

Undamped natural frequency: $\omega_n = 0.854$ rad/sec.

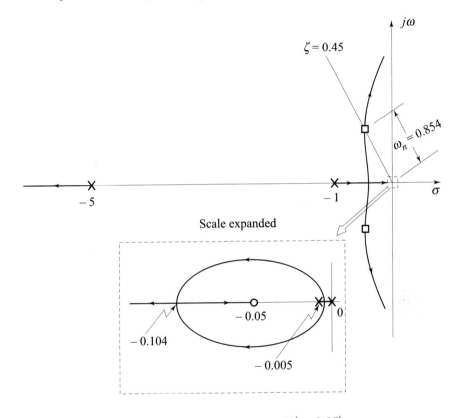

Fig. 7.30 *Root locus plot of* $1 + \dfrac{K(s+0.05)}{s(s+0.005)(s+1)(s+5)}$

A comparison of the uncompensated system and the compensated system shows that the undamped natural frequency has decreased slightly from 0.898 to 0.854 rad/sec, but there is considerable increase in velocity error constant: from 0.838 to 8.02. This increase in K_v is, in fact, approximately equal to $|z|/|p|$ where $s = -z$ is the location of the compensating zero and $s = -p$ is the location of the compensating pole.

We see from the above discussion that the compensating zero must be located to the left of the compensating pole; both the zero and the pole confined to the left half of the s-plane. The transfer function of such a first-order compensator then becomes

$$D(s) = \frac{s+z}{s+p} = \frac{s+1/\tau}{s+1/\beta\tau}; \ \beta = \frac{z}{p} > 1, \ \tau > 0 \qquad (7.48)$$

Note that $\beta > 1$ ensures that the pole is located to the right of the zero, i.e., nearer the origin than the zero. The contribution of $D(s)$ to the angle criterion of the root locus is always negative. This type of compensator is called *lag compensator*. The name 'lag compensator' has a clearer meaning with respect to frequency-domain design, which is covered later in Chapter 10.

The physical realization of a lag compensator can be accomplished in many ways. Hardware and software implementation schemes commonly used in industrial practice are given in Chapter 11.

Concluding Comments

The purpose of reshaping the root locus generally falls into one of the following categories.

1. A given system is stable and its transient response is satisfactory, but its steady-state error is too large. Thus, the corresponding error constant must be increased while nearly preserving the transient response. This can be achieved by a cascade lag compensator

$$D(s) = \frac{s+z}{s+p} = \frac{s+1/\tau}{s+1/\beta\tau} \; ; \beta = \frac{z}{p} > 1, \; \tau > 0$$

2. A given system is stable, but its transient response is unsatisfactory. Thus the root locus must be reshaped so that it is moved farther to the left, away from the imaginary axis. This can be achieved by a cascade lead compensator

$$D(s) = \frac{s+z}{s+p} = \frac{s+1/\tau}{s+1/\alpha\tau}; \; \alpha = \frac{z}{p} < 1, \; \tau > 0$$

3. A lead-compensated system has satisfactory transient response but its steady-state error is too large. The steady-state error can be decreased by cascading a lag compensator to the lead-compensated system. This is equivalent to using a second-order compensator, called *lag-lead compensator*, of the form

$$D(s) = \left(\frac{s+z_2}{s+p_2}\right)\left(\frac{s+z_1}{s+p_1}\right) = \left(\frac{s+1/\tau_2}{s+1/\beta\tau_2}\right)\left(\frac{s+1/\tau_1}{s+1/\alpha\tau_1}\right);$$

$$\beta = \frac{z_2}{p_2} > 1, \; \alpha = \frac{z_1}{p_1} < 1, \; \tau_2 > 0, \; \tau_1 > 0$$

4. A given system is unstable for all values of gain. Thus the root locus must be reshaped so that part of each branch falls in the left half of the s-plane thereby making the system stable. A double lead compensator (two compensators in cascade) may sometimes be required to obtain satisfactory transient response.

▲▲

The systems, which are type-2 or higher, are usually absolutely unstable. For these types of systems, clearly lead compensators are required, as only a lead compensator increases the margin of stability. In type-1 and type-0 systems, stable operation is always possible if the gain is sufficiently reduced. In such cases, any of the three compensators, namely, lag, lead, or lag-lead, may be used to obtain the desired performance. The particular choice is based upon transient and steady-state response characteristics of uncompensated system.

7.6 CASCADE LEAD COMPENSATION

As has been pointed out in the previous section, lead compensation generally is used to improve the transient response of a system. In this section, we consider how the root locus may be used to design a compensator so as to realize a desired improvement in transient response.

Consider a unity-feedback system with a forward-path transfer function $G(s)$. The transfer function $G(s)$ is assumed to be unalterable except for the adjustment of gain. Let the system dynamic response specifications be translated into the desired location s_d for the dominant complex closed-loop poles as shown in Fig. 7.31.

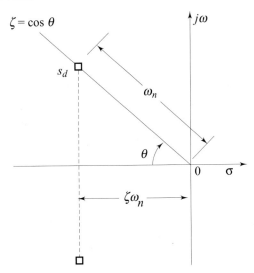

Fig. 7.31 *Desired dominant closed-loop poles*

If the angle criterion at s_d is not met, i.e., $\angle G(s_d) \neq \pm 180°$, the uncompensated root locus with variable open-loop gain will not pass through the desired root location, indicating the need for compensation. Let us introduce a first-order lead compensator with zero and pole in the left half of the complex plane:

$$D(s) = \frac{s+z}{s+p} = \frac{s+1/\tau}{s+1/\alpha\tau}; \; \alpha = \frac{z}{p} < 1, \; \tau > 0 \tag{7.49}$$

in cascade with the forward-path transfer function $G(s)$ as shown in Fig. 7.32.

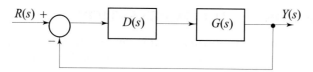

Fig. 7.32 *A feedback system with cascade compensator*

The compensator $D(s)$ has to be so designed that the compensated root locus passes through s_d. In terms of the angle criterion, this requires that

$$\angle D(s_d)G(s_d) = \angle D(s_d) + \angle G(s_d) = \pm 180°$$

or $$\angle D(s_d) = \phi = \pm 180° - \angle G(s_d) \tag{7.50}$$

Thus, for the root locus of the compensated system to pass through the desired root location, the lead compensator pole-zero must contribute an angle ϕ given by Eqn. (7.50) and shown in Fig. 7.33. For a given angle ϕ for lead compensation, there is no unique location for the pole-zero pair. Out of many possible solutions, we select the one that satisfies the following additional requirements:

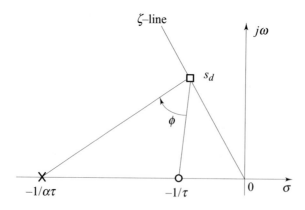

Fig. 7.33 *Angle contribution of lead compensator*

(i) The least-damped complex poles of the resulting closed-loop transfer function correspond to the desired dominant poles, and all other closed-loop poles are either located very close to the open-loop zeros or are relatively far away from the $j\omega$-axis. This ensures that the poles other than the dominant poles make a negligible contribution to the system dynamics.

(ii) Changing the locations of the compensator pole and zero can produce a range of values for the gain while maintaining the desired root s_d. The pole-zero pair location that produces maximum gain (and hence results in minimum steady-state error) is preferred.

(iii) Realization of requirements (i) and (ii) may demand a large value of the ratio p/z. If we choose this ratio to be too large, high frequency noise problems can, and probably will, become significant. A rule of thumb that is sometimes used is to limit this ratio to 10 (pole is located at a distance 10 times the value of the zero location), but this depends on the physical system under consideration and particularly on the noise present.

In the light of the above discussion, the steps for lead compensator design are summarized below.

1. Translate the transient response specifications into a pair of complex dominant roots.

2. Sketch the pole-zero plot of the uncompensated system and determine using angle criterion whether the desired root locations can be realized by gain adjustment alone. If not, calculate the angle deficiency ϕ. This angle must be contributed by the lead compensator if the root locus is to pass through the desired root locations.

3. Place the compensating zero on the real axis in the region below the desired dominant root s_d. If the uncompensated system has an open-loop pole on the real axis in the region below s_d, the compensating zero should lie to the left of this pole.

4. Determine the compensator pole location so that the total angle contributed by compensator pole-zero pair at s_d is ϕ.

5. Evaluate the gain at s_d and then calculate the error constant.

6. Repeat the steps if transient performance is unsatisfactory because of a weak dominance condition and/or if the error constant is not satisfactory.

Example 7.7

Let us first consider the example of a unity-feedback type-2 system with open-loop transfer function

$$G(s) = \frac{K}{s^2}$$

This system has zero steady-state error for both the step and ramp inputs. It can be seen from its root locus plot that the closed-loop poles always lie on the $j\omega$-axis. As explained earlier, lead compensator is the only choice for this system.

It is desired to compensate the system so as to meet the following transient response specifications:

Settling time, $t_s \leq 4$ sec

Peak overshoot for step input $\leq 20\%$

These specifications imply that

$$\zeta \geq 0.45, \quad \text{and} \quad \zeta\omega_n \geq 1$$

We choose a desired dominant root location as

$$s_d = -\zeta\omega_n + j\omega_n \sqrt{1-\zeta^2} = -1 + j2$$

Figure 7.34 shows the pole-zero map of $G(s)$, and the desired dominant root location s_d. From this figure, we find that

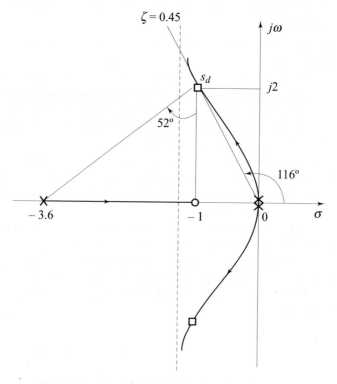

Fig. 7.34 *Cascade lead compensation (Example 7.7)*

$$\angle G(s_d) = -2 \times 116° = -232°$$

Therefore the angle contribution at s_d required of the lead compensator pole-zero pair is

$$\phi = -180° - (-232°) = 52°$$

Place the zero of the compensator on the real-axis segment directly below s_d, at $s = -z = -1$. Join the compensator zero to s_d and locate the compensator pole by making an angle of $\phi = 52°$, as shown in Fig. 7.34. The location of the pole is found to be at $s = -p = -3.6$.

With the addition of the cascade lead compensator

$$D(s) = \frac{s+1}{s+3.6},$$

the open-loop transfer function of the system becomes

$$D(s)G(s) = \frac{K(s+1)}{s^2(s+3.6)}$$

The gain K is evaluated by measuring the vector lengths from the poles and zeros to the root location s_d:

$$K = \frac{(2.23)^2 (3.25)}{2} = 8.1$$

Therefore the open-loop transfer function of the compensated system is

$$D(s)G(s) = \frac{8.1(s+1)}{s^2(s+3.6)} \tag{7.51}$$

The root locus plot of the compensated system is shown in Fig. 7.34. The third closed-loop pole introduced because of the lead compensator lies on the real-axis root locus between $s = -3.6$ and $s = -1$. Due to this closed-loop pole, there will be an exponential term in the transient response in addition to the oscillatory term due to the complex pair of closed-loop poles. The specifications for the transient response were originally expressed in terms of the overshoot and the settling time of the system. These specifications were translated on the basis of an approximation of the system by a second-order system, to an equivalent ζ and ω_n, and therefrom the desired closed-loop pole locations. However, the original specifications will be satisfied only if the poles selected are dominant. Often the designer will simulate the final design and obtain the actual transient response of the system. If the peak overshoot and settling time indices of the transient response do not compare well with the specified values, the system is redesigned.

Computer simulation of the unity-feedback system with open-loop transfer function (7.51) resulted in a peak overshoot of about 46% and a settling time of 3.8 sec for a step input. The difference in the overshoot from the specified value is due to the third closed-loop pole, which is not negligible. A second attempt to obtain a compensated system with an overshoot of 20% would utilize a compensator with zero at say $s = -2$. This approach would move the third closed-loop pole farther to the left in the s-plane, reduce the effect of the third closed-loop pole on the transient response, and reduce the overshoot.

Finally, the error constants of the system are evaluated. We find that the system under consideration is type-2, and therefore will result in zero steady-state error for step and ramp input signals. The acceleration error constant is

$$K_a = \lim_{s \to 0} s^2 D(s)G(s) = \frac{8.1}{3.6} = 2.25$$

The steady-state performance of the system is quite satisfactory. With the compensator zero shifted farther to the left in a redesign attempt, the error constant K_a will increase marginally.

Example 7.8

Now let us consider a unity-feedback type-1 system with open-loop transfer function

$$G(s) = \frac{K}{s(s + 2)}$$

It is desired to design a cascade lead compensator such that the dominant closed-loop poles provide a damping ratio $\zeta = 0.5$ and have an undamped natural frequency $\omega_n = 4$ rad/sec.

Our specifications provide the location of the desired dominant closed-loop poles. An s-plane diagram showing the desired pole location s_d and the open-loop poles of the uncompensated transfer function is given in Fig. 7.35. The desired closed-loop pole is at

$$s_d = -\zeta\omega_n + j\omega_n\sqrt{1 - \zeta^2} = -2 + j3.46$$

The angle of $G(s)$ at the desired closed-loop pole, obtained from Fig. 7.35, is

$$\angle G(s_d) = -210°$$

Thus, if we need to force the root locus to go through the desired closed-loop pole, the lead compensator must contribute $\phi = 30°$ at this point.

Let us locate the compensator zero at $s = -2.9$, i.e., in the region below the desired dominant closed-loop pole location and just to the left of the open-loop pole at $s = -2$. Join the compensator zero to s_d and locate the compensator pole by making an angle $\phi = 30°$ as shown in Fig. 7.35. The location of the pole is found to be at $s = -5.4$.

The open-loop transfer function of the compensated system becomes

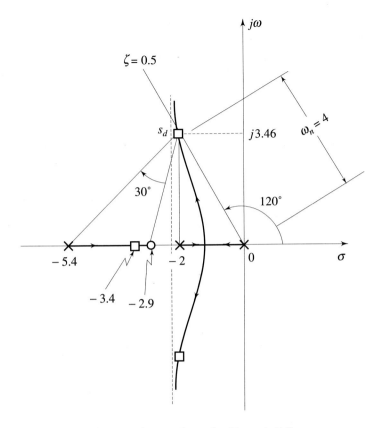

Fig. 7.35 *Root locus plot (Example 7.8)*

$$D(s)G(s) = \left(\frac{s + 2.9}{s + 5.4}\right)\left[\frac{K}{s(s + 2)}\right]$$

The gain K at s_d, evaluated using magnitude criterion, is 18.7. It follows that

$$D(s)G(s) = \frac{18.7(s + 2.9)}{s(s + 2)(s + 5.4)}$$

The root locus plot of the compensated system is shown in Fig. 7.35. The third closed-loop pole is at $s = -3.4$, which is close to the added zero at $s = -2.9$. Therefore the effect of this pole on the transient response is expected to be small. This should be verified by simulation study on the closed-loop transfer function

$$\frac{Y(s)}{R(s)} = M(s) = \frac{18.7(s + 2.9)}{(s + 2 + j3.46)(s + 2 - j3.46)(s + 3.4)}$$

The velocity error constant of the compensated system is

$$K_v = \lim_{s \to 0} sD(s)G(s) = \frac{18.7 \times 2.9}{2 \times 5.4} = 5.02 \text{ sec}^{-1}$$

Although a certain change in the value of K_v can be made by altering the pole-zero location of the lead compensator, if a large increase in the value of K_v is desired, then we must alter the lead compensator to a lag-lead compensator.

Example 7.9

A unity-feedback system with open-loop transfer function

$$G(s) = \frac{K}{s^2(s+1.5)}$$

is to be compensated to meet the following specifications:

Settling time, $t_s < 5$ sec

Peak overshoot for step input $\cong 25\%$.

For a second-order system, damping ratio $\zeta = 0.45$ gives 20% overshoot, and with undamped natural frequency $\omega_n = 2.2$ rad/sec, the settling time $t_s = 4/\zeta\omega_n = 4$ sec.

These specifications provide the location of desired dominant roots:

$$s_{1,2} = -\zeta\omega_n \pm j\omega_n \sqrt{1-\zeta^2} = -1 \pm j2$$

At $s_d = -1 + j2$ (refer Fig. 7.36), $\angle G(s_d) = -2 \times 116° - 75° = -307°$

Therefore the angle contribution required from a lead compensator is $\phi = -180° - (-307°) = 127°$.

The large value of ϕ here is an indication that a double lead compensator is appropriate. Each section of the compensator has then to contribute an angle of 63.5° at s_d.

In the region below the desired root, there is an open-loop pole at $s = -1.5$. We may place zero of the compensator at $s = -z = -1.5$, cancelling the plant pole. Join the compensator zero to s_d and locate the compensator pole by making an angle of $\phi = 63.5°$, as shown in Fig. 7.36. The location of the pole is found to be at $s = -10$.

With the cascade double lead compensator $D(s) = \dfrac{(s+1.5)^2}{(s+10)^2}$, the open-loop transfer function of the compensated system becomes

$$D(s)G(s) = \frac{K(s+1.5)^2}{s^2(s+1.5)(s+10)^2} = \frac{K(s+1.5)}{s^2(s+10)^2}$$

The gain K at s_d, evaluated using magnitude criterion, is 247. It follows that

$$D(s)G(s) = \frac{247(s+1.5)}{s^2(s+10)^2}$$

A rough root locus plot of the compensated system is shown in Fig. 7.36. By locating all the closed-loop poles and carrying out a simulation study on the closed-loop system, we can determine whether the dominance of the complex pole-pair is ensured, i.e., whether the actual transient response compared well with the specified one.

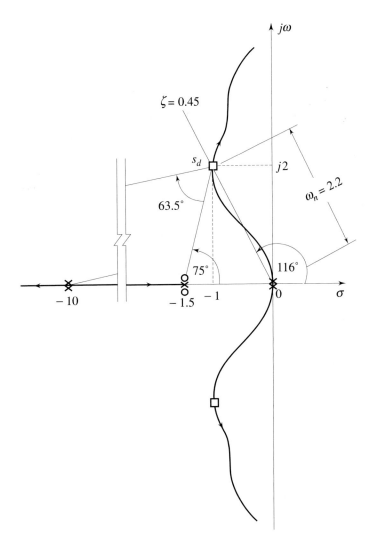

Fig. 7.36 *Root locus plot (Example 7.9)*

7.7 CASCADE LAG COMPENSATION

As pointed out earlier in Section 7.5, a lag compensator improves the steady-state behaviour of a system, while nearly preserving its transient response. In this section, we consider how the root locus may be used to design a compensator so as to realize a desired improvement in steady-state response.

Consider a unity-feedback system with a forward-path transfer function

$$G(s) = \frac{K \prod_{i=1}^{m}(s + z_i)}{s^r \prod_{j=r+1}^{n}(s + p_j)} \qquad (7.52)$$

We assume that at a certain value of K, this system has satisfactory transient response, i.e., its root locus plot passes through (or is close to) the desired closed-loop pole location s_d indicated in Fig. 7.37. It is required to improve the system error constant K_p, K_v or K_a (depending on whether the system is type-0, -1 or -2, respectively) to a specified value without impairing its transient response. This requires that after compensation, the root locus should continue to pass through s_d, while the error constant at s_d is raised to the specified value. To accomplish this, consider adding a lag compensator pole-zero pair close to origin, with zero to the left of the pole. If pole and zero of this pair are located close to each other, it will contribute a negligible angle λ at s_d such that s_d continues to lie on the root locus of the compensated system. Figure 7.37 shows the location of such a lag compensator pole-zero pair.

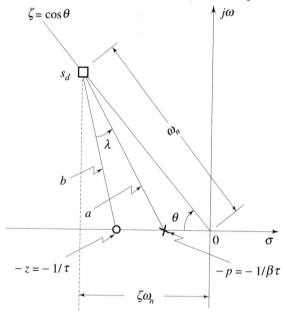

Fig. 7.37 *Locating the lag compensator pole-zero pair*

The gain of the uncompensated system at s_d is given by

$$K^{uc}(s_d) = \frac{|s_d|^r \prod_{j=r+1}^{n}|s_d + p_j|}{\prod_{i=1}^{m}|s_d + z_i|} \qquad (7.53)$$

For the system with a cascade lag compensator

$$D(s) = \frac{s+z}{s+p} = \frac{s+1/\tau}{s+1/\beta\tau}; \; \beta = \frac{z}{p} > 1, \; \tau > 0 \qquad (7.54)$$

the system gain at s_d is (refer Fig. 7.37)

$$K^c(s_d) = \frac{|s_d|^r \prod_{j=r+1}^{n} |s_d + p_j|}{\prod_{i=1}^{m} |s_d + z_i|} \left(\frac{a}{b}\right) \qquad (7.55)$$

where $a = |s_d + 1/\beta\tau|$, and $b = |s_d + 1/\tau|$.

Since the compensator pole and zero are located close to each other, they are nearly equidistant from s_d, i.e., $a \cong b$. It therefore follows from Eqns (7.53) and (7.55) that

$$K^c(s_d) \cong K^{uc}(s_d)$$

The error constant K_e (which is equal to K_p, K_v, or K_a depending on the type of the system) of the uncompensated system is given by

$$K_e^{uc} = K^{uc}(s_d) \frac{\prod_{i=1}^{m} z_i}{\prod_{j=r+1}^{n} p_j}$$

The error constant of the compensated system is given by (refer Fig. 7.37)

$$K_e^c = K^c(s_d) \frac{\prod_{i=1}^{m} z_i}{\prod_{j=r+1}^{n} p_j} \left(\frac{z}{p}\right) \cong K_e^{uc}\left(\frac{z}{p}\right)$$

Since the error constant K_e^c must equal the desired value K_e^d, we have

$$K_e^d \cong K_e^{uc}\left(\frac{z}{p}\right)$$

or

$$\beta = \left(\frac{z}{p}\right) \cong \frac{K_e^d}{K_e^{uc}} \qquad (7.56)$$

Thus the β-parameter of the lag compensator (refer Eqn. (7.54)) is nearly equal to the ratio of the desired error constant to the error constant of the uncompensated system.

Since the lag compensator does contribute a small negative angle λ at s_d, the compensated root locus will not pass through s_d. The effect of the small lag angle λ is to press the root locus slightly to the right. The intersection of the compensated root locus with the specified ζ-line will be at s_d' having slightly lower value of ω_n compared to the one corresponding to s_d. Also the actual error constant will somewhat fall short of the specified value if β obtained from Eqn. (7.56) is used.

The effects of lag angle λ can be anticipated and counteracted by taking design parameter ω_n to be somewhat larger than the specified value. Also in the design process, we may choose a β somewhat larger than that given by Eqn. (7.56).

In the light of the above discussion, the steps for lag compensator design are summarized below.

1. Draw the root locus plot for the uncompensated system.
2. Translate the transient response specifications into a pair of complex dominant roots and locate these roots on the uncompensated root locus plot. It is assumed that acceptable transient performance can be obtained by gain adjustment; the desired dominant root will therefore lie on (or close to) the uncompensated root locus.
3. Calculate the gain of the uncompensated system at the dominant root s_d and evaluate the corresponding error constant.
4. Determine the factor by which the error constant of the uncompensated system should be increased to meet the specified value. Choose the β-parameter of lag compensator to be somewhat greater than this factor.
5. Select zero $(s = -z)$ of the compensator sufficiently close to the origin. As a guide rule, we may construct a line making an angle of $10°$ (or less) with the desired ζ-line from s_d; the intersection of this line with the real axis gives location of the compensator zero.
6. The compensator pole can then be located at $s = -p = -z/\beta$. It is important to note that the compensator pole-zero pair should contribute an angle λ less than $5°$ at s_d so that the root locus plot in the region of s_d is not appreciably changed and hence satisfactory transient behaviour of the system is preserved.

Example 7.10

Reconsider the uncompensated system of Example 7.8, where the uncompensated open-loop transfer function is

$$G(s) = \frac{K}{s(s + 2)}$$

The system is to be compensated to meet the following specifications.
Damping ratio, $\zeta = 0.707$
Settling time, $t_s \leq 5$ sec
Velocity error constant, $K_v \geq 4$

The uncompensated root locus is vertical line at -1 and results in a root on the $\zeta = 0.707$ line at $s_d = -1 + j1$, as shown in Fig. 7.38. Settling time corresponding to this root is $4/\zeta\omega_n = 4$ sec. The gain at s_d is $K = 2$. Therefore, the uncompensated system with the gain adjusted to a value of 2 meets the transient response specifications. Slight reduction in ω_n due to the small lag angle of the compensator required to improve steady-state performance, is also permissible.

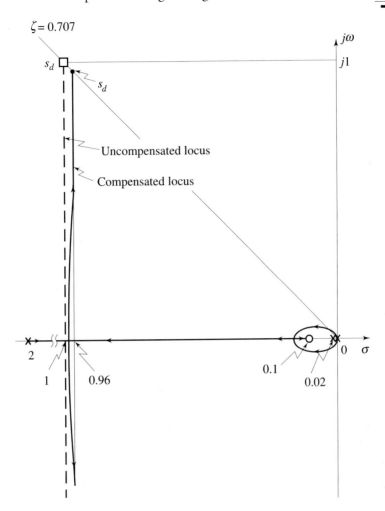

Fig. 7.38 *Root locus plot (Example 7.10)*

The velocity error constant of the uncompensated system is

$$K_v^{uc} = \lim_{s \to 0} sG(s) = K/2 = 1$$

The desired velocity error constant is

$$K_v^d \geq 4$$

Thus, the velocity error constant must be increased by at least a factor of 4. Lag compensator with $\beta = 5$ is expected to meet this requirement. We might set compensator zero at $s = -z = -0.1$. Note that $|z|$ is much smaller compared to $|s_d| = \sqrt{2}$. The compensator pole is located at $s = -p = -z/\beta = -0.02$. The difference of the angles from compensator zero and pole at the desired root s_d is about 3°; therefore $s_d = -1 + j1$ will lie close to compensated root locus.

The open-loop transfer function of the compensated system becomes

$$D(s)G(s) = \left(\frac{s + 0.1}{s + 0.02}\right)\left[\frac{K}{s(s + 2)}\right]$$

The root locus plot of the compensated system is shown in Fig. 7.38. It intersects the $\zeta = 0.707$ line at $s'_d = -0.96 + j0.96$. The gain K at s'_d, evaluated by magnitude criterion, remains approximately equal to 2. It follows that

$$D(s)G(s) = \frac{2(s + 0.1)}{s(s + 0.02)(s + 2)}$$

From Fig. 7.38, we find that corresponding to $K = 2$, the third closed-loop pole is at $s = -0.11$. Note that the real pole has a time-constant of $\tau = 1/0.11 = 9.1$ sec, which would appear to make the system so slow as to be unusable. However, there is a zero close to this additional pole. The net effect is that the settling time will increase because of the third pole, but the amplitude of the response term contributed by this pole will be very small. In system response, a long tail of small amplitude will appear which may not degrade the performance of the system appreciably. This should be verified by simulation study on the closed-loop transfer function,

$$\frac{Y(s)}{R(s)} = M(s) = \frac{2(s + 0.1)}{(s + 0.11)(s + 0.96 + j0.96)(s + 0.96 - j0.96)}$$

7.8 | CASCADE LAG-LEAD COMPENSATION

In the preceding sections, we have seen that the lead compensator is suitable for systems having unsatisfactory transient response. However, it provides only a limited improvement in steady-state response. If the steady-state behaviour is highly unsatisfactory, the lead compensator may not be the answer. On the other hand, for systems with satisfactory transient response but unsatisfactory steady-state response, the lag compensator is found to be a good choice.

When both transient and steady-state responses are unsatisfactory, we must draw upon the combined powers of lag and lead compensators in order to meet the specifications. The transfer function for the lag-lead compensator is of the form

$$D(s) = \left(\frac{s + z_2}{s + p_2}\right)\left(\frac{s + z_1}{s + p_1}\right) \tag{7.57a}$$

$$= \underbrace{\left(\frac{s + 1/\tau_2}{s + 1/\beta\tau_2}\right)}_{\text{Lag Section}}\underbrace{\left(\frac{s + 1/\tau_1}{s + 1/\alpha\tau_1}\right)}_{\text{Lead Section}}; \beta = \frac{z_2}{p_2} > 1, \alpha = \frac{z_1}{p_1} < 1, \tau_2 > 0, \tau_1 > 0$$

$$\tag{7.57b}$$

In designing a lag-lead compensator, we frequently choose $\beta = 1/\alpha$ (this is not necessary; we can, of course, choose $\beta \neq 1/\alpha$). The reason for this choice is that this makes physical realization of the compensator simpler (refer

Chapter 11). With $\beta = 1/\alpha$, the transfer function (7.57) of the lag-lead compensator reduces to

$$D(s) = \underbrace{\left(\frac{s + 1/\tau_2}{s + \alpha/\tau_2}\right)}_{\text{Lag Section}}\underbrace{\left(\frac{s + 1/\tau_1}{s + 1/\alpha\tau_1}\right)}_{\text{Lead Section}}; \tau_2, \tau_1 > 0 \qquad (7.58)$$

We first design the lead section to realize the required ζ and ω_n for the dominant closed-loop poles. The error constant is then determined for the lead-compensated system, say it is K_e^{lc}. If K_e^{lc} is sufficiently high to give the desired steady-state response, we need not go further. Lead compensation is all that is required. If, however, K_e^{lc} is not large enough, we consider adding the lag section with $\beta = 1/\alpha$. This results in an error constant

$$K_e^{llc} \cong \frac{1}{\alpha} K_e^{lc} \qquad (7.59)$$

If K_e^{llc}, as given in Eqn. (7.59), is not large enough to meet steady-state specifications, we choose $\beta > 1/\alpha$ and redesign the lag section.

Example 7.11

Consider a plant with transfer function

$$G(s) = \frac{4}{s(s + 0.5)}$$

Design a feedback system to meet the following specifications:
1. Damping ratio of dominant closed-loop poles, $\zeta = 0.5$.
2. Undamped natural frequency of dominant closed-loop poles, $\omega_n = 5$ rad/sec.
3. Velocity error constant = 80 sec.$^{-1}$

We choose the unity-feedback control configuration shown in Fig. 7.39. Root locus plot of the system with $A > 0$ and $D(s) = 1$ is shown by dashed line in Fig. 7.40. The $\zeta = 0.5$ line intersects the root locus at the point $s = -0.25 + j0.433$. The undamped natural frequency corresponding to this root is 0.5 rad/sec. Therefore the configuration in Fig. 7.39 with $D(s) = 1$ cannot meet the specifications.

We introduce a cascade lead compensator. From the performance specifications we find that the dominant closed-loop poles must be at $s = -2.5 \pm j4.33$. Consider the desired location

$$s_d = -2.5 + j4.33$$

Since (refer Fig. 7.40) $\angle G(s_d) = -120° -115° = -235°$, the lead compensator must contribute 55° so that the root locus passes through the desired root s_d. To design the lead compensator, we first determine the location of the compensator zero. There are many possible choices, but we shall here choose the zero at $s = -z = -0.5$ so that it cancels the open-loop pole at $s = -0.5$. Once the compensator zero is chosen, the compensator pole can be located such that

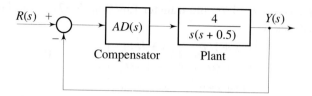

Fig. 7.39 *Control configuration (Example 7.11)*

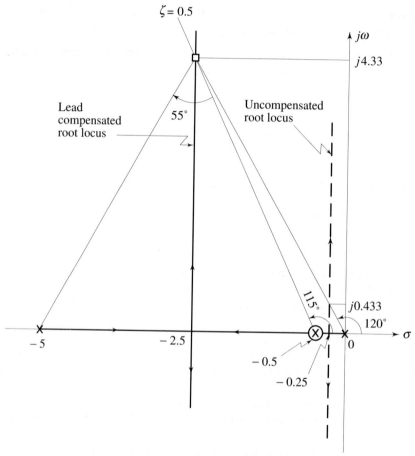

Fig. 7.40 *Root locus plot (Example 7.11)*

the angle contribution of the pole-zero pair is 55°. By simple graphical analysis (refer Fig. 7.40), we find that the pole must be located at $s = -p = -5$. Thus, with the lead compensator

$$D_1(s) = \frac{s + 1/\tau_1}{s + 1/\alpha\tau_1} = \frac{s + 0.5}{s + 5}, \quad \alpha = 0.1,$$

the open-loop transfer function of the system becomes

$$D_1(s)G(s) = \frac{K(s+0.5)}{s(s+0.5)(s+5)} = \frac{K}{s(s+5)}; K = 4A$$

The value of K obtained by magnitude criterion, is

$$K = |s_d| |s_d + 5| \cong 25$$

Root locus plot of the lead-compensated system is shown in Fig. 7.40. Let us evaluate the steady-state performance of this system.

$$K_v = \lim_{s \to 0} sD_1(s)G(s) = \frac{K}{5} = 5$$

The desired K_v is 80. A large increase in K_v cannot be obtained by adjustment of pole-zero pair of the lead compensator. We, therefore, must alter the lead compensation to a lag-lead compensation.

Let us design a lag compensator

$$D_2(s) = \frac{s + 1/\tau_2}{s + 1/\beta\tau_2}; \beta > 1$$

for the lead-compensated system. If we choose $\beta = 1/\alpha = 10$, the velocity error constant will increase by a factor of about 10, i.e., the velocity error constant of the lag-lead compensated system will become about 50. The choice $\beta = 1/\alpha$, therefore, does not meet our requirements on steady-state accuracy.

The velocity error constant of the lead-compensated system is $K_v^{lc} = 5$.

The desired velocity error constant is $K_v^d = 80$.

Thus, the velocity error constant must be increased by a factor of 16. The lag compensator with $\beta = 16$ will meet this requirement. We now choose the pole-zero pair of the lag compensator. We want that

$$|D_2(s_d)| = \left| \frac{s_d + z_2}{s_d + p_2} \right| \cong 1$$

$$-5° < \angle D_2(s_d) = \angle s_d + z_2 - \angle s_d + p_2 < 0°$$

$z_2 = 0.2$, and $p_2 = z_2/\beta = 0.2/16 = 0.0125$ meet these requirements.

The open-loop transfer function of the lag-lead compensated system becomes

$$D_2(s)D_1(s)G(s) = \frac{25(s+0.2)}{s(s+0.0125)(s+5)}$$

$$= \frac{25}{4} \frac{(s+0.2)(s+0.5)}{(s+0.0125)(s+5)} \left[\frac{4}{s(s+0.5)} \right]$$

Therefore (refer Fig. 7.39)

$$AD(s) = \frac{25}{4} \frac{(s+0.2)(s+0.5)}{(s+0.0125)(s+5)}$$

Root locus analysis of the lag-lead compensated feedback system is left as an exercise for the reader.

7.9 | MINOR-LOOP FEEDBACK COMPENSATION

The feedback control schemes discussed in the preceding sections have all utilized a compensator $D(s)$ placed in the forward path in cascade with the plant transfer function $G(s)$. The compensator $D(s)$ typically involves PI terms (lag compensator), PD terms (lead compensator), or PID terms (lag-lead compensator).

Derivative action of a compensator need not be implemented with the derivative term in the forward path, especially when there are step changes in the reference input and could produce plant input saturation. In such cases, a practical implementation of compensation is that depicted in Fig. 7.41, namely, a derivative term with a roll-off pole:

$$H_D(s) = \frac{K_D s}{\tau_D s + 1} \tag{7.60}$$

implemented by means of a *minor loop* around the plant, and a proportional (P) or a lag (PI) compensator in the forward path. Alternatively, ideal derivative (velocity) feedback with

$$H_D(s) = K_t s \tag{7.61}$$

could be used in those situations where a tachometer is employed.

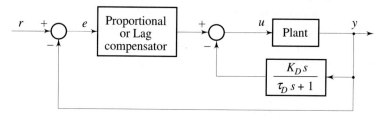

Fig. 7.41   *Minor-loop feedback compensation*

$H_D(s)$ cannot be applied as cascade controller in forward path, since it acts as open circuit in the steady-state when the frequency is zero. As a minor-loop feedback controller, the zero-transmission property to dc signals does not pose any problems.

Rate Feedback

The feedback system shown in Fig. 7.42 provides the opportunity for varying three parameters: A, K, and K_t.

The larger the number of variables inserted into a system, the better the opportunity for achieving a specified performance. However, the design problem becomes much more complex.

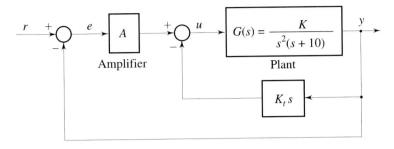

Fig. 7.42 *Rate feedback compensation*

We shall discuss two methods for the design of control systems with rate feedback; one is based on single-parameter loci and the other on multiple-parameter loci.

Single-Parameter Loci

The characteristic equation of the given system is (refer Fig. 7.42)

$$1 + \frac{AG(s)}{1 + sK_t G(s)} = 1 + \frac{AK}{s^2(s + 10) + KK_t s} = 0 \tag{7.62}$$

Rearranging, we get

$$s^3 + 10 s^2 + KK_t s + AK = 0$$

There are three variable parameters: A, K, and K_t. By appropriate partitioning of the characteristic equation, we can use single-parameter root loci for the design of three parameters (A, K, K_t) of the given system.

Consider the following partitioning:

$$1 + \frac{KK_t(s + A/K_t)}{s^2(s + 10)} = 0 \tag{7.63a}$$

This equation shows that the net effect of rate feedback is to add a zero at $s = -A/K_t$. Now the design procedure calls for a search for suitable location for this additional zero to satisfy the specifications.

Assume that the system is to be compensated to meet the following specifications:

Per cent peak overshoot $\leq 10\%$
Settling time ≤ 4 sec

The damping ζ and natural frequency ω_n of the dominant roots, obtained from the relations

$$e^{-\pi\zeta/\sqrt{1-\zeta^2}} \cong 0.1; \quad \text{and} \quad \frac{4}{\zeta\omega_n} = 4$$

are $\zeta = 0.6$, $\omega_n = 1.67$ rad/sec.

The desired dominant roots are then given as $s_d = -1 \pm j1.34$.

From Fig. 7.43, we see that the angle contribution of the open-loop poles at s_d is $-2(127°) - 8° = -262°$. Therefore, for the point s_d to be on the root locus, the compensating zero should contribute an angle of $\phi = -180° - (-262°)$ = 82°. The location of the compensating zero is thus found to be at $s = -1.2$. The open-loop transfer function of the compensated system becomes

$$F(s) = \frac{KK_t(s + 1.2)}{s^2(s + 10)} \qquad (7.63b)$$

The root locus plot of the compensated system is shown in Fig. 7.43. It is now observed that for all values of KK_t, the system is stable. The value of KK_t at s_d is found to be 17.4. The third closed-loop pole is at $s = -8$ which is far away from the imaginary axis compared to dominant closed-loop poles. Hence, its effect on the transient behaviour is negligible.

From Fig. 7.43, we observe that the root locus intersects the $\zeta = 0.6$ line at two points, P and Q. Thus, the two values of KK_t will give the damping ratio ζ of the closed-loop poles equal to 0.6. $KK_t = 17.4$ at point P results in a pair of dominant complex-conjugate closed-loop poles which satisfy the transient response specifications. The third closed-loop pole is at $s = -8$ which has insignificant contribution to system dynamics. At point Q, the dominance condition will be weakened; the third closed-loop pole on the real axis will force a slow overdamped response. It is important to point out that the zero at $s = -1.2$ is

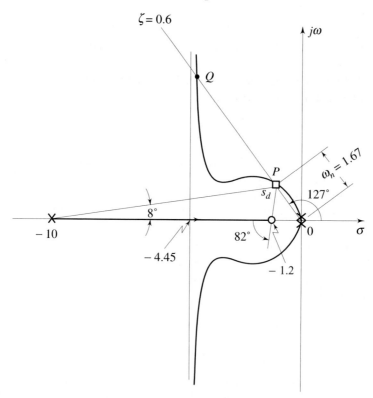

Fig. 7.43 *Root locus plot for the characteristic equation (7.63)*

not the closed-loop zero. It is the open-loop zero of $F(s)$ (refer Eqns (7.63)) which was introduced in the process of partitioning the characteristic equation such that the adjustable variable KK_t appears as a multiplying factor.

Let us now investigate the steady-state behaviour of the compensated system. From Eqn. (7.62), the velocity error constant K_v is given by

$$K_v = \lim_{s \to 0} s \left[\frac{AK}{s^2(s+10) + KK_t s} \right] = \frac{AK}{KK_t} = A/K_t = 1.2$$

If this value of K_v is acceptable, then the design is complete. Otherwise, the design procedure given above cannot satisfy the steady-state and transient specifications simultaneously. A trade-off between the steady-state and transient behaviour becomes necessary.

We have three parameters and two equations:

$$A/K_t = 1.2; \quad KK_t = 17.4$$

If we select $K_t = 0.4$, then the other two parameters become: $A = 0.48$ and $K = 43.5$. K can be decreased with no change in performance by increasing A and K_t; e.g., $K_t = 0.8$ gives $A = 0.96$ and $K = 21.75$.

Multiple-Parameter Loci (Root Contours)

The root locus method is basically a one parameter method that is used to study the effect (on root locations) of varying *any* chosen parameter. We can, however, use the method to study the total effect of varying two or more than two parameters by simply doing the calculations sequentially. The sequential process gives rise to a family of root loci called *root contours*. The root contours possess the same properties as the single-parameter root loci.

The characteristic equation of the system under consideration is (refer Eqns (7.63))

$$s^3 + 10s^2 + KK_t s + AK = 0 \qquad (7.64a)$$

The two parameters to be selected are

$$\alpha = AK, \text{ and } \beta = KK_t$$

In terms of the parameters α and β, the characteristic equation becomes

$$s^3 + 10s^2 + \beta s + \alpha = 0 \qquad (7.64b)$$

Choose one of the variables for the first stage of sequential calculations, set the other to zero and partition. The root locus equation as a function of α with $\beta = 0$, is

$$1 + \frac{\alpha}{s^2(s+10)} = 0$$

The root locus plot for α varying from 0 to ∞ is shown in Fig. 7.44 (unbroken thick lines). The points on these loci become the open-loop poles for the second stage of the sequential calculations.

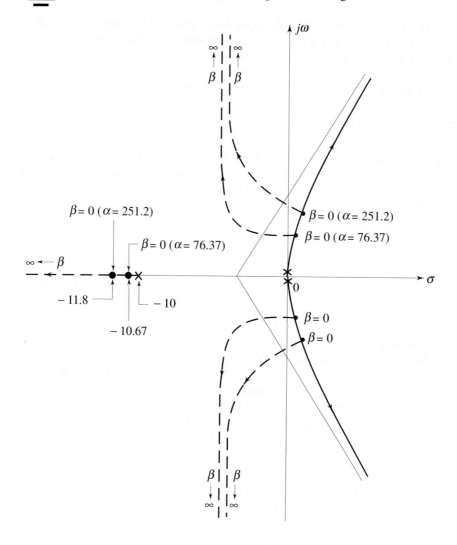

Fig. 7.44 *Root contours for the characteristic equation (7.64)*

The root locus equation as a function of β is

$$1 + \frac{\beta s}{s^3 + 10s^2 + \alpha} = 0$$

For some selected values of α, the loci for β (dotted thick lines) are sketched in Fig. 7.44. The family of root loci (the root-contour plot) illustrates the total effect of both α and β on the roots of the characteristic equation of the system.

In general, a computer solution seems preferable for multiple-parameter variations because of the amount of labour required for graphical construction.

COMPENSATION FOR PLANTS WITH DOMINANT COMPLEX POLES

We have presented lead, lag, and lag-lead compensators as being capable of providing any needed improvements in performance. The success of these designs, however, depends on the basic system dynamics being dominated by real poles. When this is not the case, the methods may fail and others are needed.

Figure 7.45a shows root locus plot of a feedback system controlling the plant

$$G(s) = \frac{K}{(\tau_1 s + 1)(\tau_2 s + 1)(As^2 + Bs + 1)}$$

It has been assumed that pair of complex poles of the plant are *not* dominant. Suppose we have set gain for desired damping ratio and find the response too slow, suggesting lead compensation. The cancellation type lead compensator $D(s) = (\tau_3 s + 1)/(\tau_4 s + 1)$; $\tau_3 = \tau_2$, appears to work as shown in Fig. 7.45a. Detailed analysis/design confirms this result.

In Fig. 7.45b, however, where the complex plant poles are dominant, we find little or no performance improvement with lead compensation. Similar difficulties may be encountered with lag compensation.

Since dominant complex poles (resonances) do arise in practice, for example, in robot manipulators, space crafts, etc., where flexibility in the structure gives rise to one or more modes of vibration, we need compensation to deal with this. Controlled-variable derivative compensation and cancellation of complex dominant poles with compensator zeros are the two useful approaches for such problems.

Example 7.12

Aircraft attitude (angular orientation) control involves three axes (pitch, roll, and yaw) of motion. However preliminary design usually considers each axis separately. A simplified Newton's analysis for the pitch axis produces the aircraft transfer function relating pitch angle θ to elevator angle δ [74]:

$$\frac{\theta(s)}{\delta(s)} = \frac{K(\tau s + 1)}{s\left(\dfrac{s^2}{\omega_n^2} + \dfrac{2\zeta}{\omega_n}s + 1\right)}$$

The nominal values of K, τ, ω_n and ζ vary from one airplane or missile to another, and for a given vehicle, with altitude and Mach number. Aerodynamic design for drag reduction often results in very poor (low) values of aircraft damping. Use of derivative control allows us to radically improve this poor stability without changing the airplane in any way.

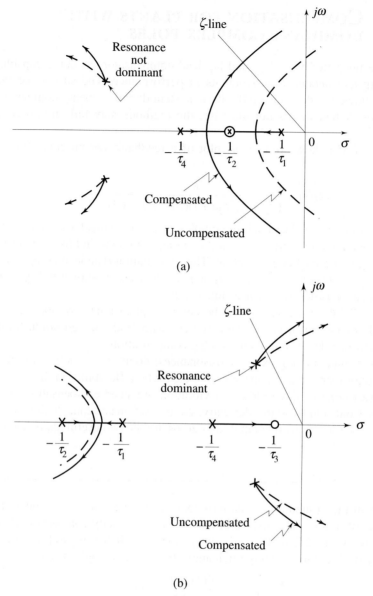

(a)

(b)

Fig. 7.45 *Lead compensation for plants with complex poles*

A basic pitch-command control system would force the aircraft pitch angle θ to follow the pilot's control stick rotation θ_r, using a position sensor (gyroscope) to measure θ, as is shown in Fig. 7.46a. The electrohydraulic servo that positions the elevator in response to voltage command $\hat{e}$ is itself a complete feedback system; however, when properly designed, its closed-loop response can be adequately modeled as first-order. We see from the root locus shown in

Fig. 7.46b that this basic system is unacceptable, since closed-loop damping is actually *worse* than that of the airplane itself, which was already bad.

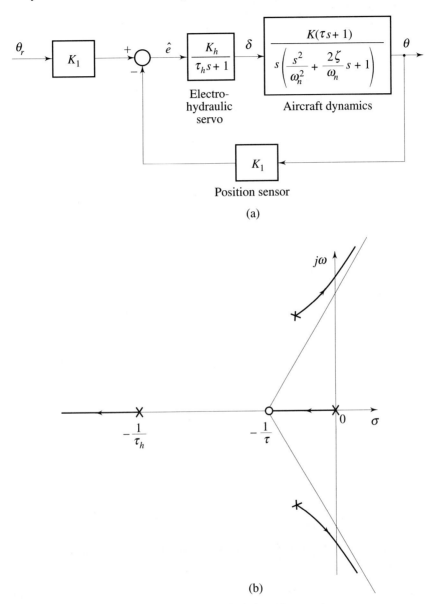

Fig. 7.46 *Aircraft pitch angle control*

By adding a rate gyroscope to provide measurement of $\dot{\theta}$, we can implement derivative control. From Fig. 7.47, we see that the closed-loop system with derivative control has *better* damping than the aircraft alone.

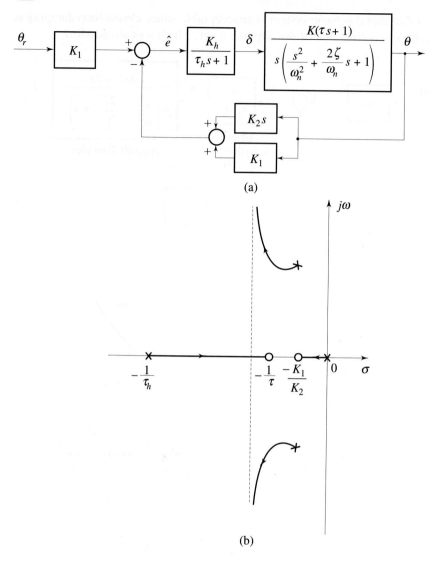

Fig. 7.47 *Aircraft pitch angle control*

Another approach uses forward-path cancellation compensation with a compensator

$$D(s) = \frac{As^2 + Bs + 1}{Es^2 + Fs + 1} \tag{7.65}$$

where A and B are chosen to cancel the complex poles of the plant and E and F are picked to give a 'more desirable' (overdamped or underdamped) pole pair than did A and B.

The transfer functions of the form (7.65) with, in general, complex poles and zeros can be realized with op amp electronics in analog systems or with appropriate software in digital systems. A $D(s)$ having complex zeros and real poles can be realized by simple passive electrical circuits containing only resistor-capacitor elements. We can use such RC circuits for cancellation of complex plant poles; then a compensator can be designed for all real-pole plants. Hardware and software realization schemes for transfer functions with complex zeros/poles are given in Chapter 11.

In practice, the poles and zeros can never exactly cancel since they are determined by two independent pieces of hardware whose numerical values are neither precisely known nor precisely fixed. Since imperfect cancellation is bound to occur, one wonders how bad the imperfection can get before we lose the essential benefits of cancellation.

Example 7.13———————————————————————————

Consider a servomechanism example from the missile guidance field. A gyro-stabilized platform using air-bearing gyros and low-friction gimbals presents an open-loop transfer function $G(s)$ containing a quadratic with essentially zero damping [74]:

$$G(s) = \frac{K}{s\left(\dfrac{s^2}{\omega_n^2} + 1\right)}$$

A simple proportional control would be unstable for any gain, as the root locus of Fig. 7.48 shows. Let us attempt the cancellation-compensation using a forward-path compensator of the form

$$D(s) = \frac{\left(\dfrac{s^2}{\omega_n^2} + 1\right)}{(\tau s + 1)^2}$$

Figure 7.48 shows the root locus plot of the compensated system, including the effect of cancellation mismatch.

From Fig. 7.48 we see that the two root locus branches near the $j\omega$-axis are very short segments. This is the result of cancellation mismatch. For any degree of mismatch, there are of course two additional closed-loop poles contributing to the total system transient response. However, if the mismatch is slight, there will be a zero very close to the pole, and the pair will make a negligible effect on system behaviour.

The extra locus near the imaginary axis should be avoided, because the locus might cross into the right-half plane making the system unstable (refer Fig. 7.49). The only safe thing to do is to place the compensator zeros well into the left-half plane and 'suck' the root loci emanating from the pure imaginary poles over to them (refer Fig. 7.50). We should never attempt to cancel poles in the right-half plane, since any inaccurate cancellation will result in an unstable closed-loop system.

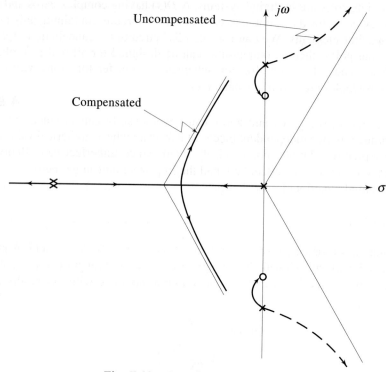

Fig. 7.48   *Cancellation compensation*

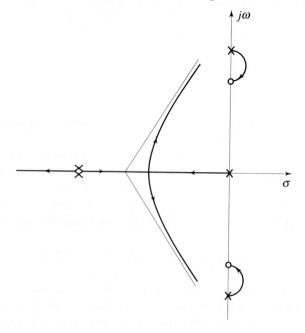

Fig. 7.49   *Cancellation compensation*

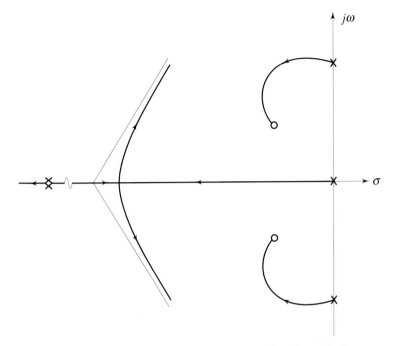

Fig. 7.50 *Compensation for undamped inertial guidance platform*

7.11 | THE ROOT LOCUS OF SYSTEMS WITH DEAD-TIME

Let us consider the problem of constructing the root locus for systems where a dead-time τ_D is involved in the loop function. Figure 7.51 shows in block diagram form two systems involving delay in the forward path and the feedback path. In either case, the characteristic equation is given by

$$1 + KG(s)H(s)e^{-\tau_D s} = 0; \; K \geq 0 \tag{7.66}$$

Equation (7.66) is not a polynomial and thus does not fall in the same class as our other examples so far. How would one plot the root locus corresponding to this equation? There are two basic approaches: direct application, and approximation of the phase criterion.

The direct application approach demands the use of angle and magnitude criteria directly on the given characteristic equation without any approximation. These criteria are not changed if the process is nonrational.

Angle criterion

$$\angle G(s)H(s)e^{-\tau_D s} = \pm 180°(2q + 1); \; q = 0,1,\ldots \tag{7.67a}$$

Magnitude criterion

$$|KG(s)H(s)e^{-\tau_D s}| = 1 \tag{7.67b}$$

One can formulate a root-locus problem as searching for locations where the angle criterion (7.67a) is satisfied. The value of the root locus gain K at any

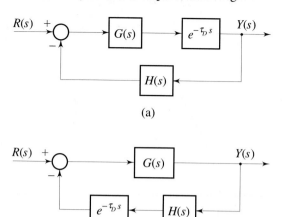

Fig. 7.51 *Closed-loop systems with time delays involved*

point on the root locus can then be determined by using the magnitude criterion (7.67b). It may however be noted that the rules given in Table 7.1 are not applicable for such a problem.

In the second approach, we reduce the given problem close to the one we have previously solved by approximating the nonrational function $e^{-\tau_D s}$ with a rational function. Since we are concerned with control systems (systems with low frequencies), we want an approximation that will be good for $s = 0$ and nearby. The most common means used to find such an approximation is attributed to Pade and is based on matching the series expansion of $e^{-\tau_D s}$ with that of a rational function, a ratio of numerator polynomial of degree p and denominator polynomial of degree q. For our purposes, we will consider only the case $p = q = 1$ (refer Eqn. (2.118)):

$$e^{-\tau_D s} \cong \frac{1 - \dfrac{\tau_D}{2} s}{1 + \dfrac{\tau_D}{2} s} = \frac{-[s - (2/\tau_D)]}{s + (2/\tau_D)} \tag{7.68}$$

With this approximation, the characteristic equation (7.66) becomes

$$1 - KG(s)H(s)\,[s - (2/\tau_D)]\,/\,[s + (2/\tau_D)] = 0 \tag{7.69}$$

Examining Eqn. (7.69), we note that the equation is of the form

$$1 - F(s) = 0 \tag{7.70}$$

where

$$F(s) = \frac{K \displaystyle\prod_{i=1}^{m} (s + z_i)}{\displaystyle\prod_{j=1}^{n} (s + p_j)}$$

This equation again is not of the standard form (7.22) used earlier to derive construction rules of Table 7.1. Therefore, the construction rules of Table 7.1

cannot be used directly even in the approach based on approximation of non-rational function $e^{-\tau_D s}$. However, only a minor modification in the rules of Table 7.1 is required to deal with characteristic equations of the form (7.70). Our discussion will be limited to second approach; the approach based on approximation given by Eqn. (7.68).

In a manner similar to the development of the root-locus method in Section 7.2, we require that the root locus of the characteristic equation (7.70) satisfy the equations:

Angle criterion

$$\angle F(s) = \sum_{i=1}^{m}(s + z_i) - \sum_{j=1}^{n}(s + p_j) = \pm\, q(360°);\ q = 0, 1, 2, \ldots \quad (7.71a)$$

Magnitude criterion

$$|F(s)| = \frac{K \prod_{i=1}^{m}|s + z_i|}{\prod_{j=1}^{n}|s + p_j|} = 1 \quad (7.71b)$$

The locus of roots follows a zero-degree locus (Eqn. (7.71a)) in contrast with the 180° locus considered previously. However, the root locus rules of Table 7.1 may be altered to account for the zero-degree phase angle requirement, and then the root locus may be obtained as in the preceding sections.

Rule (i) : No change

Rule (ii) : No change

Rule (iii) : No change in centroid calculation. Angles of asymptotes are now given by the relation $\phi_A = \dfrac{q(360°)}{n - m}$; $q = 0, 1, \ldots, (n - m - 1)$

$$(7.72)$$

Rule (iv) : A point on the real axis lies on the locus if the number of open-loop poles plus zeros on the real axis to the right of this point is even.

Rule (v) : No change

Rule (vi) : The angle of departure, ϕ_p, of a locus from a complex open-loop pole is given by

$$\phi_p = \phi \quad (7.73)$$

where ϕ is the net angle contribution at this pole of all other open-loop poles and zeros.

Rule (vii) : The angle of arrival, ϕ_z, of a locus at a complex zero is given by

$$\phi_z = -\phi \quad (7.74)$$

where ϕ is the net angle contribution at this zero of all other open-loop poles and zeros.

Rule (viii) : No change

Rule (ix) : No change

Example 7.14

Suppose that the plant in Fig. 7.51 is $G(s) = K/s$, the sensor $H(s) = 1$ and the dead-time $\tau_D = 1$ sec.

The characteristic equation of the system becomes

$$1 + \frac{Ke^{-s}}{s} = 0; \quad K \geq 0$$

With the approximation $e^{-s} \cong \dfrac{1 - s/2}{1 + s/2}$, the characteristic equation becomes

$$1 - \frac{K(s - 2)}{s(s + 2)} = 0 \tag{7.75}$$

Examining the real-axis segments of the root loci shown in Fig. 7.52, it is obvious that there will be two breakaway points. These points are the solutions

of the equation $\dfrac{dK}{ds} = 0$; where $K = \dfrac{s(s + 2)}{(s - 2)}$.

The solutions are $s = -0.83,\ 4.83$.

The characteristic equation (7.75) can equivalently be expressed as

$$s^2 + (2 - K)\,s + 2K = 0$$

Obviously, $K = 2$ results in oscillations of frequency $\omega_0 = 2$. Therefore, the root loci intersect the imaginary axis at $s = \pm j2$; the value of K corresponding to these points is 2.

The complete root locus plot is sketched in Fig.7.52. It can, in fact, be shown that the complex root branches of the root loci form a circle (refer Example 7.1).

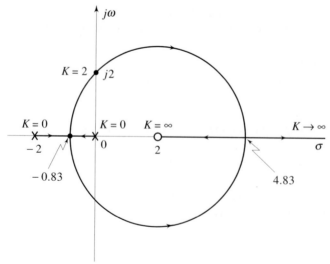

Fig. 7.52 *Root locus plot for the characteristic equation (7.75)*

7.12 SENSITIVITY AND THE ROOT LOCUS

The parameters used in the design of control systems vary due to factors such as wear and tear, aging, change in environmental conditions, variations in the operating point, model uncertainties, etc. In order to study the influence of parameter changes on the stability of the system, it is useful to determine the sensitivity of roots of the characteristic equation with respect to parameter changes.

Let $s = \lambda_1, \lambda_2,...,\lambda_n$ be the roots of the characteristic equation of a system which depend on the system parameters $\theta_1, \theta_2,..., \theta_m$. Consider the perturbation only in the parameter θ_i from its nominal value θ_{i0}. The effect of this perturbation on the root $s = \lambda_j$ with nominal value λ_{j0} is given by the following relation (refer Eqn. (4.7)):

Relative root sensitivity

$$\widetilde{S}_{\theta_i}^{\lambda_j} = \frac{\Delta\lambda_j / \lambda_{j0}}{\Delta\theta_i / \theta_{i0}} \tag{7.76}$$

If $\widetilde{S}_{\theta_i}^{\lambda_j} = 0$, then the root λ_j is insensitive to the parameter θ_i at the nominal point θ_{i0}. If $\widetilde{S}_{\theta_i}^{\lambda_j} \neq 0$, then λ_j is sensitive and the value of $\widetilde{S}_{\theta_i}^{\lambda_j}$ is a measure of the degree of dependence of λ_j on θ_i. It gives relative change $\Delta\lambda_j / \lambda_{j0}$ in the root location for a given relative change $\Delta\theta_i / \theta_{i0}$ in the parameter.

Absolute change in the root location λ_j due to change in parameters $\theta_1, \theta_2,...,\theta_m$ is, therefore, given by

$$\Delta\lambda_j = \lambda_{j0} \sum_{i=1}^{m} \widetilde{S}_{\theta_i}^{\lambda_j} \frac{\Delta\theta_i}{\theta_{i0}} \tag{7.77}$$

An alternative definition of root sensitivity is as follows.

Semirelative root sensitivity

$$S_{\theta_i}^{\lambda_j} = \frac{\Delta\lambda_j}{\Delta\theta_i / \theta_{i0}} \tag{7.78}$$

This definition gives the absolute amount of shift in the root location for a given relative change in parameters (definition (7.76) gives the relative amount of shift in the root location for a given relative change in parameters). The absolute change in the root location λ_j due to change in parameters $\theta_1, \theta_2,...,\theta_m$ is given by

$$\Delta\lambda j = \sum_{i=1}^{m} S_{\theta_i}^{\lambda_j} \frac{\Delta\theta_i}{\theta_{i0}} \tag{7.79}$$

The evaluation of the root sensitivity for a control system can be readily accomplished by utilizing the root locus method. We illustrate the procedure through an example.

Example 7.15_____

In the following, we determine and compare the root sensitivity of the roots of
a unity-feedback system with the open-loop transfer function

$$G(s) = \frac{0.5}{s(s+1)}$$

to variations (i) $\Delta\alpha$ in the open-loop pole at $s = -1$, and (ii) ΔK in the open-loop
gain of 0.5.

The characteristic equation of the nominal system is

$$s^2 + s + 0.5 = 0$$

Therefore, the nominal characteristic roots are

$$s_{1,2} = -0.5 \pm j0.5$$

Since the roots are complex conjugate, the root sensitivity for $\lambda_1 = -0.5 +
j0.5$ is the conjugate of the root sensitivity for $\lambda_2 = -0.5 - j0.5$. Therefore, we
need to evaluate only the root sensitivity of one of these roots, say λ_1.

Let us consider the root sensitivity of λ_1 to the two parameters: open-loop
pole at $s = -1$ and open-loop gain of 0.5, one by one.

Root sensitivity to open-loop pole

The open-loop transfer function

$$G(s) = \frac{0.5}{s(s+\alpha)}$$

where $\alpha = \alpha_0 + \Delta\alpha$ and $\alpha_0 = 1$. The characteristic equation as a function of
$\Delta\alpha$ is

$$s(s + 1 + \Delta\alpha) + 0.5 = 0$$

or $s^2 + s + 0.5 + (\Delta\alpha)s = 0$

The root locus for $\Delta\alpha$ is determined by using the locus equation

$$1 + \frac{(\Delta\alpha)s}{(s+0.5+j0.5)(s+0.5-j0.5)} = 0 \qquad (7.80)$$

For positive variations in α, we have

$$1 + \frac{(\Delta\alpha)s}{(s+0.5+j0.5)(s+0.5-j0.5)} = 0; \ \Delta\alpha \geq 0 \qquad (7.81)$$

The poles and zeros of Eqn. (7.81) are shown in Fig. 7.53a. The angle of
departure from the root $\lambda_1 = -0.5 + j0.5$ is

$$\phi_p = 180° + [135° - 90°] = 225°$$

Near λ_1, the locus may be approximated by a line drawn from $-0.5 + j0.5$ at
an angle of 225°, as shown in Fig. 7.53a. For a change of $\Delta\lambda_1 = 0.2 \angle 225°$
along the departure line, $\Delta\alpha$ is determined by evaluating the vector lengths from
poles and zeros:

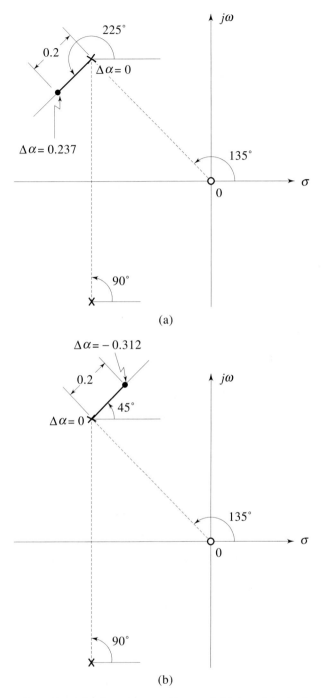

Fig. 7.53 *The root locus for the parameter (a) $\Delta\alpha \geq 0$ (b) $\Delta\alpha \leq 0$ in the characteristic equation (7.80)*

$$\Delta\alpha = 0.2 \times 0.875 / 0.7375 = 0.237$$

Therefore , the sensitivity at λ_1 to positive variations in α is

$$S_{\alpha+}^{\lambda_1} = \frac{\Delta\lambda_1}{\Delta\alpha/\alpha_0} = \frac{0.2\angle 225°}{0.237} = 0.84 \angle - 135° \qquad (7.82)$$

For negative variations in α, we have from Eqn. (7.80),

$$1 + \frac{(\Delta\alpha)s}{(s + 0.5 + j0.5)(s + 0.5 - j0.5)} = 0;\ \Delta\alpha \le 0 \qquad (7.83)$$

This equation is of the form

$$1 - F(s) = 0$$

where

$$F(s) = \frac{K \prod_{i=1}^{m}(s + z_i)}{\prod_{j=1}^{n}(s + p_j)}; K \ge 0$$

The rules given in Section 7.11 can be applied for sketching the root loci. The poles and zeros of Eqn. (7.83) are shown in Fig. 7.53b. The angle of departure from the root $\lambda_1 = - 0.5 + j\ 0.5$ is (refer Eqn. (7.73))

$$\phi_p = 135° - 90° = 45°$$

Near λ_1, the locus may be approximated by a line drawn from $- 0.5 + j0.5$ at an angle of 45° as shown in Fig. 7.53b. For a change of $\Delta\lambda_1 = 0.2\ \angle 45°$ along the departure line, $\Delta\alpha$ is determined by evaluating the vector lengths from poles and zeros:

$$\Delta\alpha = - 0.2 \times 1.15/0.7375 = - 0.312$$

Therefore the sensitivity at λ_1 to negative variations in α is

$$S_{\alpha-}^{\lambda_1} = \frac{\Delta\lambda_1}{\Delta\alpha/\alpha_0} = \frac{0.2\angle 45°}{0.312} = 0.64\angle 45° \qquad (7.84)$$

It can easily be verified that as the percentage change $(\Delta\alpha/\alpha_0)$ decreases, the sensitivity measures $S_{\alpha+}^{\lambda_1}$ and $S_{\alpha-}^{\lambda_1}$ will approach equality in magnitude and a difference in angle of 180°. Thus for small changes in $\alpha\ (\Delta\alpha/\alpha_0 \to 0)$, the sensitivity measures are related as

$$\left| S_{\alpha+}^{\lambda_1} \right| = \left| S_{\alpha-}^{\lambda_1} \right| \qquad (7.85a)$$

and

$$\angle S_{\alpha+}^{\lambda_1} = 180° + \angle S_{\alpha-}^{\lambda_1} \qquad (7.85b)$$

Usually the desired sensitivity measure is for small changes in the parameter. Therefore, we need to evaluate only one sensitivity measure, say for positive changes in parameter; the other sensitivity measure (for negative changes of parameter) can be obtained from Eqns (7.85).

Root sensitivity to open-loop gain

The open-loop transfer function

$$G(s) = \frac{K}{s(s+1)}$$

where $K = K_0 + \Delta K$ and $K_0 = 0.5$. The characteristic equation as a function of ΔK is

$$s(s+1) + 0.5 + \Delta K = 0$$

or $\quad 1 + \dfrac{\Delta K}{s^2 + s + 0.5} = 1 + \dfrac{\Delta K}{(s + 0.5 + j0.5)(s + 0.5 - j0.5)} = 0 \qquad (7.86)$

We will consider positive variations in K, i.e., $\Delta K \geq 0$.

The poles and zeros of Eqn. (7.86) are shown in Fig. 7.54. The angle of departure from the root $\lambda_1 = -0.5 + j0.5$ is

$$\phi_p = 180° + [-90°] = 90°$$

For a change of $\Delta \lambda_1 = 0.2 \angle 90°$ along the departure line, ΔK is given by

$$\Delta K = 0.2 \times 1.2 = 0.24$$

Therefore, the sensitivity at λ_1 to positive variations in K is

$$S_{K_+}^{\lambda_1} = \frac{\Delta \lambda_1}{\Delta K / K_0} = \frac{0.2 \angle 90°}{0.24 / 0.5} = 0.417 \angle 90° \qquad (7.87)$$

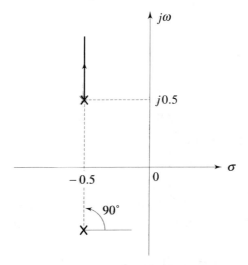

Fig. 7.54 *Root locus for the parameter $\Delta K \geq 0$ in the characteristic equation (7.86)*

▲▲

The root sensitivity measure for a parameter is useful for comparing the sensitivity for various design parameters and at different root locations. Comparing Eqns (7.82), and (7.84) for α with Eqn. (7.87) for K, we find that the sensitivity for α is greater in magnitude, and the angle for $S_{\alpha-}^{\lambda_1}$ indicates that the approach of the root toward the $j\omega$-axis is more sensitive for changes in α. Therefore, the tolerance requirements for α would be more stringent than for K. This information provides the designer with a comparative measure of the required tolerances for each parameter.

Review Examples

Review Example 7.1

The block diagram of Fig. 7.55 represents a position control system. The open-loop transfer function of the uncompensated system is

$$G(s) = \frac{K}{s(s+1)(s+4)}$$

The specifications of the system are as follows:

1. Velocity error as small as possible
2. Overshoot < 20%
3. Settling time < 5 sec

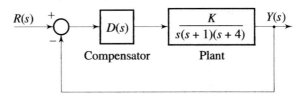

Fig. 7.55   *A position control system*

For a second-order system, damping ratio $\zeta = 0.5$ gives 16% peak over-shoot, and with undamped natural frequency $\omega_n = 2$ rad/sec, the settling time $t_s = 4/\zeta\omega_n = 4$ sec. We know that the compensated system may not behave as a perfect second-order system because of the dominance requirements; we therefore set $\zeta = 0.5$ and $\omega_n = 2$ as our design goals for dominant closed-loop poles, keeping a slight margin for degradation of transient response due to additional closed-loop poles. The desired dominant closed-loop poles are then required to be located at

$$s_{1,2} = -\zeta\omega_n \pm j\omega_n\sqrt{1-\zeta^2} = -1 \pm j1.73$$

Let us denote one of these poles by s_d:

$$s_d = -1 + j1.73$$

Figure 7.56 shows a pole-zero plot of the plant $G(s)$ and the location of the desired dominant pole s_d. From this figure, we find that

$$\angle G(s_d) = -120° - 90° - 30° = -240°$$

In order for the root locus to go through s_d, the angle contribution from the lead compensator pole-zero pair must be

$$\phi = -180° - \angle G(s_d) = -180° - (-240°) = 60°$$

Further, it is observed that the open-loop pole at $s = -1$ lies directly below the desired closed-loop pole location. Place the compensator zero close to this pole to its left, say at $s = -1.2$. Such a choice of compensator zero generally ensures the dominance condition.

Join the compensator zero to s_d and locate the compensator pole by making an angle of $\phi = 60°$, as shown in Fig. 7.56. The location of the pole is found to be at $s = -4.95$.

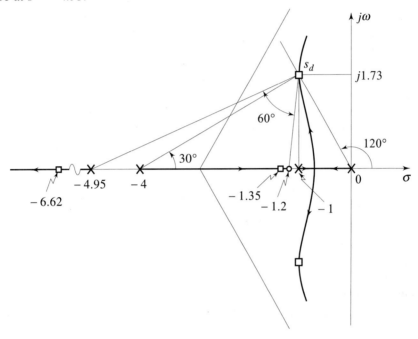

Fig. 7.56   *Root locus plot (Review Example 7.1)*

With the addition of the cascade lead compensator

$$D(s) = \frac{s + 1.2}{s + 4.95}$$

the open-loop transfer function of the system becomes

$$D(s)G(s) = \frac{K(s + 1.2)}{s(s + 1)(s + 4)(s + 4.95)}$$

The value of K at s_d, obtained from Fig. 7.56, is 30. Therefore

$$D(s)G(s) = \frac{30(s + 1.2)}{s(s + 1)(s + 4)(s + 4.95)}$$

The compensated root locus is shown in Fig. 7.56. For $K = 30$, there are two closed-loop poles on the real axis at $s = -1.35$ and $s = -6.62$. The closed-loop transfer function of the system becomes

$$\frac{Y(s)}{R(s)} = \frac{30(s+1.2)}{(s+1+j1.73)(s+1-j1.73)(s+1.35)(s+6.62)}$$

The closed-loop pole at $s = -1.35$, which is created by the introduction of the compensator zero, lies close to this zero. Its contribution to system dynamics will be insignificant. Equally, the contribution of the pole at $s = -6.62$ will be negligible as it is located far to the left of the dominant poles. The two complex poles at $s_{1,2} = -1 \pm j1.73$ should therefore dominate the response of the system. This can easily be checked by determining the step response of the closed-loop system.

The velocity error constant is

$$K_v = \lim_{s \to 0} sD(s)G(s) = \frac{30 \times 1.2}{1 \times 4 \times 4.95} = 1.82$$

Note that only a marginal increase in K_v above this value can be achieved by a slight readjustment of the compensating zero. Any large shift in the compensating zero would result in appreciable degradation of the transient performance.

Review Example 7.2 ————————————————————

Reconsider the system of Fig. 7.55. The system is to be compensated to meet the following specifications:

Damping ratio, $\zeta = 0.5$
Settling time, $t_s \le 10$ sec
Velocity error constant, $K_v \ge 5$ sec^{-1}

From the transient response specifications, it follows that undamped natural frequency

$$\omega_n = \frac{4}{10 \times 0.5} = 0.8 \text{ rad/sec}$$

The desired dominant closed-loop poles are then required to be located at

$$s_{1,2} = -\zeta\omega_n \pm j\omega_n\sqrt{1-\zeta^2} = -0.4 \pm j0.7$$

Figure 7.57 shows a pole-zero plot of the plant $G(s)$ and a desired closed-loop pole at $s_d = -0.4 + j0.7$. From this figure, we find that

$$\angle G(s_d) = -120° - 49.4° - 11° = -180.4°$$

The angle criterion is (approximately) satisfied and therefore the point s_d lies on (or close to) root locus of the uncompensated system.

At s_d, the gain K^{uc} of the uncompensated system is given by
$$K^{uc} = 0.8 \times 0.9 \times 3.7 = 2.66$$

The velocity error constant of the uncompensated system is
$$K_v^{uc} = \lim_{s \to 0} sG(s) = 2.66/4 = 0.666$$

The desired velocity error constant in $K_v^d \geq 5$.

Therefore the β-parameter of the lag compensator is given by
$$\beta = K_v^d / K_v^{uc} = 5/0.666 = 7.5$$

To counter the effect of small negative angle contributed by the lag compensator at s_d, choose a slightly higher value of β, say $\beta = 10$.

From the desired location s_d, draw a line making an angle of, say 6° with the desired ζ-line. Its intersection with the real axis determines the compensator zero at $s = -z = -0.1$ as shown in Fig. 7.57. The compensator pole is then located at $s = -p = -z/\beta = -0.01$.

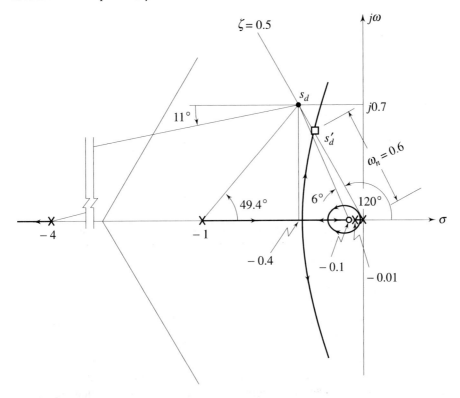

Fig. 7.57 *Root locus plot (Review Example 7.2)*

With the addition of the cascade lag compensator
$$D(s) = \frac{s + 0.1}{s + 0.01}$$

the open-loop transfer function of the system becomes

$$D(s)G(s) = \frac{K(s + 0.1)}{s(s + 0.01)(s + 1)(s + 4)}$$

The compensated root locus is shown in Fig. 7.57. Note that because of the small negative angle contributed by the lag compensator at s_d, this point does not lie on the compensated root locus. The point s'_d which lies on the $\zeta = 0.5$ line and satisfies angle criterion for the compensated root locus, gives $\omega_n = 0.6$ rad/sec. Thus, the undamped natural frequency has decreased from 0.8 to 0.6 rad/sec because of the lag compensation. This means a slight increase in the settling time. If this increase is unacceptable, the system must be redesigned by choosing s_d with a slightly higher value of ω_n than the specified value 0.8.

The value of K at s'_d, obtained from Fig. 7.57, is 2.5. Therefore

$$D(s)G(s) = \frac{2.5(s + 0.1)}{s(s + 0.01)(s + 1)(s + 4)}$$

The velocity error constant of the compensated system is

$$K_v = \frac{2.5 \times 0.1}{0.01 \times 4} = 6.25$$

which is satisfactory.

Review Example 7.3 _____

Let us again consider the system of Fig. 7.55. The system is now required to be compensated to meet the following specifications:

Damping ratio, $\zeta = 0.5$
Undamped natural frequency, $\omega_n = 2$ rad/sec
Velocity error constant, $K_v \geq 5$ sec^{-1}

The desired dominant closed-loop poles are required to be located at

$$s_{1,2} = -\zeta\omega_n \pm j\omega_n \sqrt{1 - \zeta^2} = -1 \pm j1.73$$

Figure 7.58 shows the pole-zero plot of the plant $G(s) = \dfrac{K}{s(s + 1)(s + 4)}$, and a desired closed-loop pole at $s_d = -1 + j1.7$. From this figure, we find that

$$\angle G(s_d) = -120° - 90° - 30° = -240°$$

The point s_d, therefore, does not lie on the uncompensated root locus and transient response specifications cannot be met by gain adjustment alone. We propose to add a cascade lead compensator to meet the transient response specifications. In order for the root locus to go through s_d, the angle contribution from the lead compensator pole-zero pair must be

$$\phi = -180° - \angle G(s_d) = -180° - (-240°) = 60°$$

Further, it is observed that the open-loop pole at $s = -1$ lies directly below the desired closed-loop pole location. It appears that the best transient response

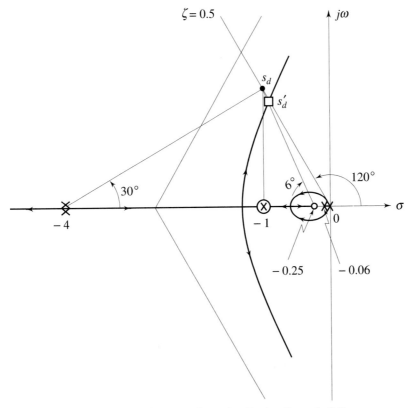

Fig. 7.58 *Root locus plot (Review Example 7.3)*

due to the complex closed-loop pole will occur when the zero of the compensator cancels the open-loop pole at $s = -1$; there will be no real closed-loop pole near the imaginary axis in this case. This ideal situation, however, cannot be realized practically because of imperfect cancellation. A real closed-loop pole near the imaginary axis will occur but a zero will be very close to it; the dominance condition will therefore be ensured.

Join the compensator zero to s_d and locate the compensator pole making an angle of $\phi = 60°$ as shown in Fig. 7.58. The location of the pole is found to be at $s = -4$.

With the addition of the cascade lead compensator

$$D_1(s) = \frac{s+1}{s+4} = \frac{s + 1/\tau_1}{s + 1/\alpha\tau_1}; \ \tau_1 = 1, \ \alpha = \frac{1}{4}$$

the open-loop transfer function of the system becomes

$$D_1(s)G(s) = \frac{K(s+1)}{s(s+1)(s+4)^2} = \frac{K}{s(s+4)^2}$$

The value of K at s_d is found to be 24. Therefore

$$D_1(s)G(s) = \frac{24}{s(s+4)^2}$$

The velocity error constant of the lead compensated system is

$$K_v^{lc} = \lim_{s \to 0} s\, D_1(s)G(s) = 1.5$$

This does not meet the specified $K_v \geq 5$. A lag section

$$D_2(s) = \frac{s + 1/\tau_2}{s + \alpha/\tau_2} = \frac{s + 1/\tau_2}{s + 1/4\tau_2}$$

will increase K_v by about four times, which then satisfies the specifications on steady-state performance.

The line drawn from s_d making an angle of 6° with the desired ζ-line intersects real axis at -0.25 which gives the location of the zero of the lag section. The pole of the lag section is then found to be at $-0.25/4 \cong -0.06$.

The open-loop transfer function of the lag-lead compensated system then becomes

$$D_2(s)D_1(s)G(s) = \frac{K^c(s + 0.25)}{s(s + 0.06)(s + 4)^2}$$

The root locus plot for the lag-lead compensated system is shown in Fig. 7.58. From this figure, the gain at s_d' (which is slightly shifted from s_d due to introduction of the lag section) is given by $K^c = 23.5$.

Therefore, the open-loop transfer function of the lag-lead compensated system is

$$D_2(s)D_1(s)G(s) = \frac{23.5(s + 0.25)}{s(s + 0.06)(s + 4)^2}$$

Review Example 7.4

Consider a plant with transfer function

$$G(s) = \frac{2}{s(s + 1)(s + 5)}$$

Design a feedback system to meet the specifications:
1. Velocity error as small as possible
2. $\zeta = 0.707$
3. Settling time < 4.5 seconds

Solution

As a first try, we choose a unity-feedback system shown in Fig. 7.59. The root locus plot of this system for $A > 0$ is shown in Fig. 7.60. In order for the feedback system to have settling time less than 4.5 seconds, all the closed-loop poles must lie on the left hand side of the vertical line passing through the point $-4/t_s = -4/4.5 = -0.9$. From the root loci in Fig. 7.60 we see that this is not possible for any $A > 0$. Therefore, the configuration in Fig. 7.59 cannot meet the specifications.

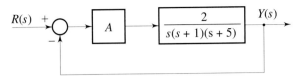

Fig. 7.59   *A control configuration (Review Example 7.4)*

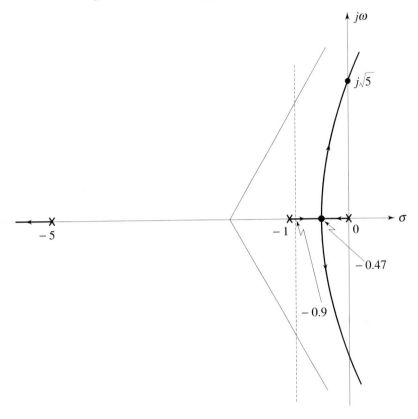

Fig. 7.60   *Root locus plot for the system of Fig. 7.59*

As a next try, we introduce an additional tachometer feedback as shown in Fig. 7.61. The characteristic equation of the system becomes

$$1 + \frac{AG(s)}{1 + sK_t G(s)} = 0 \qquad (7.88)$$

where

$$G(s) = \frac{2}{s(s + 1)(s + 5)}.$$

Rearranging, we get

$$s^3 + 6s^2 + (5 + 2K_t)\, s + 2A = 0$$

There are two variable parameters: A and K_t. We can use single-parameter root loci for the design by choosing a value for A. First we choose $A = 5$ and carry out the design. We will change the value of A appropriately if we find that the design is not possible with $A = 5$.

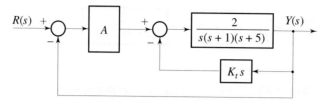

Fig. 7.61 *Tachometer feedback control configuration (Review Example 7.4)*

Partitioning of the characteristic equation with $A = 5$ gives

$$1 + \frac{2K_t s}{s^3 + 6s^2 + 5s + 10} = 0$$

or $\qquad 1 + \dfrac{Ks}{(s + 5.42)(s + 0.29 + j1.33)(s + 0.29 - j1.33)} = 0$

    The root loci of this equation are plotted in Fig. 7.62. The $\zeta = 0.707$ line intersects the root locus at two points. Both the points lie on the left-hand side of the vertical line passing through -0.9. From Fig. 7.62, we see that the point $-1.2 + j1.2$ that corresponds to $K = 6.3$ (or $K_t = 3.15$), meets the dominance requirement better compared to the other point. We therefore select $K_t = 3.15$

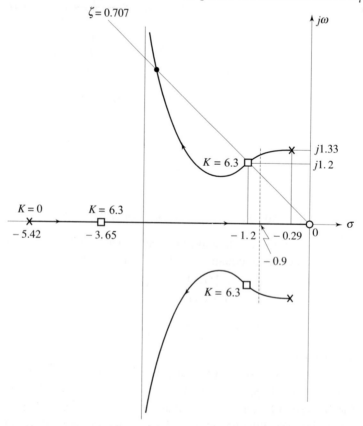

Fig. 7.62 *Root locus plot for the system of Fig. 7.61*

Let us now investigate the steady-state behaviour of the compensated system. From Eqn. (7.88), the velocity error constant K_v is given by

$$K_v = \lim_{s \to 0} s \left[\frac{AG(s)}{1 + sK_t G(s)} \right]$$

$$= \lim_{s \to 0} s \left[\frac{10}{s(s+1)(s+5) + 6.3s} \right] = \frac{10}{11.3}$$

A marginal increase in K_v above this value can be achieved by readjustment of the parameter A.

Review Questions

7.1 Discuss the compensation characteristics of cascade lag and lead compensators using root locus plots. Show that

(i) lead compensation is suitable for systems having unsatisfactory transient response, and it provides a limited improvement in steady-state performance; and

(ii) lag compensation is suitable for systems with satisfactory transient response but unsatisfactory steady-state response.

7.2 In many control systems, it is desirable to use a feedback compensator forming a minor loop around the plant, in addition to a cascade gain compensator which is used to adjust the overall performance. Discuss compensation characteristics of the minor-loop feedback scheme. (Help: Section 7.9, pp647-648)

7.3 (a) Show that a lead compensator is nothing but a PD controller with a filter. (Help: pp447-448)

(b) Show that a lag compensator has the characteristics of a PI controller. (Help: pp451-452)

(c) In a design problem using cascade lag-lead compensator, α-parameter of lead stage and β-parameter of lag stage are related by $\alpha = 1/\beta$. Is there any advantage of such a choice? (Help: p468, pp700-702)

(d) Cascade lag compensated system usually has a closed-loop pole near the origin in addition to the desired complex-conjugate pair of poles. How do you justify your claim of having achieved the desired performance? (Help: Example 7.10)

7.4 (a) A type-1 system with finite e_{ss} to ramp input has been accepted in the design problems. Why? We know that e_{ss} to parabolic input will be infinity. (Help: p366)

(b) A type-2 system has finite e_{ss} to parabolic input. Do you recommend PI controller to reduce e_{ss} to zero? Why? (Help: p455)

(c) A plant has a transfer function $K/(s-1)$. Do you recommend a controller $(s-1)/(s+1)$ in cascade with the plant? Why? (Help: p481)

7.5 Show that lead and lag compensators usually give successful design only if system dynamics is dominated by real poles. Suggest compensation schemes for plants dominated by complex conjugate poles. Give physical examples of plants where such transfer functions occur. (Help: p125, Section 7.10, p648)

7.6 A plant has transfer function $G(s)H(s)e^{-s\tau_D}$. Approximate the non-rational function with the rational one for the purpose of root-locus plotting. Are the root-locus plotting rules given in Table 7.1 directly applicable to this situation? If not, give modified rules.

7.7 λ_1, λ_2, ..., λ_n are the roots of the characteristic equation of a feedback system which depend on the plant parameters θ_1, θ_2, ..., θ_m. Consider the perturbation in the parameter θ_i from its nominal value θ_{i0}. Illustrate with the help of an example the sensitivity analysis that yields the effect of perturbation in θ_i on the root λ_j with nominal value λ_{j0}.

Problems

7.1 For each of the open-loop transfer functions $F(s)$ given below, sketch the general shape of the root locus plot of the characteristic equation $1 + F(s) = 0$, as the gain K is varied from 0 to ∞. Where applicable, the plot should include (i) the large-gain asymptotes, (ii) the angles of departure from complex poles of $F(s)$, (iii) the angles of arrival at complex zeros of $F(s)$, (iv) breakaway points, and (v) the frequency at which the root loci cross the $j\omega$-axis.

(a) $F(s) = \dfrac{K(s+2)}{(s+3)^2(s+1+j4)(s+1-j4)}$

(b) $F(s) = \dfrac{K}{s(s+3)(s^2+2s+2)}$

(c) $F(s) = \dfrac{K(s^2+6s+25)}{s(s+1)(s+2)}$

(d) $F(s) = \dfrac{K}{s(s^2+4s+5)}$

(e) $F(s) = \dfrac{K(s+1)}{s^2(s+4)}$

(f) $F(s) = \dfrac{K(s+1)}{s^2(s+12)}$

(g) $F(s) = \dfrac{K(s+4)}{(s+0.5)^2(s+2)}$

7.2 For each of the characteristic equations given below, estimate locations of multiple roots (if any), and the order of multiplicity of roots. Roughly sketch the root locus plot in each case showing clearly the directions of root loci approaching the points of multiple roots, and the directions at which the loci break away from these points.

(i) $1 + \dfrac{K}{s(s^2+6s+10)} = 0; K \geq 0$

(ii) $1 + \dfrac{K}{s(s^2+6s+12)} = 0; K \geq 0$

(iii) $1 + \dfrac{K(s+1)}{s^2(s+9)} = 0; K \geq 0$

(iv) $1 + \dfrac{K}{s(s+2)(s^2+2s+5)} = 0; K \geq 0$

(v) $1 + \dfrac{K}{s(s+2)(s^2+2s+2)} = 0; K \geq 0$

7.3 A unity-feedback control system has an open-loop transfer function

$$G(s) = \frac{K}{s(s+1)(s+2)}\ ; K \geq 0$$

Make a rough sketch of the root locus plot of the system, explicitly identifying the centroid, the asymptotes, the breakaway points and $\pm j\omega$ cross-over points. By a trial-and-error application of the angle criterion, locate a point on the locus that gives dominant closed-loop poles with $\zeta = 0.5$. Determine the value of K at this point. Corresponding to this value of K, determine the closed-loop transfer function of the system.

7.4 A unity-feedback control system has an open-loop transfer function

$$G(s) = \frac{K}{s(s+4)(s^2+8s+32)}; K \geq 0$$

Make a rough sketch of the root locus plot of the system, explicitly identifying the centroid, the asymptotes, the breakaway points, the departure angles from poles of $G(s)$, and the $\pm j\omega$ cross-over points.

By a trial-and-error application of the angle criterion, locate a point on the locus that gives dominant closed-loop poles with $\zeta = 0.707$. Determine the value of K at this point. Corresponding to this value of K, roughly locate the other two closed-loop poles and comment upon the dominance condition.

7.5 A unity-feedback control system has an open-loop transfer function

$$G(s) = \frac{K}{s(s^2+8s+32)}; K \geq 0$$

Make a rough sketch of the root locus plot of the system, explicitly identifying the centroid, the asymptotes, the departure angles from complex poles of $G(s)$, and the $\pm j\omega$ cross-over points.

By a trial-and-error application of the angle criterion, locate a point on the locus that gives dominant closed-loop poles with $\zeta = 0.5$. Determine the value of K at this point. Corresponding to this value of K, roughly locate the third closed-loop pole and comment upon the dominance condition.

7.6 Draw the root locus plot for a control system with unity feedback having the forward-path transfer function

$$G(s) = \frac{K}{s(s+1)(s+5)}; K \geq 0$$

Give all relevant characteristics of the curves that are useful in establishing the locus.

Find the least value of K to give an oscillatory response and the greatest value of K that can be used before continuous oscillations occur. Find the frequency of the continuous oscillations when K is just large enough to give this condition.

7.7 Prove that a combination of two poles $s = -a_1$ and $s = -a_2$ and one zero $s = -b$ to the left of both of them on the real axis, results in a root locus whose complex root branches form a circle centred at the zero with radius given by $\sqrt{(b - a_1)(b - a_2)}$; the root locus gain varying from 0 to ∞.

7.8 Consider a unity-feedback system with a forward path transfer function

$$G(s) = \frac{K(s + 3)}{s(s + 2)}; K \geq 0$$

Show that part of the root locus is a circle.

Construct the root locus and determine the damping ratio for maximum oscillatory response. What is the value of K at this point of the locus?

7.9 Prove that the combination of two complex-conjugate poles $s_{1,2} = -\alpha \pm j\beta$ and a real zero $s = -b$ results in a root locus whose complex root branches lie on a circle centred at the zero with radius = $\sqrt{(\alpha - b)^2 + \beta^2}$; the root locus gain varies from 0 to ∞.

7.10 Consider a unity-feedback system with open-loop transfer function

$$G(s) = \frac{K(s^2 + 1)}{s(s + 2)}; K \geq 0$$

Sketch the root locus plot. Show that the complex root branches lie on a circle.

7.11 Consider a unity-feedback system with a forward path transfer function

$$G(s) = \frac{K(s + 4)}{(s + 2)(s - 1)}; K \geq 0$$

Draw a root locus plot and find the value of K that results in $\zeta = 0.707$ and $t_s < 4$ sec. Determine the peak overshoot, the settling time, and the position error for this value of K.

7.12 Sketch the root locus plot for the system shown in Fig. P7.12 as K varies from 0 to ∞. Show that the complex root branches of the plot form a circle.

Find the value of K that results in (i) damping ratio $\zeta = 1$, and (ii) minimum steady-state error to ramp inputs.

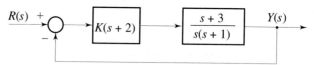

Fig. P7.12

7.13 Consider the control loop shown in Fig. P7.13. Sketch the root locus plot as K varies from 0 to ∞. Find the value of K that yields an oscillatory response of the control loop with a damping ratio of 0.707.

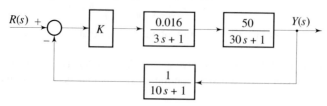

Fig. P7.13

7.14 Figure P7.14 represents a position servo with an appreciable sensor time-constant.
   (a) Plot root loci and find $K > 0$ for a damping ratio of 0.5 for unity feedback (i.e., assuming an ideal feedback sensor).
   (b) If the actual sensor has in fact an appreciable time-constant, what will be the actual damping ratio if the value of K found in part (a) is used? An approximate answer will suffice.

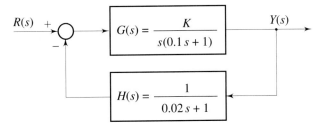

Fig. P7.14

7.15 Consider the system shown in Fig. P7.15. Sketch the root locus plot of the system as gain K varies from 0 to ∞. Determine the value of K such that the damping ratio ζ of the dominant closed-loop poles is 0.5. For the selected value of K, find all the closed-loop poles.

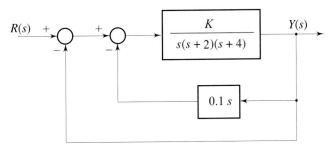

Fig. P7.15

7.16 Consider the servo system shown in Fig. P7.16. Sketch the root locus plot of the system as the velocity feedback constant K_t varies from 0 to ∞. Determine the value of K_t such that the closed-loop poles have a damping ratio of 0.7.

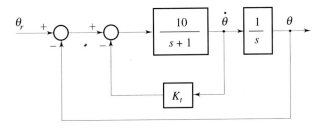

Fig. P7.16

7.17 Consider the system shown in Fig. P7.17. Draw the root locus plot of the system as K_t is varied from 0 to ∞. Determine the value of K_t such that damping

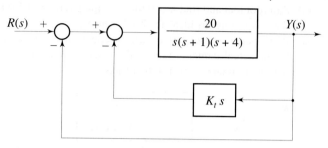

Fig. P7.17

ratio of the dominant closed-loop poles is 0.4.
If more than one solution to the above problem is possible, then select a solution that meets the dominance condition better.

7.18 Consider the system shown in Fig. P7.18. Draw the root locus plot of the system as α is varied from 0 to ∞. Determine the value of α such that damping ratio ζ of the dominant closed-loop poles is 0.5. For the selected value of α, find all the closed-loop poles.

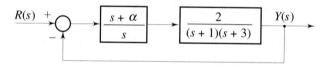

Fig. P7.18

7.19 Consider the system shown in Fig. P7.19. Draw the root locus plot of the system as α is varied from 0 to ∞. Determine the value of α such that damping ratio ζ of the dominant closed-loop poles is 0.5. For the selected value of α, find all the closed-loop poles.

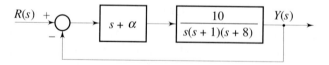

Fig. P7.19

7.20 Consider the feedback system of Fig. P7.20. Note that the plant is open-loop unstable.

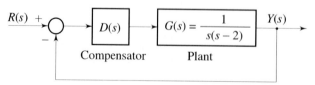

Fig. P7.20

    (a) Plot the root loci to determine whether the system can be stabilized by proportional control, i.e., $D(s) = K$.

    (b) If not, could the unstable pole of $G(s)$ be cancelled by a zero of $D(s)$ to stabilize the system, and if not, why not?

    (c) Choose a compensator $D(s) = \dfrac{K(s+1)}{s+8}$ and sketch root loci. How does this phase-lead compensator affect the transient as well as steady-state behaviour?

7.21 A unity-feedback system has an open-loop transfer function

$$G(s) = \frac{K}{s(s+1)(s+5)}$$

Draw the root locus plot and determine the value of K that yields a damping ratio of 0.3 for the dominant closed-loop poles. A phase-lag compensator having a transfer function

$$D(s) = \frac{10s+1}{100s+1}$$

is now introduced in tandem. Find the new value of K that gives the same damping ratio for the dominant closed-loop poles. Compare the velocity error constant and settling time of the original and the compensated systems.

7.22 A unity-feedback system has forward path transfer function

$$G(s) = \frac{K}{s(s+1)}$$

It is required that the closed-loop poles be located at $s_{1,2} = -1.6 \pm j4$ using a lead compensator with transfer function $D(s) = \dfrac{s+2.5}{s+\alpha}$.

Determine the values of α and K to locate the closed-loop poles as required. What is the location of the third closed-loop pole?

7.23 Consider the type-1 system of Fig. P7.23. We would like to design the compensator $D(s)$ to meet the following specifications:

    (i) Damping ratio $\zeta = 0.707$

    (ii) Settling time ≤ 2 sec

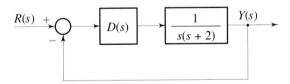

Fig. P7.23

    (a) Show that the proportional control is not adequate.

    (b) Show that proportional plus derivative control will work.

    (c) For $D(s) = K_c + K_D s$, find gains K_c and K_D to meet the design specifications.

7.24 A unity-feedback servo system has open-loop transfer function

$$G(s) = \frac{100(1 + 10\,s)}{s(1 + 0.2\,s + 0.25\,s^2)}$$

A second-order cascade compensator

$$D(s) = \frac{s^2 + 0.8s + 4}{(s + 0.384)(s + 10.42)}$$

cancels the complex poles of $G(s)$. Using root-locus analysis, compare the transient performance of compensated and uncompensated systems. What is the effect of $D(s)$ on steady-state performance?

7.25 Determine the values of K, z, and p of the system shown in Fig. P7.25, so that (i) the dominant closed-loop poles have damping ratio $\zeta = 0.45$ and (ii) velocity error constant $K_v = 20$.

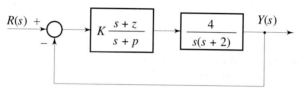

Fig. P7.25

7.26 The controlled plant of a unity-feedback system is

$$G(s) = \frac{K}{s\,(s + 1)(s + 5)}$$

It is desired to compensate the system so as to meet the following transient response specifications.

Settling time, $t_s \leq 3$ sec

Peak overshoot for step input $\leq 20\%$

Design a suitable cascade compensator (choose the compensator zero so as to cancel the plant pole at $s = -1$). What is the velocity error constant of the compensated system?

7.27 The controlled plant of a unity-feedback system is

$$G(s) = \frac{K}{s(s + 1)}$$

It is desired to compensate the system so as to meet the following transient response specifications:

Damping ratio, $\zeta = 0.707$

Settling time, $t_s = 1.4$ sec

Design a suitable first-order or second-order (two first-order sections in cascade) lead compensator for the system.

7.28 The controlled plant of a unity-feedback system is

$$G(s) = \frac{1.06}{s(s + 1)(s + 2)}$$

Sketch a root locus plot of the system, and determine the dominant closed-loop poles and the velocity error constant.

It is desired to increase the velocity error constant to about 5 sec^{-1} without appreciably changing the location of the dominant closed-loop poles. Design a first-order cascade compensator $D(s) = \dfrac{K(s+z)}{s+p}$ to meet this specification.

7.29 The controlled plant of a unity-feedback system is

$$G(s) = \frac{K}{s(s+10)(s+20)}$$

Determine the value of K so that the damping ratio of the dominant closed-loop poles is 0.6. For this value of K, determine the velocity error constant K_v.

It is desired to increase K_v by a factor of 10. It is also desired to keep the damping ratio of the dominant closed-loop poles at 0.6. A small change in the undamped natural frequency of the dominant closed-loop poles is permissible. Design a suitable cascade compensator to realize these objectives.

7.30 Consider the type-0 system of Fig. P7.30. We would like to design the compensator $D(s)$ to meet the following specifications:
  (i) Damping ratio, $\zeta = 0.6$
  (ii) Time constant $\tau = 1/\zeta\omega_n = 1/0.75$
  (iii) Zero steady-state error for a step input.
  (a) Show that the proportional control is not adequate.
  (b) Show that proportional plus integral control will work.
  (c) For $D(s) = K_c + \dfrac{K_I}{s}$, find gains K_c and K_I to meet the design specifications.

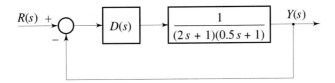

Fig. P7.30

7.31 The controlled plant of a unity-feedback system is

$$G(s) = \frac{K}{s(s+10)^2}$$

It is specified that velocity error constant of the system be equal to 20, while the damping ratio of the dominant roots be 0.707. Design a suitable cascade compensation scheme to meet the specifications.

7.32 Controlled plant of a unity-feedback system is

$$G(s) = \frac{K}{s(s+1)(s+5)}$$

It is desired to compensate the system so as to meet the following specifications:
Damping ratio of dominant roots = 0.45
Undamped natural frequency of dominant roots = 3.5 rad/sec
Velocity error constant = 30 sec^{-1}

Design a cascade lag-lead compensator to meet these objectives (choose the zero of the lead section of the compensator to cancel the plant pole at $s = -1$).

7.33 Controlled plant of a unity-feedback system is

$$G(s) = \frac{1}{s^2 + 1}$$

(a) Design a PD controller such that the dominant closed-loop poles are located at $-1 \pm j\sqrt{3}$. What is the position error constant of the compensated system?

(b) It is desired to reduce the steady-state error to step inputs to zero. Design a PID controller that meets the requirements on both the transient and the steady-state performance.

7.34 A unity-feedback system is characterized by the open-loop transfer function

$$G(s) = \frac{K}{s(s + 3)(s + 9)}$$

(a) Determine the value of K if 20% overshoot to a step input is desired.

(b) For the above value of K, determine the settling time and velocity error constant K_v.

(c) Design a cascade compensator that will give approximately 15% overshoot to a unit-step input, while the settling time is decreased by a factor of 2.5 with $K_v \geq 20$.

7.35 For a plant with transfer function $G(s) = \dfrac{K}{s(s + 2)}$, a feedback system is to be designed to satisfy the following specifications:

(i) Steady-state error for a ramp input ≤ 35 % of input slope

(ii) Damping ratio of dominant roots ≥ 0.707

(iii) Settling time of the system ≤ 3 sec

The structure of the control system is shown in Fig. P7.35. Select the parameters K and K_t to meet the given specifications.

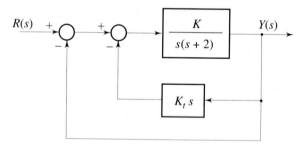

Fig. P7.35

7.36 Consider the feedback system of Fig. P7.35. Sketch a root contour plot which shows the total effect of variation of two parameters, $\alpha = K$ and $\beta = KK_t$, on the poles of the feedback system.

7.37 For a plant with transfer function $G(s) = \dfrac{K}{s(s+1)(s+5)}$, a feedback system

is to be designed to satisfy the following specifications:
  (i) Dominant closed-loop poles at $-1 \pm j2$.
  (ii) Ramp error constant, $K_v \geq 1.5$
The structure of the control system is shown in Fig. P7.37.
  (a) Select the parameters A, K, and K_t to meet the given specifications.
  (b) Find the closed-loop transfer function of the system.

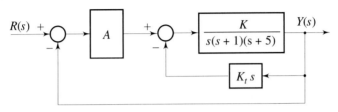

Fig. P7.37

7.38 For the feedback system of Fig. P7.37, sketch a root contour plot which shows the total effect of variation of two parameters, $\alpha = AK$ and $\beta = KK_t$, on the closed-loop poles.

7.39 A unity-feedback control system has an open-loop transfer function

$$G(s) = \frac{Ke^{-s}}{s+1}$$

Sketch a root locus plot of the system as K is varied from 0 to ∞, using the

approximation $e^{-s} = \dfrac{1 - \dfrac{1}{2}s}{1 + \dfrac{1}{2}s}$.

Show that the complex root branches form a circle.

7.40 Sketch a root locus plot for the characteristic equation

$$1 + \frac{Ks}{s^2 + s + 0.5} = 0; K \leq 0$$

Show that the complex root segments lie on a circle.

7.41 Determine and compare root sensitivity of the dominant roots of a unity-feedback system with an open-loop transfer function

$$G(s) = \frac{20.7(s+3)}{s(s+2)(s+8)}$$

to variations

  (i) $+\Delta\alpha$ in the open-loop pole at $s = -8$
  (ii) $+\Delta\beta$ in the zero at $s = -3$
Which of the two variations is dangerous?

7.42 A unity-feedback control system has an open-loop transfer function

$$G(s) = \frac{K(s+5)}{s(s+2)(s+3)}$$

(a) Sketch the root loci for varying K. Show that for $K=8$, the closed-loop poles are located at $-4, -0.5 \pm j3.12$.

(b) Sketch loci to show the effect of variation δ of the open-loop pole at $s = -2$ on the closed-loop poles for $K = 8$. Which direction of variation is dangerous?

chapter 8

The Nyquist Stability Criterion and Stability Margins

8.1 INTRODUCTION

In the preceding chapters, we have presented techniques for the analysis and design of feedback control systems based on pole-zero (root locus) formalism. An overview of the control-system design procedure is as follows.

Step 1: Construct transfer function models for the controlled process, actuator, and the sensor. Validate the models with experimental data where possible.

Step 2: Investigate the stability properties of a feedback structure of the form shown in Fig. 8.1.

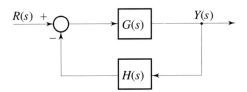

Fig. 8.1 *A feedback control system*

The stability as we know, is dictated by the poles of the closed-loop transfer function

$$\frac{Y(s)}{R(s)} = \frac{G(s)}{1 + G(s)H(s)}$$

Given the open-loop transfer function $G(s)H(s)$, the stability of the closed-loop transfer function can be determined using Routh stability criterion, without actually computing the closed-loop poles.

Step 3: Translate the performance requirements into time response, and pole-zero specifications.

A typical result of this step is a requirement that the system has a step response with specified limits on rise time, peak overshoot, and settling time. This requirement is translated into a pair of dominant poles in the specified region of the *s*-plane. The maximum allowable steady-state error in tracking standard test signals is also specified.

Step 4: Shape the root locus plot by simple cascade compensators and/or minor-loop feedback compensators. Try to meet the specifications on dominant closed-loop poles and steady-state accuracy.

Compare the trial-and-error compensators with respect to the effects of plant parameter variations, sensor noise and external disturbances. If a design seems satisfactory, go to step 6; otherwise try step 5.

Step 5: Re-evaluate the specifications, the physical configuration of the process, and the actuator and sensor selections in the light of the current design and go to step 1.

Step 6: Build a computer model and compute (simulate) the performance of the design.

The computer model of the system must include important nonlinearities such as actuator saturation, noise, and parameter variations that are expected during the operation of the system. Such a simulation of the design will confirm stability and robustness, and allow one to predict the true performance to be expected from the system. If the performance is not satisfactory, go to step 1.

Step 7: Build a prototype.

As a final test before production, a prototype can be built and tested. After these tests, one might want to reconsider the sensor, actuator, and process, and conceivably return to step 1—unless time, money, or ideas have run out.

▲▲

The root locus design technique, developed by Walter R. Evans in 1948, is highly attractive because it offers the designer the advantage of dealing directly with the poles and zeros of a closed-loop system, enabling him/her to exert direct influence on the dynamic behaviour of the system. By the judicious location of poles and zeros of compensation devices, the designer can see almost at a glance the manner in which the transient response of the closed-loop system is affected. Construction of the root locus plots to acceptable engineering accuracy is straightforward. The success of the method is, however, dependent upon the availability of reasonably accurate pole-zero models of the process, the actuator, and the sensor.

We now turn our attention to a design technique that uses only the information of $G(s)$ and $H(s)$ along the positive imaginary axis, that is, $G(j\omega)$ and $H(j\omega)$ for all $\omega \geq 0$; and is called the *frequency domain technique*. Chronologically, the frequency-domain technique was the first method developed to design control systems. Harry Nyquist in 1932 published his study of stability theory, which is the foundation of the frequency-domain approach to control system analysis and design. The Nyquist criterion is a graphical procedure for illustrating system stability, or lack thereof. The complex plots (Nyquist plots) required can usually be sketched quickly without extensive mathematical calculations. System stability and the margins by which that stability is obtained (relative stability) are readily apparent from the sketch.

The general objective in all the frequency-domain design procedures is to shape the Nyquist plot to achieve acceptable closed-loop response characteristics. Direct use of the Nyquist plot for design is not particularly convenient, since changes in parameters other than gain require extensive plot revisions. The work of Hendrik W. Bode during the 1930s led to a more efficient design procedure: the general characteristics of the Nyquist plot can be visualized with reasonable accuracy in most cases of interest from the Bode plot shape, and the Bode plot is easily constructed and modified. The frequency-domain design procedures are reduced to orderly graphical trial-and-error processes carried out using the Bode plot. Thus, although the Nyquist plot characteristics form the basis for all of our designs, the mechanics of the design procedures are readily established on the Bode plot without requiring the construction of Nyquist plot.

A preview of the frequency-domain design procedure is as follows.

Step 1: Construct transfer function models for the controlled process, actuator, and the sensor. Validate the models $G(s)$ and $H(s)$ (refer Fig. 8.1) with experimental data where possible. Compute $G(j\omega)$ and $H(j\omega)$; $\omega \geq 0$.

Major strength of frequency-domain methods is that it does not need precise mathematical models. It uses only $G(j\omega)$ and $H(j\omega)$ which, for stable devices, can be obtained by direct measurement. Once $G(j\omega)$ and $H(j\omega)$ are measured, we may proceed directly to the design without computing the transfer functions $G(s)$ and $H(s)$.

Step 2: Investigate stability properties of a feedback structure of the form shown in Fig. 8.1.

Given the data $G(j\omega)$ and $H(j\omega)$; $\omega \geq 0$, computed from $G(s)$ and $H(s)$ with s replaced by $j\omega$, or obtained by experimental measurement, the stability of the closed-loop system can be determined by the Nyquist stability criterion using Nyquist plots/Bode plots.

Step 3: Translate the performance requirements into frequency-domain specifications.

There is a definite correlation between the time-domain and frequency-domain modes of behaviour. A common procedure is to interpret desired time-domain behaviour (step response with specified limits on rise time, peak overshoot, and settling time) in terms of frequency-domain characteristics. Design is carried out in the frequency domain and is translated back into the time domain. There is a constant interplay of characteristics between the two domains. Thus the correlation between the time-domain and frequency-domain modes of behaviour plays a major role in the design procedure. Unfortunately, this correlation is not a simple one mathematically. Accordingly, in dealing with the problem of stabilizing and compensating control systems by using the frequency-domain techniques, control over the time-domain behaviour is most conveniently secured in terms of appropriate figures of merit such as gain margin, phase margin, bandwidth, etc., which although defined in frequency domain, are used as indicators of the performance in time domain. These figures of merit provide only an approximate correlation between the time-domain and frequency-domain characteristics. This is probably the major limitation of the frequency-domain approach; it sacrifices an exact description of the time-domain performance for ease of analysis and design.

Step 4: Shape the Bode plot by simple cascade compensators and/or minor-loop feedback compensators. Try to meet the specifications on transient response (given in terms of frequency-domain measures) and steady-state accuracy.

Compare the trial-and-error compensators with respect to the effects of plant parameter variations, sensor noise and external disturbances. If a design seems satisfactory, go to step 6; otherwise try step 5.

Step 5: Re-evaluate the specifications, the physical configuration of the process, and the actuator and sensor selections in the light of the current design and go to step 1.

Step 6: Build a computer model and compute (simulate) the performance of the design.

Since the preliminary design is based on the approximate correlations between time-domain and frequency-domain modes of behaviour, the time-domain specifications must be checked before final parameter choices are made. A simulation study is generally the most appropriate method for imposing time-domain specifications on the system.

Step 7: Build a prototype.

▲▲

It may be noted that no particular design method, root locus or Bode plot, can be judged superior to the other. Each has its own particular use and advantage in a particular situation. As the reader becomes fully acquainted with these methods, he/she will become aware of the potentialities of each and will know when each should be used. We normally attempt the design using both the time-domain and frequency-domain approaches; this way one can gain an additional perspective to the complex analysis and design problems of feedback control systems.

The following strengths of the frequency-domain approach will become clear as we take up the subject.

1. The method does not need precise mathematical description of systems. The root locus method needs reasonably accurate mathematical description.

2. The method is independent of the complexity of systems and is applicable to systems containing time-delay elements. The root locus method, as we know, needs an approximate description of time-delay elements.

3. The method gives a simple and orderly approach for trial-and-error design.

4. It provides a very good indication of the system bandwidth which often appears explicitly in the specifications, and can only be approximated with the root-locus method of design.

The major limitation is that the direct control on the time-domain performance is lost.

The present chapter is concerned with the stability analysis in frequency domain. A frequency-domain stability criterion was developed by H. Nyquist in 1932 and remains a fundamental approach to the investigation of the stability of linear control systems. In addition to answering the question of absolute stability, this criterion also gives some useful results on relative stability. The relative stability measures given by the Nyquist stability criterion are, in fact, central to the great importance of frequency-domain design methods.

We first develop the Nyquist stability criterion from complex variable theory. Two common types of frequency-domain plots (Nyquist plots, Bode plots) are then introduced, and using these plots, absolute and relative stability are investigated on the basis of the Nyquist stability criterion. The use of the Nyquist criterion in frequency-domain design procedures will appear in the next two chapters.

8.2 | DEVELOPMENT OF THE NYQUIST CRITERION

In order to investigate the stability of a control system, we consider the closed-loop transfer function

$$\frac{Y(s)}{R(s)} = \frac{G(s)}{1 + G(s)H(s)} \tag{8.1}$$

keeping in mind that the transfer functions of both the single-loop and the multiple-loop control systems can be expressed in this form. The characteristic equation of the closed-loop system is obtained by setting the denominator of $Y(s)/R(s)$ to zero, which is same as setting the numerator of $1 + G(s)H(s)$ to zero. Thus, the roots of the characteristic equation must satisfy

$$1 + G(s)H(s) = 0 \tag{8.2}$$

We assume at this point that $G(s)H(s)$ can be expressed by a ratio of finite algebraic polynomials in s. This assumption has been made for convenience;

the Nyquist criterion applies to more general situations, as shown subsequently. Let

$$G(s)H(s) = \frac{K(s + z_1')(s + z_2') \cdots (s + z_m')}{(s + p_1)(s + p_2) \cdots (s + p_n)} \; ; \; m \le n \qquad (8.3)$$

$G(s)H(s)$ is the product of plant, compensator, and sensor transfer functions; its pole and zero locations are assumed to be known since these transfer functions are generally available in factored form. Substituting for $G(s)H(s)$ from Eqn. (8.3) into Eqn. (8.2), we obtain

$$1 + G(s)H(s) = 1 + \frac{K(s + z_1')(s + z_2') \cdots (s + z_m')}{(s + p_1)(s + p_2) \cdots (s + p_n)}$$

$$= \frac{(s + p_1)(s + p_2) \cdots (s + p_n) + K(s + z_1')(s + z_2') \cdots (s + z_m')}{(s + p_1)(s + p_2) \cdots (s + p_n)}$$

$$= \frac{(s + z_1)(s + z_2) \cdots (s + z_n)}{(s + p_1)(s + p_2) \cdots (s + p_n)} \qquad (8.4)$$

It is apparent from Eqn. (8.4) that the poles of $1 + G(s)H(s)$ are identical to those of $G(s)H(s)$, i.e., the open-loop poles of the system; and the zeros of $1 + G(s)H(s)$ are identical to the roots of the characteristic equation, i.e., the closed-loop poles of the system. For the closed-loop system to be stable, the zeros of $1 + G(s)H(s)$ must lie in the left half of the s-plane. It is important to note that even if some of the open-loop poles lie in the right half s-plane, all the zeros of $1 + G(s)H(s)$, i.e., the closed-loop poles may lie in the left half s-plane, meaning thereby that an open-loop unstable system may lead to closed-loop stable operation.

Recall that we have introduced two methods of checking whether or not all zeros of $1 + G(s)H(s)$ have negative real parts. The zeros of $1 + G(s)H(s)$ are roots of the polynomial

$$(s + p_1)(s + p_2) \cdots (s + p_n) + K(s + z_1')(s + z_2') \cdots (z + z_m')$$

and we may apply the Routh test. Another method is to plot the root loci of

$$\frac{K(s + z_1')(s + z_2') \cdots (s + z_m')}{(s + p_1)(s + p_2) \cdots (s + p_n)} = -1$$

as a function of K. In this section, we shall introduce yet another method of checking whether or not all zeros of $1 + G(s)H(s)$ lie inside the open left half s-plane. The method, called the *Nyquist stability criterion*, is based on the *principle of argument* in the theory of complex variables. The basic concept used in the Nyquist criterion is explained below, and in more detail in Appendix A.

Consider a rational function

$$1 + G(s)H(s) = Q(s) = \frac{s + z_1}{s + p_1}$$

The pole-zero map of $Q(s)$ is shown in Fig. 8.2a. This figure also shows a closed contour Γ_1. A point or an area is said to be *enclosed* by a closed path if it is found to lie to the right of the path when the path is traversed in the clockwise direction. The pole $-p_1$ and the zero $-z_1$ are therefore enclosed by the contour Γ_1 in Fig. 8.2a.

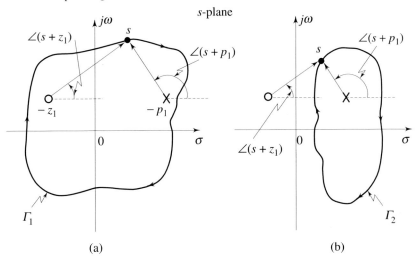

Fig. 8.2 *(a) A contour which encloses both the pole and the zero*
(b) A contour which encloses only the pole

Now we see that as the point s follows the prescribed path (i.e., clockwise direction) on the s-plane contour Γ_1, both $\angle(s + z_1)$ and $\angle(s + p_1)$ decrease continuously. For one clockwise traversal of Γ_1, we have

$$\delta_{\Gamma_1}\angle(s + z_1) = -2\pi$$
$$\delta_{\Gamma_1}\angle(s + p_1) = -2\pi$$

where $\delta_{\Gamma_1}\angle$ indicates the change in angle as Γ_1 is traversed.

$$\delta_{\Gamma_1}\angle Q(s) = \delta_{\Gamma_1}\angle(s + z_1) - \delta_{\Gamma_1}\angle(s + p_1)$$
$$= -2\pi - (-2\pi) = 0$$

Thus the change in $\angle Q(s)$ as s traverses Γ_1 (which is a completely general contour in the s-plane except that it encloses both $-z_1$ and $-p_1$) once in clockwise direction, is zero. Using these arguments on the contour Γ_2 in the s-plane which encloses only $-p_1$ and not $-z_1$, we find that (Fig. 8.2b)

$$\delta_{\Gamma_2}\angle Q(s) = 0 - (-2\pi) = 2\pi$$

We thus see that a change in $\angle Q(s)$ that one gets in traversing a contour in the s-plane, is strictly a function of how many poles and zeros of $Q(s)$ are enclosed by the s-plane contour. Let us consider a general $Q(s)$ with m zeros and n poles, given by Eqn. (8.4), for which a typical pole-zero plot might be made as shown in Fig. 8.3. The figure also shows an s-plane contour Γ_s which encloses Z zeros and P poles of $Q(s)$. Note that Γ_s does not go through any of the poles or

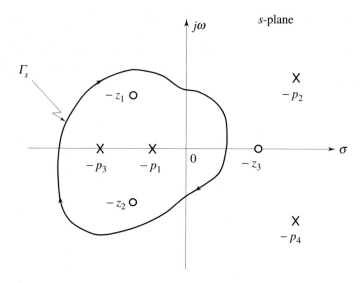

Fig. 8.3 *A general pole-zero plot with contour Γ_s which encloses Z zeros and P poles*

zeros of $Q(s)$. If we make one clockwise traversal of the contour Γ_s, it may be seen that

$$\delta_{\Gamma_s} \angle Q(s) = Z(-2\pi) - P(-2\pi)$$

$$= (P - Z)\, 2\pi \tag{8.5}$$

Another way of looking at the result of Eqn. (8.5) is to consider $Q(s)$ given by Eqn. (8.4) evaluated on the s-plane contour Γ_s of Fig. 8.3 and plotted in the $Q(s)$-plane. For every point $s = \sigma + j\omega$ on the s-plane contour Γ_s, we obtain $Q(s) = \mathrm{Re}\,Q + j\mathrm{Im}\,Q$. Alternatively, it can be stated that the function $Q(s)$ *maps* the point $\sigma + j\omega$ in the s-plane into the point $\mathrm{Re}\,Q + j\mathrm{Im}\,Q$ in the $Q(s)$-plane. It follows that for the closed contour Γ_s in the s-plane, there corresponds a closed contour Γ_Q in the $Q(s)$-plane. A typical Γ_Q is shown in Fig. 8.4. The arrowheads on this contour indicate the direction that $Q(s)$ takes as s moves on Γ_s in the clockwise direction. Now as we traverse Γ_Q once in the direction indicated by arrowheads, contour Γ_s in the s-plane is traversed once in the clockwise direction. For the example of Fig. 8.4, traversing Γ_Q once in the clockwise direction gives a change in $\angle Q(s)$ of -4π, since the origin is encircled twice in the negative direction. Thus Eqn. (8.5) gives

$$\delta_{\Gamma_s} \angle Q(s) = 2\pi(P - Z) = -4\pi$$

or $\qquad\qquad Z - P = 2$

In general,

$$Z - P = N \tag{8.6}$$

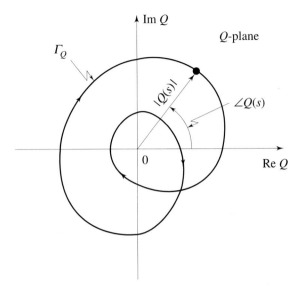

Fig. 8.4 *Q(s) evaluated on the contour Γ_s in Fig. 8.3*

where N is the number of clockwise encirclements of the origin that Γ_Q makes in the Q-plane. It may be noted that we are not interested in the exact shape of the $Q(s)$-plane contour. The important fact that concerns us is the encirclements of the origin by the $Q(s)$-plane contour.

The Principle of Argument

The relation (8.6) between the enclosure of poles and zeros of $Q(s)$ by the s-plane contour and the encirclements of the origin by the $Q(s)$-plane contour is commonly known as the *principle of argument* which may be stated as follows (refer Appendix A).

Let $Q(s)$ be a ratio of polynomials in s. Let P be the number of poles and Z be the number of zeros of $Q(s)$ which are enclosed by a simple closed contour in the s-plane, multiplicity accounted for. Let the closed contour be such that it does not pass through any poles or zeros of $Q(s)$. The s-plane contour then maps into the $Q(s)$-plane contour as a closed curve.

The number N of clockwise encirclements of the origin of the $Q(s)$-plane, as a representative point s traces out the entire contour in the s-plane in the clockwise direction, is equal to $Z - P$.

Since $\qquad Q(s) = 1 + G(s)H(s),$

we can obtain $Q(s)$-plane contour from the $G(s)H(s)$-plane contour simply by adding +1 to each point of $G(s)H(s)$-plane contour. Figure 8.5 shows a typical $G(s)H(s)$-plane contour Γ_{GH}. The effect of adding +1 to each point of Γ_{GH} to obtain $Q(s)$-plane contour Γ_Q is accomplished simply by adding +1 to the scale

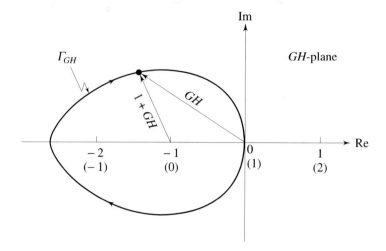

Fig. 8.5 *Evaluating 1 + G(s)H(s) from the G(s)H(s) map*

of the real axis, as shown by the numbers in parentheses in Fig. 8.5. It is seen that $-1+j0$ point of the $G(s)H(s)$ map Γ_{GH} corresponds to the origin of the $Q(s)$ map Γ_Q. For convenience, we designate the $-1+j0$ point of the $G(s)H(s)$-plane as the *critical point*. Thus the encirclements of the origin by the contour Γ_Q is equivalent to the encirclements of the critical point $-1+j0$ by the contour Γ_{GH}. In the light of these observations, we can express Eqn. (8.6) as follows:

$$Z - P = N \qquad\qquad (8.7)$$

where

Z = number of zeros of $1+G(s)H(s)$ enclosed by the s-plane contour Γ_s;

P = number of poles of $G(s)H(s)$ enclosed by the s-plane contour Γ_s; and

N = number of clockwise encirclements of the critical point $-1+j0$ made by the $G(s)H(s)$-plane contour Γ_{GH}.

In general N can be positive $(Z > P)$, zero $(Z = P)$, or negative $(Z < P)$. $N > 0$ corresponds to N encirclements of the critical point $-1+j0$ in clockwise direction by the Γ_{GH} contour. $N = 0$ indicates that Γ_{GH} contour does not encircle the critical point. $N < 0$ corresponds to N encirclements of the critical point in counterclockwise direction by the Γ_{GH} contour.

A convenient way of determining N with respect to the critical point $-1+j0$ of the $G(s)H(s)$-plane is to draw a radial line from this point. The number of *net* intersections of the radial line with the Γ_{GH} contour gives the magnitude of N. Figure 8.6 gives several examples of the method of determining N.

The Nyquist Contour

At this point the reader may place himself/herself in the position of Nyquist many years ago, confronted with the problem of stability of the closed-loop system that has the transfer function of Eqn. (8.1), which is equivalent to determining whether or not the function $1+G(s)H(s)$ has zeros in the right half s-plane. Apparently, Nyquist discovered that the principle of argument of the complex-variable theory could be applied to solve the stability problem if the s-plane contour Γ_s is taken to be one that encloses the entire right half of the s-plane. Of course, as an alternative, Γ_s can be chosen to enclose the entire left half of the s-plane, as the solution is a relative one.

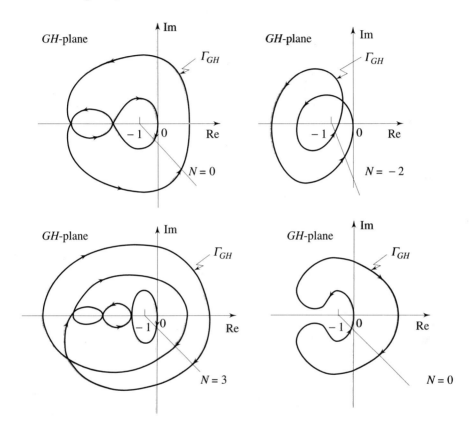

Fig. 8.6   *Examples of determination of N*

Figure 8.7 illustrates a Γ_s contour that encloses the entire right half of the s-plane. Such a contour is called the *Nyquist contour*. It is directed clockwise and comprises of an infinite line segment C_1 along the $j\omega$-axis and arc C_2 of infinite radius.

Along C_1, $s = j\omega$ with s varying from $-j\infty$ to $+j\infty$.

Along C_2, $s = Re^{j\theta}$ with $R \to \infty$ and θ varying from $+90°$ through $0°$ to $-90°$.

As the s-plane contour Γ_s must avoid all poles of $1+G(s)H(s)$, modifications in the Nyquist contour defined in Fig. 8.7 are required when $G(s)H(s)$, and therefore $1+G(s)H(s)$, has one or more poles on the imaginary axis. The basic trick, of course, is to take a small detour around the imaginary axis poles. Figure 8.8 illustrates a modified Nyquist contour when $G(s)H(s)$ has a pole at

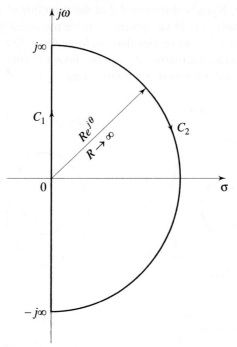

Fig. 8.7   *The Nyquist contour*

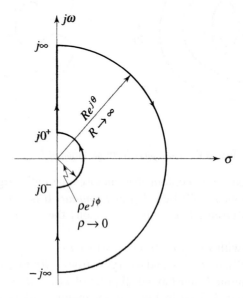

Fig. 8.8   *Indented Nyquist contour*

$s = 0$. Along the semicircular indent around the pole at the origin, $s = \rho e^{j\phi}$ with $\rho \to 0$ and ϕ varying from $-90°$ through $0°$ to $+90°$. The indented Nyquist contour in Fig. 8.8 does not enclose the pole at the origin. Of course, as an alternative, the Nyquist contour may be indented to enclose the pole at the origin.

The Nyquist Plot

The Nyquist stability criterion is a direct application of the principle of argument when the s-plane contour Γ_s is the Nyquist contour. In principle, once the Nyquist contour is specified, the stability of a closed-loop system can be determined by plotting the $G(s)H(s)$ locus when s takes on values along the Nyquist contour, and investigating the behaviour of the $G(s)H(s)$ plot with respect to the critical point $-1+j0$. The $G(s)H(s)$ plot that corresponds to the Nyquist contour is called the *Nyquist plot* of $G(s)H(s)$.

With the additional dimension added to the stability problem, we define $N, P,$ and Z as follows.

$N =$ number of clockwise encirclements of the critical point $-1+j0$ made by the $G(s)H(s)$ locus of the Nyquist plot.

$P =$ number of poles of $G(s)H(s)$, and therefore of $1+G(s)H(s)$, enclosed by the Nyquist contour.

Then (refer Eqn. (8.7))

$Z =$ number of zeros of $1+G(s)H(s)$ enclosed by the Nyquist contour

$$= N + P \tag{8.8a}$$

Closed-loop stability requires that

$$Z = 0 \tag{8.8b}$$

This condition is met if

$$N = -P \tag{8.8c}$$

In the special case (this is generally the case in most single-loop practical systems) of $P = 0$ (i.e., the open-loop transfer function $G(s)H(s)$ has no poles in right half s-plane), the closed-loop system is stable if

$$N = 0 \tag{8.8d}$$

The Nyquist Criterion

We can now state the Nyquist stability criterion as follows:

If the Nyquist plot of the open-loop transfer function $G(s)H(s)$ corresponding to the Nyquist contour in the s-plane encircles the critical point $-1+j0$ in the counterclockwise direction as many times as the number of right half s-plane poles of $G(s)H(s)$, the closed-loop system is stable.

In the commonly occurring case of $G(s)H(s)$ with no poles in right half s-plane, the closed-loop system is stable if the Nyquist plot of $G(s)H(s)$ does not encircle the $-1+j0$ point.

When the Nyquist plot of $G(s)H(s)$ passes through $-1+j0$ point, the number of encirclements N is indeterminate. This corresponds to the condition where $1+G(s)H(s)$ has zeros on the imaginary axis. A necessary condition for applying the Nyquist criterion is that the Nyquist contour must not pass through any poles or zeros of $1+G(s)H(s)$. When this condition is violated, the value for N becomes indeterminate and the Nyquist stability criterion cannot be applied.

8.3 | SELECTED ILLUSTRATIVE NYQUIST PLOTS

The following examples serve to illustrate the application of the Nyquist criterion to the stability study of control systems.

Example 8.1——————————————————————————

Consider a single-loop feedback control system with the open-loop transfer function given by

$$G(s)H(s) = \frac{K}{(\tau_1 s + 1)(\tau_2 s + 1)} \; ; \; \tau_1, \tau_2 > 0, K > 0 \qquad (8.9)$$

$G(s)H(s)$ has no poles in the right-half s-plane; therefore, stability is assured if the Nyquist plot of $G(s)H(s)$ does not encircle the $-1+j0$ point.

The Nyquist plot of $G(s)H(s)$, as we know, is the mapping of the Nyquist contour in the s-plane onto $G(s)H(s)$-plane. In Fig. 8.9a, the Nyquist contour has been divided into three sections: C_1, C_2, and C_3. Section C_1 is defined by $s = j\omega, 0 \leq \omega < \infty$; section C_2 is defined by $s = j\omega, -\infty < \omega \leq 0$; and section C_3 is defined by $s = Re^{j\theta}, R \to \infty$, and θ varies from $+90°$ through $0°$ to $-90°$.

Mapping of Section C_1 onto $G(s)H(s)$-plane

Substituting $s = j\omega$ into $G(s)H(s)$, we obtain

$$G(j\omega)H(j\omega) = \frac{K}{(j\omega\tau_1 + 1)(j\omega\tau_2 + 1)} \qquad (8.10)$$

A plot of $G(j\omega)H(j\omega)$ on polar coordinates as ω is varied from 0 to ∞ is the map of section C_1 on the $G(s)H(s)$-plane. This plot is called the *polar plot* of sinusoidal transfer function $G(j\omega)H(j\omega)$.

For application of the Nyquist stability criterion, an exact polar plot of $G(j\omega)H(j\omega)$ is not essential. Often a rough sketch is adequate for stability analysis. The general shape of the polar plot of $G(j\omega)H(j\omega)$ may be determined from the following information.

1. The behaviour of the magnitude and phase of $G(j\omega)H(j\omega)$ at $\omega = 0$ and $\omega = \infty$.
2. The points of intersection of the polar plot with the real and imaginary axes, and the values of ω at these intersections.
3. A few on-locus points in second and third quadrants in the vicinity of the critical point $-1+j0$.

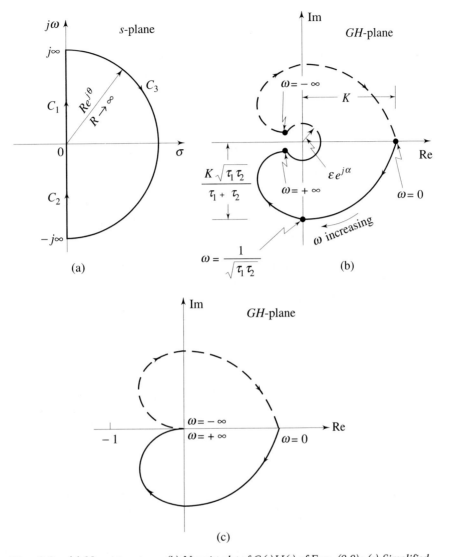

Fig. 8.9 *(a) Nyquist contour; (b) Nyquist plot of $G(s)H(s)$ of Eqn. (8.9); (c) Simplified Nyquist plot*

For $G(j\omega)H(j\omega)$ given by Eqn. (8.10), the magnitude and phase at $\omega = 0$ and $\omega = \infty$ are calculated as follows:

$$\left| G(j\omega)H(j\omega) \right|_{\omega = 0} = K$$

$$\angle G(j\omega)H(j\omega) \Big|_{\omega = 0} = 0°$$

$$\left| G(j\omega)H(j\omega) \right|_{\omega \to \infty} = \left| \frac{K}{j^2 \omega^2 \tau_1 \tau_2} \right|_{\omega \to \infty} = 0$$

$$\angle G(j\omega)H(j\omega)\Big|_{\omega \to \infty} = \angle\left(\frac{K}{j^2\omega^2\tau_1\tau_2}\right) = -180°$$

The intersections of the polar plot with the axes of $G(s)H(s)$-plane can easily be ascertained by identifying the real and imaginary parts of $G(j\omega)H(j\omega)$.

$$G(j\omega)H(j\omega) = \frac{K}{(1+j\omega\tau_1)(1+j\omega\tau_2)}\left[\frac{(1-j\omega\tau_1)(1-j\omega\tau_2)}{(1-j\omega\tau_1)(1-j\omega\tau_2)}\right]$$

$$= \frac{K\left[(1-\omega^2\tau_1\tau_2) - j\omega(\tau_1+\tau_2)\right]}{(1+\omega^2\tau_1^2)(1+\omega^2\tau_2^2)}$$

$$= \frac{K(1-\omega^2\tau_1\tau_2)}{\omega^4\tau_1^2\tau_2^2 + \omega^2(\tau_1^2+\tau_2^2)+1} - j\frac{K\omega(\tau_1+\tau_2)}{\omega^4\tau_1^2\tau_2^2 + \omega^2(\tau_1^2+\tau_2^2)+1}$$

$$= \mathrm{Re}[G(j\omega)H(j\omega)] + j\mathrm{Im}[G(j\omega)H(j\omega)]$$

When we let $\mathrm{Im}[G(j\omega)H(j\omega)]$ to zero, we get $\omega = 0$, meaning that the polar plot intersects the real axis only at $\omega = 0$. Similarly, the intersection of $G(j\omega)H(j\omega)$-plot with the imaginary axis is found by setting $\mathrm{Re}[G(j\omega)H(j\omega)]$ to zero, which gives

$$\omega = \frac{1}{\sqrt{\tau_1\tau_2}}$$

$$\left|G(j\omega)H(j\omega)\right|_{\omega=\frac{1}{\sqrt{\tau_1\tau_2}}} = \frac{K\omega(\tau_1+\tau_2)}{\omega^4\tau_1^2\tau_2^2 + \omega^2(\tau_1^2+\tau_2^2)+1}\Bigg|_{\omega=\frac{1}{\sqrt{\tau_1\tau_2}}}$$

$$= \frac{K\sqrt{\tau_1\tau_2}}{\tau_1+\tau_2}$$

Based on this information, a rough sketch of the polar plot can easily be made, as shown in Fig. 8.9b (the portion of the locus from $\omega = 0$ to $\omega = +\infty$).

Mapping of Section C_2 onto $G(s)H(s)$-plane

Given $G(j\omega)H(j\omega)$, $0 \le \omega < \infty$, $G(j\omega)H(j\omega)$ for $-\infty < \omega \le 0$ is constructed by realizing

$$G(-j\omega)H(-j\omega) = [G(j\omega)H(j\omega)]^*$$

where * denotes conjugate. Thus, given the $G(j\omega)H(j\omega)$-locus for $0 \le \omega < \infty$, we get the $G(j\omega)H(j\omega)$-locus for the negative $j\omega$-axis by simply taking the mirror image about the real axis of the locus for positive ω. The dashed portion of the locus in Fig. 8.9b from $\omega = -\infty$ to $\omega = 0$ is thus the map of section C_2 of Nyquist contour.

Mapping of Section C_3 onto $G(s)H(s)$-plane

Along section C_3, $s = Re^{j\theta}$; $R \to \infty$ and θ varies from $+90°$ through $0°$ to $-90°$. Substituting into $G(s)H(s)$, we obtain

$$G(s)H(s)\bigg|_{s=Re^{j\theta}} = \frac{K}{(\tau_1 Re^{j\theta}+1)(\tau_2 Re^{j\theta}+1)}$$

$$= \frac{K}{\tau_1\tau_2 R^2 e^{j2\theta}} = \frac{K}{\tau_1\tau_2 R^2} e^{-j2\theta}$$

The infinitesimal semicircular locus around the origin (refer Fig. 8.9b), represented by

$$G(s)H(s) = \varepsilon e^{j\alpha}$$

with $\varepsilon \to 0$ and α varying from $-180°$ through $0°$ to $+180°$, is thus the map of section C_3 of Nyquist contour.

For application of the Nyquist stability criterion, exact shape of the Nyquist plot around the origin of $G(s)H(s)$-plane is of no interest to us. We can therefore take $\varepsilon = 0$; the resulting Nyquist plot is shown in Fig. 8.9c. This plot does not encircle the critical point $-1+j0$ for any positive values of K, τ_1, and τ_2. Therefore, the system is stable for all positive values of K, τ_1, and τ_2.

Example 8.2

Consider now a feedback system whose open-loop transfer function is given by

$$G(s)H(s) = \frac{K}{s(\tau s + 1)}; \; K > 0, \; \tau > 0 \tag{8.11}$$

We note here that for this type-1 system, there is one pole on the imaginary axis, precisely at the origin. The Nyquist contour is shown in Fig. 8.10a, where a semicircular detour about the origin is indicated. The Nyquist contour has been divided into four sections: C_1, C_2, C_3 and C_4. Section C_1 is defined by $s = j\omega$, $0 < \omega < \infty$; section C_2 is defined by $s = j\omega$, $-\infty < \omega < 0$; section C_3 is defined by $s = Re^{j\theta}$, $R \to \infty$, and θ varies from $+90°$ through $0°$ to $-90°$; and section C_4 is defined by $s = \rho e^{j\phi}$, $\rho \to 0$, and ϕ varies from $-90°$ through $0°$ to $+90°$.

Mapping of section C_1 onto the $G(s)H(s)$-plane is given by the polar plot of sinusoidal transfer function

$$G(j\omega)H(j\omega) = \frac{K}{j\omega(j\omega\tau + 1)} \tag{8.12}$$

This sinusoidal transfer function can be expressed as

$$G(j\omega)H(j\omega) = -\frac{K\tau}{1+\omega^2\tau^2} - j\frac{K}{\omega(1+\omega^2\tau^2)}$$

The low-frequency portion of the polar plot becomes

$$\lim_{\omega\to 0} G(j\omega)H(j\omega) = -K\tau - j\infty$$

and the high-frequency portion is (refer Eqn. (8.12))

$$\lim_{\omega \to \infty} G(j\omega)H(j\omega) = \frac{K}{\omega^2 \tau} \angle \left(\frac{1}{j^2 \omega^2 \tau} \right) \Bigg|_{\omega \to \infty} = 0 \angle -180°$$

The general shape of the polar plot is shown in Fig. 8.10b. The $G(j\omega)H(j\omega)$-plot is asymptotic to the vertical line passing through the point $-K\tau + j0$.

Mapping of section C_2 onto $G(s)H(s)$-plane is obtained simply by taking the mirror image about the real axis of the polar plot of $G(j\omega)H(j\omega)$.

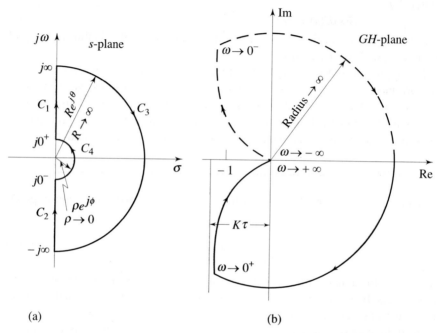

(a)   (b)

Fig. 8.10 *(a) Nyquist contour; (b) Nyquist plot of $G(s)H(s)$ of Eqn. (8.11)*

Mapping of section C_3 onto the $G(s)H(s)$-plane is obtained as follows.

$$G(s)H(s)\Bigg|_{s = Re^{j\theta}} = \frac{K}{Re^{j\theta}(\tau Re^{j\theta} + 1)} = \frac{K}{\tau R^2} e^{-j2\theta}$$

The $G(s)H(s)$-locus thus turns at the origin with zero radius from $-180°$ through $0°$ to $+180°$.

Mapping of section C_4 onto the $G(s)H(s)$-plane is obtained as follows. Along C_4, $s = \rho e^{j\phi}$; $\rho \to 0$, and ϕ varies from $-90°$ through $0°$ to $+90°$.

Substituting into $G(s)H(s)$, we obtain

$$G(s)H(s)\Bigg|_{s = \rho e^{j\phi}} = \frac{K}{\rho e^{j\phi}(\tau \rho e^{j\phi} + 1)} = \frac{K}{\rho} e^{-j\phi}$$

The value K/ρ approaches infinity as $\rho \to 0$, and $-\phi$ varies from $+90°$ through $0°$ to $-90°$ as s moves along section C_4 of the Nyquist contour. Thus the infinitesimal semicircular indent around the origin in the s-plane maps into a semicircular arc of infinite radius on the $G(s)H(s)$-plane as shown in Fig. 8.10b.

The complete Nyquist plot for $G(s)H(s)$ given by Eqn. (8.11) is shown in Fig. 8.10b. In order to investigate the stability of this second-order system, we first note that the number of poles of $G(s)H(s)$ in the right-half s-plane is zero. Therefore, for this system to be stable, we require that the Nyquist plot of $G(s)H(s)$ does not encircle the critical point $-1+j0$. Examining Fig. 8.10b, we find that irrespective of the value of the gain K and the time-constant τ, the Nyquist plot does not encircle the critical point, and the system is always stable.

Example 8.3———————————————————————

We now consider a type-2 system with open-loop transfer function

$$G(s)H(s) = \frac{K}{s^2(\tau s + 1)}; K > 0, \tau > 0 \qquad (8.13)$$

The Nyquist contour is shown in Fig. 8.10a. The Nyquist plot is shown in Fig. 8.11. Clearly the portion of the $G(s)H(s)$-locus from $\omega = 0^+$ to $\omega = +\infty$ is simply the polar plot of

$$G(j\omega)H(j\omega) = \frac{K}{j^2\omega^2(j\omega\tau + 1)} \qquad (8.14)$$

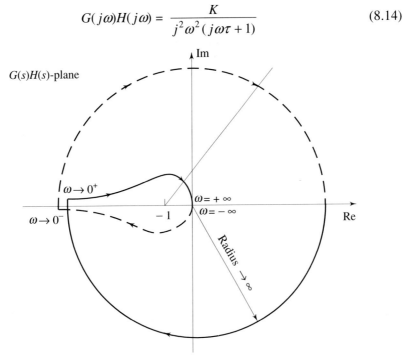

Fig. 8.11 *Nyquist plot[1] for $G(s)H(s)$ of Eqn. (8.13)*

[1]	For $K = 1, \tau = 1$;				
ω	0.01	0.05	0.1	0.5	1
$|GH|$	4×10^6	600	98.51	3.57	0.7
$\angle GH$	179.97	177.68	174.2	153.4	135

Note that

$$G(j\omega)H(j\omega)\bigg|_{\omega \to 0^+} = \left(\frac{K}{\omega^2}\bigg|_{\omega \to 0^+}\right)\angle - 180°$$

$$G(j\omega)H(j\omega)\bigg|_{\omega \to +\infty} = \left(\frac{K}{\omega^3}\bigg|_{\omega \to +\infty}\right)\angle - 270°$$

It can easily be examined that the locus of $G(j\omega)H(j\omega)$ does not intersect the real or imaginary axis; it lies in the second quadrant for all values of ω.

The $G(s)H(s)$-locus turns at the origin with zero radius from $-270°$ through $0°$ to $+270°$. This corresponds to the locus from $\omega = +\infty$ to $\omega = -\infty$. The portion of the $G(s)H(s)$-locus from $\omega = -\infty$ to $\omega = 0^-$ is the mirror image about the real axis of the locus for positive ω. From $\omega = 0^-$ to $\omega = 0^+$, $s = \rho e^{j\phi}$, $\rho \to 0$ and ϕ varies from $-90°$ through $0°$, to $+90°$. This gives

$$G(s)H(s)\bigg|_{s = \rho e^{j\phi}} = \frac{K}{\rho^2 e^{j2\phi}(\tau\rho e^{j\phi} + 1)} = \frac{K}{\rho^2}e^{-j2\phi}$$

The portion of the $G(s)H(s)$ locus from $\omega = 0^-$ to $\omega = 0^+$ is a circular arc of infinite radius ranging from $+180°$ at $\omega = 0^-$ through $0°$ to $-180°$ at $\omega = 0^+$.

From Fig. 8.11, we observe that the Nyquist plot encircles the critical point $-1+j0$ twice in the clockwise direction, i.e., $N = 2$. Since P = number of poles of $G(s)H(s)$ in right-half s-plane = 0, we have from Eqn. (8.8a), $Z = 2$; i.e, there are two roots of the closed-loop system in the right-half s-plane and the system, irrespective of the gain K and time-constant τ, is unstable.

Example 8.4

Consider now an open-loop system with the transfer function

$$G(s)H(s) = \frac{s+1}{s^2(s-2)} \tag{8.15}$$

Let us determine whether the system is stable when the feedback path is closed.

From the transfer function of the open-loop system it is observed that there is one open-loop pole in the right half s-plane. Therefore $P = 1$.

The Nyquist contour is shown in Fig. 8.10a. The Nyquist plot is shown in Fig. 8.12. Clearly, the portion of the $G(s)H(s)$-locus from $\omega = 0^+$ to $\omega = +\infty$ is simply the polar plot of

$$G(j\omega)H(j\omega) = \frac{j\omega+1}{j^2\omega^2(j\omega-2)} \tag{8.16}$$

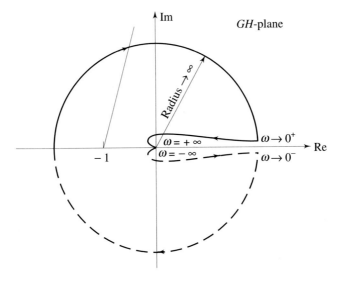

Fig. 8.12 *Nyquist plot for G(s)H(s) of Eqn. (8.15)*

The following points were used to construct the polar plot:

$$G(j\omega)H(j\omega)\Big|_{\omega \to 0^+} \to \infty \angle 0°$$

$$G(j\omega)H(j\omega)\Big|_{\omega = 0.1} = 50\angle 9°$$

$$G(j\omega)H(j\omega)\Big|_{\omega = 1} = 0.6\angle 71°$$

$$G(j\omega)H(j\omega)\Big|_{\omega = 10} = 0.01\angle 162°$$

$$G(j\omega)H(j\omega)\Big|_{\omega \to +\infty} \to 0 \angle - 180°$$

The plot of $G(j\omega)H(j\omega)$ for $\omega < 0$ is the reflection, with respect to the real axis, of the plot for $\omega > 0$. Every point on the large semicircle in Fig. 8.10a, is mapped by $G(s)H(s)$ into the origin of the $G(s)H(s)$-plane. A point $s = \rho e^{j\phi}$; $\rho \to 0$, ϕ varying from $-90°$ through $0°$ to $+90°$ is mapped by $G(s)H(s)$ into

$$G(s)H(s)\Big|_{s=\rho e^{j\phi}} = \frac{s+1}{s^2(s-2)}\Big|_{s=\rho e^{j\phi}} = -\frac{1}{2\rho^2 e^{j2\phi}} = \frac{1}{2\rho^2} \angle(180° - 2\phi)$$

This gives

$$G(s)H(s)\Big|_{s=\rho e^{j0°}} = \frac{1}{2\rho^2} \angle 180°$$

$$G(s)H(s)\Big|_{s=\rho e^{j45°}} = \frac{1}{2\rho^2} \angle 90°$$

$$G(s)H(s)\Big|_{s=\rho e^{j90°}} = \frac{1}{2\rho^2} \angle 0°$$

Figure 8.12 indicates that the critical point $-1+j0$ is encircled by the Nyquist plot once in the clockwise direction. Therefore $N = 1$, and (refer Eqn. (8.8a))

Z = number of zeros of $1+G(s)H(s)$ enclosed by the Nyquist contour

$= N + P = 2$

Hence the feedback system is unstable with two poles in the right half s-plane.

Example 8.5_____

Consider a feedback system with the following open-loop transfer function:

$$G(s)H(s) = \frac{K}{s(s + 3)(s + 5)} \tag{8.17}$$

Let us investigate the stability of this system for various values of K.

First set $K = 1$ and sketch the Nyquist plot for the system using the contour shown in Fig. 8.10a. For all points on the imaginary axis,

$$G(j\omega)H(j\omega) = \frac{K}{s(s + 3)(s + 5)}\bigg|_{\substack{K=1 \\ s = j\omega}} = \frac{-8\omega^2 - j(15\omega - \omega^3)}{64\omega^4 + \omega^2(15 - \omega^2)^2} \tag{8.18}$$

At $\omega = 0$, $G(j\omega)H(j\omega) = -0.0356 - j\infty$.

Next, find the point where the Nyquist plot intersects the negative real axis.

Setting the imaginary part of Eqn. (8.18) equal to zero, we find $\omega = \sqrt{15}$. Substituting this value of ω back into Eqn. (8.18), yields the real part of -0.0083.

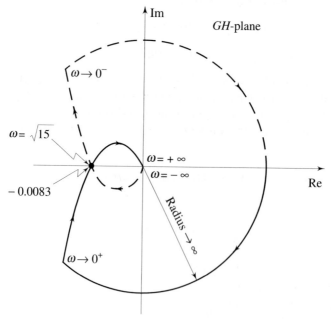

Fig. 8.13 *Nyquist plot for G(s)H(s) of Eqn. (8.17)*

Finally, at $\omega = \infty$, $G(j\omega)H(j\omega) = G(s)H(s)\big|_{s \to j\infty} = \dfrac{1}{(j\omega)^3} = 0 \angle -270°.$

The Nyquist plot for $G(s)H(s)$ of Eqn. (8.17) with $K = 1$ is shown in Fig. 8.13. Application of the Nyquist criterion shows that with $K = 1$, the closed-loop system is stable.

If we were to increase the gain by a factor $1/0.0083 = 120.48$, all points on the $G(j\omega)H(j\omega)$-locus would increase in magnitude by this factor along radial lines centred at the origin. The length of the vector $G(j\sqrt{15})H(j\sqrt{15})$ would be $0.0083\,(1/0.0083) = 1$, and therefore the curve $G(j\omega)H(j\omega)$ would go through the critical point; the closed-loop system would be at the limit of instability. Hence, for stability, K must be less than 120.48, i.e., the stability range is $0 < K < 120.48$.

Example 8.6

Let us consider the control system shown in Fig. 8.14 and determine its stability. The characteristic equation of the system is

$$1 + G(s) = 0$$

$$G(s) = \frac{K_A(1 + K_t s)}{s(s - 1)} \tag{8.19}$$

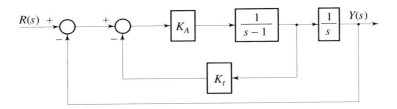

Fig. 8.14   *A feedback control system*

The open-loop transfer function has one pole in the right half s-plane, and therefore $P = 1$. In order for the closed-loop system to be stable, we require $N = -1$ (i.e., the Nyquist plot must encircle the critical point once in the counterclockwise direction).

Several important values of $G(j\omega)$-locus are given below:

$$G(j\omega)\big|_{\omega \to 0^+} = \infty \angle +90°$$

$$G(j\omega)\big|_{\omega \to +\infty} = 0 \angle -90°$$

$$G(j\omega) = \frac{K_A(1 + K_t j\omega)}{-\omega^2 - j\omega} = \frac{-K_A(\omega^2 + \omega^2 K_t) + j(\omega - K_t \omega^3)K_A}{\omega^2 + \omega^4} \quad (8.20)$$

$$G(j\omega)\Big|_{\omega^2 = 1/K_t} = -K_A K_t$$

At the semicircular detour at the origin in the s-plane (refer Fig. 8.10a), we let $s = \rho e^{j\phi}$; $\rho \to 0$ and ϕ varies from $-90°$ through $0°$ to $+90°$.

$$G(s)\Big|_{s = \rho e^{j\phi}} = \frac{K_A}{-\rho e^{j\phi}} = \frac{K_A}{\rho} \angle(-180° - \phi)$$

Therefore the semicircular detour in the Nyquist contour is mapped into a semicircle of infinite radius in the left half of $G(s)$-plane, as shown in Fig. 8.15. When $-K_A K_t < -1$ or $K_A K_t > 1$, the Nyquist plot encircles the $-1 + j0$ point once in counterclockwise direction. Thus the system is stable when $K_A K_t > 1$.

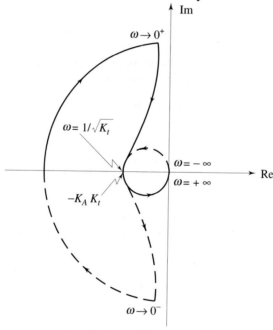

Fig. 8.15   *Nyquist plot[2] for G(s) of Eqn. (8.19)*

8.4   STABILITY MARGINS

In the preceding sections, the Nyquist plot was used to detemine if a system was stable or unstable. Of course, in general, a usable system must be stable. However, there are concerns beyond simple stability, for two reasons. First, a stable system must also have, among other characteristics, an acceptable tran-

[2]   for $K_A = 1$, $K_t = 3$;

ω	0.02	0.05	0.09	1
$|G|$	146.3	74	37.16	2.23
$\angle G$	91.57	93.1	96.14	153.56

sient response. Also, the model that is used in the analysis and design of a control system is never exact. Hence, the model may indicate that a system is stable, whereas in fact the physical system is unstable. Generally we require not only that a system be stable but also that it be stable by some margin of safety.

Measures of degree of stability of a closed-loop system that has open-loop transfer function with no poles in right half s-plane, can be conveniently created through Nyquist plot. The stability information for such a system becomes obvious by the inspection of the Nyquist plot of its open-loop transfer function $G(s)H(s)$, since the stability criterion is merely the non-encirclement of the critical point $-1+j0$. It can be intuitively imagined that as the Nyquist plot gets closer to the critical point, the system tends towards instability.

Consider two different systems whose dominant closed-loop poles are shown on the s-plane in Figs 8.16a and 8.16b. Obviously, system A is 'more stable' than system B, since its dominant closed-loop poles are located comparatively away to the left from the $j\omega$-axis. The Nyquist plots of open-loop transfer functions of systems A and B are shown in Figs 8.16c and 8.16d, respectively. Comparison of the closed-loop pole locations of these systems with their corresponding Nyquist plots reveals that as a Nyquist plot moves closer to the critical point $-1+j0$, the system closed-loop poles move closer to the $j\omega$-axis and hence the system becomes relatively less stable and *vice versa*.

Thus, the distance between the Nyquist plot of open-loop transfer function $G(s)H(s)$ and the critical point $-1+j0$ can be used as a measure of degree of stability of the closed-loop system. Generally, the larger the distance, the more stable the system. The distance can be found by drawing a circle touching the Nyquist plot as shown in Figs 8.16c and 8.16d. Such a distance, however, is not convenient for analysis and design. The measures: gain margin and phase margin, are commonly used to quantify the closeness of a Nyquist plot to the critical point.

Gain Margin

Figure 8.17 shows a 'typical' Nyquist plot of $G(j\omega)H(j\omega)$; $\omega \geq 0$. $G(s)H(s)$ is known to have no poles in the right half s-plane. A closed-loop system with the $G(s)H(s)$ as open-loop transfer function is stable.

The point at which the Nyquist plot crosses the negative real axis is marked A, and the frequency at that point is designated ω_ϕ. The point A is thus the tip of the vector $G(j\omega_\phi)H(j\omega_\phi)$ with magnitude $|G(j\omega_\phi)H(j\omega_\phi)|$ and angle $180°$. It is seen from Fig. 8.17 that $|G(j\omega_\phi)H(j\omega_\phi)| < 1$, and therefore the tip of the vector $G(j\omega_\phi)H(j\omega_\phi)$ does not reach the critical point $-1+j0$.

If we were to increase the gain of $G(j\omega)H(j\omega)$ by a factor $1/|OA|$ without altering its phase, all points on the Nyquist plot of $G(j\omega)H(j\omega)$ would increase in magnitude by this factor along radial lines centred at the origin. The length of the vector $G(j\omega_\phi)H(j\omega_\phi)$ would be $|OA|(1/|OA|) = 1$, and therefore the curve $G(j\omega)H(j\omega)$ would go through the critical point; the closed-loop system would

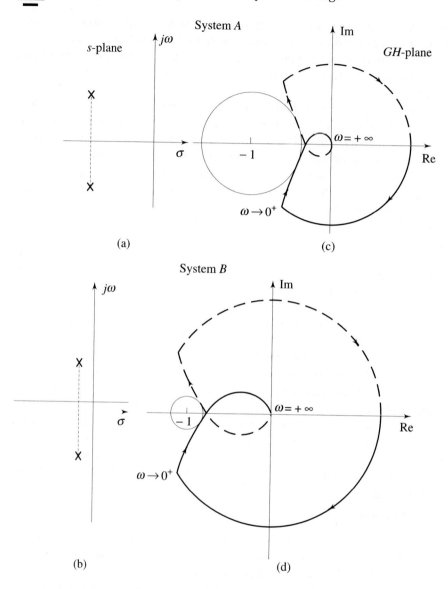

Fig. 8.16 *Correlation between the closed-loop s-plane root locations and open-loop frequency-response curves*

be at the limit of stability. We call the multiplying factor 1/|OA| the *gain margin* because it is the factor by which the gain can be increased to drive the system to the verge of instability.

From the graphical description of Fig. 8.17, we now make the following definitions.

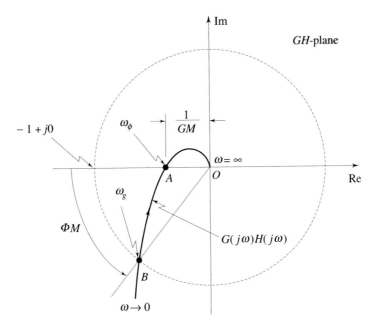

Fig. 8.17 *Typical Nyquist plot of $G(j\omega)H(j\omega)$*

Phase crossover point

It is a point on the $G(s)H(s)$-plane at which the Nyquist $G(j\omega)H(j\omega)$-plot intersects the negative real axis.

Phase crossover frequency ω_ϕ

It is the frequency at the phase crossover point, or where

$$\angle G(j\omega_\phi)H(j\omega_\phi) = -180° \tag{8.21}$$

Gain margin

The gain margin GM of the closed-loop system that has $G(s)H(s)$ as its open-loop transfer function is defined as the number

$$GM = \frac{1}{|G(j\omega_\phi)H(j\omega_\phi)|} \tag{8.22}$$

For example, if $|G(j\omega_\phi)H(j\omega_\phi)| = 0.5$, then the $GM = 2$; the loop gain magnitude could be increased by a factor of 2 before the closed-loop system would go unstable. For stable systems, GM is always a number greater than one.

Phase Margin

A unit circle centred at the origin has been drawn in Fig. 8.17 in order to identify point B at which Nyquist $G(j\omega)H(j\omega)$-plot has unity magnitude; the frequency at point B has been designated ω_g. The point B is thus the tip of the vector $G(j\omega_g)H(j\omega_g)$ with magnitude $|G(j\omega_g)H(j\omega_g)| = 1$ and angle $\angle G(j\omega_g)H(j\omega_g)$. It is seen from Fig. 8.17 that the tip of the vector $G(j\omega_g)H(j\omega_g)$ does not reach the critical point $-1 + j0$.

If we were to decrease the phase of $G(j\omega)H(j\omega)$ without altering its gain, all points on the Nyquist $G(j\omega)H(j\omega)$-plot would rotate clockwise about the origin an angular amount equal to the increase in phase lag. In the light of Fig. 8.17, we see that the tip of the vector $G(j\omega_g)H(j\omega_g)$ would be placed at the critical point if the increase in phase lag of $G(j\omega)H(j\omega)$ were made equal to the angle *ΦM*. We call the angle *ΦM*, *measured positively in the counterclockwise direction from the negative real axis to the vector* $G(j\omega_g)H(j\omega_g)$, *the phase margin* because it is the angle by which the phase of $G(j\omega)H(j\omega)$ can be decreased to drive the system to the verge of instability.

From the graphical description of Fig. 8.17, we now make the following definitions.

Gain crossover point

It is a point on the $G(s)H(s)$-plane at which the Nyquist $G(j\omega)H(j\omega)$-plot has unity magnitude.

Gain crossover frequency ω_g

It is the frequency at the gain crossover point, or where

$$|G(j\omega_g)H(j\omega_g)| = 1 \tag{8.23}$$

Phase margin

The phase margin *ΦM* of the closed-loop system that has $G(s)H(s)$ as its open-loop transfer function is defined as

$$\Phi M = 180° + \angle G(j\omega_g)H(j\omega_g) \tag{8.24}$$

For example, if $\angle G(j\omega_g)H(j\omega_g) = -135°$, then *ΦM* = 45°; an additional phase lag of 45° could be associated with $G(j\omega)H(j\omega)$ before the closed-loop system would go unstable. For stable systems, *ΦM* is always positive.

▲▲

Consider now an unstable closed-loop system with Nyquist $G(j\omega)H(j\omega)$-plot of Fig. 8.18 ($G(s)H(s)$ is known to have no poles in the right half s-plane). Applying the definition of gain margin to this plot we find that $G(j\omega_\phi)H(j\omega_\phi)$ is a number greater than one and therefore GM is a number less than one. Applying the definition of phase margin, we observe that the vector $G(j\omega_g)H(j\omega_g)$ lies in the second quadrant. The angle measured from negative real axis to this vector is negative (counterclockwise measurement is taken as positive by definition) and therefore the phase margin *ΦM* is negative.

In general, the gain margin and the phase margin are mutually independent. For example, it is possible for $G(j\omega)H(j\omega)$ to reflect an excellent gain margin but a poor phase margin. Such is the case depicted in Fig. 8.19, where the GM = ∞ but the *ΦM* < 15°. In such a case, the phase crossover frequency ω_ϕ is undefined. Conversely, $G(j\omega)H(j\omega)$ can reflect a poor gain margin but an excellent phase margin, as is the case depicted in Fig. 8.20, where the *ΦM* = ∞ but the GM is only slightly greater than 1. In such a case, the gain crossover frequency ω_g is undefined.

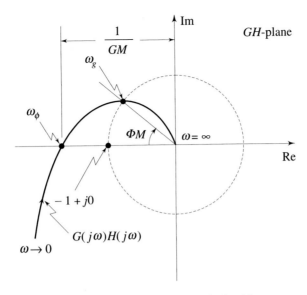

Fig. 8.18 *Nyquist plot of an unstable closed-loop system*

In the light of these observations, gain and phase margins should be used in conjunction with one another when determining the degree of stability of a closed-loop system. Together, they represent a measure of the distance of $G(j\omega)H(j\omega)$ from the critical point $-1+j0$.

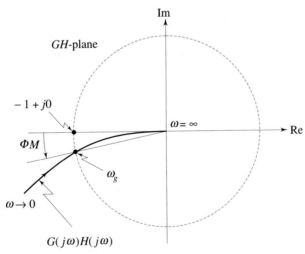

Fig. 8.19 *Infinite GM, poor ΦM*

Some Constraints and Cautions

Gain margin and phase margin are valid measures of relative stability of a closed-loop system only if its open-loop transfer function $G(s)H(s)$ has no

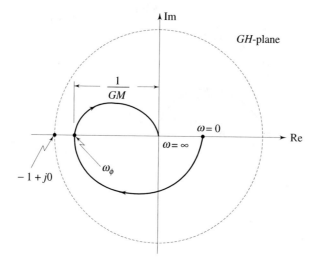

Fig. 8.20   *Poor GM, infinite ΦM*

poles in the right half *s*-plane. If the open-loop transfer function has poles in the right half *s*-plane, it is safer to examine the complete Nyquist plot and/or root locus for interpreting relative stability of the closed-loop system.

It should be observed that the sketches of Figs 8.17–8.20 each cross the negative real axis or the unit circle at most once. For systems with numerous zeros and poles, the Nyquist plot may cross the negative real axis several times, or it may cross the unit circle more than once. For such curves, several values of gain margin and phase margin are defined, as shown in Figs 8.21 (a) and (b). Caution is suggested when interpreting the stability of such systems.

It should also be observed that the sketches of Figs. 8.12–8.20 correspond to systems where increasing gain leads to instability. There are certain practical situations wherein increase in gain can make the system stable. Consider, for example, unity-feedback system with open-loop transfer function

$$G(s) = \frac{K(s+10)^2}{s^3}$$

This is a system for which increasing gain causes a transition from instability to stability. (The Routh criterion shows that the closed-loop system is unstable for $K < 5$ and stable for $K > 5$). The Nyquist plot in Fig. 8.21c has been drawn for the stable value $K = 7$. From this figure we observe that the phase margin is positive and the gain margin is less than one. According to the rules for stability discussed earlier, these two margins yield conflicting signals on system stability. Caution is suggested when interpreting the stability of such systems.

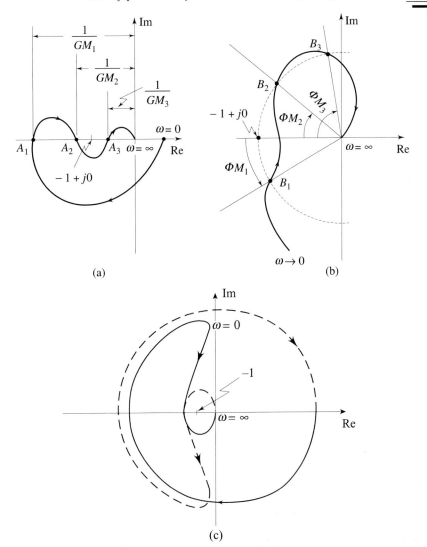

Fig. 8.21 *Nyquist plots requiring careful interpretation of GM and ΦM*

Example 8.7

A unity-feedback system has open-loop transfer function

$$G(s) = \frac{6}{(s^2 + 2s + 2)(s + 2)} \tag{8.25}$$

Since the open-loop poles are only in the left half s-plane, the Nyquist criterion tells us that we want no encirclement of $-1 + j0$ point for stability. In such cases closed-loop stability can be evaluated from Nyquist $G(j\omega)$-plot.

$$G(j\omega)\big|_{\omega = 0} = 1.5\angle 0°; \quad G(j\omega)\big|_{\omega \to \infty} = 0\angle 90°$$

$$G(j\omega) = \frac{6}{(s^2 + 2s + 2)(s + 2)}\bigg|_{s = j\omega}$$

$$= \frac{6[4(1 - \omega^2) - j\omega(6 - \omega^2)]}{16(1 - \omega^2)^2 + \omega^2(6 - \omega^2)^2} \qquad (8.26)$$

Setting the imaginary part to zero, we find the phase crossover frequency $\omega_\phi = \sqrt{6}$ rad/sec. At this frequency, the real part of $G(j\omega)$ in Eqn. (8.26) is calculated to be -0.3 (refer Fig. 8.22). Thus the gain can be increased by $(1/0.3)$ before the real part becomes -1. The gain margin is $GM = 3.33$.

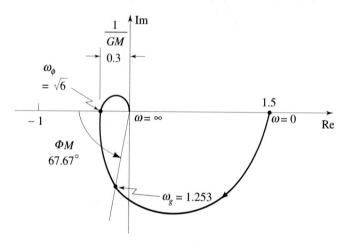

Fig. 8.22   *Nyquist plot for $G(j\omega)$ of Eqn. (8.26)*

To find the phase margin, first find the gain crossover frequency ω_g: the frequency for which the magnitude of $G(j\omega)$ in Eqn. (8.26) is unity. As the problem stands, this calculation requires computational tools. Later in this chapter, we will simplify the calculation process by using Bode plots.

The gain crossover frequency $\omega_g = 1.253$ rad/sec. At this frequency, the phase angle of $G(j\omega)$ is $-112.33°$. The difference between this angle and $180°$ is $67.67°$, which is the phase margin ΦM.

8.5 THE BODE PLOTS

A sinusoidal transfer function may be represented by two separate plots; one giving the magnitude *versus* frequency, and the other the phase angle *versus* frequency. A *Bode plot* (named after Hendrick W. Bode) consists of two graphs: one is a plot of the logarithm of the magnitude of the sinusoidal transfer function, and the other is a plot of the phase angle in degrees; both are plotted against the frequency in logarithmic scale.

In a Bode plot, the logarithmic magnitude of sinusoidal transfer function $G(j\omega)$ is represented[3] as $20 \log |G(j\omega)|$, where the base of the logarithm is 10.

---

3. There is little reason for this choice; the choice dates from Alexander Graham Bell's study of the response of the human ear. In electromagnetics and some other applications, the natural logarithm is used; the unit then is *neper*.

The unit used in this representation of the magnitude is *decibel* (one-tenth of a 'Bel': a unit named after Alexander Graham Bell), usually abbreviated as dB.

The main advantage of using the logarithmic plot is that the multiplication of magnitudes can be converted into addition. Consider a typical rational transfer function $G(s)$ factored in the time-constant form:

$$G(s) = \frac{K(1 + s\tau_a)(1 + s\tau_b)\cdots}{s^N(1 + s\tau_1)(1 + s\tau_2)\cdots[1 + (2\zeta/\omega_n)s + s^2/\omega_n^2]\cdots} \tag{8.27}$$

This transfer function has zeros at $s = -1/\tau_a, -1/\tau_b, \ldots,$ N poles at the origin, real poles at $s = -1/\tau_1, -1/\tau_2, \ldots,$ and complex poles at $-\zeta\omega_n \pm j\omega_n\sqrt{1 - \zeta^2}$. We note that the constant multiplier $K = \lim_{s \to 0} s^N G(s)$, where N is the type number for the system with open-loop transfer function $G(s)$ given by Eqn. (8.27). Thus for a type-0 system, $K_p = K$. For a type-1 system, $K_v = K$, and for a type-2 system, $K_a = K$. Any rational $G(s)$ can be factored in the form of Eqn. (8.27). If $G(s)$ has complex zeros, then even though it is not shown in Eqn. (8.27), a quadratic term of the form $[1 + (2\zeta/\omega_n)s + s^2/\omega_n^2]$ will also appear in the numerator.

The magnitude of $G(j\omega)$ in dB is obtained by multiplying the logarithm to the base 10 of $|G(j\omega)|$ by 20.

$$\begin{aligned}
|G(j\omega)|_{dB} &= 20 \log |G(j\omega)| \\
&= 20 \log K + 20 \log |1 + j\omega\tau_a| + 20 \log |1 + j\omega\tau_b| + \cdots \\
&\quad - 20N \log |j\omega| - 20 \log |1 + j\omega\tau_1| - 20 \log |1 + j\omega\tau_2| - \cdots \\
&\quad - 20 \log |1 + j2\zeta\omega/\omega_n - \omega^2/\omega_n^2| - \cdots
\end{aligned} \tag{8.28a}$$

The phase of $G(j\omega)$ is

$$\begin{aligned}
\angle G(j\omega) &= \tan^{-1}\omega\tau_a + \tan^{-1}\omega\tau_b + \cdots - N(90°) - \tan^{-1}\omega\tau_1 - \tan^{-1}\omega\tau_2 - \cdots \\
&\quad - \tan^{-1} 2\zeta\omega\omega_n/(\omega_n^2 - \omega^2) - \cdots
\end{aligned} \tag{8.28b}$$

Equations (8.28) express the magnitude and the phase of $G(j\omega)$ as linear combinations of relatively simple terms. The curves for each term can be added together graphically to get the curves for the complete transfer function.

The logarithmic scale used for frequency in Bode plots, has some interesting properties. The frequency in a typical control system application varies over many powers of ten so that most information would be compressed near the origin if a linear scale were used. The logarithmic scale is nonlinear, that is, the distance between 1 and 2 is greater than the distance between 2 and 3 and so on. As a result, use of this scale enables us to cover a greater range of frequencies; both low and high frequency behaviour of a system can be adequately displayed in one plot. The other interesting property of the use of log scale for frequency, as we shall see shortly, is that the straight-line approximation of the Bode plots becomes possible. This property allows the plotting by hand that is quick and yet sufficiently accurate for control-system design. Most control-system designers will have access to computer programs that will diminish the need for hand plotting; however, it is still important to develop good intuition so that erroneous computer results are quickly identified, and for this one needs the ability to check results by hand plotting.

The phase angle graph of the Bode plot, $\angle G(j\omega)$ *versus* $\log\omega$, has a linear scale for phase in degrees and a logarithmic scale for frequency ω. The magnitude graph[4] of the Bode plot, $|G(j\omega)|_{dB}$ versus $\log\omega$, has a linear scale for magnitude in dB and a logarithmic scale for frequency ω.

In general, a rational transfer function $G(s)$ can contain just four simple types of factors:

1. Real constant: $K > 0$
2. Poles or zeros at the origin of order N: $(s)^{\mp N}$
3. Poles or zeros at $s = -1/\tau$ of order q: $(1 + s\tau)^{\mp q}$
4. Complex poles or zeros of order r: $(1 + 2\zeta s/\omega_n + s^2/\omega_n^2)^{\mp r}$

Equations (8.28) indicate one of the unique characteristics of Bode plot —each of the four types of factors listed can be considered as a separate plot; the individual plots are then algebraically added to yield the total plot of the given transfer function. Bode plots of the four types of factors are, therefore, the basic building blocks for the construction of the Bode plot of the given transfer function.

Magnitude Plot: Straight-Line Approximation

We shall now discuss how the $|G(j\omega)|_{dB}$ *versus* $\log\omega$ graph can be sketched with very little effort using straight-line approximation. We first examine the basic building blocks, and then use these blocks to build the magnitude plot of the given transfer function.

The dB *versus* $\log\omega$ graph can be sketched on a linear rectangular coordinate graph paper. However, use of semilog graph paper is more convenient as it eliminates the need to take logarithm of many numbers. The logarithmic scale of the semilog graph paper is used for frequency and the linear scale is used for dB.

The units used to express frequency bands or frequency ratios are the *octave* and the *decade*. An octave is a frequency band from ω_1 to ω_2 where $\omega_2/\omega_1 = 2$. There is an increase of one decade from ω_1 to ω_2 when $\omega_2/\omega_1 = 10$. Semilog graph papers come in two, three, four or five cycles, indicating the range of coverage in decades (refer Fig. 8.23). It may be noted that we cannot locate the point $\omega = 0$ on the log scale since $\log 0 = -\infty$.

Real constant K

Since the constant K is frequency-invariant, the plot of

$$dB = 20\log K \qquad (8.29)$$

is a horizontal straight line. The magnitude plot for $K = 10$ is shown in Fig. 8.23 in semilog coordinates. The horizontal axis is $\log\omega$; labeled ω on logarithmic scale. The vertical axis is magnitude in decibels; labeled dB on linear scale.

---

4. An alternative presentation of the magnitude graph uses logarithmscale for frequency ω and logarithmic scale for magnitude $|G(j\omega)|$, resulting in $\log |G(j\omega)|$ *versus* $\log\omega$ locus.

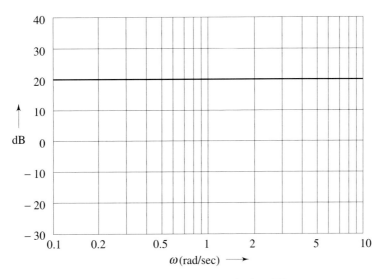

Fig. 8.23   *Bode magnitude plot of K*

Poles or zeros at the origin

The factor $1/(j\omega)$ appearing in a transfer function $G(j\omega)$ has the magnitude ·

$$\text{dB} = 20 \log\left|\frac{1}{j\omega}\right| = -20 \log \omega \qquad (8.30)$$

The dB versus $\log \omega$ plot of Eqn. (8.30) is a straight line with a slope of -20 dB per unit change in $\log \omega$. A unit change in $\log \omega$ means

$$\log(\omega_2/\omega_1) = 1 \text{ or } \omega_2 = 10\omega_1$$

This range of frequencies is called a *decade*. Thus the slope of Eqn. (8.30) is -20 dB/decade. The range of frequencies $\omega_2 = 2\,\omega_1$ is called an *octave*. Since $-20 \log 2 = -6$ dB, the slope of Eqn. (8.30) could also be expressed as -6 dB/octave. The plot of Eqn. (8.30) is shown in Fig. 8.24a; it intersects the 0-dB axis at $\omega = 1$.

For an Nth-order pole at the origin, the magnitude is

$$\text{dB} = 20 \log\left|\frac{1}{(j\omega)^N}\right| = -20N \log \omega \qquad (8.31)$$

The magnitude plot is still a straight line that intersects the 0-dB axis at $\omega = 1$, but the slope is now $-20N$ dB/decade.

For the case that a transfer function has a zero at the origin, the magnitude of the term is given by

$$\text{dB} = 20 \log |j\omega| = 20 \log \omega \qquad (8.32)$$

and the plot is the negative of that for a pole at the origin; it is a straight line with a slope of $+20$ dB/decade that intersects the 0-dB axis at $\omega = 1$ (Fig. 8.24b).

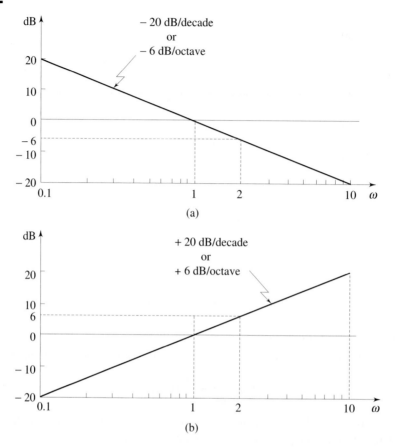

Fig. 8.24   *Bode magnitude plot of (a) pole (b) zero at the origin*

For the case of an Nth-order zero at the origin, it is seen that the plot is the negative of that for the Nth-order pole.

Example 8.8

Consider the transfer function

$$G(s) = \frac{K}{s^N}$$

There are two terms in $G(s)$: the constant K, and the repeated pole at the origin. We could add the Bode magnitude plots of the two terms to get the Bode magnitude plot of $G(s)$. However, treating K/s^N as a single term turns out to be more convenient, as is seen below.

$$dB = 20 \log \left| \frac{K}{(j\omega)^N} \right| = -20N \log \omega + 20 \log K \tag{8.33}$$

With $\log \omega$ as abscissa, the plot of Eqn. (8.33) is a straight line having a slope $-20N$ dB/decade and passing through $20 \log K$ dB when $\log \omega = 0$, i.e., when

$\omega = 1$, as shown in Fig. 8.25. Further, the plot has a value of 0 dB at the frequency of

$$20N \log \omega = 20\log K \quad \text{or} \quad \omega = (K)^{1/N}$$

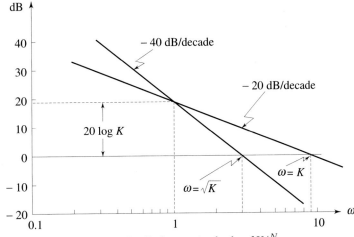

Fig. 8.25   *Bode magnitude plot of K/s^N*

Poles or zeros at s = –1/τ

The factor $1/(1+j\omega\tau)$ appearing in a transfer function $G(j\omega)$ has magnitude

$$dB = 20 \log \left| \frac{1}{1+j\omega\tau} \right| = -20 \log \sqrt{1+\omega^2\tau^2} \tag{8.34}$$

For low frequencies, such that $\omega \ll 1/\tau$, the magnitude may be approximated by
$$dB = -20 \log 1 = 0 \tag{8.35}$$
For high frequencies, such that $\omega \gg 1/\tau$, the magnitude may be approximated by
$$dB = -20 \log(\omega\tau) = -20 \log\omega - 20 \log \tau \tag{8.36}$$

The plot of Eqn. (8.35) is a straight line coincident with the 0-dB axis. The plot of Eqn. (8.36) is also a straight line having a slope of –20 dB/decade intersecting the 0-dB axis at $\omega = 1/\tau$ as shown in Fig. 8.26. We call the straightline approximations the *asymptotes*. The low-frequency approximation

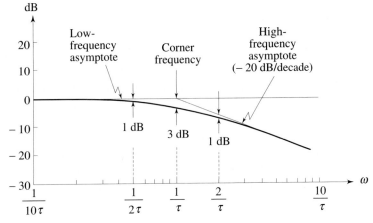

Fig. 8.26   *Bode magnitude plot of $1/(1+j\omega\tau)$*

is called the *low-frequency asymptote* and the high-frequency approximation is called the *high-frequency asymptote*. The frequency $\omega = 1/\tau$ at which the two asymptotes meet is called the *corner frequency* or *break frequency*.

Though the asymptotic approximations hold good for $\omega \ll 1/\tau$ and $\omega \gg 1/\tau$, with some loss of accuracy these could be extended for $\omega \leq 1/\tau$ and $\omega \geq 1/\tau$. Therefore, the dB *versus* $\log\omega$ curve of $1/(1 + j\omega\tau)$ can be approximated by two asymptotes, one a straight line at 0 dB for the frequency range $0 < \omega \leq 1/\tau$ and the other, a straight line with a slope -20 dB/decade (or -6dB/octave) for the frequency range $1/\tau \leq \omega < \infty$. The corner frequency divides the plot into two regions, a low-frequency region and a high-frequency region.

The error in the magnitude plot caused by the use of asymptotes can easily be calculated. The maximum error occurs at the corner frequency $\omega = 1/\tau$ and is given by (refer Eqns (8.34) and (8.35))

$$- 20 \log \sqrt{1+1} + 20 \log 1 = -3.01 \text{ dB}$$

The error at the frequency one octave below the corner frequency $(\omega = 1/(2\tau))$ is (refer Eqns (8.34) and (8.35))

$$- 20 \log \sqrt{1 + \tfrac{1}{4}} + 20 \log 1 = - 0.97 \text{ dB}$$

The error at the frequency one octave above the corner frequency $(\omega = 2/\tau)$ is (refer Eqns (8.34) and (8.36))

$$- 20 \log \sqrt{1 + 4} + 20 \log 2 = - 0.97 \text{ dB}$$

The error at the frequency one decade below the corner frequency ($\omega = 1/(10\tau)$) is

$$- 20 \log \sqrt{1 + \tfrac{1}{100}} + 20 \log 1 = - 0.04 \text{ dB}$$

The error at the frequency one decade above the corner frequency $(\omega = 10/\tau)$ is

$$- 20 \log \sqrt{1 + 100} + 20 \log 10 = - 0.04 \text{ dB}$$

Similarly, the errors at other frequencies may be calculated.

In practice, a sufficiently accurate magnitude plot is obtained by correcting the asymptotic plot by -3 dB at the corner frequency and by -1 dB one octave below and one octave above the corner frequency, and then drawing a smooth curve through these points approaching the low and high frequency asymptotes as shown in Fig. 8.26.

It is seen from Eqn. (8.28a) that the magnitude plot of the factor $1 + j\omega\tau$ is exactly of the same form as that of the factor $1/(1 + j\omega\tau)$, but with the opposite sign. The approximate plot consists of two straight line asymptotes, one a straight line at 0 dB for the frequency range $0 < \omega \leq 1/\tau$, and the other a straight line with a slope of $+20$ dB/decade (or $+ 6$ dB/octave) for the frequency range $1/\tau \leq \omega < \infty$. The frequency $\omega = 1/\tau$ is the corner frequency. A sufficiently accurate plot is obtained by correcting the asymptotic plot by $+3$ dB at the corner frequency and by $+1$ dB one octave below and one octave above the corner frequency, and then drawing a smooth curve through these points approaching the low and high frequency asymptotes as shown in Fig. 8.27.

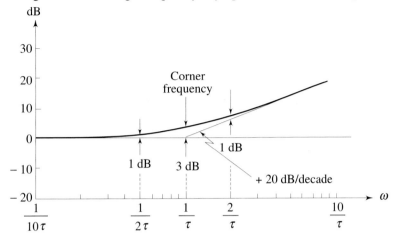

Fig. 8.27 *Bode magnitude plot of $(1 + j\omega\tau)$*

For the case when a given transfer function involves terms like $(1+j\omega\tau)^{\mp q}$, a similar asymptotic construction may be made. The corner frequency is still at $\omega = 1/\tau$ and the asymptotes are straight lines. The low-frequency asymptote is a straight line at $0\,dB$ and the high-frequency asymptote has a slope of $\mp 20q$ dB/decade (or $\mp 6q$ dB/octave). The error involved in asymptotic approximation is q times that for $(1+j\omega\tau)^{\mp 1}$; $\mp 3q$ dB at the corner frequency and $\mp q$ dB one octave below and one octave above the corner frequency.

Example 8.9

Let us draw the Bode magnitude plot for the transfer function

$$G(s) = \frac{200(s+1)}{(s+10)^2}$$

The rearrangement of the transfer function in the time-constant form gives

$$G(s) = \frac{2(1+s)}{(1+s/10)^2}$$

Therefore, the sinusoidal transfer function in the time-constant form is given by

$$G(j\omega) = \frac{2(1+j\omega)}{(1+j\omega/10)^2}$$

Our approach is to first construct an asymptotic plot and then apply corrections to it to get an accurate plot. The corner frequencies of the asymptotic plot in order of their occurrence as frequency increases, are

(i) $\omega_{c1} = 1$, due to zero at $s = -1$;
(ii) $\omega_{c2} = 10$, due to double pole at $s = -10$

At frequencies less than ω_{c1}, the first corner frequency, only the factor $K = 2$ is effective.

Pertinent characteristics of each factor of the transfer function are given in Table 8.1. By sketching the asymptotes for each factor and then algebraically adding them, we obtain the asymptotic plot for the transfer function $G(j\omega)$. We can, however, draw the composite asymptotic plot directly, as is outlined below.

Table 8.1 *Asymptotic approximation table for Bode magnitude plot of* $2(1 + j\omega)/(1 + j\omega/10)^2$

Factor	Corner frequency	Asymptotic magnitude characteristic
2	None	Constant magnitude of $+6$ dB
$1 + j\omega$	$\omega_{c1} = 1$	Straight line of 0 dB for $\omega \leq \omega_{c1}$; straight line of $+20$ dB/decade for $\omega \geq \omega_{c1}$
$1/(1 + j\omega/10)^2$	$\omega_{c2} = 10$	Straight line of 0 dB for $\omega \leq \omega_{c2}$; straight line of -40 dB/decade for $\omega \geq \omega_{c2}$

Step 1: We start with the factor $K = 2$. Its magnitude plot is the asymptote 1; a horizontal straight line at the magnitude of 6 dB.

Step 2: Let us now add to the asymptote 1, the plot of the factor $(1 + j\omega)$ corresponding to the lowest corner frequency $\omega_{c1} = 1$. Since this factor contributes zero dB for $\omega \leq \omega_{c1} = 1$, the resultant plot up to $\omega = 1$ is the same as that of the asymptote 1. For $\omega > \omega_{c1} = 1$, this factor contributes $+20$ dB/decade such that the resultant plot of the two factors is the asymptote 2 of slope $+20$ dB/decade passing through (6 dB, 1 rad/sec) point. At $\omega = \omega_{c2} = 10$, the resultant plot has a magnitude of 26 dB as shown in Fig. 8.28.

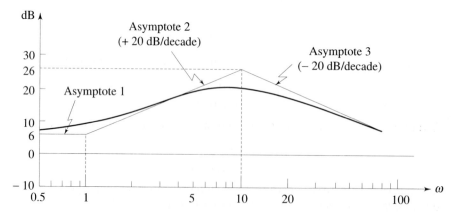

Fig. 8.28 *Bode magnitude plot for Example 8.9*

Step 3: We now add to the resultant plot of step 2, the plot of the factor $1/(1 + j\omega/10)^2$ corresponding to the corner frequency $\omega_{c2} = 10$. Since this factor contributes 0 dB for $\omega \le \omega_{c2} = 10$, the resultant plot up to $\omega = 10$ is the same as that of step 2. For $\omega > \omega_{c2} = 10$, this factor contributes -40 dB/decade such that the resultant plot of the three factors is the asymptote 3 of slope $(+ 20) + (- 40) = - 20$ dB/decade passing through (26 dB, 10 rad/sec) point. Figure 8.28 shows the asymptotic magnitude plot of given $G(j\omega)$.

To the asymptotic plot thus obtained, corrections are to be applied. The corrections at each corner frequency and at an octave above and below the corner frequency are usually sufficient. The corner frequency $\omega_{c1} = 1$ corresponds to the first-order factor $(1 + j\omega)$: the corrections are $+ 3$dB at $\omega = 1$, $+ 1$dB at $\omega = 0.5$ and $+ 1$dB at $\omega = 2$. The corner frequency $\omega_{c2} = 10$ corresponds to second-order factor $1/(1 + j\omega/10)^2$: the corrections are $- 6$dB at $\omega = 10$, $- 2$ dB at $\omega = 5$ and $- 2$ dB at $\omega = 20$. Table 8.2 lists the net corrections.

Table 8.2 *Corrections to the asymptotic magnitude plot of* $2(1 + j\omega)/(1 + j\omega/10)^2$

Frequency, ω	0.5	1	2	5	10	20
Net correction	+ 1 dB	+ 3 dB	+ 1 dB	− 2 dB	− 6 dB	− 2 dB

The corrected asymptotic magnitude plot of the given transfer function is shown in Fig. 8.28.

Example 8.10

Consider the transfer function $\quad G(j\omega) = \dfrac{10(1 + j\omega/2)}{(j\omega)^2(1 + j\omega)}$

The corner frequencies of the asymptotic Bode magnitude plot of $G(j\omega)$ in order of their occurrence as frequency increases, are

   (i) $\omega_{c1} = 1$, due to simple pole,

   (ii) $\omega_{c2} = 2$, due to simple zero.

At frequencies less than ω_{c1}, only the factor $10/(j\omega)^2$ is effective.

Asymptotic magnitude plot of $G(j\omega)$ is shown in Fig. 8.29. The plot is obtained following the steps given below:

Step 1: We start with the factor $10/(j\omega)^2$ corresponding to double pole at the origin. Its magnitude plot is the asymptote 1, having a slope of $- 40$ dB/decade and passing through the point $20 \log 10 = 20$ dB at

     $\omega = 1$. Asymptote 1 intersects the 0-dB line at $\omega = \sqrt{10}$.

Step 2: Let us now add to the asymptote 1, the plot of the factor $1/(1 + j\omega)$ corresponding to the lowest corner frequency $\omega_{c1} = 1$. Since this factor contributes zero dB for $\omega \le 1$, the resultant plot up to $\omega = 1$ is the same as that of aymptote 1. For $\omega > 1$ this factor contributes -20 dB/decade such that the resultant plot of the two factors is the asymptote 2 of slope $(-40) + (-20) = -60$ dB/decade passing through (20 dB, 1 rad/sec) point. At $\omega = \omega_{c2} = 2$, the resultant plot has a magnitude of 2 dB as shown in Fig. 8.29.

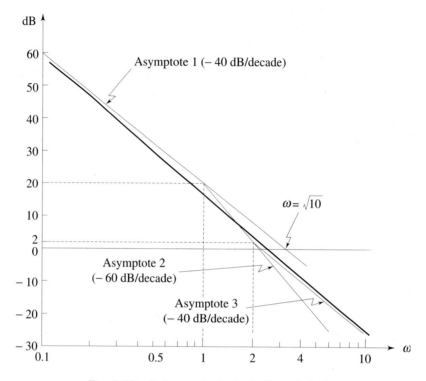

Fig. 8.29 *Bode magnitude plot for Example 8.10*

Step 3: We now add to the resultant plot of step 2, the plot of the factor $(1 + j\omega/2)$ corresponding to the corner frequency $\omega_{c2} = 2$. This gives rise to a straight line of slope $+20$ dB/decade for $\omega > 2$, which when added to asymptote 2 results in asymptote 3 of slope $(-60) + (+20) = -40$ dB/decade passing through (2 dB, 2 rad/sec) point. Figure 8.29 shows the asymptotic magnitude plot of given $G(j\omega)$.

To the asymptotic plot thus obtained, corrections are to be applied. The corrections due to asymptotic approximation of magnitude plot of the pole factor are: -3 dB at $\omega = 1$, -1 dB at $\omega = 0.5$ and -1 dB at $\omega = 2$. To these corrections, we algebraically add the corrections due to the asymptotic approximation of magnitude plot of the zero factor: $+3$ dB at $\omega = 2$, $+1$ dB at $\omega = 1$, and $+1$ dB at $\omega = 4$. Table 8.3 lists the net corrections.

Table 8.3   *Corrections to the asymptotic magnitude plot of*
$10(1 + j\omega/2)/(j\omega)^2(1 + j\omega)$

Frequency, ω	0.5	1	2	4
Net correction	-1 dB	-2 dB	$+2$ dB	$+1$ dB

The corrected asymptotic magnitude plot of the given transfer function is shown in Fig. 8.29.

Complex Poles or Zeros

Transfer functions of control systems often possess quadratic factors of the form

$$\frac{1}{1 + j(2\zeta/\omega_n)\omega - \omega^2/\omega_n^2}; 0 < \zeta \le 1 \qquad (8.37a)$$

This term is slightly more complicated since besides being a function of ω as before, it is also a function of the variable ζ. As may be expected, the shape of the Bode plot depends strongly upon what value of damping ratio ζ is being considered.

In normalized form, the quadratic factor (8.37a) may be written as

$$\frac{1}{(1 + j2\zeta u - u^2)} \qquad (8.37b)$$

where $u = \omega/\omega_n$ is the normalized frequency. The magnitude of this factor is

$$dB = 20 \log \left| \frac{1}{1 - u^2 + j2\zeta u} \right| = -20 \log \sqrt{(1 - u^2)^2 + (2\zeta u)^2} \qquad (8.38)$$

For low frequencies, such that $u \ll 1$, the magnitude may be approximated by

$$dB = -20 \log 1 = 0 \qquad (8.39)$$

For high frequencies, such that $u \gg 1$, the magnitude may be approximated by

$$dB = -20 \log (u^2) = -40 \log u \qquad (8.40)$$

Therefore an approximate magnitude plot of the quadratic factor (8.37b) consists of two straight line asymptotes, one horizontal line at 0 dB for $u \le 1$ and the other, a line with a slope -40 dB/decade for $u \ge 1$. The two asymptotes meet on 0-dB line at $u = 1$, i.e., $\omega = \omega_n$, which is the corner frequency of the plot. The asymptotic plot is shown in Fig. 8.30.

The error in the magnitude plot caused by the use of asymptotes can be calculated as follows.

For $0 < u \le 1$, the error is (refer Eqns (8.38) and (8.39))

$$-20 \log \sqrt{(1 - u^2)^2 + (2\zeta u)^2} + 20 \log 1 \qquad (8.41a)$$

and for $1 \le u < \infty$, the error is (refer Eqns (8.38) and (8.40))

$$-20 \log \sqrt{(1-u^2)^2 + (2\zeta u)^2} + 40 \log u \qquad (8.41b)$$

The error at the corner frequency ($u = 1$ or $\omega = \omega_n$) is

$$-20 \log 2\zeta \qquad (8.42)$$

For $\zeta = 1$, the error at the corner frequency is $-20 \log 2 \cong -6$ dB. Note that for $\zeta = 1$, Eqn. (8.37) has two equal real poles:

$$\left.\frac{1}{(1 + j2\zeta u - u^2)}\right|_{\zeta=1} = \frac{1}{(1 + ju)^2} = \frac{1}{(1 + j\omega/\omega_n)^2}$$

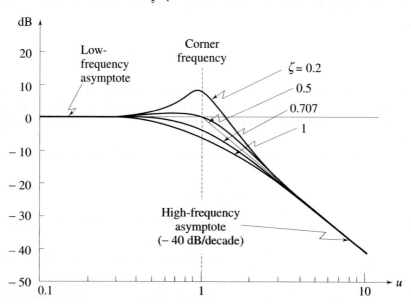

Fig. 8.30 *Bode magnitude plot of 1/(1 +j2ζu–u²)*

From expression (8.42) we see that at the corner frequency, the error is negative for $\zeta > 0.5$ and positive for $\zeta < 0.5$. The corrected magnitude curves for various values of ζ are shown in Fig. 8.30. From this figure, it is seen that for small values of ζ the magnitude curves have pronounced peak at a frequency slightly less than the corner frequency. In fact, smaller the value of ζ the higher the peak. We shall discuss this peak in some detail.

Consider Fig. 8.31, which shows what might be a typical plot of (refer Eqn. (8.38))

$$dB = -20 \log \sqrt{(1 - u^2)^2 + (2\zeta u)^2}$$

The peak value occurs at normalized frequency which is labeled u_r ($u_r = \omega_r/\omega_n$) and the height of the peak is M_r. This peak will occur at a u where $\sqrt{(1-u^2)^2 + (2\zeta u)^2}$ is at a minimum. The minimum can be found by simple differentiation.

$$\frac{d}{du}\left[\sqrt{(1-u^2)^2+(2\zeta u)^2}\right]\Bigg|_{u=u_r} = \frac{\frac{1}{2}\left[-4(1-u_r^2)u_r+8\zeta^2 u_r\right]}{[(1-u_r^2)^2+(2\zeta u_r)^2]^{1/2}} = 0$$

which gives

$$4u_r^3 - 4u_r + 8\zeta^2 u_r = 0$$

or
$$u_r = \sqrt{1-2\zeta^2} \tag{8.43}$$

The corresponding peak value M_r is then

$$M_r = -20 \log\sqrt{(1-u_r^2)^2+(2\zeta u_r)^2}$$

$$= -20 \log 2\zeta\sqrt{1-\zeta^2} \text{ dB} \tag{8.44}$$

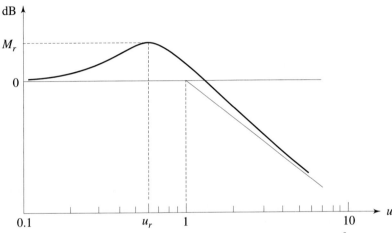

Fig. 8.31   *A typical magnitude curve of $1/(1+j2\zeta u - u^2)$*

Note that as ζ goes to zero, the peak value M_r goes off to infinity (refer Eqn. (8.44)) and frequency u_r approaches the corner frequency (refer Eqn. (8.43)). For $0 < \zeta < 1/\sqrt{2}$, u_r is less than the corner frequency. For $\zeta \geq 1/\sqrt{2}$, the errors given by expressions (8.41) are negative for all frequencies and therefore magnitude curves do not have a peak.

For given values of ζ and ω_n, an exact dB versus $\log \omega$ curve is obtained from the following expression (refer Eqn. (8.38)).

$$\text{dB} = -20 \log \sqrt{\left[1-\left(\frac{\omega}{\omega_n}\right)^2\right]^2 + \left(\frac{2\zeta\omega}{\omega_n}\right)^2} \tag{8.45}$$

Most control-system designers will have access to computer programs to do this job. The following procedure is useful for hand plotting.

Draw two straight line asymptotes: one a 0-dB line for $0 < \omega \leq \omega_n$ and the other a -40 dB/decade line for $\omega_n \leq \omega < \infty$. The two asymptotes meet at the corner frequency $\omega = \omega_n$. Correct the asymptotic plot by M_r dB at the frequency ω_r where (refer Eqns (8.44) and (8.43))

$$M_r = -20 \log 2\zeta\sqrt{1-\zeta^2} \ \text{dB} \tag{8.46a}$$

$$\omega_r = \omega_n \sqrt{1-2\zeta^2} \ \text{rad/sec} \tag{8.46b}$$

Of course, this correction is applied when $\zeta < 1/\sqrt{2}$. Correct the asymptotic plot by $-20 \log (2\zeta)$ dB at the corner frequency $\omega = \omega_n$ (refer expression (8.42)). Draw a smooth curve through these points approaching the low and high frequency asymptotes.

The accuracy of the plot can be improved by correcting the asymptotic plot at some other frequencies also; say one octave below and above the corner frequency. The errors are calculated from the following expressions (refer expressions (8.41)).

$$-20 \log \sqrt{\left[1-\left(\frac{\omega}{\omega_n}\right)^2\right]^2 + \left[2\zeta\left(\frac{\omega}{\omega_n}\right)\right]^2} \quad \text{for } 0 < \omega \le \omega_n \tag{8.47a}$$

$$-20 \log \sqrt{\left[1-\left(\frac{\omega}{\omega_n}\right)^2\right]^2 + \left[2\zeta\left(\frac{\omega}{\omega_n}\right)\right]^2} + 40 \log \left(\frac{\omega}{\omega_n}\right) \quad \text{for } \omega_n \le \omega < \infty \tag{8.47b}$$

The magnitude plot of the factor $[(1 + j(2\zeta/\omega_n)\omega - \omega^2/\omega_n^2]$ is exactly of the same form as that of the factor $1/[1 + j(2\zeta/\omega_n)\omega - \omega^2/\omega_n^2]$, but with the opposite sign. Similar asymptotic construction may be made for the case when a given transfer function involves terms like $[1 + j(2\zeta/\omega_n)\omega - \omega^2/\omega_n^2]^{\mp r}$.

Example 8.11

Let us draw the Bode magnitude plot of the transfer function

$$G(s) = \frac{200(s+2)}{s(s^2 + 10s + 100)}$$

The rearrangement of the transfer function in time-constant form gives

$$G(s) = \frac{4(1 + s/2)}{s[1 + s/10 + (s/10)^2]}$$

Therefore, the sinusoidal transfer function in time-constant form is given by

$$G(j\omega) = \frac{4(1 + j\omega/2)}{j\omega(1 + j\omega/10 - \omega^2/100)} \tag{8.48}$$

The corner frequencies of the asymptotic plot of $G(j\omega)$, in order of their occurrence as frequency increases, are

(i) $\omega_{c1} = 2$, due to zero at $s = -2$;

(ii) $\omega_{c2} = 10$, due to pair of complex conjugate poles with $\zeta = 0.5$ and $\omega_n = 10$.

At frequencies less than ω_{c1}, only the factor $4/(j\omega)$ is effective.

Asymptotic magnitude plot of $G(j\omega)$ is drawn in Fig. 8.32. The plot is obtained following the steps given below.

Step 1: We start with the factor $4/(j\omega)$ corresponding to the pole at the origin. Its magnitude plot is the asymptote 1 having a slope of -20 dB/decade passing through the point $20 \log 4 = 12$ dB at $\omega = 1$. Asymptote 1 intersects the 0-dB line at $\omega = 4$. At $\omega = \omega_{c1} = 2$, the magnitude is 6 dB.

Step 2: We now add to the asymptote 1, the plot of the factor $(1 + j\omega/2)$ corresponding to the lowest corner frequency $\omega_{c1} = 2$. Since this factor contributes 0 dB for $\omega \leq 2$, the resultant plot up to $\omega = 2$ is the same as that of asymptote 1. For $\omega > 2$, this factor contributes $+20$ dB/decade such that the resultant plot of the two factors is the asymptote 2 of slope $(-20) + (+20) = 0$ dB/decade passing through (6 dB, 2 rad/sec) point. At $\omega = \omega_{c2} = 10$, the resultant plot has a magnitude of 6 dB as shown in Fig. 8.32.

Step 3: We now add to the resultant plot of step 2, the plot of the factor $1/(1 + j\omega/10 - \omega^2/100)$ corresponding to the corner frequency $\omega_{c2} = \omega_n = 10$. This gives rise to a straight line of slope -40 dB/decade for $\omega > 10$ which when added to asymptote 2 results in asymptote 3 with a slope $0 + (-40) = -40$ dB/decade passing through the point (6 dB, 10 rad/sec).

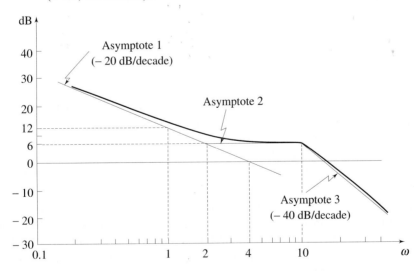

Fig. 8.32 *Bode magnitude plot for Example 8.11*

To the asymptotic plot thus obtained, corrections are to be applied. Table 8.4 lists the corrections.

Table 8.4 *Corrections to the asymptotic plot of*
$$4(1 + j\omega/2)/(j\omega)(1 + j\omega/10 - \omega^2/100)$$

Frequency	Correction	Remarks
$\omega = 2$	$+ 3$ dB	
$\omega = 1$	$+ 1$ dB	
$\omega = 4$	$+ 1$ dB	
$\omega = 10$	0 dB	Error $= -20 \log 2\zeta = 0$
$\omega = 10/\sqrt{2}$	$-20 \log(\sqrt{3}/2)$ dB	$M_r = -20 \log 2\zeta\sqrt{1 - \zeta^2}$

The corrected asymptotic plot of the given transfer function is shown in Fig. 8.32.

Phase Plot

The phase angle at any frequency can be obtained as the algebraic sum of the phase angles due to various factors in the transfer function, in a manner similar to that used for obtaining magnitude plots (refer Eqns (8.28)). To illustrate the procedure, we consider the transfer function

$$G(j\omega) = \frac{K(1 + j\omega\tau_1)}{j\omega(1 + j\omega\tau_2)(1 + (j2\zeta/\omega_n)\omega - \omega^2/\omega_n^2)} \tag{8.49}$$

The phase of $G(j\omega)$ is

$$\angle G(j\omega) = \tan^{-1}\omega\tau_1 - 90° - \tan^{-1}\omega\tau_2 - \tan^{-1}2\zeta\omega\omega_n/(\omega_n^2 - \omega^2)$$

$$= \phi_1 + \phi_2 + \phi_3 + \phi_4 \tag{8.50}$$

The first term on the right-hand side of Eqn. (8.50) is due to the real zero, and is given by

$$\phi_1 = \tan^{-1}\omega\tau_1$$

The values of ϕ_1 for various values of ω are given in Table 8.5, and these values are plotted in Fig. 8.33. We can approximate the exact curve with the straightline construction shown in Fig. 8.33. The straight line approximation for the phase characteristic breaks from $0°$ at the frequency $\omega = 1/10\tau_1$, and breaks again to a constant value of $90°$ at $\omega = 10/\tau_1$. The maximum error in the approximation is $5.7°$, and occurs at the two corners $1/10\tau_1$ and $10/\tau_1$.

The second term on the right-hand side in Eqn. (8.50) is due to the pole at the origin and is identically equal to $-90°$. The third term in Eqn. (8.50) is due to the real pole and is similar to the first term but for reversal in sign. We shall now look at the fourth term, which is due to the complex-conjugate pair of poles, and is given by

$$\phi_4 = -\tan^{-1}\frac{2\zeta\omega_n\omega}{\omega_n^2 - \omega^2}$$

Table 8.5 *Phase characteristics of $(1 + j\omega\tau_1)$*

w (rad/sec)	Exact value	Straight line approximation
$0.05/\tau_1$	2.9°	0°
$0.1/\tau_1$	5.7°	0°
$0.2/\tau_1$	11.3°	13.5°
$0.5/\tau_1$	26.6°	31.5°
$0.8/\tau_1$	38.7°	40.6°
$1/\tau_1$	45°	45°
$2/\tau_1$	63.4°	58.5°
$5/\tau_1$	78.7°	76.5°
$8/\tau_1$	82.9°	85.6°
$10/\tau_1$	84.3°	90°
$20/\tau_1$	87.1°	90°

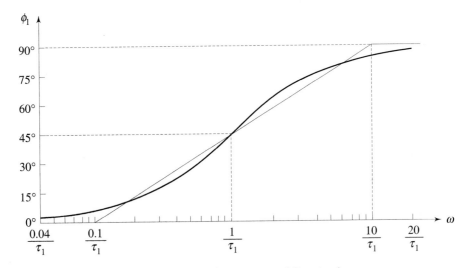

Fig. 8.33 *Phase characteristics of $(1 + j\omega\tau_1)$*

For $\omega \ll 0.1\omega_n$, we have $\phi_4 = 0$, and for $\omega \gg 10\omega_n$, we get $\phi_4 = 180°$. At the intermediate frequency $\omega = \omega_n$, we have $\phi_4 = 90°$. The plots of the asymptotic approximation and the actual curve for various values of ζ are shown in Fig. 8.34. It is seen that for small values of ζ, the actual phase angle changes very rapidly for ω near the undamped natural frequency ω_n.

The overall phase angle is now obtained as the algebraic sum of the phase angle due to each factor. The addition, however, is not as simple as in the case of the magnitude plot due to the fact that the straightline approximation consists of three parts over four decades. The only exception arises when the various poles and zeros have 'large' separation, so that frequency range of phase angle plot of one factor does not overlap with the frequency range of

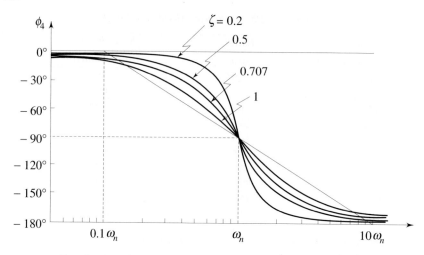

Fig. 8.34   *Phase characteristics of $1/[1 + (j\,2\zeta/\omega_n)\omega - \omega^2/\omega_n^2]$*

phase angle plot of any other factor. In this case, the phase angle plots for the various factors can be superimposed on each other to obtain the overall phase.

For a general case, it is usually advisable to make a table of phase angle against frequency for each factor and then obtain the total phase as the algebraic sum of these. Better accuracy is obtained by using the exact values in the table instead of those obtained through the asymptotic approximation. The computational effort to achieve this accuracy is not heavy.

Example 8.12

Consider the transfer function given in Eqn. (8.48) for which the magnitude plot was obtained in Fig. 8.32. We shall now plot the phase curve.

The phase angle due to each factor for different values of ω is given in Table 8.6. The plot of the total phase is shown in Fig. 8.35.

Table 8.6   *Phase angle due to different factors of the transfer function given by Eqn. (8.48)*

ω (rad/sec)	Poles at the origin	Zero at $s = -2$	Complex conjugate poles	Total phase angle, ϕ
0.1	$-90°$	$2.86°$	$-0.57°$	$-87.71°$
0.2	$-90°$	$5.71°$	$-1.15°$	$-85.44°$
0.5	$-90°$	$14.04°$	$-2.87°$	$-78.33°$
1	$-90°$	$26.57°$	$-5.77°$	$-69.20°$
2	$-90°$	$45.00°$	$-11.77°$	$-56.77°$
5	$-90°$	$68.20°$	$-33.69°$	$-55.49°$
10	$-90°$	$78.69°$	$-90.00°$	$-101.32°$
20	$-90°$	$84.29°$	$-146.31°$	$-152.02°$
50	$-90°$	$87.71°$	$-168.23°$	$-170.52°$
100	$-90°$	$88.85°$	$-174.22°$	$-175.68°$

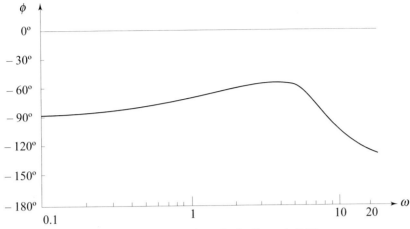

Fig. 8.35   *Bode phase plot for Example 8.12*

8.6 | STABILITY MARGINS ON THE BODE PLOTS

The general objective of the frequency-domain design procedures is to shape the Nyquist plot such that the critical point $-1 + j0$ is avoided with some reasonable stability margins, thereby providing acceptable closed-loop response characteristics. Direct use of the Nyquist plot for design is not particularly convenient, since changes in parameters other than gain require extensive plot revisions. Fortunately, general characteristics of Nyquist plots can be visualized with reasonable accuracy in most cases of interest from Bode plots, and Bode plots are easily constructed and modified.

Since the Bode plot corresponds to only the positive portion of the $j\omega$-axis from $\omega = 0$ to $\omega = \infty$ in the s-plane, its use in stability studies is limited to the determination of gain and phase crossover points and the corresponding phase and gain margins. In practice, the Bode plot is more convenient to apply when the system has open-loop transfer function with no poles in right half s-plane.

Since the straightline approximation of the Bode plot is relatively easier to construct, the data necessary for the other frequency-domain plots, such as the Nyquist plots, can be easily generated from the Bode plot.

Example 8.13———————————————————————

A unity-feedback system has open-loop transfer function

$$G(s) = \frac{K}{(s + 2)(s + 4)(s + 5)}; K = 200 \qquad (8.51a)$$

Let us determine the stability of this system implementing the Nyquist stability criterion using Bode plots.

We begin by sketching the Bode magnitude and phase plots. In the time-constant form, the transfer function $G(s)$ is expressed as

$$G(s) = \frac{5}{(1 + s/2)(1 + s/4)(1 + s/5)}$$ (8.51b)

The sinusoidal transfer function

$$G(j\omega) = \frac{5}{(1 + j\omega/2)(1 + j\omega/4)(1 + j\omega/5)}$$

Bode magnitude and phase plots for $G(j\omega)$ are shown in Fig. 8.36.

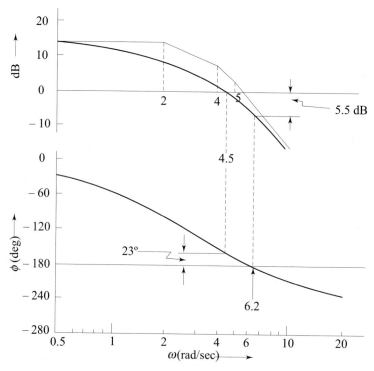

Fig. 8.36 *Bode plot for Example 8.13*

The Nyquist criterion for this example tells us that we want zero encirclements of the $-1+j0$ point for stability. Thus, we recognise that on Bode magnitude plot, the magnitude must be less than 0 dB (which corresponds to unity gain of $G(j\omega)$ on polar plane) at that frequency where the phase is $-180°$. Accordingly, we see that at a frequency of 6.2 rad/sec where the phase is $-180°$, the magnitude is -5.5 dB. Therefore, an increase in gain of $+5.5$ dB is possible before the system becomes unstable. Since the magnitude plot was drawn for a gain of 200 (refer Eqn. (8.51a)), $+5.5$ dB (20 log 1.885 $\cong$ 5.5) represents the allowed increase in gain above 200. Hence the gain for instability is $200 \times 1.885 = 377$. The closed-loop system is stable for $0 < K < 377$.

Next we show how to evaluate the gain and phase margins using Bode plots. The gain margin is found by using the phase plot to find the phase crossover frequency ω_ϕ where the phase angle is $-180°$. At this frequency, look at the magnitude plot to determine the gain margin, *GM*, which is the gain required to raise the magnitude curve to 0 dB. From Fig. 8.36, we find that

$$\omega_\phi = 6.2 \text{ rad/sec}; \ GM = 5.5 \text{ dB}$$

The phase margin is found by using the magnitude curve to find the gain crossover frequency ω_g, where the gain is 0 dB. On the phase curve at that frequency, the phase margin, *ΦM*, is the difference between the phase value and $-180°$. From Fig. 8.36, we find that

$$\omega_g = 4.5 \text{ rad/sec}; \ \Phi M = -157° - (-180°) = 23°$$

*Example 8.14*_____

Consider now a unity-feedback system with open-loop transfer function

$$G(s) = \frac{100}{s\,(1 + 0.1s)\,(1 + 0.2s)}$$

The Bode plots of $G(j\omega)$ are shown in Fig. 8.37. From this figure we find that

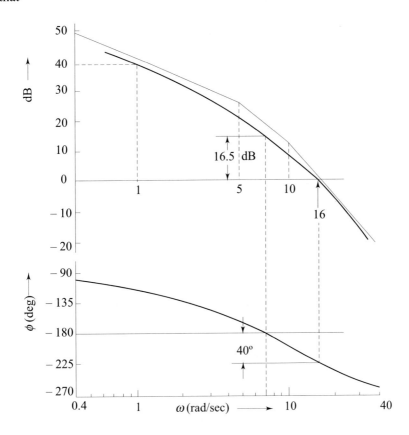

Fig. 8.37 *Bode plot for Example 8.14*

ω_ϕ = phase crossover frequency = 7 rad/sec

GM = gain margin = – 16.5 dB

ω_g = pain crossover frequency = 16 rad/sec

ΦM = phase margin = – 40°

The closed-loop system is thus unstable.

8.7 STABILITY ANALYSIS OF SYSTEMS WITH DEAD-TIME

Figure 8.38 shows the block diagram of a system with dead-time elements in the loop. Open-loop transfer function of the system is

$$G(s)H(s) = G_1(s)e^{-s\tau_D} \tag{8.52}$$

where $G_1(s)$ is a rational function.

Root locus analysis of systems with dead-time elements is possible, but the method is quite complex. In Section 7.11, root locus analysis was carried out using the following approximation:

$$e^{-s\tau_D} \cong \frac{1 - s\tau_D/2}{1 + s\tau_D/2}$$

This approximation works fairly well as long as the dead-time τ_D is small in comparison to the system time-constants.

The frequency-domain graphical methods provide a simple yet exact approach to handle the dead-time problem since the factor $e^{-s\tau_D}$ is readily interpreted in terms of either the Nyquist or the Bode plot.

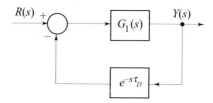

Fig. 8.38 *A closed-loop system with dead-time elements in the loop*

Assume that $G_1(s)$ in Fig. 8.38 is an integrator. Then the open-loop transfer function of the system becomes

$$G(s)H(s) = \frac{e^{-s\tau_D}}{j\omega}$$

The sinusoidal transfer function is

$$G(j\omega)H(j\omega) = \frac{e^{-j\omega\tau_D}}{j\omega}$$

Clearly

$$|G(j\omega)H(j\omega)| = 1/\omega; \quad \angle G(j\omega)H(j\omega) = -\omega\tau_D - \pi/2$$

$$G(j\omega)H(j\omega) = \frac{1}{j\omega}(\cos \omega\tau_D - j\sin \omega\tau_D)$$

$$= -\frac{\sin \omega\tau_D}{\omega} - j\frac{\cos \omega\tau_D}{\omega}$$

$$\lim_{\omega \to 0} [G(j\omega)H(j\omega)] = -\tau_D - j\infty$$

Since the magnitude decreases monotonically, and the phase angle also decreases monotonically indefinitely, the polar plot of the given transfer function will spiral into the $\omega \to \infty$ point at the origin, as shown in Fig. 8.39. The curious reader may like to find some of the intersections with real and imaginary axes. For the first intersection with the real axis, set

Im $[G(j\omega)H(j\omega)] = 0$ to obtain $\omega\tau_D = \pi/2$.

$$\text{Re}[G(j\omega)H(j\omega)]\Big|_{\omega = \frac{\pi}{2\tau_D}} = -\frac{1}{\omega}\Big|_{\omega = \frac{\pi}{2\tau_D}} = -2\tau_D/\pi$$

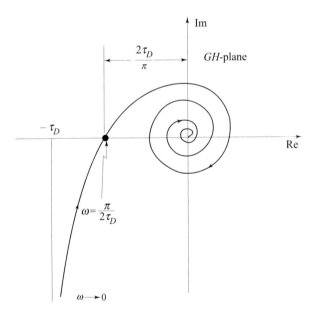

Fig. 8.39 *Polar plot of $e^{-s\tau_D}/s$*

Once the Nyquist plot is constructed, the stability of the closed-loop system is determined in the usual manner. From Fig. 8.39, we observe that relative stability of the system reduces as τ_D increases. Sufficiently large values of τ_D may drive the system to instability.

The Critical Trajectory

Thus far, we have used the point $-1+j0$ of the $G(s)H(s)$-plane as the critical point for stability analysis using Nyquist criterion. We can relax the critical-point idea by extending it into a trajectory if necessary.

The roots of the characteristic equation of the system shown in Fig. 8.38 satisfy (refer Eqn. (8.52)).

$$1 + G_1(s)\, e^{-s\tau_D} = 0$$

or
$$G_1(s)\, e^{-s\tau_D} = -1 \tag{8.53}$$

The right-hand side of the last equation points to the fact that $-1+j0$ is the critical point for stability analysis of the closed-loop system. Equation (8.53) can be written as

$$G_1(s) = -e^{+s\tau_D} \tag{8.54}$$

The corresponding condition for the system without dead-time is

$$G_1(s) = -1 \tag{8.55}$$

The comparison of Eqns (8.54) and (8.55) reveals that the effect of dead-time is simply to shift the critical stability point $-1+j0$ to $-e^{s\tau_D}$, which describes a *critical trajectory*. When $\omega = 0$, the trajectory starts at the point $-1+j0$, and as ω increases, the critical point traces out a circle with unit radius centred at the origin of $G_1(s)$-plane, in the counterclockwise direction.

*Example 8.15*_____

Let us determine, with the help of Nyquist stability criterion, the maximum value of τ_D for stability of the closed-loop system of Fig. 8.38 with

$$G_1(s) = \frac{1}{s(s+1)(s+2)}$$

From Eqn. (8.54), we have with $s = j\omega$,

$$G_1(j\omega) = \frac{1}{j\omega(j\omega+1)(j\omega+2)} = -e^{+j\omega\tau_D}$$

Figure 8.40 shows the $G_1(j\omega)$ locus together with the critical trajectory of $-e^{+j\omega\tau_D}$. The frequency at which the $G_1(j\omega)$ locus intersects the critical trajectory is found by setting the magnitude of $G_1(j\omega)$ to unity, i.e.,

$$|G_1(j\omega)| = \left| \frac{1}{-3\omega^2 + j\omega(2-\omega^2)} \right| = 1$$

which gives $\omega = 0.446$ rad/sec.

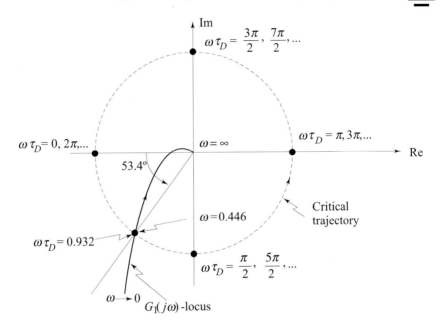

Fig. 8.40   *Critical trajectory and G_1 $(j\omega)$-locus for Example 8.15*

Since

$$\angle G_1(j\omega)\big|_{\omega\,=\,0.446} = \angle -e^{j\omega\tau_D}\big|_{\omega=\,0.446}$$

we obtain (refer Fig. 8.40)

$$53.4\,(\pi/180) = 0.932 \text{ rad} = 0.446\,\tau_D \text{ rad}$$

which gives

$$\tau_D = 2.09 \text{ sec}$$

From Fig. 8.40, we observe that the critical point on the critical trajectory is encircled by the $G_1(j\omega)$ locus for $\tau_D > 2.09$ and is not encircled for $\tau_D < 2.09$; and hence we conclude that the system under discussion is stable if $\tau_D < 2.09$ sec.

Bode Plots of Systems with Dead-Time

The stability analysis of systems with dead-time can be conducted easily using the Bode plots. Since $20 \log |e^{-j\omega\tau_D}| = 0$, the magnitude plot of a system is unaffected by the presence of dead-time. The dead-time, of course, contributes a phase angle of $-(\omega\tau_D \times 180°)/\pi$, thereby causing the modification of the phase plot. An illustrative example follows.

Example 8.16————————————————————

Consider the closed-loop system of Fig. 8.38 with

$$G_1(s) = \frac{K}{s\,(s+1)\,(s+2)} = \frac{K/2}{s(1+s)\,(1+s/2)}$$

Figure 8.41 shows the Bode plots of $G_1(j\omega)e^{-j\omega\tau_D}$ with $K = 1$ and $\tau_D = 0$. We find from this figure that

ω_g = gain crossover frequency = 0.446 rad/sec

ΦM = phase margin = 53.4°

ω_ϕ = phase crossover frequency = 1.4 rad/sec

GM = gain margin = 16 dB

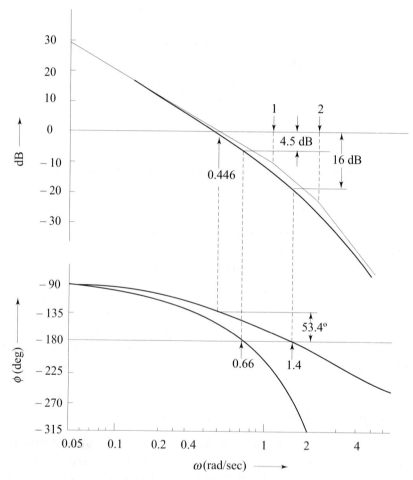

Fig. 8.41   *Bode plots of Example 8.16*

The effect of dead-time is to add the phase shift of $-(\omega\tau_D \times 180)/\pi$ degrees to the phase curve while not affecting the magnitude curve. The adverse effect of dead-time on stability is apparent since the negative phase shift caused by the dead-time increases rapidly with the increase in ω. Let us set $\tau_D = 1$ sec and find the critical value of K for stability. Figure 8.41 also shows Bode plots of $G_1(j\omega)e^{-j\omega\tau_D}$ with $K = 1$ and $\tau_D = 1$. The magnitude curve is unchanged; the phase curve drops with the increase in ω, and the phase crossover frequency is now at 0.66 rad/sec. The gain margin is 4.5 dB. Note that $20 \log 1.67 = 4.5$ dB; therefore the critical value of K for stability when $\tau_D = 1$ is 1.67.

Let us now determine the critical value of dead-time, τ_D for stability with $K = 1$. Since the phase margin with $\tau_D = 0$ and $K = 1$ is 53.4°, a phase lag of 53.4° can be introduced by dead-time before instability sets in. The critical value of dead-time is, therefore, given by the relation

$$\omega_g \tau_D \times 180/\pi = 53.4$$

which gives
$$\tau_D = 2.09 \text{ sec}$$

8.8 FREQUENCY RESPONSE MEASUREMENTS

In this section we will describe how a system responds to sinusoidal input— called the system's *frequency response*—and how the frequency response measurements can be used for design purposes.

To introduce the ideas, we consider a *stable* linear time-invariant system shown in Fig. 8.42. The input and output of the system are described by $x(t)$ and $y(t)$ respectively. The response of the system to sinusoidal input

$$x(t) = X \sin \omega t$$

will consist of two components: the transient component and the steady-state component (refer Example 2.5). The transient component will disappear as time goes by. The steady-state output that results after the transient dies out, is of the form

$$y(t) = A(\omega) \times \sin(\omega t + \phi(\omega))$$

which is a sine wave of the same frequency as the input; it differs from the sinusoidal input only in the amplitude and the phase angle. Both the amplitude and the phase angle change when we use a different frequency ω.

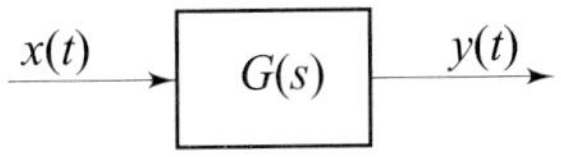

Fig. 8.42 *A stable linear time-invariant system*

The output-input amplitude ratio $A(\omega)$, and the phase angle $\phi(\omega)$ between the output and input sinusoids are given by the relations

$$A(\omega) = \frac{\text{Amplitude of the sinusoidal output}}{\text{Amplitude of sinusoidal input}}$$

$$= |G(s = j\omega)|$$

$$\phi(\omega) = \text{Phase angle of the sinusoidal output}$$
$$- \text{phase angle of the sinusoidal input}$$

$$= \angle G(s = j\omega)$$

The variation of $A(\omega)$ and $\phi(\omega)$ with frequency ω is, by definition, the *frequency response* of the system.

If the system equations are known, complete with numerical values, we can derive its transfer function $G(s)$ and therefrom the *sinusoidal transfer function* $G(j\omega)$. Frequency response of the system can be computed from $G(j\omega)$.

For example, for a system with transfer function

$$G(s) = \frac{10}{s+1}$$

$$|G(j\omega)| = A(\omega) = \frac{10}{\sqrt{1+\omega^2}} ; \angle G(j\omega) = \phi(\omega) = -\tan^{-1}\omega$$

The frequency-response data generated from these equations is given in Table 8.7. This data completely characterizes the steady-state behaviour of the system to sinusoidal inputs; for the sinusoidal input

$$x(t) = 3 \sin 5t,$$

the steady-state output

$$y(t) = 3 \times 1.96 \sin (5t - 78.7°)$$
$$= 5.28 \sin (5t - 78.7°)$$

Table 8.7   *Frequency response data for G(s) = 10/(s + 1)*

ω (rad/sac)	$|G(j\omega)|$	$\angle G(j\omega)$
0	10.00	0°
0.5	8.94	−26.6°
1.0	7.07	−45°
1.5	5.55	−56.3°
2.0	4.47	−63.4°
3.0	3.16	−71.6°
5.0	1.96	−78.7°
10.0	1.00	−84.3°

If the equations and/or parameter values are not known, but the physical system or its components exist and are available for test, we can generate the frequency-response data by experimental measurements:

(i) A sinusoidal input of known amplitude and frequency is applied to the system.

(ii) The system output is allowed to 'settle' into a steady-state pattern.

(iii) The amplitude and relative phase of the sinusoidal output are measured and recorded.

(iv) This procedure is repeated for values of ω spanning the frequency range of interest.

Obviously, no steady-state response exists for an unstable system; so a frequency-response test will directly indicate instability.

Raw measurements of the output amplitude and phase of a stable plant undergoing a sinusoidal input are sufficient to analyse feedback system stability. No intermediate processing of the data is necessary because Nyquist plot/ Bode plot can be sketched directly from experimental measurements.

Identification

Sometimes it is desirable to obtain an approximate model, in terms of a transfer function, directly from the frequency-response measurements. Determination of a transfer function $G(s)$ from measured data is an *identification problem*.

For a stable system, $|G(j\omega)|$ and $\angle G(j\omega)$ can be obtained by measurement. This is also possible if the system is marginally stable with a pole at $s = 0$. Experimental data are used to obtain the exact log-magnitude and phase angle curves of the Bode plot. Asymptotes are drawn on the exact log-magnitude curves by utilizing the fact that their slopes must be multiples of ± 20 dB/ decade. From these asymptotes, the system type and approximate time-constants are determined.

Careful interpretation of the phase angle curve is necessary to identify whether the transfer function is a *minimum phase* or a *nonminimum phase* transfer function. Let us first define these terms.

Consider the following transfer functions:

$$G_1(j\omega) = \frac{1 - j\omega\tau}{(1 + j\omega\tau_1)(1 + j\omega\tau_2)};$$

$$G_2(j\omega) = \frac{1 + j\omega\tau}{(1 + j\omega\tau_1)(1 + j\omega\tau_2)}$$

It can easily be deduced that the two transfer functions have the same magnitude characteristics:

$$|G_1(j\omega)| = |G_2(j\omega)|; \ \omega \geq 0$$

However, the phase characteristics are different for the two cases as illustrated in Fig. 8.43. The transfer function with a zero in the right half s-plane undergoes a net change in phase, when evaluated for frequency inputs between zero and infinity, which is greater than that for the transfer function with the zero in the left half s-plane; magnitude plots of two transfer functions being the same.

Based on the phase shift characteristics, transfer functions are classified as minimum phase and nonminimum phase.

The range of phase shift of a *minimum phase transfer function* is the least possible corresponding to a given magnitude curve, whereas the range of phase shift of *nonminimum phase transfer function* is greater than the minimum possible for the given magnitude curve.

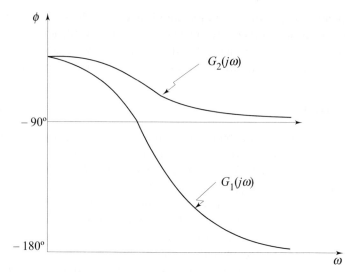

Fig. 8.43   *Phase angle characteristics of minimum phase
and nonminimum phase transfer functions*

It can easily be established that a proper rational transfer function is a minimum phase transfer function if all of its zeros lie in the left half s-plane. It is a nonminimum phase transfer function if it has one or more zeros in the right half s-plane[5].

Using the basic definition, we can easily establish the minimum phase or nonminimum phase character of irrational transfer functions as well. A nonminimum phase irrational transfer function of practical importance is one with $e^{-\tau_D s}$ as its factor, e.g.,

$$G(j\omega) = \frac{(1 + j\omega\tau)\, e^{-j\omega\tau_D}}{(1 + j\omega\tau_1)(1 + j\omega\tau_2)}$$

With these observations, we can go back to the identification problem. If the Bode plot is obtained by frequency response measurements, then, except for a possible pole at $s = 0$, all the poles must lie in the left half s-plane. However, zeros in the right half s-plane and/or presence of dead-time elements cannot be ruled out. Therefore, care must be taken in interpreting the phase angle plot to

---

5   It may be noted that there are two different definitions of minimum phase transfer functions in the literature. One requires both poles and zeros to lie in the left half s-plane; the other requires only zeros. The phrase 'minimum phase' is, however, most often applied to the case where a system is asymptotically stable (poles in the left half s-plane). Our use of the terms 'minimum phase' and 'nonminimum phase' is motivated by this consideration.

detect the presence of right half plane zeros and/or dead-time elements. We illustrate the identification procedure through examples.

Example 8.17───────────────────────────────

Table 8.8 gives experimentally-obtained frequency-response data of a system. From this data, let us determine the approximate transfer function model of the system.

    Bode plots shown in Fig. 8.44 are drawn using the data of Table 8.8. First we approximate the magnitude plot by the three straight dashed lines shown. They intersect at $\omega = 15$ and $\omega = 150$. We begin with the left most part of the magnitude plot. The low frequency asymptote is a horizontal line at 25 dB. It indicates that the transfer function represents a type-0 system with a gain K given by

$$20 \log K = 25 \text{ or } K = 17.8$$

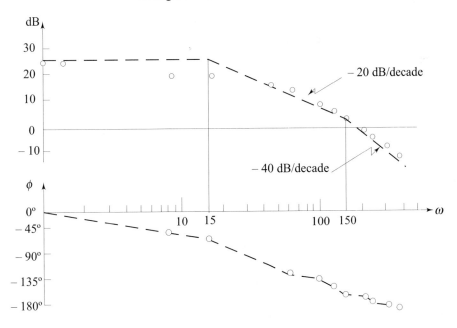

Fig. 8.44 *Experimental data in Bode coordinate system*

    At $\omega = 15$, the slope becomes -20 dB/decade. Thus there is a pole with corner frequency 15. At $\omega = 150$, the slope becomes -40 dB/decade, a decrease of 20 dB/decade. Therefore, there is another pole with corner frequency 150.

    The transfer function must be of the form: $G(s) = \dfrac{17.8}{(1 + s/15)\,(1 + s/150)}$.

Table 8.8   *Experimental frequency response data*

f(Hz)	ω(rad/sec)	Gain(dB)	Phase(deg)
60	377	−7.75	−155
50	314	−4.3	−150
40	251	−0.2	−145
35	219	0.75	−140
25	157	5.16	−135
20	126	7.97	−120
16	100	10.5	−110
10	63	15.0	−100
7	44	16.9	−85
2.5	16	20.4	−45
1.3	8	21.6	−30
0.22	1.38	24.0	−5
0.16	1.0	24.1	0

The phase characteristics calculated from this transfer function are in fair agreement with experimentally obtained characteristics shown in Fig. 8.44. Dead-time element is, therefore, not present.

Example 8.18 _____

Let us find the transfer function of the Bode plot shown in Fig. 8.45. First we approximate the magnitude plot by the three dashed lines shown. They intersect at $\omega = 1$ and $\omega = 10$. In the low-frequency range, there is an asymptote with slope − 20 dB/decade; it indicates the presence of a factor of the form $K/(j\omega)$ in the transfer function. At $\omega = 1$, the magnitude of the asymptote is 40 dB. Therefore

$$20 \log K = 40$$

This gives $$K = 100$$

At $\omega = 1$, the slope becomes − 40 dB/decade, a decrease of 20 dB/decade; thus there is a pole with corner frequency $\omega = 1$. At $\omega = 10$, the slope becomes − 20 dB/decade, an increase of 20 dB/decade; there is a zero with corner frequency $\omega = 10$. The transfer function must be of the form

$$G(s) = \frac{100\left(1 \pm \dfrac{s}{10}\right)}{s\,(1+s)}$$

We have assumed that the Bode plot of Fig. 8.45 is obtained by frequency response measurements; the pole in the right half s-plane is, therefore, not possible. However, a zero in the right half s-plane may exist, i.e., the system under experimental analysis may be a nonminimum-phase system.

Now we use the phase plot to determine the sign of the zero factor. If the sign of zero $(1 \pm 0.1s)$ is positive, the zero will introduce positive phase into

$G(s)$ or, equivalently, the phase of $G(s)$ will increase as ω passes through the corner frequency at 10. This is not the case as seen from Fig. 8.45; thus we have $(1 - 0.1s)$ and the transfer function of the Bode plot is

$$G(s) = \frac{100 \, (1 - 0.1s)}{s \, (1 + s)}$$

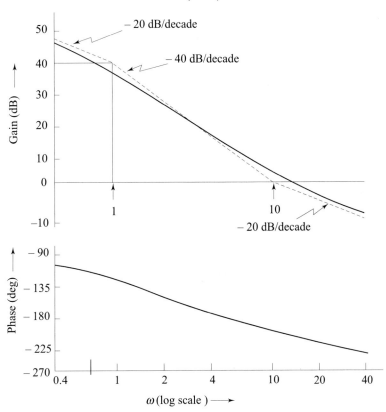

Fig. 8.45   *Experimentally obtained Bode plot*

The phase characteristics calculated from this transfer function are in fair agreement with experimentally obtained characteristics shown in Fig. 8.45.

Review Examples

Review Example 8.1

Consider a feedback system with an open-loop transfer function

$$G(s)H(s) = \frac{1 + 4s}{s^2 (1 + s) (1 + 2s)}$$

which has a double pole at the origin. The indented Nyquist contour shown in Fig. 8.46a does not enclose these poles. The Nyquist plot shown in Fig. 8.46b is obtained as follows.

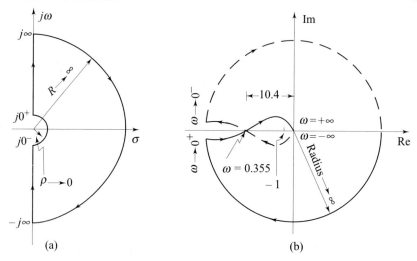

Fig. 8.46 *Nyquist contour and the corresponding mapping[6] for G(s)H(s)*
= (4s + 1)/[s²(s + 1)(2s + 1)]

The portion of the $G(s)H(s)$-locus from $\omega = 0^+$ to $\omega = +\infty$ is simply the polar plot of

$$G(j\omega)H(j\omega) = \frac{1 + j4\omega}{(j\omega)^2 (1 + j\omega)(1 + j2\omega)}$$

The following points were used to construct the polar plot:
  (i) $G(j\omega)H(j\omega)|_{\omega \to 0^+} \to \infty \angle - 180°$
  (ii) The $G(j\omega)H(j\omega)$-locus intersects the real axis at a point where

$$\angle G(j\omega)H(j\omega) = - 180°$$

or $- 180° - \tan^{-1}\omega - \tan^{-1}2\omega + \tan^{-1}4\omega = - 180°$

or $\tan^{-1}4\omega - \tan^{-1}\omega = \tan^{-1}2\omega$

Therefore $\tan(\tan^{-1}4\omega - \tan^{-1}\omega) = \tan(\tan^{-1}2\omega)$

or $\dfrac{4\omega - \omega}{1 + 4\omega^2} = 2\omega$

This gives $\omega = \dfrac{1}{2\sqrt{2}} = 0.355$ rad/sec

6

ω	0.01	0.1	0.35	0.36
$|GH|$	4×10^6	104.09	11.4	10.3
$\angle GH$	$- 179.97$	$- 175.2$	$- 179.35$	179.64

$$\left. |G(j\omega)H(j\omega)| \right|_{\omega = 0.355} = 10.4$$

(iii) $\left. G(j\omega)H(j\omega) \right|_{\omega \to +\infty} \to 0 \angle -270°$

The plot of $G(j\omega)H(j\omega)$ for $\omega < 0$ is the reflection with respect to the real axis, of the plot for $\omega > 0$. Every point on the large semicircle in Fig. 8.46a, is mapped by $G(s)H(s)$ into the origin of the $G(s)H(s)$-plane. A point $s = \rho e^{j\phi}$; $\rho \to 0$, ϕ varying from $-90°$ through $0°$ to $+90°$ is mapped by $G(s)H(s)$ into

$$\left. G(s)H(s) \right|_{s = \rho e^{j\phi}} = \left. \frac{1 + 4s}{s^2(1+s)(1+2s)} \right|_{s = \rho e^{j\phi}} = \frac{1}{\rho^2 e^{j2\phi}} = \frac{1}{\rho^2} \angle -2\phi$$

This gives $\left. G(s)H(s) \right|_{s = \rho e^{-j90°}} = \frac{1}{\rho^2} \angle 180°$; $\left. G(s)H(s) \right|_{s = \rho e^{-j45°}} = \frac{1}{\rho^2} \angle 90°$

$$\left. G(s)H(s) \right|_{s = \rho e^{j0°}} = \frac{1}{\rho^2} \angle 0°; \left. G(s)H(s) \right|_{s = \rho e^{j45°}} = \frac{1}{\rho^2} \angle -90°$$

$$\left. G(s)H(s) \right|_{s = \rho e^{j90°}} = \frac{1}{\rho^2} \angle -180°$$

Figure 8.46b indicates that the critical point $-1 + j0$ is encircled by the Nyquist plot twice in the clockwise direction. Therefore $N = 2$. From the given transfer function it is seen that no pole of $G(s)H(s)$ lies in the right half s-plane, i.e., $P = 0$. Therefore (refer Eqn. (8.8a))

Z = number of zeros of $1 + G(s)H(s)$ enclosed by the Nyquist contour

$= N + P = 2$

Hence the feedback system is unstable with two poles in the right half s-plane.

Review Example 8.2

Consider a feedback control system with open-loop transfer function

$$G(s)H(s) = \frac{K}{(s + 2)(s^2 + 4)}$$

which has a pair of imaginary poles at $s = j2$ and $s = -j2$. The indented Nyquist contour shown in Fig. 8.47a does not enclose these poles. The Nyquist plot shown in Fig. 8.47b is obtained as follows.

$$\left. G(s)H(s) \right|_{s = 0} = \frac{K}{8} \angle 0°$$

$$\left. G(s)H(s) \right|_{\substack{s = j(2-\varepsilon) \\ \varepsilon \to 0}} = \left. \frac{K}{[j(2 - \varepsilon + 2)][-(4 + \varepsilon^2 - 4\varepsilon) + 4]} \right|_{\varepsilon \to 0}$$

$$= \left. \frac{K}{4\varepsilon[2 + j(2 - \varepsilon)]} \right|_{\varepsilon \to 0}$$

$$= \infty \angle -45°$$

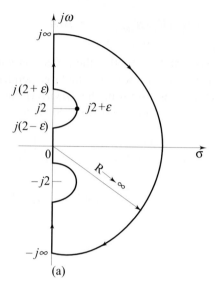

(a)

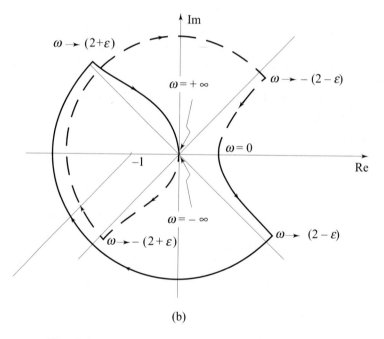

(b)

Fig. 8.47 *Nyquist contour and the corresponding mapping for*
G(s)H(s) = K/[(s + 2)(s² + 4)]

$$G(s)H(s)\bigg|_{\substack{s=j2+\varepsilon \\ \varepsilon \to 0}} = \frac{K}{(j2+\varepsilon+2)\left(-4+\varepsilon^2+j4\varepsilon+4\right)}\bigg|_{\varepsilon \to 0}$$

$$= \frac{K}{8\varepsilon(-1+j1)}\bigg|_{\varepsilon \to 0} = \infty \angle -135°$$

$$G(s)H(s)\Big|_{\substack{s = j(2+\varepsilon) \\ \varepsilon \to 0}} = \frac{K}{[j(2+\varepsilon)+2]\left[-\left(4+\varepsilon^2+4\varepsilon\right)+4\right]}\Bigg|_{\varepsilon \to 0}$$

$$= \frac{K}{4\varepsilon\left[-2-j(2+\varepsilon)\right]}\Bigg|_{\varepsilon \to 0} = \infty \angle 135°$$

The portion of the locus from $\omega = 0$ to $\omega = 2 - \varepsilon$, and from $\omega = 2 + \varepsilon$ to $\omega = +\infty$ is simply the polar plot of

$$G(j\omega)H(j\omega) = \frac{K}{(j\omega+2)(j\omega+j2)(j\omega-j2)}$$

$$= \frac{-2K}{\omega^4-16} + j\frac{K\omega}{\omega^4-16}$$

Every point on the large semicircle in Fig. 8.47a is mapped by $G(s)H(s)$ into the origin of the $G(s)H(s)$-plane.

Figure 8.47b indicates that the critical point $-1+j0$ is encircled by the Nyquist plot twice in the clockwise direction. Therefore $N = 2$. Since $P = 0$, we have (refer Eqn. (8.8a))

$Z =$ number of zeros of $1 + G(s)H(s)$ enclosed by the Nyquist contour

$\quad = N + P = 2$

Hence the feedback system is unstable with two poles in the right half s-plane.

Review Example 8.3_____

The frequency response test data for the forward-path elements of a unity-feedback control system are given in Table 8.9. These data are sufficient to analyse feedback system stability, as is seen below.

Figure 8.48 shows the frequency response data of Table 8.9 on Bode plots. From these plots we find that

phase crossover frequency $\omega_\phi = 48$ rad/sec,
gain crossover frequency $\omega_g = 3$ rad/sec,
gain margin $GM = 28$ dB, and
phase margin $\varPhi M = 49°$.

Table 8.9   *Experimental frequency response data*

ω(rad/sec)	0.5	1	2	4	10	20	30
Gain (dB)	19.75	13	5	-4	-17	-24	-26
Phase (deg)	-101	-111	-125	-134	-130	-127	-134
ω(rad/sec)	40	50	60	70	80	90	100
Gain (dB)	-27	-29	-34	-39	-43	-47	-50
Phase (deg)	-154	-189	-218	-235	-243	-249	-252

The feedback system is therefore stable.

It may be desirable to obtain a transfer function that approximates the experimental amplitude and phase characteristics. A series of straight-line asymptotes fitted to the experimentally obtained magnitude curve are shown in Fig. 8.48. The low frequency asymptote has a slope of -20 dB/decade and when extended, intersects the 0-dB axis at $\omega = 5$. Therefore, the asymptote is a plot of the factor $5/(j\omega)$. The corner frequencies are found to be located at $\omega = 2$, $\omega = 10$ and $\omega = 50$. At the first corner frequency, the slope of the curve changes by -20 dB/decade and at the second corner frequency, it changes by $+20$ dB/decade. Therefore, the transfer function has factors $1/(1 + j\omega/2)$ and $(1 + j\omega/10)$ corresponding to these corner frequencies. At $\omega = 50$, the curve changes by a slope of -40 dB/decade. At this frequency, the error between actual and approximate plots is $+4.5$ dB. The change of slope by -40 dB/decade indicates the presence of either double pole on real axis or a pair of complex conjugate poles. The error of $+4.5$ dB at the corner frequency and the peak occurring at a frequency less than the corner frequency indicate the presence of a quadratic factor with $\zeta < 0.5$. In fact, we can calculate the approximate value of ζ using expression (8.42):

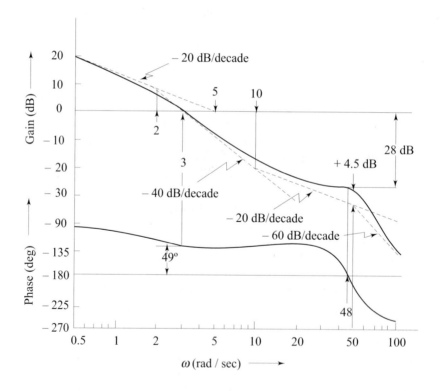

Fig. 8.48 *Experimentally obtained magnitude and phase characteristics*

$$-20 \log 2\zeta = 4.5$$

This gives $$\zeta = 0.3$$

Therefore, the transfer function has a quadratic factor

$$\frac{1}{1 + j2\zeta\,(\omega/50) + (j\omega/50)^2} \quad \text{where } \zeta = 0.3$$

Thus an approximate transfer function of the forward-path elements of the feedback system becomes

$$G(j\omega) = \frac{5\,(1 \pm j\omega/10)}{j\omega\,(1 + j\omega/2)\left[1 + j0.6\,(\omega/50) + (j\omega/50)^2\right]}$$

Now we use the phase plot to determine the sign of the zero factor. The phase characteristics calculated from the transfer function are in fair agreement with experimentally obtained characteristics shown in Fig. 8.48, when the sign of the zero factor is positive. Therefore, the transfer function of the Bode plot of Fig. 8.48 is

$$G(s) = \frac{5\,(1 + s/10)}{s\,(1 + s/2)\left[1 + 0.6s/50 + (s/50)^2\right]}$$

Review Questions

8.1 (a) Using principle of argument, derive the Nyquist stability criterion.
   (b) What is the interpretation of stability analysis when Nyquist plot crosses the $-1+j0$ point? (Help: p526)
   (c) Give an example of a physical system whose transfer function model has a pole in right-half s-plane. (Help: Fig. P2.8, Fig. 12.14a)

8.2 (a) Give an account of meaning of the terms 'gain margin' and 'phase margin', with reference to Nyquist plots.
   (b) How can a frequency response be represented by a Bode plot? Indicate what gain and phase margins are in this context.
   (c) Why do we use logarithmic scale for frequency in Bode plots? (Help: p545)

8.3 Explain the significance of dead-time transfer function $e^{-s\tau_D}$ in a closed-loop, and its effect on system stability. (Help: Section 2.13, Review Example 5.3 Section 8.7)

8.4 (a) Give the properties of minimum-phase and nonminimum-phase transfer functions.
   Describe a method of identification of transfer function model of a system using frequency-response measurements. (Help: p573)
   (b) Give an example of a physical system whose transfer function model is of nonminimum-phase type. (Help: Review Examples 3.1 and 3.5)

8.5 (a) A system has infinite *GM*. Does it imply that the relative stability of the system is high? (Help: p541)

(b) *GM* and *ΦM* are valid measures of relative stability of a closed-loop system only if open-loop transfer function $G(s)H(s)$ has no poles in right-half plane. How do you ascertain relative stability when open-loop transfer function has poles in right-half plane? (Help: pp 541-542, pp 623-625)

(c) Compared to Nyquist plots, Bode plots are easier to work with for interpreting relative stability of a closed-loop system. Can you cite some situations wherein Bode plots fail to provide relative stability analysis, while Nyquist plot does?

8.6 (a) Give examples of Nyquist plots with
  (i) poor *ΦM*, infinite *GM*
  (ii) poor *GM*, infinite *ΦM*
  (iii) undefined phase crossover frequency
  (iv) undefined gain crossover frequency (Help: Figs 8.19-8.20)

(b) *GM* and *ΦM* definitions assume that increasing gain leads to instability. Give an example of Nyquist plot wherein this condition is not satisfied. (Help: Fig. 8.21c)

(c) *GM* and *ΦM* definitions assume that the Nyquist plot crosses the negative real axis atmost once and also crosses the unit circle atmost once. Give examples of Nyquist plots wherein these conditions are not satisfied. (Help: Figs 8.21a-8.21b)

8.7 Given an asymptotic Bode plot, can you identify the transfer function model? If your answer is YES, review your answer with respect to the following points:
  (i) The transfer function may have zeros in the right-half plane.
  (ii) The transfer function may include dead-time elements.
  Do you require phase plot to identify these features? (Help: pp573-575), Example 8.18)

Problems

8.1 Sketch the general shapes of the polar plots for

(a) $G(j\omega) = \dfrac{1}{(1 + j\omega\tau_1)(1 + j\omega\tau_2)}$

(b) $G(j\omega) = \dfrac{1}{j\omega(1 + j\omega\tau)}$

(c) $G(j\omega) = \dfrac{1}{(j\omega)^2(1 + j\omega\tau)}$

(d) $G(j\omega) = \dfrac{1}{j\omega(1 + j\omega\tau_1)(1 + j\omega\tau_2)}$

(e) $G(j\omega) = \dfrac{1}{(j\omega)^2(1 + j\omega\tau_1)(1 + j\omega\tau_2)}$

based on magnitude and phase calculations at (i) $\omega = 0$, (ii) $\omega = \infty$, (iii) the point of intersection (if any) with the real axis, and (iv) the point of intersection (if any) with the imaginary axis.

8.2 Check the stability of unity-feedback systems whose Nyquist plots are shown in Fig. P8.2. $G(s)$ represents open-loop transfer function.

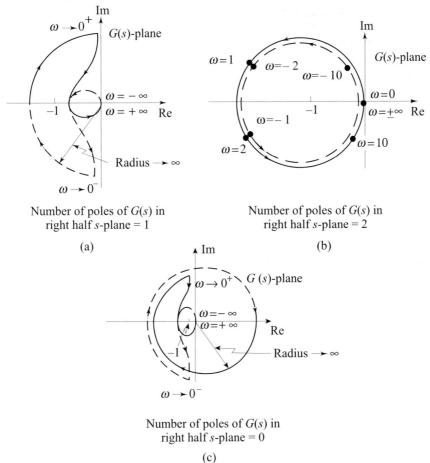

Number of poles of $G(s)$ in
right half s-plane = 1

(a)

Number of poles of $G(s)$ in
right half s-plane = 2

(b)

Number of poles of $G(s)$ in
right half s-plane = 0

(c)

Fig. P8.2

8.3 Consider the unity-feedback system shown in Fig. P8.3a. The polar plot of $G(s)$ is of the form shown in Fig. P8.3b. Assuming that the Nyquist contour in s-plane encloses the entire right half s-plane, draw a complete Nyquist plot in the $G(s)$-plane. Then answer the following questions.

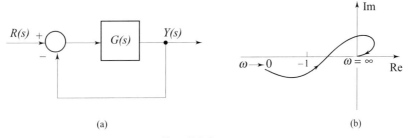

(a)

(b)

Fig. P8.3

(i) If $G(s)$ has no poles and no zeros in the right half s-plane, is the closed-loop system stable?

(ii) If $G(s)$ has one pole and no zeros in the right half s-plane, is the closed-loop system stable?

(iii) If $G(s)$ has one zero and no poles in the right half s-plane, is the closed-loop system stable?

8.4 By use of the Nyquist criterion, determine whether the closed-loop systems having the following open-loop transfer functions are stable or not. If not, how many closed-loop poles lie in the right half s-plane?

(a) $G(s)H(s) = \dfrac{180}{(s+1)\,(s+2)\,(s+5)}$

(b) $G(s)H(s) = \dfrac{2}{s\,(s+1)\,(2s+1)}$

(c) $G(s)H(s) = \dfrac{s+2}{(s+1)\,(s-1)}$

(d) $G(s)H(s) = \dfrac{8s}{(s-1)\,(s-2)}$

(e) $G(s)H(s) = \dfrac{s+2}{s^2}$

(f) $G(s)H(s) = \dfrac{1}{s^2+100}$

(g) $G(s)H(s) = \dfrac{2\,(s+3)}{s\,(s-1)}$

8.5 The stability of a closed-loop system with open-loop transfer function

$$G(s)H(s) = \frac{K(\tau_2 s + 1)}{s^2(\tau_1 s + 1)}\,;\, K,\, \tau_1,\, \tau_2 > 0$$

depends on the relative magnitudes of τ_1 and τ_2. Draw Nyquist plots and therefrom determine stability of the system when (i) $\tau_1 < \tau_2$, and (ii) $\tau_1 > \tau_2$.

8.6 Use the Nyquist criterion to determine the range of values of $K > 0$ for the stability of the system in Fig. P8.6 with

(a) $G(s) = \dfrac{8}{(s+1)\left(s^2 + 2s + 2\right)}$

(b) $G(s) = \dfrac{4\,(1+s)}{s^2(1+0.1s)}$

(c) $G(s) = \dfrac{4\,(1+0.1s)}{s^2(1+s)}$

(d) $G(s) = \dfrac{e^{-0.8s}}{s+1}$

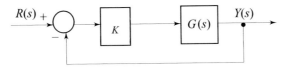

Fig. P8.6

8.7 Sketch the Nyquist plot for a feedback system with open-loop transfer function

$$G(s)H(s) = \frac{K\,(s+3)\,(s+5)}{(s-2)\,(s-4)}\,;\, K>0$$

Find the range of values of K for which the system is stable.

8.8 Sketch the Nyquist plot for a feedback system with open-loop transfer function

$$G(s)H(s) = \frac{K\,(1+0.5s)\,(s+1)}{(1+10s)\,(s-1)}\,;\, K>0$$

Find the range of values of K for which the system is stable.

8.9 Consider the control system shown in Fig. P8.9. Using the Nyquist criterion, determine the range of gain $K>0$ for stability of the system.

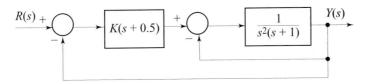

Fig. P8.9

8.10 Consider the feedback systems shown in Figs P8.10a and P8.10b. Sketch the Nyquist plot in each case and therefrom determine the maximum value of K for stability.

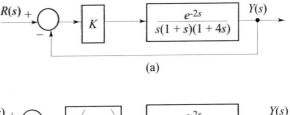

(a)

(b)

Fig. P8.10

8.11 A unity-feedback system has open-loop transfer function

$$G(s) = \frac{e^{-s\tau_D}}{s\,(s+1)}$$

Draw the Nyquist plot of $G_1(j\omega) = \dfrac{1}{j\omega\,(j\omega+1)}$, together with the critical trajectory of $e^{-j\omega\tau_D}$. Using these curves, obtain the maximum value of dead-time τ_D in seconds for the closed-loop system to be stable.

8.12 Using the Nyquist plot, determine gain crossover frequency, phase crossover frequency, gain margin, and phase margin of feedback system with open-loop transfer function

$$G(s)H(s) = \frac{10}{s\,(1+0.2s)\,(1+0.02s)}$$

8.13 Sketch the Nyquist plot for a feedback system with open-loop transfer function

$$G(s)H(s) = \frac{K\,(s+10)^2}{s^3}\,;\, K > 0$$

(a) Show that the feedback system is stable for $K > 5$.

(b) Determine the gain margin and phase margin when $K = 7$.

8.14 Sketch the Bode asymptotic plots showing the magnitude in dB as a function of log frequency for the transfer functions given below. Determine the gain crossover frequency in each case.

(a) $G(s) = \dfrac{25}{(s+1)\,(0.1s+1)\,(0.05s+1)}$

(b) $G(s) = \dfrac{50\,(0.2s+1)}{s\,(s+1)\,(0.02s+1)}$

(c) $G(s) = \dfrac{500\,(0.2s+1)\,(0.1s+1)}{s^2\,(s+1)\,(0.02s+1)}$

(d) $G(s) = \dfrac{50\,(0.05s+1)}{s\,(0.1s+1)\,(0.02s+1)\left((s/200)^2 + (0.02s/200)+1\right)}$

8.15 Using Bode plots, determine gain crossover frequency, phase crossover frequency, gain margin, and phase margin of a feedback system with open-loop transfer function

(a) $G(s) = \dfrac{10}{s\,(0.1s+1)}$

(b) $G(s) = \dfrac{10}{s\,(0.1s+1)^2}$

(c) $G(s) = \dfrac{20\,(0.2s+1)}{s\,(0.5s+1)}$

(d) $G(s) = \dfrac{20\,(0.2s+1)\,e^{-0.1s}}{s\,(0.5s+1)}$

(e) $G(s) = \dfrac{40}{(s+2)\,(s+4)\,(s+5)}$

(f) $G(s) = \dfrac{10}{s^2(0.2s+1)}$

8.16 Use Bode plots to determine the stability of the system shown in Fig. P8.16 for the two cases: (i) $K = 10$, and (ii) $K = 100$.

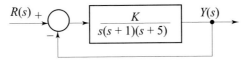

Fig. P8.16

8.17 Use Bode plots to determine the range of K within which a unity-feedback system with open-loop transfer function $G(s)$ is stable. Given:

(a) $G(s) = \dfrac{K}{(s+2)\,(s+4)\,(s+5)}$

(b) $G(s) = \dfrac{K}{s\,(1+0.2s)\,(1+0.02s)}$

(c) $G(s) = \dfrac{Ke^{-s}}{s\,(s+1)\,(s+2)}$

8.18 Open-loop transfer function of a closed-loop system is

$$G(s)H(s) = \dfrac{10e^{-s\tau_D}}{s\,(0.1s+1)\,(0.05s+1)}$$

(a) Find the gain margin and phase margin when $\tau_D = 0$.

(b) Find the gain margin and phase margin when $\tau_D = 0.04$ sec. Comment upon the effect of dead-time.

(c) Determine the maximum value of τ_D for the closed-loop system to be stable.

8.19 The experimental frequency response data of certain systems presented on Bode plots and asymptotically approximated are shown in Fig. P8.19. Find the transfer function in each case (systems are known to have minimum-phase characteristics).

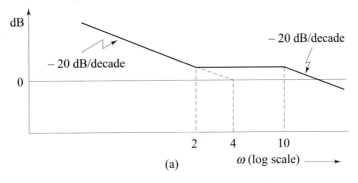

(a)

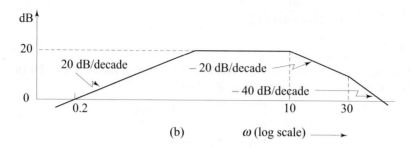

(b)

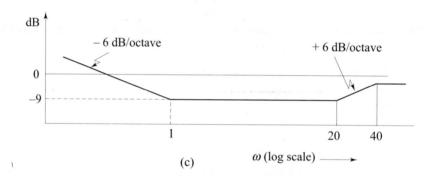

(c)

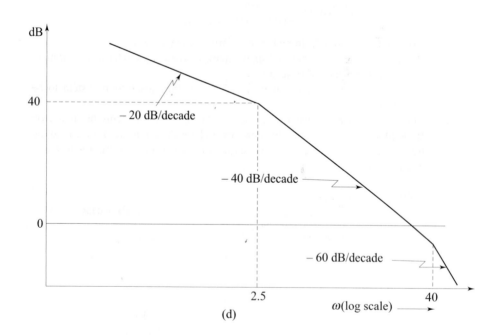

(d)

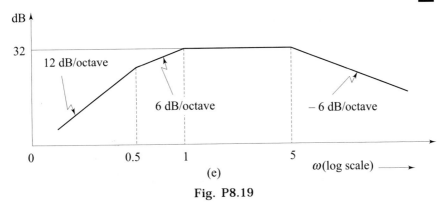

Fig. P8.19

8.20 Consider a minimum-phase system whose asymptotic amplitude frequency response is depicted in Fig. P8.20.

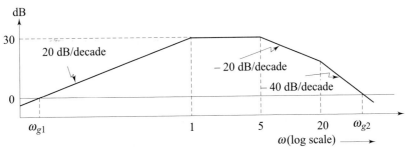

Fig. P8.20

(a) Determine the transfer function $G(s)$ of the system.

(b) Determine the two gain crossover frequencies ω_{g1} and ω_{g2}.

8.21 The asymptotic amplitude frequency response of the open path of a feedback system is shown in Fig. P8.21. Determine the gain margin of the system. The system is known to have minimum-phase characteristics.

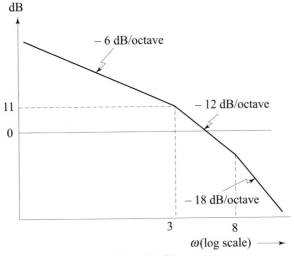

Fig. P8.21

8.22 The following frequency response test data were obtained for a system known to have minimum-phase characteristics. Plot the data on semilog graph paper and determine the transfer function of the system using asymptotic approximation.

Gain (dB)	34	28	24.6	14.2	8	1.5	− 3.5	− 7.2
Frequency (rad/sec)	0.1	0.2	0.3	0.7	1.0	1.5	2.0	2.5
Gain (dB) − 12.5	− 14.7	− 16.0	− 17.5	− 17.5	− 17.5			
Frequency (rad/sec) 4.0	5.0	6.0	9.0	20	35			

8.23 Determine an approximate transfer function model of a system for which experimental frequency response data is given in the following table.

ω	dB	Phase
0.1	− 20	0
0.5	− 21	0
1.0	− 21	− 9°
2.0	− 22	− 54°
3.0	− 24	− 90°
5.0	− 28	− 135°
10.0	− 40	− 170°
30.0	− 60	− 178°
100.0	− 84	− 180°

chapter 9

Feedback System Performance Based on the Frequency Response

9.1 INTRODUCTION

For the single-loop control system configuration shown in Fig. 9.1, the closed-loop transfer function is

$$\frac{Y(s)}{R(s)} = M(s) = \frac{G(s)}{1 + G(s)\,H(s)} \qquad (9.1a)$$

For a stable closed-loop system, the function

$$M(j\omega) = \frac{Y(j\omega)}{R(j\omega)} = \frac{G(j\omega)}{1 + G(j\omega)\,H(j\omega)} \qquad (9.1b)$$

completely characterizes the steady-state behaviour of the system to sinusoidal inputs. The variation of the magnitude $|M(j\omega)|$ and the phase angle $\angle M(j\omega)$ with frequency ω, is the frequency response of the closed-loop system.

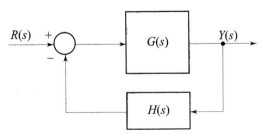

Fig. 9.1 *A single-loop control system configuration*

The concept of frequency response is especially relevant to those systems that exhibit frequency-selective characteristics, meaning that they selectively pass or reject a band of frequencies. A *lowpass filter*, for example, is a frequency-selective system which passes without appreciable change only 'low' frequencies, while severely diminishing the output amplitude at 'high' frequencies. Similarly, one can speak of *highpass* and *bandpass filters*.

Ideally, a filter should totally reject all frequencies outside its passband, and therefore an ideal filter would have a clearly defined *bandwidth*. But, sad to say, such filters are physically unrealizable, although they may be closely approximated. Real filters have more or less a gradual transition between passband and rejection, and defining the bandwidth of a real filter becomes somewhat arbitrary. A commonly used convention is to take the bandwidth as that range of positive frequencies over which the amplitude ratio drops not lower than $1/\sqrt{2}$ = 0.707 times the maximum value in the passband. Figure 9.2a shows the gain and phase characteristics of the ideal lowpass filter that has a sharp cut-off at ω_{BW}; therefore ω_{BW} defines the bandwidth of the ideal filter. Figure 9.2b shows the characteristics of a real lowpass filter:

$$|M(j\omega)|_{\max} = |M(j0)| = 1 \qquad (9.2a)$$
$$|M(j\omega_b)| = 0.707 \qquad (9.2b)$$

ω_b defines the bandwidth of the real filter.

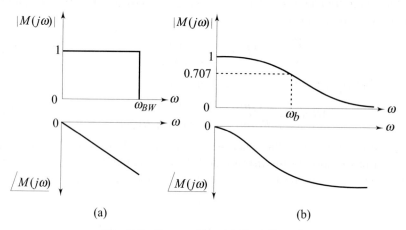

Fig. 9.2 *Lowpass filter (a) ideal (b) real*

In many ways, the design of feedback control systems is quite similar to filter design, and the control system is regarded as a signal processor. In fact, if the gain and phase characteristics shown in Fig. 9.2a were physically realizable, they would be ideal as the frequency response of a feedback control system. The output of such a system would follow all inputs with frequencies up to ω_{BW} without any error.

We know that a rapidly changing input has a large high frequency content, while a smooth slowly varying input has a relatively small high frequency content. Thus, if the control system is to faithfully follow a command that is changing rapidly, it must be capable of reproducing inputs at high frequencies, i.e., it must have a large bandwidth. On the other hand, if the command is slowly varying, the control system does not need a high bandwidth. A step change (i.e., a discontinuity) in the input has a large amount of high frequency content; to reproduce it faithfully (with a short rise time) requires a high bandwidth. If a short rise time is not required, then neither is a high bandwidth. Furthermore, all control systems are subject to noise during operation. Therefore, in addition to responding to the input signal, the system should be able to suppress noise and unwanted signals. The phase characteristics of the frequency response of a control system is also of importance, as it plays an important role in the stability of closed-loop systems. Shaping the frequency-response characteristics is the objective of the frequency-domain design methods.

When one has the frequency-response curves (obtained experimentally, or analytically using Eqn. (9.1b)) for any stable system, evaluation of the steady-state response to a sinusoidal input is straightforward. What is not obvious, but is extremely important, is that the frequency-response curves are really a *complete* description of the system's dynamic behaviour and allow one to compute the response to *any* input, not just sine waves.

The behaviour in the frequency domain of a given driving function $r(t)$ can be determined by the Fourier transform (refer Eqn. (A.26a) in Appendix A) as

$$R(j\omega) = \int_{-\infty}^{\infty} r(t)e^{-j\omega t}dt \qquad (9.3a)$$

For a given control system, the frequency response of the controlled variable is

$$Y(j\omega) = \frac{G(j\omega)}{1 + G(j\omega) H(j\omega)} R(j\omega) = M(j\omega)R(j\omega) \qquad (9.3b)$$

Inverse Fourier transformation (refer Eqn. (A.26b) in Appendix A) of $Y(j\omega)$ then gives the response

$$y(t) = \frac{1}{2\pi} \int_{-\infty}^{\infty} Y(j\omega)e^{j\omega t}d\omega \qquad (9.3c)$$

Therefore, if we know the frequency response of a stable linear system, we can compute the dynamic response to any form of input. It should thus not be surprising that the control system performance can be (and is) described in frequency-response terms.

The correlation between transient response and frequency response through the Fourier integral forms an important basis of most design procedures and criteria. Usually the desired time-domain behaviour is interpreted in terms of frequency-response characteristics, the design is carried out in frequency domain, and the frequency response is then translated back into the time domain.

In Chapter 6, the transient performance of a control system was discussed by the examination of the standard second-order feedback system shown in Fig. 9.3. This is based on the fact that the performance of many control systems is dominated by a complex-conjugate pair of poles. Fortunately, direct and simple correlations exist between the transient-response measures of performance and frequency-response measures of performance, for the standard second-order system (the general correlation between transient response and frequency response through the Fourier integral is highly laborious to compute). The design based on these correlations proceeds very fast, though it is not exact. Sound engineering skill and judgement are necessary to estimate the accuracy of such a procedure. It is in fact essential to check the exact response after the design is completed.

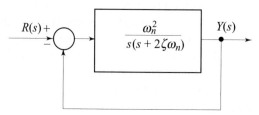

Fig. 9.3 *Standard second-order feedback system*

This chapter develops correlating relations between the frequency-domain and time-domain performance specifications, leading to design methods using the wealth of graphical information available in frequency domain. Methods for setting the gain in order to achieve a specified closed-loop frequency response are also described.

The procedure for gain adjustment may not yield a satisfactory closed-loop frequency response. In such a case, the dynamic compensation of the system is necessary. Compensation procedures are covered in the next chapter.

9.2 PERFORMANCE SPECIFICATIONS IN FREQUENCY DOMAIN

In the design of linear control systems using frequency-domain methods, it is necessary to define a set of specifications so that the quality of the system can be properly described using frequency-response characteristics. Consider the feedback system shown in Fig. 9.4. A typical plot of $M(j\omega) = Y(j\omega)/R(j\omega)$, the closed-loop frequency response, is shown in Fig. 9.5. The magnitude and phase angle approximate the ideal $1.0 \angle 0°$ for some range of 'low' frequencies but deviate for higher frequencies.

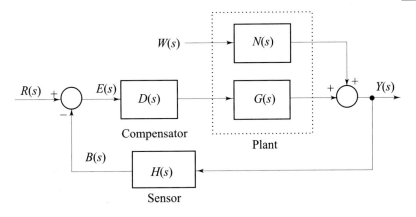

Fig. 9.4 *A feedback system*

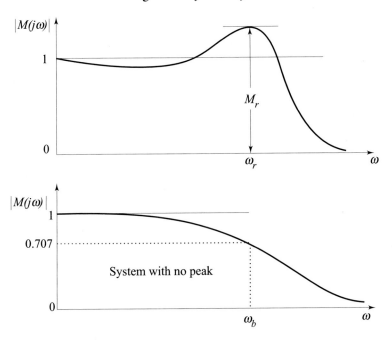

Fig. 9.5 *Closed-loop frequency response criteria*

We know that $|M(j\omega)|$ *versus* ω curve will have a pronounced peak if $M(s)$ = $Y(s)/R(s)$ has complex poles with very small damping ratio. In fact, the smaller the value of damping ratio, higher the peak. The peak occurs at a frequency slightly less than the natural frequency of the complex poles (refer Figs 8.30 and 8.31). The maximum value M_r of $|M(j\omega)|$ is termed the *resonance peak*, and the frequency ω_r at which it occurs is the *resonance frequency* (refer Fig. 9.5).

Resonance peak M_r is a very good measure of relative stability of a closed-loop system; a large M_r corresponds to a large overshoot in transient response. Many systems are designed to exhibit resonance peak in the range 1.2 to 1.4.

The resonance frequency ω_r is a measure of speed of response; the higher ω_r, the faster the system. For systems that exhibit no peak (refer Fig. 9.5) which is sometimes the case, the *bandwidth* ω_b is used for the speed of response specification. It can, of course, be specified even if there is a peak.

Alternative measures of relative stability and speed of response are stability margins and crossover frequencies. We have seen in Chapter 8 that *both* a good *gain margin* and a good *phase margin* are needed for robust stability; neither is sufficient by itself. General numerical design goals for gain margin and phase margin cannot be given since systems that satisfy other specific performance criteria may exhibit a wide range of gain and phase margins. It is possible, however, to give useful lower bounds; gain margin should usually exceed 2.5 (20 log 2.5 dB) and phase margin should exceed 30°.

Of particular importance for the speed of response analysis is the *gain crossover frequency* ω_g. Raising the gain crossover frequency increases the speed of response.

With respect to disturbances, if we set $R \equiv 0$ and let W be a sine wave (refer Fig. 9.4), we can measure or calculate $Y(j\omega)/W(j\omega)$ which should of course ideally be zero for all frequencies. A real system cannot achieve this perfection but will behave typically as in Fig. 9.6. For low frequencies, the feedback action is effective in keeping Y near the ideal value of zero. Just beyond this range, control becomes ineffective but the process is still capable of responding to W, giving the response shown. For still higher frequencies, the process itself is too slow to react to W, and response approaches zero again.

Fig. 9.6 *Closed-loop frequency response to disturbance input*

9.3 CORRELATION BETWEEN FREQUENCY-DOMAIN AND TIME-DOMAIN SPECIFICATIONS

In Chapter 6, the transient performance of a control system was discussed by the examination of the standard second-order system of Fig. 9.3, with open-loop transfer function

$$G(s) = \frac{\omega_n^2}{s \, (s + 2\zeta\omega_n)} \tag{9.4}$$

and closed-loop transfer function

$$\frac{Y(s)}{R(s)} = M(s) = \frac{\omega_n^2}{s^2 + 2\zeta\omega_n s + \omega_n^2} \tag{9.5}$$

This was based on the fact that the performance of many systems is dominated by a complex-conjugate pole pair. It is appropriate, therefore, to discuss the frequency response of this standard second-order system.

For the standard second-order system of Fig. 9.3, direct and simple correlations exist between frequency-domain specifications described in Section 9.2, and time-domain specifications described in Section 6.2. We will study these correlations in this section.

Damping Ratio and Phase Margin

In order to evaluate the phase margin, we first find the frequency for which

$$|G(j\omega)| = \frac{\omega_n^2}{\left| - \omega^2 + j2\zeta\omega_n\omega \right|} = 1 \tag{9.6}$$

The frequency, ω_g, that satisfies Eqn. (9.6) is given by

$$\omega_n^2 = \omega_g \sqrt{\omega_g^2 + (2\zeta\omega_n)^2}$$

or

$$\omega_g^4 + 4\zeta^2\omega_n^2\omega_g^2 - \omega_n^4 = 0$$

The roots of this equation follow by applying the quadratic formula in terms of ω_g^2:

$$\omega_g^2 = \omega_n^2 \left(- 2\zeta^2 \pm \sqrt{4\zeta^4 + 1} \right)$$

Fog ω_g to be real-valued, the positive root must be used so that

$$\omega_g = \omega_n \sqrt{\sqrt{4\zeta^4 + 1} - 2\zeta^2} \tag{9.7}$$

The phase angle of $G(j\omega)$ at this frequency is

$$\angle G(j\omega_g) = - 90° - \tan^{-1} \frac{\omega_g}{2\zeta\omega_n}$$

$$= - 90° - \tan^{-1} \frac{\sqrt{\sqrt{4\zeta^4 + 1} - 2\zeta^2}}{2\zeta} \tag{9.8}$$

The difference between the angle of Eqn. (9.8) and $- 180°$ is the phase margin ΦM. Thus

$$\Phi M = 90° - \tan^{-1} \frac{\sqrt{\sqrt{4\zeta^4 + 1} - 2\zeta^2}}{2\zeta}$$

$$= \tan^{-1} \frac{2\zeta}{\sqrt{\sqrt{4\zeta^4 + 1} - 2\zeta^2}} \tag{9.9}$$

Figure 9.7 shows phase margin, ΦM, in degrees *versus* damping ratio ζ. The dashed line in the figure shows a straight line approximation to the function

where
$$\zeta = \frac{\Phi M}{100} \tag{9.10}$$

It is clear that the approximation only holds for phase margin below about 70°.

For the standard second-order system under consideration, we cannot define gain margin because $|G(j\omega)| \to 0$ as $\angle G(j\omega) \to -180°$.

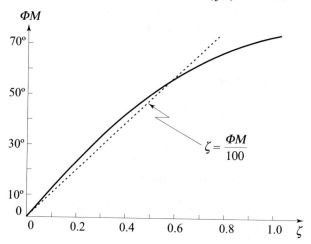

Fig. 9.7 *Phase margin versus damping ratio*

Response Speed and Gain Crossover Frequency

Equation (9.7), reproduced below, relates the gain crossover frequency to the undamped natural frequency ω_n and damping ratio ζ.

$$\omega_g = \omega_n \sqrt{\sqrt{4\zeta^4 + 1} - 2\zeta^2} \tag{9.11}$$

Figure 9.8 shows a plot of ω_g/ω_n versus ζ.

We know that when a root-locus design holds the damping ratio constant, both the rise time and the settling time decrease as the undamped natural frequency increases. Therefore, when a frequency-domain design holds the phase margin constant while increasing the gain crossover frequency, the resulting rise time and settling time would diminish in the time domain.

It should be remembered that the use of the second-order system of Fig. 9.3 as a standard for reference is based on the assumption of dominance. We are assuming that the contributions of all additional poles and zeros may be neglected. There will certainly be cases where this assumption is not valid. It is

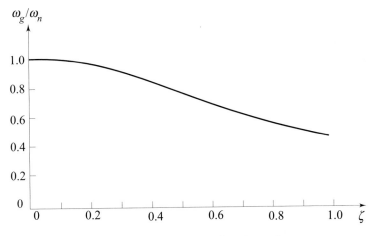

Fig. 9.8 ω_g/ω_n *versus damping ratio*

not practical to develop correlations for exceptions; so the transient response should be determined, usually by simulation, as a check.

Example 9.1 ⎯⎯⎯⎯⎯⎯⎯⎯⎯⎯⎯⎯⎯⎯⎯⎯⎯⎯⎯⎯⎯⎯

The transient behaviour of the system of Fig. 9.9 can be estimated from Bode plots of $G(j\omega)$, as is seen below.

$$G(j\omega) = \frac{0.5e^{-j\omega}}{j\omega(1 + j\omega)(1 + 0.1j\omega)}$$

Bode plots for this transfer function are shown in Fig. 9.10. Note that the magnitude plot is not affected by the dead-time; however, the phase plot is affected. The dead-time yields a decreased phase margin since at any frequency, the phase angle is more negative. Using a second-order approximation, this decrease in phase margin implies a lower damping ratio and a more oscillatory response for the closed-loop system.

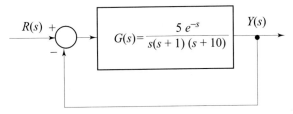

Fig. 9.9 *A feedback system*

The magnitude curve of Fig. 9.10 crosses the 0-dB axis at a frequency of 0.47 rad/sec; the corresponding phase angle is $-145°$. Therefore the gain crossover frequency $\omega_g = 0.47$ rad/sec, and the phase margin $\varPhi M = -145° - (-180°) = 35°$.

The values of ζ and ω_n to be used for approximating the transient behaviour of the system of Fig. 9.9 can be determined from Eqns (9.9)–(9.11) or Figs 9.7–9.8. The values obtained from these second-order approximations are

$$\zeta = 0.33; \quad \omega_n = 0.52 \text{ rad/sec}$$

An estimate of the transient behaviour of the system of Fig. 9.9 to step input is therefore obtained as:

$$M_p = \text{peak overshoot} = 100e^{-\pi\zeta/\sqrt{1-\zeta^2}} = 33\%$$
$$t_s = \text{settling time} = 4/\zeta\omega_n = 23.3 \text{ sec}$$

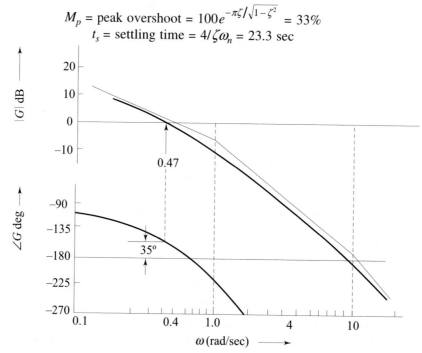

Fig. 9.10 *Bode plot for G(s) of Fig. 9.9*

Computer simulation (Fig. 9.11) shows $M_p \cong 38\%$ and $t_s \cong 24$ sec.

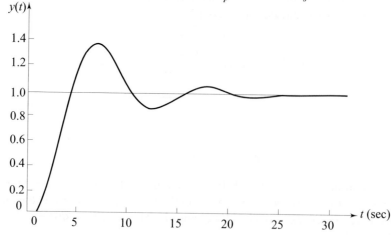

Fig. 9.11 *Step response for system of Fig. 9.9*

Gain Adjustments

From the correlation between damping ratio (equivalently, peak overshoot in step response) and phase margin developed for standard second-order systems, we observe that if we can vary the phase margin, we can vary the peak overshoot in the step response of the system. Looking at Fig. 9.12, we see that if we desire a phase margin represented by *CD*, we would have to lower the magnitude curve by *AB*. Thus, a simple gain adjustment can be used to design phase margin and hence percentage overshoot in step response. Such a design is acceptable if both the resulting gain crossover frequency (equivalently, speed of response) and gain margin are acceptable. Dynamic compensation (discussed in Chapter 10) will become necessary in cases wherein the design for specified phase margin by gain adjustment results in poor gain crossover frequency and/or gain margin.

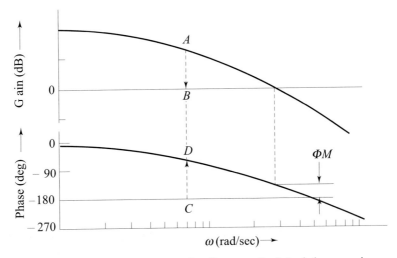

Fig. 9.12 *Bode plot showing gain adjustment for desired phase margin*

Gain adjustments can also be used to design gain margin. The resulting phase margin and gain crossover frequency are then examined to see whether the design is acceptable. Similarly, we could adjust the gain for specified gain crossover frequency and then examine the resulting gain margin and phase margin.

Example 9.2

Consider a unity-feedback system with open-loop transfer function

$$G(s) = \frac{K}{s\,(1 + 0.1s)\,(1 + 0.05s)}$$

Figure 9.13 shows the Bode plots of $G(j\omega)$ with open-loop gain $K = 10$. From this figure, it is found that gain margin $GM = 10$ dB, phase margin

$\Phi M = 33°$, and gain crossover frequency $\omega_g = 7.4$ rad/sec. The steady-state error for unit-ramp input for this type-1 system is $e_{ss} = 1/K = 1/10$.

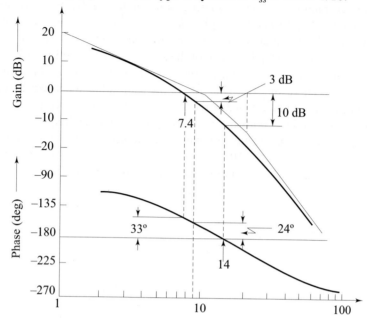

Fig. 9.13   *Bode plot of $G(j\omega) = 10/j\omega(j0.1\omega + 1)\,(j0.05\,\omega + 1)$*

Let us examine the effects of gain adjustments.

(i) Suppose that to reduce the steady-state error, a phase margin of 24° will be accepted. To obtain phase margin of 24°, we must first determine the frequency at which the phase angle of $G(j\omega)$ is $-156°$, and then adjust the value of K so that the gain at this frequency is 0 dB. From the Bode plots of Fig. 9.13, we find that for $\omega = 9$ rad/sec, we get this phase angle and a gain of -3 dB. Therefore, if the gain crossover frequency is changed to 9 rad/sec, a phase margin of 24° will be obtained. To change the gain crossover frequency to 9 rad/sec, the magnitude curve should be raised by 3 dB, i.e., the gain 10 must be raised by a factor of α given by 20 log $\alpha = 3$. Hence $\alpha = 1.4$ and the new gain is $K = 10 \times 1.4 = 14$.

From Fig. 9.13, we observe that increasing K reduces the phase margin and gain margin, and increases the gain crossover frequency. The system thus becomes relatively less stable (peak overshoot in transient response increases). The increase in gain crossover frequency will generally result in better speed of response (reduced rise time/settling time).

(ii) Suppose it is desired to find the open-loop gain for a gain margin of 20 dB. To determine the gain margin of 20 dB, first we determine the phase crossover frequency and the gain at this frequency. From the Bode plots of Fig. 9.13 we find that phase crossover frequency $\omega_\phi = 14$ rad/sec and the gain at ω_ϕ is -10 dB. Hence for the desired gain margin, we must decrease the gain by 10 dB. It means that magnitude curve must be lowered by 10 dB, i.e., the gain K must be reduced by a factor of β, given by $20 \log(1/\beta) = -10$. Hence $\beta = 3.16$ and the new gain is $K = 10/3.16 = 3.16$.

From Fig. 9.13 we observe that reducing K increases the phase margin and gain margin, and reduces the gain crossover frequency.

Damping Ratio and Resonance Peak

To evaluate resonance peak and the frequency at which it occurs, we consider the closed-loop transfer function (9.5) with $s = j\omega$:

$$M(j\omega) = \frac{1}{\left(1 - \omega^2/\omega_n^2\right) + j2\zeta\left(\omega/\omega_n\right)} \tag{9.12}$$

For particular values of ζ and ω_n, a plot of $|M(j\omega)| \triangleq M$ *versus* ω can easily be obtained. Some representative curves are shown in Fig. 9.14.

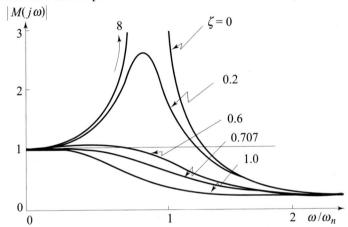

Fig. 9.14 *M versus* ω/ω_n

Next, consider the magnitude M^2 as derived from Eqn. (9.12):

$$M^2 = \frac{1}{\left(1 - \omega^2/\omega_n^2\right)^2 + 4\zeta^2\left(\omega^2/\omega_n^2\right)} \tag{9.13}$$

To find the peak value of M and the frequency at which it occurs, Eqn. (9.13) is differentiated with respect to frequency and set equal to zero:

$$\frac{dM^2}{d\omega} = -\frac{-4\left(1 - \omega^2/\omega_n^2\right)\left(\omega/\omega_n^2\right) + 8\zeta^2\left(\omega/\omega_n^2\right)}{\left[\left(1 - \omega^2/\omega_n^2\right)^2 + 4\zeta^2\left(\omega^2/\omega_n^2\right)\right]^2} = 0 \tag{9.14}$$

The frequency ω_r at which the value M exhibits a peak, as found from Eqn. (9.14), is

$$\omega_r = \omega_n \sqrt{1 - 2\zeta^2} \tag{9.15}$$

This value of frequency is substituted into Eqn. (9.13) to yield resonance peak

$$M_r = \frac{1}{2\zeta \sqrt{1 - \zeta^2}} \tag{9.16}$$

From these equations, it is seen that as ζ approaches zero, resonance frequency ω_r approaches undamped natural frequency ω_n, and the resonance peak M_r goes off to infinity. For $0 < \zeta < 1/\sqrt{2}$, the resonance frequency has a value less than ω_n and the resonance peak has a value greater than one. For $\zeta = 1/\sqrt{2}$, the peak value of M is one at zero frequency. For $\zeta > 1/\sqrt{2}$, it is seen from Eqn. (9.15) that $dM^2/d\omega$ does not become zero for any real value of ω. For the range $\zeta \geq 1/\sqrt{2}$, the magnitude M decreases monotonically from $M = 1$ at $\omega = 0$ with increasing ω, as shown in Fig. 9.14. It, therefore, follows that for $\zeta \geq 1/\sqrt{2}$, there is no resonance peak as such and the greatest value of M equals one. This limiting value of ζ for peaking on the magnitude curve of closed-loop frequency response should not be confused with the overshoot on the step response, where there is overshoot for $0 < \zeta < 1$.

It is important to note that for the standard second-order system, resonance peak M_r is a function of damping ratio only. Figure 9.15 illustrates the relationship between M_r and ζ.

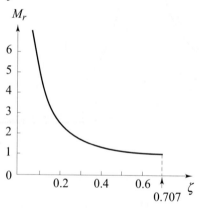

Fig. 9.15 M_r versus ζ

Response Speed and Resonance Frequency

Equation (9.15), reproduced below, relates the resonance frequency ω_r to the undamped natural frequency ω_n and damping ratio ζ.

$$\omega_r = \omega_n \sqrt{1 - 2\zeta^2} \; ; \; \zeta > 1/\sqrt{2} \tag{9.17}$$

Figure 9.16 shows a plot of ω_r/ω_n versus ζ.

From Eqns (9.16) and (9.17), we see that when a frequency-domain design holds M_r constant while increasing the resonance frequency, the resulting rise time and settling time would diminish in time domain.

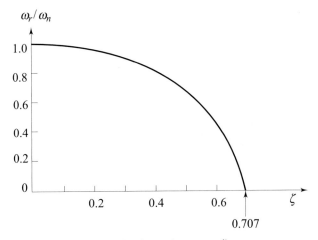

Fig. 9.16 *ω_r/ω_n versus ζ*

Response Speed and Bandwidth

Another relationship between the frequency response and time response is between the speed of time response (as measured by settling time, and rise time), and the *bandwidth* of the closed-loop frequency response, which is defined as the *frequency ω_b, at which the magnitude M is $1/\sqrt{2}$ = 0.707 times its value at zero frequency* (see Fig. 9.17a). In Bode coordinate system, the bandwidth ω_b is the frequency at which the magnitude falls off by 3 dB from its low-frequency value (see Fig. 9.17b).

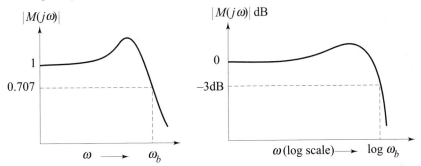

Fig. 9.17 *Definition of bandwidth*

The bandwidth of the standard second-order system can be found by finding that frequency for which $M = 1/\sqrt{2}$ in Eqn. (9.13):

$$\frac{1}{\left(1 - \omega_b^2/\omega_n^2\right)^2 + 4\zeta^2\left(\omega_b^2/\omega_n^2\right)} = \frac{1}{2}$$

Thus $\qquad (1 - \omega_b^2/\omega_n^2)^2 + 4\zeta^2(\omega_b^2/\omega_n^2) = 2$

or $\qquad (\omega_b^4/\omega_n^4) - 2(1 - 2\zeta^2)(\omega_b^2/\omega_n^2) - 1 = 0$

Solving for ω_b^2/ω_n^2, we get

$$(\omega_b^2/\omega_n^2) = (1 - 2\zeta^2) \pm \sqrt{4\zeta^4 - 4\zeta^2 + 2}$$

In the last equation the plus sign should be chosen, since ω_b/ω_n must be a positive real quantity for any ζ. Therefore, the bandwidth of the standard second-order system is

$$\omega_b = \omega_n \sqrt{\left[\left(1 - 2\zeta^2\right) + \sqrt{4\zeta^4 - 4\zeta^2 + 2}\right]} \qquad (9.18)$$

Figure 9.18 shows a plot of ω_b/ω_n versus ζ. For given ζ, ω_b is proportional to ω_n, and a measure of speed of response. Raising ω_b reduces settling time and rise time of the step response.

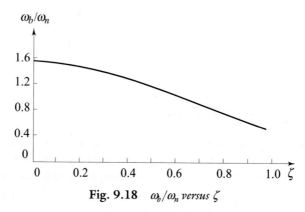

Fig. 9.18 ω_b/ω_n versus ζ

The reader is reminded here that the correlations between time-domain and frequency-domain performance specifications arrived at in this section apply only to the standard second-order system of Fig. 9.3. When other second-order or higher-order systems are involved, the correlations are different and more complex. It is not practical to develop correlations for all the cases.

Application of correlations developed for standard second-order system to other second-order and higher-order systems is based on the assumption of dominance. There will certainly be cases where this assumption is not valid; therefore, the transient response must be determined, usually by simulation, as a check.

9.4 CONSTANT-M CIRCLES

A control system is a closed-loop system. By Nyquist stability criterion, we predict its stability using plots of the open-loop transfer function. Closed-loop performance measures such as gain crossover frequency, phase margin, and gain margin are also determined using plots of open-loop transfer functions.

Other useful measures of performance of a feedback system are resonance peak, resonance frequency, and bandwidth of the closed-loop frequency response. Fortunately, these closed-loop performance indices can also be determined using plots of the open-loop transfer function, as is seen below.

Consider a single-loop unity-feedback system shown in Fig. 9.19. The closed-loop transfer function is

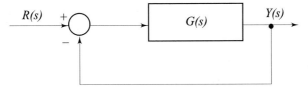

Fig. 9.19   *A unity-feedback system*

$$M(s) = \frac{G(s)}{1 + G(s)}$$

The frequency response of the closed-loop transfer function is given by

$$M(j\omega) = \frac{G(j\omega)}{1 + G(j\omega)} \qquad (9.19)$$

Figure 9.20 shows a typical plot of $G(j\omega)$ in polar coordinates. Consider the point A on this plot associated with frequency ω_1. $G(j\omega_1)$ is a vector from the origin to the point A; and $1 + G(j\omega_1)$ is a vector from $-1 + j0$ point to the point A. One point on the closed-loop frequency response can be calculated by measuring lengths and angles of these vectors:

$$|M(j\omega_1)| = \frac{|G(j\omega_1)|}{|1 + G(j\omega_1)|}$$

$$\angle M(j\omega_1) = \angle G(j\omega_1) - \angle(1 + G(j\omega_1))$$

Obviously, this calculation can be repeated at many points on the $G(j\omega)$-curve, and the entire closed-loop frequency response can be calculated in this manner.

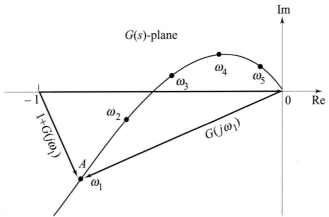

Fig. 9.20   *Polar relationship between open-loop and closed-loop frequency responses*

It is easier to prepare nomographs so that the results can be read off without additional calculations. Consider the graphical configuration of Fig. 9.20 as a problem in geometry and trigonometry, without regard to frequency response. The lines for $G(j\omega_1)$ and $1 + G(j\omega_1)$ are simply vectors which have lengths and angles associated with them when drawn from the origin and the $-1 + j0$ point, respectively, to a common point A in the complex plane.

$$G(j\omega_1) = \text{Re } G(j\omega_1) + j\text{Im } G(j\omega_1) = u + jv$$
$$1 + G(j\omega_1) = (1 + u) + jv$$

By definition,

$$\frac{|G(j\omega_1)|}{|1 + G(j\omega_1)|} = \frac{|u + jv|}{|(1 + u) + jv|} = M, \text{ a number} \tag{9.20}$$

Are there any other points in the plane such that the same value of M would be associated with vectors drawn to them? The answer to this question is *yes*. In fact, the locus of constant-M points on the polar plane is a circle. This can be proved as follows.

From Eqn. (9.20), we have

$$M^2 = \frac{u^2 + v^2}{(1 + u)^2 + v^2}$$

or
$$M^2(1 + u^2 + 2u + v^2) = u^2 + v^2$$

Rearranging, we get

$$(1 - M^2)u^2 + (1 - M^2)v^2 - 2M^2 u = M^2 \tag{9.21}$$

This equation is conditioned by dividing through by $(1 - M^2)$ and adding the term $[M^2/(1- M^2)]^2$ on both sides. We have

$$u^2 + v^2 - \frac{2M^2}{1 - M^2} u + \left(\frac{M^2}{1 - M^2}\right)^2 = \frac{M^2}{1 - M^2} + \left(\frac{M^2}{1 - M^2}\right)^2$$

which is finally simplified to

$$\left(u - \frac{M^2}{1 - M^2}\right) + v^2 = \left(\frac{M^2}{1 - M^2}\right)^2 \tag{9.22}$$

For a given M, Eqn. (9.22) represents a circle with the centre at $(M^2/(1 - M^2), 0)$. The radius of the circle is $r = M/(1 - M^2)$.

Note that Eqn. (9.22) is invalid for $M = 1$. For $M = 1$, Eqn. (9.21) gives

$$u = -\frac{1}{2} \tag{9.23}$$

which is the equation of a straight line parallel to the imaginary axis and passing through the point $\left(-\frac{1}{2}, 0\right)$ in the $G(s)$-plane.

When M takes on different values, Eqn. (9.22) describes in the $G(s)$-plane a family of circles that are called *constant-M circles*. A representative family of constant-M circles is shown in Fig. 9.21. The following conclusions are easily drawn regarding these circles.

Case I: M > 1

As M increases, the radii of constant-M circles reduce monotonically, and the centres located on negative real axis progressively shift towards $(-1+j0)$ point. $M = \infty$ circle has a radius zero and is centred at $(-1+j0)$.

Case II: M = 1

It follows that $M = 1$ circle is of infinite radius with centre at infinity on the real axis, i.e., it is a straight line parallel to the imaginary axis of the $G(s)$-plane. It intersects the real axis at $-1/2$.

Case III: M < 1

As M decreases, the radii of constant-M circles reduce monotonically, and centres located on positive real axis shift towards the origin. $M = 0$ circle has a radius zero and is centred at the origin.

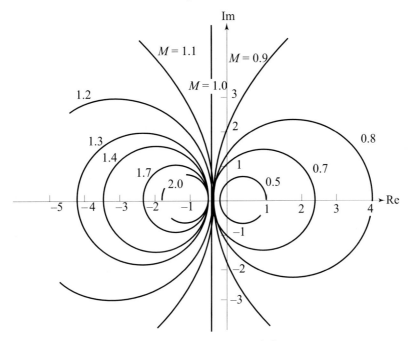

Fig. 9.21   *Constant-M circles*

The constant-M circles are useful when overlaid on the polar plot of $G(j\omega)$ as shown in Fig. 9.22. The intersection of $G(j\omega)$ plot with M_1 circle at frequencies ω_1 and ω_4 indicates that

$$\frac{|G(j\omega_1)|}{|1 + G(j\omega_1)|} = |M(j\omega_1)| = M_1$$

$$\frac{|G(j\omega_4)|}{|1 + G(j\omega_4)|} = |M(j\omega_4)| = M_1$$

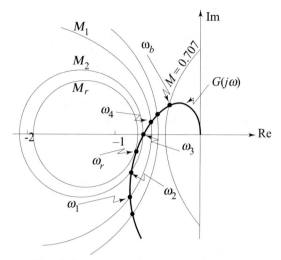

Fig. 9.22   *Constant-M circles and G(jω)-plot*

Similarly, the intersection of $G(j\omega)$ plot with M_2 circle at frequencies ω_2 and ω_3 indicates that

$$\left|M(j\omega_2)\right| = \left|M(j\omega_3)\right| = M_2$$

Note that the circle tangent to the $G(j\omega)$ plot provides us with the peak magnitude M_r of the closed-loop frequency response and the corresponding frequency ω_r. Using Fig. 9.22, we can also read the bandwidth; it is the frequency ω_b associated with the point of intersection of $G(j\omega)$ plot with the $M = 0.707$ circle. A typical magnitude curve of closed-loop frequency response is shown in Fig. 9.23.

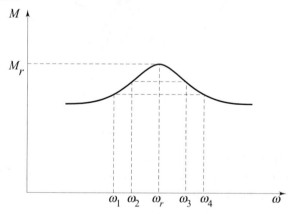

Fig. 9.23   *Closed-loop frequency response*

It is also possible to plot loci of constant phases of $M(j\omega)$ on the $G(s)$-plane. The plot consists of a family of circles called *constant-N circles*; $N = \tan \alpha$, $\alpha = \angle M(j\omega)$. When overlaid on the $G(j\omega)$ plot, the constant-N circles give the phase curve of closed-loop frequency response in a manner similar to that used for obtaining magnitude curve.

It may be noted that instead of using constant-M and constant-N circles, we can compute closed-loop frequency response directly from Eqn. (9.19) by use of a computer program. However, as we shall see shortly, the graphical method allows the design of a system with specified values of M_r, ω_r and/or ω_b. These performance measures are associated with only the magnitude curve of closed-loop frequency response and can be read off directly from a plot of $G(j\omega)$ superimposed on constant-M circles. Constant-N circles are not used in this text and, therefore, will not be discussed.

As is evident from the above discussion, the constant-M circles can be used only for systems with unity feedback. For nonunity feedback systems, we will translate the performance requirements into specifications on gain margin, phase margin, and gain crossover frequency, and then carry out the design using Bode plots. To check the design for requirements on resonance peak and resonance frequency/bandwidth, the magnitude curve of the closed-loop frequency response may be generated using a computer program.

Example 9.3

A unity-feedback control system has an open-loop frequency response $G(j\omega)$ with properties as follows:

ω (rad/sec)	2	3	4	5	6
$\lvert G(j\omega)\rvert$	2.7	1.7	0.97	0.63	0.4
$\angle G(j\omega)$ (degrees)	-115	-126	-138	-150	-163

The open-loop frequency response, plotted in polar coordinates, is shown in Fig. 9.24. The $G(j\omega)$-plot is tangential to the $M = 1.4$ circle at a frequency $\omega = 4$ rad/sec. Therefore, the resonance peak $M_r = 1.4$, and the resonance frequency $\omega_r = 4$ rad/sec.

The values of ζ and ω_n to be used for approximating the transient behaviour of the system can be determined from Eqns (9.16)–(9.17) or Figs 9.15–9.16. Rearranging Eqn. (9.16), we obtain

$$\zeta^4 - \zeta^2 + (1/4\ M_r^2) = 0 \tag{9.24}$$

Since $M_r = 1.4$, we have $\zeta = 0.39$ and 0.92. A damping ratio larger than 0.707 yields no peak above zero frequency. Thus, use select $\zeta = 0.39$. Using Eqn. (9.17) with $\omega_r = 4$ and $\zeta = 0.39$, we get $\omega_n = 4.8$ rad/sec.

The bandwidth of a system is defined as the frequency at which the magnitude of the closed-loop frequency response is 0.707 of its magnitude at $\omega = 0$. From Fig. 9.24, we see that $M = 0.707$ circle intersects the $G(j\omega)$-plot at $\omega = 6$ rad/sec. This frequency can be taken as the bandwidth if it is assumed that the closed-loop gain is unity at $\omega = 0$.

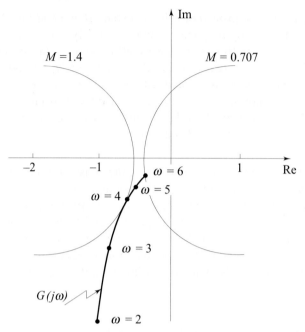

Fig. 9.24   *Constant-M circles and G(jω)-plot for Example 9.3*

9.5 | THE NICHOLS CHART

In the previous section, we have seen that closed-loop frequency response of a unity-feedback system (refer Fig. 9.19) can easily be determined from polar plot of open-loop transfer function $G(j\omega)$ superimposed on constant-M circles. Use of constant-M circles on polar plane is straightforward but seldom used because Nyquist analysis is normally carried out on the Bode plots and it is more efficient to use a nomograph compatible with Bode data. The *Nichols Chart*, introduced by N.B. Nichols in the 1940s, is such a nomograph.

The Nichols chart consists of curves that are maps of the constant-M and constant-N circles on a new coordinate system. The Nichols coordinate system plots $|G(j\omega)|$ in dB as ordinate *versus* $\angle G(j\omega)$ in degrees as abscissa, with origin at $|G(j\omega)| = 0$ dB and $\angle G(j\omega) = -180°$. This origin is the map of the critical point $-1 + j0$ of the polar coordinate (Nyquist) plot. Figure 9.26 illustrates the coordinate system (not the nomograph) with a plot of Bode data from Fig. 9.25. Note that the phase and gain margins are readily identified.

The constant-M and constant-N circles in polar coordinates do not remain circles when mapped onto dB *versus* phase plane. A typical constant-M circle is shown in Fig. 9.27. The magnitude ρ and angle λ of a vector drawn to any point on this circle are shown. The equation of the M circle is (refer Eqn. (9.22))

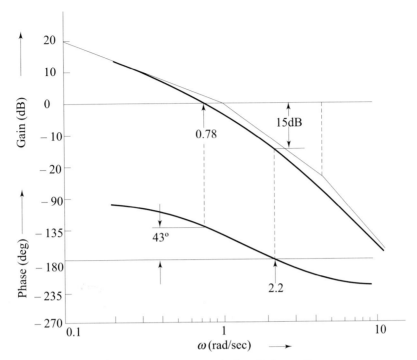

Fig. 9.25 *Frequency-response plot in a Bode coordinate system*

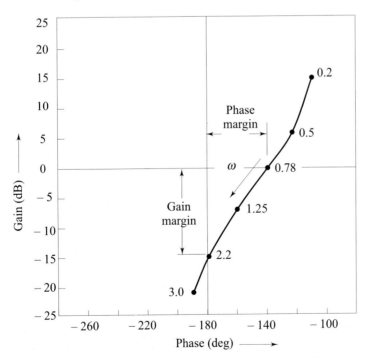

Fig. 9.26 *Frequency-response plot in a Nichols coordinate system*

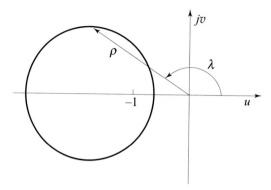

Fig. 9.27 *A constant-M circle*

$$\left(u - \frac{M^2}{1 - M^2} \right)^2 + v^2 = \left(\frac{M^2}{1 - M^2} \right)^2$$

where $u = \rho \cos \lambda$, and $v = \rho \sin \lambda$. Combining these equations produces

$$\left(\rho \cos \lambda - \frac{M^2}{1 - M^2} \right)^2 + \rho^2 \sin^2 \lambda = \left(\frac{M}{1 - M^2} \right)^2$$

or

$$\rho^2 - 2 \cos \lambda \left(\frac{M^2}{1 - M^2} \right) \rho - \frac{M^2}{1 - M^2} = 0 \qquad (9.25)$$

For any value of M, a series of values of λ can be inserted in Eqn. (9.25) to solve for ρ. This magnitude must be changed to dB. The data thus generated when plotted in Nichols coordinate system, gives a constant-M locus. When M takes on different values, Eqn. (9.25) describes in the Nichols system a family of loci. A representative family of constant-M loci is shown in Fig. 9.28. The constant-N circles can be transferred on Nichols chart in a similar manner, if needed.

Note that the $M = 1$ curve is asymptotic to $-90°$ and $-270°$ lines of Nichols coordinate system. The curves for $M > 1$ are closed curves inside the limits of $-90°$ and $-270°$ lines. The curves for $M < 1$ cross these limits. The curves are symmetrical about $-180°$ line.

The Nichols charts were commercially available until the middle 1970s. These charts cannot be purchased any more. They can, however, be easily generated with the help of a computer. An expanded section of the Nichols chart with selected constant-M loci is shown in Fig. 9.29; the values of M are given in dB.

Superimposing the dB versus phase angle curve of $G(j\omega)$ shown in Fig. 9.26, on the Nichols chart we obtain the plot of Fig. 9.30. The intersection of $G(j\omega)$-curve with $M = 1$ dB locus at frequencies ω_1 and ω_2 indicates that

$$\frac{|G(j\omega_1)|}{|1 + G(j\omega_1)|} = |M(j\omega_1)| = 1 \text{ dB}$$

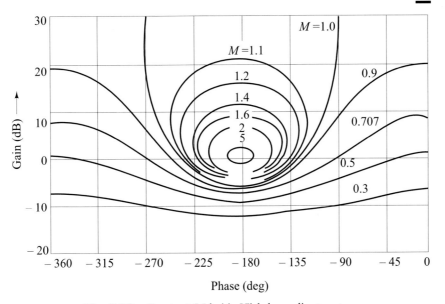

Fig. 9.28 *Constant-M loci in Nichols coordinate system*

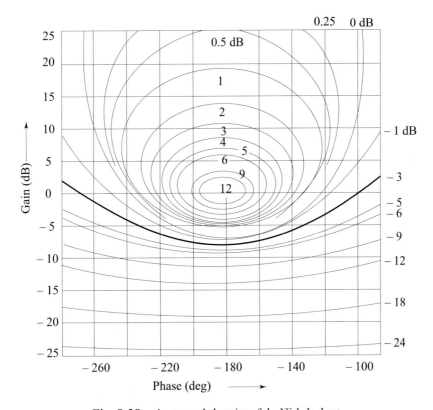

Fig. 9.29 *An expanded section of the Nichols chart*

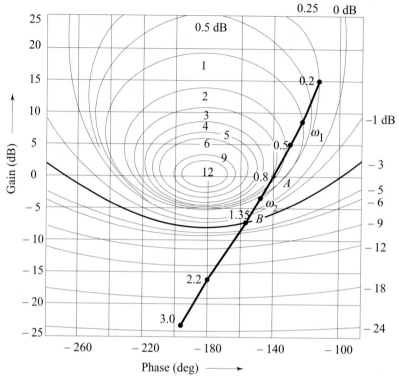

Fig. 9.30 *The curve of Fig. 9.26 superimposed on the Nichols chart*

$$\frac{|G(j\omega_2)|}{|1 + G(j\omega_2)|} = |M(j\omega_2)| = 1 \text{ dB}$$

Similarly, the intersections of $G(j\omega)$-curve with other constant-M loci determine the magnitude (in dB) of the closed-loop frequency response for various frequencies. The data so generated when plotted with magnitude in dB as ordinate and frequency ω (log scale) as abscissa, gives the Bode magnitude plot of the closed-loop frequency response.

Note that the constant-M locus tangent to the $G(j\omega)$-curve provides us with the peak magnitude M_r (in dB) of the closed-loop frequency response and the corresponding frequency ω_r. We can also directly read off the bandwidth from the Nichols chart; it is the frequency associated with the point of intersection of $G(j\omega)$-curve with $M = -3$ dB locus.

The Nichols chart of Fig. 9.30 has 2 dB and 3 dB closed-loop gain curves; the M_r value lies between 2 dB and 3 dB. One must do a little interpolation to determine M_r. From Fig. 9.30 we see that an approximate value of M_r is 2.5 dB and it occurs at a frequency $\omega_r = 0.8$ (the frequency ω_r corresponding to the point A has been determined from Fig. 9.25).

Point B represents the intersection of $G(j\omega)$-curve with $M = -3$ dB contour. The frequency corresponding to this point (read from Fig. 9.25) is the bandwidth $\omega_b = 1.35$ rad/sec.

Gain Adjustments

The concept of constant-M circles will now be applied to the design of control systems. In obtaining acceptable performance, the adjustment of gain is usually the first consideration. The adjustment may be based on a desirable value for the resonance peak. In what follows, we shall demonstrate how the Nichols chart can be used to determine the gain K so that the system will have a desired value of M_r. Such a design is usually acceptable if the resulting bandwidth ω_b is satisfactory.

Example 9.4_____

Let us reconsider the system discussed in Example 9.2. The system has an open-loop transfer function

$$G(j\omega) = \frac{K}{j\omega \, (j0.1\omega + 1) \, (j0.05\omega + 1)} ; K = 10$$

Figure 9.13 shows the Bode plots of $G(j\omega)$. Transferring the Bode data to a Nichols chart, we get the dB versus phase angle plot of $G(j\omega)$. This is shown in Fig. 9.31. From the figure, it is seen that

$$M_r = 5.3 \text{ dB, and } \omega_r = 8.14 \text{ rad/sec}$$

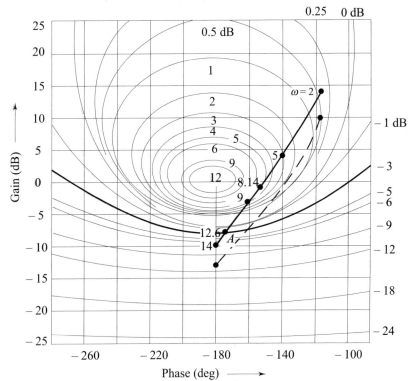

Fig. 9.31 *The Nichols chart for Example 9.4*

The dB versus phase angle plot of $G(j\omega)$ intersects the -3 dB M-locus at the point A. The frequency parameter at this point can be easily determined by transferring the open-loop dB data at A to the Bode plot of Fig. 9.13. We find the frequency to be 12.6 rad/sec. Therefore, bandwidth $\omega_b = 12.6$ rad/sec.

Let us examine the effects of gain adjustments. Suppose it is desired to find the open-loop gain for resonance peak of 2 dB. From Fig. 9.31, it is found that the dB versus phase angle plot of $G(j\omega)$ must be moved downwards by 3.5 dB in order that it be tangent to the 2 dB M-locus. It means that the gain $K = 10$ must be reduced by a factor of β, given by 20 log $(1/\beta) = -3.5$. Hence $\beta = 1.5$ and the new gain is $K = 10/1.5 = 6.33$.

From Fig. 9.31, we observe that reducing K reduces the resonance peak M_r; it also reduces the bandwidth ω_b. The system thus becomes relatively more stable (peak overshoot in transient response reduces). The reduced bandwidth will generally result in increased rise time/settling time of the transient response.

9.6 | SENSITIVITY ANALYSIS IN FREQUENCY DOMAIN

Consider the unity feedback system shown in Fig. 9.32, with the plant $G(s)$ and the compensator $D(s)$. The system has the following inputs:

$$r = \text{reference (or command input),}$$
$$w = \text{disturbance input, and}$$
$$w_n = \text{measurement noise.}$$

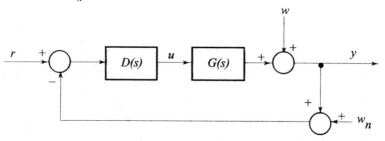

Fig. 9.32   *Block diagram of a feedback system including disturbance and measurement noise inputs*

From the block diagram, we may write

$$Y(s) = W(s) + D(s)G(s)[R(s) - Y(s) - W_n(s)]$$

or $$[1 + D(s)G(s)]Y(s) = W(s) + D(s)G(s)R(s) - D(s)G(s)W_n(s)$$

Therefore, the total output of the closed-loop system is

$$Y(s) = \frac{D(s)\,G(s)}{1 + D(s)\,G(s)}\,R(s) + \frac{1}{1 + D(s)\,G(s)}\,W(s) \qquad (9.26)$$

$$-\frac{D(s)\,G(s)}{1 + D(s)\,G(s)}\,W_n(s)$$

If we define the tracking error as $e = r - y$, we get

$$E(s) = \frac{1}{1 + D(s)\,G(s)}\,R(s) - \frac{1}{1 + D(s)\,G(s)}\,W(s)$$

$$+ \frac{D(s)\,G(s)}{1 + D(s)\,G(s)}\,W_n(s) \qquad (9.27)$$

Finally, the controller output (i.e., the plant input) is given by

$$U(s) = \frac{D(s)}{1 + D(s)\,G(s)}\,R(s) - \frac{D(s)}{1 + D(s)\,G(s)}\,W(s)$$

$$- \frac{D(s)}{1 + D(s)\,G(s)}\,W_n(s) \qquad (9.28)$$

The following quantities appear in these relationships.

Loop Gain

In the light of Fig. 9.32, the open-loop transfer function of the feedback system is $D(s)G(s)$ (it is the transfer function between $R(s)$ and $Y(s)$ if the feedback loop is broken at the summing point).

Note that $D(s)G(s)$ is the transfer function product around the entire feedback loop. We call it *loop gain*, and denote it by $L(s)$:

$$L(s) \triangleq D(s)G(s) \qquad (9.29)$$

Return Difference

The term return difference, first introduced by Bode, means the following. Suppose a feedback loop is broken at a given point. Inject a 1 volt signal at the entrance of the broken loop and measure the signal returned at the exit; the difference between the injected signal and the returned signal is called the *return difference*. In the light of Fig. 9.32, the return difference is

$$1 - (- D(s)G(s)) = 1 + D(s)G(s) \qquad (9.30)$$

Sensitivity Function

In the light of Fig. 9.32, the sensitivity function $S(s)$ (refer Eqn. (4.12)) is given by

$$S(s) = \frac{1}{1 + D(s)\,G(s)} \qquad (9.31a)$$

$$= \frac{1}{1 + L(s)} \qquad (9.31b)$$

Complimentary Sensitivity Function

In the light of Fig. 9.32, the complimentary sensitivity function $M(s)$ (refer Eqn. (4.14)) is given by

$$M(s) = \frac{D(s)\,G(s)}{1 + D(s)\,G(s)} \tag{9.32a}$$

$$= \frac{L(s)}{1 + L(s)} \tag{9.32b}$$

Note that $M(s)$ is the closed-loop transfer function between $R(s)$ and $Y(s)$.

The sum of the two sensitivity functions always obeys the relation

$$S(s) + M(s) = 1 \tag{9.33}$$

As a consequence of Eqn. (9.33), the choice of a particular sensitivity function $S(s)$ directly implies a corresponding unique choice for the complimentary sensitivity function $M(s)$, and *vice versa*. This observation underlines an important factor in design; namely the trade offs that must be made when selecting these two mutually dependent transfer functions.

In the analysis to follow, it will always be assumed that the feedback system is stable; therefore S and M are stable, proper transfer functions. Equations (9.26)–(9.28) may be expressed in terms of sensitivity functions as follows.

$$Y(s) = M(s)R(s) + S(s)W(s) - M(s)W_n(s) \tag{9.34}$$

$$E(s) = S(s)R(s) - S(s)W(s) + M(s)W_n(s) \tag{9.35}$$

$$U(s) = D(s)S(s)R(s) - D(s)S(s)W(s) - D(s)S(s)W_n(s) \tag{9.36}$$

We are now ready to draw the following conclusions from these relations:

1. *Disturbance rejection:* $S(s)$ must be kept small to minimize the effect of disturbances. From the definition of S, this can be met if the loop gain is large.
2. *Tracking:* $S(s)$ must be kept small to keep the tracking errors small.
3. *Noise suppression:* $M(s)$ must be kept small to reduce the effects of measurement noise on the output and error. From the definition of M, this is met if loop gain is small.
4. *Actuator limits:* $D(s)S(s)$ must be bounded to ensure that the actuating signal driving the plant does not exceed plant tolerances. Another reason for taking this into consideration is to reduce the control energy so that we can use smaller actuators (such as motors). Note that

$$D(s)S(s) = \frac{D(s)}{1 + D(s)\,G(s)} = \frac{M(s)}{G(s)} \tag{9.37}$$

Hence, by keeping M small, we can reduce control energy.

Tracking and disturbance rejection require small sensitivity. Noise suppression and reduction in control energy require small complimentary sensitivity. As these two transfer functions add up to unity, we cannot reduce both the transfer functions to zero simultaneously. We can, however, avoid the conflict by noting that in practice, command inputs and disturbances are low-frequency signals (i.e., they vary slowly with time) whereas measurement noise is a high-frequency signal. Therefore we can meet both the objectives by keeping S small in the low-frequency range and M small for high frequencies. Figure 9.33

depicts typical plots of both the sensitivity function and the complimentary sensitivity function that are consistent with our goals.

The intermediate frequencies typically control the gain and phase margins, as is seen below.

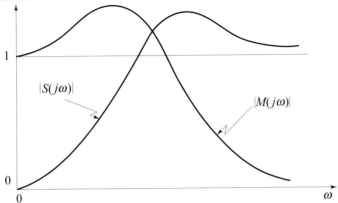

Fig. 9.33   *Typical magnitude plots of S(jω) and M(jω)*

Stability Margins from the Sensitivity Function

The maximum amplitude of $S(s = j\omega)$ for all $\omega \geq 0$; that is, $\overset{max}{\omega}|S(j\omega)|$, can be used to obtain simple bounds on both the gain margin (*GM*) and phase margin (*ΦM*) of stable closed-loop systems. Indeed a simple bound on $\overset{max}{\omega}|S(j\omega)|$ can be used as a measure of robust stability in virtually all closed-loop stable cases, including the nonminimum-phase systems, and systems with open-loop poles in right-half *s*-plane for which both the *GM* and *ΦM* are ill-defined.

We begin with the so-called 'infinity norm' of a stable, proper, rational, transfer function $F(s)$. As shown by Francis [141], the (*Hardy space*) H_∞–norm, or simply the ∞-norm of $F(s)$ is defined by the relationship

$$\|F\|_\infty \overset{\Delta}{=} \overset{max}{\omega}|F(j\omega)| \tag{9.38}$$

and simply represents the maximum amplitude obtained by its frequency response.

Consider the Nyquist plot of Fig. 9.34. We observe that the magnitude of the return difference, $|1 + D(j\omega)G(j\omega)|$, equals the length of a vector drawn from $-1 + j0$ point to a point on the $D(j\omega)G(j\omega)$-locus in the complex $D(s)G(s)$-plane. For convenience, we define α to be the distance from $-1 + j0$ point to a point on the $D(j\omega)G(j\omega)$-locus. Therefore

$$\alpha = |1 + D(j\omega)G(j\omega)| = [|S(j\omega)|]^{-1} \tag{9.39}$$

The minimum distance from $D(j\omega)G(j\omega)$-locus to the $-1 + j0$ point is

$$\alpha_{min} = \overset{min}{\omega}|1 + D(j\omega)G(j\omega)|$$

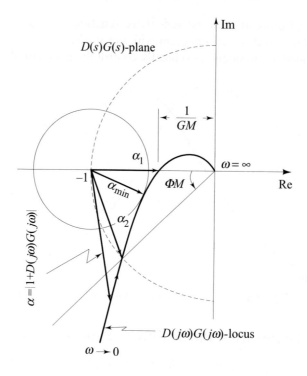

Fig. 9.34 *Nyquist plot showing stability margins*

$$= \frac{1}{\max\limits_{\omega} |S(j\omega)|} = \frac{1}{||S||_{\infty}} \qquad (9.40)$$

Note that α_{min} is the radius of the circle with the centre at $-1 + j0$ and tangent to the Nyquist plot as shown in Fig. 9.34. From this figure, we see that

$$GM = \frac{1}{1 - \alpha_1} \qquad (9.41a)$$

$$\Phi M = 2 \sin^{-1}(\alpha_2/2) \qquad (9.41b)$$

and because α_1 and α_2 must both be greater than α_{min}, we see that the ∞-norm of the sensitivity function yields information about the phase and gain margins. One could use α_{min} in Eqns (9.41) to yield conservative estimates of GM and ΦM:

$$GM \geq \frac{||S||_{\infty}}{||S||_{\infty} - 1} \qquad (9.42a)$$

$$\Phi M \geq 2 \sin^{-1}\left(\frac{1}{2||S||_{\infty}}\right) \qquad (9.42b)$$

To ensure an acceptable nominal design that attains a $GM \geq 2$ and a $\Phi M \geq 30°$, we may require that

$$||S||_{\infty} \leq 2 \qquad (9.43)$$

Note that the single sensitivity function requirement defined in (9.43) can be used to replace both the *GM* and the *ΦM* requirements not only in the minimum phase cases but also in not defined cases, and in systems with open-loop poles in right-half *s*-plane. In particular, (9.43) will ensure that $D(j\omega)G(j\omega)$ remains at an acceptable 'marginal' distance away from the critical $-1+j0$ point, irrespective of the number and the direction of encirclements required for closed-loop stability; that is, (9.43) will ensure robust stability with respect to plant parameter variations once nominal closed-loop stability has been obtained.

Example 9.5

A unity-feedback system has open-loop transfer function

$$G(s) = \frac{10}{s(1+0.1s)(1+0.05s)}$$

Let us find the sensitivity of the closed-loop transfer function with respect to *G*.

Sensitivity function given by Eqns (9.31) can be evaluated using the Nichols chart as follows

$$S(j\omega) = \frac{1}{1+G(j\omega)} = \frac{G^{-1}(j\omega)}{1+G^{-1}(j\omega)} \tag{9.44}$$

This indicates that magnitude of $S(j\omega)$ can be obtained by plotting $G^{-1}(j\omega)$ on the Nichols chart. For the given $G(s)$, a plot of $G^{-1}(j\omega)$ on the Nichols chart is shown in Fig. 9.35. The intersection of $G^{-1}(j\omega)$ curve with the constant-*M* loci

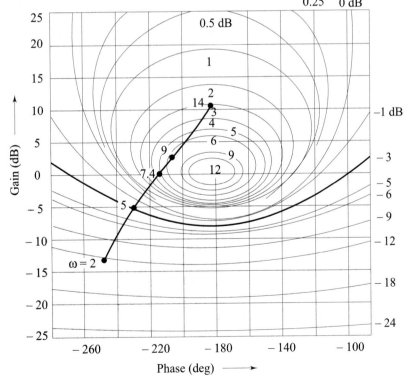

Fig. 9.35 *Determination of the sensitivity function from the Nichols chart*

gives $|S(j\omega)|$ at the corresponding frequencies. From Fig. 9.35, it is observed that peak value of $|S(j\omega)|$ is 7 dB at $\omega = 9$ rad/sec.

Review Examples

Review Example 9.1

Consider the unity-feedback system shown in Fig. 9.36. Let the compensator $D(s)$ be simply a constant K. Find a gain K such that
  (i) phase margin $\geq 60°$, and
  (ii) bandwidth is as large as possible.

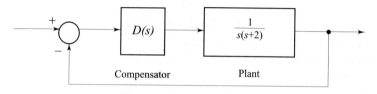

Fig. 9.36   *Unity-feedback system*

Solution

The system under consideration is a standard second-order system. Correlations derived in Section 9.3 are applicable without any approximation. Using Eqns (9.11) and (9.18), we obtain the ratio of gain crossover frequency ω_g and bandwidth ω_b as a function of ζ. Table 9.1 shows this ratio for a range of values of ζ. It is quite interesting to note that the ratio is rather constant. Raising the gain crossover frequency increases the bandwidth of the system.

Table 9.1   *Bandwidth-gain crossover frequency correlation*

ζ	0.3	0.4	0.6	0.707	0.8
ω_g/ω_b	0.63	0.62	0.63	0.64	0.68

The Bode plots of

$$G(j\omega) = \frac{1}{j\omega\,(j\omega + 2)} = \frac{0.5}{j\omega\,(j0.5\omega + 1)}$$

are shown in Fig. 9.37. The magnitude plot crosses the 0-dB line roughly at 0.46; thus the gain crossover frequency is 0.46 rad/sec. The phase margin is then measured from the plot as 77°. The specification on phase margin is, thus, met without the need for a compensator $D(s)$.

Now we shall adjust K to make gain crossover frequency as large as possible. If we increase K from 1, the magnitude plot will move upward and the gain crossover frequency will increase. This will cause the phase margin to decrease, as can be seen from Fig. 9.37. In other words, as the gain crossover frequency increases, the phase margin will decrease. The largest permissible gain crossover frequency corresponds to a phase margin of 60°. It is seen from Fig. 9.37 that if magnitude plot is shifted up by 9 dB, then 1.15 rad/sec becomes the new gain crossover frequency and the phase margin is 60°. Therefore, the required gain K is given by 20 log K = 9, which implies K = 2.8.

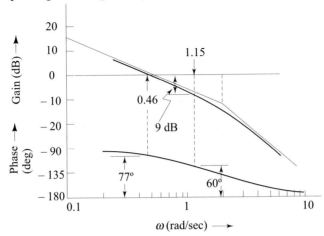

Fig. 9.37 *Bode Plot of* $G(j\omega) = 0.5/j\omega(j0.5\omega + 1)$

We may determine the bandwidth of the gain-compensated closed-loop system using the Nichols chart. Transferring the Bode data from Fig. 9.37 corresponding to K = 2.8 to the Nichols coordinate system, we obtain Fig. 9.38. The – 3dB M-locus has been constructed using Table 9.2, obtained from the Nichols chart of Fig. 9.29. The dB versus phase angle curve of $KG(j\omega)$ intersects the –3dB M-locus at point A. The frequency parameter at this point can be easily determined by transferring the open-loop dB data at A to the Bode plot of Fig. 9.37. We find this frequency to be 2; therefore the bandwidth ω_b = 2 rad/sec.

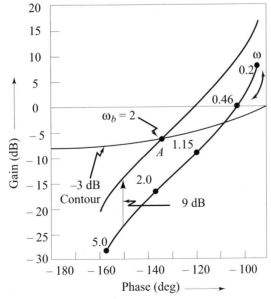

Fig. 9.38 *Determination of bandwidth*

Table 9.2 *Data for construction of – 3dB M-locus of the Nichols chart*

Degrees	– 90	– 100	– 120	– 140	– 160	– 180	– 200	– 220
dB	0	– 1.5	– 4.18	– 6.13	– 7.28	– 7.66	– 7.28	– 6.13

Note that the above design problem could also be solved analytically using correlations developed in Section 9.3; we opted for the graphical tools to illustrate a design procedure applicable to second-order as well as higher-order systems.

Review Example 9.2

Let us consider a unity-feedback system with open-loop transfer function

$$G(s) = \frac{0.64}{s\left(s^2 + s + 1\right)}$$

The $G(j\omega)$ plot in polar coordinate system is shown in Fig. 9.39. From this figure, we find that

$$\Phi M = 30°, M_r = 2.8$$

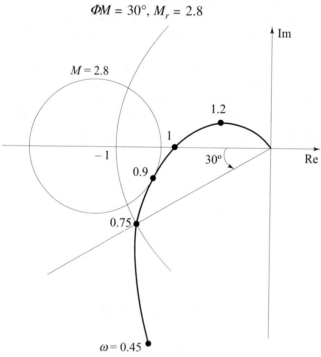

Fig. 9.39 *Nyquist plot for $G(j\omega) = 0.64/j\omega\,[(j\omega)^2 + j\omega + 1)]$*

On the basis of phase margin, we estimate the system damping ratio as $\zeta \cong 0.30$ (refer Eqn (9.10)), and on the basis of resonance peak we find that $\zeta \cong 0.175$ (refer Eqn (9.16)). The apparent conflict discovered in this example clearly indicates that a designer must use the frequency-domain to time-domain correlations with caution. The correlations arrived at in Section 9.3 apply to standard second-order systems. Use of these correlations for higher-order systems where dominance condition is not satisfied, can lead to unclear and uncertain estimates. One is usually safe if the lesser of the two values of ζ resulting from ΦM and M_r relations is utilized for analysis and design purposes.

Review Questions

9.1 (a) Describe a set of performance specifications characterizing desired frequency response, that are frequently used in the design of linear control systems using Bode plots.

   (b) Frequency response of a feedback control system should be similar to that of an ideal low pass filter. Justify this statement. (Help: p594)

   (c) Most of the plants we have encountered so far have low-pass filtering characteristic. Do you agree with this statement? Examine filtering characteristic of some typical transfer function models of plants.

9.2 (a) Show that if we know the frequency response of a stable linear system, we can compute the dynamic response for any form of input. (Help: p595)

   (b) Given the following measures of frequency response of a unity feedback system with open-loop transfer function $G(s) = \dfrac{\omega_n^2}{s\left(s + 2\zeta\omega_n\right)}$:

   (i) phase margin, ΦM; (ii) gain crossover frequency, ω_g; (iii) resonance peak, M_r; (iv) resonance frequency, ω_r; (v) bandwidth, ω_b.
   Through graphical plots, explain the correlation of these functions with ζ and ω_n.

9.3 Given a unity feedback system with forward-path transfer function $G(j\omega)$. Resonance peak M_r, resonance frequency ω_r, and bandwidth ω_b of the closed-loop frequency response can be obtained by generating plot of $|M(j\omega)| = |G(j\omega)| / |1 + G(j\omega)|$ vs ω. As we know, these closed-loop frequency response parameters can be determined using frequency-response plot of $G(j\omega)$, without the need to generate frequency-response plots of $M(j\omega)$. How do we determine M_r, and ω_b of the closed-loop system from frequency-responce plot of $G(j\omega)$?

9.4 (a) Define the terms resonance peak M_r, and the bandwidth ω_b of a closed-loop control system. (Help: pp556–557, p594, p606, p607)

   (b) What is the Nichols chart? How can we identify resonance peak and bandwidth from the Nichols chart?

   (c) Nichols chart can be used only for systems with unity feedback. Suggest a suitable design procedure for non-unity feedback systems. (Help: p613)

9.5 All our control system designs are based on a model of the plant; however, it is inevitable that the model we use is only an approximation of the true dynamics of the system. In general, a good plant model $G(s)$ will be well-known at low frequencies and less well-known at high frequencies. Illustrate with the help of an example the sensitivity analysis that yields the effect of uncertainty in $G(j\omega)$ on the closed-loop transfer function $M(j\omega)$. How do you determine the frequency at which M is most sensitive to uncertainties in G? (Help: Example 9.5)

9.6 (a) What does it mean when a control system is described as being robust? (Help: pp243-244, Section 10.6)

    (b) Show that both a good GM and a good ΦM are needed for robust stability. (Help: p541)

    (c) GM and ΦM may be used as measures of robust stability for closed-loop systems only if the open-loop transfer function has no poles in right-half s-plane. Give a measure of robust stability for closed-loop systems with open-loop poles in right-half s-plane. (Help: pp623-625)

Problems

9.1 Consider a unity-feedback system with open-loop transfer function

$$G(s) = \frac{\omega_n^2}{s\left(s + 2\zeta\omega_n\right)}$$

Show that the phase margin (relative stability measure in frequency domain) is given by

$$\Phi M = \tan^{-1} \frac{2\zeta}{\sqrt{\sqrt{4\zeta^4 + 1} - 2\zeta^2}}$$

9.2 For the standard second-order system

$$\frac{Y(s)}{R(s)} = \frac{\omega_n^2}{s^2 + 2\zeta\omega_n s + \omega_n^2},$$

show that the bandwidth is given by

$$\omega_b = \omega_n \sqrt{\left[\left(1 - 2\zeta^2\right) + \sqrt{4\zeta^4 - 4\zeta^2 + 2}\right]}$$

9.3 Show that when $0 < \zeta < 0.707$, the frequency response of a system defined by a transfer function

$$M(s) = \frac{\omega_n^2}{s^2 + 2\zeta\omega_n s + \omega_n^2}$$

has a peak amplitude given by

$$M_r = \frac{1}{2\zeta\sqrt{1 - \zeta^2}}$$

which occurs at the resonance frequency

$$\omega_r = \omega_n \sqrt{1 - \zeta^2}$$

9.4 Consider the feedback system shown in Fig. P9.4.

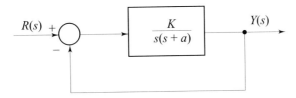

Fig. P9.4

(a) Find the values of K and a to satisfy the following frequency-domain specifications:
$$M_r = 1.04; \ \omega_r = 11.55 \ \text{rad/sec}$$

(b) For the values of K and a determined in part (a), calculate the settling time and bandwidth of the system.

9.5 Unit-step response data of a second-order system is given below. Obtain the corresponding frequency response indices $(M_r, \ \omega_r, \ \omega_b)$ for the system.

$t(\text{sec})$	0	0.05	0.10	0.15	0.20	0.25	0.30	0.35	0.40	0.45	0.50
$y(t)$	0	0.25	0.8	1.08	1.12	1.02	0.98	0.98	1.0	1.0	1.0

9.6 Phase margin for a second-order system is given by

$$\Phi M = \tan^{-1} \frac{2\zeta}{\sqrt{\sqrt{4\zeta^4 + 1} - 2\zeta^2}}$$

Write the approximate expression for ΦM for low values of ζ. Using the approximate expression, find the value of gain K such that the system shown in Fig. P9.6. has a phase margin of ϕ_m degrees.

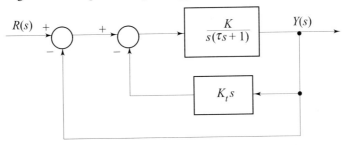

Fig. P9.6

9.7 The open-loop transfer function of a unity-feedback system is given by

$$G(s) = \frac{K}{s(\tau_1 s + 1)(\tau_2 s + 1)}$$

Derive an expression for gain K in terms of τ_1 and τ_2 and specified gain margin G_m.

9.8 Feedback system of Fig. P9.8 has open-loop transfer function

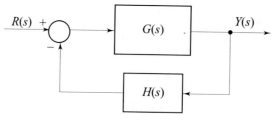

Fig. P9.8

$$G(s)H(s) = \frac{199}{s\,(s+1.71)(s+100)}$$

(a) Using Bode plots, determine the gain crossover frequency and phase margin.

(b) Using second-order correlations between time-domain and frequency-domain measures, estimate the peak overshoot and settling time of the transient response to step input.

9.9 The Bode magnitude plot of a system (known to have minimum-phase characteristics) is shown in Fig. P9.9. Deduce approximate Bode phase plot of the system.

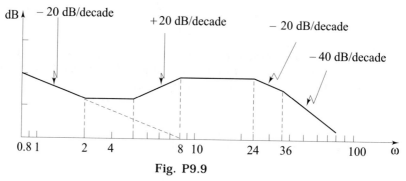

Fig. P9.9

Determine phase margin and gain margin of the system when operating in the closed-loop mode with unity feedback. From the frequency-domain performance measures, estimate the peak overshoot in transient response of the feedback system to step input.

9.10 Suppose that for the system of Fig. P9.8,

$$G(s)H(s) = \frac{4}{s(s+1)\,(s+2)}$$

(a) Using Bode plots of $G(j\omega)H(j\omega)$, determine the phase margin of the system.

(b) How should the gain be adjusted so that phase margin is 50°?

(c) Using second-order correlation between phase margin and damping ratio, estimate the peak overshoot in transient response of the system to step input.

9.11 Figure P9.11 shows block diagram of a control system. Determine the gain K such that the phase margin is 50°. What is the gain margin in this case?

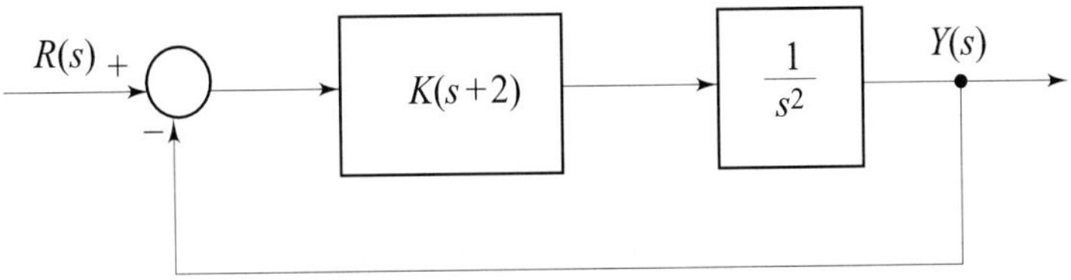

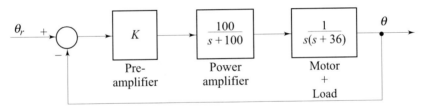

Fig. P9.11

9.12 A unity-feedback system has the following open-loop frequency response.

ω (rad/sec)	2	3	4	5	6	8	10
$\|G(j\omega)\|$	7.5	4.8	3.15	2.25	1.70	1.00	0.64
$\angle G(j\omega)$	$-118°$	$-130°$	$-140°$	$-150°$	$-157°$	$-170°$	$-180°$

(a) Using Bode plots, evaluate the gain margin and phase margin of the system.
(b) Determine the change in gain required so that the gain margin of the system is 20 dB.
(c) Determine the change in gain required so that the phase margin of the system is 60°.

9.13 For the position control system shown in Fig. P9.13, find the value of the preamplifier gain K to yield a 9.48% overshoot in the transient response for a step input. For the gain-compensated system, determine t_p: the time to peak overshoot. Use only frequency-domain techniques based on Bode plots.

$$\theta_r \xrightarrow{+} \bigotimes \xrightarrow{} \boxed{K} \xrightarrow{} \boxed{\dfrac{100}{s+100}} \xrightarrow{} \boxed{\dfrac{1}{s(s+36)}} \xrightarrow{} \theta$$

Pre-amplifier · Power amplifier · Motor + Load

Fig. P9.13

9.14 The open-loop transfer function of a unity-feedback system is given by

$$G(s) = \frac{5}{s(s+1)\left(s^2 + 2s + 5\right)}$$

(a) Using Bode plots, evaluate the gain margin, the phase margin, and the gain crossover frequency.
(b) How should the gain be adjusted in the system so that the gain margin becomes 10 dB?
(c) How should the gain be adjusted so that the gain crossover frequency becomes 1.27 rad/sec?
(d) How should the gain be adjusted so that the phase margin becomes 45°?

9.15 The open-loop transfer function of a unity-feedback system is

$$G(s) = \frac{K}{s(s+2)(s+10)}$$

Determine the value of K so that the system is stable with (i) a phase margin $\geq 45°$, and (ii) gain crossover frequency as large as possible.

9.16 (a) The open-loop system with transfer function

$$G(s) = \frac{5e^{-s}}{s(s+1)(s+10)}$$

is used in unity-feedback configuration. Estimate the peak overshoot in transient response to step input. Use frequency-domain techniques based on Bode plots.

(b) Repeat part (a) for the system without dead-time.

9.17 The open-loop system with transfer function

$$G(s) = \frac{31.5e^{-s\tau_D}}{(s+1)(30s+1)\left[\left(s^2/9\right)+(s/3)+1\right]}$$

is used in unity-feedback configuration.

(a) Find phase margin when $\tau_D = 0$.

(b) Find phase margin when $\tau_D = 1$. Adjust the gain to obtain phase margin of $30°$.

(c) Compare steady-state errors of the two cases with the same phase margin.

9.18 A unity-feedback system has open-loop transfer function

$$G(s) = \frac{50}{s(s+3)(s+6)}$$

(a) Using constant-M circles and polar plot of $G(j\omega)$, determine resonance peak M_r and bandwidth ω_b of the closed-loop frequency response.

(b) Using second-order correlations between time-domain and frequency-domain measures, estimate the peak overshoot and settling time of the transient response to step input.

9.19 A unity-feedback control system has the following open-loop frequency response.

ω (rad/sec)	2	3	4	5	6
$\|G(j\omega)\|$	2.7	1.7	0.97	0.63	0.4
$\angle G(j\omega)$	$-115°$	$-126°$	$-138°$	$-150°$	$-163°$

(a) Plot the open-loop frequency response in polar coordinates.

(b) Find the resonance peak M_r and the resonance frequency ω_r of the closed-loop frequency response.

(c) From the frequency-domain performance measures, estimate the peak overshoot and settling time of the transient response of the feedback system to step input.

9.20 The open-loop transfer function of a unity-feedback system is

$$G(s) = \frac{11.7}{s\,(1 + 0.05s)\,(1 + 0.1s)}$$

(a) Draw Bode plots of $G(j\omega)$, and therefrom determine gain crossover frequency, phase crossover frequency, gain margin and phase margin.

(b) Transfer the Bode data to a Nichols chart and determine the resonance peak, resonance frequency and bandwidth.

9.21 The open-loop frequency response of a unity-feedback system is given below.

ω (rad/sec)	1	2	3	4	5
$\|G(j\omega)\|$ (dB)	12.6	3.92	-2.22	-7	-11
$\angle G(j\omega)$ (degree)	$-127°$	$-152°$	$-168°$	$-179°$	$-188°$

Transfer the frequency-response data to a Nichols chart and therefrom determine the gain margin, phase margin, resonance peak, resonance frequency and bandwidth.

9.22 A unity-feedback system has open-loop transfer function

$$G(s) = \frac{4}{s\,(s + 1)\,(s + 2)}$$

(a) Using Bode plots of $G(j\omega)$, determine the phase margin of the system.

(b) How should the gain be adjusted so that phase margin is $50°$?

(c) Determine the bandwidth of the gain-compensated system.

The -3dB contour of the Nichols chart may be constructed using the following table.

Phase, degrees	0	-30	-60	-90	-120	-150	-180	-210
Magnitude, dB	7.66	6.8	4.18	0	-4.18	-6.8	-7.66	-6.8

(d) Using second-order correlations between frequency-domain measures (phase margin, bandwidth) and time-domain measures (damping ratio, undamped natural frequency), estimate the peak overshoot and settling time of the transient response of gain-compensated system to step input.

9.23 A unity-feedback system has open-loop transfer function

$$G(s) = \frac{54}{(1 + 0.1s)\left(s^2 + 8s + 25\right)}$$

(a) Using Nichols chart, determine M_r and ω_r.

(b) What value of ζ and ω_n should be used to approximate the transient behaviour of the system.

9.24 For the system shown in Fig. P9.24, the transfer function $G(s)$ is

$$G(s) = \frac{100}{(1 + 0.1s)\left(s^2 + 8s + 25\right)}$$

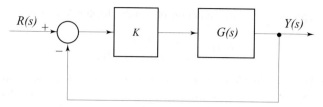

Fig. P9.24

(a) Using Nichols chart, determine the factor K by which the gain of the system should be changed so that the resulting system will have an M_r of 1.4.

(b) Find the bandwidth of the gain-compensated system.

9.25 The open-loop transfer function of a unity-feedback system is

$$G(s) = \frac{Ke^{-0.1s}}{s(1+0.1s)(1+s)}$$

By use of Bode plots and/or Nichols chart, determine the following.
(a) The value of K so that the gain margin of the system is 20 dB.
(b) The value of K so that the phase margin of the system is 60°.
(c) The value of K so that the resonance peak M_r of the system is 1 dB. What are the corresponding values of ω_r and ω_b?
(d) The value of K so that the bandwidth ω_b of the system is 1.5 rad/sec.

9.26 The following experimental results were obtained from an open-loop frequency response test of a unity-feedback control system.

ω	4	5	6	8	10
Gain	0.66	0.48	0.36	0.23	0.15
Phase angle	$-134°$	$-143°$	$-152°$	$-167°$	$-180°$

Plot the locus of the loop transfer function in Nichols coordinates (dB versus angle) and measure the gain and phase margins.

By what factor should the gain be increased so that the resonance peak in closed-loop frequency response is 1.4, and what would then be the gain and phase margins?

9.27 The open-loop frequency response of a unity-feedback system is given below.

ω (rad/sec)	0.8	1.0	1.2	1.4	1.6
$\text{Re}[KG(j\omega)]$	-3.5	-2.9	-2.3	-2.0	-1.2
$\text{Im}[KG(j\omega)]$	-4.4	-3.2	-1.9	-1.2	-0.5

Determine the change in gain K required to make the resonance peak $M_r = 1.4$. For this value of gain, determine the phase margin of the system. Using second-order correlation between resonance peak and damping ratio, determine the value of ζ that approximates the transient behaviour of the gain-compensated system. Repeat the calculation for ζ using second-order correlation between phase margin and damping ratio, and comment on the result.

9.28 A unity-feedback system has open-loop transfer function

$$G(s) = \frac{10}{s\,(1 + 0.02s)\,(1 + 0.2s)}$$

Find the peak sensitivity of the closed-loop transfer function with respect to G, and determine the frequency at which it occurs.

chapter 10

Compensator Design Using Bode Plots

10.1 | INTRODUCTION

The design of feedback control systems in industry is probably accomplished using frequency-domain methods more often than any other method. The popularity of these methods with practising engineers has remained high over the years despite the development of alternate design methods, such as root locus, pole placement by state feedback, and optimal control. The primary reason for the popularity of frequency-domain design is that the effects of disturbances, sensor noise, and plant uncertainties are relatively easy to visualize and assess in the frequency domain. Disturbance rejection can be specified in terms of low-frequency gain, and sensor-noise rejection can be specified in terms of high-frequency attenuation. For systems with known high-frequency resonances, a *band reject filter* can easily be designed in frequency domain to alleviate the effects of these uncertainties.

Another advantage of using frequency response is the ease with which experimental information can be used for design purposes. Raw measurements of the output magnitude and phase of a plant undergoing sinusoidal input are sufficient to design a suitable feedback control.

A disadvantage of frequency-response design is that it gives us information on closed-loop system's transient response indirectly, while the root locus design gives this information directly. The value of resonance peak M_r in closed-loop frequency response essentially describes the damping ratio ζ, and therefore is an indicator of relative stability of the system. For a specific value of M_r, ω_r—the frequency at which the resonance peak occurs, or ω_b—the bandwidth, determines the undamped natural frequency which in turn determines the speed of response of the system. The gain margin and phase margin, given by the open-loop frequency response, are indicators of relative stability. The objective of the frequency-response design is to reshape, by means of a compensator, the frequency-response plot of the basic system and achieve the performance specifications in terms of M_r, ω_r, ω_b, gain margin, phase margin, etc. We can obtain the transient-response parameters from the frequency-response parameters using the correlations developed in the previous chapter. These correlations are, however, approximate and give only qualitative information about the transient response.

The root-locus design provides very good indicators of the transient response of a system. However, we do need a relatively accurate model of the system to obtain these benefits from the root locus plots. In fact, various design techniques supplement each other, rather than one method excluding others; the control engineer must therefore be familiar with all the design methods.

This chapter is concerned with the changes that can be made in the frequency-response characteristics of a given system by various types of compensators. Design procedures to obtain improvement in the system performance are described.

10.2 | RESHAPING THE BODE PLOT

The performance of a closed-loop system may be described in terms of the following frequency-domain specifications:

1. Phase margin ΦM/resonance peak M_r—indicative of relative stability.
2. Gain crossover frequency ω_g/bandwidth ω_b/resonance frequency ω_r—indicative of speed of response.
3. Error constants K_p/K_v/K_a—indicative of steady-state error to step/ramp/parabolic input.

In case the transient-response specifications are given in time domain, we must first translate these into frequency domain to carry out frequency-domain compensation. This translation is carried out by using the explicit correlations between the two domains for the standard second-order system. These correlations are valid approximations for higher-order systems dominated by a pair of complex conjugate poles. The correlations, developed earlier in chapter 9, are reproduced below for convenience of use.

$$\Phi M = \tan^{-1} \frac{2\zeta}{\sqrt{\sqrt{4\zeta^4 + 1} - 2\zeta^2}} \cong 100\zeta \tag{10.1}$$

$$\omega_g = \omega_n \sqrt{\sqrt{4\zeta^4 + 1} - 2\zeta^2} \tag{10.2}$$

$$M_r = \frac{1}{2\zeta\sqrt{1 - \zeta^2}} \tag{10.3}$$

$$\omega_r = \omega_n \sqrt{1 - 2\zeta^2} \tag{10.4}$$

$$\omega_b = \omega_n \sqrt{\left[(1 - 2\zeta^2) + \sqrt{4\zeta^4 - 4\zeta^2 + 2} \right]} \tag{10.5}$$

After completing the compensation design in frequency domain, one must recheck the time response specifications by computing the exact time response of the compensated system. Based on the results of this check, it may sometimes be necessary to repeat the complete design process.

The frequency-domain compensation may be carried out using Nyquist plots, Bode plots, or Nichols chart. The advantages of the Bode plots are that they are easier to draw and modify. Further the gain adjustments are conveniently carried out and the error constants are always clearly in evidence. We shall discuss in this chapter mainly the design procedures using Bode plots. Nichols chart is used to check the values of M_r, ω_r, and ω_b wherever necessary.

The design procedure usually starts with the gain adjustments to meet the performance specifications. If the desired specifications are not met by gain adjustments alone, compensating devices must be used. These devices alter the shape of the frequency-domain plot to meet the performance specifications.

The compensating device may be inserted into the system either in cascade with the forward portion of the loop as shown in Fig. 10.1 or as part of minor feedback loop as shown in Fig. 10.2. We have seen in Chapter 7 that cascade compensation is usually concerned with the addition of lead, lag, or lag-lead active/passive network. The minor-loop feedback compensation is primarily concerned with the addition of rate feedback.

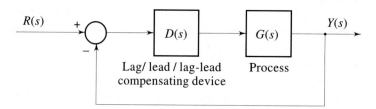

Fig. 10.1   *Illustration of cascade compensation*

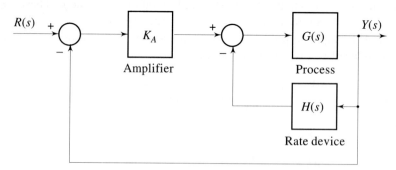

Fig. 10.2   *Illustration of minor-loop feedback compensation*

Cascade Compensation

The transfer function of a simple first-order compensator is

$$D(s) = K_c\left(\frac{s+z}{s+p}\right); \quad p, z > 0 \tag{10.6}$$

where K_c is a constant; $s = -z$, and $s = -p$ are, respectively, zero and pole of the compensator. Recall that a *lead compensator* has a single zero and a single pole with the pole lying to the left of the zero on negative real axis of the complex plane (refer Chapter 7). The first-order compensator given by Eqn. (10.6) is therefore a lead compensator if $p > z$. A *lag compensator* has a single zero and a single pole with the pole lying to the right of the zero on the negative real axis of the complex plane. The first-order compensator given by Eqn. (10.6) is therefore a lag compensator if $p < z$.

In the following, we study the frequency-domain characteristics of lead and lag compensators. Realization of these basic cascade compensators will be discussed in Chapter 11.

Lead Compensation for Reshaping the Bode Plot

The transfer function of a lead compensator may be expressed in the pole-zero form as

$$D(s) = K_c\left(\frac{s+z}{s+p}\right) = K_c\left(\frac{s+1/\tau}{s+1/\alpha\tau}\right); \quad \alpha = \frac{z}{p} < 1, \; \tau > 0, \; K_c > 0 \tag{10.7a}$$

Rearranging this transfer function in time-constant form, we obtain

$$D(s) = K_c\alpha\left(\frac{\tau s+1}{\alpha\tau s+1}\right) \tag{10.7b}$$

Note that the lead compensator has a zero-frequency gain of $K_c\alpha$. For the purpose of simplifying the design procedure, we normally associate the gain $K_c\alpha$ with the plant transfer function and design a compensator with unity zero-frequency gain:

$$D(s) = \frac{\tau s+1}{\alpha\tau s+1}; \; a < 1, \; \tau > 0 \tag{10.8}$$

based on the new plant transfer function. At the implementation stage, the total required gain is appropriately taken care of.

The sinusoidal transfer function of the lead compensator with unity zero-frequency gain is given by

$$D(j\omega) = \frac{1+j\omega\tau}{1+j\omega\alpha\tau}; \; a < 1, \; \tau > 0 \tag{10.9}$$

Figure 10.3 shows the Bode plot of $D(j\omega)$ for $\tau = 0.36$ and $\alpha = 1/6$. Note that the name 'lead' refers to the property that the compensator adds positive phase to the system over some appropriate frequency range.

To visualize the basic philosophy of reshaping the Bode plot by lead compensation, consider the unity-feedback control system of Fig. 10.4. The design parameters are K, τ, and α. The design problem may be viewed as follows.

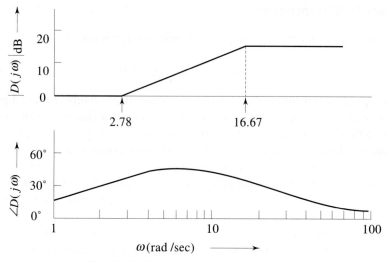

Fig. 10.3 *Bode plot of a lead compensator*

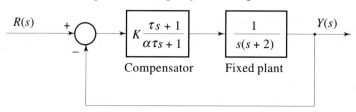

Fig. 10.4 *A unity-feedback control system*

Obtain the unity zero-frequency gain compensator,

$$D(s) = \frac{\tau s + 1}{\alpha \tau s + 1}; \ \alpha < 1$$

for the plant with adjustable gain,

$$G(s) = \frac{K}{s(s + 2)}$$

so that the closed-loop system meets the performance specifications. We will assume that the phase margin ΦM and the velocity error constant K_v are our major design specifications. Impose the requirements of (i) $K_v \geq 10$, and (ii) $\Phi M \geq 60°$.

First we examine whether or not adjustment of gain alone can achieve the design.

$$K_v = \lim_{s \to 0} sG(s) = \frac{K}{2}$$

In order to meet the K_v specification, we require that $K \geq 20$. We choose $K = 20$ and sketch the Bode plot of

$$G(s) = \frac{20}{s(s+2)} = \frac{10}{s(0.5s+1)}$$

in Fig. 10.5. We plot only the asymptotes. We see that the gain crossover frequency roughly equals 4.4 rad/sec, and the phase margin roughly equals 24°. This phase margin does not meet the specification. If K is the only parameter that can be adjusted to achieve the design, the only way to increase the phase margin is to decrease K. Decreasing K to 2.5 results in gain crossover frequency of 1.2 rad/sec and phase margin of 59° (refer Fig. 10.5). This, however, will violate the K_v specification. Thus for this problem, both the steady-state and transient performance requirements cannot be met by adjusting K alone.

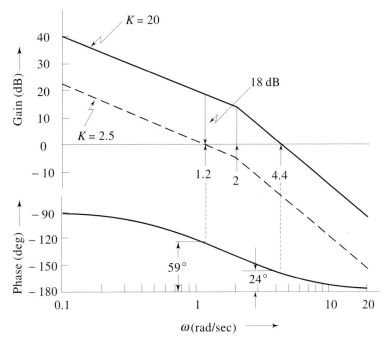

Fig. 10.5 *Reshaping of the Bode plot by gain adjustment*

The steady-state performance of the system is governed by low-frequency characteristics of the transfer function, and the transient performance of the system is governed by high-frequency characteristics. To simultaneously satisfy the transient and the steady-state performance requirements, the Bode plot of $G(j\omega)$ must be reshaped so that the high-frequency portion of the plot satisfies the phase margin requirement and the low-frequency portion satisfies the K_v requirement. When we inspect the Bode plot of Fig. 10.5 for $K = 20$, we see that we can meet the design objectives by adding more phase to the system in the positive direction in the high-frequency range around gain crossover frequency 4.4 rad/sec, while keeping the low-frequency region relatively unaltered. This reshaping of the Bode plot can be achieved using a cascade lead compensator. Figure 10.6 serves to illustrate the principle of lead compensation. This figure shows Bode plots of $G(j\omega) = 10/j\omega(j0.5\omega + 1)$ and $D(j\omega)G(j\omega)$ where $D(j\omega)$ is given by Fig. 10.3. The uncompensated system has a phase margin of 24° and gain crossover frequency of 4.4 rad/sec. Using lead compensator $D(j\omega)$, the phase angle plot is raised for higher frequencies. Since the positive phase in the lead compensator is accompanied by an additional gain at high frequencies, the gain crossover frequency increases when lead compensation is employed. From Fig. 10.6 we see that the compensated system has gain crossover frequency of 6.8 rad/sec, phase margin of 62° and $K_v = 10$.

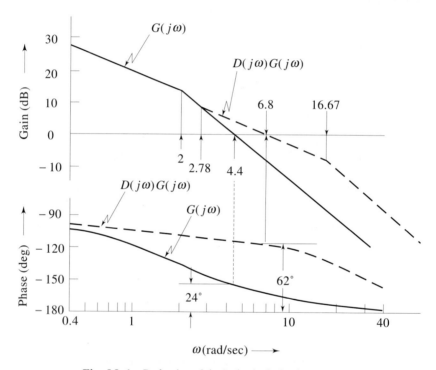

Fig. 10.6 *Reshaping of the Bode plot by lead compensation*

Lag Compensation for Reshaping the Bode Plot

The transfer function of a lag compensator may be expressed in the pole-zero form as

$$D(s) = K_c\left(\frac{s+z}{s+p}\right) = K_c\left(\frac{s+1/\tau}{s+1/\beta\tau}\right); \quad \beta = \frac{z}{p} > 1, \ \tau > 0, \ K_c > 0 \quad (10.10a)$$

Rearranging this transfer function in time-constant form, we obtain

$$D(s) = K_c\beta\left(\frac{\tau s + 1}{\beta\tau s + 1}\right) \quad\quad (10.10b)$$

Note that the lag compensator has a zero-frequency gain of $K_c\beta$. For the purpose of simplifying the design procedure, we normally associate the gain $K_c\beta$ with the plant transfer function and design a compensator with unity zero-frequency gain:

$$D(s) = \frac{\tau s + 1}{\beta \tau s + 1}; \ \beta > 1, \ \tau > 0 \qquad (10.11)$$

based on the new plant transfer function. At the implementation stage, the total required gain is appropriately taken care of.

The sinusoidal transfer function of the lag compensator with unity zero-frequency gain is given by

$$D(j\omega) = \frac{1 + j\omega\tau}{1 + j\omega\beta\tau}; \ \beta > 1, \ \tau > 0 \qquad (10.12)$$

Figure 10.7 shows the Bode plot of $D(j\omega)$ for $\tau = 11.1$ and $\beta = 10$. The compensator gets its name for a reason similar to the lead compensator; it introduces phase lag.

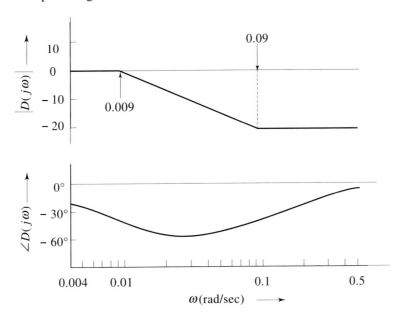

Fig. 10.7 *Bode plot of a lag compensator*

To visualize the basic philosophy of reshaping the Bode plot by lag compensation, reconsider the unity-feedback system of Fig. 10.4. The design problem now becomes:

Obtain the unity zero-frequency gain compensator

$$D(s) = \frac{\tau s + 1}{\beta \tau s + 1}; \ \beta > 1$$

for the plant with adjustable gain,

$$G(s) = \frac{K}{s(s+2)}$$

so that the closed-loop system meets the performance requirements of (i) $K_v \geq 10$, and (ii) $\Phi M \geq 60°$.

In Fig. 10.5, we have seen that $K = 2.5$ meets the phase margin requirement. Apparently, we cannot set K to 2.5, since the velocity error constant would only be 1.25, and the steady-state performance requirement would not be satisfied. When we inspect the Bode plot of Fig. 10.5 for $K = 2.5$, we see that we can meet both the phase margin and the K_v requirements by reshaping the low-frequency portion of the plot to obtain $K_v = 10$, while keeping the plot near gain crossover frequency relatively unaltered. This reshaping requires increasing the gain in the low-frequency region. This is equivalent to increasing the gain for the entire frequency range and then attenuating the magnitude curve in the high-frequency region. We can therefore meet the design objectives for the problem under consideration by starting with the plot of $G(j\omega)$ for $K = 20$, reducing the magnitude of $G(j\omega)$ in the high-frequency region in order to shift the gain crossover frequency to a lower value to meet the phase margin requirement, while keeping the low-frequency region of $G(j\omega)$ relatively unaltered. This reshaping of the Bode plot can be achieved using a lag compensator. Figure 10.8 serves to illustrate the principle of lag

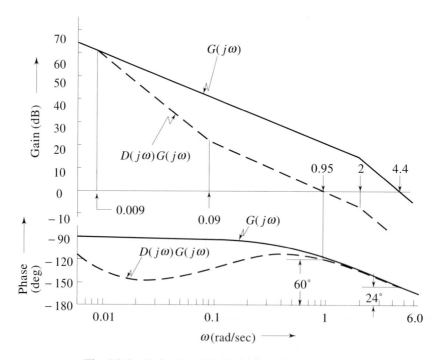

Fig. 10.8 *Reshaping of the Bode plot by lag compensation*

compensation. This figure shows Bode plots of $G(j\omega) = 10/j\omega$ ($j0.5\omega + 1$) and $D(j\omega)G(j\omega)$ where $D(j\omega)$ is given by Fig. 10.7. The uncompensated system has a phase margin of 24° and gain crossover frequency of 4.4 rad/sec. Using lag compensator $D(j\omega)$, the gain crossover frequency reduces to 0.95 rad/sec, and the requirements on both the ΦM and the K_v are met.

It should be noted that the attenuation characteristic of the lag compensator is accompanied by phase lag that tends to offset the increase in phase margin achieved due to reduction in gain crossover frequency. The loss in phase margin due to the phase lag characteristic of the compensator can be minimized by placing the frequency band over which the compensator has large phase lag much below the new gain crossover frequency. From Fig. 10.7 we see that the upper corner frequency of the lag compensator is 0.09 rad/sec, which is nearly one decade below the new gain crossover frequency 0.95 rad/sec.

The examples given are simply for the purpose of illustrating the principle of design of control systems in the frequency domain using compensators with phase-lead and phase-lag characteristics. In general, it may not be possible to satisfy all the design specifications by simply using a lead or a lag compensator. Situations often arise when both the low-frequency and the high-frequency portions of the Bode plot of the controlled process need to be reshaped by using a *lag-lead compensator*, which is basically a lag compensator and a lead compensator in cascade.

It should be pointed out that the design of linear control systems is not an exact science. A number of compensation schemes and parameter values may satisfy the given set of performance specifications. Some degree of trial-and-error and fine tuning is inevitable. Therefore, a CAD facility for frequency-domain analysis should be invaluable [176–179].

Minor-Loop Feedback Compensation

The decision to use a minor-loop feedback scheme (refer Section 7.9) is sometimes a matter of convenience, sometimes a matter of necessity, and for some problems it can be shown that minor-loop feedback scheme will do a better job. For example, use of velocity feedback for damping is very effective and consequently quite popular. Servomotors with builtin tachometers are shelf items; so the use of velocity feedback can be very convenient. When designing compensation for process controls, it becomes necessary to take derivative action on controlled variable and not on error variable in order to avoid the derivative 'kick' on set-point changes. Finally, in systems subjected to frequent load disturbances, feedback compensation may be preferred as it provides greater stiffness against load disturbances. Besides all these factors, the available components, and designer's experience and preferences influence the choice between a cascade and a feedback compensation scheme.

A basic point of view that is helpful in developing techniques for analysis and design is to realize that either method, cascade or feedback compensation, ultimately replaces the forward-path transfer function $G(s)$ with a new transfer function $G_{eq}(s)$. The design process then can be thought of as converting a $G(s)$ that is not suitable to $G_{eq}(s)$ that is more satisfactory for the proposed system.

Parameter values of minor-loop compensation scheme, that satisfy the given frequency-domain specifications, can easily be determined by trial-and-error using CAD facility.

Compensation for Plants with Dominant Complex Poles

Lead and lag compensators usually give successful design only if system dynamics is dominated by real poles. Since dominant complex poles (resonances) do arise in practice, we need compensation to deal with this (refer Section 7.10).

From the frequency-domain standpoint, the design of compensation for systems with dominant complex poles involves cascading a second-order controller with complex zeros that provides required attenuation at the resonance frequency. Physical realization of a simple second-order controller with complex zeros and its frequency-domain characteristics are given in Chapter 11 (Figs 11.11–11.13). The magnitude plot of the controller typically has a 'notch' at the resonance frequency. The phase plot is negative below and positive above the resonance frequency, while passing through zero degrees at the resonance frequency. The attenuation of the magnitude curve and the positive-phase characteristics can be used effectively to improve the stability of a linear system. Because of the 'notch' characteristic in the magnitude curve, the controller is also referred to in the industry as *notch filter* or *notch controller*. From the frequency-domain standpoint, the notch controller has advantages over the phase-lead and phase-lag controllers in certain design conditions, since the magnitude and phase characteristics do not affect the high and low-frequency properties of the system.

The frequency-domain design of the notch controller can easily to carried out using CAD facility.

An alternative approach to design of compensation for plants with dominant complex poles uses forward-path cancellation compensation with a compensator

$$D_1(s) = \frac{As^2 + Bs + 1}{Es^2 + Fs + 1}$$

where A and B are chosen to cancel the complex poles of the plant, and E and F are picked up to give real pole pair. A lead or lag compensator $D_2(s)$ can then be designed for all real-pole plant (Problem 10.16).

10.3 | CASCADE LEAD COMPENSATION

The primary function of a lead compensator is to reshape the frequency-domain plot by providing sufficient phase lead angle over some appropriate frequency range to offset the excessive phase lag associated with the plant.

Lead Compensator Frequency Response

Let us first look at the frequency-response characteristics of a lead compensator and derive some valuable relationships that will help us in the design process. The transfer function of a lead compensator with unity zero-frequency gain is of the form

$$D(s) = \frac{\tau s + 1}{\alpha \tau s + 1}; \ \alpha < 1, \ \tau > 0 \tag{10.13}$$

The sinusoidal transfer function

$$D(j\omega) = \frac{1 + j\omega\tau}{1 + j\omega\alpha\tau} \tag{10.14}$$

The Bode plot of $D(j\omega)$, shown in Fig. 10.9, has two corner frequencies at $\omega = 1/\tau$ and $\omega = 1/\alpha\tau$. The phase lead at any frequency ω is given by

$$\phi = \tan^{-1}\omega\tau - \tan^{-1}\omega\alpha t \tag{10.15}$$

Differentiating with respect to ω, we obtain

$$\frac{d\phi}{d\omega} = \frac{\tau}{1 + (\omega\tau)^2} - \frac{\alpha\tau}{1 + (\omega\alpha\tau)^2}$$

Setting $d\phi/d\omega$ equal to zero, we find that the frequency ω_m at which the maximum phase lead ϕ_m occurs, is

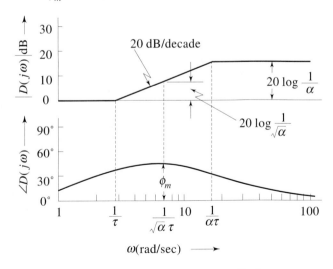

Fig. 10.9 *Frequency response characteristics of lead compensators*

$$\omega_m = \frac{1}{\tau\sqrt{\alpha}} = \sqrt{\frac{1}{\tau}\left(\frac{1}{\alpha\tau}\right)} \qquad (10.16)$$

As seen from Eqn. (10.16), ω_m is the geometric mean of the two corner frequencies of the compensator.

At $\omega = \omega_m$, the maximum phase lead ϕ_m is given by (refer Eqn. (10.15))

$$\phi_m = \tan^{-1}\frac{1}{\sqrt{\alpha}} - \tan^{-1}\sqrt{\alpha}$$

Making use of the relation

$$\tan(\theta_1 - \theta_2) = \frac{\tan\theta_1 - \tan\theta_2}{1 + \tan\theta_1\tan\theta_2},$$

we obtain

$$\tan\phi_m = \frac{1}{\sqrt{\alpha}} - \sqrt{\alpha} = \frac{1-\alpha}{\sqrt{\alpha}}$$

or

$$\sin\phi_m = \frac{1-\alpha}{1+\alpha} \qquad (10.17)$$

This gives α in terms of ϕ_m as

$$\alpha = \frac{1 - \sin\phi_m}{1 + \sin\phi_m} \qquad (10.18)$$

The magnitude of $D(j\omega)$ at $\omega = \omega_m$, the frequency of maximum phase lead, is

$$|D(j\omega_m)| = \frac{|1 + j\omega_m\tau|}{|1 + j\omega_m\alpha\tau|} = \frac{1}{\sqrt{\alpha}} \qquad (10.19)$$

An important consideration governing the choice of α is the inherent noise in control systems. The noise is generally of high frequency nature relative to the frequencies of control signals that appear in the loop. We see from Fig. 10.9 that in a lead compensator, the high-frequency noise signals are amplified by a factor $(1/\alpha) > 1$, while the low-frequency control signals undergo unit amplification (0 dB gain). This means that the lead compensator boosts the noise signal level relative to the control signal, and the lower the value of α, the higher this boost. Thus, if noise is a problem in a particular system, one must be careful about choosing a value of α for a lead compensator. It is recommended that the value of α should not be less than 0.07. A common choice is $\alpha = 0.1$. Limiting the value of α amounts to limiting an increase in gain crossover frequency of the system due to addition of a lead compensator.

We are now ready to enumerate a design procedure for lead compensation.

Design Procedure

To illustrate the lead compensator design procedure, we reconsider the unity-feedback system of Fig. 10.4 which was discussed earlier in Section 10.2. The design problem is to obtain the unity zero-frequency gain compensator

$$D(s) = \frac{\tau s + 1}{\alpha \tau s + 1}; \ \alpha < 1, \ \tau > 0$$

for the plant with adjustable gain,

$$G(s) = \frac{K}{s(s + 2)}$$

so that the closed-loop system has (i) $\Phi M \geq 60°$, and (ii) $K_v \geq 10$.

Since the lead compensator has negligible effect at low frequencies, we set the gain of the uncompensated system to a value that satisfies the steady-state error requirement. It is seen that $K = 20$ meets the K_v specification. The Bode plot of $G(j\omega)$ for $K = 20$ is shown in Fig. 10.10. From the plot we see that the uncompensated system has gain crossover frequency $\omega_g = 4.4$ rad/sec and

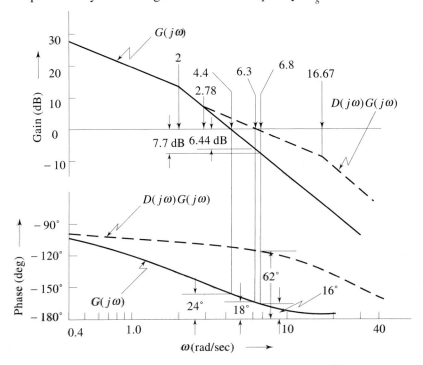

Fig. 10.10 *Cascade lead compensation*

phase margin = 24°. The required phase margin is 60°. If it were possible to simply add phase without affecting the magnitude, we would only need an additional 36° phase at the gain crossover frequency of $\omega_g = 4.4$. However, we know that insertion of lead compensator will maintain the same low-frequency gain but will affect the gain in high-frequency range; the gain crossover frequency will increase to a value $\omega_g' > \omega_g$. As the phase of most control processes decreases with increase in frequency, the phase of $G(j\omega)$ at ω_g' will be less than that at ω_g. Let this inevitable phase drop be equal to ε degrees. Therefore, to realize the specified phase margin, the lead compensator must provide a lead angle of $36° + \varepsilon$ at new gain crossover frequency ω_g'.

The value of ε depends upon ω_g', which in turn depends upon the parameters of the lead compensator. In the trial-and-error design procedure, we make a guess on the value of ε and design a lead compensator. If the characteristics of the feedback system are not acceptable after the design, then a redesign with a different value of ε may be necessary. The initial guess on ε depends upon the slope of the magnitude plot of the uncompensated system in the region of gain crossover frequency ω_g. For a slope of -40 dB/decade, as in the present example, $\varepsilon = 3°$ is a good guess. The guessed value may have to be as high as $15-20°$ for a slope of -60 dB/decade.

In order to provide a phase lead angle of $36° + \varepsilon$ at ω_g' with the largest value of parameter α (this is desirable from signal/noise considerations), the frequency ω_m at which maximum phase lead occurs, must be made to coincide with ω_g'. Thus we get

$$\omega_m = \omega_g'$$

$$\phi_m = 36° + \varepsilon = 36° + 3° = 39°$$

The α-parameter of the compensator can then be computed from Eqn. (10.18).

$$\alpha = \frac{1 - \sin 39°}{1 + \sin 39°} = \frac{0.37}{1.63} = 0.227$$

Since at ω_m, the compensator provides a gain of $20 \log\left(1/\sqrt{\alpha}\right)$ dB (see Fig. 10.9), the new gain crossover frequency $\omega_g' = \omega_m$ can be determined as that frequency at which the uncompensated system has a gain of $-20 \log\left(1/\sqrt{\alpha}\right)$ dB. We draw a horizontal line at $-20\log\left(1/\sqrt{\alpha}\right) = -6.44$ dB as shown in Fig. 10.10; its intersection with the magnitude plot yields the new gain crossover frequency as $\omega_g' = 6.3$. The corresponding phase margin of the uncompensated system is then read from the plot as $18°$. The phase margin of uncompensated system at $\omega_g = 4.4$ was determined as $24°$. Because $24° - 18° = 6°$, which is larger than $\varepsilon = 3°$, the choice of $\varepsilon = 3°$ is not satisfactory. As a next try, we choose $\varepsilon = 7°$. Then we have $\phi_m = 36° + 7° = 43°$ and the corresponding α-parameter computed from Eqn. (10.18) is 0.17. Intersection of the horizontal line at $-20 \log \left(1/\sqrt{0.17}\right)$ dB $= -7.7$ dB with the magnitude plot yields $\omega_g'' = 6.8$ rad/sec. The phase margin of the uncompensated system at ω_g'' is $16°$. The phase drop due to increase in gain crossover frequency is $24° - 16° = 8°$ which nearly equals ε. Thus the choice of $\varepsilon = 7°$ is satisfactory and the corresponding $\alpha = 0.17$ can be used in the design.

Now we let $\omega_m = \omega_g''$. Using Eqn. (10.16),

$$\omega_m = \frac{1}{\sqrt{\alpha\tau}} = 6.8$$

which implies

$$\tau = \frac{1}{\sqrt{0.17 \times 6.8}} = 0.36$$

Thus, the required lead compensator is

$$D(s) = \frac{\tau s + 1}{\alpha \tau s + 1} = \frac{0.36 s + 1}{0.06 s + 1}$$

The open-loop transfer function of the compensated system becomes

$$D(s)G(s) = \frac{10(0.36 s + 1)}{s(0.5 s + 1)(0.06 s + 1)}$$

The frequency-response characteristics of $D(s)G(s)$ in Fig. 10.10 can be seen to yield a phase margin of 62°. The compensated system, therefore, meets both the steady-state and the relative stability requirements.

The lead-compensation design procedure given above has been tailored to the set of two specifications: phase margin (measure of relative stability), and error constant (measure of steady-state performance). The resulting compensated system must be evaluated with respect to other performance requirements. It may become necessary to repeat the design procedure several times to meet all the specifications within acceptable bounds.

In many design problems, relative stability is adequately specified by the phase margin alone. However, if gain margin is also specified, we must check the gain margin from the Bode plot of $D(s)G(s)$ and repeat the design if the requirement is not satisfied. For the problem under consideration, specification on gain margin is not useful because the phase never crosses the $-180°$ line and the gain margin is always infinite.

Gain crossover frequency read from the Bode plot of $D(s)G(s)$ is an estimate of speed of response of the compensated system. We have seen that introduction of cascade lead compensator increases the gain crossover frequency and, consequently, the speed of response of the resulting system.

Bandwidth of the feedback system may be determined by transferring the data from Bode plot to Nichols chart. Since the gain crossover frequency is a rough measure of the bandwidth of a feedback system, we can say that the lead compensation increases the system bandwidth. It must of course be noted that too large an increase in system bandwidth so as to include some of the noise frequencies is undesirable and must be guarded against in lead compensation design.

A summary of the lead-compensation design procedure for designing compensator $D(s) = (\tau s + 1)/(\alpha \tau s + 1)$ for the plant $G(s)$ with adjustable gain K, is given below. This design procedure will apply to many cases; however, the designer should keep in mind that the specific procedure followed in any particular design may need to be tailored to its particular set of specifications.

1. Sketch the Bode plot of the uncompensated system with the gain K set according to the steady-state error requirement. Measure the gain crossover frequency ω_g, and phase margin of the uncompensated system.
2. Using the relation given below, determine the additional amount of phase lead needed at the new gain crossover frequency ω_g' to realize the specified phase margin.

Additional phase lead required

= specified phase margin – phase margin of the uncompensated system

at $\omega_g + \varepsilon$

ε is a margin of safety required by the fact that the gain crossover frequency will increase due to compensation. A guess is made on the value of ε depending upon the slope of the magnitude plot in the region of gain crossover frequency. For a slope of – 40 dB/decade, $\varepsilon = 5°$ is a good guess. The guessed value may have to be as high as 15–20° for a slope of – 60 dB/decade.

3. Set the maximum phase of the lead compensator,

ϕ_m = additional phase lead required,

and compute parameter α of the compensator using the following equation:

$$\alpha = \frac{1 - \sin\phi_m}{1 + \sin\phi_m}$$

4. Locate the frequency at which the uncompensated system has a gain of $-20\log\left(1/\sqrt{\alpha}\right)$ dB. Select this frequency as the new gain crossover frequency ω_g'. Measure the phase margin of the uncompensated system at ω_g'. If the difference in phase margins of $G(j\omega)$ at ω_g and ω_g' is less than ε, go to the next step. Otherwise, choose a larger ε in step 2 and repeat steps 3 and 4.

5. Set $\omega_m = \omega_g'$ and compute parameter τ of the compensator using the following equation:

$$\omega_m = \frac{1}{\sqrt{\alpha}\tau}$$

6. Sketch the frequency-response plots of compensated system in Bode and Nichols coordinate systems. Check any additional specifications on system performance, e.g., gain margin, bandwidth, etc. Redesign for another choice of ω_g', till all specifications are met. It may be noted that the additional specifications can only be met if they are consistent.

*Example 10.1*_____

Consider a type-1 unity-feedback system with an open-loop transfer function

$$G(s) = \frac{K}{s(s + 1)}$$

It is desired to have the velocity error constant $K_v = 10$. Furthermore we desire that the phase margin of the system be atleast 45°.

The first step in the design procedure is to sketch the Bode plot of the uncompensated system with the gain K set according to the steady-state error requirement. $K = 10$ meets the K_v specification. The Bode plot of

$$G(j\omega) = \frac{10}{j\omega(j\omega + 1)}$$

is drawn in Fig. 10.11. The gain crossover frequency of the uncompensated system is $\omega_g = 3.16$ rad/sec, and the phase margin is $18°$.

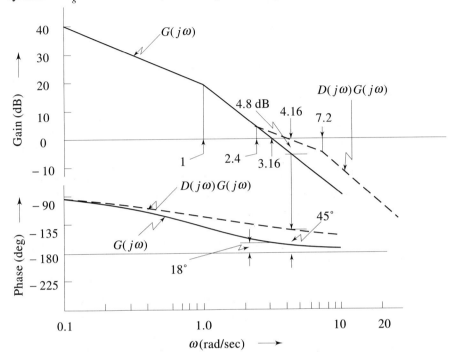

Fig. 10.11 *Bode plot for Example 10.1*

If cascade lead compensation scheme is employed to increase the phase margin to the specified value, the additional phase lead required at the new gain crossover frequency ω_g' is given by the following relation.
Additional phase lead required
= specified phase margin – phase margin of the uncompensated
$$\text{system at } \omega_g + \varepsilon$$
$$= 45° - 18° + 3° = 30°$$
Setting the maximum phase ϕ_m of the lead compensator equal to the additional required phase lead of $30°$, we obtain the α parameter of the lead compensator:

$$\alpha = \frac{1 - \sin\phi_m}{1 + \sin\phi_m} = \frac{1 - \sin 30°}{1 + \sin 30°} = 0.333$$

The uncompensated system has a gain of $-20\log\left(1/\sqrt{\alpha}\right) = -4.8$ dB at $\omega_g' = 4.16$ rad/sec. Setting ω_m, the frequency at which the lead compensator has maximum phase ϕ_m, equal to ω_g', we obtain the τ parameter of the lead compensator:

$$\omega_m = \frac{1}{\sqrt{\alpha\tau}} = \omega'_g = 4.16$$

This gives $\tau = 0.416$

Therefore the lead compensator

$$D(s) = \frac{\tau s + 1}{\alpha\tau s + 1} = \frac{0.416\,s + 1}{0.139\,s + 1}$$

and the compensated open-loop transfer function

$$D(s)G(s) = \frac{10(0.416\,s + 1)}{s(s+1)(0.139\,s + 1)}$$

The frequency-response plots of uncompensated and compensated systems in Bode and Nichols coordinate systems are shown in Figs. 10.11 and 10.12, respectively. From these plots we observe the following:

1. Phase margin is increased from 18° to 45°.
2. Resonance peak is reduced from 10 dB to 3 dB.
3. Bandwidth is increased from 5 rad/sec to 7 rad/sec.

Thus, in general, the effect of the lead compensation is to increase the margin of stability and speed of response (the design has been done here with the straightline asymptotic plots rather than the exact curves for the magnitude).

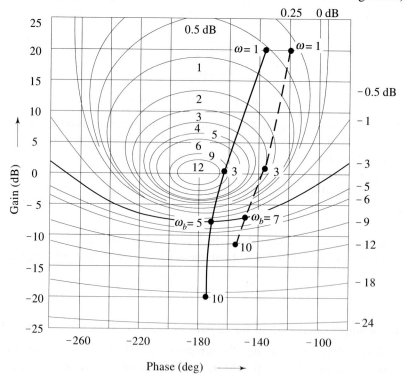

Fig. 10.12 *Nichols chart for Example 10.1*

Example   10.2

Let us consider a unity-feedback control system with open-loop transfer function

$$G(s) = 1/s^2$$

The uncompensated system is a type-2 system and at first appears to possess a satisfactory steady-state error for both step and ramp input signals. However, when uncompensated, the response of the system is an undamped oscillation, because the closed-loop transfer function

$$M(s) = \frac{Y(s)}{R(s)} = \frac{1}{s^2 + 1}$$

Gain adjustment alone cannot change the nature of transient response; the system, therefore, requires compensation. We assume that a transient response with $\zeta \geq 0.45$ is desired. By using Eqn. (10.1), the phase margin of the system is required to be approximately 45°. In order to provide a margin of safety, we will design a compensation scheme to realize a phase margin of 50°.

The phase margin of the uncompensated system is 0° because the double integrator results in a constant 180° phase lag. Therefore we must add a 50° phase-lead angle at the gain crossover frequency of the compensated system. This can be achieved by adding a cascade lead compensator

$$D(s) = \frac{\tau s + 1}{\alpha \tau s + 1}$$

Evaluating the value of parameter α (refer Eqn. (10.18)), we have

$$\alpha = \frac{1 - \sin 50°}{1 + \sin 50°} = 0.1325$$

The frequency at which the uncompensated system has a magnitude of $-20 \log\left(1/\sqrt{\alpha}\right) = -8.77\text{dB}$ is 1.7 rad/sec (refer Fig. 10.13). Selecting this frequency as the new gain crossover frequency ω_g', we set

$$\omega_m = \frac{1}{\sqrt{\alpha \tau}} = \omega_g' = 1.7$$

This gives $\tau = 1.61$

The open-loop transfer function of the lead-compensated system becomes

$$D(s)G(s) = \frac{(1.61 s + 1)}{s^2 (0.214\, s + 1)}$$

Figure 10.13 shows the Bode plot of $D(j\omega)G(j\omega)$. The phase margin requirement is satisfied. Steady-state error of the lead-compensated system for both step and ramp input signals will be zero.

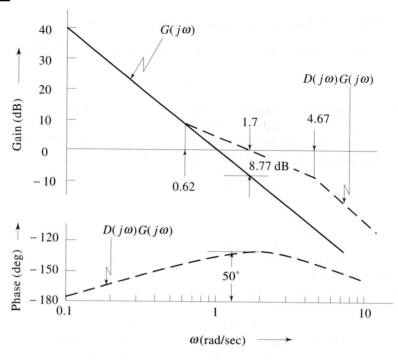

Fig. 10.13 *Bode plot for Example 10.2*

Example 10.3

Consider now a unity-feedback control system with open-loop transfer function

$$G(s) = \frac{K}{s^2(0.2\,s + 1)}$$

Assume that the system is required to be compensated to meet the following specifications:

1. Acceleration error constant $K_a = 10$.
2. Phase margin $\geq 35°$.

From the steady-state requirement, we set $K = 10$. The Bode plot of $G(j\omega)$ when $K = 10$ is shown in Fig. 10.14. As observed from this plot, the gain crossover frequency $\omega_g = 3.16$ rad/sec, and the phase margin is $-32°$, which means that the uncompensated system is unstable. In fact, the uncompensated system is unstable for all values of K.

The phase lead needed at the new gain crossover frequency ω_g' is obtained as follows:

Additional phase lead required

= specified phase margin − phase margin of the uncompensated
system at $\omega_g + \varepsilon$

= $35° + 32° + 15° = 82°$

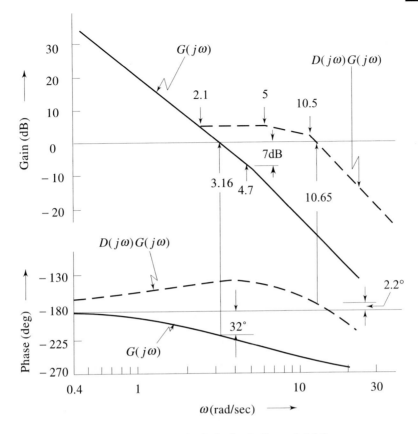

Fig. 10.14 *Bode plot for Example 10.3*

A large value of ε has been selected in this example because of rapid decrease of $\angle G(j\omega)$ in the region of gain crossover frequency ω_g.

Setting the maximun phase ϕ_m of the lead compensator equal to the additional required phase lead of 82°, we obtain the α parameter of the compensator as

$$\alpha = \frac{1 - \sin 82°}{1 + \sin 82°} = 0.005$$

Since the high-frequency noise signals are amplified by a factor of $1/\alpha$, the use of $\alpha = 0.005$ may not be acceptable.

Figure 10.15 shows the plot of ϕ_m *versus* $1/\alpha$, from which it is observed that to obtain phase leads more than 60° ($\alpha \cong 0.07$), $1/\alpha$ increases rather sharply, quite out of proportion to the increase in phase lead. Therefore, for phase leads greater than 60°, it is advisable to use two or more cascaded stages of lead compensator (described by Eqn. (10.13)) with moderate values of α rather than a single-stage lead compensator with too small a value of α.

For the design problem under consideration, using a single-stage lead compensator to give a phase lead of 82° is not advisable. We shall design a two-

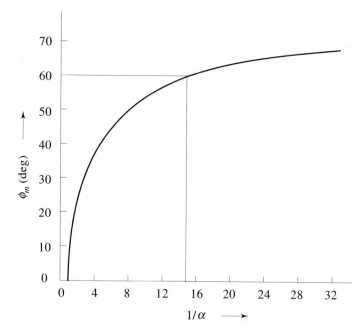

Fig. 10.15 ϕ_m *versus $1/\alpha$ for a lead compensator*

stage lead compensator (with an isolating amplifier), so that each stage has to provide maximum phase lead of $82/2 = 41°$. The α parameter of each stage is

$$\alpha = \frac{1 - \sin 41°}{1 + \sin 41°} \cong 0.2$$

From the Bode plot of uncompensated system, it is seen that the gain $-20 \log \left(1/\sqrt{\alpha}\right) = -7\,\mathrm{dB}$ occurs at $\omega_g' = 4.7$ rad/sec (Fig. 10.14). This should be the gain crossover frequency of the system with single-stage lead compensator. Choosing $\omega_m = \omega_g'$, we obtain the τ parameter of one stage:

$$\omega_m = \frac{1}{\sqrt{\alpha}\,\tau} = \omega_g' = 4.7$$

This gives $\tau = 0.474$

By adding another identical stage of lead compensator, the open-loop transfer function of the compensated system becomes

$$D(s)G(s) = \frac{10(0.474\,s + 1)^2}{s^2(0.2\,s + 1)(0.095\,s + 1)^2}$$

The Bode plot of $D(j\omega)G(j\omega)$ in shown in Fig. 10.14, from which it is found that the phase margin of the compensated system is 2.2°. This indicates that the system has become stable but the desired phase margin is not yet fully achieved. This is because of the excessive lag of the fixed part of the system at the new gain crossover frequency. If this phase margin is not acceptable, then the compensator should be redesigned with a higher value of ε.

Concluding Remarks

1. The steady-state error of a feedback system is not affected by introduction of a unity zero-frequency gain lead compensator.
2. The phase of the open-loop transfer function in the vicinity of the gain crossover frequency is increased by lead compensation. This improves the phase margin of the closed-loop system.
3. Lead compensation increases the gain crossover frequency and bandwidth; consequently, the speed of response of the closed-loop system is increased.
4. The value of the α parameter of the lead compensator should not be smaller than 0.07, nor should the maximum phase lead ϕ_m be more than 60°, because such choices will need an additional gain of excessive value. If more than 60° phase lead is required, two (or more) lead networks may be used in series with an isolating amplifier.
5. If the uncompensated system has low stability margin, the additional phase lead required to obtain a certain desired phase margin may be excessive. This requires a relatively small value of α parameter of the compensator, which, as a result, will give rise to large bandwidth for the compensated system. Such a compensator may not be acceptable because of considerations of noise transmission. As we shall see later in this chapter, a lead compensator cascaded with a lag compensator may realize a large phase margin while limiting the increase in bandwidth of the closed-loop system.
6. If the phase angle of the uncompensated system decreases rapidly near the gain crossover frequency, lead compensation becomes ineffective because the shift in the gain crossover frequency to the right makes it difficult to provide enough phase lead at the new gain crossover frequency.

   The following situations may give rise to rapidly changing phase curve near the gain crossover frequency:
   (a) The open-loop transfer function has two or more poles close to each other and are close to the gain crossover frequency.
   (b) The open-loop transfer function has one or more pairs of complex-conjugate poles near the gain crossover frequency.
7. The steady-state performance of a feedback system can be improved to any desired level by appropriately raising the open-loop gain K. Raising K results in amplification of signals at all frequencies. Introduction of a lead compensator provides additional gain for high-frequency signals, thereby boosting the noise signal level relative to the control signal. This imposes a limit on the improvement of steady-state error by raising gain K in a lead-compensated system.

10.4   CASCADE LAG COMPENSATION

The primary function of a lag compensator is to reshape the frequency-domain plot by providing sufficient attenuation over some appropriate frequency range. The phase lag characteristic is of no consequence in lag compensation.

Lag Compensator Frequency Response

The transfer function of a lag compensator with unity zero-frequency gain is of the form

$$D(s) = \frac{\tau s + 1}{\beta \tau s + 1} \quad \beta > 1, \ \tau > 0 \tag{10.20}$$

The sinusoidal transfer function

$$D(j\omega) = \frac{1 + j\omega\tau}{1 + j\omega\beta\tau} \tag{10.21}$$

The Bode plot of $D(j\omega)$, shown in Fig. 10.16, has two corner frequencies at $\omega = 1/\beta\tau$ and $\omega = 1/\tau$. The phase lag mainly occurs within and around the two corner frequencies. It must be recognized here that any phase lag at the gain crossover frequency of the compensated system is undesirable. To prevent detrimental effects of phase lag due to the lag compensator, the corner frequencies of the lag compensator must be located substantially lower than the gain crossover frequency of the compensated system.

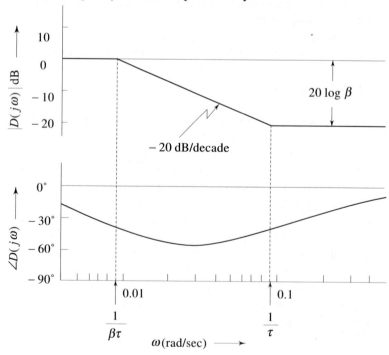

Fig. 10.16 *Frequency response characteristics of lag compensators*

Figure 10.16 also shows that in the high-frequency range, the lag compensator has an attenuation of 20 log β dB, which is the property that is utilized to give a system sufficient phase margin.

The addition of a lag compensator results in an improvement in the ratio of control signal to noise signal in the loop. The high-frequency noise signals are attenuated by a factor $\beta > 1$, while the low-frequency control signals undergo unit amplification (0 dB gain). The choice of β is usually restricted because a very large β will appreciably reduce the gain crossover frequency and consequently speed of response of the system. A typical choice of β is 10.

We are now ready to enumerate a design procedure for lag compensation.

Design Procedure

To illustrate the lag-compensator design procedure, we reconsider the unity-feedback system of Fig. 10.4 which was discussed earlier in Section 10.2. The design problem is to obtain the unity zero-frequency gain compensator

$$D(s) = \frac{\tau s + 1}{\beta \tau s + 1}; \beta > 1, \ \tau > 0$$

for the plant with adjustable gain,

$$G(s) = \frac{K}{s(s + 2)}$$

so that the closed-loop system has (i) $\Phi M \geq 60°$, and (ii) $K_v \geq 10$.

The steady-state error requirement sets $K = 20$. The Bode plot of $G(j\omega)$ for $K = 20$ is shown in Fig. 10.17. From this plot we see that the uncompensated

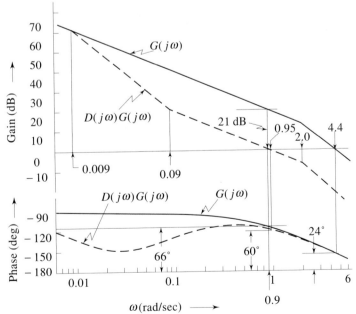

Fig. 10.17 *Cascade lag compensation*

system has gain crossover frequency $\omega_g = 4.4$ rad/sec and phase margin = 24°. The required phase margin of 60° can be achieved by lowering the gain crossover frequency to a region where $G(j\omega)$ has more favourable phase characteristics. This can be achieved by introducing a lag compensator.

First we search for a new gain crossover frequency that has a phase margin of 60° plus 6° (this will be explained later), or 66°. This can be found by drawing a horizontal line with 66° phase margin. Its intersection with the phase plot yields the new gain crossover frequency. It is read from Fig. 10.17 as $\omega_g' = 0.9$. We then draw a vertical line upward to the magnitude plot. We see that the magnitude at $\omega = \omega_g'$ is 21dB. To bring the magnitude curve down to 0 dB at ω_g', the lag compensator must provide 21 dB attenuation at ω_g'. From Fig. 10.16, we see that a lag compensator provides an attenuation of 20 log β for $\omega > 1/\tau$, the upper corner frequency. Therefore, a lag compensator with upper corner frequency $1/\tau < \omega_g'$, and the β parameter given by

$$20 \log \beta = 21 \tag{10.22}$$

will provide the required attenuation. From Eqn. (10.22), we get $\beta = 11$. We take $\beta = 10$ as the initial trial value.

Once the value of β is determined, it is necessary only to select the proper value of τ to complete the design. If the upper corner frequency $1/\tau$ is close to ω_g', the phase margin at ω_g' will be greatly reduced by the phase lag of the compensator. If the upper corner frequency is very far away from ω_g' (on the left-hand side), then the phase margin will be hardly affected by the phase lag of the compensator. Therefore, it seems that we should choose τ so that $1/\tau$ is as small as possible. However, this will cause a different problem. If $1/\tau$ is very small, then $D(s)$ has a pole very close to the origin. If we plot the root locus of $1 + D(s)G(s)$, then we can see that the closed-loop system will have a pole very close to the origin and the corresponding time-constant will be very large. Due to this additional closed-loop pole, the speed of response of the resulting system may become slow. The magnitude of the response term contributed by the additional pole will not be too large because of the presence of compensator zero close to the additional closed-loop pole.

Usually, as a general guideline, the upper corner frequency, $1/\tau$, of the compensator should be approximately one octave to one decade below the new gain crossover frequency ω_g'. Taking

$$\frac{1}{\tau} = \frac{\omega_g'}{10}$$

we obtain

$$\tau = \frac{10}{0.9} = 11.1$$

Thus, the required lag compensator is

$$D(s) = \frac{\tau s + 1}{\beta \tau s + 1} = \frac{11.1s + 1}{111s + 1}$$

This lag compensator has a phase lag of 5.7° at $\omega'_g = 0.9$. Thus the phase of $G(s)$ will be reduced by roughly 6° after introducing $D(s)$. This is the reason for adding 6° to the required phase margin in determining ω'_g.

The open-loop transfer function of the compensated system becomes

$$D(s)G(s) = \frac{10(11.1s + 1)}{s(0.5s + 1)(111s + 1)}$$

The frequency-response characteristics of $D(s)G(s)$ in Fig. 10.17 can be seen to yield a phase margin of 60°. The compensated system, therefore, meets both the steady-state and the relative stability requirements.

A summary of the lag-compensation design procedure for designing compensator $D(s) = (\tau s + 1)/(\beta \tau s + 1)$ for the plant $G(s)$ with adjustable gain K, is given below.

1. Sketch the Bode plot of the uncompensated system with the gain K set according to the steady-state error requirement. Measure the gain crossover frequency ω_g, and the phase margin of the uncompensated system.

2. Determine the frequency at which the phase angle of the uncompensated system is:

   $$- 180° + \text{specified phase margin} + \varepsilon$$

   Select this frequency as new gain crossover frequency ω'_g.

   ε is a margin of safety required by the fact that the compensator will contribute phase lag at ω'_g. A guess is made on the value of ε depending upon the value of ω'_g. If we can place upper corner frequency, $1/\tau$, of the compensator far below ω'_g, a small value of ε is taken. If ω'_g is fairly low, the upper corner frequency $1/\tau$ cannot be taken far to its left to avoid large time-constants. In such cases, phase lag contribution of the compensator at ω'_g will be considerable; a large value of ε is taken to compensate for this detrimental effect.

   Allow for ε from 5° to 15° for phase lag contribution of the compensator at ω'_g.

3. To bring the magnitude curve down to 0 dB at ω'_g, the lag compensator must provide the amount of attenuation equal to the value of gain of the uncompensated system at ω'_g. Measure the gain of the uncompensated system at ω'_g and equate it to 20 log β. Calculate therefrom, the parameter β of the compensator.

4. Choose the upper corner frequency of the compensator one octave to one decade below ω'_g. This gives the parameter τ of the compensator.

5. Calculate the phase lag of the compensator at ω'_g. If it is less than ε, go to the next step. Otherwise, choose a larger ε in step 2 and repeat steps 3 and 4.

6. Sketch the frequency-response plots of compensated system in Bode and Nichols coordinate system. Check any additional specification on system performance. Redesign for another choice of $1/\tau$ till all specifications are met. It may be noted that the additional specifications can only be met if they are consistent.

Example 10.4

Consider a type-1 unity-feedback system with an open-loop transfer function

$$G(s) = \frac{K}{s(s + 1)}$$

It is desired to have the velocity error constant $K_v = 10$. Furthermore, we desire that the phase margin of the system be atleast 45°. Earlier in Example 10.1, a lead compensator was used to realize these specifications. We now attempt a lag compensation scheme.

The first step in the design procedure is to sketch the Bode plot of the uncompensated system with the gain K set according to the steady-state error requirement. $K = 10$ meets the K_v specification. The Bode plot of

$$G(j\omega) = \frac{10}{j\omega(j\omega + 1)}$$

is drawn in Fig. 10.18. The gain crossover frequency of the uncompensated system is $\omega_g = 3.16$ rad/sec, and the phase margin is 18°.

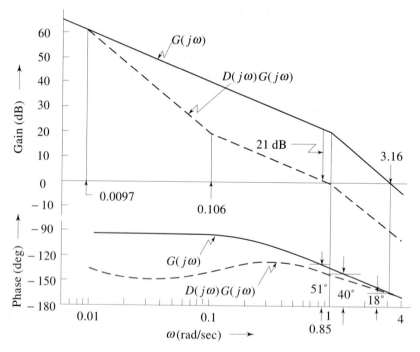

Fig. 10.18 *Bode plot for Example 10.4*

To realize a phase margin of 45°, the gain crossover frequency should be moved to ω_g' where the phase angle of the uncompensated system is:

$$- 180° + \text{specified phase margin} + \varepsilon = - 180° + 45° + 6° = - 129°$$

From Fig. 10.18, we find that $\omega_g' = 0.85$. The gain of the uncompensated system at ω_g' is 21 dB. Therefore, to bring the magnitude curve down to 0dB at

ω'_g, the lag compensator must provide an attenuation of 21 dB. The β parameter of the lag compensator can now be calculated.

$$20 \log \beta = 21$$

This gives $\qquad \beta = 11$

Placing the upper corner frequency of the compensator three octaves below ω'_g, we obtain,

$$\frac{1}{\tau} = \frac{\omega'_g}{(2)^3} = \frac{0.85}{8}$$

which gives $\qquad \tau = 9.4$

The lower corner frequency is $\dfrac{1}{\beta\tau} = \dfrac{1}{103.4}$. Therefore the lag compensator

$D(s) = \dfrac{9.4s + 1}{103.4s + 1}$, and the compensated open-loop transfer function

$$D(s)G(s) = \frac{10(9.4\,s + 1)}{s(s + 1)(103.4\,s + 1)}$$

The Bode plot of the compensated system is shown in Fig. 10.18. It is seen that the phase margin of the compensated system is approximately 40°. If this phase margin is not acceptable, then the compensator should be redesigned with a higher value of ε.

In Fig. 10.19, the log-magnitude *versus* phase shift plots of original and compensated systems are plotted on the Nichols chart. These plots are obtained by

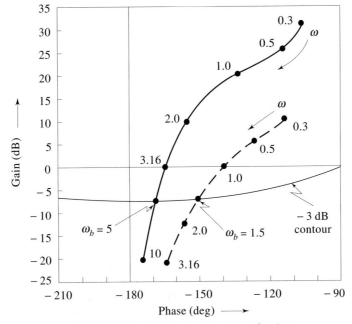

Fig. 10.19 *Nichols chart for Example 10.4*

taking the values of magnitude and phase shift directly from the Bode plot of Fig. 10.18. From the Nichols chart, the bandwidth without compensation is found to be 5 rad/sec. The bandwidth after compensation is found to be 1.5 rad/sec, which means that the time response is slower with lag compensation.

*Example 10.5*_____

A unity-feedback control system has open-loop transfer function

$$G(s) = \frac{K}{s(0.1s + 1)(0.2s + 1)}$$

The system is required to satisfy the following performance specifications:
1. $K_v = 30$.
2. Phase margin $\geq 40°$.
3. Bandwidth $\omega_b = 5$ rad/sec.

From the steady-state requirement, we set $K = 30$. The Bode plot of $G(j\omega)$, when $K = 30$ is shown in Fig. 10.20, from which it is found that the gain crossover frequency is $\omega_g = 11$ rad/sec, and phase margin is $-23°$. The uncompensated system is therefore unstable.

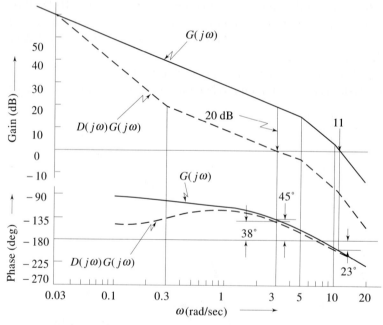

Fig. 10.20 *Bode plot for Example 10.5*

The rapid decrease in phase of $G(j\omega)$ near the gain crossover frequency ω_g implies that lead compensation will not be effective for this system. The phase lead required at the gain crossover frequency of the compensated system will be too large. Although we can realize this phase lead by two stages of lead compensator described by Eqn. (10.13), the resulting system will have a large bandwidth and will be sensitive to noise. Let us try lag compensation for the given system.

To realize a phase margin of 40°, the gain crossover frequency should be moved to ω'_g where the phase angle of the uncompensated system is:

$$-180° + \text{specified phase margin} + \varepsilon = -180° + 40° + 5° = -135°.$$

From Fig. 10.20, we find that $\omega'_g = 3$ rad/sec. The gain of the uncompensated system at ω'_g is 20 dB. Therefore, to bring the magnitude curve down to 0 dB at ω'_g, the lag compensator must provide an attenuation of 20 dB. The β parameter of the lag compensator can now be calculated.

$$20 \log \beta = 20$$

This gives $\beta = 10$. Placing the upper corner frequency of the compensator one decade below ω'_g, we obtain

$$\frac{1}{\tau} = \frac{\omega'_g}{10} = \frac{3}{10}$$

which gives

$$\tau = 3.33$$

The lower corner frequency is $\dfrac{1}{\beta\tau} = \dfrac{1}{33.3}$. Therefore the lag compensator

$D(s) = \dfrac{3.33\,s + 1}{33.3\,s + 1}$, and the compensated open-loop transfer function

$$D(s)G(s) = \frac{30(3.33\,s + 1)}{s(0.1\,s + 1)(0.2\,s + 1)(33.3\,s + 1)}$$

The Bode plot of the compensated system is shown in Fig. 10.20. It is seen that the phase margin of the compensated system is approximately 38°.

In Fig. 10.21, the magnitude *versus* phase shift plot of the compensated system is drawn on the Nichols chart. It is seen that the bandwidth of the compensated system is 4.65 rad/sec. Since this value lies in the acceptable range, our design is complete.

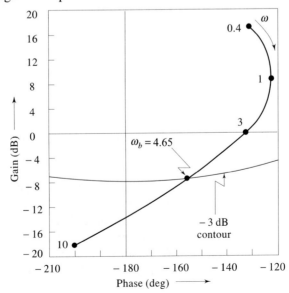

Fig. 10.21 *Nichols chart for Example 10.5*

Concluding Remarks

1. We utilize the attenuation characteristic of the lag compensator rather than its phase lag characteristic. The phase lag characteristic has no use for compensation purposes.
2. The steady-state error of a feedback system is not affected by introduction of a unity zero-frequency gain lag compensator.
3. Lag compensation reduces high-frequency gain for better phase margin.
4. Lag compensation decreases the gain crossover frequency and bandwidth; consequently, the closed-loop system becomes more sluggish.
5. Attenuation of high-frequency gain by lag compensation improves signal/noise ratio of the system.
6. If the uncompensated system has low stability margin, the high-frequency attenuation required to obtain a certain desired phase margin may be excessive. Such a compensator may not be acceptable because of consideration of speed of response. As we shall see later in this chapter, a lag compensator cascaded with a lead compensator may realize a large phase margin while limiting the loss of speed of response of the closed-loop system.
7. Steady-state performance of a feedback system can be improved to any desired level by appropriately raising the open-loop gain K. Raising K results in amplification of signals at all frequencies. Introduction of a lag compensator results in attenuation of the high-frequency signals, thereby reducing the noise signal level relative to the control signal. This feature of lag compensation allows a large value of K for significant improvement in steady-state performance of the feedback system.

10.5 | CASCADE LAG-LEAD COMPENSATION

In general, there are two situations in which the compensation is required. In the first case, the system is absolutely unstable and the compensation is required to stabilize it, as well as to achieve a specified performance. In the second case, the system is stable but the compensation is required to obtain the desired performance. The systems which are type-2 or higher, are usually absolutely unstable. The phase curve of such systems may lie entirely below the $-180°$ line in the Bode coordinate system. Under such situations, lag compensation cannot provide stability and required performance; lead compensation is the only answer.

In type-1 and type-0 systems, stable operation is always possible if the gain is sufficiently reduced. For such systems, phase margin can be improved to any level for a specified error constant by either lead or lag compensation. Decision on the choice of lead or lag compensation is based on performance requirements other than the relative stability and steady-state error. The lead compensation results in increased bandwidth and, consequently, faster speed of response. For higher-order systems and for systems with large specified error constants, large lead angles are required for compensation, resulting in excessively large bandwidth which is undesirable from noise transmission point of view. For such systems, lag compensation is preferred.

The lag compensation, on the other hand, reduces system bandwidth and, consequently, slows down the speed of response. For large specified error constant and moderately large desired bandwidth, it may not be possible to meet the specifications through either lead or lag compensation. Under such circumstances, we can use a lag-lead compensator.

Lag-Lead Compensator Frequency Response

As the name implies, the lag-lead compensator is basically just a lag compensator and a lead compensator in cascade. The transfer function of a lag-lead compensator with unity zero-frequency gain is of the form

$$D(s) = \underbrace{\left(\frac{\tau_1 s + 1}{\beta \tau_1 s + 1} \right)}_{\text{Lag section}} \underbrace{\left(\frac{\tau_2 s + 1}{\alpha \tau_2 s + 1} \right)}_{\text{Lead section}}; \ \beta > 1, \ \alpha < 1; \ \tau_1, \ \tau_2 > 0 \qquad (10.23)$$

The lead section alters the frequency-domain plot by adding phase lead angle and increasing the phase margin at the gain crossover frequency. The lag section provides attenuation near and above the gain crossover frequency and thereby allows an increase of gain in the low-frequency range to improve the steady-state performance.

The transfer function in Eqn. (10.23) can be realized by a single network if $\alpha = 1/\beta$ (discussed later in Chapter 11). Thus, for applications where independent choice of α and β is not essential, a lag-lead compensator of the form

$$D(s) = \frac{(\tau_1 s + 1)(\tau_2 s + 1)}{(\beta \tau_1 s + 1)\left(\frac{1}{\beta} \tau_2 s + 1 \right)}; \ \beta > 1 \ \tau_1, \ \tau_2 > 0 \qquad (10.24)$$

may be used. The sinusoidal transfer function of this compensator is

$$D(j\omega) = \frac{(1 + j\omega \tau_1)(1 + j\omega \tau_2)}{(1 + j\omega \beta \tau_1)(1 + j\omega \tau_2 / \beta)} \qquad (10.25)$$

Figure 10.22 shows the Bode plot of $D(j\omega)$. Note that the phase shift is a function of input frequency; phase angle varies from lag to lead as the frequency is increased. Thus, phase lag and phase lead occur in different frequency bands.

Design Procedure

To start with design, we check the phase margin and bandwidth of the uncompensated system with gain adjusted to meet the error constant specification. If the bandwidth is smaller than the specified value, lead compensation may be tried. However, if the bandwidth is larger than

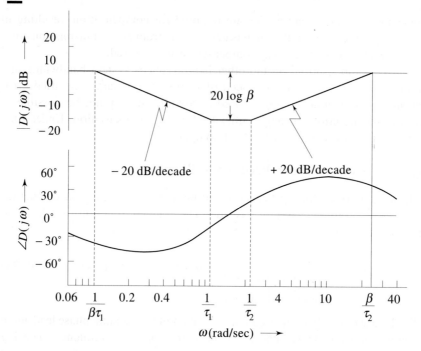

Fig. 10.22 *Frequency response characteristics of lag-lead compensators*

acceptable, lead compensation would not be desirable; so we try lag compensation provided that the uncompensated system is not absolutely unstable. If the lag compensator design results in too low a bandwidth, the need for a lag-lead compensation is indicated.

Let us demonstrate the design procedure with an example.

Example 10.6

Consider the unity-feedback system whose open-loop transfer function is

$$G(s) = \frac{K}{s(0.1\,s + 1)(0.2\,s + 1)}$$

The system is to be compensated to meet the following specifications:
1. Velocity error constant $K_v = 30$.
2. Phase margin $\Phi M \geq 50°$.
3. Bandwidth $\omega_b = 12$ rad/sec.

It easily follows that $K = 30$ satisfies the specification on K_v. The Bode plot of $G(j\omega)$ with $K = 30$ is shown in Fig. 10.23 from which it is found that the uncompensated system has a gain crossover frequency $\omega_g = 11$ rad/sec and phase margin $= -23°$.

If lag compensation is employed for this system, the bandwidth will decrease sufficiently so as to fall short of the specified value of 12 rad/sec, result-

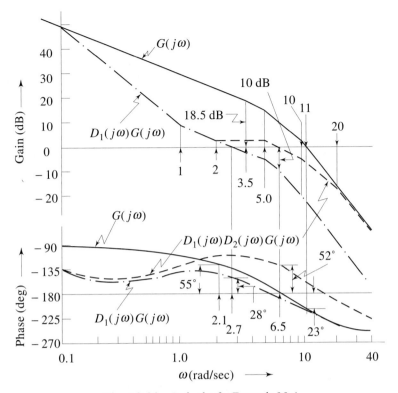

Fig. 10.23 *Bode plot for Example 10.6*

ing in a sluggish system. This fact can be verified by designing a lag compensator. If on the other hand, lead compensation is attempted, the bandwidth of the resulting system will be much higher than the specified value; the closed-loop system will be sensitive to noise which is undesirable.

This fact can also be verified by designing a lead compensation scheme. Owing to the large phase lead needed at the gain crossover frequency of the compensated system, two stages of lead compensator described by Eqn. (10.13), may be used.

Let us design a lag-lead compensator to overcome the difficulties mentioned above. Since a full lag compensator would reduce the system bandwidth excessively, the lag section of the lag-lead compensator must be designed to provide partial compensation only. The lag section design therefore proceeds by making a choice of the new gain crossover frequency which must be higher than the crossover frequency if the system were fully lag compensated. Full lag compensation demands that the gain crossover frequency should be shifted to a point where the phase angle of the uncompensated system is:

$-180° +$ specified phase margin $+ \varepsilon = -180° + 50° + 5° = -125°$

From Fig. 10.23, we find that this requirement is met at 2.1 rad/sec. For the design of lag section of lag-lead compensator, the selected gain crossover frequency should be higher than 2.1. The choice is made as $\omega_g' = 3.5$ rad/sec to start with.

From Fig. 10.23, we find that the gain of the uncompensated system at ω_g' is 18.5 dB. Therefore to bring the magnitude curve down to 0 dB at ω_g', the lag section must provide an attenuation of 18.5 dB. This gives the β parameter of the lag section as

$$20 \log \beta = 18.5$$

or $$\beta = 8.41, \text{ say } 10$$

Let us now place the upper corner frequency of the lag section at 1 rad/sec. This gives the lag-section transfer function

$$D_1(s) = \frac{\tau_1 s + 1}{\beta \tau_1 s + 1} = \frac{s + 1}{10 s + 1}$$

Bode plot of lag-section compensated system is shown in Fig. 10.23; the phase margin is 28°.

We now proceed to design the lead section. We choose $\alpha = 1/\beta = 0.1$. The maximum lead provided by the lead section is therefore (refer Eqn. (10.17)).

$$\phi_m = \sin^{-1}\left(\frac{1 - \alpha}{1 + \alpha}\right) = 55°$$

The lag-compensated system has a gain of $-20 \log (1/\sqrt{\alpha}) = -10$ dB at $\omega_g'' = 6.5$ rad/sec. Setting ω_m, the frequency at which the lead section has maximum phase ϕ_m, equal to ω_g'', we obtain

$$\omega_m = \frac{1}{\sqrt{\alpha} \tau_2} = \omega_g'' = 6.5$$

This gives $$\tau_2 = 0.5$$

The transfer function of the lead section, therefore, is

$$D_2(s) = \frac{\tau_2 s + 1}{\alpha \tau_2 s + 1} = \frac{0.5 s + 1}{0.05 s + 1}$$

Combining the transfer functions of the lead and lag sections, we obtain

$$D(s) = \frac{(s + 1)(0.5 s + 1)}{(10 s + 1)(0.05 s + 1)}$$

The open-loop transfer function of the lag-lead compensated system is

$$D(s)G(s) = \frac{30(s + 1)(0.5 s + 1)}{s(0 \cdot 1 s + 1)(0.2 s + 1)(10 s + 1)(0.05 s + 1)}$$

The Bode plot of $D(j\omega)G(j\omega)$ is shown in Fig. 10.23. The phase margin is found to be 52°.

The magnitude *versus* phase angle curve of the lag-lead compensated system is drawn on the Nichols chart in Fig. 10.24, from which the bandwidth of the system is found to be 9.6 rad/sec.

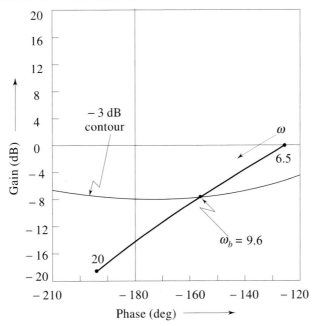

Fig. 10.24   *Nichols chart for Example 10.6*

The design, therefore, does not meet the specifications laid down. We must, therefore, redesign by adjusting the initial choice of β and τ_1.

10.6 | ROBUST CONTROL SYSTEMS

Most control system designs are based on a model of the plant; however, it is inevitable that the model we use is only an approximation of true system dynamics. The difference between the model on which the design is based and the true system used in the actual control is referred to generally as *model uncertainty*. If the design performs well for substantial variations in the dynamics of the plant from the design values, we say the design is *robust*.

Model uncertainties may be described by some parameters $\{\theta_1, \ldots, \theta_N\}$ that vary over ranges. This leads to a family $\mathscr{P}$ of perturbed plant models $\hat{P}$, where each member of the family may represent the nominal plant P, but it remains unknown which member does.

$$\mathscr{P} = \{\hat{P}(\theta_1, \ldots, \theta_N) | L_1 \le \theta_1 \le U_1, \ldots, L_N \le \theta_N \le U_N\}$$

Parameterized plant perturbation set can be used to model different types of plant variations:

(i) Errors in Parameter Identification

In a model developed from physical principles, θ_i may represent physical parameters such as lengths, masses, heat conduction coefficients, etc.; the bounds L_i and U_i are then the minimum and maximum values that could be expected to occur.

(ii) Externally Induced Changes

The system to be controlled may be well modelled as a linear time-invariant system that depends upon external operating conditions which change slowly compared to the system dynamics. Examples include temperature-induced variations in a process, effects of varying aerodynamic pressure on aircraft dynamics, load changes on a robot manipulator, etc.

(iii) Component Drift or Aging

Some plant pertubations cannot be described by the variation of a small number of real parameters. The family $\mathscr{P}$ of perturbed plant models may in such cases be described by a set of frequency responses; for every frequency, the frequency response of the nominal plant lies in the set.

Frequency-dependent plant perturbation set may be used to model the following types of plant variations:

(i) Errors in Plant Identification Experiments

Experimentally obtained plant transfer functions may inaccurately model the system to be controlled because of measurement errors.

(ii) Model Simplification

Fast dynamic modes and some nonlinear phenomena are usually neglected to simplify the model.

(iii) High Frequency Dynamics

A model of the system to be controlled may become less accurate at high frequencies because of unknown and unmodelled dynamics. For example, the elasticity of structural members that comprise many mechanical systems, such as aircraft and space structures, are characterized by resonance or bending modes which often are ignored in nominal system representation because their exact frequencies are difficult to determine.

With respect to the knowledge available about the causes of uncertainties, unstructured and structured uncertainties are distinguished. In case of *unstructured uncertainties*, it is only known that there are some discrepancies between the model and the real plant, and probably, how large the resulting deviations in input-output behaviour may be. Contrary to this, *structured uncertainties* are known insofar as that particular points within the plant are made responsible for the uncertainties. The deviation of the model from the original plant can be described by some specified tolerance of certain elements.

All control system examples in Chapter 3 contained physical parameters; the plant models were functions of these parameters. A parameter θ_i may be thought to lie between two limits with a specific midrange value used for the nominal plant (very often these bounds are really educated guesses). This gives us a simple model for structured uncertainties.

A simple model for unstructured uncertainties is obtained as follows:

A nominal plant P has the transfer function $G(j\omega)$, and the family $\mathscr{P}$ consists of perturbed plants $\hat{P}$ with transfer functions of the form

$$\hat{G}(j\omega) = (1 + \Delta W(j\omega)) \, G(j\omega)$$

Here $W(j\omega)$ is a fixed *stable* transfer function—the weighting function, and Δ is a scaling factor on the weighting function; $0 \leq \Delta \leq 1.0$.

The idea behind this uncertainty model is that ΔW is the normalized plant pertubation away from 1:

$$\frac{\hat{G}}{G} - 1 = \Delta W$$

Therefore

$$\left| \frac{\hat{G}(j\omega)}{G(j\omega)} - 1 \right| \leq |W(j\omega)| \; \forall \; \omega$$

This inequality describes a disk in the complex plane. At each frequency, the point $\hat{G}/G$ lies in the disk with centre 1 and radius $|W|$.

How does one get the weighting function W in practice? Let us take an example. Suppose that the plant is stable and its transfer function is arrived at by means of frequency-response measurements. The experiment is repeated, say, n times. Let A_{ik} and ϕ_{ik}, respectively, represent the amplitude and phase measurements for frequency ω_i and experiment k. Based on these data, we select nominal magnitude-phase pairs (A_i, ϕ_i) for each frequency ω_i and fit a nominal transfer function $G(j\omega)$ to these pairs. We then fit a weighting function $W(j\omega)$ so that

$$\left| \frac{A_{ik} e^{j\phi_{ik}}}{A_i e^{j\phi_i}} - 1 \right| \leq |W(j\omega)| \; \forall \; \omega \text{ and } \forall k$$

Linear control methods (presented in this book) presuppose that sufficiently accurate model of the process to be controlled is available; meeting the specifications on steady-state accuracy, transient-response characteristics, and disturbance rejection is the primary aim of design. In these design methods, the treatment of model uncertainties appears only qualitatively through sensitivity analysis (note that sensitivity analysis deals with (infinitesimally) small perturbations in plant model and does not refer to the amount of perturbations). Robustness properties are investigated by simulation of the closed-loop system; no effort is made to give quantitative bounds on the permissible model uncertainties.

As opposed to linear control in general, robust control methods consider the robustness requirement as the primary aim of design. Quantitatively specified relations between the amount of uncertainties and the properties to be attained dominate the design process. Quantitative robustness has regard to the amount of model uncertainties and concerns the question whether the properties of interest are preserved under completely specified class of plant perturbations. *A robust controller is a linear time-invariant controller that satisfies the design requirements in connection with all plants of a given set $\mathscr{P}$.*

Adaptive control theory provides another approach to the design of uncertain systems. Adaptation is the ability of a system to (asymptotically) behave in a prescribed way even if the parameter vector is altered. As opposed to sensitivity and robustness, adaptation assumes that the system is able to actively respond to changes of the parameter vector by changing its own properties. The controller compensates for the effects of a parameter deviation within the plant. This leads to nonlinear control laws.

The above discussion explains the difference between robust control and insensitive, and adaptive control respectively. In the robustness approach, the design specifications must be fulfilled with certainty for the whole set $\mathscr{P}$ of possible plant dynamics. It contrasts the sensitivity approach in which the effects of differentially small parameter variations on the quality of the closed-loop system is considered. The difference to adaptive control becomes obvious by the restriction to linear time-invariant control laws.

Presentation of robust-control design methods is beyond the scope of this book. A survey of known principles and methods could be useful. Even this intention turns out to be very intricate, because in the current state of research there is no general theoretical background of all the methods. On the contrary, the known approaches are highly divergent. They presuppose different assumptions concerning the form of model uncertainties and the information available to describe them. They deal with different design requirements and aspects of robustness, and—last but not the least—they are based on different systems theoretical concepts. We, therefore, direct the reader to references [135–144] on the subject.

In fact, all the feedback-control designs given in this book are robust to a certain degree, because feedback reduces sensitivity of the closed-loop system with respect to uncertainties in the plant transfer function on which the design is based. Deviations in the transfer function over a certain range are taken care of by performance specifications: gain margin and phase margin. Large gain/phase margins give the feedback system the capability to perform satisfactorily under uncertainties in the plant. Uncertainty models are not used implicitly in the design process; however the robustness properties may be checked by simulation for a given uncertainty model. Re-entering the design cycle may become necessary if the robustness requirements are not satisfied.

In fact building of uncertainty model itself is subject to uncertainties; the industry, by and large, continue to rely on frequency-domain design methods with gain margin and phase margin specifications for robustness.

*Example 10.7*_____

The block diagram representation of an electromechanical servomechanism is sketched in Fig. 10.25. We assume that the servo has a mission requiring accurate positioning of the load.

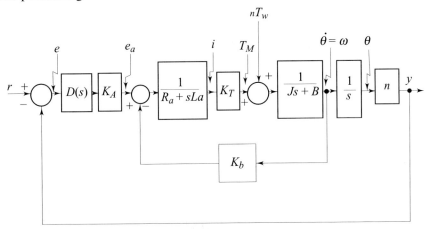

Fig. 10.25 *Block diagram of an electromechanical servomechanism*

The power amplifier is characterized by the parameter K_A. The possibility of loading problem is evident. We assume here that the amplifier has been tested and qualified for its $e(t)$ to $e_a(t)$ performance when it is loaded by the motor. In a position control application, the amplifier must be capable of supplying both positive and negative $e_a(t)$. This requirement demands careful electronic design to achieve a smooth transition between the positive and negative regions of operation without a *deadzone* [180] in the static e_a–e relation in the transition region. The amplifier must also be capable of supplying the instantaneous power required to move the load. The current output of the amplifier is usually limited (*saturation* [180]) in order to prevent damage to amplifier and motor.

R_a is the resistance of the circuit in which armature current circulates which includes the resistance of armature winding plus the contact resistance of the brushes wiping the sliding contacts. We assume R_a to be constant when the motor is turning (speed $\omega(t)$). L_a denotes the self-inductance of the armature circuit. $K_b\omega(t)$ is the back emf.

Let us now look at the mechanical side of the motor. Torque developed on the shaft is $K_T i(t)$. It drives the load through a single-mesh gear train of ratio n (We will neglect *backlash* [180] introduced by the gear train). The load torque is assumed to be contributed by a rotating mass with moment of inertia J_L

about the load axis. In addition to the load, the controlled plant will be subjected to unwanted disturbance T_w on the output shaft.

J_M is the moment of inertia of the motor shaft and all massive parts that are rigidly attached to it, excluding those of the load. B_M is viscous-damping coefficient resulting in velocity-dependent torque $B_M \omega(t)$ on the shaft. Note that the velocity-dependent torque is, in general, a nonlinear function of $\omega(t)$. Its approximation by a linear function is based on the following justification: servomotors which are machines intended for position control applications, are designed with low-friction bearings and with attention given to minimizing brush friction (*Coulomb friction* [180]). In many operating environments, the servomotor is subject to vibration, which also has the effect of reducing static friction (*stiction* [180]). In the moderate speed range, the torque-speed curve is nearly a straight line for most servomotors.

The numerical values of the physical parameters of the system are:

$$K_A = 4.1545 \text{ V/V}$$
$$R_a = 3.086 \text{ }\Omega$$
$$L_a = 0.01 \text{ H}$$
$$K_T = 0.0952 \text{ N-m/amp}$$
$$K_b = 0.0952 \text{ V/(rad/sec)}$$
$$J_M = 2.119 \times 10^{-5} \text{ kg-m}^2$$
$$B_M = B = 47.5 \times 10^{-5} \text{ N-m/(rad/sec)}$$
$$n = 1/10.5$$
$$J_L = 227.272 \times 10^{-5} \text{ kg-m}^2$$

Moment of inertia reflected on the motor shaft

$$J = J_M + n^2 J_L = 4.1804 \times 10^{-5}$$

The moments of inertia of the gears are negligible. The position transducer on the output shaft has a scale factor of 1 V/rad.

Figure 10.26 shows the reduced block diagram model of the servo-mechanism (numerical values have been rounded slightly). This linear model produces analytical results that predict experimental behaviour to a satisfactory degree. Nevertheless in some cases, the presence of *nonlinearities* and *uncertainties* in model parameters yields experimental dynamic behaviour that is substantially different from that predicted by analytical results based on linear model of the form shown in Fig. 10.25.

The nonlinearities we have neglected, are:
- Deadzone in amplifier characteristics
- Saturation in amplifier output
- Backlash in gears
- Static and Coulomb friction

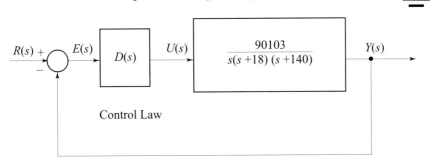

Fig. 10.26 *Reduced block diagram obtained from Fig. 10.25 with $T_w = 0$*

Simulation of the system model that includes one or more nonlinearities listed above may be used to predict experimental dynamic behaviour. Refer [180] for details.

In the model of Fig. 10.25, we have assumed that the physical parameters of the amplifier, motor, gears and load are known and fixed. In many practical cases, the numerical values of these parameters are not precisely known; also after the system is placed in service, the parameters may change owing to wear or variations in the operating environment. The system is *robust* if its performance remains satisfactory in the event of such uncertainties and changes. Considerable research effort is being expanded on the difficult problem of analytically representing the effect of uncertainties and changes in physical parameters in order to quantitatively assess the robustness of a control system.

In some cases, only a single parameter changes over a known range of values, and in such a case it is possible to calculate the robustness of the system with respect to the changes in the parameter if these changes occur slowly. As an example, consider the servomechanism of Fig. 10.25. One of the parameters is the moment of inertia of the load J_L, which is 227.272×10^{-5} kg-m^2. We consider this to be uncertain parameter whose actual value is $J_L = 227.272\Delta \times 10^{-5}$ kg-m^2.

$\Delta = 1$ corresponds to the nominal plant model. For the nominal plant, the lag compensator

$$D(s) = \frac{17.05(s + 5)}{s + 0.2}$$

gives satisfactory solution. The system will be required to follow a family of tracking functions. The steady-state error will be nearly zero if the tracking function is less severe and can be approximated by step functions ('staircase' function). If the tracking function is more severe, then we may approximate it by ramp functions. For a ramp of unit slope, the steady-state error is $1/K_v$. The proposed design gives velocity error constant $K_v = 1519.63$. The large value of K_v results in acceptable tracking performance. Still more severe tracking functions may be approximated by parabolic functions. If such tracking functions

are expected, the proposed design will not yield acceptable tracking performance. A redesign becomes necessary. Usually the tracking functions for position servos can be approximated by step/ramp functions. We, therefore, accept
this design from tracking performance point of view.

The load shaft in our application is subjected to extraneous torque T_w due to
environmental conditions. This torque will displace the load shaft from its
desired position. The proposed design reduces this error to acceptable level for
quite large values of disturbance torque.

From Fig. 10.25, we get (numerical values have been rounded slightly)

$$\frac{Y(s)}{T_w(s)}\bigg|_{R(s)=0} = \frac{217(s+309)}{s(s+140)(s+180)+90105\,D(s)}$$

The steady-state error resulting from a step disturbance torque $T_w(s) = A/s$,
can be determined by inspection of the equation:

$$y_{ss} = \frac{0.74 \times A}{D(0)} = 1.75 \times 10^{-3} \times A$$

The proposed design gives the following transient performance (obtained
from Nichols chart):

    Phase margin = 46.9°
    Gain margin = 13.9 dB
    Bandwidth   = 98.5 rad/sec

Variations in performance parameters for Δ ranging from 0.25 to 3 are given
below (obtained from Nichols chart).

    Phase margin : 57.5° to 31.5°
    Gain margin : 14.3 dB to 13.2 dB
    Bandwidth   : 113 rad/sec to 74.5 rad/sec.

This gives a useful analysis of the robustness of the system with respect to
a wide variation in the design value of J_L.

Review Examples

Review Example 10.1 _____

Consider a unity-feedback type-1 system with open-loop transfer function

$$G(s) = \frac{K}{s(s+1)(s+4)}$$

The system is to be compensated to meet the following specifications:
    Velocity error constant $K_v = 5$
    Peak overshoot $M_p = 25\%$
    Settling time $t_s = 10$ sec

Peak overshoot of 25% and settling time of 10 sec imply $\zeta = 0.4$ and $\omega_n = 1$ for the closed-loop dominant poles (refer Eqns (6.14) and (6.19)). Equation (10.1) yields a 40° phase margin for a damping ratio of 0.4, and from Eqn. (10.5), with $\zeta = 0.4$ and $\omega_n = 1$, a closed-loop bandwidth of $\omega_b = 1.375$ rad/sec is required.

In order to meet the specification of $K_v = 5$, K must be set at 20, yielding

$$G(s) = \frac{5}{s(s+1)(0.25s+1)}$$

Bode plot of uncompensated system for $K = 20$ is shown in Fig. 10.27, from which it is found that the gain crossover frequency $\omega_g = 2.2$ rad/sec and the phase margin is $-4°$. If lead compensation is employed for this system, the gain crossover frequency of the compensated system will be more than 2.2 rad/sec and the bandwidth will exceed the specified value, making the system sensitive to noise. We, therefore, try lag compensation.

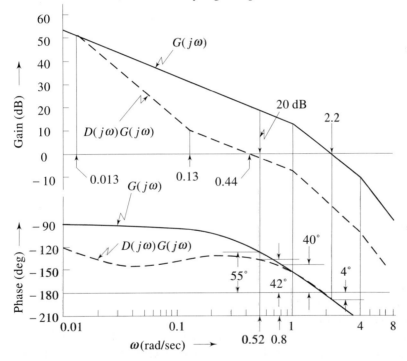

Fig. 10.27 *Bode plot for Review Example 10.1*

It is seen from the Bode plot that neglecting the phase-lag contribution of the compensator, the specified phase margin of 40° is obtained if the gain cross over frequency is 0.8 rad/sec. Since this is fairly low, the upper corner frequency of the lag compensator cannot be taken far to its left to avoid large time-constants. This indicates that phase-lag contribution of the compensator at the new gain crossover frequency ω_g will be considerable and may be guessed at $\varepsilon = 15°$. The uncompensated system must, therefore, have a phase angle of

$$-180° + \text{specified phase margin} + \varepsilon = -180° + 40° + 15° = -125°$$

at ω_g', which is found to be 0.52 rad/sec.

The gain of the uncompensated system at ω_g' is 20 dB. Therefore, to bring the magnitude curve down to 0 dB at ω_g', the lag compensator must provide an attenuation of 20 dB. The β parameter of the lag compensator can now be calculated.

$$20 \log \beta = 20$$

This gives $\beta = 10$

Placing the upper corner frequency of the compensator two octaves below ω_g', we have

$$\frac{1}{\tau} = \frac{\omega_g'}{(2)^2} = 0.13 \text{ rad/sec} = \frac{1}{7.7}$$

The lower corner frequency of the compensator is then fixed at

$$\frac{1}{\beta\tau} = 0.013 \text{ rad/sec} = \frac{1}{77}$$

The transfer function of the lag compensator is then

$$D(s) = \frac{7.7\,s + 1}{77\,s + 1}$$

Phase-lag introduced by the lag compensator at ω_g' is

$$\tan^{-1}(7.7\,\omega_g') - \tan^{-1}(77\,\omega_g') = 76° - 88° = -12°$$

Therefore, the safety margin of $\varepsilon = 15°$ is justified.

The open-loop transfer function of the compensated system becomes

$$D(s)G(s) = \frac{5(7.7\,s + 1)}{s(s + 1)(0.25\,s + 1)(77\,s + 1)}$$

The Bode plot of $D(j\omega)G(j\omega)$ is shown in Fig. 10.27, from where the phase margin of the compensated system is found to be 42°.

In Fig. 10.28, the magnitude *versus* phase shift plot of the compensated system is drawn on the Nichols chart. It is seen that the bandwidth of the compensated system is 1 rad/sec. We must redesign by adjusting the initial choice of β and τ if an improvement in bandwidth is required.

Review Example 10.2

Consider the system shown in Fig. 10.29. Design a suitable compensator such that the closed-loop system will have the phase margin of 50°, the gain margin of not less than 10 dB and the gain crossover frequency of 1 rad/sec.

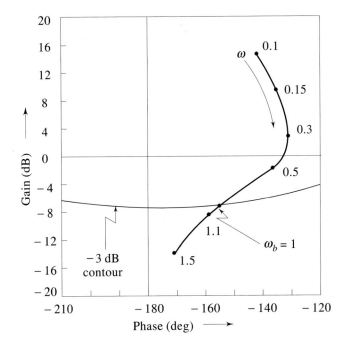

Fig. 10.28 *Nichols chart for Review Example 10.1*

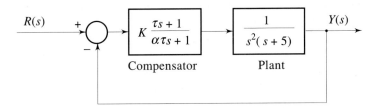

Fig. 10.29 *Feedback system for Review Example 10.2*

Solution

The design problem may be reformulated as follows:
Design the unity zero-frequency gain compensator

$$D(s) = \frac{\tau s + 1}{\alpha \tau s + 1}$$

for the plant with adjustable gain,

$$G(s) = \frac{K}{s^2 (s + 5)}$$

so that the closed-loop system meets the performance specifications.

Since the uncompensated system is unstable for all values of K, lag compensation scheme cannot be used. We attempt lead compensation. The gain crossover frequency of the compensated system is given to be $\omega_g = 1$ rad/sec. At ω_g, the phase angle of $G(j\omega)$ is $-191.3°$.

To realize a phase margin of 50°, the lead compensator must provide a phase lead of $50° + 11.3° = 61.3°$ at $\omega_g = 1$. Setting the maximum phase lead ϕ_m of the compensator equal to 61.3°, we obtain the α parameter of the lead compensator:

$$\alpha = \frac{1 - \sin\phi_m}{1 + \sin\phi_m} = 0.065$$

Noting that the maximum phase lead angle ϕ_m occurs at the geometric mean of the two corner frequencies of the compensator, we have

$$\omega_m = \sqrt{\frac{1}{\tau}\left(\frac{1}{\alpha\tau}\right)} = 1 = \frac{1}{\sqrt{\alpha}\,\tau}$$

This gives $\tau = 3.9$

Therefore the lead compensator $D(s) = \dfrac{\tau s + 1}{\alpha\tau s + 1} = \dfrac{3.9\,s + 1}{0.25\,s + 1}$

and the compensated open-loop transfer function

$$D(s)G(s) = \frac{K(3.9\,s + 1)}{s^2(s + 5)(0.25\,s + 1)} = \frac{0.2K(3.9\,s + 1)}{s^2(0.2\,s + 1)(0.25\,s + 1)}$$

A Bode plot of $D(j\omega)G(j\omega)/(0.2K)$ is shown in Fig. 10.30. From this plot we find that the magnitude curve must be lowered by 11.7 dB so that the magnitude equals 0 dB at $\omega = 1$ rad/sec. Hence

20 log $(0.2\,K) = -11.7$ or $0.2\,K = 0.26$

which yields $K = 1.3$

The Bode plot of compensated system (Fig. 10.30) shows that the system has phase margin of 50° and gain margin of $4.3 + 11.7 = 16$ dB. Hence the design specifications are satisfied.

Review Example 10.3 _____

The transfer function of the controlled process of a unity-feedback system is

$$G(s) = \frac{1.57e^{-0.785s}}{s(s + 1)}$$

The Bode plot of $G(j\omega)$ is shown in Fig. 10.31. From the plot we see that the phase margin of the uncompensated system is approximately $-5°$ and gain crossover frequency is $\omega_g = 1.1$ rad/sec.

Let us assume that the design specification calls for a phase margin of at least 45°. From Fig. 10.31 we see that the phase of $G(j\omega)$ decreases rapidly

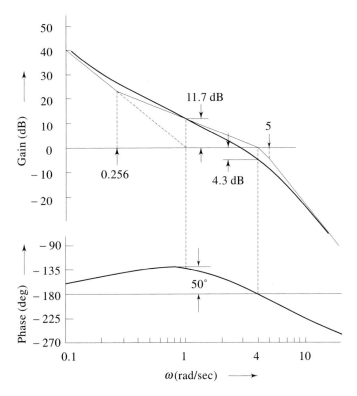

Fig. 10.30 *Bode plot for Review Example 10.2*

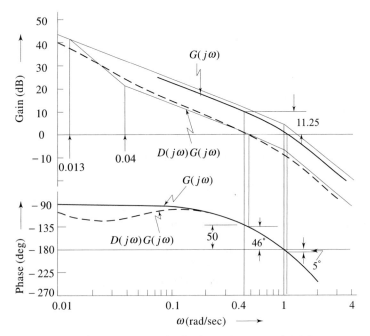

Fig. 10.31 *Bode plot for Review Example 10.3*

beyond 1 rad/sec. Therefore a cascade lead compensator may not be effective in improving the phase margin of the system. A cascade lag compensator seems to be more appropriate for this system.

To realize a phase margin of 45°, the gain crossover frequency should be moved to ω_g' where the phase angle of the uncompensated system is:

$$- 180° + \text{specified phase margin} + \varepsilon = - 180° + 45° + 5° = -130°$$

From Fig. 10.31 we find that $\omega_g' = 0.4$ rad/sec. The gain of the uncompensated system at ω_g' is 11.25 dB. Therefore, to bring the magnitude curve down to 0 dB at ω_g', the lag compensator must provide an attenuation of 11.25 dB. The β parameter of the lag compensator can now be calculated.

$$20 \log \beta = 11.25$$

This gives $\qquad \beta = 3.65$

Placing the upper corner frequency of the compensator one decade below ω_g', yields

$$\frac{1}{\tau} = \frac{\omega_g'}{10} = 0.04 \quad \text{or} \quad \tau = 25$$

Therefore the lag compensator $D(s) = \dfrac{25 s + 1}{91.25 s + 1}$

The Bode plot of the compensated system transfer function $D(j\omega)G(j\omega)$ is sketched in Fig. 10.31. The phase margin of the compensated system is as per specifications.

Review Questions

10.1 Discuss the compensation characteristics of cascade lag and lead compensators using Bode plots. Show that
   (i) lead compensation is suitable for systems having unsatisfactory transient response, and it provides a limited improvement in steady-state performance; and
   (ii) lag compensation is suitable for systems with satisfactory transient response but unsatisfactory steady-state response.
10.2 (a) The lead compensator transfer function is given by

$$D(s) = \frac{\tau s + 1}{\alpha \tau s + 1}; \; \alpha < 1, \tau > 0$$

   What does the name 'lead' refer to? (Help: p641, p697)
   (b) The lag compensator transfer function is given by

$$D(s) = \frac{\tau s + 1}{\beta \tau s + 1}; \; \beta > 1, \tau > 0$$

   What does the name 'lag' refer to? (Help: p 645, p 700)
10.3 (a) On what factors does the choice of bandwidth depend?(Help: pp594-595)

(b) A type-1 system can be designed to obtain desired K_v and phase margin by either lead or lag compensation. How? On what factors does the decision on choice of lead or lag compensation depend?(Help: pp670-671)

10.4 (a) Phase lag compensator has phase lag at all frequencies, still it can be used to improve phase margin. Explain. (Help: p647)

(b) When is it advisable to use two or more cascaded stages of lead compensator? (Help: p455, p462, pp659-660)

(c) Lag-lead compensation is useful for systems with high demands on speed of response, margin of stability, and steady-state accuracy. Justify the statement. (Help: p468, pp670-671)

10.5 Show that from the filtering standpoint,

(i) the lead empensator is a highpass filter; (Help: p697)

(ii) the lag compensator is a low pass filter; and (Help: p700)

(iii) the lag-lead compensator is a band reject filter. (Help: p702)

Problems

10.1 The open-loop transfer function of a control system is

$$G(s)H(s) = \frac{1}{s(1 + 0.5s)(1 + 2s)}$$

(a) Determine approximate values of gain margin and phase margin.

(b) If a lag compensator with transfer function $D(s) = K_c(1 + 3s)/(1 + 5s)$ is inserted in the forward path, find the value of K_c to keep the gain margin unchanged.

10.2 The open-loop transfer function of a control system is

$$G(s)H(s) = \frac{10}{s(1 + 0.5s)(1 + 0.1s)}$$

(a) Draw the Bode plot and determine gain crossover frequency, and phase and gain margins.

(b) A lead compensator with transfer function
$D(s) = (1 + 0.23s)/(1 + 0.023s)$ is now inserted in the forward path. Determine the new gain crossover frequency, and phase and gain margins. Comment upon the effects of lead compensation on system performance.

10.3 The block diagram of Fig. P10.3 represents a position control system. You have been given the task of designing the compensation $D(s)$.

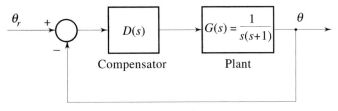

Fig. P10.3

(a) Consider first $D(s) = K$. What value of K would provide velocity error constant $K_v = 12$?

(b) For the value of K in part (a), determine phase margin ΦM, bandwidth ω_b, resonance peak M_r, and resonance frequency ω_r.

(c) Next consider $D(s) = K\dfrac{\tau s + 1}{\alpha\tau s + 1}$. With the parameter K set for K_v of 12, choose $\tau > 0$, and $\alpha < 1$ so that ΦM is greater than 40°.

(d) For the value of $D(s)$ in part (c), determine ΦM, ω_b, M_r, and ω_r.

10.4 Consider the system shown in Fig. P10.3. It is desired to obtain a phase margin greater than 45°, and steady-state error less than 0.1 for a unit ramp input.

(a) Design a cascade lead compensator that meets the given specifications.

(b) Design a cascade lag compensator that meets the given specifications.

(c) Since an identical set of specifications can be met by lead as well as lag compensation, how do we make a choice of the compensation scheme?

10.5 A unity-feedback control system has open-loop transfer function
$$G(s) = 1/s^2$$
The specifications for the system are:

Settling time $t_s \le 4$ sec

Peak overshoot for a step input $\le 20\%$

Design a suitable compensation scheme.

10.6 An uncompensated control system with unity feedback has a plant transfer function

$$G(s) = \frac{K}{s(s + 2)}$$

It is desired to have a steady-state error for a ramp input less than five per cent of the magnitude of ramp. It is also desired that the phase margin of the system be at least 45° and the closed-loop bandwidth greater than 10 rad/sec. Design a cascade lead compensator to yield the desired specifications.

10.7 For the system of Problem 10.6, design a cascade lag compensator to yield the desired specifications, with the exception that a bandwidth equal to or greater than 2 rad/sec will be acceptable.

10.8 An uncompensated control system with unity feedback has a plant transfer function

$$G(s) = \frac{K}{s(1 + 0.1s)(1 + 0.2s)}$$

The system must satisfy the following performance specifications:

(i) The magnitude of the steady-state error of the system due to a unit ramp function input is 0.01.

(ii) Phase margin $\ge 40°$.

Use two identical cascaded lead compensators to compensate the system. Justify the use of two-stage lead compensator.

10.9 Consider the problem of design of angular control system of a robot's joint. A block diagram of the system is shown in Fig. P10.9. The performance specifications of the system are as follows:

(i) The steady-state error due to ramp input should be less than or equal to one per cent.

(ii) The phase margin of the system should be greater than 45°.
Design a cascade lead compensator to yield the desired specifications.
Determine the resonance peak M_r, and the bandwidth ω_b of the
compensated system.

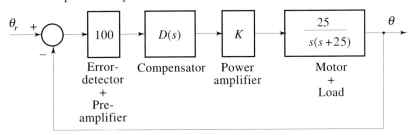

θ_r θ

Error-detector   Compensator   Power   Motor
\+   amplifier   \+
Pre-   Load
amplifier

Fig. P10.9

10.10 For the system of Problem 10.9, design a cascade lag compensator to yield the
desired specifications. Determine the resonance peak M_r, and the bandwidth
ω_b of the compensated system.

10.11 A unity-feedback system has an open-loop transfer function

$$G(s) = \frac{5}{s(s+1)(0.5s+1)}$$

It is desired to obtain the phase margin of at least 40° and the gain margin of
atleast 10 dB without sacrificing the velocity error constant of the system.
Design a suitable cascade compensator. Give reasons for your choice of the
compensation scheme.

10.12 The block diagram of Fig. P10.12 represents a position control system. You
have been given the task of designing the compensation $D(s)$ to meet the
following specifications:
Velocity error constant, $K_v = 30$.
Phase margin, $\Phi M \geq 50°$.
Bandwidth, $\omega_b = 12$ rad/sec.
(a) Show that if lead compensation is employed to meet the K_v and ΦM
requirements, the bandwidth will be larger than the specified value,
resulting in a system sensitive to noise.
(b) Show that if lag compensation is attempted to meet the K_v and ΦM
requirements, the bandwidth will fall short of the specified value,
resulting in a sluggish system.
(c) Design a suitable lag-lead compensator that meets the specifications on
K_v, ΦM, and ω_b.

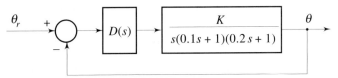

θ_r θ

Fig. P10.12

10.13 For the position control system shown in Fig. P10.13, design a lead compensator to yield a $K_v = 40$, and a 20% overshoot in the transient response for a

step input with a peak time of 0.1 second. Use only frequency domain methods.

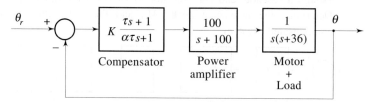

Fig. P10.13

10.14 The open-loop transfer function of a unity-feedback system is

$$G(s) = \frac{K}{s(s+10)^2}$$

It is specified that the velocity error constant of this system be equal to 20, while the damping ratio of the dominant roots be equal to 0.707.
   (a) It is not advisable to compensate this system by a single-stage cascade lead compensator. Why?
   (b) Design a cascade lag compensator to meet the given performance specifications. Use only frequency-domain methods.
   (c) Determine the bandwidth of the compensated system.
The -3 dB contour of the Nichols chart may be constructed using the following table.

Phase, degrees	0	-30	-60	-90	-120	-150	-180	-210
Magnitude, dB	7.66	6.8	4.18	0	-4.18	-6.8	-7.66	-6.8

10.15 A unity-feedback type-0 system with dead-time has a forward path transfer function

$$G(s) = \frac{10 e^{-0.02 s}}{(0.5 s + 1)(0.1 s + 1)(0.05 s + 1)}$$

Design a suitable compensation scheme so that the system acquires a damping ratio of 0.4 without loss of steady-state accuracy. Use only frequency-domain methods.

Estimate the bandwidth and the settling time of the compensated system.

10.16 Consider the servo system shown in Fig. P10.16.

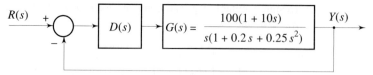

Fig. P10.16

   (a) Sketch the Bode plot of $G(s)$ when $D(s) = 1$. Find the phase margin of the uncompensated system.
   (b) The second-order compensator

$$D(s) = \frac{s^2 + 0.8\,s + 4}{(s + 0.384)(s + 10.42)}$$

cancels the complex poles of the process transfer function $G(s)$. Find the phase margin of the compensated system. What is the effect of $D(s)$ on the steady-state performance of the system?

(c) The closed-loop system is required to have a phase margin of at least 70° without sacrificing the steady-state performance of the system. If the cancellation-compensation proposed in part (b) cannot meet the phase-margin requirement, add a stage of lead compensator to further improve the relative stability of the system.

10.17 Consider the position control system of Fig. P10.17.

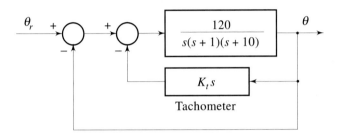

Fig. P10.17

Show that $K_t = \dfrac{1}{8}$ provides approximately 25° phase margin. Find K_v of the compensated system.

chapter 11

Hardware and Software Implementation of Common Compensators

11.1 INTRODUCTION

Various forms of devices have been used for the mechanization of industrial automatic controllers. As error detectors, gear differential for comparing rotational displacements; linkages for comparing translational displacements; pneumatic bellows for comparing pressures; potentiometers, synchro devices, and op amps for comparing electrical quantities, etc., have been used. To implement control logic (compensators), pneumatic systems made up of restrictors, bellows, flapper amplifiers, and other elements have been extensively used in process industries. Hydraulic systems made up of springs, dashpots, hydraulic servomotors and other elements; passive electric networks made up of resistors and capacitors; and active electric networks made up of resistors, capacitors, and op amps are the other forms of implementation of compensators. Passive electric networks can be converted to active networks just by tacking an op amp to the output of the passive network. Since an op amp has a high input and low output impedance, it provides network isolation. An arbitrary amount of gain is an added bonus.

Industrial automatic controllers based on op amp circuits (electronic controllers) are more versatile and flexible than the other forms of controllers—hydraulic and pneumatic. Every proper transfer function is synthesizable by using op amp circuits; this is, however, not the case with other forms. This gives us more design freedom; our design need not be constrained because of problems of physical realization. In fact, many designs different from conventional PID, and its approximations, have been successfully implemented.

Electronic controllers are compatible with electromechanical systems; the signal from sensor/error detector is electrical in nature, and the actuator needs an electrical input signal. In process control applications where pneumatic actuators are used to position the control valves, electropneumatic valves provide the necessary interface. In servo systems where hydraulic motors are used as actuators, the interface is provided by electrohydraulic valves. In carrier (ac) control systems, modulators and demodulators are used to interface ac devices with op amp circuits.

With the ever-increasing reliability of integrated circuits, electronic controllers are now commonly used in industrial applications. In process industry, electronic controllers have generally replaced pneumatic controllers. The development is fast moving towards computer-based controllers. Pneumatic controllers are now used in special situations, such as in environments prone to explosions.

In this chapter, we restrict our attention to implementation of common compensators using passive and active electric networks. For a smooth transition to a digital control environment, a modest investment in computer-based implementation is also made.

Some useful passive and active circuit models were given in Section 2.9; revisiting this section will be helpful.

11.2   PASSIVE ELECTRIC NETWORKS

There are obvious advantages of using only passive electrical components—resistors, capacitors, and inductors—for the implementation of a compensator. However, since the inductor is a very bulky component at low frequencies, passive networks made up of only resistors and capacitors are used in practice. Condition for realizability of transfer function $D(s)$ with passive resistor-capacitor (RC) networks is that all finite poles of $D(s)$ must be simple and lie on the negative real axis, the zeros of $D(s)$ may lie anywhere in the s-plane [42]. By tacking an op amp on to the output of a passive RC network, it is possible to realize a specified gain of the compensator.

The transfer function of a simple first-order compensator that can be implemented by passive RC networks is

$$D(s) = \frac{K(s + z)}{(s + p)} \tag{11.1}$$

where K is a constant; $s = -z$, and $s = -p$ are, respectively, the zero and pole of the compensator.

Recall that a lead compensator has a single pole and a single zero with the pole lying to the left of the zero on negative real axis of the complex plane. The first-order compensator given by Eqn. (11.1) is therefore a lead compensator if $p > z$. A lag compensator has a single pole and a single zero with the pole lying to the right of the zero on negative real axis of the complex plane. The first-order compensator given by Eqn. (11.1) is therefore a lag compensator if $p < z$.

Lead Compensator Implementation

Consider the RC network shown in Fig. 11.1. Assume that this network sees a small source impedance and that the output load impedance is large. Sometimes an isolating amplifier is inserted to ensure the validity of this assumption.

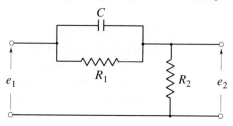

Fig. 11.1   *A lead network*

Taking these impedances to be zero and infinity, respectively, the transfer function of the network is derived as follows.

The equivalent impedance of R_1 and C is

$$Z(s) = \frac{R_1\left(\dfrac{1}{Cs}\right)}{R_1 + \dfrac{1}{Cs}} = \frac{R_1}{R_1 Cs + 1}$$

The transfer function between the output $E_2(s)$ and the input $E_1(s)$ is

$$\frac{E_2(s)}{E_1(s)} = \frac{R_2}{Z(s) + R_2} = \frac{R_2}{R_1 + R_2}\left(\frac{R_1 Cs + 1}{\dfrac{R_1 R_2}{R_1 + R_2}Cs + 1}\right)$$

Define
$$R_1 C = \tau \tag{11.2a}$$

$$\frac{R_2}{R_1 + R_2} = \alpha < 1$$

Then the transfer function becomes

$$\frac{E_2(s)}{E_1(s)} = \alpha\left(\frac{\tau s + 1}{\alpha \tau s + 1}\right) = \frac{s + 1/\tau}{s + 1/\alpha\tau} \tag{11.2b}$$

This transfer function has a real zero at $s = -1/\tau$ and a real pole at $s = -1/\alpha\tau$ with the pole to the left of the zero, as is shown in Fig. 11.2. The network of Fig. 11.1 thus realizes a lead compensator. The values of the three parameters R_1, R_2, and C are determined from the two compensator parameters τ and α using Eqns (11.2a). There is an additional degree of freedom in the choice of the values of the network components which is used to set the impedance level of the network.

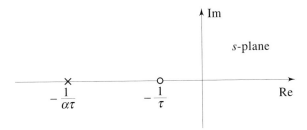

Fig. 11.2 *Pole-zero map for a lead compensator*

It is important to note that the lead compensator in Eqn. (11.2b) has a zero-frequency gain of $\alpha < 1$, i.e., a zero-frequency attenuation of $1/\alpha$. This attenuation is detrimental to the steady-state performance since it will reduce the error constant. Thus, when using the lead network of Fig. 11.1, it is important to increase the loop gain by an amount $1/\alpha$. The realization of a lead compensator is then visualized as a combination of a network and an amplifier as shown in Fig. 11.3.

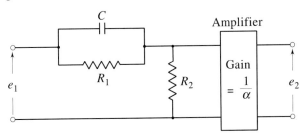

Fig. 11.3 *A lead network with an amplifier*

The sinusoidal transfer function of the lead compensator with unity zero-frequency gain is given by

$$D(j\omega) = \frac{1 + j\omega\tau}{1 + j\omega\alpha\tau}; \ \alpha < 1, \ \tau > 0 \qquad (11.3)$$

Figure 11.4 shows the Bode plots of $D(j\omega)$. Note that the name 'lead' refers to the property that the compensator adds positive phase to the system over some appropriate frequency range. From Fig.11.4, it is observed that from the filtering standpoint, the lead compensator is a *highpass filter*.

Some Practical Considerations in the Choice of α

In choosing parameter values for the compensator, it may be seen from Eqns (11.2a) that τ depends solely upon R_1 and C. The range of resistance and capacitance values allows the designer to choose practically any value of τ. One does not have quite as free a choice with the parameter α. An important consideration governing the choice of α is the inherent noise in control systems. The noise is generally of a high-frequency nature relative to the frequencies of control signals that appear in the loop. We see from Fig.11.4 that in a lead network, the high-frequency noise signals are amplified by a factor

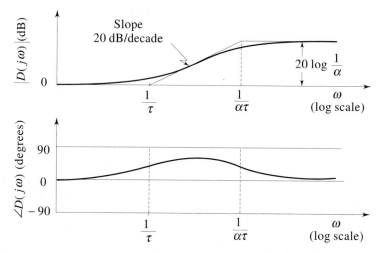

Fig. 11.4 *Bode plots of a lead compensator*

$(1/\alpha) > 1$, while the low-frequency control signals undergo unit amplification (0 dB gain). This means that the lead compensator boosts the noise signal level in the loop relative to the control signal, and the lower the value of α, the higher this boost. Thus, if noise is a problem in a particular system, one must be careful about choosing a value of α for a lead compensator. It is recommended that value of α should not be less than 0.07. A common choice is $\alpha = 0.1$. Limiting the value of α amounts to limiting an increase in the bandwidth of the system due to addition of a lead compensator.

*Example 11.1*_____

In this example, we design a passive RC network to realize the lead compensator

$$D(s) = \frac{s + 1.15}{s + 4.3}$$

Comparing this transfer function with the one given in Eqn. (11.2b), we see that the elements of network of Fig. 11.3 must satisfy the equations

$$R_1 C = \tau = \frac{1}{1.15} = 0.87$$

$$\frac{R_2}{R_1 + R_2} = \alpha = \frac{1.15}{4.3} = 0.267$$

Since there are three unknowns and only two equations to be satisfied, we choose $C = 1\,\mu\text{F}$. The other elements are then found to be $R_1 = 0.87$ MΩ and $R_2 = 0.317$ MΩ.

Lag Compensator Implementation

Consider the RC network shown in Fig. 11.5. Assume that the input and the output impedance seen by the network are zero and infinite respectively. Under this assumption, the transfer function of the network is derived as follows.

The equivalent impedance of R_2 and C is

$$Z(s) = R_2 + \frac{1}{Cs}$$

The transfer function between the output $E_2(s)$ and input $E_1(s)$ is

$$\frac{E_2(s)}{E_1(s)} = \frac{Z(s)}{R_1 + Z(s)} = \frac{R_2 Cs + 1}{(R_1 + R_2)Cs + 1}$$

Define
$$R_2 C = \tau$$
$$\frac{R_1 + R_2}{R_2} = \beta > 1$$
(11.4a)

Then the transfer function becomes

$$\frac{E_2(s)}{E_1(s)} = \frac{\tau s + 1}{\beta \tau s + 1} = \frac{1}{\beta}\left(\frac{s + 1/\tau}{s + 1/\beta\tau}\right)$$
(11.4b)

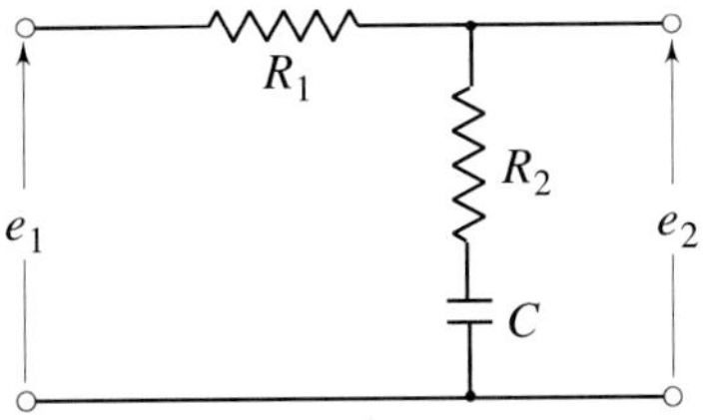

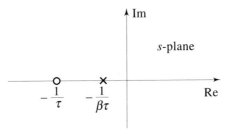

Fig. 11.5 *A lag network*

This transfer function has a real zero at $s = -1/\tau$ and a real pole at $s = -1/\beta\tau$, with the pole to the right of the zero, as shown in Fig. 11.6. The network of Fig. 11.5 thus realizes a lag compensator. The values of the three network parameters R_1, R_2 and C are determined from the two compensator parameters τ and β from Eqns (11.4a). As in the case of lead compensator realization, we have an additional degree of freedom in the lag compensator realization also, which is used for impedance matching.

Fig. 11.6 *Pole-zero map for a lag compensator*

The sinusoidal transfer function of the lag network is given by

$$D(j\omega) = \frac{1 + j\omega\tau}{1 + j\omega\beta\tau}; \ \beta > 1, \ \tau > 0 \tag{11.5}$$

Figure 11.7 shows the Bode plots of this $D(j\omega)$. The network gets its name for a reason similar to the lead network; it introduces phase lag. From the filtering standpoint, a lag compensator is a *lowpass filter*.

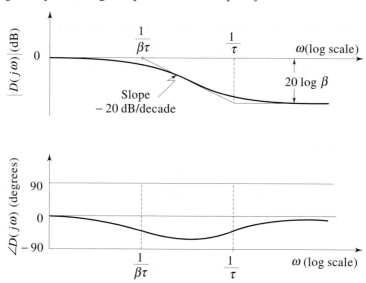

Fig. 11.7   *Bode plots of a lag compensator*

Some Practical Considerations in the Choice of β

The lag compensator, in contrast to the lead compensator, attenuates high-frequency noise signals in the control loop. We see from Fig. 11.7 that in a lag network, the high-frequency noise signals are attenuated by a factor $\beta > 1$, while the low-frequency control signals are not attenuated (0 dB gain). The addition of a lag compensator, thus, results in an improvement in the ratio of the control to noise signal in the loop.

The parameter τ for the lag compensator may be chosen almost arbitrarily; however, the choice of β is usually restricted because a very large β will appreciably reduce the bandwidth of the system. A typical choice of β is 10.

Lag-lead Compensator Implementation

As the name implies, the lag-lead compensator is basically just a lag compensator and a lead compensator in cascade. It has one pole-zero pair corresponding to the lag section, and another pole-zero pair corresponding to the lead section of the compensator. The transfer function for the lag-lead compensator is of the form

$$D(s) = \left(\frac{\tau_1 s + 1}{\beta \tau_1 s + 1}\right)\left(\frac{\tau_2 s + 1}{\alpha \tau_2 s + 1}\right); \ \beta > 1, \ \alpha < 1, \ \tau_1, \ \tau_2 > 0 \qquad (11.6)$$

$$\underbrace{\phantom{\frac{\tau_1 s + 1}{\beta \tau_1 s + 1}}}_{\text{Lag section}} \underbrace{\phantom{\frac{\tau_2 s + 1}{\alpha \tau_2 s + 1}}}_{\text{Lead section}}$$

The attenuation factor α of the lead compensator is not included in the equation assuming that adequate loop gain is available in the system to compensate for this attenuation.

A lag-lead compensator can be realized by cascading the lead and the lag networks. However, a single network can be used to realize the transfer function in Eqn. (11.6) if α and β need not be specified independently.

Let us examine the RC network shown in Fig. 11.8, to see whether it realizes a lag-lead compensator. With the usual impedance assumptions, the transfer function of the network is derived as follows.

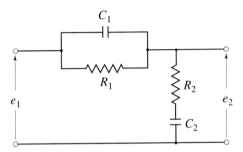

Fig. 11.8 *A lag-lead network*

The equivalent impedance of R_1 and C_1 is

$$Z_1(s) = \frac{R_1\left(\dfrac{1}{C_1 s}\right)}{R_1 + \dfrac{1}{C_1 s}} = \frac{R_1}{R_1 C_1 s + 1},$$

and the equivalent impedance of R_2 and C_2 is

$$Z_2(s) = R_2 + \frac{1}{C_2 s}$$

The transfer function between the output $E_2(s)$ and the input $E_1(s)$ is

$$\frac{E_2(s)}{E_1(s)} = \frac{Z_2(s)}{Z_1(s) + Z_2(s)} = \frac{(R_1 C_1 s + 1)(R_2 C_2 s + 1)}{(R_1 C_1 s + 1)(R_2 C_2 s + 1) + R_1 C_2 s}$$

The denominator of the transfer function can be factored into two real terms. Let us define

$$R_1 C_1 = \tau_1; \quad R_2 C_2 = \tau_2$$

$$R_1 C_1 + R_2 C_2 + R_1 C_2 = \beta \tau_1 + \frac{1}{\beta} \tau_2; \ \beta > 1$$

$$\hspace{10cm} (11.7a)$$

Then $E_2(s)/E_1(s)$ can be simplified to

$$\frac{E_2(s)}{E_1(s)} = \frac{(\tau_1 s + 1)(\tau_2 s + 1)}{(\beta \tau_1 s + 1)\left(\frac{1}{\beta}\tau_2 s + 1\right)} \qquad (11.7b)$$

The pole-zero map of this transfer function is shown in Fig. 11.9. The network of Fig. 11.8, thus, realizes a lag-lead compensator given by Eqn. (11.6) with $\alpha = 1/\beta$. The values of the four network parameters R_1, R_2, C_1, and C_2 are determined from the three compensator parameters τ_1, τ_2, and β using Eqns (11.7a); the additional degree of freedom is used for impedance matching.

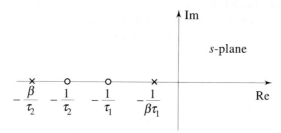

Fig. 11.9 *Pole-zero map for a lag-lead compensator*

The sinusoidal transfer function of the lag-lead network is given by

$$D(j\omega) = \frac{(1 + j\omega\tau_1)(1 + j\omega\tau_2)}{(1 + j\omega\beta\tau_1)(1 + j\omega\tau_2/\beta)}; \; \beta > 1, \tau_1, \; \tau_2 > 0 \qquad (11.8)$$

Figure 11.10 shows the Bode plots of this $D(j\omega)$. Note that the phase shift is a function of input frequency; phase angle varies from lag to lead as the frequency is increased. Thus phase lag and phase lead occur in different frequency bands. From the filtering standpoint, the compensator with frequency response of Fig. 11.10 may be called a *band reject filter*.

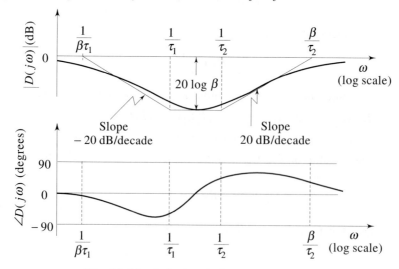

Fig. 11.10 *Bode plots of a lag-lead compensator*

Implementation of a Compensator with Complex Zeros

Consider the bridged-T network shown in Fig. 11.11, which has only RC elements. With the usual impedance assumptions, the transfer function of the network is derived as follows.

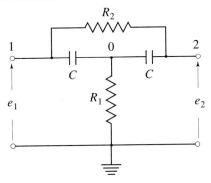

Fig. 11.11   *A bridged-T network*

The nodal equations are

$$\frac{E_2 - E_1}{R_2} + \frac{E_2 - E_0}{1/Cs} = 0$$

$$\frac{E_0 - E_2}{1/Cs} + \frac{E_0 - E_1}{1/Cs} + \frac{E_0}{R_1} = 0$$

Rearranging yields

$$-CsE_0 + \left(\frac{1}{R_2} + Cs\right)E_2 = \frac{1}{R_2}E_1$$

$$\left(\frac{1}{R_1} + 2Cs\right)E_0 - CsE_2 = CsE_1$$

This set is solved for E_2 by *Cramer's rule*:

$$E_2 = \begin{vmatrix} -Cs & E_1/R_2 \\ \dfrac{1}{R_1}+2Cs & Cs\,E_1 \end{vmatrix} \Bigg/ \begin{vmatrix} -Cs & \dfrac{1}{R_2}+Cs \\ \dfrac{1}{R_1}+2Cs & -Cs \end{vmatrix}$$

$$= \frac{[1 + 2R_1Cs + R_1R_2C^2s^2]E_1}{1 + (2R_1 + R_2)Cs + R_1R_2C^2s^2}$$

Therefore

$$\frac{E_2(s)}{E_1(s)} = \frac{s^2 + \dfrac{2}{R_2C}s + \dfrac{1}{R_1R_2C^2}}{s^2 + \dfrac{2R_1+R_2}{R_1R_2C}s + \dfrac{1}{R_1R_2C^2}} \tag{11.9}$$

Passive RC networks have transfer functions with simple (non-repeated) poles on the negative real axis; therefore, Eqn. (11.9) can be expressed as

$$\frac{E_2(s)}{E_1(s)} = \frac{s^2 + 2\zeta\omega_0 s + \omega_0^2}{(s + p_1)(s + p_2)} \tag{11.10}$$

where

$$\omega_0 = \frac{1}{C\sqrt{R_1 R_2}}; \; \zeta = \sqrt{R_1/R_2}$$

and

$$p_1, p_2 = \zeta\omega_0\left[1 + \frac{1}{2\zeta^2} \mp \left(1 + \frac{1}{(2\zeta^2)^2}\right)^{\frac{1}{2}}\right] \tag{11.11}$$

For sufficiently small ζ, the poles go to

$$p_1 \cong \zeta\omega_0$$

and

$$p_2 \cong \omega_0/\zeta$$

Evidently, a pole near the origin comes with lightly damped zeros. Figure 11.12 shows a pole-zero map of a bridged-T network.

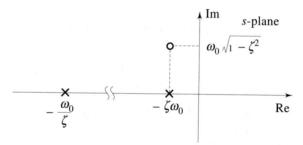

Fig. 11.12 *Pole-zero map for a bridged-T network*

Figure 11.13 shows Bode plots of the transfer function of a typical bridged-T network. Notice that the magnitude plot has a 'notch' at the resonance frequency ω_0. The phase plot is negative below and positive above the resonance frequency, while passing through zero degrees at the resonance

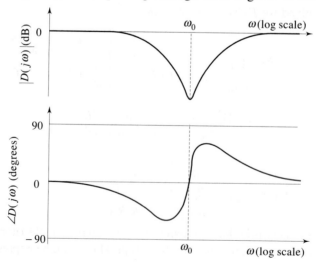

Fig. 11.13 *Bode plots of a bridged-T network*

frequency. Due to the 'notch' characteristic in the amplitude curve, the bridged-T network is also referred to as *notch filter* (It is also called a *band reject filter* in electric network theory).

11.3 | OPERATIONAL AMPLIFIER USAGE

Since the advent of semiconductor operational amplifiers, inductors have been largely replaced by combinations of resistors, capacitors, and op amps in circuits operating at low frequencies—low-frequency inductors usually have iron cores and are large compared to integrated circuit packages. Every proper transfer function is realizable using active RC networks [42]; therefore, compensators with complex conjugate poles can be implemented (recall that compensators with complex conjugate poles cannot be implemented using passive RC networks). Even in situations where passive RC network realization is possible, an op amp based realization permits the use of reasonable-valued resistors and capacitors (passive RC networks at low frequencies can become rather bulky because of capacitor sizes). The primary advantage of active compensators is their small size and weight for low-frequency applications and their ruggedness. There are, of course, problems like offsets, noise, etc., which are introduced because of op amp usage; an alert designer can, however, take care of these aspects while doing a practical design.

Consider the network shown in Fig. 11.14. The transfer function for this network can be obtained as follows.

The equivalent impedance of R_1 and C_1 is

$$Z_1(s) = \frac{R_1}{R_1 C_1 s + 1}$$

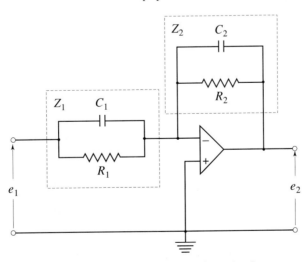

Fig. 11.14 *Operational amplifier circuit*

The equivalent impedance of R_2 and C_2 is

$$Z_2(s) = \frac{R_2}{R_2 C_2 s + 1}$$

The transfer function between the output $E_2(s)$ and the input $E_1(s)$ is

$$\frac{E_2(s)}{E_1(s)} = -\frac{Z_2(s)}{Z_1(s)} = -\frac{R_2}{R_1}\left(\frac{R_1 C_1 s + 1}{R_2 C_2 s + 1}\right) \qquad (11.12)$$

Notice that the transfer function in Eqn. (11.12) contains a minus sign. If this sign is not acceptable in the actual application, a sign inverter may be connected to either the input or the output of the network of Fig. 11.14. An example is shown in Fig. 11.15. The sign inverter has the transfer function

$$\frac{E_3(s)}{E_2(s)} = -\frac{R_4}{R_3}$$

Hence, the network shown in Fig. 11.15 has the following transfer function.

$$\frac{E_3(s)}{E_1(s)} = \frac{R_2 R_4}{R_1 R_3}\left(\frac{R_1 C_1 s + 1}{R_2 C_2 s + 1}\right) = \frac{R_4 C_1}{R_3 C_2}\left(\frac{s + \dfrac{1}{R_1 C_1}}{s + \dfrac{1}{R_2 C_2}}\right) \qquad (11.13)$$

The network is a lead compensator if $R_1 C_1 > R_2 C_2$. It is a lag compensator if $R_1 C_1 < R_2 C_2$. A lag-lead compensator may be realized by cascading two active networks as shown in Fig. 11.16. Rather than introducing both a lead compensator and a lag compensator as separate units, however, it may be preferable in terms of cost and simplicity, to design a single lag-lead network for the combined modes (refer Problem 11.4).

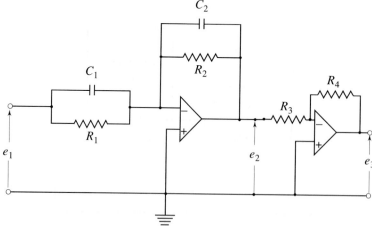

Fig. 11.15 *Operational amplifier circuit used as a lead or a lag compensator*

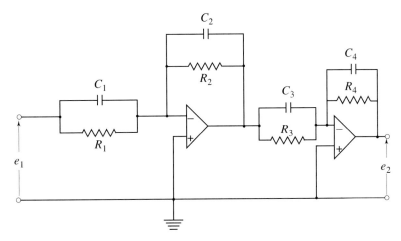

Fig. 11.16 *Operational amplifier circuit used as a lag-lead compensator*

Example 11.2

In this example, we design a circuit for the lead compensator

$$D(s) = \frac{16(s + 1)}{s + 6}$$

Comparing this transfer function with that given in Eqn. (11.12), we see that the circuit elements of Fig. 11.14 must satisfy the equations

$$R_1 C_1 = 1; \quad R_2 C_2 = \frac{1}{6}; \quad \frac{C_1}{C_2} = 16$$

Since there are four unknowns and only three equations to be satisfied, we choose $R_1 = 100$ kΩ. The other circuit elements are then found to be $R_2 = 266.7$ kΩ, $C_1 = 10$ μF, and $C_2 = 0.625$ μF. The required circuit is shown in Fig. 11.17, where the unity-gain inverting amplifier has been added to the circuit to give the correct sign to the transfer function.

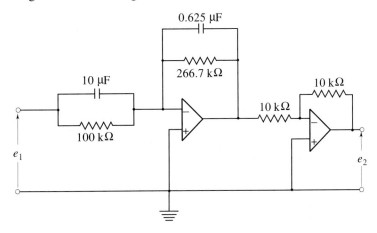

Fig. 11.17 *A lead compensator circuit for Example 11.2*

11.4 | USE OF DIGITAL COMPUTER AS A COMPENSATOR DEVICE

In recent years, there has been a rapid increase in the use of digital computers in control systems. In fact, many industrial control systems include digital computers as an integral part of their operation. Also the availability of low-cost microprocessors and microcomputers has established a new trend towards the use of digital computers even in small-scale control systems, including those for automobiles and household appliances.

Advantages Offered by Digital Control

1. The accuracy of analog control systems is often limited. For example, if an analog compensator is to be built using a resistor with resistance 980.5 ohms and a capacitor with capacitance 81.33 microfarads, it would be difficult and expensive to obtain components with exactly these values. In digital control systems, the accuracy of a digital compensator can be increased simply by increasing the number of bits.

2. Digital signals are coded in sequences of '0' and '1', which represent ranges of voltages (for example, '0' from 0 to 1 volt, and '1' from 2 to 4 volts). This representation is less susceptible to noise and drift of power supply.

3. Due to the growth of very large scale integration (VLSI) technology, the price of digital systems has been constantly decreasing during the last decade. Now the use of a digital computer or microprocessor is cost-effective even for small control systems.

4. An important advantage offered by digital control is in flexibility of modifying controller characteristics, or of adapting the controller if plant dynamics change with operating conditions. The ability to 'redesign' the controller by changing software (rather than hardware) is an important feature of digital control over analog control.

5. If a digital computer is used, it can be used not only as a compensator but also to collect data, to carry out complex computations, and to monitor the status of the control system. To enable the computer to meet the variety of demands imposed on it, it is time-shared among its tasks.

6. Implementation of nonlinear and/or time-varying control laws, and adaptive control schemes was earlier constrained by the limitations of analog controllers and high cost of digital computers. However, with the advent of inexpensive digital computers with virtually limitless computing power, advanced control techniques may now be put to practice.

7. The study of emerging applications shows that artificial-intelligence (AI) will affect design and application of control systems as profoundly as

the impact of microprocessor has been in the last decade. It is clear that future generation control systems will have a significant AI component; the list of applications of computer-based control will continue to expand.

Implementation Problems in Digital Control

The main problems associated with the implementation of digital control are related to the effects of sampling and quantization.

Most processes that we are called upon to control operate in continuous time. This implies that we are dealing largely with an analog environment; to this environment we must interface the digital computer through which we seek to influence the process.

The interface is accomplished by a system of the form shown in Fig. 11.18. It is a cascade of the A/D conversion system followed by a computer followed by a D/A conversion system. The A/D conversion process involves deriving samples of the analog signal at discrete instants of time separated by sampling period T sec. The D/A conversion process involves reconstructing a continuous-time signal from the samples given out by the digital computer.

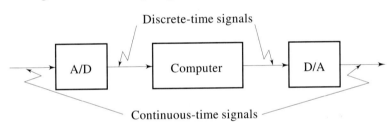

Fig. 11.18   *Discrete-time processing of continuous-time signals*

Quantization Effects

The conversion of signals from analog into digital form and *vice versa* is performed by electronic devices (A/D and D/A converters) of finite resolution. A device of n-bit resolution has 2^n quantization levels and the analog signal gets tied to these finite number of quantization levels in the process of conversion to digital form. Therefore, by the sheer act of conversion, a valuable part of information about the signal is lost.

Furthermore, any computer employed as a real-time controller must perform all of the necessary calculations with a limited precision, thus introducing a truncation error after each arithmetic operation has been performed. As the computational accuracy is normally much higher than the resolution of real converters, a further truncation must take place before the computed data are converted into the analog form. The repeated process of approximate conversion—computation—conversion may be costly, if not disastrous, in terms of control system performance.

Sampling Effects

Selection of sampling period T is a fundamental problem in digital control systems. The *sampling theorem*[1] states that a continuous-time signal whose frequency spectrum is bounded by upper limit ω_m, can be completely reconstructed from its samples when the sampling frequency $\omega_s = 2\pi/T > 2\omega_m$. There are two problems associated with the use of sampling theorem in practical control systems.

1. Frequency spectra of real signals do not possess strictly defined bandwidth ω_m. There are almost always frequency components outside the 3 dB-bandwidth ω_b. Therefore, the selection of the sampling frequency ω_s using the sampling theorem on the basis of system bandwidth ($\omega_b = \omega_m$) will result in information loss due to sampling.

2. Ideal lowpass filter needed for distortionless reconstruction of the continuous-time signal from its samples, is not physically realizable. Practical devices, such as D/A converters, introduce distortions.

Thus the process of sampling and reconstruction affects the amount of information available to the plant, and degrades control system performance. The ill-effects of sampling can be reduced, if not eliminated completely, by sampling at a very high rate. As a signal is sampled more frequently, adjacent samples have more or less similar magnitudes. In order to realize the beneficial effects of shorter sampling, longer word lengths are needed to resolve the differences between adjacent samples. Excessively fast sampling ($T \to 0$) may, however, result in numerical ill-conditioning in implementation of recursive control algorithms.

With the availability of low-cost, high-performance digital computers and interfacing hardware, the implementation problems in digital control do not pose a serious threat to its usefulness; the advantages of digital control outweigh its disadvantages for most of the applications.

11.5 CONFIGURATION OF THE BASIC COMPUTER-CONTROL SCHEME

Figure 11.19 depicts a block diagram of a computer-controlled system showing a configuration of the basic control scheme. The basic elements of the system are shown by the blocks.

The analog feedback signal coming from the sensor is usually of low frequency. It may often include higher frequency 'noise'. Such noise signals are too fast for control system to correct; lowpass filtering is often needed to allow good control performance. The filter shown in Fig. 11.19 serves this purpose.

The analog feedback signal coming from the sensor is converted into digital form by an A/D conversion system. The conversion system usually consists of an A/D converter preceded by a sample-and-hold (S/H) device. The A/D

---

1. Chapter 2 of reference [180].

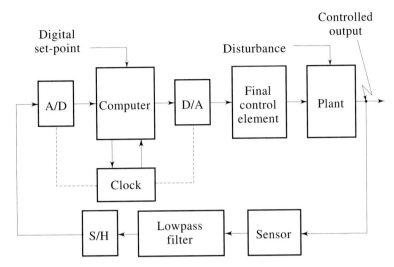

Fig. 11.19 *Configuration of the basic digital control scheme*

converter converts a voltage (or current) amplitude at its input into a binary code representing a quantized amplitude value closest to the amplitude of the input. However, the conversion is not instantaneous. Input signal variation during the conversion time of an A/D converter can lead to erroneous results. For this reason, high performance A/D conversion system includes a S/H device which keeps the input to the A/D converter constant during its conversion time.

The digital computer processes the sequence of numbers by means of an algorithm and produces a new sequence of numbers. Since data conversions and computations take time, there will always be a delay when a control law is implemented using a digital computer. The delay, which is called the *computational delay*, degrades the control system performance. It should be minimized by a proper choice of hardware and by a proper design of software for the control algorithm. Floating-point operations take a considerably longer time to perform (even when carried out by arithmatic co-processor) than the fixed-point ones. We therefore try to execute fixed-point operations whenever possible.

The D/A conversion system in Fig.11.19 converts the sequence of numbers in numerical code into a piecewise continuous-time signal. The output of the D/A converter is fed to the plant through the actuator (final control element) to control its dynamics.

The basic control scheme of Fig.11.19 assumes a uniform sampling operation, i.e., only one sampling rate exists in the system and the sampling period is constant. The real-time clock in the computer synchronizes all the events of A/D conversion $\rightarrow$ computation $\rightarrow$ D/A conversion.

The overall system in Fig. 11.19 is hybrid in nature; the signals are in a *sampled form (discrete-time signals/digital signals)* in the computer and in continuous-time form in the plant. Such systems have traditionally been called sampled-data control systems; we will use this term as a synonym to *computer control systems/digital control systems*.

11.6 PRINCIPLES OF SIGNAL CONVERSION

Figure 11.20a shows an analog signal $y(t)$—it is defined at a continuum of times, and its amplitudes assume a continuous range of values. Such a signal cannot be stored in digital computers; the signal therefore must be converted to a form that will be accepted by digital computers. One very common way to do this is to record sample values of this signal at equally spaced instants. If we sample the signal every 10 msec, for example, we obtain the *discrete-time signal* sketched in Fig. 11.20b. This *sampling interval* corresponds to a *sampling rate* of 100 samples/sec. The choice of sampling rate is an important one, since it determines how accurately the discrete-time signal can represent the original signal.

Notice that the time axis of the discrete-time signal in Fig.11.20b is labelled simply 'sample number' and index k has been used to denote this number $k = 0, 1, 2, \ldots$. Corresponding to different values of sample number k, the discrete-time signal assumes the same continuous range of values assumed by

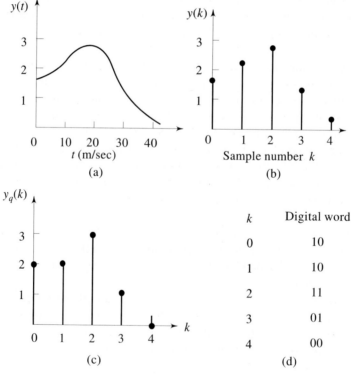

Fig. 11.20 *Sampling, quantization, and coding of an analog signal*

the analog signal $y(t)$. We can represent the sample values by a sequence of numbers y_s (refer Fig.11.20b):

$$y_s = \{1.7,\ 2.4,\ 2.8,\ 1.4,\ 0.4,\ \ldots\}$$

In general,

$$y_s = \{y(k)\},\ 0 \le k < \infty$$

where $y(k)$ denotes the kth number in the sequence.

The sequence defined above is a *one-sided sequence*; $y_s = 0$ for $k < 0$. In digital control applications, we normally encounter one-sided sequences.

Although, strictly speaking, $y(k)$ denotes the kth number in the sequence, the notation given above is often unnecessarily cumbersome, and it is convenient and unambiguous to refer to $y(k)$ itself as a sequence.

Throughout our discussion on digital control, we will assume *uniform sampling*, i.e., sample values of the analog signal are extracted at equally spaced sampling instants. If the physical time corresponding to the sampling interval is T seconds, then the kth sample $y(k)$ gives the value of the discrete-time signal at $t = kT$ seconds. We may, therefore, use $y(kT)$ to denote a sequence wherein the independent variable is physical time.

The signal of Fig.11.20b is defined at discrete instants of time; the sample values are however tied to a continuous range of numbers. Such a signal, in principle, can be stored in an infinite-bit machine because a finite-bit machine can store only a finite set of numbers.

A simplified hypothetical two-bit machine can store four numbers given below:

Binary number	Decimal equivalent
00	0
01	1
10	2
11	3

The signal of Fig.11.20b can therefore be stored in such a machine if the sample values are quantified to four *quantization levels*. Figure 11.20c shows a quantized discrete-time signal for our hypothetical machine. We have assumed that any value in the interval [0.5, 1.5) is rounded to 1, and so forth. The signals for which both time and amplitude are discrete, are called *digital signals*.

After sampling and quantization, the final step required in converting an analog signal to a form acceptable to digital computer is *coding* (or *encoding*). The encoder maps each quantized sample value into a digital word. Figure 11.20d gives a coded digital signal corresponding to the analog signal of Fig. 11.20a for our hypothetical two-bit machine.

The device that performs the sampling, quantization and coding is an *analog-to-digital* (A/D) *converter*. Figure 11.21 is a block diagram representation of the operations performed by an A/D converter.

It may be noted that the quantized discrete-time signal of Fig. 11.20c and the coded signal of Fig. 11.20d carry exactly the same information. For the purpose

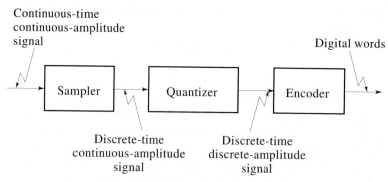

Fig. 11.21 *Operations performed by an A/D converter*

of an analytical study of digital systems, we will use the quantized discrete-time form for digital signals.

The number of binary digits carried by a device is its *word length*, and this is obviously an important characteristic related to the *resolution* of the device — the smallest change in the input signal that will produce a change in the output signal. The A/D converter that generates signals of Fig.11.20 has two binary digits and thus four quantization levels. Any change, therefore, in the input over the interval [0.5, 1.5) produces no change in the output. With three binary digits, 2^3 quantization levels can be obtained, and the resolution of the converter would improve.

The A/D converters in common use have word length of 8 to 16 bits. For an A/D converter with a word length of eight-bits, an input signal can be resolved to one part in 2^8, or 1 in 256. If the input signal has a range of 10 V, the resolution is 10/256, or approximately 0.04 V. Thus, the input signal must change by at least 0.04 V in order to produce a change in the output.

With the availability of converters with resolution ranging from 8 to 16 bits, the quantization errors do not pose a serious threat in computer control of industrial processes. In our treatment of the subject, we assume quantization errors to be zero. This is equivalent to assuming infinite-bit digital devices. Thus, we treat digital signals as if they are discrete-time signals with amplitudes assuming a continuous range of values. In other words, we make no distinction between the words 'discrete-time' and 'digital'.

A typical topology of a single-loop digital control system is shown in Fig. 11.19. It has been assumed that the measuring transducer and the actuator (final control element) are analog devices, requiring respectively A/D and D/A conversion at the computer input and output. The D/A conversion is a process of producing an analog signal from a digital signal and is, in some sense, the reverse of the sampling process discussed above.

The *digital-to-analog* (D/A) *converter* performs two functions; first, generation of output samples from the binary-form digital signals produced by the machine, and second, conversion of these samples to analog form. Figure 11.22 is a block diagram representation of the operations performed by a D/A

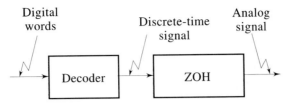

Fig. 11.22 *Operations performed by a D/A converter*

converter. The decoder maps each digital word into a sample value of the signal in discrete-time form. It is usually not possible to drive a load, such as a motor, with these samples. In order to deliver sufficient energy, the sample amplitude might have to be so large that it is infeasible to be generated. Also, large-amplitude signals might saturate the system being driven.

The solution to this problem is to smooth the output samples to produce a signal in analog form. The simplest way of converting a sample sequence into a continuous-time signal is to hold the value of the sample until the next one arrives. The net effect is to convert a sample to a pulse of duration T, the sampling period. This function of a D/A converter is referred to as a *zero-order hold* (ZOH) operation. The term *zero order* refers to the zero-order polynomial used to extrapolate between the sampling times. Figure 11.23 shows a typical sampled sequence produced by the decoder, and the analog signal resulting from the ZOH operation.

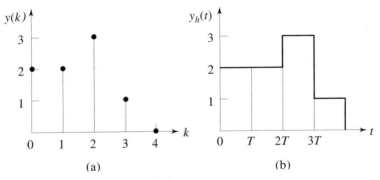

Fig. 11.23 *(a) Sampled sequence*
(b) Analog output from ZOH

Figure 11.24 represents a model of a unity-feedback digital control system. This representation is useful for the purpose of analytical study of digital control systems. The sampler which samples continuous-time signal $e(t)$ every T secs, is a model of A/D converter, and the ZOH which constructs a continuous-time signal from a discrete-time output of digital control algorithm, is a model of D/A converter.

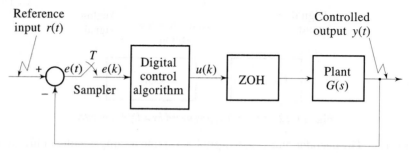

Fig. 11.24 *Analytical model of a unity-feedback digital control system*

11.7 | DIGITAL IMPLEMENTATION OF ANALOG COMPENSATORS

Plants of control systems are mostly analog systems. However, because digital compensators have many advantages over analog ones, we may be asked to design digital compensators to control analog plants. There are two approaches to carrying out the design. The first approach uses the design methods discussed in the preceding chapters to design an analog compensator and then transforms it into a digital one. The second approach first transforms analog plants into digital plants and then carries out design using digital techniques. We consider here the first approach.

Consider the analog compensator with a proper transfer function $D(s)$ shown in Fig. 11.25a. The arrangement in Fig. 11.25b implements the analog compensator digitally. It consists of three parts: a sampler, a digital control algorithm, and a ZOH . The problem is to find a digital algorithm such that for any input $e(t)$, the output $u(t)$ of the analog compensator and the output $u^+(t)$ of the digital compensator are roughly equal. From Fig. 11.25b, we see that the output of the sampler is $e(k) \triangleq e(t = kT)$, the sample of $e(t)$ with sampling

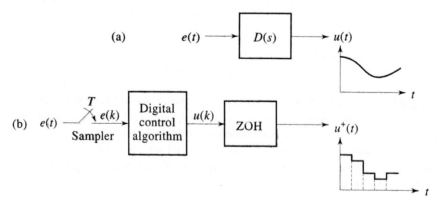

Fig. 11.25 *(a) Analog compensator*
(b) Digital compensator

period T. We then search for a digital algorithm which operates on $e(k)$ to yield a sequence $u(k)$. The ZOH then holds the value of u constant until the arrival of next data. Thus, the output $u^+(t)$ of the digital compensator is stepwise as shown. The output of analog compensator is generally not stepwise; the best we can achieve is that $u^+(t)$ approximately equals $u(t)$.

Computer processing of input samples $e(k)$ to produce output samples $u(k)$ may be described by difference equations, analogous to differential equations that characterize continuous-time systems. The general form of nth-order linear difference equation relating output $u(k)$ to input $e(k)$ is given below.

$$u(k + n) + a_1 u(k + n - 1) + \cdots + a_n u(k) =$$
$$b_0 e(k + m) + b_1 e(k + m - 1) + \cdots + b_m e(k)$$

The coefficients a_i and b_j are real constants; k, m, and n are integers with $m \le n$.

We will derive our results for the case of $m = n$, i.e., we consider the general linear difference equation in the following form:

$$u(k + n) + a_1 u(k + n - 1) + \cdots + a_n u(k) =$$
$$b_0 e(k + n) + b_1 e(k + n - 1) + \cdots + b_n e(k) \qquad (11.14)$$

There is no loss of generality in this assumption: the results for $m = n$ can be used for the case of $m < n$ by setting appropriate b_i coefficients to zero.

To solve an equation of the form (11.14) is an elementary matter. Substituting $k = 0$ we observe that the output at instant n is expressed in terms of n values of the past outputs: $u(0)$, $u(1)$, ..., $u(n - 1)$, and n terms of inputs: $e(0)$, $e(1)$, ..., $e(n - 1)$. If k is incremented to take on values $k = 0, 1, 2, ...,$ etc., the $u(k)$; $k = n, n + 1, ...,$ can easily be generated by iterative procedure.

Since the difference equation model (11.14) represents a time-invariant system, the choice of the initial point on the time scale is simply a matter of convenience in analysis. Shifting the origin from $k = n$ to $k = 0$, we get the equivalent difference equation model:

$$u(k) + a_1 u(k - 1) + \cdots + a_n u(k - n) =$$
$$b_0 e(k) + b_1 e(k - 1) + \cdots + b_n e(k - n) \qquad (11.15)$$

If the input is assumed to be switched on at $k = 0$ ($e(k) = 0$ for $k < 0$), then the difference equation model (11.15) gives the output at instant '0' in terms of the past values of the output: $u(-1)$, $u(-2)$, ..., $u(-n)$, and the present input $e(0)$. The sequence $\{u(-1), u(-2), ..., u(-n)\}$, thus, gives the *initial conditions* of the process initiated at $k = 0$.

Consider, for example, the computer processing of the input samples $e(k) \triangleq e(kT)$ to generate output sequence $u(k) \triangleq u(kT)$ as per the algorithm described by second-order difference equation

$$u(k + 2) - 3u(k + 1) + 2u(k) = 2e(k + 1) - e(k) \qquad (11.16)$$

The input is applied at $k = 0$ ($e(k) = 0$ for $k < 0$). We assume zero initial conditions, i.e., $u(k) = 0$ for $k < 0$.

If we write Eqn. (11.16) as

$$u(k) = 3u(k - 1) - 2u(k - 2) + 2e(k - 1) - e(k - 2)$$

then its response to the given input sequence $e(k)$; $k \geq 0$, can be computed recursively as

$$u(0) = 0$$
$$u(1) = 3u(0) + 2e(0)$$
$$u(2) = 3u(1) - 2u(0) + 2e(1) - e(0)$$
$$u(3) = 3u(2) - 2u(1) + 2e(2) - e(1)$$

and so forth.   ⋮

The discretization problem, therefore, amounts to conversion of the transfer function

$$\frac{U(s)}{E(s)} = D(s)$$

to an equivalent difference equation. There is no exact solution to this problem because $D(s)$ responds to the complete history of $e(t)$, whereas the digital control algorithm has access only to the samples $e(k)$. In a sense, various discretization procedures simply make different assumptions about what happens to $e(k)$ between the sample points.

A simple discretization approach is based on finite-difference approximations of derivatives and integrals.

Finite-Difference Approximations of Derivatives

This approach is based on transforming a continuous-time system into a discrete-time one by approximating derivatives in a differential equation representation of the continuous-time system by finite differences. This is a common procedure in digital simulations of analog systems and is motivated by the intuitive notion that the derivative of a continuous-time function can be approximated by the difference between consecutive samples of the signal to be differentiated. The *forward difference* approximation of $du(t)/dt$ is given by

$$\left. \frac{du(t)}{dt} \right|_{t=kT} = \frac{u(k+1) - u(k)}{T} \tag{11.17}$$

and the *backward-difference* approximation is given by

$$\left. \frac{du(t)}{dt} \right|_{t=kT} = \frac{u(k) - u(k-1)}{T} \tag{11.18}$$

To illustrate the procedure, consider the first-order compensator

$$\frac{U(s)}{E(s)} = D(s) = \frac{1}{s+a}$$

We can represent $D(s)$ by the first-order differential equation

$$\frac{du(t)}{dt} + au(t) = e(t) \tag{11.19}$$

The *backward-difference* method consists of replacing $e(t)$ by $e(k)$, $u(t)$ by $u(k)$, and the first derivative $du(t)/dt$ by $[u(k) - u(k-1)]/T$. This yields the difference equation

$$\frac{u(k) - u(k-1)}{T} + au(k) = e(k)$$

or
$$u(k+1) = \frac{1}{1+aT} u(k) + \frac{T}{1+aT} e(k+1) \qquad (11.20)$$

Finite-Difference Approximations of Integrals

Consider the continuous-time system (11.19):

$$\frac{du(t)}{dt} = -au(t) + e(t) \qquad (11.21a)$$

which upon integration gives

$$u(t) = u(0) - a\int_0^t u(\tau)d\tau + \int_0^t e(\tau)d\tau \qquad (11.21b)$$

Rectangular Rules for Integration

In numerical analysis, the procedure known as the rectangular rule for integration proceeds by approximating the continuous-time function by contiguous rectangles, as illustrated in Fig. 11.26, and then adding their areas to compute the total integral. We thus approximate the area as given below.

Forward rectangular rule for integration

$$\int_{(k-1)T}^{kT} u(t)dt = [u(k-1)]T \qquad (11.22)$$

Backward rectangular rule for integration

$$\int_{(k-1)T}^{kT} u(t)dt = [u(k)]T \qquad (11.23)$$

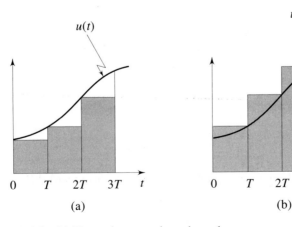

(a)   (b)

Fig. 11.26 *(a) Forward rectangular rule, and*
(b) backward rectangular rule for integral approximation

With the backward rectangular rule for integration, the continuous-time system (11.21b) is converted to the following recursive algorithm:

$$u(k) = u(k-1) - aTu(k) + Te(k)$$

or
$$u(k+1) = \frac{1}{1+aT}u(k) + \frac{T}{1+aT}e(k+1) \qquad (11.24)$$

which is same as that obtained by backward-difference approximation of derivative.

Example 11.3

The simplest formula for the PID or three-mode controller is the addition of the proportional, integral, and derivative modes:

$$u(t) = K_c\left[e(t) + \frac{1}{T_I}\int_0^t e(t)dt + T_D\frac{de(t)}{dt}\right] \qquad (11.25)$$

where

$u =$ controller output signal
$e =$ error (controller input) signal
$K_c =$ controller gain
$T_I =$ integral or reset time
$T_D =$ derivative or rate time

For the digital realization of the PID controller, it is necessary to approximate each mode in Eqn. (11.25) using the sampled values of $e(t)$.

The proportional mode requires no approximation since it is purely static part:

$$u_P(k) = K_c e(k)$$

The integral mode may be approximated by backward rectangular rule for integration. If $S(k-1)$ approximates the area under the $e(t)$ curve upto $t = (k-1)T$, then the approximation to the area under the $e(t)$ curve up to $t = kT$ is given by (refer Eqn. (11.23))

$$S(k) = S(k-1) + Te(k)$$

A digital realization of the integral mode of control is as follows:

$$u_I(k) = \frac{K_c}{T_I}S(k)$$

where

$S(k) =$ sum of the areas under the error curve
$\quad = S(k-1) + Te(k)$

The derivative mode may be approximated by the backward-difference approximation:

$$\left.\frac{de(t)}{dt}\right|_{t=kT} = \frac{e(k) - e(k-1)}{T}$$

Therefore, $\quad u_D(k) = \dfrac{K_c T_D}{T}[e(k) - e(k - 1)]$

Bringing all the three modes together results in the following PID algorithm:

$$u(k) = u_P(k) + u_I(k) + u_D(k)$$

$$= K_c\left[e(k) + \frac{1}{T_I}S(k) + \frac{T_D}{T}[e(k) - e(k - 1)]\right] \quad (11.26a)$$

where

$$S(k) = S(k - 1) + Te(k) \quad (11.26b)$$

Trapezoidal Rule for Integration

Let us consider a continuous-time system for which the describing equation is (Eqn. (11.19))

$$\dot{u}(t) = -au(t) + e(t) \quad (11.27a)$$

or $\quad u(t) = u(0) - a\displaystyle\int_0^t u(\tau)d\tau + \int_0^t e(\tau)d\tau \quad (11.27b)$

In numerical analysis, the procedure known as the trapezoidal rule for integration proceeds by approximating the continuous-time function by contiguous trapezoids, as illustrated in Fig. 11.27, and then adding their areas to compute the total integral. We thus approximate the area

$$\int_{(k-1)T}^{kT} u(t)dt \text{ by } \frac{1}{2}[u(k) + u(k - 1)]T \quad (11.28)$$

With this approximation, Eqn. (11.27b) can be converted to the following recursive algorithm:

$$u(k) = u(k - 1) - \frac{aT}{2}[u(k) + u(k - 1)] + \frac{T}{2}[e(k) + e(k - 1)]$$

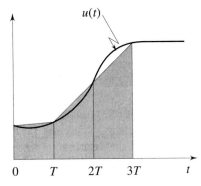

Fig. 11.27 *Trapezoidal rule for integral approximation*

or $\quad u(k+1) = \dfrac{1 - \dfrac{aT}{2}}{1 + \dfrac{aT}{2}} \, u(k) + \dfrac{T/2}{1 + \dfrac{aT}{2}} \, e(k+1) + \dfrac{T/2}{1 + \dfrac{aT}{2}} \, e(k)$ (11.29)

Sampling Rate Selection

The selection of the best sampling rate for a digital control system is the result of a compromise among many factors. The basic motivation to lower the sampling rate is cost. A decrease in sampling rate means more time is available for the control calculations; hence slower computers can be used for a given control function or more control capability can be achieved from a given computer. Either way, the cost per function is lowered. For systems with A/D converters, less demand on conversion speed will also lower cost. These economic arguments indicate that the best engineering choice is the slowest possible sampling rate that still meets all performance specifications.

With excessive reduction in sampling rate, a number of potentially degrading effects start to become significant. For a particular application, one or more of these degrading effects set the lower limit for the sampling rate. The process dynamics, the type of algorithm and control requirements, and the characteristics of input and noise signals all interact to set the maximum usable value for sampling period T.

How to find an adequate sampling interval, has been widely discussed in the literature. Some commonly used empirical rules are reported below.

Empirical Rules for the Selection of Sampling Rate

Practical experience and simulation results have produced a number of useful approximate rules for the specification of minimum sampling rate/maximum sampling interval.

1. The following recommendations for the most common process variables follow from the experience of process industries:

Type of variable	Sampling time (sec)
Flow	1–3
Level	5–10
Pressure	1–5
Temperature	10–20

2. Fast-acting electromechanical systems require much shorter sampling intervals, perhaps down to a few milliseconds.

3. A rule of thumb says that select a sampling period that is much shorter than any of the time-constants in the continuous-time plant to be controlled digitally. Sampling interval equal to one-tenth of the smallest time-constant or the inverse of the largest real pole (or real part of complex pole) has been recommended.

4. For complex poles with imaginary part ω_d, the frequency of transient oscillations corresponding to the poles is ω_d. A convenient rule suggests sampling at the rate of 6 to 10 times per cycle. Thus, if the largest imaginary part in the poles of the continuous-time plant is 1 rad/sec, which corresponds to transient oscillations with a frequency of 1/6.28 cycles per second, $d = 1$ sec may be satisfactory.

5. Rules of thumb based on open-loop plant model are full of danger under the conditions where high closed-loop performance is forced from a plant with a low open-loop performance. The rational choice of the sampling rate should be based on an understanding of its influence on the closed-loop performance of the control system. It seems reasonable that the highest frequency of interest should be closely related to the 3 dB-bandwidth of the closed-loop system. The selection of sampling rates can then be based on the bandwidth of the closed-loop system. Reasonable sampling rates are 10 to 30 times the bandwidth.

6. Another rule of thumb based on closed-loop performance is to select sampling interval T equal to or less than one-tenth of the desired settling time.

*Example 11.4*_____

Consider the analog control system shown in Fig. 11.28. The specifications for the system are that the damping ratio ζ of the pair of dominant closed-loop poles be 0.7, and the natural frequency ω_n be 0.3 rad/sec. The specifications can be met with

$$D(s) = \frac{0.81(s + 0.2)}{s + 2}$$

as can be verified by the root locus plot.

To digitize this $D(s)$, we first need to select a sampling rate. For a system with $\omega_n = 0.3$ rad/sec, a very 'safe' sampling rate would be a factor of 20 faster than ω_n, yielding $\omega_s = 0.3 \times 20 = 6$ rad/sec, or 1 Hz

Thus, let us pick $T = 1$ sec. Using the trapezoidal rule for integration, a digital control algorithm is obtained as follows:

$$D(s) = \frac{0.81(s + 0.2)}{s + 2} = \frac{U(s)}{E(s)} \qquad (11.30)$$

gives $\qquad \dot{u}(t) + 2u(t) = 0.81\,\dot{e}(t) + 0.162\ e(t)$

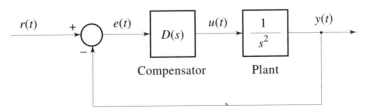

Fig. 11.28 *An analog control system*

or $\qquad \dot{u}(t) = -2\,u(t) + 0.81\dot{e}(t) + 0.162\,e(t)$

Therefore $\quad u(t) = u(0) - 2\int_0^t u(\tau)\,d\tau + 0.81e(t) - 0.81e(0) + 0.162\int_0^t e(\tau)\,d\tau$

Using the trapezoidal rule for integration, the following recursive algorithm follows from this equation.

$$u(k) = u(k-1) - 2\left[\frac{u(k)+u(k-1)}{2}\right]T + 0.81e(k) - 0.81e(k-1)$$

$$+ 0.162\left[\frac{e(k)+e(k-1)}{2}\right]T$$

or $\qquad u(k) = 0.4455\,e(k) - 0.3645\,e(k-1)$ $\qquad\qquad$ (11.31)

where $\qquad e(k) = r(k) - y(k)$

This completes the digital algorithm design. The complete digital control system is shown in Fig. 11.29.

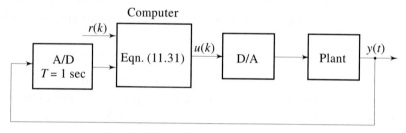

Fig. 11.29 *A digital control system*

Applicability Limits of Digital Implementation of Analog Compensators

When a continuous-time signal is sampled at regular intervals of time and is then reconstructed by holding the sampled values constant for each sampling interval, the reconstructed signal is effectively delayed by approximately one half of the sampling interval, as shown in Fig. 11.30.

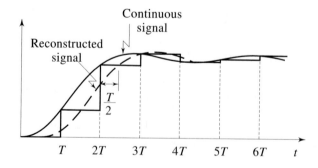

Fig. 11.30 *Time delay introduced by sampling and reconstruction*

In digital control configuration of Fig. 11.24, the ZOH holds the output of the digital controller constant between updates, thus introducing a delay of $T/2$ sec into the loop. This dead-time introduces a phase lag, and thus reduces the stability margin in a closed-loop system. If an exact discrete-time analysis or a simulation of a digital control system obtained by discretization of analog design were performed, and the discretization determined for a wide range of sampling rates, the system would be unstable for sampling rates lower than approximately $5 \times \omega_b$, and the damping would be substantially degraded for sampling rates slower than $10 \times \omega_b$. At sampling rates of the order of $20 \times \omega_b$, this design method will yield reasonable results, and can be used with confidence for sampling rates of $30 \times \omega_b$ or higher.

Thus, a fictitious limit on the sampling rate occurs when using digital implementation of analog design. The inherent approximation in the method may give rise to system instabilities as the sampling rate is lowered, and this can lead the designer to conclude that a lower limit on ω_s has been reached when, in fact, the proper conclusion is that the approximations are invalid; the solution is not to sample faster but to refine the design.

A simple way to refine the design is to account for the lagging effect of the ZOH in the analog design itself. We introduce the transfer function

$$G_h(s) = e^{-sT/2} \qquad (11.32)$$

in analog control loop (refer Fig. 11.31) in anticipation of the conversion from an analog controller to a digital controller. Note that $G_h(s)$ is a pure time delay with dead time of $T/2$ and a dc gain of unity. Considering $G_h(s)G(s)$ as the plant model, we design the analog compensator $D(s)$. Discretization of this $D(s)$ will allow for higher values of sampling interval.

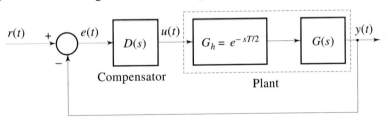

Fig. 11.31 *Analog compensator design for digital implementation*

One of the advantages of using the analog design method, however, is that the sampling rate need not be selected until after the basic feedback design is completed. We carry out analog design and then discretize the analog compensator. If the discretized compensator does not yield a satisfactory result, we select a different sampling period and again discretize the analog compensator. There is no need to repeat the design. Use of Eqn. (11.32) eliminates this advantage, although it does partially alleviate a primary disadvantage: the approximate nature of the method.

In the *direct digital design* approach, we first discretize the plant and then carry out design using digital techniques. If the result is found to be unsatisfactory, we must select a different sampling period, again discretize the analog plant and then repeat the design. This approach allows a longer sampling interval without the introduction of unacceptable error.[2]

Example 11.5

Consider the first-order continuous-time system shown in Fig. 11.32a. This feedback system is stable for all values of $K > 0$.

Introduce now a sampler and ZOH in the forward path of the system, converting it to a sampled-data system of Fig. 11.32b. Due to the action of the ZOH, the control signal during the kth sampling interval is

$$u^+(t) = u(kT); \quad kT \le t < (k + 1)T$$

The output $y(t)$ during this period due to the action of the integrator is given by

$$y(t) = y(kT) + \int_{kT}^{t} u(kT)d\tau; \quad kT \le t < (k + 1)T$$

At $t = (k + 1)T$,

$$y[(k + 1)T] = y(kT) + \left[\int_{kT}^{(k+1)T} d\tau \right] u(kT)$$

$$= y(kT) + Tu(kT) = y(kT) + KT[r(kT) - y(kT)]$$

$$= (1 - KT)y(kT) + KT\, r(kT)$$

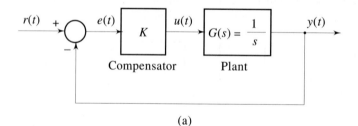

(a)

(b)

Fig. 11.32 *(a) A first-order continuous-time system*
(b) A first-order sampled-data system

2. Chapter 4 of reference [180].

or $\qquad y(kT) = (1 - KT)y(kT - T) + KT\, r(kT - T)$

Assume that $r(kT) = y(kT) = 0$ for $k < 0$. The response $y(kT)$ for $k \geq 0$ can be computed recursively as

$$y(0) = 0; \quad y(T) = KT\, r(0); \quad y(2T) = (1 - KT)KT\, r(0) + KT\, r(T); \; \dots$$

The closed-form solution is given by

$$y(kT) = KT \sum_{i=0}^{k-1} (1 - KT)^{k-i-1} r(iT); \; k > 0$$

For a bounded input, the output is bounded (i.e., the system is stable) if

$$|1 - KT| < 1$$

or $\qquad\qquad 0 < KT < 2$

or $\qquad\qquad K < \dfrac{2}{T}$

It may be recalled that the corresponding continuous-time system of Fig. 11.32a is stable for all values of K. Sampling, thus, has detrimental effect on the relative stability of the system.

Consider now the steady-state behaviour. The type-1 continuous-time system of Fig. 11.32a has a zero steady-state error to unit-step input. Unit-step response of the sampled-data system of Fig. 11.32b is[3]

$$
\begin{aligned}
y(k)\big|_{k \to \infty} &= \lim_{k \to \infty} KT \sum_{i=0}^{k-1} (1 - KT)^{k-1-i} r(iT) \\
&= \lim_{k \to \infty} KT \sum_{i=0}^{k-1} (1 - KT)^{k-1-i} \\
&= KT \sum_{j=0}^{\infty} (1 - KT)^{j} = 1
\end{aligned}
$$

Sampling, thus, has no effect on steady-state error of the type-1 system to unit-step input (this, in fact, is true for all types of systems, under all input conditions[4]).

▲▲

From Example 11.5, we observe that a poor selection of sampling interval may result in considerable reduction in stability margin. Therefore, discretization of an analog control scheme performing satisfactorily, may lead to a digital control system with an unacceptable degradation in performance. Analysis of the control loop containing a digital compensator must be carried out to evaluate the performance degradation. State variable technique for analysis of sampled-data systems is given in Chapter 12.

---

3. $\displaystyle \sum_{k=0}^{\infty} x^k = \frac{1}{1-x}; \, |x| < 1.$

4. Section 4.2 of reference [180].

11.8 | TUNABLE PID CONTROLLERS

In servomechanism applications, mathematical models of systems are often close enough to reality that controller parameters for optimum response can be fairly well predicted at the design stage and only a minor 'tweaking' of adjustments is needed during experimental development. In the process-control field, however, it is not uncommon for a controller to be installed on a process with little analytical study being done beforehand. Such a practice may not be as irrational as it first seems. Industrial processes are relatively slow and complex which in many cases can be expensive and time-consuming to analyse, if meaningful analysis is possible at all. Also many years of experience have shown that a PID controller is versatile enough to control a wide variety of processes. Thus an approach that selects a certain class (P, PI, PID) of controller based on past experience with certain classes of processes (pressure, flow, liquid-level, temperature, composition, etc.), and then sets controller parameters by experiment once the controller is installed, is not unreasonable. This experimental 'design' of controller settings has come to be known as *controller tuning*.

Tuning is thus the procedure of adjusting the parameters of a feedback controller to obtain a specific closed-loop response. The difficulty of the problem increases with the number of parameters that must be adjusted. For example, tuning procedure for a P controller is simple because only one parameter, the controller gain, needs to be adjusted to obtain the desired response. The next degree of difficulty is the tuning of the PI controller; since two parameters, the gain and the integral time, must be adjusted, the tuning procedure is significantly more complicated than when only one parameter needs to be adjusted. Finally the tuning of the PID controller represents the next higher degree of difficulty since three parameters, the gain, the integral time, and the derivative time must be adjusted.

Another difficulty inherent in the tuning of process loops arises because of the slow response of most of the industrial processes. We may have to wait for several minutes and may be even hours to observe the response that results from our tuning adjustments. This makes the tuning of feedback controllers by trial-and-error a tedious and time-consuming task. Yet this happens to be the most common method used in process industry. A number of tuning rules have been introduced to tune controllers for various response criteria. Tuning rules mathematically define the trial parameter values; this is often followed by a manual fine tuning by a process engineer. Auto-tuners, which automate some of the tasks manually performed by a process engineer, are also commercially available. In this section we will study commonly used methods of manual tuning of analog and digital controllers.

The values of the tuning parameters depend on the desired closed-loop response and on the dynamic characteristics of the process. Dynamic characteristics of most of the industrial processes exhibit nonlinear behaviour. For most of the temperature and composition loops, for example, the process gain decreases as the throughput increases. Another common nonlinearity is the exponential dependence of reaction rates on temperature. Besides non-linear behaviour, many process characteristics vary with time due to catalyst deactivation in the reactors, fouling of heat exchanger tubes, choking of furnace tubes, and the like. A particular set of tuning parameters can provide the desired response at only one operating point, given that standard feedback controllers are basically linear devices. However, recalling that feedback control is usually a very robust strategy, small variations in process operating conditions would normally not change the closed-loop behaviour. Whenever process non-linearities and/or time-dependent characteristics cause a significant change in the process dynamic parameters, *adaptive control* is needed. We will not be able to accommodate adaptive control techniques (refer [180]). It may, however, be noted that because of the robustness property of feedback control, very few processes require adaptive control although almost all processes are nonlinear/time-varying.

Another limitation of our presentation is that tuning procedures for process control systems with only single feedback loops are considered. *Cascade control* strategy, which is commonly used for improving the performance of process control systems, results in a multiloop design. In its simplest form, cascade control implies closing a feedback loop inside the primary control loop by measuring an intermediate process variable. MIMO processes also give rise to multiloop control configurations if each controlled variable is affected by more than one manipulated variable. Knowledge-base required for tuning multiloop process control systems consists of tuning procedures for single loop designs and experts' knowledge, mostly learned on the job. Many of the books exclusively devoted to process control [5–13] give some tuning tips for multiloop designs.

A Brief Review of Analog PID Controllers

Approximately 75% of feedback controllers in the process industry are PI controllers; most of the balance are PID controllers. Some applications require only I, only P, or PD controllers, but these are few.

Basic characteristics of proportional, integral and derivative modes of feedback control have already been discussed in Chapter 4. A brief review is presented here with the objective of identifying tuning parameters, and other adjustment features of process controllers.

Proportional Controller

The equation that describes the proportional controller is:

$$u(t) = K_c e(t) \tag{11.33a}$$

or

$$U(s) = K_c E(s) \tag{11.33b}$$

where K_c is the *controller gain*, e is the error, and u is the perturbation in controller output signal from the bias or base value corresponding to the normal operating conditions; the base value on the controller is adjusted to produce zero error under the conditions of no disturbance and/or set-point change.

Some instrument manufacturers calibrate the controller gain as *proportional band (PB)*. A 10% *PB* means that a 10% change in the controller input causes a full-scale (100%) change in controller output. The conversion relation is thus

$$K_c = \frac{100}{PB} \tag{11.34}$$

A proportional controller has only one adjustable or tuning parameter: K_c or *PB*.

As we shall see later in this section, it is rare for industrial processes to include an integration property. A proportionally controlled process with no integration property will always exhibit error at steady-state in the presence of disturbances and changes in set-point. The error, of course, can be made negligibly small by increasing the gain of the proportional controller. However, as the gain is increased, the performance of the closed-loop system becomes more oscillatory and takes longer to settle down after being disturbed. Further, most process plants have a considerable amount of dead-time which severely restricts the value of the gain that can be used. In processes where the control within a band from the set-point is acceptable, proportional control is sufficient. However, in processes which require perfect control at the set-point, proportional controllers will not provide satisfactory performance.

Proportional–Integral Controller

To remove the steady-state offset in the controlled variable of a process, an extra amount of intelligence must be added to the proportional controller. This extra intelligence is the integral or reset action; consequently the controller becomes a PI controller. The equation describing a PI controller is as follows:

$$u(t) = K_c \left[e(t) + \frac{1}{T_I} \int_0^t e(t)dt \right] \tag{11.35a}$$

or

$$U(s) = K_c \left[1 + \frac{1}{T_I s} \right] E(s) \tag{11.35b}$$

where T_I is the *integral* or *reset time*.

A PI controller has thus two adjustable or tuning parameters: K_c (or *PB*) and T_I. The integral or reset action in this controller removes the steady-state offset in the controlled variable. However, the integral mode of control has a considerable destabilizing effect which, in most of the situations, can be compensated by adjusting the gain K_c.

Some instrument manufacturers calibrate the integral mode parameter as the *reset rate*, which is simply the reciprocal of the reset time.

Proportional–Integral–Derivative Controller

Sometimes a mode faster than the proportional mode is added to the PI controller. This new mode of control is the derivative action, also called the rate action, which responds to the rate of change of error with time. This speeds up the controller action. The equation describing the PID controller is as follows:

$$u(t) = K_c\left[e(t) + \frac{1}{T_I}\int_0^t e(t)dt + T_D\frac{de(t)}{dt} \right] \qquad (11.36a)$$

or

$$U(s) = K_c\left[1 + \frac{1}{T_I s} + T_D s \right]E(s) \qquad (11.36b)$$

where T_D is the *derivative* or *rate time*.

A PID controller has thus three adjustable or tuning parameters: K_c (or PB), T_I, and T_D. The derivative action anticipates the error, initiates an early corrective action, and tends to increase the stability of the system. It does not affect the steady-state error directly. A derivative control mode in isolation produces no corrective effort for any constant error, no matter how large, and would therefore allow uncontrolled steady-state errors. Thus, we cannot consider derivative modes in isolation; they will always be considered as augmenting some other mode.

The block diagram implementation of Eqn. (11.36b) is sketched in Fig. 1133a. The alternative form, Fig. 11.33b, is more commonly used because it avoids taking the rate of change of the set-point input to the controller, thus preventing the undesirable derivative 'kick' on set-point changes by the process operator.

Due to the noise-accentuating characteristics of derivative operations, the lowpass-filtered derivative $T_D s/(\alpha T_D s + 1)$ is actually preferred in practice (Fig. 11.33c). The value of the filter parameter α is not adjustable but is built into the design of the controller. It is usually of the order of 0.05 to 0.3 (refer Problem 11.1a).

The controller of Fig. 11.33 is considered to be *noninteracting* in that its derivative and integral modes operate independently of each other (although proportional gain affects all the three modes). Noninteraction is provided by the parallel functioning of integral and derivative modes. By contrast, many controllers have derivative and integral action applied serially to the controlled variable resulting in interaction between them. Many of the analog industrial controllers commercially available today realize the following *interacting* PID control action (it is claimed that this form of controller is easier to tune manually).

$$U(s) = K'_c\left[\frac{T'_D s + 1}{\alpha T'_D s + 1} \right]\left[1 + \frac{1}{T'_I s} \right]E(s) \qquad (11.37)$$

The first term in brackets is a derivative unit (refer Problem 11.1b) attached to the standard PI controller serially to create the PID controller (Fig. 11.34a).

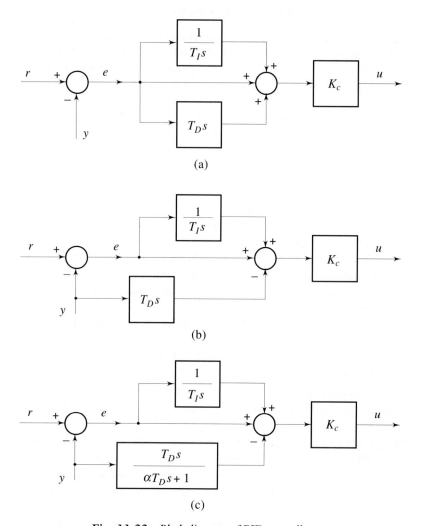

(a)

(b)

(c)

Fig. 11.33 *Block diagram of PID controller*

The derivative unit is installed on the controlled variable input to the controller in order to avoid the derivative kick (Fig. 11.34b).

From Figs 11.33a and 11.34a, the following equivalence can easily be established between the parameters of idealized versions of noninteracting PID controller and interacting PID controller ($\alpha = 0$):

$$F_{12} = 1 + (T'_D/T'_I) \tag{11.38}$$

$$K_c = K'_c F_{12}; \; T_I = T'_I F_{12}; \; T_D = T'_D/F_{12}$$

or $$F_{21} = 0.5 + [0.25 - (T_D/T_I)]^{1/2} \tag{11.39}$$

$$K'_c = K_c F_{21}; \; T'_I = T_I F_{21}; \; T'_D = T_D/F_{21}$$

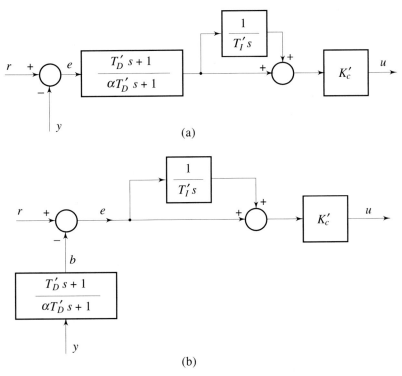

Fig. 13.34 *Alternative realization schemes for PID control action*

Functions of a PID Controller

For adjusting the output signal $u(t)$ from a PID controller, the following features are normally provided in industrial controllers.

1. Adjusting (tuning) the parameters of proportional, integral, and derivative control modes.
2. Direct/reverse action switch.
3. Adjusting lower and upper bounds on the control signal for protection against integral (reset) wind up.

Tuning the Proportional, Integral and Derivative Control Modes

We have already reviewed the basic characteristics of proportional, integral, and derivative modes of feedback control. These characteristics can be controlled by adjusting the parameters—K_c(controller gain), T_I (integral time), and T_D (derivative time).

Direct/Reverse Action Switch

The position of the direct/reverse action switch of the controller depends upon the action of control valves of the process plant.

Two types of control valves are available on the market—the 'fail-open' type and the 'fail-closed' type. A 'fail-open' valve opens its restriction to flow when energy supply (air pressure/current) to the valve fails, and a 'fail-closed' valve closes its restriction to flow on the failure of energy supply.

The great majority of control valves are pneumatically operated and consequently the energy supply is air pressure. A 'fail-closed' valve requires energy to open it; they are also referred to as 'air-to-open' (A–O) valves (Fig. 11.35a). The 'fail-open' valves that require energy to close are also referred to as 'air-to-close' (A–C) valves (Fig. 11.35b).

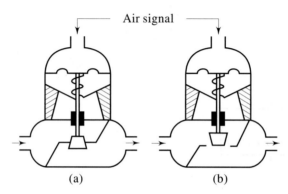

Fig. 11.35 *Pneumatic control valves*

The choice of a control valve for a particular application is based on safety considerations. Consider, for example, the process shown in Fig. 11.36a. In this process, the outlet temperature of process fluid is controlled by manipulating the steam flow to the heat exchanger. The question is: what do we want the steam valve to do when the air supply to it fails? We want the steam valve to move to the safest position. It seems that the safest condition may be the one that stops the steam flow. This means that fail-closed (A–O) valve should be used. In making this decision we have not taken into account the effect of not heating the process fluid by closing the valve. In some cases, this may not cause any problems; however, in other cases, it may have to be considered. For example, consider the case when the steam is maintaining the temperature of a certain polymer. If the steam valve closes, the temperature will drop and the polymer may solidify in the exchanger. In this case, it might be decided that a fail-open (A-C) valve provides the safest condition.

Assume that the A-O control valve has been selected for the heat exchanger control loop shown in Fig. 11.36a. The objective of the control loop is to maintain the outlet temperature of the process fluid, $\theta(t)$, at its desired value (set-point θ_r) in the presence of variations of the process fluid flow $q_m(t)$ and inlet temperature $\theta_i(t)$. The steam flow $q_{ms}(t)$ is the variable that can be adjusted to control the outlet temperature.

If the outlet temperature moves above the set-point, the controller must close the steam valve. Since the valve is A-O valve, the controller must reduce its output (air pressure/current) signal. To make this decision, the direct/reverse action switch must be set to *reverse action*.

Consider now the level control loop shown in Fig. 11.36b. The system shown is designed to maintain tank level $h(t)$ at desired value h_r in the face of disturbance in the inlet flow $q_i(t)$.

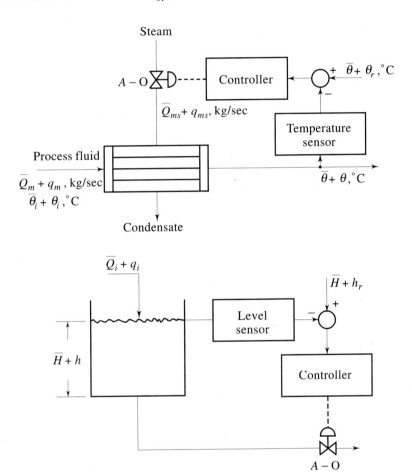

Fig. 11.36 *(a) A temperature control loop*
(b) A liquid-level control loop

If the liquid level moves above the set-point, the controller must open the valve to bring the level back to the set-point. Since the valve is an A-O valve, the controller must increase its output (air pressure/current) signal. To make this decision, the direct/reverse action switch must be set to *direct action*[1].

▲▲

---

5. A reverse-acting controller will be required if an air-to-close (A-C) valve is used.

The equation $\qquad u(t) = K_c e(t) = K_c[y_r - y(t)]$ $\qquad$ (11.40)

describes a *reverse-acting controller*: if the controlled variable $y(t)$ increases above the set-point y_r, the error becomes negative and the output $u(t)$ from the controller decreases.

The equation $\qquad u(t) = K_c[y(t) - y_r]$

describes a *direct-acting controller*: if the controlled variable increases above the set-point y_r, the output from the controller increases.

The usual way to show a *direct-acting controller* mathematically is by Eqn. (11.40) treating the controller gain K_c as negative. We must, however, remember that there are no negative gains in industrial controllers; the direct/reverse action switch takes care of the control requirement arising from the selection of control valves. The negative K_c is used when doing a mathematical analysis of a control system that requires a direct-acting controller.

Integral (reset) Wind-up

A properly tuned controller will behave well as long as its output remains in a range where it can change the manipulated flow. However it will behave poorly if, for any reason, the effect of the controller output on the manipulated flow is lost. A gap between the limit on the controller output and the operational limit of the control valve is the most common cause of integral (reset) wind-up. The heat exchanger control loop shown in Fig. 11.36a is used to explain this problem. The block diagram for the temperature control loop is shown in Fig. 11.37.

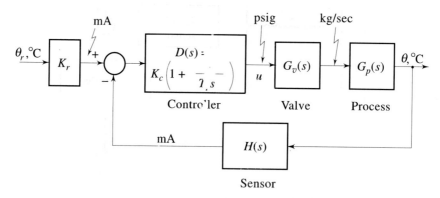

Fig. 11.37 *A block diagram for the temperature control loop of Fig. 11.36a*

Assume that a PI controller is used to control the temperature θ by adjusting the steam control valve. The instrumentation is electropneumatic.

The controlled variable θ is measured with a sensor that generates a signal (mA) that is proportional to the temperature. The measurement is sent to the controller where it is compared with the set-point (the term K_r on the set-point signal is included to indicate the conversion of the set-point scale). The controller then generates a control signal (mA) on the basis of the error between the measurement and the set-point. The controller output signal is then connected to the actuator of the steam control valve through a current-to-pressure transducer. To keep the diagram simple, we have included the constant gain of the current-to-pressure transducer in the controller transfer function $D(s)$.

The nominal pressure range of the valve is 3 to 15 psig and the supply pressure is 20 psig.

Assume that a command signal for a step change θ_r in the set-point is given. Initially the temperature θ is much below its set-point value; because of the large error the controller output is driven to a large value by integral action. A typical time recording of the experiment is shown in Fig. 11.38. At $t = t_1$, the controller output pressure is 15 psig. The control valve (sized to be wide open at 15 psig) saturates at this pressure.

Figure 11.38 shows that at $t = t_1$ (when the control valve is fully open), the controlled variable θ has not reached its set-point. Since there is still an error, the controller will try to correct for it by further increasing (integrating the error) its output pressure, even though the valve will not open more after 15 psig. The output of the controller can, in fact, integrate up to the supply pressure 20 psig. In Fig. 11.38, the point $t = t_2$ corresponds to this situation. The controller cannot increase its output pressure for $t > t_2$, its output having saturated at $t = t_2$. Although the controller is saturated, it keeps the steam valve fully open. This is the correct strategy to force the temperature θ to set-point value in minimum time. The point $t = t_3$ corresponds to this situation in Fig. 11.38.

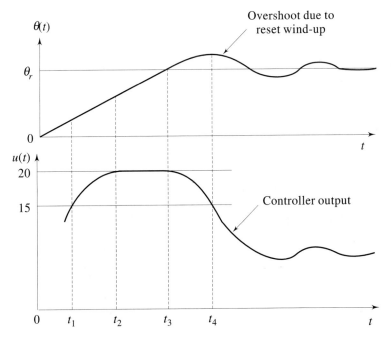

Fig. 11.38 *Reset wind-up in heat exchanger*

The wind-up problem begins to show up when the controlled variable θ reaches its set-point. At that instant ($t = t_3$) the controller output is 20 psig. The error reverses at $t = t_3$; the valve cannot respond to this change, until the integral signal (which has 'wound-up' to 20 psig) is 'unwound' back to the 15 psig level at $t = t_4$. This delayed response effect is called *reset wind-up* or *integral wind-up*. Note that this delay is in addition to the normal lagging behaviour of integral control and can thus cause excessive overshooting and stability problems.

▲▲

One way to prevent the large overshoot caused by reset wind-up is to keep the controller on *manual* until the temperature reaches the set-point, and then switch it to *automatic*. In this case the steam valve is kept fully open by manually setting the controller output to 15 psig. This ensures that the control valve will start to close as soon as the controller is switched to automatic.

A second alternative is to install a limiter on the controller output to keep it from going beyond the operating range of the control valve, i.e., above 15 psig or below 3 psig. Figure 11.39a shows a straightforward scheme of a PI controller with a limiter. Note that this implementation, where the limiter is placed on the controller output, does not prevent the wind-up problem: the output of the integral action $u_I(t)$ will still be driven beyond the controller output limits and cause wind-up. In order to prevent wind-up, the output of the integral action must somehow be limited. In pneumatic and electronic controllers, this limiting is accomplished in a very ingenious way.

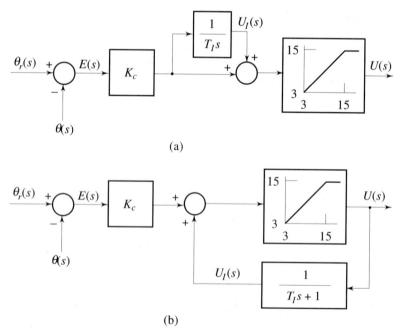

(a)

(b)

Fig. 11.39 *Anti-reset wind-up for PI controller*

A PI controller is described by the equation (refer Eqn. (11.35b))

$$U(s) = K_c \left[1 + \frac{1}{T_I s} \right] E(s)$$

or

$$U(s) = K_c E(s) + \frac{K_c}{T_I s} E(s) = K_c E(s) + U_I(s)$$

where

$$U_I(s) = \frac{K_c}{T_I s} E(s)$$

Rearranging these equations, yields

$$U_I(s) = \left[\frac{1}{T_I s + 1} \right] U(s) \qquad (11.41)$$

This implementation of integral action is represented in the block diagram of Fig. 11.39b. We can see from this diagram that if we place the limiter as shown, $U_I(s)$ will be automatically limited. This is because $U_I(s)$ is always lagging $U(s)$ with a gain of 1.0 and adjustable time-constant T_I; thus it can never get outside the range within which $U(s)$ is limited.

Reset wind-up occurs most commonly during start-up and shut-down, but it can also occur during product grade switches, and large disturbances during continuous operation. Reset wind-up is, of course, not a problem in every application of integral control.

Adjustment Features in Industrial Controllers

A great number of manufacturers are now making available in the market process controllers (electronic, pneumatic, and computer-based) with features that permit adjusting the set-point, transferring between manual and automatic control modes, adjusting the output signal from the control-action unit (tuning the parameters K_c, T_I, and T_D), and displaying the controlled variable, set-point, and control signal. Figure 11.40 shows the basic structure of an industrial controller. The controller has been broken down into three main units:

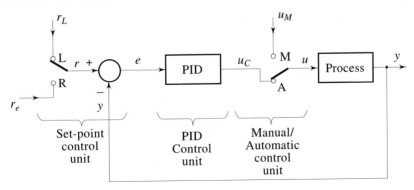

Fig. 11.40 *Basic structure of an industrial controller*

1. The set-point control unit
2. The PID control unit
3. The manual/automatic control unit.

The set-point control unit receives the measurement y of controlled variable of the process together with the set-point r of the control. A switch gives an option of choosing between local and remote (external) set-point operation. If the set-point to the controller is to be set by the operating personnel, then the local option r_L is chosen. If the set-point to the controller is to be set by another control module, then remote (external) option r_e is chosen. This is the case, for example, in cascade control where the drive of the controller in the major loop constitutes the set-point of the minor-loop controller.

The PID control unit receives the error signal e developed by the set-point control unit and generates an appropriate control signal u_C. Adjustment features provided in the control unit for generating appropriate control signals are: tuning of the three parameters K_c, T_I, and T_D; direct/reverse action switch; and setting of the upper and lower bounds of the closed-loop control.

The manual/automatic control unit has a switch which determines the mode of control action. When the switch is in the auto (A) position, the control signal u_C calculated by PID control unit is sent to the process (in such a case, the process is controlled in closed loop). When the switch is in the manual (M) position, the PID control unit 'freezes' its output. The control signal u_M can then be changed manually by the operating personnel (the process is then controlled in open loop).

The basic structure of a process controller shown in Fig. 11.40 is common for pneumatic, electronic, and computer-based controllers. These controllers are different in terms of realization of adjustment features.

For a long time, PID controllers were pneumatic. This technology is still used in special cases (in an explosive atmosphere, for instance). It should also be observed that the simplicity of maintenance of pneumatic modules, for a long time, made them preferable to electronic modules; but with the development of operational amplifiers and the ever-increasing reliability of integrated circuits, electronic controllers have gradually replaced pneumatic controllers. This development is now moving towards computer-based controllers. The interface between commonly used pneumatically-operated diaphragm actuators for control valves and electronic/computer-based controllers is achieved through electropneumatic transducers (refer Section 3.8).

*Example 11.6*_____

The PI controller shown in Fig. 11.41 becomes a *reverse acting* controller when the direct/reverse action switch is in position R (it becomes a *direct-acting* controller when the switch is thrown to position D).

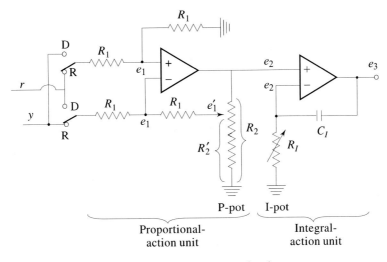

Fig. 11.41 *PI control unit*

The proportional-action unit is governed by the following relations (revisiting Section 2.9 will be helpful):

$$\frac{r - e_1}{R_1} = \frac{e_1}{R_1}; \; r = \text{reference input}$$

$$\frac{y - e_1}{R_1} = \frac{e_1 - e_1'}{R_1}; \; y = \text{controlled variable}[6]$$

Manipulation of these equations, gives

$$e_1' = r - y$$

Neglecting the loading effect on the potentiometer R_2, we get

$$e_1' = e_2 \frac{R_2'}{R_2}$$

Therefore,
$$E_2(s) = \frac{R_2}{R_2'}[R(s) - Y(s)] = K_c[R(s) - Y(s)] \qquad (11.42)$$

The proportional-action unit therefore establishes the difference of the two voltages r and y, and multiplies it by the gain $K_c = R_2/R_2'$. The gain K_c can be adjusted by means of a potentiometer which causes R'_2 to vary.

The integral action is carried out as follows:

$$\frac{e_2}{R_I} = C_I \frac{d}{dt}(e_3 - e_2)$$

---

6. If the output of the sensor measuring the controlled variable is a current signal, it is converted into a voltage signal y and then fed.

Therefore, $\qquad \dfrac{E_3(s)}{E_2(s)} = 1 + \dfrac{1}{T_I s}; \; T_I = R_I C_I$ $\qquad\qquad$ (11.43)

The integral time T_I can be adjusted by means of a potentiometer that causes R_I to vary.

From Eqns (11.42) and (11.43), we get[7]

$$E_3(s) = K_c\left(1 + \frac{1}{T_I s}\right)[R(s) - Y(s)] \qquad\qquad (11.44)$$

Figure 11.42 shows the manual/automatic switch unit of an industrial PI controller. This unit uses the op amp of the integral stage to construct the manual control. This circuit is intended to avoid any bumps on the controller output when switching from automatic to manual or from manual to automatic.

In the 'automatic' position, the structure in Fig. 11.42a is, in fact, equivalent to that of Fig. 11.42b. From this figure we observe that

$$e_3(t) = e_2(t) + \frac{1}{R_I C_I}\int e_2(\tau)d\tau \qquad\qquad (11.45)$$

and the voltage across the capacitor C_M is $e(t) = e_3(t)$. If at the instant t_0, the operator flicks the switch to the 'manual' position, $e = e_3(t_0)$ and the voltage remains constant (and therefore e_3 remains constant) as long as there is no voltage e_M applied on the manual control.

In the 'manual' position, the structure in Fig. 11.42a is equivalent to that in Fig. 11.42c. From this figure, we observe that

$$C_M \frac{de_3}{dt} = -\frac{e_M}{R_M}$$

or $\qquad\qquad e_3(t) = e_3(t_0) - \dfrac{1}{R_M C_M}\displaystyle\int e_M(\tau)d\tau \qquad\qquad$ (11.46)

Depending on the sign of e_M, an increase or decrease in output voltage $e_3(t)$ can be achieved.

Note that any variation in e_2 has no effect on e_3 for the output voltage of an operational amplifier depends only on the voltage applied at its '+' and '−' inputs. However, the capacitance C_I, which isolates e_2 from e_3, memorizes the difference between the voltages all the time:

$$e'(t) = e_3(t) - e_2(t); \; t \geq t_0$$

If at the instant t_1, the operator flicks the switch to automatic position, then

$$e'(t_1) = e_3(t_1) - e_2(t_1) \qquad\qquad (11.47a)$$

and $\qquad\qquad e_3(t) = e'(t_1) + e_2(t) + \dfrac{1}{R_I C_I}\displaystyle\int e_2(\tau)d\tau, \; t \geq t_1 \qquad\qquad$ (11.47b)

So the switch is made without bumps.

---

7. If the electronic controller is required to release a current signal, a voltage to current converter is used to convert $e_3(t)$ into current.

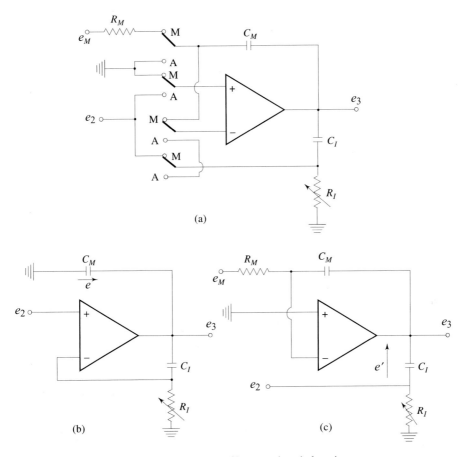

Fig. 11.42 *Manual/automatic switch unit*

Example 11.7

The PD controller shown in Fig. 11.43 consists of three basic units:

   (i) set-point control unit;

   (ii) derivative-action unit; and

   (iii) proportional-action unit.

The set-point control unit receives the set-point signal r (local or external), the controlled variable y, and develops the difference of these two measurements.

$$\frac{r - e_1}{R} = \frac{e_1 - e_2}{R}; \frac{y - e_1}{R} = \frac{e_1}{R}$$

Manipulation of these equations gives

$$e_2 = y - r \tag{11.48}$$

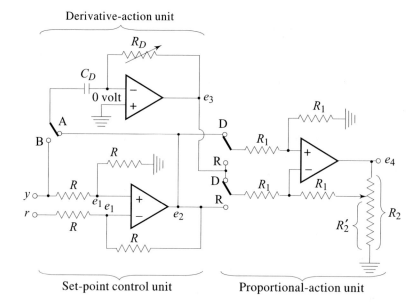

Fig. 11.43 *PD control unit*

It may be noted that the set-point control unit given in Fig. 11.43 constructs sign-inverted error variable.

The derivative-action unit given in Fig. 11.43 calculates the derivative either from the error variable developed by the set-point control unit, or directly from the controlled variable. The choice between these two possibilities depends on the position of a switch. When the switch is in position A, the circuit is governed by the following relation:

$$C_D \frac{de_2}{dt} = \frac{0 - e_3}{R_D}$$

Therefore,[8]
$$\frac{E_3(s)}{E_2(s)} = -T_D s; \; T_D = R_D C_D \tag{11.49}$$

The transfer function of the proportional-action unit has already been derived in Example 11.6. With the direct/reverse action switch in position D,

$$E_4(s) = \frac{R_2}{R_2'} [E_2(s) - E_3(s)] \tag{11.50}$$

From Eqns (11.48)–(11.50), we get
$$E_4(s) = K_c(1 + T_D s)[Y(s) - R(s)]; \tag{11.51a}$$

---

8. A lowpass filter may be inserted in cascade with the ideal differentiator to filter out high-frequency signals. Alternatively, the differentiator circuit may be redesigned. Refer Problems 11.1a – 11.1b.

$$K_c = \frac{R_2}{R_2'}, \; T_D = R_D C_D$$

With the direct/reverse action switch thrown to position R, we obtain

$$E_4(s) = K_c(1 + T_D s)[R(s) - Y(s)] \qquad (11.51b)$$

Digital PID Controllers

Most process industries today use computers to carry out the basic feedback control calculations. The formulas that are programmed to calculate the controller output are mostly the discrete versions of the analog controllers presented earlier in this section. This practice allows the use of established experience with analog controllers and, in principle, their well-known tuning rules could be applied.

As there is no extra cost in programming all the three modes of control, most computer-based algorithms contain all the three and then use flags and logic to allow the process engineer to specify any single mode or a combination of two or three modes. Many computer controllers use the noninteracting version of PID control (refer Eqn. (11. 36b)) and some computer control systems allow the option of either noninteracting or interacting (refer Eqn. (11.37)) version of PID control.

Noninteracting Position PID Algorithm

The equation describing the idealized noninteracting PID controller is as follows (refer Eqn. (11.36a)):

$$u(t) = K_c \left[e(t) + \frac{1}{T_I} \int_0^t e(t) dt + T_D \frac{de(t)}{dt} \right] \qquad (11.52)$$

with parameters

$\quad\quad K_c$ = controller gain;
$\quad\quad T_I$ = integral time; and
$\quad\quad T_D$ = derivative time.

For small sample times T, this equation can be turned into a difference equation by discretization. Various methods of discretization were presented in Section 11.7.

Approximating the derivative mode by the backward-difference approximation and the integral mode by backward integration rule, we obtain (refer Eqns (11.26))

$$u(k) = K_c \left[e(k) + \frac{1}{T_I} S(k) + \frac{T_D}{T}(e(k) - e(k-1)) \right]; \qquad (11.53)$$

$$S(k) = S(k-1) + Te(k)$$

where $\quad u(k)$ = the controller output at sample k;
$\quad\quad\quad S(k)$ = the sum of the errors; and
$\quad\quad\quad T$ = the sampling interval.

This is a nonrecursive algorithm. For the formation of the sum, all past errors $e(\cdot)$ have to be stored.

Equation (11.53) is known as the 'absolute form' or 'position form' of the PID algorithm, since the absolute value of the control variable calculated from the error sequence determines the actual value of the manipulated variable (valve position; Fig. 11.36).

In addition to the normal operation of the PID control algorithm given by Eqn. (11.53), the following supplementary functions are required in practical applications.

1. *Prevention of integral wind-up*

For large deviations $e(k)$, the actuator element (control valve; Fig. 11.37) is driven to its saturation level and the integral term of the control algorithm (11.53) produces continually increasing values of the control variable $u(k)$. When the controlled (output) variable reaches the reference value and the error sign is reversed, the algorithm takes long to integrate backwards and to quit the saturation range of the actuator element. This therefore results in undesired long and large overshoots.

A simple measure taken against this undesired property is to include *conditioned integration* in the programming of the algorithm: the integration is executed only if $|e(k)| < e_{max}$.

2. *Bumpless transfer from manual to automatic operation*

Equation (11.53) suffers from one particular disadvantage which is manifest when the process it is controlling is switched from manual to automatic control (refer Fig. 11.40). The initial value of the control variable u will simply be

$$u(0) = K_c\left[1 + \frac{T}{T_I} + \frac{T_D}{T}\right]e(0)$$

Since the controller has no knowledge of the previous sample values, it is not likely that this output value will coincide with that previously available under manual control. As a result, the transfer of control will cause a 'bump' which may seriously disturb the plant operation. This can only be overcome by laboriously aligning the manual and computer outputs or by adding complexity to the controller so that it will automatically 'track' the manual controller.

Practical implementation of the PID algorithm includes the following additional features.

1. It is seldom desirable for the derivative mode of the controller to respond to set-point changes. This is because the set-point changes cause large changes in the error that last for only one sample; when the derivative mode acts on this error, undesirable pulses or 'derivative kicks' occur on the controller output right after the set-point is changed. These pulses, which last for one sampling interval, can be avoided by having the derivative mode act on the controlled variable rather than on the error.

2. A pure derivative term should not be implemented because it will give a very large amplification of the measurement noise. The gain of the derivative must thus be limited. This can be done by approximating the transfer function $T_D s$ as follows:

$$T_D s \cong \frac{T_D s}{\alpha T_D s + 1}$$

where α is the filter parameter whose value is not adjustable, but is built into the design of the controller. It is usually of the order of 0.05 to 0.3. The PID controller, therefore, takes the form (refer Fig. 11.33c):

$$U(s) = K_c \left[E(s) + \frac{1}{T_I s} E(s) - \frac{T_D s}{\alpha T_D s + 1} Y(s) \right] \qquad (11.54)$$

Discretization of this equation results in the following PID algorithm:

$$u(k) = K_c \left[e(k) + \frac{1}{T_I} S(k) + D(k) \right] \qquad (11.55)$$

$$S(k) = S(k-1) + Te(k)$$

$$D(k) = \frac{\alpha T_D}{\alpha T_D + T} D(k-1) - \frac{T_D}{\alpha T_D + T} [y(k) - y(k-1)]$$

Noninteracting Velocity PID Algorithm

This is a recursive algorithm characterized by the calculation of the current control variable $u(k)$ based on the previous control variable $u(k-1)$ and correction terms. To derive the recursive algorithm, we subtract from Eqn. (11.53)

$$u(k-1) = K_c \left[e(k-1) + \frac{1}{T_I} S(k-1) + \frac{T_D}{T} (e(k-1) - e(k-2)) \right]$$

This gives

$$u(k) - u(k-1) = K_c \left[e(k) - e(k-1) + \frac{T}{T_I} e(k) + \frac{T_D}{T} [e(k) \right.$$
$$\left. - 2e(k-1) + e(k-2)] \right] \qquad (11.56)$$

Now, only the current change in the control variable

$$\Delta u(k) = u(k) - u(k-1)$$

is calculated. This algorithm is known as the 'incremental form' or 'velocity form' of the PID algorithm, since the incremental value of the control variable determines the change in the manipulated variable (change in the valve position; Fig. 11.36). The distinction between the position and velocity algorithms is significant only for controllers with integral effect.

The velocity algorithm provides a simple solution to the requirement of bumpless transfer. The problem of bumps arises mainly from the need for an 'initial condition' on the integral, and the solution adopted is to externalize the integration as shown in Fig. 11.44. The external integration may take the form of an electronic integrator but frequently the type of actuating element is changed so that recursive algorithm is used with actuators which, by their very nature, contain integral action. Stepper motor is one such actuating element. These devices will retain the last calculated position of the control valve.

Notice that in the velocity algorithm, the controller output can be directly limited, while in the position algorithm the error sum must be limited to prevent wind-up.

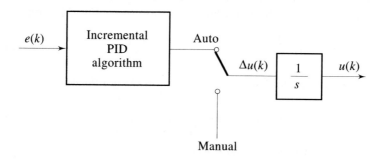

Fig. 11.44 *Control scheme for bumpless transfer*

Compared to 'position form', the 'velocity form' provides a more efficient way to program the PID algorithm from the standpoints of handling the initialization when the controller is switched from 'manual' to 'automatic', and of limiting the controller output to prevent reset wind-up. Practical implementation of this algorithm includes the features of avoiding derivative kicks/filtering measurement noise. Using Eqn. (11.55) we obtain

$$\Delta u(k) = K_c \left[e(k) - e(k-1) + \frac{T}{T_I} e(k) - \frac{T}{\alpha T_D + T} D(k-1) \right.$$

$$\left. - \frac{T_D}{\alpha T_D + T} (y(k) - y(k-1)) \right] \qquad (11.57)$$

$$D(k) = \frac{\alpha T_D}{\alpha T_D + T} D(k-1) - \frac{T_D}{\alpha T_D + T} [y(k) - y(k-1)]$$

where $y(k)$ = controlled variable;

$\Delta u(k)$ = incremental control variable = $u(k) - u(k-1)$;

$e(k)$ = error variable; K_c = controller gain;

T_I = integral time; T_D = derivative time; and

T = sampling interval.

Interacting PID Algorithms

The interacting PID controller is described by the equation (refer Fig. 11.34b)

$$U(s) = K'_c \left[E(s) + \frac{1}{T'_I s} E(s) \right] \tag{11.58}$$

where $\quad E(s) = R(s) - B(s) = R(s) - \dfrac{T'_D s + 1}{\alpha T'_D s + 1} Y(s)$

Discretization of this equation results in the following interacting PID algorithm in 'position form':

$$u(k) = K'_c \left[e(k) + \frac{1}{T'_I} S(k) \right] \tag{11.59}$$

where $\quad S(k) = S(k - 1) + Te(k); \quad e(k) = r(k) - b(k);$

$$b(k) = \frac{\alpha T'_D}{\alpha T'_D + T} b(k - 1) + \frac{T}{\alpha T'_D + T} y(k) + \frac{T'_D}{\alpha T'_D + T} [y(k) - y(k - 1)]$$

The interacting PID algorithm in 'velocity form' is given by

$$\Delta u(k) = u(k) - u(k - 1) = K'_c \left[e(k) - e(k - 1) + \frac{T}{T'_I} e(k) \right] \tag{11.60}$$

where $e(k) = r(k) - b(k);$

$$b(k) = \frac{\alpha T'_D}{\alpha T'_D + T} b(k - 1) + \frac{T}{\alpha T'_D + T} y(k) + \frac{T'_D}{\alpha T'_D + T} [y(k) - y(k - 1)]$$

11.9 ZIEGLER-NICHOLS METHODS FOR CONTROLLER TUNING

From Examples 11.6 and 11.7 we observe that the parameters K_c, T_I, and T_D of a PID controller can easily be adjusted by adjusting potentiometer settings. A commonly used approach for controlling industrial processes is to interface a PID controller (with adjustment features) to the process and adjust the parameters of the controller on-line by trial-and-error to obtain acceptable performance. The following is a collection of tuning tips that should be useful in selecting a suitable combination of the three basic control modes for the process, and in making the controller tuning task more efficient.

Self-regulating Processes

All *self-regulating* processes reach a new steady-state when driven by a step change in input. A simple self-regulating process has single time-constant with insignificant dead-time. The transfer function model of such a process is of the form:

$$G(s) = \frac{K}{\tau s + 1}$$

The responses shown in Fig. 11.45a illustrate the typical behaviour of a simple self-regulating process after a step change in the load disturbance occurs (refer

Fig. 6.1). The controlled variable y is shown as a deviation from the set-point value. In process control applications where the offsets can be tolerated, P control is attractive because of its simplicity. For example, in some level control problems, maintaining the liquid level at the set-point is not important as long as the storage tank does not overflow or run dry.

The qualitative effects of changing the controller gain K_c are as follows. In general, increasing K_c tends to make the response faster and reduces the offset. However, as the closed-loop system response gets faster and faster, at some point, the neglected dynamics (such as in the sensor, electropneumatic transducer, and/or valve positioner) are no longer negligible, and the system response becomes oscillatory. If too large a value of K_c is used, the response may exhibit an undesirable degree of oscillation or even become unstable.

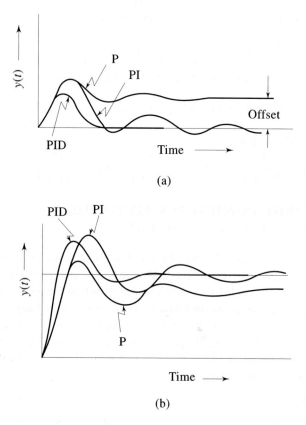

Fig. 11.45 *Typical process responses with feedback control*

If the objective is 'to maintain the controlled variable at its set-point', an integral mode to eliminate the offset is required. The I control eliminates the offset but reduces the speed of response of the process; the closed-loop response becomes sluggish. Decreasing the value of the reset time T_I makes the response relatively less sluggish; however, with too small a value of T_I, the response becomes oscillatory.

If the process time-constant is small (the process a fast compared to the desired transient response), pure I control should give acceptable performance. Some flow control loops have been determined to be fast enough to require only I control.

In a large number of industrial processes, I control action is employed in conjunction with P control. Theoretically, the offset will be eliminated for all values of T_I between ∞ and 0, and the speed of response can be increased by increasing K_c and decreasing T_I. However, as we have seen earlier, increasing K_c and decreasing T_I makes the response of the closed-loop system more sensitive and such trends may lead to instability. Proper tuning of the controller parameters K_c and T_I gives an acceptable performance in a large number of industrial processes. A limited amount of oscillation can usually be tolerated (refer Fig. 11.45a).

The PI control is very often used in flow control loops and gas-pressure control loops because the response times of these processes are usually quite small, and the speed of the closed-loop systems remains satisfactory despite the slow down caused by the integral control mode.

Addition of the derivative mode to the P/PI controller brings a stabilizing effect to the system and allows the use of higher gains which produce faster responses without excessive oscillations (refer Fig. 11.45a).

It is difficult to generalize about the effect of the derivative time T_D. Increasing T_D tends to improve the response by reducing the peak overshoot, response time, and degree of oscillation. However, if T_D is too large, measurement noise tends to be amplified and the response may become oscillatory.

The PID control is recommended for processes with very sluggish response. The sluggish response of a process is attributed to:

   (i) the presence of dead-time elements in the feedback loop (process model

     is of the form $G(s) = \dfrac{Ke^{-s\tau_D}}{\tau s + 1}$),

  (ii) the presence of many significant simple lags in the feedback loop

     (process model is of the form $G(s) = \dfrac{K}{(\tau_1 s + 1)(\tau_2 s + 1)}$), and/or

 (iii) the presence of two opposing effects (which give rise to inverse response) in the process (process model is of the form

    $G(s) = \dfrac{K(1 - \tau_2 s)}{\tau_1 s + 1}$; refer Review Example 3.5)

Responses shown in Fig. 11.45b illustrate the typical behaviour to a set-point change of a process with two simple lags and a dead-time element:

$$G(s) = \frac{Ke^{-s\tau_D}}{(\tau_1 s + 1)(\tau_2 s + 1)}$$

The P control gives an oscillatory response with an offset. The addition of integral action eliminates the offset at the expense of a more oscillatory response. When derivative action is also included, the response is much faster and much less oscillatory. The large overshoots shown in all the three cases are characteristic of processes with relatively large time delays.

Temperature control loops are usually characterized by many sub-processes involving heat transfer. We expect, therefore, that the overall response will be rather sluggish and a PI controller will make it even more so. We have a similar situation in composition control loops; slow composition sensors cause a very slow response. PID controllers are, therefore, recommended for temperature and composition control.

Integrating Processes

Processes characterized by models having the term $1/s$ in their transfer function are the *integrating processes*. When controlled with proportional controller, such processes do not exhibit offset for set-point changes but they do so for sustained load changes (refer Problem 4.7). If we are interested in maintaining the controlled variable not exactly at the set-point but within a certain range, P control is quite effective. The derivative mode is added when significant lags in sensor, control valve, etc., are present. Some liquid-level control loops in industrial processes are controlled by PD controllers.

For processes requiring all the three control modes, a successful approach is to select the integral time first, set the derivative time to about one-fourth of the integral time, and then adjust the proportional gain to obtain required control on the controlled variable. If the response is still too oscillatory, double the integral and derivative times; or, if it is too slow in approaching the set-point, halve the integral and derivative times; then re-adjust the gain.

It may be noted that experimental adjustment of controller settings (tuning) is applied to processes whose dynamics are not precisely known. For processes whose dynamics are known, the use of trial-and-error tuning is not justified since many analytical approaches to the design of PID controllers are available (some of these approaches have been discussed in the earlier chapters) which predict the controller parameters fairly well at the design stage itself; only a minor 'tweaking' of adjustments is needed during experimental development.

For trial-and-error tuning, enough information about the process equipment may be gathered to estimate the dynamic characteristics of the process. Information can also be gathered during various trials of the tuning process.

A number of *tuning methods* have been introduced to obtain trial parameter values for various response criteria. Some of these methods, which have been successfully used in process industry, will be described in this section. If application of the tuning rules gives excessive overshoot, it is always possible to make *fine tuning* so that the closed-loop system will exhibit satisfactory transient response. In fact, the tuning rules give an educated guess for paremeter values, and provide a starting point for trial-and-error fine tuning.

All tuning methods consist of the following two steps:

(i) experimental determination of the dynamic characteristics of the control loop; and

(ii) estimation of the controller tuning parameters that produce a desired response for the dynamic characteristics determined in first step.

It may be noted that industrial processes are relatively slow and complex; identification of process dynamics precisely (through experiments or otherwise) can be expensive if meaningful identification is possible at all. For tuning purposes, simple experiments are performed to estimate important dynamic attributes of the process. The approximate models have proven to be quite useful to process control applications.

Tuning Method Based on Ultimate Gain and Period

This pioneer method, also known as the closed-loop or on-line tuning method, was proposed by J.G. Ziegler and N.B. Nichols around 1940. In this method, the parameters by which the dynamic characteristics of the process are represented are the ultimate gain and period. These parameters are used in tuning the controller for a specified response: the quarter-decay ratio (QDR) response.

Determination of Ultimate Gain and Period

When the process is under closed-loop P control, the gain of the P controller at which the loop oscillates with constant amplitude has been defined as the *ultimate gain K_{cu}*. *Ultimate period T_u* is the period of these sustained oscillations. The ultimate gain is thus a measure of difficulty in controlling a process; the higher the ultimate gain, the easier it is to control the process loop. The ultimate period is, in turn, a measure of speed of response of the loop; the larger the period, the slower the loop.

By its definition, it can be deduced that the ultimate gain is the gain at which the loop is at the threshold of instability. At gains just below the ultimate, the loop signals will oscillate with decreasing amplitude, and at gains above the ultimate, the amplitude of the oscillations will grow with time.

For experimental determination of K_{cu} and T_u, the controller is set in 'auto' mode and the following procedure is followed (refer Fig. 11.40).

1. Remove the integral mode by setting the integral time to its highest value. Alternatively, if the PID controller allows for switching off the integral mode, switch it off.

2. Switch off the derivative mode or set the derivative time to its lowest value, usually zero.

3. Increase the proportional gain in steps. After each increase, disturb the loop by introducing a small step change in set-point and observe the response of the controlled variable, preferably on a trend recorder.

The controlled variable should start oscillating as the gain is increased. When the amplitude of the oscillations remains approximately constant, the ultimate controller gain has been reached. Record it as K_{cu}.

4. Measure the period of the oscillations from the trend recording. This parameter is T_u.

The procedure just outlined is simple and requires a minimum upset to the process, just enough to be able to observe the oscillations. Nevertheless, the prospect of taking a process control loop to the verge of instability is not an attractive one from a process operation standpoint.

It is also important to realize that some loops cannot be made to oscillate with constant amplitude with only a P controller. Fortunately, these are usually very simple loops and can be tuned very easily by trial-and-error.

Tuning for Quarter-Decay Ratio Response

Ziegler and Nichols proposed that the parameters K_{cu} and T_u characterizing a process be used in tuning the controller for QDR response. The QDR response is illustrated in Fig. 11.46 for a step change in disturbance and for a step change in set-point. Its characteristic is that each oscillation has an amplitude that is one-fourth of the previous oscillation.

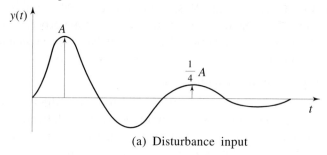

(a) Disturbance input

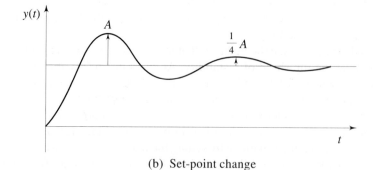

(b) Set-point change

Fig. 11.46 *QDR response*

Empirical relations [7] for calculating the QDR tuning parameters of P, PI and PID controllers from the ultimate gain K_{cu} and period T_u are given in Table 11.1.

PI and PID tuning parameters that produce quarter-decay response are not unique. For each setting of the integral and derivative times, there will usually be a setting of the controller gain that produces quarter-decay response. The settings given in Table 11.1 are the figures based on experience; these settings have produced fast response for most industrial loops.

Table 11.1 *QDR tuning formulas based on ultimate gain and period*

Controller	Gain	Integral time	Derivative time
P	$K_c = 0.5K_{cu}$	—	—
PI	$K_c = 0.45K_{cu}$	$T_I = T_u/1.2$	—
PID(noninteracting)	$K_c = 0.75K_{cu}$	$T_I = T_u/1.6$	$T_D = T_u/10$
PID(interacting)	$K_c' = 0.6K_{cu}$	$T_I' = T_u/2$	$T_D' = T_u/8$

Tunning Method Based on Process Reaction Curve

Although the tuning method based on ultimate gain and period is simple and fast, other methods of characterizing the dynamic response of feedback control loops have been developed over the years. The need for these alternative methods is based on the fact that it is not always possible to determine the ultimate gain and period of a loop; some loops would not exhibit sustained oscillations with a proportional controller. Also, the ultimate gain and period do not give insight into which process or control system characteristics could be modified to improve the feedback controller performance. A more fundamental method of characterizing process dynamics is needed to guide such modifications. In the following, we present an open-loop method for characterizing the dynamic response of the process in the loop (Wherever applicable, closed-loop tuning method is expected to give better trial values for fine tuning. However, using more than one tuning method is helpful in trial-and-error approach of parameter selection).

Process Reaction Curve

Process control is characterized by systems which are relatively slow and complex and which in many cases include an element of pure time delay (dead-time). Even where a dead-time element is not present, the complexity of the system which will typically contain several first-order sub-systems, will often result in a *process reaction curve* (dynamic response to a step change in input) which has the appearance of pure time delay.

Process reaction curve may be obtained by carrying out the following step-test procedure.

With the controller on 'manual', i.e., the loop opened (refer Fig. 11.40), a step change of magnitude Δu in the control signal $u(t)$ is applied to the process which includes the control valve and the sensor for the process output variable

$y(t)$. The magnitude Δu should be large enough for the consequent change $\Delta y(t)$ in the process output variable to be measurable, but not so large that the response will be distorted by process nonlinearities. The process output is recorded for a period from the introduction of the step change in the input until the process reaches a new steady state.

A typical process reaction curve is sketched in Fig. 11.47. The most common model used to characterize the process reaction curve is the following:

$$\frac{Y(s)}{U(s)} = G(s) = \frac{Ke^{-\tau_D s}}{\tau s + 1} \tag{11.61}$$

where K = the process steady-state gain;

τ_D = the effective process dead-time; and

τ = the effective process time-constant

This is a *first-order plus dead-time model*. The model response for a step change in the input signal of magnitude Δu, is given by

$$Y(s) = \frac{Ke^{-\tau_D s}}{\tau s + 1} \frac{\Delta u}{s} = K\Delta u\, e^{-\tau_D s}\left[\frac{1}{s} - \frac{\tau}{\tau s + 1}\right]$$

Inverting with the help of a Laplace transform table given in Appendix A, and applying the real translation theorem of Laplace transforms (Eqn. (A.34) in Appendix A), we get

$$\Delta y(t) = K\Delta u\left[1 - e^{-(t - \tau_D)/\tau}\right]\mu(t - \tau_D) \tag{11.62}$$

or $\Delta y(t) = K\Delta u\left[1 - e^{-(t - \tau_D)/\tau}\right]; t > \tau_D$

$\qquad\qquad = 0 \qquad\qquad\qquad\quad ; t \le \tau_D$

The term Δy is the perturbation or change in the output from its initial value:

$$\Delta y(t) = y(t) - y(0)$$

Figure 11.48 shows the model response to a step change of magnitude Δu in the input signal. Δy_{ss} is the steady-state change in the process output (refer Eqn. (11.62)):

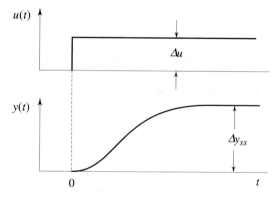

Fig. 11.47   *A process reaction curve*

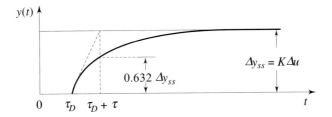

Fig. 11.48 *Step-response of first-order plus dead-time model*

$$\Delta y_{ss} = \lim_{t \to \infty} \Delta y(t) = K\Delta u$$

At the point $t = \tau_D$ on the time axis, the process output variable leaves the initial steady-state with a maximum rate of change (refer Eqn. (11.62)):

$$\frac{d}{dt}\Delta y(t)\bigg|_{t = \tau_D} = K\Delta u\left(\frac{1}{\tau}\right) = \frac{\Delta y_{ss}}{\tau}$$

The time-constant τ is the distance on the time axis between the point $t = \tau_D$, and the point at which the tangent to the model response curve drawn at $t = \tau_D$ crosses the new steady-state.

Note that the model response at $t = \tau_D + \tau$ is given by

$$\Delta y(\tau_D + \tau) = K\Delta u(1 - e^{-1}) = 0.632\,\Delta y_{ss}$$

The process reaction curve of Fig. 11.47 can be matched to the model response of Fig. 11.48 by the following estimation procedure.

The model parameter K is given by

$$K = \frac{\text{Change in process output at steady-state}}{\text{Step change in process input}} = \frac{\Delta y_{ss}}{\Delta u} \qquad (11.63a)$$

The estimation of the model parameters τ_D and τ can be done by at least three methods, each of which results in different values.

Tangent method

This method makes use of the line that is tangent to the process reaction curve at the point of maximum rate of change. The time-constant is then defined as the distance on the time axis between the point where the tangent crosses the initial steady-state of the output variable, and the point where it crosses the new steady-state value. The dead-time is the distance on the time axis between the occurrence of the input step change and the point where the tangent line crosses the initial steady-state. These estimates are indicated in Fig. 11.49a.

Tangent-and-po int method

In this method, τ_D is determined in the same manner as in the earlier method, but the value of τ is the one that forces the model response to coincide with the actual response at $t = \tau_D + \tau$. Construction for this method is shown in Fig. 11.49b. The value of τ obtained by this method is usually less than that obtained by the earlier method, and the process reaction curve is usually closer to the response of the model obtained by this method compared to the one obtained by the earlier method.

Two-points method

The least precise step in the determination of τ_D and τ by the previous two methods is the drawing of the line tangent to the process reaction curve at the point of maximum rate of change. To eliminate this dependence on the tangent line, it is proposed that the values of τ_D and τ be selected such that the model and the actual responses coincide at two points in the region of high rate of change. The two points recommended are $(\tau_D + \frac{1}{3}\tau)$ and $(\tau_D + \tau)$. To locate these points, we make use of Eqn. (11.62):

$$\Delta y\left(\tau_D + \tfrac{1}{3}\tau\right) = K\Delta u[1 - e^{-1/3}] = 0.283\,\Delta y_{ss}$$

$$\Delta y(\tau_D + \tau) = K\Delta u[1 - e^{-1}] = 0.632\,\Delta y_{ss}$$

These two points are labelled t_1 and t_2 in Fig. 11.49c. Knowing t_1 and t_2, we can obtain the values of τ_D and τ.

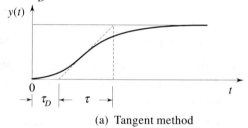

(a) Tangent method

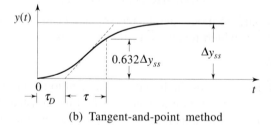

(b) Tangent-and-point method

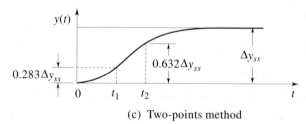

(c) Two-points method

Fig. 11.49 *Estimation of model parameters*

$$\tau_D + \tau = t_2; \quad \tau_D + \tfrac{1}{3}\tau = t_1$$

which reduces to

$$\tau = \tfrac{3}{2}(t_2 - t_1); \quad \tau_D = t_2 - \tau \tag{11.63b}$$

where t_1 = time at which $\Delta y(t) = 0.283\,\Delta y_{ss}$

t_2 = time at which $\Delta y(t) = 0.632\,\Delta y_{ss}$

Tuning for QDR response

Besides the formulas for QDR response tuning based on the ultimate gain and period of the loop (refer Table 11.1), Ziegler and Nichols also developed tuning formulas based on the parameters of a first-order model fit to the process reaction curve. These formulas are given in Table 11.2 [7].

Table 11.2 *QDR tuning formulas based on process reaction curve; process model*

$$G(s) = \frac{Ke^{-\tau_D s}}{\tau s + 1}$$

Controller	Gain	Integral time	Derivative time
P	$K_c = \tau/K\tau_D$	—	—
PI	$K_c = 0.9\,\tau/K\tau_D$	$T_I = 3.33\,\tau_D$	—
PID(noninteracting)	$K_c = 1.5\,\tau/K\tau_D$	$T_I = 2.5\,\tau_D$	$T_D = 0.4\,\tau_D$
PID(interacting)	$K'_c = 1.2\,\tau/K\tau_D$	$T'_I = 2.0\,\tau_D$	$T'_D = 0.5\,\tau_D$

Three major conclusions can be drawn from this table.

1. The controller gain is inversely proportional to the process gain K which represents the product of gains of all the elements in the loop other than the controller (control valve, process equipment, and sensor). It means that if the gain of any of the elements were to change because of recalibration, resizing, or nonlinearity, the response of the feedback loop will change unless the controller gain is readjusted.

2. The controller gain must be reduced when the ratio of the process dead-time to its time-constant increases. This means that the difficulty in controlling the loop increases when the ratio of the process dead-time to its time-constant increases. This ratio, which can be used as a measure of difficulty in controlling a process, will be called the *normalized dead-time* τ_{ND}.

$$\frac{\text{Apparent dead-time } \tau_D}{\text{Apparent time-constant } \tau} = \text{Normalized dead-time } \tau_{ND} \tag{11.64}$$

τ_{ND} can be estimated from the process reaction curve. Processes with small τ_{ND} are easy to control and processes with large τ_{ND} are difficult to control.

Notice that having a long dead-time parameter means that the loop is difficult to control only if the time-constant is short. In other words, a loop with a dead-time of several minutes would be just as difficult to control as one with a dead-time of a few seconds if the normalized dead-time for both the loops is the same.

3. The speed of response of the controller, which is determined by integral and derivative times, must match the speed of response of the process. The formulas in Table 11.2 match these response speeds by relating the integral and derivative times of the controller to the process dead-time.

These three conclusions can be very helpful in guiding the tuning of feedback controllers, even in such cases when the tuning formulas cannot be used directly because the process parameters cannot be determined (e.g., for integrating processes, process reaction curve is not *S*-shaped (Fig.11.47), and some integrating process loops cannot be made to oscillate with constant amplitude with only a P controller).

In using the formulas of Table 11.2, we must keep in mind that they were developed empirically for the most common range of the normalized dead-time parameter, which is between 0.1 and 0.3, based on the fact that most processes do not exhibit significant transportation lag (rather, the dead-time is the result of several first-order lags in series).

As was pointed out in the earlier discussion on QDR tuning based on ultimate gain and period, the difficulty of the QDR performance specification for PI and PID controllers is that there is an infinite set of values of the controller parameters that can produce it; i.e., for each setting of the integral time on a PI controller and for each reset–derivative time combination on a PID controller, there is a setting of the gain that results in QDR response. The settings given in Table 11.2 are the figures based on experience; these settings have produced fast response for most industrial loops.

Tuning Rules for Digital Controllers

Though tuning formulas that are specifically applicable to digital control algorithms have been developed [7, 89], the most popular and widely used tuning approach for digital PID controllers is to apply rules of Tables 11.1–11.2 with a simple correction to account for the effect of sampling. When a continuous-time signal is sampled at regular intervals of time and is then reconstructed by holding the sampled values constant for each sampling interval, the reconstructed signal is effectively delayed by approximately one half of the sampling interval, as shown in Fig. 11.30. In the digital control configuration of Fig. 11.24, the D/A converter holds the output of the digital controller constant between updates, thus adding one half the sampling time to the dead-time of the process components. The correction for sampling is then simply to add one half the sampling time to the dead-time obtained from the process reaction curve.

$$\tau_{CD} = \tau_D + \tfrac{1}{2} T \qquad\qquad (11.65)$$

where τ_{CD} is the corrected dead-time, τ_D is the dead-time of the process, and T is the sampling interval.

The tuning formulas given in Table 11.2 can directly be used for digital PID controllers with τ_D replaced by τ_{CD}.

Notice that the on-line tuning method based on ultimate gain and period inherently incorporates the effect of sampling when the ultimate gain and period are determined with the digital controller included in the loop. Tuning rules of Table 11.1 can therefore be applied to digital control algorithms without any correction.

Review Examples

Review Example 11.1

A PID controller is described by the following relation between input $e(t)$ and output $u(t)$:

$$u(t) = K_c\left[e(t) + \frac{1}{T_I}\int_0^t e(t)dt + T_D\frac{de(t)}{dt}\right] \tag{11.66a}$$

Obtain PID control algorithm by the discretization of the equation

$$\dot{u}(t) = K_c\left[\dot{e}(t) + \frac{1}{T_I}e(t) + T_D\ddot{e}(t)\right] \tag{11.66b}$$

using backward-difference approximation of the derivatives.

Solution
By backward-difference approximation,

$$\dot{u}(t)\Big|_{t=kT} = \frac{u(k) - u(k-1)}{T} \tag{11.67}$$

$$\dot{e}(t)\Big|_{t=kT} \triangleq \dot{e}(k) = \frac{e(k) - e(k-1)}{T} \tag{11.68}$$

$$\ddot{e}(t)\Big|_{t=kT} = \frac{\dot{e}(k) - \dot{e}(k-1)}{T} = \frac{1}{T^2}\left[e(k) - 2e(k-1) + e(k-2)\right] \tag{11.69}$$

Substituting Eqns (11.67)–(11.69) into Eqn. (11.66b) at $t = kT$, we obtain

$$\frac{1}{T}[u(k) - u(k-1)] = \frac{K_c T_D}{T^2}\left[e(k) - 2e(k-1) + e(k-2)\right]$$

$$+ \frac{K_c}{T}[e(k) - e(k-1)] + \frac{K_c}{T_I}e(k)$$

or

$$u(k) = u(k-1) + K_c\left[1 + \frac{T}{T_I} + \frac{T_D}{T}\right]e(k) - K_c\left[1 + \frac{2T_D}{T}\right]e(k-1)$$

$$+ \frac{K_c T_D}{T}e(k-2) \tag{11.70}$$

Review Example 11.2 _____

Figure 11.50 shows the block diagram of an analog position control system; $\theta(t)$ is the controlled position, $\theta_R(t)$ is the commanded position, and $u(t)$ is the control variable.

   We wish to replace the analog control scheme by a digital one. Design an equivalent digital control scheme.

Solution

The analog control scheme of Fig. 11.50 requires feedback of shaft speed and position. Shaft speed is usually measured by a tachogenerator attached to the motor shaft, and shaft position by potentiometer or synchro devices.

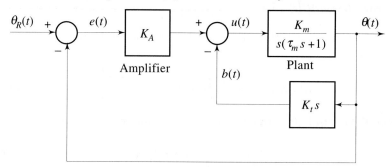

Fig. 11.50   *A position control system*

   In digital control systems, we normally use the shaft encoder for digital measurement of shaft position/speed. The shaft encoder consists of a rotary disk made of a transparent material. The disk is divided into a number of equal angular sectors depending on the resolution required. Every alternate sector is made opaque. The device has a light source sending a beam on the disk on one side, and on opposite side a photoelectric sensor receiving the beam. As the disk moves relative to the sensor, a pulse train is generated, and is fed to a counter to record how much motion has occurred.[9]

   Once the position data is available from shaft encoder, it is fairly straightforward to carry out step-by-step calculation of the slope of the position-time curve to obtain the speed measurement.

   For digital implementation of analog control scheme of Fig. 11.50, the following digital control algorithm may be used.

$$u(k) = K_A e(k) - b(k) \qquad\qquad (11.71)$$

where $$e(k) = \theta_R(k) - \theta(k)$$

and $$b(k) = \frac{K_t}{T}[\theta(k) - \theta(k-1)]; \; T = \text{sampling interval.}$$

A block diagram of the digital position control system is shown in Fig. 11.51

_____

9. Chapters 3 of reference[180].

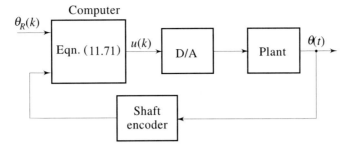

Fig. 11.51 *A digital position control system*

Review Example 11.3 _____

Consider the residential heating system shown in Fig. 1.9a. A typical experimental curve obtained by opening the steam valve at $t = 0$ from fully closed position to a position that allows a flow Q_m of 1 kg/min with initial senosr temperature θ of 0°C, is shown in Fig. 11.52. Approximate the process reaction curve by a first-order plus dead-time model using two-points method of approximation.

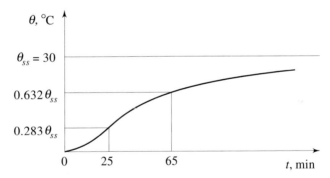

Fig. 11.52 *Experimental response curve of a residential heating system*

Solution

Process steady-state gain, $K = \dfrac{\theta_{ss}}{Q_m} = \dfrac{30}{1} = 30\,°C/(kg/min)$

$\theta(t) = 0.283\,\Delta\theta_{ss}$ at $t_1 = 25$ min

$\theta(t) = 0.632\,\Delta\theta_{ss}$ at $t_2 = 65$ min

Therefore (refer Eqns (11.63b))

$$\tau_D + \tfrac{1}{3}\,\tau = t_1 = 25 \tag{11.72}$$

$$\tau_D + \tau = t_2 = 65 \tag{11.73}$$

where

$$\tau_D = \text{effective dead-time of the process}$$

$$\tau = \text{effective time-constant of the process}$$

Solving Eqns (11.72)–(11.73), we get

$$\tau_D = 5 \text{ min}$$

$$\tau = 60 \text{ min}$$

The process reaction curve of the residential heating system is thus represented by the model

$$G(s) = \frac{\theta(s)}{Q_m(s)} = \frac{Ke^{-\tau_D s}}{\tau s + 1} = \frac{30e^{-5s}}{60s + 1} \, ^\circ C/kg/min)$$

Review Questions

11.1 Draw circuit diagrams of passive RC networks capable of providing
(a) phase lead;
(b) phase lag;
(c) phase lead and lag over different frequency bands.
Determine transfer function model for each network and draw Bode plots for each model.

11.2 Sketch op amp circuits capable of providing
(a) phase lead;
(b) Phase lag; and
(c) phase lead and lag over different frequency bands.
Determine transfer function model of each network and draw Bode plots for each model.

11.3 (a) The transfer function of a lag-lead compensator is given by

$$D(s) = \underbrace{\left(\frac{\tau_1 s + 1}{\beta \tau_1 s + 1} \right)}_{\substack{\text{Lag} \\ \text{section}}} \underbrace{\left(\frac{\tau_2 s + 1}{\alpha \tau_2 s + 1} \right)}_{\substack{\text{Lead} \\ \text{section}}}; \ b > 1, a < 1, \tau_1, \tau_2 > 0$$

Give an operational amplifier circuit that realizes this $D(s)$.
(b) We have a passive RC network that realizes the lag section and another passive RC network that realizes the lead section. Can we cascade the two units to obtain realization for lag-lead compensator? Justify your answer. (Help: p696, Section 2.14)

11.4 (a) Inductors are not used for implementation of compensators. Why? (Help: p695, p 705)
(b) We often prefer op amp based realization for compensators over the passive network realization. Why? (Help: p705)
(c) State the conditions for realizability of a proper transfer function $D(s)$ with passive RC networks. (Help: p695)

(d) Can we use passive RC networks to implement compensators with complex conjugate poles? If not, suggest suitable implementation schemes. (Help: p705)

11.5 Describe important advantages offered by the use of digital computer as compensator device in a control system. What are the main problems associated with implementation of digital control?

11.6 Sketch a schematic diagram of a speed control system using the following units: motor, tachogenerator, A/D converter, digital computer, D/A converter, and power amplifier. Explain the function of each section of the diagram. How do we select the sampling rate? (Help: Fig. 1.17; pp722-723)

11.7 (a) The sampling theorem states that a continuous-time signal whose frequency spectrum is bounded by upper limit ω_m, can be completely reconstructed from its samples when the sampling frequency $\omega_s > 2\omega_m$. What are the problems associated with the use of sampling theorem in practical control systems? (Help: p710)

(b) What is a zero-order hold device and what is it used for? (Help: pp715-716)

11.8 Investigate methods of conversion of analog compensator $D(s)$ to an equivalent digital compensator.

11.9 Using appropriate examples, show that sampling usually has detrimental effect on the transient response and the relative stability of a closed-loop system.

What is the effect of sampling on the steady-state error of a closed-loop system? (Help: Example 11.5)

11.10 (a) Explain with the help of block diagrams, important features of non-interacting and interacting PID controllers used for controlling industrial processes.

(b) What is derivative kick in a process control system? How is it prevented?
(Help: p731, p746)

11.11 (a) Using schematic diagrams, explain the operational features of A-O and A-C pneumatic control valves. On what factors is the choice of a control valve for a particular application based?

(b) What is the typical symptom of reset wind-up in a process control system? What causes it? How can it be prevented?

11.12 Explain using a block diagram, the basic structure of an industrial controller with features that permit adjusting the set-point, transferring between manual and automatic modes, and tuning of control-action parameters. Give op amp based circuits for an industrial PI controller with these features.

11.13 (a) Consider a feedback loop comprising plant with transfer function $K_1/[(\tau_1 s + 1)(\tau_2 s + 1)]$, sensor with transfer function K_2, electropneumatic transducer with transfer function K_3, control valve with transfer function K_4, and a proportional controller with transfer function K_c. Basic analysis shows that the system is stable for all $K_c > 0$. However, the actual system shows highly oscillatory response (may even become unstable) for large values of K_c. Comment on this statement. (Help: p267, p750)

(b) Replace the P-controller by a PD-controller $K_c(1 + T_D s)$. Increasing T_D tends to reduce response time and degree of oscillation. Can we take very large values of T_D? Why? (Help: p356, p751)

11.14 (a) Give an example of a process control system with a dead-time element in feedback loop. (Help: Fig. 3.59)

   (b) Give an example of a process control system having many significant simple lags in feedback loop. (Help: Fig. 4.6)

   (c) Give an example of a process with inverse response characteristics.
                                                              (Help: Fig. 3.67)
   Show that the sluggish response of a process is attributed to dead-time element in feedback loop, and/or many significant lags in feedback loop, and/or inverse response characteristics.

11.15 A process control system has the following controller in feedback loop:

$$D(s) = K_c \left(1 + \frac{1}{T_I s} + T_D s \right)$$

   Discuss the effects of changing the parameters K_c, T_I and T_D between 0 and ∞.
                                                              (Help: pp749-752)

11.16 (a) Sketch a typical process reaction curve for an industrial process and explain how it can be used to obtain a first-order plus dead-time model of the process.

   (b) How is control of a feedback loop affected by the ratio of the process dead-time and its time-constant? (Help: p759)

11.17 (a) What is QDR response? (Help: p754)

   (b) We have two tuning methods, one based on ultimate gain and period and the other based on process reaction curve. How do we make a selection for a process control application? (Help: p754, p755, p760)

   (c) Why do we need fine tuning after setting controller parameters as per Ziegler-Nichols tuning methods? (Help: p753)

   (d) Given the tuning rules for analog controllers, how do we obtain tuning rules for digital controllers? (Help: pp760-761)

11.18 Discretize the PID controller

$$u(t) = K_c \left| e(t) + \frac{1}{T_I} \int_0^t e(\tau) \, d\tau + T_D \, \frac{de(t)}{dt} \right|$$

   to obtain noninteracting PID algorithm in
   (a)   position form; and
   (b) velocity form.
   What are the advantages of velocity PID algorithm over the position algorithm? (Help: pp 747-748)

Problems

11.1a Prove that the differentiator shown in Fig. P11.1a has transfer function of the form

$$G(s) = -\frac{T_D s}{\alpha T_D s + 1}$$

Determine the values of α and T_D in terms of the parameters R, C_D and R_D.

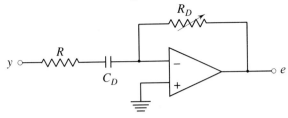

Fig. 11.1a

11.1b Prove that the controller shown in Fig. P11.1b has transfer function of the form

$$G(s) = -\frac{K_c(T_D s + 1)}{\alpha T_D s + 1}$$

Determine the values of K_c, α and T_D in terms of the parameters R, R_1, R_2 and C.

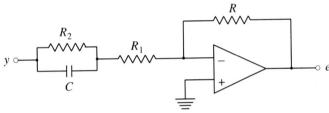

Fig. P11.1b

11.2 Show that the transfer function of the network in Fig. P11.2 is given by the standard form of lead compensator. Sketch the Bode plot of the network and comment upon its filtering properties.

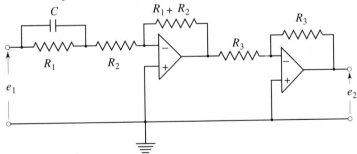

Fig. P11.2

11.3 Find the transfer function of the op amp circuit shown in Fig. P11.3. Modify the circuit to realize a standard lag compensator. Sketch the Bode plot for the modified circuit and comment upon its filtering properties.

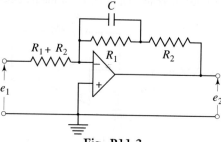

Fig. P11.3

11.4 The network shown in Fig. P11.4 realizes the lag-lead compensator

$$D(s) = \frac{K_c\left(s + \dfrac{1}{\tau_1}\right)\left(s + \dfrac{1}{\tau_2}\right)}{\left(s + \dfrac{1}{\alpha\tau_1}\right)\left(s + \dfrac{1}{\beta\tau_2}\right)}$$

Find the expressions for the compensator parameters K_c, τ_1, τ_2, α, and β in terms of network paramete rs R_1, R_2, R_3, R_4, R_5, R_6, C_1 and C_2.

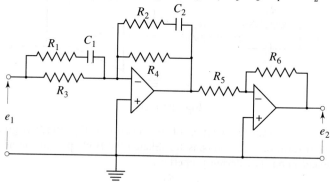

Fig. P11.4

11.5 In the network of Fig. P11.5, $C_1 = C_2 = 10\ \mu F$, and $R_3 = 10\ k\Omega$. Determine the values of R_1, R_2, and R_4 such that the network realizes the transfer function

$$D(s) = 39.42\left[1 + \frac{1}{3.077s} + 0.7692s\right]$$

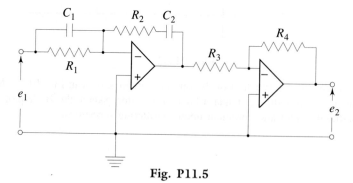

Fig. P11.5

11.6 Consider the network shown in Fig. P11.6. Given: $C_1 = C_2 = 10\ \mu\text{F}$, and $R_3 = 10\ \text{k}\Omega$. Determine the values of R_1, R_2, and R_4 such that the network realizes the transfer function

$$D(s) = 2.51\left(\frac{0.345s + 1}{0.185s + 1}\right)$$

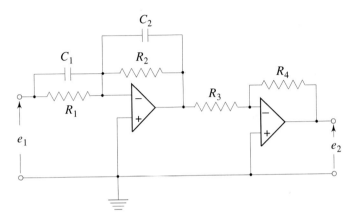

Fig. P11.6

11.7 A PID controller is described by the following relation between input $e(t)$ and output $y(t)$:

$$u(t) = K_c\left[e(t) + \frac{1}{T_I}\int_0^t e(t)dt + T_D\frac{de(t)}{dt}\right]$$

Using the trapezoidal rule for integration and backward-difference approximation for the derivative, obtain the difference equation model for the PID algorithm.

11.8 Consider the analog control system shown in Fig. P11.8. By root-locus analysis, it is found that the closed-loop natural frequency $\omega_n \cong 0.6$ rad/sec, and damping ratio $\zeta = 0.5$.

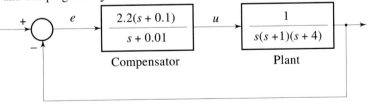

Fig. P11.8

We wish to replace the analog compensator by a digital one. Select a suitable sampling interval and obtain an equivalent digital control algorithm using backward-difference approximation for derivatives. Give a block diagram of the digital control system.

11.9 For $\dfrac{U(s)}{E(s)} = \dfrac{K(s+b)}{s+a}$,

    (a) show that backward-difference approximation for derivatives, and backward rectangular rule for integration lead to the same computer algorithm.

    (b) Find the algorithm based on the trapezoidal rule for integration.

11.10 Testing of the servo system shown in Fig. P11.10 gave the following performance:

          Closed-loop damping ratio   = 0.66
          Settling time   = 0.25 sec
          Bandwidth   = 38 rad/sec

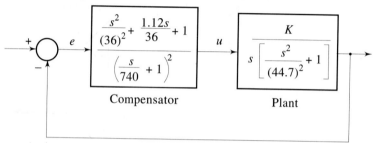

Fig. P11.10

Select a suitable sampling interval and obtain a digital control algorithm by the discretization of analog compensator using backward-difference approximation of the derivatives.

Is there a need to refine the design by the direct digital design method? If yes, why?

11.11 Figure P11.11 shows a minor-loop feedback compensation scheme. We wish to realize the control action by a digital controller with a uniform sampling interval of T sec. Obtain digital control algorithm using trapezoidal rule for integration. Give a block diagram of the digital control system.

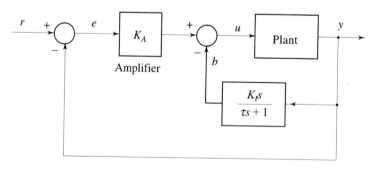

Fig. P11.11

11.12 An electronic controller comprises of

    (i) a set-point control unit,

    (ii) proportional-action unit,

    (iii) derivative-action unit, and

(iv) an integral-action unit.

Op amp circuits for these units are given in Fig. 11.41 and Fig. 11.43. Make a sketch of the controller showing how the units are connected to realize a PID control action given by the following transfer function model:

$$D(s) = K_c(1 + T_D s)\left(1 + \frac{1}{T_I s}\right)[Y(s) - R(s)]$$

11.13 Figure 11.43 shows an op amp circuit for a PD controller. Determine the transfer function of the controller when the switch of the derivative-action unit is in position B and the direct/reverse action switch is in position R. Give block diagram representation of the controller.

11.14 From a test conducted on a temperature control loop, it is determined that the controller gain required to cause sustained oscillations is 1.2 and the period of oscillations is 4.5 min. Determine the QDR tuning parameters for
   (a) a PI controller
   (b) a noninteracting PID controller

Report the controller gain as a proportional band and the reset rate in repeats per minute.

11.15 The curve in Fig. P11.15 gives the measured open-loop response of a process to a unit-step input. Approximate the process reaction curve by a first-order plus dead-time model using tangent-and-point method. Use this model to obtain QDR tuning parameters for a PI controller.

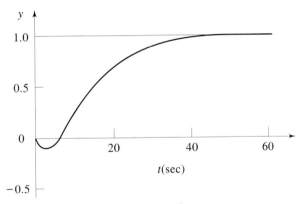

Fig. P11.15

11.16 The following table gives the measured open-loop response of a process using unit-step input. Approximate this response curve by a first-order plus dead-time model using two-points method of approximation.

Time (min) t	0	0.5	1.0	1.5	2.0	2.5	3.0	3.5
Response y	0	0.009	0.056	0.15	0.28	0.428	0.572	0.7
t	4.0	4.5	5.0	5.5	6.0	7.0		
y	0.802	0.876	0.924	0.953	0.967	0.973		

(a) Tune a proportional-only controller for QDR response.

(b) Tune a PI controller for QDR response.

11.17 Calculate normalized dead-time for the three processes described by first-order plus dead-time models given in the table below. Using normalized dead-time as a measure of difficulty in control, compare the three processes.

	Process A	Process B	Process C
Process gain	2	2	0.5
Time-constant	10 min	3 min	10 sec
Dead-time	2 min	1.5 min	5 sec

11.18 Consider the process A given in table of Problem 11.17.

(a) Calculate the QDR tuning parameters for an interacting PID controller.

(b) Readjust the tuning parameters calculated in (a) if the PID control is to be carried out with a processing period of 8 sec on a computer control installation.

11.19 A process has a gain of 1.6, a time-constant of 10 min, and a dead-time of 2.5 min. Calculate the tuning parameters for a noninteracting PID algorithm tuned for QDR response if the sample time is (a) 4 sec (b) 1 min (c) 10 min, and (d) 50 min. Comment upon the effect of increase in sample time.

11.20 In a lowpass process, the following critical quantities were determined by an oscillation test conducted on a computer-controlled loop with sample time T = 4 sec.

Ultimate gain, $K_{cu} = 5$

Ultimate period, $T_u = 34$ sec

Determine tuning parameters for a digital PI controller.

chapter 12

Control System Analysis Using State Variable Methods

12.1 | INTRODUCTION

In the preceding chapters, we showed that the root-locus method and the frequency-response methods are quite powerful for the analysis and design of feedback control systems. The analysis and design are carried out using transfer functions, together with a variety of graphical tools such as root-locus plots, Nyquist plots, Bode plots, Nichols chart, etc. These techniques of the so-called *classical control theory* have been greatly enhanced by the availability and low cost of digital computers for system analysis and simulation. The graphical tools can now be more easily used with computer graphics.

The classical design methods suffer from certain limitations due to the fact that the transfer function model is applicable only to linear time-invariant systems, and there too it is generally restricted to SISO systems as the classical design approach becomes highly cumbersome for use in MIMO systems. Another limitation of the transfer function technique is that it reveals only the system output for a given input and provides no information about the internal behaviour of the system. There may be situations where the output of a system is stable and yet some of the system elements may have a tendency to exceed their specified ratings. In addition to this, it may sometimes be necessary and advantageous to provide a feedback proportional to the internal variables of a system, rather than the output alone, for the purpose of stabilizing and improving the performance of a system.

The limitations of classical methods based on transfer function models, have led to the development of a state-variable approach of analysis and design. It is a direct time-domain approach which provides a basis for *modern control theory*. It is a powerful technique for the analysis and design of linear and nonlinear, time-invariant or time-varying MIMO systems. The organization of the state variable approach is such that it is easily amenable to solution through digital computers.

It will be incorrect to conclude from the foregoing discussion that the state variable design methods can completely replace the classical design methods. In fact, the classical control theory comprising a large body of use-tested knowledge is going strong. State variable design methods prove their mettle in applications which are intractable by classical methods.

The state variable formulation contributes to the application areas of classical control theory in a different way. It is the most efficient form of system representation from the standpoint of computer simulation. To compute the response of $G(s)$ to an input $R(s)$ requires expansion of $\{G(s)R(s)\}$ into partial fractions; which, in turn, requires computation of all the poles of $\{G(s)R(s)\}$, or all the roots of a polynomial. The roots of a polynomial are very sensitive to their coefficients (refer Section 7.12). Furthermore, to develop a computer program to carry out partial fraction expansion is not simple. On the other hand, the response of state variable equations is easy to program. Its computation does not require computation of roots or eigenvalues; therefore, it is less sensitive to parameter variations. For these reasons, it is desirable to compute the response of $G(s)$ through state variable equations.

Many CAD packages handling both the classical and the modern tools of control system design use this notation. It is, therefore, helpful for the control engineer to be familiar with state variable methods of system representation and analysis. This chapter introduces the main concepts of state variable analysis. This material may be used as a brief terminating study or as an introduction to a more in-depth discussion of state variable methods in another course[1] to follow.

We have been mostly concerned with SISO systems in the text so far. In this chapter also our emphasis will be on SISO systems. However, many of the methods based on state variable concepts are applicable to both SISO and MIMO systems with almost equal convenience; the only difference being the additional computational effort for MIMO systems which is taken care of by CAD packages.

12.2 | MATRICES

This section is intended to be a concise summary of facts about matrices[2] that the reader will need to know in reading the present chapter. Having them all at hand will minimize the need to consult a book on matrix theory. It also serves to define the notation and terminology which are, regrettably, not entirely standard.

---

1. Reference [180]
2. We will use upper case bold letters to represent matrices and lower case bold letters to represent vectors.

No attempt has been made at proving every statement made in this section. The interested reader is urged to consult a suitable book (for example [32, 33]) for details of proofs.

Basic definitions and algebraic operations associated with matrices are given below.

Matrix

The matrix
$$\mathbf{A} = \begin{bmatrix} a_{11} & a_{12} & \cdots & a_{1m} \\ a_{21} & a_{22} & \cdots & a_{2m} \\ \vdots & \vdots & & \vdots \\ a_{n1} & a_{n2} & \cdots & a_{nm} \end{bmatrix} = \begin{bmatrix} a_{ij} \end{bmatrix} \tag{12.1}$$

is a rectangular array of nm elements. It has n rows and m columns. a_{ij} denotes (i, j)th element, i.e., the element located in ith row and jth column. $\mathbf{A}$ is said to be a *rectangular matrix* of order $n \times m$.

When $m = n$, i.e., the number of columns is equal to that of rows, the matrix is said to be a *square matrix* of order n.

An $n \times 1$ matrix, i.e., a matrix having only one column is called a *column matrix*. A $1 \times n$ matrix, i.e., a matrix having only one row is called a *row matrix*.

Diagonal matrix

A diagonal matrix is a square matrix whose elements off the *principal diagonal* are all zeros ($a_{ij} = 0$ for $i \neq j$). The following matrix is a diagonal matrix.

$$\Lambda = \begin{bmatrix} a_{11} & 0 & \cdots & 0 \\ 0 & a_{22} & \cdots & 0 \\ \vdots & \vdots & & \vdots \\ 0 & 0 & \cdots & a_{nn} \end{bmatrix} = \mathrm{diag}[a_{11}\ a_{22} \cdots a_{nn}] \tag{12.2}$$

Unit (identity) matrix

A unit matrix $\mathbf{I}$ is a diagonal matrix whose diagonal elements are all equal to unity ($a_{ii} = 1$, $a_{ij} = 0$ for $i \neq j$).

$$\mathbf{I} = \begin{bmatrix} 1 & 0 & \cdots & 0 \\ 0 & 1 & \cdots & 0 \\ \vdots & \vdots & & \vdots \\ 0 & 0 & \cdots & 1 \end{bmatrix}$$

Whenever necessary, an $n \times n$ unit matrix will be denoted by $\mathbf{I}_n$.

Null (zero) matrix

A null matrix $\mathbf{0}$ is a matrix whose elements are all equal to zero.

$$\mathbf{0} = \begin{bmatrix} 0 & 0 & \cdots & 0 \\ 0 & 0 & \cdots & 0 \\ \vdots & \vdots & & \vdots \\ 0 & 0 & \cdots & 0 \end{bmatrix}$$

Whenever necessary, the dimensions of the null matrix will be indicated by two subscripts: $\mathbf{0}_{nm}$.

Lower-triangular matrix

A lower-triangular matrix $\mathbf{L}$ has all its elements *above* the principal diagonal equal to zero; $l_{ij} = 0$ if $i < j$ for $1 \le i \le n$ and $1 \le j \le m$.

$$\mathbf{L} = \begin{bmatrix} l_{11} & 0 & \cdots & 0 \\ l_{21} & l_{22} & \cdots & 0 \\ \vdots & \vdots & & \vdots \\ l_{n1} & l_{n2} & \cdots & l_{nm} \end{bmatrix}$$

Upper-triangular matrix

An upper-triangular matrix $\mathbf{U}$ has all its elements *below* the principal diagonal equal to zero; $u_{ij} = 0$ if $i > j$ for $1 \le i \le n$ and $1 \le j \le m$.

$$\mathbf{U} = \begin{bmatrix} u_{11} & u_{12} & \cdots & u_{1m} \\ 0 & u_{22} & \cdots & u_{2m} \\ \vdots & \vdots & & \vdots \\ 0 & 0 & \cdots & u_{nm} \end{bmatrix}$$

Matrix transpose

If the rows and columns of an $n \times m$ matrix $\mathbf{A}$ are interchanged, the resulting $m \times n$ matrix, denoted as $\mathbf{A}^T$, is called the *transpose* of the matrix $\mathbf{A}$. Namely, if $\mathbf{A}$ is given by Eqn. (12.1), then

$$\mathbf{A}^T = \begin{bmatrix} a_{11} & a_{21} & \cdots & a_{n1} \\ a_{12} & a_{22} & \cdots & a_{n2} \\ \vdots & \vdots & & \vdots \\ a_{1m} & a_{2m} & \cdots & a_{nm} \end{bmatrix}$$

Some properties of the matrix transpose are

   (i) $(\mathbf{A}^T)^T = \mathbf{A}$
   (ii) $(k\mathbf{A})^T = k\mathbf{A}^T$, where k is a scalar
   (iii) $(\mathbf{A} + \mathbf{B})^T = \mathbf{A}^T + \mathbf{B}^T$
   (iv) $(\mathbf{AB})^T = \mathbf{B}^T\mathbf{A}^T$

Determinant of a matrix

Determinants are defined for square matrices only. The determinant of the $n \times n$ matrix $\mathbf{A}$, written as $|\mathbf{A}|$ or $det\ \mathbf{A}$, is a scalar-valued function of $\mathbf{A}$. It is found through the use of minors and cofactors.

The *minor* m_{ij} of the element a_{ij} is the determinant of a matrix of order $(n-1) \times (n-1)$ obtained from $\mathbf{A}$ by removing the row and the column containing a_{ij}.

The *cofactor* c_{ij} of the element a_{ij} is defined by the equation

$$c_{ij} = (-1)^{i+j}\ m_{ij}$$

Determinants can be evaluated by the method of *Laplace expansion*. If **A** is an $n \times n$ matrix, any arbitrary row k can be selected and $|\mathbf{A}|$ is then given by

$$|\mathbf{A}| = \sum_{j=1}^{n} a_{kj}\, c_{kj}$$

Similarly, Laplace expansion can be carried out with respect to any arbitrary column l, to obtain

$$|\mathbf{A}| = \sum_{i=1}^{n} a_{il}\, c_{il}$$

Laplace expansion reduces the evaluation of an $n \times n$ determinant down to the evaluation of a string of $(n-1) \times (n-1)$ determinants, namely the cofactors. Some properties of determinants are
- (i) $det\ \mathbf{AB} = (det\ \mathbf{A})(det\ \mathbf{B})$
- (ii) $det\ \mathbf{A}^{T} = det\ \mathbf{A}$
- (iii) $det\ k\mathbf{A} = k^{n} det\ \mathbf{A}$; **A** is $n \times n$ matrix and k is scalar
- (iv) The determinant of any diagonal or triangular matrix is the product of its diagonal elements.

Singular matrix
A square matrix is called singular if the associated determinant is zero.

Nonsingular matrix
A square matrix is called nonsingular if the associated determinant is non-zero.

Adjoint matrix
The adjoint matrix of a square matrix **A** is found by replacing each element a_{ij} of matrix **A** by its cofactor c_{ij} and then transposing.

$$adj\ \mathbf{A} = \mathbf{A}^{+}$$

$$= \begin{bmatrix} c_{11} & c_{21} & \cdots & c_{n1} \\ c_{12} & c_{22} & \cdots & c_{n2} \\ \vdots & \vdots & & \vdots \\ c_{1n} & c_{2n} & \cdots & c_{nn} \end{bmatrix} = [c_{ji}]$$

Note that

$$\mathbf{A}(adj\ \mathbf{A}) = (adj\ \mathbf{A})\mathbf{A} = |\mathbf{A}|\ \mathbf{I} \tag{12.3}$$

Matrix inverse
The inverse of a square matrix is written as $\mathbf{A}^{-1}$, and is defined by the relation

$$\mathbf{A}^{-1}\mathbf{A} = \mathbf{A}\mathbf{A}^{-1} = \mathbf{I}$$

From Eqn. (12.3) and the definition of the inverse matrix, we have

$$\mathbf{A}^{-1} = \frac{adj\ \mathbf{A}}{|\mathbf{A}|} \tag{12.4}$$

Some properties of matrix inverse are

(i) $(\mathbf{A}^{-1})^{-1} = \mathbf{A}$

(ii) $(\mathbf{A}^{T})^{-1} = (\mathbf{A}^{-1})^{T}$

(iii) $(\mathbf{AB})^{-1} = \mathbf{B}^{-1}\mathbf{A}^{-1}$

(iv) $det\ \mathbf{A}^{-1} = \dfrac{1}{det\ \mathbf{A}}$

(v) $det\ \mathbf{P}^{-1}\mathbf{AP} = det\ \mathbf{A}$

(vi) Inverse of diagonal matrix given by Eqn. (12.2) is

$$\Lambda^{-1} = \begin{bmatrix} 1/a_{11} & 0 & \cdots & 0 \\ 0 & 1/a_{22} & \cdots & 0 \\ \vdots & \vdots & & \vdots \\ 0 & 0 & \cdots & 1/a_{nn} \end{bmatrix} = \text{diag}\ \begin{bmatrix} \dfrac{1}{a_{11}} & \dfrac{1}{a_{22}} & \cdots & \dfrac{1}{a_{nn}} \end{bmatrix}$$

Rank of a matrix

The rank $\rho(\mathbf{A})$ of a matrix $\mathbf{A}$ is the dimension of the largest array in $\mathbf{A}$ with a non-zero determinant. Some properties of rank are

(i) $\rho(\mathbf{A}^{T}) = \rho(\mathbf{A})$

(ii) The rank of a rectangular matrix cannot exceed the lesser of the number of rows or the number of columns. A matrix whose rank is equal to the lesser of the number of rows and number of columns is said to be of *full rank*.

$$\rho(\mathbf{A}) \le \min\ (n, m);\ \mathbf{A}\ \text{is}\ n \times m\ \text{matrix}$$

(iii) The rank of a product of two matrices cannot exceed the rank of the either:

$$\rho(\mathbf{AB}) \le \min\ [\rho(\mathbf{A}), \rho(\mathbf{B})]$$

Partitioned matrix

A matrix can be partitioned into submatrices. Broken lines are used to show the partitioning when the elements of the submatrices are explicitly shown. For example

$$\mathbf{A} = \begin{bmatrix} a_{11} & a_{12} & a_{13} \\ a_{21} & a_{22} & a_{23} \\ a_{31} & a_{32} & a_{33} \end{bmatrix} \tag{12.5}$$

The broken lines indicating the partitioning are sometimes omitted when the context makes it clear that partitioned matrices are being considered. For example, the matrix $\mathbf{A}$ given above may be expressed as

$$\mathbf{A} = \begin{bmatrix} \mathbf{A}_{11} & \mathbf{A}_{12} \\ \mathbf{A}_{21} & \mathbf{A}_{22} \end{bmatrix} \tag{12.6}$$

We will be frequently using the following forms of partitioning.

(i) Matrix $\mathbf{A}$ partitioned into its columns:

$$\mathbf{A} = [\mathbf{a}_1 \quad \mathbf{a}_2 \quad \cdots \quad \mathbf{a}_m]$$

where

$$
\mathbf{a}_i = \begin{bmatrix} a_{1i} \\ a_{2i} \\ \vdots \\ a_{ni} \end{bmatrix} = i\text{th column in } \mathbf{A}
$$

(ii) Matrix **A** partitioned into its rows:

$$
\mathbf{A} = \begin{bmatrix} \alpha_1 \\ \alpha_2 \\ \vdots \\ \alpha_n \end{bmatrix}
$$

where

$$
\alpha_i = [\ a_{i1} \quad a_{i2} \cdots a_{im}\ ] = i\text{th row in } \mathbf{A}
$$

(iii) A *block diagonal matrix* is a square matrix that can be partitioned so that the non-zero elements are contained only in square submatrices along the main diagonal,

$$
\mathbf{A} = \begin{bmatrix} \mathbf{A_1} & \mathbf{0} & \cdots & \mathbf{0} \\ \mathbf{0} & \mathbf{A_2} & \cdots & \mathbf{0} \\ \vdots & \vdots & & \vdots \\ \mathbf{0} & \mathbf{0} & \cdots & \mathbf{A}_m \end{bmatrix} \tag{12.7}
$$

$$
= \text{diag}\,[\mathbf{A_1} \quad \mathbf{A_2} \quad \cdots \quad \mathbf{A}_m\,]
$$

For this case

(i) $|\mathbf{A}| = |\mathbf{A_1}|\,|\mathbf{A_2}| \quad \cdots \quad |\mathbf{A}_m|$

(ii) $\mathbf{A}^{-1} = \text{diag}\,[\mathbf{A_1}^{-1}\mathbf{A_2}^{-1} \quad \cdots \quad \mathbf{A}^{-1}_m]$, provided that $\mathbf{A}^{-1}$ exists.

12.3 STATE VARIABLE REPRESENTATION

We have already seen in Chapter 2 (refer Eqns (2.4)) that the application of physical laws to mechanical, electrical, thermal, liquid-level, and other physical processes results in state variable models of the form

$$
\dot{\mathbf{x}}(t) = \mathbf{A}\mathbf{x}(t) + \mathbf{b}u(t); \mathbf{x}(t_0) \overset{\Delta}{=} \mathbf{x}^0 : \textit{State equation} \tag{12.8a}
$$
$$
y(t) = \mathbf{c}\mathbf{x}(t) + du(t): \textit{output equation} \tag{12.8b}
$$

where

$\mathbf{x}(t) = n \times 1$ state vector of nth-order dynamic system

$u(t) =$ system input

$y(t) =$ defined output

$\mathbf{A} = n \times n$ matrix

$\mathbf{b} = n \times 1$ column matrix

c = $1 \times n$ row matrix

d = scalar, representing direct coupling between input and output (direct coupling is rare in control systems, i.e., usually $d = 0$)

Example 12.1 _____

Two very usual applications of dc motors are in speed and position control systems.

Figure 12.1 gives the basic block diagram of a speed control system. A separately excited dc motor drives the load. A dc tachogenerator is attached to the motor shaft; speed signal is fedback and the error signal is used to control the armature voltage of the motor.

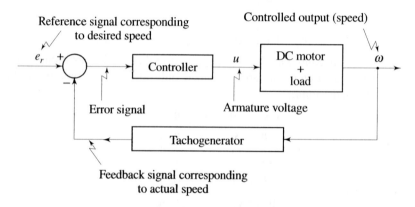

Fig. 12.1 *Basic block diagram of a closed-loop speed control system*

In the following, we derive the plant model for the speed control system. A separately excited dc motor with armature voltage control is shown in Fig. 12.2.

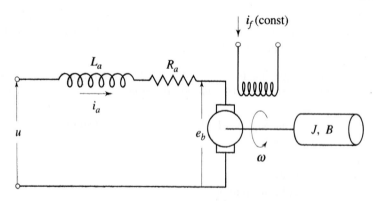

Fig. 12.2 *Model of a separately excited dc motor*

The voltage loop equation is

$$u(t) = L_a \frac{d\,i_a(t)}{d\,t} + R_a\,i_a(t) + e_b(t) \qquad (12.9a)$$

where

L_a = inductance of armature winding (henrys)
R_a = resistance of armature winding (ohms)
i_a = armature current (amperes)
e_b = back emf (volts)
u = applied armature voltage (volts)

The torque balance equation is

$$T_M(t) = J \frac{d\omega(t)}{dt} + B\,\omega(t) \qquad (12.9b)$$

where

T_M = torque developed by the motor (newton-m)
J = equivalent moment of inertia of motor and load referred to motor shaft (kg-m^2)
B = equivalent viscous friction coefficient of motor and load referred to

motor shaft $\left(\dfrac{\text{newton-m}}{\text{rad/ sec}} \right)$

ω = angular velocity of motor shaft (rad/sec)

In servo applications, the dc motors are generally used in the linear range of the magnetization curve. Therefore, the air gap flux ϕ is proportional to the field current. For the armature controlled motor, the field current i_f is held constant. Therefore, the torque T_M developed by the motor, which is proportional to the product of the armature current and the air gap flux, can be expressed as

$$T_M(t) = K_T\,i_a(t) \qquad (12.9c)$$

where

K_T = motor torque constant $\left(\dfrac{\text{newton-m}}{\text{amp}} \right)$

The counter electromotive force e_b, which is proportional to ϕ and ω, can be expressed as

$$e_b(t) = K_b\,\omega(t) \qquad (12.9d)$$

where

K_b = back emf constant[3] $\left(\dfrac{\text{volts}}{\text{rad / sec}} \right)$

Equations (12.9) can be reorganized as

---

3. In MKS units, $K_b = K_T$. Refer Section 3.5.

$$\frac{di_a(t)}{dt} = -\frac{R_a}{L_a} i_a(t) - \frac{K_b}{L_a} \omega(t) + \frac{1}{L_a} u(t)$$

(12.10)

$$\frac{d\omega(t)}{dt} = \frac{K_T}{J} i_a(t) - \frac{B}{J} \omega(t)$$

$x_1(t) = \omega(t)$, and $x_2(t) = i_a(t)$ is the obvious choice for state variables. The output variable is $y(t) = \omega(t)$.

The plant model of the speed control system organized into the vector-matrix notation is given below:

$$\begin{bmatrix} \dot{x}_1(t) \\ \dot{x}_2(t) \end{bmatrix} = \begin{bmatrix} -\dfrac{B}{J} & \dfrac{K_T}{J} \\ -\dfrac{K_b}{L_a} & -\dfrac{R_a}{L_a} \end{bmatrix} \begin{bmatrix} x_1(t) \\ x_2(t) \end{bmatrix} + \begin{bmatrix} 0 \\ \dfrac{1}{L_a} \end{bmatrix} u(t)$$

$$y(t) = x_1(t)$$

Let us assign numerical values to the system parameters.

For the parameters[4]

$$R_a = 1 \text{ ohm}, \ L_a = 0.1 \text{ H}, \ J = 0.1 \text{ kg-m}^2,$$

(12.11)

$$B = 0.1 \ \frac{\text{newton-m}}{\text{rad/sec}}, \ K_b = K_T = 0.1$$

the plant model becomes

$$\dot{\mathbf{x}}(t) = \mathbf{A}\mathbf{x}(t) + \mathbf{b}u(t)$$

$$y(t) = \mathbf{c}\mathbf{x}(t)$$

(12.12)

where

$$\mathbf{A} = \begin{bmatrix} -1 & 1 \\ -1 & -10 \end{bmatrix}; \ \mathbf{b} = \begin{bmatrix} 0 \\ 10 \end{bmatrix}; \ \mathbf{c} = \begin{bmatrix} 1 & 0 \end{bmatrix}$$

Example 12.2

Figure 12.3 gives the basic block diagram of a position control system. The controlled variable is now the angular position $\theta(t)$ of the motor shaft:

$$\frac{d\theta(t)}{dt} = \omega(t)$$

(12.13)

We make the following choice for state and output variables.

$$x_1(t) = \theta(t), \ x_2(t) = \omega(t), \ x_3(t) = i_a(t), \ y(t) = \theta(t)$$

For this choice, we obtain the following plant model from Eqns (12.10) and (12.13).

---

4. These parameters have been chosen for computational convenience.

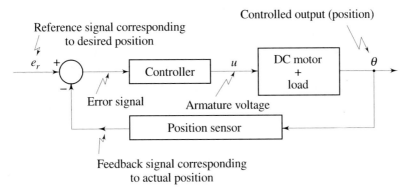

Fig. 12.3 *Basic block diagram of a closed-loop position control system*

$$
\begin{bmatrix} \dot{x}_1(t) \\ \dot{x}_2(t) \\ \dot{x}_3(t) \end{bmatrix} = \begin{bmatrix} 0 & 1 & 0 \\ 0 & -\dfrac{B}{J} & \dfrac{K_T}{J} \\ 0 & -\dfrac{K_b}{L_a} & -\dfrac{R_a}{L_a} \end{bmatrix} \begin{bmatrix} x_1(t) \\ x_2(t) \\ x_3(t) \end{bmatrix} + \begin{bmatrix} 0 \\ 0 \\ \dfrac{1}{L_a} \end{bmatrix} u(t)
$$

$$
y(t) = x_1(t)
$$

For the system parameters given by (12.11), the plant model for position control system becomes

$$
\dot{\mathbf{x}}(t) = \mathbf{A}\mathbf{x}(t) + \mathbf{b}u(t) \tag{12.14}
$$
$$
y(t) = \mathbf{c}\mathbf{x}(t)
$$

where

$$
\mathbf{A} = \begin{bmatrix} 0 & 1 & 0 \\ 0 & -1 & 1 \\ 0 & -1 & -10 \end{bmatrix}; \mathbf{b} = \begin{bmatrix} 0 \\ 0 \\ 10 \end{bmatrix}; \mathbf{c} = \begin{bmatrix} 1 & 0 & 0 \end{bmatrix}
$$

▲▲

In Examples 12.1 and 12.2 discussed above, the selected state variables are the physical quantities of the systems which can be measured. It may sometimes be necessary and advantageous to provide a feedback proportional to the state variables of a system, rather than the output alone, for the purpose of stabilizing and improving the performance of a system[5]. The implementation of design with state variable feedback becomes straightforward if the state variables are available for feedback. The choice of physical variables of a system as state variables therefore helps in the implementation of design. Another advantage of selecting physical variables for state variable formulation is that the solution of state equation gives time variation of variables which have direct relevance to the physical system.

---

5. Chapter 7 of reference [180].

Transformation of State Variables

It frequently happens that the state variables used in the original formulation of the dynamics of a system are not as convenient as another set of state variables. Instead of having to reformulate the system dynamics, it is possible to transform the set $\{\mathbf{A}, \mathbf{b}, \mathbf{c}, d\}$ of the original formulation (12.8) to a new set $\{\overline{\mathbf{A}}, \overline{\mathbf{b}}, \overline{\mathbf{c}}, \overline{d}\}$. The change of variables is represented by a linear transformation

$$\mathbf{x} = \mathbf{P}\overline{\mathbf{x}} \tag{12.15a}$$

where $\overline{\mathbf{x}}$ is a state vector in the new formulation and $\mathbf{x}$ is the state vector in the original formulation. It is assumed that the transformation matrix $\mathbf{P}$ is a nonsingular $n \times n$ matrix, so that we can always write

$$\overline{\mathbf{x}} = \mathbf{P}^{-1}\mathbf{x} \tag{12.15b}$$

We assume, moreover, that $\mathbf{P}$ is a constant matrix.

The original dynamics are expressed by

$$\dot{\mathbf{x}}(t) = \mathbf{A}\mathbf{x}(t) + \mathbf{b}u(t); \; \mathbf{x}(t_0) \triangleq \mathbf{x}^0 \tag{12.16a}$$

and the output by

$$y(t) = \mathbf{c}\mathbf{x}(t) + du(t) \tag{12.16b}$$

Substitution of $\mathbf{x}$ as given by Eqn. (12.15a) into these equations, gives

$$\mathbf{P}\dot{\overline{\mathbf{x}}}(t) = \mathbf{A}\mathbf{P}\overline{\mathbf{x}}(t) + \mathbf{b}u(t)$$

$$y(t) = \mathbf{c}\mathbf{P}\overline{\mathbf{x}}(t) + du(t)$$

or

$$\dot{\overline{\mathbf{x}}}(t) = \overline{\mathbf{A}}\,\overline{\mathbf{x}}(t) + \overline{\mathbf{b}}u(t); \; \overline{\mathbf{x}}(t_0) = \mathbf{P}^{-1}\mathbf{x}(t_0) \tag{12.17a}$$

$$y(t) = \overline{\mathbf{c}}\,\overline{\mathbf{x}}(t) + \overline{d}\,u(t) \tag{12.17b}$$

with

$$\overline{\mathbf{A}} = \mathbf{P}^{-1}\mathbf{A}\mathbf{P}, \; \overline{\mathbf{b}} = \mathbf{P}^{-1}\mathbf{b}, \; \overline{\mathbf{c}} = \mathbf{c}\mathbf{P}, \; \overline{d} = d$$

In the next section we will prove that both the linear systems (12.16) and (12.17) have identical output responses for the same input. The linear system (12.17) is said to be *equivalent* to the linear system (12.16), and $\mathbf{P}$ is called an *equivalence* or *similarity transformation*.

It is obvious that there exist an infinite number of equivalent systems since the transformation matrix $\mathbf{P}$ can be arbitrarily chosen. Some transformations have been extensively used for the purposes of analysis and design. Five of such special (*canonical*) transformations will be introduced in this chapter.

Example 12.3 —————————————————————————

Example 12.1 revisited

For the system of Fig. 12.2, we have taken angular velocity $\omega(t)$ and armature current $i_a(t)$ as state variables:

$$\mathbf{x} = \begin{bmatrix} x_1 \\ x_2 \end{bmatrix} = \begin{bmatrix} \omega \\ i_a \end{bmatrix}$$

We now define new state variables as

$$\bar{x}_1 = \omega, \ \bar{x}_2 = -\omega + i_a$$

or

$$\bar{\mathbf{x}} = \begin{bmatrix} \bar{x}_1 \\ \bar{x}_2 \end{bmatrix} = \begin{bmatrix} x_1 \\ -x_1 + x_2 \end{bmatrix} = \begin{bmatrix} 1 & 0 \\ -1 & 1 \end{bmatrix} \begin{bmatrix} x_1 \\ x_2 \end{bmatrix}$$

We can express velocity $x_1(t)$ and armature current $x_2(t)$ in terms of the variables $\bar{x}_1(t)$ and $\bar{x}_2(t)$:

$$\mathbf{x} = \mathbf{P}\bar{\mathbf{x}} \tag{12.18}$$

with

$$\mathbf{P} = \begin{bmatrix} 1 & 0 \\ 1 & 1 \end{bmatrix}$$

Using Eqns (12.17) and (12.12), we obtain the following state variable model for the system of Fig. 12.2 in terms of the transformed state vector $\bar{\mathbf{x}}(t)$:

$$\dot{\bar{\mathbf{x}}}(t) = \bar{\mathbf{A}}\bar{\mathbf{x}}(t) + \bar{\mathbf{b}}u(t)$$
$$y(t) = \bar{\mathbf{c}}\,\bar{\mathbf{x}}(t) \tag{12.19}$$

where

$$\bar{\mathbf{A}} = \mathbf{P}^{-1}\mathbf{A}\mathbf{P} = \begin{bmatrix} 1 & 0 \\ -1 & 1 \end{bmatrix} \begin{bmatrix} -1 & 1 \\ -1 & -10 \end{bmatrix} \begin{bmatrix} 1 & 0 \\ 1 & 1 \end{bmatrix} = \begin{bmatrix} 0 & 1 \\ -11 & -11 \end{bmatrix}$$

$$\bar{\mathbf{b}} = \mathbf{P}^{-1}\mathbf{b} = \begin{bmatrix} 1 & 0 \\ -1 & 1 \end{bmatrix} \begin{bmatrix} 0 \\ 10 \end{bmatrix} = \begin{bmatrix} 0 \\ 10 \end{bmatrix}$$

$$\bar{\mathbf{c}} = \mathbf{c}\mathbf{P} = \begin{bmatrix} 1 & 0 \end{bmatrix} \begin{bmatrix} 1 & 0 \\ 1 & 1 \end{bmatrix} = \begin{bmatrix} 1 & 0 \end{bmatrix}$$

$$\bar{x}_1(t_0) = x_1(t_0); \ \bar{x}_2(t_0) = -x_1(t_0) + x_2(t_0) \tag{12.20}$$

Equations (12.19) give an alternative state variable model of the system previously represented by Eqns (12.12). $\bar{\mathbf{x}}(t)$ and $\mathbf{x}(t)$ both qualify to be state vectors of the given system (the two vectors individually characterize the system completely at time t), and the output $y(t)$, as we shall see shortly, is uniquely determined from either of the models (12.12) and (12.19). State variable model (12.19) is thus *equivalent* to the model (12.12), and the matrix $\mathbf{P}$ given by Eqn. (12.18) is an equivalence or similarity transformation.

The state variable model given by Eqns (12.19) is in a *canonical* (special) form.

12.4 CONVERSION OF STATE VARIABLE MODELS TO TRANSFER FUNCTIONS

We shall derive the transfer function of a SISO system from the Laplace-transformed version of the state and output equations. Refer Section 12.2 for the matrix operations used in the derivation.

Consider the state variable model (Eqns (12.8)):

$$\dot{\mathbf{x}}(t) = \mathbf{A}\mathbf{x}(t) + \mathbf{b}u(t); \ \ \mathbf{x}(t_0) \triangleq \mathbf{x}^0$$

$$y(t) = \mathbf{c}\mathbf{x}(t) + du(t)$$

(12.21)

Taking the Laplace transform of Eqns (12.21), we obtain

$$s\mathbf{X}(s) - \mathbf{x}^0 = \mathbf{A}\mathbf{X}(s) + \mathbf{b}U(s)$$

$$Y(s) = \mathbf{c}\mathbf{X}(s) + dU(s)$$

where

$$\mathbf{X}(s) \triangleq \mathscr{L}[\mathbf{x}(t)]; U(s) \triangleq \mathscr{L}[u(t)]; Y(s) \triangleq \mathscr{L}[y(t)]$$

Manipulation of these equations gives

$$(s\mathbf{I} - \mathbf{A})\mathbf{X}(s) = \mathbf{x}^0 + \mathbf{b}U(s); \ \mathbf{I} \text{ is } n \times n \text{ identity matrix}$$

or

$$\mathbf{X}(s) = (s\mathbf{I} - \mathbf{A})^{-1}\mathbf{x}^0 + (s\mathbf{I} - \mathbf{A})^{-1}\mathbf{b}U(s)$$

(12.22a)

$$Y(s) = \mathbf{c}(s\mathbf{I} - \mathbf{A})^{-1}\mathbf{x}^0 + [\mathbf{c}(s\mathbf{I} - \mathbf{A})^{-1}\mathbf{b} + d]U(s)$$

(12.22b)

Equations (12.22) are algebraic equations. If $\mathbf{x}^0$ and $U(s)$ are known, $\mathbf{X}(s)$ and $Y(s)$ can be computed from these equations.

In the case of a zero initial state (i.e., $\mathbf{x}^0 = \mathbf{0}$), the input–output behaviour of the system (12.21) is determined entirely by the transfer function

$$\frac{Y(s)}{U(s)} = G(s) = \mathbf{c}(s\mathbf{I} - \mathbf{A})^{-1}\mathbf{b} + d$$

(12.23)

We can express the inverse of the matrix $(s\mathbf{I} - \mathbf{A})$ as

$$(s\mathbf{I} - \mathbf{A})^{-1} = \frac{(s\mathbf{I} - \mathbf{A})^+}{|s\mathbf{I} - \mathbf{A}|}$$

(12.24)

where

$$|s\mathbf{I} - \mathbf{A}| = \text{determinant of the matrix } (s\mathbf{I} - \mathbf{A})$$

$$(s\mathbf{I} - \mathbf{A})^+ = \text{adjoint of the matrix } (s\mathbf{I} - \mathbf{A})$$

Using Eqn. (12.24), the transfer function $G(s)$ given by Eqn. (12.23) can be written as

$$G(s) = \frac{\mathbf{c}(s\mathbf{I} - \mathbf{A})^+\mathbf{b}}{|s\mathbf{I} - \mathbf{A}|} + d$$

(12.25)

For a general nth-order matrix

$$\mathbf{A} = \begin{bmatrix} a_{11} & a_{12} & \cdots & a_{1n} \\ a_{21} & a_{22} & \cdots & a_{2n} \\ \vdots & \vdots & & \vdots \\ a_{n1} & a_{n2} & \cdots & a_{nn} \end{bmatrix},$$

the matrix $(s\mathbf{I} - \mathbf{A})$ has the following appearance:

$$(s\mathbf{I} - \mathbf{A}) = \begin{bmatrix} s - a_{11} & - a_{12} & \cdots & - a_{1n} \\ - a_{21} & s - a_{22} & \cdots & - a_{2n} \\ \vdots & \vdots & & \vdots \\ - a_{n1} & - a_{n2} & \cdots & s - a_{nn} \end{bmatrix}$$

If we imagine calculating $det(s\mathbf{I} - \mathbf{A})$, we see that one of the terms will be product of diagonal elements of $(s\mathbf{I} - \mathbf{A})$:

$$(s - a_{11})(s - a_{22}) \cdots (s - a_{nn}) = s^n + \alpha_1' s^{n-1} + \cdots + \alpha_n',$$

a polynomial of degree n with the leading coefficient of unity. There will be other terms coming from the off-diagonal elements of $(s\mathbf{I} - \mathbf{A})$, but none will have a degree as high as n. Thus $|s\mathbf{I} - \mathbf{A}|$ will be of the following form:

$$|s\mathbf{I} - \mathbf{A}| = \Delta(s) = s^n + \alpha_1 s^{n-1} + \cdots + \alpha_n \qquad (12.26)$$

where α_i are constant scalars.

This is known as the *characteristic polynomial* of the matrix $\mathbf{A}$. It plays a vital role in the dynamic behaviour of the system. The roots of this polynomial are called the *characteristic roots* or *eigenvalues* of matrix $\mathbf{A}$. These roots, as we shall see in Section 12.6, determine the essential features of the unforced dynamic behaviour of the system (12.21).

The adjoint of an $n \times n$ matrix is itself an $n \times n$ matrix whose elements are the cofactors of the original matrix. Each cofactor is obtained by computing the determinant of the matrix that remains when a row and a column of the original matrix are deleted. It thus follows that each element in $(s\mathbf{I} - \mathbf{A})^+$ is a polynomial in s of maximum degree $(n - 1)$. Adjoint of $(s\mathbf{I} - \mathbf{A})$ can therefore be expressed as

$$(s\mathbf{I} - \mathbf{A})^+ = \mathbf{Q}_1 s^{n-1} + \mathbf{Q}_2 s^{n-2} + \cdots + \mathbf{Q}_{n-1} s + \mathbf{Q}_n \qquad (12.27)$$

where $\mathbf{Q}_i$ are constant $n \times n$ matrices. We can express transfer function $G(s)$ given by Eqn. (12.25) in the following form:

$$G(s) = \frac{\mathbf{c}[\mathbf{Q}_1 s^{n-1} + \mathbf{Q}_2 s^{n-2} + \cdots + \mathbf{Q}_{n-1} s + \mathbf{Q}_n]\mathbf{b}}{s^n + \alpha_1 s^{n-1} + \cdots + \alpha_{n-1} s + \alpha_n} + d \qquad (12.28)$$

$G(s)$ is thus a rational function of s. When $d = 0$, the degree of numerator polynomial of $G(s)$ is strictly less than the degree of the denominator polynomial and therefore the resulting transfer function is a *strictly proper transfer function*. When $d \neq 0$, the degree of numerator polynomial of $G(s)$ will be equal to the degree of the denominator polynomial, giving a *proper transfer function*. Further,

$$d = \lim_{s \to \infty} [G(s)] \qquad (12.29)$$

From Eqns (12.26) and (12.28) we observe that the characteristic polyno-mial of matrix $\mathbf{A}$ of the system (12.21) is same as the denominator polynomial of the corresponding transfer function $G(s)$. If there are no cancellations between the numerator and denominator polynomials of $G(s)$ in Eqn. (12.28), the *eigenvalues* of matrix $\mathbf{A}$ are same as the *poles* of $G(s)$. We will take up in Section 12.8, this aspect of the correspondence between state variable models and transfer functions. It will be proved that for a completely controllable and completely observable state variable model, the eigenvalues of matrix $\mathbf{A}$ are same as the poles of the corresponding transfer function.

Invariance Property

It is recalled that the state variable model for a system is not unique, but depends on the choice of a set of state variables. A transformation

$$\mathbf{x}(t) = \mathbf{P}\overline{\mathbf{x}}(t); \mathbf{P} \text{ is a nonsingular matrix} \tag{12.30}$$

results in the following alternative state variable model (refer Eqns (12.17)) for the system (12.21):

$$\dot{\overline{\mathbf{x}}}(t) = \overline{\mathbf{A}}\,\overline{\mathbf{x}}(t) + \overline{\mathbf{b}}\,u(t); \ \overline{\mathbf{x}}(t_0) = \mathbf{P}^{-1}\mathbf{x}(t_0) \tag{12.31a}$$

$$y(t) = \overline{\mathbf{c}}\,\overline{\mathbf{x}}(t) + du(t) \tag{12.31b}$$

where $\quad\quad\quad \overline{\mathbf{A}} = \mathbf{P}^{-1}\mathbf{AP}, \ \overline{\mathbf{b}} = \mathbf{P}^{-1}\mathbf{b}, \ \overline{\mathbf{c}} = \mathbf{cP}$

The definition of new set of internal state variables should evidently not affect the eigenvalues or input-output behaviour. This may be verified by evaluating the characteristic polynomial and the transfer function of the transformed system.

(i) $\quad |s\mathbf{I} - \overline{\mathbf{A}}| = |s\mathbf{I} - \mathbf{P}^{-1}\mathbf{AP}| = |s\mathbf{P}^{-1}\mathbf{P} - \mathbf{P}^{-1}\mathbf{AP}|$

$$= |\mathbf{P}^{-1}(s\mathbf{I} - \mathbf{A})\mathbf{P}| = |\mathbf{P}^{-1}| \, |s\mathbf{I} - \mathbf{A}| \, |\mathbf{P}| = |s\mathbf{I} - \mathbf{A}| \tag{12.32}$$

(ii) System output in response to input $u(t)$ is given by the transfer function

$$\overline{G}(s) = \overline{\mathbf{c}}(s\mathbf{I} - \overline{\mathbf{A}})^{-1}\overline{\mathbf{b}} + d$$

$$= \mathbf{cP}(s\mathbf{I} - \mathbf{P}^{-1}\mathbf{AP})^{-1}\mathbf{P}^{-1}\mathbf{b} + d$$

$$= \mathbf{cP}(s\mathbf{P}^{-1}\mathbf{P} - \mathbf{P}^{-1}\mathbf{AP})^{-1}\mathbf{P}^{-1}\mathbf{b} + d$$

$$= \mathbf{cP}[\mathbf{P}^{-1}(s\mathbf{I} - \mathbf{A})\mathbf{P}]^{-1}\mathbf{P}^{-1}\mathbf{b} + d$$

$$= \mathbf{cPP}^{-1}(s\mathbf{I} - \mathbf{A})^{-1}\mathbf{PP}^{-1}\mathbf{b} + d$$

$$= \mathbf{c}(s\mathbf{I} - \mathbf{A})^{-1}\mathbf{b} + d = G(s) \tag{12.33}$$

(iii) System output in response to initial state $\overline{\mathbf{x}}(t_0)$ is given by (refer Eqn. (12.22b))

$$\bar{\mathbf{c}}(s\mathbf{I} - \bar{\mathbf{A}})^{-1}\bar{\mathbf{x}}(t_0) = \mathbf{c}\mathbf{P}(s\mathbf{I} - \mathbf{P}^{-1}\mathbf{A}\mathbf{P})^{-1}\mathbf{P}^{-1}\mathbf{x}(t_0)$$

$$= \mathbf{c}(s\mathbf{I} - \mathbf{A})^{-1}\mathbf{x}(t_0) \qquad (12.34)$$

The input-output behaviour of the system (12.21) is thus *invariant* under the transformation (12.30).

*Example 12.4*_____

Consider the position control system of Example 12.2. The plant model of the system is reproduced below:

$$\dot{\mathbf{x}}(t) = \mathbf{A}\mathbf{x}(t) + \mathbf{b}u(t)$$
$$y(t) = \mathbf{c}\mathbf{x}(t) \qquad (12.35)$$

with
$$\mathbf{A} = \begin{bmatrix} 0 & 1 & 0 \\ 0 & -1 & 1 \\ 0 & -1 & -10 \end{bmatrix}; \mathbf{b} = \begin{bmatrix} 0 \\ 0 \\ 10 \end{bmatrix}; \mathbf{c} = \begin{bmatrix} 1 & 0 & 0 \end{bmatrix}$$

The characteristic polynomial of matrix $\mathbf{A}$ is

$$|s\mathbf{I} - \mathbf{A}| = \begin{vmatrix} s & -1 & 0 \\ 0 & s+1 & -1 \\ 0 & 1 & s+10 \end{vmatrix} = s(s^2 + 11s + 11)$$

The transfer function

$$G(s) = \frac{Y(s)}{U(s)} = \frac{\mathbf{c}(s\mathbf{I} - \mathbf{A})^+ \mathbf{b}}{|s\mathbf{I} - \mathbf{A}|}$$

$$= \frac{\begin{bmatrix} 1 & 0 & 0 \end{bmatrix} \begin{bmatrix} s^2 + 11s + 11 & s+10 & 1 \\ 0 & s(s+10) & s \\ 0 & -s & s(s+1) \end{bmatrix} \begin{bmatrix} 0 \\ 0 \\ 10 \end{bmatrix}}{s(s^2 + 11s + 11)}$$

$$= \frac{10}{s(s^2 + 11s + 11)} \qquad (12.36)$$

Alternatively, we can draw the state diagram (refer Fig. 2.33) of the plant model in signal flow graph form and from there obtain the transfer function using Mason's gain formula. For the plant model (12.35), the state diagram is shown in Fig. 12.4. Application of Mason's gain formula yields

$$\frac{Y(s)}{U(s)} = G(s) = \frac{10\,s^{-3}}{1 - (-10\,s^{-1} - s^{-1} - s^{-2}) + 10\,s^{-2}}$$

$$= \frac{10}{s^3 + 11s^2 + 11s} = \frac{10}{s(s^2 + 11s + 11)}$$

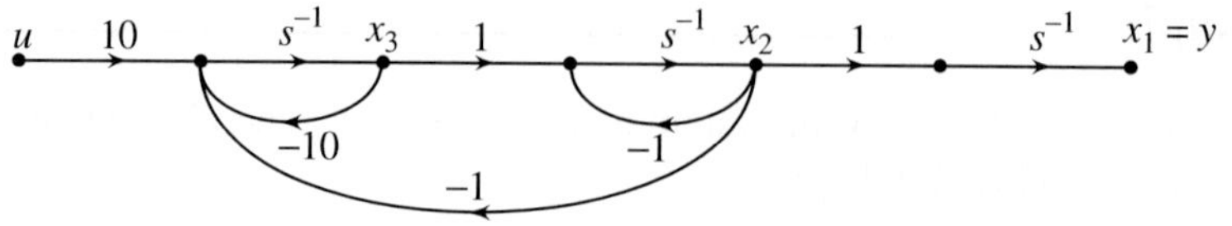

Fig. 12.4 *State diagram for the system (12.35)*

12.5 | CONVERSION OF TRANSFER FUNCTIONS TO CANONICAL STATE VARIABLE MODELS

In the last section, we studied the problem—finding the transfer function from the state variable model of a system. The converse problem—finding a state variable model from the transfer function of a system, is the subject of discussion in this section. This problem is quite important because of the following reasons:

(i) Quite often the system dynamics is determined experimentally using standard test signals like a step, impulse, or sinusoidal signal. A transfer function is conveniently fitted to the experimental data in some best possible manner.

There are, however, many design techniques developed exclusively for state variable models. In order to apply these techniques, experimentally obtained transfer function descriptions must be realized into state variable models.

(ii) Realization of transfer functions into state variable models is needed even if the control system design is based on frequency-domain design methods. In these cases the need arises for the purpose of transient response simulation. Many algorithms and numerical integration computer programs designed for solution of systems of first-order equations are available, but there is not much software for the numerical inversion of Laplace transforms. Thus, if a reliable method is needed for calculating the transient response of a system, one may be better off converting the transfer function of the system to state variable description and numerically integrating the resulting differential equations rather than attempting to compute the inverse Laplace transform by numerical methods.

We shall discuss here the problem of realization of transfer function into state variable models. Note the use of the term 'realization'.

A state variable model that has a prescribed rational function $G(s)$ as its transfer function, is the *realization* of $G(s)$. The term 'realization' is justified by the fact that by using the *state diagram,* a pictorial representation of the state variable model, the system with the transfer function $G(s)$ can be built in the real world by an op amp circuit (we shall see this shortly).

The following three problems are involved in the realization of a given transfer function into state variable models:

(i) Is it possible at all to obtain state variable description from the given transfer function?

(ii) If yes, is the state variable description unique for a given transfer function?

(iii) How do we obtain the state variable description from the given transfer function?

The answer to the first problem has been given in the last section. A rational function $G(s)$ is realizable by a finite dimensional linear time-invariant state model if and only if $G(s)$ is a proper rational function. A proper rational function will have state model of the form:

$$\dot{\mathbf{x}}(t) = \mathbf{A}\mathbf{x}(t) + \mathbf{b}u(t)$$
$$y(t) = \mathbf{c}\mathbf{x}(t) + du(t) \qquad (12.37)$$

where $\mathbf{A}$, $\mathbf{b}$, $\mathbf{c}$ and d are constant matrices of appropriate dimensions. A strictly proper rational function will have state model of the form

$$\dot{\mathbf{x}}(t) = \mathbf{A}\mathbf{x}(t) + \mathbf{b}u(t)$$
$$y(t) = \mathbf{c}\mathbf{x}(t) \qquad (12.38)$$

Let us now turn to the second problem. In the last section, we saw that there are innumerable systems that have the same transfer function. Hence, the representation of a transfer function in state variable form is obviously not unique. However, all these representations will be equivalent.

In the remaining part of this section, we deal with the third problem. We shall develop three standard, or 'canonical' representations of transfer functions.

A linear time-invariant SISO system is described by transfer function of the form

$$G(s) = \frac{\beta_0 s^m + \beta_1 s^{m-1} + \cdots + \beta_m}{s^n + \alpha_1 s^{n-1} + \cdots + \alpha_n} \; ; m \le n$$

where the coefficients α_i and β_i are real constant scalars. Note that there is no loss in generality to assume the coefficient of s^n to be unity.

In the following, we derive results for $m = n$; these results may be used for the case $m < n$ by setting appropriate β_i coefficients equal to zero. Therefore, our problem is to obtain a state variable model corresponding to the transfer function

$$G(s) = \frac{\beta_0 \, s^n + \beta_1 \, s^{n-1} + \cdots + \beta_n}{s^n + \alpha_1 \, s^{n-1} + \cdots + \alpha_n} \qquad (12.39)$$

First Companion Form

Our development starts with a transfer function of the form

$$\frac{Z(s)}{U(s)} = \frac{1}{s^n + \alpha_1 \, s^{n-1} + \cdots + \alpha_n} \qquad (12.40)$$

which can be written as

$$(s^n + \alpha_1 \, s^{n-1} + \cdots + \alpha_n) \, Z(s) = U(s)$$

The corresponding differential equation is

$$p^n z(t) + \alpha_1 p^{n-1} z(t) + \cdots + \alpha_n z(t) = u(t)$$

where

$$p^k z(t) \overset{\Delta}{=} \frac{d^k z(t)}{dt^k}$$

Solving for highest derivative of $z(t)$, we obtain

$$p^n z(t) = -\alpha_1 p^{n-1} z(t) - \alpha_2 p^{n-2} \, z(t) - \cdots -\alpha_n z(t) + u(t) \qquad (12.41)$$

Now consider a chain of n integrators as shown in Fig. 12.5. Suppose that the output of the last integrator is $z(t)$. Then the output of the just previous integrator is $pz = dz/dt$, and so forth. The output from the first integrator is $p^{n-1} z(t)$, and the input to this integrator is thus $p^n z(t)$. This leaves only the problem of obtaining $p^n z(t)$ for use as input to the first integrator. In fact, this is already specified by Eqn. (12.41). Realization of this equation is shown in Fig. 12.5.

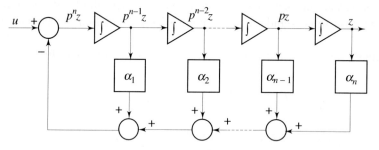

Fig. 12.5 *Realization of the system (12.41)*

Having developed a realization of the simple transfer function (12.40), we are now in a position to consider the more general transfer function (12.39). We decompose this transfer function into two parts, as shown in Fig. 12.6. The output $Y(s)$ can be written as

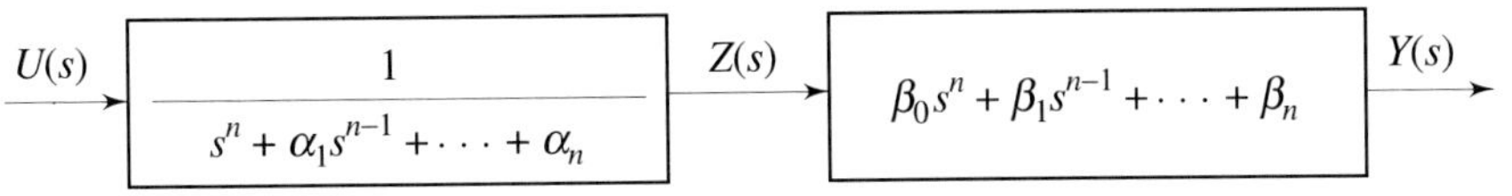

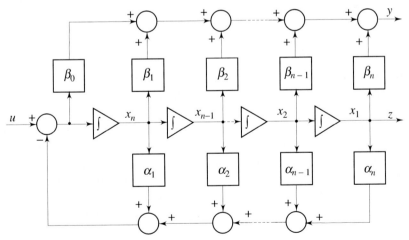

Fig. 12.6 *Decomposition of the transfer function (12.39)*

$$Y(s) = (\beta_0 s^n + \beta_1 s^{n-1} + \cdots + \beta_n) Z(s) \qquad (12.42a)$$

where $Z(s)$ is given by

$$\frac{Z(s)}{U(s)} = \frac{1}{s^n + \alpha_1 s^{n-1} + \cdots + \alpha_n} \qquad (12.42b)$$

A realization of the transfer function (12.42b) has already been developed. Figure 12.5 shows this realization. The output of the last integrator is $z(t)$ and the inputs to the integrators in the chain from the last to the first are the n successive derivatives of $z(t)$.

Realization of the transfer function (12.42a) is now straightforward. The output

$$y(t) = \beta_0 p^n z(t) + \beta_1 p^{n-1} z(t) + \cdots + \beta_n z(t),$$

is nothing but the sum of the scaled versions of the inputs to the n integrators. Figure 12.7 shows complete realization of the transfer function (12.39). All that remains to be done is to write the corresponding differential equations.

To get one state variable model of the system, we identify the output of each integrator in Fig. 12.7 with a state variable, starting at the right and proceeding to the left. The corresponding differential equations using this identification of state variables are

Fig. 12.7 *Realization (state diagram) of the system (12.39)*

$$\dot{x}_1 = x_2$$

$$\dot{x}_2 = x_3$$

$$\vdots$$

$$\dot{x}_{n-1} = x_n$$ (12.43a)

$$\dot{x}_n = -\alpha_n x_1 - \alpha_{n-1} x_2 - \cdots - \alpha_1 x_n + u$$

The output equation is found by careful examination of the block diagram of Fig. 12.7. Note that there are two paths from the output of each integrator to the system output—one path upward through the box labelled β_i, and a second path down through the box labelled α_i and thence through the box labelled β_0. As a consequence,

$$y = (\beta_n - \alpha_n\beta_0) x_1 + (\beta_{n-1} - \alpha_{n-1}\beta_0) x_2 + \cdots$$

$$+ (\beta_1 - \alpha_1\beta_0) x_n + \beta_0 u$$ (12.43b)

The state and output equations (12.43), organized in vector-matrix form, are given below:

$$\dot{\mathbf{x}}(t) = \mathbf{A}\mathbf{x}(t) + \mathbf{b}u(t)$$

$$y(t) = \mathbf{c}\mathbf{x}(t) + du(t)$$ (12.44)

with

$$\mathbf{A} = \begin{bmatrix} 0 & 1 & 0 & \cdots & 0 \\ 0 & 0 & 1 & \cdots & 0 \\ \vdots & \vdots & \vdots & & \vdots \\ 0 & 0 & 0 & \cdots & 1 \\ -\alpha_n & -\alpha_{n-1} & -\alpha_{n-2} & \cdots & -\alpha_1 \end{bmatrix}; \mathbf{b} = \begin{bmatrix} 0 \\ 0 \\ \vdots \\ 0 \\ 1 \end{bmatrix}$$

$$\mathbf{c} = [\beta_n - \alpha_n\beta_0, \quad \beta_{n-1} - \alpha_{n-1}\beta_0, \ldots, \beta_1 - \alpha_1\beta_0]; \, d = \beta_0$$

If the direct path through β_0 is absent (refer Fig. 12.7), then the scalar d is zero and the row matrix $\mathbf{c}$ contains only the β_i coefficients.

The matrix $\mathbf{A}$ in Eqns (12.44) has a very special structure: the coefficients of the denominator of the transfer function preceded by minus signs form a string along the bottom row of the matrix. The rest of the matrix is zero except for the 'superdiagonal' terms which are all unity. In matrix theory, a matrix with this structure is said to be in *companion form*. For this reason, we identify the realization (12.44) as *companion-form realization* of the transfer function (12.39). We call this the *first companion form*: another companion form follows.

Second Companion Form

In the first companion form, the coefficients of the denominator of the transfer function appear in one of the rows of the $\mathbf{A}$ matrix. There is another companion form in which the coefficients appear in a column of the $\mathbf{A}$ matrix. This can be obtained by writing Eqn. (12.39) as

$$(s^n + \alpha_1 s^{n-1} + \cdots + \alpha_n)\, Y(s) = (\beta_0 s^n + \beta_1 s^{n-1} + \cdots + \beta_n)\, U(s)$$

or
$$s^n\,[Y(s) - \beta_0 U(s)] + s^{n-1}\,[\alpha_1 Y(s) - \beta_1 U(s)] + \cdots$$
$$+ [\alpha_n Y(s) - \beta_n U(s)] = 0$$

On dividing by s^n and solving for $Y(s)$, we obtain

$$Y(s) = \beta_0 U(s) + \frac{1}{s}\,[\beta_1 U(s) - \alpha_1 Y(s)] + \cdots + \frac{1}{s^n}\,[\beta_n U(s) - \alpha_n Y(s)] \quad (12.45)$$

Note that $1/s^n$ is the transfer function of a chain of n integrators. Realization of

$\dfrac{1}{s^n}\,[\beta_n U(s) - \alpha_n Y(s)]$ requires a chain of n integrators with an input $[\beta_n u - \alpha_n y]$

to the first integrator in the chain from left-to-right. Realization of

$\dfrac{1}{s^{n-1}}\,[\beta_{n-1} U(s) - \alpha_{n-1} Y(s)]$ requires a chain of $(n-1)$ integrators with input

$[\beta_{n-1} u - \alpha_{n-1} y]$ to the first integrator in the chain from left-to-right, and so forth. This immediately leads to the structure shown in Fig. 12.8. The signal y is fed back to each of the integrators in the chain and the signal u is fed forward. Thus the signal $[\beta_n u - \alpha_n y]$ passes through n integrators; the signal $[\beta_{n-1} u - \alpha_{n-1} y]$ passes through $(n-1)$ integrators and so forth to complete the realization of Eqn. (12.45). The structure retains the ladder-like shape of the first companion form, but the feedback paths are in different directions.

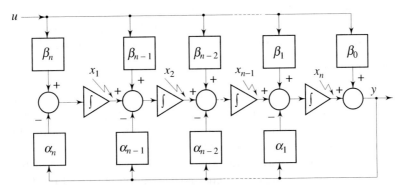

Fig. 12.8   *Realization (state diagram) of Eqn. (12.45)*

We can now write differential equations for the realization given by Fig. 12.8. To get one state variable model, we identify the output of each integrator in Fig. 12.8 with a state variable starting at the left and proceeding to the right. The corresponding differential equations are

$$\dot{x}_n = x_{n-1} - \alpha_1(x_n + \beta_0 u) + \beta_1 u$$
$$\dot{x}_{n-1} = x_{n-2} - \alpha_2(x_n + \beta_0 u) + \beta_2 u$$
$$\vdots$$
$$\dot{x}_2 = x_1 - \alpha_{n-1}(x_n + \beta_0 u) + \beta_{n-1} u$$
$$\dot{x}_1 = -\alpha_n(x_n + \beta_0 u) + \beta_n u$$

and the output equation is

$$y = x_n + \beta_0 u$$

The state and output equations organized in vector-matrix form are given below:

$$\dot{\mathbf{x}}(t) = \mathbf{A}\mathbf{x}(t) + \mathbf{b}u(t)$$
$$y(t) = \mathbf{c}\mathbf{x}(t) + du(t) \tag{12.46}$$

with
$$\mathbf{A} = \begin{bmatrix} 0 & 0 & \cdots & 0 & -\alpha_n \\ 1 & 0 & \cdots & 0 & -\alpha_{n-1} \\ 0 & 1 & \cdots & 0 & -\alpha_{n-2} \\ \vdots & \vdots & & \vdots & \vdots \\ 0 & 0 & \cdots & 1 & -\alpha_1 \end{bmatrix} ; \quad \mathbf{b} = \begin{bmatrix} \beta_n - \alpha_n\beta_0 \\ \beta_{n-1} - \alpha_{n-1}\beta_0 \\ \vdots \\ \beta_1 - \alpha_1\beta_0 \end{bmatrix}$$

$$\mathbf{c} = [0 \ 0 \ \cdots \ 0 \ 1]; \ d = \beta_0$$

Compare $\mathbf{A}$, $\mathbf{b}$, and $\mathbf{c}$ matrices of the second companion form with that of the first. We observe that $\mathbf{A}$, $\mathbf{b}$, and $\mathbf{c}$ matrices of one companion form correspond to the transpose of the $\mathbf{A}$, $\mathbf{c}$, and $\mathbf{b}$ matrices, respectively, of the other.

There are many benefits derived from the companion forms of state variable models. One obvious benefit is that both the companion forms lend themselves easily to simple analog computer models. Both the companion forms also play an important role in pole-placement design through state feedback[6].

Jordan Canonical Form

In the two canonical forms (12.44) and (12.46), the coefficients of the denominator of the transfer function appear in one of the rows or columns of matrix $\mathbf{A}$. In another of the canonical forms, the poles of the transfer function form a string along the main diagonal of the matrix. This canonical form follows directly from the partial fraction expansion of the transfer function.

The general transfer function under consideration is (refer Eqn. (12.39))

$$G(s) = \frac{\beta_0 s^n + \beta_1 s^{n-1} + \cdots + \beta_n}{s^n + \alpha_1 s^{n-1} + \cdots + \alpha_n}$$

6. Chapter 7 of reference [180].

By long division, $G(s)$ can be written as

$$G(s) = \beta_0 + \frac{\beta_1' s^{n-1} + \beta_2' s^{n-2} + \cdots + \beta_n'}{s^n + \alpha_1 s^{n-1} + \cdots + \alpha_n} = \beta_0 + G'(s)$$

The results are simplest when the poles of the transfer function are all distinct. The partial fraction expansion of the transfer function then has the form (refer Eqns (A.3)–(A.5) in Appendix A):

$$G(s) = \frac{Y(s)}{U(s)} = \beta_0 + \frac{r_1}{s - \lambda_1} + \frac{r_2}{s - \lambda_2} + \cdots + \frac{r_n}{s - \lambda_n} \qquad (12.47)$$

The coefficients $r_i(i = 1, 2, ..., n)$ are the residues of the transfer function $G'(s)$ at the corresponding poles at $s = \lambda_i$ $(i = 1, 2, ..., n)$. In the form of Eqn. (12.47), the transfer function consists of a direct path with gain β_0, and n first-order transfer functions in parallel. A block diagram representation of Eqn. (12.47) is shown in Fig. 12.9. The gains corresponding to the residues have been placed at the outputs of the integrators. This is quite arbitrary. They could have been located on the input side, or indeed split between the input and the output.

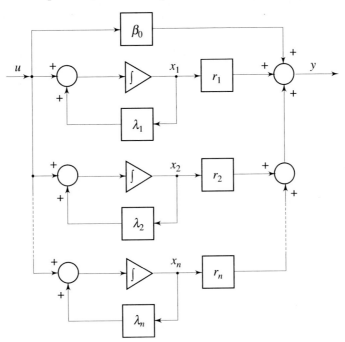

Fig. 12.9   *Realization (state diagram) of G(s) in Eqn. (12.47)*

Identifying the outputs of the integrators with the state variables results in the following state and output equations:

$$\dot{\mathbf{x}}(t) = \Lambda \mathbf{x}(t) + \mathbf{b}u(t)$$
$$y(t) = \mathbf{c}\mathbf{x}(t) + du(t) \qquad (12.48)$$

with
$$\Lambda = \begin{bmatrix} \lambda_1 & 0 & \cdots & 0 \\ 0 & \lambda_2 & \cdots & 0 \\ \vdots & \vdots & & \vdots \\ 0 & 0 & \cdots & \lambda_n \end{bmatrix}; \mathbf{b} = \begin{bmatrix} 1 \\ 1 \\ \vdots \\ 1 \end{bmatrix}$$

$$\mathbf{c} = \begin{bmatrix} r_1 & r_2 & \cdots & r_n \end{bmatrix}; d = \beta_0$$

It is observed that for this canonical state variable model, the matrix Λ is a diagonal matrix with the poles of $G(s)$ as its diagonal elements. The unique *decoupled* nature of the canonical model is obvious from Eqns (12.48); the n first-order differential equations are independent of each other:

$$\dot{x}_i(t) = \lambda_i\, x_i(t) + u(t); \; i = 1, 2, ..., n \tag{12.49}$$

This decoupling feature greatly helps in system analysis (refer [180]).

The block diagram representation of Fig. 12.9 can be turned into hardware only if all the poles at $s = \lambda_1, \lambda_2, ..., \lambda_n$ are real. If they are complex, the feedback gains and the gains corresponding to the residues are complex. In this case, the representation must be considered as being purely conceptual; valid for theoretical studies, but not physically realizable. A realizable representation can be obtained by introducing an equivalence transformation.

Suppose that $s = \sigma + j\omega$, $s = \sigma - j\omega$ and $s = \lambda$ are the three poles of a transfer function. The residues at the pair of complex conjugate poles must be themselves complex conjugates. Partial fraction expansion of the transfer function with a pair of complex conjugate poles and a real pole has the form

$$G(s) = d + \frac{p + jq}{s - (\sigma + j\omega)} + \frac{p - jq}{s - (\sigma - j\omega)} + \frac{r}{s - \lambda}$$

A state variable model for this transfer function is given below (refer Eqns (12.48)):

$$\dot{\mathbf{x}} = \Lambda\mathbf{x} + \mathbf{b}u$$
$$y = \mathbf{c}\mathbf{x} + du \tag{12.50}$$

with
$$\Lambda = \begin{bmatrix} \sigma + j\omega & 0 & 0 \\ 0 & \sigma - j\omega & 0 \\ 0 & 0 & \lambda \end{bmatrix}; \mathbf{b} = \begin{bmatrix} 1 \\ 1 \\ 1 \end{bmatrix}$$

$$\mathbf{c} = \begin{bmatrix} p + jq & p - jq & r \end{bmatrix}$$

Introducing an equivalence transformation

$$\mathbf{x} = \mathbf{P}\bar{\mathbf{x}}$$

with
$$\mathbf{P} = \begin{bmatrix} 1/2 & -j1/2 & 0 \\ 1/2 & j1/2 & 0 \\ 0 & 0 & 1 \end{bmatrix}$$

we obtain (refer Eqns (12.17))

$$\dot{\bar{\mathbf{x}}}(t) = \overline{\mathbf{A}}\,\bar{\mathbf{x}}(t) + \overline{\mathbf{b}}\,u(t)$$
$$y(t) = \overline{\mathbf{c}}\,\bar{\mathbf{x}}(t) + du(t)$$

$$(12.51)$$

where

$$\overline{\mathbf{A}} = \mathbf{P}^{-1}\Lambda\mathbf{P} = \begin{bmatrix} 1 & 1 & 0 \\ j & -j & 0 \\ 0 & 0 & 1 \end{bmatrix} \begin{bmatrix} \sigma + j\omega & 0 & 0 \\ 0 & \sigma - j\omega & 0 \\ 0 & 0 & \lambda \end{bmatrix} \begin{bmatrix} 1/2 & -j1/2 & 0 \\ 1/2 & j1/2 & 0 \\ 0 & 0 & 1 \end{bmatrix}$$

$$= \begin{bmatrix} \sigma & \omega & 0 \\ -\omega & \sigma & 0 \\ 0 & 0 & \lambda \end{bmatrix}$$

$$\overline{\mathbf{b}} = \mathbf{P}^{-1}\mathbf{b} = \begin{bmatrix} 2 \\ 0 \\ 1 \end{bmatrix}$$

$$\overline{\mathbf{c}} = \mathbf{c}\mathbf{P} = \begin{bmatrix} p & q & r \end{bmatrix}$$

When the transfer function $G(s)$ has repeated poles, the partial fraction expansion will not be as simple as Eqn. (12.47). Assume that $G(s)$ has m distinct poles at $s = \lambda_1, \lambda_2, \ldots, \lambda_m$ of multiplicity $n_1, n_2, \ldots, n_m$ respectively; $n = n_1 + n_2 + \cdots + n_m$. That is, $G(s)$ is of the form

$$G(s) = \beta_0 + \frac{\beta_1' s^{n-1} + \beta_2' s^{n-2} + \cdots + \beta_n'}{(s - \lambda_1)^{n_1}(s - \lambda_2)^{n_2} \cdots (s - \lambda_m)^{n_m}}$$

$$(12.52)$$

The partial fraction expansion of $G(s)$ is of the form (refer Eqns (A.9)-(A.14) in Appendix A)

$$G(s) = \beta_0 + H_1(s) + \cdots + H_m(s) = \frac{Y(s)}{U(s)}$$

$$(12.53)$$

where

$$H_i(s) = \frac{r_{i1}}{(s - \lambda_i)^{n_i}} + \frac{r_{i2}}{(s - \lambda_i)^{n_i - 1}} + \cdots + \frac{r_{in_i}}{(s - \lambda_i)} = \frac{Y_i(s)}{U(s)}$$

The first term in $H_i(s)$ can be synthesized as a chain of n_i identical, first-order systems, each having transfer function $1/(s - \lambda_i)$. The second term can be synthesized by a chain of $(n_i - 1)$ first-order systems, and so forth. The entire $H_i(s)$ can be synthesized by the system having the block diagram shown in Fig. 12.10.

We can now write differential equations for the realization of $H_i(s)$ given by Fig. 12.10. To get one state variable formulation, we identify the output of each integrator with a state variable starting at the right and proceeding to the left. The corresponding differential equations are

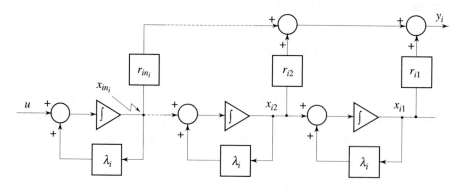

Fig. 12.10 *Realization (state diagram) of $H_i(s)$ in Eqn. (12.53)*

$$\begin{aligned}
\dot{x}_{i1} &= \lambda_i\, x_{i1} + x_{i2} \\
\dot{x}_{i2} &= \lambda_i\, x_{i2} + x_{i3} \\
&\ \ \vdots \\
\dot{x}_{in_i} &= \lambda_i\, x_{in_i} + u
\end{aligned} \tag{12.54a}$$

and the output is given by

$$y_i = r_{i1}\, x_{i1} + r_{i2}\, x_{i2} + \cdots + r_{in_i}\, x_{in_i} \tag{12.54b}$$

If the state vector for the subsystem is defined by

$$\mathbf{x}_i = [\,x_{i1} \quad x_{i2} \cdots x_{in_i}\,]^T$$

then Eqns (12.54) can be written in the standard form

$$\begin{aligned}
\dot{\mathbf{x}}_i &= \Lambda_i \mathbf{x}_i + \mathbf{b}_i\, u \\
y_i &= \mathbf{c}_i \mathbf{x}_i
\end{aligned} \tag{12.55}$$

where

$$\Lambda_i = \begin{bmatrix}
\lambda_i & 1 & 0 & \cdots & 0 & 0 \\
0 & \lambda_i & 1 & \cdots & 0 & 0 \\
\vdots & \vdots & \vdots & & \vdots & \vdots \\
0 & 0 & 0 & \cdots & \lambda_i & 1 \\
0 & 0 & 0 & \cdots & 0 & \lambda_i
\end{bmatrix}; \quad \mathbf{b}_i = \begin{bmatrix} 0 \\ 0 \\ \vdots \\ 0 \\ 1 \end{bmatrix}$$

$$\mathbf{c}_i = \begin{bmatrix} r_{i1} & r_{i2} & \cdots & r_{in_i} \end{bmatrix}$$

Note that matrix Λ_i has two diagonals—the principal diagonal has the corresponding characteristic root (pole) and the superdiagonal has all 1's. In matrix theory, a matrix having this structure is said to be in *Jordan form*. For this reason, we identify the realization (12.55) as *Jordan canonical form*.

According to Eqn. (12.53), the overall transfer function $G(s)$ consists of a direct path with gain β_0 and m subsystems, each of which is in the Jordan canonical form as shown in Fig. 12.11. The state vector of the overall system consists of the concatenation of the state vectors of each of the *Jordan blocks*:

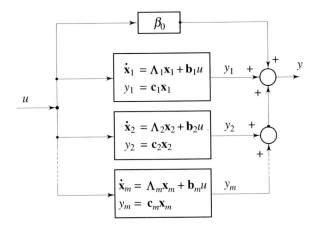

Fig. 12.11 *Subsystems in Jordan canonical form combined into overall system*

$$\mathbf{x} = \begin{bmatrix} \mathbf{x}_1 \\ \mathbf{x}_2 \\ \vdots \\ \mathbf{x}_m \end{bmatrix} \tag{12.56a}$$

Since there is no coupling between any of the subsystems, the Λ matrix of the overall system is 'block diagonal':

$$\Lambda = \begin{bmatrix} \Lambda_1 & 0 & \cdots & 0 \\ 0 & \Lambda_2 & \cdots & 0 \\ \vdots & \vdots & & \vdots \\ 0 & 0 & \cdots & \Lambda_m \end{bmatrix} \tag{12.56b}$$

where each of the submatrices Λ_i is in the Jordan canonical form (12.55). The **b** and **c** matrices of the overall system are the concatenations of the $\mathbf{b}_i$ and $\mathbf{c}_i$ matrices respectively of each of the subsystems:

$$\mathbf{b} = \begin{bmatrix} \mathbf{b}_1 \\ \mathbf{b}_2 \\ \vdots \\ \mathbf{b}_m \end{bmatrix} ; \mathbf{c} = [\mathbf{c}_1 \quad \mathbf{c}_2 \cdots \mathbf{c}_m] ; d = \beta_0 \tag{12.56c}$$

The state variable model (12.48) derived for the case of distinct poles, is a special case of Jordan canonical form (12.56) where each Jordan block is of 1×1 dimension.

Example 12.5

In the following, we obtain three different realizations for the transfer function

$$G(s) = \frac{s + 3}{s^3 + 9s^2 + 24s + 20} = \frac{Y(s)}{U(s)}$$

First companion form

Note that the given $G(s)$ is a strictly proper fraction; the realization will there-fore be of the form (12.38), i.e., the parameter d in the realization $\{\mathbf{A}, \mathbf{b}, \mathbf{c}, d\}$ is zero.

The state variable formulation in the first companion form can be written just by inspection of the given transfer function. Referring to Eqns (12.44), we obtain

$$\begin{bmatrix} \dot{x}_1 \\ \dot{x}_2 \\ \dot{x}_3 \end{bmatrix} = \begin{bmatrix} 0 & 1 & 0 \\ 0 & 0 & 1 \\ -20 & -24 & -9 \end{bmatrix} \begin{bmatrix} x_1 \\ x_2 \\ x_3 \end{bmatrix} + \begin{bmatrix} 0 \\ 0 \\ 1 \end{bmatrix} u$$

$$y = \begin{bmatrix} 3 & 1 & 0 \end{bmatrix} \begin{bmatrix} x_1 \\ x_2 \\ x_3 \end{bmatrix}$$

Figure 12.12a shows the state diagram in signal flow graph form.

Second companion form

Referring to Eqns (12.46), we obtain

$$\begin{bmatrix} \dot{x}_1 \\ \dot{x}_2 \\ \dot{x}_3 \end{bmatrix} = \begin{bmatrix} 0 & 0 & -20 \\ 1 & 0 & -24 \\ 0 & 1 & -9 \end{bmatrix} \begin{bmatrix} x_1 \\ x_2 \\ x_3 \end{bmatrix} + \begin{bmatrix} 3 \\ 1 \\ 0 \end{bmatrix} u$$

$$y = x_3$$

Figure 12.12b shows the state diagram.

Jordan canonical form

The given transfer function $G(s)$ in the factored form:

$$G(s) = \frac{s+3}{(s+2)^2(s+5)}$$

Using partial fraction expansion, we obtain

$$G(s) = \frac{1/3}{(s+2)^2} + \frac{2/9}{s+2} + \frac{-2/9}{s+5}$$

A matrix of the state variable model in Jordan canonical form will be block-diagonal; consisting of two Jordan blocks (refer Eqns (12.55)):

$$\Lambda_1 = \begin{bmatrix} -2 & 1 \\ 0 & -2 \end{bmatrix},$$

$$\Lambda_2 = [-5]$$

The corresponding $\mathbf{b}_i$ and $\mathbf{c}_i$ vectors are (refer Eqns (12.55)):

$$\mathbf{b}_1 = \begin{bmatrix} 0 \\ 1 \end{bmatrix}; \mathbf{c}_1 = \begin{bmatrix} \frac{1}{3} & \frac{2}{9} \end{bmatrix}$$

$$\mathbf{b}_2 = [1] ; \mathbf{c}_2 = \begin{bmatrix} -\frac{2}{9} \end{bmatrix}$$

The state variable model of the given $G(s)$ in Jordan canonical form is therefore given by (refer Eqns (12.56))

$$\begin{bmatrix} \dot{x}_1 \\ \dot{x}_2 \\ \dot{x}_3 \end{bmatrix} = \begin{bmatrix} -2 & 1 & 0 \\ 0 & -2 & 0 \\ 0 & 0 & -5 \end{bmatrix} \begin{bmatrix} x_1 \\ x_2 \\ x_3 \end{bmatrix} + \begin{bmatrix} 0 \\ 1 \\ 1 \end{bmatrix} u$$

$$y = \begin{bmatrix} \frac{1}{3} & \frac{2}{9} & \frac{2}{9} \end{bmatrix} \begin{bmatrix} x_1 \\ x_2 \\ x_3 \end{bmatrix}$$

Figure 12.12c shows the state diagram. We note that Jordan canonical state variables are not completely decoupled. The decoupling is blockwise; state variables of one block are independent of state variables of all other blocks. However, the state variables of one block among themselves are coupled; the coupling is unique and simple.

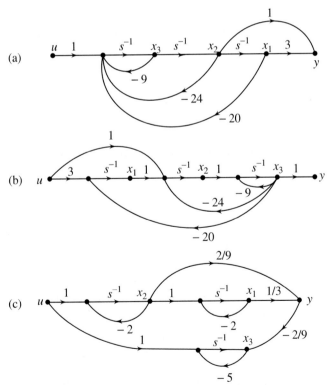

Fig. 12.12 *Three realizations of given G(s)*

12.6 | SOLUTION OF STATE EQUATIONS

In this section, we investigate the solution of the state equation

$$\dot{\mathbf{x}}(t) = \mathbf{A}\mathbf{x}(t) + \mathbf{b}u(t); \ \mathbf{x}(t_0) \triangleq \mathbf{x}^0 \tag{12.57}$$

where $\mathbf{x}$ is $n \times 1$ state vector, u is a scalar input, $\mathbf{A}$ is $n \times n$ constant matrix, and $\mathbf{b}$ is $n \times 1$ constant vector.

Matrix Exponential

Functions of square matrices arise in connection with the solution of vector differential equations. Of immediate interest to us are matrix infinite series.

Consider the infinite series in a scalar variable x:

$$f(x) = \alpha_0 + \alpha_1 x + \alpha_2 x^2 + \cdots = \sum_{i=0}^{\infty} \alpha_i x^i \tag{12.58a}$$

with the radius of convergence r.

We can define infinite series in a matrix variable $\mathbf{A}$ as

$$f(\mathbf{A}) = \alpha_0 \mathbf{I} + \alpha_1 \mathbf{A} + \alpha_2 \mathbf{A}^2 + \cdots = \sum_{i=0}^{\infty} \alpha_i \mathbf{A}^i \tag{12.58b}$$

An important relation between the scalar power series (12.58a) and the matrix power series (12.58b) is that if the absolute values of eigenvalues of $\mathbf{A}$ are smaller than r, then the matrix power series (12.58b) converges (for proof, refer Lefschetz [36]).

Consider, in particular, the scalar power series

$$f(x) = 1 + x + \frac{1}{2!}x^2 + \cdots + \frac{1}{k!}x^k + \cdots = \sum_{i=0}^{\infty} \frac{1}{i!}x^i \tag{12.59a}$$

It is well-known that this power series converges on to the exponential e^x for the finite x, so that

$$f(x) = e^x \tag{12.59b}$$

It follows from this result that the matrix power series

$$f(\mathbf{A}) = \mathbf{I} + \mathbf{A} + \frac{1}{2!}\mathbf{A}^2 + \cdots + \frac{1}{k!}\mathbf{A}^k + \cdots = \sum_{i=0}^{\infty} \frac{1}{i!}\mathbf{A}^i$$

converges for all $\mathbf{A}$. By analogy with the power series in Eqns (12.59) for the ordinary exponential function, we adopt the following nomenclature:

If $\mathbf{A}$ is an $n \times n$ matrix, the *matrix exponential* of $\mathbf{A}$ is

$$e^{\mathbf{A}} \triangleq \mathbf{I} + \mathbf{A} + \frac{1}{2!}\mathbf{A}^2 + \cdots + \frac{1}{k!}\mathbf{A}^k + \cdots = \sum_{i=0}^{\infty} \frac{1}{i!}\mathbf{A}^i$$

The following matrix exponential will appear in the solution of state equations:

$$e^{\mathbf{A}t} = \mathbf{I} + \mathbf{A}t + \frac{1}{2!}\mathbf{A}^2 t^2 + \cdots + \frac{1}{k!}\mathbf{A}^k t^k + \cdots = \sum_{i=0}^{\infty} \frac{1}{i!}\mathbf{A}^i t^i \quad (12.60)$$

It converges for all $\mathbf{A}$ and all finite t.

In the following we examine some of the properties of the matrix exponential.

1.
$$e^{\mathbf{A}0} = \mathbf{I} \quad (12.61)$$

This is easily verified by setting $t = 0$ in Eqn. (12.60).

2.
$$e^{\mathbf{A}(t+\tau)} = e^{\mathbf{A}t}e^{\mathbf{A}\tau} = e^{\mathbf{A}\tau}e^{\mathbf{A}t} \quad (12.62)$$

This is easily verified by multiplying out the first few terms for $e^{\mathbf{A}t}$ and $e^{\mathbf{A}\tau}$.

3.
$$(e^{\mathbf{A}t})^{-1} = e^{-\mathbf{A}t} \quad (12.63)$$

Setting $\tau = -t$ in Eqn. (12.62), we obtain
$$e^{\mathbf{A}t}e^{-\mathbf{A}t} = e^{\mathbf{A}0} = \mathbf{I}$$

Thus the inverse of $e^{\mathbf{A}t}$ is $e^{-\mathbf{A}t}$.

Since the inverse of $e^{\mathbf{A}t}$ always exists, the matrix exponential is nonsingular for all finite values of t.

4.
$$\frac{d}{dt}e^{\mathbf{A}t} = \mathbf{A}e^{\mathbf{A}t} = e^{\mathbf{A}t}\mathbf{A} \quad (12.64)$$

Term-by-term differentiation of Eqn. (12.60) gives

$$\frac{d}{dt}e^{\mathbf{A}t} = \mathbf{A} + \mathbf{A}^2 t + \frac{1}{2!}\mathbf{A}^3 t^2 + \cdots + \frac{1}{(k-1)!}\mathbf{A}^k t^{k-1} + \cdots$$

$$= \mathbf{A}[\mathbf{I} + \mathbf{A}t + \frac{1}{2!}\mathbf{A}^2 t^2 + \cdots + \frac{1}{(k-1)!}\mathbf{A}^{k-1} t^{k-1} + \cdots] = \mathbf{A}e^{\mathbf{A}t}$$

$$= [\mathbf{I} + \mathbf{A}t + \frac{1}{2!}\mathbf{A}^2 t^2 + \cdots + \frac{1}{(k-1)!}\mathbf{A}^{k-1} t^{k-1} + \cdots]\mathbf{A} = e^{\mathbf{A}t}\mathbf{A}$$

Solution of Homogeneous State Equation

The simplest form of the general differential equation (12.57) is the homogeneous, i.e., unforced equation

$$\dot{\mathbf{x}}(t) = \mathbf{A}\mathbf{x}(t); \ \mathbf{x}(t_0) \triangleq \mathbf{x}^0 \quad (12.65)$$

We assume a solution $\mathbf{x}(t)$ of the form
$$\mathbf{x}(t) = e^{\mathbf{A}t}\mathbf{k} \quad (12.66)$$

where $e^{\mathbf{A}t}$ is the matrix exponential function defined in Eqn. (12.60) and $\mathbf{k}$ is a suitably chosen constant vector.

The assumed solution is, in fact, the true solution since it satisfies the differential equation (12.65) as is seen below.

$$\dot{\mathbf{x}}(t) = \frac{d}{dt}[e^{\mathbf{A}t}\mathbf{k}] = \frac{d}{dt}[e^{\mathbf{A}t}]\mathbf{k}$$

Using property (12.64) of the matrix exponential, we obtain

$$\dot{\mathbf{x}}(t) = \mathbf{A}e^{\mathbf{A}t}\,\mathbf{k} = \mathbf{A}\mathbf{x}(t)$$

To evaluate the constant $\mathbf{k}$ in terms of the known initial state $\mathbf{x}(t_0)$, we substitute $t = t_0$ in Eqn. (12.66):

$$\mathbf{x}(t_0) = e^{\mathbf{A}t_0}\,\mathbf{k}$$

Using property (12.63) of the matrix exponential, we obtain

$$\mathbf{k} = (e^{\mathbf{A}t_0})^{-1}\mathbf{x}(t_0) = e^{-\mathbf{A}t_0}\mathbf{x}(t_0)$$

Thus the general solution to Eqn. (12.65) for the state $\mathbf{x}(t)$ at time t, given the state $\mathbf{x}(t_0)$ at time t_0, is

$$\mathbf{x}(t) = e^{\mathbf{A}t}e^{-\mathbf{A}t_0}\,\mathbf{x}(t_0) = e^{\mathbf{A}(t-t_0)}\,\mathbf{x}(t_0) \qquad (12.67a)$$

We have used the property (12.62) of the matrix exponential to express the solution in this form.

If the initial time $t_0 = 0$, i.e., the initial state $\mathbf{x}^0$ is known at $t = 0$, we have from Eqn. (12.67a):

$$\mathbf{x}(t) = e^{\mathbf{A}t}\mathbf{x}(0) \qquad (12.67b)$$

From Eqn. (12.67b) it is observed that the initial state $\mathbf{x}(0) \triangleq \mathbf{x}^0$ at $t = 0$ is driven to a state $\mathbf{x}(t)$ at time t. This transition in state is carried out by the matrix exponential $e^{\mathbf{A}t}$. Due to this property, $e^{\mathbf{A}t}$ is known as the *state transition matrix*, and is denoted by $\phi(t)$.

Properties of state transition matrix

Properties of the matrix exponential, given earlier in Eqns (12.61)–(12.64), are restated below in terms of state transition matrix $\phi(t)$.

1. $$\frac{d}{dt}\phi(t) = \mathbf{A}\phi(t); \ \phi(0) = \mathbf{I}$$

2. $$\phi(t_2 - t_1)\phi(t_1 - t_0) = \phi(t_2 - t_0) \text{ for any } t_0, t_1, t_2$$

This property of the state transition matrix is important since it implies that a state transition process can be divided into a number of sequential transitions. The transition form t_0 to t_2:

$$\mathbf{x}(t_2) = \phi(t_2 - t_0)\,\mathbf{x}(t_0);$$

is equal to the transition from t_0 to t_1 and then from t_1 to t_2:

$$\mathbf{x}(t_1) = \phi(t_1 - t_0)\mathbf{x}(t_0)$$

$$\mathbf{x}(t_2) = \phi(t_2 - t_1)\mathbf{x}(t_1)$$

3. $$\phi^{-1}(t) = \phi(-t)$$

4. $\phi(t)$ is a nonsingular matrix for all finite t.

Evaluation of state transition matrix

Taking the Laplace transform on both sides of Eqn. (12.65) yields

$$s\mathbf{X}(s) - \mathbf{x}^0 = \mathbf{A}\mathbf{X}(s)$$

where $\qquad \mathbf{X}(s) \triangleq \mathcal{L}[\mathbf{x}(t)]$

$\qquad \mathbf{x}^0 \triangleq \mathbf{x}(0)$

Solving for $\mathbf{X}(s)$, we get

$$\mathbf{X}(s) = (s\mathbf{I} - \mathbf{A})^{-1}\mathbf{x}^0$$

The state vector $\mathbf{x}(t)$ can be obtained by inverse transforming $\mathbf{X}(s)$:

$$\mathbf{x}(t) = \mathcal{L}^{-1}[(s\mathbf{I} - \mathbf{A})^{-1}]\mathbf{x}^0$$

Comparing this equation with Eqn. (12.67b), we get

$$e^{\mathbf{A}t} = \phi(t) = \mathcal{L}^{-1}[(s\mathbf{I} - \mathbf{A})^{-1}] \qquad (12.68)$$

The matrix $(s\mathbf{I} - \mathbf{A})^{-1} = \Phi(s)$ is known in mathematical literature as the resolvent of $\mathbf{A}$. The entries of the resolvent matrix $\Phi(s)$ are rational functions of s.

Example 12.6——————————————————————————————

Consider the system

$$\dot{\mathbf{x}} = \begin{bmatrix} 0 & 0 & -2 \\ 0 & 1 & 0 \\ 1 & 0 & 3 \end{bmatrix}\mathbf{x} \; ; \; \mathbf{x}(0) = \begin{bmatrix} 0 \\ 1 \\ 0 \end{bmatrix}$$

The resolvent matrix

$$\Phi(s) = (s\mathbf{I} - \mathbf{A})^{-1} = \begin{bmatrix} s & 0 & 2 \\ 0 & s-1 & 0 \\ -1 & 0 & s-3 \end{bmatrix}^{-1} = \frac{(s\mathbf{I} - \mathbf{A})^+}{|s\mathbf{I} - \mathbf{A}|}$$

$$|s\mathbf{I} - \mathbf{A}| = (s-1)^2(s-2)$$

$$(s\mathbf{I} - \mathbf{A})^+ = \begin{bmatrix} (s-1)(s-3) & 0 & -2(s-1) \\ 0 & (s-1)(s-2) & 0 \\ (s-1) & 0 & s(s-1) \end{bmatrix}$$

$$e^{\mathbf{A}t} = \mathcal{L}^{-1}[\Phi(s)] = \mathcal{L}^{-1}[(s\mathbf{I} - \mathbf{A})^{-1}]$$

$$= \mathcal{L}^{-1} \begin{bmatrix} \dfrac{(s-3)}{(s-1)(s-2)} & 0 & \dfrac{-2}{(s-1)(s-2)} \\ 0 & \dfrac{1}{(s-1)} & 0 \\ \dfrac{1}{(s-1)(s-2)} & 0 & \dfrac{s}{(s-1)(s-2)} \end{bmatrix}$$

$$= \begin{bmatrix} 2e^t - e^{2t} & 0 & 2e^t - 2e^{2t} \\ 0 & e^t & 0 \\ -e^t + e^{2t} & 0 & 2e^{2t} - e^t \end{bmatrix}$$

Consequently, the free response of the system is

$$\mathbf{x}(t) = e^{\mathbf{A}t}\mathbf{x}(0) = \begin{bmatrix} 0 \\ e^t \\ 0 \end{bmatrix}$$

Note that $\mathbf{x}(t)$ could be more easily computed by taking the inverse Laplace transform of

$$\mathbf{X}(s) = [(s\mathbf{I} - \mathbf{A})^{-1}\mathbf{x}(0)]$$

Solution of Nonhomogeneous State Equation

When an input $u(t)$ is present, the complete solution $\mathbf{x}(t)$ is obtained from the nonhomogeneous equation (12.57).

By writing Eqn. (12.57) as

$$\dot{\mathbf{x}}(t) - \mathbf{A}\mathbf{x}(t) = \mathbf{b}u(t)$$

and premultiplying both sides of this equation by $e^{-\mathbf{A}t}$, we obtain

$$e^{-\mathbf{A}t}[\dot{\mathbf{x}}(t) - \mathbf{A}\mathbf{x}(t)] = e^{-\mathbf{A}t}\mathbf{b}u(t) \tag{12.69}$$

By applying the rule for the derivative of the product of two matrices, we can write (refer Eqn. (12.64))

$$\frac{d}{dt}[e^{-\mathbf{A}t}\mathbf{x}(t)] = e^{-\mathbf{A}t}\frac{d}{dt}(\mathbf{x}(t)) + \frac{d}{dt}(e^{-\mathbf{A}t})\mathbf{x}(t)$$

$$= e^{-\mathbf{A}t}\dot{\mathbf{x}}(t) - e^{-\mathbf{A}t}\mathbf{A}\mathbf{x}(t)$$

$$= e^{-\mathbf{A}t}[\dot{\mathbf{x}}(t) - \mathbf{A}\mathbf{x}(t)]$$

Use of this equality in Eqn. (12.69) gives

$$\frac{d}{dt}[e^{-\mathbf{A}t}\mathbf{x}(t)] = e^{-\mathbf{A}t}\mathbf{b}u(t)$$

Integrating both sides with respect to t between the limits 0 and t, we get

$$e^{-\mathbf{A}t}\mathbf{x}(t)\Big|_0^t = \int_0^t e^{-\mathbf{A}\tau}\mathbf{b}u(\tau)d\tau$$

or

$$e^{-\mathbf{A}t}\mathbf{x}(t) - \mathbf{x}(0) = \int_0^t e^{-\mathbf{A}\tau}\mathbf{b}u(\tau)d\tau$$

Now premultiplying both sides by $e^{\mathbf{A}t}$, we have

$$\mathbf{x}(t) = e^{\mathbf{A}t}\mathbf{x}(0) + \int_0^t e^{\mathbf{A}(t-\tau)}\mathbf{b}u(\tau)d\tau \tag{12.70}$$

If the initial state is known at $t = t_0$, rather than $t = 0$, Eqn. (12.70) becomes

$$\mathbf{x}(t) = e^{\mathbf{A}(t-t_0)}\mathbf{x}(t_0) + \int_{t_0}^{t} e^{\mathbf{A}(t-\tau)}\mathbf{b}u(\tau)d\tau \qquad (12.71)$$

Equation (12.71) can also be written as

$$\mathbf{x}(t) = \phi(t-t_0)\,\mathbf{x}(t_0) + \int_{t_0}^{t} \phi(t-\tau)\,\mathbf{b}u(\tau)\,d\tau \qquad (12.72)$$

where $\qquad \phi(t) = e^{\mathbf{A}t}$

Equation (12.72) is the solution of Eqn. (12.57). This equation is called the *state transition equation*. It describes the change of state relative to the initial conditions $\mathbf{x}(t_0)$ and the input $u(t)$.

Example 12.7

For the speed control system of Fig. 12.1, following plant model was derived in Example 12.1 (refer Eqns (12.12)):

$$\dot{\mathbf{x}} = \mathbf{A}\mathbf{x} + \mathbf{b}u$$
$$y = \mathbf{c}\mathbf{x}$$

with

$$\mathbf{A} = \begin{bmatrix} -1 & 1 \\ -1 & -10 \end{bmatrix}; \mathbf{b} = \begin{bmatrix} 0 \\ 10 \end{bmatrix}; \mathbf{c} = [\,1 \quad 0\,]$$

State variables x_1 and x_2 are the physical variables of the system:

$$x_1(t) = \omega(t),\ \text{angular velocity of the motor shaft}$$
$$x_2(t) = i_a(t),\ \text{armature current}$$

The output

$$y(t) = x_1(t) = \omega(t)$$

In the following, we evaluate the response of this system to a unit step input under zero initial conditions.

$$(s\mathbf{I} - \mathbf{A})^{-1} = \begin{bmatrix} s+1 & -1 \\ 1 & s+10 \end{bmatrix}^{-1}$$

$$= \frac{1}{s^2 + 11s + 11} \begin{bmatrix} s+10 & 1 \\ -1 & s+1 \end{bmatrix}$$

$$= \begin{bmatrix} \dfrac{s+10}{(s+a_1)(s+a_2)} & \dfrac{1}{(s+a_1)(s+a_2)} \\ \dfrac{-1}{(s+a_1)(s+a_2)} & \dfrac{s+1}{(s+a_1)(s+a_2)} \end{bmatrix}; a_1 = 1.1125,\ a_2 = 9.8875$$

$$e^{\mathbf{A}t} = \mathscr{L}^{-1}[(s\mathbf{I} - \mathbf{A})^{-1}]$$

$$= \begin{bmatrix} 1.0128e^{-a_1 t} - 0.0128e^{-a_2 t} & 0.114e^{-a_1 t} - 0.114e^{-a_2 t} \\ -0.114e^{-a_1 t} + 0.114e^{-a_2 t} & -0.0128e^{-a_1 t} + 1.0128e^{-a_2 t} \end{bmatrix}$$

$u(t) = 1; \ t \geq 0$

$\mathbf{x}(0) = \mathbf{0}$

Therefore,

$$\mathbf{x}(t) = \int_0^t e^{\mathbf{A}(t-\tau)}\mathbf{b}d\tau = \int_0^t \begin{bmatrix} 1.14\left(e^{-a_1(t-\tau)} - e^{-a_2(t-\tau)}\right) \\ 1.14\left(-0.1123e^{-a_1(t-\tau)} + 8.8842e^{-a_2(t-\tau)}\right) \end{bmatrix} d\tau$$

$$= \begin{bmatrix} 0.9094 - 1.0247e^{-a_1 t} + 0.1153e^{-a_2 t} \\ -0.0132 + 0.1151e^{-a_1 t} - 0.1019e^{-a_2 t} \end{bmatrix}$$

The output

$$y(t) = \omega(t) = 0.9094 - 1.0247 \ e^{-1.1125t} + 0.1153e^{-9.8875t}; \ t \geq 0$$

Discrete-Time Solution

As illustrated in Fig. 12.13, the time axis is discretized into intervals of width T, and $u(t)$ is approximated by a staircase function, constant over the intervals. For the kth interval.

$$u(t) = u(kT); \ kT \leq t < (k+1)T; \ k = 0, 1, 2, \ldots \qquad (12.73)$$

Using Eqn. (12.71) for $t_0 = kT$,

$$\mathbf{x}(t) = e^{\mathbf{A}(t-kT)}\mathbf{x}(kT) + \left[\int_{kT}^t e^{\mathbf{A}(t-\tau)}\mathbf{b}d\tau \right] u(kT); \ kT \leq t < (k+1)T \qquad (12.74)$$

In response to the input $u(kT)$, the state settles to the value $\mathbf{x}((k+1)T)$, where

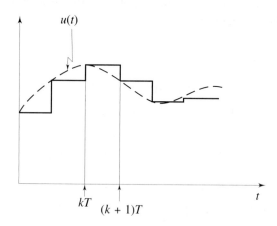

Fig. 12.13   *Time discretization*

$$\mathbf{x}((k+1)T) = e^{\mathbf{A}T}\mathbf{x}(kT) + \left[\int_{kT}^{(k+1)T} e^{\mathbf{A}[(k+1)T-\tau]}\mathbf{b}d\tau\right]u(kT)$$

Letting $\sigma = (\tau - kT)$, we have

$$\mathbf{x}((k+1)T) = e^{\mathbf{A}T}\mathbf{x}(kT) + \left[\int_{0}^{T} e^{\mathbf{A}(T-\sigma)}\mathbf{b}d\sigma\right]u(kT)$$

With $\theta = T - \sigma$, we get

$$\mathbf{x}((k+1)T) = e^{\mathbf{A}T}\mathbf{x}(kT) + \left[\int_{0}^{T} e^{\mathbf{A}\theta}\mathbf{b}d\theta\right]u(kT)$$

Therefore, for the kth interval,

$$\mathbf{x}((k+1)T) = \mathbf{F}\mathbf{x}(kT) + \mathbf{g}u(kT) \tag{12.75a}$$

where

$$\mathbf{F} = e^{\mathbf{A}T} \tag{12.75b}$$

$$\mathbf{g} = \int_{0}^{T} e^{\mathbf{A}\theta}\mathbf{b}d\theta \tag{12.75c}$$

This permits the solution to be calculated forward in time.

The infinite series (12.60) may be used to compute $\mathbf{F}$ and $\mathbf{g}$.

$$\mathbf{F} = e^{\mathbf{A}T} = \mathbf{I} + \mathbf{A}T + \frac{1}{2!}\mathbf{A}^2 T^2 + \frac{1}{3!}\mathbf{A}^3 T^3 + \cdots$$

$$= \sum_{i=0}^{\infty} \frac{\mathbf{A}^i T^i}{i!}; \quad \mathbf{A}^0 = \mathbf{I} \tag{12.76}$$

For a finite T, this series is uniformly convergent. It is therefore possible to evaluate $\mathbf{F}$ within prescribed accuracy. If the series is truncated at $i = N$, then we may write the finite series sum as

$$\mathbf{F} \cong \sum_{i=0}^{N} \frac{\mathbf{A}^i T^i}{i!} \tag{12.77}$$

which represents the infinite series approximation. The larger the N, the better is the approximation.

The integral in Eqn. (12.75c) can be evaluated term by term to give

$$\mathbf{g} = \left[\int_{0}^{T}\left(\mathbf{I} + \mathbf{A}\theta + \frac{1}{2!}\mathbf{A}^2\theta^2 + \cdots\right)d\theta\right]\mathbf{b}$$

$$= \sum_{i=0}^{\infty} \frac{\mathbf{A}^i T^{i+1}}{(i+1)!}\mathbf{b} \tag{12.78}$$

$\mathbf{g}$ may also be computed by the approximation technique described above.

*Example 12.8*_____

Consider the state variable model

$$\dot{x}(t) = \mathbf{A}x(t) + \mathbf{b}\,u(t)$$

$$y(t) = \mathbf{c}x(t)$$

with

$$\mathbf{A} = \begin{bmatrix} 0 & 1 \\ 0 & -5 \end{bmatrix}; \ \mathbf{b} = \begin{bmatrix} 0 \\ 1 \end{bmatrix}; \ \mathbf{c} = \begin{bmatrix} 1 & 0 \end{bmatrix}$$

The state transition matrix

$$e^{\mathbf{A}t} = \mathcal{L}^{-1}[(s\mathbf{I} - \mathbf{A})^{-1}]$$

$$= \mathcal{L}^{-1}\begin{bmatrix} \frac{1}{s} & \frac{1}{s(s+5)} \\ 0 & \frac{1}{s+5} \end{bmatrix} = \begin{bmatrix} 1 & \frac{1}{5}(1-e^{-5t}) \\ 0 & e^{-5t} \end{bmatrix}$$

Discretizing time axis into intervals of width $T = 0.1$ sec, we get the following state transition equation, that yields discrete-time solution:

$$x((k+1)T) = \mathbf{F}x(kT) + \mathbf{g}u(kT)$$

where

$$\mathbf{F} = e^{\mathbf{A}t} = \begin{bmatrix} 1 & \frac{1}{5}(1-e^{-5T}) \\ 0 & e^{-5T} \end{bmatrix}$$

$$= \begin{bmatrix} 1 & 0.0787 \\ 0 & 0.6065 \end{bmatrix}$$

$$\mathbf{g} = \int_0^T e^{\mathbf{A}\theta}\mathbf{b}\,d\theta$$

$$= \begin{bmatrix} \int_0^T \frac{1}{5}(1-e^{-5\theta})d\theta \\ \int_0^T e^{-5\theta}\,d\theta \end{bmatrix} = \begin{bmatrix} \frac{1}{5}(T - \frac{1}{5} + \frac{1}{5}e^{-5T}) \\ \frac{1}{5}(1-e^{-5T}) \end{bmatrix}$$

$$= \begin{bmatrix} 0.0043 \\ 0.0787 \end{bmatrix}$$

For a given initial state $x(0)$, and input $u(t)$; $t \geq 0$,

$$x(T) = \mathbf{F}x(0) + \mathbf{g}u(0)$$

$$x(2T) = \mathbf{F}x(T) + \mathbf{g}u(T)$$

$$x(3T) = \mathbf{F}x(2T) + \mathbf{g}u(2T)$$

$$\vdots$$

The output

$$y(kT) = \mathbf{c}x(kT)$$

12.7 | CONCEPTS OF CONTROLLABILITY AND OBSERVABILITY

Controllability and observability are properties which describe structural features of a dynamic system. These properties play an important role in modern control system design theory; the conditions on controllability and observability often govern the control solution.

To illustrate the motivation of investigating controllability and observability properties, we consider the problem of the stabilization of an inverted pendulum on a motor-driven cart.

*Example 12.9*_____

Figure 12.14a shows an inverted pendulum with its pivot mounted on a cart. The cart is driven by an electric motor. The motor drives a pair of wheels of the cart; the whole cart and the pendulum become the 'load' on the motor. The motor at time t exerts a torque $T(t)$ on the wheels. The linear force applied to the cart is $u(t)$; $T(t) = R u(t)$, where R is the radius of the wheels.

The pendulum is obviously unstable. It can, however, be kept upright by applying a proper control force $u(t)$. This somewhat artificial system example represents a dynamic model of a space booster on take off—the booster is balanced on top of the rocket engine thrust vector.

From inspection of Fig. 12.14a, we construct the differential equations describing the dynamics of the inverted pendulum and the cart. The horizontal displacement of the pivot on the cart is $z(t)$, while the rotational angle of the pendulum is $\theta(t)$. The parameters of the system are as follows.

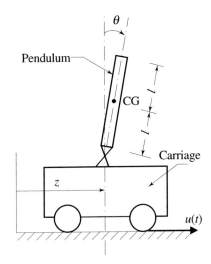

Fig. 12.14a *Inverted pendulum system*

$M =$ the mass of the cart
$L =$ the length of the pendulum $= 2l$
$m =$ the mass of the pendulum
$J =$ the moment of inertia of the pendulum with respect to centre of gravity (CG)

The horizontal and vertical positions of the CG of the pendulum are given by $(z + l \sin\theta)$ and $(l \cos\theta)$ respectively.

The forces exerted on the pendulum are the force mg on the centre of gravity, a horizontal reaction force H and a vertical reaction force V (Fig. 12.14b). Taking moments around CG of the pendulum, we get

$$J\frac{d^2\theta(t)}{dt^2} = V(t)\, l \sin\theta(t) - H(t)\, l \cos\theta(t) \tag{12.79a}$$

Summing up all forces on the pendulum in vertical and horizontal directions, we obtain

$$m\frac{d^2}{dt^2}(l \cos\theta(t)) = V(t) - mg \tag{12.79b}$$

$$m\frac{d^2}{dt^2}(z(t) + l \sin\theta(t)) = H(t) \tag{12.79c}$$

Summing up all forces on the cart in the horizontal direction (Fig. 12.14b), we get

$$M\frac{d^2 z(t)}{dt^2} = u(t) - H(t) \tag{12.79d}$$

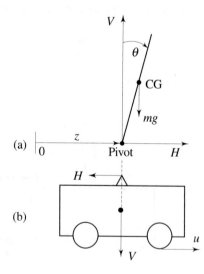

Fig. 12.14b

In our problem, since the objective is to keep the pendulum upright, it seems reasonable to assume that $\dot\theta(t)$ and $\theta(t)$ will remain close to zero. In view of this, we can set with sufficient accuracy $\sin\theta \cong \theta$; $\cos\theta \cong 1$. With this approximation, we get from Eqns (12.79),

$$ml\,\ddot\theta(t) + (m + M)\ddot z(t) = u(t)$$

$$(J + ml^2)\ddot\theta(t) + ml\,\ddot z(t) - mgl\,\theta(t) = 0$$

These equations may be rearranged as

$$\ddot\theta(t) = \frac{ml(M + m)g}{\Delta}\,\theta(t) - \frac{ml}{\Delta}u(t) \qquad (12.80a)$$

$$\ddot z(t) = -\frac{m^2 l^2 g}{\Delta}\,\theta(t) + \frac{(J + ml^2)}{\Delta}u(t) \qquad (12.80b)$$

where

$$\Delta = (M + m)J + Mml^2$$

Suppose that the system parameters are $M = 1$ kg, $m = 0.15$ kg, and $l = 1$ m. Recall that

$$g = 9.81 \text{ m/sec}^2$$

$$J = \tfrac{1}{3}mL^2 = \tfrac{4}{3}ml^2 = 0.2 \text{ kg-m}^2$$

For these parameters, we have from Eqns (12.80),

$$\ddot\theta(t) = 4.4537\,\theta(t) - 0.3947\,u(t) \qquad (12.81a)$$

$$\ddot z(t) = -0.5809\,\theta(t) + 0.9211\,u(t) \qquad (12.81b)$$

Choosing the states $x_1 = \theta$, $x_2 = \dot\theta$, $x_3 = z$, and $x_4 = \dot z$ we obtain the following state model for the inverted pendulum on moving cart.

$$\dot{\mathbf{x}} = \mathbf{A}\mathbf{x} + \mathbf{b}u \qquad (12.82)$$

with

$$\mathbf{A} = \begin{bmatrix} 0 & 1 & 0 & 0 \\ 4.4537 & 0 & 0 & 0 \\ 0 & 0 & 0 & 1 \\ -0.5809 & 0 & 0 & 0 \end{bmatrix} ; \mathbf{b} = \begin{bmatrix} 0 \\ -0.3947 \\ 0 \\ 0.9211 \end{bmatrix}$$

The plant (12.82) is said to be *completely controllable* if every state $\mathbf{x}(t_0)$ can be affected or controlled to reach a desired state in finite time by some unconstrained control $u(t)$. Shortly we will see that the plant (12.82) satisfies this condition and therefore a solution exists to the following control problem:

   Move the cart from one location to another without causing the pendulum to fall.

   The solution to this control problem is not unique. We normally look for a feedback control scheme so that the destabilizing effects of disturbance forces (due to wind, for example) are filtered out. Figure 12.15a shows a state-feedback control scheme for stabilizing the inverted pendulum. The closed-loop system is formed by feeding back the state variables through a real constant matrix $\mathbf{k}$;

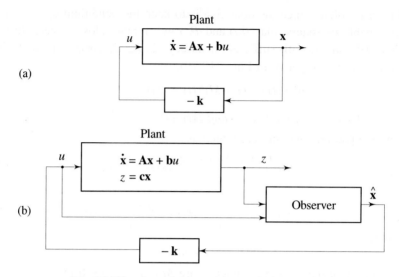

Fig. 12.15 *Control system with state feedback*

$$u(t) = - \mathbf{kx}(t)$$

The closed-loop system is thus described by

$$\dot{\mathbf{x}}(t) = (\mathbf{A} - \mathbf{bk})\mathbf{x}(t)$$

The design objective in this case is to find the feedback matrix **k** such that the closed-loop system is stable. The existence of solution to this design problem is directly based on the controllability property of the plant (12.82).

Implementation of the state-feedback control solution requires access to all the state variables of the plant model. In many control situations of interest, it is possible to install sensors to measure all the state variables. This may not be possible or practical in some cases. For example, if the plant model includes non-physical state variables, measurement of these variables using physical sensors is not possible. Accuracy requirements or cost considerations may prohibit the use of sensors for some physical variables also.

The input and the output of a system are always physical quantities, and are normally easily accessible to measurement. We therefore need a subsystem that performs the estimation of state variables based on the information received from the input $u(t)$ and the output $y(t)$. This subsystem is called an *observer* whose design is based on *observability property* of the controlled system.

The plant (12.82) is said to be *completely observable* if all the state variables in $\mathbf{x}(t)$ can be observed from the measurements of the output $y(t) = \theta(t)$ and the input $u(t)$. Shortly we will see that the plant (12.82) does not satisfy this condition, and therefore a solution to the observer-design problem does not exist when the inputs to the observer subsystem are $u(t)$ and $\theta(t)$.

Cart position $z(t)$ is easily accessible to measurement and, as we shall see, the observability condition is satisfied with this choice of input information to the observer subsystem. Figure 12.15b shows the block diagram of the closed-loop system with an observer that estimates the state vector from measurements of $u(t)$ and $z(t)$. The observed or estimated state vector, designated as $\hat{\mathbf{x}}$, is then used to generate the control u through the feedback matrix $\mathbf{k}$.

A study of controllability and observability properties, presented in this section, provides a basis for the state-feedback design problems. Further, these properties establish the conditions for complete equivalence between the state variable and transfer function representations.

Definitions of Controllability and Observability

In this section, we study the controllability and observability of linear time-invariant systems described by state variable model of the following form:

$$\dot{\mathbf{x}}(t) = \mathbf{A}\mathbf{x}(t) + \mathbf{b}u(t) \tag{12.83a}$$
$$y(t) = \mathbf{c}\mathbf{x}(t) + du(t) \tag{12.83b}$$

where $\mathbf{A}$, $\mathbf{b}$, $\mathbf{c}$ and d are respectively $n \times n$, $n \times 1$, $1 \times n$ and 1×1 matrices, $\mathbf{x}(t)$ is $n \times 1$ state vector, $y(t)$ and $u(t)$ are respectively output and input variables.

Controllability

For the linear system given by (12.83), if there exists an input $u_{[0,\ t_1]}$ which transfers the initial state $\mathbf{x}(0) \triangleq \mathbf{x}^0$ to the state $\mathbf{x}^1$ in a finite time t_1, the state $\mathbf{x}^0$ is said to be controllable. If all initial states are controllable, the system is said to be *completely controllable*, or simply *controllable*. Otherwise, the system is said to be *uncontrollable*.

From Eqn. (12.70), the solution of Eqn. (12.83a) is

$$\mathbf{x}(t) = e^{\mathbf{A}t}\mathbf{x}^0 + \int_0^t e^{\mathbf{A}(t-\tau)}\mathbf{b}u(\tau)\,d\tau$$

To study the controllability property, we may assume without loss of generality that $\mathbf{x}^1 \equiv \mathbf{0}$. Therefore if the system (12.83) is controllable, there exists an input $u_{[0,\ t_1]}$ such that

$$-\mathbf{x}^0 = \int_0^{t_1} e^{-\mathbf{A}\tau}\mathbf{b}u(\tau)\,d\tau \tag{12.84}$$

From this equation, we observe that complete controllability of a system depends on $\mathbf{A}$ and $\mathbf{b}$, and is independent of output matrix $\mathbf{c}$. The controllability of the system (12.83) is frequently referred to as the controllability of the pair $\{\mathbf{A}, \mathbf{b}\}$.

It may be noted that according to the definition of controllability, there is no constraint imposed on the input or on the trajectory that the state should follow. Further, the system is said to be uncontrollable although it may be 'controllable in part'.

From the definition of controllability, we observe that by complete controllability of a plant, we mean that we can make the plant do whatever we please. Perhaps this definition is too restrictive in the sense that we are asking too much of the plant. But if we are able to show that system equations satisfy this definition, certainly there can be no intrinsic limitation on the design of the control system for the plant. However, if the system turns out to be uncontrollable, it does not necessarily mean that the plant can never be operated in a satisfactory manner. Provided that a control system will maintain the important variables in an acceptable region, the fact that the plant is not completely controllable is immaterial.

Another important point which the reader must bear in mind is that almost all physical systems are nonlinear in nature to a certain extent and a linear model is obtained after making certain approximations. Small perturbations of the elements of $\mathbf{A}$ and $\mathbf{b}$ may cause an uncontrollable system to become controllable.

A common source of uncontrollable state variable models arises when redundant state variables are defined. No one would intentionally use more state variables than the minimum number needed to characterize the behaviour of the dynamic system. In a complex system with unfamiliar physics, one may be tempted to write down differential equations for everything in sight and in doing so, may write down more equations than are necessary. This will invariably result in an uncontrollable model for the system.

Observability

For the linear system given by Eqns (12.83), if the knowledge of the output y and the input u over a finite interval of time $[0, t_1]$ suffices to determine the state $\mathbf{x}(0) \triangleq \mathbf{x}^0$, the state $\mathbf{x}^0$ is said to be observable. If all initial states are observable, the system is said to be *completely observable*, or simply *observable*. Otherwise, the system is said to be *unobservable*.

The output of the system (12.83) is given by

$$y(t) = \mathbf{c}\,e^{\mathbf{A}t}\mathbf{x}^0 + \mathbf{c}\int_0^t e^{\mathbf{A}(t-\tau)}\mathbf{b}u(\tau)d\tau + du(t)$$

The output and the input can be measured and used, so that following signal $\eta(t)$ can be obtained from u and y.

$$\eta(t) \triangleq y(t) - \mathbf{c}\int_0^t e^{\mathbf{A}(t-\tau)}\mathbf{b}u(\tau)d\tau - du(t) = \mathbf{c}\,e^{\mathbf{A}t}\mathbf{x}^0 \tag{12.85}$$

Premultiplying by $e^{\mathbf{A}^T t}\mathbf{c}^T$ and integrating from 0 to t_1, gives

$$\left\{\int_0^{t_1} e^{\mathbf{A}^T t}\mathbf{c}^T\mathbf{c}e^{\mathbf{A}t}dt\right\}\mathbf{x}^0 = \int_0^{t_1} e^{\mathbf{A}^T t}\mathbf{c}^T\eta(t)dt \tag{12.86}$$

When the signal $\eta(t)$ is available over a time interval $[0, t_1]$, and the system (12.83) is observable, then the initial state $\mathbf{x}^0$ can be uniquely determined from Eqn. (12.86).

From Eqn. (12.86) we see that complete observability of a system depends on $\mathbf{A}$ and $\mathbf{c}$, and is independent of $\mathbf{b}$. The observability of the system (12.83) is frequently referred to as the observability of the pair $\{\mathbf{A}, \mathbf{c}\}$.

Note that the system is said to be unobservable, although it may be 'observable in part'. For plants that are not completely observable, one may examine feedback control schemes which do not require complete state feedback.

Controllability Test

It is difficult to guess whether a system is controllable or not from the defining equation (12.84). Some simple mathematical tests which answer the question of controllability have been developed. The following theorem gives a simple controllability test[7].

Theorem 12.1
The necessary and sufficient condition for the system (12.83) to be completely controllable is that the $n \times n$ *controllability matrix*

$$\mathbf{U} \triangleq [\mathbf{b} \quad \mathbf{Ab} \quad \mathbf{A}^2\mathbf{b} \cdots \mathbf{A}^{n-1}\mathbf{b}] \qquad (12.87)$$

has rank equal to n, i.e., $\rho(\mathbf{U}) = n$.

Example 12.10

Recall the inverted pendulum of Example 12.9, shown in Figs 12.14, in which the object is to apply a force $u(t)$ so that the pendulum remains balanced in the vertical position. We found the linearized equations governing the system to be:

$$\dot{\mathbf{x}} = \mathbf{Ax} + \mathbf{b}u$$

where
$$\mathbf{x} = [\theta \ \dot{\theta} \ z \ \dot{z}]^T$$

$$\mathbf{A} = \begin{bmatrix} 0 & 1 & 0 & 0 \\ 4.4537 & 0 & 0 & 0 \\ 0 & 0 & 0 & 1 \\ -0.5809 & 0 & 0 & 0 \end{bmatrix} ; \mathbf{b} = \begin{bmatrix} 0 \\ -0.3947 \\ 0 \\ 0.9211 \end{bmatrix}$$

$z(t) =$ horizontal displacement of the pivot on the cart

$\theta(t) =$ rotational angle of the pendulum.

To check the controllability of this system, we compute the controllability matrix $\mathbf{U}$:

---

7. For proof, refer Chapter 5 of reference [180].

$$\mathbf{U} = [\mathbf{b} \ \ \mathbf{Ab} \ \ \mathbf{A}^2\mathbf{b} \ \ \mathbf{A}^3\mathbf{b}] = \begin{bmatrix} 0 & -0.3947 & 0 & -1.7579 \\ -0.3947 & 0 & -1.7579 & 0 \\ 0 & 0.9211 & 0 & 0.2293 \\ 0.9211 & 0 & 0.2293 & 0 \end{bmatrix}$$

Since $|\mathbf{U}| = 2.3369$, $\mathbf{U}$ has full rank, and by Theorem 12.1, the system is completely controllable. Thus if the angle θ departs from equilibrium by a small amount, a control always exists which will drive it back to zero.[8] Moreover, a control also exists which will drive both θ and z, as well as their derivatives, to zero.

Example 12.11 _____

Consider the electrical network shown in Fig. 12.16. Differential equations governing the dynamics of this network can be obtained by various standard methods. By use of nodal analysis, for example, we get

$$C_1 \frac{de_1}{dt} + \frac{e_1 - e_2}{R_3} + \frac{e_1 - e_0}{R_1} = 0$$

$$C_2 \frac{de_2}{dt} + \frac{e_2 - e_1}{R_3} + \frac{e_2 - e_0}{R_2} = 0$$

The appropriate state variables for the network are the capacitor voltages e_1 and e_2. Thus, the state equations of the network are

$$\dot{\mathbf{x}} = \mathbf{Ax} + \mathbf{b}e_0$$

where $\quad\quad\quad \mathbf{x} = [e_1 \ \ e_2]^T$

$$\mathbf{A} = \begin{bmatrix} -\left(\dfrac{1}{R_1} + \dfrac{1}{R_3}\right)\dfrac{1}{C_1} & \dfrac{1}{R_3 C_1} \\ \dfrac{1}{R_3 C_2} & -\left(\dfrac{1}{R_2} + \dfrac{1}{R_3}\right)\dfrac{1}{C_2} \end{bmatrix} ; \mathbf{b} = \begin{bmatrix} \dfrac{1}{R_1 C_1} \\ \dfrac{1}{R_2 C_2} \end{bmatrix}$$

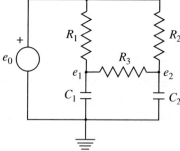

Fig. 12.16

_____

8. This justifies the assumption that $\theta(t) \cong 0$, provided we choose an appropriate control strategy.

The controllability matrix of the system is

$$\mathbf{U} = [\mathbf{b} \ \ \mathbf{Ab}] = \begin{bmatrix} \dfrac{1}{R_1 C_1} & -\dfrac{1}{(R_1 C_1)^2} + \dfrac{1}{R_3 C_1}\left(\dfrac{1}{R_2 C_2} - \dfrac{1}{R_1 C_1}\right) \\ \dfrac{1}{R_2 C_2} & -\dfrac{1}{(R_2 C_2)^2} + \dfrac{1}{R_3 C_2}\left(\dfrac{1}{R_1 C_1} - \dfrac{1}{R_2 C_2}\right) \end{bmatrix}$$

We see that under the condition

$$R_1 C_1 = R_2 C_2,$$

$\rho(\mathbf{U}) = 1$ and the system becomes 'uncontrollable'. This condition is the one required to balance the bridge, and in this case, the voltage across the terminals of R_3 cannot be influenced by the input e_0.

Observability Test

The following theorem gives a simple observability test[9].

Theorem 12.2
The necessary and sufficient condition for the system (12.83) to be completely observable is that the $n \times n$ *observability matrix*

$$\mathbf{V} \triangleq \begin{bmatrix} \mathbf{c} \\ \mathbf{cA} \\ \vdots \\ \mathbf{cA}^{n-1} \end{bmatrix} \tag{12.88}$$

has rank equal to n, i.e., $\rho(\mathbf{V}) = n$.

Example 12.12 ────────────────────────────

We now return to the inverted pendulum of Example 12.10. Assuming that the only output variable for measurement is $\theta(t)$, the position of the pendulum, then the linearized equations governing the system are

$$\dot{\mathbf{x}} = \mathbf{Ax} + \mathbf{b}u$$
$$y = \mathbf{cx}$$

where

$$\mathbf{A} = \begin{bmatrix} 0 & 1 & 0 & 0 \\ 4.4537 & 0 & 0 & 0 \\ 0 & 0 & 0 & 1 \\ -0.5809 & 0 & 0 & 0 \end{bmatrix} ; \mathbf{b} = \begin{bmatrix} 0 \\ -0.3947 \\ 0 \\ 0.9211 \end{bmatrix}$$

$$\mathbf{c} = [\,1 \ \ 0 \ \ 0 \ \ 0\,]$$

The observability matrix

───────────────

9. For proof, refer Chapter 5 of reference [180].

$$V = \begin{bmatrix} \mathbf{c} \\ \mathbf{cA} \\ \mathbf{cA}^2 \\ \mathbf{cA}^3 \end{bmatrix} = \begin{bmatrix} 1 & 0 & 0 & 0 \\ 0 & 1 & 0 & 0 \\ 4.4537 & 0 & 0 & 0 \\ 0 & 4.4537 & 0 & 0 \end{bmatrix}$$

$|V| = 0$, and therefore by Theorem 12.2, the system is not completely observable.

Consider now the displacement $z(t)$ of the cart as the output variable. Then

$$\mathbf{c} = [0 \ 0 \ 1 \ 0]$$

and the observability matrix

$$V = \begin{bmatrix} 0 & 0 & 1 & 0 \\ 0 & 0 & 0 & 1 \\ -0.5809 & 0 & 0 & 0 \\ 0 & -0.5809 & 0 & 0 \end{bmatrix}$$

$|V| = 0.3374 \neq 0$; the system is therefore completely observable. The values of $\dot{z}(t)$, $\theta(t)$ and $\dot{\theta}(t)$ can all be determined by observing $z(t)$ over an arbitrary time interval.

Invariance Property

It is recalled that the state variable model for a system is not unique, but depends on the choice of a set of state variables. A transformation

$$\mathbf{x}(t) = \mathbf{P}\bar{\mathbf{x}}(t); \ \mathbf{P} \text{ is a nonsingular constant matrix,}$$

results in the following alternative state variable model (refer Eqns (12.17)) for the system (12.83):

$$\dot{\bar{\mathbf{x}}}(t) = \bar{\mathbf{A}}\bar{\mathbf{x}}(t) + \bar{\mathbf{b}}u(t); \ \bar{\mathbf{x}}(t_0) = \mathbf{P}^{-1}\mathbf{x}(t_0)$$

$$y(t) = \bar{\mathbf{c}}\bar{\mathbf{x}}(t) + du(t)$$

where

$$\bar{\mathbf{A}} = \mathbf{P}^{-1}\mathbf{A}\mathbf{P}, \ \bar{\mathbf{b}} = \mathbf{P}^{-1}\mathbf{b}, \ \bar{\mathbf{c}} = \mathbf{c}\mathbf{P}$$

The definition of new set of internal state variables should evidently not affect the controllability and observability properties. This may be verified by evaluating the controllability and observability matrices of the transformed system.

I. $$\bar{\mathbf{U}} = [\bar{\mathbf{b}} \ \ \bar{\mathbf{A}}\bar{\mathbf{b}} \ \ \cdots \ \ (\bar{\mathbf{A}})^{n-1}\bar{\mathbf{b}}]$$

$$\bar{\mathbf{b}} = \mathbf{P}^{-1}\mathbf{b}$$

$$\bar{\mathbf{A}}\bar{\mathbf{b}} = \mathbf{P}^{-1}\mathbf{A}\mathbf{P}\mathbf{P}^{-1}\mathbf{b} = \mathbf{P}^{-1}\mathbf{A}\mathbf{b}$$

$$(\bar{\mathbf{A}})^2\bar{\mathbf{b}} = \bar{\mathbf{A}}(\bar{\mathbf{A}}\bar{\mathbf{b}}) = \mathbf{P}^{-1}\mathbf{A}\mathbf{P}\mathbf{P}^{-1}\mathbf{A}\mathbf{b} = \mathbf{P}^{-1}\mathbf{A}^2\mathbf{b}$$

$$\vdots$$

$$(\bar{\mathbf{A}})^{n-1}\bar{\mathbf{b}} = \mathbf{P}^{-1}\mathbf{A}^{n-1}\mathbf{b}$$

Therefore,

$$\overline{\mathbf{U}} = [\mathbf{P}^{-1}\mathbf{b} \quad \mathbf{P}^{-1}\mathbf{A}\mathbf{b} \cdots \mathbf{P}^{-1}\mathbf{A}^{n-1}\mathbf{b}] = \mathbf{P}^{-1}\mathbf{U}$$

where

$$\mathbf{U} = [\mathbf{b} \quad \mathbf{A}\mathbf{b} \cdots \mathbf{A}^{n-1}\mathbf{b}]$$

Since $\mathbf{P}^{-1}$ is nonsingular,

$$\rho(\overline{\mathbf{U}}) = \rho(\mathbf{U})$$

II. A similar relationship can be shown for the observability matrices.

12.8 | EQUIVALENCE BETWEEN TRANSFER FUNCTION AND STATE VARIABLE REPRESENTATIONS

In frequency-domain analysis, it is tacitly assumed that the dynamic properties of a system are completely determined by the transfer function of the system. That this is not always the case is illustrated by the following examples.

*Example 12.13*_____

Consider the system

$$\dot{\mathbf{x}} = \mathbf{A}\mathbf{x} + \mathbf{b}u \tag{12.89}$$
$$y = \mathbf{c}\mathbf{x}$$

with

$$\mathbf{A} = \begin{bmatrix} -2 & 1 \\ 1 & -2 \end{bmatrix}; \mathbf{b} = \begin{bmatrix} 1 \\ 1 \end{bmatrix}; \mathbf{c} = [0 \quad 1]$$

The controllability matrix

$$\mathbf{U} = [\mathbf{b} \quad \mathbf{A}\mathbf{b}] = \begin{bmatrix} 1 & -1 \\ 1 & -1 \end{bmatrix}$$

Since $\rho(\mathbf{U}) = 1$, the second-order system (12.89) is not completely controllable. The eigenvalues of matrix $\mathbf{A}$ are the roots of the characteristic equation

$$|s\mathbf{I} - \mathbf{A}| = \begin{vmatrix} s+2 & -1 \\ -1 & s+2 \end{vmatrix} = 0$$

The eigenvalues are obtained as $-1, -3$. The *modes* of the transient response are therefore e^{-t} and e^{-3t}.

The transfer function of the system (12.89) is calculated as

$$G(s) = \mathbf{c}(s\mathbf{I} - \mathbf{A})^{-1}\mathbf{b} = [0 \quad 1] \begin{bmatrix} s+2 & -1 \\ -1 & s+2 \end{bmatrix}^{-1} \begin{bmatrix} 1 \\ 1 \end{bmatrix}$$

$$= [0 \quad 1] \begin{bmatrix} \dfrac{s+2}{(s+1)(s+3)} & \dfrac{1}{(s+1)(s+3)} \\ \dfrac{1}{(s+1)(s+3)} & \dfrac{s+2}{(s+1)(s+3)} \end{bmatrix} \begin{bmatrix} 1 \\ 1 \end{bmatrix} = \dfrac{1}{s+1}$$

We find that because of pole-zero cancellation, both the eigenvalues of matrix **A** do not appear as poles in $G(s)$. The dynamic mode e^{-3t} of the system (12.89) does not show up in input-output characterization given by the transfer function $G(s)$. Note that the system under consideration is not a completely controllable system.

*Example 12.14*_____

Consider the system

$$\dot{\mathbf{x}} = \mathbf{A}\mathbf{x} + \mathbf{b}u$$
$$y = \mathbf{c}\mathbf{x} \qquad\qquad (12.90)$$

with

$$\mathbf{A} = \begin{bmatrix} -2 & 1 \\ 1 & -2 \end{bmatrix};\ \mathbf{b} = \begin{bmatrix} 1 \\ 0 \end{bmatrix};\ \mathbf{c} = [1\ \ -1]$$

The observability matrix

$$\mathbf{V} = \begin{bmatrix} \mathbf{c} \\ \mathbf{c}\mathbf{A} \end{bmatrix} = \begin{bmatrix} 1 & -1 \\ -3 & 3 \end{bmatrix}$$

Since $\rho(\mathbf{V}) = 1$, the second-order system (12.90) is not completely observable.

The eigenvalues of matrix **A** are $-1, -3$. The transfer function of the system (12.90) is calculated as

$$G(s) = \mathbf{c}(s\mathbf{I} - \mathbf{A})^{-1}\mathbf{b}$$

$$= [1\ \ -1] \begin{bmatrix} \dfrac{s+2}{(s+1)(s+3)} & \dfrac{1}{(s+1)(s+3)} \\ \dfrac{1}{(s+1)(s+3)} & \dfrac{s+2}{(s+1)(s+3)} \end{bmatrix} \begin{bmatrix} 1 \\ 0 \end{bmatrix} = \dfrac{1}{s+3}$$

The dynamic mode e^{-t} of the system (12.90) does not show up in the input-output characterization given by the transfer function $G(s)$. Note that the system under consideration is not a completely observable system.

In the following, we give two specific state transformations to reveal the underlying structure imposed upon a system by its controllability and observability properties (for proof, refer [102]). These results are then used to establish equivalence between transfer function and state variable representations.

Theorem 12.3

Consider an nth-order system

$$\dot{\mathbf{x}} = \mathbf{A}\mathbf{x} + \mathbf{b}u$$
$$y = \mathbf{c}\mathbf{x} \qquad\qquad (12.91a)$$

Assume that

$$\rho(\mathbf{U}) = \rho[\mathbf{b}\ \ \mathbf{A}\mathbf{b}\ \cdots\ \mathbf{A}^{n-1}\mathbf{b}] = m < n$$

There exists an equivalence transformation

$$\mathbf{x} = \mathbf{P}\bar{\mathbf{x}} \qquad (12.91b)$$

that transforms the system (12.91a) to the following form:

$$\begin{bmatrix} \dot{\bar{\mathbf{x}}}_1 \\ \dot{\bar{\mathbf{x}}}_2 \end{bmatrix} = \begin{bmatrix} \bar{\mathbf{A}}_c & \bar{\mathbf{A}}_{12} \\ \mathbf{0} & \bar{\mathbf{A}}_{22} \end{bmatrix} \begin{bmatrix} \bar{\mathbf{x}}_1 \\ \bar{\mathbf{x}}_2 \end{bmatrix} + \begin{bmatrix} \bar{\mathbf{b}}_c \\ \mathbf{0} \end{bmatrix} u$$

$$= \bar{\mathbf{A}}\,\bar{\mathbf{x}} + \bar{\mathbf{b}}u \qquad (12.91c)$$

$$y = [\bar{\mathbf{c}}_1 \quad \bar{\mathbf{c}}_2] \begin{bmatrix} \bar{\mathbf{x}}_1 \\ \bar{\mathbf{x}}_2 \end{bmatrix} = \bar{\mathbf{c}}\,\bar{\mathbf{x}}$$

where the m-dimensional subsystem

$$\dot{\bar{\mathbf{x}}}_1 = \bar{\mathbf{A}}_c\,\bar{\mathbf{x}}_1 + \bar{\mathbf{b}}_c\,u + \bar{\mathbf{A}}_{12}\,\bar{\mathbf{x}}_2$$

is controllable from u (the additional driving term $\bar{\mathbf{A}}_{12}\bar{\mathbf{x}}_2$ has no effect on controllability), and the $(n-m)$ dimensional subsystem

$$\dot{\bar{\mathbf{x}}}_2 = \bar{\mathbf{A}}_{22}\,\bar{\mathbf{x}}_2$$

is not affected by the input, and is therefore entirely uncontrollable.

This theorem shows that any system which is not completely controllable can be decomposed into controllable and uncontrollable subsystems shown in Fig. 12.17. The state model (12.91c) is said to be in *controllability canonical form*.

In Section 12.4, it was shown that the characteristic equations and transfer functions of equivalent systems are identical. Thus the set of eigenvalues of matrix $\mathbf{A}$ of system (12.91a) is same as the set of eigenvalues of matrix $\mathbf{A}$ of system (12.91c), which is a union of the subsets of eigenvalues of matrices $\bar{\mathbf{A}}_c$

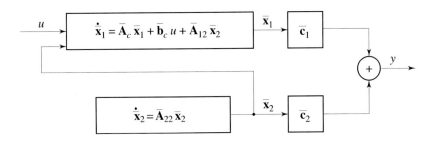

Fig. 12.17   *The controllability canonical form of a state variable model*

and $\overline{\mathbf{A}}_{22}$. Also the transfer function of system (12.91a) must be the same as that of (12.91c). The transfer function of (12.91a) is calculated from Eqn. (12.91c) as[10]

$$G(s) = [\overline{\mathbf{c}}_1 \quad \overline{\mathbf{c}}_2] \begin{bmatrix} s\mathbf{I} - \overline{\mathbf{A}}_c & -\overline{\mathbf{A}}_{12} \\ \mathbf{0} & s\mathbf{I} - \overline{\mathbf{A}}_{22} \end{bmatrix}^{-1} \begin{bmatrix} \overline{\mathbf{b}}_c \\ \mathbf{0} \end{bmatrix}$$

$$= [\overline{\mathbf{c}}_1 \quad \overline{\mathbf{c}}_2] \begin{bmatrix} (s\mathbf{I} - \overline{\mathbf{A}}_c)^{-1} & (s\mathbf{I} - \overline{\mathbf{A}}_c)^{-1}\overline{\mathbf{A}}_{12}(s\mathbf{I} - \overline{\mathbf{A}}_{22})^{-1} \\ \mathbf{0} & (s\mathbf{I} - \overline{\mathbf{A}}_{22})^{-1} \end{bmatrix} \begin{bmatrix} \overline{\mathbf{b}}_c \\ \mathbf{0} \end{bmatrix}$$

$$= \overline{\mathbf{c}}_1 (s\mathbf{I} - \overline{\mathbf{A}}_c)^{-1}\mathbf{b}_c$$

Therefore, the input–output relationship for the system is dependent only on the controllable part of the system. We will refer to the eigenvalues of $\overline{\mathbf{A}}_c$ as *controllable poles* and the eigenvalues of $\overline{\mathbf{A}}_{22}$ as *uncontrollable poles*.

Only the controllable poles appear in the transfer function model; the uncontrollable poles are cancelled by the zeros.

Theorem 12.4

Consider the nth order system

$$\dot{\mathbf{x}} = \mathbf{A}\mathbf{x} + \mathbf{b}u$$
$$y = \mathbf{c}\mathbf{x} \tag{12.92a}$$

Assume that

$$\rho(\mathbf{V}) = \rho \begin{bmatrix} \mathbf{c} \\ \mathbf{c}\mathbf{A} \\ \vdots \\ \mathbf{c}\mathbf{A}^{n-1} \end{bmatrix} = l < n$$

There exits an equivalence transformation

$$\overline{\mathbf{x}} = \mathbf{Q}\mathbf{x} \tag{12.92b}$$

that transforms the system (12.92a) to the following form:

$$\begin{bmatrix} \dot{\overline{\mathbf{x}}}_1 \\ \dot{\overline{\mathbf{x}}}_2 \end{bmatrix} = \begin{bmatrix} \overline{\mathbf{A}}_0 & \mathbf{0} \\ \mathbf{A}_{21} & \mathbf{A}_{22} \end{bmatrix} \begin{bmatrix} \overline{\mathbf{x}}_1 \\ \overline{\mathbf{x}}_2 \end{bmatrix} + \begin{bmatrix} \overline{\mathbf{b}}_1 \\ \mathbf{b}_2 \end{bmatrix} u = \overline{\mathbf{A}}\,\overline{\mathbf{x}} + \overline{\mathbf{b}}u \tag{12.92c}$$

---

10. $\begin{bmatrix} \mathbf{A}_1 & \mathbf{A}_2 \\ \mathbf{0} & \mathbf{A}_3 \end{bmatrix} \begin{bmatrix} \mathbf{B}_1 & \mathbf{B}_2 \\ \mathbf{B}_3 & \mathbf{B}_4 \end{bmatrix} = \begin{bmatrix} \mathbf{I} & \mathbf{0} \\ \mathbf{0} & \mathbf{I} \end{bmatrix}$

gives $\begin{bmatrix} \mathbf{B}_1 & \mathbf{B}_2 \\ \mathbf{B}_3 & \mathbf{B}_4 \end{bmatrix} = \begin{bmatrix} \mathbf{A}_1^{-1} & -\mathbf{A}_1^{-1}\mathbf{A}_2\mathbf{A}_3^{-1} \\ \mathbf{0} & \mathbf{A}_3^{-1} \end{bmatrix}$

$$y = \begin{bmatrix} \overline{\mathbf{c}}_0 & \mathbf{0} \end{bmatrix} \begin{bmatrix} \overline{\mathbf{x}}_1 \\ \overline{\mathbf{x}}_2 \end{bmatrix} = \overline{\mathbf{c}}\,\overline{\mathbf{x}}$$

where the l-dimensional subsystem

$$\dot{\overline{\mathbf{x}}}_1 = \overline{\mathbf{A}}_0 \overline{\mathbf{x}}_1 + \overline{\mathbf{b}}_1 u$$

$$y = \overline{\mathbf{c}}_0\,\overline{\mathbf{x}}_1$$

is observable from y, and the $(n-l)$-dimensional subsystem

$$\dot{\overline{\mathbf{x}}}_2 = \overline{\mathbf{A}}_{22}\,\overline{\mathbf{x}}_2 + \overline{\mathbf{b}}_2\,u + \overline{\mathbf{A}}_{21}\,\overline{\mathbf{x}}_1$$

has no effect upon the output y, and is therefore entirely unobservable, i.e., nothing about $\overline{\mathbf{x}}_2$ can be inferred from output measurement.

This theorem shows that any system which is not completely observable can be decomposed into the observable and unobservable subsystems shown in Fig. 12.18. The state model (12.92c) is said to be in *observability canonical form*.

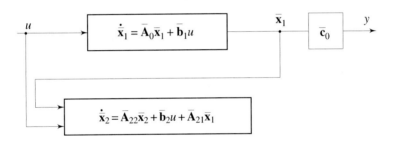

Fig. 12.18 *The observability canonical form of a state variable model*

Since systems (12.92a) and (12.92c) are equivalent, the set of eigenvalues of matrix $\mathbf{A}$ of system (12.92a) is same as the set of eigenvalues of matrix $\overline{\mathbf{A}}$ of system (12.92c), which is a union of the subsets of eigenvalues of matrices $\overline{\mathbf{A}}_0$ and $\overline{\mathbf{A}}_{22}$. The transfer function of the system (12.92a) may be calculated from (12.92c) as follows:

$$G(s) = \begin{bmatrix} \overline{\mathbf{c}}_0 & \mathbf{0} \end{bmatrix} \begin{bmatrix} s\mathbf{I} - \overline{\mathbf{A}}_0 & \mathbf{0} \\ -\overline{\mathbf{A}}_{21} & s\mathbf{I} - \overline{\mathbf{A}}_{22} \end{bmatrix}^{-1} \begin{bmatrix} \overline{\mathbf{b}}_1 \\ \overline{\mathbf{b}}_2 \end{bmatrix}$$

$$= \begin{bmatrix} \overline{\mathbf{c}}_0 & \mathbf{0} \end{bmatrix} \begin{bmatrix} (s\mathbf{I} - \overline{\mathbf{A}}_0)^{-1} & \mathbf{0} \\ (s\mathbf{I} - \overline{\mathbf{A}}_{22})^{-1}\,\overline{\mathbf{A}}_{21}\,(s\mathbf{I} - \overline{\mathbf{A}}_0)^{-1} & (s\mathbf{I} - \overline{\mathbf{A}}_{22})^{-1} \end{bmatrix} \begin{bmatrix} \overline{\mathbf{b}}_1 \\ \overline{\mathbf{b}}_2 \end{bmatrix}$$

$$= \overline{\mathbf{c}}_0 (s\mathbf{I} - \overline{\mathbf{A}}_0)^{-1}\,\overline{\mathbf{b}}_1 \qquad\qquad (12.93)$$

which shows that the unobservable part of the system does not affect the input–output relationship. We will refer to the eigenvalues of $\overline{\mathbf{A}}_0$ as *observable poles* and the eigenvalues of $\mathbf{A}_{22}$ as unobservable poles.

We now examine the use of state variable and transfer function models of a system to study its dynamic properties.

We know that a system is asymptotically stable if all the eigenvalues of the characteristic matrix $\mathbf{A}$ of its state variable model are in the left-half of complex plane. Also we know that a system is (bounded-input bounded-output) BIBO stable if all the poles of its transfer function model are in the left-half of complex plane. Since, in general, the poles of the transfer function model of a system are a subset of the eigenvalues of the characteristic matrix $\mathbf{A}$ of the system, *asymptotic stability always implies BIBO stability.*

The reverse, however, may not always be true because the eigenvalues of the uncontrollable and/or unobservable part of the system are hidden from the BIBO stability analysis. These may lead to instability of a BIBO stable system. When a state variable model is both controllable and observable, all the eigenvalues of characteristic matrix $\mathbf{A}$ appear as poles in the corresponding transfer function. Therefore *BIBO stability implies asymptotic stability only for completely controllable and completely observable system.*

To conclude, we may say that the transfer function model of a system represents its complete dynamics only if the system is both controllable and observable.

Review Examples

Review Example 12.1

A feedback system has a closed-loop transfer function

$$\frac{Y(s)}{R(s)} = \frac{10(s+4)}{s(s+1)(s+3)}$$

Construct three different state models for this system:
(a) One where the system matrix $\mathbf{A}$ is a diagonal matrix.
(b) One where $\mathbf{A}$ is in first companion form.
(c) One where $\mathbf{A}$ is in second companion form.

Solution
(a) The given transfer function can be expressed as

$$\frac{Y(s)}{R(s)} = \frac{10(s+4)}{s(s+1)(s+3)} = \frac{40/3}{s} + \frac{-15}{s+1} + \frac{5/3}{s+3}$$

Therefore,

$$Y(s) = \frac{40/3}{s} R(s) + \frac{-15}{s+1} R(s) + \frac{5/3}{s+3} R(s)$$

Let $\quad X_1(s) = \dfrac{40/3}{s} R(s)$; this gives $\dot{x}_1 = \frac{40}{3} r$

$$X_2(s) = \frac{-15}{s+1} R(s); \text{ this gives } \dot{x}_2 + x_2 = -15\,r$$

$$X_3(s) = \frac{5/3}{s+3} R(s); \text{ this gives } \dot{x}_3 + 3x_3 = \tfrac{5}{3}r$$

In terms of x_1, x_2 and x_3, the output $y(t)$ is given by

$$y(t) = x_1(t) + x_2(t) + x_3(t)$$

A state variable formulation for the given transfer function is defined by the following matrices:

$$\Lambda = \begin{bmatrix} 0 & 0 & 0 \\ 0 & -1 & 0 \\ 0 & 0 & -3 \end{bmatrix}; \mathbf{b} = \begin{bmatrix} 40/3 \\ -15 \\ 5/3 \end{bmatrix}; \mathbf{c} = [\,1 \;\; 1 \;\; 1\,]; d = 0$$

Note that the coefficient matrix Λ is diagonal, and the state model is in Jordan canonical form.

We now construct two state models for the given transfer function in companion form. To do this, we express the transfer function as

$$\frac{Y(s)}{R(s)} = \frac{10(s+4)}{s(s+1)(s+3)} = \frac{10s+40}{s^3+4s^2+3s} = \frac{\beta_0 s^3 + \beta_1 s^2 + \beta_2 s + \beta_3}{s^3 + \alpha_1 s^2 + \alpha_2 s + \alpha_3};$$

$$\beta_0 = \beta_1 = 0, \; \beta_2 = 10, \; \beta_3 = 40, \; \alpha_1 = 4, \; \alpha_2 = 3, \; \alpha_3 = 0$$

(b) With reference to Eqns (12.44), we obtain the following state model in the first companion form:

$$\mathbf{A} = \begin{bmatrix} 0 & 1 & 0 \\ 0 & 0 & 1 \\ 0 & -3 & -4 \end{bmatrix}; \mathbf{b} = \begin{bmatrix} 0 \\ 0 \\ 1 \end{bmatrix}; \mathbf{c} = [40 \;\; 10 \;\; 0]; d = 0$$

(c) With reference to Eqns (12.46), the state model in second companion form becomes

$$\mathbf{A} = \begin{bmatrix} 0 & 0 & 0 \\ 1 & 0 & -3 \\ 0 & 1 & -4 \end{bmatrix}; \mathbf{b} = \begin{bmatrix} 40 \\ 10 \\ 0 \end{bmatrix}, \mathbf{c} = [0 \;\; 0 \;\; 1]; \; d = 0$$

Review Example 12.2 ─────────────────────────────

A linear time-invariant system is characterized by the homogeneous state equation

$$\begin{bmatrix} \dot{x}_1 \\ \dot{x}_2 \end{bmatrix} = \begin{bmatrix} 0 & 1 \\ 0 & -2 \end{bmatrix} \begin{bmatrix} x_1 \\ x_2 \end{bmatrix}$$

(a) Compute the solution of the homogeneous equation assuming the initial state vector

$$\mathbf{x}(0) = \begin{bmatrix} 1 \\ 0 \end{bmatrix}$$

(b) Consider now that the system has a forcing function and is represented by the following nonhomogeneous state equation:

$$\begin{bmatrix} \dot{x}_1 \\ \dot{x}_2 \end{bmatrix} = \begin{bmatrix} 0 & 1 \\ 0 & -2 \end{bmatrix} \begin{bmatrix} x_1 \\ x_2 \end{bmatrix} + \begin{bmatrix} 0 \\ 1 \end{bmatrix} u$$

where u is a unit step input.

Compute the solution of this equation assuming initial conditions of part (a).

Solution

(a) Since

$$(s\mathbf{I} - \mathbf{A}) = \begin{bmatrix} s & -1 \\ 0 & s+2 \end{bmatrix}$$

we obtain

$$(s\mathbf{I} - \mathbf{A})^{-1} = \begin{bmatrix} \dfrac{1}{s} & \dfrac{1}{s(s+2)} \\ 0 & \dfrac{1}{s+2} \end{bmatrix}$$

Hence

$$e^{\mathbf{A}t} = \mathcal{L}^{-1}[(s\mathbf{I} - \mathbf{A})^{-1}] = \begin{bmatrix} 1 & \frac{1}{2}(1 - e^{-2t}) \\ 0 & e^{-2t} \end{bmatrix}$$

$$\mathbf{x}(t) = e^{\mathbf{A}t}\mathbf{x}(0) = \begin{bmatrix} 1 \\ 0 \end{bmatrix}$$

(b)

$$\mathbf{x}(t) = e^{\mathbf{A}t}\mathbf{x}(0) + \int_0^t e^{\mathbf{A}(t-\tau)} \mathbf{b}u(\tau)d\tau$$

Now

$$\int_0^t e^{\mathbf{A}(t-\tau)} \mathbf{b}u(\tau)d\tau = \begin{bmatrix} \frac{1}{2}\int_0^t [1 - e^{-2(t-\tau)}]d\tau \\ \int_0^t e^{-2(t-\tau)}d\tau \end{bmatrix} = \begin{bmatrix} -\frac{1}{4} + \frac{1}{2}t + \frac{1}{4}e^{-2t} \\ \frac{1}{2}(1 - e^{-2t}) \end{bmatrix}$$

Therefore,

$$x_1(t) = \frac{3}{4} + \frac{1}{2}t + \frac{1}{4}e^{-2t}$$

$$x_2(t) = \frac{1}{2}(1 - e^{-2t})$$

Review Example 12.3

The motion of a satellite in the equatorial (r, θ) plane is given by the state equation [109]

$$\begin{bmatrix} \dot{x}_1 \\ \dot{x}_2 \\ \dot{x}_3 \\ \dot{x}_4 \end{bmatrix} = \begin{bmatrix} 0 & 1 & 0 & 0 \\ 3\omega^2 & 0 & 0 & 2\omega \\ 0 & 0 & 0 & 1 \\ 0 & -2\omega & 0 & 0 \end{bmatrix} \begin{bmatrix} x_1 \\ x_2 \\ x_3 \\ x_4 \end{bmatrix} + \begin{bmatrix} 0 \\ 1 \\ 0 \\ 0 \end{bmatrix} u_1 + \begin{bmatrix} 0 \\ 0 \\ 0 \\ 1 \end{bmatrix} u_2$$

where ω is the angular frequency of the satellite in circular, equatorial orbit, $x_1(t)$ and $x_3(t)$ are, respectively, the deviations in position variables $r(t)$ and $\theta(t)$ of the satellite, and $x_2(t)$ and $x_4(t)$ are, respectively, the deviations in velocity variables $\dot{r}(t)$ and $\dot{\theta}(t)$. The inputs $u_1(t)$ and $u_2(t)$ are the thrusts u_r and u_θ in the radial and tangential directions respectively, applied by small rocket engines or gas jets (**u** = **0** when **x** = **0**). Sensors have been installed for measuring $r(t)$ and $\theta(t)$

(a) Suppose that the tangential thruster becomes inoperable. Determine the controllability of the system with the radial thruster alone.

(b) Suppose that the radial thruster becomes inoperable. Determine the controllability of the system with the tangential thruster alone.

(c) Suppose that the tangential measuring device becomes inoperable. Determine the observability of the system from radial position measurement ($x_1 = r$) alone.

(d) Suppose that the radial measurements are lost. Determine the observability of the system from tangential position measurement ($x_3 = \theta$) alone.

Solution

(a) With $u_2 = 0$,

$$\mathbf{b} = \begin{bmatrix} 0 \\ 1 \\ 0 \\ 0 \end{bmatrix}$$

The controllability matrix

$$\mathbf{U} = [\mathbf{b} \quad \mathbf{Ab} \quad \mathbf{A^2b} \quad \mathbf{A^3b}] = \begin{bmatrix} 0 & 1 & 0 & -\omega^2 \\ 1 & 0 & -\omega^2 & 0 \\ 0 & 0 & -2\omega & 0 \\ 0 & -2\omega & 0 & 2\omega^3 \end{bmatrix}$$

$$|\mathbf{U}| = - \begin{vmatrix} 1 & 0 & -\omega^2 \\ 0 & -2\omega & 0 \\ -2\omega & 0 & 2\omega^2 \end{vmatrix} = -[-2\omega(2\omega^3 - 2\omega^3)] = 0$$

Therefore, $\rho(\mathbf{U}) < 4$, and the system is not completely controllable with u_1 alone.

(b) With $u_1 = 0$,

$$\mathbf{b} = \begin{bmatrix} 0 \\ 0 \\ 0 \\ 1 \end{bmatrix}$$

The controllability matrix

$$
\mathbf{U} = \begin{bmatrix} 0 & 0 & 2\omega & 0 \\ 0 & 2\omega & 0 & -2\omega^3 \\ 0 & 1 & 0 & -4\omega^2 \\ 1 & 0 & -4\omega^2 & 0 \end{bmatrix}
$$

$$
|\mathbf{U}| = 2\omega \begin{vmatrix} 0 & 2\omega & -2\omega^3 \\ 0 & 1 & -4\omega^2 \\ 1 & 0 & 0 \end{vmatrix} = -12\omega^4 \neq 0
$$

Therefore, $\rho(\mathbf{U}) = 4$, and the system is completely controllable with u_2 alone.

(c) With $\qquad y = x_1,$

$$
\mathbf{c} = [1 \quad 0 \quad 0 \quad 0]
$$

The observability matrix

$$
\mathbf{V} = \begin{bmatrix} \mathbf{c} \\ \mathbf{c}\mathbf{A} \\ \mathbf{c}\mathbf{A}^2 \\ \mathbf{c}\mathbf{A}^3 \end{bmatrix} = \begin{bmatrix} 1 & 0 & 0 & 0 \\ 0 & 1 & 0 & 0 \\ 3\omega^2 & 0 & 0 & 2\omega \\ 0 & -\omega^2 & 0 & 0 \end{bmatrix}
$$

$$
|\mathbf{V}| = 0
$$

Therefore, $\rho(\mathbf{V}) < 4$, and the system is not completely observable from $y = x_1$ alone.

(d) With $y = x_3,$

$$
\mathbf{c} = [0 \ 0 \ 1 \ 0]
$$

The observability matrix

$$
\mathbf{V} = \begin{bmatrix} 0 & 0 & 1 & 0 \\ 0 & 0 & 0 & 1 \\ 0 & -2\omega & 0 & 0 \\ -6\omega^3 & 0 & 0 & -4\omega^2 \end{bmatrix}
$$

$$
|\mathbf{V}| = -12\omega^4 \neq 0
$$

Therefore, $\rho(\mathbf{V}) = 4$, and the system is completely observable from $y = x_3$ alone.

Review Example 12.4

Consider state equation of a single-input system which includes delay in control action:

$$
\dot{\mathbf{x}}(t) = \mathbf{A}\mathbf{x}(t) + \mathbf{b}u(t - \tau_D) \tag{12.94a}
$$

where $\mathbf{x}$ is $n \times 1$ state vector, u is scalar input, τ_D is the dead-time, and $\mathbf{A}$ and $\mathbf{b}$ are respectively $n \times n$ and $n \times 1$ real constant matrices.

For discrete-time solution, the time axis is discretized (sampled) into intervals of width T; $t = kT, k = 0, 1, 2, ...$; and $u(t)$ is approximated by a staircase function, constant over the intervals. For the kth interval,

$u(k) = u(kT);\ kT \le t < (k + 1)\ T;\ k = 0,1\ 2,\dots;$ the solution of Eqn. (12.94a) with t_0 as initial time is

$$\mathbf{x}(t) = e^{\mathbf{A}(t-t_0)}\mathbf{x}(t_0) + \int_{t_0}^{t} e^{\mathbf{A}(t-\tau)}\mathbf{b}u(\tau - \tau_D)d\tau \qquad (12.94b)$$

If we let $t_0 = kT$ and $t = kT + T$ in Eqn. (12.94b), we obtain

$$\mathbf{x}(kT + T) = e^{\mathbf{A}T}\mathbf{x}(kT) + \int_{kT}^{kT+T} e^{\mathbf{A}(kT+T-\tau)}\mathbf{b}u(\tau - \tau_D)d\tau$$

With $\sigma = kT + T - \tau$, we get

$$\mathbf{x}(kT + T) = e^{\mathbf{A}T}\mathbf{x}(kT) + \int_{0}^{T} e^{\mathbf{A}\sigma}\mathbf{b}u(kT + T - \tau_D - \sigma)d\sigma \qquad (12.95)$$

If N is the largest integer number of sampling intervals in τ_D, we can write

$$\tau_D = NT + \Delta T;\ 0 \le \Delta < 1 \qquad (12.96a)$$

Substituting in Eqn. (12.95), we get

$$\mathbf{x}(kT + T) = e^{\mathbf{A}T}\mathbf{x}(kT) + \int_{0}^{T} e^{\mathbf{A}\sigma}\mathbf{b}u(kT + T - NT - \Delta T - \sigma)d\sigma$$

We introduce a parameter m such that

$$m = 1 - \Delta \qquad (12.96b)$$

Then

$$\mathbf{x}(kT + T) = e^{\mathbf{A}T}\mathbf{x}(kT) + \int_{0}^{T} e^{\mathbf{A}\sigma}\mathbf{b}u(kT - NT + mT - \sigma)d\sigma \qquad (12.97)$$

The nature of the integral in Eqn. (12.97) with respect to variable σ becomes clear from the sketch of the piecewise constant input u over a segment of time axis near $t = kT - NT$ (Fig. 12.19). The integral runs for σ from 0 to T which corresponds to t from $kT - NT + mT$ backward to $kT - NT - T + mT$.

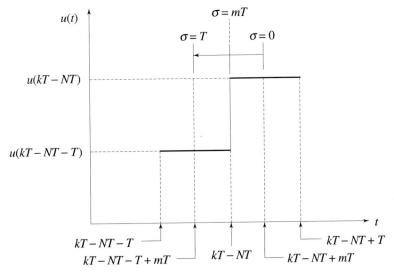

Fig. 12.19

Over this period, the control first takes on the value $u(kT - NT)$ and then the value $u(kT - NT - T)$. Therefore we can break the integral in Eqn. (12.97) into two parts as follows:

$$\mathbf{x}(kT + T) = e^{\mathbf{A}T}\mathbf{x}(kT) + \left[\int_0^{mT} e^{\mathbf{A}\sigma}\mathbf{b}\,d\sigma \right] u(kT - NT)$$

$$+ \left[\int_{mT}^{T} e^{\mathbf{A}\sigma}\mathbf{b}\,d\sigma \right] u(kT - NT - T)$$

$$= \mathbf{F}\mathbf{x}(kT) + \mathbf{g}_1 u(kT - NT - T) + \mathbf{g}_2 u(kT - NT) \qquad (12.98a)$$

where $\qquad \mathbf{F} = e^{\mathbf{A}T} \qquad\qquad\qquad\qquad\qquad\qquad\qquad\qquad (12.98b)$

$$\mathbf{g}_1 = \int_{mT}^{T} e^{\mathbf{A}\sigma}\mathbf{b}\,d\sigma \qquad\qquad\qquad\qquad\qquad (12.98c)$$

$$\mathbf{g}_2 = \int_0^{mT} e^{\mathbf{A}\sigma}\mathbf{b}\,d\sigma \qquad\qquad\qquad\qquad\qquad (12.98d)$$

Setting $\theta = \sigma - mT$ in Eqn. (12.98c), we get

$$\mathbf{g}_1 = \int_0^{\varDelta T} e^{\mathbf{A}(mT + \theta)}\mathbf{b}\,d\theta = e^{\mathbf{A}mT} \int_0^{\varDelta T} e^{\mathbf{A}\theta}\mathbf{b}\,d\theta \qquad (12.98e)$$

The matrices/vectors $\mathbf{F}$, $\mathbf{g}_1$ and $\mathbf{g}_2$ can be evaluated by series truncation method discussed in Eqns (12.76)-(12.78).

As an example, consider the state variable model

$$\dot{x}_1(t) = -x_1(t) + u(t - \tau_D); \quad \tau_D = 1.5 \qquad\qquad (12.99)$$

Assume that the time axis is sampled with interval $T = 1$ sec. From Eqns (12.96), we have

$$N = 1, \ \varDelta = 0.5, \ m = 0.5$$

Equations (12.98b), (12.98d), and (12.98e) give

$$\mathbf{F} = e^{-1} = 0.3679$$

$$\mathbf{g}_2 = \int_0^{0.5} e^{-\sigma}\,d\sigma = e^{-0.5} = 0.3935$$

$$\mathbf{g}_1 = e^{-0.5} \int_0^{0.5} e^{-\theta}\,d\theta = e^{-0.5} - e^{-1} = 0.2387$$

The following state transition equation yields discrete-time solution of the system (12.99).

$$x_1(k + 1) = 0.3679\,x_1(k) + 0.2387\,u(k - 2) + 0.3935\,u(k - 1) \qquad (12.100)$$

Review Questions

12.1 Given a single-input single-output state variable model

$$\dot{\mathbf{x}} = \mathbf{A}\mathbf{x} + \mathbf{b}u$$

$$y = \mathbf{c}\mathbf{x}$$

Prove that eigenvalues of matrix $\mathbf{A}$ are invariant under state transformation $\mathbf{x} = \mathbf{P}\bar{\mathbf{x}}$; $\mathbf{P}$ is a constant nonsingular matrix.

12.2 Given a single-input single-output state variable model

$$\dot{\mathbf{x}} = \mathbf{A}\mathbf{x} + \mathbf{b}u$$

$$y = \mathbf{c}\mathbf{x}$$

(a) Prove that $\dfrac{Y(s)}{U(s)} = G(s) = \mathbf{c}(s\mathbf{I} - \mathbf{A})^{-1}\mathbf{b}$.

(b) Prove that $G(s)$ is strictly proper transfer function. (Help: p787)

(c) Prove that $G(s)$ is invariant under state transformation $\mathbf{x} = \mathbf{P}\bar{\mathbf{x}}$; $\mathbf{P}$ is a constant nonsingular matrix.

12.3 For the single-input single-output state variable model

$$\dot{\mathbf{x}} = \mathbf{A}\mathbf{x} + \mathbf{b}u$$

$$y = \mathbf{c}\mathbf{x} + du$$

find an expression for determination of the transfer function $G(s) = Y(s)/U(s)$. Show that (Help: p787)

$$d = \lim_{s \to \infty} [G(s)]$$

12.4 Is the state variable description for a given transfer function

$$G(s) = \frac{\beta_0 s^n + \beta_1 s^{n-1} + \cdots + \beta_{n-1} s + \beta_n}{s^n + \alpha_1 s^{n-1} + \cdots + \alpha_{n-1} s + \alpha_n}$$

unique? If not, explain how three different state variable descriptions for the given transfer function can be obtained.

12.5 (a) Many CAD packages use state variable equations to compute the response of $G(s)$ to an input $R(s)$; inverse Laplace transformation is not preferred. Why? (Help: p774, p790)

(b) Why are some state variable models called canonical? (Help: p784)

(c) A state variable model that has a prescribed rational function $G(s)$ as its transfer function, is called the realization of $G(s)$. Explain the use of the term 'realization'. (Help: pp790-791)

12.6 (a) Write two $n \times n$ general matrices, one having companion form and the other having Jordan form structure.

(b) An nth order state variable model in Jordan canonical form always yields n decoupled first-order differential equations. Is the statement true? Justify your answer.

12.7 Given a single-input state variable equation

$$\dot{\mathbf{x}} = \mathbf{A}\mathbf{x} + \mathbf{b}u$$

Prove that

$$\mathbf{x}(t) = e^{\mathbf{A}t}\,\mathbf{x}(0) + \int_0^t e^{\mathbf{A}(t-\tau)}\mathbf{b}\,u(\tau)\,d\tau$$

Comment upon the convergence property of the infinite series (Help: pp804-805)

$$e^{\mathbf{A}t} = \mathbf{I} + \mathbf{A}t + \frac{1}{2!}\,\mathbf{A}^2t^2 + \cdots + \frac{1}{k!}\,\mathbf{A}^kt^k + \cdots$$

12.8 List the properties of the state transition matrix

$$\phi(t) = e^{\mathbf{A}t}$$

of the system

$$\dot{\mathbf{x}} = \mathbf{A}\mathbf{x}; \mathbf{x}(0) \overset{\Delta}{=} \mathbf{x}^0$$

Prove that

$$e^{\mathbf{A}t} = \mathscr{L}^{-1}\,|(s\mathbf{I} - \mathbf{A})^{-1}|$$

Why is the matrix exponential $e^{\mathbf{A}t}$ called the state transition matrix? (Help: p806)

12.9 Given a single-input state equation

$$\dot{\mathbf{x}} = \mathbf{A}\mathbf{x} + \mathbf{b}u$$

For discrete-time solution, the equation can be discretized to the following form:

$$\mathbf{x}(kT + T) = \mathbf{F}\mathbf{x}(kT) + \mathbf{g}u(kT); \ T = \text{sampling interval.}$$

Find the matrices $\mathbf{F}$ and $\mathbf{g}$.

12.10 Consider the state equation of a single-input system which includes delay in control action:

$$\dot{\mathbf{x}} = \mathbf{A}\mathbf{x} + \mathbf{b}u(t - \tau_D)$$

For discrete-time solution, the equation can be discretized to the following form:

$$\mathbf{x}(kT + T) = \mathbf{F}\mathbf{x}(kT) + \mathbf{g}_1u(kT - NT - T) + \mathbf{g}_2u\,(kT - NT);$$

T = sampling interval; $\tau_D = NT + \Delta T, 0 \le \Delta < 1$. Find the matrices $\mathbf{F}$, $\mathbf{g}_1$ and $\mathbf{g}_2$.

12.11 A system is described by the single-input single-output state variable model

$$\dot{\mathbf{x}} = \mathbf{A}\mathbf{x} + \mathbf{b}u$$

$$y = \mathbf{c}\mathbf{x}$$

What is the motivation behind the concept of controllability of the system? Give a precise definition of controllability and describe a controllability test in terms of matrices $\mathbf{A}$ and $\mathbf{b}$.

Prove that controllability property is invariant under state transformation $\mathbf{x} = \mathbf{P}\bar{\mathbf{x}}$; $\mathbf{P}$ is a constant nonsingular matrix.

12.12 A system is described by the single-input single-output state variable model

$$\dot{\mathbf{x}} = \mathbf{A}\mathbf{x} + \mathbf{b}u$$

$$y = \mathbf{c}\mathbf{x}$$

What is the motivation behind the concept of observability? Give a precise definition of observability and describe an observability test in terms of matrices $\mathbf{A}$ and $\mathbf{c}$.

Prove that observability property is invariant under state transformation $\mathbf{x} = \mathbf{P\bar{x}}$; $\mathbf{P}$ is a constant nonsingular matrix.

12.13 (a) Show that if a continuous-time linear time-invariant system is asymptotically stable, it is also BIBO stable. (Help: p828)

(b) Show that a BIBO stable continuous-time linear time-invariant system is asymptotically stable only if the system is completely controllable and completely observable. (Help: p828)

12.14 Prove that the transfer function model of the single-input single-output system

$$\dot{\mathbf{x}} = \mathbf{Ax} + \mathbf{b}u$$

$$y = \mathbf{cx}$$

is a complete characterization of the system only if the system is both controllable and observable. (Help: p828)

12.15 (a) An nth order single-input single-output system

$$\dot{\mathbf{x}} = \mathbf{Ax} + \mathbf{b}u$$

$$y = \mathbf{cx}$$

is found to be uncontrollable. On further analysis, it is found that m eigenvalues of $\mathbf{A}$ are controllable and $(n-m)$ eigenvalues of $\mathbf{A}$ are uncontrollable. Both the subsets of eigenvalues, controllable and uncontrollable, have some unstable eigenvalues. Can you design a stabilizing controller for such a system? Justify your answer.

(b) If the uncontrollable eigenvalues of the system are found to be stable, then a stabilizing controller can always be designed. Do you agree with this statement? Justify your answer.

(c) If the system turns out to be unobservable, it means that the plant can never be operated in a satisfactory manner. Do you agree with this statement? Justify your answer.

Problems

12.1 Figure P12.1 shows a control scheme for controlling the azimuth angle of a rotating antenna. The plant consists of an armature-controlled dc motor with dc generator used as an amplifier. The parameters of the plant are given below:

Motor torque constant, $K_T = 1.2$ N-m/amp

Motor back emf constant, $K_b = 1.2$ V/(rad/sec)

Generator gain constant, $K_g = 100$ V/amp

Motor to load gear ratio, $n = \left(\dot{\theta}_L / \dot{\theta}_M\right) = 1/2$

$R_f = 21\,\Omega, L_f = 5\text{H}, R_g = 9\,\Omega, L_g = 0.06\,\text{H}, R_a = 10\,\Omega, L_a = 0.04\,\text{H},$
$J = 1.6$ N-m/(rad/sec^2), $B = 0.04$ N-m/(rad/sec), motor inertia and friction are negligible.

Taking physically meaningful and measurable variables as state variables, derive a state model for the system.

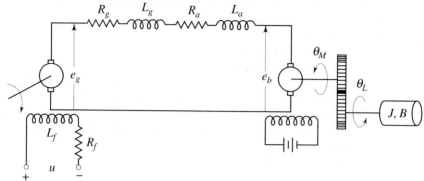

Fig. P12.1

12.2 Figure P12.2 shows a position control system with state variable feedback. The plant consists of a field-controlled dc motor with a dc amplifier. The parameters of the plant are given below:

Amplifier gain, $K_A = 50$ volt/volt
Motor field resistance, $R_f = 99\ \Omega$
Motor field inductance, $L_f = 20\ \text{H}$
Motor torque constant, $K_T = 10\ \text{N-m/amp}$
Moment of inertia of load, $J = 0.5\ \text{N-m/(rad/sec}^2)$
Coefficient of viscous friction of load, $B = 0.5\ \text{N-m/(rad/sec)}$
Motor inertia and friction are negligible.

Taking $x_1 = \theta$, $x_2 = \dot{\theta}$, and $x_3 = i_f$ as the state variables, $u = e_f$ as the input, and $y = \theta$ as the output, derive a state variable model for the plant.

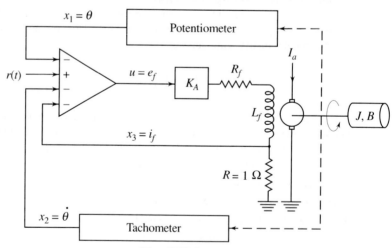

Fig. P12.2

12.3 Figure P12.3 shows the block diagram of a motor-driven single-link robot manipulator with position and velocity feedback. The drive motor is an armature controlled dc motor; e_a is armature voltage, i_a is armature current, θ_M is the motor shaft position and $\dot{\theta}_M$ is motor shaft velocity. θ_L is the position of the robot arm.

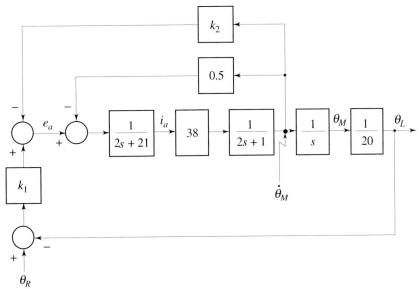

Fig. P12.3

Taking θ_M, $\dot{\theta}_M$ and i_a as state variables, derive a state model for the feedback system.

12.4 Figure P12.4 shows the block diagram of a speed control system with state variable feedback. The drive motor is an armature-controlled dc motor with armature resistance R_a, armature inductance L_a, motor torque constant K_T, inertia referred to motor shaft J, viscous friction coefficient referred to motor shaft B, back emf constant K_b, and tachometer constant K_t. The applied armature voltage is controlled by a three-phase full-converter. We have assumed a linear relationship between the control voltage e_c and the armature voltage e_a. e_r is the reference voltage corresponding to the desired speed.

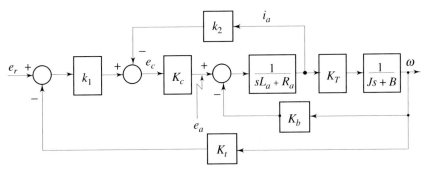

Fig. P12.4

Taking $x_1 = \omega$ (speed) and $x_2 = i_a$ (armature current) as the state variables, $u = e_r$ as the input, and $y = \omega$ as the output, derive a state variable model for the feedback system.

12.5 Consider the system

$$\dot{\mathbf{x}} = \begin{bmatrix} -3 & 1 \\ -2 & 0 \end{bmatrix} \mathbf{x} + \begin{bmatrix} 0 \\ 1 \end{bmatrix} u$$

$$y = [1 \quad 0] \, \mathbf{x}$$

A similarity transformation is defined by

$$\mathbf{x} = \mathbf{P}\bar{\mathbf{x}} = \begin{bmatrix} 2 & -1 \\ -1 & 1 \end{bmatrix} \bar{\mathbf{x}}$$

(a) Express the state model in terms of the states $\bar{\mathbf{x}}(t)$.

(b) Draw state diagrams in signal flow graph form for the state models in $\mathbf{x}(t)$ and $\bar{\mathbf{x}}(t)$.

(c) Show by Mason's gain formula that the transfer functions for the two state diagrams in (b) are equal.

12.6 Consider a double-integrator plant described by the differential equation

$$\frac{d^2\theta(t)}{dt^2} = u(t)$$

(a) Develop a state equation for this system with u as the input, and θ and $\dot{\theta}$ as the state variables x_1 and x_2 respectively.

(b) A similarity transformation is defined as

$$\mathbf{x} = \mathbf{P}\bar{\mathbf{x}} = \begin{bmatrix} 1 & 0 \\ 1 & 1 \end{bmatrix} \bar{\mathbf{x}}$$

Express the state equation in terms of the states $\bar{\mathbf{x}}(t)$.

(c) Show that the eigenvalues of the system matrices of the two state equations in (a) and (b) are equal.

12.7 A system is described by the state equation

$$\dot{\mathbf{x}} = \begin{bmatrix} 0 & 1 & 0 \\ 0 & 0 & 1 \\ -1 & 0 & -3 \end{bmatrix} \mathbf{x} + \begin{bmatrix} 0 \\ 0 \\ 1 \end{bmatrix} u \; ; \mathbf{x}(0) = \mathbf{x}^0$$

Using the Laplace transform technique, transform the state equation into a set of linear algebraic equations in the form

$$\mathbf{X}(s) = \mathbf{G}(s)\mathbf{x}^0 + \mathbf{H}(s) \, U(s)$$

12.8 Give a block diagram for the programming of the system of Problem 12.7 on an analog computer.

12.9 The state diagram of a linear system is shown in Fig. P12.9. Assign the state variables and write the dynamic equations of the system.

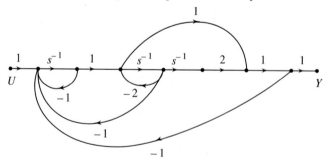

Fig. P 12.9

12.10   Derive transfer functions corresponding to the following state models:

(a)
$$\dot{\mathbf{x}} = \begin{bmatrix} 0 & 1 \\ -2 & -3 \end{bmatrix} \mathbf{x} + \begin{bmatrix} 1 \\ 0 \end{bmatrix} u; \, y = [1 \ 0] \, \mathbf{x}$$

(b)
$$\dot{\mathbf{x}} = \begin{bmatrix} -3 & 1 \\ -2 & 0 \end{bmatrix} \mathbf{x} + \begin{bmatrix} 0 \\ 1 \end{bmatrix} u; \, y = [1 \ 0] \mathbf{x}$$

12.11   Figure P12.11 shows the block diagram of a control system with state variable
feedback and integral control. The plant model is:

$$\begin{bmatrix} \dot{x}_1 \\ \dot{x}_2 \end{bmatrix} = \begin{bmatrix} -3 & 2 \\ 4 & -5 \end{bmatrix} \begin{bmatrix} x_1 \\ x_2 \end{bmatrix} + \begin{bmatrix} 1 \\ 0 \end{bmatrix} u$$

$$y = [\, 0 \qquad 1\,] \mathbf{x}$$

(a)   Derive a state model of the feedback system.

(b)   Derive the transfer function $Y(s)/R(s)$.

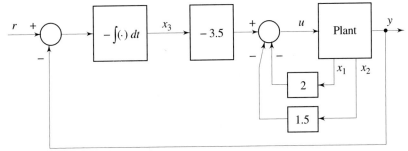

Fig. P12.11

12.12   Construct state models for the systems of Fig. P12.12a and Fig. P12.12b, taking
outputs of simple lag blocks as state variables.

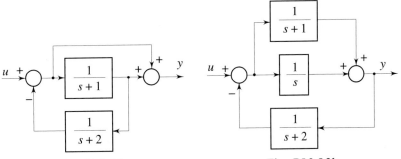

Fig. P12.12a   **Fig. P12.12b**

12.13   Construct state models for the following transfer functions. Obtain different
canonical form for each system.

(i) $\dfrac{s+3}{s^2 + 3s + 2}$

(ii) $\dfrac{5}{(s+1)^2 (s+2)}$

(iii) $\dfrac{s^3 + 8s^2 + 17s + 8}{(s+1)(s+2)(s+3)}$

Give block diagrams for the analog computer simulation of these transfer functions.

12.14   Construct state models for the following differential equations. Obtain a different canonical form for each system.

     (i) $\dddot{y} + 3\ddot{y} + 2\dot{y} = \dot{u} + u$

     (i) $\dddot{y} + 6\ddot{y} + 11\dot{y} + 6y = u$

     (iii) $\dddot{y} + 6\ddot{y} + 11\dot{y} + 6y = \ddot{u} + 8\dot{u} + 17\dot{u} + 8u$

12.15   Derive two state models for the system with transfer function

$$\frac{Y(s)}{U(s)} = \frac{50(1 + s/5)}{s(1 + s/2)(1 + s/50)}$$

     (a)   One for which the system matrix is a companion matrix.

     (b)   One for which the system matrix is diagonal.

12.16   (a)   Obtain state variable model in Jordan canonical form for the system with transfer function

$$\frac{Y(s)}{U(s)} = \frac{2s^2 + 6s + 5}{(s+1)^2(s+2)}$$

     (b)   Find the response $y(t)$ to a unit-step input using the state variable model in (a)

     (c)   Give a block diagram for analog computer simulation of the transfer function.

12.17   Consider a continuous-time system

$$\dot{\mathbf{x}}(t) = \begin{bmatrix} -2 & 2 \\ 1 & -3 \end{bmatrix} \mathbf{x}(t) + \begin{bmatrix} -1 \\ 5 \end{bmatrix} u(t)$$

$$y(t) = [2 \quad -4]\, \mathbf{x}(t) + 6u(t)$$

Discretizing time axis into intervals of $T = 0.2$ sec, obtain state transition and output equations that yield discrete-time solutions for $\mathbf{x}(t)$ and $y(t)$.

12.18   The mathematical model of the plant of a control system is given below:

$$\frac{Y(s)}{U(s)} = G(s) = \frac{e^{-0.4s}}{s+1}$$

For digital simulation of the plant, obtain a difference equation model with $T = 1$ sec as the sampling interval.

12.19   Given the system

$$\dot{\mathbf{x}} = \begin{bmatrix} -2 & 1 \\ 1 & -2 \end{bmatrix} \mathbf{x} + \begin{bmatrix} 1 \\ 1 \end{bmatrix} u$$

     (a)   Obtain a state diagram in signal flow graph form.

     (b)   From the signal flow graph, determine the state equation in the form

$$\mathbf{X}(s) = \mathbf{G}(s)\mathbf{x}(0) + \mathbf{H}(s)U(s)$$

     (c)   Using inverse Laplace transformation, obtain the

         (i)   zero-input response to initial condition

$$\mathbf{x}(0) = \begin{bmatrix} x_1^0 & x_2^0 \end{bmatrix}^T ; \text{ and}$$

         (ii)   zero-state response to unit-step input.

12.20 Consider the system

$$\dot{\mathbf{x}} = \begin{bmatrix} 0 & 1 \\ -2 & -3 \end{bmatrix} \mathbf{x} + \begin{bmatrix} 0 \\ 1 \end{bmatrix} u \; ; \; \mathbf{x}(0) = \begin{bmatrix} 1 \\ 1 \end{bmatrix}$$

$$y = [1 \; 0]\mathbf{x}$$

(a) Determine the stability of the system.

(b) Find the output response of the system to unit-step input.

12.21 Figure P12.21 shows the block diagram of a control system with state variable feedback and feedforward control. The plant model is

$$\dot{\mathbf{x}} = \begin{bmatrix} -3 & 2 \\ 4 & -5 \end{bmatrix} \mathbf{x} + \begin{bmatrix} 1 \\ 0 \end{bmatrix} u$$

$$y = [0 \; 1]\mathbf{x}$$

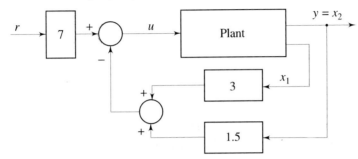

Fig. P12.21

(a) Derive a state model for the feedback system.

(b) Find the output $y(t)$ of the feedback system to a unit-step input $r(t)$; the initial state is assumed to be zero.

12.22 Consider the state equation

$$\dot{\mathbf{x}} = \begin{bmatrix} 0 & 1 \\ -1 & -2 \end{bmatrix} \mathbf{x}$$

Find a set of states $x_1(1)$ and $x_2(1)$ such that $x_1(2) = 2$.

12.23 The following facts are known about the linear system

$$\dot{\mathbf{x}}(t) = \mathbf{A}\mathbf{x}(t)$$

If $\mathbf{x}(0) = \begin{bmatrix} 1 \\ -2 \end{bmatrix}$, then $\mathbf{x}(t) = \begin{bmatrix} e^{-2t} \\ -2e^{-2t} \end{bmatrix}$

If $\mathbf{x}(0) = \begin{bmatrix} 1 \\ -1 \end{bmatrix}$, then $\mathbf{x}(t) = \begin{bmatrix} e^{-t} \\ -e^{-t} \end{bmatrix}$

Find $e^{\mathbf{A}t}$ and hence $\mathbf{A}$.

12.24 Show that the pair $\{\mathbf{A}, \mathbf{c}\}$ is completely observable for all values of α_i's.

$$\mathbf{A} = \begin{bmatrix} 0 & 0 & 0 & \cdots & 0 & -\alpha_n \\ 1 & 0 & 0 & \cdots & 0 & -\alpha_{n-1} \\ 0 & 1 & 0 & \cdots & 0 & -\alpha_{n-2} \\ \vdots & \vdots & \vdots & & \vdots & \vdots \\ 0 & 0 & 0 & \cdots & 0 & -\alpha_2 \\ 0 & 0 & 0 & \cdots & 1 & -\alpha_1 \end{bmatrix}$$

$$\mathbf{c} = [0 \; 0 \; \cdots \; 0 \; 1]$$

12.25   Show that the pair {**A**, **b**} is completely controllable for all values of α_i's.

$$\mathbf{A} = \begin{bmatrix} 0 & 1 & 0 & \cdots & 0 \\ 0 & 0 & 1 & \cdots & 0 \\ \vdots & \vdots & \vdots & & \vdots \\ 0 & 0 & 0 & \cdots & 1 \\ -\alpha_n & -\alpha_{n-1} & -\alpha_{n-2} & \cdots & -\alpha_1 \end{bmatrix}; \mathbf{b} = \begin{bmatrix} 0 \\ 0 \\ \vdots \\ 0 \\ 1 \end{bmatrix}$$

12.26   Determine the controllability and observability properties of the following systems:

(i) $\mathbf{A} = \begin{bmatrix} -2 & 1 \\ 1 & -2 \end{bmatrix}; \mathbf{b} = \begin{bmatrix} 1 \\ 0 \end{bmatrix}; \mathbf{c} = \begin{bmatrix} 1 & -1 \end{bmatrix}$

(ii) $\mathbf{A} = \begin{bmatrix} -1 & 0 \\ 0 & -2 \end{bmatrix}; \mathbf{b} = \begin{bmatrix} 2 \\ 5 \end{bmatrix}; \mathbf{c} = \begin{bmatrix} 0 & 1 \end{bmatrix}$

(iii) $\mathbf{A} = \begin{bmatrix} 0 & 1 & 0 \\ 0 & 0 & 1 \\ 0 & -2 & -3 \end{bmatrix}; \mathbf{b} = \begin{bmatrix} 0 \\ 0 \\ 1 \end{bmatrix}; \mathbf{c} = \begin{bmatrix} 10 & 0 & 0 \end{bmatrix}$

(iv) $\mathbf{A} = \begin{bmatrix} 0 & 0 & 0 \\ 1 & 0 & -3 \\ 0 & 1 & -4 \end{bmatrix}; \mathbf{b} = \begin{bmatrix} 40 \\ 10 \\ 0 \end{bmatrix}; \mathbf{c} = \begin{bmatrix} 0 & 0 & 1 \end{bmatrix}$

12.27   The following models realize the transfer function $G(s) = \dfrac{1}{s+1}$.

(i) $\mathbf{A} = \begin{bmatrix} -2 & 1 \\ 1 & -2 \end{bmatrix}; \mathbf{b} = \begin{bmatrix} 1 \\ 1 \end{bmatrix}; \mathbf{c} = \begin{bmatrix} 0 & 1 \end{bmatrix}$

(ii) $\mathbf{A} = \begin{bmatrix} -1 & 0 \\ 0 & -3 \end{bmatrix}; \mathbf{b} = \begin{bmatrix} 1 \\ 1 \end{bmatrix}; \mathbf{c} = \begin{bmatrix} 1 & 0 \end{bmatrix}$

(iii) $\mathbf{A} = \begin{bmatrix} -2 & 0 \\ 0 & -1 \end{bmatrix}; \mathbf{b} = \begin{bmatrix} 0 \\ 1 \end{bmatrix}; \mathbf{c} = \begin{bmatrix} 0 & 1 \end{bmatrix}$

Investigate the controllability and observability properties of these models. Find a state variable model for the given transfer function which is both controllable and observable.

12.28   Consider the systems

(i) $\mathbf{A} = \begin{bmatrix} 0 & -2 \\ 1 & -3 \end{bmatrix}; \mathbf{b} = \begin{bmatrix} 1 \\ 1 \end{bmatrix}; \mathbf{c} = \begin{bmatrix} 0 & 1 \end{bmatrix}$

(ii) $\mathbf{A} = \begin{bmatrix} 0 & 1 & 0 \\ 0 & 0 & 1 \\ -6 & -11 & -6 \end{bmatrix}; \mathbf{b} = \begin{bmatrix} 0 \\ 0 \\ 1 \end{bmatrix}; \mathbf{c} = \begin{bmatrix} 4 & 5 & 1 \end{bmatrix}$

Determine the transfer function in each case. What can we say about controllability and observability properties without making any further calculations?

12.29 Consider the system

$$\dot{\mathbf{x}} = \begin{bmatrix} 1 & 1 & 0 \\ 0 & -2 & 1 \\ 0 & 0 & -1 \end{bmatrix} \mathbf{x} + \begin{bmatrix} 0 \\ 1 \\ -2 \end{bmatrix} u \; ; y = \begin{bmatrix} 1 & 0 & 0 \end{bmatrix} \mathbf{x}$$

(a) Find the eigenvalues of **A** and from there determine the stability of the system.
(b) Find the transfer function model and from there determine the stability of the system.
(c) Are the two results same? If not, why?

12.30 Given a transfer function

$$G(s) = \frac{10}{s(s+1)} = \frac{Y(s)}{U(s)}$$

Construct three different state models for this system:
(a) One which is both controllable and observable.
(b) One which is controllable but not observable.
(c) One which is observable but not controllable.

Appendix A

Mathematical Background

A.1 INTRODUCTION

In an attempt to make the book reasonably self-contained, we present in this appendix the background material that is needed for the analysis and design of control systems. Our treatment will be fairly rapid, as we shall assume that the reader has been exposed to some of the mathematical notions we need. Also, our treatment will be incomplete in the sense that mathematical rigour will be missing. The appendix should serve as a working reference.

A.2 FUNCTIONS OF A COMPLEX VARIABLE

As many of the techniques used in the analysis of time-invariant linear systems have their foundations in the theory of functions of a complex variable, we shall state the properties and prove the theorems that are of use to us in this book. However, a complete coverage of the subject is not attempted, and the reader is referred to any standard text for further coverage, e.g., Churchill *et al.* [35].

Let $s = \sigma + j\omega$ denote a complex variable. Another complex variable $W = U + jV$ is said to be *function of the complex variable s* if, to each value of s in some set, there corresponds a value, or a set of values, of W. We denote the rule of correspondence between s and W by writing $W = F(s)$. If for each value of s there is only one value of W, then $F(s)$ is said to be a *single-valued* function of s. Complex functions commonly encountered in control systems are single-valued functions. Our work will be limited to three classes of functions: polynomials, rational functions (ratios of polynomials), and exponentials.

The functional relationship $W = F(s)$ can be interpreted as a mapping of points in the s-plane into points in the W-plane, or the $F(s)$-plane. Figure A.1 shows a point P in the s-plane and a corresponding point P' in the $F(s)$-plane. We call P' the image of P.

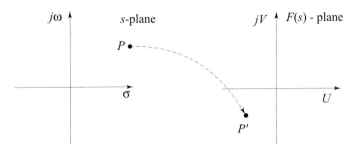

Fig. A.1 *Single-valued mapping from the s-plane to the F(s)-plane*

A function $F(s)$ is said to be *analytic (regular)* at a point s_0 if it is defined at $s = s_0$ and the derivative dF/ds is continuous at every point in neighbourhood of s_0. A function $F(s)$ that is analytic at every point of a domain D in the s-plane, is said to be analytic in D.

It can be proved that the sum and product of functions that are analytic in some domain are also analytic. As the function $F(s) = s$ is analytic everywhere in the finite s-plane, it follows that all polynomials in s are analytic everywhere in the finite s-plane. Furthermore, it can be shown that the quotient to two analytic functions is analytic everywhere except at those points for which the denominator vanishes. Hence, any rational function of s is analytic everywhere except at the roots of the denominator polynomial.

Points in the s-plane at which a function $F(s)$ is analytic are the *ordinary points*, while the points at which the function is not analytic are referred to as *singularities*. If $F(s)$ has a singularity at the point s_0 but is analytic everywhere else in the neighbourhood of the point, then s_0 is said to be an *isolated singularity*. We shall concern ourselves exclusively with this type of singular points.

A function $F(s)$ is said to have a *pole* of order n at $s = s_0$ if it is analytic in the neighbourhood of s_0 except at s_0, and

$$\lim_{s \to s_0} [(s - s_0)^n F(s)]$$

has a finite nonzero value. In other words, the denominator of $F(s)$ must include the factor $(s - s_0)^n$, so that when $s = s_0$ the function becomes infinite. If $n = 1$, the pole at $s = s_0$ is called a *simple pole*.
For example,

$$F(s) = \frac{10(s + 1)}{s(s + 2)^2} \tag{A.1}$$

has a second-order pole at $s = -2$ and a simple pole at $s = 0$. $F(s)$ is analytic in the s-plane except at these singularities.

A function $F(s)$ is said to have a *zero* of order m at $s = s_1$ if it approaches zero as s approaches s_1, and

$$\lim_{s \to s_1} [(s - s_1)^{-m} F(s)]$$

has a finite nonzero value. If $m = 1$, the zero at $s = s_1$ is called a *simple zero*. For example, the function of Eqn. (A.1) has a simple zero at $s = -1$.

If $F(s)$ is a rational function of s, i.e., a ratio of two polynomials of s, the total number of poles equals the total number of zeros (counting the multiple-order poles and zeros) when the s-palne includes the points at infinity. The function $F(s)$ given by Eqn. (A.1) has two zeros at infinity, since

$$\lim_{s \to \infty} F(s) = \lim_{s \to \infty} \frac{10}{s^2} = 0$$

Therefore $F(s)$ of Eqn. (A.1) has three poles and three zeros (one finite zero at $s = -1$, and two zeros at infinity).

Partial Fraction Expansion

In the analysis of linear time-invariant systems, we very often encounter rational fractions of the form:

$$F(s) = \frac{b_0 s^m + b_1 s^{m-1} + \cdots + b_{m-1} s + b_m}{s^n + a_1 s^{n-1} + \cdots + a_{n-1} s + a_n} = \frac{N(s)}{\Delta(s)} \qquad (A.2)$$

where the coefficients a_i and b_i are real constants, and m and n are integers with $m < n$.

A fraction of the form given in Eqn. (A.2) can be expanded into partial fractions. To do this, first of all we factorize the polynomial $\Delta(s)$ into n first-order factors. The roots of $\Delta(s)$, which are the poles of $F(s)$, can be real, complex, distinct or repeated. Various cases are discussed below.

Case I: $\Delta(s)$ has distinct roots

For this case, Eqn. (A.2) can be written as

$$F(s) = \frac{N(s)}{\Delta(s)} = \frac{N(s)}{(s + p_1)(s + p_2) \cdots (s + p_k) \cdots (s + p_n)} \qquad (A.3)$$

which when expanded, gives

$$F(s) = \frac{A_1}{s + p_1} + \frac{A_2}{s + p_2} + \cdots + \frac{A_k}{s + p_k} + \cdots + \frac{A_n}{s + p_n} \qquad (A.4)$$

The coefficient A_k is called the *residue* of $F(s)$ at the pole $s = -p_k$.
Multiplying both sides of Eqn. (A.4) by $(s + p_k)$ and letting $s = -p_k$, gives

$$A_k = [(s + p_k) F(s)]|_{s = -p_k} \qquad (A.5)$$

Case II: $\Delta(s)$ has complex conjugate roots

Suppose that there is a pair of complex conjugate roots in $\Delta(s)$ given by $s = -a - j\omega$, and $s = -a + j\omega$.

Then $F(s)$ can be written as

$$F(s) = \frac{N(s)}{\Delta(s)} = \frac{N(s)}{(s + a + j\omega)(s + a - j\omega)(s + p_3)\cdots(s + p_n)} \qquad (A.6)$$

which when expanded, gives

$$F(s) = \frac{A_1}{s + a + j\omega} + \frac{A_1^*}{s + a - j\omega} + \frac{A_3}{s + p_3} + \cdots + \frac{A_n}{s + p_n} \qquad (A.7)$$

where A_1 and A_1^* are residues of $F(s)$ at the poles $s = -a - j\omega$ and $s = -a + j\omega$ respectively. These residues form a complex conjugate pair.

As per Eqn. (A.5), the residue A_1 is given by

$$A_1 = [(s + a + j\omega)\, F(s)]|_{s = -(a + j\omega)} \qquad (A.8)$$

A_1^* is obtained by taking complex conjugate of A_1.

The residues $A_3, \ldots, A_n$ of $F(s)$ at the simple real poles $s = -p_3, \ldots, -p_n$, respectively, can be evaluated using the relation (A.5).

Case III: $\Delta(s)$ has repeated roots

Assume that the root p_1 of $\Delta(s)$ is of multiplicity r and all other roots are distinct. The function $F(s)$ can then be written as

$$F(s) = \frac{N(s)}{\Delta(s)} = \frac{N(s)}{(s + p_1)^r (s + p_{r+1})\cdots(s + p_n)} \qquad (A.9)$$

which when expanded, gives

$$F(s) = \frac{A_{1(r)}}{(s + p_1)^r} + \frac{A_{1(r-1)}}{(s + p_1)^{r-1}} + \cdots + \frac{A_{12}}{(s + p_1)^2}$$

$$+ \frac{A_{11}}{s + p_1} + \frac{A_{r+1}}{s + p_{r+1}} + \cdots + \frac{A_n}{s + p_n} \qquad (A.10)$$

$A_{r+1}, \ldots, A_n$ are the residues of $F(s)$ at the simple poles $s = -p_{r+1}, \ldots, -p_n$, respectively, and can be evaluated using the relation (A.5).

Multiplying both sides of Eqn. (A.10) by $(s + p_1)^r$, we obtain

$$(s + p_1)^r F(s) = A_{1(r)} + (s + p_1) A_{1(r-1)} + \cdots + (s + p_1)^{r-2} A_{12}$$

$$+ (s + p_1)^{r-1} A_{11} + \cdots \qquad (A.11)$$

Letting $s = -p_1$ in Eqn. (A.11), gives

$$A_{1(r)} = [(s + p_1)^r F(s)]|_{s = -p_1} \qquad (A.12)$$

Taking derivative of both sides of Eqn. (A.11) and letting $s = -p_1$, we obtain

$$A_{1(r-1)} = \frac{d}{ds} [(s + p_1)^r F(s)]|_{s = -p_1}$$

Following relations easily follow from Eqn. (A.11).

$$A_{1(r-2)} = \frac{1}{2!} \frac{d^2}{ds^2} [(s + p_1)^r F(s)]|_{s = -p_1} \qquad (A.13)$$

$$\vdots$$

$$A_{11} = \frac{1}{(r-1)!} \frac{d^{r-1}}{ds^{r-1}} [(s+p_1)^r F(s)]\Big|_{s=-p_1}$$

The general term is

$$A_{1(r-i)} = \frac{1}{i!} \frac{d^i}{ds^i} [(s+p_1)^r F(s)]\Big|_{s=-p_1}; \qquad (A.14)$$

$$i = 0, 1, 2, \ldots, r-1$$

A_{11} is the residue of $F(s)$ at the multiple-order pole $s = -p_1$.

Mapping of s-plane Contours

An analytic function $F(s)$ maps points, paths or domains of s-plane onto $F(s)$-plane. The mapping is *conformal* in the sense that the $F(s)$-plane image 'conforms' with the s-plane counterpart: a continuous path from s_1 to s_2 in the s-plane has a continuous image from $F(s_1)$ to $F(s_2)$ in the $F(s)$-plane; for a sharp turn in the s-plane path, there is a corresponding sharp turn in the $F(s)$-plane image; for a closed contour in the s-plane, the image in the $F(s)$-plane is also a closed contour. It is however necessary that the contours in the s-plane do not pass through the singularities of $F(s)$.

Figure A.2 gives a simple example of conformal mapping. The mapping function is

$$F(s) = \frac{s+2}{s}$$

The s-plane contours in Fig. A.2 do not pass through the singularity (the pole at $s = 0$) of $F(s)$.

A point or an area is said to be *enclosed* by a closed path if it is found to lie to the right of the path when the path is traversed in the clockwise direction[1].

As per this convention, the pole of $F(s)$ at $s = 0$ is enclosed by the s-plane contour shown in Fig. A.2a while the zero of $F(s)$ at $s = -2$ is not enclosed. The s-plane contour of Fig. A.2b encloses both the pole and the zero of $F(s)$. The s-plane contour of Fig. A.2c encloses the zero of $F(s)$ but does not enclose the pole. Figure A.2d shows an s-plane contour which does not enclose either the pole or the zero of $F(s)$.

From the mapping of s-plane contour shown in Fig. A.2, it is obvious that $F(s)$-plane contours conform to the corresponding s-plane contours in terms of the sense of angles; the overall shape, of course, gets distorted.

One feature of $F(s)$-plane contours is of special interest to us: whether the contour encircles the origin of the $F(s)$-plane or not. In Fig. A.2a, the $F(s)$-plane contour encircles the origin of the $F(s)$-plane once in the counter-clock-

---

1. This convention is opposite to that usually employed in complex variable theory, but is equally applicable and is generally used in control system theory.

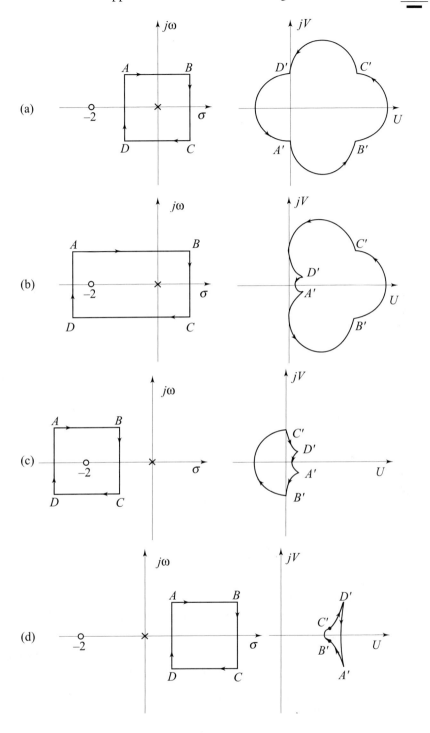

Fig. A.2 *Mapping of s-plane contours by F(s) = (s + 2)/s*

wise direction. In Fig. A.2b, the $F(s)$-plane contour does not encircle the origin of the $F(s)$-plane. In Fig. A.2c, the $F(s)$-plane contour encircles the origin of the $F(s)$-plane once in the clockwise direction. The $F(s)$-plane contour in Fig. A.2d does not encircle the origin of the $F(s)$-plane.

The well-known principle of argument in complex variable theory gives a relation between the enclosure of poles and zeros of $F(s)$ by an s-plane contour and the encirclements of the origin of the $F(s)$-plane image. In the following, we establish this relation for rational functions. The results are, however, valid for other analytic functions also.

The Principle of Argument

Let $F(s)$ be a ratio of polynomials in s. Let P be the number of poles and Z be the number of zeros of $F(s)$ which are enclosed by a simple[2] closed contour in the s-plane, multiplicity accounted for. Let the closed contour be such that it does not pass through any poles or zeros of $F(s)$. The s-plane contour then maps into the $F(s)$-plane as a closed curve.

The number N of clockwise encirclements of the origin of $F(s)$-plane, as a representative point s traces out the entire contour in the s-plane in the clockwise direction, is equal to $Z–P$.

The proof needs Cauchy's integral theorem, and residue theorem.

Cauchy's Integral Theorem

Let $F(s)$ be analytic everywhere on and within a simple closed contour C. Then

$$\oint_C F(s)ds = 0 \qquad \text{(A.15)}$$

where $\oint_C$ denotes the line integral in clockwise direction along C.

Residue Theorem

Let $F(s)$ be analytic everywhere on and within a simple closed contour C except at the isolated singular points $s_1, s_2, \ldots, s_N$. Then

$$\oint_C F(s)ds = -2\pi j \sum_{n=1}^{N} A_n \qquad \text{(A.16)}$$

where $A_1, A_2, \ldots, A_n$ are the residues of $F(s)$ at $s_1, s_2, \ldots, s_N$ respectively. These singularities are poles of $F(s)$.

If the direction of integration is reversed, the sign of right hand side of Eqn. (A.16) must be reserved.

▲▲

Since $F(s)$ is a rational function of s, it can be written as

$$F(s) = \frac{(s + z_1)^{r_1} (s + z_2)^{r_2} \cdots}{(s + p_1)^{m_1} (s + p_2)^{m_2} \cdots} G(s) \qquad \text{(A.17)}$$

2. By simple, we mean that the contour does not cross itself.

where $G(s)$ is analytic in the area enclosed by simple closed contour in the s-plane and all the multiple-order poles at $s = -p_1, -p_2, \ldots$, and multiple-order zeros at $s = -z_1, -z_2, \ldots$, are enclosed by the s-plane contour.

The ratio $F'(s)/F(s); F'(s) \triangleq \dfrac{dF(s)}{ds}$, can be written as

$$\frac{F'(s)}{F(s)} = \left(\frac{r_1}{s + z_1} + \frac{r_2}{s + z_2} + \cdots \right) - \left(\frac{m_1}{s + p_1} + \frac{m_2}{s + p_2} + \cdots \right) + \frac{G'(s)}{G(s)} \qquad (A.18)$$

This may be seen from the following consideration:

If $F(s)$ is given by

$$F(s) = (s + z)^r G(s) \qquad (A.19)$$

then $F(s)$ has a zero of rth-order at $s = -z$. Differentiating $F(s)$ with respect to s yields

$$F'(s) = r(s + z)^{r-1} G(s) + (s + z)^r G'(s)$$

Hence,

$$\frac{F'(s)}{F(s)} = \frac{r}{s + z} + \frac{G'(s)}{G(s)} \qquad (A.20)$$

We see that by taking the ratio $F'(s)/F(s)$, the rth-order zero of $F(s)$ becomes a simple pole of $F'(s)/F(s)$. Since the last term on the right-hand side of Eqn. (A.20) is analytic in the area enclosed by the s-plane closed contour, $F'(s)/F(s)$ is analytic in this area except at the singularity at $s = -z$. Then

$$\oint_C \frac{F'(s)}{F(s)} ds = \oint_C \frac{r}{s + z} ds + \oint_C \frac{G'(s)}{G(s)} ds = -2\pi j r$$

Referring to Eqn. (A.18), we obtain the following relationship:

$$\oint_C \frac{F'(s)}{F(s)} ds = -2\pi j[(r_1 + r_2 + \cdots) - (m_1 + m_2 + \cdots)]$$

$$= -2\pi j(Z - P) \qquad (A.21)$$

where $Z = r_1 + r_2 + \cdots$ = total number of zeros of $F(s)$ enclosed by the s-plane contour.

$P = m_1 + m_2 + \cdots$ = total number of poles of $F(s)$ enclosed by the s-plane contour.

Since $F(s)$ is a complex variable, it can be written as

$$F(s) = |F(s)|e^{j\theta}$$

and

$$\ln F(s) = \ln |F(s)| + j\theta$$

Noting that $F'(s)/F(s)$ can be expressed as

$$\frac{F'(s)}{F(s)} = \frac{d \ln F(s)}{ds}$$

we obtain $\dfrac{F'(s)}{F(s)} = \dfrac{d}{ds}\,[\ln\,|F(s)|] + j\,\dfrac{d\theta}{ds}$

$$\oint_C \frac{F'(s)}{F(s)}\,ds = \oint_C d[\ln\,|F(s)|] + j\oint_C d\theta \qquad\qquad (A.22)$$

The first integral on the right-hand side of Eqn. (A.22) is zero since the magnitude $|F(s)|$ is the same at the initial point and the terminal point of the contour C. $\angle F(s)$ at the terminal point will differ from $\angle F(s)$ at the initial point by an integer multiple of 2π radians if the contour in the $F(s)$-plane encircles the origin, and the two angles will be equal if the origin is not encircled. Noting that N is the number of clockwise encirclements of the origin of the $F(s)$-plane, we obtain

$$\oint_C \frac{F'(s)}{F(s)}\,ds = -\,2\pi j N \qquad\qquad (A.23)$$

Finally, the argument principle results if the right-hand sides of Eqns (A.21) and (A.23) are equated to give

$$N = Z - P \qquad\qquad (A.24)$$

We can easily relate the mapping shown in Fig. A.2 to Cauchy's principle of argument.

A.3 | LAPLACE TRANSFORMS

A time function $y(t)$ can be expressed as a continuous sum of exponential functions of the from $e^{j\omega t}$:

$$y(t) = \frac{1}{2\pi}\int_{-\infty}^{\infty} Y(j\omega)e^{j\omega t}\,d\omega \qquad\qquad (A.25a)$$

where

$$Y(j\omega) = \int_{-\infty}^{\infty} y(t)e^{-j\omega t}\,dt \qquad\qquad (A.25b)$$

This representation is valid for any time function for which the integrals exist.

Integration over all time given by Eqn. (A.25b) is referred to as the *Fourier transform* of $y(t)$, and is frequently denoted symbolically as $\mathscr{F}\,[y(t)]$.

Conversion back to the time domain by means of integration over all frequency given by Eqn. (A.25a) is referred to as the *inverse Fourier transform* and is often denoted symbolically as $\mathscr{F}^{-1}\,[Y(j\omega)]$. Taken together, these two integrals are referred to as the *Fourier transform pair:*

$$\mathscr{F}\,[y(t)] = Y(j\omega) \triangleq \int_{-\infty}^{\infty} y(t)e^{-j\omega t}\,dt \qquad\qquad (A.26a)$$

$$\mathscr{F}^{-1}[Y(j\omega)] = y(t) \triangleq \frac{1}{2\pi} \int_{-\infty}^{\infty} Y(j\omega)e^{j\omega t} \, d\omega \qquad (A.26b)$$

Unfortunately, there are many signals of interest that arise in linear system analysis problems for which Fourier transforms do not exist. To extend the transform technique to such signals, the signal is expressed as a continuous sum of exponentials of the type e^{st} with $s = \sigma + j\omega$. As is seen below, this introduces a convergence factor $e^{-\sigma t}$; this factor, in effect, makes the product $y(t)e^{-\sigma t}$ Fourier transformable even if Fourier transform of $y(t)$ itself does not exist, thereby expanding the class of transformable functions.

The technique of expressing a signal as a continuous sum of exponentials e^{st} is known as the *Laplace transform* technique. The Laplace transform of $y(t)$, denoted symbolically as $\mathscr{L}[y(t)]$, is defined as follows:

$$\mathscr{L}[y(t)] = Y(s) \triangleq \int_{-\infty}^{\infty} y(t) \, e^{-st} \, dt \qquad (A.27)$$

By writing Eqn. (A.27) as

$$Y(s) = \int_{-\infty}^{\infty} [y(t) \, e^{-\sigma t}]e^{-j\omega t} \, dt$$

and comparing it with Eqn. (A.26a), we can see a strong similarity to the Fourier transform; the signal $y(t)$ possesses a Laplace transform if $\{y(t)e^{-\sigma t}\}$ possesses a Fourier transform.

Restricting our consideration to functions that are zero for $t < 0$, the transform integral in Eqn. (A.27) reduces to

$$Y(s) = \mathscr{L}[y(t)] = \int_{0}^{\infty} y(t)e^{-st}dt \qquad (A.28)$$

The integral in Eqn. (A.28) does not converge for all functions. And when it converges, it does so for restricted values of s in the s-plane. Therefore, for each function for which Laplace transform exists, there is an associated *convergence region* in the complex s-plane.

Consider the exponential function

$$y(t) = 0 \text{ for } t < 0$$
$$= e^{-at} \text{ for } t \geq 0$$

where a is a constant.

The Laplace transform of this exponential can be obtained as follows:

$$Y(s) = \int_{0}^{\infty} e^{-at} \, e^{-st} \, dt = \frac{-1}{s+a} \, e^{-(s+a)t} \, \Big|_{0}^{\infty}$$

$$= \frac{1}{s+a} ; \text{ Re}(s) > -a$$

The ability to recover a signal uniquely from its Laplace transform rests upon there being at least one value of s for which the infinite integral converges. For exponential function, the integral converges for any complex value of s for which

$$\text{Re}(s) = \sigma > -a$$

There are similar regions of convergence on the s-plane for the Laplace transforms of other time functions.

▲▲

The operation that changes $Y(s)$ back to $y(t)$ is referred to as the *inverse Laplace transformation* and is symbolized by $\mathscr{L}^{-1}[Y(s)]$. We observe from the inverse Fourier transform integral in Eqn. (A.26b) that

$$y(t)e^{-\sigma t} = \mathscr{F}^{-1}[Y(\sigma + j\omega)] = \frac{1}{2\pi} \int_{-\infty}^{\infty} Y(\sigma + j\omega)e^{j\omega t}\, d\omega$$

Multiplying both sides by $e^{\sigma t}$ and assuming s constant, we obtain the inverse Laplace transform:

$$y(t) = \mathscr{L}^{-1}[Y(s)] = \frac{1}{2\pi j} \int_{\sigma - j\infty}^{\sigma + j\infty} Y(s)e^{st}\, ds \qquad (A.29)$$

where the change of variable: $s = \sigma + j\omega$ and $ds = j d\omega$, has been used.

The inverse Laplace transform operation involves closed contour integration on the complex plane within the region of convergence of $Y(s)$. We may make use of the residue theorem of the theory of complex variables to evaluate the integral.

Since comprehensive tables of *Laplace transform pairs* have been published, it is rarely necessary for a transform user to actually work out integrals in Eqns (A.28) and (A.29). A short table given in Section A.4 is adequate for the purposes of this text.

It may be noted that in the transform table of Section A.4, regions of convergence have not been specified. In our applications of system analysis which involve transformation from time-domain to s-domain and inverse transformation, the variable s acts as a dummy operator; if transform pairs for functions of interest to us are available, we are not concerned with the regions of convergence[3].

Transform Inversion by Partial Fractions The inversion of Laplace transform plays an important role in the study of control systems, primarily because

---

3. Unlike *one-sided* Laplace transform (defined by Eqn. (A.28)), the *two-sided* Laplace transform (defined by Eqn. (A.27)) is not generally unique. That is, two different time functions can have the same two-sided Laplace transform, each with a different region of convergence. It is then necessary to additionally specify the region of convergence in order to specify the time function. We will not use two-sided transforms in this book.

of the emphasis on transient response. We frequently encounter transforms that are rational functions, i.e., the ratio of two polynomials in s. For simple rational functions, inverse Laplace transform is directly given by transform tables. For functions not listed in transform tables, an approach based on partial fraction expansion is widely used for inverse transformation. This approach is based on the *linearity property* of the Laplace transforms:

$$\mathcal{L}^{-1}[a_1 Y_1(s) + a_2 Y_2(s)] = a_1 \mathcal{L}^{-1}[Y_1(s)] + a_2 \mathcal{L}^{-1}[Y_2(s)]$$

where a_1 and a_2 are constants.

The given rational function $Y(s)$ is expanded into partial fractions (refer Eqns (A.3)–(A.14)) such that the inverse Laplace transform of each fraction is available directly from the transform tables. The algebraic sum of the inverse Laplace transforms of the partial fractions yields the inverse Laplace transform of the given rational function.

Some Laplace Transform Properties

In addition to Laplace transform pairs, some Laplace transform properties are also used in control system analysis. Properties of interest to us are given below.

Multiplication by t

From the basic definition (A.28),

$$\frac{dY(s)}{ds} = \int_0^\infty \frac{d}{ds}(y(t)e^{-st})dt$$

$$= \int_0^\infty (-t)y(t)e^{-st}\,dt$$

Consequently,

$$\mathcal{L}[ty(t)] = \frac{dY(s)}{ds} \tag{A.30}$$

Transforms of Derivatives

From the basic definition (A.28),

$$\mathcal{L}\left[\frac{dy(t)}{dt}\right] = \int_0^\infty \frac{dy(t)}{dt}\,e^{-st}\,dt$$

Integrating by parts, we get

$$\mathcal{L}\left[\frac{dy(t)}{dt}\right] = y(t)e^{-st}\Big|_0^\infty + s\int_0^\infty y(t)\,e^{-st}\,dt$$

We assume that the function $y(t)$ is transformable; the existence of $Y(s)$ guarantees that $y(t)e^{-st}\big|_{t \to \infty} = 0$. Hence

$$\mathcal{L}\left[\frac{dy(t)}{dt}\right] = sY(s) - y(0)$$

Use of this result in a recursive manner results in the family of transform formulas:

$$\mathscr{L}\left[\frac{d^2 y(t)}{dt^2}\right] = s^2 Y(s) - sy(0) - \frac{dy}{dt}(0)$$

$$\vdots$$

$$\mathscr{L}\left[\frac{d^n y(t)}{dt^n}\right] = s^n Y(s) - s^{n-1} y(0) - s^{n-2} \frac{dy}{dt}(0) - \cdots$$

$$- s \frac{d^{n-2} y}{dt^{n-2}}(0) - \frac{d^{n-1} y}{dt^{n-1}}(0) \qquad (A.31)$$

Transform of an Integral

By definition,

$$\mathscr{L}\left[\int_{-\infty}^{t} y(\tau)\, d\tau\right] = \int_{0}^{\infty}\left[\int_{-\infty}^{t} y(\tau)\, d\tau\right] e^{-st}\, dt$$

Integrating by parts, we get

$$\mathscr{L}\left[\int_{-\infty}^{t} y(\tau)\, d\tau\right] = \frac{e^{-st}}{-s}\left[\int_{-\infty}^{t} y(\tau)d\tau\right]\Bigg|_0^{\infty} + \frac{1}{s}\int_0^{\infty} y(t)e^{-st} dt$$

$$= \frac{Y(s)}{s} + \frac{\displaystyle\int_{-\infty}^{0} y(\tau)d\tau}{s} \qquad (A.32)$$

Complex Frequency Shift

The Laplace transform of

$$y(t) = x(t)e^{-\alpha t} \qquad (A.33a)$$

is

$$Y(s) = X(s + \alpha) \qquad (A.33b)$$

where $X(s) = \mathscr{L}[x(t)]$, and α is a real constant.

The proof easily follows by substituting Eqn. (A.33a) into the definition of the Laplace transform and noting that the integral is the Laplace transform of $x(t)$ with the variable $s + \alpha$:

$$\mathscr{L}[x(t)e^{-\alpha t}] = \int_0^{\infty} e^{-\alpha t} x(t)e^{-st}\, dt$$

$$= \int_0^{\infty} x(t)e^{-(s + \alpha)t}\, dt = X(s + \alpha)$$

Time-delay

If the Laplace transform of $y(t)\mu(t)$ is $Y(s)$, then

$$\mathscr{L}\left[y(t - t_0)\mu(t - t_0)\right] = e^{-st_0} Y(s); \; t_0 > 0 \qquad \text{(A.34)}$$

where $\mu(t)$ is a unit step function.

The proof follows easily by using the definition of Laplace transform. Since

$$\mu(t - t_0) = 0 \text{ for } t < t_0. \text{ we obtain}$$

$$\mathscr{L}\left[y(t - t_0)\,\mu(t - t_0)\right] = \int_{t_0}^{\infty} y(t - t_0)e^{-st}\,dt$$

Letting $\tau = t - t_0$ in the integrand, we get

$$\mathscr{L}\left[y(t - t_0)\,\mu(t - t_0)\right] = \int_{0}^{\infty} y(\tau)e^{-s(\tau + t_0)}\,d\tau = e^{-st_0} Y(s)$$

Final-Value Theorem

In the analysis of dynamic systems, one often desires to know the value that a variable approaches as $t \to \infty$, assuming, of course, that it does approach a limit. Using partial fraction expansions, it is a simple matter to show that $y(t)$ approaches a limit as $t \to \infty$ if all the poles of $Y(s)$ lie in the left half s-plane with the possible exception of a simple pole at the origin. A more compact way of phrasing this condition is to say that $sY(s)$ must be analytic on the imaginary axis and in the right-half s-plane. The final-value theorem states that when this condition on $sY(s)$ is satisfied, then

$$\lim_{t \to \infty} y(t) = \lim_{s \to 0} [sY(s)] \qquad \text{(A.35)}$$

The proof is as follows:

$$\mathscr{L}\left[\frac{dy}{dt}\right] = \int_{0}^{\infty} \frac{dy}{dt} e^{-st}\,dt$$

or $\qquad sY(s) - y(0) = \displaystyle\int_{0}^{\infty} \frac{dy}{dt} e^{-st}\,dt$

Letting $s \to 0$ on both sides, we have

$$\lim_{s \to 0} [sY(s)] = y(0) + \int_{0}^{\infty} \frac{dy}{dt}\,dt = y(0) + y(t)\Big|_{0}^{\infty} = y(\infty)$$

It is noted that when $y(t)$ is sinusoidal function $\sin \omega t$, $sY(s)$ has poles on $\pm j\omega$ and $\lim_{t \to \infty} y(t)$ does not exist. Therefore, the final value theorem is not valid for such a function. We must make sure that all the conditions for the final value theorem are satisfied before applying it to a given problem.

A.4 TABLE OF TRANSFORMS

For convenient reference, this section gives an abbreviated table of transforms. The table lists Laplace transforms of commonly encountered functions $f(t)$; $t \geq 0$.

$F(s)$	$f(t)$: $t \geq 0$
1	Unit impulse $\delta(t)$
$\dfrac{1}{s}$	Unit step $\mu(t)$
$\dfrac{1}{s^2}$	t
$\dfrac{2}{s^3}$	t^2
$\dfrac{1}{s+a}$	e^{-at}
$\dfrac{1}{(s+a)^2}$	te^{-at}
$\dfrac{a}{s(s+a)}$	$1 - e^{-at}$
$\dfrac{b-a}{(s+a)(s+b)}$	$e^{-at} - e^{-bt}$
$\dfrac{a^2}{s^2(s+a)}$	$at - 1 + e^{-at}$
$\dfrac{a(s+b)}{s^2(s+a)}$	$\dfrac{a-b}{a} + bt - \left(\dfrac{a-b}{a}\right)e^{-at}$
$\dfrac{ab}{s(s+a)(s+b)}$	$1 + \dfrac{b}{a-b}e^{-at} - \dfrac{a}{a-b}e^{-bt}$
$\dfrac{a}{s^2+a^2}$	$\sin at$
$\dfrac{s}{s^2+a^2}$	$\cos at$
$\dfrac{b}{(s+a)^2+b^2}$	$e^{-at}\sin bt$
$\dfrac{s+a}{(s+a)^2+b^2}$	$e^{-at}\cos bt$

MATLAB Environment

MATLAB, an abbreviation for MATrix LABoratory, is a high-performance language for technical computing. It integrates computation, visualization, and programming in an easy-to-use environment where problems and solutions are expressed in familiar mathematical notation.

The MATLAB family of programs includes the base program plus a variety of application-specific solutions called toolboxes. Toolboxes are comprehensive collections of MATLAB functions (M-files) that extend the MATLAB environment to solve particular classes of problems. Together, the base program plus the *Control System Toolbox* provide the capability to use MATLAB for control system analysis and design problems at the level of the text. Whenever MATLAB is referred to in this book, you can interpret that to mean the base program plus the control system toolbox.

If you are new to MATLAB and want to learn it quickly, start by reading the document "Getting Started with MATLAB", a publication of the MATH WORKS, Inc. [177]. After you learn the basics—how to enter matrices, how to use the colon (:) operator, and how to invoke functions—you can access the rest of the documentation as needed, and/or you can use online **help** facility to learn other commands. MATLAB provides extensive documentation in both printed and online format to help you learn about and use all of its features. The online **help** provides task-oriented, and function-reference information. The documentation is also available in PDF format. See either the online documentation if it is installed or the Math Works website at www.mathworks.com.

MATLAB manuals are self-contained; it is infact not necessary to give additional material to teach how to use MATLAB with a text book. The only purpose this appendix will probably serve is to give a "starting kick" to the students who need to be kicked to action. The appendix has not been designed as a substitute to the MATLAB manuals; its intent is to lead the reader to the routine in MATLAB that can be used to carry out a specific calculation. In some cases, it may eliminate the need to look at the manual or **help file**, but in most cases it will primarily point the reader to the right routine.

All our work has been performed on the Windows Platform with MATLAB version 6 and Control System Toolbox version 5.

On the Windows desktop, the installer usually creates a shortcut icon for starting MATLAB; double-clicking on this icon opens MATLAB Command Window. The MATLAB interpreter displays prompt (>>) indicating that it is ready to accept commands. To end your MATLAB session, type **quit** in the Command Window, or select **Exit MATLAB** from the **File** menu in the desktop.

Basic data element of MATLAB is an array that does not require dimensioning. Consider a polynomial "$s^3 + 3s^2 + 4$", to which we attach the *variable* name **p**. MATLAB represents the variable **p** as a row vector containing coefficients of the polynomial ordered by descending powers. To create this variable in MATLAB workspace, you can type the *statement* (any operation that assigns a value to a variable, creates the variable or overwrites its current value if it already exists)

>> p = [1   3   0   4]

The blank spaces (or commas) around the elements of the row vector separate the elements.

When you press the **Enter** key, MATLAB executes the statement (command) and responds with the display

p =
  1   3   0   4

When the variable name and "=" are omitted from a statement, the result is assigned to the generic variable **ans**.

>> [1   3   0   4]

ans =
  1   3   0   4

If the statement is followed by a semicolon,

>> p = [1   3   0   4];

the display of the polynomial **p** is suppressed. The assignment of the variable **p** has been carried out even though the display is suppressed by the semicolon. It is often the case that your MATLAB sessions will include intermediate calculations whose display is of little interest. Output display management has the added benefit of increasing the execution speed of the calculations, since display screen output takes time.

Variable names begin with a letter and are followed by any number of letters or numbers (including underscore). Keep the name length to 31 characters, since MATLAB remembers only the first 31 characters. Generally we do not use extremely long variable names even though they may be legal MATLAB names. Since MATLAB is case sensitive, the variables **P** and **p** are not the same; they are recognized as different quantities. To view the assignment of a variable, simply enter the variable name.

For numbers, MATLAB uses conventional decimal notation, with an optional decimal point and leading plus or minus sign; letter e specifies a power-of-ten scale factor. Some examples of numbers accepted by MATLAB are

$$3 \qquad -99 \qquad 0.001$$
$$9.6397238 \qquad 1.60210e{-}20 \qquad 6.02252e23$$

To enter a 3-by-3 matrix with variable name **A**, you can type the statement

`>> A = [1    2    3    ;    4    5    6    ;    7    8    9]`

MATLAB response on execution is

A =

$$\begin{matrix} 1 & 2 & 3 \\ 4 & 5 & 6 \\ 7 & 8 & 9 \end{matrix}$$

Elements of a row are separated with blanks (or commas), and semicolon indicates the end of each row.

MATLAB has several predefined variables, including **pi, inf, NaN, i** and **j**. **NaN** stands for Not-a-Number and results from undefined operations like 0/0. **inf** represents $+\infty$, and **pi** represents π. The variable $\mathbf{i} = \sqrt{-1}$ is used to represent complex numbers. The variable $\mathbf{j} = \sqrt{-1}$ can be used for complex arithmetic by those who prefer it over **i**.

The variables in the MATLAB workspace (predefined and those created by the user) can be manipulated from the MATLAB command line:

`>> x = 3 - 4*j + 10/pi + 5.678 ...`
$$\text{+ 7.890 + 5\textasciicircum2;}$$

+ addition, − subtraction, * multiplication, / division, ^ power, are usual arithmetic operators. When a statement being entered is too long for one line, use three periods, ..., followed by **Enter** to indicate that the statement continues on the next line.

Several statements can be placed on one line if they are separated by commas/semicolons.

`>> p = [1    3    0    4], z = 3 + 4*j;`

The use of colon (**:**) operator plays an important role in MATLAB. This operator may be used to generate a row vector containing the numbers from a given starting value **xi**, to the final value **xf**, with a specified increment **dx**.

$$\mathbf{x = [xi : dx : xf]}$$

>> x = [0 : 0.1 : 1]' % apostrophe ,', represents transpose operator

The MATLAB response to this command is

x =

     0
  0.1000
  0.2000
  0.3000
  0.4000
  0.5000
  0.6000
  0.7000
  0.8000
  0.9000

  1.0000

By default increment is taken as unity.

>> x = [0 : 10]

MATLAB response is

x =

  0   **1**   **2**   **3**   **4**   **5**   **6**   **7**   **8**   **9**   **10**

The colon vector can be used to subscript matrices. For example, $A(:, j)$ is the jth column of A, and $A(i, :)$ is the ith row of A.

(Note that command lines beginning with "%" are not executed; such lines are programmer's comments)

All computations in MATLAB are performed in *double precision*. The screen output can be displayed in several formats. The default output format contains four digits past the decimal point for nonintegers. This can be changed by using the **format** command. Remember that the **format** command affects only how numbers are displayed, not how MATLAB computes or saves them.

MATLAB has a vast collection of mathematical and graphics functions. In addition, MATLAB features a family of application-specific solutions called toolboxes—comprehensive collection of MATLAB functions that extend the MATLAB environment to solve particular classes of problems. Our focus will be on simple mathematical functions, graphical functions for two-dimensional presentations, and application-specific functions specialized to control engineering.

Files that contain MATLAB language code have been named as **M-files**. All the built-in functions of the interpreter are MATLAB supplied **M-files**. For functions that are not built into the interpreter, you can create **M-files** using the Editor/Debugger and then use them as you would use any other MATLAB function or command. The Editor/Debugger provides basic text editing operations as well as access to M-file debugging tools. To start the Editor/Debugger, select **New** from the **File** menu, or click the **New M-File** (page icon) button on the toolbar. Select **Save As...** from the **File** menu or click the **Save** (page icon) button on the toolbar to save the M-file you have created.

Because of extensive use of graphics in control engineering, description of some of the MATLAB graphics functions is in order here.

MATLAB directs graphics output to a window separate from the command window, called a figure window. Graphics functions automatically create figure windows. Multiple plots may be displayed in the same figure window. Utilities exist for linear and logarithmic scales. Autoscaling is selected by default, although the user is free to scale axes. A title, axis labels and arbitrary text may be placed on the graph. Displayed graphs may be saved to data files or sent directly to a printer.

If **x** and **y** are vectors of the same length, the command **plot** (**x,y**) plots the values in **y** against the values in **x**. The axes scales are automatically chosen. The axes may be labeled with the **xlable** and **ylabel** functions; the title of the graphical plot may be printed with the **title** function. A grid can be placed on the plot by using **grid** function. A text string may be placed at defined location of the plot using the **text** function. The function **gtext** accepts a string as an argument and waits while you select a location of the graph with the mouse. MATLAB then displays the text string at the indicated location. Thus a basic *x-y* plot is generated with the combination of functions : **plot**, **xlabel**, **ylabel**, **title**, **grid** and **text/gtext**. Multiple *x-y* pair arguments create multiple graphs with a single call to **plot**. MATLAB automatically cycles through a predefined (but user settable) list of colours to allow discrimination between each set of data. The **legend** command provides an easy way to identify the individual plots.

The **plot** function accepts character-string arguments that specify various line styles, marker symbols, and colours. You can add plots to an existing graph using the **hold** command. When you set **hold** to **on**, MATLAB does not remove the existing graph; it adds the new data to the current graph, rescaling if the new data falls outside the range of the previous axis limits.

MATLAB automatically selects axis limits based on the range of the plotted data. However, you can specify the limits using the **axis** command. Call **axis** with the new limits defined as a four-element vector:

$$\textbf{axis ([xmin, xmax, ymin, ymax])}$$

By default, MATLAB displays graphs in a rectangular axes that has the same aspect ratio as the figure window. This makes optimum use of space available for plotting. MATLAB provides control over the aspect ratio with the **axis** command. The command **axis square** makes the *x-* and *y-***axis equal** in length. The command **axis equal** produces an axes that is rectangular in shape, but has equal scaling along each axis.

Graphing functions automatically open a new figure window if there are no figure windows already on the screen. If a figure window exists, MATLAB uses that window for graphics output. If there are multiple figure windows open, MATLAB targets the one that is designated the "current figure". To make an existing figure window the current figure, you can type **figure** (n) where **n** is the number in the figure toolbar. The results of subsequent graphics commands are displayed in this window. To open a new figure window and make it the current figure, type **figure**.

The subplot command enables you to display multiple plots in the same window. Typing **subplot (m, n, p)** partitions the figure window into an $m \times n$ matrix of small subplots and selects the pth subplot for the current plot. The plots are numbered along first the top row of the figure window, then the second row, and so on.

MATLAB has a large number of built-in functions for working with polynomials. These functions operate primarily on vectors (MATLAB represents polynomials as row vectors containing the coefficients ordered by descending powers). We give some examples here.

>> p = [3   2   1]; q = [1   4];

>> n = conv(p, q)

MATLAB response

n =
   3   14   9   4

The function **conv** has been used to multiply two polynomials $p(s) = 3s^2 + 2s + 1$, $q(s) = s + 4$, to get the result $n(s) = 3s^3 + 14s^2 + 9s + 4$.

The function **roots (p)** gives a column vector containing the roots of the polynomial **p**. Given a column vector **r** representing the roots of a polynomial, the function **poly(r)** assembles the polynomial.

A large number of built-in matrix functions are available in MATLAB. Some examples follow. If **A** is an $n \times n$ matrix, **poly(A)** gives the characteristic equation represented by the $(n + 1)$-element row vector whose elements are the coefficients of the characteristic equation. The function **eig(A)** outputs the eigenvalues of matrix **A**. The **expm(A)** function outputs the matrix exponential e^A. The functions **det(A)**, **rank(A)**, and **size(A)** yield determinant of matrix **A**, rank of matrix **A**, and row and column dimensions of matrix **A.** The function **inv(A)** outputs the inverse of matrix **A**.

Some of the commonly used utility matrices are : **ones(m,n), zeros (m,n), eye(n), rand(m,n), randn(m,n). ones(m,n)** produces an $m \times n$ matrix whose each element is 1. Similarly **zeros(m, n)** produces an $m \times n$ matrix whose each element is 0. **eye(n)** gives an $n \times n$ identity matrix. **rand(m,n)** is an $m \times n$ matrix with random entries, chosen from a uniform distribution on the interval (0.0, 1.0). The sequence of numbers generated is determined by the state of the generator. Since MATLAB resets the state at start-up, the sequence of numbers generated will be the same unless state is changed. **rand('state', S)** resets the state to **S. rand('state', 0)** resets the generator to its initial state. **randn(m, n)** is an $m \times n$ matrix with random entries chosen from a normal distribution with mean zero, variance one and standard deviation one.

The basic matrix operations can be modified for element-by-element operations by preceding the operator with a period. The modified matrix operations are called *array-operations*. For example

$$\mathbf{A} = \begin{bmatrix} a_{11} & a_{12} \\ a_{21} & a_{22} \end{bmatrix}, \mathbf{B} = \begin{bmatrix} b_{11} & b_{12} \\ b_{21} & b_{22} \end{bmatrix}$$

$$\mathbf{A.*B} = \begin{bmatrix} a_{11}\,b_{11} & a_{12}\,b_{12} \\ a_{21}\,b_{21} & a_{22}\,b_{22} \end{bmatrix}$$

Operators of interest to use are: **+**, **−**, matrix multiply *****, array multiply **.***, matrix power **^**, array power **.^**, array divide **./**.

There are many flow control functions in MATLAB.

The **for** function in MATLAB provides a mechanism for repeatedly executing a series of statements a given number of times. The **for** function connected to an **end** statement sets up a repeating circulation loop.

Consider the characteristic polynomial

$$q(s) = s^3 + 2s^2 + 4s + K; \, 0 < K < 20$$

The following **script** computes the roots of $q(s)$ (Script is an M-file that can be created using Editor/Debugger. When you invoke a script, MATLAB simply executes the commands found in the file. Scripts can operate on existing data in the workspace, or they can create new data that remains in work space. Scripts do not accept input arguments or return output arguments).

```
>> K = [0 : 0.5 : 20];
>> for i = 1 : length (K)
       q = [1   2   4   K(i)];
       p (:, i) = roots (q);
   end
```

The loops can be nested. An important point is that each **for** must be matched with an **end**. The **break** statement provides exit jump out of loop.

The **while** function in MATLAB allows a mechanism for repeatedly executing a series of statements an indefinite number of times, under control of a logical condition.

The function **if** evaluates a logical expression and executes a group of statements based on the value of the expression. The **else** statement further conditionalizes the **if** statement.

We conclude our brief description of MATLAB Environment with an example on MATLAB Graphics.

Consider the following differential equation:

$$\ddot{y}(t) + 2\zeta\omega_n\dot{y}(t) + \omega_n^2 y(t) = 0; \ \dot{y}(0) = 0, \ y(0) = y0$$

The unforced dynamic response $y(t)$ is:

$$y(t) = \frac{y0}{\sqrt{1-\zeta^2}} \ e^{-\zeta\omega_n t} \sin\left(\omega_n\left(\sqrt{1-\zeta^2}\right)t + \theta\right)$$

where

$$\theta = \cos^{-1}\zeta$$

The MATLAB Script B.1 generates the plot of the unforced response for given values of $y0$, ζ, and ω_n. The description of the MATLAB functions used in the script can easily be accessed from the **help file** using **help** command.

The **input** function displays a prompt, waits for a keyboard input, and then returns the value from the keyboard. The graphics function **plot** creates a figure window, automatically selects appropriate axis ranges and draws a graph of y versus t. Thickness, linestyle and colour of the graph have been selected using **set** function. The functions **xlabel**, **ylabel**, **legend**, and **title** annotate the graph.

The command **hold on** holds the current graph so that subsequent graphing commands add to the existing graph. To add new data, the function **plot** has been used again, but this time it plots multiple graphs in one call; also the linestyles and colours are specified in its arguments (on the monitor, you will see these graphs in red colour). The function **line** prominently displays the $y = 0$ line.

Script B.1

```
clear all
close all
%Using MATLAB Graphics
y0=input('Enter initial condition y0:')
zeta=input('Enter value of zeta:')
wn=input('Enter value of wn:')
t=[0:0.1:10];theta=acos(zeta)*ones(1,length(t));
c=y0/sqrt(1-zeta^2);
y=c*exp(-zeta*wn*t).*sin(wn*sqrt(1-zeta^2)*t+theta);
env1=c*exp(-zeta*wn*t);env2=-env1;
h=plot(t,y);
set(h,'linewidth',1.5,'linestyle','-','color','k');
hold on
plot(t,env1,'-r',t,env2,'-r');grid;
line(t,0*ones(length(t),1));
xlabel('Time[sec]');ylabel('Output y');
title('Using MATLAB Graphics')
legend('Unforced response')
```

After creating a plot, you can make changes to it and annotate it with the **Plot Editor**, which is an easy-to-use graphical interface. Click the button ↖ in the figure window to enable plot editor mode. Annotating, zooming, and rotating the plot are some of the features you can play with. In plot editing mode, you can use a graphical user interface, called the **Property Editor**, to edit the properties of the objects in the graph. MATLAB response to Script B.1 for $y0 = 0.15$, $\zeta = 0.35$, and $\omega_n = 4$, is given in Fig. B.1. Plot Editor was used to place text strings with arrows at suitable locations on the plot.

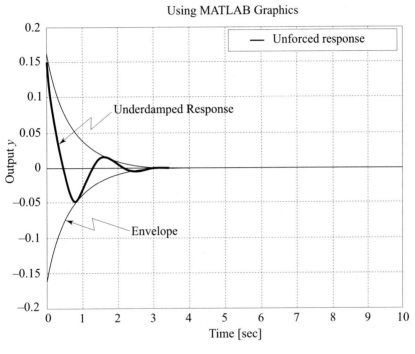

Fig. B.1

Matlab Functions for Control Design

If you are a new user, start by reading the document "Getting Started with the Control System Toolbox". After you learn the basics—how to build and manipulate time-invariant models of the dynamical systems, how to analyze such models and plot their time and frequency responses, and how to design compensators—you can access the rest of the documentation as needed, and/or you can use the online "Control System Toolbox Function Reference" for reference information on functions and tools (LTI Viewer and SISO Design Tool are graphical user interfaces (GUIs) that you can use to analyze systems and design SISO compensators).

Our presentation has a limited objective of helping the reader to learn the toolbox quickly.

Models

When a control engineer is given a control problem, often one of the first tasks that he undertakes is the development of the mathematical model of the process to be controlled. We can use first principles of physics to write down a model. Another way is to perform "system identification" via the use of real plant data to produce a model of the system.

For linear time-invariant systems, mathematical model building based on physical laws normally results in a set of (first-order, and second-order) differential equations. These equations, when rearranged as a set of first-order differential equations, result in a state-space model of the following from for single-input, single-output (SISO) systems:

$$\dot{\mathbf{x}} = \mathbf{A}\mathbf{x} + \mathbf{b}u$$
$$y = \mathbf{c}\mathbf{x} + du \tag{B.1}$$

where $\mathbf{x}(t)$ is the $n \times 1$ internal state vector, $u(t)$ is the control input, $y(t)$ is the measured output. Overdot represents differentiation with respect to time t.

Complex processes and machines often have several manipulated inputs available to provide this control (multivariable or MIMO system). In many situations, one input affects primarily one output and has only weak effect on other outputs; it becomes possible to ignore weak interactions (coupling) and design controllers under the assumption that one input affects only one output. Input-output pairing to minimize the effect of interactions and application of SISO control schemes to obtain separate controllers for each input-output pair, results in an acceptable performance. This, in fact, amounts to considering the MIMO system as consisting of an appropriate number of separate SISO systems. Coupling effects are considered as disturbances to the separate control systems. Though MATLAB has a provision for both the SISO and MIMO models, we will limit our discussion to SISO models.

For the state-space representation (B.1), the data for the model consists of four matrices. For convenience, the MATLAB provides customized data structure. This is called the **SS** object. This object encapsulates the model data and enables you to manipulate linear time-invariant (LTI) system as single entity, rather than collection of data vectors and matrices.

An LTI object of the type **SS** is created whenever you invoke the construction function **ss**. For example, type

```
>> A = [- 8   - 16   - 6;   1   0   0 ; 0   1   0];
>> b = [1;   0;   0];
>> c = [2   8   6];
>> d = 0;
>> sys = ss(A, b, c, d)
```

and MATLAB responds with

a =

	x1	x2	x3
x1	− 8.0000	− 16.0000	− 6.0000
x2	1.0000	0	0
x3	0	1.0000	0

b =

	u1
x1	1.0000
x2	0
x3	0

c =

	x1	x2	x3
y1	2.0000	8.0000	6.0000

d =

	u1
y1	0

Controllability and observability of a system in state variable form can be checked using the MATLAB functions **ctrb** and **obsv**, respectively. The input to the **ctrb** function are the system matrix **A** and the input matrix **b**; the output of **ctrb** function is the controllability matrix **U**. Similarly, the input to the **obsv** function are the system matrix **A** and the output matric **c**; the output is observability matrix **V**. The functions **det(U)/rank(U) and det(V)/rank(V)** give, respectively, the controllability and observability properties.

Our next step is to make a design model. Since our focus is going to be on frequency-domain design methods, a transfer function model will be required. A transfer function

$$G(s) = \frac{n(s)}{d(s)} \tag{B.2}$$

is characterized by the numerator $n(s)$ and denominator $d(s)$, both polynomials of the Laplace variable s. MATLAB provides LTI object **TF** for transfer functions. The object **TF** is created whenever you invoke the construction function **tf**. For example, for

$$G(s) = (8 + 12s + 4s^3) \big/ (17s^5 + 23s^3 + 8s^2 + 6), \text{ type}$$

>> **num = [4 0 12 8]; den = [17 0 23 8 0 6];**

>> **sys = tf(num, den)**
and MATLAB responds with
Transfer function:

$$\frac{4s^3 + 12s + 8}{17s^5 + 23s^3 + 8s^2 + 6}$$

Quite often, the transfer function in hand is in zero-pole-gain form,

$$G(s) = \frac{10\,(s-3)\,(s+4.5)\,(s+100)}{(s+40)^3\,(s+80)}$$

MATLAB provides construction function **zpk** to create **ZPK** object. We can, however, create **TF** object for this transfer function using construction function **tf**.

>> r1 = [3; – 4.5; – 100]; r2 = [– 40; – 40; – 40; – 80];

>> num = 10* poly(r1); den = poly(r2);

>> sys = tf(num, den);

r1 is a column vector containing the roots of a polynmial. The function **poly(r1)** assembles the polynomial.

Some more examples of construction of **TF** object follow.

$$G(s) = \frac{10\,(s+2)\,(s+5)}{\left(s^2+2s+5\right)(s+3)}$$

with real as well as complex poles.

>> r = [– 2; – 5];

>> num = 10 * poly(r);

>> p = [1 2 5]; q = [1   3];

>> den = conv(p, q);

>> sys = tf(num, den);

The function **conv** has been used to multiply two polynomials $p(s) = s^2 + 2s + 5$, and $q(s) = s + 3$.

$$G(s) = \frac{100\,(5s+1)\,(15s+1)}{s(3s+1)\,(10s+1)}$$

is a transfer function in time-constant form.

>> n1 = [5   1]; n2 = [15   1];   d1 = [1   0]; d2 = [3   1];

>> d3 = [10   1]; num = 100 * conv(n1, n2);

>> den = conv(d1, conv(d2, d3));

>> sys = tf(num, den);

To create the object **TF** directly, use these commands:

>> s = tf('s');

>> sys = 100*(5*s+1)*(15*s+1)/[s*(3*s+1)*(10*s+1)];

In cases where our knowledge of the system under study is limited, or the theoretical model turns out to be highly complex, the only reliable information on which to base the control design is the experimental data. MATLAB has a provision of creating an LTI object called **FRD** which stores frequency response data (complex frequency response, alongwith a corresponding vector of frequency points) that you obtain experimentally.

MATLAB has the means to perform model conversions. Given the **SS** model *sys_ss*, the syntax for conversion to **TF** model is

$$\text{sys\_tf} = \text{tf(sys\_ss)}$$

Common pole-zero factors of the **TF** model must be cancelled before we can claim that we have the transfer function representation of the system. To assist us in pole-zero cancellation, MATLAB provides **minreal** function.

$$\text{sysr} = \text{minreal(sys\_tf)}$$

Given the **TF** model **sys_tf**, the syntax for conversion to **SS** model is

$$\text{sys\_ss} = \text{ss(sys\_tf)}$$

Process transfer function models frequently have dead-time (input-output delay). **TF** object for transfer functions with dead-time can be created using the syntax

$$\text{sys} = \text{tf(num, den, 'InputDelay', value)}$$

For $\quad G(s) = (6.6\ e^{-7s})\big/(10.9s + 1)$, type

```
>> num = [6.6]; den = [10.9   1];
>> sys = tf(num, den, 'InputDelay', 7);
```

Two cascaded blocks with transfer functions $G_1(s)$ and $G_2(s)$ can be multiplied using the **series** function.

$$\text{sys1} = \text{tf(num1, den1)} \ \% \ \mathbf{G_1(s)}$$
$$\text{sys2} = \text{tf(num2, den2)} \ \% \ \mathbf{G_2(s)}$$
$$\text{sys} = \text{series(sys1, sys2)} \ \% \ \mathbf{G_1(s)G_2(s)}$$

or $\qquad\qquad\quad$ sys = sys1 *sys2

If **sys1** and **sys2** are in parallel, then

$$\text{sys} = \text{parallel(sys1, sys2)} \ \% \ \mathbf{G_1(s) + G_2(s)}$$

or $\qquad\qquad\quad$ sys = sys1 + sys2

For a negative feedback loop with forward path transfer function $G(s)$ and feedback path transfer function $H(s)$, the function **feedback** results in closed-loop transfer function.

$$\text{sys1} = \text{tf(num1, den1)} \ \% \ \mathbf{G(s)}$$
$$\text{sys2} = \text{tf(num2, den2)} \ \% \ \mathbf{H(s)}$$
$$\text{sys} = \text{feedback(sys1, sys2)} \ \% \ \mathbf{G(s)}\big/(\mathbf{1 + G(s)H(s)})$$

For a unity-feedback system, the closed-loop transfer function is given by

$$\text{sys} = \text{feedback(sys1, 1)} \ \% \ \mathbf{G(s)}\big/(\mathbf{1 + G(s)})$$

Time Response

For the **SS** object of the model (B.1):

$$\text{sys} = \text{ss(A, b, c, d)}$$

the function **step(sys)** will generate a plot of unit-step response $y(t)$ (with zero initial conditions). The time vector is automatically selected when **t** is not explicitly included in the **step** command.

If you wish to supply the time vector **t** at which the response will be computed, the following command is used.

step(sys, t)

You can specify either a final time **t = Tfinal,** or a vector of evenly spaced time samples of the form

t = 0 : dt : Tfinal

When invoked with left-hand arguments such as

[y,t] = step(sys)

[y,t,X] = step(sys)

y = step(sys, t)

no plot is generated on the screen. Hence it is necessary to use a **plot** command to see the response curves. The vector **y** and matrix **X** contain the output and state response of the system, respectively, evaluated at the computation points returned in the time vector **t** (**X** has as many columns as states and one row for each element in vector **t**).

Other time-response functions of interest to use are:

impulse(sys)	**% impulse response**
initial(sys,x0)	**% free response to initial state vector x0**
lsim(sys,u,t)	**% response to input time history**
lsim(sys,u,t,x0)	**% in vector u having length (t) rows**

For the **TF** object of the model (B.2):

sys = tf(num, den)

the function **step(sys)** will generate a unit-step response $y(t)$. The time vector is automatically selected when **t** is not explicitly included in the **step** command. If you wish to supply the time vector **t** at which the response will be computed, the following command is used.

step (sys,t)

When invoked with left-hand arguments such as

[y,t] = step(sys)

y = step(sys,t)

no plot is generated on the screen. Hence it is necessary to use a **plot** command to see the response curve. The vector **y** has one column and one row for each element in time vector **t**.

Other time-response functions of interest to us are:

impulse(sys) % impulse response

lsim(sys,u,t) % response to input time history in vector u having
% length (t) rows.

Place your mouse on any point along a plot line (step, impulse, lsim, initial). Left-clicking on this point opens data with relevant information displayed.

As the nature of the transient response of a control system is dependent upon the system poles only and not on the type of the input, it is sufficient to analyze the transient response to one of the standard test signals; a step is generally used. In specifying the steady-state response characteristics, it is common to specify the steady-state error of the system to one or more of the standard test signals—step, ramp, parabola. Theoretically, it is desirable for a control system to have the capability of responding with zero error to all the polynomial inputs of degree k: $r(t) = (t^k/k!)$; $t \geq 0$, $k = 0, 1, 2, \ldots$ Higher the value of k, more stringent is the steady-state requirement, making it difficult to satisfy other specifications on the performance of the system. It is therefore necessary that tracking commands which a control system is expected to be subjected to be carefully examined and steady-state specifications be formulated for inputs with minimum possible value of k.

Typical design specifications demand that the system have (when subjected to command/disturbance inputs)

(i) a step response inside some constraint boundaries—specified by settling time, peak overshoot, etc; and

(ii) steady-state error to step/ramp/parabolic input within prescribed limits, under the constraints imposed by physical limitations of the selected plant, actuator, and sensor.

You can analyze the time response using the **LTI Viewer**, which is a graphical user interface for viewing and manipulating response plots of LTI models. For example

Itiview('step',sys)

will open a window displaying the step response of the LTI model **sys**. Once initialized, the **LTI Viewer** assists you with the analysis of the response by facilitating such functions as zooming into regions of the response plots; calculating response characteristics such as peak response, settling time, rise time, steady state; toggling the grid on or off the plot; and many other useful features.

Right-click anywhere in the plot region of the step response plot. This opens a menu list (Plot Type, Systems, Characteristics, Grid, Zoom, Properties) in the plot region. Select the **Grid** menu item with left mouse button. A grid for the graph appears. Now right-click again and place the pointer in the **Characteristics** menu item. The submenu items (Peak Response, Settling Time, Rise Time, Steady-State) of the Characteristics menu are displayed. Select **Settling Time** with left mouse button. The settling time marker appears on the graph. Place your mouse on the marker. This opens data with relevant information displayed. To make it persistent, left-click on the marker.

In addition to right-click menus, the LTI Viewer provides plot-data markers. Left-click anywhere on a plot line; a data marker appears with the response values of the plot at that point displayed. You can move the data marker along the plot line. Move the mouse pointer over the marker. The pointer becomes a hand. Grab the marker by holding down the left mouse button when the hand appears. Drag the marker with your mouse and release the mouse button at a point of your interest along the plot line. Response values at the selected point are displayed.

You may want to zoom in on one region of the given plot in order to inspect the response behaviour in that region more closely. Move the pointer on the **Zoom** menu item. The submenu items (ln-X, ln-Y, X-Y, Out) are displayed. Select **X-Y** to zoom in both the horizontal and vertical directions. Use your mouse to create the rectangular rubber band that indicates the zoom region (Point your mouse to any corner of the rectangle of the region you want to zoom in on. Left-click there and hold the mouse button down. Drag the mouse pointer until the rectangle covers the region you want to zoom in on. Release your mouse).

You can use the **Property Editor** to customize various attributes of your plot Move the pointer on the **Properties** menu item to open the editor.

Frequency Response

For the **TF** object of the model (B.2):

$$sys = tf(num, den)$$

the function **bode(sys)** generates the Bode frequency-response plots. This function automatically selects the frequency values by placing more points in regions where the frequency response is changing quickly. This range is user-selectable using the command **bode(sys,w)**. Since the Bode diagram has log scale, if we choose to specify the frequencies explicitly, it is desirable to generate the vector **w** using the **logspace** function. When invoked with left-hand arguments,

$$[mag,phase,w] = bode(sys)$$
$$[mag,phase] = bod(sys,w)$$

return the magnitude and phase of frequency response at the frequencies **w**. **nyquist(sys)** plots the real and imaginary parts of the frequency response of an arbitrary LTI models **sys**. **nyquist (sys,w)** explicitly specifies the frequency range to be used for the plot. To focus on a particular frequency interval, set **w = {wmin,wmax}**. When invoked with left-hand arguments

$$[re,im,w] = nyquist(sys)$$
$$[re,im] = nyquist(sys,w)$$

return the real and imaginary parts of the frequency response at the frequencies **w**.

Sometimes in the course of using the **nyquist** function, we may find that a Nyquist plot looks nontraditional or that some information appears to be missing. It may be necessary, in these cases, to override the automatic scaling and focus in on the $-1 + j0$ point region for stability analysis.

In practice, Nyquist diagrams are commonly plotted on the Nichols coordinate system with rectangular coordinate axes for the phase (in degrees) and the gain (in dB). On the Nichols coordinate system, the critical point for stability becomes (180°, 0dB).

The Nyquist diagram on the Nichols coordinate system can be generated using the **nichols** function. **nichols(sys)** produces a Nyquist plot of the LTI model **sys**. **nichols(sys,w)** explicitly specifies the frequency range to be used for the plot. When invoked with left-hand arguments,

$$[\text{mag,phase,w}] = \text{nichols(sys)}$$

$$[\text{mag,phase}] = \text{nichols(sys,w)}$$

return the magnitude (in dB) and phase (in degrees) of the frequency response at the frequencies **w** (in rad/sec). Nichols chart grid is drawn on the existing plot using **ngrid** function.

Requirements that a control system have a step response inside some constraint boundaries—specified by settling time, peak overshot, etc., can equivalently be represented as requirements that the system have a frequency response satisfying certain constraints specified by gain margin, phase margin, bandwidth, etc. The function **margin** determines gain margin, phase margin, gain crossover frequency, and phase crossover frequency. Resonance peak, resonance frequency, and bandwidth of a closed-loop system may be obtained from the plot generated by **nichols** and **ngrid** functions.

You can analyze the frequency response using the **LTI Viewer**, which is a graphical user interface for viewing and manipulating response plots of LTI models. For example,

Itiview('Nichols',sys)

will open a window displaying the Nichols plot of the LTI system **sys**. Once initialized, the **LTI Viewer** assists you with the analysis of the response by facilitating such functions as zooming into regions of response plot; calculating response characteristics such as resonance peak, resonance frequency, bandwidth, stability margins; and many other useful features.

Right-click anywhere in the plot region of the Nichols plot. This opens a menu list (Plot Type, Systems, Characteristics, Grid, Zoom, Properties) in the plot region. Select the **Grid** menu item with left mouse button. A grid for the graph appears. Now right-click again and place the pointer on the **Characteristics** menu item. The submenu items (Peak Response, Stability Margins,...) are displayed. Select **Peak Response** with left mouse button. The marker for resonance peak appears on the graph. Left-click the marker to read the values of resonance peak and resonance frequency off the plot (Zooming in on certain region of the plot may be required). Similarly, stability margins can be read. Left-clicking anywhere on the plot line gives the response values of the plot at that point. Identify the −3 dB contour on the grid. Zoom in on the region of intersection of this contour with the plot. Click on the point of intersection; hold the mouse button down to read the value of bandwidth.

Root Locus

If **sys** models a transfer function

$$G(s) = \frac{n(s)}{d(s)}$$

rlocus adaptively selects a set of positive gains K and produces a smooth plot of the roots of

$$d(s) + Kn(s) = 0$$

Alternatively, **rlocus(sys,K)** uses the user-specified vector **K** of gains to plot the root locus. Left-click anywhere on the root loci to see the relevant information about the locus at that point.

The function **rlocfind** returns the feedback gain associated with a particular set of poles on the root locus. **[K,poles] = riocfind(sys)** is used for interactive gain selection. The function **rlocfind** puts up a cross hair cursor on the root locus plot that you use to select a particular pole location. The root locus gain associated with this point is returned in **K** and the column vector **poles** contains the closed-loop poles for this gain. To use this command, the root locus must be present in the current figure window.

The function **sgrid/spchart** is used for ω_n and ζ grid on the root locus.

Note that LTI functions are available in figure windows of the commands **margin, bode, nyquist, nichols, rlocus**. Left-click anywhere an a particular plot line to see the response values of that plot at that point. You can drag the data marker along a plot line. Also right-click menus are available.

Lag/Lead Design

To form an initial estimate of the complexity of the design problem, sketch frequency response (Bode plot) and root-locus plot with respect to plant gain. Try to meet the specifications with a simple controller of lag/lead variety. Do not overlook feedforward of the disturbances if the necessary sensor information is available. Consider the effect of sensor noise, and compare a lead network in the forward path to minor-loop feedback structure having direct feedback from velocity sensor, to see which gives a better design.

For design by root-locus method, the design specifications are translated into desired dominant closed-loop poles. Other closed-loop poles are required to be located at a large distance from the $j\omega$-axis. It may be noted that pole-placement methods do not allow the designer to judge how close the system performance is to the best possible. Also, there is lack of visibility into low-frequency disturbance rejection. This can cause many problems: the disturbance rejection may not be optimized, and the plant-parameter variations may cause large closed-loop response variations. Stability margins on Nyquist/Bode plot give a better robustness measure. For this reason, though the specifications on the closed-loop performance are often formulated in time domain, it is worthwhile to convert them into frequency-domain specifications and then design the compensator with frequency-domain methods. Root-locus plots are very impressive analysis tools for systems that have been designed by frequency-domain methods. For example, these plots can be valuable for the analysis of the effects of certain parameter variations on stability.

Note that the above comments reflect the opinion of practising engineers. Teaching in universities relies heavily on both the methods; our textbook also follows this standard pattern.

You can design a compensator using the SISO Design Tool, which is a graphical user interface (GUI). To initialize this GUI, type

sisotool(sys)

This command opens the SISO Design Tool with the root locus and open-loop Bode diagrams for the system **sys** plotted by default. Gain and phase margins are also displayed. By default, the compensator **C(s)** = 1 is in the forward path of the unity feedback structure. Alternative feedback structures are user selectable.

Some important features of the GUI that facilitate the design of compensators using root locus plots are as follows (Refer Chapter 7 for the design procedure).

1. As you iterate on a compensator design, you may find it convenient to be able to examine the various loop responses. To view, for example, the closed-loop step response, select **Plant Output (Step)** under **Loop Responses** from the **Tools** menu. This opens an LTI Viewer with closed-loop step response of **sys**.

2. Right-click anywhere in the plot region of the root locus plot. This opens a menu list (Add, Delete Pole/Zero, Edit Compensator, Design Constraints, Grid, Zoom, Properties). Select **X-Y** under **Zoom**. Hold down your mouse's left button to select a rectangular region for zooming in. When you let go off the button, the SISO Design Tool replots the root locus with the new axis boundaries.

3. Select **Design Constraints** from this right-click menu. Enter the design specifications (Settling time/Natural frequency, Peak overshoot/ Damping ratio) in the appropriate text fields. After you press OK, the GUI calculates and displays the specifications.

4. Select **Edit Compensator** from the right-click menu. Use the Edit Compensator window to edit the locations of the compensator poles and zeros, add compensator poles and zeros, and delete compensator poles and zeros.

   Select trial values of compensator pole and zero and click OK. Root locus plot of the compensated system appears in the plot region. Keep on trying with different compensator pole and zero values till you meet the performance specifications.

5. To get the gain value at s_d (the desired dominant closed-loop pole), click at this point. This completes the design.

6. To see that this design meets the performance requirements, take a look at the step response of the closed-loop system.

There are many other features of the GUI you may use. For example, you may use the zoom icons on the toolbar. You can change the compensator gain by grabbing the red squares on the root locus plot (the closed-loop poles) and moving them along the curve. Alternatively, you can change the compensator gain by entering values into the **C(s)** field in the **Current Compensator** panel. You may add poles or zeros to the compensator by selecting **Add** (Real pole, Complex Pole, Integrator, Real Zero, Complex Zero, Differentiator, Lead, Lag, Notch) from the right-click menu. **Delete Pole/Zero** in the right-click menu helps you to delete poles or zeros. You can use buttons on the toolbar to add/delete compensator pole/zero at any location of the root locus plot. As you know, the compensator design process can involve some trail and error; you can try dragging the compensator poles or compensator zeros around the root locus until you meet the design criteria.

If you want to specify the precise numerical values, you should use the **Edit Compensator** window to change the gain value, and the pole and zero locations of your compensator. You can open **Edit Compensator** window by selecting **Edit Compensator** under the **Edit** menu on the menu bar, selecting the **Edit compensator** in the right-click menu, or double-clicking your mouse in the **Current Compensator** panel.

For these and many other features, refer MATLAB documentation on Control System Toolbox.

Some important features of the GUI that facilitate the design of the compensator using Bode plots are as follows (Refer Chapter 10 for the design procedure).

1. Set the gain K as per the steady-state error requirement by entering value into the **C(s)** field in the **Current Compensator** panel. Read the values of gain crossover frequency ω_g, and the phase margin of the uncompensated system.

2. Determine the additional amount of phase lead needed at the new gain crossover frequency ω_g' to realize the specified phase margin. Setting this equal to the maximum phase of the lead compensator, calculate parameter α of the compensator.

3. Locate the frequency ω_g' at which the uncompensated system has a gain of $-20 \log (1/\sqrt{\alpha})$dB.

   Note that the plots in the Bode diagram window do not have the facility provided by an LTI Viewer. We cannot get the relevant data at an arbitrary point on the plot lines by left-clicking. By repeated application of **Zoom**, we can adjust the scales to read ω_g'; the value, however, will be an approximation.

   Alternatively, we can open LTI Viewer by selecting **Open-Loop Nichols** under **Loop Responses** from the **Tools** menu. Left-clicking along the plot line, we can accurately locate the point having gain of $-20 \log (1/\sqrt{\alpha})$dB; the corresponding frequency can then be read from the data marker.

4. Setting ω_g' equal to frequency at which maximum phase lead of the compensator occurs, calculate parameter τ of the compensator.

5. Select **Edit Compensator** from the right-click menu and enter the values of the compensator pole and zero. When you click OK, the Bode plots of the compensated system appear. Keep on trying with different compensator pole and zero values till you meet the specifications on the phase margin (and gain margin).

6. Select **Open-Loop Nichols** under **Loop Responses** from the **Tools** menu to determine the bandwidth of the compensated system (You may, alternatively, select **Closed-Loop Bode** under **Loop Responses** from the **Tools** menu to determine the bandwidth. For non-unity feedback system, only **Closed-Loop Bode** will give the bandwidth). Iterate on the compensator design if the performance specification on bandwidth is not met.

7. Take a look at the step response of the closed-loop system (Select **Plant Output (Step)** under the **Loop Responses** from the **Tools** menu).

A procedure similar to the one given above may be followed for lag compensator design.

Controller Implementation

Should the compensator be analog or digital? There are many factors to consider. A digital compensator has the advantage that it can be reprogrammed in response to known changes in the plant. A primary disadvantage of the digital compensators is that they reduce the available feedback when the computational delay in the loop is significant. For this reason, analog compensators are the first choice for fast feedback loops.

Suppose analog compensator $D(s)$ has been created in MATLAB as **sysc**. The command

sysd = c2d(sysc,T,'tustin') % Tustin approximation

% T is sampling interval

converts the continuous-time system $D(s)$ to discrete-time system using trapezoidal rule for integration. The object **sysc** may be an **SS** object or a **TF** object. Refer [180] for more details.

Simulation of the Performance of the Design

After reaching the best compromise among process modification, actuator and sensor selection, and controller design choice, run a computer model of the feedback system. This model should include important nonlinearities—such as actuator saturation, and parameter variations you expect to find during operation of the system. The simulation will confirm stability and robustness, and allow you to predict the true performance you can expect from the system.

MATLAB provides many Runge Kutta numerical integration routines for solving ordinary differential equations; the function **ode23** usually suffices for

our applications. The feedback system is represented by a set of linear/
nonlinear state-space equations; the system is coded in an **M-file**, and then **ode**
solver function such as **ode23** is applied to solve the system on a given time
interval with a particular initial condition vector. Refer [180].

   Simulink, a companion program to MATLAB, is an interactive system for
simulating nonlinear dynamic systems. It is a graphical mouse-driven program
that allows you to model a system by drawing a block diagram on the screen
and manipulating it dynamically. Refer [180].

Problems

Each problem covers an important area of control-system analysis or design.
Important MATLAB commands are included as help to these problems, in the
form of script files. In MATLAB, script files are called **M-files**. In attempting
a problem, the reader can type the MATLAB commands in the script file in an
interactive manner, or use the script file as an **M-file**.

   Following each problem, one or more what-if's may be posed to examine
the effect of variations of the key parameters. Comments to alert the reader to
the special features of MATLAB commands are included in the script files to
enhance the learning experience. Partial answers to the problems are also included.

   The description of the MATLAB functions used in the script files can easily
be accessed from the **help file** using **help** command.

B.1 Figure 4.7 shows the model of a heat exchanger control loop. Plot
     response of the system to unit-step input θ_r, for $K_A = 10$, and for $K_A = 5$.
     Comment on the effect of amplifier gain on transient and steady-state
     accuracy.

B.2 Figure 4.7 shows the model of a heat exchanger control loop. Plot re-
     sponse of the system to unit-step disturbance θ_i, for $K_A = 10$, and for K_A
     = 5.
     Comment on the effect of amplifier gain on transient and steady-state
     accuracy.

B.3 Figure 4.7 shows the model of a heat exchanger control loop. Determine
     the closed-loop poles of the system. Sketch a pole-zero map and
     therefrom comment upon stability.

B.4 *Review Example 5.3 revisited.*
     A non-unity feedback system has process transfer function

$$G(s) = \frac{K}{s(s+1)}$$

     and feedback transfer function

$$H(s) = \frac{1-Ts}{1+Ts}$$

What are the combinations of K and T for which the system is stable?

B.5 *The Script PB.4 revisited.*

The MATLAB response to this script shows the stability region for a non-unity feedback system. Take a point in this region and determine the response of the resulting feedback system to a unit-ramp input.

B.6 *Review Example 6.2 revisited.*

A unity-feedback system is characterized by the open-loop transfer function

$$G(s) = \frac{1}{s(0.5\,s + 1)\,(0.2\,s + 1)}$$

(a) Determine the damping ratio and natural frequency of dominant closed-loop poles.

(b) Determine the error constants K_p, K_v, and K_a.

(c) Determine peak overshoot, time to peak, and settling time of the step response of the feedback system. Are your results different from the ones given in the text? Why?

(Ans: M_p = 12.1186%; t_p = 3 sec; t_s = 4.52 sec)

B.7 *Examples 6.2 and 6.4 revisited.*

A unity-feedback position control system has open-loop transfer function

$$G(s) = \frac{4500}{s(s + 361.2)}$$

Plot step response of the system with a cascade controller $D(s)$ with

(a) $D(s) = 184.1$

(b) $D(s) = 184.1 + 0.324s$

(c) $D(s) = 14.728 + 147.28/s$

Compare the responses for (a) and (b), and those for (a) and (c). Comment upon the effects of derivative and integral control actions.

B.8 *Examples 9.2 and 9.4 revisited.*

A unity-feedback system has open-loop transfer function

$$G(s) = \frac{10}{s(1 + 0.1s)\,(1 + 0.05s)}$$

(a) Determine gain margin, phase margin, gain crossover frequency and phase crossover frequency.

(b) Determine resonance peak, resonance frequency, and bandwidth. The answers will be slightly different from the ones given in the text. The text answers are based upon Bode plot obtained using asymptotic approximation.

B.9 *Design Example 1 in Section 7.5 revisited.*

A unity-feedback system has open-loop transfer function

$$G(s) = \frac{K}{s(s+1)(s+5)}$$

Relative stability specification calls for a peak overshoot of 14%. Find the value of K to meet this specification and the resulting closed-loop poles. What is the natural frequency of dominant pair of poles?

Using LTI Viewer, determine the peak overshoot and settling time of the closed-loop step response. (Ans: 19%; 9.51 sec)

B.10 *Example 7.8 revisited.*

A unity-feedback system has open-loop transfer function

$$G(s) = \frac{K}{s(s+2)}$$

It is desired that dominant closed-loop poles provide damping ratio $\zeta = 0.5$ and have an undamped natural frequency $\omega_n = 4$ rad/sec. Velocity error constant K_v is required to be greater than 4.

(a) Verify that only gain adjustment can't meet these objectives.
(b) Design a lead compensator to meet the objectives.
(c) Using LTI Viewer, determine the peak overshoot and settling time of the lead-compensated system (Ans: $M_p = 21\%$; $t_s = 0.02$ sec)
(d) Design a lag compensator to meet the objectives (Refer Example 7.10).

B.11 *Example 10.4 revisited.*

A unity-feedback system has open-loop transfer function

$$G(s) = \frac{K}{s(s+1)}$$

It is desired to have the velocity error constant $K_v = 10$. Furthermore, we desire that the phase margin of the system be atleast 45°. Design a phase-lag compensator to achieve these specifications.

Are your results different from the ones given in the text? Why?

Using LTI Viewer, determine the peak overshoot and settling time of the lag-compensated system. (Ans: $M_p = 28\%$; $t_s = 14$ sec)

B.12 *Example 10.1 revisited.*

Repeat Problem B.11 under the constraint that we use phase-lead compensation to achieve the performance specifications. (Ans: $M_p = 29\%$; $t_s = 1.77$ sec)

B.13 *Example 8.16 revisited.*

A unity-feedback system has open-loop transfer function

$$G(s) = \frac{e^{-s\tau_D}}{s(s+1)(s+2)}$$

Determine gain crossover frequency, phase crossover frequency, phase margin and gain margin when (i) $\tau_D = 0$ (ii) $\tau_D = 1$.

B.14 *Example 11.4 revisited.*

For a unity-feedback system with plant transfer function $G(s) = 1/s^2$, show that the cascade compensator $D(s) = 0.81(s + 0.2)/(s + 2)$ meets the specifications: $\zeta = 0.7$, $\omega_n = 0.3$. Plot step response of the compensated system.

Now discretize the compensator (sampling time $T = 1$ sec) and plot step response of the discretized system with digital compensator. Comment upon the discrepancy with respect to performance achieved using analog design.

(Help: The response of the MATLAB script gives the digital compensator as

$$D(z) = \frac{0.4458\,z - 0.3648}{z}$$

Therefore,

$$\frac{U(z)}{E(z)} = \frac{0.4458 - 0.3648\,z^{-1}}{1}$$

or

$$u(k) = 0.4458\,e(k) - 0.3648\,e(k{-}1)$$

B.15 *Example 12.9 revisited*

Show that the Inverted Pendulum described in this example is unstable. Also show that state-feedback

$$u(t) = -\,\mathbf{k}\,\mathbf{x}(t)$$
$$\mathbf{k} = [-\,27 \quad -\,12.544 \quad -\,0.258 \quad -\,1.033]$$

stabilizes this system.

For initial conditions

$$\mathbf{x}(0) = [0.1 \quad 0 \quad 0 \quad 0]^T$$

and zero external input, simulate the feedback system.

Script PB.1

```
clear all;
close all;
disp('Refer Fig.4.7 ')
%Step response of heat exchanger control system
%Block diagram manipulation
D1=10;Gv=tf(0.1,[3 1]);Gp=tf(50,[30 1]);
H=tf(0.16,[10 1]);
Gfw1=D1*Gv*Gp;
M1=0.16*feedback(Gfw1,H);
%Step response
t=[0:0.1:300];
y1=step(M1,t);
```

```
plot(t,y1,'r');title('Step response')
xlabel('time[sec]');ylabel('temp[degC]');grid
%Steady-state error
yss1=y1(length(t));
line(t,yss1*ones(length(t),1));line(t,ones(length(t),1));
text(23,1.7,'K_A=10')
hold on
%Change in amplifier gain
D2=5;Gfw2=D2*Gv*Gp;
M2=0.16*feedback(Gfw2,H);
y2=step(M2,t);
plot(t,y2,'r-');
yss2=y2(length(t));
line(t,yss2*ones(length(t),1));line(t,ones(length(t),1));
text(28,1.15,'K_A=5')
hold off
```

Script PB.2

```
clear all
close all
disp('Refer Fig.4.7 ')
%Response of heat exchanger control system to
%step disturbance
%Block diagram manipulation
N1=tf(3,[30 1]);
D1=10;Gv=tf(0.1,[3 1]);Gp=tf(50,[30 1]);
Hs=tf(0.16,[10 1]);
H1=Hs*D1*Gv*Gp;
Mw1=-1*feedback(1,H1)*N1;
%Response to step disturbance
t=[0:0.1:300];
y1=step(Mw1,t);subplot(2,1,1);plot(t,y1,'r')
legend('Disturbance step response for K_A=10');
xlabel('time[sec]');ylabel('temp[degC]');grid
%Steady-state error
yss1=y1(length(t));
line(t,yss1*ones(length(t),1))
text(225,yss1-0.02,'Steady-state error')
%Change in amplifier gain
D2=5;H2=Hs*D2*Gv*Gp;Mw2=-1*feedback(1,H2)*N1;
y2=step(Mw2,t);subplot(2,1,2);plot(t,y2,'r')
legend('Disturbance step response for K_A=5')
xlabel('time[sec]');ylabel('temp[degC]');grid
```

```
yss2=y2(length(t));
line(t,yss2*ones(length(t),1))
text(225,yss2-0.02,'Steady-state error')
```

Script PB.3

```
clear all
close all
disp('Refer Fig.4.7 ')
%Stability analysis of heat exchanger control system
%Block diagram manipulation
D=10;
Gv=tf(0.1,[3 1]);
Gp=tf(50,[30 1]);
H=tf(0.16,[10 1]);
Gfw=D*Gv*Gp;
M=0.16*feedback(Gfw,H);
%Stability test
Closed_loop_Poles=pole(M)
pzmap(M)
```

Script PB.4

```
clear all
close all
disp('Refer Review Example 5.3 ')
%Stability region for a feedback system
T=[0.1:0.05:10];K=[0:0.05:10];
x=0*T;y=0*T;
n=length(T);
m=length(K);
for i=1:n
   for j=2:m
      G=tf([K(j)],[1 1 0]);
      H=tf([-T(i) 1],[T(i) 1]);
      [num,den]=tfdata(feedback(G,H),'v');
      p=roots(den);
      if max(real(p))>0,
         x(i)=T(i);
         y(i)=K(j-1);
         break
      end
   end
end
```

```
%Wait for the response
plot(x,y);
grid;
xlabel('T');
ylabel('K');
gtext('Stability Region')
%gtext puts up a cross hair.Position the cross hair
%on the graph with the mouse & click.
```

Script PB.5

```
clear all;
close all;
disp('Refer the Script ME 4.')
%Ramp response of a feedback system
%Select a point in the stability region
T=0.5;K=1;
G=tf(K,[1 1 0]);H=tf([-T 1],[T 1]);
M=feedback(G,H);
%Ramp response
t=[0:0.1:30];
u=t;
[y,t]=lsim(M,u,t);
plot(t,y,t,u);grid
xlabel('time[sec]');ylabel('y(t)');
```

Script PB.6

```
clear all
close all
disp('Refer Review Example 6.2')
%Performance specifications in time-domain
%Open-loop transfer function
den=conv(conv([1 0],[0.5 1]),[0.2 1]);
G=tf(1,den);
%Unity-feedback system
M=feedback(G,1);
%Damping ratio & natural frequency
[wn,zeta,p]=damp(M);
%Position,velocity & acceleration error constants
Kp=dcgain(G);
Gv=tf([1 0],1)*G;
Kv=dcgain(Gv);
Ga=tf([1 0],1)*Gv;
```

```
Ka=dcgain(Ga);
%Peakovershoot,time to peak,& settling time
t=[0:0.01:10];
y=step(M,t);
[Mp,i]=max(y);tp=t(i);
%OR operation
j=max(find((y<=0.98)|(y>=1.02)));
ts=t(j);
%Output the results
wn=wn(1)
zeta=zeta(1)
Kp=Kp
Kv=Kv
Ka=Ka
Mp=(Mp-1)*100
tp=tp
ts=ts
%Obtain performance specs using LTI Viewer
ltiview('step',M)
```

Script PB.7

```
clear all
close all
disp('Refer Examples 6.2 & 6.4')
%PID control of a position servo
%Unity-feedback system
G=tf(4500,[1 361.2 0]);
Kc=184.1;
M1=feedback(Kc*G,1);
%Step response with P & PD controllers
t=[0:0.0001:0.04];
y1=step(M1,t);
KD=0.324;
D1=tf([KD Kc],1);
M2=feedback(D1*G,1);
y2=step(M2,t);
figure(1);
plot(t,y1,t,y2);grid;xlabel('t');ylabel('y(t)');
text(0.005,1.4,'With P control')
text(0.003,1.07,'With PD control')
%Step response with P & PI controllers
Kc=14.728;KI=147.28;
```

```
D2=tf([Kc KI],[1 0]);
M3=feedback(D2*G,1);
y3=step(M3,t);
figure(2);
plot(t,y1,t,y3);grid;
xlabel('t');ylabel('y(t)');
text(0.005,1.5,'With P control')
text(0.02,1.15,'With PI control')
```

Script PB.8

```
clear all
close all
disp('Refer Examples 9.2 & 9.4 ')
%Performance specifications in frequency-domain
%Open-loop transfer function
den=conv(conv([1 0],[0.1 1]),[0.05 1]);
G=tf(10,den);
figure(1);
%Unity-feedback system
M=feedback(G,1);
%Read Phase margin & Gain margin from figure 1.
margin(G);
w=[1:0.001:100]';
[mag,phase]=bode(M,w);
%Frequency-response of feedback system
figure(2);
bode(M,w);
magdB=20*log10(mag);
%Resonance peak
[Mr,i]=max(magdB);
wr=w(i);
Resonancepeak=Mr
Resonancefrequecny=wr
%Bandwidth
%Select proper frequency range.Function interp1q
%requires monotonic increasing data.
w1=[wr:0.001:100]';
[mag1,phase1]=bode(M,w1);
mag1dB=20*log10(mag1);
wb=interp1q(-mag1dB,w1,3);
Bandwidth=wb
%LTI Viewer functions are available in figure 2
%window.Obtain resonance peak,resonance frequency,
%and bandwidth using these functions.
```

```
%Obtain performance specs from Nichols chart
figure(3)
%LTI Viewer functions are available in figure 3
%window.Zoom the -3dB contour region,and region
%of tangency to an M-contour.Read off the values
%of bandwidth & resonance frequency by clicking
%at appropriate places.Read the resonance peak
% from the ngrid.
ngrid;nichols(G);
pause
%The gain-phase plot of G(s) is not tangent to any
%of the M-contours available in ngrid.Using ginput
%fuction,read the values of phase & gain of G(s) at
%the expected point of tangency & calculate Mr.Come
%out of pause state by pressing any key.
[theta,dB]=ginput(1);
%dB to absolute value
rp=10.^(dB./20);
theta=theta*pi/180;
[x,y]=pol2cart(theta,rp);
%Refer Eqns.(9.20-9.21)
Mr=((x.^2+y.^2)./(((1+x).^2)+y.^2)).^0.5;
Mr=20*log10(Mr)
```

Script PB.9

```
close all
clear all
disp('Refer Section 7.5(Design Example 1)')
% Root locus gain for specified zeta
den=conv(conv([1 1],[1 5]),[1 0]);
G=tf(1,den);
Mp=0.14;
zeta=sqrt((((log(Mp)/pi)^2))/{1+((log(Mp)/pi)^2)});
figure(1);
rlocus(G);
axis equal;axis([-7 2 -5 5]);
%Draw zeta-line.To get a longer line,we have used
%large value of wn in spchart function.
spchart(gca,zeta,10);
%Replace spchart command by sgrid(zeta,wn) if working with
%MATLAB 5.3 version.
[KK polesCL]=rlocfind(G)
%Position crosshair cursor on point of intersection
```

```
%of root locus with zeta-line & click.
M=feedback(KK*G,1);
[wn zeta p]=damp(M);
wn=wn(1)
%Analysis using LTI Viewer
ltiview('step',M)
```

Script PB.10

```
close all
clear all
disp('Refer Example 7.8 ')
%Compensator design on root locus plots
%Plant model
G=tf(1,[1 2 0]);
%Uncompensated root locus
figure(1)
rlocus(G);
axis equal;axis([-7 2 -5 5]);
%Replace spchart command by sgrid(zeta,wn) if working with
%MATLAB 5.3 version.
spchart(gca,[0.5 1],4);
%Gain adjustment does not satisfy specs.
%Lead compensator zero in the region below desired
%dominant pole,just to the left of open-loop pole.
%Take zero at -2.9 and pole at - beta.
beta=input('Enter trial value of beta:')
D=tf([1 2.9],[1 beta]);
figure(2)
rlocus(D*G)
axis equal;axis([-7 2 -5 5]);
spchart(gca,[0.5 1],4);
[KK polesCL]=rlocfind(D*G)
%Place the crosshair cursor at sd point & click.
Gv=tf([1 0],1)*KK*D*G;
Kv=dcgain(Gv)
%Perform simulation study on closed-loop TF
%using LTI Viewer.
M=feedback(KK*D*G,1);
ltiview('step',M)
%Carry out the design on GUI using the command
% sisotool(G)
```

Script PB.11

```
clear all;close all
disp('Refer Example 10.4')
%Lag compensation on Bode plots
%Uncompensated system
den=[1 1 0];
G=tf(10,den);
figure(1);
margin(G);
%Read uncompensated phase margin from figure 1.
w=logspace(-1,1,100)';
[mag ph]=bode(G,w);
% mag & ph are arrays;the function interp1 does
%not accept these arrays.Reshape the arrays
%into column vectors.
ph=reshape(ph,100,1);
mag=reshape(mag,100,1);
%Phi=-180+specified phase margin+epsilon=-129
Phi=input('Enter phase angle Phi :')
%Select frequency range properly;function interp1
%requires monotonic data.
wg=interp1(ph,w,Phi)
% wg is the desired gain crossover wg'.
beta=interp1(ph,mag,Phi)
%Upper corner frequency at wg'/8.
wcu=input('Enter upper corner frequency :')
tau=1/wcu;
D=tf([tau 1],[beta*tau 1]);
figure(2);
%Read phase margin of compensated system
%from figure 2.
margin(D*G);
%Bandwidth(uncompensated & compensated)
w=[1:0.1:10];
[mag,ph,w]=bode(feedback(G,1));
magdB=20*log10(mag);
wb=interp1q(-magdB,w,3)
[mag1,ph1,w]=bode(feedback(D*G,1));
mag1dB=20*log10(mag1);
wb1=interp1q(-mag1dB,w,3)
%Analysis on Nichols chart
figure(3)
Gc=D*G;
```

```
ngrid;nichols(G,Gc);
%Step-response analysis using LTI Viewer
M=feedback(D*G,1);
ltiview('step',M)
%Carry out the design on GUI using command
% sisotool(G)
```

Script PB.12

```
clear all;close all
disp('Refer Example 10.1')
%Lead compensation on Bode plots
%Uncompensated system
den=[1 1 0];
G=tf(10,den);
figure(1);
margin(G);
%Read uncompensated phase margin from figure 1.
%phiM=specified phase margin-uncompensated phase margin
%+epsilon=30
phiM=input('Enter required phase lead :');
alpha=(1-sin(phiM*pi/180))/(1+sin(phiM*pi/180));
w=logspace(-1,1,100)';
[mag,ph]=bode(G,w);
magdB=20*log10(mag);
magdB=reshape(magdB,100,1);
wm=interp1(magdB,w,-20*log10(1/sqrt(alpha)));
tau=1/(wm*sqrt(alpha));
D=tf([tau 1],[alpha*tau 1]);
figure(2);
%Read compensated phase margin from figure 2.
margin(D*G);
%Bandwidth(uncompensated & compensated)
w=[1:0.1:10];
[mag,ph,w]=bode(feedback(G,1));
magdB=20*log10(mag);
wb=interp1q(-magdB,w,3)
[mag1,ph1,w]=bode(feedback(D*G,1));
mag1dB=20*log10(mag1);
wb1=interp1q(-mag1dB,w,3)
%Analysis on Nichols chart
figure(3)
Gc=D*G;
ngrid;nichols(G,Gc);
```

```
pause
%The gain-phase plot of G(s) is not tangent
%to any M-contour available in ngrid.Using ginput
%function,read the values of gain & phase of G(s)
%at the expected point of tangency & calculate Mr.
%Come out of the pause state by pressing any key.
[theta,dB]=ginput(1);
%dB to absolute value
rp=10.^(dB./20);
theta=theta*pi/180;
[x,y]=pol2cart(theta,rp);
%Refer Eqns.(9.20-9.21)
Mr=((x.^2+y.^2)./(((1+x).^2)+y.^2)).^0.5;
Mr=20*log10(Mr)
%Step-response analysis using LTI Viewer
M=feedback(D*G,1);
ltiview('step',M)
%Carry out the design on GUI using command
% sisotool(G)
```

Script PB.13

```
clear all;close all
disp('Refer Example 8.16')
% System with dead-time
den=conv(conv([1 0],[1 1]),[1 2]);
G=tf(1,den);
figure(1);
%GM & PM without deadtime.
margin(G);
tauD=1;
G1=tf(1,den,'InputDelay',tauD);
%Function margin does not accept deadtime model.
G11=pade(G1,2);
figure(2);
%GM & PM with deadtime
margin(G11);
```

Script PB.14

```
clear all
close all
disp('Refer Example 11.4')
%Discretization of analog design
```

```
%Analog design
G=tf(1,[1 0 0]);
D=tf([1 0.2],[1 2]);
figure(1)
rlocus(D*G);
axis equal;axis([-2.5,0.5,-2,2])
%Replace spchart command by sgrid(zeta,wn) if working with
%MATLAB 5.3 version.
spchart(gca,[0.7 1],0.3);
[K,polesCL]=rlocfind(D*G)
%Move the crosshair at intersection point
%of zeta-line & wn-circle and click.
figure(2)
%Step response with analog controller.
step(feedback(K*D*G,1));
hold on
%Discretization
Dz=c2d(K*D,1,'tustin')
%Dz is a z-transform TF;it can easily be
%converted into a difference equation.
%Refer[180].
Gz=c2d(G,1);
%Step response with digital controller.
step(feedback(Dz*Gz,1));
%Comparison of the plots shows that sampling
%rate needs to be increased.
```

Script PB.15

```
clear all
close all
disp('Refer Example 12.9')
%State variable analysis(Inverted Pendulum)
%Inverted pendulum system
A=[0 1 0 0;4.4537 0 0 0;0 0 0 1;-0.5809 0 0 0];
b=[0;-0.3947;0;0.9211];c=[1 0 0 0];
sys=ss(A,b,c,0);
%State feedback
polesOL=eig(A)
k=[-27 -12.544 -0.258 -1.033];
sysCL=ss(A-b*k,[0; 0; 0; 0],c,0);
polesCL=eig(A-b*k)
%Simulation
t=[0:0.1:20];
x0=[0.1,0,0,0]';
```

```
[y,t,X]=initial(sysCL,x0,t);
figure(1)
subplot(2,2,1);plot(t,X(:,1));grid;legend('x_1')
subplot(2,2,2);plot(t,X(:,2));grid;legend('x_2')
subplot(2,2,3);plot(t,X(:,3));grid;legend('x_3')
subplot(2,2,4);plot(t,X(:,4));grid;legend('x_4')
```

Appendix C

Control Theory Quiz

A set of questions with multiple answer choices is given here. These questions have been designed to capture important aspects of Control Theory covered in the book. For each of these questions, identify the best of the given answer choices. Compare your answers with the master key given at the end of the session. This quiz should serve the purpose of a self-appraisal test for the reader.

1. A linear time-invariant system initially at rest, when subjected to a unit-step input, gives a response $y(t) = te^{-t}; t > 0$. The transfer function of the system is

   (A) $\dfrac{1}{(s+1)^2}$ (B) $\dfrac{1}{s(s+1)^2}$ (C) $\dfrac{s}{(s+1)^2}$ (D) $\dfrac{1}{s(s+1)}$

2. The system shown in Fig. Q2 is of
   (A) zero order
   (C) second order
   (B) first order
   (D) third order

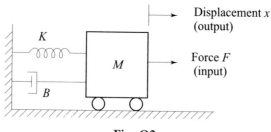

Fig. Q2

3. Time-constant of the circuit of Fig. Q3 is

(A) 0.25 sec   (B) 0.5 sec   (C) 1 sec   (D) 2 sec

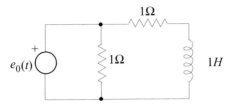

Fig. Q3

4. The step response of a system with transfer function $G(s) = 1/(\tau s + 1)$ attains more than 98% of its final value in time t equal to
   (A) τ (B) 2τ (C) 3τ (D) 4τ

5. The response of the system of Fig. Q5a to an input $r(t) = 8\mu(t)$ is shown in Fig. Q5b. The time-constant τ is equal to
   (A) 0.535 msec   (B) 0.32 msec   (C) 0.09 msec   (D) 11.25 msec

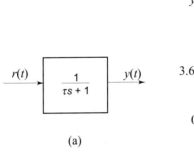

(a)

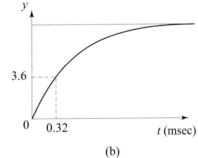

(b)

Fig. Q5

6. Closed-loop transfer function of a unity-feedback system is given by $Y(s)/R(s) = 1/(\tau s + 1)$. Steady-state error to unit-ramp input is
   (A) ∞ (B) τ (C) 1   (D) $1/\tau$

7. The series RLC circuit shown in Fig. Q7 is underdamped if

   (A) $\left(\dfrac{R}{2L}\right)^2 < \dfrac{1}{LC}$

   (B) $\left(\dfrac{R}{2L}\right)^2 = \dfrac{1}{LC}$

   (C) $\left(\dfrac{R}{2L}\right)^2 > \dfrac{1}{LC}$

   (D) None of the answers in (A), (B), and (C) is correct

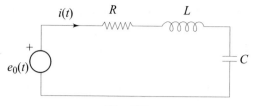

Fig. Q7

8. Closed-loop transfer function of a unity-feedback system is given by

$$\frac{Y(s)}{R(s)} = \frac{\omega_n^2}{s^2 + 2\zeta\omega_n s + \omega_n^2}.$$ Steady-state error to unit-ramp input is

(A) ∞ (B) $2\zeta/\omega_n$ (C) 1   (D) $4/\zeta\omega_n$

9. When two networks shown in Fig. Q9 are cascaded in tandem, the overall transfer function $E_4(s)/E_1(s)$ is
   (A) $H_1(s)\,H_2(s)$
   (B) $H_1(s) + H_2(s)$
   (C) $H_1(s)/H_2(s)$
   (D) None of the answers in (A), (B), and (C) is correct

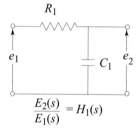

$$\frac{E_2(s)}{E_1(s)} = H_1(s)$$

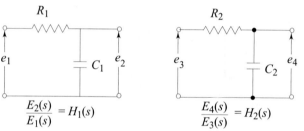

$$\frac{E_4(s)}{E_3(s)} = H_2(s)$$

Fig. Q9

10. Dead-time model $e^{-s\tau_D}$ may be approximated by the transfer function

(A) $\dfrac{1 - \dfrac{\tau_D}{2}s}{1 + \dfrac{\tau_D}{2}s}$ (B) $\dfrac{1 + \dfrac{\tau_D}{2}s}{1 - \dfrac{\tau_D}{2}s}$ (C) $\dfrac{1 - \tau_D s}{1 + \tau_D s}$ (D) $\dfrac{1 + \tau_D s}{1 - \tau_D s}$

11. Consider the block diagram shown in Fig. Q11. The transfer function between $Y(s)$ and $W(s)$ is

(A) $\dfrac{D(s)\,G(s)\,N(s)}{1 + D(s)\,G(s)\,H(s)}$

(B) $\dfrac{N(s)}{1 + D(s)\,G(s)\,H(s)}$

(C) $\dfrac{N(s)}{1 - D(s)\,G(s)\,H(s)}$

(D) None of the answers in (A), (B), and (C) is correct

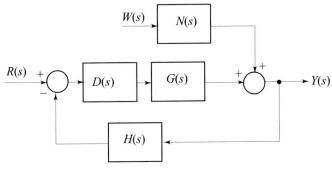

Fig. Q11

12. The gear train shown in Fig. Q12
    (A) reduces the speed and the torque
    (B) increases the speed and the torque
    (C) reduces the speed and increases the torque
    (D) increases the speed and reduces the torque

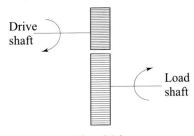

Fig. Q12

13. Effect of back emf in an armature-controlled dc servomotor is
    (A) to increase effective motor friction, thereby reducing motor time-constant
    (B) to increase effective motor friction, thereby increasing motor time-constant
    (C) to increase motor inertia, thereby increasing motor time-constant
    (D) to increase motor inertia, thereby reducing motor time-constant

14. Electrical time-constant of an armature-controlled dc servomotor is
    (A) equal to mechanical time-constant
    (B) smaller than mechanical time-constant
    (C) larger than mechanical time-constant
    (D) None of the answers in (A), (B), and (C) is correct

15. Consider the following statements:
    (i) Characteristics of ac servomotors are quite linear, and these motors are easier to control.
    (ii) Characteristics of dc servomotors are quite nonlinear and these motors are difficult to control.
    Which of the following is the correct answer?

(A) None of the above statements is true

(B) Statement (i) is true but statement (ii) is false

(C) Statement (i) is false but statement (ii) is true

(D) Both the statements are true

16. Ratio of the rotor reactance X to the rotor resistance R for a two-phase servomotor

(A) is equal to that of a normal induction motor

(B) is less than that of a normal induction motor

(C) is greater than that of a normal induction motor

(D) may be less or greater than that of a normal induction motor

17. Consider the following statements:

(i) The stator windings S_1, S_2 and S_3 of a synchro control transformer are connected to a three-phase power source.

(ii) The rotor of a synchro control transformer is cylindrically shaped. Which of the following is the correct answer?

(A) None of the above statements is true

(B) Statement (i) is true but statement (ii) is false

(C) Statement (i) is false but statement (ii) is true

(D) Both the statements are true

18. Feedback control systems are

(A) insensitive to both forward- and feedback-path parameter changes

(B) less sensitive to feedback-path parameter changes than to forward-path parameter charges

(C) less sensitive to forward-path parameter changes than to feedback-path parameter changes

(D) equally sensitive to forward- and feedback-path parameter charges

19. In the system of Fig. Q19, sensitivity of $M(s) = Y(s)/R(s)$ with respect to parameter K_1 is

(A) $\dfrac{1}{1 + K_1 K_2}$

(B) $\dfrac{1}{1 + K_1 G(s)}$

(C) 1

(D) None of the answers in (A), (B), and (C) is correct

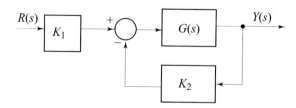

Fig. Q19

20. In the system of Fig. Q19, sensitivity of $M(s) = Y(s)/R(s)$ with respect to parameter K_2 is

   (A) $\dfrac{1}{1 + K_2 K_1}$

   (B) $\dfrac{1}{1 + K_2 G(s)}$

   (C) $\dfrac{-K_2 G(s)}{1 + K_2 G(s)}$

   (D) None of the answers in (A), (B), and (C) is correct

21. A speed control system is represented by the signal flow graph shown in Fig. Q21. The nominal value of the parameter K is 10. Sensitivity of $M(s) = \omega(s)/\omega_r(s)$ to changes in K is

   (A) $\dfrac{s + 0.1}{s + 11}$

   (B) $\dfrac{s + 0.1}{s + 0.2}$

   (C) $\dfrac{-0.1}{s + 0.2}$

   (D) None of the answers in (A), (B), and (C) is correct

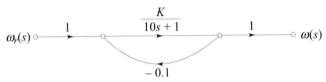

Fig. Q21

22. A speed control system is represented by the block diagram of Fig. Q22. The system is subjected to a step disturbance $\omega(s)$. $\omega_{ss}^{CL}/\omega_{ss}^{OL}$ (the steady-state speed under closed-loop operation/steady-state speed under open-loop operation) is equal to

   (A) 1/2

   (B) 1

   (C) 2

   (D) None of the answers in (A), (B), and (C) is correct

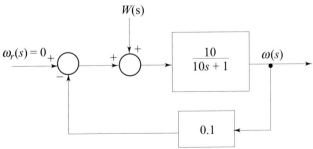

Fig. Q22

23. For the negative feedback system shown in Fig. Q23, the effective time-constant is

(A) L/R

(B) Less than L/R

(C) more than L/R

(D) zero

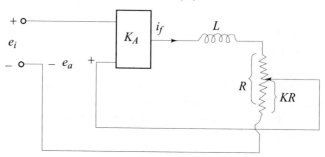

Fig. Q23

24. The time response of the system of Fig. Q24a to an input $r(t) = 10\ \mu(t)$ is shown in Fig. Q24b. The gain K is equal to

(A) 10

(B) 8

(C) 4

(D) None of the answers in (A), (B), and (C) is correct

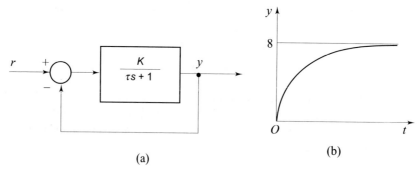

(a)   (b)

Fig. Q24

25. An inertial and a frictional load are driven by a dc motor with torque T_M. The dynamic model of the system is

$$T_M(t) = J\ \frac{d\omega(t)}{dt} + B\omega(t)$$

The steady-state speed of the motor for step input will be doubled when

(A) inertia J is doubled

(B) friction B is doubled

(C) both the inertia J and friction B are doubled

(D) None of the answers in (A), (B), and (C) is correct

26. Consider the following statements:
    (i) If an open-loop system is unstable, applying feedback will always improve its stability.
    (ii) If an open-loop system is subject to parameter variations, applying feedback will always improve robustness.
    Which of the following is the correct answer?
    (A) None of the above statements is true
    (B) Statement (i) is true but statement (ii) is false
    (C) Statement (i) is false but statement (ii) is true
    (D) Both the statements are true

27. The condition that all the roots of the polynomial
$$\Delta(s) = a_0 s^3 + a_1 s^2 + a_2 s + a_3; \; a_i > 0$$
    have negative real parts, is given by
    (A) $a_1 a_3 > a_0 a_2$ (B) $a_1 a_0 > a_2 a_3$
    (C) $a_1 a_2 > a_0 a_3$ (D) $a_2 a_0 > a_1 a_3$

28. Consider the following statements:
    (i) All the roots of the polynomial
$$\Delta_1(s) = 3s^4 + 10s^3 + 5s^2 + 2$$
    have negative real parts.
    (ii) All the roots of the polynomial
$$\Delta_2(s) = s^4 + 4s^3 + 6s^2 + 4s - 5$$
    have negative real parts.
    Which of the following is the correct answer?
    (A) None of the above statements is true
    (B) Statement (i) is true but statement (ii) is false
    (C) Statement (i) is false but statement (ii) is true
    (D) Both the statements are true

29. The characteristic equation of a feedback control system is given by
$$2s^4 + s^3 + 2s^2 + 5s + 10 = 0$$
    The number of roots in the right half of s-plane are
    (A) zero   (B) 1   (C) 2   (D) 3

30. The polynomial
$$\Delta(s) = s^3 + 3s^2 + 2s + 6$$
    has
    (A) two roots in left half s-plane and one root in right half
    (B) two roots in right half s-plane and one root in left half
    (C) two roots on $j\omega$-axis of s-plane and one root in right half
    (D) two roots on $j\omega$-axis of s-plane and one root in left half.

31. The characteristic equation of a feedback control system is
$$s^3 + \alpha_1 s^2 + \alpha_2 s + K\alpha_2 = 0; \; \alpha_1, \, \alpha_2, \, > 0,$$
    where K is a variable positive scalar parameter. The system is stable for all values of K given by

(A) $K > \alpha_2$ (B) $K < \alpha_2$ (C) $K > \alpha_1$ (D) $K < \alpha_1$

32. The open-loop transfer function of a unity feedback system is

$$G(s) = K/[s^2(s + 5)]; \quad K > 0$$

The system is unstable for
(A) $K > 5$
(B) $K < 5$
(C) $K > 0$
(D) All the answers in (A), (B) and (C) are correct

33. A unity feedback system has open-loop transfer function

$$G(s) = K/[s(s + 1)(s + 2)]; \quad K > 0$$

The value of K that results in oscillatory response to step input, is
(A) 2   (B) 6   (C) 20   (D) 60

34. Consider the following statements:
   (i) When a row of Routh tabulation contains all zeros before the tabulation ends, this means that the characteristic equation necessarily has roots on the imaginary axis of the s-plane.
   (ii) When a row of Routh tabulation contains a zero pivot element with atleast one nonzero element, this means that the characteristic equation necessarily has roots on the imaginary axis of the s-plane.
   Which of the following is the correct answer?
   (A) None of the above statements is true
   (B) Statement (i) is true but statement (ii) is false
   (C) Statement (i) is false but statement (ii) is true
   (D) Both the statements are true

35. The first two rows of Routh tabulation of a third-order system are

$$\begin{array}{c|cc} s^3 & 2 & 2 \\ s^2 & 4 & 4 \end{array}$$

   (A) The characteristic equation has one root in right half s-plane
   (B) The characteristics equation has two roots on the $j\omega$-axis at $s = \pm j$
   (C) The characteristic equation has two roots on the $j\omega$-axis at $s = \pm 2j$
   (D) None of the answers in (A), (B), and (C) is correct

36. Presence of transportion lag in the forward path of a closed-loop control system
   (A) decreases margin of stability
   (B) increases margin of stability
   (C) does not affect its margin of stability

37. A unity feedback system has open-loop transfer function $G(s) = 9/[s(s + 3)]$. The system has

   (A) damping ratio $= \dfrac{1}{2}$, and natural frequency $= 9$

   (B) damping ratio $= \dfrac{1}{6}$, and natural frequency $= 3$

(C) damping ratio = $\dfrac{1}{6}$, and natural frequency = 9

(D) damping ratio = $\dfrac{1}{2}$, and natural frequency = 3

38. A unity feedback system has open-loop transfer function $G(s) = 25/[s(s + 6)]$. The time t_p at which the peak of the step-input response occurs, is

(A)11/7 sec   (B)11/4 sec   (C)11/14 sec   (D)11/28 sec

39. Peak overshoot of step-input response of an underdamped second-order system is explicitly indicative of
   (A) settling time   (B) rise time
   (C) natural frequency   (D) damping ratio

40. Consider the following statements:
   (i) The peak overshoot of step-input response of $G(s)$ will never exceed 100% when ζ and ω_n are both positive.

$$G(s) = \frac{Y(s)}{R(s)} = \frac{\omega_n^2}{s^2 + 2\zeta\omega_n s + \omega_n^2}$$

   (ii) The peak overshoot of step-input response of $G(s)$ will never exceed 100% when ζ, ω_n and α are all positive.

$$G(s) = \frac{Y(s)}{R(s)} = \frac{\omega_n^2(1 + \alpha s)}{s^2 + 2\zeta\omega_n s + \omega_n^2}$$

   Which of the following is the correct answer?
   (A) None of the statements is true
   (B) Statement (i) is true but statement (ii) is false
   (C) Statement (i) is false but statement (ii) is true
   (D) Both the statements are true

41. A unity feedback system has open-loop transfer function $G(s) = 25/[s(s + 6)]$. The peak overshoot in the step-input response of the system is approximately equal to
   (A) 5%   (B) 10%   (C) 15%   (D) 20%

42. The step-input response of the system of Fig. Q42a is shown in Fig. Q42b. The value of damping ratio of the system is
   (A) 0.39   (B) 0.49   (C) 0.59   (D) 0.69

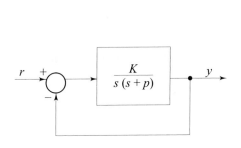

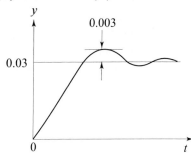

Fig. Q42

43. A unity feedback system with open-loop transfer function $G(s) = 4/[s(s + p)]$ is critically damped. The value of the parameter p is
   (A) 4   (B) 3   (C) 2   (D) 1

44. Consider the following statements:

   (i) The transfer function $G(s)$ can be approximated by $\hat{G}(s)$ since the pole at $s = -20$ is much larger than the dominant pole at $s = -1$.

   $$G(s) = \frac{10}{s(s+1)(s+20)} ; \hat{G}(s) = \frac{10}{s(s+1)}$$

   (ii) The transfer function $G(s)$ can be approximated by $\hat{G}(s)$ since the pole at $s = -1$ is very close to the zero at $s = -1.1$.

   $$G(s) = \frac{s+1.1}{(s+1)(s+2)} ; \hat{G}(s) = \frac{1}{s+2}$$

   Which of the following is the correct answer?
   (A) None of the statements is true
   (B) Statement (i) is true but statement (ii) is false
   (C) Statement (i) is false but statement (ii) is true
   (D) Both the statements are true

45. A unity feedback system has open-loop transfer function $G(s)$. The steady-state error is zero for
   (A) step input and type-1 $G(s)$
   (B) ramp input and type-1 $G(s)$
   (C) step input and type-0 $G(s)$
   (D) ramp input and type-0 $G(s)$

46. A unity feedback system with forward path transfer function $G(s) = 1/[s^2(s + 1)]$ is subjected to an input $r(t) = K_1 + K_2 t + \frac{1}{2}t^2$. The steady-state error of the system is
   (A) infinity
   (B) 1
   (C) zero
   (D) None of the answers in (A), (B), and (C) is correct

47. A closed-loop speed control system is set up using a dc servomotor, a dc tachogenerator, and a differential amplifier. System steady-state error to unit-step input is expected to be
   (A) zero
   (B) infinity
   (C) constant-amplitude oscillation
   (D) constant finite value

48. Closed-loop transfer function of a unity feedback system is given by

   $$\frac{Y(s)}{R(s)} = \frac{1}{\tau s + 1}$$

System K_v is
(A) τ (B) $1/\tau$ (C) 1   (D) ∞

49. Closed-loop transfer function of a unity feedback system is given by

$$\frac{Y(s)}{R(s)} = \frac{\omega_n^2}{s^2 + 2\zeta\omega_n s + \omega_n^2}$$

System K_v is
(A) $\omega_n/2\zeta$ (B) 1   (C) ∞ (D) $2\zeta/\omega_n$

50. Consider the position control system of Fig. Q50. The value of K such that the steady-error is 10° for input $\theta_r = 400t\,\mu(t)$ rad/sec, is
(A) 104.5
(B) 114.5
(C) 124.5
(D) None of the answers in (A), (B), and (C) is correct

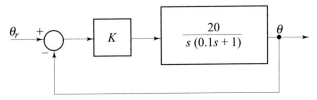

Fig. Q50

51. Consider the speed control system shown in Fig. Q51. Parameter variations occurring during operating conditions cause K_A to modify to $K_A' = 0.9K_A$. The value of K_A that limits the change in steady-state motor speed due to parameter variations to 0.1%, is
(A) 25   (B) 35   (C) 45   (D) 55

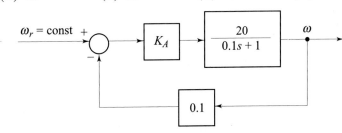

Fig. Q51

52. Derivative error compensation is employed in feedback control systems to
(A) increase the effective damping in the system
(B) decrease the effective damping in the system
(C) improve the steady-state response of the system

53. Tachometric feedback is sometimes used in position control systems to
(A) increase the effective damping in the system

(B) decrease the effective damping in the system

(C) improve the steady-state response of the system

54. Integral error compensation is employed in feedback control systems to

(A) improve damping

(B) improve speed of response

(C) reduce steady-state error

55. Which of the following control schemes will be employed to improve the steady-state performance of a position control system?

(A) Cascade PD

(B) Cascade PI

(C) Tachometric feedback

(D) None of the answers in (A), (B), and (C) is correct

56. A unity feedback system has open-loop poles at $s = -2 \pm j2$, $s = -1$, and $s = 0$; and a zero at $s = -3$. The angles made by the root-locus asymptotes with the real axis, and the point of intersection of the asymptotes are, respectively,

(A) $(60°, -60°, 180°)$ and $-3/2$

(B) $(60°, -60°, 180°)$ and $-2/3$

(C) $(45°, -45°, 180°)$ and $-2/3$

(D) $(45°, -45°, 180°)$ and $-4/3$

57. In a root locus plot,

(i) there is only one intersect of the asymptotes and it is always on the real axis;

(ii) the breakaway points always lie on the real axis.

Which of the following is the correct answer?

(A) None of the statements is true

(B) Statement (i) is true but statement (ii) is false

(C) Statement (i) is false but statement (ii) is true

(D) Both the statements are true

58. Which of the root locus plots shown in Fig. Q58 is the correct plot for a unity feedback system with open-loop poles at $s = -1 \pm j1$, and a zero at $s = -2$?

(A) Fig. Q58a   (B) Fig. Q58b   (C) Fig. Q58c   (D) Fig. Q58d

59. Which of the root locus plots shown in Fig. Q59 is the correct plot for a unity feedback system with open-loop transfer function $G(s) = K/[s^2(s + 5)]$?

(A) Fig. Q59a   (B) Fig. Q59b   (C) Fig. Q59c

60. A unity feedback system has open-loop transfer function $G(s) = K(s + 1)(s + 2)/[s(s + 3)(s + 4)]$. For $K = 10$, the closed-loop poles are

(A) all real and distinct

(B) one real and two complex conjugate

(C) all real and repeated

(D) None of the answers in (A), (B), and (C) is correct

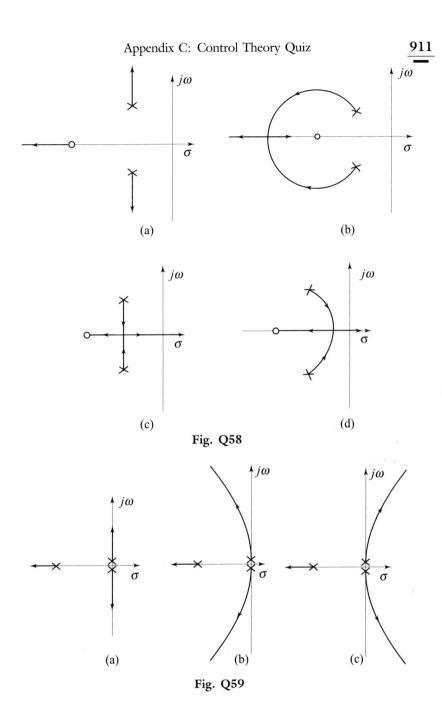

(a)   (b)

(c)   (d)

Fig. Q58

(a)   (b)   (c)

Fig. Q59

61. Root locus plot of a feedback system as gain K is varied, is shown in Fig. Q61. The system response to step input is nonoscillatory for
    (A) $0 < K < 0.4$
    (B) $0.4 < K < 6$
    (C) $6 < K < \infty$
    (D) None of the answers in (A), (B), and (C) is correct

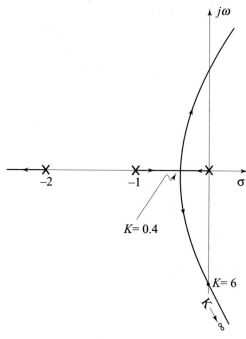

Fig. Q61

62. Consider the root locus plot shown in Fig. Q61.
    (i) Adding a zero between $s = -1$ and $s = -2$ would move the root locus to the left.
    (ii) Adding a pole at $s = 0$ would move the root locus to the right.
    Which of the following is the correct answer?
    (A) None of the above statements is true
    (B) Statement (i) is true but statement (ii) is false
    (C) Statement (i) is false but statement (ii) is true
    (D) Both the statements are true
63. Consider the following statements:
    (i) Given the characteristics equation

    $$s^3 + 3s^2 + 2s + K = 0$$

    Increasing K will improve damping.
    (ii) Given the characteristic equation

    $$s^2 + 2s + K(0.2s + 1) = 0$$

    Increasing K will improve damping.
    Which of the following is the correct answer?
    (A) None of the statements is true
    (B) Statement (i) is true but statement (ii) is false
    (C) Statement (i) is false but statement (ii) is true
    (D) Both the statements are true

64. For a plant with dominant complex poles, a useful compensation approach is to cancel complex poles with compensator zeros. Such a cancellation can be achieved using a
    (A) lead network
    (B) lag network
    (C) lag-lead network
    (D) bridged-T network

65. A type-1 plant is changed to type-2 feedback system by the following cascade control action:
    (A) PD
    (B) PI
    (C) Either PD or PI
    (D) Neither PD nor PI

66. A process control system has type-0 plant. For an accurate step-command following, a recommended cascade compensation scheme for the system employs
    (A) a lag compensator
    (B) a lead compensator
    (C) either a lag or a lead compensator
    (D) neither a lag nor a lead compensator

67. Figure Q67 shows the Nyquist plot of a unity feedback system having open-loop transfer function $G(s)$ with one pole in right half of s-plane. The feedback system is
    (A) stable
    (B) unstable
    (C) marginally stable

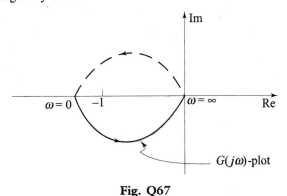

Fig. Q67

68. Figure Q68 shows the Nyquist plot of a unity feedback system having open-loop transfer function $G(s)$ with one pole in right half of s-plane. The feedback system is
    (A) stable
    (B) unstable
    (C) marginally stable

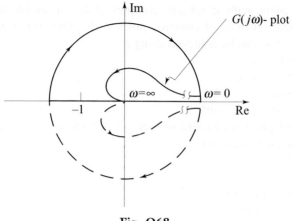

Fig. Q68

69. The transfer function of a system is $G(s) = 10(1+0.2s)/(1+0.5s)$. The phase shifts at $\omega = 0$ and $\omega = \infty$, will be respectively
   (A) 90° and 0°
   (B) $-$ 180° and 180°
   (C) $-$ 90° and 90°
   (D) None of the answers in (A), (B), and (C) is correct
70. Polar plot of $G(j\omega) = 1/[j\omega(1 + j\omega\tau)]$
   (A) crosses the negative real axis
   (B) crosses the negative imaginary axis
   (C) crosses the positive imaginary axis
   (D) None of the answers in (A), (B), and (C) is correct
71. Which of the polar plots shown in Fig. Q71 is the correct plot for $G(j\omega)$
   $= 1/[(j\omega)^2(1 + j\omega\tau)]$?
   (A) Fig. Q71a   (B) Fig. Q71b   (C) Fig. Q71c   (D) Fig. Q71d

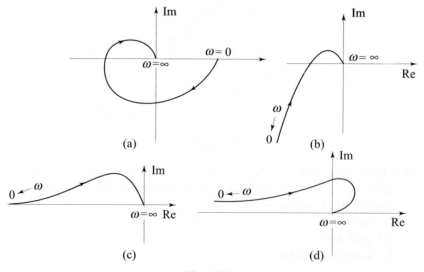

Fig. Q71

72. Which of the Bode asymptotic plots shown in Fig. Q72 is the correct plot for $G(s) = K/[s^2(s + 5)]$?
    (A) Fig. Q72a (B) Fig. Q72b (C) Fig. Q72c (D) Fig. Q72d

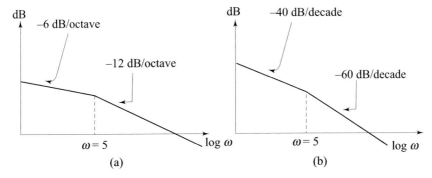

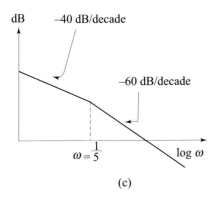

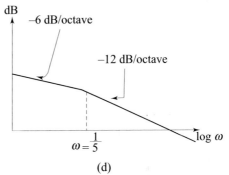

Fig. Q72

73. The Bode asymptotic plot of a transfer function is given in Fig. Q73. There

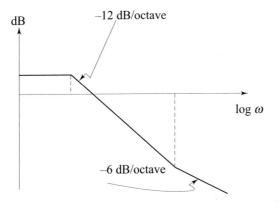

Fig. Q73

(A) are no poles at the origin

(B) is one pole at the origin

(C) are two poles at the origin

74. The Bode asymptotic plot of a transfer function is given in Fig. Q74. The transfer function has

(A) one pole and one zero

(B) two poles and one zero

(C) one pole and two zeros

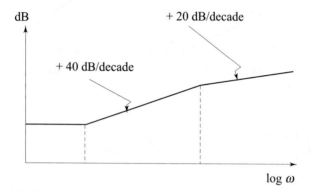

Fig. Q74

75. The minimum-phase transfer function that corresponds to the Bode asymptotic plot shown in Fig. Q75, is

(A) $\dfrac{1}{2s+1}$ (B) $2s+1$ (C) $\dfrac{1}{\dfrac{1}{2}s+1}$ (D) $\dfrac{1}{2}s+1$

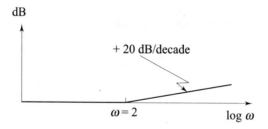

Fig. Q75

76. A unity feedback system has open-loop transfer function $G(s)$. Polar plot of $G(j\omega)$ is shown in Fig. Q76. The gain margin (GM) and the phase margin $(\varPhi M)$ of the feedback system are

(A) $GM = -0.3$; $\varPhi M = 112.33°$

(B) $GM = 0.3$; $\varPhi M = 112.33°$

(C) $GM = 3.33$; $\Phi M = 67.67°$

(D) None of the answers in (A), (B), and (C) is correct

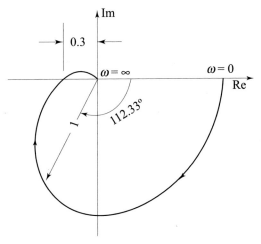

Fig. Q76

77. A unity feedback system has open-loop transfer function $G(s) = K/[s(1 + s\tau)]$. The gain margin of the feedback system is
   (A) ∞
   (B) 0
   (C) 1
   (D) None of the answers in (A), (B), and (C) is correct

78. A unity feedback system has open-loop transfer function $G(s)$. Bode plot of $G(j\omega)$ is shown in Fig. Q78. The feedback system has
   (A) positive phase margin and negative gain margin
   (B) positive phase margin and positive gain margin
   (C) negative phase margin and negative gain margin
   (D) negative phase margin and positive gain margin

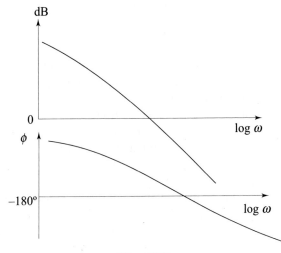

Fig. Q78

79. Consider the following statements for an underdamped second-order system:
   (i) Peak overshoot in step-input response reduces as damping is increased from 0.2 to 0.6.
   (ii) Resonance peak in frequency response reduces as damping is increased from 0.2 to 0.6.
   Which of the following is the correct answer?
   (A) None of the above statements is true
   (B) Statement (i) is true but statement (ii) is false
   (C) Statement (i) is false but statement (ii) is true
   (D) Both the statements are true

80. Undamped natural frequency ω_n and resonance frequency ω_r of a unity feedback system with open-loop transfer function

$$G(s) = \frac{\omega_n^2}{s\left(s + 2\zeta\omega_n\right)}; \; \zeta < \frac{1}{\sqrt{2}},$$

   are related as
   (A) $\omega_n = \omega_r$
   (B) $\omega_n > \omega_r$
   (C) $\omega_r < \omega_r$
   (D) None of the answers in (A), (B), and (C) is correct

81. Undamped natural frequency ω_n and bandwidth ω_b of a unity feedback system with open-loop transfer function

$$G(s) = \frac{\omega_n^2}{s\left(s + 2\zeta\omega_n\right)}$$

   are related as
   (A) $\omega_n = \omega_b$
   (B) $\omega_n > \omega_b$
   (C) $\omega_n < \omega_b$
   (D) None of the answers in (A), (B), and (C) is correct

82. For a unity feedback system with open-loop transfer function $G(s)$

$$= \frac{\omega_n^2}{s\left(s + 2\zeta\omega_n\right)}, \; \zeta < 0.7;$$

   (i) phase margin is explicitly indicative of damping ratio;
   (ii) resonance peak is explicitly indicative of damping ratio.
   Which of the following answers is correct?
   (A) None of the above statements is true
   (B) Statement (i) is true but statement (ii) is false
   (C) Statement (i) is false but statement (ii) is true
   (D) Both the statements are true

83. Open-loop transfer function of a unity feedback system is $G(s) = K/[s(s + 5)]$. The gain K that results in a phase margin of $50°$ is approximately
   (A) 15   (B) 20   (C) 25   (D) 30

84. A motion control system has type-2 plant. A recommended cascade compensation scheme for this system employs
    (A) a lag compensator
    (B) a lead compensator
    (C) either a lag or a lead compensator
    (D) neither a lag nor a lead compensator

85. An uncompensated feedback control system has a phase margin of 10°, and the required phase margin is 40°. A cascade compensator for this system employs
    (A) a lag compensator only
    (B) a lead compensator only
    (C) either a lag or a lead compensator
    (D) neither a lag nor a lead compensator

86. Maximum phase-lead of the compensator $D(s) = (0.5s + 1)/(0.05s + 1)$, is
    (A) 52° at 4 rad/sec
    (B) 52° at 10 rad/sec
    (C) 55° at 12 rad/sec
    (D) None of the answers in (A), (B), and (C) is correct

87. Consider the following statements:
    (i) Cascade lead compensation decreases the bandwidth.
    (ii) Cascade lag compensation increases the bandwidth.
        Which of the following is the correct answer?
    (A) None of the above statements is true
    (B) Statement (i) is true but statement (ii) is false
    (C) Statement (i) is false but statement (ii) is true
    (D) Both the statements are true

88. Bandwidth of a feedback system can be increased by introducing the following cascade control action:
    (A) PD   (B) PI
    (C) Either PD or PI   (D) Neither PD nor PI

89. In control systems
    (i) reduction in bandwidth results in sluggish response;
    (ii) reduction in bandwidth results in better signal/noise ratio.
        Which of the following is the correct answer?
    (A) None of the above statements is true
    (B) Statement (i) is true but statement (ii) is false
    (C) Statement (i) is false but statement (ii) is true
    (D) Both the statements are true

90. Which of the following control schemes will be employed for systems with high demands on speed of response, margin of stability and steady-state accuracy?
    (A) Cascade Lag
    (B) Cascade Lead

(C) Lead network in minor-loop feedback

(D) Cascade Lag-Lead

91. Consider the following statements:

   (i) Lead compensation is suitable for systems having unsatisfactory transient response. It also provides a limited improvement in steady-state response.

   (ii) lag compensation is suitable for systems with satisfactory transient response but unsatisfactory steady-state response.

   Which of the following is the correct answer?

   (A) None of the statements is true

   (B) Statement (i) is true but statement (ii) is false

   (C) Statement (i) is false but statement (ii) is true

   (D) Both the statements are true

92. From the filtering standpoint, the network shown in Fig. Q92 is a

   (A) low pass filter   (B) high pass filter

   (C) band pass filter   (D) band reject filter

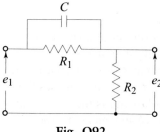

Fig. Q92

93. From the filtering standpoint, the network shown in Fig. Q93 is a

   (A) low pass filter   (B) high pass filter

   (C) band pass filter   (D) band reject filter

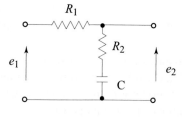

Fig. Q93

94. The network shown in Fig. Q93 is a

   (A) phase lead network with a pole-zero pair in left half of s-plane; zero to the right of the pole

   (B) phase lead network with a pole-zero pair in left half of s-plane; pole to the right of the zero

   (C) phase lag network with a pole-zero pair in left half of s-plane; zero to the right of the pole

    (D) phase lag network with a pole-zero pair in left half of s-plane; pole to the right of the zero

95. From the filtering standpoint, the network shown in Fig. Q95 is a
    (A) low pass filter   (B) high pass filter
    (C) band pass filter   (D) band reject filter

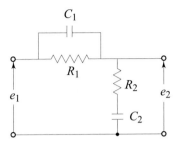

Fig. Q95

96. Consider the op amp circuit shown in Fig. Q96. It can be used as
    (A) a lead compensator only
    (B) a lag compensator only
    (C) either a lead or a lag compensator
    (D) neither a lead nor a lag compensator

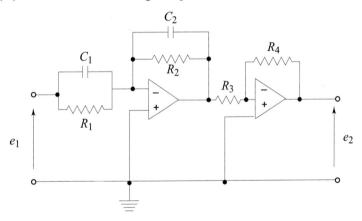

Fig. Q96

97. For a compensator

$$\frac{U(s)}{E(s)} = \frac{1}{s+a},$$

the algorithm (with sampling period T), based on backward-difference approximation for derivatives, is given by

(A) $u(k + 1) = (1 - aT)\, u(k) + Te(k)$

(B) $u(k + 1) = \dfrac{1}{1 + aT}\, u(k) + \dfrac{1}{1 + aT}\, e(k + 1)$

(C) $u(k + 1) = (1 + aT)\, u(k) + Te(k)$

98. A PI controller given by

$$u(t) = K_c \left[e(t) + \frac{1}{T_I} \int e(\tau)\, d\tau \right]$$

has been approximated by the following algorithm (with sampling period T):

$$u(k) = K_c \left[e(k) + \frac{1}{T_I} S(k) \right]; \quad S(k) = S(k - 1) + Te(k)$$

The discretization is based on
(A) backward rectangular rule for integration
(B) forward rectangular rule for integration
(C) trapezoidal rule for integration

99. Consider the sampled-data system shown in Fig. Q99. Steady-state error for unit-ramp input is

(A) $\dfrac{1}{KT}$

(B) $\dfrac{T}{K}$

(C) $\dfrac{1}{K}$

(D) None of the answers in (A), (B), and (C) is correct

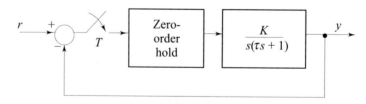

Fig. Q99

100. In a digital control system, selection of a large sampling period
(A) increases the stability margin
(B) decreases the stability margin
(C) has no effect on stability
(D) has an effect on stability that depends on plant parameters

101. In a digital control scheme, selection of a large sampling interval
    (A) improves the steady-state performance
    (B) deteriorates the steady-state performance
    (C) has no effect on steady-state performance
    (D) has an effect on steady-state performance that depends on plant parameters
102. In a sampled-data control system, delay introduced by sampling and reconstruction process is approximately equal to
    (A) sampling interval
    (B) twice the sampling interval
    (C) half the sampling interval
    (D) None of the answers in (A), (B), and (C) is correct
103. Consider the proportional control scheme for a self-regulating process. Increasing the proportional band of the controller
    (A) increases the offset error
    (B) reduces the offset error
    (C) has no effect on the offset error
    (D) has an effect on the offset error that depends on process parameters
104. The following feedback control scheme is recommended for a self-regulating process with very sluggish response:
    (A) P   (B) PI   (C) PD   (D) PID
105. Which of the following feedback control schemes will be employed to eliminate the offset to a step change in set-point of a self-regulating process:
    (A) P
    (B) PD
    (C) PI
    (D) None of the answers in (A), (B), and (C) is correct
106. Which of the following control schemes will be employed to obtain faster response without excessive oscillations and with zero offset to a step change in set-point of an integrating process:
    (A) P
    (B) PD
    (C) PI
    (D) None of the answers in (A), (B), and (C) is correct
107. Figure Q107 shows feedback control scheme for an integrating process. The steady-state error in output y due to a unit-step disturbance, is
    (A) 0
    (B) 1
    (C) $\dfrac{1}{K}$
    (D) None of the answers in (A), (B), and (C) is correct

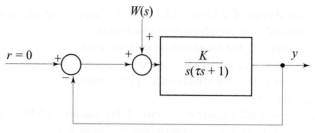

Fig. Q107

108. The process transfer function of a unity-feedback loop is

$$G(s) = \frac{(s+2)(s+3)}{s(s+1)(s+5)}$$

   (A) The tuning method based on process reaction curve is not applicable for this process

   (B) The tuning method based on ultimate gain and period is not applicable for this process

 Which of the following answers is correct?

   (A) None of the above statements is true.

   (B) Statement (i) is true but statement (ii) is false.

   (C) Statement (i) is false but statement (ii) is true.

   (D) Both the statements are true.

109. A process was subjected to a step input of magnitude 0.8, and the reaction curve shown in Fig. Q109 was obtained. The parameters K, τ_D and τ of the process model $G(s) = Ke^{-s\tau_D}/(\tau s + 1)$ are, respectively,

   (A) 0.64, 7, 62   (B) 0.64, 7, 55

   (C) 0.8, 7, 62   (D) 0.8, 7, 55

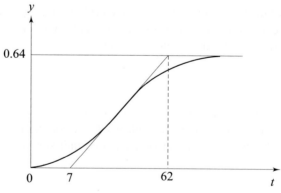

Fig. Q109

110. Given a state variable model

$$\dot{\mathbf{x}} = \mathbf{A}\mathbf{x} + \mathbf{b}u$$

$$y = \mathbf{c}x + du$$

Under the transformation $\mathbf{x} = \mathbf{P}\overline{\mathbf{x}}$; $\mathbf{P}$ a constant nonsingular matrix, the model becomes

$$\dot{\overline{\mathbf{x}}} = \overline{\mathbf{A}}\,\overline{\mathbf{x}} + \overline{\mathbf{b}}u$$

$$y = \overline{\mathbf{c}}\,\overline{\mathbf{x}} + du$$

(A) $\overline{\mathbf{A}} = \mathbf{PAP}^{-1}$; $\overline{\mathbf{b}} = \mathbf{P}^{-1}\mathbf{b}$; $\overline{\mathbf{c}} = \mathbf{cP}$

(B) $\overline{\mathbf{A}} = \mathbf{P}^{-1}\mathbf{AP}$; $\overline{\mathbf{b}} = \mathbf{P}^{-1}\mathbf{b}$; $\overline{\mathbf{c}} = \mathbf{cP}$

(C) $\overline{\mathbf{A}} = \mathbf{P}^{-1}\mathbf{AP}$; $\overline{\mathbf{b}} = \mathbf{Pb}$; $\overline{\mathbf{c}} = \mathbf{cP}$

(D) $\overline{\mathbf{A}} = \mathbf{P}^{-1}\mathbf{AP}$; $\overline{\mathbf{b}} = \mathbf{Pb}$; $\overline{\mathbf{c}} = \mathbf{cP}^{-1}$

111. A state variable formulation of a system is given by the equations

$$\begin{bmatrix} \dot{x}_1 \\ \dot{x}_2 \end{bmatrix} = \begin{bmatrix} -1 & 0 \\ 0 & -3 \end{bmatrix} \begin{bmatrix} x_1 \\ x_2 \end{bmatrix} + \begin{bmatrix} 1 \\ 1 \end{bmatrix} u$$

$$y = [1 \; 0] \begin{bmatrix} x_1 \\ x_2 \end{bmatrix}$$

The transfer function of the system is

(A) $\dfrac{1}{(s+1)(s+3)}$

(B) $\dfrac{1}{s+1}$

(C) $\dfrac{1}{s+3}$

(D) None of the answers in (A), (B), and (C) is correct

112. A state variable formulation of a system is given by the equations

$$\begin{bmatrix} \dot{x}_1 \\ \dot{x}_2 \end{bmatrix} = \begin{bmatrix} -1 & 0 \\ 0 & -3 \end{bmatrix} \begin{bmatrix} x_1 \\ x_2 \end{bmatrix} + \begin{bmatrix} 1 \\ 1 \end{bmatrix} u; \; x_1(0) = x_2(0) = 0$$

$$y = [1 \; 0] \begin{bmatrix} x_1 \\ x_2 \end{bmatrix}$$

The response $y(t)$ to unit-step input is

(A) $1 + e^{-t}$

(B) $\dfrac{1}{3}(1 - e^{-3t})$

(C) $1 - e^{-t}$

(D) None of the answers in (A), (B), and (C) is correct

113. The eigenvalues of the matrix

$$A = \begin{bmatrix} 0 & 1 & 0 \\ 0 & 0 & 1 \\ 0 & -3 & -4 \end{bmatrix}$$

are
(A) $0, -1, -3$
(B) $0, -3, -4$
(C) $0, 0, -4$
(D) None of the answers in (A), (B), and (C) is correct

114. Given the system

$$\dot{x} = \begin{bmatrix} 0 & 0 & -20 \\ 1 & 0 & -24 \\ 0 & 1 & -9 \end{bmatrix} x + \begin{bmatrix} 3 \\ 1 \\ 0 \end{bmatrix} u$$

$$y = [0\ 0\ 1]x$$

The characteristic equation of the system is
(A) $s^3 + 20s^2 + 24s + 9 = 0$
(B) $s^3 + 9s^2 + 24s + 20 = 0$
(C) $s^3 + 24s^2 + 9s + 20 = 0$
(D) None of the answers in (A), (B), and (C) is correct

115. A state variable model of a system is given by

$$\begin{bmatrix} \dot{x}_1 \\ \dot{x}_2 \end{bmatrix} = \begin{bmatrix} 1 & 1 \\ -2 & -1 \end{bmatrix} \begin{bmatrix} x_1 \\ x_2 \end{bmatrix} + \begin{bmatrix} 0 \\ 1 \end{bmatrix} u$$

$$y = [1\ 0] \begin{bmatrix} x_1 \\ x_2 \end{bmatrix}$$

The system is
(A) controllable and observable
(B) controllable but unobservable
(C) observable but uncontrollable
(D) uncontrollable and unobservable

116. The transfer function

$$G(s) = c(sI - A)^{-1}b$$

of the system

$$\dot{x} = Ax + bu$$
$$y = cx + du$$

has pole-zero cancellation. The system
(A) is uncontrollable and unobservable
(B) is observable but uncontrollable
(C) is controllable but unobservable
(D) may be any one of (A), (B), and (C)

117. The transfer function

$$G(s) = \mathbf{c}(s\mathbf{I} - \mathbf{A})^{-1}\mathbf{b}$$

of the system

$$\dot{\mathbf{x}} = \mathbf{A}\mathbf{x} + \mathbf{b}u$$
$$y = \mathbf{c}\mathbf{x} + du$$

has no pole-zero cancellation. The system
(A) is controllable and observable
(B) is observable but uncontrollable
(C) is controllable but unobservable
(D) may be any one of (A), (B), and (C).

118. Consider the system

$$\mathbf{A} = \begin{bmatrix} 0 & 1 & 0 \\ 0 & 0 & 1 \\ -6 & -11 & -6 \end{bmatrix}; \mathbf{b} = \begin{bmatrix} 0 \\ 0 \\ 1 \end{bmatrix}; \mathbf{c} = [4\ 5\ 1]$$

The transfer function of the system has pole-zero cancellation. The system is
(A) controllable and observable
(B) uncontrollable and unobservable
(C) controllable but unobservable
(D) observable but uncontrollable

119. Consider the system

$$\mathbf{A} = \begin{bmatrix} 0 & -2 \\ 1 & -3 \end{bmatrix}; \mathbf{b} = \begin{bmatrix} 1 \\ 1 \end{bmatrix}; \mathbf{c} = [0\ 1]$$

The transfer function of the system has pole-zero cancellation. The system is
(A) controllable and observable
(B) uncontrollable and unobservable
(C) controllable but unobservable
(D) observable but uncontrollable

120. For all finite values of t, the matrix exponential $e^{\mathbf{A}t}$ is nonsingular for
(A) singular $\mathbf{A}$
(B) nonsingular $\mathbf{A}$
(C) all $\mathbf{A}$
(D) nothing can be said, in general, about nonsingularity of $e^{\mathbf{A}t}$ for a given $\mathbf{A}$

MASTER KEY

1. (C)	2. (C)	3. (C)	4. (D)
5. (A)	6. (B)	7. (A)	8. (B)

9. (D)	10. (A)	11. (B)	12. (C)
13. (A)	14. (B)	15. (A)	16. (B)
17. (C)	18. (C)	19. (C)	20. (C)
21. (B)	22. (A)	23. (B)	24. (C)
25. (D)	26. (C)	27. (C)	28. (A)
29. (C)	30. (D)	31. (D)	32. (D)
33. (B)	34. (A)	35. (B)	36. (A)
37. (D)	38. (C)	39. (D)	40. (B)
41. (B)	42. (C)	43. (A)	44. (C)
45. (A)	46. (B)	47. (D)	48. (B)
49. (A)	50. (B)	51. (D)	52. (A)
53. (A)	54. (C)	55. (B)	56. (B)
57. (B)	58. (B)	59. (C)	60. (A)
61. (A)	62. (D)	63. (C)	64. (D)
65. (B)	66. (A)	67. (A)	68. (B)
69. (D)	70. (D)	71. (C)	72. (B)
73. (A)	74. (C)	75. (D)	76. (C)
77. (A)	78. (B)	79. (D)	80. (B)
81. (C)	82. (D)	83. (C)	84. (B)
85. (C)	86. (D)	87. (A)	88. (C)
89. (D)	90. (D)	91. (D)	92. (B)
93. (A)	94. (D)	95. (D)	96. (C)
97. (B)	98. (A)	99. (C)	100. (B)
101. (C)	102. (C)	103. (A)	104. (D)
105. (C)	106. (B)	107. (B)	108. (D)
109. (D)	110. (B)	111. (B)	112. (C)
113. (A)	114. (B)	115. (A)	116. (D)
117. (A)	118. (C)	119. (D)	120. (C)

References

APPLICATIONS

1. Bogler, P.L., *Radar Principles with Applications to Tracking Systems*, New York: John Wiley and Sons, 1990.
2. Bose, B.K., *Power Electronics and AC Drives*, Englewood Cliffs, New Jersey: Prentice-Hall, 1986.
3. Sen, P.C., *Thyristor DC Drives*, New York: Wiley Interscience Publication, 1981.
4. Geiger, D.F., *Phaselock Loops for DC Motor Speed Control*, New York: Wiley Interscience Publication, 1981.
5. Rao, M., and H. Qiu, *Process Control Engineering*, Amsterdam: Gordon and Breach Science Publishers, 1993.
6. Coughanower, D.R., *Process Systems Analysis and Control*, 2nd Edition, Singapore: McGraw-Hill Book Company, 1991.
7. Corripio, A.B., *Tuning of Industrial Control Systems*, Research Triangle Park, North Carolina: Instrument Society of America, 1990.
8. Deshpande, P.B., and R.H. Ash, *Computer Process Control*, 2nd Edition, Research Triangle Park, North Carolina: Instrument Society of America, 1989.
9. Seborg, D.E., T.F. Edgar, and D.A. Mellichamp, *Process Dynamics and Control*, New York: John Wiley and Sons, 1989.
10. Shinskey, F.G., *Process Control Systems*, 3rd Edition, New York: McGraw-Hill Book Company, 1988.
11. Astrom, K.J., and T. Hagglund, *Automatic Tuning of PID Regulators*, Research Triangle Park, North Carolina: Instrument Society of America, 1988.
12. Smith, C.A., and A.B. Corripio, *Principles and Practice of Automatic Process Control*, New York: John Wiley and Sons, 1985.
13. Stephanopoulos, G., *Chemical Process Control—An Introduction to Theory and Practice*, Englewood Cliffs, New Jersey: Prentice-Hall 1984.

14. Mclean, D., Automatic *Flight Control Systems*, Hemel Hempstead: Prentice-Hall International, 1990.

15. Ashley, H., *Engineering Analysis of Flight Vehicles*, Reading, Massachusetts: Addison-Wesley Publishing Company, 1974.

16. McRuer, D.T., I. Askenas, and D. Graham, *Aircraft Dynamics and Automatic Control*, Princeton, New Jersey: Princeton University Press, 1973.

17. Blakelock, J.H., *Automatic Control of Aircraft and Missiles*, New York: John Wiley and Sons, 1965.

18. Etkin, B., *Dynamics of Flight: Stability and Control*, New York: John Wiley and Sons, 1959.

19. Koivo, A.J., *Fundamentals for Control of Robotics Manipulators*, New York: John Wiley and Sons, 1989.

20. Spong, W., and M. Vidyasagar, *Robot Dynamics and Control*, New York: John Wiley and Sons, 1989.

21. Fu, K.S., R.C. Gonzalez, and C.S.G. Lee, *Robotics: Control, Sensing, Vision and Intelligence*, New York: McGraw-Hill Book Company, 1987.

22. Asada, H., and K. Youcef-Toumi, *Direct Drive Robots: Theory and Practice*, Cambridge, Massachusetts: The MIT Press, 1987.

23. Craig, J.J., *Introduction to Robotics: Mechanics and Control*, Reading, Massachusetts: Addison-Wesley Publishing Company, 1986.

24. Dorf, R.C., *Robotics and Automated Manufacturing*, Reston, Virginia: Reston Publishing Company, 1983.

25. Pessen, D.W., *Industrial Automation*, Singapore: John Wiley and Sons (SEA), 1990.

26. Hughes, T.A., *Programmable Controllers*, Research Triangle Park, North Carolina: Instrument Society of America, 1989.

27. Bryan, L.A., and E.A. Bryan, *Programmable Controllers: Theory and Implementation*, Chicago: Industrial Text Co., 1988.

28. Johnson, D.G., *Programmable Controllers for Factory Automation*, New York: Marcel Dekker, 1987.

29. Koren, Y., *Computer Control of Manufacturing Systems,* Singapore: McGraw-Hill Book Company, 1983.

30. Patton, W.J., *Numerical Control: Practice and Applications*, Reston, Virginia: Reston Publishing Company, 1970.

31. Beards, C.F., *Vibrations and Control Systems*, Chichester: Ellis Horwood Publishers, 1988.

MATHEMATICAL BACKGROUND

32. Noble, B., and J.W. Daniel, *Applied Linear Algebra*, 3rd Edition, Englewood Cliffs, New Jersey: Prentice-Hall, 1988.

33. Lancaster, P., and M. Tismenetsky, *The Theory of Matrices*, 2nd Edition, Orlando, Florida; Academic Press, 1985.

34. Oppenheim, A.V., A.S. Willsky, and I.T. Young, *Signals and Systems*, Englewood Cliffs, New Jersey: Prentice-Hall, 1983.

35. Churchil, R.V., J.W. Brown, and R.F. Verhev, *Complex Variables and Applications*, 3rd Edition, New York: McGraw-Hill Book Company, 1976.

36. Lefschetz, S., *Differential Equations: Geometric Theory*, New York: Wiley Interscience Publication, 1957.

MODELLING OF PHYSICAL SYSTEMS

37. Clark, R.N., *Control System Dynamics*, New York: Cambridge University Press, 1996.
38. Palm, W.J., III, *Modelling, Analysis and Control of Dynamic Systems*, New York: John Wiley and Sons, 1983.
39. Nagrath, I.J., and M. Gopal, *Systems: Modelling and Analysis*, New Delhi: Tata McGraw-Hill, 1982.
40. Doebelin, E.O., *System Modelling and Response*, New York: John Wiley and Sons, 1980.
41. Ogata, K., *System Dynamics*, Englewood Cliffs, New Jersey: Prentice-Hall, 1978.
42. Moschytz, G.S., *Linear Integrated Networks: Fundamentals*, New York: Van Nostrand Reinhold Company, 1974.
43. Schwarz, R.J., and B. Friendland, *Linear Systems*, New York: McGraw-Hill Book Company, 1965.
44. Mason, S.J., "Feedback Theory: Further Properties of Signal Flow Graphs", *Proc. IRE*, Vol. 44, No. 7, pp. 920–926, July 1956.
45. Mason, S.J., "Feedback Theory: Some Properties of Signal Flow Graphs", *Proc. IRE*, Vol. 41, No. 9, pp. 1144–1156, Sept. 1953.

INDUSTRIAL CONTROL DEVICES

46. De Silva, C.W., *Control Sensors and Actuators*, Englewood Cliffs, New Jersey: Prentice-Hall, 1989.
47. Anderson, W.R., *Controlling Electrohydraulic Systems*, New York: Marcel Dekker, 1988.
48. Parr, E.A., *Industrial Control Handbook*, Vol.1—Vol.3, Oxford: BSP Professional Books, 1987.
49. Schuler., C.A., and W.L. McNamee, *Industrial Electronics and Robotics*, New York: McGraw-Hill Book Company, 1986.
50. Kenjo, T., and S. Nagamori, *Permanent-magnet and Brushless DC Motors*, Oxford: Clarendon Press, 1985.
51. Kenjo. T., *Stepping Motors and their Microprocessor Controls*, Oxford: Clarendon Press, 1984.
52. Morris, N.M., *Control Engineering*, 3rd Edition, London: McGraw-Hill Book Company, 1983.
53. Doebelin, E.O., *Measurement Systems*, 3rd Edition, New York: McGraw-Hill Book Company, 1983.
54. Singh, M.G., J-P Elloy, R. Mezencev, and N. Munro, *Applied Industrial Control*, Oxford: Pergamon Press, 1980.
55. Kuo. B.C. (ed.), *Incremental Motion Control*, Vol. 2: *Step Motors and Control Systems*, Champaign, Illinois: SRL Publishing Co., 1980.
56. Kuo, B.C., *Theory and Applications of Step Motors*, St. Paul, Minnesota: West Publishing Co., 1974.

57. Ahrendt, W.R., and C.J. Savant, Jr., *Servomechanism Practice*, 2nd Edition, New York: McGraw-Hill Book Company, 1960.

FEEDBACK CONTROL THEORY

58. Raven, F.H., *Automatic Control Engineering*, 5th Edition, New York: McGraw-Hill Book Company, 1995.

59. Wolovich, W.A., *Automatic Control Systems: Basic Analysis and Design*, Orlando, Florida: Saunders College Publishing, 1994.

60. Stafani, R.T., C.J. Savant, Jr., B. Shahran, and G.H. Hostetter, *Design of Feedback Control Systems*, 3rd Edition, Orlando, Florida: Saunders College Publishing, 1994.

61. Van De Vegte, J., *Feedback Control Systems*, 3rd Edition, Englewood Cliffs, New Jersey: Prentice-Hall, 1993.

62. Chen, C-T, *Control System Design*, Orlando, Florida: Saunders College Publishing, 1993.

63. Shinners, S.M., *Modern Control System Theory and Design*, New York: John Wiley and Sons, 1992.

64. Kuo, B.C., *Automatic Control Systems*, 6th Edition, Englewood Cliffs, New Jersey: Prentice-Hall, 1991.

65. Ogata, K., *Modern Control Engineering*, 2nd Edition, Englewood Cliffs, New Jersey: Prentice-Hall, 1990.

66. Dorf, R.C., *Modern Control Systems*, 5th Edition, Reading, Massachusetts: Addison-Wesley Publishing Company, 1989.

67. Thaler, G.J., *Automatic Control Systems*, St. Paul, Minnesota: West Publishing Co., 1989.

68. D'Azzo, J.J., and C.H. Houpis, *Linear Control System Analysis and Design*, 3rd Edition, New York: McGraw-Hill Book Company, 1988.

69. D' Souza, A.F., *Design of Control Systems*, Englewood Cliffs, New Jersey: Prentice-Hall, 1988.

70. Phillips, C.L., and R.D. Harbor, *Feedback Control Systems*, Englewood Cliffs, New Jersey: Prentice-Hall, 1988.

71. Franklin, G.F., J.D. Powell, and Abbas Emami-Naeini, *Feedback Control of Dynamic Systems*, Reading, Massachusetts: Addison-Wesley Publishing Company, 1986.

72. Nagrath, I.J., and M. Gopal, *Control Systems Engineering*, 2nd Edition, Singapore: John Wiley and Sons (SEA), 1986.

73. Palm, W.J., III, *Control Systems Engineering*, New York: John Wiley and Sons, 1986.

74. Doebelin, E.O., *Control System Principles and Design*, New York: John Wiley and Sons, 1985.

75. Kurman, K.J., *Feedback Control: Theory and Design*, Amsterdam: Elsevier Science Publishers, 1984.

76. Phelan, R.M., *Automatic Control Systems*, London: Cornell University Press, 1977.

77. Truxal, J.G., *Automatic Feedback Control System Synthesis*, New York: McGraw-Hill Book Company, 1955.

DIGITAL CONTROL

78. Santina, M.S., A.R. Stubberud, and G.H. Hostetter, *Digital Control System Design*, 2nd Edition, Orlando, Florida: Saunders College Publishing, 1994.

79. Jacquot, R.G., *Modern Digital Control Systems*, 2nd Edition, New York: Marcel Dekker, 1994.

80. Kau, B.C., *Digital Control Systems*, 2nd Edition, Orlando, Florida; Saunders College Publishing, 1992.

81. Dote, Y., *Servo Motor and Motion Control Using Digital Signal Processors*, Englewood Cliffs, New Jersey: Prentice-Hall, 1990.

82. Astrom, K.J., and B. Wittenmark, *Computer Controlled Systems: Theory and Design*, 2nd Edition, Englewood Cliffs, New Jersey: Prentice-Hall, 1990.

83. Phillips, C.L., and H.T. Nagle, Jr., *Digital Control System Analysis and Design*, 2nd Edition, Englewood Cliffs, New Jersey: Prentice-Hall, 1990.

84. Franklin, G.F., J.G. Powell, and M.L. Workman, *Digital Control of Dynamic Systems,* 2nd Edition, Reading, Massachusetts: Addison-Wesley, 1990.

85. Isermann, R., *Digital Control Systems*, Vol. I, 2nd Edition, Berlin: Springer-Verlag, 1989.

86. Zikic, A.M., *Practical Digital Control*, Chichester: Ellis Horwood Publishers, 1989.

87. Gayakwad, R., and L. Sokoff, *Analog and Digital Control Systems*, Englewood Cliffs, New Jersey: Prentice-Hall, 1988.

88. Gopal, M., *Digital Control Engineering*, New Delhi: Wiley Eastern, 1988.

89. Warwick, K. and D. Rees (eds.), *Industrial Digital Control Systems*, Revised Edition, London: Peter Peregrinus, 1988.

90. Kuc, Roman, *Introduction to Digital Signal Processing*, New York: McGraw-Hill Book Company, 1988.

91. Ogata, K., *Discrete-Time Control Systems*, Englewood Cliffs, New Jersey: Prentice-Hall, 1987.

92. Sinha, N.K. (ed.), *Microprocessor-Based Control Systems*, Dordrecht: D. Reidel Publishing Company, 1986.

93. Van Landingham, H.F., *Introduction to Digital Control Systems*, New York: MacMillan Publishing Company, 1985.

94. Ackermann, J., *Sampled-Data Control Systems*, Berlin: Springer-Verlag, 1985.

95. Leigh, J.R., *Applied Digital Control*, Englewood Cliffs, New Jersey: Prentice-Hall, 1985.

96. Houpis, C.H., and G.B. Lamont, *Digital Control Systems: Theory, Hardware, Software*, New York: McGraw-Hill Book Company, 1985.

97. Moroney, P., *Issues in the Implementation of Digital Feedback Compensators*, Cambridge, Massachusetts: The MIT Press, 1983.

98. Katz, P., *Digital Control Using Microprocessors*, Englewood Cliffs, New Jersey: Prentice-Hall, 1981.

99. Rao, G.V., *Complex Digital Control Systems*, New York: Van Nostrand Reinhold Company, 1979.

100. Rao, M.V.C., and A.K. Subramanium "Elimination of singular cases in Jury's test", *IEEE Trans. Automatic Control*, Vol. AC-21, pp. 114–115, February 1976.

101. Jury, E.I., and J. Blanchard, "A Stability Test for Linear Discrete-time Systems in Table Form", *Proc. IRE*, Vol. 49, pp. 1947–1948, 1961.

STATE VARIABLE METHODS

102. Gopal M., *Modern Control System* Theory, 2nd Edition, New Delhi: Wiley Eastern, 1993.
103. Callier, F.M., and C.A. Desoer, *Linear System Theory*, New York: Springer-Verlag, 1991.
104. DeCarla, R.A., *Linear Systems: A State Variable Approach with Numerical Implementation*, Englewood Cliffs, New Jersey: Prentice-Hall, 1989.
105. Furuta, K., A Sano, and D. Atherton, *State Variable Methods in Automatic Control*, Chichester: John Wiley and Sons, 1988.
106. Friedland, B., *Control System Design: An Introduction to State-Space Methods*, New York: McGraw-Hill Book Company 1986.
107. Brogan, W.L., *Modern Control Theory*, 2nd Edition, Englewood Cliffs, New Jersey: Prentice-Hall, 1985.
108. Chen, C-T., *Linear System Theory and Design*, New York: Holt, Rinehart and Winston, 1984.
109. Fortman, T.E., and K.L. Hitz, *An Introduction to Linear Control Systems*, New York: Marcel Dekker, 1977.
110. Wiberg, D.M., *State Space and Linear Systems* (Schaum's Outline Series), New York: McGraw-Hill Book Company, 1971.
111. Ogata, K., *State Space Analysis of Control Systems*, Englewood Cliffs, New Jersey: Prentice-Hall, 1967.
112. Schultz, D.G., and J.L. Melsa, *State Functions and Linear Control Systems*, New York: McGraw-Hill Book Company, 1967.
113. DeRusso, P.M., R.J. Roy, and C.M. Close, *State Variables for Engineers*, New York; John Wiley and Sons, 1965.
114. Dorf, R.C., *Time Domain Analysis and Design of Control Systems*, Reading, Massachusetts: Addison-Wesley Publishing Company, 1965.
115. Zadeh, L.A., and C.A. Desoer, *Linear System Theory: A State Space Approach*, New York: McGraw-Hill Book Company, 1963.

NONLINEAR CONTROL

116. Ching-Fang Lin, *Advanced Control Systems Design*, Englewood Cliffs, New Jersey: PTR Prentice-Hall, 1994.
117. Slotine, J-J.E., and W.Li, *Applied Nonlinear Control*, Englewood Cliffs, New Jersey: Prentice-Hall, 1991.
118. Mohler, R.R., *Nonlinear Systems*, Vol. I: *Dynamics and Control*, Englewood Cliffs, New Jersey: Prentice-Hall, 1991.
119. Atherton, D.P., *Stability of Nonliner Systems*, New York: John Wiley and Sons, 1981.
120. Itkis, U., *Control Systems of Variable Structure*, New York: John Wiley and Sons, 1976.
121. Atherton, D.P., *Nonlinear Control Engineering*, London: Van Nostrand Reinhold Company, 1975.

122. Minorsky, N., *Theory of Nonlinear Control Systems*, New York: McGraw-Hill Book Company, 1969.

MULTIVARIABLE AND OPTIMAL CONTROL

123. Anderson, B.D.O., and J.B. Moore, *Optimal Control: Linear Quadartic Methods*, Englewood Cliffs, New Jersey: Prentice-Hall, 1990.
124. Grimble, M.J., and M.A. Johnson, *Optimal Control and Stochastic Estimation: Theory and Applications*, Vol. I, Chichester: John Wiley and Sons, 1988.
125. Kwakernaak, H., and R. Sivan, *Linear Optimal Control Systems*, New York: Wiley Interscience Publication, 1972.
126. Kirk, D.E., *Optimal Control Theory: An Introduction*, Englewood Cliffs, New Jersey: Prentice-Hall, 1970.
127. Sage, A.P., *Optimum Systems Control*, Englewood Cliffs, New Jersey: Prentice-Hall, 1968.
128. Kautsky, J., N.K. Nichols, and P. Dooren, "Robust pole assignment by linear state feedback", *Int. J. Control*, Vol. 41, No, 5, pp. 1129–1155, 1985.
129. Titli, A., and J. Bernussou, *Interconnected Dynamical Systems: Stability Decomposition and Decentralization*, System and Control Series, Vol. 5, Amsterdam: North Holland Publishing Company, 1982.
130. Patel, R.V., and N. Munro, *Multivariable System Theory and Design*, Oxford: Pergamon Press, 1982.
131. MacFarlane, A.J.G. (ed.), *Frequency Response Methods in Control Systems*, New York: IEEE Press, 1979.
132. Fisher, D.G., and D.E. Seborg (eds), *Multivariable Computer Control: A Case Study*, Amsterdam: North Holland Publishing Company, 1976.
133. Layton, J.M., *Multivariable Control Theory*, London: Peter Peregrinus, 1976.
134. Wolovich, W.A., *Linear Multivariable Systems*, New York: Springer-Verlag, 1974.

ROBUST CONTROL

135. Zhou, K., J.C. Doyle, and K. Glover, *Robust and Optimal Control,* New Jersey: Prentice Hall, 1996.
136. Belanger, P.R., *Control Engineering: A Modern Approach*, Florida: Saunders College Publishing, 1995.
137. Saberi, A., B.M. Chen, and P. Sannuti, *Loop Transfer Recovery: Analysis and Design*, London: Springer-Verlag, 1993.
138. Doyle, J.C., B.A. Francis, and A.R. Tannenbaum, *Feedback Control Theory*, New York: MacMillan Publishing Company, 1992.
139. Morari, M., and E. Zafiriou, *Robust Process Control*, Englewood Cliffs, New Jersey: Prentice-Hall, 1989.
140. Bhattacharyya, S.P., *Robust Stabilization Against Structured Perturbations*, New York: Springer-Verlag, 1987.
141. Francis, B.A., *A Course in H_∞ Control Theory, Lecture Notes in Control and Information Sciences*, No. 88, Berlin: Springer-Verlag, 1987.

142. Doyle, J.C., and G. Stein, "Robustness with Observers", *IEEE Trans. Automatic Control*, Vol. AC-24, No. 4, pp. 607–611, Aug. 1979.

143. Dorato, P., L. Fortuna, and G. Muscato, *Robust Control for Unstructured Perturbations—An Introduction*, Lecture notes in Control and Information Sciences, No. 168, Berlin: Springer-Verlag, 1992.

144. Frank, P.M., *Introduction to System Sensitivity Theory*, New York: Academic Press, 1978.

IDENTIFICATION AND ADAPTIVE CONTROL

145. Isermann, R., *Digital Control Systems*, Vol. II, 2nd Edition, Berlin: Springer-Verlag, 1991.

146. Landau, I.D., *System Identification and Control Design*, Englewood Cliffs, New Jersey: Prentice-Hall, 1990.

147. Sastry, S., and M. Bodson, *Adaptive Control: Stability, Convergence and Robustness*, Englewood Cliffs, New Jersey: Prentice Hall, 1989.

148. Middleton, R.H., and G.C. Goodwin, *Digital Control and Estimation: A Unified Approach*, Englewood Cliffs, New Jersey: Prentice-Hall, 1989.

149. Narendra, K.S., and A.M. Annaswamy, *Stable Adaptive Systems*, Englewood Cliffs, New Jersey: Prentice-Hall, 1989.

150. Astrom, K.J., and B. Wittenmark, *Adaptive Control*, Reading, Massachusetts: Addison-Wesley Publishing Company, 1989.

151. Soderstrom, T., and P. Stoica, *System Identification*, Hemel Hempstead: Prentice-Hall International, 1989.

152. Grimble, M.J., and M.A. Johnson, *Optimal Control and Stochastic Estimation: Theory and Applications*, Vol. II, Chichester: John Wiley and Sons, 1988.

153. Ljung, L., *System Identification: Theory for the User*, Englewood Cliffs, New Jersey: Prentice-Hall, 1987.

154. Goodwin, G.C., and K.S. Sin, *Adaptive Filtering Prediction and Control*, Englewood Cliffs, New Jersey: Prentice-Hall, 1984.

155. Harris, C.J., and S.A. Billings (eds), *Self-Tuning and Adaptive Control: Theory and Applications*, London: Peter Peregrinus, 1981.

156. Narendra, K.S., and R.V. Monopoli (eds), *Applications of Adaptive Control*, New York: Academic Press, 1980.

157. Landau, Y.D., *Adaptive Control: The Model Reference Approach,* New York: Marcel Dekker, 1979.

INTELLIGENT CONTROL

158. Norgaard, M., O. Ravn, N.K. Poulsen, and L.K. Hansen, *Neural Networks for Modelling and Control of Dynamic Systems*, London : Springer-Verlag, 2000.

159. Lewis, F.L., S. Jagannathan, and A. Yesildirek, *Neural Network Control of Robot Manipulators and Nonlinear Systems*, London: Taylor and Francis, 1999.

160. Haykin, S., *Neural Networks: A Comprehensive Foundation*, 2nd Edition, Prentice-Hall, 1998.

161. Lin C-T, and C.S. George Lee, *Neural Fuzzy Systems*, Upper Saddle River, NJ: Prentice Hall, 1996.

162. Zurada, J.M., *Introduction to Artificial Neural Systems*, St Paul MN : West Publishing Company, 1992.

163. Ying, Hao., *Fuzzy Control and Modeling: Analytical Foundations and Applications*, New York: IEEE Press, 2000.

164. Passion, K.M., and S. Yurkovich, *Fuzzy Control,* California: Addison-Wesley, 1998.

165. Wang Li-Xin, *A Course in Fuzzy Systems and Control,* New Jersey : Prentice-Hall International, 1997.

166. Ross, T.J., *Fuzzy Logic with Engineering Applications,* New York, McGraw-Hill, 1995.

167. Driankov, D., H. Hellendoorn, and M. Reinfrank, *An Introduction to Fuzzy Control*, Berlin: Springer-Verlag, 1993.

168. Goldberg, D.E., *Genetic Algorithms in Search, Optimization, and Machine Learning*, Reading, Massachusetts: Addison-Wesley, 1989.

COMPUTER AIDED DESIGN

169. Linkens, D.A. (ed), *CAD for Control Systems*, New York: Marcel Dekker, 1993.

170. Chipperfield, A.J., and P.J. Fleming (eds), *MATLAB toolboxes and applications for control*, London: Peter Peregrinus, 1993.

171. Jamshidi, M., and C.J. Herget (eds). *Advances in Computer-Aided Control Systems Engineering*, Amsterdam: North-Holland, 1985.

172. Korn, G.A., and J.V. Wait, *Digital Continuous System Simulation*, Englewood Cliffs, New Jersey: Prentice-Hall, 1978.

173. Speckhart, F.H., and W.L. Green, *A Guide to Using CSMP—The Continuous System Modelling Program (IBM Crop,)*, Englewood Cliffs, New Jersey: Prentice-Hall, 1976.

174. Program ACSL
    Features: Advanced Continuous Simulation Language. The software has a section for simulation of sampled-data systems.
    Source: Mitchell and Gauthier Associates, 73, Junction Square Drive, Concord, MA 01742-9990.

175. Program SIMNON
    Features: Simulation of linear and nonlinear systems operating in continuous-time or discrete-time.
    Source: Engineering Software Concepts, 436 Palo Alto Avenue, P.O. Box 66, Palo Alto, CA 94301.

176. Program CTRL-C
    Features: Analysis and design of control systems; both the classical and the modern approaches. Permits direct interface to users pre-existing FORTRAN and C programs and to program ACSL.
    Source: Systems Control Technology, Inc., 2300 Geng Road, P.O. Box 10180, Palo Alto, CA 94303-0888.

177. Program PC-MATLAB (with Control System Tool Box and SIMULAB)
    Features: Classical and modern control tools; dynamic system simulation.
    Source: The Math Works, Inc. Cochituate Place, 24 Prime Park Way, Natick, MA 01760.

The Student Edition of MATLAB, Englewood Cliffs, New Jersey: Prentice-Hall, 1992.

178. Program MATRIX/PC
Features: Modelling, simulation and control design.
Source: Integrated Systems, Inc., Jay Street, Santa Clara, California 95054.

179. Program CC
Features: Analysis and design of linear control systems, analysis of stochastic systems; no facility for simulation of nonlinear systems.
Source: Systems Technology, Inc., 13766 South Hawthorne Blvd, Hawthorne, CA 90250-7083.

COMPANION BOOK

180. Gopal, M., *Digital Control and State Variable Methods: Conventional and Neural-Fuzzy Control Systems,* 2nd edition, New Delhi: Tata McGraw-Hill, 2002.

Companion Book

Gopal, M., *Digital Control and State Variable Methods, Conventional and Neural-Fuzzy Control Systems,* 2nd edition, New Delhi: Tata McGraw-Hill, 2002.

1. **Introduction**

   1.1 Control System Terminology; 1.2 Computer-Based Control: History and Trends; 1.3 Control Theory: History and Trends; 1.4 An Overview of the Classical Approach to Analog Controller Design; 1.5 Scope and Organization of the Book

2. **Signal Processing in Digital Control**

   2.1 Why use Digital Control; 2.2 Configuration of the Basic Digital Control Scheme; 2.3 Principles of Signal Conversion; 2.4 Basic Discrete-Time Signals; 2.5 Time-Domain Models for Discrete-Time Systems; 2.6 Transfer Function Models; 2.7 Stability on the z-Plane and the Jury Stability Criterion; 2.8 Sampling as Impulse Modulation; 2.9 Sampled Spectra and Aliasing; 2.10 Filtering; 2.11 Practical Aspects of the Choice of Sampling Rate; 2.12 Principles of Discretization; 2.13 The Routh Stability Criterion on the r-Plane

3. **Models of Digital Control Devices and Systems**

   3.1 Introduction; 3.2 z-Domain Description of Sampled Continuous-Time Plants; 3.3 z-Domain Description of Systems with Dead-Time; 3.4 Implementation of Digital Controllers; 3.5 Tunable PID Controllers; 3.6 Digital Temperature Control System; 3.7 Digital Position Control System; 3.8 Stepping Motors and Their Control; 3.9 Programmable Logic Controllers

4. **Design of Digital Control Algorithms**

   4.1 Introduction; 4.2 z-Plane Specifications of Control System Design; 4.3 Digital compensator Design Using Frequency Response Plots; 4.4 Digital Compensator Design Using Root Locus Plots; 4.5 z-Plane Synthesis

5. **Control System Analysis Using State Variable Methods**

   5.1 Introduction; 5.2 Vectors and Matrices; 5.3 State Variable Representation; 5.4 Conversion of State Variable Models to Tranfer Functions; 5.5 Conversion of

Transfer Functions to Canonical State Variable Models; 5.6 Eigenvalues and Eigenvectors; 5.7 Solution of State Equations; 5.8 Concepts of Controllability and Observability; 5.9 Equivalence Between Transfer Function and State Variable Representation; 5.10 Multivariable Systems

6. State Variable Analysis of Digital Control Systems

6.1 Introduction; 6.2 State Descriptions of Digital Processors; 6.3 State Description of Sampled Continuous-Time Plants; 6.4 State Description of Systems with Dead-Time; 6.5 Solution of State Difference Equations; 6.6 Controllability and Observability; 6.7 Multivariable Systems

7. Pole-Placement Design and State Observers

7.1 Introduction; 7.2 Stability Improvement by State Feedback; 7.3 Necessary and Sufficient Conditions for Arbitrary Pole Placement; 7.4 State Regulator Design; 7.5 Design of State Observers; 7.6 Compensator Design by the Separation Principle; 7.7 Servo Design: Introduction of the Reference Input by Feedforward Control; 7.8 State Feedback with Integral Control; 7.9 Digital Control Systems with State Feedback; 7.10 Deadbeat Control by State Feedback and Deadbeat Observers; 7.11 Introduction to System Identification and Adaptive Control

8. Lyapunov Stability Analysis

8.1 Introduction; 8.2 Basic Concepts; 8.3 Stability Definitions; 8.4 Stability Theorems; 8.5 Lyapunov Functions for Nonlinear Systems; 8.6 Lyapunov Functions for Linear Systems; 8.7 A Model Reference Adaptive System; 8.8 Discrete-Time Systems

9. Linear Quadratic Optimal Control

9.1 Parameter Optimazation and Optimal Control Problems; 9.2 Quadratic Performance Index; 9.3 Control Configurations; 9.4 State Regulator Design Through the Lyapunov Equation; 9.5 Optimal State Regulator Through the Matrix Riccati Equation; 9.6 Optimal Digital Control Systems; 9.7 Critique of Linear Quadratic Control

10. Nonlinear Control Systems

10.1 Introduction; 10.2 A Class of Nonlinear Systems: Separable Nonlinearties; 10.3 Filtered Nonlinear System; The Describing Function Analysis; 10.4 Describing Functions of Common Nonlinearities; 105. Stability Analysis by the Describing Function Method; 10.6 Nonlinear Sampled-Data Systems; 10.7 Second-Order Nonlinear System on the Phase Plane; 10.8 Fundamental types of Phase Portraits; 10.9 System Analysis on the Phase Plane; 10.10 Optimal Switching in Bang-Bang Control Systems

11. Neural Networks For Control

11.1 Introduction; 11.2 Neuron Models; 11.3 Network Architectures; 11.4 Learning in Neural Networks; 11.5 Training the Multilayer Neural Network—Backpropagation Tuning; 11.6 Function Approximation with Neural Networks; 11.7 System Identification with Neural Networks; 11.8 Control with Neural Networks

Answers to Problems

2.1 (a) $y(t) = \dfrac{KA}{\tau}\, e^{-t/\tau}$; $y_{ss} = 0$

(b) $y(t) = KA(1 - e^{-t/\tau})$; $y_{ss} = KA$

(c) $y(t) = KA(t - \tau + \tau e^{-t/\tau})$; $y_{ss} = KA(t - \tau)$

(d) $y(t) = \dfrac{KA\omega\tau}{\tau^2\omega^2 + 1}\, e^{-t/\tau} + \dfrac{KA}{\sqrt{\tau^2\omega^2 + 1}}\,\sin(\omega t - \tan^{-1}\omega\tau)$

$y_{ss} = \dfrac{KA}{\sqrt{\tau^2\omega^2 + 1}}\,\sin(\omega t - \tan^{-1}\omega\tau)$

2.2 (a) $y(t) = 1 - \dfrac{e^{-\zeta\omega_n t}}{\sqrt{1 - \zeta^2}}\,\sin\left(\omega_d t + \tan^{-1}\dfrac{\sqrt{1 - \zeta^2}}{\zeta}\right)$

$\omega_d = \omega_n\sqrt{1 - \zeta^2}$

$y_{ss} = 1$

(b) $y(t) = t - \dfrac{2\zeta}{\omega_n} + \dfrac{e^{-\zeta\omega_n t}}{\omega_d}\,\sin\left(\omega_d t + 2\tan^{-1}\dfrac{\sqrt{1 - \zeta^2}}{\zeta}\right)$

$y_{ss} = t - \dfrac{2\zeta}{\omega_n}$

2.3 $R = 10\ \text{k}\Omega$; $C = 0.01\ \mu\text{F}$; Steady-state error = 0.001

2.4 Steady-state error = 1.5

2.5 $\zeta = 0.5$; $\omega_n = 10$; $\omega_d = 5\sqrt{3}$

$$y(t) = 0.01 \left[1 - \frac{2}{\sqrt{3}} e^{-5t} \sin \left(5\sqrt{3}\, t + \tan^{-1} \sqrt{3} \right) \right]$$

2.6 $y_{ss} = \frac{3}{50} \sin 2t - \frac{21}{50} \cos 2t$

2.7 (a) $y(t) = \frac{1}{2} e^{-t} - \frac{1}{3} e^{-2t} - \frac{1}{6} e^{-5t}$

  (b) $y(t) = \frac{1}{2} e^{-t} + \frac{3}{2} e^{-2t} - e^{-5t}$

2.8 (a) $\bar{I} = 0.6$ amp; $\bar{X} = 0.27$ cm

  (b) $\dfrac{X(s)}{I(s)} = \dfrac{47.6}{s^2 - 16.17}$

2.9 $\dfrac{X(s)}{I(s)} = \dfrac{0.1667}{(0.0033s + 1)(0.0217s + 1)}$; $x(\text{peak}) = 1.2113$ cm

2.10 (a) Peak amplitude of the force transmitted to the foundation

$$= \frac{A \sqrt{1 + \left(\dfrac{B\omega}{K} \right)^2}}{\sqrt{\left(1 - \dfrac{M\omega^2}{K} \right)^2 + \left(\dfrac{B\omega}{K} \right)^2}}$$

  (b) Peak amplitude of machine vibration

$$= \frac{A \sqrt{1 + \left(\dfrac{B\gamma}{K} \right)^2}}{\sqrt{\left(1 - \dfrac{M\gamma^2}{K} \right)^2 + \left(\dfrac{B\gamma}{K} \right)^2}}$$

2.11 $M_1 \ddot{y}_1 + K_1(y_1 - y_0) + B_1(\dot{y}_1 - \dot{y}_0) + K_2(y_1 - y_2) + B_2(\dot{y}_1 - \dot{y}_2) = 0$

  $M_2 \ddot{y}_2 + K_2(y_2 - y_1) + B_2(\dot{y}_2 - \dot{y}_1) = 0$

2.12 (a) $\dfrac{E_0(s)}{E_i(s)} = \dfrac{1 + 2RC_2 s + R^2 C_1 C_2 s^2}{1 + R(C_1 + 2C_2)s + R^2 C_1 C_2 s^2}$

  (b) $\dfrac{E_0(s)}{E_i(s)} = \dfrac{1 + 2R_1 Cs + R_1 R_2 C^2 s^2}{1 + (2R_1 + R_2)Cs + R_1 R_2 C^2 s^2}$

2.15 $x_1 = \phi,\ x_2 = \dot{\phi},\ x_3 = z,\ x_4 = \dot{z},\ r = F(t)$

  $\dot{\mathbf{x}} = \mathbf{Ax} + \mathbf{b}r$

$$\mathbf{A} = \begin{bmatrix} 0 & 1 & 0 & 0 \\ 4.4537 & 0 & 0 & 0 \\ 0 & 0 & 0 & 1 \\ -0.5809 & 0 & 0 & 0 \end{bmatrix}; \mathbf{b} = \begin{bmatrix} 0 \\ -0.3947 \\ 0 \\ 0.9211 \end{bmatrix}$$

2.16 $\dfrac{\theta(s)}{\theta_i(s)} = \dfrac{e^{-1.5s}}{s+1}$

$x(t) = K\theta_i(t); \; K = Q/[K_v(\theta_H - \theta_C)]$

2.17 $\dot{\theta}_1 = -1.92\theta_1 + 1.92\theta_2 + 4.46q_m$

$\dot{\theta}_2 = 0.078\theta_1 - 0.2\theta_2 + 0.125\theta_i$

2.18 $\overline{Q}_m = 17.26$ kg/min

2.19 $\dfrac{\theta_2(s)}{Q_1(s)} = -\dfrac{557.6}{100.5 \times 10^3 s^2 + 729s + 0.8}$

2.20 $\dot{h}_1 = -3h_1 + 2h_2 + r_1$

$\dot{h}_2 = 4h_1 - 5h_2 + r_2$

2.21 (i) $q(t) = \dfrac{\overline{Q}}{2\overline{H}} h(t)$

(ii) $\dot{h} = -0.01h + 0.133q_1 + 0.133q_2$

$\dot{c} = -0.02c - 0.004q_1 + 0.002q_2$

3.1 $\dfrac{Y(s)}{R(s)} = \dfrac{G_1(G_2G_3 + G_4)}{1 + (G_2G_3 + G_4)(G_1 + H_2) + G_1H_1G_2}$

3.2 $\dfrac{Y(s)}{R(s)} = G_4 + \dfrac{G_1G_2G_3}{1 + G_2G_3H_2 + G_2H_1(1 - G_1)}$

3.3 $\dfrac{Y(s)}{R(s)} = \dfrac{(1 + G_4H_2)(G_2 + G_3)G_1}{1 + G_1H_1H_2(G_2 + G_3)}$

3.4 $M(s) = \dfrac{G_1G_2G_3}{1 + G_2H_3 + G_3H_2 + G_1G_2G_3 H_1}$

$M_w(s) = \dfrac{G_3(1 + H_3G_2)}{1 + H_3G_2 + G_3(G_1H_1G_2 + H_2)}$

3.5 $\mathbf{G}(s) = \begin{bmatrix} G_{11}(s) & G_{12}(s) \\ G_{21}(s) & G_{22}(s) \end{bmatrix}$

$G_{11} = G_1G_2G_3(1 + G_4)/\Delta$

$G_{21} = G_1G_4G_5G_6H_2/\Delta$

$G_{12} = G_1G_2G_3G_4G_5H_1/\Delta$

$G_{22} = G_4G_5G_6(1 + G_1G_2)/\Delta$

$\Delta = (1 + G_1G_2)(1 + G_4) - G_1G_4G_5H_1H_2$

3.6 $\dfrac{\omega(s)}{E_r(s)} = \dfrac{50}{s + 10.375}$

$\omega(t) = 481.8\,(1 - e^{-10.375t})$

3.7 $\dfrac{\theta_L(s)}{\theta_R(s)} = \dfrac{1}{s(0.1s + 1)(0.2s + 1) + 1}$

3.8 $\dfrac{\theta_L(s)}{E_c(s)} = \dfrac{1}{s(0.32s + 1)}$

3.9 (i) $\dfrac{\theta_M(s)}{\theta_a(s)} = \dfrac{16.7}{s\left(s^2 + 100s + 19.2\right)}$

3.10 $\dfrac{\theta_M(s)}{\theta_R(s)} = \dfrac{13.33}{s^2 + 3.55s + 13.33}$

3.11 $\dfrac{\theta_L(s)}{\theta_R(s)} = \dfrac{15 \times 10^3}{s^3 + 54s^2 + 200s + 15 \times 10^3}$

3.12 (a) $\dfrac{\omega(s)}{E_r(s)} = \dfrac{K}{\dfrac{1}{\omega_n^2}s^2 + \dfrac{2\zeta}{\omega_n}s + 1}$; $K = 17.2,\ \zeta = 1.066,\ \omega_n = 61.2$

3.13 (b) $\dfrac{\theta_L(s)}{\theta_R(s)} = \dfrac{K_P K_A K_T\, G(s)}{1 + K_P K_A K_T\, G(s)}$

$\dfrac{\theta_L(s)}{-T_w(s)} = \dfrac{N(s)}{1 + K_P K_A K_T\, G(s)}$

$G(s) = \dfrac{Bs + K}{s^2\left[J_M J_L s^2 + (J_M + J_L)Bs + (J_M + J_L)K\right]}$

$N(s) = \dfrac{J_M s^2 + Bs + K}{s^2\left[J_M J_L s^2 + (J_M + J_L)Bs + (J_M + J_L)K\right]}$

3.14 $\dfrac{Y(s)}{R(s)} = \dfrac{2}{s^2 + 0.02s + 2}$

3.15 $\dfrac{Y(s)}{Y_r(s)} = \dfrac{K_A K_v K_1 A K_r / K_2}{Ms^2 + \left(B + A^2/K_2\right)s + K_A K_v K_1 K_s\, A/K_2}$

3.16 $\dfrac{Y(s)}{Y_r(s)} = \dfrac{b K_r A K_1 /(a + b)K_2}{Ms^2 + \left(B + A^2/K_2\right)s + K + a A K_1/(a + b)K_2}$

3.17 $\dfrac{Y(s)}{E_r(s)} = \dfrac{G(s)}{1 + G(s)\,H(s)}$

$$G(s) = \frac{(K_A\,K_v\,K_1\,A/K_2)\,e^{-s\tau_D}}{s\left(Ms + B + A^2/K_2\right)}\; ; \; \tau_D = d/v$$

$H(s) = K_s$

4.1 $\left|S_G^M\right| = 0.0289 ; \; \left|S_H^M\right| = 1.02$

4.2 $\dfrac{Y(s)}{R(s)} = M(s) = \dfrac{5K_1}{s^2\left(s + 1 + 5K_1\right) + 5K_1 + 5}\; ; \; S_{K_1}^M = 0.5$

4.3 $y(t)\Big|_{\text{open-loop}} = 20(1 - e^{-t})$

$y(t)\Big|_{\text{closed-loop}} = \dfrac{20}{21}\,(1 - e^{-21t})$

$y'(t)\Big|_{\text{open-loop}} = 50(1 - e^{-0.4t})$

$y'(t)\Big|_{\text{closed-loop}} = \dfrac{20}{20.4}\,(1 - e^{-20.4t})$

4.4 $e_{ss}\Big|_{\text{open-loop}} = 0$

$e_{ss}\Big|_{\text{closed-loop}} = 0.0099$

$e'_{ss}\Big|_{\text{open-loop}} = -0.1$

$e'_{ss}\Big|_{\text{closed-loop}} = 0.009$

4.5 $\tau_f\Big|_{\text{open-loop}} = 0.04$ sec; $K = 4.99$

4.6 $K = 3.9$

4.7   Case I: $y_{ss} = 0$; Case II: $y_{ss} = 1$

4.8   (i) $e_{ss} = 1/3$ (ii) $e_{ss} = 0$ (iii) $e_{ss} = 1/3$

4.9   (i) Oscillatory (ii) stable (iii) unstable

4.10   (a) $e_r = 1.5$ volts

(b) $S_{K_e}^M = \dfrac{(s+1)(5s+1)}{(s+1)(5s+1) + 9.75}$; $M(s) = \dfrac{V(s)}{E_r(s)}$

(c) 25%

4.11 (b) $K = 0.1$; change in terminal voltage = 15 volts;
$e_r = 53$ volts

(c) $e_r = 25$ volts; change in terminal voltage = 30 volts

4.12 (a) $\omega_0(t) = \frac{125}{13} (1 - e^{-130t})$; $\omega_{0ss} = 9.61$ rad/sec

(b) $\omega_0(t) = 9.61(1 - e^{-5t})$

(c) $\dfrac{\omega_0(s)}{\omega_r(s)} = M(s)$ with feedback

$= G(s)$ without feedback

$$S_{K_A}^M = \frac{2s + 10}{2s + 10 + K_A K_g} = S_{\omega_g}^M$$

$$S_{K_A}^G = 1 = S_{\omega_g}^G$$

4.13 (b) $\left| S_{K_g}^M \right| = 4 \times 10^{-4}$

(c) $\theta_{Lss} = 0.1$ rad

4.14 (a) $\dfrac{\theta(s)}{\theta_r(s)} = M(s)$ with feedback

$= G(s)$ without feedback

$$S_K^M = \frac{s(0.25s^2 + 0.02s + 1)}{s(0.25s^2 + 0.02s + 1) + K_P K_A K_e \, K(25s + 1)}$$

$$S_K^G = 1$$

4.15 (a) $\theta_{ss} = \dfrac{K_w R_a}{K_T K_A}$

(b) $S_J^M = \dfrac{(-J/B)s^2}{s\left(\dfrac{J}{B} s + 1\right) + s \dfrac{K_b K_T}{B R_a} + \dfrac{K_T K_A}{B R_a}}$; $M(s) = \dfrac{\theta(s)}{\theta_r(s)}$

4.16 (c) $S_R^M = \dfrac{1}{1 + K R}$; $M(s) = \dfrac{H(s)}{H_r(s)}$

(d) $e_{ss} = \dfrac{1}{1 + K R}$

4.17 $c_{ss} = \dfrac{A \overline{Q_i}}{Q + K \overline{C_i}}$

With integral control, $c_{ss} = 0$

4.18 (b) Open-loop case:

(i) $S_K^G = 1$, $G(s) = \dfrac{\theta(s)}{E_r(s)}$ (ii) $\theta_{ss} = 1$ (iii) $\tau = R_1 C$

Closed-loop case:

(i) $S_K^M = \dfrac{R_1 Cs + 1}{R_1 Cs + 1 + KK_t R_1}$, $M(s) = \dfrac{\theta(s)}{E_r(s)}$

(ii) $\theta_{ss} = \dfrac{1}{1 + KK_t R_1}$ (iii) $\tau = \dfrac{R_1 C}{1 + KK_t R_1}$

(c) $\left. \theta_{ss} \right|_{\text{open-loop}} = \dfrac{R_1}{R_1 + R_2}$; $R_2 = \dfrac{1}{UA}$

$\left. \theta_{ss} \right|_{\text{closed-loop}} = \dfrac{R_1}{R_1 + R_2 + KK_t R_1 R_2}$

4.19 (a) $y_{ss} = 0.089$ (c) $K_f = 0.8$

4.20 (a) $\left. \tau \right|_{\text{without current feedback}} = \dfrac{L_f}{R_f + 1}$

$\left. \tau \right|_{\text{with current feedback}} = \dfrac{L_f}{R_f + K_A + 1}$

4.21 (a) $K_c = 4$; $T_D = 0.5$

4.22 $\left| S_K^M \right| = 1.41$ for Fig. P4.22a

         $\left| S_K^M \right| = 1$ for Fig. P4.22b

5.1 (a) All roots in the left-half plane
   (b) Two roots in the right-half plane, and the rest in the left-half plane
   (c) Two roots in the right-half plane, and the rest in the left-half plane
   (d) Two roots on the imaginary axis, and the rest in the left-half plane
   (e) One root in the right-half plane, and the rest in the left-half plane
   (f) Two roots in the right-half plane, and the rest in the left-half plane

5.2 (a) $(s + j3)(s - j3)(s + 1 + j1)(s + 1 - j1) = 0$
   (b) $(s + 2)(s + 1)(s - 1)(s + j5)(s - j5) = 0$
   (c) $(s + 1)(s + 2)(s + j1)(s - j1)(s + j\sqrt{2})(s - j\sqrt{2}) = 0$

5.3 The largest time-constant is equal to 1.0 sec.

5.4 (a) Unstable for all values of K
   (b) Unstable for all values of K
   (c) $K < 14/9$
   (d) $K > 0.528$

5.5 $K > 0.528$

5.6 $K < 43.3$

5.7 (i) $K < 45$
   (ii) $K < 7.5$

(iii) $K < 10.1$

5.8 (a) (i) $K < 70$ (ii) $K = 70$ (iii) $\Delta(s) = (s + j9.54)(s - j9.54)(s + 10)$
   (b) (i) $K > 7.5$ (ii) $K = 7.5$ (iii) $\Delta(s) = (s + j1.223)(s - j1.223)(s + 5)$
   (c) (i) $K < 28.1$ (ii) $K = 28.1$
       (iii) $\Delta(s) = (s + j2.75)(s - j2.75)(s + 5.7)(s + 1.3)$

5.9 (a) System stable for $K < 666.25$. Oscillations of frequency 4.06 rad/sec when $K = 666.25$.
   (b) System stable for $23.3 < K < 35.7$. Oscillations of frequency 1.56 rad/sec when $K = 23.3$, and 2.56 rad/sec when $K = 35.7$.

5.10 $K = 2$; $a = 0.75$

5.11 (a) $K < 15$
   (b) 7.07 rad/sec for $K = 15$
   (c) Two characteristic roots have time-constants larger than 1 sec.

5.12 (a) Unstable for all K_c
   (b) For stability, $T_D > \tau$

5.13 (a) $K < 30$
   (b) $\tau < 0.2$
   (c) $K < \left(\dfrac{2}{\tau} + 10\right)$

5.14 $K_c < (30 - 25/T_I)$

5.15 $K < (7.5 + 15K_t)$

6.1 (b) (i) $\omega_n = 10$ rad/sec; $\zeta = 0.5$; $\omega_d = 8.66$ rad/sec
       (ii) $t_r = 0.242$ sec; $t_p = 0.363$ sec; $M_p = 16.32\%$; $t_s = 0.8$ sec
       (iii) $K_p = \infty$; $K_v = 10$; $K_a = 0$
       (iv) $e_{ss} = 0$; $e_{ss} = 0.1$; $e_{ss} = \infty$

6.2 (a) $K_A = 2.5$
   (b) $e_{ss} = 0.4$

6.3 (a) (i) $e_{ss} = 0$ (ii) $e_{ss} = 2$
   (b) The system of Fig. P6.3b is unstable

6.4 $e_{ss} = 7/3$

6.5 (a) $K_A < 23.84$
   (b) $K_A = 11.25$

6.6 (b) $0 < K_I < 3$

6.7 (a) $K_c = 10$; $K_D = 0.09$
   (b) ζ is not an accurate estimate of M_p.

6.8 (a) $K_I = 10$
   (b) $K_c = 0.41$
   (c) $-1 \pm j\,11.14$; $\zeta = 0.09$
   (d) ζ approximately represents M_p.

6.9 (a) $T_D = 0.216$
   (c) $T_I > 0.0198$

6.10 (a) $\zeta = 0.158$
   (b) $K_t = 0.216$; $e_{ss} = 0.316$
   (c) $K_t = 0.9$; $K_A = 10$

6.11 (a) $K_1 = 735.39$; $K_2 = 0.31$

    (b) $K_p = \infty$; $K_v = 114.9$; $K_a = 0$

6.12 $K = 8$; $K_t = 0.79$

6.13 $M = 79.71$ kg; $B = 182.47$ N/(m/sec); $K = 300$ N/m

6.14 $J = 2.5$ kg-m^2; $B = 40$ N-m/(rad/sec); $K_T = 1000$ N-m/rad

6.15 $\omega(t) = 1.5\pi\,(1 - e^{-0.5t})$ rad/sec

    $e_{ss} = 5$ rpm

6.16 $\theta(t) = \dfrac{\pi}{3}\left[1 - 1.1547e^{-2t}\sin\left(3.464\,t + \dfrac{\pi}{3}\right)\right]$ rad

    $M_p = 16.3\%$

6.17 (b) $K_A = 904.5$; $M_p = 0.85\%$; $t_s = 0.0796$ sec

    (d) $M_p = 0.772\%$; $t_s = 0.08$ sec

6.18 $K_A = 2.67$; fraction of the tachogenerator voltage fedback = 0.024

6.19 (b) $K_A = 1010$; $\zeta = 0.355$; $M_p = 30.33\%$

    (c) $K_D = 6.95$; $M_p = 9.5\%$

6.20 (a) $e_{ss} = 0.01/K_A$

    (b) $y_{ss} = 0.1/K_A$

    (c) Minimum $e_{ss} = 7.81 \times 10^{-3}$

    Minimum $y_{ss} = 0.078$

6.21 (b) $K_c > 3.5 \times 10^{-3}$; $T_D > 0$

    (c) $D(s) = K_c(1 + T_D s) = 0.1045\,(1 + 0.04s)$

6.22 (a) System-type number = 2

    (b) $K_c > 10$; $K_D > 0.1\,K_c$

6.23 $K_1 = 3$; $K_2 = 19.237$

7.2 (i) Two roots at $s = -1.1835$

    Two roots at $s = -2.8165$

  (ii) Three roots at $s = -2$

 (iii) Three roots at $s = -3$

 (iv) Two roots at $s = -1$

    Two roots at $s = -1 + j1.22$

    Two roots at $s = -1 - j1.22$

  (v) Four roots at $s = -1$

7.3 $K = 1.04$

Closed-loop transfer function

$$= \frac{1.04}{(s + 0.33 + j0.58)(s + 0.33 - j0.58)(s + 2.33)}$$

7.4 $K = 130$; real part of complex pair away from $j\omega$-axis is approximately four times as large as that of the pair near $j\omega$-axis.

7.5 $s_d = -2 + j3.4$

    $K = 65$

Third pole at $s = -4$

7.6 $K = 1.128$; oscillations of $\sqrt{5}$ rad/sec when $K = 30$

7.8 $\zeta = 0.82$; $K = 2.1$

7.10 There exists a circular root locus with centre at $\left(\frac{1}{2}, 0\right)$ and the radius equal to $\sqrt{5}/2$.

7.11 $K = 5$; $M_p = 4.3\%$, $t_s = \frac{4}{3}$ sec, $e_{ss} = 11.11\%$

7.12 $K = 14$

7.13 $K = 1.475$

7.14 (a) $K = 10$ (b) $\zeta = 0.4$

7.15 $K = 10.154$

      $s_d = -0.75 + j1.3$

      Third pole at $s = -4.5$

7.16 $K_t = 0.3427$

7.17 $K_t = 0.449$

7.18 $\alpha = 2.16$; closed-loop poles: $-0.63 \pm j1.09$, -2.75

7.19 $\alpha = 2.8$; closed-loop poles: $-1 \pm j1.732$, -7.

7.20 (c) System is stable for $K > 19.2$; steady-state error to unit-ramp input $= -16/K$.

7.21 Uncompensated system: $K = 7.0$, $K_v = 1.4$, $t_s = 11.6$ sec

      Compensated system: $K = 60$, $K_v = 12.0$, $t_s = 12.7$ sec

7.22 $\alpha = 5.3$; $K = 23.2$; third pole at $s = -3.1$

7.23 (c) $K_c = 8$; $K_D = 2$

7.24 $D(s)$ improves transient performance considerably; no effect on steady-state performance

7.28 $-0.33 \pm j0.58$; $K_v = 0.53$

7.29 $K = 820$; $K_v = 4.1$

7.33 (a) $D(s) = 3 + 2s$; $K_p = 3$

7.34 (a) $K = 56$

      (b) $t_s = 3.6$ sec; $K_v = 2.07$

7.39 There exists a circular root locus with centre at $(2, 0)$ and the radius equal to $\sqrt{12}$.

7.40 There exists a circular root locus with centre at $(0, 0)$ and the radius equal to 0.707.

7.41 Dominant roots of the feedback system are $\lambda_{1,2} = -2.36 \pm j2.48$

      (i) $S_\alpha^{\lambda_1} = 3.34 \angle -80°$

      (ii) $S_\beta^{\lambda_1} = 2.84 \angle +50°$

7.42 $\delta < 0$ is dangerous.

8.2 (a) Unstable	(b) Stable	(c) Stable	
8.3 (i) Yes	(ii) No	(iii) Yes	
8.4 (a) Two	(b) Two	(c) Stable	(d) Stable

(e) Stable   (f) Nyquist criterion not applicable

(g) Stable

8.5   (i) Stable (ii) Unstable

8.6   (a) Stable for $K < 5/4$ (b) Stable for all K (c) Unstable for all K

    (d) Stable for $K < 2.65$

8.7 $K > 0.75$

8.8 $K > 6$

8.9 $K > 2$

8.10 (a) $K = 0.385$ (b) Unstable for all values of K

8.11 $\tau_D = 1.2$ sec

8.12 $\omega_g = 6.2$ rad/sec; $\omega_\phi = 15.9$ rad/sec

      $\Phi M = 31.7°$; $GM = 5.5$

8.13 $GM = 0.7$; $\Phi M = 10°$

8.14 (a) 16 rad/sec (b) 10.2 rad/sec (c) 10 rad/sec (d) 26 rad/sec

8.15 (a) $\omega_g = 7.86$ rad/sec; ω_ϕ: phase never reaches $-180°$

        $\Phi M = 51.8°$; $GM = \infty$

    (b) $\omega_g = 6.8$ rad/sec; $\omega_\phi = 10$ rad/sec

        $\Phi M = 21.4°$; $GM = 6$ dB

    (c) $\omega_g = 9$ rad/sec; ω_ϕ: Phase never reaches $-180°$

        $\Phi M = 73.4°$; $GM = \infty$

    (d) $\omega_g = 9$ rad/sec; $\omega_\phi = 13.65$ ras/sec

        $\Phi M = 22°$; $GM = 4.2$ dB

    (e) ω_g: gain never reaches 0 dB; $\omega_\phi = 7$ rad/sec

        $\Phi M = \infty$; $GM = 20$ dB

    (f) $\omega_g = 3.16$ rad/sec; ω_ϕ: phase never reaches $-180°$

        $\Phi M = -33°$: $GM = -\infty$

8.16 (i) Stable system with $\Phi M = 21°$ and $GM = 8$ dB

    (ii) Unstable system with $\Phi M = -30°$, and $GM = -12$ dB

8.17 (a) $K < 400$ (b) $K < 55$ (c) $K < 1.67$

8.18 (a) $GM = 12$ dB; $\Phi M = 33°$

    (b) $GM = 2.5$ dB; $\Phi M = 18°$

    (c) $\tau_D = 0.078$ sec

8.19 (a) $\dfrac{4(1 + s/2)}{s(1 + s/10)}$; (b) $\dfrac{5s}{(1 + s/2)(1 + s/10)(1 + s/30)}$

    (c) $\dfrac{0.355(1 + s)(1 + 0.05s)}{s(1 + 0.025s)}$

    (d) $\dfrac{250}{s(1 + 0.4s)(1 + 0.025s)}$

(e) $\dfrac{79.6s^2}{(1+2s)(1+s)(1+0.2s)}$

8.20 (a) $\dfrac{31.623s}{(1+s)\left(\dfrac{1}{5}s+1\right)\left(\dfrac{1}{20}s+1\right)}$

(b) $\omega_{g1} = 0.0316$ rad/sec;

(c) 56.234 rad/sec

8.21 $GM = -2.5$ dB

8.22 $G(s) = \dfrac{5\left(1+\dfrac{1}{10}s\right)}{s\left(1+\dfrac{1}{2}s\right)\left[1+\dfrac{0.6}{50}s+\dfrac{1}{2500}s^2\right]}$

8.23 $G(s) = \dfrac{0.1}{\left(\dfrac{1}{3}s+1\right)^2}$

9.4 (a) $K = 475$; $a = 26.2$

(b) $t_s = 0.305$ sec; $\omega_b = 25.1$ rad/sec

9.5 $M_r = 1.11$; $\omega_r = 13.25$ rad/sec; $\omega_b = 24.6$ rad/sec

9.6 $\zeta = 0.01\ \phi_m$

$$K = \dfrac{1}{K_t^2}\left[\begin{array}{c} 2\times10^{-4}\phi_m^2\,\tau - K_t \\[2mm] \pm 2\times10^{-2}\phi_m\sqrt{\tau}\ \sqrt{10^{-4}\phi_m^2\,\tau - K_t} \end{array}\right]$$

9.7 $K = \dfrac{1}{G_m}\left(\dfrac{1}{\tau_1}+\dfrac{1}{\tau_2}\right)$

9.8 (a) $\omega_g = 1$ rad/sec; $\varPhi M = 59.2°$

(b) $M_p = 9.48\%$; $t_s = 4.76$ sec

9.9 $\varPhi M = 50°$; $GM = 24$ dB; $M_p \cong 18\%$

9.10 (a) $\varPhi M = 12°$ (b) Reduce the gain by a factor of 3.5

(C) $M_p \cong 18\%$

9.11 $K = 1.826$; $GM = \infty$

9.12 (a) $GM = 3.88$ dB; $\varPhi M = 10°$

(b) Gain should be changed by a factor of 0.156

(c) Gain should be changed by a factor of 0.147

9.13 $K = 582.51$; $t_p = 0.19$ sec

9.14 (a) $GM = 5$ dB, $\varPhi M = 30°$, $\omega_g = 0.83$ rad/sec

(b) Gain should be reduced by 5 dB

(c) Gain should be increased by 4.8 dB

(d) Gain should be reduced by 3.5 dB

9.15 $K = 37.67$

9.16 (a) $M_p = 33\%$ (b) $M_p = 7.3\%$

9.17 (a) $\Phi M = 40°$ (b) $\Phi M = -3°$; Reduce the gain by a factor of 1.78
   (c) Increase in steady-state error as the loop gain is reduced

9.18 (a) $M_r = 1.8$; $\omega_b = 3.61$ rad/sec
   (b) $M_p = 38.6\%$; $t_s = 5.58$ sec

9.19 (b) $M_r = 1.4$; $\omega_r = 4$ rad/sec
   (c) $M_p = 26.43\%$; $t_s = 2.14$ sec

9.20 (a) $\omega_g = 8.3$ rad/sec, $\omega_\phi = 14.14$ rad/sec
      $GM = 8.2$ dB, $\Phi M = 27.7°$
   (b) $M_r = 6.7$ dB, $\omega_r = 9$ rad/sec,
      $\omega_b = 13.6$ rad/sec

9.21 $GM = 7$ dB; $\Phi M = 17°$; $M_r = 10$ dB
   $\omega_r = 2.75$ rad/sec; $\omega_b = 4.2$ rad/sec

9.22 (a) $\Phi M = 12°$
   (b) Gain should be reduced to the value 4/3.5
   (c) 0.911 rad/sec
   (d) $M_p = 18\%$; $t_s = 11.93$ sec

9.23 (a) $M_r = 1.4$; $\omega_r = 6.9$ rad/sec
   (b) $\zeta = 0.39$; $\omega_n = 8.27$ rad/sec

9.24 (a) $K = 0.54$
   (b) $\omega_b = 9.2$ rad/sec

9.25 (a) $K = 0.5$ (b) $K = 0.446$
   (c) $K = 0.63$, $\omega_r = 0.5$ rad/sec, $\omega_b = 1$ rad/sec (d) $K = 1.35$

9.26 $GM = 16.5$ dB; $\Phi M = 59°$
   Gain should be increased by a factor of 1.75. The gain compensated system has $GM = 11.6$ dB, $\Phi M = 42.5°$.

9.27 K should be reduced by a factor of 3.5.
   $\Phi M = 42.5°$
   $M_r = 1.4$ gives $\zeta = 0.387$
   $\Phi M = 42.5°$ gives $\zeta = 0.394$

9.28 $\left| S_G^M(j\omega) \right|_{max} = 2.18$; 7 rad/sec

10.1 (a) $GM = 6$ dB; $\Phi M = 17°$
   (b) $K_c = 1.2$

10.2 (a) $\omega_g = 4.08$ rad/sec; $\Phi M = 3.9°$, $GM = 1.6$ dB
   (b) $\omega_g = 5$ rad/sec; $\Phi M = 37.6°$, $GM = 18$ dB

10.3 (a) $K = 12$
   (b) $\Phi M = 15°$; $\omega_b = 5.5$ rad/sec; $M_r = 12$ dB; $\omega_r = 3.5$ rad/sec

10.16 (a) $\Phi M = 0.63°$

(b) $\Phi M = 9.47°$; no effect on steady-state performance

10.17 $K_v = 4.8$

11.1 (a) $\alpha = R/R_D$; $T_D = R_D C_D$

(b) $K_c = R/(R_1 + R_2)$; $T_D = R_2 C$; $\alpha = R_1/(R_1 + R_2)$

11.3 $\dfrac{E_2(s)}{E_1(s)} = -\dfrac{\tau s + 1}{\beta \tau s + 1}$; $\tau = \dfrac{R_1 R_2}{R_1 + R_2} C$; $\beta = \dfrac{R_1 + R_2}{R_2}$

11.4 $K_c = \dfrac{R_2 R_4 R_6}{R_1 R_3 R_5}\left(\dfrac{R_1 + R_3}{R_2 + R_4}\right)$; $\tau_1 = (R_1 + R_3)C_1$; $\tau_2 = R_2 C_2$

$\alpha = \dfrac{R_1}{R_1 + R_3}$; $\beta = \dfrac{R_2 + R_4}{R_2}$

11.5 $R_1 = R_2 = 153.85$ kΩ; $R_4 = 197.1$ kΩ

11.6 $R_1 = 34.5$ kΩ; $R_2 = 18.5$ kΩ; $R_4 = 46.8$ kΩ

11.7 $u(k) = K_c\left[e(k) + \dfrac{T}{T_I}\displaystyle\sum_{i=1}^{k}\dfrac{e(i-1)+e(i)}{2} + \dfrac{T_D}{T}\left\{e(k) - e(k-1)\right\}\right]$

11.8 $T = 0.5$ sec

$u(k) = \dfrac{2}{2.01}u(k-1) + \dfrac{4.62}{2.01}e(k) - \dfrac{4.4}{2.01}e(k-1)$

11.9 (b) $u(k) = \dfrac{1 - \dfrac{aT}{2}}{1 + \dfrac{aT}{2}}u(k-1) + \dfrac{K\left(1 + \dfrac{bT}{2}\right)}{1 + \dfrac{aT}{2}}e(k) - \dfrac{K\left(1 - \dfrac{bT}{2}\right)}{1 + \dfrac{aT}{2}}e(k-1)$

11.10 $T = 0.015$ sec

$1.1881\,u(k) - 0.1962\,u(k-1) + 0.0081\,u(k-2)$
$= 6.42\,e(k) - 8.84\,e(k-1) + 3.42\,e(k-2)$

11.11 $b(k) = \dfrac{1 - T/2\tau}{1 + T/2\tau}b(k-1) + \dfrac{K_t/\tau}{1 + T/2\tau}y(k) - \dfrac{K_t/\tau}{1 + T/2\tau}y(k-1)$

11.13 $D(s) = K_c[R(s) - (1 + T_D s)\,Y(s)]$

$K_c = R_2/R'_2$; $T_D = R_D C_D$

11.14 (a) 185%, 0.266 repeats/min

(b) 110%, 0.355 repeats/min, 0.45 min

11.15 $K_c = 1.8$; $T_I = 19.98$ sec

11.16 $K = 1$; $\tau = 1.875$; $\tau_D = 1.375$

(a) $K_c = 1.36$

(b) $K_c = 1.23$; $T_I = 4.58$ min

11.17 Control of process A is less difficult compared to processes B and C, which have equal measure of difficulty in control.

11.18 (a) $K'_c = 3$; $T'_I = 4$ min; $T'_D = 1$ min

(b) $K'_c = 2.9$; $T'_I = 4.13$ min; $T'_D = 1.03$ min

11.20 $K_c = 2.25$; $T_I = 28.33$ sec

12.1 $x_1 = \theta_M$, $x_2 = \dot{\theta}_M$, $x_3 =$ motor armature current i_a,

    $x_4 =$ generator field current i_f; $y = \theta_L$

$$\mathbf{A} = \begin{bmatrix} 0 & 1 & 0 & 0 \\ 0 & -0.025 & 3 & 0 \\ 0 & -12 & -190 & 1000 \\ 0 & 0 & 0 & -4.2 \end{bmatrix}; \mathbf{b} = \begin{bmatrix} 0 \\ 0 \\ 0 \\ 0.2 \end{bmatrix}$$

$$\mathbf{c} = [0.5\ 0\ 0\ 0]$$

12.2 $$\mathbf{A} = \begin{bmatrix} 0 & 1 & 0 \\ 0 & -1 & 20 \\ 0 & 0 & -5 \end{bmatrix}; \mathbf{b} = \begin{bmatrix} 0 \\ 0 \\ 2.5 \end{bmatrix}$$

$$\mathbf{c} = [1\ 0\ 0]$$

12.3 $x_1 = \theta_M$, $x_2 = \dot{\theta}_M$, $x_3 = i_a$

$$\mathbf{A} = \begin{bmatrix} 0 & 1 & 0 \\ 0 & -0.5 & 19 \\ \dfrac{-k_1}{40} & \dfrac{-(k_2 + 0.5)}{2} & \dfrac{-21}{2} \end{bmatrix}; \mathbf{b} = \begin{bmatrix} 0 \\ 0 \\ \dfrac{k_1}{2} \end{bmatrix}$$

$$\mathbf{c} = \begin{bmatrix} \frac{1}{20} & 0 & 0 \end{bmatrix}$$

12.4 $$\mathbf{A} = \begin{bmatrix} \dfrac{-B}{J} & \dfrac{K_T}{J} \\ \dfrac{-(k_1 K_t K_c + K_b)}{L_a} & \dfrac{-(R_a + k_2 K_c)}{L_a} \end{bmatrix}; \mathbf{b} = \begin{bmatrix} 0 \\ \dfrac{k_1 K_c}{L_a} \end{bmatrix}$$

$$\mathbf{c} = [1\ 0]$$

12.5 (a) $\overline{\mathbf{A}} = \begin{bmatrix} -11 & 6 \\ -15 & 8 \end{bmatrix}$; $\overline{\mathbf{b}} = \begin{bmatrix} 1 \\ 2 \end{bmatrix}$; $\overline{\mathbf{c}} = [2\ \ -1]$

    (b) $\dfrac{Y(s)}{U(s)} = \dfrac{1}{s^2 + 3s + 2}$

12.6 (a) $\mathbf{A} = \begin{bmatrix} 0 & 1 \\ 0 & 0 \end{bmatrix}$; $\mathbf{b} = \begin{bmatrix} 0 \\ 1 \end{bmatrix}$

    (b) $\overline{\mathbf{A}} = \begin{bmatrix} 1 & 1 \\ -1 & -1 \end{bmatrix}$; $\overline{\mathbf{b}} = \begin{bmatrix} 0 \\ 1 \end{bmatrix}$

    (c) $|\lambda \mathbf{I} - \mathbf{A}| = |\lambda \mathbf{I} - \overline{\mathbf{A}}| = \lambda^2$

12.7 $\quad \mathbf{G}(s) = \dfrac{1}{\Delta} \begin{bmatrix} s(s+3) & s+3 & 1 \\ -1 & s(s+3) & s \\ -s & -1 & s^2 \end{bmatrix}; \; \mathbf{H}(s) = \dfrac{1}{\Delta} \begin{bmatrix} 1 \\ s \\ s^2 \end{bmatrix}$

$\Delta = s^3 + 3s^2 + 1$

12.9 $\quad x_1, x_2, x_3$: outputs of integrators starting at the right and proceeding to the left.

$$\mathbf{A} = \begin{bmatrix} 0 & 1 & 0 \\ 0 & -2 & 1 \\ -2 & 1 & -2 \end{bmatrix}; \; \mathbf{b} = \begin{bmatrix} 0 \\ 0 \\ 1 \end{bmatrix}; \; \mathbf{c} = [2 \; -2 \; 1]$$

12.10 (a) $G(s) = \dfrac{s+3}{(s+1)(s+2)}$

    (b) $G(s) = \dfrac{1}{(s+1)(s+2)}$

12.11 (a) $\mathbf{A} = \begin{bmatrix} -5 & 0.5 & -3.5 \\ 4 & -5 & 0 \\ 0 & 1 & 0 \end{bmatrix}; \; \mathbf{b} = \begin{bmatrix} 0 \\ 0 \\ -1 \end{bmatrix}$

    $\mathbf{c} = [0 \; 1 \; 0]$

    (b) $G(s) = \dfrac{14}{(s+1)(s+2)(s+7)}$

12.12 (a) x_1 = output of lag $1/(s+2)$; x_2 = output of lag $1/(s+1)$

$$\mathbf{A} = \begin{bmatrix} -2 & 1 \\ -1 & -1 \end{bmatrix}; \; \mathbf{b} = \begin{bmatrix} 0 \\ 1 \end{bmatrix}; \; \mathbf{c} = [-1 \; 1]; \; d = 1$$

    (b) x_1 = output of lag $1/(s+2)$; x_2 = output of lag $1/s$;
    x_3 = output of lag $1/(s+1)$

$$\mathbf{A} = \begin{bmatrix} -2 & 1 & 1 \\ -1 & 0 & 0 \\ -1 & 0 & -1 \end{bmatrix}; \; \mathbf{b} = \begin{bmatrix} 0 \\ 1 \\ 1 \end{bmatrix}; \; \mathbf{c} = [0 \; 1 \; 1]$$

12.13 (i) $\Lambda = \begin{bmatrix} -1 & 0 \\ 0 & -2 \end{bmatrix}; \; \mathbf{b} = \begin{bmatrix} 1 \\ 1 \end{bmatrix}; \; \mathbf{c} = [2 \; -1]$

    (ii) $\mathbf{A} = \begin{bmatrix} 0 & 0 & -2 \\ 1 & 0 & -5 \\ 0 & 1 & -4 \end{bmatrix}; \; \mathbf{b} = \begin{bmatrix} 5 \\ 0 \\ 0 \end{bmatrix}; \; \mathbf{c} = [0 \; 0 \; 1]$

(iii) $\mathbf{A} = \begin{bmatrix} 0 & 1 & 0 \\ 0 & 0 & 1 \\ -6 & -11 & -6 \end{bmatrix}$; $\mathbf{b} = \begin{bmatrix} 0 \\ 0 \\ 1 \end{bmatrix}$; $\mathbf{c} = [2 \quad 6 \quad 2]$

12.14 (i) $\mathbf{A} = \begin{bmatrix} 0 & 0 & 0 \\ 1 & 0 & -2 \\ 0 & 1 & -3 \end{bmatrix}$; $\mathbf{b} = \begin{bmatrix} 1 \\ 1 \\ 0 \end{bmatrix}$; $\mathbf{c} = [0 \quad 0 \quad 1]$

(ii) $\mathbf{A} = \begin{bmatrix} 0 & 1 & 0 \\ 0 & 0 & 1 \\ -6 & -11 & -6 \end{bmatrix}$; $\mathbf{b} = \begin{bmatrix} 0 \\ 0 \\ 1 \end{bmatrix}$; $\mathbf{c} = [1 \quad 0 \quad 0]$

(iii) $\Lambda = \begin{bmatrix} -1 & 0 & 0 \\ 0 & -2 & 0 \\ 0 & 0 & -3 \end{bmatrix}$; $\mathbf{b} = \begin{bmatrix} 1 \\ 1 \\ 1 \end{bmatrix}$

$\mathbf{c} = [-1 \quad 2 \quad 1]$; $d = 1$

12.15 (a) $\mathbf{A} = \begin{bmatrix} 0 & 1 & 0 \\ 0 & 0 & 1 \\ 0 & -100 & -52 \end{bmatrix}$; $\mathbf{b} = \begin{bmatrix} 0 \\ 0 \\ 1 \end{bmatrix}$

$\mathbf{c} = [5000 \quad 1000 \quad 0]$

(b) $\Lambda = \begin{bmatrix} 0 & 0 & 0 \\ 0 & -2 & 0 \\ 0 & 0 & -50 \end{bmatrix}$; $\mathbf{b} = \begin{bmatrix} 50 \\ -31.25 \\ -18.75 \end{bmatrix}$

$\mathbf{c} = [1 \quad 1 \quad 1]$

12.16 (a) $\Lambda = \begin{bmatrix} -1 & 1 & 0 \\ 0 & -1 & 0 \\ 0 & 0 & -2 \end{bmatrix}$; $\mathbf{b} = \begin{bmatrix} 0 \\ 1 \\ 1 \end{bmatrix}$; $\mathbf{c} = [1 \quad 1 \quad 1]$

(b) $y(t) = 2.5 - 2e^{-t} - 0.5\ e^{-2t} - te^{-t}$

12.17 $\mathbf{F} = \begin{bmatrix} 0.696 & 0.246 \\ 0.123 & 0.572 \end{bmatrix}$; $\mathbf{g} = \begin{bmatrix} -0.021 \\ 0.747 \end{bmatrix}$

$\mathbf{c} = [2 \quad -4]$; $d = 6$

12.18 $x_1(k) = y(k)$; $x_2(k) = u(k-1)$

$\mathbf{F} = \begin{bmatrix} 0.3679 & 0.1809 \\ 0 & 0 \end{bmatrix}$; $\mathbf{g} = \begin{bmatrix} 0.4512 \\ 0 \end{bmatrix}$; $\mathbf{c} = [1 \quad 0]$

12.19 (b) $\dfrac{X_1(s)}{x_1^0} = G_{11}(s) = \dfrac{1/2}{s+1} + \dfrac{1/2}{s+3}$

$\dfrac{X_1(s)}{x_2^0} = G_{12}(s) = \dfrac{1/2}{s+1} + \dfrac{-1/2}{s+3}$

$\dfrac{X_2(s)}{x_1^0} = G_{21}(s) = \dfrac{1/2}{s+1} + \dfrac{-1/2}{s+3}$

$\dfrac{X_2(s)}{x_2^0} = G_{22}(s) = \dfrac{1/2}{s+1} + \dfrac{1/2}{s+3}$

$\dfrac{X_1(s)}{U(s)} = H_1(s) = \dfrac{1}{s+1}; \dfrac{X_2(s)}{U(s)} = H_2(s) = \dfrac{1}{s+1}$

(c) (i) $\mathbf{x}(t) = \dfrac{1}{2}\begin{bmatrix} e^{-t}\left(x_1^0 + x_2^0\right) + e^{-3t}\left(x_1^0 + x_2^0\right) \\ e^{-t}\left(x_1^0 + x_2^0\right) + e^{-3t}\left(-x_1^0 + x_2^0\right) \end{bmatrix}$

(ii) $\mathbf{x}(t) = \begin{bmatrix} 1 - e^{-t} \\ 1 - e^{-t} \end{bmatrix}$

12.20 (a) Asymptotically stable

(b) $y(t) = \frac{1}{2} + 2e^{-t} - \frac{3}{2}e^{-2t}$

12.21 (a) $\mathbf{A} = \begin{bmatrix} -6 & 0.5 \\ 4 & -5 \end{bmatrix}; \mathbf{b} = \begin{bmatrix} 7 \\ 0 \end{bmatrix}; \mathbf{c} = [0 \quad 1]$

(b) $y(t) = \dfrac{28}{3}\left[\frac{1}{4}\left(1 - e^{-4t}\right) - \frac{1}{7}\left(1 - e^{-7t}\right)\right]$

12.22 $\begin{bmatrix} x_1(1) \\ x_2(1) \end{bmatrix} = \begin{bmatrix} 2.7183 - k \\ 2k \end{bmatrix}$ for any $k \neq 0$

12.23 $e^{\mathbf{A}t} = \begin{bmatrix} 2e^{-t} - e^{-2t} & e^{-t} - e^{-2t} \\ 2e^{-2t} - 2e^{-t} & 2e^{-2t} - e^{-t} \end{bmatrix}$

$\mathbf{A} = \begin{bmatrix} 0 & 1 \\ -2 & -3 \end{bmatrix}$

12.26 (i) Controllable but not observable

(ii) Controllable but not observable

(iii) Both controllable and observable

(iv) Both controllable and observable

12.27 (i) Observable but not controllable

(ii) Controllable but not observable

    (iii) Neither controllable nor observable

$A = -1;\ b = 1;\ c = 1$

12.28 (i) $G(s) = \dfrac{1}{s+2}$

The state model is not controllable

    (ii) $G(s) = \dfrac{s+4}{(s+2)(s+3)}$

The state model is not observable

12.29 (a) $\lambda_1 = 1;\ \lambda_2 = -2;\ \lambda_3 = -1;$ unstable

    (b) $G(s) = \dfrac{1}{(s+1)(s+2)};$ stable

12.30 (a) $\mathbf{A} = \begin{bmatrix} 0 & 1 \\ 0 & -1 \end{bmatrix};\ \mathbf{b} = \begin{bmatrix} 0 \\ 1 \end{bmatrix};\ \mathbf{c} = [10 \quad 0]$

    (b) $\mathbf{A} = \begin{bmatrix} 0 & 1 & 0 \\ 0 & 0 & 1 \\ 0 & -2 & -3 \end{bmatrix};\ \mathbf{b} = \begin{bmatrix} 0 \\ 0 \\ 1 \end{bmatrix};\ \mathbf{c} = [20 \quad 10 \quad 0]$

    (c) $\mathbf{A} = \begin{bmatrix} 0 & 0 & 0 \\ 1 & 0 & -2 \\ 0 & 1 & -3 \end{bmatrix};\ \mathbf{b} = \begin{bmatrix} 20 \\ 10 \\ 1 \end{bmatrix};\ \mathbf{c} = [0 \quad 0 \quad 1]$

Index